More information about this series at http://www.springer.com/series/8197

Touhid Bhuiyan · Md. Mostafijur Rahman ·
Md. Asraf Ali (Eds.)

Cyber Security and Computer Science

Second EAI International Conference, ICONCS 2020
Dhaka, Bangladesh, February 15–16, 2020
Proceedings

Editors
Touhid Bhuiyan
Daffodil International University
Dhaka, Bangladesh

Md. Mostafijur Rahman
Daffodil International University
Dhaka, Bangladesh

Md. Asraf Ali
Daffodil International University
Dhaka, Bangladesh

ISSN 1867-8211 ISSN 1867-822X (electronic)
Lecture Notes of the Institute for Computer Sciences, Social Informatics and Telecommunications Engineering
ISBN 978-3-030-52855-3 ISBN 978-3-030-52856-0 (eBook)
https://doi.org/10.1007/978-3-030-52856-0

This Springer imprint is published by the registered company Springer Nature Switzerland AG
The registered company address is: Gewerbestrasse 11, 6330 Cham, Switzerland

Preface

We are pleased to introduce the proceedings of the 2nd International Conference on Computer Science and Cyber Security (ICONCS 2020). This conference has brought researchers, industry (both public and private) practitioners, and academics in the field of computer science in general and cyber security in particular from around the world and has provided a platform for them to discuss state-the-art technologies that have significant impact on society.

The technical program of ICONCS 2020 consisted of 16 sessions with oral presentations from authors of 58 full-length papers. The conference sessions were: Session 1–Optimization Problems, Session 2–Image Steganography and Risk Analysis on Web Applications, Session 3–Data Mining, Session 4–Machine Learning in Disease Diagnosis and Monitoring, Session 5–Computer Vision and Image Processing in Health Care, Session 6–Text and Speech Processing, Session 7–Machine Learning in Health Care, Session 8–Blockchain Applications, Session 9–Computer Vision and Image Processing in Health Care, Session 10–Malware Analysis, Session 11–Computer Vision, Session 12–Future Technology Applications, Session 13–Computer Networks, Session 14–Machine Learning on Imbalanced Data, Session 15–Computer Security, and Session 16–Bangla Language Processing. Aside from the high-quality technical paper presentations, the technical program also featured two keynote speeches and two plenary sessions. The two keynote speeches were Dr. Oguz Findik from Karabuk University, Turkey, and Dr. Jemal Abawajy from Deakin University, Australia. While the first keynote discussed techniques for Spam Mail Detection using Hierarchical Temporal Memory, the second keynote touched upon a broader area "Cyber Physical System Cybersecurity Challenges and Opportunities." The two plenary sessions on the other hand were aimed at a larger and more general audience by bringing in ideas such as organizational and national cyber security challenges and opportunities. The first of these sessions were conducted by Dr. Md. Abdur Razzaque from Green University of Bangladesh and the second was conducted by various practitioners and policy-makers from academia, industry, and the government.

Organizing a high-quality peer-reviewed conference is indeed a difficult task and for this we sincerely appreciate everyone in both the Technical Program Committee and the Organizing Committee for their dedication and hard work. We would also like to thank all the reviewers and the session chairs who helped us in completing the peer-review process in time and who contributed in producing a high-quality technical program. Last but not the least, we are grateful to all the authors who submitted their works to ICONCS 2020.

We strongly believe that ICONCS 2020 provided a good forum for all the researchers and practitioners to discuss cutting-edge research in the fields of computer science in general and cyber security in particular. We also expect that the future editions of ICONCS conference will be as successful and stimulating as indicated by the contributions presented in this volume.

June 2020

Touhid Bhuiyan
Md. Mostafijur Rahman
Asraf Ali

Organization

Chief Patron

Md. Sabur Khan	DIU, Bangladesh

Patrons

Yousuf Mahbubul Islam	DIU, Bangladesh
Refik Polat	Rector Karabük University, Turkey
S. M. Mahbub Ul Haque Majumder	DIU, Bangladesh

General Chair

Touhid Bhuiyan	DIU, Bangladesh

General Co-chairs

Md. Kabirul Islam	DIU, Bangladesh
Mehmet Akbaba	Karabük University, Turkey

Secretary, Program Chair and Publication Chair

Md. Mostafijur Rahman	DIU, Bangladesh

Technical Program Chairs

Md. Asraf Ali	DIU, Bangladesh
Muhammet Tahir Guneser	Karabuk University, Turkey
Md. Maruf Hassan	DIU, Bangladesh

Technical Program Committee

Md. Ismail Jabiullah	DIU, Bangladesh
Shaikh Muhammad Allayear	DIU, Bangladesh
Imran Mahmud	DIU, Bangladesh
Sheak Rashed Haider Noori	DIU, Bangladesh
İdris Kahraman	Karabuk University, Turkey
Kadir Ileri	Karabuk University, Turkey
Caner Özcan	Karabuk University, Turkey
Ameer Ali	BUBT, Bangladesh

Md. Mijanur Rahman	Uttara University, Bangladesh
Kasım Özacar	Karabuk University, Turkey
Emrullah Sonuc	Karabuk University, Turkey
Ferhat Atasoy	Karabuk University, Turkey
Zafer Albayrak	Karabuk University, Turkey
Khan Iftekharuddin	Old Dominion University, USA
Rasib Khan	Northern Kentucky University, USA
Nizam U. Ahamed	University of Pittsburgh, USA
Md. Anamul Islam	City University of New York, USA
Robert S. Laramee	Swansea University, UK
Kaniz Fatema	University of Derby, UK
Ljiljana Trajkovic	Simon Fraser University, Canada
Mohammad Rashid	Massey University, New Zealand
Fakhrul Alam	Massey University, New Zealand
Nasim Ahmed	Massey University, New Zealand
Yuvaraj Rajamanickam	Nanyang Technological University, Singapore
A. R. Jac Ferodo	Nanyang Technological University, Singapore
Mahdi H. Miraz	CFRED, CUHK, Hong Kong
Hamed Vahdat-Nejad	University of Birjand, Iran
Zaid Ameen Abduljabbar	University of Basrah, Iraq
Zaid Alaa Hussien	Southern Technical University, Iraq
Muhammad Imran Ahmad	UniMap, Malaysia
Zahereel Ishwar Abdul Khalib	UniMap, Malaysia
Sathees Kumar Nataraj	AMA International University, Bahrain
Rajkumar Palaniappan	AMA International University, Bahrain
Mohammad Nurul Huda	United International University, Bangladesh
Surendran Rajendran	AMA International University, Bahrain
V. Rajesh Kumar	VIT University, India
V. Nithish Kumar	VIT University, India
Md. Masbaul Alam Polash	Jagannath University, Bangladesh
Md. Abu Layek	Jagannath University, Bangladesh
Mohammad Ismat Kadir	Khulna University, Bangladesh
Md. Shamim Ahsan	Khulna University, Bangladesh
G. M. Atiqur Rahaman	Khulna University, Bangladesh
Mostafa Zaman Chowdhury	KUET, Bangladesh
Md. Salah Uddin Yusuf	KUET, Bangladesh
K. M. Azharul Hasan	KUET, Bangladesh
Mohiuddin Ahmad	KUET, Bangladesh
Monir Hossen	KUET, Bangladesh
Md. Foisal Hossain	KUET, Bangladesh
Md. Shahjahan	KUET, Bangladesh
Mohammad Osiur Rahman	University of Chittagong, Bangladesh
Jamal Uddin Ahamed	University of Chittagong, Bangladesh
Md. Shahjahan Ali	Islamic University, Bangladesh
Md. Manjur Ahmed	University of Barishal, Bangladesh

Md. Sajjadur Rahman	JU, Bangladesh
Md. Mahabub Hossain	HSTU, Bangladesh
Mohammad Abdur Rouf	DUET, Bangladesh
Md. Nasim Akhtar	DUET, Bangladesh
Brenda Scholtz	Nelson Mandela University, South Africa
André Calitz	Nelson Mandela University, South Africa
Md. Motaharul Islam	BRAC University, Bangladesh
Hasan Sarwar	United International University, Bangladesh
Md. Khalilur Rahman	BRAC University, Bangladesh
Imtiaz Mahmud	Kyungpook National Universtiy, South Korea
You-Ze Cho	Kyungpook National University, South Korea
Teoh Ai Ping	USM, Malaysia
Yulita Hanum P. Iskandar	USM, Malaysia
Mathias Hatakka	Orebro University, Sweden
Vito Veneziano	University of Hertfordshire, UK
Ghossoon Mohammed Waleed AlSadoon	AMA International University, Bahrain
Mohammad Kamrul Islam	Google Inc., USA

Organizing Chair

K. M. Imtiaz-Ud-Din — DIU, Bangladesh

Logistics and Venue Management Chair

Md. Shohel Arman — DIU, Bangladesh

Technical Sessions Chair

Md. Anwar Hossen — DIU, Bangladesh

Refreshment and Food Management Chair

Khalid Been Badruzzaman Biplob — DIU, Bangladesh

Proceedings Preparation Chair

Farzana Sadia — DIU, Bangladesh

Sponsorship Chair

M. Khaled Sohel — DIU, Bangladesh

Finance Chair

Md. Fahad Bin Zamal DIU, Bangladesh

Invitation Chair

Nusrat Jahan DIU, Bangladesh

Public Relation Chair

Afsana Begum DIU, Bangladesh

International Guest Management Chair

Fatama Binta Rafiq DIU, Bangladesh

Certificate and Crests Preparation Chair

Md. Mushfiqur Rahman DIU, Bangladesh

Website Management Chair

Sheikh Shah Mohammad Motiur Rahman DIU, Bangladesh

Design Support Chair

Shaikh Muhammad Allayear DIU, Bangladesh

Transport Management Chair

Md. Sanzidul Islam DIU, Bangladesh

IT Support Chair

Raiyan Mostofa DIU, Bangladesh

Conference Support Chairs

Sayed Asaduzzaman DIU, Bangladesh
Bikash Kumar Paul DIU, Bangladesh

Contents

Machine Learning in Disease Diagnosis and Monitoring

Text and Speech Processing

Bangla Language Processing

Computer Vision and Image Processing in Health Care

Computer Networks

Computer Security

Framework for the Optimal Design of an Information System to Diagnostic the Enterprise Security Level and Management the Information Risk Based on ISO/IEC-27001

Christopher A. Kanter-Ramirez[1,2], Josue A. Lopez-Leyva[1(✉)], Lucia Beltran-Rocha[1], and Dominica Ferková[3]

[1] CETyS University, 22860 Ensenada, BC, Mexico
josue.lopez@cetys.mx
[2] Softtek S.A. de C.V., 22760 Ensenada, BC, Mexico
[3] University of Applied Sciences Upper Austria, 4600 Wels, Austria

Abstract. This paper presents the framework for the optimized development of a digital platform based on ISO/IEC-27001 with the objective of making an initial diagnosis regarding the informatics security level in any company. In addition, the optimization process considers that the diagnostic results should be clear and direct, to making possible the fast security risk mitigation. In particular, the optimization process is based on the analysis of a conventional Management Information System framework in order to propose a novel customized framework for ISO/IEC-27001 applications. Thus, an optimized Management Information System is proposed which is the basis of the optimized digital platform. As preliminary results, the reduction of needed elements for the initial diagnosis for the informatics security promotes the simplicity of the application and thus, increases the possibility of applying the ISO/IEC-27001 to a greater amount of users, which means that it is promoted cybersecurity.

Keywords: Security level · ISO/IEC-27001 · Optimal design

1 Introduction

Information security is an extremely important aspect in any organization, whether it is considered the information in digital or physical form. Thus, the enterprises have been used methodologies and standards aiming to meet the requirements for security, particularly for Industry 4.0 [1, 2]. In fact, the lack of consideration for protecting the information can cause significant damage not only to the company directly, but can also cause collateral damage. In this way, several research groups and companies have focused on the design and development of hardware and software that allow increasing the level of information security, whether using traditional concepts and techniques, as well as high-end options [3–6]. For example, computational algorithms based on complex mathematical formulations have been proposed, tested and widely used in various

T. Bhuiyan et al. (Eds.): ICONCS 2020, LNICST 325, pp. 3–13, 2020.
https://doi.org/10.1007/978-3-030-52856-0_1

current telecommunications systems [7, 8]. In addition, as a high-end option, information security systems based on quantum mechanics laws have also been investigated and developed, although such technological options are not as common in traditional communications systems [9, 10]. However, the main problem when trying to protect the information is not related to the type of technology used, in fact, the main problem lies in the not knowing a clear and precise process that allows analyzing the information risks and proposing the minimum and necessary controls to maintain a desired level of security. In particular, today is clear that numerous activities (e.g. development and execution of information security-policy, compliance training, awareness, among others) related to the management within the companies have a significant impact on the quality of management of information security [11, 12]. Thus, the optimum way to promote a particular informatics security level must be based on the correct use of an Information Security Management System (ISMS) that allows the holistic analysis of the information risk in order to propose adequate controls [13]. In particular, the aforementioned it is considered in detail by the ISO/IEC-27001 standard.

Although the ISO/IEC-27001 is intended to be applied by any company, it is important to clarify that a certain level of technical knowledge is required in order to produce adequate results related to an information security level desired. Also, there exist some challenges that avoid the correct implementation of the ISO/IEC-27001, e.g. gap analysis and communication, stakeholder investment, risk assessment, among others. These allow that many companies are not protecting their computer resources, therefore, these companies are vulnerable to various types of cyberattacks [14]. In addition, this lack of information security also has an impact on the reduction of global or regional competitiveness [15]. In order to clarify the information security importance, McAfee revealed that cybercrime has a global impact on the economy of five hundred billion dollars per year. In addition, the complexity of computer assaults is measured based on the level of importance of the data involved and the amount of money required to amend the problems. Among the greatest attacks registered are the following: 1) PlayStation Network (2011), for 23 days, the PlayStation online service remained unworked, 77 million users were affected without the possibility of generating transactions generating losses of approximately 180 million dollars [16], 2) LinkedIn (2012), the social network of professional contacts suffered a computer attack in which 117 million accounts were affected, from the theft of confidential data to the elimination of accounts and passwords. Some days after the attack, the information obtained was put up for sale on the dark web in exchange for five bitcoins [17], 3) Yahoo (2013), this company was a victim of the theft of personal information (birth dates, email addresses, phone numbers and passwords) of one billion accounts [18] and, 4) eBay (2014), in May, the online buying and selling company was the victim of an attack against 145 million accounts [19]. In this paper, a framework for designing and developing a digital platform based on ISO/IEC-27001 is presented with the objective of mitigating the challenges for its correct implementation. In particular, this paper is organized as follows: Sect. 2 presents the theoretical background. Section 3 shows the technical proposal and Sect. 4 presents the conclusions.

2 Theoretical Background

2.1 General Aspects of ISO/IEC-27001

The ISO/IEC-27001 is a family of standards that supports and helps to maintain and reach the security for the information resources of any company. In particular, the correct application depends on many factors such as the elaboration of a contingency plan for incidents, risk analysis, enterprise capabilities, the degree of involvement of managers, security investments, the degree of implementation of controls, among others. Also, ISO/IEC-27001 is based on the model Plan-Do-Check-Act (PDCA), which means that it is a continuous improvement process [20]. Therefore, the degree of progress and achievement of objectives must be monitored along the time in an effective way. However, although the ISO/IEC-27001 provides administrative and technical details related to the aspects and processes to be evaluated in order to improve the security of information resources, in addition to mentioning that it can be applied for any type and size of industry, optimization aspects of resources and processes to achieve a certain information security level according to particular users are not considered. In fact, ISO/IEC-27001 does not directly propose the optimization of resources, although it could be understood inherently in the same process, so on it is ambiguous. It is important to mention that the optimization process has to comprise complementary state-of-the-art decision support tools and technologies in order to minimize cost and maximize resource utilization [21]. These tools and technologies are not considered by the ISO/IEC-27001.

As was mentioned above, there are many commercial digital platforms that support the ISO/IEC-27001 processes, but also they have many constraints, being the main constraint the not optimization of the resources, i.e. they were designed considering a certain type of users as a potential market, which it is valid, but on the other hand, they do not guarantee the service for other types of users that require a true optimization of resources. Hence, an optimized digital platform is required not only regarding the ISO/IEC-27001 but also regarding the digital platform itself. In general, the software development optimized can consider a lot of levels of optimization such as design level, algorithms and data structures, source code level, build level, among others. For example, respect to the design level, several aspects are highly considered, e.g. ensuring the best use of the available resources, given goals, and expected load, detailed architectural design, among others. In addition, Client-Side (CSO) and Server-Side (SSO) Optimization are also considered in an overall optimization design process [22]. Because there are several optimization parameters, this paper only will be focus on the design level and algorithms & data structures. The aforementioned in order to propose an optimized and simplified digital platform to manage the information risk based on ISO/IEC-27001. It is important to mention that such optimization is not trivial, because ISO/IEC-27001 already establishes certain processes and documents that are necessary within the conventional framework. Therefore, prior work related to the analysis of ISO/IEC-27001 itself is necessary.

2.2 General Aspects of Management Information System

In general, a Management Information System (MIS) is an informatics system that can consist of hardware and software, in the case of the most advanced MIS, or, for those basic MIS, they consist of only software. In particular, the main objective of an MIS is to support the process of intelligent decision making in a company [23]. In order to reach this, the MIS needs to acquire information from different resources, perform an analysis process and then, generate technical reports as evidence or supporting documents for future smart decision making [24–27]. In this way, MIS offers certain advantages for any improvement process, in our case, the implementation of ISO/IEC-27001. For example, using an MIS it is possible to detect strengths and weaknesses in the security of informatics resources, it allows us to obtain an overall picture of the security level of the company, among many other advantages. Considering the aforementioned, it means that the correct implementation of MIS in relation to ISO/IEC-27001 can help to increase the competitiveness of the company [28–31].

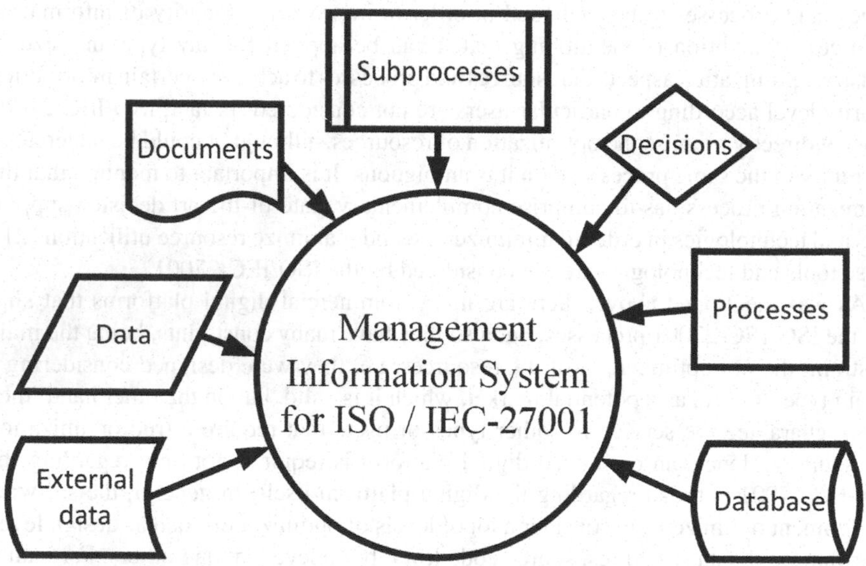

Fig. 1. Management Information Systems proposal for ISO/IEC-27001.

Figure 1 shows some elements that MIS requires to achieve its objective mentioned, such elements are processes, sub-processes, decision-making actions, documentation, data, external data, databases, among others. Also, a generic MIS should use various rules and tools for the analysis of information considering the elements mentioned [32–34]. In order to clarify, the conventional applications of ISO/IEC-27001 do not consider the uses of MIS. In fact, it is possible that only large companies with sufficient financial resources could implement an MIS to support the ISO/IEC-27001 process. In this case, small and medium-sized companies will not have the possibility of providing security to their information resources at the same or similar security level as large companies [35–37].

3 Technical Proposal

Considering the above, this paper proposes to develop a digital platform where a generic user can self-evaluate in order to obtain a diagnosis regarding the level of information security of your company. Then, based on the results obtained, process and practice options will be shown that can be used to improve the integrity and security of the information. In particular, this digital tool will be developed as a multiplatform mobile application, it will have a repository which will store information that will be used by the application, in turn, a user-friendly interface and user experience will be highly considered. Also, Lean with Kanban development methodology will be used, using ZenHub tools for the activity board with sprint kind meetings. Regarding the code version control, GitHub will be used. Figure 2 shows the flowchart of the first stage of the development process for the digital platform. The first step is reviewing the general requirements of the ISO/IEC-27001 for general purposes and users. Next, the analysis of such requirements is needed in order to begin the optimization process for the future custom application. In this case, the requirements have to be prioritized as a principal aspect of the optimized design and development. In addition, as Fig. 2 shows, each step in the process requires particular and specialized technical reports, which will be related to those technical reports that are necessary for the implementation of ISO/IEC-27001 in conventional scenarios.

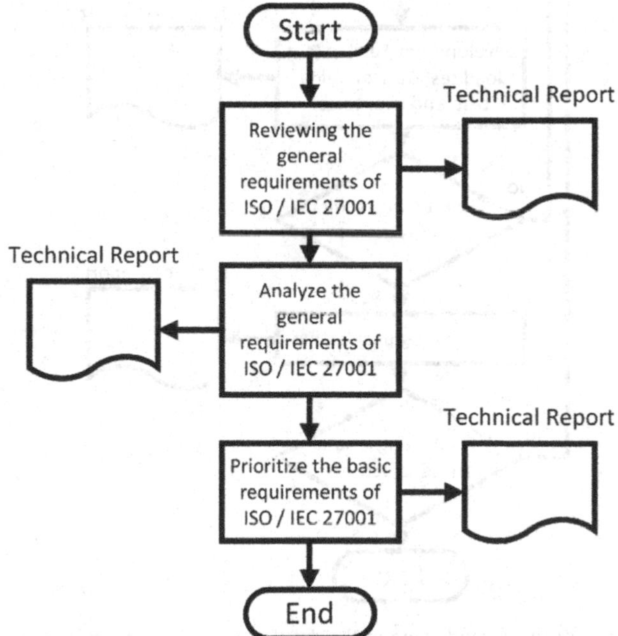

Fig. 2. Flowchart of the first stage of the development process for the digital platform.

Then, Fig. 3 shows the flowchart of the second stage of the development process for the digital platform considering the optimization process shown in Fig. 2. In particular, the first step is to propose the user interface and system flow diagram in order to simplify the conventional ISO/IEC-27001 process. Next, the interface is developed considering the flow diagram proposed. It is important to clarify that, as at stage 1, the technical reports are highly important. At this moment, the development testing and Beta testing have to be performed in order to ensure the correct functionality. If the performance of the optimized digital platform is not satisfactory, a redesign will be necessary.

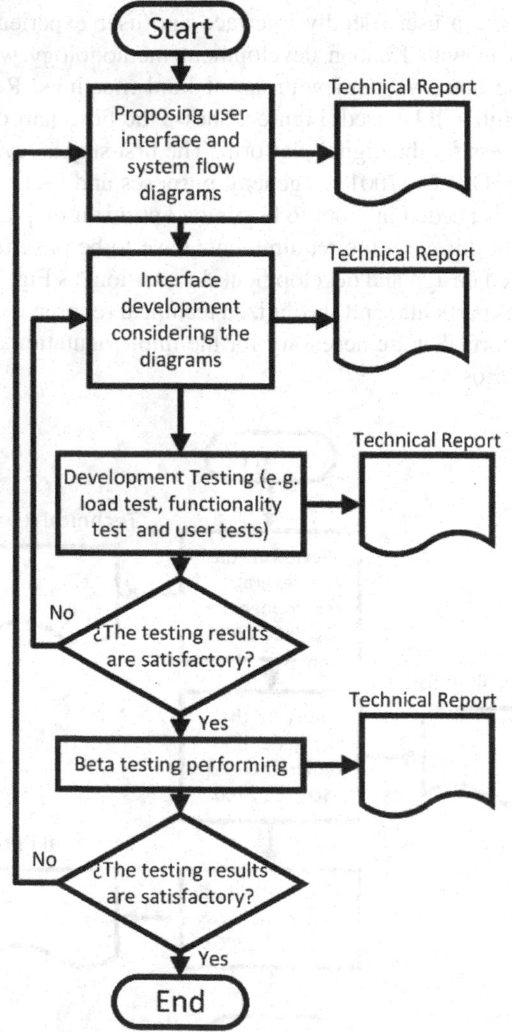

Fig. 3. Flowchart of the second stage of the development process for the digital platform.

Until now, Fig. 2 and 3 show the flowcharts of the first and second stages, where can be seen the optimization related to the basic requirements of ISO/IEC-27001 and aspects related to platform development and testing. Next, Fig. 4 shows the MIS scheme that only considers the basic and priority requirements necessary to develop the initial diagnosis. In particular, the MIS only requires information related to the documentation, processes and sub processes directly related to the basic aspects prioritized above. It is true that many elements present in Fig. 1 are not considered in Fig. 4, the reason is that the data, external data, decision rules and database elements were considered unnecessary and probably non-existent for certain types of users. Thus, it is possible to generate an initial diagnosis related to the level of security of a company's resources (mainly, small or medium-sized companies).

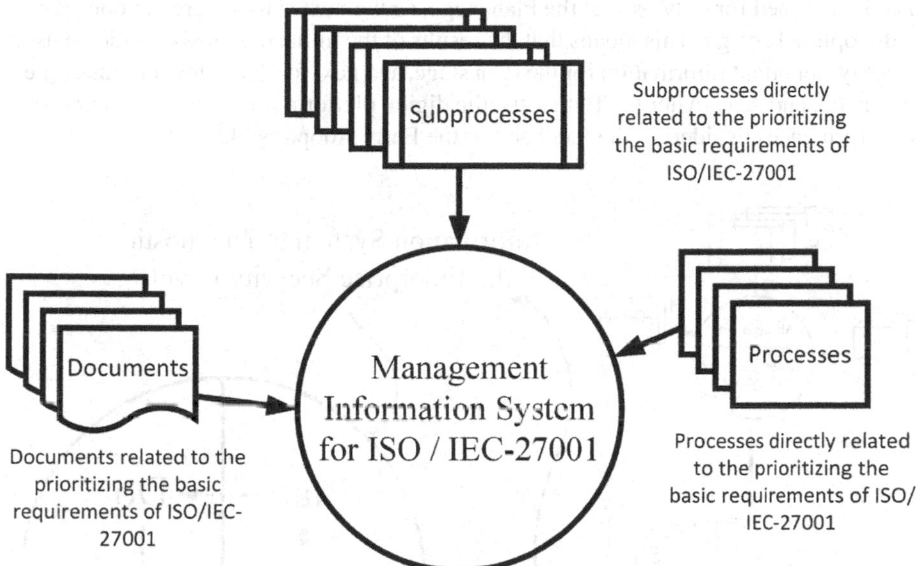

Fig. 4. Management Information Systems proposal for ISO/IEC-27001 considering the prioritized requirements to perform the initial security diagnostic.

It is important to clarify that, the proposal presented in Fig. 4 is highly dependent on the quality of the organizational structure of the company that promotes the performing of the information security diagnosis. In particular, the Management Information Systems proposal for ISO/IEC-27001 shown in Fig. 4 considers the prioritization of requirements to perform the initial security diagnostic for any company, which means the existent of well-defined and accessible documentation, sub-processes and processes related to the business core and model for each company. Otherwise, the absence of documents, and evidence of well-defined processes and sub processes, will not allow the correct management of the information in order to analyze the risks of the informatics resources of a particular company. Therefore, before executing the Management Information Systems proposal for ISO /IEC-27001, it is recommended to carry out an analysis of the company's conventional processes, in order to ensure the success of the application of ISO /IEC-27001 through the proposed digital platform [38–41].

Finally, Fig. 5 shows the overall framework related to the future application of ISO/IEC-27001. As can be seen, the Management Information Systems proposal for

ISO/IEC-27001 firstly considers relevant requirements to perform the initial security diagnostic. Then, using the aforementioned prioritized requirements, various activities are carried out to develop the digital platform, e.g., script, programs, diagrams, projects, databases, among others. Therefore, the information system to diagnostic the security level of the company is almost ready. Now, such a digital platform should be used as part of the Plan-Do-Check-Act model, particularly at the planning stage. In particular, the framework mentioned until now is related to the optimal design of an information system to diagnostic the enterprise security level based on the management of the information risk of particular activities, documents, and processes of the company. However, this proposal is designed for only uses at the Plan stage, so the next stages were not considered for the optimal design. This means that the results of the initial diagnosis should be used as highly important information for the Plan stage, and next for the following stages (i.e., Do, Check, and Act). After the Beta tests, the digital platform proposed should improve its performance considering the feedback of the Early Adopters [42–45].

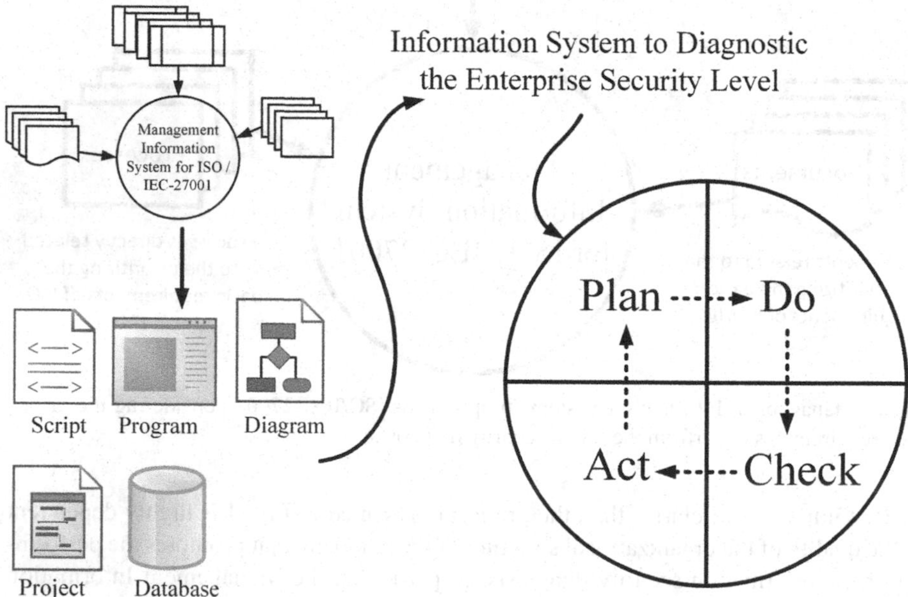

Fig. 5. The final framework proposed for using an information system to diagnostic the enterprise security level and manage the information risk based on ISO/IEC-27001.

4 Conclusions

In this paper, the framework for the optimal design of an information system to diagnostic the enterprise security level and management of the information risk based on ISO/IEC-27001 has been proposed. In particular, the digital platform should improve cybersecurity, which it is related to the definition of the access controls, the correct application of security policy, the optimum design and deployment of secure services, information risk management, the adequate selection for security automation tools and system security, the analysis related to the vulnerability detection model/techniques (i.e. ethical hacking), among others aspect that the ISO/IEC-27001 considers. In addition, the proposal pretends to improve the support to the enterprises based on a customization process, fast and low cost for implementation of the ISO/IEC-27001. As future work, various activities related to the digital platform development are already being carried out as well as some software testing. The above is in order to perform some initial tests, called Beta testing with the Early Adopters. In fact, the goal of the Beta tests is that Early Adopters provide feedback regarding the design of the digital platform, functionality, and impact on conventional computer security processes or services. With this, the platform will gradually increase the level of security in terms of diagnosing the security of company information. In addition, it is important to clarify that the technical contribution presented in this paper has important implications in the conventional processes that provide information security in the companies. That is, although the aspects considered by ISO/IEC-27001 are used for the design of the framework of the digital platform, the company that intends to use such a platform must modify its conventional processes. In this way, the addition and use of the said platform can be defined with an innovation process for the management of secure information for end-users. In addition, the technical contribution shown in this paper can help significantly to increase the competitiveness of companies by adding value to their processes and services. In fact, the analysis of risks related to the information, precisely attempts to prevent such malicious actions that affect the integrity and accessibility of important information. It is also important to remember that, the technical proposal considers small and medium-sized companies, so the technical and financial capabilities are not insured, as would be the case with large companies. This means that, although the digital platform and framework presented apparently are very simple, it was tried to optimize the aspects of the ISO/IEC-27001 with the objective of providing a level of security to the information of the companies with fewer resources.

References

1. Dotsenko, S., Illiashenko, O., Kamenskyi, S., Kharchenko, V.: Integrated security management system for enterprises in industry 4.0. Inf. Secur. Int. J. **43**(3), 294–304 (2019)
2. Almeida, F., Carvalho, I., Cruz, F.: Structure and challenges of a security policy on small and medium enterprises. KSII Trans. Internet Inf. Syst. **12**(2), 747–763 (2018)
3. Liu, Z., Zeng, Y., Yan, Y., Zhang, P., Wang, Y.: Machine learning for analyzing malware. J. Cyber Secur. Mob. **6**(3), 227–244 (2017)
4. Varadharajan, V., Karmakar, K., Tupakula, U., Hitchens, M.: A policy-based security architecture for software-defined networks. IEEE Trans. Inf. Forensics Secur. **14**(4), 897–912 (2019)
5. Polian, I.: Hardware-oriented security. it Inf. Technol. **61**(1), 1–2 (2019)
6. Wagner, M.: The hard truth about hardware in cyber-security: it's more important. Netw. Secur. **2016**(12), 16–19 (2016)
7. Verma, M., Dhamal, P.: High security of data using steganography with hybrid algorithm. Int. J. Sci. Res. **4**(11), 2469–2473 (2015)

8. Ahmed, S., Nader, M.: New algorithm for wireless network communication security. Int. J. Cryptogr. Inf. Secur. **6**(3/4), 01–08 (2016)
9. Dong, H., Song, Y., Yang, L.: Wide area key distribution network based on a quantum key distribution system. Appl. Sci. **9**(6), 1073 (2019)
10. Mehic, M., Maurhart, O., Rass, S., Voznak, M.: Implementation of quantum key distribution network simulation module in the network simulator NS-3. Quantum Inf. Process. **16**(10), 253 (2017)
11. Soomro, Z.A., Shah, M.H., Ahmed, J.: Information security management needs more holistic approach: a literature review. Int. J. Inf. Manag. **36**(2), 215–225 (2016)
12. Albrechtsen, E., Hovden, J.: Improving information security awareness and behaviour through dialogue, participation and collective reflection. An intervention study. Comput. Secur. **29**(4), 432–445 (2010)
13. Nazareth, D.L., Choi, J.: A system dynamics model for information security management. Inf. Manag. **52**(1), 123–134 (2015)
14. Phirke, A., Ghorpade-Aher, J.: Best practices of auditing in an organization using ISO 27001 standard. Int. J. Recent Technol. Eng. **8**(2S3), 691–695 (2019)
15. Yunis, M.M., Koong, K.S., Liu, L.C., Kwan, R., Tsang, P.: ICT maturity as a driver to global competitiveness: a national level analysis. Int. J. Account. Inf. Manag. **20**(3), 255–281 (2012)
16. Milian, M.: Sony: Hacker stole PlayStation users' personal info. http://www.cnn.com/2011/TECH/gaming.gadgets/04/26/playstation.network.hack/index.html. Accessed 21 Nov 2019
17. Gunaratna, S.: LinkedIn: 2012 data breach much worse than we thought. https://www.cbsnews.com/news/linkedin-2012-data-breach-hack-much-worse-than-we-thought-passwords-emails/. Accessed 21 Nov 2019
18. Perlroth, N.: All 3 Billion Yahoo Accounts Were Affected by 2013 Attack. The New York Times. https://www.nytimes.com/2017/10/03/technology/yahoo-hack-3-billion-users.html. Accessed 21 Nov 2019
19. Kelion, L.: EBay makes users change passwords. https://www.bbc.com/news/technology-27503290. Accessed 21 Nov 2019
20. Anon: Implementing an Information Security Management System—Plan-Do-Check-Act, How to Achieve 27001 Certification, Auerbach Publications (2007)
21. Smith, P.C.: Decision support systems: tools and techniques. Inf. Process. Manage. **23**(6), 651 (1987)
22. Singh, R., Singhrova, A., Bhatia, R.: Optimized test case generation for object oriented systems using weka open source software. Int. J. Open Source Softw. Process. **9**(3), 15–35 (2018)
23. Sabarguna, B.S.: Management Functions of Information System Components as an Integration Model, Management of Information Systems, InTech (2018)
24. Ada, Ş., Ghaffarzadeh, M.: Decision making based on management information system and decision support system. Eur. Res. **93**(4), 260–269 (2015)
25. Oppl, S.: Articulation of work process models for organizational alignment and informed information system design. Inf. Manag. **53**(5), 591–608 (2016)
26. Gill, A.Q., Chew, E.: Configuration information system architecture: Insights from applied action design research. Inf. Manag. **56**(4), 507–525 (2019)
27. Caserio, C., Trucco, S.: Relationship between information system and information overload. A preliminary analysis. Int. J. Manag. Inf. Technol. **11**(5), 3040–3050 (2016)
28. Agustino, D.P.: Information Security Management System Analysis Menggunakan ISO/IEC 27001 (Studi Kasus: STMIK STIKOM Bali). Eksplora Informatika **8**(1), 1–5 (2018)
29. Mantra, I.: Implementation: Information Security Management System (ISMS) ISO 27001:2005 at Perbanas University. ACMIT Proc. **1**(1), 46–58 (2014)
30. Disterer, G.: ISO/IEC 27000, 27001 and 27002 for information security management. J. Inf. Secur. **4**(2), 92–100 (2013)

31. Makupi, D.: A design of information security maturity model for universities based on ISO 27001. Int. J. Bus. Manag. **7**(6), 134–139 (2019)
32. Chai, D.T., Wier, J.M.: Information management system: interactive information management systems. Bell Syst. Tech. J. **52**(10), 1681–1689 (1973)
33. Heindel, L.E., Roberto, J.T.: Information management system: the off-the-shelf system-a packaged information management system. Bell Syst. Tech. J. **52**(10), 1743–1763 (1973)
34. Campbell, R.H., Grimshaw, M.: User resistance to information system implementations: a dual-mode processing perspective. Inf. Syst. Manag. **33**(2), 179–195 (2016)
35. Jagodzińska, N.: Key changes to the ISO 9001, ISO 14001, ISO 27001 management standards in the approach to the organizational context including risk management. Transp. Econ. Logist. **78**, 103–112 (2018)
36. Rosa, F.D.F., Jino, M., Bueno, P.M.S., Bonacin, R.: Applying heuristics to the selection and prioritisation of security assessment items in software assessment: the case of ISO/IEC 27001 the case of ISO/IEC 27001. ACTA IMEKO **8**(2), 12–20 (2019)
37. Everett, C.: Is ISO 27001 worth it? Comput. Fraud Secur. **2011**(1), 5–7 (2011)
38. Hoy, Z., Foley, A.: A structured approach to integrating audits to create organisational efficiencies: ISO 9001 and ISO 27001 audits. Total Qual. Manag. Bus. Excell. **26**(5–6), 690–702 (2015)
39. Wahab, M.H.A.-A.A., Ismail, M., Muhayiddin, M.N.: Factors influencing the operational excellence of small and medium enterprise in Malaysia. Int. J. Acad. Res. Bus. Soc. Sci. **6**(12), 285–297 (2016)
40. Nehete, R., Narkhede, B.E., Raut, R.D.: Manufacturing performance and relevance of operational performance to small and medium scale enterprises - literature review. Int. J. Bus. Excell. **10**(3), 354–391 (2016)
41. Choubey, S., Bhargava, A.: Significance of ISO/IEC 27001 in the implementation of governance, risk and compliance. Int. J. Sci. Res. Netw. Secur. Commun. **6**(2), 30–33 (2018)
42. Elbanna, A., Sarker, S.: The risks of agile software development: learning from adopters. IEEE Softw. **33**(5), 72–79 (2016)
43. Roumani, Y., Nwankpa, J.K., Roumani, Y.F.: Adopters' trust in enterprise open source vendors: an empirical examination. J. Syst. Softw. **125**, 256–270 (2017)
44. Panda, P.S.: Implementation of Information Security Management System (ISMS) aligned with ISO 27001. Int. J. Res. Appl. Sci. Eng. Technol. **7**(5), 218–227 (2019)
45. Makupi, D., Masese, N.: Determining Information Security Maturity Level of an organization based on ISO 27001. Int. J. Comput. Sci. Eng. **6**(7), 5–11 (2019)

Performance Optimization of Layered Signature Based Intrusion Detection System Using Snort

Noor Farjana Firoz, Md. Taslim Arefin(✉), and Md. Raihan Uddin

Department of ETE, Daffodil International University, Dhaka 1207, Bangladesh
noorfarjana01@gmail.com, arefin@diu.edu.bd, mkraihan13@gmail.com

Abstract. Intrusion Detection System (IDS) is used to protect a system or a computer network from different kinds of anomaly attacks. Different detection techniques have been discussed on network-based IDS. The study has been done on the operational procedures of network based open source IDS tool Snort based intrusion detection system, which can read every incoming or outgoing packet through a network and alert the admin accordingly. In this paper, Different types of IDS are compared and criticized which explores the vulnerability of the system. To check every packet, Snort uses a central database system of signature. A layered database system has been proposed to upgrade system performance. An analytical operation has been conveyed on the proposed solution and compared with the existing standard system. After applying the proposed solution the number of packets analyzed rate has been increasing remarkably from 86% to 98%.

Keywords: Snort · IDS · Signature based IDS · Intrusion · Detection

1 Introduction

The intrusion detection system monitors various networks and systems for network packets, rootkit analysis, intrusions, or even analyze system logs and reports to the main server or keeps a record in a machine. It may be a hardware or/and software solution. The system always looks on network and system for various attacks [8] (i.e. Scanning Attack, DoS Attack, and Penetration Attack). Apart from the Intrusion Detection System, a firewall can also be used, but firewalls are not dynamic. They follow some simple rules to allow or deny protocols, IPs or requests. On the other hand, IDS is used to deal with complex attacks, it's a dynamic system as well as update while required [1]. The basic diagram of the IDS is shown in Fig. 1. IDS can be differentiated into two categories such as Network based IDS (NIDS) and Host based IDS. NIDS works by analyzing network traffic and make decision based on the severity of the attack, either inform the administrator or block the source IP. There are open-source tools for NIDS which work on different logic to identify as well as prevent the network from

T. Bhuiyan et al. (Eds.): ICONCS 2020, LNICST 325, pp. 14–27, 2020.
https://doi.org/10.1007/978-3-030-52856-0_2

intrusion. In this paper, the operating procedure of open source NIDS Snort has been discussed. A Simple NIDS based Network Architecture is shown in Fig. 2. There are two main techniques on which NIDS works. One is Signature based NIDS and another is Anomaly based NIDS. In this paper, a layered signature based NIDS has been proposed and evaluated. Network based IDS works on two techniques.

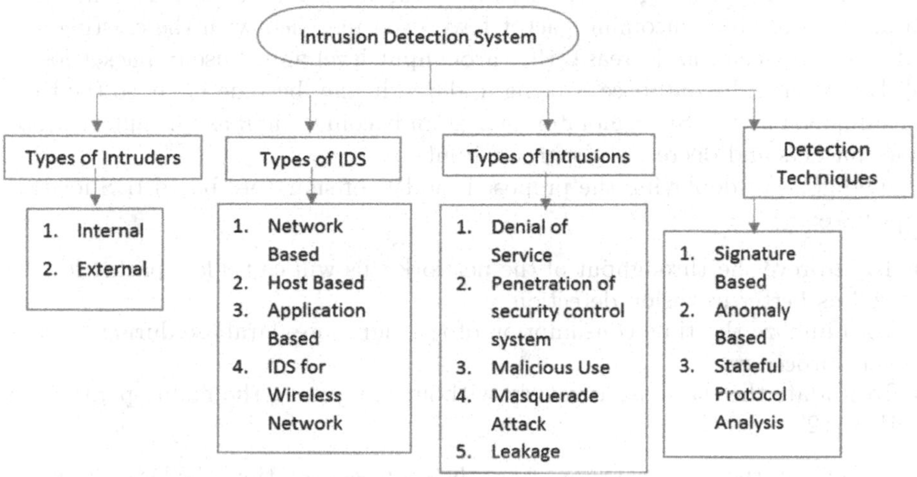

Fig. 1. Basic diagram of Intrusion Detection System.

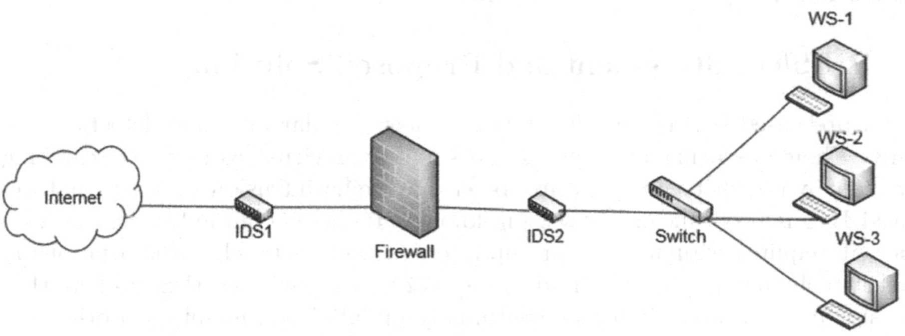

Fig. 2. Simple NIDS based Network Architecture.

The very well-known and popular method is pattern matching, which means "signature" based and "misuse" or anomaly based detection. Signature is nothing but a known pattern of strings or characters in the payload section of a packet. For this type of detection system, normal traffic knowledge is not required but a signature database is essential [2]. Signature based IDS works on the known pattern of attacks. The sensor looks for traffic that matches the pattern of known attacks. The effectiveness depends on the database where the pattern has been stored. The analogy is simple, it's like you know the fingerprint of a predefined criminal and match it at the crime scene whether the known criminal is involved or not. Now the main problem with this fingerprint analysis is, it fails to identify new attacks if it's not a defined signature in its database. Both, signature based and anomaly based system have their limitations which make none better than others. A typical signature based IDS maintains a large database where the parameters of every incoming packet have been matched with the existing signatures. The scenario decreases the throughput level and cause of packet losses [3]. Every time the database is being updated it may become large, so the time consumption by the SIDS monitoring system becomes high, as a result, it drops more packets and decreases the throughput.

The goals of deploying the proposed models of signature based IDS for this paper are:

- To improve the throughput of the network this will cause less packet loss as well as better intrusion detection.
- To minimize the time consumption of the signature database during the update procedure.
- To update the database regularly without hampering the main operation of IDS [12].

To achieve the expected result from the proposed solution, the large database of the signatures has been broken in parts after analyzing the network traffic flow. The small databases are connected to a central system that maintains the due time up-gradation and the small databases replicate the deployed parts without hampering the operation of the system.

2 Problem Statement and Proposed Solution

Signature-based IDS is considered as the most popular intrusion detection systems. Their operating principle is the same as a virus scanner, by searching for a known identity or signature for each specific intrusion event. Signature-based IDS is very efficient at sensing known attacks like an anti-virus software does, it requires regular signature updates, to keep in touch with variations in hacker technique [4]. So the disadvantages of Signature based IDS lies here that the signature database must be continually updated and maintained otherwise Signature based IDS may fail to identify unique attacks. But the continuous update may cause a regular increase of the database, which may force the system to compare the packets with lots of signatures that lead to packet loss, poor throughput, and vulnerable service [13].

2.1 Proposed Model

As it was stated that a large signature database may lead to several vulnerabilities. The below given Fig. 3 shows the block diagram of the existing standard intrusion detection system using Snort, where there is only one master signature database which resides with the sensor and matches every in/out packets to and from the local network. If the signature database can be layered, then the packets need to be matched with less number of signatures that will decrease the computational time. Moreover, in the layered system, the mostly occurred pattern may prioritize, like if the system communicates via specific protocols then the admin can generate the signature database by activating or writing or customizing the relevant rules only and the other less occurred attack may place in another database, based on position and priority.

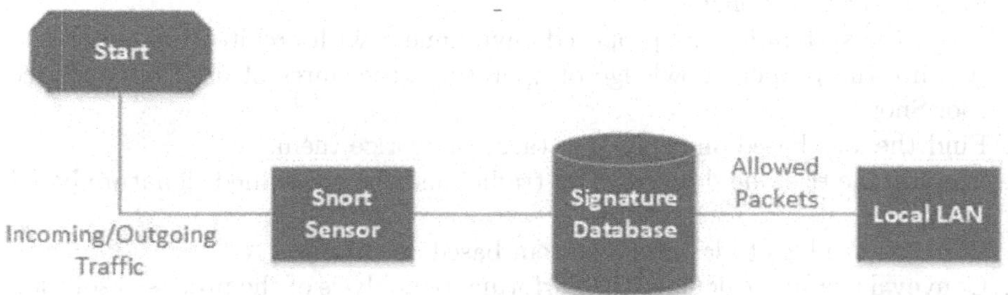

Fig. 3. Network traffic flow diagram through signature based IDS.

This proposed system shown in Fig. 4, at first, a test phase has been run to trace the regular pattern of traffic. After analyzing the logged traffic, the mostly occurred attack patterns have been classified from other minor attacks. Then the system has been layered base on the analysis. The performance has been measured and com-pared to ensure a step up and a better security system.

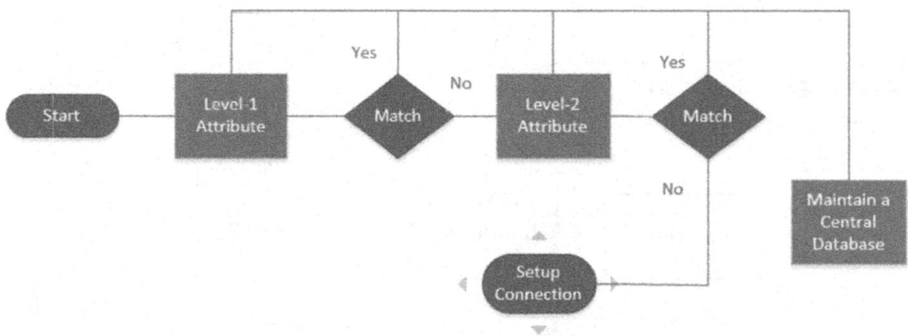

Fig. 4. Network traffic flow diagram through proposed layered signature based IDS.

2.2 Work Flow

The workflow of this research initiated with various literature reviews related to the topic. More than 25 scholarly articles and paper works have been reviewed which have the discussion and research work on anomaly based IDS, signature based IDS, different open source tools, different architectural models, different types of attacks, etc.

The workflow is given below:

1. Conduct literature and article searches on data breaches and a different security system.
2. Making the IDS policy.
3. Setup the system for the proposed environment with architecture analysis.
4. Acquire the proper knowledge of operating procedures of used open source tool Snort.
5. Find the logs based on types of attack, categorize them.
6. Prepare the training data (normal traffic) and the predefined signature based database.
7. Work on the logs to layer the system based on priority
8. Convey a test and calculate the performance analysis of the proposed solution model.
9. Compare the result with the existing default model.

3 Configuring SNORT

Snort is an open source IDS that can do real time traffic analysis of the data flow in the network. It detects the attack pattern depending on the rules written by the admin. This kind of method has some obligations, such as it won't able to detect any unknown pattern. But, as Snort can analyze packet in real time, the obligation has overcome in most of the cases.

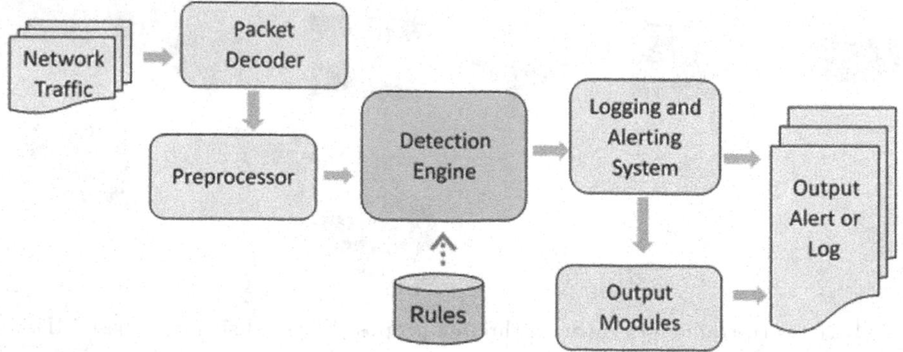

Fig. 5. SNORT data flow.

Snort monitor the network performance, if there is any degradation due to any traffic pattern then it discards the packets. [14] We can think Snort as a combination of different components as shown in Fig. 5. Depending on this component it takes the necessary action against an attack [5]. Firstly, packets from different network interfaces are collected by Packet and are sent to the next level (pre processor or detection engine). Snort must decode the particular protocol elements for each packet. Here a series of decoders are used where everyone is decoded with specific protocol elements. A packet follows the below given data flow as it moves through the packet decoder [9]. Snort decoder always makes sure that all packets are assembled according to the specification by looking into the structure of each packet. If any packet has been found with unusual settings, size or options, the decoder will generate an alert [10]. The flow of packets through the Snort Decoder is shown in Fig. 6.

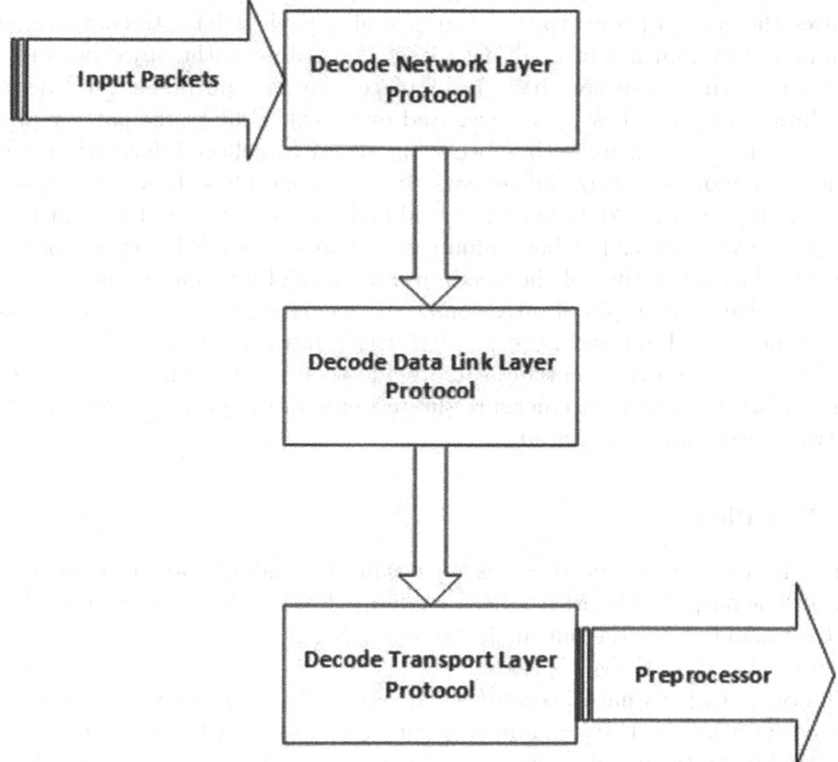

Fig. 6. Flow of packets through Snort decoder.

If the admin is not concerned about these alerts or it generates a large number of false positives which is not expected, then the generated alert can be disabled by customizing the snort.conf file. By default, all such alerts are enabled.

To disable a particular type of alert, remove the comment character (*) at the beginning of the line. The Snort decoder configuration options are [10]:

config disable-decode-alerts
config disable-tcpopt-experimental-alerts
config disable-tcpopt-alerts
config disable-tcpopt-obsolete-alerts
config disable-tcpopt-ttcp-alerts
config disable-ipopt-alerts

4 Simulation and Analysis

The system proposed in this paper is motivated by the fact that it is easy, less time consuming and more efficient to update small signature databases compare to update large signature database continuously from time to time. The efficiency increases the system throughput as the incoming packets have to compare with less number of signatures in small databases. According to the objective and the network pattern two sensors have been placed for test purposes. And here in this solution, the data-base has segregated by checking the traffic pattern of the system. At first, a test phase has been conducted to collect information about the most common threats of the network. In the second phase based on the usage patterns, the signature databases are updated. In this proposed system traffic pattern to a web server has been monitored from few hours to several days, in weekends, during the time of the maximum number of hits and off pick hours to make sure that what types of intrusions have occurred to the web server. Based on this report the database of the very 1st sensor has been updated by activated the rules against mostly occurring threats and then few tools have been used to make test intrusion traffic to measure the response of the proposed system. Here only two sensors have been used.

4.1 Test Phase

During the test phase, the IDS has been run in standard form to capture the packets. The output of Snort has been configured to log the alerts in several text files. Command to log the output in txt mode is

- snort -l C: Snort log - L test1

The output alerts have been logged to a text file named test1.txt, which is analyzed later by the network analyzer software "Wireshark" shown in Fig. 8.

According to traffic analysis, the maximum probable number of attacks has been figured out. The Types of attack occurred during the test period have been classified and given below:

ICMP Tunneling: Between client and server an ICMP channel is established which forces a firewall not to generate any alarm if data are sent via ICMP [11]. In a normal ICMP echo request, the packet length is 42 bytes, where the data length is 0, and if we append any data into the ICMP data field then the size

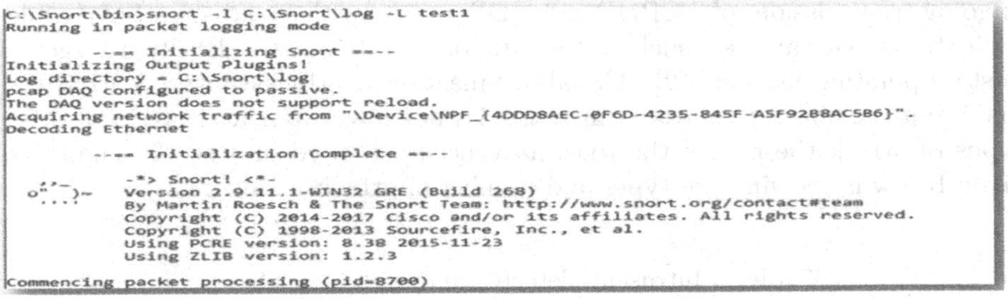

```
C:\Snort\bin>snort -l C:\Snort\log -L test1
Running in packet logging mode

        --== Initializing Snort ==--
Initializing Output Plugins!
Log directory = C:\Snort\log
pcap DAQ configured to passive.
The DAQ version does not support reload.
Acquiring network traffic from "\Device\NPF_{4DDD8AEC-0F6D-4235-845F-A5F92B8AC5B6}".
Decoding Ethernet

        --== Initialization Complete ==--

   ,,_     -*> Snort! <*-
  o"  )~   Version 2.9.11.1-WIN32 GRE (Build 268)
   ''''    By Martin Roesch & The Snort Team: http://www.snort.org/contact#team
           Copyright (C) 2014-2017 Cisco and/or its affiliates. All rights reserved.
           Copyright (C) 1998-2013 Sourcefire, Inc., et al.
           Using PCRE version: 8.38 2015-11-23
           Using ZLIB version: 1.2.3

Commencing packet processing (pid=8700)
```

Fig. 7. Test Traffic logging in text mode.

of the packet increases [6]. So to detect ICMP tunneling using Snort a rule has been written or activated stating that if any data is present in the data header of the ICMP, then fire an alert.

DoS Attack: DoS is a malicious attempt to make a service unavailable to the users. It is different from DDoS in a way that DDoS attacks occur by using a distributed ser-vice whereas DoS occurs from a specific source. In DoS a single Internet-connected device to flood a target with malicious traffic [7]. During the test phase, SYN flood packets have been detected which may cause the total bandwidth occupied [15] (Fig. 7).

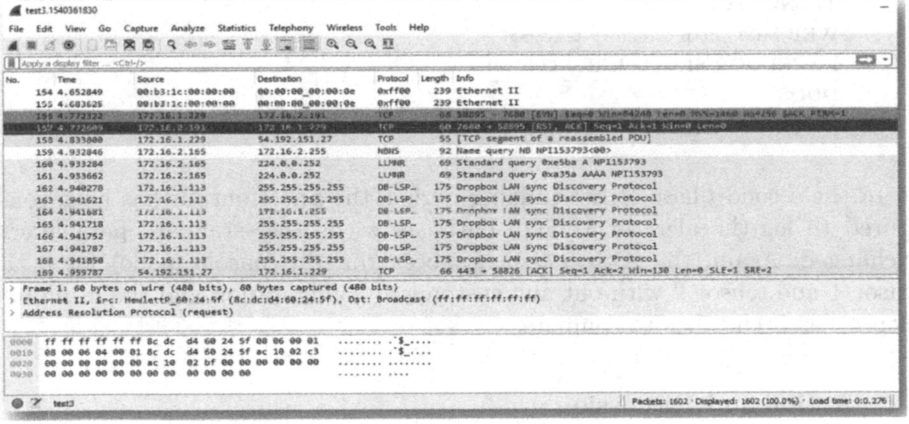

Fig. 8. Test traffic analyzing with a network analyzer (Wireshark).

Web CGI-Way Board: Way-board CGI program allows remote attackers to read arbitrary files by specifying the filename in the DB parameter and terminating the filename with a null byte. TCP/IP and UDP Network with source Port of 0: Port 0 is used for requesting system-allocated, dynamic ports. So, any malformed TCP/IP and UDP network traffic may have a source port of 0. This type of ongoing transmissions of TCP/IP and UDP packets with a source port of 0 could indicate ongoing attacks, such as spoofing or an attempt to identify a targeted host's operating system [12]. The above-mentioned attacks have occurred the maximum number of times, so in sensor1 rules have been activated for these types of attack the rest of the rules have been activated in sensor2. The table given below is showing the types and number of attacks (Table. 1):

Table 1. Intrusions detected during the test phase.

Signature name	Number of occurrences
FTP command overflow attempt	120
http_inspect	20
(http_inspect) WEB ROOT DIRECTORY TRAVERSAL	39
UDP Portscan	12
(spp_rpc_decode) Incomplete RPC segment	89
Invalid UDP header, length field	2197
TTL Limit Exceeded (reassemble) detection	8
SNMP request UDP	40
BAD-TRAFFIC (UDP port 0 traffic)	896
ICMP Destination Unreachable Communication	18
BAD-TRAFFIC TCP port 0 traffic	75
Administratively Prohibited	21
BACKDOOR Q access	26
ICMP Echo Reply	789
TELNET SGI	32
WEB-MISC http directory traversal	29
BACKDOOR SIGNATURE - Q ICMP	28
DDOS	29

In the second phase of the training period, the Snort output has been configured to log the alert in MySQL database with other standard parameters unchanged. Again, the IDS system has been run (in console mode) for both sensor 1 and sensor 2 with-out any customized configuration and the resultant output has been taken to compare.

4.2 Action and Discussion

During the training period, the threat was taken, happened most frequently. So, after completing the training period the Signature rules for those types of intrusion have been dump in a single rules file named local Rule, and these rules are activated in sensor 1. Whereas the other classifications (of rules for web service) have been activated in the second sensor, Sensor 2. To make the frequency level of intrusion high, few tools have been used and the operational phase has been run around 2 h and 27 min.

The result of the proposed system is stated in the below given table:

Table 2. Results before and after application of the proposed system

Test phase (All rules enabled)	Most frequent signature enabled in Sensor 1
Packet received: 520136	Packet received: 555267
Packet analyzed: 450612	Packet analyzed: 548120
Packet dropped: 20124	Packet dropped: 1209
Percentage of packet drop: 1.580%	Percentage of packet drop: 0.220%

Test-1: Command prompt Output – Test Phase (All Rules Enabled)

```
Select C:\WINDOWS\system32\cmd.exe
===============================================================================
Run time for packet processing was 8860.958000 seconds
Snort processed 450612 packets.
Snort ran for 0 days 2 hours 27 minutes 40 seconds
   Pkts/hr:        198158
  Pkts/min:          3057
  Pkts/sec:            53
===============================================================================
Packet I/O Totals:
  Received:        520136
  Analyzed:        450612 ( 86.633%)
   Dropped:         20124 (  4.465%)
```

Command prompt Output – Most Frequent Signature Enabled

```
Select C:\WINDOWS\system32\cmd.exe
===============================================================================
Run time for packet processing was 8860.958000 seconds
Snort processed 548120 packets.
Snort ran for 0 days 2 hours 27 minutes 40 seconds
   Pkts/hr:        274060
  Pkts/min:          3728
  Pkts/sec:            61
===============================================================================
Packet I/O Totals:
  Received:        555267
  Analyzed:        548120 ( 98.713%)
   Dropped:          1209 (  0.220%)
```

Table 2 shows that after applying the proposed solution the number of packets analyzed rate has been increasing remarkably from 86% to 98%, thus the packet received rate also increases and the percentage of packets drops has been decreased to almost 0% from 4% which leads to increase the overall system throughput.

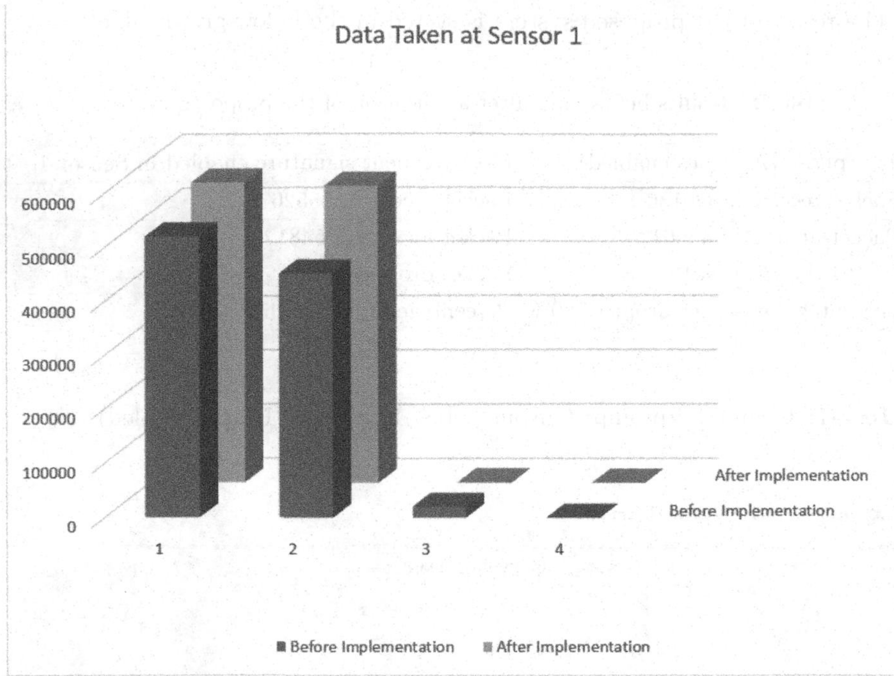

Fig. 9. Performance graph for SNORT layered DB solution (at Sensor-1). (Color figure online)

The results have been plotted in Fig. 9 to make some comparisons. Here the blue bar shows the parameters achieved in test phase with all rules enabled in sensor 1 and the orange bar shows the parameters achieved after implementation of the pro-posed solution. Y-axis represents the number of packets.

Test-2: The second phase has been conveyed by monitoring the 2nd sensor where the rest of rules have been enabled.

Table 3. Results before and after application of the proposed system

Test phase (All rules enabled)	Most frequent signature enabled in Sensor 2
Packet received: 320456	Packet received: 380864
Packet analyzed: 230591	Packet analyzed: 379932
Packet dropped: 89865	Packet dropped: 932
Percentage of packet drop: 28.042%	Percentage of packet drop: 0.245%

Command prompt Output – Test Phase (All Rules Enabled)

```
===============================================================================
Run time for packet processing was 4430.197000 seconds
Snort processed 230591 packets.
Snort ran for 0 days 1 hours 13 minutes 50 seconds
    Pkts/hr:         230591
   Pkts/min:           3158
   Pkts/sec:             52
===============================================================================
Packet I/O Totals:
   Received:         320456
   Analyzed:         230591 ( 71.957%)
    Dropped:          89865 ( 28.042%)
```

Command prompt Output – Other Signatures (except most frequent) Enabled

```
===============================================================================
Run time for packet processing was 4430.167000 seconds
Snort processed 379932 packets.
Snort ran for 0 days 1 hours 13 minutes 20 seconds
    Pkts/hr:         379932
   Pkts/min:           5197
   Pkts/sec:             86
===============================================================================
Packet I/O Totals:
   Received:         380864
   Analyzed:         379932 ( 99.755%)
    Dropped:            932 (  0.245%)
```

Table 3 shows that in second sensor the resulting output comes in the same manner and even better where the other signatures (except the most frequent) have been applied, thus the packet received rate also increase and the percentage of packets drops has been decreased which leads to increase the overall system throughput as like as we observed in sensor 1. The percentage of analyzed packets has been increased from 719% to 99% that's why the packet drop fall to almost 0% from 28%.

The resultant parameters have been plotted in Fig. 10 where the Y-axis represents the number of packets and the X-axis represents nothing but the number of parameters taken to compare the outcomes.

The central database mentioned earlier (Fig. 3) has been updated when the SNORT update available there. Then the sensor databases have been updated accordingly (for activated rules only) by running a cron script at a specific time of the day. In such a manner the time consumption of updating the large signature database has been saved. And the admin can run the cron script at

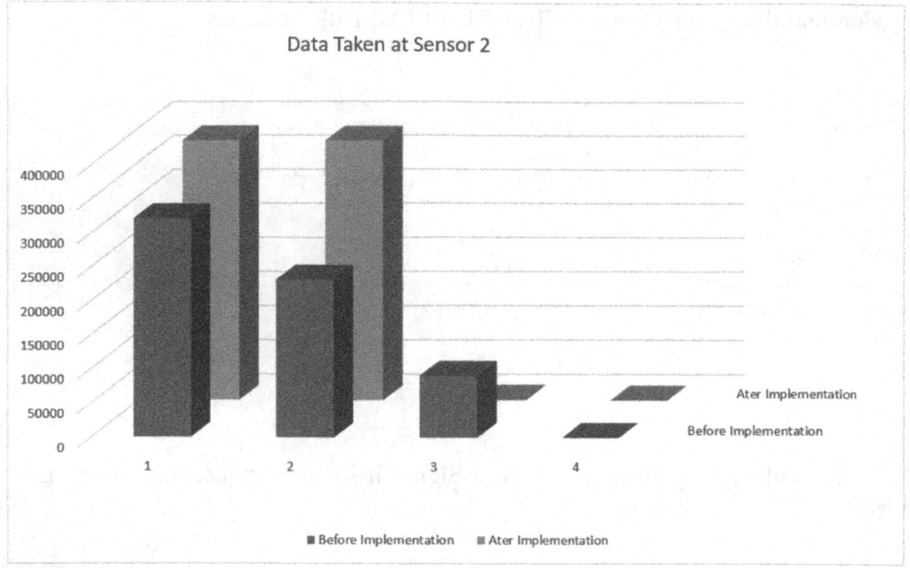

Fig. 10. Performance graph for SNORT layered DB solution (at Sensor-2).

any preferable time (off-peak) to update the sensors small signature databases without hampering the core operation.

5 Conclusion

The proposed architecture is nothing but a slight change in implementation which improves the overall system throughput remarkably. The sensors are being used does not need very high-end configuration so the implementation cost may have compromised. There are many more solutions working on increasing system throughput and decreasing operational time. Here in this system, the central database has been managed for a proper update without hampering the core operation, which may also be used for updating anomaly based IDS if the admin prefers to use any hybrid solution for further development. Every system has vulnerabilities and scope for further progress and research. Though the proposed model increases the system efficiency it is important in any environment to know what types of threats we might be facing in a very frequent manner as intruders always improving their techniques. So, the test phase should be done in a regular basis to activate the appropriate rules in the appropriate sensor. The proposed system can be improved by implementing dynamic updated of every small signature database of the system, which will dynamically update, add or remove the signatures in a regular manner. There are scopes of work to improve the training period traffic analysis (test phase) and multiple IDS database updated procedure of the proposed system.

References

1. Gigatux. Chapter-5-Section-3. http://books.gigatux.nl/mirror/snortids/0596006616/snortids-CHP-5-SECT-3.html. Accessed Apr 2019
2. Uddin, M., Rahman, A.A.: Dynamic multi-layer signature-based intrusion detection system using mobile agents. arXiv preprint arXiv:1010.5036 (2010)
3. Bronte, R. N.: A framework for hybrid intrusion detection systems (2016)
4. Uddin, M., Rahman, A.A., Uddin, N., Memon, J., Alsaqour, R.A., Kazi, S.: Signature base multilayer IDS sytem using mobile agent. Int. J. Netw. Secur. **15**(1), 79–87 (2013)
5. Uddin, M., Rahman, A.A., Uddin, N., Memon, J., Alsaqour, R.A., Kazi, S.: Signature-based multi-layer distributed intrusion detection system using mobile agents. Int. J. Netw. Secur. **15**(2), 97–105 (2013)
6. Cepheli, Ö., Büyükçorak, S., Karabulut Kurt, G.: Hybrid intrusion detection system for DDoS attacks. J. Electr. Comput. Eng. **2016** (2016). 8 pages
7. "Snort Resource Page" Cited on April, 2019. https://www.adrew.cmu.edu/user/rdanyliw/snort. Accessed 20 Oct 2019
8. Singh, A.P., Singh, M.D.: Analysis of host-based and network-based in-trusion detection system. Int. J. Comput. Netw. Inf. Secur. **8**, 41–47 (2014)
9. Koziol, J.: Intrusion Detection with Snort. Sams Publishing, Indianapolis (2003)
10. Cox, K.J., Gerg, C.: Managing Security with Snort & IDS Tools: Intrusion Detection with Open Source Tools. O'Reilly Media Inc., Sebastapol (2004)
11. Mazerik, R.: ICMP attacks in web servers: Infosec Institute web resource USA. https://resources.infosecinstitute.com/icmp-attacks/?cv=1. Accessed 23 Oct 2019
12. Greene, B. R., Smith, P.: Cisco ISP essentials. Cisco Press. https://resources.infosecinstitute.com/icmp-attacks/?cv=1. Accessed 23 Oct 2019
13. Ajeena, R.K.K., Yaqoob, S.J.: The integer sub-decomposition method to improve the elliptic ElGamal digital signature algorithm. In: 2017 International Conference on Current Research in Computer Science and Information Technology (ICCIT), pp. 14–20. IEEE (2017)
14. Baldi, M., et al.: Design and implementation of a digital signature scheme based on low-density generator matrix codes. arXiv preprint arXiv:1807.06127 (2018)
15. Gaddam, R., Nandhini, M.: An analysis of various snort based techniques to detect and prevent intrusions in networks proposal with code refactoring snort tool in Kali Linux environment. In: 2017 International Conference on Inventive Communication and Computational Technologies (ICICCT), pp. 10–15. IEEE (2017)

Designing a New Hybrid Cryptographic Model

Burhan Selçuk(✉) and Ayşe Nur A. Tanküll

Karabuk University, 78050 Karabük, Turkey
bselcuk@karabuk.edu.tr

Abstract. With the rapid development of technology, one of the most important requirements in today's systems is the reliable transfer of information and confidentiality. Thus, military, electronics, banking systems and many other places have become the fields of use of cryptography science. Cryptology methods are used to solve these problems and need of secure information transfer resulted in the development of reliable encryption techniques. In this study, a new poly-alphabetic substitution cipher is designed using the coordinate axes. The proposed method of a hybrid encryption method is a mix of the Polybius square cipher and the Vigenère cipher, reinforced with the RSA cryptography algorithm. For each letter in the alphabet, there is more than one point on Cartesian coordinate system and in the calculation of these points random chosen values are used. Values used to calculate alphabet and start index of alphabet are send to receiver using RSA algorithm with cipher text. So, with multiple security stages the proposed method is a strong encryption method that is difficult to decode.

Keywords: Poly-alphabetic substitution cipher · Vigenère cipher · Polybius square cipher · RSA · Coordinate axis

1 Introduction

Cryptology is a set of techniques and applications based on mathematically challenging problems that enable communicating parties to exchange information securely. The science of cryptology has two main sub-branches called cryptography and cryptanalysis. Cryptography investigates the methods used to encrypt and decrypt documents; cryptoanalysis examines the mechanisms established by crypto logical systems and tries to find unknown keys [1–3].

In terms of key encryption, there are two categories for cryptography, symmetric and asymmetric cryptography. The main difference between these two encryption methods is the use of a key in the encryption algorithm. While symmetric encryption algorithms use the same key for both encryption and decryption, an asymmetric encryption algorithm, by contrast, uses another key to decrypt a key to encrypt data. In asymmetric systems, the key used for encryption is known as the public key and can be easily shared with other people. On the other hand, the key used for decryption is a private key and must be kept confidential [4]. Although such a difference is seemingly simple, it determines

T. Bhuiyan et al. (Eds.): ICONCS 2020, LNICST 325, pp. 28–42, 2020.
https://doi.org/10.1007/978-3-030-52856-0_3

the functional differences between the two cryptographic techniques and how they are used.

Advanced Encryption Standards (AES) and Data Encryption Standards (DES) are examples of symmetric key cryptography. DES was accepted as a standard by the National Institute of Standards and Technology (NIST) in 1977 and published as the Federal Information Processing Standards (FIPS) [5]. DES is an example of block encryption. In other words, by simply splitting a plaintext into pieces (blocks), it encrypts each part independently and performs the same operation on blocks to open a ciphertext. The length of these blocks is 64 bits. DES also receives a 64-bit key. However, the valid length of this key is 56 bits because it is spent on an 8-bit parity. DES algorithm has been used as a standard for many years, but in 2001 AES is announced by the NIST as a new standard. The basis of the emergence of AES is that DES encryption algorithm is vulnerable to attacks. AES algorithm is a block cipher algorithm that encrypts 128-bit data blocks with 128, 192 or 256-bit key options [6]. The difference between the key length bit numbers changes the number of AES tour cycles. This algorithm is more efficient both in software and hardware implementations.

RSA and Elliptical Curve Cryptography (ECC) are an asymmetric block coder used to encrypt and decrypt information. In 1977, Ron Rivest, Adi Shamir and Leonard Aldeman [7] developed the RSA algorithm and used the initials of the surnames as the name of the algorithm. The RSA logic is based on the fact that it is more difficult to factor an integer than to find it by multiplying new integers. The base value is obtained by multiplying the two sufficiently large prime numbers. Other key parameters are derived from the same two prime numbers [8]. For ECC, to find the discrete logarithm of a randomly chosen element of an elliptic curve by using a known point is not feasible [9]. The problem difficulty is determined by the elliptic curve size.

In cryptography, a hash function is a branch like encryption. The difference of a hash function from encryption is that a hash function does not use a key to do the encoding as it does for encryption. A hash function maps plaintext with different sizes into a sequence of bits of a certain length, a fixed-length hash value also called a hash code. For hashing, any change in the data changes the hash value [10]. There are many types of hash algorithms. Message Digest 5 (MD5) and Secure Hash Algorithm (SHA) algorithms are the most commonly used cryptographic hash algorithms. MD5 was proposed by Ron Rivest in 1991 [11]. This algorithm takes an input and gives a 128 bits output in a digest form. Input processed in 512 bits block size which is divided into 16 subblocks with the size of 32 bits. SHA was first announced by the NIST in 1993, and the algorithm was modified to improve security in 1995 is called SHA1. In 2001, SHA2 was proposed which is the revised version of SHA1. SHA2 is more powerful against attacks and can be used with larger data entries [12]. The SHA-2 hash function is used in some common security applications and protocols, such as TLS and SSL, PGP, SSH, S/MIME, and IPsec. It is also used in digital signature and crypto money such as bitcoin.

In this study, we focus to improve our previous work [13]. Section 2 provides information about poly-alphabetic substitution cipher. Section 3 introduces star coordinates that form coordinates on axis and their properties are examined. In Sect. 4, a new encryption model is designed using star coordinates. In Sect. 5, the developed application is explained, and examples to better understand the proposed encryption model. Finally, the results obtained in this study are examined.

2 Poly-Alphabetic Substitution Cipher

In Caesar and a substitution cipher, a key is first selected and then each character is mapped to a single character. These are good examples of a monoalphabetic cipher. The best example for substitution cipher is Polybius square cipher [14]. Let's give a simple example in Table 1;

Table 1. Polybius square cipher example

	1	2	3	4	5
1	a	b	c	d	e
2	f	g	h	i, j	k
3	l	m	n	o	p
4	q	r	s	t	u
5	v	w	x	y	z

In the above table, every number pairs denote one letter. Using the above matrix, if we use encryption operation on plaintext which is "thischannelisnotsafe", then we get ciphertext is {44, 23, 24, 43, 13, 23, 11, 33, 33, 15, 31, 24, 43, 33, 34, 44, 43, 11, 21, 15}.

The disadvantage of Cesar cipher is that it has a small key space. As for substitution cipher, even if the number of permutations is high, it is weak against statistical attack as in the case of a dictionary attack. To overcome the disadvantage of these two ciphers, the polyalphabetic substitution cipher approach has emerged as a powerful method of statistical attack with large key space.

Vigenère cipher is a good example. Every letter in English alphabet is denoted one number as 0, 1, …, 25, respectively. Let P is a plain text, C is a cipher text and K is key set. If plain text is given "thisexampleisaboutpolyalphabeticcipher" and key set K is given {2, 8, 15, 7, 4, 17}, the ciphertext is obtained as "vpxziocuesizuiqvykrwafecrppiikkkrpty" using the formula $C_i = P_i + K_{i\%m},\ i = 1, \ldots, 26,\ m = 6$. In this cipher, the same letter is replaced by another letter in different places. When the key sequence is finished, the encryption starts again. The length of the key is called the period of encryption.

In the matrix array symmetric key method, a two-dimensional array is initialized with plaintext character codes and manipulated using a 128-bit secret key to obtain the mapping process [15]. This method is fast in terms of working time and also reliable. With a 128-bit key, it is necessary to try 2^{128} different combinations to decrypt without a secret key in encryption, which takes centuries to solve. The Infinite Number of Alphabetical Tables method is another Polyalphabetic Substitution method [16]. This method is similar to the Vigenère cipher method. Differently, the key sequence is generated randomly and a new key sequence for encryption is generated when each key sequence is used. This method is more reliable and complex than the Vigenère method. The drawback of the method is the need to generate a large number of key sequences for a long text. In addition to monoalphabetic and polyalphabetic methods, the methods obtained by combining these two different methods are used for encryption. Vigenère cipher with Affine cipher method is a new method that the polyalphabetic Vigenère method and monoalphabetic Affine method have been combined to provide for better results [17]. Similarly, Vigenère and Caesar cipher methods have been used together for more secure encryption [18].

The proposed method is a polyalphabetic method and the motivation of this method is Polybius square cipher, Vigenère cipher and the RSA encryption algorithm. This hybrid method is a combination of Polybius square cipher and Vigenère cipher algorithm, and it is enhanced with the RSA encryption algorithm that strengthens the method against attacks.

3 Star Coordinates

In this section, we focus on a new sequence of numbers called star coordinates in XY coordinate axes. We descript the following algorithm to introduce star coordinates. Selcuk et al. studied the following algorithm in [13]. To increase randomness, they selected the first three steps as the RSA algorithm. Here, we will add operation mod$n$ and switch-case blocks and in step 4. Thus, we increase randomness as using inverse of the points according to mod$n$.

Algorithm 1. Construct of Star Coordinates

Step 1. Choose p and q randomly large two prime numbers,
Step 2. Compute $n = p * q$ and $\phi(n) = (p-1)(q-1)$,
Step 3. Choose at random e, $\gcd(e, \phi(n)) = 1$ where $1 < e < \phi(n)$,
Step 4. Divide an array with n elements into four parts

if $mod(n,4) = 1$, then
  $m = (n-1)/4$
  $n = [1, \ldots, m+1, -1, \ldots, -m, m+2, \ldots, 2m+1, -m-1, \ldots, -2m]$ mod$n$
  switch(select)
    case 1: // all positive
      $n = [1, \ldots, m+1, n-1, \ldots, n-m, m+2, \ldots, 2m+1, n-m-1, \ldots, n-2m]$
    case 2: // all negative
      $n = [-n+1, \ldots, -n+m+1, -1, \ldots, -m, -n+m+2, \ldots, -n+2m+1, -m-1, \ldots, -2m]$
    case 3: // reverse of original
      $n = [-n+1, \ldots, -n+m+1, n-1, \ldots, n-m, -n+m+2, \ldots, -n+2m+1, n-m-1, \ldots, n-2m]$
    case 4:
      default:

if $mod(n,4) = 3$, then
  $m = (n-3)/4$
  $n = [1, \ldots, m+1, -1, \ldots, -m-1, m+2, \ldots, 2m+2, -m-2, \ldots, -2m-1]$ mod$n$
  switch(select)
    case 1: // all positive
      $n = [1, \ldots, m+1, n-1, \ldots, n-m-1, m+2, \ldots, 2m+2, n-m-2, \ldots, n-2m-1]$
    case 2: // all negative
      $n = [-n+1, \ldots, -n+m+1, -1, \ldots, -m-1, -n+m+2, \ldots, -n+2m+2, -m-2, \ldots, -2m-1]$
    case 3: // reverse
      $n = [-n+1, \ldots, -n+m+1, n-1, \ldots, n-m-1, -n+m+2, \ldots, -n+2m+2, n-m-2, \ldots, n-2m-1]$
    case 4:
      default:

Step 5. Construct 2 dimensions array using n such that $\{n/e\} = \left[\begin{smallmatrix} n \\ n \end{smallmatrix}\right]$,
Step 6. In the {n/e} sequences, e step goes back from the end in the second column. We match the first element of the new line of arrays with first element in the first column, and then all points are matched.

Remark 1 (See [13]). In Table 2, we divide the array into four parts with n elements as step 4 in Algorithm 1. If we also reconstruct the Table 2 with different version of their parts, then we get Table 3;

Table 2. Division of the array into four parts with n elements

Cases	n value	Part I	Part II	Part III	Part IV
Case I	$n = 4m + 1$	$m + 1$	m	m	m
Case II	$n = 4m + 3$	$m + 1$	$m + 1$	$m + 1$	m

Table 3. Different version of Table 2

Cases	n value	Part I	Part II	Part III	Part IV
Case I	$n = 4m + 1$	m	m	m	$m + 1$
Case II	$n = 4m + 3$	m	$m + 1$	$m + 1$	$m + 1$

A total number of different versions of Table 2 is $C(4, 1).C(4, 3)$ i.e. 16. Indeed, Case I has four alternative separations, $C(4, 1)$, via new extra one element of an array with $n = 4m + 1$, and Case II has four alternative separations, $C(4, 3)$, via new extra three elements of an array with $n = 4m + 3$. If we divide the array into five parts with n elements as step 4 in Algorithm 1, then we get a division simple in Table 4;

Table 4. Division of the array into five parts with n elements

Cases	n value	Part I	Part II	Part III	Part IV	Part V
Case I	$n = 5m$	m	m	m	m	m
Case II	$n = 5m + 1$	m	$m + 1$	m	m	m
Case III	$n = 5m + 2$	$m + 1$	$m + 1$	m	m	m
Case IV	$n = 5m + 3$	$m + 1$	$m + 1$	m	$m + 1$	m
Case V	$n = 5m + 4$	$m + 1$	m	$m + 1$	$m + 1$	$m + 1$

A total number of different versions of Table 4 is $C(5, 0).C(5, 1).C(5, 2).C(5, 3).C(5, 4)$ i.e. 2500. In fact, case 1 in Table 4 does not occur. Because, p and q were chosen as randomly large prime numbers in step 1 in Algorithm 1. Also, the result does not change from $C(5, 0) = 1$.

If we generalize and divide an array with n elements into l parts, then we get a total number of different versions is

$$\text{if } l \text{ is even, } C(l,1).C(l,3)\ldots C(l,l-1),$$
$$\text{if } l \text{ is odd, } C(l,0).C(l,1)\ldots C(l,l-1).$$

A general subroutine to calculate alternative cases of step 4 is given appendix in [13].

Remark 2. **(i)** As seen in Remark 1, our alternative number for the design of step 4 of algorithm 1 is quite high. Although this is a positive phenomenon, it has a disadvantage. If the algorithm 1 will be used in an encryption system, the sender and the receiver form step 4 with the same strategy. This, in fact, implies the existence of a secret key for this encryption system. It is very important to transmit the key to the other party through a secure channel. We cope with this difficulty in [13].

(ii) In algorithm 1, since the selection of parameters n and e is made with the RSA key generation subroutine;

- All selections and constraints for n and e are the same as for RSA,
- Runtime of algorithm 1 is equal to the number of points in star coordinates (n)
- Eliminates all possible situations for the selection of points on the coordinate axis.

Example 1. For ease of operation, we select $p = 7, q = 3$. Compute $n = pq = 21$ and $\phi(n) = 12$. We may select $e = 7$ sincc $\gcd(e, \phi(n)) = \gcd(7, 12) = 1$.

Let us find the star coordinates {21/7} and select = 4 using the Algorithm 1 as in Table 5;

Table 5. Star coordinates {21/7} of Example 1 with select = 4

X	1	2	3	4	5	6	−1	−2	−3	−4	−5	7	8	9	10	11	−6	−7	−8	−9	−10
Y	10	11	−6	−7	−8	−9	−10	1	2	3	4	5	6	−1	−2	−3	−4	−5	7	8	9

and

$$\{(1,10),(2,11),(3,-6),(4,-7),(5,-8),(6,-9),(-1,-10),(-2,1),(-3,2),(-4,3),(-5,4)$$
$$(7,5),(8,6),(9,-1),(10,-2),(11,-3),(-6,-4),(-7,-5),(-8,7),(-9,8),(-10,9)\}$$

where $n = 21$ satisfies the Case I in Table 2.

Let us find the star coordinates {21/7} and select = 1 using the Algorithm 1 as in Table 6;

Table 6. Star coordinates {21/7} of Example 1 with select = 1

X	1	2	3	4	5	6	20	19	18	17	16	7	8	9	10	11	15	14	13	12	11
Y	10	11	15	14	13	12	11	1	2	3	4	5	6	20	19	18	17	16	7	8	9

and

$\{(1, 10), (2, 11), (3, 15), (4, 14), (5, 13), (6, 12), (20, 11), (19, 1), (18, 2), (17, 3), (16, 4)$
$(7, 5), (8, 6), (9, 20), (10, 19), (11, 18), (15, 17), (14, 16), (13, 7), (12, 8), (11, 9)\}$

where $n = 21$ satisfies the Case I in Table 2.

4 A New Model

In this section, new poly-alphabet cipher method has been developed by using star coordinates obtained from the Algorithm 1. Since the same letter is represented by a different coordinate in different places, a powerful method against statistical attacks is presented.

Example 2. We let the alphabet $\Omega = \{A, C, D, E, K, L, P, R, T, Y\}$ and follow alphabetical order for simplicity. Using the alphabet Ω, the star coordinates of the $\{21/7\}$, (19, 1) initial coordinate, and initial letter is E and select parameter is 1, encrypt the following words;

(a) "CYPERATTACK" and (b) "ACYPERATTACKDETECTED".
In Example 1, if we place the letters of the alphabet in the star coordinates of the $\{21/7\}$, we obtained as in Table 7;

Table 7. Star coordinates $\{21/7\}$ of Example 1 with select = 1 and assigned letters

X	1	2	3	4	5	6	20	19	18	17	16	7	8	9	10	11	15	14	13	12	11
Y	10	11	15	14	13	12	11	1	2	3	4	5	6	20	19	18	17	16	7	8	9
Letter	Y	T	R	P	L	K	E	E	K	L	P	R	T	Y	A	C	D	E	D	C	A

Let z be the quotient of $sn/(s(\Omega))$ and $r = n - s(\Omega)z$. Number of repetitions of the alphabet and number of elements remaining is found as $z = 2$ and $r = 2$, respectively, where $n = 21$ and $s(\Omega) = 10$. The alphabet repeats exactly 2 times and the rest of the 1 element, E, continue to repeat operations. Thus, the first element in the alphabet repeats 3 times, the remaining 9 elements repeats 2 times.

(a) If we encrypt the word "CYPERATTACK" using the alphabet Ω, we get;
"$C_1Y_1P_1E_1R_1A_1T_1T_2A_2C_2K_1$"

$(11, 18), (9, 20), (16, 4), (19, 1), (7, 5), (10, 19), (8, 6), (2, 11), (11, 9), (12, 8), (18, 2)$

(b) If we encrypt the word "ACYPERATTACKDETECTED" using the alphabet Ω, we get;
"$A_1C_1Y_1P_1E_1R_1A_2T_1T_2A_1C_2K_1D_1E_2T_1E_3C_1T_2E_1D_2$"

$(10, 19), (11, 18), (9, 20), (16, 4), (19, 1), (7, 5), (11, 9), (8, 6), (2, 11), (10, 19), (12, 8),$
$(18, 2), (15, 17), (14, 16), (8, 6), (20, 11), (11, 18), (2, 11), (19, 1), (13, 7)$

See Fig. 1.

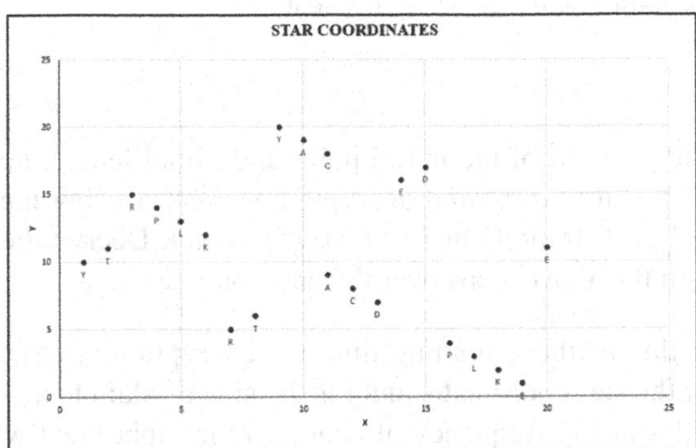

Fig. 1. Star coordinates in Example 2

4.1 Proposed Method

The star coordinates are found as mentioned in Algorithm 1, and any initial point is selected from these points. All letters in the alphabet are placed in sequence from the initial point [13]. Unlike [13], the alphabet will be assigned normally and reverse order in step 3 of encryption process in this paper.

I. Key Generation

Sender and receiver agree with Ω, p and q. Ω is the alphabet to be used for cipher. p and q are randomly large prime numbers.

II. Encryption

Step 1. Sender to calculate star coordinates puts p and q in Algorithm 1. Sender chooses a random e, it satisfies $\gcd(e, \phi(n)) = 1$ where $1 < e < \phi(n)$, and s^* is a select parameter for using step 4. Sender calculates star coordinates by following the other steps of the Algorithm 1.

Step 2. Sender chooses S and A are randomly parameters, which store the position of the initial coordinate (point) in the star coordinates and the position of the initial letter in the alphabet, respectively.

Step 3. Sender assigns alphabet letters to star coordinates. After the alphabet is finished, assignment of alphabet is started again in reverse order with same initial letter. This process is continued until n points are used (in the last round, the alphabet does not have to end completely). Let z be the quotient of $n/(s(\Omega))$. The alphabet repeats exactly z times, the rest of the r elements continue to repeat operations. Thus, an initial letter and if z is even, the first $r-1$ letter after the initial letter, if z is odd, the first $r-1$ letter before the initial letter in the alphabet repeats $z+1$ times, the remaining $s(\Omega) - r$ element repeats z times (see Example 2).

Step 4. The star coordinates of the letters of the text we will encrypt.

Step 5. Sender encrypts S, A and s^* using the RSA algorithm as $CS = S^e \text{mod} n$, $CA = A^e \text{mod} n$ and $cs^* = (s^*)^e \text{mod} n$. Sender transmits receiver $\{n, e, CS, CA, cs^*\}$ and the ciphertext. Sender's public keys are $\{n, e, CS, CA, cs^*\}$.

III. Decryption

A receiver to get the position of the initial point and initial letter calculates the secret key d such that $ed \equiv 1 \bmod \phi(n)$ and decrypts CS *and* CA using the RSA algorithm as $S = CS^d \text{mod} n$, $A = CA^d \text{mod} n$ and $s^* = (cs^*)^d \text{mod} n$. Decryption is performed in reverse order through the above steps over the encrypted text.

Remark 3. **(i)** For this method, running time for encryption is O(nt) where n is the number of points in the star coordinate, and t is the size of plain text.

(ii) For large values of n, frequency of characters in cipher text will be one. Since the runtime depends on n, the minimum value of n must be selected to get the frequency as 1 for each character. The minimum limit of n can be calculated as size of alphabet multiplied by the highest character frequency of plain text.

(iii) If the text to be encrypted is too long, the working time will be long accordingly. Therefore, several repetitions of the assigned points for some high frequency characters can be accepted for shorter run time and the method still remains secure.

(iv) For encryption and decryption, since symmetric encryption is used proposed method is a fast method.

(v) The key generation and key exchange is done with asymmetric encryption that ensures a high level of security.

The strengths of the two encryption methods were used in the proposed method.

5 Application

We developed an application that uses the star coordinates to encrypt and decrypt text with a given the alphabet. Using the MATLAB R2017_a program and a computer with 1.6 GHz Intel Core i5 processor, this application was developed.

In the application, 'n' is the number of star coordinates, 'e' and 'step' are the parameters to construct star coordinates, alphabet, initial letter in the alphabet, initial point of star coordinates and plaintext used for encryption are inputs in the encryption section. When the encryption process is finished, outputs will be seen on the screen which are the calculated star coordinates, the index of first letter used in the alphabet and the encrypted text. Also, on the XY coordinate plane, the star coordinates for with letters are shown in a new window. A star coordinate point is assigned to each letter in the resulting encrypted text. In Fig. 2, example of encryption on the application with parameters $n = 38$, $e = 3$, start index is 1, step is 4, initial letter is 'A', alphabet is $\Omega = \{$A, C, D, E, H, I, J, M, N, O, R, S, T$\}$ and plain text is 'COORDINATES' is shown.

In the application, in the decryption section inputs are 'n' the number of star coordinates, 'e' and 'step' parameters for construction of star coordinates, start index of alphabet on the star coordinates, the alphabet, initial letter in the alphabet and ciphertext to decrypt. The decrypted text and the calculated star coordinates are outputs. As

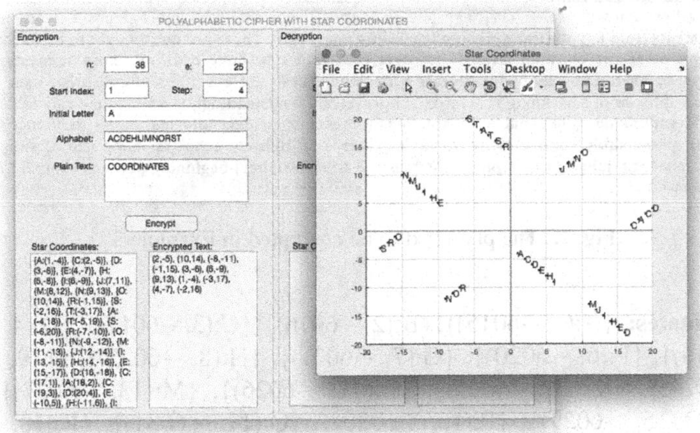

Fig. 2. The encryption operation on the application

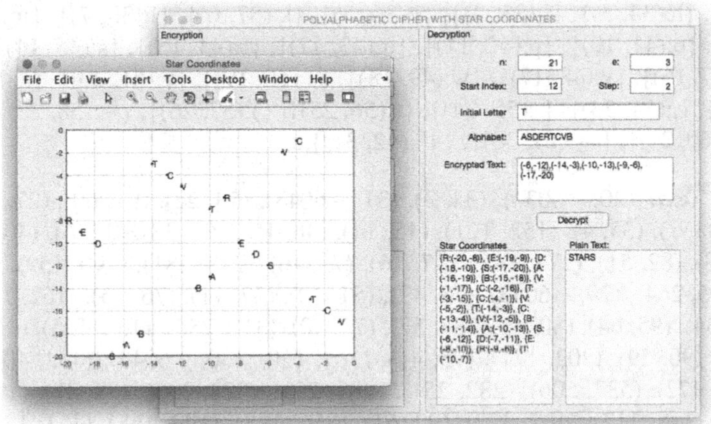

Fig. 3. The decryption operation on the application

in the encryption section, the star coordinates with alphabet characters are shown on XY axis in a new window. Figure 3 shows an example of decryption with parameters $n = 21, e = 3$, initial letter is 'T', start index is 12, step is 2, alphabet is $\Omega = \{$A, S, D, E, R, T, C, V, B$\}$ on the application and the resulted text is 'STARS'.

In practice, encryption and decryption are working separately. The encryption and decryption can be done with different alphabets and different parameter values.

Example 3. Encryption of the given text (Fig. 4) with values: p = 107, q = 113, n = 12091, e = 31, d = 383, r = 11872, step = 4, start index = 1, initial letter = A and Ω = {ABCDEFGHIJKLMNOPQRSTUVWXYZabcdefghijklmnopqrstuvwxyz,. ()-'+—}

The earliest known use of cryptography is found in non-standard hieroglyphs carved into monuments from Egypt's Old Kingdom (ca 4500+ years ago). These are not thought to be serious attempts at secret communications, however, but rather to have been attempts at mystery, intrigue, or even amusement for literate onlookers. These are examples of still other uses of cryptography, or of something that looks (impressively if misleadingly) like it. Some clay tablets from Mesopotamia, somewhat later are clearly meant to protect information — they encrypt recipes, presumably commercially valuable. Later still, Hebrew scholars made use of simple monoalphabetic substitution ciphers (such as the Atbash cipher) beginning perhaps around 500 to 600 BC.

Fig. 4. The plain text to be encrypted in Example 3

Star Coordinates: {A:(1, −6015)}, {B:(2, −6016)}, {C:(3, −6017)}, {D:(4, −6018)}, {E:(5, −6019)}, {F:(6, −6020)}, {G:(7, −6021)}, {H:(8, −6022)}, {I:(9, −6023)}, {J:(10, −6024)}, {K:(11, −6025)}, {L:(12, −6026)}, {M:(13, −6027)}, {N:(14, −6028)}, {O:(15, −6029)}, {P:(16, −6030)}, {Q:(17, −6031)}, {R:(18, −6032)}, {S:(19, −6033)}, {T:(20, −6034)}, {U:(21, −6035)}, {V:(22, −6036)}, {W:(23, −6037)}, {X:(24, −6038)}, {Y:(25, −6039)}, {Z:(26, −6040)}, {a:(27, −6041)}, {b:(28, −6042)}, {c:(29, −6043)}, {d:(30, −6044)}, {e:(31, −6045)}, {f:(32, 1)}, {g:(33, 2)}, {h:(34, 3)}, {i:(35, 4)}, {j:(36, 5)}, {k:(37, 6)}, {l:(38, 7)}, {m:(39, 8)}, {n:(40, 9)}, {o:(41, 10)}, {p:(42, 11)}, {q:(43, 12)}, {r:(44, 13)}, {s:(45, 14)}, {t:(46, 15)}, {u:(47, 16)}, {v:(48, 17)}, {w:(49, 18)}, {x:(50, 19)}, {y:(51, 20)}, {z:(52, 21)}, { :(53, 22)}, {,:(54, 23)}, {.:(55, 24)}, {(:(56, 25)}, {):(57, 26)}, {−:(58, 27)}, {':(59, 28)}, {+ :(60, 29)}, {—:(61, 30)}, {+ :(62, 31)},...

Encrypted Text: (20, −6034), (34, 3), (31, −6045), (53, 22), (91, 60), (27, −6041), (44, 13), (38, 7), (35, 4), (152, 121), (45, 14), (46, 15), (69, 38), (37, 6), (40, 9), (41, 10), (49, 18), (82, 51), (174, 143), (47, 16), (77, 46), (212, 181), (190, 159), (81, 50), (32, 1), (295, 264), (29, −6043), (78, 47), (51, 20), (42, 11), (76, 45), (162, 131), (33, 2), (165, 134), (95, 64), (80, 49), (88, 57), (71, 40), (311, 280), (156, 125), (166, 135), (416, 385), (90, 59), (202, 171), (75, 44), (161, 130), (30, −6044), (432, 401), (277, 246), (203, 172), (537, 506), (282, 251), (283, 252), (324, 293), (58, 27), (198, 167), (167, 136), (148, 117), (403, 372), (92, 61), (216, 185), (199, 168), (151, 120), (553, 522), (155, 124), (398, 367), (273, 242), (286, 255), (323, 292), (89, 58), (84, 53), (172, 141), (163, 132), (209, 178), (287, 256), (658, 627), (93, 62), (269, 238), (320, 289), (48, 17), (333, 302), (213, 182), (674, 643), (519, 488), (445, 414), (197, 166), (404, 373), (779, 748), (39, 8), (444, 413), (524, 493), (168, 137), (83, 52), (394, 363), (566, 535), (288, 257), (319, 288), (795, 764), (153, 122), (407, 376), (525, 494), (160, 129), (900, 869), (5, −6019), (154, 123), (192, 161), (201, 170), (318, 287), (408, 377), (916, 885), (15, −6029), (159, 128), (272, 241), (1021, 990), (11, −6025), (640, 609), (645, 614), (210, 179), (334, 303), (565, 534), (204, 173), (1037, 1006), (56, 25), (150, 119), (337, 306), (1142, 1111), (60, 29), (1158, 1127), (293, 262), (454, 423), (390, 359), (441, 410), (440, 409), (1263, 1232), (458, 427), (275, 244), (646, 615), (57, 26), (55, 24), (1279, 1248), (102, 71), (276, 245), (515, 484), (529, 498), (575, 544), (1384, 1353), (511, 480), (528, 497), (636, 605), (1400, 1369), (687, 656), (686, 655), (409, 378), (1505, 1474), (439, 408), (330, 299), (767, 736), (196, 165), (331, 300), (397, 366), (530, 499), (1521, 1490), (560, 529), (807, 776), (1626, 1595), (28, −6042), (696, 665), (1642, 1611), (561, 530), (757, 726), (562, 531), (761, 730), (888, 857), (289, 258), (650, 619), (1747,

1716), (579, 548), (651, 620), (681, 650), (817, 786), (281, 250), (284, 253), (772, 741), (682, 651), (1763, 1732), (632, 601), (802, 771), (1868, 1837), (771, 740), (878, 847), (214, 183), (649, 618), (938, 907), (893, 862), (1884, 1853), (271, 240), (928, 897), (325, 294), (402, 371), (317, 286), (766, 735), (882, 851), (335, 304), (700, 669), (923, 892), (1003, 972), (1009, 978), (808, 777), (803, 772), (54, 23), (1989, 1958), (451, 420), (1049, 1018), (73, 42), (999, 968), (74, 43), (1059, 1028), (683, 652), (68, 37), (2005, 1974), (94, 63), (410, 379), (1014, 983), (2110, 2079), (770, 739), (753, 722), (1044, 1013), (518, 487), (1120, 1089), (804, 773), (2126, 2095), (1135, 1104), (1130, 1099), (2231, 2200), (572, 541), (821, 790), (169, 138), (1180, 1149), (2247, 2216), (149, 118), (1241, 1210), (1301, 1270), (887, 856), (2352, 2321), (874, 843), (1165, 1134), (1256, 1225), (1362, 1331), (446, 415), (322, 291), (1286, 1255), (892, 861), (2368, 2337), (942, 911), (1377, 1346), (2473, 2442), (523, 492), (313, 282), (924, 893), (1407, 1376), (1422, 1391), (891, 860), (414, 383), (175, 144), (2489, 2458), (1124, 1093), (929, 898), (1498, 1467), (925, 894), (1245, 1214), (396, 365), (438, 407), (1483, 1452), (189, 158), (2594, 2563), (1170, 1139), (1012, 981), (2610, 2579), (1543, 1512), (195, 164), (1604, 1573), (1008, 977), (2715, 2684), (995, 964), (567, 536), (531, 500), (1013, 982), (1664, 1633), (644, 613), (1725, 1694), (1050, 1019), (1528, 1497), (2731, 2700), (211, 180), (1251, 1220), (1046, 1015), (2836, 2805), (205, 174), (1366, 1335), (1619, 1588), (1785, 1754), (1133, 1102), (1063, 1032), (1649, 1618), (1846, 1815), (2852, 2821), (1291, 1260), (1129, 1098), (280, 249), (1372, 1341), (1412, 1381), (85, 54), (1906, 1875), (1167, 1136), (1045, 1014), (67, 36), (2957, 2926), (141, 110), (639, 608), (1967, 1936), (1134, 1103), (2027, 1996), (2973, 2942), (1116, 1085), (1254, 1223), (2088, 2057), (−55, −24), (2148, 2117), (50, 19), (1184, 1153), (688, 657), (405, 374), (326, 295), (2209, 2178), (1166, 1135), (−71, −40), (1493, 1462), (274, 243), (−176, −145), (1255, 1224), (1740, 1709), (1487, 1456), (401, 370), (447, 416), (−192, −161), (1533, 1502), (1770, 1739), (693, 662), (2269, 2238), (1288, 1257), (−297, −266), (559, 528), (1287, 1256), (2330, 2299), (1376, 1345), (−313, −282), (1614, 1583), (332, 301), (−418, −387), (392, 361), (1375, 1344), (434, 403), (443, 412), (1861, 1830), (1654, 1623), (452, 421), (1409, 1378), (1237, 1206), (526, 495), (760, 729), (535, 504), (296, 265), (−434, −403), (1735, 1704), (1496, 1465), (−539, −508), (1775, 1744), (395, 364), (−555, −524), (1408, 1377), (1856, 1825), (765, 734), (2390, 2359), (1891, 1860), (814, 783), (1608, 1577), (1171, 1140), (517, 486), (−660, −629), (1982, 1951), (881, 850), (1305, 1274), (2012, 1981), (−676, −645), (522, 491), (1896, 1865), (1977, 1946), (158, 127), (1497, 1466), (−781, −750), (66, 35), (1729, 1698), (809, 778), (564, 533), (1530, 1499), (2451, 2420), (1529, 1498), (1618, 1587), (1850, 1819), (290, 259), (2511, 2480), (568, 537), (555, 524), (−797, −766), (1971, 1940), (453, 422), (−902, −871), (886, 855), (2092, 2061), (1650, 1619), (643, 612), (2572, 2541), (1358, 1327), (393, 362), (2213, 2182), (1250, 1219), (573, 542), (689, 658), (656, 625), (65, 34), (−918, −887), (764, 733), (2334, 2303), (206, 175), (2632, 2601), (−1023, −992), (2455, 2424), (2103, 2072), (176, 145), (−1039, −1008), (19, −6033), (2017, 1986), (930, 899), (2693, 2662), (−1144, −1113), (456, 425), (810, 779), (1426, 1395), (676, 645), (−1160, −1129), (2133, 2102), (1479, 1448), (215, 184), (885, 854), (2753, 2722), (2224, 2193), (1739, 1708), (−1265, −1234), (516, 485), (1617, 1586), (2098, 2067), (1007, 976), (−1281, −1250), (13, −6027), (2814, 2783), (1771, 1740), (2138, 2107), (647, 616), (2219, 2188), (2254, 2223), (1547, 1516), (1051, 1020), (2576, 2545),

(1600, 1569), (310, 279), (−1386, −1355), (1860, 1829), (2259, 2228), (1128, 1097), (2874, 2843), (170, 139), (935, 904), (1668, 1637), (2345, 2314), (−1402, −1371), (931, 900), (1721, 1690), (2375, 2344), (2935, 2904), (1651, 1620), (−1507, −1476), (1789, 1758), (1738, 1707), (2995, 2964), (−1523, −1492), (513, 482), (1006, 975), (−33, −2), (1842, 1811), (1772, 1741), (1052, 1021), (777, 746), (−1628, −1597), (1172, 1141), (−93, −62), (1910, 1879), (1292, 1261), (2466, 2435), (−1644, −1613), (2496, 2465), (2340, 2309), (−1749, −1718), (685, 654), (1859, 1828), (2380, 2349), (2587, 2556), (−154, −123), (577, 546), (2617, 2586), (−1765, −1734), (2697, 2666), (1371, 1340), (574, 543), (2461, 2430), (1893, 1862), (1249, 1218), (1963, 1932), (2708, 2677), (2818, 2787), (2501, 2470), (1413, 1382), (−1870, −1839), (61, 30), (−1886, −1855), (2738, 2707), (1002, 971), (−214, −183), (797, 766), (−1991, −1960), (−275, −244), (1492, 1461), (634, 603), (1980, 1949), (898, 867), (768, 737), (2829, 2798), (−2007, −1976), (2014, 1983), (−335, −304), (698, 667), (2939, 2908), (806, 775), (−396, −365), (1892, 1861), (417, 386), (−2112, −2081), (889, 858), (2101, 2070), (−456, −425), (1981, 1950), (652, 621), (1293, 1262), (2031, 2000), (270, 239), (1127, 1096), (918, 887), (−2128, −2097), (755, 724), (2582, 2551), (1370, 1339), (1414, 1383), (−517, −486), (2135, 2104), (819, 788), (−37, −6), (2084, 2053), (1173, 1142), (1248, 1217), (1019, 988), (−2233, −2202), (316, 285), (2152, 2121), (1294, 1263), (680, 649), (2205, 2174), (336, 305), (1369, 1338), (−577, −546), (188, 157), (−2249, −2218), (12, −6026), (2273, 2242), (2859, 2828), (−638, −607), (2222, 2191), (−2354, −2323), (2013, 1982), (2950, 2919), (−158, −127), (1415, 1384), (1490, 1459), (431, 400), (−2370, −2339), (8, −6022), (−698, −667), (391, 360), (2256, 2225), (−759, −728), (194, 163), (−2475, −2444), (2102, 2071), (876, 845), (1056, 1025), (2622, 2591), (1536, 1505), (2326, 2295), (2343, 2312), (2134, 2103), (−2491, −2460), (1491, 1460), (2394, 2363), (455, 424), (−819, −788), (−2596, −2565), (773, 742), (2223, 2192), (−880, −849), (−2612, −2581), (2703, 2672), (637, 606), (−2717, −2686), (2255, 2224), (−279, −248), (1535, 1504), (927, 896), (1611, 1580), (−940, −909), (−2733, −2702), (1612, 1581), (2743, 2712), (1534, 1503), (2824, 2793), (2447, 2416), (1657, 1626), (1010, 979), (1123, 1092), (2515, 2484), (457, 426), (−1001, −970), (2980, 2949), (−400, −369), (940, 909), (−2838, −2807), (2344, 2313), (801, 770), (512, 481), (2376, 2345), (−48, −17), (−521, −490), (−78, −47), (894, 863), (−169, −138), (−642, −611), (2864, 2833), (1613, 1582), (−2854, −2823), (997, 966), (−763, −732), (1048, 1017), (1177, 1146), (−1061, −1030), (2377, 2346), (2465, 2434), (−2959, −2928), (177, 146), (2497, 2466), (922, 891), (1061, 1030), (1244, 1213), (−2975, −2944), (2568, 2537), (2586, 2555), (3080, 3049), (−199, −168), (1298, 1267), (−1122, −1091), (3096, 3065), (1, −6015), (−290, −259), (578, 547), (2636, 2605), (2618, 2587), (1365, 1334), (3201, 3170), (1118, 1087), (−884, −853), (1131, 1100), (1419, 1388), (−1182, −1151), (2464, 2433), (178, 147) (3217, 3186) (633, 602) (−1243, −1212) (638, 607), (−1005, −974), (1655, 1624), (1734, 1703), (−1126, −1095), (1776, 1745), (694, 663), (3322, 3291), (1169, 1138), (−1303, −1272), (2498, 2467), (1486, 1455), (2689, 2658), (1252, 1221), (2707, 2676), (3338, 3307), (2757, 2726), (2585, 2554), (2945, 2914), (1015, 984), (1855, 1824), (514, 483), (3443, 3412), (3459, 3428), (−320, −289), (2985, 2954), (3564, 3533), (3580, 3549), (2, −6016), (3, −6017), (297, 266)

In this example large prime numbers are used for encryption. Elapsed time is 0.259863 s for calculation of encryption in developed application. The character with the largest frequency is 110 and the alphabet has 61 characters in total. If we select the value n greater than 61 * 110 = 6710, the frequency of each point in the encrypted text will be 1. We choose n = 12091 that is more than enough.

6 Conclusion and Future Work

In this paper, based on Vigenère cipher, Polybius square cipher and the RSA algorithm a new text decryption and encryption algorithm is designed and developed an application for implementation of this algorithm. The proposed method is a hybrid poly-alphabet cipher method that maps characters of an alphabet multiple times on different star coordinates. If the number of coordinate points is selected large, in ciphertext, the frequency for each character will be one. Also, if the initial letter in the alphabet and the initial coordinate point is randomly chosen in the star coordinates, then in the definition space, the probability of choosing each element is nearly the same. It makes it approach successful against statistical attacks. Security is enhanced by one time by using the RSA and a highly secure method is achieved. New hybrid methods can be developed by revising the proposed method and using S-box for image encryption.

References

1. Katz, J., Lindell, Y.: Introduction to Modern Cryptography: Principles and Protocols. Chapman & Hall, London (2008)
2. Koç, Ç.: Cryptographic Engineering. Springer, Heidelberg (2009)
3. Paar, C., Pelzl, J.: Understanding Cryptography: A Textbook for Student and Practitioners. Springer, Heidelberg (2010). https://doi.org/10.1007/978-3-642-04101-3
4. Kumar, Y., Munjal, R., Sharma, H.: Comparison of symmetric and asymmetric cryptography with existing vulnerabilities and countermeasures. IJCSMS Int. J. Comput. Sci. Manag. Stud. **11**(03), 60–63 (2011)
5. FIPS 46–3, Data Encryption Standard. National Institute of Standarts and Technology (NIST) (1999)
6. FIPS 197, Announcing the ADVANCED ENCRYPTION STANDARD (AES). National Institute of Standarts and Technology (NIST) (2001)
7. Rivest, R.L., Shamir, A., Adleman, L.M.: A method for obtaining digital signatures and public-key cryptosystems. CACM **21**(2), 120–126 (1978)
8. Chaudhury, P., et al.: ACAFP: asymmetric key based cryptographic algorithm using four prime numbers to secure message communication. A review on RSA algorithm. In: 8th Annual Industrial Automation and Electromechanical Engineering Conference (IEMECON), Bangkok, pp. 332–337(2017)
9. Miller, V.S.: Use of elliptic curves in cryptography. In: Williams, Hugh C. (ed.) CRYPTO 1985. LNCS, vol. 218, pp. 417–426. Springer, Heidelberg (1986). https://doi.org/10.1007/3-540-39799-X_31
10. Ratna, A. A. P., Purnamasari, P. D., Shaugi, A., Salman, M.: Analysis and comparison of MD5 and SHA-1 algorithm implementation in simple-O authentication based security system. In: 2013 International Conference on QiR, pp. 99–104 (2013)

11. Rivest, R.: The MD5 Message-Digest Algorithm. Network Working Group, MIT Laboratory for Computer Science and RSA Data Security, Inc., April 1992
12. Chaves, R., Sousa, L., Sklavos, N., Fournaris, A.P., Kalogeridou, G., Kitsos, P., Sheikh, F.: Secure Hashing: SHA-1, SHA-2, and SHA-3. Taylor & Francis Group, LLC, Milton Park (2016)
13. Selcuk, B, Tankul, A.N.A., Dundar, A., Akkus, Z., Arslan, M.: Designing a new hybrid cryptographic model using coordinate axes. Anatolian J. Comput. Sci. (accepted)
14. Highland, H.J.: Data encryption: a non-mathematical approach. Comput. Sec. **16**(5), 369–386 (1997)
15. Paul, A.J., Mythili, P.: Poly-alphabetic substitution mapping for cryptographic transformations. In: Conference: National Conference on Recent Innovations in Technology, March 2009
16. Kartha, R.S., Paul, V.: An efficient algorithm for polyalphabetic substitution using infinite number of alphabetical tables. Int. J. Appl. Eng. Res. **13**(4), 14–20 (2018)
17. Aung, T.M., Naing, H.H., Hla, N.N.: A complex transformation of monoalphabetic cipher to polyalphabetic cipher: (Vigenère-Affine cipher). Int. J. Mach. Learn. Comput. **9**(3), 296–303 (2019)
18. Saraswat, A., Khatri, C., Thakral, P., Biswas, P.: An extended hybridization of vigenère and caesar cipher techniques for secure communication. Proc. Comput. Sci. **92**, 355–360 (2016)

RP-DMAC: Receiver Pivotal Directional MAC with Multichannel for IoT Based WSN

Arpita Howlader[1(✉)] and Samrat Kumar Dey[2]

[1] Dhaka University of Engineering and Technology, Gazipur 1700, Bangladesh
arpita.toma@gmail.com

[2] Dhaka International University, 66 Green Road, Dhaka 1205, Bangladesh

Abstract. In the construction of the wireless sensor network; MAC protocols are considered as a foremost element of IoT based devices that are used for data transmission and greater scalability with simple executions. Furthermore, most of the researches on WSN conduct directional antenna to provide substantial progresses in communication. However, numerous types of problems such as deafness, deadlock, and head of line blocking problems irrespective of a number of channels are introducing inherently in directional MAC protocols. Some proposed asynchronous multichannel MAC protocol is based on RIT or RI mechanisms that escape those prevalent problems. Using a multichannel directional MAC with RP is proposed in this article that referred to as Receiver Pivotal DMAC (RP-DMAC). We propose RP-DMAC as a state-of-the-art protocol for IoT based WSN to separate deafness and other problem by using directional RTR (Ready to Receive) packet, data channel, and guard band. As like most of the DMAC protocols, in default mode, our RP-DMAC is sender-initiated. When deafness problem is recognized then as our RP protocol manner; nodes will initiate with DRTR negotiation in its unused sector expending through guard band to received data from desire sender. To solve the deadlock and packet loss, our proposed RP protocol performs better results than DA-MAC and circular RTR MAC in terms of packet drop ratio, overhead, and throughput.

Keywords: Ad hoc networks · Receiver-initiated · Throughput · Directional antenna · Deafness

1 Introduction

MAC plays an important part in WSN. It is primarily effective for the construction of communication links between nodes that are central to the creation of a network infrastructure. The MAC system then uses multiple nodes to monitor the access of the shared wireless channel [1]. Compared with the existing networks where the main priority is given to the bandwidth efficiency and Quality of Service (QoS), energy efficiency is the major objective of WSNs, rendering conventional MAC methods inapplicable [2]. Meanwhile, the sensor node transceiver takes advantage of the maximum power compared to other node components controlled by the duty cycle [3]. Regarding of WSN

T. Bhuiyan et al. (Eds.): ICONCS 2020, LNICST 325, pp. 43–55, 2020.
https://doi.org/10.1007/978-3-030-52856-0_4

an essential network infrastructure can be generated for reliable establishment of communication link among nodes and controls the access of the shared wireless channel. In WSN, an IoT network clearly show the existence of a few numbers of wireless sensor nodes in a wide range of important applications such as healthcare, transport, oceanographic data collection, pollution detection, and so on. Wireless sensor nodes are used to exchange or collect data that are limited for power, memory and for that reason power, energy consumption and different types of losses needs to be controlled [4]. Therefore, industries around the globe are highly interested in one of the principal technologies in recent time is directional antennas by which consumer devices can obtain benefits, likely better spatial reuse and a longer transmission range [5].

Many existing MSC protocol for WSN use either synchronous or asynchronous approach for finding a specific rendezvous point between two nodes where nodes are in active state and a communication link can be established between sender and receiver [6]. According to [7] synchronize schemes are quite planned or prearranged but at the same time other nodes must be in sleep zone or ideal. In asynchronous technique nodes acts wake-up and sleep in a way that is free from outside influence of other nodes since this scheme is not synchronous and follows two technique for communication: sender initiative or receiver initiative [6–8].

Omni-directional or directional antenna-based MAC protocols which are the major elements of IoT networks involve various sustainable techniques for WSN. Most of the directional antenna MAC is sender-initiated in default mode but experienced some popular problem like hidden terminal problem and deafness problem which reduces throughput of the network.

On the other hand, when sender realizes that receiver is not responding, then in few protocols, sender increase back off time and wait to resend RTS. During this increasing period of time, the data for another node are blocked. However, receiver deaf node become ideal, this sender cannot immediately initiate RTS because of the long back off and receiver can be busy with another communication which causes of deadlock and packets loss problem. According to the existing solution to the deafness problem, some approaches are as follows: CRDMAC protocol circular RTR packet in the control channel to notify neighbors [9], tone-based approaches, and approaches that allow RTR frame to notify potential sender.

However, most of the proposal scheme still unable to resolve the deafness problem and the complication created for deafness. RP-DMAC is a combination of sender and receiver-initiated operations. We evaluate our work through extensive simulation study with different values of parameters such as the number of nodes, data size, and beam width.

2 Relevant Work

In this section, we will briefly discuss some of the relevant work that has performed previously in order to address the problem of deafness in directional MAC protocol. Authors in [5] proposed DA-MAC protocol that is capable of distinguish deafness from a collision by exploiting two channels likely data and control. By using the support of these two channels, DA-MAC sender can identify deafness, and collision cases. The proposed CRDMAC protocol [9] which used an RTR frame to inform potential neighbor as senders to wait until a node finishes transmission. To avoids deafness this protocol circular RTR packet in the control channel to notify neighbors.

In protocol RC-MAC [10] avoids data collision by adding another CCA before data transmission and with ACK in beacon. Though this protocol gives better performance in throughput, it is unable to solve deafness problem. For avoiding Early Wake-up a new MAC protocol for IoT applications, called Bird-MAC, which is highly energy efficient in the applications where IoT sensors report monitoring status in a quasi-periodic manner is proposed by authors in [11].

Another approach by using ready-to-receive (RTR) frame to solve the deafness problems was proposed by authors in [12]. Whenever a node finishes a transmission to another node it expects to receive data from its potential senders and tries to minimize the deafness duration.

Authors in [13] proposed a protocol which used additional RTS (A-RTS) frame to inform potential senders to wait until a node finishes transmission so that it avoids deafness. Although, it tries to evade the deafness problem by the advance notice, in some cases they cannot resolve the deafness problems [13].

A neighbor-initiated approach in [14] proposed by authors to avoid deaf and hidden node problems by transmitting RTS and CTS to its vicinity through its all remaining beams. In addition, idle neighbor of the nodes send NIP to communicate other node after finishing the communication. Following Table 1 represent the comparison of previous work with our proposed solution.

Table 1. Comparative analysis with existing works

Protocol name	Channel	Control packet	Antenna	Protocol description and problems
DA-MAC [5]	Data channel as control channel	Minimum	Directional	node starts new communicate after recognizing receiver as deaf node
CRDMAC [9]	Data channel as control channel	Maximum	Omni-directional and Directional	Use circular RTR packet in control channel to notify neighbors
RI-DMAC [12]	Data channel as control channel	Medium	Directional	Use unverified polling table
Neighbor initiated approach [14]	Data channel as control channel	Maximum	Directional	Transmit RTS and CTS to all beams and this protocol cause line blocking problem
RP-DMAC (Proposed)	Guard band as control channel	Minimum	Directional	Initiate with DRTR negotiation in its unused sector expending through guard band but do not consider power consumption

From the above discussion, it is evident that existing schemes and different protocols are still impotent to resolve the deafness and packet drop as well as deadlock problems. In that case, our proposed architecture will help us by providing either our desire nodes are engaged with communication or not and the number of times it will be deaf during communication. Based on this deaf time, sender will decide either to hold or drop the packet and deaf node will take action for receiving data which will reduce the severe packet loss and overhead. Deaf node will then use RTR and guard band which will also increase the throughput and channel utilization.

3 Problem Definition

In this section we will briefly discuss about our problem statement and also propose a possible solution to overcome the defined problem. RI model-based technique is existing in both synchronous and asynchronous communication with omni-directional and directional antenna MAC protocols. However, asynchronous MAC protocols with directional antenna are popular because of its high gain, low duty cycle and low communication overhead.

Figure 1 shows an example of the deafness problem that occurred in [5]. Suppose sender node S wants to send data to node D directionally. Sender node S then send DRTS to node D and aware its neighbor about this negotiation. Consequently, node transmit

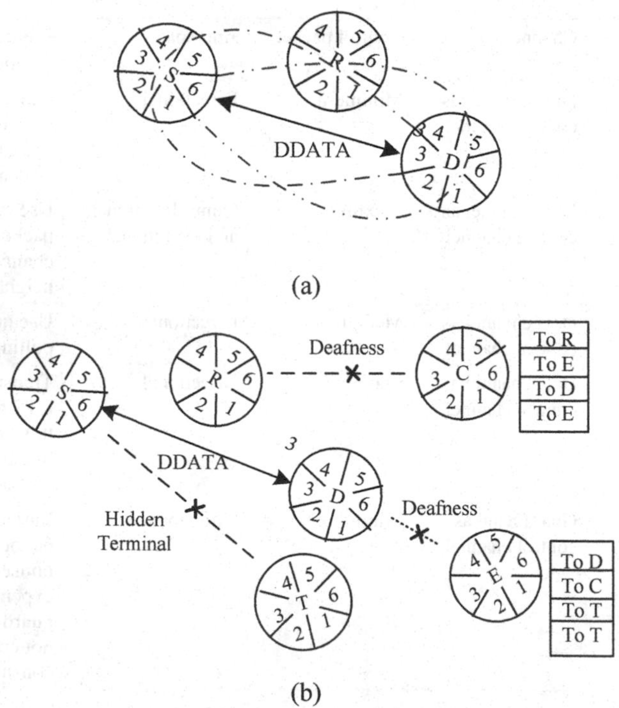

Fig. 1. Established problem in Directional MAC

DCTS to reply the sender and aware its neighbor about the successful communication. Consequently, node D and its neighbors answer with DCTS frames.

At the same time neighbor node update DNAV and beam of any node that can be causes of interference to transmission of S and D are blocked loke as Fig. 1(a) show that, the beam sector 1,2,3 and 6 of node R become blocked. Now if node C has data for node R and then node C with beam 3 try to send data to beam 6 of node R, node R will not respond because of its beam 6 is blocked, which can identify as deafness problem.

Figure 1(b) shows, since beam 3 of node D is engaged in communication, then node D will not receive DRTS from node E, which is another deafness condition. On the other hand, after completing own communication if node T send DRTS to beam 6 of node S, it will then be the causes of collision refer to as hidden terminal problem.

The RI-MAC paradigm of communication is shown in Fig. 2. Here each node wakes-up periodically to check for incoming data packets. In RI model-based MAC, as like Fig. 2 the sender S^{Tx} and C^{Tx} awake and wait random time for receiver beacon packet. The intended nodes immediately transmit after receiving the receiver beacon packet from receiver node D^{Rx}. The collision occurs when sender S^{Tx} and C^{Tx} listen the beacon at the same time and immediately transmit their data to the target receiver D^{Rx}.

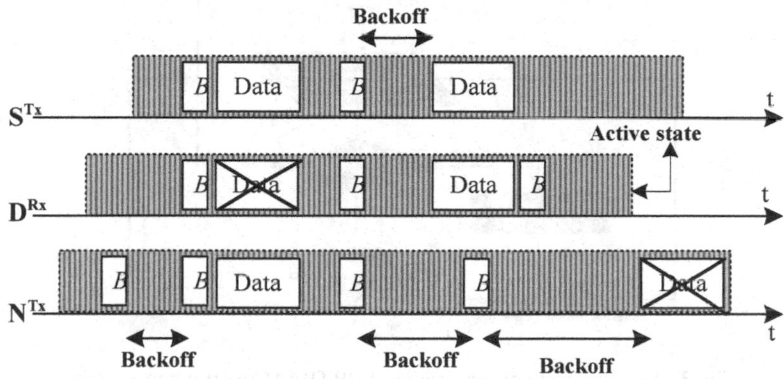

Fig. 2. RI-MAC mechanism with beacon and backoff window

Usually, the beacon packet serves two purposes, one: it mentioning that the transmitted packet is not successfully received and second: it holds a backoff value to indicate that transmit again after taking this backoff. If a sender node C^{Tx} is failed for a successful transmission then again take a binary exponential backoff. The backoff mechanism in RI-MAC shows poor performance in case of throughput and consumes much energy for lot of packet retransmission.

4 Proposed RP-DMAC

4.1 Basic System Model

The directional antenna radio has different sectors to transmit or receive gain in different directions as well as reduces interference from undesired sources. Based on 360-degree surroundings each of directional antenna has s sectors. We also assume that, when a node transmits using one beam, the other beams cannot receive due to the use of a single channel. Here, we assume that our directional antenna has dual radios of which one for data communication and one for Busy packet (BP). According to antenna theory and design [15], the main lobes area size has large gain with beam-width Φ and minor lobe beam-width will be 2Π - Φ; however, it can be ignored.

The main idea of RP-DMAC is that it will use guard-band for informing neighbor with the busy packet as Common Control Channel (CCC) and all data-channels will use for data communication (Fig. 3).

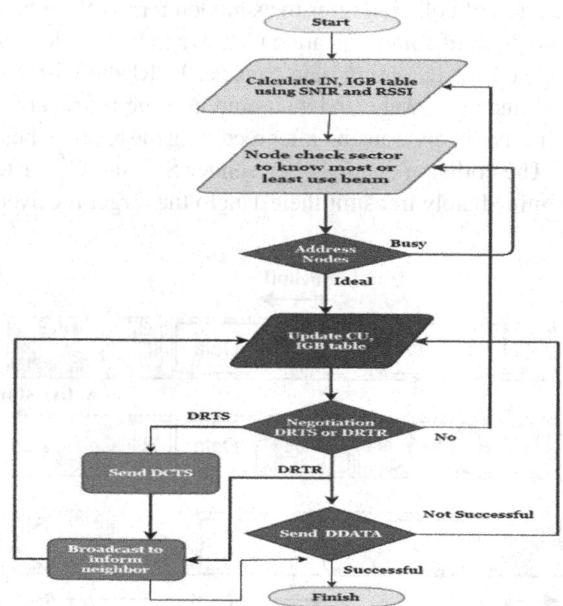

Fig. 3. Flow diagram of our proposed RP-DMAC working procedure

4.2 List of Channel Utilization and Discovery Neighbor Node

By using table of list of channels utilization, nodes can check information about all channels like "how many pair are using a channel directionally" and "which channels are fully unused". In Table 2, pair of senders (Tx) and receiver (Rx), status of channel availability, and number of channel uses are included.

Without wasting bandwidth, it is possible to discover neighbor node through guard band subcarrier. All nodes will generate IN table (Information of Neighbor) which will consist of Information Index (Beam, Accessible/TL, Space (M)). Table 3 contains information of Neighbor as like for node C and node R (B3, TL, SCR), where beam 3 of node C use to communicate with node R; Present of TL means node is busy or block, and SCR indicate the space between these two nodes.

Table 2. List of Channel Utilization

Channel	Tx Rx	Usage	Status
Ch-1	S, D	1	1
Ch-2	–	–	0
Ch-2	(T, E), (R, C)	2	1
–	–	–	0
Ch-N	–	–	0

Table 3. Information of Neighbor (IN)

Node	Information index (Beam, Accessible/T_L, Space(M))
C	R(B_3, T_L, S_{CR}), E(B_1, 0, S_{CE}), D(B_2, T_L, S_{CD})
D	R(B_3, T_L, S_{DR}), E(B_6, 0, S_{DE}), C(B_5, T_L, S_{DC}), T(B_2, 0, S_{CE}),
E	T(B_3, T_L, S_{CR}), C(B_5, 0, S_{CE}), D(B_4, T_L, S_{CD})
R	S(B_3, T_L, S_{CR}), C(B_6 0, S_{CE}), D(B_1, T_L, S_{CD})
S	R(B_5, T_L, S_{CR}), T(B_6, 0, S_{CE}), D(B_6, T_L, S_{CD})
T	R(B_4, T_L, S_{CR}), E(B_6, 0, S_{CE}), D(B_5, T_L, S_{CD}),S(B_4, T_L, S_{CD})

4.3 Information Guard-Band (IGB)

Information of guard band and distance between nodes can be calculated by measuring Signal to Noise and Interference Ratio (SINR) and Received Signal Strength Indication (RSSI) values. Free node regulates guard-band SINR value, which is calculated as:

$$\mathrm{SINR} = \mathrm{P}\,(\frac{I}{I+N}) \tag{1}$$

Moreover, receiver signal strength and space between nodes can be calculated based on RSSI value as:

$$\mathrm{P_r} = \mathrm{P_s}(1/\mathrm{d})^{\mathrm{n}} \tag{2}$$

$$10\,\mathrm{lg}\,\mathrm{P_r} = 10\mathrm{n}\,\mathrm{lg}\,\mathrm{P_s} - 10\mathrm{n}\,\mathrm{lg}\,\mathrm{d} \tag{3}$$

$$\mathrm{P_R}(\mathrm{dB_m}) = \mathrm{A} - 10\mathrm{n}\,\mathrm{lg}\,\mathrm{d} \tag{4}$$

Status is 0 when all subcarrier is unused and status is 1 when subcarrier ID contain used subcarrier. After this calculation, information's of node C Guard-band is stored in IGB table and from this table nodes choose perfect subcarrier from guard band and use it for broadcasting BP to neighbor. Following Table 4 represent Guard Band Information.

Table 4. Guard Band Information table

Guard Band (Id)	Status (0–1)	Subcarrier Id
G1	1	4
G2	0	–
G3	1	2,4
–	–	–
G*m*-1	0	–

4.4 Control Packet

In RP-DMAC, protocol has used different control frames those are shown in Fig. 4. The busy packet (BP) control packet is used to aware neighbor node and hearing this, deal neighbor update DNAVE, IN table, list of CU table and IGB table.

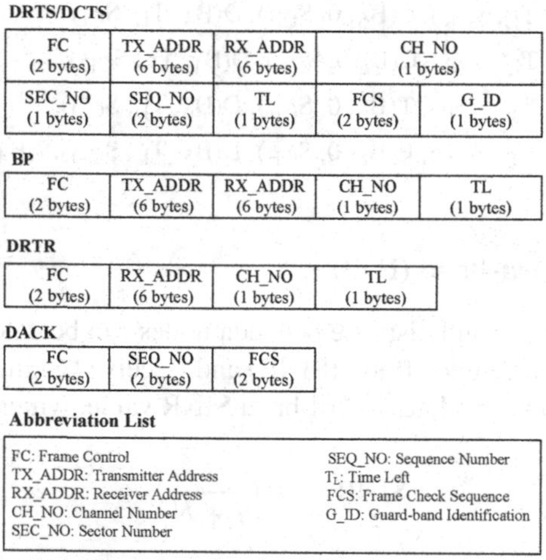

DRTS/DCTS

FC (2 bytes)	TX_ADDR (6 bytes)	RX_ADDR (6 bytes)	CH_NO (1 bytes)	
SEC_NO (1 bytes)	SEQ_NO (2 bytes)	TL (1 bytes)	FCS (2 bytes)	G_ID (1 bytes)

BP

FC (2 bytes)	TX_ADDR (6 bytes)	RX_ADDR (6 bytes)	CH_NO (1 bytes)	TL (1 bytes)

DRTR

FC (2 bytes)	RX_ADDR (6 bytes)	CH_NO (1 bytes)	TL (1 bytes)

DACK

FC (2 bytes)	SEQ_NO (2 bytes)	FCS (2 bytes)

Abbreviation List

FC: Frame Control
TX_ADDR: Transmitter Address
RX_ADDR: Receiver Address
CH_NO: Channel Number
SEC_NO: Sector Number
SEQ_NO: Sequence Number
T_L: Time Left
FCS: Frame Check Sequence
G_ID: Guard-band Identification

Fig. 4. Structure of a control frame

4.5 RP-DMAC

The proposed RP-DMAC is an asynchronous, multi-channel; dual-antenna based directional protocol. Here, we use dual radio; though one radio antenna sender and receiver transmit data and second radio used to aware neighbor node through BP. Busy packet to inform neighbor nodes about the data communication through suitable sub-carriers of the guard-band. RP-DMAC provide following feature:

- **Deafness-consciousness:** By checking IN table and overhearing BP; any node can identify deafness node and where communication can be failed.

- **Data hold or drop:** Sender will check IN table to know whether receiver node busy or ideal. When desire receiver node is busy then sender will check waiting time. If T_L < (Data transmitting time/2), then sender will hold data for receiver, otherwise drop or keep data in last of packet queue. In this way RP-DMAC protocol reduce packet drop.
- **Scheduling queue:** When deaf node become free or ideal from block mode or after finishing communication it will send DRTR to receive data from waiting sender. During this time deaf node will check it's IN table and will send DRTR directionally using most recent usage beam to another node accept recent sender node.
  Assume that the probability of receiving data from most recent usage beam is high. It will wait DIFS time to receive data otherwise send DRTR to other less use beam. Table 5 shows beam number and no-usage value indicates how many times a beam is used. In this way RP-DMAC protocol reduce packet drop, and deadlock problem, and improving the aggregate throughput.

Table 5. Node Beam Usage

Beam	No-usage
B_1	0
B_2	2
B_3	3
–	–
–	–
B_m	5

- **Decrease Control overhead:** Sender and receiver do not transmit the DRTS or DCTS frame to their neighbors. Neighbors are informed through BP. To increase the throughput, it reduces the control packet overhead to all neighbors.

Sender S has data for receiver node D. To start communication, node S will check all tables and wait for TDIFS time to notify receiver either it is busy or ideal. At the time of communication; BP will be send through second radio in the sub-carrier oriented common channel guard band to inform neighbor. Neighbor node will update DNAV and all other table. As in timing diagram shows in Fig. 5, suppose node Q is busy for data communication in different data channel.

For communication between node S and node D, node R is blocked and update DNAVE table including all tables. Through this RP-DMAC protocol neighbor nodes are able to know about ongoing communication and deaf node. After finishing communication node S, node D and node R will become ideal and node S and node R will send DRTR after waiting DIFS time. During this time node T will receive DRTR from node S and will send DDATA and node C will send DDATA to node R

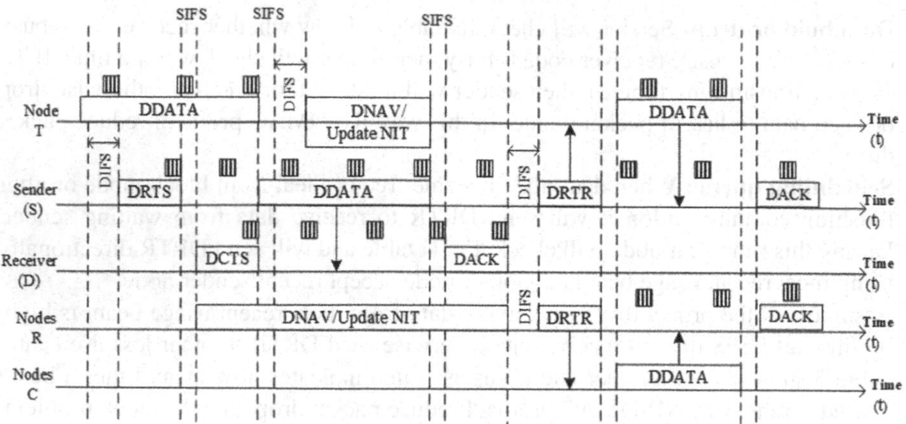

Fig. 5. Proposed RP-DMAC protocol

5 Performance Analysis

In this section, we will present the results of performance analysis of our proposed protocol. After simulating our protocol, we compared it with RI-MAC, RC-MAC, DA-MAC, and CRDMAC. Here we have considered some parameter as the randomly distributed including area $\pi \times 10^2\,m^2$, transmission range is 250 m and carrier sensing range 500 m, Data Packet size is 512 byte. In this protocol, number of simulations is 10 with 100 s simulation time and the result place in average number of collision of packets and average throughput in kbps. The simulations result of average throughput and collision is shown in Fig. 6 and Fig. 7. Throughput result are shown in Fig. 6, where RI-MAC and CRD-MAC shows small amount of throughput.

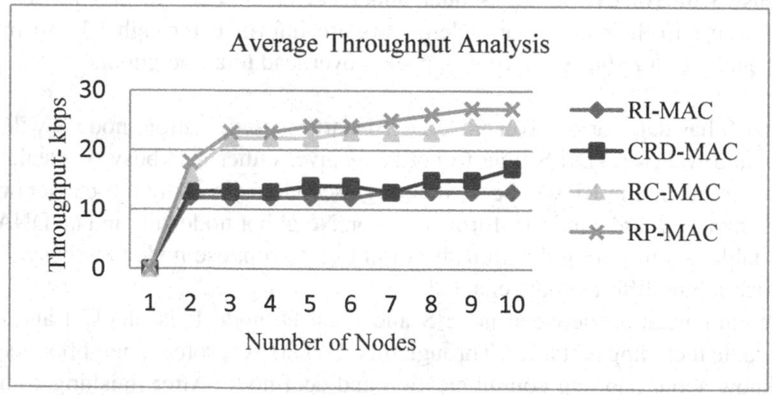

Fig. 6. Average throughput comparison

RC-MAC throughput is improved by the use of CCA before communication in order to avoid collision. The result is more improved in RP-DMAC. However, in Fig. 7, it is evident that the possibility of collision is greater in RI-MAC but collision result for CRD and RC-MAC is mostly related. Among them again our RP-DMAC protocol shows improved result because average collision is also significantly low. Figure 8 clearly illustrate that the comparison of RI-MAC, CRDMAC and RP-DMAC protocol depends on Control packet overhead where COP generally increases in all protocol with respect to data payload size.

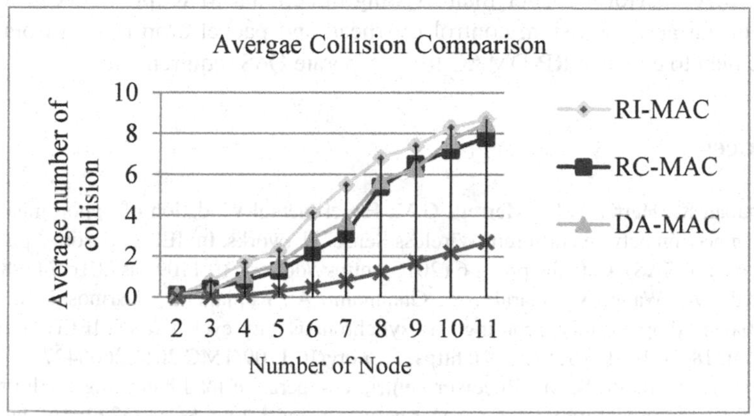

Fig. 7. Average Collison comparison

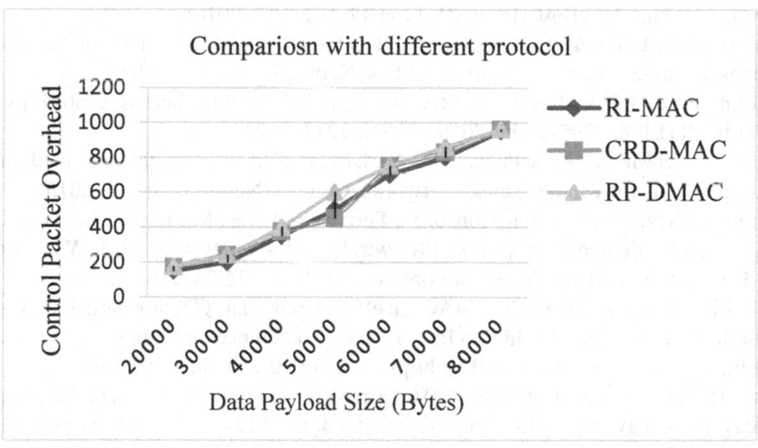

Fig. 8. Comparison of RI-MAC, CRD-MAC, and RP-DMAC based on CPO

6 Conclusion and Future Work

In this article, deafness issue in directional MAC protocol is addressed by proposing RP-DMAC protocol to solve the problem. RP-DMAC is a novel receiver pivotal mechanism that takes action for deafness problem reactively using DRTR and uses BP in guard band to inform the neighbor. The potential deaf node can recognize that in which sector it was absent for long time and when receiver becomes idle; deliver DRTR packet immediately. The awaited send also can identify that receiver is ideal and if get DRTR then directly send data; otherwise go through the default process. The experimental results show that RP-DMAC performs better than existing directional MAC protocols in terms of throughput, fairness, collision, control overhead and packet drop ratio. In our future work, we plan to enhance RP-DMAC to incorporate QoS requirements.

References

1. Singhanat, K., Harris, N.R., Merrett, G.V.: Experimental validation of opportunistic direct interconnection between different Wireless Sensor Networks. In: IEEE Sensors Applications Symposium (SAS), Catania, pp. 1–6 (2016). https://doi.org/10.1109/sas.2016.7479814
2. Hawbani, A., Wang, X., Sharabi, Y., Ghannami, A., Kuhlani, H., Karmoshi, S.: LORA: load-balanced opportunistic routing for asynchronous duty-cycled WSN. IEEE Trans. Mob. Comput. **18**(7), 1601–1615 (2019). https://doi.org/10.1109/TMC.2016.2606427
3. Gowda, D.M., Illahi, S. M.: Receiver centric co-operative load balancing medium access control layer protocol for wireless sensor networks. Int. J. Eng. Sci. **6632** (2016). https://doi.org/10.4010/2016.1592
4. Renato, F., Brandão, D.: Proposal of receiver initiated MAC protocol for WSN in urban environment using IoT. IFAC-PapersOnLine **49**, 102–107 (2016)
5. Woongsoo, N., Laihyuk, P., Sungrae, C.: Deafness-aware MAC protocol for directional antennas in wireless ad hoc networks. Ad Hoc Netw. **24**, 121–134 (2015)
6. Rachelin Sujae, P., Arulselvi, S.: Receiver-initiated medium access control (RI-MAC) protocols. IJITEE **8**, 2395–2398 (2019). ISSN: 2278–3075
7. Fafoutis, X., Di Mauro, A., Vithanage, M.D., Dragoni, N.: Receiver initiated medium access control protocols for wireless sensor networks. Comput. Netw. **76**, 55–74 (2015)
8. Rodríguez-Pérez, M., Herrería-Alonso, S., Fernández-Veiga, M., López-García, C.: A self-tuning receiver-initiated MAC protocol for wireless sensor networks. IEEE Wirel. Commun. Lett. **4**(6), 601–604 (2015). https://doi.org/10.1109/lwc.2015.2472398
9. Lu, H., Li, J., Dong, Z., Ji, Y.: CRDMAC: an effective circular RTR directional MAC protocol for wireless ad hoc networks. In: 7th International Conference on Mobile Ad-hoc and Sensor Networks, pp. 231–237. IEEE (2011). https://doi.org/10.1109/msn.2011.30
10. Huang, P., Wang, C., Xiao, L.: RC-MAC: a receiver-centric mac protocol for event-driven wireless sensor networks. IEEE Trans. Comput. **64**(4), 1149–1161 (2015). https://doi.org/10.1109/tc.2014.2308174
11. Kim, D., Jung, J., Koo, Y., Yi, Y.: Bird-MAC: energy-efficient MAC for quasi-periodic IoT applications by avoiding early wake-up. IEEE Trans. Mob. Comput. (2019). https://doi.org/10.1109/tmc.2019.2899572
12. Takata, M., Bandai, M., Watanabe, T.: RI-DMAC: a receiver-initiated directional MAC protocol for deafness problem. Int. J. Sensor Netw. **5**(2), 79 (2009). https://doi.org/10.1504/ijsnet.2009.024678

13. Feng, J., Ren, P., Yan, S.: A deafness free MAC protocol for ad hoc networks using directional antennas. In: 4th IEEE Conference on Industrial Electronics and Applications, pp. 449–454. IEEE (2009)
14. Alam, M.N., Hussain, M.A., Kwak, K.S.: Neighbor initiated approach for avoiding deaf and hidden node problems in directional MAC protocol for ad-hoc networks. Wireless Netw. **19**, 933 (2013). https://doi.org/10.1007/s11276-012-0510-8
15. Stutzman, W., Thiele, G.: Antenna Theory and Design, pp. 1051–1056. Wiley, New York (1998)

Malware Analysis

Android Malware Detection by Machine Learning Apprehension and Static Feature Characterization

Md Rashedul Hasan, Afsana Begum(✉), Fahad Bin Zamal, Lamisha Rawshan, and Touhid Bhuiyan

Department of Software Engineering, Daffodil International University, 1207 Dhaka, Bangladesh
{rashedul35-1556,afsana.swe,fahad.swe,lamisha.swe}@diu.edu.bd,
t.bhuiyan@daffodilvarsity.edu.bd

Abstract. The increased usage and popularity of Android devices encourage malware developers to generate newer ways to launch malware in different packaged forms in different applications. These malware causes various information leakage and money lost. For example, only in Canada, McAfee, which surveyed 1,000 Canadians and found 65% of them, had lost more than $100 and almost a third had lost more than $500 to various cyber scams so far this year. Moreover, after identifying software as malware, unethical developer repackages the detected one and again launches the software. Unfortunately, repackaged software remains undetected mostly. In this research three different tasks were done. Comparing to the existing work we have used source code based analysis using bag-of words algorithm in machine learning. By modifying Bag-of-word procedure and adding some additional preprocessing of dataset the evaluation results represent 0.55% better than the existing work in this field. In that case re-packaging was included and this is a new edition in this field of research. Moreover in this research, a vocabulary was also created to identify the malicious code. Here with existing 69 malicious patterns more 12 malicious patterns were added. In addition to these two contributions, we have also implemented our model in a web application to test. This paper represents such a model, which will help the developers or antivirus launcher to detect malware if it is repackaged. This vocabulary will also help to do so.

Keywords: Malware analysis · Android malware · Source code · Text processing · Repackaging · Bag-of-Words

1 Introduction

As our world is being connected at a swift pace numbers of cellular devices are on the rise. The abundance of private information preserved on or accessible through these devices has made them an attractive target for cyber criminals [1]. From different types of studies researches revealed users are not accustomed to install anti-virus or anti-malwares on their mobile devices as the efficiency of such applications are debatable.

T. Bhuiyan et al. (Eds.): ICONCS 2020, LNICST 325, pp. 59–71, 2020.
https://doi.org/10.1007/978-3-030-52856-0_5

Malware developers or Exploit writers concentrates their focus on platforms or operating systems possessing rather a larger market share [2]. From the business perspective mobile devices are to be regarded as “feeble links” of consortium security. Who doesn"t realize Androids permission based security infrastructure offers defense in a lesser extent when it comes to application permissions [3]. In multiple instances malicious applications were approved by Google Play store, which made Android a prudent platform for malware developers [4]. Again repackaging of Malware source code intensifies the probability and the likelihood for a Malware to exist in different variants. The urged reasons create a plea for more efficient Malware analysis capabilities and methods for to be taken into consideration. Conclusive studies represent that malware detection engines can only detect a malicious behavior when an application is labeled and in a packaged form, they cannot be detected when they are in raw form. For example: if a malicious apk file is detected by an antivirus engine the developer could decompile his .apk file to get the core source file and from those source files he may collect some portion or functionalities and can implement them in a specialized form in another .apk file to evade detection. As the form of that particular source code has been restated in another file in another form it will not be detected as malicious even if it was before. The reason is malicious functionality like collecting sms, or spying on call records has been implemented in the new .apk file but as a specialized form. Which makes a perception of insecurity and a probability of that malware being repackaged in another form or as an another application. It is to be anticipated such phenomena is an inception which is a major setback for an efficient detection. So, the research concentration has been focused in this particular area to find out a constructive solution. The objectives which had been focused on to achieve the goal are:

a. To propose a new approach of static analysis for better detection and accuracy referencing a similar work conducted in the field.
b. To propose and execute an efficient methodology combining both static and dynamic analysis techniques to address repackaging.
c. Implantation of text processing (Bag of words algorithm) with static analysis and performing machine learning to understand the effectiveness and accuracy of the proposed method. Create a vocabulary based on it.
d. Implement the proposed model in a simple system to test the result.

To conduct the task raw coding in Python was used, virus total, JD-gui, Dex to jar tools and for web application PHP, HTML, CSS, Mysql Database were used.

2 Literature Review

Android malwares are presenting a serious challenge due to their rapid growth to researchers. The researchers constantly suggest countermeasures and build instruments to combat these attacks [5]. The detection of deviations on battery usage was the foundation for early approaches to detecting mobile malware [6]. Server operating events, such as API calls, Input/Output demands, and resource locks, have also been used in flexible malware detection approaches. For example, TaintDroid is an uncontrollable variables-based malware detection system for the data use behavior of the app [7]. The researchers developed an anomaly monitoring system for the identification of malicious apps for Android Dalvik op-coding frequencies. Machine learning was used to classify malware according to their behavior. The researchers relied for example on runtime activity and classified Android malware in malware families using inter process communications with SVM [8]. In Android malware detection, a random forest strategy is used with a set of 42 vectors, including battery, CPU and memory usage, and network interaction [9]. System calls and regular expressions have been used by authors to detect data leakage, deploy and use destructive apps [10]. To order to avoid mobile device deterioration, mechanisms for both static and dynamic malware analysis focused on distributed computing and collaborative analysis are also advocated. For example, M0Droid is a malware-resistant Android solution which explores and produces signatures for system calls of Android apps on the network, which are pointed to threat detection devices [11]. static malware identification are believed to reduce investigation speed and interoperability because the techniques are taken consideration as manual practice. Numerous methods have also been introduced for streamlining the static analysis process. Researchers recommended the need for comprehensive methods to test the software's activities to convert malware-source code into CCS statements [12]. The authors implied a fingerprinting method for applications that capture the binary and structural functionalities of the [13]. Techniques for automatic malware analysis can be used in machine learning. Even pattern recognition techniques are used to detect malware [14]. while other works use generic algorithms for machine learning, such as perception, SVM, locality-sensitive hatching and decision trees [15]. Before the various machine learning algorithms were used to classify malicious programs, the authors extracted network Access Functions, process execution, string handling, file manipulation and information reading [16]. 100 features had been extracted from API calls, permissions, actions, and related strings of numerous Android apps and space analysis through Eigen for the identification of malicious programs were applied [17]. Sahs and Khan have used Androguard to get Android apps' permission and flow charts and have established an SVM-based model for characterizing Android malware [18].In The work by researchers - Nikola Milosevic a, Ali Dehghantanha b, Kim-Kwang Raymond Choo [19] they implemented an Android malware detection machine-learning model based on device allowances. This was a light, computer-intensive solution that could be used on various mobile phones. They also introduced a new approach to code assessment using machine learning. The work basically focused Android malware analysis approaches based on permission and source code. In their source code assessment approach they obtained accuracy results with multiple algorithms however their source code based approach did not address repackaging. The source code based approach basically focused extraction of features from raw source code using the M0Droid dataset and processing that with a text processing algorithm like Bag of Words and obtaining results through machine learning, where each application from that dataset was extracted to develop their own dataset. Malware repackaging is a conspicuous issue where the raw source code of a malware is reused as in another form. Android malwares in packaged form can be detected easily with antivirus engines but as in raw form they remain undetected. Moreover, when repackaged then for which code pattern one code could be malicious should be identified. Lots of researcher worked on android application malware pattern and by combing all of it total 69 code pattern was already established till now. So it may happen that there exists more code pattern. Moreover, there was not found any tool if repacked any malware remains undetected by virus detector.

3 Methodology

This entire research was divided into three separate portions. First of all by considering the existing research work, modify the general Bag of Words algorithm and propose a modified model with better accuracy. Secondly, construct a unique vocabulary containing malicious code patterns or keywords. Finally develop a system or tool to check whether a code pattern is malicious or not, only if the source code are reused in repackaging process. The work by researchers Nikola Milosevic a, Ali Dehghantanha b, Kim-Kwang Raymond Choo [19] was considered as a base paper in this research because it focused on Android malware analysis with raw source code however the issue of repackaging was not addressed there. It is a vital issue and addressing repackaging in a proper way, better efficiency and accuracy can be obtained on the source code based approach.

3.1 Method Representation

The base paper for this research focused on addressing analysis process through raw source code where apk file is transformed into zip file and zip file is extracted into .dex file (dalvik executable file), where dex is converted to jar file, jar to class files to obtain java codes and merging the java codes to process with bag of words algorithm and construct a dataset for machine learning to obtain results. This paper follows the basic procedure as them with some modification. In the Fig. 1 the proposed model is shown. Relating to the base paper the dataset is collected from M0Droid dataset. This dataset contain package names and systems calls. Relating to our base paper, as they extracted 368 source codes, same has been done here. To conduct this procedure .apk files were collected accordingly as stated in the M0droid dataset. Then .apk files were converted to .zip format and classes.dex file was obtained from the package. This proposed method suggests to analyze the dex file through VirusTotal and identify the core file with VT graph to understand the core location of the infection. To obtain the jar file dex-to-jar was utilized as jar files were extracted using another windows based tool jd-gui. Java codes only from infected files has been merged for a dataset and machine learning but for to obtain better results from the base paper a customization of Bag of Words have been implanted and malicious patterns have been categorized by the means of a filtering process through a customized version of the algorithm. From the results obtained from the custom Bag of Words algorithm another filtered dataset was constructed to conduct machine learning on the dataset. The below Fig. 1 represents the methodology diagram.

After obtaining the .dex files they were provided on the online version of VirusTotal [20]. It analyzes the .dex files and provides results of their status based on the antivirus engines on VirusTotal. VirusTotal has a unique feature called VT graph which shows the exact location of infected file which is causing the maliciousness. After obtaining the exact file location, .java files from only that exact location were merged for the first dataset. In the base paper researches utilized all the source code to create dataset and applied Bag-of-Words algorithm, however in this paper some preprocessing were made to construct the final dataset. As some keywords and library functions never could be a part of malicious activities, thus it was focused to remove those from dataset. Moreover in this research when the Bag-of-Words algorithm was applied before that fresh keywords and malicious keywords were separated.

Stop Words such as "the", "is", "in", "for", "where", "when", "how", "to", "txt", "png", ".jpg", "A-Z", "a-z" and similar file extensions. Variables, Numbers, Default keywords such as "public", "super", "catch", "throws", "protected", "extends", "java", "io", "private", "system", "super", "float", "integer", "Boolean", "import","using" and finally Unicode and special characters such as '0x7f', '0xff', '0d', "{",'}", "@", "#", "%", "+", "-", "*", "%", "^", $, ~, !, ?, /, ___, Blank Space, Line Gaps and more special characters were considered as fresh keywords. Malicious source codes of java system calls packages and methods were obtained from the work of different researchers. References of API calls were obtained from reference no 21 [21]. References of functions were obtained from reference no 22 [22]. Again few classes were identified from the context of Examining Features for Android Malware Detection [23]. Another research GroddDroid [24] categorized malicious classes by categories. For obtaining the rest of possible java API calls, functions, methods and classes source code which were identified malicious by VirusTotal was inspected and manually separated. Results were obtained from a survey to identify few more malicious java API calls, functions, methods and classes.

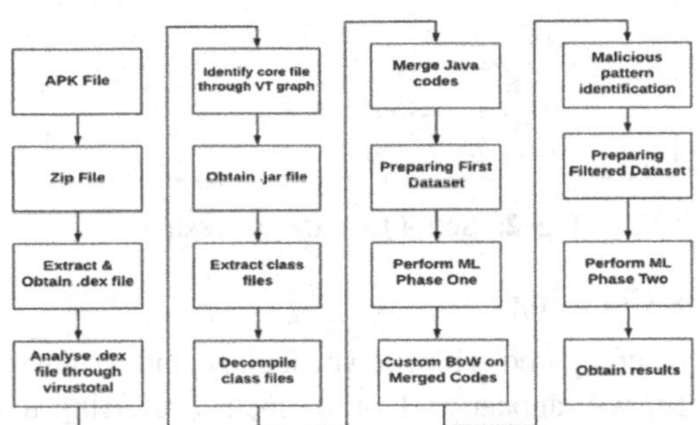

Fig. 1. Step by step method representation

3.2 Customizing Bag of Words and Practical Implementation

Bag of words model [25] is a technique of Natural Language Processing or NLP to extract features from text or perhaps words from sentences. The way it is performed is counting the frequency of words in a document. For the proposed model - after studying the generalized algorithm and implantation of it in base paper it was decided to customize the algorithm. Particularly customizations were made on three segments, let them be sequentially discussed:

3.2.1 The Process of Collecting Data

Basically the obtained data was the raw source code, which has been fetched as a particular line to compare it with the vocabulary. Each line has to be minimal by quotation marks and separated by comma. So a python script was prepared to take each line in the file into consideration and separate them accordingly. After it was completed the script would generate an output file for it. The below figure shows the script:

3.2.2 Generating and Managing the Vocabulary

After assessing the basic Bag of Words a customized script was prepared according to the research necessity as shown in Fig. 2. It has three segments, Tokenizing sentences, extracting words from sentences and generating a format of Bag of Words. Python modules like Numpy and re were utilized in the script. Words would be extracted from sentences where words would be ignored which will not appear in the vocabulary. The cleaned text would appear in the corpora for tokenizing and sorting the words and finally bag of words will be generated based on the given input what is in this case are the source codes. The prepared script can be viewed here [26].

```
import sys

fname= sys.argv[1]


file= open(fname.replace('.txt','')+"_result.txt",'w')


with open(fname) as f:
    lines = f.readlines()
for line in lines:
        line=line.replace('\n','')
        wr='"'+line+'",'
        file.write(wr+'\n')
```

Fig. 2. Script for data processing

3.2.3 The Process of Counting

Each line given will be compared with the vocabulary and a matrix will be generated, if the word is present it will appear as 1 in the matrix referring to its presence in the vocabulary; if it is not present it will be represented as 0, as shown Fig. 3.

Let"s consider Bag of Words is to be performed with the script to a piece of code which has been prepared as comma separated with by the previous script, Considering if any listener class implemented in the code such as android.telephony.PhoneStateListener in generic and specialized form then it will be considered as malicious as it has been refereed and found in multiple malicious instances (Palmer, D, 2017) and put its result on the second dataset, here words and characters can be ignored in the code such as 'import', 'extends', '{', 'try', 'return', 'String', 'Log', 'exception', '0', '32', 'ctx','e', 'this', 'util', 'void' etc. So, from the generated as output where it can be seen.

The vocabulary list and the matrix comparison by sentences and the words ignored will be excluded in the corpora. It can be seen that **android.telephony.PhoneStateListener** has been identified in multiple instances as a generic form and in specialized from

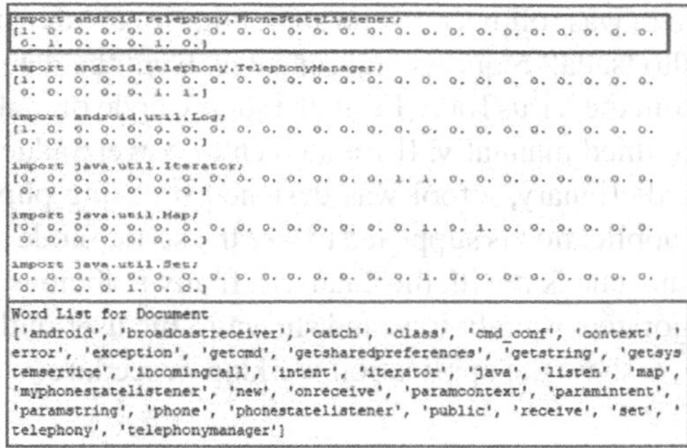

Fig. 3. Pattern identification with BoW

3.2.4 Malicious Keywords Categorization

All malicious code patterns which were found in various research paper are categorized here depending on their behavior. Malicious keywords were categorized based on few segments such as API calls on privacy such as getSimSerialNumber(), getSubscriberId(), getCellLocation(), getNetworkOperator(), API calls on Network, httpclient.execute(), getOutputStream(), getInputStream(), getNetworkInfo(), HttpURLConnection.connect(),openStream(), setDataAndType(), setRequestMethod(). API calls on SMS such as sendTextMessage(),sendTextData() etc. API calls on Wifi such as setWifiEnabled(), getWifiState() etc. Functions such as GlobalAlloc, GetModuleFileName, UnmapViewOfFile CreateFile, GlobalFree, GetFileSize, CreateFileMapping, CloseHandle etc. Classes based on SMS such as android.telephony.SmsManager, android.telephony.SmsMessage. Classed based on telephony such as android.telephony.TelephonyManager, android.os.IBinder, android.os.IBinder, android.location.LocationListener etc. Classes based on security and connection such as javax.crypto.*, java.security.spec.*, java.net.Proxy, java.util.Hashtable java.net.Socket, java.net.ServerSocket, java.net.MalformedURLException,java.net.SocketTimeoutException, java.net.proxy, java.security.Signature, java.security.SecureRandom etc. Classes based on android.net.NetworkInfo, android.net.NetworkInfo.State, android.net.Proxy, and based on few other classes, methods and call requests. Table 1 shows one additional keyword based on class, methods and call requests. These all data are collected from existing research work. As in this field only one keyword was found, so it was followed some procedures to find out some additional keyword to add in the vocabulary.

Table 1. Malicious keyword categories based class, methods and call requests

Methods and call requests	Based on network class and other
getVirusesIndexesDao()	android.view.View.OnClickListener

The procedure which was followed to add some additional keyword in the dictionary was to select few methods, call requests and functions from the dataset developed from the results obtained from the VirusTotal. From the source code of malware variants these were selected and examined manually. If found then they were added to the dictionary.

To implement the dictionary, a tool was designed by using php, CSS, HTML and mySql database. This application is supposed to take the source code as user input, search for malicious pattern and check it with the database. If any malicious pattern is identified then it would be categorized as malicious and shown to the user in the application front end. Below Figs. 4, 5, 6 show the application working procedure.

4 Result and Discussion

As stated before the dataset of M0Droid was utilized from where application packages were extracted and collected, source codes for 368 samples were successfully decompiled. Both of the datasets were constructed based on that.

For evaluating the dataset Support Vector Machine (SVM) has been utilized with Support Vector classified complimented by linear kernel. Then a dataset was prepared. After that, the dataset was preprocessed with proposed methodology and the result is stated at Table 2. Here it is shown that the accuracy is 95.65%, precision, recall and f1 score is around 0.5, 0.5, and 0.5 respectively. This indicates that the modification process of Bag-of-word Algorithm or additional prepossessing which was done in this paper is effective.

Table 2. ML results from the filtered dataset

Algorithm	Accuracy	Precision	Recall	F1
SVM	95.65	0.5	0.5	0.5

Machine learning aided Android malware classification [19] obtained their best results for source code based classification with SVM was 95.1%, as the following Table 3 represents. And the value of precision, recall and F1 score was 0.952, 0.951 and 0.951 respectively.

Table 3. Results from existing work

Algorithm	Accuracy	Precision	Recall	F1
SVM	95.1	0.952	0.951	0.951

Comparison with obtained results from this proposed methodology is given in Table 4. From the result comparison it can be clearly stated that the proposed model has a better accuracy than the existing model, which displays at least a 0.55% better accuracy than the best accuracy results obtained in the similarly existing model. As the value of precision is decreased by 0.452, the reason behind it is, the data set was not exactly. Again as recall is decreased by 0.451, again the same reasons exist behind it. As the accuracy is increasing than the existing work, so this model would provide better result.

Table 4. Results comparison

Parameters	Existing model	Proposed model	Comparison
Algorithm	**SVM**	**SVM**	
Accuracy	95.1	95.65	0.55% better

As stated above, this modified model is performing relatively better, so by checking the dataset we have added the following keywords in the existing vocabulary list. Table 5 shows the list of added keywords in the existing dictionary.

Table 5. List of added keywords in the existing vocabulary

Collected Entities from Observation
MessagesContentSender
fetchContact()
GetappInfo()
IMAdTrackerReceiver()
onStartCommand()
onTerminate()
PendingIntent.getService()
InstallActivity.this.startActivity()
getPassword()
getPasswordAuthentication()
fetchContacts()
Android.telephony.phoneStateListener

MessagesContentSender, retrieves Message Content and sends it to third party, **fetchContact()** fetches and sends information to third party, **GetappInfo()** obtains application information **IMAdTrackerReceiver()** is an external broadcast receiver to invoke other classes **onStartCommand()** has been identified as an initialization command **onTerminate()** was identified in multiple instances terminating a course of action for subduing malicious, **PendingIntent.getService()** It is a token is given to a foreign application that enables foreign application to use the permission from the application to perform a default code piece, **InstallActivity.this.startActivity()** focuses on installing a particular activity installing it at a sheath fashion, **getPassword()** has been utilized as malicious intent, **getPasswordAuthentication()** invokes password authentication multiple times. **fetchContacts()** has been identified retrieving contacts from the infected device. Finally **android.telephony.PhoneStateListener** has been distinguishes in generic and specialized form which is considered malicious from multiple instance.

Thus after adding all these twelve words to the vocabulary, it will help the researcher to find out more patterns.

Moreover a system is already developed to test it. The system works as following: Any source code of Java Platform from any Android Application can be copied here and paste here. A button is there "Check Source" to submit it as given in Fig. 4. The system will check it by using the prepared vocabulary. If the vocabulary matched were found, then it will show the system is vulnerable, otherwise it is not vulnerable. Figure 5 and Fig. 6 shows the result of malicious pattern recognition.

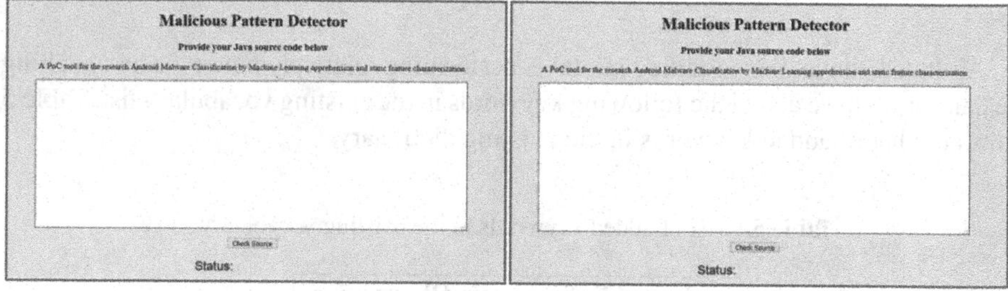

Fig. 4. Outlook of Implemented tool

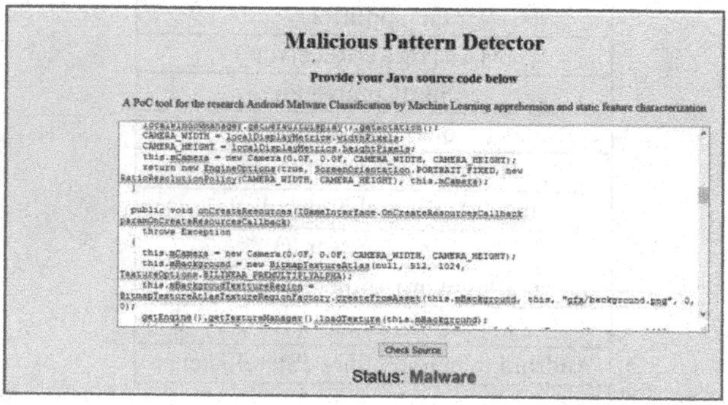

Fig. 5. Output of implemented tool after inserting malicious pattern

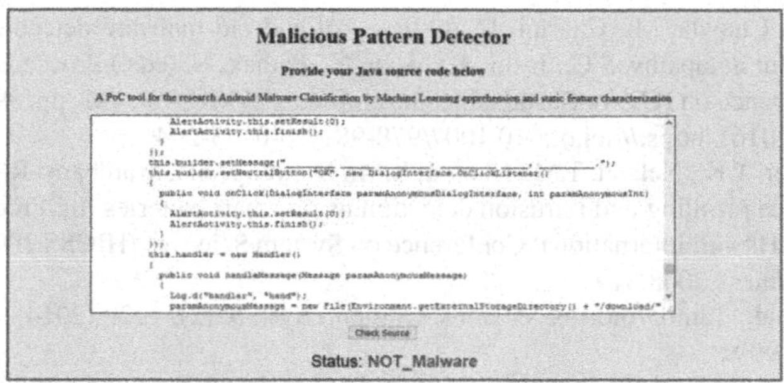

Fig. 6. Output of implemented tool after inserting non malicious pattern

5 Conclusion and Future Research Direction

The whole research basically focused on the overall mechanism of static analysis and addressing the prevention of source code repackaging of malwares. Existing works in the field provided scheme for the development of a model which may provide better results in case of efficiency and accuracy. The proposed model addresses repackaging in a proper way. Normal static analysis does not properly addresses the issue which has been the main goal of this research. Automating static analysis method by the means of classification algorithm (SVM) was another agenda in terms of accuracy and performance with comparison with few of the similar research in the field. As the comparing paper used SVM that is why this paper used SVM only. This approach takes focus on API calls, functions, classes, methods and statements in generic and specialized forms to detect malicious pattern rather than few fixed defined features what has been observed in similar researches. Moreover the proposed model has obtained 0.55% better accuracy than a similar classification based adaptation on source code. Moreover, this research added 12 additional malicious patterns to the vocabulary which will help to identify the vulnerable android application when repackaged. This research shows a tool to check the malicious pattern of android application source code when repackaged. This application will help to identify a source code whether it is vulnerable or not. In future this research could be enhanced by adding more malicious pattern to the vocabulary. Practical implementation of the proposed model was done as a web application. In future it could be implement by using Artificial Platform (AI).

References

1. Dehghantanha, A., Franke, K.: Privacy-respecting digital investigation
2. Twelfth Annual International Conference on Privacy, Security and Trust (2014). https://doi.org/10.1109/pst.2014.6890932
3. Kitagawa, M., Gupta, A., Cozza, R., Durand, I., Glenn, D., Maita, K., et al.: Market share: final pcs, ultramobiles and mobile phones, all countries, 2q15 update, Technical report (2015)
4. Chia, C., Choo, K.-K., Fehrenbacher, D.: How cyber-savvy are older mobile device users? Mob. Secur. Priv. 67–83 (2017). https://doi.org/10.1016/b978-0-12-804629-6.00004-3
5. Viennot, N., Garcia, E., Nieh, J.: A measurement study of google play. ACM SIGMETRICS Perform. Eval. Rev. **42**(1), 221–233 (2014). https://doi.org/10.1145/2637364.2592003

6. Sharma, M., Chawla, M., Gajrani, J.: A survey of android malware detection strategy and techniques. In: Satapathy, S.C., Joshi, A., Modi, N., Pathak, N. (eds.) Proceedings of International Conference on ICT for Sustainable Development. AISC, vol. 409, pp. 39–51. Springer, Singapore (2016). https://doi.org/10.1007/978-981-10-0135-2_4
7. Buennemeyer, T.K., Nelson, T.M., Clagett, L.M., Dunning, J.P., Marchany, R.C., Tront, J.G.: Mobile device profiling and intrusion detection using smart batteries. In: Proceedings of the 41st Annual Hawaii International Conference on System Sciences (HICSS 2008). https://doi.org/10.1109/hicss.2008.319
8. Enck, W., et al.: TaintDroid. ACM Trans. Comput. Syst. **32**(2), 1–29 (2014). https://doi.org/10.1145/2619091
9. Dash, S.K., et al.: DroidScribe: classifying android malware based on runtime behavior. In: 2016 IEEE Security and Privacy Workshops (SPW) (2016). https://doi.org/10.1109/spw.2016.25
10. Alam, M.S., Vuong, S.T.: Random forest classification for detecting android malware. In: 2013 IEEE International Conference on Green Computing and Communications and IEEE Internet of Things and IEEE Cyber, Physical and Social Computing (2013). https://doi.org/10.1109/greencom-ithings-cpscom.2013.122
11. Isohara, T., Takemori, K., Kubota, A.: kernel-based behavior analysis for android malware detection. In: 2011 Seventh International Conference on Computational Intelligence and Security (2011). https://doi.org/10.1109/cis.2011.226
12. Damshenas, M., Dehghantanha, A., Choo, K.-K.R., Mahmud, R.: M0Droid: an android behavioral-based malware detection model. J. Inf. Priv. Secur. **11**(3), 141–157 (2015). https://doi.org/10.1080/15536548.2015.1073510
13. Mercaldo, F., Nardone, V., Santone, A., Visaggio, C.A.: Download malware? No, thanks. In: Proceedings of the 4th FME Workshop on Formal Methods in Software Engineering – FormaliSE 2016 (2016). https://doi.org/10.1145/2897667.2897673
14. Karbab, E.B., Debbabi, M., Mouheb, D.: Fingerprinting android packaging: generating DNAs for malware detection. Digit. Invest. **18**, S33-S45 (2016). https://doi.org/10.1016/j.diin.2016.04.013
15. Nataraj, L., Karthikeyan, S., Jacob, G., Manjunath, B.S.: Malware images. In: Proceedings of the 8th International Symposium on Visualization for Cyber Security - VizSec 2011 (2011). https://doi.org/10.1145/2016904.2016908
16. Nath, H.V., Mehtre, B.M.: Static malware analysis using machine learning methods. In: Martínez Pérez, G., Thampi, S.M., Ko, R., Shu, L. (eds.) SNDS 2014. CCIS, vol. 420, pp. 440–450. Springer, Heidelberg (2014). https://doi.org/10.1007/978-3-642-54525-2_39
17. Afonso, V.M., de Amorim, M.F., Grégio, A.R.A., Junquera, G.B., de Geus, P.L.: Identifying android malware using dynamically obtained features. J. Comput. Virol. Hacking Tech. **11**(1), 9–17 (2014). https://doi.org/10.1007/s11416-014-0226-7
18. Yerima, S.Y., Sezer, S., Muttik, I.: Android malware detection: an eigenspace analysis approach. In: 2015 Science and Information Conference (SAI) (2015). https://doi.org/10.1109/sai.2015.7237302
19. Sahs, J., Khan, L.: A machine learning approach to android malware detection. In: 2012 European Intelligence and Security Informatics Conference (2012). https://doi.org/10.1109/eisic.2012.34
20. Milosevic, N., Dehghantanha, A., Choo, K.-K.R.: Machine learning aided android malware classification. Comput. Electr. Eng. **61**, 266–274 (2017). https://doi.org/10.1016/j.compeleceng.2017.02.013
21. VirusTotal. http://www.virustotal.com/
22. Chan, P.P.K., Song, W.-K.: Static detection of Android malware by using permissions and API calls. In: 2014 International Conference on Machine Learning and Cybernetics (2014). https://doi.org/10.1109/icmlc.2014.7009096

23. Patanaik, C.K., Barbhuiya, F.A., Nandi, S.: Obfuscated malware detection using API call dependency. In: Proceedings of the First International Conference on Security of Internet of Things - SecurIT 2012 (2012). https://doi.org/10.1145/2490428.2490454
24. Leeds, M., Keffeler, M., Atkison, T.: A comparison of features for android malware detection. In: Proceedings of the SouthEast Conference on - ACM SE 2017 (2017). https://doi.org/10.1145/3077286.3077288
25. Abraham, A., Andriatsimandefitra, R., Brunelat, A., Lalande, J.-F., Tong, V.V.T. GroddDroid: a gorilla for triggering malicious behaviors. In: 2015 10th International Conference on Malicious and Unwanted Software (MALWARE) (2015). https://doi.org/10.1109/malware.2015.7413692
26. Bag-of-words model. https://en.wikipedia.org/wiki/Bag-of-words_model

Analysis of Agent-Based and Agent-Less Sandboxing for Dynamic Malware Analysis

Md. Zaki Muzahid(✉), Mahsin Bin Akram, and A. K. M. Alamgir

Department of Computer Science and Engineering, University of Dhaka, Dhaka, Bangladesh
emonssj7@gmail.com

Abstract. Observing and experimenting with malware with full user control have been complex and difficult to say the least. As time goes on, malwares are becoming more advanced and has the ability to realize that the environment they are targeting is virtual, thus shutting their process and leaves the testers unable to analyze further. To combat this problem, a sandbox can be used to test these malwares through modifications. The sandbox is needed to create a dummy virtual environment to test the malwares on, and modifications on the said environment will allow more controlled and specified testing. Bypassing intelligent Malware for in depth analysis will be successful. Dynamic analysis will be performed, specifically agent-based using Cuckoo open-source sandbox and agent-less using DRAKVUF by hypervisor and virtualization extension. Analysis result will be classified over few pre-defined criteria including network requests, system injections and modifications, security measures and kernel alteration; ultimately proving which technique is appropriate and reliable for prominent malware analysis.

Keywords: Malware · Sandbox · Virtualization · Agent-based · Agent-less · Hypervisor · Analysis

1 Introduction

Malwares are programs specifically designed to disrupt, damage, or gain unauthorized access to a computer system. Everyday more advanced malwares are being developed that can bypass already existing analysis methods becoming more evasive and diversified. Henceforth, new techniques to withstand them are required.

Two types of analyses are performed for detection: Firstly - Static Analysis, where malware samples are not executed, instead their binary executables are analyzed. The binary sequence is then recorded as "signatures" used as reference to indicate if an application is a malware or not. However, Static Analysis is proven to be less effective by malwares that obfuscate their source binary making it very difficult to translate. For Dynamic Analysis, there are Agent-based and Agent-less Sandboxing. Where, agent-based sandboxes already have built-in or installable "agents" that monitors the target system and collects information from observing the sample. Whereas agent-less sandboxes uses hypervisor-based approach which creates, runs and manages virtual environments on the underlying hardware. However, evasive malwares are more intelligent and are able to detect an agent; thus shuts down or disguises as benign processes [1].

T. Bhuiyan et al. (Eds.): ICONCS 2020, LNICST 325, pp. 72–84, 2020.
https://doi.org/10.1007/978-3-030-52856-0_6

1.1 Motivation

The motivation behind this experiment is the alarming increase of malwares in recent years as shown in Fig. 1, which uses different evasion techniques to probe and identify the malware detection and analysis systems [2]. Conventional techniques such as antivirus and antimalware softwares are not adequate to stop these evasive techniques such as Memory Injection, Malicious Document Files, and Environment Testing etc. One third of today's advance malwares are hyper-evasive malwares as introduced in [3]. These malwares have multiple layers of detection evasion techniques and runs more than twenty processes to detect agent or sandbox existence such as Cerber ransomware. Moreover, some of these malwares can detect the existence of a single sandbox and easily evades the sandbox [4].

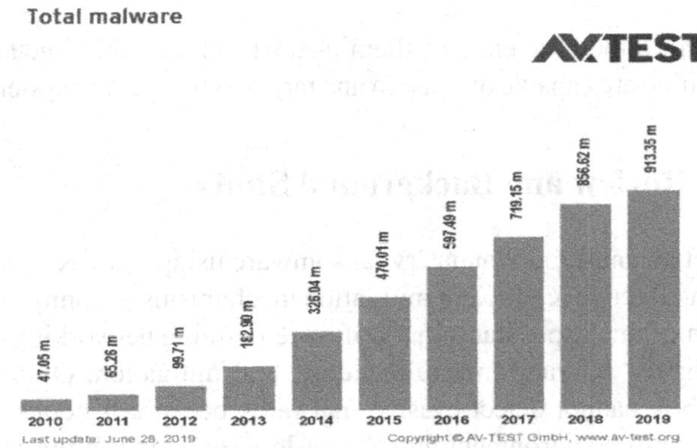

Fig. 1. Increase of malware development over years 2010 to 2019 [5]

1.2 Problem Definition

In this paper, focus has been given on agent-based sandboxing and agent-less sandboxing; while comparing the two methods ultimately determining which one is more adept at analyzing malware threats.

1.3 Research Objectives

The focal objective of this paper is to compare the two existing techniques of dynamic behavioral analysis and to determine which method is better at detecting evasive malwares.

(i) **Agent-based Sandbox for Dynamic Behavioral Analysis**

a. Implementing a virtual sandbox
b. Setting up a target system

c. Setting up an agent inside the target system
d. Infecting the system and capturing malicious processes
e. Analyzing the threat level of malware detected by behavioral analysis

(ii) **Agent-less Sandbox for Dynamic Behavioral Analysis**

a. Implementing a virtual sandbox (using hyper-visor)
b. Setting up a target system
c. Infecting the system and agent-less monitoring of Windows internal kernel functions (using hardware virtualization extensions found in Intel CPUs)
d. Analyzing the threat level of malware detected by behavioral analysis

(iii) **A comparison between the process of two different techniques**

a. Determining the efficiency of them against polymorphic, metamorphic malwares which are capable of evasion and targeted for specific system weaknesses

2 Literature Review and Background Study

Maxat Akbanov et al. analyzed WannaCry ransomware using static & dynamic analysis methods to design effective & efficient mitigation mechanisms to combat ransom-wares [6]. The limitation of this paper states that Software-defining networking (SDN) should have been investigated for ransomware detection and mitigation. On the other hand, agent-based sandbox cannot detect evasive malwares because it hooks data by dropping the agent in control environment thus Agent-less sandbox is preferred [7]. Feature sets of malwares need to be converted into binary vectors and analyzed using deep-learning algorithm using n-gram NLP techniques [8]. Victor Marchetto et al. used the similar technique and defense strategies to combat cryptojacking which includes objective, behavior, and indicators of cryptojacking attacks; where the defense strategies are deployed by mainly studying malware behaviors and building a mitigation obstructer [9]. Moreover, correlation based systems detect botnets on the basis of network behavior correlation such as communications with C&C (command and control) servers and attacks by infected hosts; statistics based systems extract statistical features from not only communications with C&C servers and attacks but also other communications and classify them with machine learning [10]. Tamas K. Lengyel et al. used DRAKVUF sandbox to improve the scalability, fidelity and stealth of malware analysis by using latest hypervisor technology and hardware virtualization extensions. The improvement of the sandbox includes the need to support multi-vCPU and Linux, including ability to stall code, record & replay, branch exploration, and timing attacks [11]. Chih-Hung Lin et al. proposed a system called VTCSandbox employs virtual time controller (VTC) mechanics to provide efficient hypervisor-based security monitoring [12]. Moreover, Satoshi Tanda and I. Korkin stated that system activities can be monitored via the hypervisor including kernel-mode thus malware interaction with the kernel can be observed [13]. According to Michael Brengel, low level timing-based mechanism can be utilized to detect hardware virtualized systems [14].

3 Proposed Approach

The approach taken elaborates the process of two different techniques (Agent-based & Agent-less) used to analyze modern malwares and ultimately conclude which method will yield better result. To specify further, here is a dataflow diagram as depicted in Fig. 2 for better representation of the proposed approach.

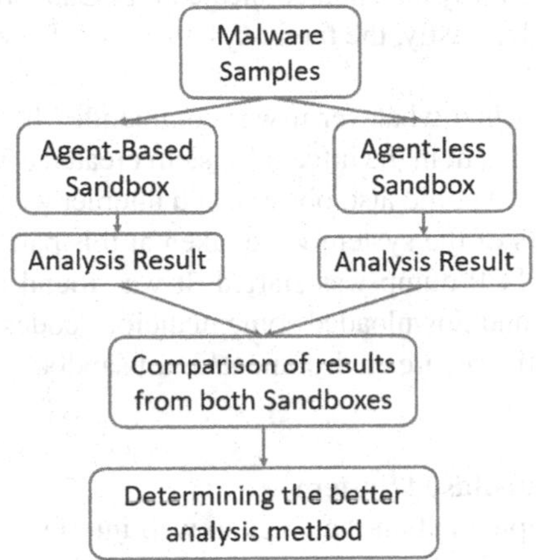

Fig. 2. Data-flow diagram of the proposed methods.

3.1 Proposed Architecture for Agent-Based System

The first part of objective was to create testbed sandbox and infecting it with malware. Then agent-based dynamic malware analysis was allowed to run in three steps: the preprocessing, infecting the target system, and dump collection and analysis.

To go in depth, at first MongoDB was employed on Linux Environment in order to use Django based web-interface. Next Volatility was installed for the extraction of digital artifacts from volatile memory (RAM) samples. Then M2Crypto was selected to access different cryptography tools. Afterwards, Cuckoo Sandbox was chosen for a safe environment for analysis of malwares [15]. It is used because Cuckoo is open source and highly malleable for different experimental purposes. Next, distrom3 was appointed to decode x86/AMD64 binary streams and return a structure that describes each instruction. Subsequently, a Blackhole Internet was set up so the malwares cannot access the internet without user permission so it acts as a sink for all activities the infected system takes.

For this research, some malware samples were collected from GIT repository such as ransomware WannaCry, Locky, and botnet Kelihos [16]. Firstly, a secure environment was required to create. The Oracle VirtualBox was used to create the target system, in this case, a Windows 7 (Service Pack 1) operating system. To monitor what malwares does once it is activated in a target system, a virtual environment was created and made it intentionally vulnerable by disabling the firewall and user account access and windows defender system. A network was also created that allows to monitor and analyze the target system by installing an agent in the target OS. The agent captured and made a log of every network/API request that was sent by the target system (which is vulnerable). Some applications were pre-installed in the target system such as outdated Mozilla Firefox Browser, Adobe Flash Player, and Acrobat Reader DC etc. which are already known to be quiet vulnerable to malwares beforehand. This was done to make the system more vulnerable and trigger the malware to exploit the vulnerable system. Then a snapshot was created of the system and connected it to Cuckoo servers in order to run the infected executable file. Lastly, the target system was infected with one malware at a time.

After the malware finished whatever it was commanded by the C&C server (command and control server), agent in the infected system created a TCP dump and returned it for further analysis [17]. It could also observe and interact with the infected system in real time. Some snapshots of the system were taken at this particular timestamp. Then further analyzing of the TCP dump was started. It was found that the malwares contacted their C&C servers and downloaded some malicious codes and file in the infected system. This proved that the secure environment/smart sandbox for analyzing malwares is effective.

Initial Analysis for Agent-Based System

The malware sample is uploaded on the Cuckoo web interface for infecting the target system (Windows 7 SP1). After the sample was uploaded, the parameters of the analysis were configured in Cuckoo. Some examples include, "Enable Injection" which is selected because if the C&C server tries to remotely inject any malwares, then it will be allowed and the outcome will be observed. "Process Memory Dump" was selected because a copy of all the processes was wanted to keep that was running during the analysis period in the target system. Similarly, "Full Memory Dump" was selected to save a copy of the physical memory during analysis. "Enable Simulated Human Interaction" was selected to deceive malwares into thinking that the environment was not simulated.

```
C:\Python27\python.exe
2019-04-16 17:12:39,530 [analyzer] DEBUG: Pipe server name: \??\PIPE\XekLUYuXzSz
jdeKBofM
2019-04-16 17:12:39,530 [analyzer] DEBUG: Log pipe server name: \??\PIPE\wIFggXG
UUYUKJXkUvSeAIAQkIcaOuTII
2019-04-16 17:12:40,201 [analyzer] DEBUG: Started auxiliary module DbgView
2019-04-16 17:12:40,622 [analyzer] DEBUG: Started auxiliary module Disguise
2019-04-16 17:12:40,632 [modules.auxiliary.dumptls] WARNING: You're not running
the Cuckoo Agent as Administrator. Doing so will improve your analysis results!
2019-04-16 17:12:40,632 [analyzer] DEBUG: Started auxiliary module DumpTLSMaster
Secrets
2019-04-16 17:12:40,642 [analyzer] DEBUG: Started auxiliary module Human
2019-04-16 17:12:40,782 [modules.auxiliary.installcert] INFO: Successfully insta
lled PFX certificate.
2019-04-16 17:12:40,782 [analyzer] DEBUG: Started auxiliary module InstallCertif
icate
2019-04-16 17:12:40,782 [analyzer] DEBUG: Started auxiliary module Reboot
2019-04-16 17:12:40,862 [analyzer] DEBUG: Started auxiliary module RecentFiles
2019-04-16 17:12:40,862 [analyzer] DEBUG: Started auxiliary module Screenshots
2019-04-16 17:12:40,862 [analyzer] DEBUG: Started auxiliary module LoadZer0m0n
2019-04-16 17:12:41,513 [lib.api.process] INFO: Successfully executed process fr
om path u'C:\\Users\\cuckoo\\AppData\\Local\\Temp\\ed01ebfbc9eb5bbea545af4d01bf5
f1071661840480439c6e5babe8e080e41aa.exe' with arguments '' and pid 2568
2019-04-16 17:12:41,765 [modules.auxiliary.human] INFO: Found button u'OK', clic
king it
```

Fig. 3. Agent in target system

The console shows that an agent is sending malware artifacts to Cuckoo server and simulating the virtual environment and deluding malware shown in Fig. 3. This console shows the connection between agent and server. The next console shows Cuckoo completing the analysis steps such as matching signatures, looking for MITM (Man in the middle) attack, behavioral analysis, suspicious TCP connections, creating process and memory dump and completing the analysis.

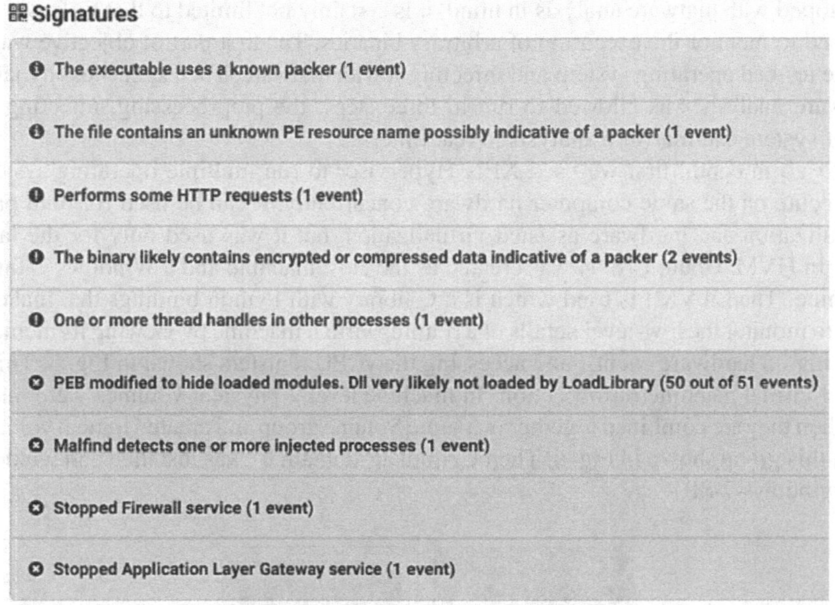

Fig. 4. Malware signatures

After the analysis is completed, the web interface displays the summary of the result. Moreover, the signatures that matches with the already known signatures saved in multiple repositories such as VirusTotal [18] are displayed in Fig. 4.

In the analysis period, carefully monitored the changes occurring in the target system resources for e.g. DNS requests, HTTP requests, API calls, files and registry related activities, service activities and process trees. This helped us to get a better understanding the behavior of malware. The TCP dump was uploaded to Cuckoo analyzer and it performed both behavioral and static analysis and found some signatures and was able to identify these malwares as threats.

Initial Observation for Agent-based System

During the analysis, closely monitored the changes occurring in the operating resource for e.g. DNS requests, HTTP requests, file related activities, registry related activities, API calls and their return values, service activities, IRC commands, and process tree that were observed during the experiment. Whenever the malware tried to execute some features, the leftover artifacts were appeared to be helpful in understanding the behavior of malware [19]. The TCP dump was uploaded to Cuckoo analyzer and it performed both behavioral and static analyses and found some signatures for identification of these malwares as threats.

3.2 Proposed Architecture for Agent-Less System

DRAKVUF provides a perfect platform for stealthy malware analysis as its footprint is nearly undetectable from the malware's perspective. While DRAKVUF has been mainly developed with malware analysis in mind, it is certainly not limited to that task as it can be used to monitor the execution of arbitrary binaries. The first part of objective was to create testbed operating system and infecting it with malware. Then agent-less dynamic malware analysis was allowed to run in three steps: the preprocessing, infecting the target system and malware analysis in real time.

To go in depth, first we used XEN Hypervisor to run multiple operating systems to execute on the same computer hardware concurrently. It can be used for both para-virtualization and hardware assisted virtualization, but it was used only for the latter case. In HVM, Ubuntu 18.04 was created as the Host machine and a Windows 7 Target machine. The LibVMI is used which is a C library with Python bindings that makes it easy to monitor the low-level details of a running virtual machine by viewing its memory, trapping on hardware events, and accessing the vCPU registers shown in Fig. 5. This is called virtual machine introspection. In machine level 2 physical volumes were made, and then they are combined together in a same Volume group and created logical volumes upon this group shown in Fig. 6. Then Ubuntu at "domain 0" was installed and windows 7 at windows-7-SP1.

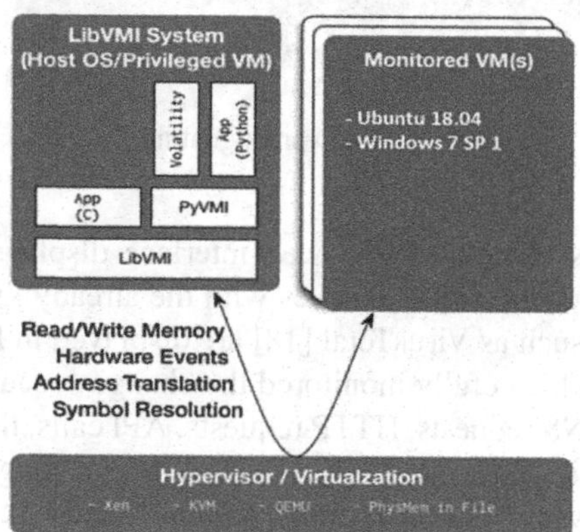

Fig. 5. LibVMI architecture

Rekall was used as the memory forensic tool. It is an advanced forensic and incident response framework. Rekall Agent is a complete endpoint incident response and forensic tool. The Rekall Agent extends Rekall's advanced capabilities to a scalable, distributed environment. Its approach to memory analysis is unique - Rekall leverages exact debugging information provided by the operating system vendors to precisely locate significant kernel data structures.

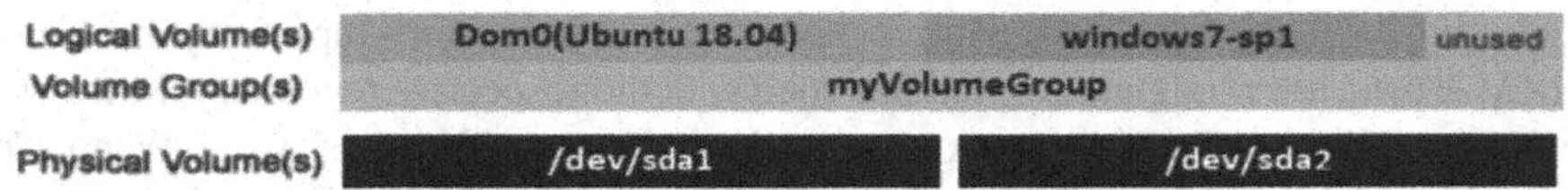

Fig. 6. Out system logical group architecture

Then installed DRAKVUF was installed to start the agent-less malware analysis as it provides a perfect platform for stealthy malware analysis as its footprint is nearly undetectable from the malware's perspective.

4 Performance Evaluation

4.1 Observation of Agent-Based Analysis Results

The result of the agent-based analysis shows the comparison of three different malwares over pre-defined criteria, such as threat level, signatures, network requests, process injection etc. displayed in Table 1. The threat level is evaluated by matching the malware signatures from community repository [20]. Higher the rating, higher the potential to harm a vulnerable system; in this case KPOT malware had the highest rating of 11.4. The PEiD detects most common packers, cryptors and compilers for PE files, for WannaCry and Locky, "Armadillo v1.71" identifier was detected. For none of the malwares, there was no match with Antivirus repository.

Table 1. Comparison based on known signatures and packers and artifacts

	WannaCry	Kelihos	Locky	KPOT
Known Signature Matching				
Threat rating (out of 10)	6.2	5.8	5.8	11.4
PEiD signatures	1	None	1	None
Antivirus signature	None	None	None	None
IRMA signatures	None	None	None	None
YARA signatures	None	None	None	None
Known Packers Detected				
In binaries	2	2	1	None
In executables	1	None	1	None
Unknown Packers Detected				
In binaries	None	None	None	None
In executables	1	None	None	None
Dropped Artifacts				
Dropped files/buffers	None	None	None	None

Moving on, there were no signatures matching with Yara tool's repository. Likewise, for IRMA there are no signatures that matched with the respective repository. Moreover, WannaCry & Kelihos had the most known packer's detected "binaries" while WannaCry and Locky had most packers in "executables". Consequently, WannaCry had 1 unknown packer that was detected. The leftover artifacts count dropped from a successful malware attack was none for all four malwares.

The next criterion represents how many "hosts" the malwares tried to connect with as shown in Table 2. WannaCry malware initiated the most host connection with total of 68. For 16 among these, no DNS query was performed. Moreover, the network connection portion of the criteria includes DNS, TCP, UDP and HTTPS requests. Once again WannaCry takes the first place with the highest number of these said requests. Moreover, KPOT is the only malware that sent a single data using HTTPS POST method. Kelihos had the highest IP address connections of 11 however these were unresponsive, which is even more suspicious. KPOT is the only malware that made 14 repeated searches for browser processes while others made none. Other than WannaCry, all three malwares utilized potentially malicious URLS. Moving on to network trafficking, all of them made no effort to move data across a network at a given point of time via ICMP or IRC traffic. Also, none of the malwares caused any alerts for both intrusion systems (Suricata and Snort).

Table 2. Comparison based on analysis detection/evasion.

	WannaCry	Kelihos	Locky	KPOT
Connections to hosts	68	20	2	6
DNS requests	89	13	11	7
TCP requests	78	9	None	12
UDP requests	114	31	20	22
HTTPS requests/suspicious	22/5	0/0	0/0	18/2
Sent Data using HTTPS POST method	None	None	None	1
Potentially malicious URLs found	None	50 out of 509	50 out of 138	50 out of 509
Connects to unresponsive IP addresses	3	11	1	2
Repeated searches for browser process	None	None	None	14
ICMP traffic	None	None	None	None
IRC traffic	None	None	None	None
Suricata alert	None	None	None	None
Snort alert	None	None	None	None

Table 3. Comparison based on System Modification Detected.

	WannaCry	Kelihos	Locky	KPOT
Malfind injected process detection	1	1	1	1
PEB modified to hide loaded modules (DLLs)	50	50	39	50
Stopped firewall service	Yes	Yes	Yes	Yes
Stopped application layer gateway service	Yes	Yes	Yes	Yes
Modified WPAD proxy auto-configuration for traffic interception	None	None	None	8
Thread handles in other processes	1	1	1	1

The next group of criteria is the detection of system modification malwares shown in Table 3. As it can be seen, all the malwares injected at least one process which was detected by Volatility's Malfind plug-in. The system dll files modification was also detected in most occasions. All of the malwares stopped the Firewall Service as well as stopped Application Layer Gateway Service to get uninterrupted network access. KPOT modified the WPAD proxy auto-configuration to intercept and steal network packets.

Now it is time to discuss the most important part of this analysis, detection of virtualization and evasion of analysis tools by the malwares shown in Table 4. From the previous table, it is seen that only KPOT malware to be aware of the virtualized operating system via Registry Key and target system memory mount. Detection of virtual network was done by checking the network adapter address. It also collected credentials from FTP client softwares, local email clients (such as MS Outlook), and fingerprint of the system (by making query in registry of MachineGUID, DigitalProductId and SystemBiosData). It collected information about installed applications such as Google Chrome, Mozilla Firefox, Oracle VirtualBox, Python, and Updater etc.

Table 4. Comparison based on Analysis Detection/Evasion.

	WannaCry	Kelihos	Locky	KPOT
Virtual environment detection	None	None	None	Yes
Check for available memory space	None	None	None	Yes
Check adapter address to detect virtual network	None	None	None	1
Harvests credentials from local FTP client softwares	None	None	None	2
Harvests credentials from local Email clients	None	None	None	2
Collects info to fingerprint the system	None	None	None	1
Collects information about installed application	None	None	None	7

4.2 Observation of Agent-Less Analysis Results

It can be monitored the execution of arbitrary malicious binary files as well as extract deleted files from memory before they are actually discarded by the operating system.

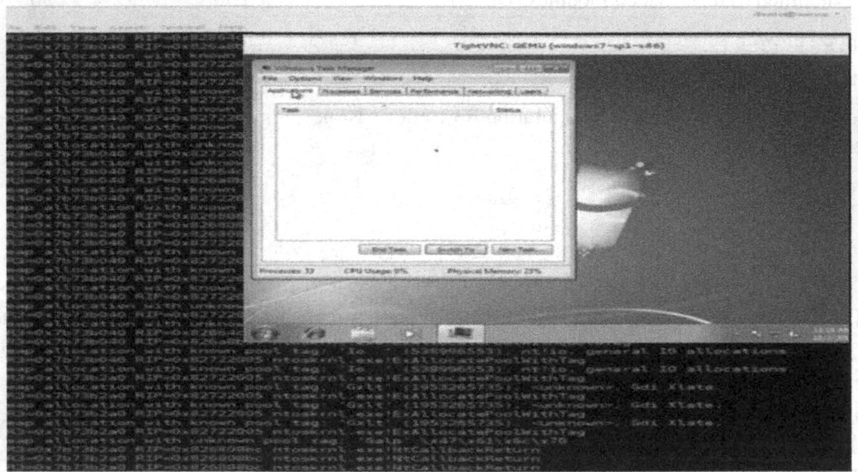

Fig. 7. Capturing kernel functions via XEN hypervisor

Many files created by malware droppers are only present in memory and never show up on disk. Also it can be monitored some system aspects such as, tracing heap allocations, tracing files being accessed, and extracting files from memory before they are deleted, tracing UDP and TCP connections. After the collection is done the files were submitted to VirusTotal for secondary analysis. The console shows the agent-less monitoring of kernel processes in the target system (Windows 7 SP1) with hypervisor technology as shown in Fig. 7. Though the system is not yet complete; the overview of the experiment gives some basic ideas how the problems would ultimately be figured out.

5 Future Work

The next step of evolution is the analysis of malwares using agent-less sandbox for dynamic analysis. We can also enhance this work for later version of Windows. It could be done by using hypervisor technology, which can monitor the malware from outside the target system, without any agent running inside. Furthermore, a detailed comparison between both agent-based and agent-less sandboxing techniques over some pre-selected criteria including HTTP, DNS requests captured, API calls monitored, IDS Signatures matched, files and registry related suspicious activities monitored, suspicious service activities monitored, zero-day activities, and true positive detection of evasive malwares.

6 Conclusion

Although this work is not yet fully completed, significant result is acquired such as detection evasive malware using agent-based sandboxing technique. In this study, we focused on agent-based sandboxing and its effectiveness while detecting evasive malwares. We implemented the Agent-based Sandbox and ran dynamic malware analysis as we intended. We further analyzed the results gained from our system and presented them in previous chapter. From the findings of Chapter 4, it is evident that some modern malwares do have internal process to detect dynamic analysis techniques such as malware KPOT. Although it did not stop its harmful activities, we were able to properly analyze the sample. However it may not always be the case, thus it is necessary to implement a technique which can analyze the malwares without being detected or update the existing technique so that it may be able to do so. The successful part of this study was the detection of evasive malware. Also as we checked our results for reconfirmation at VirusTotal, we alarmingly found a lot of antivirus engine completely failing to detect evasive malwares.

References

1. DuPaul, N.: Common malware types: Cybersecurity 101 (2019). https://www.veracode.com/blog/2012/10/common-malware-types-cybersecurity-101. Accessed 24 Jan 2020
2. Bulazel, A., Yener, B.: A survey on automated dynamic malware analysis evasion and counter-evasion: PC, Mobile, and Web. In: Proceedings of the 1st Reversing and Offensive-oriented Trends Symposium (ROOTS), pp. 1–21. Association for Computing Machinery, New York (2017). Article 2. https://doi.org/10.1145/3150376.3150378
3. Stefnisson, S.: Evasive malware now a commodity (2018). https://www.security-week.com/evasive-malware-now-commodity. Accessed 24 Jan 2020
4. Maass, M.: A Theory and Tools for Applying Sandboxes Effectively (2018). https://doi.org/10.1184/R1/6714425
5. AV-TEST GmbH: Malware statistics & trends reportlav-test (2019). https://www.av-test.org/en/statistics/malware.html. Accessed 24 Jan 2020
6. Akbanov, M., Vassilakis, V., Logothetis, M.D.: Ransomware detection and mitigation using software-defined networking: the case of WannaCry. Comput. Electr. Eng. **76**, 111–121 (2019). https://doi.org/10.1016/j.compeleceng.2019.03.012
7. Chailytko, A., Skuratovich, S.: Defeating sandbox evasion: how to increase the successful emulation rate in your virtual environment. In: ShmooCon (2017)
8. Muhammad, A., Shiaeles, S., Ghita, B.V. and Papadaki, M.: Agent-based vs agent-less sandbox for dynamic behavioral analysis (2018). https://doi.org/10.1109/GIIS.2018.8635598
9. Marchetto, V., Liu, X.: An investigation of cryptojacking: malware analysis and defense strategies. J. Strateg. Innov. Sustain. **14**(1) (2019). https://doi.org/10.33423/jsis.v14i1.987
10. Rubio-Ayala, S.: An automated behaviour-based malware analysis method based on free open source software, p. 111 (2017)
11. Lengyel, T.K., Maresca, S., Payne, B.D., Webster, G.D., Vogl, S., Kiayias, A.: Scalability, fidelity and stealth in the DRAKVUF dynamic malware analysis system (2014). https://doi.org/10.1145/2664243.2664252
12. Lin, C., Pao, H., Liao, J.: Efficient dynamic malware analysis using virtual time control mechanics. Comput. Secur. **73**, 359–373 (2018). https://doi.org/10.1016/j.cose.2017.11.010. ISSN 0167-4048

13. Tanda, S.: Monitoring & controlling kernel-mode events by hyperplatform. In: REcon Conference, Montreal, Canada (2016). https://doi.org/10.5446/32745
14. Brengel, M., Backes, M., Rossow, C.: Detecting hardware-assisted virtualization. In: Caballero, J., Zurutuza, U., Rodríguez, Ricardo J. (eds.) DIMVA 2016. LNCS, vol. 9721, pp. 207–227. Springer, Cham (2016). https://doi.org/10.1007/978-3-319-40667-1_11
15. Bolzoni, D., Schade, C., Etalle, S.: A cuckoo's egg in the malware nest: on-the-fly signature-less malware analysis, detection, and containment for large networks. In: The Past, Present, and Future of System Administration: Proceedings of the 25th Large Installation System Administration Conference, LISA 2011, 4–9 December 2011, Boston, MA, USA (2011)
16. Nativ, Y.: The Zoo – A Live Malware Repository (2019). https://github.com/ytisf/theZoo. Accessed 24 Jan 2020
17. Botacin, M.F., de Geus, P.L., Grégio, A.R.A.: The other guys: automated analysis of marginalized malware. J. Comput. Virol. Hack. Tech. **14**(1), 87–98 (2017). https://doi.org/10.1007/s11416-017-0292-8
18. Sistemas, H.: VirusTotal (2020). https://www.virustotal.com/gui/home/upload. Accessed 24 Jan 2020
19. Berlin, K., Slater, D., Saxe, J: Malicious behavior detection using windows audit logs (2015). https://doi.org/10.1145/2808769.2808773
20. Shibahara, T., Yagi, T., Akiyama, M., Chiba, D., Yada, T.: Efficient dynamic malware analysis based on network behavior using deep learning, pp. 1–7 (2016). https://doi.org/10.1109/glocom.2016.7841778

A Large-Scale Investigation to Identify the Pattern of Permissions in Obfuscated Android Malwares

Md. Omar Faruque Khan Russel,
Sheikh Shah Mohammad Motiur Rahman(✉), and Takia Islam

Department of Software Engineering,
Daffodil International University, Dhaka, Bangladesh
{russel35-1170,motiur.swe,takia35-1014}@diu.edu.bd

Abstract. This paper represents a simulation-based investigation of permissions in obfuscated android malware. Android malware detection has become a challenging and emerging area to research in information security because of the rapid growth of android based smartphone users. To detect malwares in android, permissions to access the functionality of android devices play an important role. Researchers now can easily detect the android malwares whose patterns have already been identified. However, recently attackers started to use obfuscation techniques to make the malwares unintelligible. For that reason, it's necessary to identify the pattern used by attackers to obfuscate the malwares. In this paper, a large-scale investigation has been performed by developing python scripts to extract the pattern of permissions from an obfuscated malwares dataset named Android PRAGuard Dataset. Finally, the patterns in a matrix form has been found and stored in a Comma Separated Values (CSV) file which will lead to the fundamental basis of detecting the obfuscated malwares.

Keywords: Android malware · Obfuscated malware · Permission pattern · Pattern identification

1 Introduction

Android smart phones have turned out to be trendy by expanding the number and complicated nature of their capacities than other platforms. Current mobile phones offer a lot of administrations and applications than those offered by PCs. Unfortunately, to obtain users sensitive information illegally being the attackers ultimate goal. They target the mobile devices to be financially benefited [1]. Through malicious application, an android device can be affected. That's why one of the popular ways is malware infection in android devices. The main reason to get access is in android, it is possible to allow unknown and unverified sources for installing Android Application Packages (APKs). Third party sources are responsible in most cases to make an easier way for distributing malware [2]. Using background service, malicious activities can be performed

T. Bhuiyan et al. (Eds.): ICONCS 2020, LNICST 325, pp. 85–97, 2020.
https://doi.org/10.1007/978-3-030-52856-0_7

those are the threat of the sensitive information and user's privacy. Some generic activities have been performed by malware. For example: stealing text messages, stealing user's contacts, login credentials, do subscription with premium services without users acknowledgement [3]. In the first quarter of 2018, worldwide 86% smartphones sold with the Android operating system [4]. As a result, an increasing number of smartphone users, the expanding number of security dangers that objective mobile phones have risen. Malevolent clients and programmers are exploiting both the restricted abilities of cell phones and the absence of standard security instruments to structure portable explicit malware that entrance touchy information, take the client's phone credit, or deny access to some device functionalities.In March 2019, around 121 thousand of new variations of portable malware were seen on Android mobiles in China. Because of the growth of android malware [5], Android Malware Detection has been gigantic area to research. Solutions are also increasing day by day by various researchers. To enforce the data security, security policies being applied [6]. Privacy specific [7], privilege escalation [8] typed specific attacks are focused on those studies. That's why some significant drawbacks still exist to those proposed solutions. Rapid variability of new smart attacks [9], the usage of machine learning techniques has been increased in cyber security domain [10]. Static analysis [11] and dynamic analysis [12] are the two major categories of android malware detection mechanisms [13]. Identifying the suspicious pattern is called Static analysis by inspecting the source code. Static Analysis has been performed in maximum antivirus companies. And, behavior based detection is known as dynamic analysis [14] . The core contribution of this paper is given below:

- Static analysis has been performed on obfuscated Android malware application.
- Proposed an approach to extract the used permissions from obfuscated malwares in android.
- The seven obfuscated techniques such as Trivial Encryption, String Encryption, Reflection Encryption, Class Encryption, Combination of Trivial and String Encryption, Combination of Trivial, String and Reflection Encryption, Combination of Trivial, String, Reflection and Class Encryption has been considered.
- The pattern of used permission has been represented in matrix.
- Identify the usage trends of permissions by Obfuscated Android Malware.

The structure of this paper is organized as follows. The Literature Review is described in Sect. 2. Research methodology is illustrated and described in Sect. 3. Section 4 presents the result analysis and discussion. Section 5 concludes the paper.

2 Literature Review

A huge piece of Android's worked in security is its permissions framework [15]. Protecting privacy of Android user is most important in online world.

This important task is done by permission. To access sensitive user data (Contacts, SMS), moreover explicit system features (Camera, Location) permission must be requested by android apps. Based on feature, system allow the permission automatically or might provoke the user to allow the appeal. All permission present publicly in <uses-permission> tags in the manifest file. Android app that requires normal permission (do not harm to user's privacy or device operation) system automatically allow these permission to app. App that requires dangerous permission (permission that can harmful for user's privacy or device normal operation) the user must explicitly allow to accept those permissions [16]. Permissions enable an application to get to possibly perilous API calls. Numerous applications need a few authorizations to work appropriately and client must acknowledge them at install time. Permission gives a more top to bottom view on the functional qualities of an application. Malware authors include dangerous permission in manifest that is not relevant to app and also declare much more permissions than literally required [17,18]. Therefore, the significance of permission pattern has been observed from state-of-art tabulated in table 1.

Table 1. Recent works on android permission to detect malware.

Ref.	Feature set	Samples	Accuracy	Year
[19]	Permission	7400	91.95%	2019
[20]	Permission	1740	98.45%	2019
[21]	Permission	2,000+	90%	2018
[22]	Permission	7553	95.44%	2019
[23]	Network Traffic, System Permissions	1124	94.25%	2018
[24]	Permission	399	92.437%	2018
[25]	Permission	100	94%	2018
[26]	8 features including permission	5560	97%	2019
[27]	8 features including permission	5560	97.24%	2018

From Table 1, it's been stated that permission pattern analysis has significant effect to develop anti-malware tools or to detect the malwares in android devices.

There are four fundamental obfuscated techniques along with the combination of those techniques in total seven techniques according to dataset are considered in this study including Trivial Encryption, String Encryption, Reflection and Class Encryption [28].

3 Methodology

The strategy and approach used in this research work has illustrated in Fig. 1 and described in this section.

Dataset Used. The dataset of obfuscated android malware named PRAGuard [28,29] has been investigated here. There are total 10479 samples. The samples with seven obfuscation techniques (each sample has 1497 samples) has obtained by obfuscating the MalGenome [30] and the Contagio Minidump datasets [31].

Environment Setup. For analysis, HP i5 2.30 GHz 8 GB computing environment has been used. Operating system is Windows 10, Programming language is Python 3.7 and python packages Matplotlib, Pandas, Androguard [32].

Data Preprocessing. As a preprocessing part, APKs are check whether APKs are in good format or not. After preprocessing, there were 62 APKs were corrupted. And the final dataset contains 10,417 obfuscated malware applications where Trivial, String, Reflection, Class, Trivial + String, Trivial + String + Reflection and Trivial + String + Reflection + Class encryption (enc.) with the number of samples 1485, 1486, 1486, 1486, 1492, 1492, and 1492 accordingly.

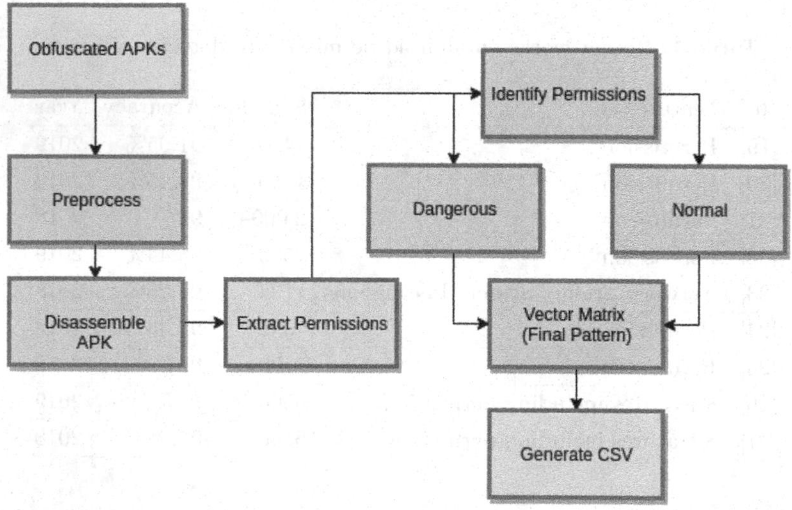

Fig. 1. Overview of proposed approach

Permission Extraction. A python script with Androguard has developed to disassemble the APKs. This script can disassemble APKs and extract the permissions from the APKs. APKs extraction time of every obfuscation techniques has taken average 40 mins time on the experimental environment.

Vector Metrics (Final Pattern). In this part a 2D vector metrics pattern are generated from the extraction process of permission. This metric pattern consists of rows and columns. Columns represent the names of the permissions and rows are labeled as a 0 or 1. If the permission found in APKs related to column, it will be 1 otherwise 0. A comma-separated values file (CSV) has generated to represent the pattern. For every APK, one vector matrix has found. A vector is a list of 0 or 1 which are in a row format. By combining all of the vector, a final CSV file has generated which represent a matrix of all the APKs in each obfuscated techniques.

4 Results and Discussion

This section represents the results obtained from experiments. The name of the permissions, for example INTERNET, READ_PHONE_STATE, READ_CONTACTS, ACCESS_NETWORK_STATE,SEND_SMS,..,WRITE_EXTERNAL_STORAGE has been denoted as PR_1, PR_2, PR_3, PR_4, $PR_5 \ldots\ldots\ldots$, PR_N . The maximum usage of permissions those found from this study are: READ_PHONE_STATE, WRITE_EXTERNAL_STORAGE, READ_SMS, SEND_SMS, RECEIVE_SMS, ACCESS_COARSE_LOCATION, READ_CONTACTS, ACCESS_FINE_LOCATION, CALL_PHONE, WRITE_CONTACTS, READ_EXTERNAL_STORAGE, PROCESS_OUTGOING_CALLS, GET_ACCOUNTS, RECEIVE_MMS, RECEIVE_WAP_PUSH, RECORD_AUDIO, CAMERA and WRITE_CALENDAR.

Trivial Encryption (enc.). The APKs which have used only trivial obfuscation techniques are analyzed and got in total 152 permissions are used where 18 were dangerous permissions. Top 50 permissions from 152 are depicted in Fig. 2. Figure 2. represents the top 50 permissions extracted from android APKs those used the trivial encryption technique. The trends of dangerous permissions used in trivial encryption technique mentioned above found in total 1359,1000, 810, 691, 529, 520, 488, 474, 439, 383, 174, 82, 75,72,69,38,26 and 14 APKs accordingly. Table 2 represents the vector structure of permission from a sample malware in trivial obfuscation techniques APKs.

Table 2. The extracted pattern sample in vector matrix of one APKs (Trivial Encryption).

PR_1	PR_2	PR_3	PR_4	PR_5	———————	PR_N
1	1	0	1	1	———————	1

Table 3 represents the matrix structure pattern of the usage of permission from some samples of malware families in trivial obfuscation techniques APKs.

Table 3. The extracted pattern sample of family wise APKs (Trivial Encryption).

Family	PR_1	PR_2	PR_3	PR_4	PR_5	———	PR_N
jSMSHider	1	1	1	1	0	———	0
AnserverBot	1	1	1	1	1	———	0
Geinimi	1	1	1	0	1	———	1

String Encryption (enc.). From the investigation, It's found that String Encryption technique has the same number of normal permissions and dangerous permissions as like as Trivial encryption. But the number of APKs those are using dangerous permission is less where the number of samples is little more than trivial technique. The top 50 permissions of the string encryption technique has depicted in Fig. 3. The usage of dangerous permissions by string encryption mentioned above are used in around 1354, 996, 810, 685, 528, 523, 488, 476, 439, 382, 174, 82, 76, 72, 69, 38, 26, 14 number of APKs respectively. Table 4 represents the vector structure of permission from a sample malware in string encryption techniques APKs. Table 5 represents the matrix structure pattern of the usage of permission from some samples of malware families in string encryption APKs.

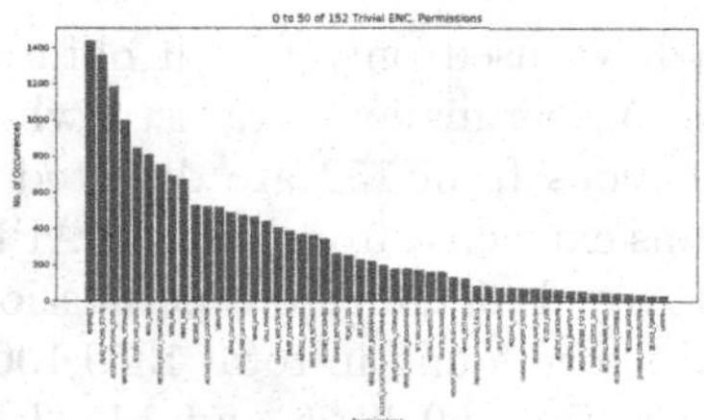

Fig. 2. Top 50 permissions used in trivial encryption technique

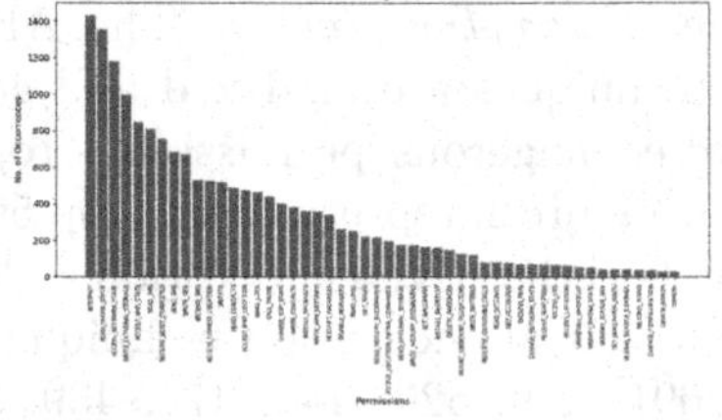

Fig. 3. Top 50 permissions used in String encryption technique

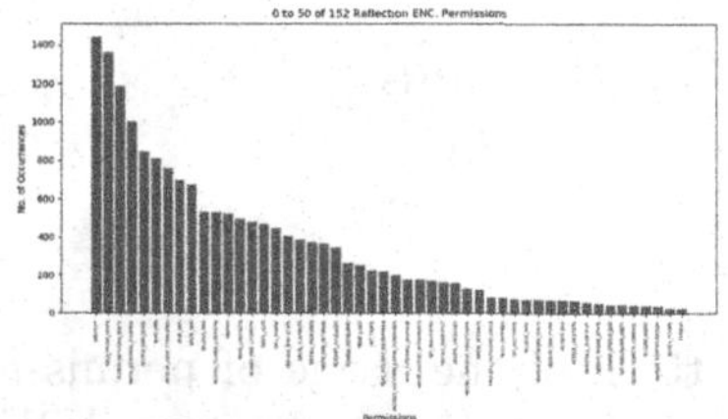

Fig. 4. Top 50 permissions used in reflection encryption technique

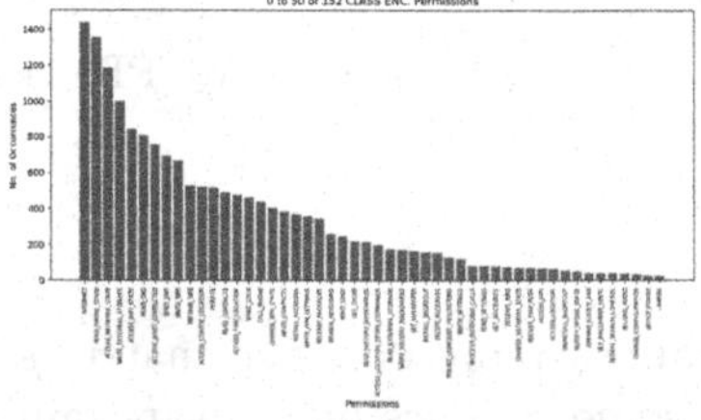

Fig. 5. Top 50 permissions used in class encryption technique

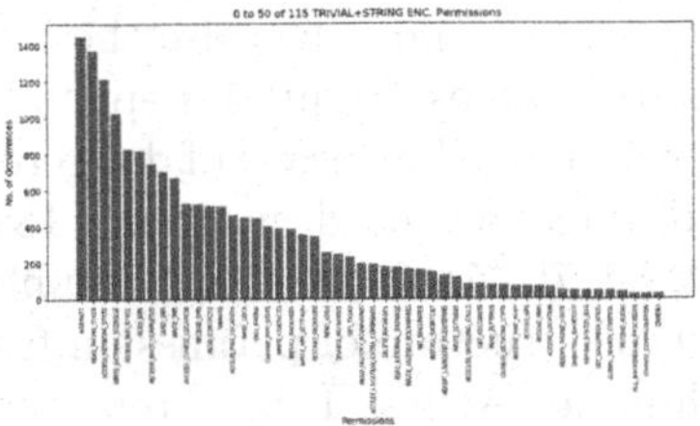

Fig. 6. Top 50 permissions used in Trivial + String encryption technique

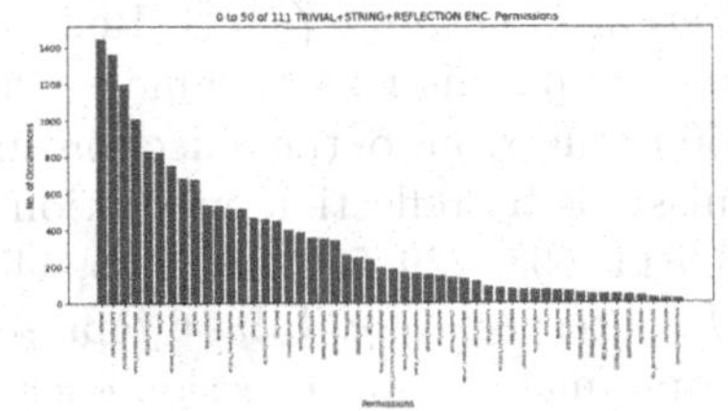

Fig. 7. Top 50 permissions used in Trivial + String + Reflection enc. technique

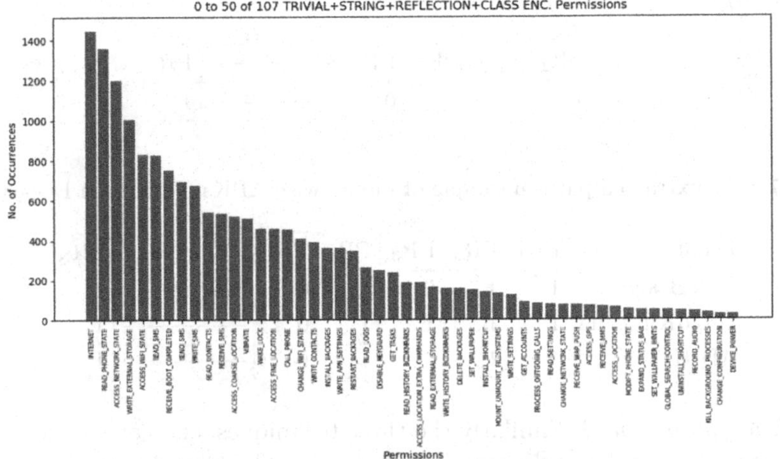

Fig. 8. Top 50 permissions used in Trivial + String + Reflection + Class enc. technique

Table 4. The extracted pattern sample in vector matrix of one APKs (String Encryption).

PR_1	PR_2	PR_3	PR_4	PR_5	————	PR_N
1	1	1	0	0	————	0

Table 5. The extracted pattern sample of family wise APKs (String Encryption).

Family	PR_1	PR_2	PR_3	PR_4	PR_5	————	PR_N
DroidKungFu1	1	1	0	1	0	————	1
KMin	1	1	1	1	1	————	1
Plankton	1	1	1	0	0	————	1

Reflection Encryption (enc.). Reflection Encryption technique has also the same number of permissions as same as the previous techniques. Figure 4. depicts the top 50 permissions of the reflection encryption technique. The usage of dangerous permissions by reflection encryption mentioned above are used in around 1362, 1003, 811, 693, 529, 523, 489, 476, 440, 383, 174, 82, 76, 72, 69, 38, 26, 14 number of APKs respectively. Table 6 represents the vector structure of permission from a sample malware in reflection encryption techniques APKs. Table 7 represents the matrix structure pattern of the usage of permission from some samples of malware families in reflection encryption APKs.

Table 6. The extracted pattern sample in vector matrix of one APKs (Reflection Encryption)

PR_1	PR_2	PR_3	PR_4	PR_5	————	PR_N
1	1	0	1	0	————	1

Table 7. The extracted pattern sample of family wise APKs (Reflection Encryption).

Family	PR_1	PR_2	PR_3	PR_4	PR_5	————	PR_N
BaseBridge	1	1	0	1	0	————	1
DroidKungFu3	1	1	1	1	0	————	1
ADRD	1	1	0	1	0	————	1

Class Encryption (enc.). Similarly the three techniques, class encryption has an equal number of total and dangerous permissions.The top 50 permissions of the class encryption technique has depicted in Fig. 5. The usage of dangerous permissions by class encryption are found mentioned above are used in around 1359, 1000, 809, 692, 529, 521, 488, 474, 440, 382, 174, 82, 76, 72, 69, 38, 26, 14 number of APKs respectively. Table 8 represents the vector structure of permission from a sample malware in class encryption techniques APKs.

Table 8. The extracted pattern sample in vector matrix of one APKs (Class Encryption)

PR_1	PR_2	PR_3	PR_4	PR_5	————	PR_N
1	1	0	1	1	————	1

Table 9 represents the matrix structure pattern of the usage of permission from some samples of malware families in class encryption APKs. From the above four basic encryption techniques, it's been observed that the same number of total 152 permissions and among them total 18 dangerous permissions have been found. However, the trends of the usage and the pattern of the permissions by each APK is different.

Table 9. The extracted pattern sample of family wise APKs (Class Encryption).

Family	PR_1	PR_2	PR_3	PR_4	PR_5	————	PR_N
DroidDream	1	1	1	1	0	————	1
GoldDream	1	0	0	1	0	————	0
YZHC	1	1	0	1	1	————	1

Combination of Trivial and String Encryption (enc.). 115 normal permissions including 18 dangerous permissions have been found from the Trivial + String enc. Above four fundamental techniques have 152 permissions where this combination techniques have only 115 permissions. However, the number of dangerous permissions with other techniques are the same. Figure 6 depicts the top 50 permissions of the reflection encryption technique. The usage of dangerous permissions by reflection encryption mentioned above are used in around 1023, 1023, 813, 701, 524, 520, 511, 461, 442, 385, 170, 80, 78, 69, 67, 38, 24, 13 number of APKs respectively. Table 10 represents the vector structure of permission from a sample malware in Trivial + String enc. techniques APKs.

Table 10. The extracted pattern sample in vector matrix of one APKs (Trivial + String enc. Encryption)

PR_1	PR_2	PR_3	PR_4	PR_5	————	PR_N
1	1	0	1	1	————	1

Table 11 represents the matrix structure pattern of the usage of permission from some samples of malware families in Trivial + String enc. APKs.

Table 11. The extracted pattern sample of family wise APKs (Trivial + String enc. Encryption).

Family	PR_1	PR_2	PR_3	PR_4	PR_5	————	PR_N
FakePlayer	0	0	0	0	1	————	0
Geinimi	1	1	1	0	1	————	1
Pjapps	1	1	1	1	1	————	1

Combination of Trivial, String and Reflection Encryption (enc.). Compared to previous technique, number of permissions has been decreased to 111. Figure 7 represents the top 50 permissions extracted from android APKs those used the Trivial + String + Reflection technique. The trends of dangerous permissions used in Trivial + String + Reflection technique above mentioned found in total 1358, 1006, 825, 685, 536, 531, 516, 459, 446, 389, 165, 81, 81, 70, 68, 40, 22 and 13 APKs accordingly. Table 12 represents the vector structure of permission from a sample malware in Trivial + String + Reflection enc. techniques APKs.

Table 12. The extracted pattern sample in vector matrix of one APKs (Trivial + String + Reflection enc.)

PR_1	PR_2	PR_3	PR_4	PR_5	———	PR_N
1	1	1	0	0	———	1

Table 13 represents the matrix structure pattern of the usage of permission from some samples of malware families in Trivial + String + Reflection enc. APKs.

Table 13. The extracted pattern sample of family wise APKs (Trivial + String + Reflection enc.)

Family	PR_1	PR_2	PR_3	PR_4	PR_5	———	PR_N
DroidDreamLight	1	1	1	1	0	———	1
DroidKungFu4	1	1	1	1	0	———	1
AnserverBot	1	1	1	1	1	———	0

Combination of Trivial, String, Reflection and Class Encryption (enc.). With contrast of other techniques, most a smaller number of permissions found from this technique. Only 107 permissions found this combination. The top 50 permissions of the Trivial + String + Reflection + Class encryption technique has depicted in Fig. 8. The usage of dangerous permissions by Trivial + String + Reflection + Class encryption mentioned above are used in around 1358, 1002, 825, 691, 541, 534, 520, 457, 452, 387, 164, 88, 81, 72, 67, 41, 21, 15 number of APKs respectively. Table 14 represents the vector structure of permission from a sample malware in Trivial + String + Reflection + Class enc. techniques APKs.

Table 14. The extracted pattern sample in vector matrix of one APKs (Trivial + String + Reflection + Class enc.)

PR_1	PR_2	PR_3	PR_4	PR_5	———	PR_N
1	0	1	1	0	———	1

Table 15 represents the matrix structure pattern of the usage of permission from some samples of malware families in Trivial + String + Reflection + Class enc. APKs.

Table 15. The extracted pattern sample of family wise APKs (Trivial + String + Reflection + Class enc.)

Family	PR_1	PR_2	PR_3	PR_4	PR_5	———	PR_N
GoldDream	1	1	0	1	1	———	1
Bgserv	1	1	0	1	1	———	1
jSMSHider	1	1	1	1	0	———	0

5 Conclusion

From the above investigation, it's been recapitulated that obfuscated android malwares has trends to use 18 dangerous permissions in total. It's also been observed that the total number of permission usage are same for four basic obfuscation techniques but it has been decreased accordingly with the combination of those techniques. However, the pattern of the permissions are different on every obfuscation techniques and also malware family wise. The final pattern obtained from these obfuscation techniques will lead a strong basement to detect the obfuscated android malwares in future.

References

1. Sen, S., Aysan, A.I., Clark, J.A.: SAFEDroid: using structural features for detecting android malwares. In: Lin, X., Ghorbani, A., Ren, K., Zhu, S., Zhang, A. (eds.) SecureComm 2017. LNICSSITE, vol. 239, pp. 255–270. Springer, Cham (2018). https://doi.org/10.1007/978-3-319-78816-6_18
2. Arp, D., Spreitzenbarth, M., Hubner, M., Gascon, H., Rieck, K., Siemens, C.E.R.T.: DREBIN: effective and explainable detection of android malware in your pocket. In: Ndss, vol. 14, pp. 23–26 (2014)
3. Saracino, A., Sgandurra, D., Dini, G., Martinelli, F.: Madam: Effective and efficient behavior-based android malware detection and prevention. IEEE Trans. Dependable Secure Comput. **15**, 83–97 (2016)
4. Number of smartphones sold to end users worldwide from 2007 to 2020 (in million units). https://www.statista.com/statistics/263437/global-smartphone-sales-to-end-users-since-2007/
5. Reina, A., Fattori, A., Cavallaro, L.: A system call-centric analysis and stimulation technique to automatically reconstruct android malware behaviors. In: EuroSec, April 2013
6. Backes, M., Gerling, S., Hammer, C., Maffei, M., von Styp-Rekowsky, P.: AppGuard – fine-grained policy enforcement for untrusted android applications. In: Garcia-Alfaro, J., Lioudakis, G., Cuppens-Boulahia, N., Foley, S., Fitzgerald, W.M. (eds.) DPM/SETOP -2013. LNCS, vol. 8247, pp. 213–231. Springer, Heidelberg (2014). https://doi.org/10.1007/978-3-642-54568-9_14
7. Gibler, C., Crussell, J., Erickson, J., Chen, H.: AndroidLeaks: automatically detecting potential privacy leaks in android applications on a large scale. In: Katzenbeisser, S., et al. (eds.) Trust 2012. LNCS, vol. 7344, pp. 291–307. Springer, Heidelberg (2012). https://doi.org/10.1007/978-3-642-30921-2_17

8. Viswanath, H., Mehtre, B.M.: U.S. Patent No. 9,959,406. Washington, DC: U.S. Patent and Trademark Office (2018)
9. Aafer, Y., Du, W., Yin, H.: DroidAPIMiner: mining API-level features for robust malware detection in android. In: Zia, T., Zomaya, A., Varadharajan, V., Mao, M. (eds.) SecureComm 2013. LNICST, vol. 127, pp. 86–103. Springer, Cham (2013). https://doi.org/10.1007/978-3-319-04283-1_6
10. Demontis, A., Melis, M., Biggio, B., Maiorca, D., Arp, D., Rieck, K., Roli, F.: Yes, machine learning can be more secure! a case study on android malware detection. IEEE Trans. Dependable Secure Comput. **16**(4), 711–724 (2017)
11. Papadopoulos, H., Georgiou, N., Eliades, C., Konstantinidis, A.: Android malware detection with unbiased confidence guarantees. Neurocomputing **280**, 3–12 (2017)
12. Shabtai, A., Moskovitch, R., Elovici, Y., Glezer, C.: Detection of malicious code by applying machine learning classifiers on static features: a state-of-the-art survey. Inf. Secur. Tech. Rep. **14**(1), 16–29 (2009)
13. Egele, M., Scholte, T., Kirda, E., Kruegel, C.: A survey on automated dynamic malware-analysis techniques and tools. ACM Comput. Surv. (CSUR) **44**(2), 6 (2012)
14. Burguera, I., Zurutuza, U., Nadjm-Tehrani, S.: Crowdroid: behavior-based malware detection system for android. In: Proceedings of the 1st ACM Workshop on Security and Privacy in Smartphones and Mobile Devices, pp. 15–26. ACM (2011)
15. Fereidooni, H., Moonsamy, V., Conti, M., Batina, L.: Efficient classification of android malware in the wild using robust static features. In: Meng, W., Luo, X., Furnell, S., Zhou, J. (eds.) Protecting Mobile Networks and Devices: Challenges and Solutions, vol. 1, pp. 181–209. CRC Press, Boca Raton (2016)
16. Permissions overview. https://developer.android.com/guide/topics/permissions/overview
17. Huang, C.Y., Tsai, Y.T., Hsu, C.H.: Performance evaluation on permission-based detection for android malware. In: Pan, J.S., Yang, C.N., Lin, C.C. (eds.) Advances in Intelligent Systems and Applications - Volume 2. Smart Innovation, Systems and Technologies, vol. 21. Springer, Heidelberg (2013). https://doi.org/10.1007/978-3-642-35473-1_12
18. Felt, A.P., Chin, E., Hanna, S., Song, D., Wagner, D.: Android permissions demystified. In: Proceedings of the 18th ACM Conference on Computer and Communications Security, pp. 627–638. ACM (2011)
19. Arslan, R.S., Doğru, İ.A., Barişçi, N.: Permission-based malware detection system for android using machine learning techniques. Int. J. Softw. Eng. Knowl. Eng. **29**(01), 43–61 (2019)
20. Yildiz, O., Doğru, I.A.: Permission-based android malware detection system using feature selection with genetic algorithm. Int. J. Softw. Eng. Knowl. Eng. **29**(02), 245–262 (2019)
21. Li, J., Sun, L., Yan, Q., Li, Z., Srisa-an, W., Ye, H.: Significant permission identification for machine-learning-based android malware detection. IEEE Trans. Ind. Inf. **14**(7), 3216–3225 (2018)
22. Arora, A., Peddoju, S.K., Conti, M.: PermPair: android malware detection using permission pairs. IEEE Trans. Inf. Forensics Secur. **15**, 1968–1982 (2019)
23. Arora, A., Peddoju, S. K.: NTPDroid: a hybrid android malware detector using network traffic and system permissions. In: 2018 17th IEEE International Conference on Trust, Security and Privacy in Computing and Communications/12th IEEE International Conference on Big Data Science and Engineering (TrustCom/BigDataSE), pp. 808–813. IEEE (2018)

24. Şahın, D.Ö., Kural, O.E., Akleylek, S., Kiliç, E.: New results on permission based static analysis for android malware. In: 2018 6th International Symposium on Digital Forensic and Security, ISDFS, pp. 1–4. IEEE (2018)
25. Wang, C., Xu, Q., Lin, X., Liu, S.: Research on data mining of permissions mode for android malware detection. Cluster Comput. **22**(6), 13337–13350 (2018). https://doi.org/10.1007/s10586-018-1904-x
26. Motiur Rahman, S.S.M., Saha, S.K.: StackDroid: evaluation of a multi-level approach for detecting the malware on android using stacked generalization. In: Santosh, K.C., Hegadi, R.S. (eds.) RTIP2R 2018. CCIS, vol. 1035, pp. 611–623. Springer, Singapore (2019). https://doi.org/10.1007/978-981-13-9181-1_53
27. Rana, M.S., Rahman, S.S.M.M., Sung, A.H.: Evaluation of tree based machine learning classifiers for android malware detection. In: Nguyen, N.T., Pimenidis, E., Khan, Z., Trawiński, B. (eds.) ICCCI 2018. LNCS (LNAI), vol. 11056, pp. 377–385. Springer, Cham (2018). https://doi.org/10.1007/978-3-319-98446-9_35
28. Maiorca, D., Ariu, D., Corona, I., Aresu, M., Giacinto, G.: Stealth attacks: an extended insight into the obfuscation effects on android malware. Comput. Secur. **51**, 16–31 (2015)
29. Android PRAGuard Dataset. http://pralab.diee.unica.it/en/AndroidPRAGuard-Dataset
30. MalGenome. http://www.malgenomeproject.org/
31. Contagio. http://contagiominidump.blogspot.com/
32. Androguard. https://github.com/androguard/androguard

Image Steganography and Risk Analysis on Web Applications

A New 8-Directional Pixel Selection Technique of LSB Based Image Steganography

Sheikh Thanbir Alam[1,2], Nusrat Jahan[1], and Md. Maruf Hassan[1,2(✉)]

[1] Daffodil International University, Dhaka, Bangladesh
maruf.swe@diu.edu.bd
[2] Cyber Security Center, DIU, Dhaka, Bangladesh

Abstract. Pixel selection for data hiding becomes crucial for the solutions in spatial domain of steganography to ensure imperceptibility. This paper presents an efficient approach of pixel selection technique for hiding secret data in cover object of image steganography. After reviewing recent literature, it has been observed that most of the works on pixel selection uses zig-zag technique for their solution. However, it becomes very prone to steganalysis based attacks by the intruders. In this study, 8-directions pixel selection technique is proposed to embed data in the cover image where Least Significant Bit (LSB) method has been used on Red, Green and Blue (RGB) color image especially focused on JPG, JPEG, and PNG. Since this projected procedure avoids the known steganalysis techniques, it will be challenging for the attacker to recognize the presence of secret information from the stego image. To measure the quality, statistical analysis has been performed where the value of the quality measurement matrices has provided better results.

Keywords: Image steganography · Pixel selection technique · Least Significant Bit (LSB) · RGB

1 Introduction

With rapid advancement in technologies a lot of secret data is transmitted over the internet but at the same time security is a major issue of today's world. The information which is transacted between sender and receiver through over internet need to secure from attacks caused by intruders. A number of cyber security techniques have been developed under information encryption and information hiding to address the security of information. Information encryption technique is known as cryptography that convert the secret message into unintelligible message. However, it's not only measure to secure data while steganography hides the existence of message by using another cover media without noticing to anyone. "Steganography" is a Greek word which is combined into two parts: Steganos which means "covered" (where a technique hides the secret messages)

T. Bhuiyan et al. (Eds.): ICONCS 2020, LNICST 325, pp. 101–115, 2020.
https://doi.org/10.1007/978-3-030-52856-0_8

and the Graphic which means "writing". The very first steganographic [1] approach was developed in antique Greece around 440 B.C. In recent years, many researchers have been introduced different image steganography approaches in digital media [2–10] to hide secret information. It is used in different organizations like military or intelligence agents to communicate with the members. There are several image steganography techniques we found which are used in RGB images, like Least Significant Bit (LSB), Pixel Value Differencing (PVD), Discrete Cosine Transformation Technique (DCT), Edges Based Data Embedding Method (EBE), Random Pixel Embedding Method (RPE), Mapping Pixel to Hidden Data Method, Labelling or Connectivity Method, Pixel Intensity Based Method etc [11–13]. Therefore, LSB is the most popular and widely used technique for image steganography [14–16] that hides secret bits in the LSB of some pixels of the RGB cover image based on it its binary coding. The advantage of LSB is better as there is less chance for degradation of the original image and more information can be stored in an image [17], [18] also it is to embed the bits of the message directly and easily into the LSB of cover-image [19] and stego-image quality is better in LSB. The key benefit of this technique that it provides high embedding capacity. Many researchers work on the same approaches [20–28] which are started embedding from the left most corner pixel of an image as the beginning pixel into cover images. With the advancement of technology, different steganalysis algorithms are developed to compromise those approaches of pixel selection technique in LSB based image steganography. Therefore, pixel selection is an important factor for data embedding [29] and these selection should be done in such a way that the image will result in minimum distortion. That is, if image quality is not better then it makes the image calm to attack [15]. The main motivation to develop a secure approach that is hard to reveal and can minimize gap of pixel selection technique. So, the objective of this approach is to make new pixel selection technique with better image quality and less embedding time. Contribution of this paper is given as follows:

- The proposed approach come out from traditional pixel selection technique where 8-directional pixel selection technique is used that is difficult to attackers to recognize the presence of secret data..
- This approach is also used LSB embedding approach where it is embedded three bits into a single pixel that provides good image quality than other existing techniques.

In this paper, we propose a technique for digital image steganography where 8 directional pixel selection technique of LSB is used with hash. The rest of this paper is organized as follows: literature survey of recent LSB based image steganography are described in Sect. 2, in 3, our proposed 8 directional pixel selection technique with hash is described and experiments and results are described in Sect. 4. Concluding remarks is described in Sect. 5.

2 Literature Review

In this section, we present an overview of prior research in the domain of image steganography based on LSB. A well-known LSB based image steganography [29] presented a method that utilized the secret key to hide the information into a pixel of cover image where a bit of secret information was placed in either LSB of Green or Blue matrix of a specific pixel was decided by the secret key. However, they used traditional pixel selection technique and they calculated only two image quality measures for a distorted image with a cover image. In [30], provided a method that was able to perform steganography and cryptography at the same time which used 8 * 8 pixel blocks of an image as a cover object for steganography and as key for cryptography also used Huffman coding for embedding but their proposed ISC (Image-based Steganography and Cryptography) algorithm's performance have measured by comparing with only one well-known model [31]. In [32], they discussed about different types of cover file format of LSB technique to hide secret information although they did not discuss about different types of file format's pixel selection techniques. A technique was proposed [33] to hide message in least significant area of pixel of an image where they used edge adaptive image steganography based on LSBMR (least significant bit matching revisited) which utilize the sharper regions within the cover images and embed secret message with higher security, although, in their research article, they did not clarify why the PVD histogram of a stego-image will abnormally decrease on the threshold. A system was provided in [34] where they develop a technique in which cryptography and steganography were used as integrated part along with newly developed enhanced security module. For Cryptography they used AES (Advanced Encryption Standard) algorithm to encrypt a message and a part of the message was hidden in DCT (Discrete Cosine Transform) of an image. In [35], a generic algorithm was proposed where they used AES to encrypt secret data and used RSA (Rivest–Shamir–Adleman) to encrypt key which was embedded a large number of secret messages into LSB in cover image but their proposed method takes more time to hide message than the standard LSB technique, told by them which is weak point of this model. In [36], they also proposed LSB based image steganography technique with encryption to improve security using AES-128, they replaced a secret bit into least significant bit of blue portion of a single pixel. However, AES has key dependent weakness that was proved in [37] also it has bit distribution weakness shown in [38]. Khan et al. represented an LSB technique [20] which hides information in the cover image taking into the pixel value of color or gray level of every pixel and embedded one to four secret message bits into a single pixel by checking several conditions. However, they use several conditions that may take a longer time for embedding. A way of pixel selection is proposed in [39] where they firstly selected middle region, then used four diagonal pixels of middle region as successive pixels and embedded the data into four edges of quadrilateral which was created by four diagonal pixels of cover image and finally reached towards the four corners of images. But in their model, as they just used an image quality matric (that was PSNR), as a result the detailed information of image distortion was not known clearly.

T. Bhuiyan et al. proposed a data hiding technique in the spatial domain of image steganography [21] where they proposed a scheme that takes the message bit and performed XOR operation with the 7th bit of every RGB component and, after then, the produced output was embedded within the 8th bit of each component of RGB. However, they used zig-zag pixel selection technique which is traditional/common [39] pixel selection method, where pixels are selected from the beginning (upper left corner) of images that's why it's might easy to recognize the presence of secret data. In [40], a hash based LSB technique was proposed where their model used random hash key for encoding and decoding secret message and the model was embedded 3-bit secret message for RED, 2 bits for GREEN and 3 bits for BLUE portion but their technique provided low image quality. In the above-mentioned schemes most of the researchers worked on traditional zig zag pixel selection technique where attackers can easily recognize the presence of secret data. Even, most of the researchers use only PSNR and MSE to determine the quality between stego and cover image. They did not use different metrics to prove their model well.

To solve those problems, we have used LSB technique with 8 directional-based pixel selection where we use Peak Signal-to-Noise Ratio (PSNR), Mean Absolute Error (MAE), Signal to Noise Ratio (SNR), Mean Square Error (MSE), Root Mean Square Error (RMSE) and embedding time metrics which can be provide us better technique than four diagonal pixel selection technique [39], XOR techniques [21], Thresholding technique [20] and other techniques. Our proposed technique also gives us better image quality than other techniques.

3 Proposed Approach

In this study, an 8-directional pixel selection technique has been proposed where secret data is hiding initially into the center point followed by the direction of up, up-right, right, underneath-right, underneath, underneath-left, left, and up-left respectively. Unlike to the zig-zag pixel selection technique, this approach will choose center pixel by selecting the middle point of width and height of the cover image.

Number of pixels where the secret data will be embedded, is depended on the length of the secret message and also identify the required pixels for each direction. To satisfy the goal of proposed 8-directional pixel selection technique, it will calculate the Total Number of Secret Message Bit Length (B_L) using binary value of each character. Then, it will calculate the Total Number of Pixels (T_{np}) for embedding using Eq. (1).

$$T_{np} = \frac{B_L}{3} \tag{1}$$

By using the value of Tnp, it will focus to get the value of Pixels Number for Each Direction (P_{pn}) using Eq. (2)

$$P_{pn} = \frac{T_{np} - 1}{8} \tag{2}$$

The technique will then start embedding secret message from Center Pixel (C_x, C_y). To calculate (C_x, C_y), it requires to find out the Height (H) and Width (W) of the cover image using Eq. (3).

$$(C_x, C_y) = |(\frac{H}{2}, \frac{W}{2})| \tag{3}$$

Here, || denotes as ceil function. Once the $\frac{H}{2}$ and/or $\frac{W}{2}$ in Eq. (3) provides the fraction value, || will consider only upper limit value.

The proposed approach will embed message in the Center Pixel (C_x, C_y) and then find out 8 directions' pixel for embedding in rest of the message. Each direction embedding will follow the straight line equation that is given in Eq. (4).

$$y = mx + c \qquad [where, m = -1, 0, 1] \tag{4}$$

Here, y denotes the length of vertical axis, x represents the length of horizontal axis, m defines the slope of straight line, and c is the value of y when x = 0. In Fig. 1 proposed approach presents 8 directional pixel selection technique following Eq. (5).

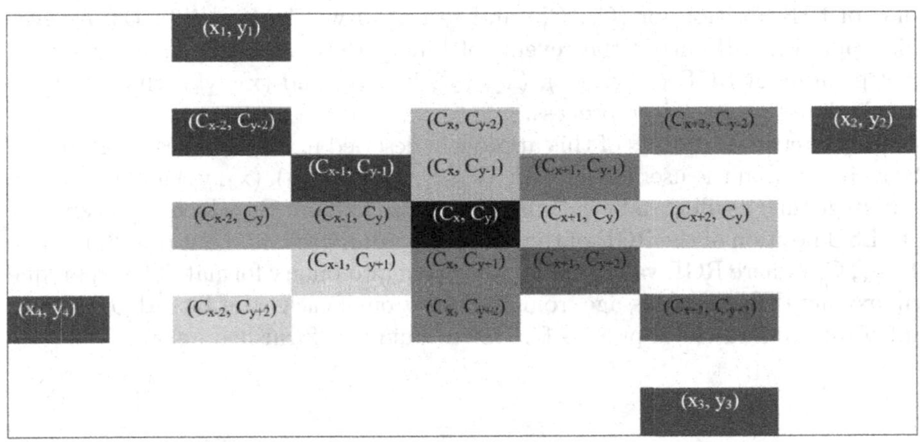

Fig. 1. 8 directional pixel selection of a cover image

Equation (5) is used to find out the 8-directional Pixel Position (D_s),

$$D_s = (C_{x\pm a}, C_{y\pm a}) \qquad [where, a = 0 \; to \; Ppn] \tag{5}$$

From the Eq. (5), pixel position will be selected e.g. the Upward equation will be (C_x,C_{y-a}) whereas Upward-right direction will be denoted as (C_{x+a},C_{y-a}).

Equation (6, 7, 8, 9) is used to find out the 4 pixels' position where this approach will embed the secret message bit size number which will use for retrieve message from stego image.

$$1^{st} \; pixel's \; position, (x_1, y_1) = (\frac{W}{2} - 2, 1) \tag{6}$$

$$2^{nd}\ pixel's\ position, (x_2, y_2) = (W, \frac{H}{2} - 2) \tag{7}$$

$$3^{rd}\ pixel's\ position, (x_3, y_3) = (\frac{W}{2} + 2, H) \tag{8}$$

$$4^{th}\ pixel's\ position, (x_4, y_4) = (1, \frac{H}{2} + 2) \tag{9}$$

Using Eq. (10) this approach will find out the value of B_L from the stego image using Secret Message Size (S_m).

$$B_L = (S_m * 8) \tag{10}$$

3.1 Embed and Retrieve Technique

Figure 2 depicts the embedding process of the proposed technique that takes Secret Message (M) and Cover Image (I) as input from the user. It will then find out the H, W, and (C_x, C_y) from that cover image following Eq. (3). This cover image consists of 24-bit which is the mixer of three core colors i.e. red, green, and blue and each color has eight bit of length. It embeds a bit in each color of LSB position for (C_x, C_y) and rest of M will be kept into Ds. At last, this approach will embed the reverse of binary value of secret message size in LSB position of RGB of (x_1, y_1), (x_2, y_2), (x_3, y_3) and (x_4, y_4) which will use to calculate B_L in retrieve process.

In the retrieval process of this approach, descried in Fig. 3, takes Stego Image (S) as input from the user initially. H, W, (x_1, y_1), (x_2, y_2), (x_3, y_3) and (x_4, y_4) of that stego image will then be calculated and also find out B_L which has been kept into LSB position of the RGB of these 4 pixels. Afterward, find out the RGB value of (C_x, C_y) where RGB value will be converted into binary format. The technique will extract the secret message from LSB position of each color bit. Algorithm for embedding and retrieval process for this technique is furnished below.

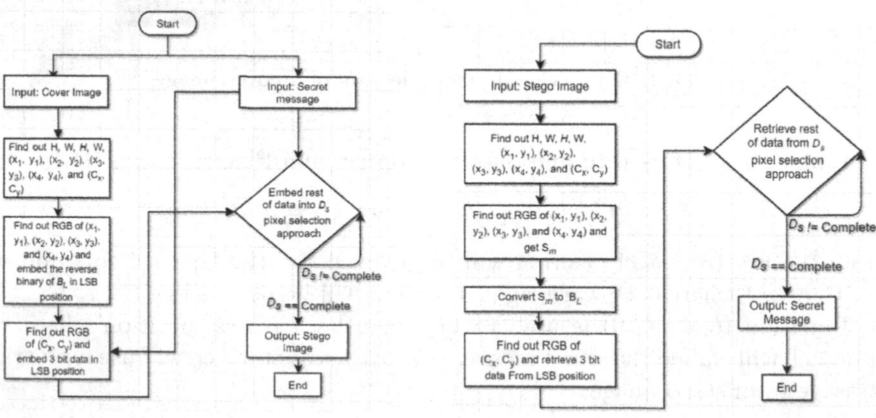

Fig. 2. Embedding technique

Fig. 3. Retrieving technique

Embedding Algorithm	Retrie ving Algorithm

Result: Stego Image
M ⟵ input
I ⟵ input
W = Image Width;
H = Image Height;
(C_x, C_y) = (H/2, W/2);
embed $((C_x, C_y))$;
B_L= Length of M;
T_{np}= B_L/3;
P_{pn}= (T_{np}-1)/8;
B_L ⟵ reverse(binary(B_L))
$(x_1, y_1), (x_2, y_2), (x_3, y_3), (x_4, y_4) \longleftarrow B_L$
a = 0;
while a $\leq P_{pn}$ do
    $D_s = (C_{x\pm a}, C_{y\pm a})$
    embed(D_s);
    a++;
function embed (position):
    RGB⟵ position
    UpdateRGB⟵ message
	Result: Secret Message
	S⟵ input
	$S_m \longleftarrow (x_1, y_1), (x_2, y_2), (x_3, y_3), (x_4, y_4)$
	S_m⟵ decimal(reverse(S_m))
	B_L⟵ (S_m*8))
	W = Image Width;
	H = Image Height;
	(C_x, C_y) = (H/2, W/2);
	retrieve $((C_x, C_y))$;
	B_L= Length of M;
	T_{np}= B_L/3;
	P_{pn}= (T_{np}-1)/8;
	a = 0;
	while a $\leq P_{pn}$ do
	    $D_s = (C_{x\pm a}, C_{y\pm a})$
	    retrieve(D_s);
	    a++;
	function retrieve (position):
	    RGB⟵ position
	    message[]⟵ RGB

3.2 Example

At first, this technique takes secret message and cover image from the user. Suppose, the size of secret message is 75 bits which has converted from a string. Here, total no. of pixel will be $\frac{75}{3} = 25$ and each direction's pixel no. will be $\frac{25-1}{8} = 3$. Assume that, height, H = 7 & width, W = 7 of a cover image and the center pixel will be $(C_x, C_y) = (\frac{H}{2}, \frac{W}{2}) = (4, 4)$. Then calculate the RGB which is (4, 4) and last bit of Red, Green, and Blue will replace by 3 secret message bits (showed (a) in Fig. 4). By following 8 directional approach, it will embed rest of secret bits from upward, upward-right, etc. directions. At last this approach will embed the secret message size into (x_1, y_1), (x_2, y_2), (x_3, y_3) and (x_4, y_4) using Eqs. (6, 7, 8, 9) with same technique (showed (b) in Fig. 4).

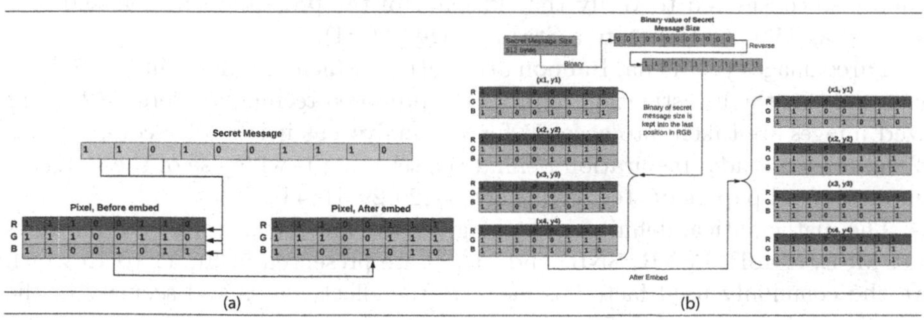

Fig. 4. Secret message and message size embedding technique

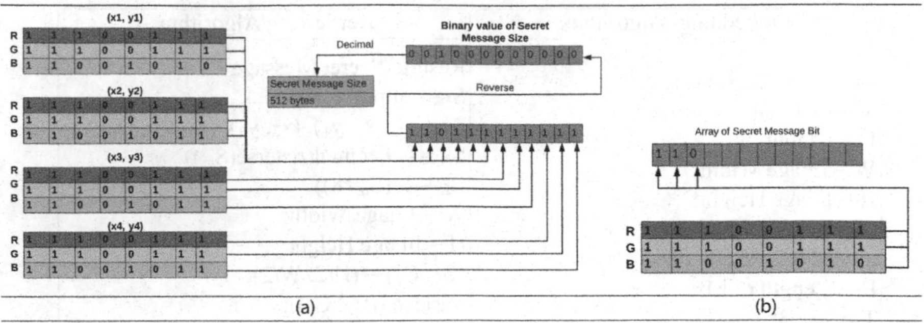

Fig. 5. Secret message and message size retrieving technique

In retrieving process, this technique takes stego image from the user. Assume that, height, H = 7 & width, W = 7 of a cover image. The (x_1, y_1), (x_2, y_2), (x_3, y_3) and (x_4, y_4) will be calculate using Eqs. (6, 7, 8, 9) which provide 12-bit binary value that will be reversed and convert to decimal value (showed (a) in Fig. 5). Afterward get the value of Sm, it will calculate the value of BL using Eq. (10). The center pixel will then be calculated which is (C_x, C_y) = $(\frac{H}{2}, \frac{W}{2})$ = (4, 4). The RGB will be calculated of (4, 4) position and last bit of Red, Green, and Blue will be taken which will keep in array (showed (b) in Fig. 5). By following D_s, it will take rest of secret bits from upward, upward-right, etc. directions. And at last that array will convert into a string and that string will be the secret message.

4 Experiments and Results

In this section, the results are presented in term of visual interpretation and comparison between cover and stego image. Also, outcomes of the proposed technique are also compared with other known methods to verify the effectiveness. The statistical analysis of the study is furnished with five quality measurement metrics that includes Mean-Square Error (MSE), Root Mean Square Error (RMSE), Signal-to-Noise Ratio (SNR), Mean Absolute Error (MAE), Peak Signal-to-Noise Ratio (PSNR), Structural Similarity Index (SSIM). Embedding Time also considered to verify the efficiency of the proposed solution and it is denoted as Time to Generate a Stego Image (TGSI).

Three images (i.e. Lena, Baboon and Nature) which are shown in Fig. 6, have been used for the investigation to proof the proposed technique. Here, 512 × 512 sized images are taken into account for the analysis as it is mostly common size of the related study. Inspiration behind the selection is wide use of these figures among several papers of steganography [17,20,29,41–44].

The mathematical definition for the given five quality measurement matrices (i.e. MSE, RMSE, PSNR, SNR, and MAE) are presented in Eq. 11 to 15 which are the commonly used factor to measure the effectiveness and security of the steganography process [45–50].

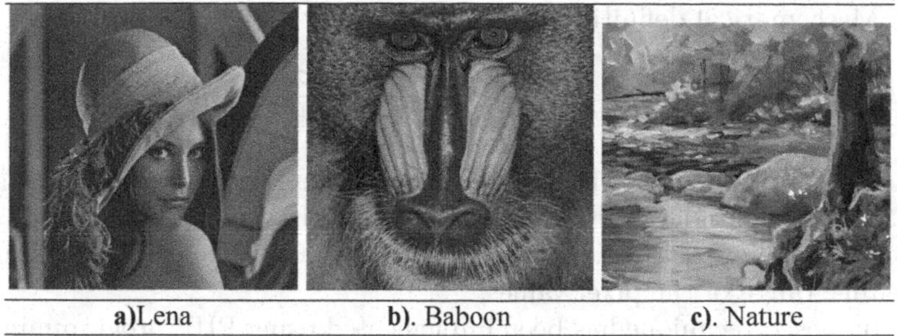

Fig. 6. Cover images

The Mathematical definition for MSE is

$$MSE = (1xMxN)\sum_{i=1}^{M}\sum_{j=1}^{N}(a_{ij} - b_{ij})^2 \tag{11}$$

In this equation, a_{ij} refers to the pixel value of the position i and j of the cover image where b_{ij} refers to the pixel value of the position i and j of stego image.

The Mathematical definition for RMSE is

$$RMSE = \sqrt{MSE} \tag{12}$$

The Mathematical definition for PSNR is

$$PSNR = 10log_{10}\frac{255^2}{MSE} \tag{13}$$

Unit of PSNR is dB, PSNR depends on MSE. Several researches prove that if the value of PSNR between cover and stego image become more than 40 dB then it can be considered as high quality.

The Mathematical definition for SNR is

$$SNR = \frac{\sum_{x=0}^{M-1}\sum_{y=0}^{N-1}\hat{f}(x,y)^2}{\sum_{x=0}^{M-1}\sum_{y=0}^{N-1}[f(x,y) - \hat{f}(x,y)]^2} \tag{14}$$

The formula is from Digital Image Processing [50] where $\hat{f}$ refers is the noisy image, f refers the original image and x, y refers the position of a pixel.

The Mathematical definition for MAE is

$$MAE = \frac{1}{3MN}\sum_{i=1}^{M}\sum_{j=1}^{N}[C(x,y) - S(x,y)]_1 \tag{15}$$

Where M&N denote the image dimension, (x, y) refers the position of pixel. C represents the cover image and S denotes the stego image and []1 denotes the city-block norm.

The Mathematical definition for SSIM is

$$\mathrm{SSIM}(x,y) = \frac{(2\mu_x\mu_y + C_1) + (2\sigma_{xy} + C_2)}{(\mu_x^2 + \mu_y^2 + C_1)(\sigma_x^2 + \sigma_y^2 + C_2)} \tag{16}$$

Where, x and y denotes the image dimension. μ_x and μ_y are the average of x, y. C1 = $(k_1L)2$ and C2 = $(k_2L)2$ are two variables to stabilize the division with weak denominator where $K_1 = 0.01$ and $k_2 = 0.03$ by default and L means the dynamic range of the pixel-values.

The proposed technique has been implemented using PHP programming language for data hiding, extracting information, and figure out the embedding time where microtime() function is used. MATLAB R2016a is used to find the value of quality measurement matrics and also to create histogram for both cover and stego image.

Result of the proposed technique are measured with three different sized payload such as 512 bytes, 256 bytes, and 128 bytes on the selected three images. Table 1. represents the results of five quality measurement matrices for given images and embedding time of the stego image.

Table 1. Quality measurement metrics of the proposed technique using different standard sized payload

Image	size	Payload	MSE	RMSE	SNR	MAE	PSNR	SSIM	TGSI (Second)
Lenna	512 * 512	512 bytes	0.0027	0.0519	68.6906	0.0027	73.8282	0.99996	0.08507
		256 bytes	0.0013	0.0363	71.8004	0.0013	76.9380	0.99997	0.06055
		128 bytes	0.0007	0.0260	74.6989	0.0007	79.8365	0.99998	0.03479
Baboon	512 * 512	512 bytes	0.0026	0.0512	68.6393	0.0026	73.9487	0.99996	0.09543
		256 bytes	0.0013	0.0356	71.7910	0.0013	77.1005	0.99998	0.06168
		128 bytes	0.0006	0.0252	74.7883	0.0006	80.0977	0.99999	0.04086
Nature	512 * 512	512 bytes	0.0017	0.0417	71.0757	0.0017	75.7208	0.99997	0.09701
		256 bytes	0.0009	0.0298	74.0117	0.0009	78.6569	0.99998	0.06307
		128 bytes	0.0004	0.0212	76.9490	0.0004	82.5942	0.99999	0.05905

In this table, 512 × 512 sized image were used for Lena, Baboon, and Nature where payload size of 512 bytes, 256 bytes, and 128 bytes respectively had been taken for consideration. The proposed technique's MSE values for Lena were 0.0027, 0.0013, and 0.0007 respectively where 0.0026, 0.0013, and 0.0006 were found for Baboon. For Nature, the MSE value were 0.0017, 0.0009, and 0.0004 consecutively. RMSE is shown in another vital parameter to assess the quality of an image. The value of RMSE for Lina were 0.0519, 0.0363, and 0.0260 where it were observed 0.0512, 0.0356, and 0.0252 sequentially for Baboon and 0.0417, 0.0298, and 0.0212 respectively were found for Nature. The values of SNR for Lena were 68.6906, 71.8004, and 74.6989 consecutively and it were 68.6393, 71.7910, and 74.7883 for Baboon. For Nature, the SNR values were 71.0757,

74.0117, and 76.9490 respectively. The seventh column represents the parameter, MAE where its values for Lena were 0.0027, 0.0013, and 0.0007 sequentially where 0.0026, 0.0013, and 0.0006 were detected for Baboon and 0.0017, 0.0009, 0.0004 were found for Nature. PSNR values for Lena were 73.8282, 76.9380, and 79.8365 but the same value for Baboon were 73.9487, 77.1005, 80.0977 accordingly. PSNR value of 75.7208, 78.6569, and 82.5942 were observed for Nature. SSIM values for Lena were 0.99996, 0.99997, and 0.99998 but the same matrix's value for Baboon were 0.99996, 0.99998, 0.99999 accordingly. SSIM value of 0.99997, 0.99998, and 0.99999 were observed for Nature. TGSI is also an important factor that represents the embedding time in second. For Lena, the values of TGSI were 0.08507 s, 0.06055 s, and 0.03479 s where it were 0.09543 s, 0.06168 s, and 0.04086 s for Baboon. The TGSI value for Nature were 0.09701 s, 0.06307 s, and 0.05905 s respectively.

4.1 Comparison with Existing Algorithms

This sub-section represents the experimental output, analysis and comparison among other recent steganographic techniques [20,21,39].

Table 2. Comparison among four techniques

Techniques	Size	Payload	MSE	RMSE	SNR	MAE	PSNR	SSIM	TGSI (Second)	Image name
Thresholding model	512 * 512	128 bytes	0.0040	0.0636	66.9215	0.0008	72.0590	0.99996	0.04536	Lenna
4 direction model	512 * 512	128 bytes	0.0007	0.0258	74.7731	0.0007	79.9107	0.99998	0.05791	
XOR model	512 * 512	128 bytes	0.0007	0.0259	74.7400	0.0007	79.8776	0.99998	0.04644	
Proposed model	512 * 512	128 bytes	0.0007	0.0260	74.6989	0.0007	79.8365	0.99998	0.03479	
Thresholding model	512 * 512	128 bytes	0.0056	0.0746	65.3612	0.0010	70.6707	0.99994	0.05486	Baboon
4 direction model	512 * 512	128 bytes	0.0007	0.0257	74.6347	0.0007	79.9441	0.99998	0.04748	
XOR model	512 * 512	128 bytes	0.0007	0.0256	74.6683	0.0007	79.9778	0.99998	0.04644	
Proposed model	512 * 512	128 bytes	0.0006	0.0252	74.7883	0.0006	80.0977	0.99999	0.03479	
Thresholding model	512 * 512	128 bytes	0.0037	0.0610	67.7825	0.0005	72.4277	0.99996	0.08748	Nature
4 direction model	512 * 512	128 bytes	0.0005	0.0242	76.4490	0.0005	81.0073	0.99998	0.07098	
XOR model	512 * 512	128 bytes	0.0005	0.0220	76.6237	0.0005	81.2689	0.99998	0.07199	
Proposed model	512 * 512	128 bytes	0.0004	0.0212	76.9490	0.0004	82.5942	0.99999	0.05905	

Here, [39] is represented 4 direction-based model, T. Bhuiyan et al. proposed XOR based model [21], Thresholding based model is represented in [20]. The comparison is done on the basis of number of image performance metrics which are given above in Subsect. 4.1. The first column name is techniques and the value for MSE, RMSE, SNR, MAE, PSNR, SSIM and Embedding time (TGSI) are shown in 4th, 5th, 6th, 7th, 8th, 9th and 10th columns. Payload is shown in 3rd column and image size are shown in 2nd column. Table 2. shows the comparison among four techniques for Lena, Baboon and Nature cover image. Proposed technique provides 0.0007, 0.0260, 74.6989, 0.0007, 79.8365, 0.99998 and 0.03479 for MSE, RMSE, SNR, MAE, PSNR, SSIM and TGSI respectively for Lena. Here, the value of TGSI for proposed technique shows the less embedding time among other related techniques mentioned in the above table and it is evident that the given proposed technique is more efficient compared to other concurrent approaches where the image quality remain almost same. For Baboon, proposed technique provides 0.0006, 0.0252, 74.7883, 0.0006, 80.0977, 0.99999 and 0.04086 for MSE, RMSE, SNR, MAE, PSNR, SSIM and TGSI respectively and these values are indicating better output than other related techniques. For Nature, it provides 0.0004, 0.0212, 76.9490, 0.0004, 82.5942, 0.99999 and 0.05905 for MSE, RMSE, SNR, MAE, PSNR, SSIM and TGSI consecutively which provide more efficient results than other techniques.

The Table 3 shows the histogram for both 512 × 512 sized cover and stego images for the above three images.

Table 3. Comparative histogram for cover and stego images

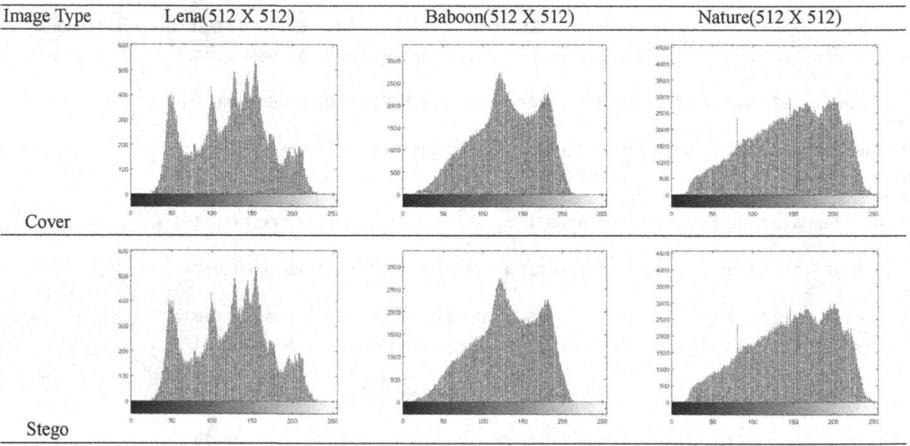

Image Type	Lena(512 X 512)	Baboon(512 X 512)	Nature(512 X 512)
Cover			
Stego			

At first, it is converted the color image into the grayscale image to see the change of RGB component in a single plot where it is used "rgb2gray". Here, "imhist" method in MATLAB is used to create the histogram. There is no major changes between cover and stego images are observed based on histogram analysis. As per result of histogram, the difference between two images is insignificant which variance cannot be recognized by naked eye.

This data hiding approach is applied in this experiment which shows proposed algorithm works better as compared to other related algorithms.

5 Conclusion

A new 8 directional pixel selection technique with LSB is presented in this paper which embed secret information in the cover image. The above discussion and comparative result analysis proves that proposed steganography data hiding technique provides extra security and less imperceptibility over some other existing data hiding techniques. However, this model keeps maximum 765 bytes' secret data in 512 × 512 cover image and max 4095 bytes' of the size of secret message. In our future work, we will fix those limitations, which will be able to handle more than 765 bytes' into 512 × 512 cover image.

References

1. Judge, J.C.: Steganography: past, present, future. No. UCRL-ID-151879. Lawrence Livermore National Lab., CA (US) (2001)
2. Singla, S., Bala, A.: A review: cryptography and steganography algorithm for cloud computing. In: 2018 Second International Conference on Inventive Communication and Computational Technologies, ICICCT, pp. 953–957. IEEE, April 2018
3. Feng, B., Lu, W., Sun, W.: Binary image steganalysis based on pixel mesh markov transition matrix. J. Vis. Commun. Image Represent. **26**, 284–295 (2015)
4. Chen, J., Lu, W., Fang, Y., Liu, X., Yeung, Y., Xue, Y.: Binary image steganalysis based on local texture pattern. J. Vis. Commun. Image Represent. **55**, 149–156 (2018)
5. Kadhim, I.J.: A new audio steganography system based on auto-key generator. Al-Khwarizmi Eng. J. **8**(1), 27–36 (2012)
6. Feng, B., Weng, J., Lu, W., Pei, B.: Steganalysis of content-adaptive binary image data hiding. J. Vis. Commun. Image Represent. **46**, 119–127 (2017)
7. Ashwin, S., Ramesh, J., Kumar, S.A., Gunavathi, K.: Novel and secure encoding and hiding techniques using image steganography: a survey. In: 2012 International Conference on Emerging Trends in Electrical Engineering and Energy Management, ICETEEEM, pp. 171–177. IEEE, December 2012
8. Awad, A.: A survey of spatial domain techniques in image steganography. J. Educ. Coll. Wasit Univ. **1**(26), 497–510 (2017)
9. Odeh, A., Elleithy, K., Faezipour, M., Abdelfattah, E.: Novel steganography over HTML code. In: Sobh, T., Elleithy, K. (eds.) Innovations and Advances in Computing, Informatics, Systems Sciences, Networking and Engineering. LNEE, vol. 313, pp. 607–611. Springer, Cham (2015). https://doi.org/10.1007/978-3-319-06773-5_81
10. Thomas, P.: Literature survey on modern image steganographic techniques. Int. J. Eng. Res. Technol. **2**, 107–111 (2013)
11. Nagpal, K.D., Dabhade, P.D.S.: A survey on image steganography and its techniques in spatial and frequency domain. Int. J. Recent Innov. Trends Comput. Commun. **3**(2), 776–779 (2015)
12. Beroual, A., Al-Shaikhli, I.F.: A review of steganographic methods and techniques. Int. J. Perceptive Cogn. Comput. **4**(1), 1–6 (2018)
13. Biradar, R.L., Umashetty, A.: A survey paper on steganography techniques. High Impact Factor **9**(1), 721–722 (2016)
14. Saleh, M.A.: Image steganography techniques - a review paper. Ijarcce **7**(9), 52–58 (2018)

15. Al-Shatnawi, A.M.: A new method in image steganography with improved image quality. Appl. Math. Sci. **6**(79), 3907–3915 (2012)
16. Swain, G.: Very high capacity image steganography technique using quotient value differencing and LSB substitution. Arab. J. Sci. Eng. **44**(4), 2995–3004 (2019)
17. Mahimah, P., Kurinji, R.: Zigzag pixel indicator based secret data hiding method. In: 2013 IEEE International Conference on Computational Intelligence and Computing Research, pp. 1–5. IEEE, December 2013
18. Sahu, A.K., Swain, G.: A review on LSB substitution and PVD based image steganography techniques. Indonesian J. Electr. Eng. Comput. Sci. **2**(3), 712–719 (2016)
19. Pavani, M., Naganjaneyulu, S., Nagaraju, C.: A survey on LSB based steganography methods. Int. J. Eng. Comput. Sci. **2**(8), 2464–2467 (2013)
20. Khan, Z., Shah, M., Naeem, M., Mahmood, T., Khan, S., Amin, N.U., Shahzad, D.: Threshold-based steganography: a novel technique for improved payload and SNR. Int. Arab J. Inf. Technol. **13**(4), 380–386 (2016)
21. Bhuiyan, T., Sarower, A.H., Karim, M.R., Hassan, M.M.: An image steganography algorithm using LSB replacement through XOR substitution. In: 2019 International Conference on Information and Communications Technology, ICOIACT, pp. 44–49. IEEE, July 2019
22. Wu, D.C., Tsai, W.H.: A steganographic method for images by pixel-value differencing. Pattern Recogn. Lett. **24**, 1613–1626 (2003)
23. Mandal J.K., Debashis D.: Colour image steganography based on pixel value differencing in spatial domain, Int. J. Inf. Sci. Tech. (IJIST) **2**(4) (2012)
24. Wu, H.C., Wu, N.I., Tsai, C.S., Hwang, M.S.: Image steganographic scheme based on pixel value differencing and LSB replacement method. In: IEEE Proceedings on Vision, Image and Signal processing, vol. 152, no. 5, pp. 611–615 (2005)
25. Bharti, P., Soni, R.: A new approach of data hiding in images using cryptography and steganography. IJOCA **58**(8), 0975–8887 (2012)
26. Ali, A.N.: An image steganography method with high hiding capacity based on RGB image. Int. J. Signal Image Process. **1**(4), 238–241 (2010)
27. Ran, Z.W., Chi, F.L., Ja, C.L.: Image hiding by optimal LSB substitution and genetic algorithm. Pattern Recogn. Soc. **34**, 671–683 (2001)
28. Li, B., Wang, M., Li, X., Tan, S., Huang, J.: A strategy of clustering modification directions in spatial image steganography. IEEE Trans. Inf. Forensics Secur. **10**(9), 1905–1917 (2015)
29. Karim, S.M., Rahman, M.S., Hossain, M.I.: A new approach for LSB based image steganography using secret key. In: 14th international conference on computer and information technology, ICCIT 2011, pp. 286–291. IEEE, December 2011
30. Bloisi, D.D., Iocchi, L.: Image based steganography and cryptography. In: VISAPP, no. 1, pp. 127–134 (2007)
31. Westfeld, A.: F5—a steganographic algorithm. In: Moskowitz, I.S. (ed.) IH 2001. LNCS, vol. 2137, pp. 289–302. Springer, Heidelberg (2001). https://doi.org/10.1007/3-540-45496-9_21
32. Thangadurai, K., Devi, G.S.: An analysis of LSB based image steganography techniques. In: 2014 International Conference on Computer Communication and Informatics, pp. 1–4. IEEE, January 2014
33. Zhu, Z., Zhang, T., Wan, B.: A special detector for the edge adaptive image steganography based on LSB matching revisited. In: 2013 10th IEEE International Conference on Control and Automation, ICCA, pp. 1363–1366. IEEE, June 2013
34. Sarmah, D.K., Bajpai, N.: Proposed system for data hiding using cryptography and steganography. Int. J. Comput. Appl. **8**(9), 7–10 (2010)

35. Gowda, S.N.: Advanced dual layered encryption for block based approach to image steganography. In: 2016 International Conference on Computing, Analytics and Security Trends, CAST, pp. 250–254. IEEE, December 2016
36. Lokhande, U.: An effective way of using LSB steganography in images along with cryptography. Int. J. Comput. Appl. **88**(12), 0975–8887 (2014)
37. Nakasone, T., Li, Y., Sasaki, Y., Iwamoto, M., Ohta, K., Sakiyama, K.: Key-dependent weakness of AES-based ciphers under clockwise collision distinguisher. In: Kwon, T., Lee, M.-K., Kwon, D. (eds.) ICISC 2012. LNCS, vol. 7839, pp. 395–409. Springer, Heidelberg (2013). https://doi.org/10.1007/978-3-642-37682-5_28
38. Riasat, R., Bajwa, I.S., Ali, M.Z.: A hash-based approach for colour image steganography. In: International Conference on Computer Networks and Information Technology, pp. 303–307. IEEE, July 2011
39. Sarkar, A., Karforma, S.: A new pixel selection technique of LSB based steganography for data hiding. Int. Res. J. Comput. Sci. (IRJCS) **5**(03), 120–125 (2018)
40. Aqeel, I., Raheel, M.: Digital image steganography by using a hash based LSB (3-2-3) technique. In: Bajwa, I.S., Kamareddine, F., Costa, A. (eds.) INTAP 2018. CCIS, vol. 932, pp. 713–724. Springer, Singapore (2019). https://doi.org/10.1007/978-981-13-6052-7_61
41. Bhardwaj, R., Sharma, V.: Image steganography based on complemented message and inverted bit LSB substitution. Proc. Comput. Sci. **93**, 832–838 (2016)
42. Huang, L., Cai, S., Xiong, X., Xiao, M.: On symmetric color image encryption system with permutation-diffusion simultaneous operation. Opt. Lasers Eng. **115**, 7–20 (2019)
43. Roy, R., Changder, S., Sarkar, A., Debnath, N.C.: Evaluating image steganography techniques: future research challenges. In: 2013 International Conference on Computing, Management and Telecommunications, ComManTel, pp. 309–314. IEEE, January 2013
44. Jassim, F.A.: A novel steganography algorithm for hiding text in image using five modulus method. arXiv preprint arXiv:1307.0642 (2013)
45. Hore, A., Ziou, D.: Image quality metrics: PSNR vs. SSIM. In: 2010 20th International Conference on Pattern Recognition, pp. 2366–2369. IEEE, August 2010
46. Kellman, P., McVeigh, E.R.: Image reconstruction in SNR units: a general method for SNR measurement. Magn. Reson. Med. **54**(6), 1439–1447 (2005)
47. Vora, V.S., Suthar, A.C., Makwana, Y.N., Davda, S.J.: Analysis of compressed image quality assessments. M. Tech Student in E & C Dept, CCET, Wadhwan-Gujarat (2010)
48. Jain, A., Bhateja, V.: A full-reference image quality metric for objective evaluation in spatial domain. In: 2011 International Conference on Communication and Industrial Application, pp. 1–5. IEEE, December 2011
49. Liu, Z., Laganière, R.: Phase congruence measurement for image similarity assessment. Pattern Recogn. Lett. **28**(1), 166–172 (2007)
50. Gonzalez, R.C., Woods, R.E., Eddins, S.L.: Digital Image Processing Using MATLAB. Pearson Education India, Chennai (2004)

An Enhancement of Kerberos Using Biometric Template and Steganography

Munira Tabassum[1,2], Afjal H. Sarower[1], Ashrafia Esha[2], and Md. Maruf Hassan[1,2](✉)

[1] Daffodil International University, Dhaka, Bangladesh
maruf.swe@diu.edu.bd
[2] Cyber Security Center, DIU, Dhaka, Bangladesh

Abstract. Kerberos, a renowned token based authentication protocol, which is famous since mid-80's for its cryptographic process, assurance of privacy, and data security for identifying appropriate users. Due to its versatile characteristics, users of the system often need to remember complex passwords as the good practice of the method requires update of the same within a defined time-frame which becomes bit difficult for users to cope up with. At the same time, it also not provides adequate channel security to transmit the user credential between the pathway of the client and server. Therefore, researchers are trying to find out a simple solution where user does not necessitate to memorize the passwords where it could guarantee better user validation. In this paper, an enhancement of Kerberos authentication model has been proposed where biometric template and Steganography are incorporated to solve the existing weaknesses. Instead of taking username and password, the new solution will take a pair of random fingerprints from the user and convert it into a hash. It will then embed the hash in the randomized image and send it to the server for authentication. A security analysis of the proposed protocol is proven using BAN logic in this article where it ensures reliability, practicability and security of the enhanced Kerberos protocol.

Keywords: Cyber Security · Authentication · Kerberos protocol · Image steganography

1 Introduction

In this modern era, the demand of online applications are increasing dramatically at all domains especially in business due to its manageable, flexible, usable, and portable characteristics to satisfy the consumer's expectation. The web applications are hosting through a web server and it communicates and also provides services to its user through the public channel. There may have a chance for the attacker to intercept and modify the messages transmitted between the server and user if any vulnerability exists in the system [1]. Different types of users such as end users, support user, privileged user, admin user, etc. are working in the

T. Bhuiyan et al. (Eds.): ICONCS 2020, LNICST 325, pp. 116–127, 2020.
https://doi.org/10.1007/978-3-030-52856-0_9

same platform to execute their roles for the smooth operation of the business. Therefore, it requires proper user authentication to ensure the right access for the valid stakeholders in the system as no intruders from cyberspace can claim themselves as legal user.

In the last 50 years researchers gave different solution of secure authentication using multiple complex authentication factors or credential protection mechanisms like as text based password, hard and soft token, biometric fingerprint and palm-print, behavioral and contextual authentication, keystroke dynamics and so on [2–7]. Including these existing solutions, biometric authentication factors are giving more accurate clarification of legal users where other solution has remains flaws for the improvement of security, user experience, unnecessary remembering and reduced operating costs. In the other hand, the solution with biometric fingerprint is also extensively used in the identity authentication system due to its unique, stable and irreplaceable physical characteristics [8].

In every solutions, it is must need to evaluate security protocols. To evaluate security protocols, Burrows, Abadi and Needham produced a formal logic of authentication called BAN logic in 1989 [35]. Kerberos is one of the most common key distribution protocols that has a full BAN guarantee to analyze the cryptographic protocols [9]. Lo is concluded that Kerberos is the strongest form of authentication [10]. Though Kasslin and Tikkanen proved that in some cases Kerberos suffers from replay attack [11,12].

The manuscript is organized as follows. Section 2 outlines the previous related researches to the concept of Biometric fingerprint scanning issues, multi factor Kerberos protocol and specific contributions. It is followed by a discussion on the proposed template protection concept and architecture for remote authentication is presented in Sect. 3 also the analysis of the BAN logic into the proposed model. The technique is experimentally discussed in Sect. 4 with security and privacy issues. Section 5 concludes the study with future work.

2 Related Work

In order to maintain secure communication through public channels and to ensure information security for sensitive online transactions, the user needs to be validated through an effective authentication mechanism. As an active identification process, three types of authentication schemes have been widely used as text-based, two-factor token-based, biometric template-based authentication in our daily lives over the past decades where these schemes have been configured for multi-server environments [13–16]. The following sections discuss details of conventional authentication schemes since the middle of the 19th century.

Text-Based Authentication. The perspective of computer systems and applications, text-based schemes based on passwords, PINs, code words are commonly used for being authentication that have been conducted with the past researches. As instance, Durbadal Chattaraj et al. proposed key exchange mechanism by dint of both public and private key cryptography and a dynamic password-based two-server authentication [17], where they could not clarify the protection public channels from attack. Traditional password-based remote user authentication is not much secure as biometric-based remote user authentication which is proved by AKA protocol [18].

Two-Factor Token Based Authentication. Two-factor authentication based on keys, smart cards, USB drives, token devices adds an additional security layer to the authentication process by making it harder for hackers to access a user's devices or online accounts. Many researchers proposed robust solution about two-factor token-based authentication such as Hassina Nacer et al. developed a decentralized and completely distributed model for composite b services using two-way authentication, three party key establishments, and a distributed certificate authority, where they could not measures the security issues of paths [19].

Biometric Template Authentication. To design a defensive and reliable, two-factor user and/or machine identification and validation biometric technologies are turning out the cornerstone of an extensive array of highly secured solution. In past researches of biometric template authentication, has been conducted with several solution like fingerprints, palm scanning, facial recognition, iris scans, retina scans, lip recognition and voice verification [20–23]. Srijan Das et al. developed a Lip biometric template security framework using spatial Steganography for improving the local features of the lip images [20].

Image Steganography Technique. Steganography is used to conceal messages into more complex information forms including images, audio, or videos. Several researchers conducted that, through the network, Steganography techniques added additional protection to data transmission [24–26]. Nevertheless, researchers have suggested a large number of solutions using Steganography techniques to mitigate the lack of attacks when transmitting data like as Yoon-Su Jeong et al. proposed a mutual authentication method in a situation where device A communicates with device B, which is an in heterogeneous environment, using biometric information from each device user [27].

After reviewing the above literature, it is found that the conventional text-based and token-based approaches are not significantly provide positive user identification because they rely on surrogate representations of user's identity. Now-a-days, the most widely used biometric techniques are fingerprint and iris scans [29–31,33,34].

3 Proposed Model

The proposed system uses biometric authentication, Cryptography and Steganography to ensure data security and presence hiding. The mechanism also use a portable device with biometric Fingerprints to add extra factor. Let's assume that there are three different roles in this proposed scheme which are the User, Authentication server and Application server. Application server is responsible for providing service to authorized user. On the other hand, the authentication server is responsible for verifying the authenticity of the user.

The Proposed system is based on the shared-keys between three principals and a Database with an Authentication server and an Application Server that makes use of Timestamp as nonce (Fig. 1).

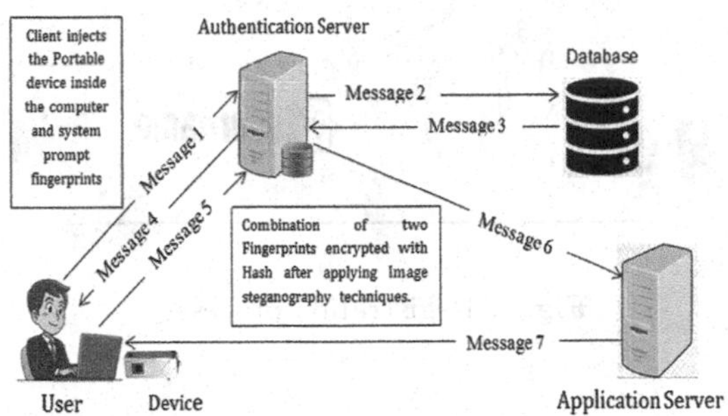

Fig. 1. Enhancement model of kerberos using biometric template and stegenography

The model is given below with the help of three principals as U, AU and AP. K_{UAU}, K_{UAP}, K_{AUAP} are the shared keys where the K_U, K_{AU} and K_{AP} are the public keys and DB as the Authentication server Database. In this phase U generates the timestamp T_U, A_U generates the timestamp T_{AU}, AP generates the timestamp T_{AP} and U generates the Lifetime L respectively. The fifth, sixth and seventh messages are used only if the mutual authentication is required. Here, OTP as One time image (fingerprint) which is generated by Stego Validation and POTP as previously used OTP where it stored in Stego Validation. The Messages are given below sequentially-

Message 1. $U \rightarrow AU : \{T_U L, D_{ID}\}_{K_{CAU}}$

Message 2. $AU \rightarrow DB : \{T_{AU}, D_{ID}, \{T_{AU}, DB \xleftrightarrow{K_{AUDB}} AU\}_{K_{DB}}\}_{K_{AUDB}}$

Message 3. $DB \rightarrow AU : \{T_{AU}, D_{ID}, \{T_{AU}, U, OTP, DB \xleftrightarrow{K_{AUDB}} AU\}_{K_{AU}}\}_{K_{AUDB}}$

Message 4. $AU \rightarrow U : \{T_{AU}, U, \{T_{AU}, POTP, (Fg_1, Fg_2), AU \xleftrightarrow{K_{UAU}} U\}_{K_U}\}_{K_{UAU}}$

Message 5. $U \rightarrow AU : \{T_U, K_{UAP}, \{T_U, (Fg_1, Fg_2), AU \xleftrightarrow{K_{UAU}} U\}_{K_{AU}}\}_{K_{UAU}}$

Message 6. $AU \rightarrow AP : \{T_{AU}, U, D_{ID}, \{T_{AU}, AU \xleftrightarrow{K_{AUAP}} AP\}_{K_{AP}}\}_{K_{AUAP}}$

Message 7. $AP \rightarrow AU : \{T_{AP}, U, D_{ID}, \{T_{AU}, AP \xleftrightarrow{K_{UAP}} U\}_{K_U}\}_{K_{UAP}}$

Application Server receives access request to U.

Now, The Model will be proved with the help of greatest BAN logic and the concept of Kerberos protocol.

3.1 Registration Process

At first, User's need to enter the Portable device into the Server for assigning Device ID. For every single Device's, Server Database will provide a key as a private key that will stored in the database. After that user have to provide every (10) finger's print sequentially according to the direction of that device. In this case, User needs to provide Username for additional security (Fig. 2).

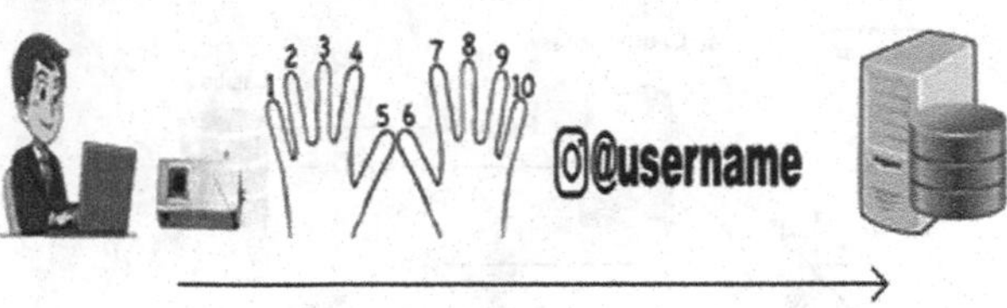

Fig. 2. Registration process

3.2 Login Process

In login process, at first user enters the portable device then with the help of database server, authentication server tries to match with the Device ID. If the Device ID matched, authentication server wants two fingerprints randomly (One from left hand and one from right hand). According to the query of Authentication Server, user will provide two fingerprints. Then, the combination of two fingerprints will go to the channel with image Steganography. After that, by the help of hash algorithm these texts will be encrypted. However, the login process will complete in 3 phases describe below:

Request Phase. First phase is the Request phase. In this phase, login request will send through the channel from client side to server side. In Request phase-

1. User U Request for login to the system by entering the portable device to the system. It reads D_{ID}.
2. The Server side matches the D_{ID} with the help of Server Database, If matches then AU pick the Username U_{NM} from the Database and pick two finger-prints (One is from Left and one is from Right) from the corresponding D_{ID} and send to the Client side.
3. User U provides these two specific fingerprints with the given instruction.
4. Client side Hash the following combination of two fingerprints by using hashing algorithm. Client side encrypts Fingerprints Fg_x using asymmetric algorithm.
5. Embed the hash into the selected image using suitable and effective Steganography technique.

Authentication Phase. Second phase is the Authentication phase. In that phase, server authenticate the client with legal identity. In Authentication phase-

1. AU receive the image files and $En(Fg_x)$.
2. First retrieve the $En(Fg_x)$ from Steganography.

3. Matches that received En(Fg_x) with the previous En(Fg_x).
4. Perform HASH operation on H.
5. Fg_1 && Fg_2 = = expected (Fg_{x_1}&&Fg_{x_2})
6. If it is TRUE. Redirect to AS.
   *$DB_h \rightarrow$ Hash stored in Database.
   *$DB_{Fg_x} \rightarrow Fg_x$ stored in database for previous authentication.

Response Phase. The last phase is the Response phase. In this phase, the server will give response to the client by creating a session. In Response phase-

1. AP receives access request to U.
2. AP creates session and provides access to U

After all these phases, login process will be completed and authentication process also be formalized.

3.3 Proposed Implementation Technologies

For our solution, we propose SHA-512 algorithm for hashing operation of user's fingerprint and LSB replacement through XOR substitution will be used for image steganography.

3.4 Notation

Several types of objects have been defined in this model as principals, encryption keys, notation and statements. Where the symbols U, AU, AP and DB denoted as User, Authentication Server, Application Server and Server Database sequentially. D_{ID} as Device ID and U_{NM} as Username. $K_{UAU}, K_{UAP}, K_{AUAP}$ denotes as Shared key between U and AU, U and AP and AU and AP respectively. K_U, K_{AU}, K_{AP} denotes specific public keys of the principals U, AU and AP and K_U^-, K_{AU}^- and K_{AP}^- denotes the corresponding secret keys where T_U, T_{AU} and T_{AP} denotes specific nonce timestamp. Here, OTP denotes One Time Image generated by Stego validation and POTP as Previously One Time Image generated by Stego validation. Fg_X denotes the combination of two fingerprints where $Fg_1, Fg_2, \ldots, Fg_{10}$ denotes every single Fingerprints sequentially.

3.5 Analysis

To analyze this protocol, the first assumptions are given here:

AU believes AU $\xleftrightarrow{K_{UAU}}$ U	AU believes fresh (T_U)
DB believes DB $\xleftrightarrow{K_{AUDB}}$ U	DB believes fresh (T_{AU})
AP believes AP $\xleftrightarrow{K_{AUAP}}$ AU	AP believes fresh (T_{AU})
AU believes U controls AU $\xleftrightarrow{K}$ U	U believes fresh (T_{AP})
DB believes AU controls DB $\xleftrightarrow{K}$ AU	
AP believes AU controls AP $\xleftrightarrow{K}$ AU	

The first left three, is about Shared keys between the three principals and Database. The right four assumptions show that the directors and the Database server believe that the timestamps generated elsewhere are fresh; this indicates that the model relies heavily on synchronized clocks. The next group of three which indicates the trust that the principles and DB has in the server to generate a good encryption key. In Message 1, U sends its device id where AU contact with the DB for conforming the D_{ID} and then AU pick the U_{NM} which generated the OTP for further identification of U, in message 2 and 3. And in Message 4, AU requested for the combination of two random Fingerprints from U. However, it is possible to skip Message 1, Message 2, message 3 and Message 4 respectively. If it is possible to build the belief between U and AU and between AU and AP then it can be claimed that AP have believe to U. After analyzing the idealized model by applying the rules it can be assume that the analysis is straightforward. In the interests of brevity, give many of the formal details necessary for this machine assisted proof only for Message 5, Message 6 and Message 7. And it will omit similar details later on. The main steps of the proof are as follows:

AU receives Message 5. The annotation rules yield that-

$$AU sees\{T_U, L, D_{ID}\}_{K_{CAU}}$$

holds afterward. Since it has the hypothesis-

$$\text{AU believes (AU} \xleftrightarrow{K_{UAU}} \text{U)}$$

Applying Rule and yields the following:-

$$\text{AU believes U said } \{T_U, (\text{AU} \xleftrightarrow{K_{UAU}} \text{U}), \{T_U, \text{AU} \xleftrightarrow{K_{UAU}} \text{U}\}K_{AU}\}K_{UAU}$$

One of the rules to break Conjunctions (Omitted here) then produces -

$$\text{AU believes U said } (T_U, (\text{AU} \xleftrightarrow{K_{UAU}} \text{U}))$$

Moreover, it has the following hypothesis:

$$AU believes fresh(T_U)$$

Rule applies and yields -

$$\text{AU believes U believes } (T_U, (\text{AU} \xleftrightarrow{K_{UAU}} \text{U}))$$

Again, breaking the conjunction, to obtain the following:

$$\text{AU believes U believes (AU} \xleftrightarrow{K} \text{U)}$$

deriving the more concrete-

$$\text{AU believes U believes (AU} \xleftrightarrow{K_{UAU}} \text{U)}$$

Finally, the Rule applies and yields the following:

$$\text{AU believes } (\text{AU} \xleftrightarrow{K_{UAU}} \text{U})$$

Therefore it concludes the analysis of Message 5.

U passes the expected Finger-prints POTP on to AU, together with a message containing a timestamp. Initially, AU can decrypted only this message:

$$\text{U believes } (\text{AU} \xleftrightarrow{K_{UAU}} \text{U})$$

This result is logically obtained in the same way that it was acquired for Message 5. Through the postulates of message, nonce-verification and jurisdiction.

Knowledge of new key allows AU to decrypted this message. Through the message-meaning and the nonce-verification postulates, deduct the following:

$$\text{U believes AU believes } (\text{AU} \xleftrightarrow{K_{UAU}} \text{U})$$

According to previous, DB also believes AU and gives replay with confirmation.

To next, AU sends message to AP for confirming the identity of U and give access U with generating session for U.

Applying these three rules according to previous it also prove that-

$$\text{AU believes AP believes } (\text{AP} \xleftrightarrow{K_{AUAP}} \text{AU})$$

Now, it can be deduced that:

$$\text{AP believes AU believes } (\text{AP} \xleftrightarrow{K_{AUAP}} \text{AU})$$

Here with that $(AP \xleftrightarrow{K_{AUAP}} \text{AU})$, AU sends message to AP that can be replaced by U. (Message that will actually send it about U's $\text{D}_{\text{ID}}, \text{U}_{\text{NM}}$). Now it deduced that:

$$APbelievesAUbelievesU$$

And, it has the following hypothesis –

$$\text{AP believes AU controls } (\text{AP} \xleftrightarrow{K} \text{AU})$$

Here with that $(\text{AP} \xleftrightarrow{K} \text{AU})$, AU sends message to AP that can be replaced by U. (Message that will actually send it about U's $\text{D}_{\text{ID}}, \text{U}_{\text{NM}}$). Now it deduce that-

$$APbelievesAUcontrolsU$$

Lastly, the jurisdiction rule applies and yields the following:

$$APbelievesU$$

And for that AP creates a session for User U. However, it is possible to build the belief between U, AU and AU, AP then it can be claimed that AP has believe on U.

4 Discussion and Security Analysis

After applying the Kerberos Protocol, BAN logic and Biometric Authentication, it was unable to ensure the data security because the path was not enough secure or data properly encrypted. Therefore, most of the attacks such as - Man in the Middle (MITM) attack, spyware, trojan-horse, phishing attack, hash-injection are mainly disrupt the security system when transmission of data via communication channels. Though it is quite impossible to protect a server from MITM attack for the cause of uses proxy server, it can be possible to secure data by effective data hiding techniques. To ensure the data security, this model uses image Steganography technique to secure data by data hiding in the stego image during transmission [28,32]. The SHA-512 hash algorithm will be used in our proposed authentication system to secure the combination of fingerprints.

The proposed model has been evaluated from a security perspective by considering possibilities for the attack. The enhancement of the proposed model provides protection against some common attacks. Apart from this, it mitigates risk caused by very certain and crucial– Man in The Middle Attack. Details explanation regarding how proposed method defends against some of the very harmful attack is given below.

Replay Attack. A replay attack occurs when a cyber-criminal eavesdrops into a secure network email, intercepts it, senses a transmission of data and has it delayed or replicated fraudulently. To do this, the attacker can retrieve image files from Stego. However, this attacker must resend the packet to the server in order to log in to the server and in this case the attacker will not be successful because the session has already been cancelled for the cause of session time limitation. As the POTP will be placed by new OTP for every successful authentication and the fingerprint will choose by random function thus it will protect against the replay attack.

Man-in-the-Middle Attack. The Man-in-the-middle attack takes place into the conversation between the user and server where the attacker can listen their conversation illegally that they should not to be listened. The intruder may be able to intercept new messages transmitting between the user and the server. However, this proposed scheme creates a strong barrier to the assault on MITM and reduces the risk of Man in the middle attack. This scheme uses steganography to conceal the credentials within stego object which hides the presence of existence of credentials. Even though a proxy server is compromised or SSL is broken the attacker may need a very long time to detect and extract the cre- dentials from stego object. However our proposed model doesn't guarantee defense against MITM attack but mitigate the risk and damage caused by the same.

Impersonating, Password Guessing and Brute Force Attack. An intruder can attempt to impersonate the original user as a legitimate credential by stealing username/password/PIN/fingerprint and login to the server using these. In that case it is the point to be noted that, our model doesn't use any password. Instead of password this scheme has used user's combinational fingerprint for authentication that will choose randomly by the system while a login attempt take places. That can reduce both of the impersonating, password guessing, and brute force attack.

Session Hijacking Attack. Hijacking of a TCP session is a security attack against a user session over a secure network. The most common session hijacking method is called IP spoofing, when an attacker uses source-routed IP packets to inject commands into an active connection between two nodes on a network and disguise themselves as one of the authenticated users. In this model, it reduces the possibilities of this session hijacking attack for the use of hashing and image steganography techniques where the OTP will create for a limited session time.

Above analysis highlights the efficiency and security of proposed authentication model. Detail study proves that this authentication mechanism is very defensive against mentioned attacks and threats. However, this research provides a theoretical concept about authentication using biometric fingerprint and unique device. No data has been shown here for proving as the implementation. According to the observation and conceptual accommodation it can be said that this model ensures more security, reliability and flexibility as compared to other authentication mechanism discussed in literature review of this paper. Moreover, implementation with manual data organization will be tested in our future work with actual comparison.

5 Conclusion

Biometric based multi-factor authentication protocol has proposed in this paper to enhance the existing Kerberos authentication protocol where the Image Steganography technique has used to ensure the data security over the public channel. The proposed solution has been proved its rules through the renowned proofing tool of authentication protocol, BAN logic that ensures the belief between both the server and the user. The advantage of this system is to authenticate the user without remembering the username and password which has made this system more unique with comparing other researches. Furthermore, the complexity of changing or remembering passwords is completely avoided in this proposed system, which ensures the effectiveness of this solution. The proposed scheme has also the advantage of better combining secrecy with biometric data that can reduce the impact of the stolen identity attacks. Theoretically the model has been proved using BAN logic in this study; however, known attacks against this solution will be tested to verify the effectiveness of the solution in future.

Acknowledgement. The authors would like to express their gratitude to the authority of Cyber Security Center, DIU (CSC, DIU) for the cooperation and support to execute the study.

References

1. Kumar, A., Ome, H.: An improved and secure multiserver authentication scheme based on biometrics and smartcard. Digit. Commun. Netw. **4**(1), 27–38 (2018)
2. Van Dijk, M., et al.: Providing authentication codes which include token codes and biometric factors. U.S. Patent No. 8,752,146, 10 June 2014
3. Shanmugapriya, D., Padmavathi, G.: A survey of biometric keystroke dynamics: approaches, security and challenges. arXiv preprint arXiv:0910.0817 (2009)
4. Brostoff, S., Sasse, M.A.: Are passfaces more usable than passwords? A field trial investigation. In: McDonald, S., Waern, Y., Cockton, G. (eds.) People and Computers XIV – Usability or Else!, pp. 405–424. Springer, London (2000). https://doi.org/10.1007/978-1-4471-0515-2_27
5. Kesanupalli, R.: Fingerprint sensor device and system with verification token and methods of using. U.S. Patent Application No. 12/561,186
6. Hessler, C.J.: Method for mobile security via multi-factor context authentication. U.S. Patent No. 8,935,769, 13 January 2015
7. Ashibani, Y., Kauling, D., Mahmoud, Q.H.: Design and implementation of a contextual-based continuous authentication framework for smart homes. Appl. Syst. Innov. **2**(1), 4 (2019)
8. Koong, C.-S., Yang, T.-I., Tseng, C.-C.: A user authentication scheme using physiological and behavioral biometrics for multitouch devices. Sci. World J. **2014**, 1–12 (2014)
9. Mukhamedov, A.: Full agreement in BAN kerberos. In: 2005 Workshop of the 1st International Conference on Security and Privacy for Emerging Areas in Communication Networks, pp. 218–223. Citeseer (2005)
10. Lo, G.: A hierarchy of authentication specifications. In: Proceedings of the 10th Computer Security Foundations Workshop (CSFW 1997). IEEE Computer Society (1997)
11. Kasslin, K., Tikkanen, A.: Kerberos V Security: ReplayAttacks. Enhancing Trust, Citeseer, p. 191
12. Fan, K., Li, H., Wang, Y.: Security analysis of the kerberos protocol using BAN logic. In: 2009 Fifth International Conference on Information Assurance and Security (2009). https://doi.org/10.1109/ias.2009.320
13. Leu, J.-S., Hsieh, W.-B.: Efficient and secure dynamic ID-based remote user authentication scheme for distributed systems using smart cards. IET Inf. Secur. **8**(2), 104–113 (2013)
14. Tsai, J.-L., Lo, N.-W., Tzong-Chen, W.: Novel anonymous authentication scheme using smart cards. IEEE Trans. Ind. Inform. **9**(4), 2004–2013 (2012)
15. Yang, G., et al.: Two-factor mutual authentication based on smart cards and passwords. J. Comput. Syst. Sci. **74**(7), 1160–1172 (2008)
16. Chen, B.-L., Kuo, W.-C., Wuu, L.-C.: Robust smart-card-based remote user password authentication scheme. Int. J. Commun Syst **27**(2), 377–389 (2014)
17. Chattaraj, D., Sarma, M., Das, A.K.: A new two-server authentication and key agreement protocol for accessing secure cloud services. Comput. Netw. **131**, 144–164 (2018)
18. Chaturvedi, A., et al.: A privacy preserving biometric-based three-factor remote user authenticated key agreement scheme. J. Inf. Secur. Appl. **32**, 15–26 (2017)
19. Nacer, H., et al.: A distributed authentication model for composite web services. Comput. Secur. **70**, 144–178 (2017)

20. Das, S., et al.: Lip biometric template security framework using spatial steganography. Pattern Recogn. Lett. **126**, 102–110 (2019)
21. Bhatnagar, G., Wu, Q.M.J., Raman, B.: Biometric template security based on watermarking. Procedia Comput. Sci. **2**, 227–235 (2010)
22. Bedi, P., Bansal, R., Sehgal, P.: Multimodal biometric authentication using PSO based watermarking. Procedia Technol. **4**, 612–618 (2012)
23. Sajjad, M., et al.: CNN-based anti-spoofing two-tier multi-factor authentication system. Pattern Recogn. Lett. **126**, 123–131 (2019)
24. Kadhim, I.J., et al.: Comprehensive survey of image steganography: techniques, evaluations and trends in future research. Neurocomputing **335**, 299–326 (2019)
25. Minz, K.S., Yadav, P.S.: A review on secure communication method based on encryption and steganography. Complexity **6**(01) (2019)
26. Sharma, U.: A review on various approaches of data hiding for secure data transmission (2019)
27. Jeong, Y.-S., Lee, B.-K., Lee, S.-H.: An efficient device authentication protocol using bioinformatic. In: Wang, Y., Cheung, Y., Liu, H. (eds.) CIS 2006. LNCS (LNAI), vol. 4456, pp. 567–575. Springer, Heidelberg (2007). https://doi.org/10.1007/978-3-540-74377-4_59
28. Alturki, F., Mersereau, R.: A novel approach for increasing security and data embedding capacity in images for data hiding applications. In: Proceedings International Conference on Information Technology: Coding and Computing. IEEE (2001)
29. Ali, S.S., et al.: Polynomial vault: a secure and robust fingerprint based authentication. IEEE Trans. Emerg. Top. Comput. (2019)
30. Lee, J.K., Ryu, S.R., Yoo, K.Y.: Fingerprint-based remote user authentication scheme using smart cards. Electron. Lett. **38**(12), 554–555 (2002)
31. Wangkeeree, N., Boonkrong, S.: Finding a suitable threshold value for an iris-based authentication system. Int. J. Electr. Comput. Eng. **9**, 3558 (2019). (2088–8708)
32. Mare, S.F., Vladutiu, M., Prodan, L.: Secret data communication system using Steganography, AES and RSA. In: 2011 IEEE 17th International Symposium for Design and Technology in Electronic Packaging (SIITME). IEEE (2011)
33. Korukonda, V.R., Reddy, E.S.: Iris based texture analysis for verification and detection: revisit (2019)
34. Kannavara, R., Bourbakis, N.: Iris biometric authentication based on local global graphs: an FPGA implementation. In: 2009 IEEE Symposium on Computational Intelligence for Security and Defense Applications. IEEE (2009)
35. Burrows, M., Abadi, M., Needham, R.: A logic of authentication. In: ACM Transactions on Computer Systems (TOCS), pp. 18–36. ACM, New York (1990)

A Vulnerability Detection Framework for CMS Using Port Scanning Technique

Md. Asaduzzaman(✉), Proteeti Prova Rawshan, Nurun Nahar Liya, Muhmmad Nazrul Islam, and Nishith Kumar Dutta

Department of Computer Science and Engineering, Military Institute of Science and Technology, Dhaka 1216, Bangladesh
asadbd45@gmail.com

Abstract. In the era of technology, attack on computer infrastructure is considered as the most severe threat. Web server is one of the most important components of this infrastructure. Preventive measures must be taken to deal with these attacks on the web servers. For this reason, vulnerability detection needs to be carried out in an effective way and should be mitigated as soon as possible. In this paper, an effective framework for vulnerability detection of web application is proposed. This framework targets the web applications developed with content management systems (CMSs). It obtains prior knowledge of the vulnerable extensions of a specific CMS from its contributors. The framework is run against a target web server using a well-known port scanning tool, Nmap. It checks if there is any existing matches for the vulnerable extension installed in that web application. Finally, the framework gives an output comprised of the installed extensions along with the installed vulnerable extensions in that web application. Although the output result is shown in the Nmap console, the framework is a segregated entity that works in collaboration with Nmap. Thus this framework can be well-utilized by the security specialists to assess the security of a web application in an easier and effective way and also to evaluate vulnerability of web servers; hence shielding the web applications from various kinds of security threats.

Keywords: Security scanner · Port scanning · Content management system · CMScan · Nmap scripting engine

1 Introduction

Nowadays, there is an increasing dependency on web applications. From an individual to an organization, almost every transaction is available, stored or traded in the web. Because of ease of access and its increasing nature of productivity and operational efficiency, reliability on web services has increased, which in turn has raised the security issue of the web applications. Web vulnerability refers to the system flaw or weakness through which the security can be compromised and resources can be exploited. Attacker can access the flaw; thereafter breach the

T. Bhuiyan et al. (Eds.): ICONCS 2020, LNICST 325, pp. 128–139, 2020.
https://doi.org/10.1007/978-3-030-52856-0_10

system integrity through exploitation. This can be easily detected by using network vulnerability scanners, which identify the security loopholes in a computer network by inspecting the most potential targets. Network vulnerability scanners like: SARA [1], SAINT [2], VLAD [3] and Nessus [4] are very effective but most of them are paid and require technical knowledge to use. Whereas, Nmap [5] is a multipurpose utility tool and a port scanner, which is used by millions of beginner users for its easy usability. It discovers services and hosts running in a computer network, including host and port discovery. An NSE script [6] allows doing a wide variety of network assessment tasks.

A widely used application for managing web contents is the Content Management System (CMS). It supports a modular and adaptable framework with the installation of plugins, so that new features can be added and thus the main functionalities of the CMS can be achieved. Amongst all, the most widely used CMS platforms are: WordPress (58.8%), WeBex (12%), Joomla (6.5%) and Drupal (4.8%) [7]. Kaluža et al. [8] carried out a survey on a number of companies and found that 61.11% of the companies used CMS, where 48.48% of the respondents used free CMS, 6.06% answered commercial, 18.18% answered custom CMS and 27.27% of the respondents failed to provide an answer. The CMSs can be kept secured if all the extensions and the plugins can be updated regularly. But the most common problem is that amongst the huge number of plugins, maximum are getting outdated thus compatibility issues are created while using the latest versions.

The main vulnerability issue of CMS lies within its feature-easy identification. Outdated plugins are the entry points for most of the attackers. Cernica et al. [9] showed that from the top ten million websites, 16% of them used WordPress. The paper also conveys that from the total of 21 backup plugins, 12 were found to be vulnerable that can lead to 'Sensitive Data Exposure'. Martinez-Caro et al. [10] conducted an extensive study on CMS alongside some basic security analysis on Joomla and Drupal and found some security vulnerabilities in the extensions of Joomla and Drupal which can be dangerous. Studies show that in 2018, 90% of the hacked CMS based websites used WordPress, then Magento taking up to 4.6% of the data sample, 4.3% of the websites with joomla then consecutively Drupal and ModX [11]. With these kinds of publicly disclosed exposures, it is easier for the attackers to exploit. Network security professionals often have to depend on the other paid vulnerability assessment tools in order to assess the security of web applications (including CMS). Besides, almost all network-security professionals along with network administrators are experts on using open source port scanners. So, an advanced framework can be incorporated in the port scanner that will allow the users to assess vulnerabilities of CMSs.

Therefore, the objective of this paper is to integrate the most required functionalities of a vulnerability scanner for CMSs with a popular port scanner. In order to attain this objective, this research proposes to build an open source framework which incorporates an NSE script in a port scanner (Nmap). It can detect the installed extensions in a CMS; hence it can detect the vulnerable extensions along with the affected versions.

The remaining sections of this paper are organized as follows: a brief overview of the related work is presented in Sect. 2, the conceptual framework is discussed in Sect. 3. In Sect. 4, the design and development of the framework is discussed. Further, the evaluation of the framework is presented in Sect. 5, followed by a discussion and conclusion in Sect. 6.

2 Literature Review

This research focused on the field of CMS based web applications, their vulnerabilities, security aspects and contextual threats and also the ways they can be exploited. To find out the related literature, a search was conducted in the major scholar databases including ACM Scholar, Google Scholar, IEEE Explorer and ScienceDirect using suitable search strings. The related literatures are presented briefly below.

Most of the CMSs are customizable, adaptable and built-in open source frameworks (WordPress, Joomla or Drupal) [12], hence they are vulnerable by their nature. Also, a shared environment provides the users with shared flaws which encourages the security researchers and the hacker community. Once these vulnerable loopholes are found, they are used for mass attacks. Yu et al. [13] made a model of mapping these vulnerabilities and attack patterns by analyzing the attack targets. He also developed a methodology to test and detect them in web services. Scott et al. [14] introduced a Secured Web Applications Project (SWAP) against various application level attacks. It protects against a large class of attacks than existing web methodologies. In addition, Kals et al. [15] proposed SecuBat, another vulnerability scanner to analyze web sites for exploitable SQL and XSS vulnerabilities.

As the most common format of exploit is SQL injections, Wassermann et al. [16] approached an automated and precise solution. It characterizes the values of string variable assuming with a context free grammar and tracks the user modifiable data by modeling string operations. It is implemented in PHP, discovers both known and unknown vulnerabilities as well as scales to large sized programs. Huang et al. [17] created a static analysis algorithm and a tool named WebSSARI, which statistically verifies CMSs' code where run time overhead is reduced to zero with sufficient annotations. After verifying, it automatically secures the potentially vulnerable sections of the code. Jovanovic et al. [18] introduced another static analysis tool (Pixy). For detecting XSS vulnerabilities in PHP, as well as detecting taint-style algorithms like SQL or command injections Pixy uses data-flow analysis and is written in Java. Fu et al. [19] proposed another static analysis tool which automatically generates test cases exploiting SQL injection vulnerabilities in ASP.NET web applications.

Few researches are conducted using Nmap NSE scripts. Rosa et al. [20] developed a number of open-source tools for analysis of PCOM security aspects that includes a Nmap NSE PCOM scan. In [21], Nmap NSE is used for testing authentication servers for malware infection. But no research is conducted for the CMS scan.

There is a number of existing Nmap NSE scripts that serve different purposes during vulnerability assessment [22]. Two of the scripts named *http-wordpress-enum.nse* and *http-drupal-enum.nse* can be used to detect the vulnerabilities of websites that are developed with WordPress and Drupal [22]. These scripts only allow users to detect vulnerabilities of WordPress (*http-wordpress-enum.nse*) and Drupal (*http-drupal-enum.nse*) respectively based on a limited number of extensions listed in *wp-plugins.lst*, *wp-themes.lst*, *drupal-modules.lst* and *drupal-themes.lst* [23]. But these are two different scripts and unable to accommodate new CMS.

In sum, though there are numerous existing methods of detecting vulnerabilities of web based applications, almost all of them are paid. The most required functionalities of vulnerability scanner and port scanner are not integrated together yet. Although some functionalities are integrated, these only cover two specific CMSs. Thus this research work will focus to develop an open-source framework that will achieve these features using port scanning technique in the context of CMSs.

3 Conceptual Framework

The proposed conceptual framework for vulnerability detection is depicted in Fig. 1. The whole design process consists of two stages: Information Gathering Stage and Operational Stage. In the Information Gathering Stage, informational details about a new CMS will be collected. Based on the information achieved, the main framework will be run to detect the vulnerabilities during the Operational Stage.

One of the major concerns is to accurately detect the vulnerable extensions or vulnerable core CMS and to minimize the security risks. Another concern is to adapt a newly developed CMS in the framework. It is needed to enrich the list of information of the CMSs in order to maximize the accuracy. So, the repository is made public so that contributors can enrich the information of existing CMS and append information about a new CMS in the Information Gathering Stage. Each of the contribution will be highly appreciated in the contribution section. The information contains details (i.e CMSs' name and common directory structure for the extensions) list of extensions available to install and list of vulnerable extensions which are publicly available in JSON format. Conventions to contribute in the repository are documented in the development process.

In the Operational Stage, the framework is run against a web server (the target host). The framework constructs a URL using the directory structure which resides in the aforementioned JSON file. It checks for the existence of the directory (HTTP response: 200) and takes decision accordingly. If the directory exists, it goes for further operation. Following the similar process, extensions are extracted from the web server those are already installed in the CMS. Vulnerability checking of this CMS is performed by analyzing the installed extensions with respect to the vulnerable extensions' list.

The scanner returns a list of vulnerable extensions. It can also return the affected versions, provided that the installed extension and vulnerable extension contain version information.

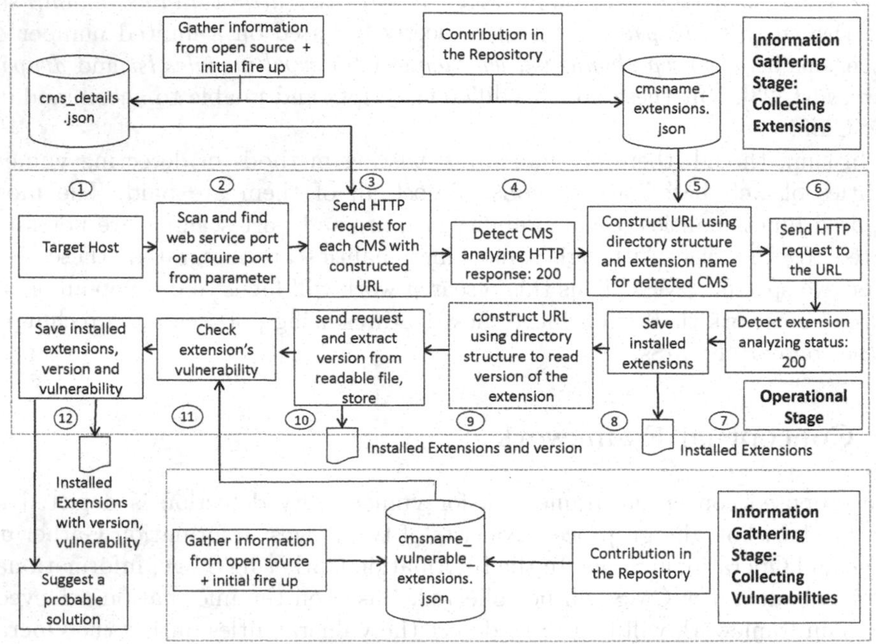

Fig. 1. Working process of the proposed framework

4 Development of the Framework

The framework can accommodate any newly released CMS. This framework works in two phases - *firstly*, it gathers the list of CMSs' details along with the list of all the extensions and vulnerable extensions that is referred to as the *Information Gathering Stage*. *Secondly*, a website is scanned with vulnerability detection framework based on the gathered information in the first stage, using a port scanning technique (*Nmap*) that is referred to as the *Operational Stage*.

Information Gathering Stage. This part of the framework is open to all the contributors. Any contribution to this open source tool will be highly appreciated in the contributors section of GitHub. Initially, the GitHub repository contains information of WordPress and Joomla which can be updated through the proper pull requests and verification. Anytime, new CMSs can be added to the repository by appending the lists of information by following the instructed conventions. There is a *cms_details.json* file which contains the details about the CMS in an array. In order to append a new CMS in the framework, the *cms_details.json* must be updated with the new CMS name, CMS version file directory and array of CMS extension file directory. A new CMS entry can be appended to the array according to the following syntax:

```
[{
  "cms_name": "example",
  "cms_version_file_directory": "/example.txt",
  "cms_extension_directory": [
      "/directory_1",
      "/directory_2"
    ]
}]
```

The cms_version_directory is the directory path of a file that contains version of the installed CMS and the cms_plugin _directory contains the array of the directories those contain the installed extensions.

There are two other files to be created for each CMS. One is the *cmsname_extension.json* that contains all the extensions available for installation in the *cmsname* CMS using the following syntax:

```
[{
  "extension": ["example_1","example_2"],
  "directory": ["dir_1/{ext}/{ext}.txt",
  "dir_2/{ext}/{ext}.txt"]
}]
```

Here, *directory* denotes the file paths those contain version of the extensions. In the Operational Stage *ext* will be replaced with the extension name. Another file to be created for each CMS with the name *cmsname_vulnerable_extensions.json* that contains all the vulnerable extensions along with the list of affected versions for *cmsname* CMS using the following syntax:

```
[{
    "vulnerable_plugin":"vulnerable_plugin_name",
    "affected_version":["4.5","2.1"],
    "description_of_vulnerability":"SQLInjection",
    "code_type":["cve","exploitdb"],
    "code":[{"cve":"xxxxx","exploitdb":"xxxxx"}],
    "source_url":["https://example.com/xxxx/",
    "https://example.com/xxxx"]
    }]
```

The above syntax may be changed and will be updated accordingly in the GitHub documentation in case of any change in the framework.

Operational Stage. In this stage, the framework works like an operational tool using the gathered information from the previous stage. In this paper, the

Operational Stage for the proposed framework is developed with an Nmap script written in *Lua programming language*. Name of the script is *cmscan.nse*. When the *nmap –script cmscan target* command is run in the terminal, the script is called and it starts working. At first, it detects the CMS looking into the *cms_details.json* and thereby recognizing the directory structure. It reads the version file, provided that the file is available in order to check the vulnerability of the core CMS. Then it takes the directory path of installed extensions from the same file. It looks for the *cmsname_extension.json* file to check an extension's existence in the CMS. A URL is constructed from the directory path of extensions and it is appended after the host. Then it checks for the URL's existence using the *http request*. If the extension exists in the CMS, the version is extracted by reading the file, a URL is constructed using the directory given, that looks up on the *cmsname_vulnerable_extensions.json* file to check whether any version of the extension is vulnerable or not. If the version is not found, it is suggested that the user should look for the extension manually.

In this way, the vulnerable plugins are detected along with its CVE, description of the vulnerability and source URL. The process is made faster and efficient using the concept of multi-threading and parallelism. Initially the framework has a base of huge list of information that contains two CMSs: WordPress and Joomla for the initial fire up. However, more CMSs can be accommodated in the framework.

5 Performance Evaluation of the Framework

To evaluate the performance of the framework, a simple experiment is conducted in two phases. Firstly, two web servers are set up with two different CMSs (i.e WordPress and Joomla) to evaluate the performance. Secondly, the framework is run against a number of web servers within a private network, where the servers are mostly operated with CMSs. In the first phase, WordPress and Joomla are installed in two different servers. Some extensions are installed in both of the servers. Some vulnerable extensions are installed in the servers intentionally. The two applications are hosted in the servers with IPs *192.168.0.10* and *192.168.0.12* for Joomla and WordPress respectively. The Nmap scan is performed against these two IP addresses by running the following commands in terminal-

```
nmap --script http-cmscan -p80 192.168.0.10
nmap --script http-cmscan -p80 192.168.0.12
```

Figure 2 shows the scan result for WordPress based web application. The scan result finds 6 plugins, 2 of the plugins are vulnerable. The names of the vulnerable plugins are *loco-translate 2.2.1* and *wp-cerber 8.0*. The scan returns result in 1.25 s. While Fig. 3 shows the installed plugins and plugin details from the WordPress admin panel. Another snapshot of scan result for Joomla based web application is depicted in Fig. 4 and the extensions page of Joomla admin

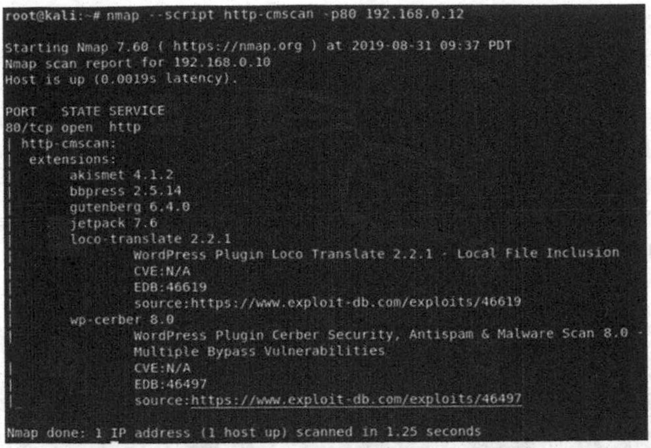

```
root@kali:~# nmap --script http-cmscan -p80 192.168.0.12

Starting Nmap 7.60 ( https://nmap.org ) at 2019-08-31 09:37 PDT
Nmap scan report for 192.168.0.10
Host is up (0.0019s latency).

PORT   STATE SERVICE
80/tcp open  http
| http-cmscan:
|  extensions:
|        akismet 4.1.2
|        bbpress 2.5.14
|        gutenberg 6.4.0
|        jetpack 7.6
|        loco-translate 2.2.1
|                WordPress Plugin Loco Translate 2.2.1 - Local File Inclusion
|                CVE:N/A
|                EDB:46619
|                source:https://www.exploit-db.com/exploits/46619
|        wp-cerber 8.0
|                WordPress Plugin Cerber Security, Antispam & Malware Scan 8.0 -
|                Multiple Bypass Vulnerabilities
|                CVE:N/A
|                EDB:46497
|_               source:https://www.exploit-db.com/exploits/46497

Nmap done: 1 IP address (1 host up) scanned in 1.25 seconds
```

Fig. 2. Passive scan result of the WordPress host

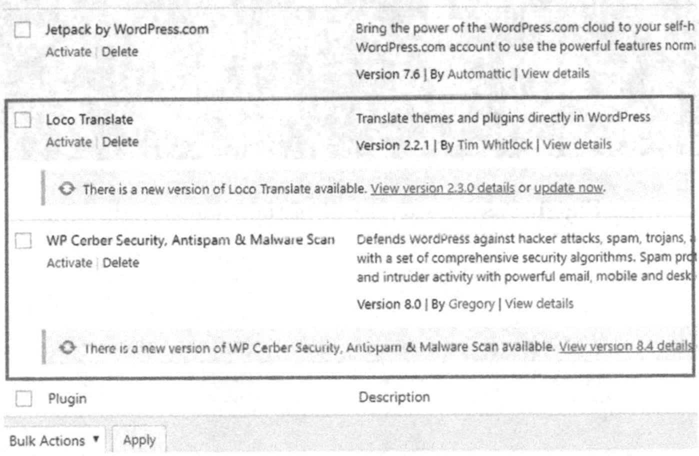

Fig. 3. WordPress extension page from admin panel

panel is depicted in Fig. 5. In this scenario four extensions are found in the server, one of the extensions is found to be vulnerable.

In the next phase, the script is run against a block of IP address (172.16.0.0/24) where a number of CMSs are hosted. Nine hosts are found those run CMSs in web server, most of the servers are run with WordPress. The result summary is given in the Table 1.

As per Table 1, the framework detects nine web servers. Two of the servers are using Joomla CMS and another seven servers are using WordPress CMS. Total number of plugins is shown in the #plugins column and total number of vulnerable plugins is shown in the #vulnerability column. Required time for the scan process is also shown for the different target IPs. The framework gives output based on the extension's information list. If the list is rich and accurate, the output will be accurate, otherwise it can be misled. The output delay depends on the number of extensions installed in the target web application and on the link speed. The result shows that using the stated port scanning technique, the framework can work efficiently and accurately based on the information list. Thus the proposed framework will help the security specialists to figure out the serious vulnerabilities which are potential to cause huge damages.

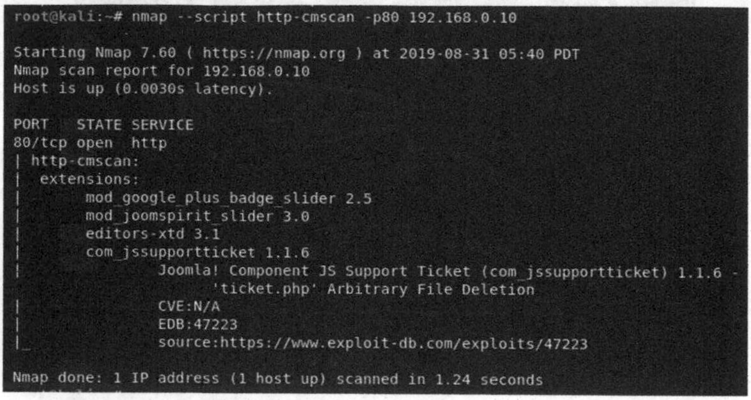

```
root@kali:~# nmap --script http-cmscan -p80 192.168.0.10

Starting Nmap 7.60 ( https://nmap.org ) at 2019-08-31 05:40 PDT
Nmap scan report for 192.168.0.10
Host is up (0.0030s latency).

PORT   STATE SERVICE
80/tcp open  http
| http-cmscan:
|   extensions:
|        mod_google_plus_badge_slider 2.5
|        mod_joomspirit_slider 3.0
|        editors-xtd 3.1
|        com_jssupportticket 1.1.6
|                Joomla! Component JS Support Ticket (com_jssupportticket) 1.1.6 -
|                      'ticket.php' Arbitrary File Deletion
|                CVE:N/A
|                EDB:47223
|_               source:https://www.exploit-db.com/exploits/47223

Nmap done: 1 IP address (1 host up) scanned in 1.24 seconds
```

Fig. 4. Passive scan result of the Joomla host

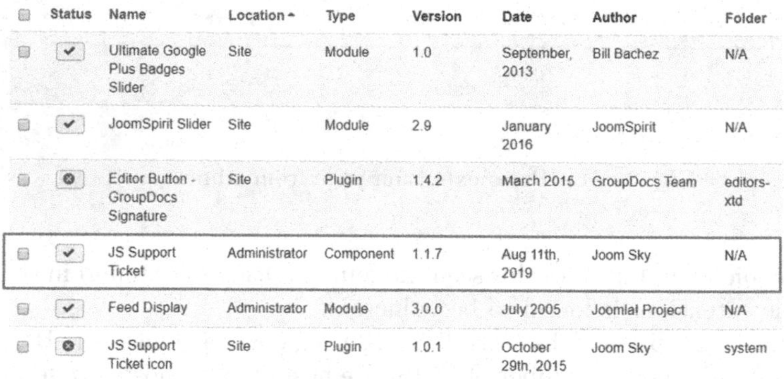

	Status	Name	Location ▴	Type	Version	Date	Author	Folder
☐	✔	Ultimate Google Plus Badges Slider	Site	Module	1.0	September, 2013	Bill Bachez	N/A
☐	✔	JoomSpirit Slider	Site	Module	2.9	January 2016	JoomSpirit	N/A
☐	✖	Editor Button - GroupDocs Signature	Site	Plugin	1.4.2	March 2015	GroupDocs Team	editors-xtd
☐	✔	JS Support Ticket	Administrator	Component	1.1.7	Aug 11th, 2019	Joom Sky	N/A
☐	✔	Feed Display	Administrator	Module	3.0.0	July 2005	Joomla! Project	N/A
☐	✖	JS Support Ticket icon	Site	Plugin	1.0.1	October 29th, 2015	Joom Sky	system

Fig. 5. Joomla extension page from admin panel

Table 1. Sample time and vulnerability of target websites.

Target	CMS	Time(Sec)	#plugins	#vulnerability
172.16.0.12	Wordpress	24.08	5	1
172.16.0.13	Wordpress	27.11	10	2
172.16.0.32	Joomla	257.14	98	14
172.16.0.33	Joomla	165.75	61	11
172.16.0.34	Wordpress	100.45	47	5
172.16.0.42	Wordpress	25.79	6	0
172.16.0.78	Wordpress	59.98	21	1
172.16.0.74	Wordpress	41.841	13	0
172.16.0.61	Wordpress	28.44	8	1

6 Discussion and Conclusions

In this paper, a framework is proposed that integrates the most important components of a vulnerability scanner with a port scanner in the context of CMS. Knowledge base of this framework is CMSs' information which is mostly dependent on the contributors. But the information will be updated from servers as well, which minimizes the framework's dependency on the contributors. As a result the framework will help in vulnerability assessment by detecting the vulnerabilities of a CMS efficiently.

The main implication of the framework is that it requires less effort to operate. Also, it is not needed to go through the hassle of paid and full-fledged vulnerability scanners. The network administrator can also use this to know about the possible vulnerabilities.

There are a number of existing tools to serve the purpose of vulnerability assessment. Most of the tools are heavy and paid. There is a shortage of open source tools that can help to assess the vulnerabilities. Most of the open source tools are not dedicated for the CMSs and so fails to detect the vulnerabilities of most of the CMSs. These tools are good for only specific CMSs. Although Nmap is a popular multipurpose tool for vulnerability assessment, there is no script or framework of Nmap to assess the vulnerabilities of CMSs [22]. In this paper, an open source framework is proposed that can be used for the vulnerability assessment of all the CMSs using Nmap. The framework serves the purpose of vulnerability assessment for a broader range of websites developed with CMSs.

The framework is currently being operated using port scanning technique and is dependent on Nmap. Also the knowledge base of this framework is mostly dependent on the contributors. The run time of the framework varies with the configuration of machine and network connectivity with the target host. The machine needs internet connection to perform the scan.

In future, the main initiative is to make the framework independent and as well as to incorporate in the other popular security tools. Also the aim is to minimize the dependency on the contributors by deploying servers for the purpose of gathering and updating the information about CMS. The scan can also be performed without internet connection; in that case the information lists are to be downloaded to the local machine in the same directory of the script. This process does not ensure the updated repository to be resided in the user's machine. Although a number of network scanning tools exist in the open source, but few of those are developed for CMSs scan. Also the tools are developed for a specific CMS. Some tools have support to scan all kind of CMSs, but the users are to pay a heavy cost for the tools. Performance evaluation can be carried out by comparing the output for a specific CMS with the existing open source tools and also with the paid tools. In future, a detailed performance evaluation and comparison will be conducted with the existing frameworks.

In this new course of technological evolution where everyone uses devices which is more or less connected to common or private networks. Access, misuse and hacking of files and directories are happening more than ever. The framework can help to find these vulnerabilities and detect the ways through which network interrogation is possible to inform the users or the administrator, thus protecting from further attacks by making a more integrated and rigid network.

References

1. Security auditor's research assistant. http://www-arc.com/sara/. Accessed 29 Nov 2019
2. Saint cybersecurity solution. http://www.saintcorporation.com/. Accessed 29 Nov 2017
3. VLAD the scanner. http://www.decuslib.com/decus/vmslt00b/net/vlad_readme.html. Accessed 29 Nov 2017
4. Nessus vulnerability scanner. https://www.tenable.com/products/nessus-vulnerability-scanner. Accessed 29 Nov 2017
5. Lyon, G.F.: NMAP network scanning: the official NMAP project guide to network discovery and security scanning. Insecure (2009)
6. NSE-NMAP scripting engine. https://nmap.org/book/nse.html. Accessed 29 Nov 2017
7. Market share: top website platforms and example sites. https://websitesetup.org/popular-cms/. Accessed 29 Nov 2017
8. Kaluža, M., Vukelić, B., Rojko, T.: Content management system security. Zbornik Veleučilišta u Rijeci **4**(1), 29–44 (2016)
9. Cernica, I.C., Popescu, N., Tiganoaia, B.: Security evaluation of WordPress backup plugins, pp. 312–316, May 2019. https://doi.org/10.1109/CSCS.2019.00056
10. Martinez-Caro, J.M., Aledo-Hernández, A.J., Guillen-Perez, A., Sanchez-Iborra, R., Cano, M.D.: A comparative study of web content management systems. Information **9**, 27 (2018). https://doi.org/10.3390/info9020027
11. Website hacked trend report 2018. https://sucuri.net/reports/19-sucuri-2018-hacked-report.pdf. Accessed 24 Jan 2020
12. Meike, M., Sametinger, J., Wiesauer, A.: Security in open source web content management systems. IEEE Secur. Privacy **7**(4), 44–51 (2009)

13. Yu, W.D., Aravind, D., Supthaweesuk, P.: Software vulnerability analysis for web services software systems. In: 2006 Proceedings of the 11th IEEE Symposium on Computers and Communications (ISCC 2006), pp. 740–748. IEEE (2006)
14. Scott, D., Sharp, R.: Developing secure web applications. IEEE Internet Comput. **6**(6), 38–45 (2002)
15. Kals, S., Kirda, E., Kruegel, C., Jovanovic, N.: SecuBat: a web vulnerability scanner. In: Proceedings of the 15th International Conference on World Wide Web, pp. 247–256. ACM (2006)
16. Wassermann, G., Su, Z.: Sound and precise analysis of web applications for injection vulnerabilities. In: ACM SIGPLAN Notices, vol. 42, pp. 32–41. ACM (2007)
17. Huang, Y.W., Yu, F., Hang, C., Tsai, C.H., Lee, D.T., Kuo, S.Y.: Securing web application code by static analysis and runtime protection. In: Proceedings of the 13th International Conference on World Wide Web, pp. 40–52. ACM (2004)
18. Jovanovic, N., Kruegel, C., Kirda, E.: Pixy: a static analysis tool for detecting web application vulnerabilities. In: 2006 IEEE Symposium on Security and Privacy, pp. 6-pp. IEEE (2006)
19. Fu, X., Lu, X., Peltsverger, B., Chen, S., Qian, K., Tao, L.: A static analysis framework for detecting SQL injection vulnerabilities. In: 31st Annual International Computer Software and Applications Conference (COMPSAC 2007), vol. 1, pp. 87–96. IEEE (2007)
20. Rosa, L., de Freitas, M.B., Mazo, S., Monteiro, E., Cruz, T., Simoes, P.: A comprehensive security analysis of a scada protocol: from OSINT to mitigation. IEEE Access **7**, 42156–42168 (2019). https://doi.org/10.1109/ACCESS.2019.2906926
21. Basam, D., Ransbottom, J., Marchany, R., Tront, J.: Strengthening MT6D defenses with LXC-based honeypot capabilities. J. Electr. Comput. Eng. **2016**, 1–13 (2016). https://doi.org/10.1155/2016/5212314
22. Rahalkar, S.: Introduction to NMAP. In: Rahalkar, S. (ed.) Quick Start Guide to Penetration Testing, pp. 20–39. Springer, Berkeley (2019). https://doi.org/10.1007/978-1-4842-4270-4_1
23. List of data in NSE libraries. https://svn.nmap.org/nmap/nselib/data/. Accessed 04 Sept 2019

A Risk Based Analysis on Linux Hosted E-Commerce Sites in Bangladesh

Rejaul Islam Royel[1], Md. Hasan Sharif[1], Rafika Risha[1], Touhid Bhuiyan[1], Md. Maruf Hassan[1(✉)], and Md. Sharif Hassan[2]

[1] Daffodil International University, Dhaka, Bangladesh
maruf.swe@diu.edu.bd
[2] University of Asia Pacific, Dhaka, Bangladesh
hassan@uap-bd.edu

Abstract. E-commerce plays a significant role to grow its business globally by satisfying the modern consumer's expectations. Without the help of Operating System (OS), e-commerce applications cannot be operated as well as broadcasted on the web. It is evident after analyzing this study that web administrators of the business are sometimes being careless, in some cases unaware about the risk of cyber-attack due the lack of vulnerability research on their OS. Therefore, a good number of the e-commerce applications are faced different type of OS exploitations through different types of attack e.g. denial of service, bypass, DECOVF, etc. that breaches the OS's confidentiality, integrity and availability. In this paper, we analyzed 140 e-commerce sites servers' information and its related 1138 vulnerabilities information to examine the risks and risky versions of the OS in e-commerce business. The probabilities of vulnerability are calculated using Orange 3 and feature selection operation has been performed using Weka through IBM statistical tool SPSS. This study identifies few versions of Ubuntu that are found in critical status in terms of risk position.

Keywords: Cyber Security · Operating system · OS vulnerability · E-commerce website · Risk analysis

1 Introduction

To keep pace with the world modernized technology, the number of users of web applications is vastly growing up. Within last few years, the popularity of electronic commerce (e-commerce), Facebook commerce (f-commerce) and other online services are increasing rapidly in Bangladesh due to having its cost efficiency and time saving services. As a computational marketplace, most of the company has given an advantage of online transaction to its consumers, especially in acquiring goods or services [1]. However, due to having open internet and operating system, security issues are being emerged which has become the barrier of e-commerce development [2–4].

T. Bhuiyan et al. (Eds.): ICONCS 2020, LNICST 325, pp. 140–151, 2020.
https://doi.org/10.1007/978-3-030-52856-0_11

According to the study of Ngai and Wat [5], among 42% of the research article topics were found on technology issues where e-commerce security was the main highlighted area. Besides, OS vulnerabilities were pointed out a major crucial hindering region on the development of e-commerce [5]. The weakness in OS generally encourages intruders doing the illegal activity on the system. In recent years, most of the computer security related studies focused on e-commerce attacks such as Denial of Service (DoS), DoS Overflow (DOVF), Broken links (BL), Bypass, Directory Traversal (DT), Overflow (OVF), Dos Execute Code Overflow (DECOVF), Execute Code (EC), Execute Code Overflow (ECOVF), Cross-Site Scripting (XSS) and Unencrypted Password (UP) etc. [6,7]. A security threat assessment focuses on perceived flaws such as the unencrypted Wi-Fi link or the user control of the GNU/Linux operating system running on the drone [8]. A research analyzes the security problems of modern computer systems caused by vulnerabilities in OSs and examines the vulnerabilities found across a variety of OSs that lead to understand how different intrusion-tolerant architectures deploy the availability, integrity and confidentiality effect of OS diversity [9].

In a study, the different features of legitimate, suspicious and phishing websites were identified using the built-in machine learning algorithms from WEKA to compare and verify the accuracy of the algorithm [10]. A platform analysis presents the potential computer intrusion and violation of privacy which occurs due to anonymous web browsing, technologies and programs [11]. However, some studies focused not only vulnerabilities, but also policies [12]. Those studies enforce that good policy making could be a perfect solution for e-commerce security as well as suggest using self-regulation policy to provide consumer's information security [13,14]. Song and Jihong's study focusing on not only business policy and software policy, but also focusing on system security policy to avoid illegal access to computer resources, because all kinds of user's operations are controlled by the operating system [15].

There is a way to mitigate the risk by applying administrator patch. If an administrator patch is applied on all the systems at risk to correct the flow or if attackers and the media lose the interest in the vulnerability, the vulnerability could die. Yet in practice, the administrator can never patch all the systems risk, only they can remove such systems at some points to make losing the interest of attacker's and media's in the vulnerability [16]. About 25% of all UNIX and Linux vulnerabilities are contingent on enablers, and 98% of those enablers are under the security engineer's control and single vulnerability information is only published when the patch fixes [17,18]. As an instant of having a third party operating system, it takes long time to fix a single vulnerability [19]. Accordingly, the best strategy is to address the security and risk of internet based content, building the security in platform rather than attempt to introduce security patches [20].

A study presented a hybrid framework of analytic hierarchy process and Intuitionistic Fuzzy Technique in order of preference solution for the assessment and evaluation of e-commerce web site (EWS) performances [21,22]. The decision-making testing and evaluation laboratory (DEMATEL) method is introduced to develop a causal relationship between e-commerce factors. This decision-making approach develops two groups of factors known as causes and effect groups to enhance the significance of e-commerce [23]. An investigation is presented on android kernel by modeling a function-call network whereof nodes and edges are respectively functions and relations between the extractions of kernel source code [24]. For four different operating systems - windows (Microsoft), Mac (apple), IOS (Cisco) and Linux as well as four web browsers - internet explorer (Microsoft), safari (apple), Firefox (mozilla), and chrome (google), an approach is presented to compare a power-law model without clustering issued for a family of SRMs that gives more accurate curve fittings and predictions in all analyzed cases [25].

Any system is not effective and efficient to use once it's OS has weakness in it; however, people are often found in using those vulnerable OS without considering their major losses of the intellectual and confidential asset due to lack of information security awareness [26]. A research discussed the issues of liability in electronic transactions when security or privacy breaches arise by concentrating on appropriate social welfare obligations for both sides – the consumer and the business (or service provider) [27]. Infringements of privacy and security occur as information is transmitted using various devices such as PCs, mobile phones, tablets, sensors and various technologies such as internet, IoT and well-defined network architectures for e-commerce. There have been many incidents of security breaches, such as the safety and payment process of Target Organization (2013), eBay's cyberattack (2014), Uber's hacking incident (2016), Facebook's personal data use and breach of privacy (2018), and many others due to have vulnerable system [28]. As Linux is an open source platform, users generally thinks that it is secure; however, after studying, it is found that Linux has vulnerability issues [29]. Therefore, this paper decided to examine the risks associated with e-commerce business that are hosted on the operating system of Linux.

Previous research apparently showed different types of work on risk analysis which occurs separately on the Linux operating system and e-commerce. The data breaches, procedures and remedies were also discussed; however, there are lacking in risk analysis of e-commerce those are hosted in Linux operating system. This research will focus on Bangladeshi e-commerce server site vulnerabilities which are hosted in Linux operating system to analyze the risks. It will also focus on figuring out the most vulnerable operating system which is alarming for e-commerce business.

2 Methodology

This section presents the step by step working process on risk analysis of e-commerce websites those are hosted in Linux operating system with the possible mechanisms and finding out which Linux operating system can be more vulnerable.

2.1 Data Collection

This study used 140 Bangladeshi e-commerce server site's (Ubuntu-based server) information. To detect the most vulnerable server for e-commerce businesses, this work collected total 1138 vulnerable data between the years of 1999 to 2018 [30]. This data collection process is done with five steps which presented in Fig. 1.

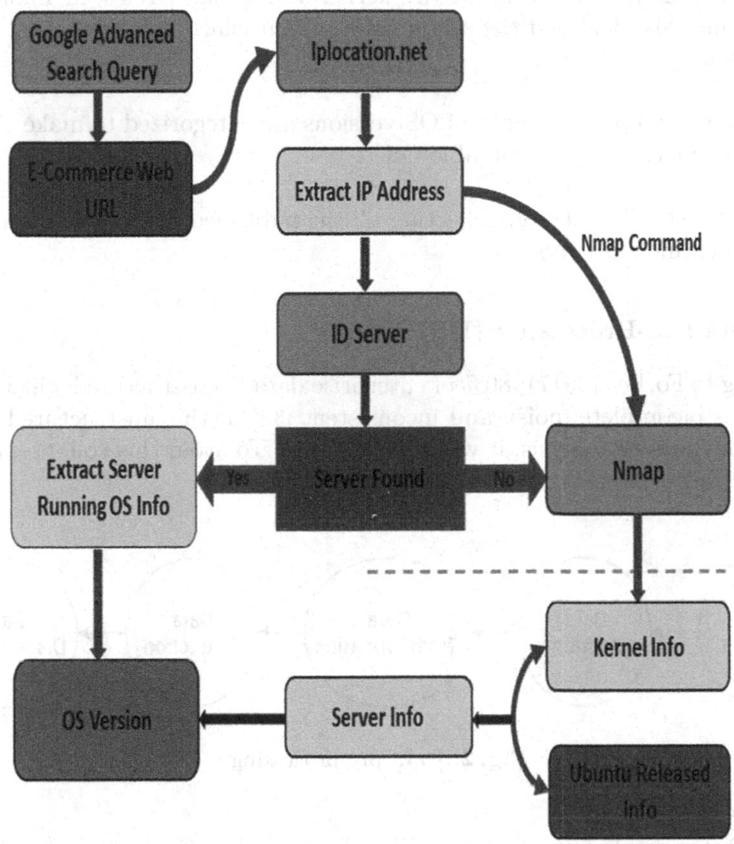

Fig. 1. Working flowchart of data collection

Step 1. Collect E-Commerce Web URL. Firstly, some popular e-commerce sites are collected using Google Search Query such as inurl, intitle, domain and the rest of the sites are picked from e-cab.net that enusers the growth of e-commerce sector in Bangladesh [31].

Step 2. Extract IP and Server Information. The filtered e-commerce application URLs are given for extracting the IP address to iplocation.net that provides IP geolocation and IP resources [32]. The extracted IP address is sent to the ID server tool to find out the running server information. If the ID server tool is able to discover the running server for the provided IP address, it will be sent to step 4 to extract the server running OS information.

Step 3. Extract Kernel Information. If the ID server tool is not able to find out the server information, the IP address is sent to the Nmap tool. To obtain the kernel and Ubuntu released information, a command "Nmap -O IP address" run on the Nmap console. From the kernel and Ubuntu released information list, this analysis identified the server information which helps to reveal the OS information.

Step 4. In this step, the identified OS versions are categorized to make a proper analysis about the more vulnerable OS.

Step 5. This step focused on collecting all the published vulnerable information from all identified OS versions.

2.2 Data Pre-Processing (DPP)

According to Forbes (2017), 80% of enterprise data is unstructured which means the data is incomplete, noisy and inconsistent [33]. If this unstructured data is used in any kind of analysis, it will be a collapse. To avoid this collapse, there is a process called Data Pre-Processing (DPP) (Fig. 2).

Fig. 2. Data pre-processing

DPP is the combination of five tasks called cleaning, integration, transformation, reduction and discretization. To obtain a proper outcome, completeness of these five tasks is mandatory. Firstly, in cleaning stage, all the inconsistent data are gotten corrected, incomplete data are gotten completed using server history, and noisy data are managed using binary method, clustering, and regression function. The integration and transformation of data are maintained strongly to manage the relationship between the e-commerce and vulnerability information. Normalization is applied to make the data smooth. Finally, the reduction and discretization is performed to analyze the future outcome.

2.3 Feature Selection

The feature selection operation is performed through correlation based feature selection and chi-square feature selection process.

Correlation-Based Feature Selection. Through a heuristic search strategy of Ranker search method, a correlation based feature selection process measures the correlation between the subset of features which are highly correlated with the class [34]. Thus, it is clear that if the ID rank's value is high, then subsets are highly correlated with each other otherwise there is no relation among them. The criteria used for accessing a subset of features can be expressed out as follows:

$$M_s = l\overline{t_c f} / \sqrt{l + l(l-1)\overline{t_f f}} \tag{1}$$

Where:

M = evaluation of a subset of S consisting of l features;
$\overline{t_c f}$ = average correlation value between features and class labels;
$\overline{t_f f}$ = average correlation value between two features.

Chi-square Feature Selection (CFS). Chi-square feature selection method uses a statistic to find out highly correlated features between the subset of features and the classes while bearing low inter correlation based on X^2 [35].

$$Chi - square(t_k, c_i,) = (N(AD - CB)^2)/((A|C)(B|D)(A|B)(C|D)) \tag{2}$$

Equation (2) demonstrate Chi-square statistics, where:

N = Total number of records in dataset;
A = Number of records in class ci that contain the term t_k;
B = Number of records in other classes that contain the term t_k ;
C = Number of records in class ci that do not contain the term t_k;
D = Number of records in other classes that do not contain the term t_k.

Each feature in each class is assigned one score.

3 Result

In the result section, the data of 1138 vulnerabilities from 140 e-commerce sites (server related information) in Bangladesh are analyzed. This study focused on discovering which vulnerabilities are highly arising in OS and which OS is in a most risky stage of e-commerce. To perform this, the feature selection methods are used [using weka version 3.7] to find out the best features of vulnerabilities. Then the highest probability values are calculated among the features observation [using orange3 version 3.14.0]. After that, a risk matrix is established to determine the level of risk for each vulnerability. Lastly, a relational table of OS vs. vulnerability has been implemented by IBM Statistical Package for Social Sciences (SPSS version 21) to get the most risky OS for e-commerce. In this investigation, the total analysis process has been performed on four separate tables with a risk matrix. The analysis is discussed below.

Table 1 represents the feature selection process. Two filtering methods are applied to find out the best relevant features for vulnerabilities where Ranker

Table 1. Feature selection using ranker and greedy stepwise method

No	Correlation attribute evaluator	CFS subset evaluator
01	Integrity	Confidentiality
02	Confidentiality	Integrity
03	Availability	Availability
04	Gained Access Level	—
05	Complexity	—
06	Access	—
07	Authentication	—

method is applied with correlation attribute evaluator and Greed Step Wise method is applied with Chi-square feature selection (CFS) subset evaluator. Integrity, confidentiality, availability, gained access level, complexity, access and authentication features are shown in the table; among them confidentiality, integrity, and availability are found as most common features.

Table 2. Vulnerabilities Probability among Confidentiality, Integrity and Availability

Vulnerability	Confidentiality	Integrity	Availability
DOS	None (0.617 ± 0.043)	None (0.662 ± 0.043)	Partial (0.397 ± 0.034)
Bypass	Partial (0.127 ± 0.030)	Partial (0.184 ± 0.034)	None (0.539 ± 0.097)
DT	Partial (0.033 ± 0.016)	Partial (0.040 ± 0.017)	None (0.157 ± 0.071)
DEC	Complete (0.123 ± 0.047)	Complete (0.124 ± 0.048)	Complete (0.094 ± 0.037)
DECOVF	Partial (0.183 ± 0.035)	Partial (0.170 ± 0.033)	Partial (0.106 ± 0.021)
DOVF	Partial (0.186 ± 0.036)	None (0.240 ± 0.039)	Partial (0.228 ± 0.029)
EC	Complete (0.214 ± 0.059)	Complete (0.216 ± 0.059)	Complete (0.163 ± 0.046)
ECOVF	Complete (0.150 ± 0.051)	Complete (0.151 ± 0.059)	Complete (0.122 ± 0.041)
OVF	Partial (0.092 ± 0.026)	Partial (0.067 ± 0.022)	None (0.147 ± 0.069)
XSS	None (0.022 ± 0.012)	Partial (0.020 ± 0.012)	None (0.098 ± 0.058)

Table 2 presents the maximum probability of vulnerability concerning the three different groups Confidentiality, Integrity, and Availability. Each group has three subgroups; those are None, Partial and Complete. Here DoS vulnerability gets maximum "None" probability with error (0.617 ± 0.043) in confidentiality, it means DoS cannot destroy servers confidentiality; however DoS gets maximum "partially" probability with error (0.397 ± 0.034) on availability, it means that DoS can partially damage server's information on demand. DEC gets maximum "Complete" probability with the error of (0.123 ± 0.047), (0.124 ± 0.048) and (0.094 ± 0.037) in confidentiality, integrity and availability respectively which declared DEC can destroy the servers confidentiality, integrity and availability completely. Further, EC gets maximum "Complete" probability with the error of (0.214 ± 0.059), (0.216 ± 0.059) and (0.163 ± 0.046) and ECOVF get maximum "Complete" probability with the error of (0.150 ± 0.051), (0.151 ± 0.059)

Table 3. Vulnerabilities risk calculation table

Vulnerability	Risk score				Average	Decision
	Confidentiality	Integrity	Availability	Total score		
DoS	0	0	4	4	1.3	Low risk
Bypass	2	2	0	4	1.3	Low risk
DT	2	2	0	4	1.3	Low risk
DEC	3	3	3	9	3	Medium risk
DECOVF	2	2	2	6	2	Low risk
DOVF	2	0	2	4	1.3	Low risk
EC	3	3	3	9	3	Medium risk
ECOVF	3	3	3	9	3	Medium risk
OVF	2	2	0	4	1.3	Low Risk
XSS	0	2	0	2	0.667	Pretty low risk

and (0.122 ± 0.041) respectively in confidentiality, integrity and availability; this shows EC and ECOVF can also ruin the servers confidentiality, integrity and availability completely.

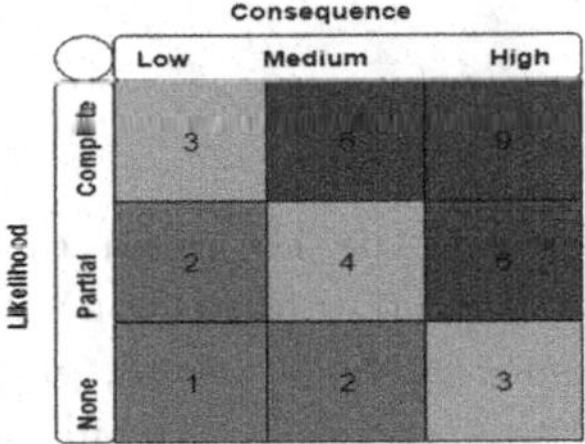

Fig. 3. Risk matrix

Figure 3 presents a three cross three matrix that is used to analyze the risk of each vulnerability type. This matrix shows the likelihood of subgroups as "None", "Partial", and "Complete"; where "None" denotes "no drawbacks" with the consequence of Low, "Partial" designates "average drawbacks" with the consequence of Medium, and "Complete" stand for "maximum drawbacks" with the consequence of the High. In this matrix, the range of 1 to 2 is Low, 3 to 4 is Medium, and 6 to 9 is denoted as High.

Table 3 serves the damage level of all vulnerabilities by calculating the value of every vulnerability risk. The risk level is determined as low, medium, and high based on the probabilities of vulnerabilities from Table 2. Table 3 shows that DEC, EC, and ECOVF are in the medium level risk. Contrarily DoS, Bypass, DT, DECOVF, DVOF, and OVF are found in low level risk and XSS is found in pretty low level risk. In this analysis, no vulnerability is found in high level risk.

Table 4 provide the vulnerabilities which are available on different versions of Ubuntu OS. DoS, DOVF, EC, DEC, and DECOVF are widely available on

Table 4. Vulnerability versus operating system cross tabulation

		Vulnerability										Total
		DoS	OVF	Bypass	DOVF	DT	EC	DEC	ECOVF	DECOVF	XSS	
OS Version	Ubuntu 6.06 LTS	19	5	5	0	1	9	3	13	5	1	61
	Ubuntu 8.04.1 LTS	16	4	5	1	2	7	9	13	5	0	62
	Ubuntu 9.10	1	0	2	0	1	0	3	0	0	0	7
	Ubuntu 10.04 LTS	5	3	10	4	3	3	2	4	3	0	37
	Ubuntu 10.10	0	0	3	0	4	2	3	0	0	0	12
	Ubuntu 11.10	3	0	7	4	2	6	1	0	1	0	24
	Ubuntu 12.04 LTS	17	3	15	5	1	4	5	4	8	0	62
	Ubuntu 13.04	23	6	15	8	0	5	2	0	6	0	65
	Ubuntu 14.04 LTS	188	21	34	110	12	30	22	21	44	5	487
	Ubuntu 15.04 LTS	37	5	10	34	0	8	2	6	14	1	117
	Ubuntu 16.04 LTS	87	10	16	41	5	13	5	5	19	3	204
Total		396	57	122	207	31	87	57	66	105	10	1138

Ubuntu 14.04 LTS, Ubuntu 15.04 LTS, and Ubuntu 16.04 LTS. After that, DoS and Bypass are present in Ubuntu 12.04 LTS widely. DoS and ECOVF are also present with good amount in Ubuntu 6.06 LTS and Ubuntu 8.04.1 LTS.

4 Discussion

The study has been conducted over the data of 1138 vulnerabilities from 140 e-commerce sites (server related information) in Bangladesh. This analysis observed some critical issues such as access, gain access level, complexity, authentication, confidentiality, integrity, and availability that are experiencing when vulnerability is available on the OSs. In Table 1, this analysis uses the feature selection technique through ranker [13] and greedy stepwise method [14] to evaluate which issues are more prone to be the most dangerous for OS security. Through the feature selection technique, it is found that confidentiality, integrity, and availability are highly associated with the vulnerabilities among the seven features.

From Table 2, this study has evaluated the vulnerability's probability of occurrence to assess the level of occurrence in confidentiality, integrity, and availability. DEC, EC, and ECOVF are classified the probability of occurrence as "Complete" which can destroy a system's confidentiality, integrity, and availability completely. DECOVF is determined the probability of occurrence as "Partial" which indicates that it can ruin system's confidentiality, integrity, and availability partially. In Table 3, risk level of every vulnerability is generated where DEC, EC, and ECOVF are classified as medium risky vulnerability. DoS, Bypass, DT, DECOVF, DOVF, and OVF are identified as low risk vulnerability whereas XSS is determined as pretty low risky vulnerability. Thus, it can be said that any OS is hazardous once the above vulnerabilities exist in such OS. From Table 4, it is clear that a large amount of DoS, DOVF, DECOVF, and Bypass vulnerabilities are available on Ubuntu 14.04 LTS, Ubuntu 15.04 LTS and Ubuntu 16.04 LTS among eleven Ubuntu OS version. Besides, DoS and Bypass are present on

Ubuntu 12.04 LTS broadly. DoS and ECOVF are accessible with a good amount in Ubuntu 6.06 LTS and Ubuntu 8.04.1 LTS.

It is evident from the analysis that Ubuntu 14.04 LTS is the most risky OS where Ubuntu 16.04 LTS and Ubuntu 15.04 are also critical OS to host e-commerce web applications. Besides, this study found 808 vulnerabilities among 1138 are existed on the given three versions of Ubuntu OSs in our sample 140 e-commerce sites.

5 Conclusion

Since e-commerce sites are associated with a large number of consumers and different stakeholders of businesses, it encourages the threat agent to send attack(s) for receiving maximum benefits. Intruders initially figure out the vulnerabilities of such applications and exploit it with all possible malicious payloads. This study will provide a valuable information for web owner to select right OS for hosting their applications for being safe from known attacks as this study identifies the risk factors, vulnerabilities, and list of probable attacks of individual Linux versions. This study found that Ubuntu 14.04 LTS is the top risky OS in our investigation where Ubuntu 16.04 LTS and Ubuntu 15.04 LTS are also revealed as second and third risky OS respectively. Unfortunately, it is alarming that these three OSs has been used in 71.002% of our sample data. This review also suggests that e-commerce owners should avoid those risky OSs and use security patches to overcome the known flaws of the given three OSs that are using in e-commerce host in Bangladesh. This study only focused on the risk analysis for Linux based e-commerce host in Bangladesh. In future, other OSs and different domains will be considered for further analysis.

Acknowledgment. The author of this paper would like to acknowledge Cyber Security Center, DIU for the support to execute the study. Also appreciate the authorities of the organizations who have given us the permission to conduct the examination on their websites.

References

1. Rosaci, D., Sarnè, G.: Multi-agent technology and ontologies to support personalization in B2C e-commerce. Electron. Commer. Res. Appl. **13**, 13–23 (2014)
2. Gerber, M., Solms, R.V.: From risk analysis to security requirements. Comput. Secur. **20**, 577–584 (2001)
3. Wang, W., Lu, N.: Security risk analysis and security technology research of government public data center. In: 2018 IEEE International Conference on Energy Internet (ICEI) (2018)
4. Xiao, G., Zheng, Z., Yin, B., Trivedi, K.S., Du, X., Cai, K.: Experience report: fault triggers in Linux operating system: from evolution perspective. In: 2017 IEEE 28th International Symposium on Software Reliability Engineering (ISSRE) (2017)
5. Ngai, E., Wat, F.: A literature review and classification of electronic commerce research. Inf. Manag. **39**, 415–429 (2002)

6. Ahmed, G., Khan, M.N.A., Bashir, M.S.: A Linux-based IDPS using Snort. Comput. Fraud Secur. **2015**, 13–18 (2015)
7. Mouli, V.R., Jevitha, K.: Web services attacks and security - a systematic literature review. Procedia Comput. Sci. **93**, 870–877 (2016)
8. Kang, J., Joe, I.: Security vulnerability analysis of Wi-Fi connection hijacking on the Linux-based robot operating system for drone systems. In: Park, J.H., Shen, H., Sung, Y., Tian, H. (eds.) PDCAT 2018. CCIS, vol. 931, pp. 473–482. Springer, Singapore (2019). https://doi.org/10.1007/978-981-13-5907-1_49
9. Gorbenko, A., Romanovsky, A., Tarasyuk, O., Biloborodov, O.: From analyzing operating system vulnerabilities to designing multiversion intrusion-tolerant architectures. IEEE Trans. Reliab. **69**, 22–39 (2020)
10. Latif, R.M.A., Umer, M., Tariq, T., Farhan, M., Rizwan, O., Ali, G.: A smart methodology for analyzing secure e-banking and e-commerce websites. In: 2019 16th International Bhurban Conference on Applied Sciences and Technology (IBCAST) (2019)
11. Coelho, N.M., Peixoto, M., Cruz-Cunha, M.M.: Prototype of a paranoid mobile operating system distribution. In: 2019 7th International Symposium on Digital Forensics and Security (ISDFS) (2019)
12. Awoleye, O.M., Ojuloge, B., Ilori, M.O.: Web application vulnerability assessment and policy direction towards a secure smart government. Gov. Inf. Q. **31**, S118–S125 (2014)
13. Barkatullah, A.H., Djumadi, : Does self-regulation provide legal protection and security to e-commerce consumers? Electron. Commer. Res. Appl. **30**, 94–101 (2018)
14. Song, B., Yan, W., Zhang, T.: Cross-border e-commerce commodity risk assessment using text mining and fuzzy rule-based reasoning. Adv. Eng. Inform. **40**, 69–80 (2019)
15. Song, J., Hu, G., Xu, Q.: Operating system security and host vulnerability evaluation. In: 2009 International Conference on Management and Service Science (2009)
16. Mchugh, J., Fithen, W., Arbaugh, W.: Windows of vulnerability: a case study analysis. Computer **33**, 52–59 (2000)
17. Ghosh, A.K., Swaminatha, T.M.: Software security and privacy risks in mobile e-commerce. Commun. ACM **44**, 51–57 (2001)
18. Pradhan, P.L.: A literature survey on risk assessment for Unix operating system. Int. J. Adv. Pervasive Ubiquit. Comput. **11**, 13–32 (2019)
19. Huang, A.: A risk detection system of e-commerce: researches based on soft information extracted by affective computing web texts. Electron. Commer. Res. **18**(1), 143–157 (2017). https://doi.org/10.1007/s10660-017-9262-y
20. Lee, S., Davis, L.: Learning from experience: operating system vulnerability trends. IT Prof. **5**, 17–24 (2003)
21. Zhang, Y., Deng, X., Wei, D., Deng, Y.: Assessment of e-commerce security using AHP and evidential reasoning. Expert Syst. Appl. **39**, 3611–3623 (2012)
22. Rouyendegh, B.D., Topuz, K., Dag, A., Oztekin, A.: An AHP-IFT integrated model for performance evaluation of e-commerce web sites. Inf. Syst. Front. **21**(6), 1345–1355 (2018). https://doi.org/10.1007/s10796-018-9825-z
23. Abdullah, L., Ramli, R., Bakodah, H., Othman, M.: Developing a causal relationship among factors of e-commerce: a decision making approach. J. King Saud Univ. - Comput. Inf. Sci. (2019)
24. Sun, P., Yang, S., Lai, Z., Li, D., Yao, A.: Function-call network reliability of kernel in android operating system. In: 2019 IEEE International Symposium on Circuits and Systems (ISCAS) (2019)

25. Tambunan, B., Sihombing, H., Doloksaribu, A., Muda, I.: The effect of security transactions, easy of use, and the risk perception of interest online buying on the e-commerce Tokopedia site (Study on Tokopedia.id site users in Medan city). In: IOP Conference Series: Materials Science and Engineering, vol. 420, p. 012118 (2018)
26. Wang, Y., Herrando, C.: Does privacy assurance on social commerce sites matter to millennials? Int. J. Inf. Manag. **44**, 164–177 (2019)
27. Chun, S.-H.: E-commerce liability and security breaches in mobile payment for e-business sustainability. Sustainability **11**, 715 (2019)
28. The 18 Biggest Data Breaches of the 21st Century. https://www.csoonline.com/article/2130877/the-biggest-data-breaches-of-the-21st-century.html
29. The Top 10 Linux Kernel Vulnerabilities. https://resources.whitesourcesoftware.com/blog-whitesource/top-10-linux-kernel-vulnerabilities
30. Current CVSS Score Distribution For All Vulnerabilities. https://www.cvedetails.com/
31. e-Commerce Association of Bangladesh. http://e-cab.net/
32. IP Location Finder. https://www.iplocation.net/
33. The Big (Unstructured) Data Problem. https://www.forbes.com/sites/forbestechcouncil/2017/06/05/the-big-unstructured-data-problem/#3c80e827493a
34. Ko, S.J., Lee, J.H.: User preference mining through collaborative filtering and content based filtering in recommender system. In: Bauknecht, K., Tjoa, A.M., Quirchmayr, G. (eds.) EC-Web 2002. LNCS, vol. 2455, pp. 244–253. Springer, Heidelberg (2002). https://doi.org/10.1007/3-540-45705-4_26
35. Bahassine, S., Madani, A., Al-Sarem, M., Kissi, M.: Feature selection using an improved Chi-square for Arabic text classification. J. King Saud Univ. - Comput. Inf. Sci. **32**, 225–231 (2020)

[illegible] B., Schmutzing, H., [illegible]: The effect of [illegible] transactions [illegible] and the risk perception [illegible] online buying [illegible] (2020)

[illegible]: Deep perspectives on social commerce [illegible]. [illegible] Manag. [illegible] (2019)

[illegible] H.: [illegible] and [illegible] in mobile payment [illegible] (2018)

[illegible] of the 21st Century. https://www.[illegible].com/[illegible]

[illegible] https://[illegible]

[illegible]

[illegible] https://[illegible]

[illegible]: [illegible] https://www.[illegible]

[illegible] and [illegible] based [illegible] In: [illegible] (eds.) [illegible] Springer [illegible]

[illegible] feature selection using [illegible] Comput. [illegible] (2020)

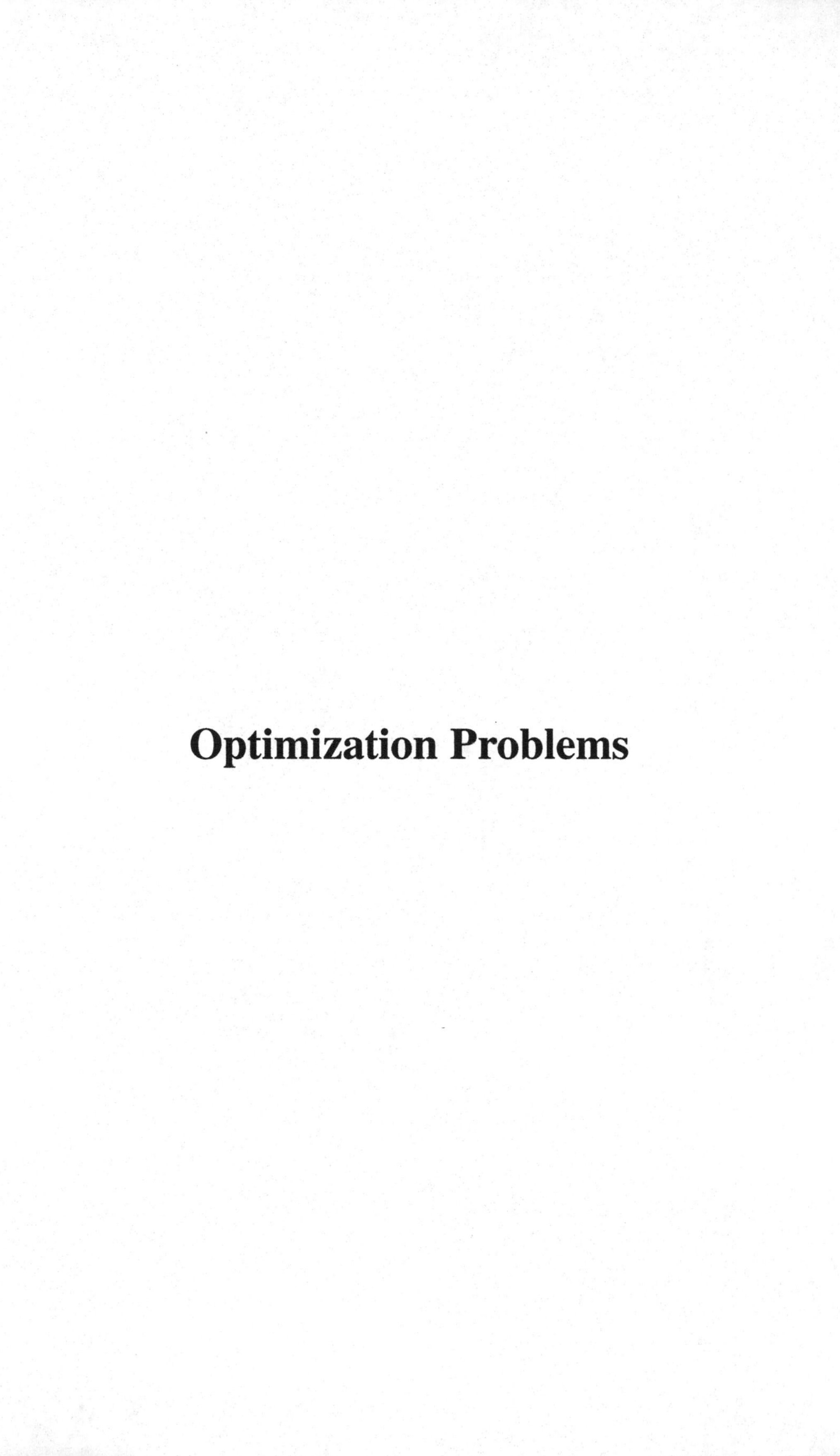

Optimization Problems

T-way Strategy for (Sequence Less Input Interaction) Test Case Generation Inspired by Fish Swarm Searching Algorithm

Mostafijur Rahman[1(✉)], Dalia Sultana[1], Khandker M Qaiduzzaman[1], Md. Hasibul Hasan[1], R. B. Ahmad[2], and Rozmie Razif Othaman[2]

[1] Department of Software Engineering, Daffodil International University, Dhaka, Bangladesh
mostafijur.cse@gmail.com

[2] School of Computer and Communication Engineering, Universiti Malaysia Perlis, Arau, Malaysia

Abstract. Since twenty years, several t-way strategies have been developed for Combinatorial Input Interaction (CII) based system to reduce the number of test cases in the test suite. The t-way strategy can be applied to Sequence-less CII system, where all inputs are parameterized and parallel. From the literature, the searching methods used in t-way strategies are divided into deterministic and non-deterministic for reducing test cases for all test configurations. It is found that t-way strategy is an NP-hard problem; no deterministic and non-deterministic t-way strategies claim that their strategy can generate the optimal number of test cases for all test configurations. In this research, an Interactive t-way Test Case Generation (ITCG) algorithm is proposed inspiring fish swarm searching algorithm to integrate with t-way strategy and evaluate the generated number of test cases comparing with existing renown t-way strategies. The results show that the proposed t-way test case generation inspiring Fish Swarm Searching Algorithm for sequence-less CII able to generate optimal and feasible results for different test configurations.

Keywords: Software testing · Combinatorial input interaction · T-way test strategy · Sequence less input interaction · Fish swarm search

1 Introduction

Nowadays, software systems have a greater impact on modern society. The multi-functional and complex software systems have multiple inputs. To improve the quality and correctness of a software product it is necessary to test different aspects of the software system [1]. Therefore, sufficient software testing is needed for software verification and validation while considering multiple numbers of input interactions. It is investigated that the insufficient software testing may cause mistake [2]. To illustrate the t-way testing problem for sequence less input interaction, consider the online shoe ordering in eBay online ordering system, shown in Fig. 1 [3]. The system consists of five parameters,

T. Bhuiyan et al. (Eds.): ICONCS 2020, LNICST 325, pp. 155–166, 2020.
https://doi.org/10.1007/978-3-030-52856-0_12

each parameter has its associated configurations or values (i.e., the parameter values of Brand are Adidas, Nike, ASICS, Cole Haan, New Balance; the values of US Shoe Size (Men's) are five like 8.5, 9, 9.5, 10, 10.5).

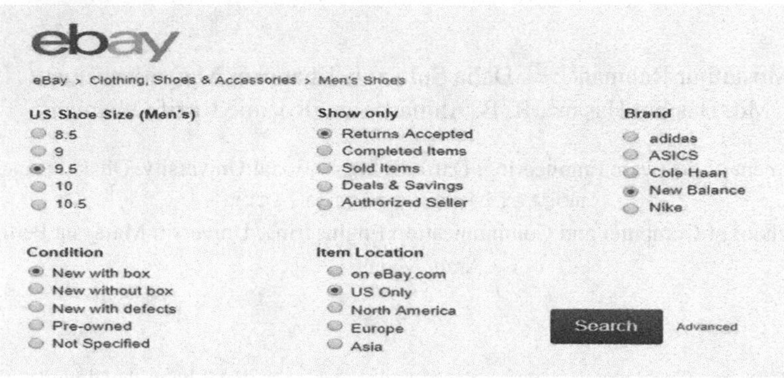

Fig. 1. eBay online ordering system [3]

A user can select the preferred values for each parameter and click the search button. Now, in this particular example (as shown in Table 1), there are five parameters and each parameter has five values. Hence, the exhaustive testing requires 3125 test cases (i.e., $5 \times 5 \times 5 \times 5 \times 5$) for testing input parameters, which is hardly feasible in practice. In this case, Sequence less t-way strategy minimize the tests systematically. Considering the above example, for $t = 2$, the exhaustive and reduced generated test cases are found 3125 and 34 respectively. This paper propose a unified t-way strategy for sequence less t-way test generation. In the field of interaction testing, many deterministic and non-deterministic algorithms have been adopted as the basis of the t-way strategy implementation. There are many existing search based researches (used in t-way testing) have focused in the literature including Simulated Annealing (SA) [4], Genetic Algorithm (GA) [5], Particle Swarm Test Generator (PSTG) [6, 7], Harmony Search Strategy (HSS) [8], Cuckoo Search Strategy (CSS) [9], Test Vector Generator TVG [10], In Parameter Order Generator (IPOG) [11], Tconfig [12], Jenny [13], etc. It is found from the literature, the adoption of the aforementioned strategies are effective to get a good quality solution [6, 14].

In combinatorial input interaction testing, the t-way test strategy focus is to reduce the number of test cases. A number of researchers, doing research on t-way test strategy for sequence-less input interaction, found that it is an NP-hard problem [5, 15–17]. Another limitation is that no researcher can claim their strategy able to produce the optimum number of test cases for all test configurations.

This section provides an overview of the existing works for generating a t-way test suite. Harmony Search Strategy (HSS) is also an effective algorithm for solving highly interactive combinatorial problems [8]. In [9], it is concluded that the Cuckoo Search Strategy (CSS) can show optimality by balancing the local intensification with the global diversification. It uses Lévy flights to efficiently explore all the search space. In [18], Bat Algorithm is proposed that can be applied to t-way strategy by modeling

Table 1. eBay online ordering system options

Show only	Condition	Brand	US shoe size Men's	Item location
Returns accepted	New with box	Adidas	8.5	On ebay.com
Completed items	New without box	Nike	9	US only
Sold items	Pre-owned	ASICS	9.5	North America
Deals & savings	New with defects	New balance	10	Europe
Authorized seller	Not specified	Cole haan	10.5	Asia

the bats' position as the potential solution. The AETG-SAT [19, 20] algorithm uses an SAT solverl to check the validity of the resulting partial test case. The mAETG is the modified version of Automatic Efficient Test Generator (AETG), proposed in [21].

The mAETG algorithm uses rank to select input parameters to search the t-set and the algorithm can handle arbitrary t-way coverage. Test Vector Generator (TVG) [10] is a project based Multiple Document Interface (MDI) application and T-Reduced, Plus-One or Random Sets algorithms are used to generate final test cases. Some swarm-based strategies such as PSTG, ACO are adopted to generate test-suite size in paper [6, 7]. PICT is a test case generation tool based on t-way test strategy, proposed in [22]. It is designed to consider the speed of test case generation, user-friendliness, and extensibility of the core engine facilities. The T-way Input Interaction Test (TWIIT) strategy is an integrated strategy supporting sequence-less and sequence input interactions [2]. The TWIIT strategy for sequence-less input interaction supports both uniform and non-uniform parameter values. In this research an extensive evaluation with different benchmarks and experimental cases has been presented to determine the strengths and threats of the proposed strategy. The TWIIT strategy (for sequence-less and sequence input interactions) able to generate minimum number of test cases compared with its counterpart strategies.

In this research, a Covering Array (CA) is used for mapping the test cases. The CA can be defined as CA (N; t, k, v), where N is the number of final test cases, t is the strength, k is the number of the independent input parameter, and v is the discrete value. The size of the CA can be defined as N × k, where each column represents a parameter and each row represents a test case. The t is any t columns of the array and each of the v^t possible t-way tuples appears at least once [2]. For example, suppose a system consists k parameter, $p_1, p_2, \ldots\ldots, p_k$. Each p_i consists of v_i values, where $1 \leq i \leq k$. The number of test candidate can be found from $v_1 \times v_2 \times v_3 \times \ldots\ldots \times v_k$. It represents a test suite consisting an array of 12 rows of test cases, 4 columns of parameters with three parameters having 2 values and one parameter having 3 values. Here, there is a need to cover all the t-way tuples but it is too expensive to test all the input combination. Therefore, the method is needed to apply and solve some testing criterion.

2 Methodology

In this work, a new uniform sequence-less strategy is proposed that is inspired by Fish Swarm Searching Algorithm (FSSA) [23]. The proposed strategy uses the concept of finding the best fish within a range and jump between the exhaustive test cases. The details of FSSA and our proposed strategy are described in Sect. 2.1 and Sect. 2.2 respectively.

2.1 Fish Swarm Searching Algorithm (FSSA)

Fish Swarm Searching Algorithm is a recently developed non-deterministic algorithm based on finding more food. In this algorithm the swarm technology is used according to its rules. In FSSA, the fishes are moved for better positions based on the hypothesis. In this algorithm, the better positions in the problem space contain more food. The fish moves towards the better positions without losing their integrity. Fishes are moved as the uniform distribution. Based on the availability of foods the fishes follow some other fishes that find more food. In FSSA, this behavior is simulated using the Eq. (1) [24]. Here the fish tries to approach its position. In this equation each fish *i* (*Fi*) choose one fish in a better position randomly.

$$Y_{\mathrm{i,d}} = X_{\mathrm{i,d}} + \left(\left(X_{\mathrm{i,d}} - X_{\mathrm{i,d}}\right) \times rand(0, 2)\right) \tag{1}$$

In Eq. (1), X(i,d) is equal to the dth component of the position vector of fish Fi, and rand (L, R) generates a random number with a uniform distribution in the range [L, R]. The Y vector is a buffer vector. The schematic of the movement of one fish toward a better one is illustrated [23].

2.2 Proposed Interactive T-way Test Case Generation (ITCG) Strategy

In this research, FSSA is adopted for solving sequence-less t-way test generation problems. In case of sequence-less interaction elements, for a set of parameters and their values v, all t-combinations of P that meet the interaction strength requirement are generated. Then, the interaction elements are generated based on these combinations. Consider a system CA with CA (N; 2, 2^4). The t-way combinations of this system are P_1P_2, P_1P_3, P_1P_4, P_2P_3, and P_2P_4, where $P = [P_1, P_2, P_3, P_4]$. For our running example, P_1, P_2, P_3 and P_4 have two values (i.e., 0 and 1). For instance, P_1P_2 has 2×2 possible interaction elements (i.e., 0:0, 0:1, 1:0, and 1:1). So, the total interaction elements be $(2 \times 2) + (2 \times 2) + (2 \times 2) + (2 \times 2) = 16$.

According to theory, the optimal test case can be found if the condition value and the total number of generated t-way tuples is known. Initially the first test case is taken as a pivot. A search strategy is set to jump from left and right side on the test candidates within a given range. All of the elements (test candidates) are checked according to the given conditions. The jump size is decremented or incremented by 1. In this search space all the t-way tuples are need covered. The condition value (*d*) is 0, indicating is completed to traverse. Balance of test candidate refers incorrect test cases generation. Otherwise, the t-way tuples are considered covered and correct test cases generation. In this search space the first test case always cover the maximum number of tuples (as the *d* value is highest). The search process is needed to repeat until the maximum number of improvements is satisfied. The proposed algorithm adds the best test case into the final test suite. Covering all t-way tuples indicate the final test suit is ready to use, i.e., the interaction list is empty and the iteration stops. The proposed strategy is shown in Algorithm 1.

Algorithm 1. ITCG

```
input: t, v, and jump size
output: optimized test cases after searching
initialize pivot and jump size
while Tuple is not empty do
  mark pivot element as taken and store into list
  find all tuples of pivot and store in TempTuple[pivot]
  for i ← 0 to size of TempTuple[pivot] do
    if i-th tuple exists in Tuple then
      delete i-th tuple from Tuple
    end if
    k ← pivot + 1, d ← 0, cv ← 0, idx ← 0
    while k < Exhaustive and cv < jump size do
      if k is marked as taken then
        k ← k + 1
      end if
      cnt ← 0
      for i ← 0 to size of TempTuple[k] do
        if i-th tuple exists in Tuple then
          cnt ← cnt + 1
        end if
      end for
      if cnt > d then
        d ← cnt, idx ← k
      end if
      k ← k + 1, cv ← cv + 1
   end while
   k ← pivot − 1, cv ← 0
  while k ≥ 0, cv < jump size do
       if k is marked as taken then
         k ← k − 1
       end if
       if cnt = d then
         if pivot − k < idx − pivot then
           idx ← k
         end if
         k ← k + 1, cv ← cv + 1
    end while
    pivot ← idx
end while
```

2.3 Results and Discussion

To perform the experiments, the Intel (R) Core (TM) i7-3770 CPU@ 3.40 GHz, 4 GB of RAM, Windows 10 professional, and 64-bit operating system are used. In this work, we have focused ITCG and TWIIT [2] algorithms for which we can represent the concrete result analysis. Since other existing strategies were not implemented in this work, to allow meaningful comparison, followed the relationship $\Delta = \beta - \alpha$, where β = our solution and α = the known best solution from the existing strategies [24].

<0; our solution is better than the known best solution. If $\Delta = \{$>0; our solution is poorer than the known best solution

=0; our solution matches with the known best solution

In this work, we recorded the minimum test suite size for each of the existing strategies. To better understand the result, we used several symbols in the experimental result Tables 2, 3, 4, 5 and 6.

Table 2. Comparison between TWIIT [2] and proposed ITCG for Experiment 1.

Test No.	System Configuration	TWIIT [2]				Proposed ITCG			
		Best	Worst	Average	Std. Dev.	Best	Worst	Average	Std. Dev.
1	CA (N; 2, 3^4)	**9***	9	9	0	**9***	17	10.6	2.76
2	CA (N; 2, 2^13)	19	26	21.3	2.41	**9**	9	9	0
3	CA (N; 3, 3^4)	**27**	32	29	1.67	33	33	33	0
4	CA (N; 3, 3^6)	**34**	45	42.1	3.5	43	46	44.7	1.19
5	CA (N; 3, 4^6)	**64***	68	64.8	1.6	**64***	64	64	0
6	CA (N; 4, 5^5)	**711**	738	726.2	6.79	749	763	753.4	4.18
7	CA (N; 4, 3^6)	**131***	139	133.5	2.24	**131***	135	134.5	1.27
8	CA (N; 4,2^10)	42	44	43.8	0.6	**38**	45	41.7	2.93
9	CA (N; 5, 2^6)	**32***	41	33.4	2.93	**32***	32	32	0
10	CA (N; 5, 2^8)	**64***	68	64.8	1.6	**64***	74	66.8	3.79
11	CA (N; 6, 2^7)	**64***	83	67.8	5.7	**64***	64	64	0
12	CA (N; 6, 3^7)	**848***	883	850	13.3	**848***	866	852.9	7.31
Average standard deviation					3.5				1.95

* value indicates the optimal solution i.e. it is the minimum possible test suit size, Bold value indicates the best result among all other strategies, but not the optimal one and – denotes unavailability of the results in the literature for that particular system configuration.

Benchmarking of Sequence-Less T-way Strategies

In this research, various system configuration for sequence-less t-way strategies are

Table 3. Benchmarking of proposed ITCG strategy (uniform values) with existing deterministic based t-way strategies for Experiment 1

Test No.	System configuration	Deterministic based strategies								
		IPO-N [17]	mAETG [21]	IPOG [11]	Jenny [13]	TVG [10]	Tconfig [12]	GTWay [26]	Density [25]	PICT [22]
1	CA (N; 2, 3^4)	–	**9***	–	–	–	–	–	–	–
2	CA (N; 2, 2^13)	–	17	–	–	–	–	–	–	–
3	CA (N; 3, 3^4)	–	–	39	34	32	32	–	–	34
4	CA (N; 3, 3^6)	47	38	–	51	48	48	–	63	48
5	CA (N; 3, 4^6)	**64***	77	–	112	120	**64***	–	**64***	111
6	CA (N; 4, 5^5)	–	–	784	837	849	773	771	–	–
7	CA (N; 4, 3^6)	–	–	–	140	–	141	–	–	142
8	CA (N; 5, 2^8)	–	–	–	74	–	70	–	–	**64***
9	CA (N; 6, 2^7)	–	–	–	87	–	**64***	–	–	72

* value indicates the optimal solution i.e. it is the minimum possible test suit size, Bold value indicates the best result among all other strategies, but not the optimal one and – denotes unavailability of the results in the literature for that particular system configuration.

considered. In Tables 2, 3, 4, 5 and 6, each system configuration was denoted by a test no. and was evaluated by a particular algorithm for 10 trials. Finally, the best, the worst, the average test suit size and the standard deviation were calculated. The benchmarking is considered with the t-way strategies selected from the reference [2]. Two experiments were done based on the following system configuration details,

- Experiment 1: Benchmarking of ITCG strategy (uniform values) system configuration with existing deterministic and non-deterministic strategies.
- Experiment 2: Generated test suite for the system configuration CA (N; t,2^{10}) with $2 \leq t \leq 9$.

Experiment 1. In this experiment, several interaction strengths (t = 2, 3, 4, 5, 6) are taken to the account and we compared the experimental result between TWIIT [2] and ITCG in Table 2. From the table, it is seen that both of the algorithms are equally capable of finding solutions for the given system configurations starting from test 1 to 12. TWIIT was able to find the best test suite size for 10 test cases whereas ITCG was able to find for

Table 4. Benchmarking of proposed ITCG strategy (uniform values) with existing non-deterministic based t-way strategies for Experiment 1

Test No.	System configuration	Non-deterministic based strategies								$\Delta_{ITCG} = \beta - \alpha$
		HSS [8]	PSTG [6, 7]	CSS [9]	SA [4]	GA [5]	BTS [18]	TWIIT [2]	ITCG	
1	CA (N; 2, 3^4)	**9***	**9***	**9***	**9***	**9***	–	**9***	**9***	0
2	CA (N; 2, 2^13)	–	17	–	16	17	–	19	**9**	−7
3	CA (N; 3, 3^4)	**27**	**27**	**27**	–	–	–	**27**	33	6
4	CA (N; 3, 3^6)	39	42	43	**33**	**33**	–	34	43	10
5	CA (N; 3, 4^6)	–	102	105	**64***	**64***	–	**64***	**64***	0
6	CA (N; 4, 5^5)	–	783	–	–	–	–	**711**	749	38
7	CA (N; 4, 3^6)	134	–	–	–	–	132	**131***	**131***	0
8	CA (N; 4,2^10)	–	–	–	–	–	–	42	**38**	−1
9	CA (N; 5, 2^6)	–	–	–	–	–	–	**32***	**32***	0
10	CA (N; 5, 2^8)	66	65	–	–	–	**64***	**64***	**64***	0
11	CA (N; 6, 2^7)	**64***	67	–	–	–	**64***	**64***	**64***	0
12	CA (N; 6, 3^7)	–	–	–	–	–	–	**848***	**848***	0

* value indicates the optimal solution i.e. it is the minimum possible test suit size, Bold value indicates the best result among all other strategies, but not the optimal one and denotes unavailability of the results in the literature for that particular system configuration.

9 test cases. However, ITCG has the average standard deviation of 1.95 whereas TWIIT has 3.5. It indicates that TWIIT has the tendency to give fluctuated solutions on each run whereas ITCG gives comparatively stable solutions. The standard deviation for each test illustrates that ITCG always has less standard deviation than TWIIT except the test no. 2, 3, 5, 9 and 11. For test no. 13, the standard deviation of TWIIT is very large (13.3).

In Table 3 and Table 4, we benchmarked the ITCG strategy with other deterministic and non-deterministic strategies for test 1 to 12. As for the overall performance, ITCG and TWIIT appears to produce the best overall test suite size with SA, ACA and GA, coming in as the closest runner up. Density performed the poorest overall. Referring to

Table 5. Comparison between TWIIT [2] and proposed ITCG for Experiment 2.

Test No.	T	TWIIT [2]				Proposed ITCG			
		Best	Worst	Average	Std. Dev.	Best	Worst	Average	Std. Dev.
1	2	9	9	9	0	**8**	9	8.5	0.5
2	3	**16***	16	16	0	**16***	18	16.3	0.64
3	4	42	44	43.8	0.8	**38**	45	41.4	2.65
4	5	**87**	92	89.8	1.24	89	89	89	0
5	6	158	174	165.3	6.24	**156**	175	167.4	7.26
6	7	**264**	300	289.9	13.63	**264**	302	281.5	11.91
7	8	**488**	549	513.1	19.1	**488**	538	513.7	14.15
8	9	**512**	548	516.5	10.83	**512**	562	527.3	16.1
Average standard deviation					6.5				6.7

* value indicates the optimal solution i.e. it is the minimum possible test suit size, Bold value indicates the best result among all other strategies, but not the optimal one and – denotes unavailability of the results in the literature for that particular system configuration.

Table 6. Benchmarking of proposed ITCG strategy with existing deterministic and non-deterministic based t-way strategies for Experiment 2.

Test No.	T	Deterministic					Non-deterministic					$\Delta = \beta - \alpha$
		TVG [10]	Jenny [13]	Tconfig [12]	ITCH [27]	IPOG [11]	PSO [28]	HSS [8]	CSS [9]	TWIIT [2]	ITCG	
1	2	10	10	9	**6***	10	8	7	8	9	8	2
2	3	17	18	20	18	19	17	**16***	**16***	**16***	**16***	0
3	4	41	39	45	58	49	37	37	**36**	42	38	2
4	5	84	87	95	–	128	82	81	**79**	87	89	10
5	6	168	169	183	–	352	158	158	157	158	**156**	−1
6	7	302	311	–	–	–	–	298	–	**264**	**264**	0
7	8	514	521	–	–	–	–	498	–	**488**	**488**	0
8	9	651	788	–	–	–	–	**512**	–	**512**	**512**	0

* value indicates the optimal solution i.e. it is the minimum possible test suit size, Bold value indicates the best result among all other strategies, but not the optimal one and – denotes unavailability of the results in the literature for that particular system configuration.

the ΔITCG values in Table 3 and Table 4, ITCG found the best test suit size for the test no. 2 and 8. But it performed poorer than the existing strategies for the test no. 3, 4 and 6, still better than several other strategies. For rest of the tests, the values of **ΔITCG** are 0; indicating that ITCG performed as well as the other best-known strategies.

Experiment 2. In Experiment 2, we generated test suit for the system configurations CA (N; t, 2^{10}) where, $2 \leq t \leq 9$. Referring to the Table 5, It is found that ITCG was more successful in finding the best solutions (for all test cases except test no. 4) than TWIIT. The standard deviations for both of the algorithms are almost identical, 6.5 and 6.7. However, for the test no. 7 and 8 the standard deviation for TWIIT fluctuates. On the other hand TWIIT is good for test no. 3. We presented the benchmarking of our strategy with the other existing strategies in Table 6 for Experiment 2. It is found that ITCG performed the best, and TWIIT and HSS performed better than the other existing strategies. However, ITCH showed the worst performance. Referring to the value of ΔITCG in Table 6, it is seen that ITCG out performed all of the other strategies for test no. 5. The poorer result generated by ITCG is for the test no. 1, 5 and 7, which is still better than other known strategies. For test no. 2, 6, 7 and 8, ITCG was able to find the best solution along with other strategies such as TWIIT, HSS and CSS.

3 Conclusion and Future Work

In this research a new ITCG is designed and developed successfully using Fish Swam Searching Algorithm. Benchmarking have done between ITCG and the other renowned strategies for sequence less input interaction. It is found that the developed strategy ITCG is compatible and efficient (for some test configurations) compared to other strategies. However, the ITCG is able to produce feasible results. In this research the time to get the output is not taken as a crucial part; however, the lower number of test cases are the major concern. During the result analysis, it is found that the increasing number of input, slower the test case generation algorithm and the deterministic searches are producing better result than the non-deterministic Search algorithms. This research can be extended for variable and input/output strategy.

References

1. Esfandyari, S., Rafe, V.: A tuned version of genetic algorithm for efficient test suite generation in interactive t-way testing strategy. Inf. Softw. Technol. **1**(94), 165–185 (2018)
2. Rahman, M.: Design of a new T-way strategy for test case generation supporting sequence-less and sequence input interaction. Ph.D. thesis, Universiti Malaysia Perlis (UNIMAP) (2017)
3. Ebay. https://www.ebay.com. Accessed 20 Nov 2019
4. Cohen, M.B., Colbourn, C.J., Ling, A.C.: Augmenting simulated annealing to build interaction test suites. In: 14th International Symposium on Software Reliability Engineering (ISSRE 2003), pp. 394–405 (2003)
5. Shiba, T., Tsuchiya, T., Kikuno, T.: Using artificial life techniques to generate test cases for combinatorial testing. In: Proceedings of the 28th Annual International Computer Software and Applications Conference (COMPSAC 2004), pp. 72–77 (2004)
6. Ahmed, B.S., Zamli, K.Z., Lim, C.P.: Application of particle swarm optimization to uniform and variable strength covering array construction. Appl. Soft Comput. **12**(4), 1330–1347 (2012)
7. Ahmed, B.S., Zamli, K.Z., Lim, C.P.: Constructing a T-way interaction test suite using the particle swarm optimization approach. Int. J. Innov. Comput. Inf. Control **8**(1), 431–452 (2012)

8. Alsewari, A.A., Zamli, K.Z.: Interaction test data generation using harmony search algorithm. In: 2011 IEEE Symposium on Industrial Electronics and Applications, pp. 559–564, 25 Sept 2011
9. Nasser, A.B., Alsewari, A.R., Zamli, K.Z.: Tuning of cuckoo search based strategy for T-way testing. In: International Conference on Electrical and Electronic Engineering, vol. 9, p. 10 (2015)
10. Arshem, J.: Test vector generator (2004). http://sourceforge.net/projects/tvg. Accessed 5 Apr 2017
11. Lei, Y., Kacker, R., Kuhn, D.R.: IPOG: a general strategy for T-way software testing. In: Proceedings of the 14th Annual IEEE International Conference and Workshops on the Engineering of Computer-Based Systems (ECBS 2007), pp. 549–556 (2017). https://doi.org/10.1109/ecbs.2007.47
12. Williams, A.W.: Determination of test configurations for pair-wise interaction coverage. In: Ural, H., Probert, R.L., Bochmann, G.V. (eds.) Testing of Communicating Systems. IAICT, vol. 48, pp. 59–74. Springer, Boston (2000). https://doi.org/10.1007/978-0-387-35516-0_4
13. Jenkins, B.: Jenny test tool. http://www.burtleburtle.net/bob/math/jenny.html. Accessed 5 Apr 2017
14. Alsewari, A.R., Zamli, K.Z.: Design and implementation of a harmony-search-based variable-strength T-way testing strategy with constraints support. Inf. Softw. Technol. **54**(6), 553–568 (2012)
15. Younis, M.I., Zamli, K.Z.: MIPOG-an efficient T-way minimization strategy for combinatorial testing. Int. J. Comput. Theory Eng. **3**(3), 388 (2011)
16. Othman, R.R., Zamli, K.Z.: T-way strategies and its applications for combinatorial testing. Int. J. New Comput. Archit. Appl. **1**(2), 459–473 (2011)
17. Nie, C., Xu, B., Shi, L., Dong, G.: Automatic test generation for N-way combinatorial testing. In: Reussner, R., Mayer, J., Stafford, J.A., Overhage, S., Becker, S., Schroeder, P.J. (eds.) QoSA/SOQUA -2005. LNCS, vol. 3712, pp. 203–211. Springer, Heidelberg (2005). https://doi.org/10.1007/11558569_15
18. Alsariera, Y.A., Zamli, K.Z.: A bat-inspired strategy for t-way interaction testing. J. Adv. Sci. Lett. **21**(8), 2281–2284 (2015). https://doi.org/10.1166/asl.2015.6316
19. Cohen, D.M., Dalal, S.R., Kajla, A., Patton, G.C.: The automatic efficient test generator (AETG) system. In: Proceedings of 1994 IEEE International Symposium on Software Reliability Engineering, 6 Nov 1994, pp. 303–309
20. Cohen, D.M., Dalal, S.R., Fredman, M.L., Patton, G.C.: The AETG system: an approach to testing based on combinatorial design. IEEE Trans. Softw. Eng. **23**(7), 437–444 (1997)
21. Cohen, M.B.: Designing test suites for software interaction testing. University of Auckland (2004)
22. Czerwonka, J.: Pairwise testing in real world. In: 24th Pacific Northwest Software Quality Conference, vol. 200 (2006)
23. Yazdani, D., Sadeghi-Ivrigh, S., Sepas-Moghaddam, A., Meybodi, M.R.: Fish swarm search algorithm: a new algorithm for global optimization. Int. J. Artif. Intell. **13**(2), 17–45 (2015)
24. Nasser, A.B., Zamli, K.Z., Alsewari, A.A., Ahmed, B.S.: An elitist-flower pollination-based strategy for constructing sequence and sequence-less t-way test suite. Int. J. Bio-Inspired Comput. **12**(2), 115–127 (2018)
25. Bryce, R.C., Colbourn, C.J.: One-test-at-a-time heuristic search for interaction test suites. In: Proceedings of the 9th Annual Conference on Genetic and Evolutionary Computation, pp. 1082–1089. ACM (2007)
26. Zamli, K.Z., Klaib, M.F., Younis, M.I., Isa, N.A., Abdullah, R.: Design and implementation of a T-way test data generation strategy with automated execution tool support. Inf. Sci. **181**(9), 1741–1758 (2011)

27. Hartman, A., Klinger, T., Raskin, L.: IBM intelligent test case handler (2005). http://ibm-intelligent-test-case-handler.updatestar.com/en. Accessed 5 Apr 2017
28. Kennedy, J., Eberhart, R.: Particle swarm optimization. In: Proceedings of the IEEE International Conference on Neural Networks, pp. 1942–1948 (1995). https://doi.org/10.1109/icnn.1995.488968

Chemical Reaction Optimization for Solving Resource Constrained Project Scheduling Problem

Ohiduzzaman Shuvo[1(✉)] and Md Rafiqul Islam[2]

[1] Green University of Bangladesh, Dhaka, Bangladesh
oheduzzamanshuvo@gmail.com
[2] Khulna University, Khulna, Bangladesh
dmri1978@gmail.com

Abstract. In this paper, a renowned metaheuristic algorithm named chemical reaction optimization (CRO) is applied to solve the resource constrained project scheduling problem (RCPSP). This work employed chemical reaction optimization to schedule project tasks to minimize makespan concerning resource and precedence constraints. Chemical reaction optimization is a population-based metaheuristic algorithm. CRO is applied to RCPSP by redesigning its basic operators and taking solutions from the search space using priority-based selection to achieve a better result. The proposed algorithm based on CRO is then tested on large benchmark instances and compared with other metaheuristic algorithms. The experimental results have shown that our proposed method provides better results than other states of art algorithms in terms of both the qualities of result and execution time.

Keywords: Chemical reaction optimization · Priority based selection · Resource constrained project scheduling problem · NP-hard

1 Introduction

Scheduling has a congenital impact in the field of business, product, management and engineering. Scheduling problems are strenuous to solve because of their large search space, constrained dependency, variation in problem based on application and domain. Many real life scheduling problems like generation plant building, software development, military projects and building nuclear submarine comes under the domain of the scheduling problems [1]. There are many other real life applications like Transport scheduling problem [2], Satellite scheduling problem [3], Academic time scheduling problem [4], Resource constrained project scheduling problem [5] which are an augmentation of the scheduling problem. Every project is comprised of numerous tasks that must be concluded in minimum time or minimum cost. The main task of project management is scheduling the project. The scheduling of a project consists of resource

T. Bhuiyan et al. (Eds.): ICONCS 2020, LNICST 325, pp. 167–179, 2020.
https://doi.org/10.1007/978-3-030-52856-0_13

allocation for each task of the project, assigning start and end time for each task and considering precedence constraints arrange these tasks in such a way so that the completion time of each project is minimum. Resource constrained project scheduling (RCPSP) is a classic type of scheduling optimization and NP-hard problem [6]. The RCPSP exhibit a very large space for the entire estimation to achieve an optimal solution. Time duration is an important factor in RCPSP. Moreover, the computational expense is increased with the larger problem size and addition of resource constraints. Practically, it is very difficult to search the entire solution space, which means minimization of time duration becomes tiresome. The fixed amount of resources and precedence constrained makes RCPSP a difficult problem to solve. Many researchers tried to solve RCPSP using the exact method but yet none of them are able to produce an optimal solution or near optimal solution. Several heuristic methods were applied to solve RCPSP and most of them either belong to priority rule-based approaches or metaheuristic approaches [7].

Metaheuristic methods start with an initial search space that contains several initial solutions. The solutions are improved by executing different types of operations on them. The most commonly used metaheuristic methods are genetic algorithm (GA), simulated annealing algorithm (SA), particle swarm optimization algorithm (PSO) and chemical reaction optimization algorithm (CRO).

One of the most earlier suggestion is made by Davis [8] for using GA to solve scheduling problems. In their paper, Davis illustrated that the importance of using a stochastic search method for a large search space and recommended an indirect depiction in which the GA operated on a list which was then decoded to articulate the actual schedule. Hartmann [9] proposed the implementation of GA for solving RCPSP. A variation was used in his paper where every gene composing a chromosome is a delivery rule and the criteria are those genes to break the tie inside the outline of the generation of sequences.

Anantathanvit proposed an extended version of particle swarm optimization named radius particle swarm optimization (R-PSO) to solve resource constrained project scheduling problem [10]. They used lbest circle topology to find the agent particle. The optimal solution or gbest particle is calculated from the agent particle. Although the proposed algorithm provides better result but the performance of the algorithm almost depends on the radius of the circle. Thus an improper value of radius may lead the algorithm to be trapped in local optima.

Chemical Reaction Optimization (CRO) is a population-based metaheuristic algorithm that has been applied to many optimization problems and it shows its efficient performance. Several applications area are vertex coloring [11], RNA structure prediction [12], Academic time scheduling problem [4]. In this paper, we present chemical reaction optimization (CRO) to solve the RCPSP using makespan as the objective function. We select molecules or schedules from the population according to the priority of them and we also redesigned the basic operators of CRO by following the objective function.

2 Chemical Reaction Optimization

Chemical Reaction Optimization (CRO) is a population-based metaheuristic that inspired by the nature of the chemical reaction. Four elementary reactions take place in each iteration of CRO. These include on-wall ineffective collision, decomposition, synthesis, and intermolecular ineffective collision. The number of molecules before the reactions and after the reactions remains the same in case of an on-wall ineffective or intermolecular ineffective collision. Besides, In the case of decomposition and synthesis, the number of molecules changes after the collision. The elementary reactions only can take place when it ensures the energy conversion condition as given below [13].

$$\sum_{i=1}^{k}(PE_{\omega i} + KE_{\omega i}) \geq \sum_{i=0}^{l} PE_{\omega' i} \tag{1}$$

Here, ω and ω' are the structures of input and output molecules k denotes the number of molecules that take part in the reaction. In the initial stage, CRO initiates its population (solution space) then it calculates the value of objective function as PE for each solution and initialize other attributes of each molecule such as population size (popsize), loss rate, collision rate (collrate), energy buffer, decomposition threshold (α), and synthesis threshold (β). CRO generates a number between 0 and 1 which is compared with collision rate and for a smaller value of this number on-wall ineffective collision or decomposition occurs conversely intermolecular ineffective collision and synthesis takes place for a large value of this number. After that, CRO generates the new molecule according to the corresponding reaction. If the new molecule is acceptable then replace the old one with the new molecule and also updates the value of KE. The solution is obtained after meeting the termination condition. Every solution of RCPSP is a sequence of activities. The variable potential energy (PE) of CRO determines the fitness value of the solution. Following the principles defined above, the steps of the CRO algorithm can be summarized by Algorithm 1.

3 Resource Constrained Project Scheduling Problem

A classical resource constrained project scheduling problem comprises a set of activities $A\{x_0, x_1, x_2, \ldots, x_{n+1}\}$ with a set of limited resource R and the constraint of resource availability is where C_r, $\forall r \in R$. Each activity x requires some resources for its execution. During the execution of an activity, the amount of resources held by that activity is unavailable for other activities but after completing the execution of that activity that resource can be used by another activity. Therefore, the resources are renewable. For the execution of each activity, the duration is fixed and known. Duration is represented by a vector $D\{d_1, d_2, d_3, \ldots, d_n\}$ where d_i represents the duration for an activity x_i. The start and end activities of a project are known as dummy activities. The duration for this dummy activities x_0 and $x_n + 1$ are $d_0 = d_{n+1} = 0$. The activities are bound by the precedence relationship. For example if an activity x_2 can not

Algorithm 1: CRO

```
Input: Objective function f and the parameter values
Set PopSize, KELossRate, MoleColl, buffer, InitialKE, α, and β.
Create PopSize number of molecules.
while stop criterion is not met do
    Generate buff ϵ [0, 1]
    if buff > MoleColl then
        Randomly select one molecule M_w.
        if Decomposition criterion is met then
            Trigger Decomposition
        end
        else
            Trigger OnwallIneffectiveCollision
        end
    end
    else
        Randomly select two molecules M_w1 and M_w2. if Synthesis criterion is
          met then
            Trigger Synthesis
        end
        else
            Trigger IntermolecularIneffectiveCollision
        end
    end
    Check for any new minimum solution
end
```

be completed before completion of an activity x_1 then activity x_1 is known as the predecessor of activity x_2 and activity x_2 is the successor of activity x_1. This type of relationship between these activities is known as precedence relation.

RCPSP involves two types of constraints one is precedence constraints and another one is resource constraints. Precedence constraints refer that all the predecessors of an activity x must be completed before the execution of x. Resource constraints refer that the project must be completed with the given type and fixed amount of resources.

The properties of a typical RCPSP is explained through a graphical representation in Fig. 1. We assume there are $0, 1 \ldots, N + 1$ activities where activity 0 and N + 1 are dummy activities with duration zero. The start time and end time of the project are also represented by these dummy activities. The activities are represented by the nodes of a graph where the precedence relationship is indicated by the directed edges among the nodes of the graph. The basic assumption for this problem instance is that the activities under a project are non-preemptive. That means an activity cannot be interrupted during the middle of execution. An arrangement of activities may be defined as a schedule. When both the precedence and resource constraints are satisfied by a schedule then it is said to be a feasible schedule. The execution time requires to complete all the activities of a schedule is known as the makespan of that schedule. From Fig. 1 we can see that a graph with 13 activities where first and last node represents dummy activities. The duration and required resources for each activity are given. The RCPSP instances under consideration have a type of resource and the amount of given resource is 3. A feasible schedule for this example is given in Fig. 2 which requires 17 times to complete its execution.

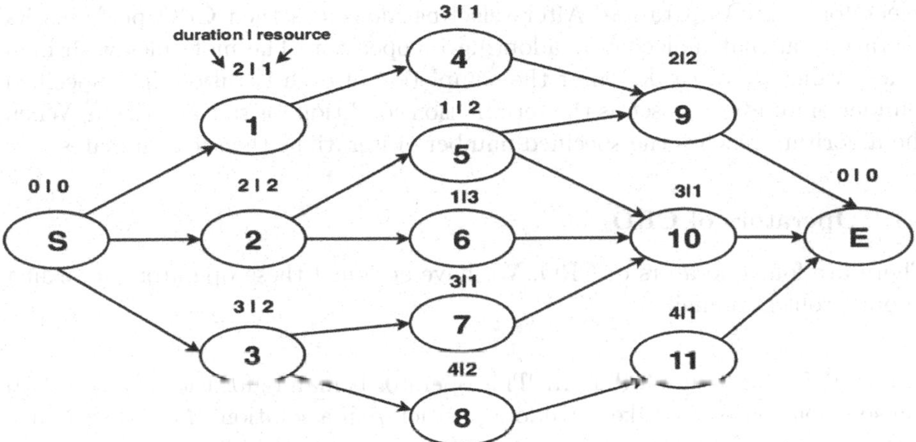

Fig. 1. A RCPSP example

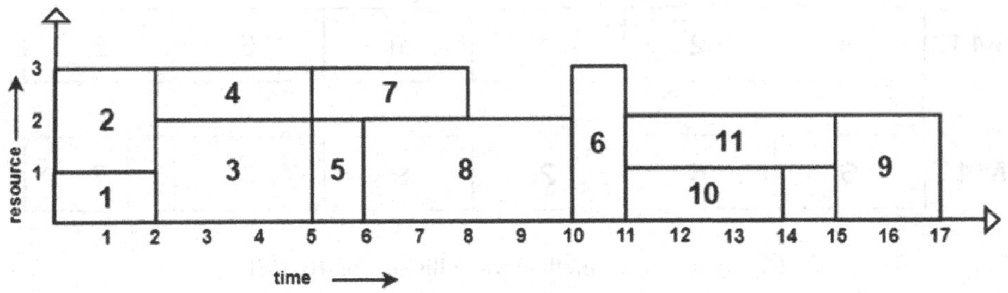

Fig. 2. A feasible schedule

For the given set of activities, the objective of this work is to produce a feasible schedule with minimum makespan. The objective function of RCPSP is to minimize the makespan concerning all constraints. Let x be a feasible solution of RCPSP, the project duration of x will be calculated using the makespan function. The objective function for solving RCPSP can be formulated as follows:

$$\phi(x) = makespan(x) \tag{2}$$

Where makespan function returns the duration of the project scheduled according to input solution activity sequences.

4 CRO for RCPSP

In the proposed model, CRO selects molecules from the population according to their priorities. The molecules are prioritized by using their fitness value. A molecule with lower fitness value (makespan value) has a higher probability to select for a CRO operation. After selecting molecules then CRO performs its operation on that molecule by adopting its operator. The molecules with high fitness value are discarded after the completion of each iteration. The specified number of iterations is set as the termination condition for this algorithm. When the algorithm reaches the specified number of iterations then it terminates.

4.1 Operators of CRO

There are four operators of CRO. We have designed these operators according to our problem domain.

On-wall Ineffective Collision. This operator is mainly for the local search in the solution space. We take a random position p in a solution $M1$ and exchange with the value of $p+1$ or $p-1$ position. By comparing the fitness values of both solutions we keep the solution with less fitness value. The on-wall ineffective collision for a feasible molecule of RCPSP is shown in Fig. 3.

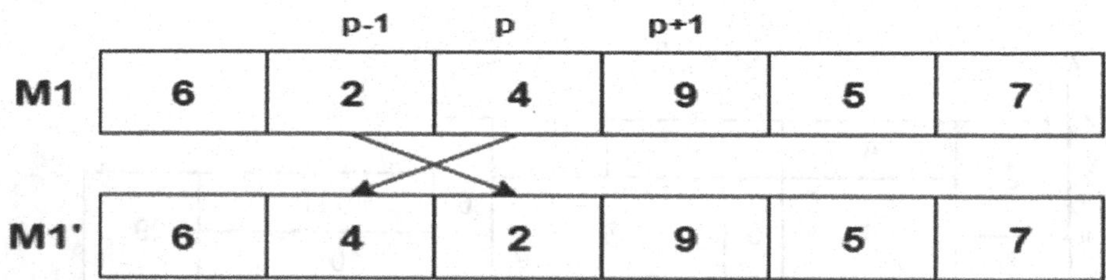

Fig. 3. On-wall ineffective collision for RCPSP

Decomposition. The decomposition operator is used for another exploration in the search space. Two molecules are produced after performing decomposition operator on a molecule and the newly generated molecule got an enormous change in their structures. Molecules M1 and M2 can be found by applying decomposition operator on a molecule M. We choose a midpoint in the parent molecule M. The output molecule M1 gets the last part of it from the first portion of parent molecule M and molecule M2 gets its first part from the last portion of M. The rest empty portions of molecule M1 and M2 are filled by shuffling the activities in the parent molecule by following the precedence relationship. The solution with minimum fitness value is kept in the solution space from the molecules M1 and M2. Figure 4 represents the decomposition reaction for RCPSP.

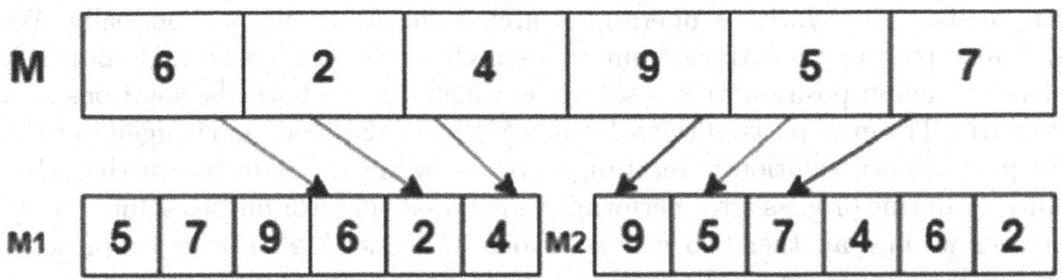

Fig. 4. Decomposition for RCPSP

Inter Molecular Ineffective Collision. This operator performs on two molecules. We randomly pick two molecules M1 and M2 from the solution space. Solutions $M1'$ and $M2'$ are produced after performing intermolecular ineffective collision operator on M1 and M2. Select two random positions t1 and t2 in both M1 and M2.

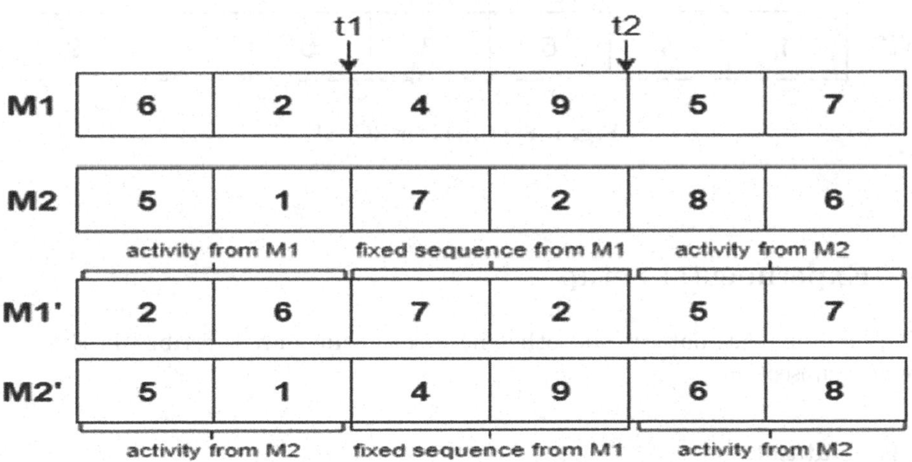

Fig. 5. Inter molecular ineffective collision for RCPSP

The positions t1 and t2 should be selected in a way so that the molecules got divided into three parts. The activities lie in the range of t1 and t2 in M2 is placed in the middle of $M1'$. The first part and last parts of $M1'$ are placed using the activities from solution M1 by following the activity sequence of M2. Solution $M2'$ is also formed using the same approach as $M1'$ has formed. After performing this operator the solution with minimum fitness value is kept in the solution space. Figure 5 represents intermolecular ineffective collision operator.

Synthesis. The synthesis operator searches the solution space globally. We randomly pick two solutions from the search space to suppose M1 and M2. Select a random position in two solutions which divides both the solutions into two parts. The even parts of the solutions M1 and M2 remain unchanged but the odd part of each solution is rearranged by following the sequence of the other solution. In this process after performing synthesis operator on two solutions M1 and M2 we find another two new solutions $M1'$ and $M2'$. Figure 6 represents the synthesis operator.

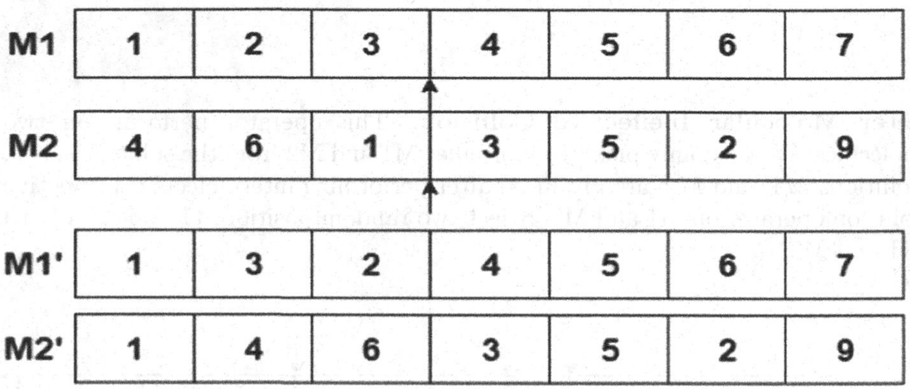

Fig. 6. Synthesis for RCPSP

5 Experimental Setup

The environment, dataset and other necessary things are described in the following subsections.

5.1 Dataset

For evaluating our proposed algorithm, we have used four standard data sets from the project scheduling library PSLIB. The benchmark data set contains 480 instances of each from j30, j60 and j120. Each j30, j60 and j120 instance consists of 30, 60 and 120 jobs respectively. Hence, total $480 + 480 + 600 = 1560$ instances have been adopted.

5.2 Parameter Setting

We have implemented the proposed CRO algorithm in Python 3.6 and tested on a personal computer with Intel Core i5 (2.30 GHz) with 8 GB RAM under Windows 10 operating system (64 bit). The parameters of our CRO algorithm are Alpha, PopSize, KELossRate, MolColl, InitialKE, and Beta. These parameters are tuned by setting different values for each to achieve the best results. The parameters used in the proposed algorithm have been shown with their values in Table 1. The termination condition for each instance is the limit of the number generated schedule such as 1000 or 5000. The number of generated schedules can be calculated using the following equation.

$$Number\ of\ Schedules = PopSize \times iteration\ number \tag{3}$$

Table 1. Parameters used in CRO.

Symbol	Description	Value
PopSize	Population size	200
Alpha	On-wall and decomposition criteria	2.9
Iteration	No. of execution	1000
KELossRate	Kinetic energy loss rate	0.5
MolColl	Uni and intermolecular criteria	0.7
InitialKE	Initial kinetic energy	0.51
Beta	Synthesis criteria	0.6

6 Results and Discussion

We have applied our algorithm on the given benchmark instances. The effectiveness of our algorithm is measured by considering the value of average deviation and the number of optimal solutions found. We run the CRO algorithm 40 times independently on each instance and set the maximum number of schedules to 1000 and 5000. The optimal solution for j30 and the lower bound value for j60 and j120 instances are provided in PSLIB. In our work, we have calculated the average percentage deviation with respect to project duration and the number of optimum instances found for every dataset. Since the optimal solution is given for the j30 dataset the deviation from the optimal solution is known as the average percentage deviation from the optimum. The deviation from lower bound for j60 and j120 dataset is known as the average percentage deviation from the lower bound. The average percentage deviation from optimum and average percentage deviation from lower bound is represented by *Avg_Dev_Opt* and the average percentage deviation from lower bound is represented by *Avg_Dev_Lowb* and calculated using Eq. 4.

$$Avg\_Dev\_Opt \textbf{ or } Avg\_Dev\_Lowb = \frac{1}{T}\sum_{i=1}^{T}\frac{n_i - n'_i}{n'_i} \times 100 \quad (4)$$

Here,

n_i represents makespan calculated for each instance.
n'_i represents optimal or lower bound value given for each instance.
T represents total number of instances. The number of optimal solutions is calculated using Eq. 5.

$$Number\_of\_optimal = \frac{Optimum\ instance}{Total\ instances} \times 100 \quad (5)$$

Table 2 presents the average percentage deviation from lower bound optimal and Table 3 presents the number of optimal solution found in case of j30, j60 and j120 dataset. The CRO algorithm is best for both 1000 and 5000 schedules, i.e for j30 average percentage deviation is 0.21% with 1000 schedules and 0.08% with 5000 schedules and optimal rates is 90.43% and 95.53% respectively. Thus, the makespan obtained by CRO is much closer to the optimal solution than other metaheuristics. We can also analyze the performance of our algorithm by a comparative study with other metaheuristics including radius particle swarm optimization algorithm (R-PSO), artificial bee colony algorithm (ABC) and simulated annealing algorithm (SA) in terms of average percentage deviation. The results show that in the case of medium and large scale CRO performs better than other metaheuristic methods. We can see that from Table 2 while the number of schedules is increasing along with it the average percentage deviation is decreasing. So increasing the number of schedules has a positive impact on the result. From the results shown in Table 2 we can state that our proposed CRO algorithm is more effective since the deviation value is small for all the datasets.

The performance analysis of CRO against other metaheuristics in terms of the optimum number of schedules is shown in Table 3. The proposed CRO also outperforms other metaheuristics including radius particle swarm optimization (R-PSO), bee swarm optimization (BSO) and artificial bee colony (ABC) algorithm.

It is shown that the chemical reaction optimization algorithm presented in this paper is robust in terms of both the average percentage deviation and the optimum number of schedules.

Table 2. Comparison between CRO and other metaheuristics algorithm.

Algorithm	Dataset	Average percentage deviation (%)	
		1000 schedules	5000 schedules
CRO (present work)	J30	0.21	0.08
	J60	11.90	11.23
	J120	33.96	33.05
R-PSO [10]	J30	0.38	0.12
	J60	12.20	11.83
	J120	34.75	33.60
PABC [14]	J30	0.34	0.17
	J60	12.35	11.96
	J120	36.84	35.79
SA [15]	J30	0.38	0.23
	J60	12.75	11.90
	J120	42.81	37.68

Table 3. Comparison between CRO against other metaheuristics in terms of optimum rate.

Algorithm	Dataset	Optimum rate (%)	
		1000 schedules	5000 schedules
CRO (present work)	J30	90.43	95.53
	J60	71.81	74.15
	J120	33.96	35.07
R-PSO [10]	J30	89.79	94.79
	J60	69.16	74.79
	J120	20.16	23.0
ABC [14]	J30	86.60	91.74
	J60	72.50	74.03
	J120	29.50	31.20
BSO [16]	J30	77.30	85.63
	J60	64.38	70.63
	J120	17.00	22.50

7 Conclusions

In this paper, we have proposed a novel metaheuristic algorithm based on CRO which is adapted for solving resource constrained project scheduling problems.The adaption was gained by redesigning some of the basic operators of CRO and using priority base molecules selection. The performance of the CRO algorithm has been investigated on a set of benchmark instances. The comparative study showed that our proposed method obtains optimal or near-optimal solutions which are better than the results of other metaheuristic algorithms. The priority selection approach plays a significant role in the case of the convergence of the algorithm. The algorithm works good but convergence rate is slightly slow in for relatively long projects. Moreover, in the future complete study on population generation, more efficient parameter generation and more efficient hybrid technique for CRO may provide higher excellence in this field.

Acknowledgement. This paper is partially funded by Green University of Bangladesh.

References

1. González, F.B.: Nuevos métodos de resolución del problema de secuenciación de proyectos con recursos limitados. Ph.D. Dissertation, Universitat de Valància (2004)
2. Islam, M.R., Mahmud, M.R., Pritom, R.M.: Transportation scheduling optimization by a collaborative strategy in supply chain management with TPL using chemical reaction optimization. Neural Comput. Appl. **32**(8), 3649–3674 (2019). https://doi.org/10.1007/s00521-019-04218-5
3. Sun, B., Wang, W., Qi, Q.: Satellites scheduling algorithm based on dynamic constraint satisfaction problem. In: 2008 International Conference on Computer Science and Software Engineering, vol. 4, pp. 167–170. IEEE (2008)
4. Ciscon, L.A., De Oliveira, H.C.B., Andrade, M.C.A., Alvarenga, G.B., Esmin, A.A.A.: The school timetabling problem: a focus on elimination of open periods and isolated classes. In: 2006 Sixth International Conference on Hybrid Intelligent Systems (HIS 2006), p. 70. IEEE (2006)
5. Drexl, A., Gruenewald, J.: Nonpreemptive multi-mode resource-constrained project scheduling. IIE Trans. **25**(5), 74–81 (1993)
6. Hartmann, S., Briskorn, D.: A survey of variants and extensions of the resource-constrained project scheduling problem. Eur. J. Oper. Res. **207**(1), 1–14 (2010)
7. Kolisch, R., Schwindt, C., Sprecher, A.: Benchmark instances for project scheduling problems. In: Węglarz, J. (ed.) Project Scheduling. International Series in Operations Research & Management Science, vol. 14, pp. 197–212. Springer, Boston (1999). https://doi.org/10.1007/978-1-4615-5533-9_9
8. Davis, L.: Hybrid genetic algorithms for machine learning. In: IEE Colloquium on Machine Learning, pp. 1–9. IET (1990)
9. Wang, H., Lin, D., Li, M.-Q.: A competitive genetic algorithm for resource-constrained project scheduling problem. In: 2005 International Conference on Machine Learning and Cybernetics, vol. 5, pp. 2945–2949. IEEE (2005)
10. Anantathanvit, M., Munlin, M.-A.: Radius particle swarm optimization for resource constrained project scheduling problem. In: 16th International Conference on Computer and Information Technology, pp. 24–29. IEEE (2014)
11. Islam, M.R., Arif, I.H., Shuvo, R.H.: Generalized vertex cover using chemical reaction optimization. Appl. Intell. **49**(7), 2546–2566 (2019). https://doi.org/10.1007/s10489-018-1391-z
12. Kabir, R., Islam, R.: Chemical reaction optimization for RNA structure prediction. Appl. Intell. **49**(2), 352–375 (2018). https://doi.org/10.1007/s10489-018-1281-4

13. Lam, A.Y.S., Li, V.O.K.: Chemical reaction optimization: a tutorial. Memet. Comput. **4**(1), 3–17 (2012). https://doi.org/10.1007/s12293-012-0075-1
14. Jia, Q., Seo, Y.: Solving resource-constrained project scheduling problems: conceptual validation of FLP formulation and efficient permutation-based ABC computation. Comput. Oper. Res. **40**(8), 2037–2050 (2013)
15. Bouleimen, K., Lecocq, H.: A new efficient simulated annealing algorithm for the resource-constrained project scheduling problem and its multiple mode version. Eur. J. Oper. Res. **149**(2), 268–281 (2003)
16. Ziarati, K., Akbari, R., Zeighami, V.: On the performance of bee algorithms for resource-constrained project scheduling problem. Appl. Soft Comput. **11**(4), 3720–3733 (2011)

A Modified Particle Swarm Optimization for Autonomous UAV Path Planning in 3D Environment

Golam Moktader Nayeem[1(✉)], Mingyu Fan[1(✉)], Shanjun Li[2], and Khalil Ahammad[3]

[1] School of Computer Science and Engineering, University of Electronic Science and Technology of China, Chengdu 611731, People's Republic of China
gmnayeem@std.uestc.edu.cn, ff98@163.com

[2] Key Laboratory of Information Network Security, Ministry of Public Security, Shanghai 201804, People's Republic of China
shanjunli@yahoo.com

[3] Department of Computer Science and Engineering, Comilla University, Cumilla, Bangladesh
khalil.cou.cse@gmail.com

Abstract. Path planning is an important aspect of an autonomous Unmanned Ariel Vehicle (UAV). As finding the best path is a non-deterministic problem, meta-heuristic algorithms proved to be a better choice in recent years. Particle Swarm Optimization (PSO) is one of the widely applied meta-heuristic algorithms for non-deterministic problem due to simplicity and ease of implementation. However, the lack of diversity in the particles in PSO algorithm generates a low-quality path for UAV. In this paper, we presented a modified PSO algorithm called n-PSO. In the algorithm, a dynamic neighborhood approach is proposed to improve the diversity of the particles. The n-PSO algorithm is applied to UAV path planning and simulated in a 3D environment. We compared the algorithm with two widely used versions of PSO for UAV path planning. The proposed algorithm showed significant improvement in particles diversity that plays an important role to produce better UAV path. At the end, we presented a time cost analysis of the algorithm for UAV path planning.

Keywords: PSO · UAV · Path planning · 3D environment

1 Introduction

The development of Autonomous Unmanned aerial vehicles (UAV) is of high interest to many researchers in recent years due to its diverse application in both military and civilian environment [1]. Some widely used applications are surveillance, search and rescue, disaster management, target search, goods delivery, wildlife research, etc. [2]. Path planning is an indispensable part of an

T. Bhuiyan et al. (Eds.): ICONCS 2020, LNICST 325, pp. 180–191, 2020.
https://doi.org/10.1007/978-3-030-52856-0_14

autonomous UAV system and aims to find the optimum path from start point to end point while satisfying the required constraints such as distance, time, power consumption, safety, etc. Path planning algorithm can be classified as offline and online. In offline path planning, an optimized path is planned before UAV fly for the known destination. On the other hand, online path planning aims to generate a dynamic path on the basis of offline reference path and real-time data of the track [3]. In this work, we considered offline path planning. In conventional path planning problem, one of the basic parameter used to calculate the best path is using the minimum distance traveled like as Traveling Salesman Problem (TSP). But constraints such as obstacle, average altitude, maximum turning angle, etc. is considered in UAV path planning. Therefore the problem becomes complex and characterized as a multi-objective optimization problem [4].

Meta-heuristic methods have been evolved to solve multi-objective optimization problem more efficiently than other available methods such as classical method, heuristic method, etc. [5]. PSO is a nature-inspired population-based meta-heuristic approach that has gained much attention in solving multi-objective optimization problems [6]. PSO deals with a set of solutions inspired by a group of an agent called particle [7]. The major advantages of using PSO are: (a) computationally inexpensive; (b) simple and easy implementation; (c) minimum interaction between particles as it uses its local best and global best information to calculate the new position; and (d) distributed processing as no mutation operation is required to generate the next generation of solution [8]. However, one of the major issues of PSO is the lack of diversity in the particle. Lack of diversity in the particles causes premature convergence and fall for local minima. As a result, a low quality solution is generated for UAV path planning [9]. In this paper, we focus on this particular problem of PSO in UAV path planning. We presented a modified PSO that produces a better solution for UAV path planning by increasing particles diversity. The main contributions of this work are: (a) We introduced a modified version of PSO named n-PSO; (b) We applied the n-PSO algorithm for UAV path planning with static obstacles in a 3D environment; and (c) We compared the n-PSO with other standard versions of PSO used for UAV path planning.

In the subsequent sections, we first give an overview of existing algorithms. In Sect. 3, we present a detailed mathematical model of the problem. An overview of the proposed model is described in Sect. 4. In Sect. 5, we present the experimental outcome of the proposed model. Lastly, we conclude the paper in Sect. 6.

2 Related Work

In recent years, a number of offline UAV path planning algorithms have been proposed based on PSO. Garcia *et al.* proposed a distributed PSO algorithm for exploration purpose for a search and rescue mission [10]. In the proposed model, PSO is used to generate the waypoints for the UAVs whereas lawnmower algorithm is used for the exploration task for UAVs. Also a new parameter is introduced instead of r_1 and r_2 to decrease the randomness of the algorithm in order to speed up the searching task of multiple targets. However, the author did not consider the diversity factor of the particles in the algorithm and the algorithm is implemented in a 2D environment without any obstacle. Huang *et al.* proposed a modified PSO called GBPSO for UAV path planning [4]. A competition strategy is introduced for selecting the global best position that helps to increase the diversity in the particles and speed up the global search process. A variant of PSO named CPSO for 2D offline path planning is proposed in [11]. In the proposed model, chaotic maps such as Singer map is used to determine the values of two basic parameters of PSO i.e. exploration and exploitation which create more diversity among the particles. However, the author did not provide the effect of a chaotic map in the particles diversity. Roberge *et al.* proposed a mathematical model and a cost function for UAV in a 3D environment and developed a parallel implementation method for UAV path planning [12]. In [9], a modified PSO named vPSO is proposed that uses Gaussian probability density function for mutation strategy in Gaussian mutation based PSO algorithm [13]. The author showed that increased diversity in the particles produces a good quality solution for UAV path planning. In addition, a number of variation of standard PSO have been proposed so far to increase the diversity in the particle for general purpose. A new parameter named constriction factor is introduced to improve the stability of PSO by Clerc [14]. Shi *et al.* introduced a time-varying inertia weight to improve the particle diversity and to avoid premature convergence [15]. To improve the diversity in the particles Sugathan *et al.* added a dynamic neighborhood parameter in PSO [16]. However, the author did not explicitly define the parameter and the algorithm is simulated with a general cost function. From the above discussion, we conclude that the effect of particle diversity in generating a good quality solution for UAV path planning requires more research attention. In our work, we introduced a dynamic neighborhood parameter named *nhbest* that increases the diversity in the particles and generates a better path for an autonomous UAV. We provided a comprehensive comparison with existing well-known versions of PSO used for UAV path planning. i.e. c-PSO [14], w-PSO [15].

3 Mathematical Model

3.1 Unmanned Ariel Vehicle (UAV)

A UAV can be classified as an autonomous robot that can move in a 3-Dimensional Space [17]. Let consider U represent UAV and S is a 3D terrain or search space where the UAV is going to move around at discrete time step t. The UAV at time state t can be expressed in 3-dimensional space and can be presented as $U_t = (x_t, y_t, z_t)$ where x_t, y_t represent axis position and z_t represent the altitude of the UAV at time t. However, the UAV flight dynamics is ignored in this work.

3.2 Environment

Defining the environment is an important part of UAV path planning. In this paper, we considered a 3D environment with multiple spherical static obstacles treated as a no-fly zone (NFZ). The environment is represented in a discrete form in the algorithm [18]. We consider a rectangular matrix $S \in R^3$ represented by $X \cdot Y \cdot Z$ where X and Y represent the x-axis and y-axis respectively and Z represent the altitude. Each cell is represented by $C = x_i, y_i, z_i$ where $x_i \in X$, $y_i \in Y$ and $z_i \in Z$. The NFZ is represented as follows:

$$NFZ = \begin{bmatrix} x_1 \; y_1 \; z_1 \; d_1 \\ x_2 \; y_2 \; z_2 \; d_2 \\ \dots\dots\dots\dots \\ x_n \; y_n \; z_n \; d_n \end{bmatrix} \tag{1}$$

where d_i represent the diameter of the ith object.

3.3 UAV Path

Path planning refers to generating the waypoints for UAVs. The waypoints are separated by equal time steps [12]. However, the discrete path generated by the algorithm is not follow-able by the UAV dynamics and kinematics. Therefore, the generated path needs to be smoothed before it is fed to the UAV flight controller. In this work, we used basis spline or bspline cubic interpolation formula with smoothing factor 0.2 to smooth the path generated by the algorithm [19]. The path is denoted by a matrix where each row represents the ith waypoint.

$$trajectory = \begin{bmatrix} x_1 \; y_1 \; z_1 \\ x_2 \; y_2 \; z_2 \\ \dots\dots\dots \\ x_n \; y_n \; z_n \end{bmatrix} \tag{2}$$

3.4 Cost Function

Defining the appropriate cost function is an import part of UAV path planning. The optimization algorithm finds the best solution based on the cost function. Optimization problem like TSP uses path length to find the shortest path that traverses all the cities. In the case of UAV path planning, the problem becomes more complex due to multiple constraints such as shortest path, obstacle avoidance, minimum altitude, sharp turn, etc. The algorithm searches for a solution with minimum cost. In this work, we have considered two constraints for UAV path planning i.e. shortest path and obstacle avoidance. We define our cost function as follows:

$$F_{cost} = C_{Path} + C_{NFZ} \tag{3}$$

where C_{Path} calculates the generated path length and C_{NFZ} penalize if the path collide with the no-fly zone. The path length is calculated using the following

Euclidean distance formula:

$$C_{Path} = \sum_{i=1}^{n-1} \sqrt{(x_{i+1} - x_i)^2 + (y_{i+1} - y_i)^2 + (z_{i+1} - z_i)^2} \tag{4}$$

where n is the number of waypoints generated, x_i, y_i, z_i are the axis position of UAV in 3D space. To evaluate whether the generated path collides with NFZ, we first calculate the distance from each waypoint from the NFZ center. If the distance is less than the diameter of the NFZ, then the function penalize heavily. The C_{NFZ} function is calculated using the following equations:

$$Collide = 1 - \sum_{i=1}^{n_{NFZ}} \frac{\sum_{j=1}^{n-1} \sqrt{(x_j - NFZ_i^x)^2 + (y_j - NFZ_i^y)^2 + (z_j - NFZ_i^z)^2}}{d_i} \tag{5}$$

$$C_{NFZ} = argMax(Collide, 0) \tag{6}$$

where NFZ_i^x, NFZ_i^y and NFZ_i^z are 3D center coordinate of ith NFZ, n_{NFZ} is total number of NFZ and d_i is the diameter of ith NFZ.

4 n-PSO for Path Planning

4.1 PSO Framework

PSO is a population-based evolutionary algorithm which was first introduced in [20]. The algorithm is inspired by animal common social behavior found in nature like as birds flock. The basic idea of PSO is as stated: *"people learn to make sense of the world by talking with other people about it"* [7]. The major advantage of PSO is simplicity and problem-solving ability. Since its introduction, PSO has been used in numerous applications for solving optimization problem. The idea of PSO is a number of candidate solutions called particles are taken into consideration and the position of each particle have been updated on the basis of particle best position (local best) and neighbors or swarms best (global best) position iteratively until all the particles converge to an optimal solution. More precisely we can describe that in PSO each particle has treated as a point in an N-dimensional space. The position of each particle is updated or adjusted on the basis of its flying experience and other particles flying experience. Each particle modifies its position on the basis of the information such as current position, current velocity, distance between particle best positions with the current position and distance between global best positions with the current position [14]. Let $P(t)$ is a population of n particles is a multidimensional space at time step t, where $P(t) = \{P_1(t), P_2(t), \ldots, P_i(t), \ldots, P_n(t)\}$. $P_i(t)$ is the ith particle in d-dimensional space at time step t, where $P_i(t) = \{X_{i,1}(t), X_{i,2}(t), \ldots, X_{i,d}(t)\}$ is ith particle position in d-dimensional space. The velocity of ith particle at time step t can be represented as $V_i(t) = \{V_{i,1}(t), V_{i,2}(t), \ldots, V_{i,d}(t)\}$. As outlined in [7], the equation for calculating the new position of ith particle $P_i(t)$ are as follows:

$$X_i(t+1) = X_i(t) + V_i(t+1) \tag{7}$$

$$V_i(t+1) = \omega(t)V_i(t) + c_1 r_1(P_l(t) - X_i(t)) + c_2 r_2(P_g(t) - X_i(t)) \tag{8}$$

where the terms are as follows:

- $V_i(t)$: Particle velocity at time t.
- $\omega(t)$: Inertia at time t.
- c_1 and c_2: Constants that used for personal influence and social influence respectively.
- r_1 and r_2: Random values between 0 and 1.
- $P_l(t)$: Particle local best.
- $P_g(t)$: Particle global best.

The value of $\omega(t)$ is calculated using the following formula:

$$\omega(t) = \omega_{max} - t \cdot \frac{\omega_{max} - \omega_{min}}{MaxIter} \tag{9}$$

where ω_{max}, ω_{min} and $MaxIter$ are final inertia, initial inertia and maximum number of iterations respectively. The particle local best position and global best position vector is computed using the following equations:

$$P_l(t) = \begin{cases} P_l(t-1) & \text{if } F_{cost}(X_i(t)) \geq F_{cost}P_l(t-1)) \\ X_i(t) & \text{if } F_{cost}(X_i(t)) \leq F_{cost}(P_l(t-1)) \end{cases} \tag{10}$$

$$P_g(t) = argmin_{P_l(t)} F_{cost}(P_l(t)) \tag{11}$$

4.2 Improved PSO

The two most well-known improvements of PSO are constriction factor PSO (c-PSO) [14] and time-varying inertia weight PSO (w-PSO) [15]. Both these methods are proposed to balance between two important characteristics of PSO algorithm i.e. exploitation and exploration. However, PSO still lacks particles diversity. Diversity in the particles is an important part of PSO in order to produce a good quality solution. In the proposed model called n-PSO, we introduced a new parameter based on the neighborhood approach proposed in [16]. The basic idea of our proposed algorithm is, instead to directly jump into the global best position; the particle creates a dynamic neighborhood and uses the neighborhood best position for exploration. The radius of the neighborhood is initially set to 1 and will increase linearly until all particles become a single neighborhood. As a result, the particles converge to the solution in a distributed manner and able to avoid local minima. The time-varying size of the neighborhood is calculated by the following equations:

$$nhsize = nhsize + \frac{N_{pop}}{MaxIt} \tag{12}$$

$$nhbest_i = min_{P_{nh_i}} F_{cost}(P_{nh_i}) \tag{13}$$

where $nhsize$, N_{pop} and $MaxIt$ are neighborhood size, total number of population and maximum number of iterations. The neighborhood best position can be calculated by equation no. (13) where P_{nh_i} is the particle position of ith neighborhood. The proposed algorithm is presented as follows:

Algorithm 1. n-PSO Algorithm

```
Create model with n static particles
Evaluate the cost based on initial particles position
Calculate the particle local best position P_l(t)
Set nhsize = 1 and update the nhbest_i from P_l(t)
Set the parameter ω_max, ω_min, c_1 and c_2
for It = 1 to MaxIter do,
    for i = 1 to N_pop do
        Calculate ω(t)
        Calculate particle velocity V_i(t)
        Calculate particle new position X_i(t + 1)
        Calculate the cost of particle new position F_cost
        Update particle local best position P_l(t)
        Update global best position P_g(t)
    for i = 1 to N_pop/nhsize do
        for nhp = 1 to nhsize do
            Evaluate nhbest_i
        Select the nhbest_i
    Update nhsize
Output the best path
```

5 Experiment and Discussion

We implemented our algorithm using Python 3.7 in a PC (CPU Core i5 3.3 GHz & RAM 8 GB). In the c-PSO algorithm, we have set the value of constriction factor (k) to 0.729 to generate better result [9]. In the w-PSO algorithm, the range of inertia weight (ω) is set from 0.6 to 0.2 [15]. In n-PSO, we kept the similar inertia parameter to incorporate the advantages of w-PSO. The value of c_1 and c_2 were set to 2.05 for c-PSO, 2.0 and 1.5 respectively in w-PSO and n-PSO. We first implemented the algorithm in a 2D environment. Figure 1, shows a 2D UAV path generated by the proposed n-PSO algorithm.

Table 1. Parameter settings for test cases.

Test case	Search space dimension	No. of NFZ	No. of populations	No. of iterations
1	20 × 20	9	100	100
2	20 × 20	9	200	150
3	40 × 40	15	100	100
4	40 × 40	15	200	150
5	60 × 60	20	100	100
6	60 × 60	20	200	150
7	80 × 80	30	100	100
8	80 × 80	30	200	150
9	100×100	40	100	100
10	100×100	40	200	150

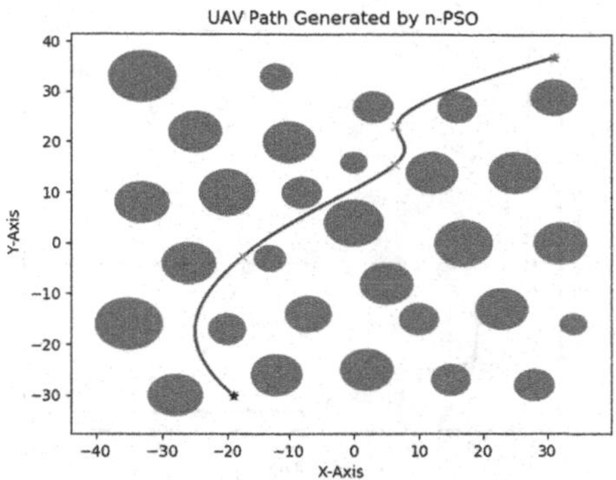

Fig. 1. A 2D UAV path generated by n-PSO algorithm

In order to compare the proposed algorithm with the other two algorithms, we have set 10 test cases for the simulation. We run each test cases 5 times for each of the algorithms and calculated the average best cost and diversity. The parameters for the test cases are given in Table 1. The performance of the proposed algorithm is presented in Table 2. In every case, n-PSO have generated a better solution than other two algorithms for UAV path planning. The improvement become more significant for larger search space size, number of iterations and number of populations.

Table 2. Comparison of different algorithm with respect to Best Cost.

Test case	c-PSO	w-PSO	n-PSO
1	20.565	20.507	20.451
2	20.465	20.557	20.453
3	67.256	49.169	45.515
4	59.571	42.031	39.966
5	90.811	63.839	62.929
6	68.895	64.940	57.845
7	114.045	94.864	94.494
8	103.443	93.145	91.761
9	140.929	138.029	136.131
10	135.557	134.456	120.599

In Fig. 2, a comparison is presented to show the convergence rate of the algorithms. From the figure, we can see that n-PSO converges slowly compared to both c-PSO and w-PSO. But, eventually it has converged to more accurate solution for an equal number of iterations. In order to measure the particles

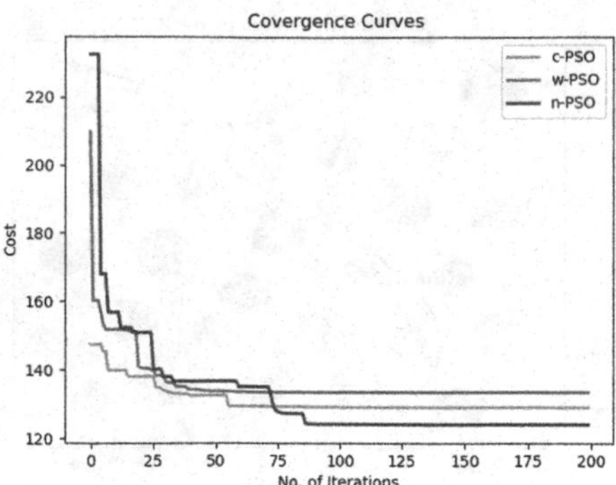

Fig. 2. Comparisons of n-PSO with c-PSO and w-PSO with respect to the convergence rate

diversity of the proposed algorithm, we used the following formula proposed by Olorunda [21]:

$$Diversity\ D(t) = \frac{1}{N_{pop}} \sum_{i=1}^{N_{pop}} \sqrt{\sum_{j=1}^{Dim} (x_{ij}(t) - \overline{x_j(t)})^2} \tag{14}$$

where N_{pop} is the total population size, $x_{ij}(t)$ is ith particle in j dimension and $\overline{x_j(t)}$ is average of jth dimension. The value of $\overline{x_j(t)}$ is can be calculated by following equation:

$$\overline{x_j(t)} = \frac{1}{N_{pop}} \sum_{i}^{N_{pop}} x_{ij} \tag{15}$$

In Table 3, we presented a comparison of particle diversity between n-PSO with others. It shows that the particles diversity of the proposed algorithm has increased significantly. The dynamic neighborhood approach prevent the algorithm to converge quickly to the global optima and increases the particles diversity. Figure 3 shows a comparison of particles diversity variation with respect to a number of iterations between three algorithms. It shows that the diversity in the particles has increased significantly in n-PSO.

In Fig. 4, we presented a time cost comparison of our proposed algorithm with the other two methods. From the figure, we can conclude that the new parameter did not put any significant computational load to the algorithm. Finally, we implement the n-PSO algorithm in a 3D environment with static obstacles. Figure 5 shows a UAV path generated by n-PSO in a 3D environment.

Table 3. Comparison of different algorithm with respect to Best Cost.

Test case	c-PSO	w-PSO	n-PSO
1	1.638	0.567	2.981
2	1.723	0.259	2.262
3	2.978	2.291	9.524
4	4.015	2.776	8.928
5	3.458	3.647	13.501
6	8.625	2.023	11.453
7	7.355	5.165	16.718
8	9.834	6.726	13.071
9	14.304	3.828	20.956
10	12.035	3.355	17.033

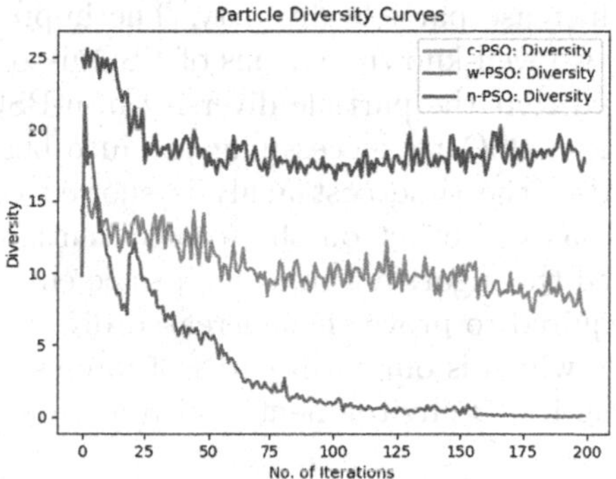

Fig. 3. Diversity variation versus no. of iterations

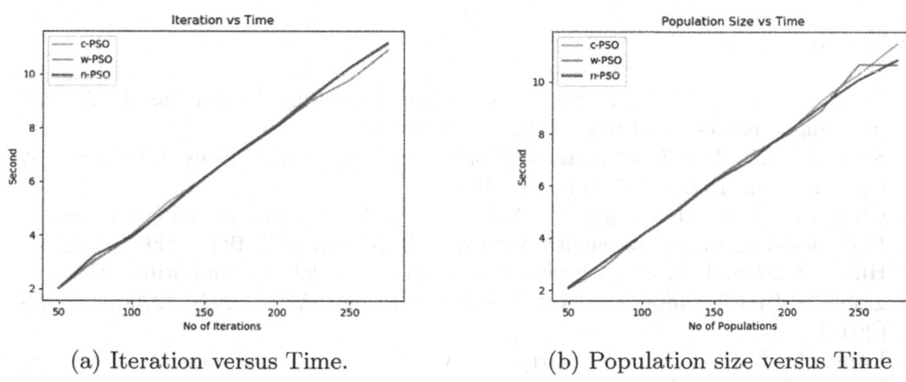

(a) Iteration versus Time.

(b) Population size versus Time

Fig. 4. Time cost analysis of n-PSO

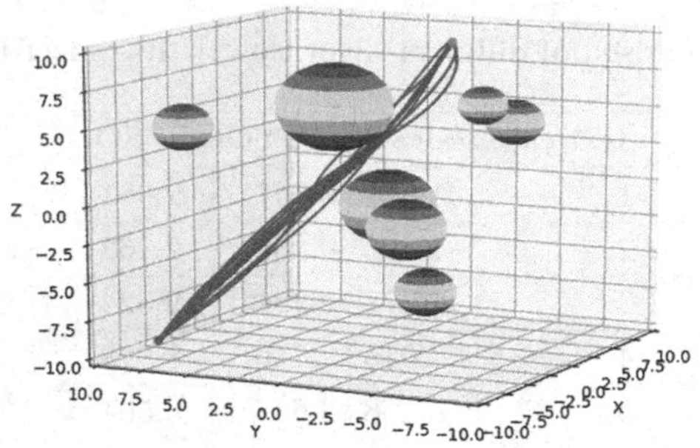

Fig. 5. An UAV path generated by n-PSO in 3D environment.

6 Conclusion

This paper presents a modified PSO based path planning solution for autonomous UAV in a 3D environment. A dynamic neighborhood-based approach is proposed to increase particle diversity. The improvement of the algorithm is verified with two well-known versions of PSO used for UAV path planning. The result showed that the particle diversity in n-PSO has increased significantly which enable n-PSO to successfully produce better UAV path than c-PSO and w-PSO. Also, the time cost analysis showed that the new parameter in the algorithm has less effect on the total execution time. However, we implemented and tested the algorithm in a small scale environment. Also, more rigorous analysis is required to prove that increased diversity in PSO will guarantee better UAV path which is our future area of interest. In addition to that, real-time path planning in 3D environment is also a key research area of UAV path planning.

Acknowledgment. This work is supported by Key Lab of Information Network Security, Ministry of Public Security, Shanghai 201804, China.

References

1. Zhao, Y., Zheng, Z., Liu, Y.: Survey on computational-intelligence-based UAV path planning. Knowl.-Based Syst. **158**, 54–64 (2018)
2. Sebbane, Y.B.: Intelligent Autonomy of UAVs: Advanced Missions and Future Use. Chapman and Hall/CRC, London (2018)
3. Cheng, Z., Wang, E., Tang, Y., Wang, Y.: Real-time path planning strategy for UAV based on improved particle swarm optimization. JCP **9**(1), 209–214 (2014)
4. Huang, C., Fei, J.: UAV path planning based on particle swarm optimization with global best path competition. Int. J. Pattern Recogn. Artif. Intell. **32**(06), 1859008 (2018)
5. BoussaïD, I., Lepagnot, J., Siarry, P.: A survey on optimization metaheuristics. Inf. Sci. **237**, 82–117 (2013)
6. Zhang, Y., Wang, S., Ji, G.: A comprehensive survey on particle swarm optimization algorithm and its applications. Math. Probl. Eng. **2015**, 1–38 (2015)

7. Kennedy, J.: Swarm intelligence. In: Zomaya, A.Y. (ed.) Handbook of Nature-Inspired and Innovative Computing, pp. 187–219. Springer, Boston (2006). https://doi.org/10.1007/0-387-27705-6_6
8. Zafar, M.N., Mohanta, J.: Methodology for path planning and optimization of mobile robots: a review. Procedia Comput. Sci. **133**, 141–152 (2018)
9. Pehlivanoğlu, Y.V.: A new particle swarm optimization method for the path planning of UAV in 3D environment. J. Aeronaut. Space Technol. **5**(4), 1–14 (2012)
10. Sanchez-Garcia, J., Reina, D., Toral, S.: A distributed PSO-based exploration algorithm for a UAV network assisting a disaster scenario. Future Gener. Comput. Syst. **90**, 129–148 (2019)
11. Tharwat, A., Elhoseny, M., Hassanien, A.E., Gabel, T., Kumar, A.: Intelligent Bézier curve-based path planning model using chaotic particle swarm optimization algorithm. Cluster Comput. **22**(2), 4745–4766 (2018). https://doi.org/10.1007/s10586-018-2360-3
12. Roberge, V., Tarbouchi, M., Labonté, G.: Comparison of parallel genetic algorithm and particle swarm optimization for real-time UAV path planning. IEEE Trans. Ind. Inform. **9**(1), 132–141 (2013)
13. Higashi, N., Iba, H.: Particle swarm optimization with Gaussian mutation. In: Proceedings of the 2003 IEEE Swarm Intelligence Symposium (SIS 2003) (Cat. No. 03EX706), pp. 72–79. IEEE (2003)
14. Clerc, M., Kennedy, J.: The particle swarm-explosion, stability, and convergence in a multidimensional complex space. IEEE Trans. Evol. Comput. **6**(1), 58–73 (2002)
15. Shi, Y., Eberhart, R.: A modified particle swarm optimizer. In: 1998 IEEE International Conference on Evolutionary Computation Proceedings. IEEE World Congress on Computational Intelligence (Cat. No. 98TH8360), pp. 69–73. IEEE (1998)
16. Suganthan, P.N.: Particle swarm optimiser with neighbourhood operator. In: Proceedings of the 1999 Congress on Evolutionary Computation (CEC 1999) (Cat. No. 99TH8406), vol. 3, pp. 1958–1962. IEEE (1999)
17. Howden, D.J.: Bushfire surveillance using dynamic priority maps and swarming unmanned aerial vehicles. Ph.D. thesis, Ph.D. dissertation, Swinburne University of Technology, Hawthorn, Victoria (2013)
18. Khan, A.: Coordinated unmanned aerial vehicles for surveillance of targets. Ph.D. thesis, Queen Mary University of London (2015)
19. Ravankar, A., Ravankar, A., Kobayashi, Y., Hoshino, Y., Peng, C.C.: Path smoothing techniques in robot navigation: state-of-the-art, current and future challenges. Sensors **18**(9), 3170 (2018)
20. Eberhart, R., Kennedy, J.: A new optimizer using particle swarm theory. In: Proceedings of the Sixth International Symposium on Micro Machine and Human Science (MHS 1995), pp. 39–43. IEEE (1995)
21. Olorunda, O., Engelbrecht, A.P.: Measuring exploration/exploitation in particle swarms using swarm diversity. In: 2008 IEEE Congress on Evolutionary Computation (IEEE World Congress on Computational Intelligence), pp. 1128–1134. IEEE (2008)

A New Approach to Solve Quadratic Equation Using Genetic Algorithm

Bibhas Roy Chowdhury[1], Md. Sabir Hossain[1(✉)], Alve Ahmad[1], Mohammad Hasan[2], and Md. Al-Hasan[2]

[1] Chittagong University of Engineering and Technology, Chittagong, Bangladesh
sabir.cse@cuet.ac.bd

[2] Bangladesh Army University of Science and Technology, Saidpur, Bangladesh

Abstract. Solving quadratic equation efficiently is a real-world challenge nowadays, due to its wide applications in the task of determining a product's profit, calculating areas or formulating the speed of an object. The general approach of finding the roots of a quadratic equation is not enough efficient due to the requirement of high computation time. Because of the Genetic Algorithm's stochastic characteristics and efficiency in solving problems it can be used to find roots of quadratic equation precisely. In modern athletics reducing the computation time of solving the quadratic equation has been so inevitable where using a genetic algorithm can find a quick solution that doesn't violate any of the constraints and with high precision also. Optimization has been done in the Crossover and Mutation process which has reduced the number of iterations for solving the equation. It reduces the time complexity of the existing approach of solving the quadratic equation and reaches towards the goal efficiently.

Keywords: Genetic algorithms · Crossover · Mutation · Chromosomal fitness · Population · Quadratic equation

1 Introduction

The approach we are going to follow to solve 2nd order linear equation is the Genetic Algorithm [2]. The Genetic Algorithm [2] is an efficient way to solve both unconstrained & constrained optimization problems that are based on natural selection. The Genetic Algorithm [2] repeatedly modifies a population of individual solutions. The basic features on which the Genetic Algorithm [2] stands are:

i) Competition in individual populations for resources and mates.
ii) Successful individuals are allowed to create more offspring.
iii) The propagation of the gene flows from fittest parent to generation.
iv) Survival of the fittest.

The basic outcome of the Genetic Algorithm [2] is a Chromosome and the collection of the chromosomes is known as a population. The process of the fitness function is

T. Bhuiyan et al. (Eds.): ICONCS 2020, LNICST 325, pp. 192–204, 2020.
https://doi.org/10.1007/978-3-030-52856-0_15

applied to chromosomes to check their stability and select them for going to the next stage. With the participation of selected chromosomes in the crossover stage, they produce offspring (child chromosomes) combining with the parent's gene. In the later stage, few chromosomes will undergo the mutation process. After that selected chromosomes which will shift to the next generation for a repeated procedure which will be determined from fitness value that indicates Darwin's theory of evolution [16]. After completing several generations following the above steps, the best and precise value of the mathematical equality problem can be gained. The whole process can be summarized by the following steps:

1. Initialization of random value to each chromosome
2. Evaluation of objective function
3. Selection based on fitness probability
4. Crossover the chromosomes
5. Mutation

We will go through these repeatedly until we get the best value of the chromosome. Hence, we find the best solution for each variable of the equation by finding the best fittest chromosome using the Genetic Algorithm [2].

There exists a local solution of generating two equations from the given quadratic equations containing the two roots and solving those which require severely increased computation time given a large Datasets and requires further data training. Another approach can be found the roots using all the coefficients of variables and constants of the equation and which is also inefficient when a root becomes imaginary. So using the genetic algorithm can be the best approach to overcome these limitations.

The sequential arrangement of the following part of this paper is as follows. Section 2 of the paper contains the background of related works. The proposed Genetic Algorithm model is described in Sect. 3. Section 4 contains implementation details. And Sect. 5 holds our experimental result. Section 6 gives the conclusion and lastly Sect. 7 finishes with all possible future works. Lastly, we included all the references we used.

2 Related Works

We adapted the idea of solving a quadratic equation in Nayak [1] using the Genetic Algorithm [2]. In this paper, they have used the generalized Schur form of genetic algorithm. To solve the 2nd order linear equation, they were limited to real-valued arithmetic & real-valued variables. So in their solutions, the probability to get a correct answer is high. By using the Hybridized Genetic Algorithm [3], their solution is not the most efficient one.

S. D. Bapon et al. [4] have shown improvement from the existing method using a new algorithm about solving a 1 st linear equation using a genetic algorithm. In their algorithm, they encoded solutions as chromosomes. It was presented by Roulette Wheel [5] in the selection after the process of evaluation. They also worked with the mutation rate to get the optimal solution more quickly.

Solving a linear equation using the evolutionary algorithm was also discussed in [6]. This paper also solved the equation but not as efficient as the previous method.

The even structural improvement in the genetic algorithm was discussed in [7]. These improvements assist in reducing complexity. A fixed point is also used in [12].

In the product recommendation system [8], U. Janjarassuk and S. Puengrusme provide a method to get the best guess for the crossover to increase efficiency. In this paper [9] they solved non-linear equations using a genetic algorithm. Their proposed technique is applied to the benchmark problem adopted from Grosan [10]. They have made a comparative analysis to substantiate the effectiveness and reliability of the proposed method in handling nonlinear systems which involved transcendental functions. Sensitivity analysis was also made to validate the selection of parameters of GA. We have also studied some optimization techniques using a genetic algorithm in [13–15].

3 Proposed Methodology

In most of the cases, we get optimal solutions from the genetic algorithm. It's because of some exclusive features of the genetic algorithm like adaptive characteristics. Mutation, crossover, and selection method are behind this algorithm's character.

3.1 Initial Population

The process begins with the Population which is nothing but a set of an individual. Individuals are a solution to the problem we want to solve. An individual is characterized by a set of parameters (variables) known as Genes. Genes are joined into a string to form a Chromosome (solution). In a genetic algorithm, the individual's set of genes is represented, in terms of an alphabet, using a string. Most of the time binary values are used (a string of 1 s and 0 s). First, we encode the gene in a chromosome then we decode it before evaluating their fitness. Only the fittest chromosomes move to the next generation (Fig. 1).

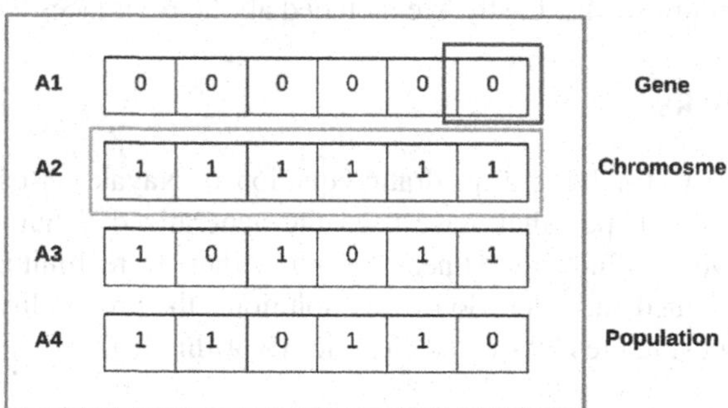

Fig. 1. Initial population.

3.2 Fitness Evaluation

Evaluation Function also is known as the Fitness Function finds how close is a given solution compared to the optimum solution of the problem. How much fit a solution is stated by it. Each of the solutions is generally represented by a chromosome as a string of binary numbers in the Genetic Algorithm. We have to test these chromosomes and come up with the best solution to solve a given problem. Each of the problems has its fitness function. The fitness function is used depends on the given problem. In our problem the fitness function that we have considered is (Fig. 2):

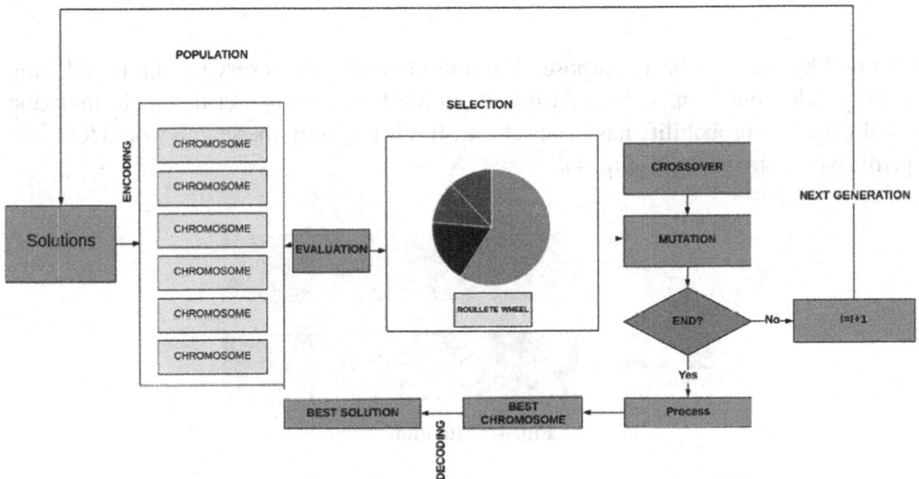

Fig. 2. The methodology of our proposed system.

$$\text{Func\_fit} = \frac{1}{1 + \text{objective function}}$$

3.3 Cross-Over

Here "par_chromosome" chromosome will be selected as parent chromosome. Here, the set of randomized numbers Random [par_chromosome] < ρc will be selected. Now, as the crossover rate is set to 35% so randomly taken chromosomes which are less than 0.35 are selected for crossover (Fig. 3).

3.4 Mutation

In the mutation process, a significant change in the chromosome has been done.

Here, Total gene = number of genes in Chromosome × the number of populations. The mutation is a process of change and so if the mutation rate or changing rate is kept low (in a range of 0.01 to 0.1) than it provides the fittest result. The mutation rate 12

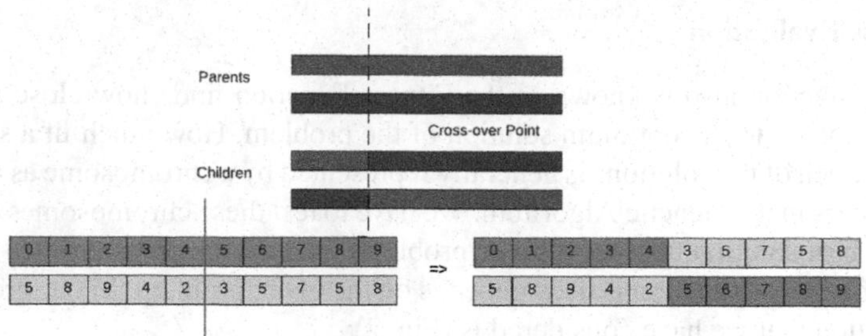

Fig. 3. Cross-over [11].

is defined by ρm. The basic purpose of mutation in GAs is preserving and introducing diversity. The mutation is done during evolution based on a user-definable mutation probability. The probability has to be set low. If it is too high, the search would turn into a primitive random search (Fig. 4).

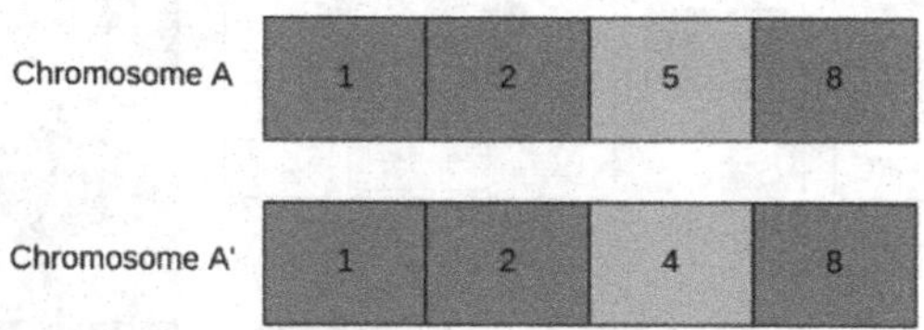

Fig. 4. Mutation.

The Pseudocode for Genetic Algorithm. The parameters of our genetic algorithm are the initial population, Max-Iteration, Best fitness, Max-fitness.

```
1: Generation =0
2: Initialize Population
3: While Generation < Max Generation
4:      Evaluate fitness of population members
5:          for i to 1 to elitist
5.1:            Select best individual
5.2:        end for
6:          for i from elites to population_ size
6.1.1:          for j to 1 from tournament size
6.1.2:              select best parents
6.1.3:          end for
6.1.4:      end for
6.2.1:      for k from elites to population_size * (1-mutation rate)
6.2.2:              crossover parents → child  (Just add this tick mark)
6.3.1:          for k from population_size*(1-mutation rate) to population_size
6.3.2:          mutant parents → child
6.3.3:      end for
6.2:            insert child for next generation's population
6.3:        end for
7:      update current population
8:      generation ++
9: end while
```

4 Implementation Details

Let, there is a quadratic equation to be like $x^2 - 8x + 15 = 0$. Here, the Genetic algorithm is used to find the root of the equation x1 and x2. Five steps will be needed such as initialization, evaluation, selection, crossing over and mutation to execute the whole process.

4.1 Initialization

At first, we take the total number of 6 chromosomes as the initial population. Then, we initialize the random values of gene x1 in each chromosome.

Chromo [1] = [x1] = [00000010]
Chromo [2] = [x1] = [00000100]
Chromo [3] = [x1] = [00000110]
Chromo [4] = [x1] = [00000111]
Chromo [5] = [x1] = [00001001]
Chromo [6] = [x1] = [00001000]

It can be decoded as follows:

Chromo [1] = [x1] = [2]

Chromo [2] = [x1] = [4]
Chromo [3] = [x1] = [6]
Chromo [4] = [x1] = [7]
Chromo [5] = [x1] = [9]
Chromo [6] = [x1] = [8]

4.2 Evaluation

In this step of evaluation, the value of the objective function for each chromosome is computed.

Func_Objective[1] = $\text{Abs}(2^2 - 2 * 8 + 15) = 3$
Func_Objective[2] = $\text{Abs}(4^2 - 4 * 8 + 15) = 1$
Func_Objective[3] = $\text{Abs}(6^2 - 6 * 8 + 15) = 3$
Func_Objective[4] = $\text{Abs}(7^2 - 7 * 8 + 15) = 8$
Func_Objective[5] = $\text{Abs}(9^2 - 9 * 8 + 15) = 24$
Func_Objective[6] = $\text{Abs}(8^2 - 8 * 8 + 15) = 15$

In the next generation, the fittest chromosomes with higher probability will get selected. To determine fitness probability at first, we determine the fitness function of each chromosome. Then, 1 will be divided by (the objective function of each chromosome + 1) to get the fitness probability.

Func_Fit [1] = 1/(1 + **Func_ objective** [1]) = 1/4 = .25
Func_Fit [2] = 1/(1 + **Func_ objective** [2]) = 1/2 = .5
Func_Fit [3] = 1/(1 + **Func_ objective** [3]) = 1/4 = .25
Func_Fit [4] = 1/(1 + **Func_ objective** [4]) = 1/9 = .11
Func_Fit [5] = 1/(1 + **Func_ objective** [5]) = 1/25 = .04
Func_Fit [6] = 1/(1 + **Func_ objective** [6]) = 1/16 = .0625
Total = 1.212

The rule for determining probability of each chromosome is:

Probability[i] = Func_Fit[i] / Total

Probability [1] = .25 / 1.212 = .206	**Probability** [4] = .11/ 1.212 = .090
Probability [2] = .5/ 1.212 = .412	**Probability** [5] = .04 / 1.212 = .033
Probability [3] = .25 / 1.212= .206	**Probability** [6] = 0.0625 / 1.212 = .0515

Seeing the above probabilities, it is seen that Chromo [2] has the highest probability of going to the next generation. A roulette wheel is used for this selection procedure. For the computation in the roulette wheel, we should compute the values of cumulative probability.

C_Probability [1] = .206
C_Probability [2] = 0.206 + .412 = .618
C_Probability [3] = 0.206 + .412 +.206 = .824

C_Probability [4] = 0.206 + .412 +.206 + .090 = .914
C_Probability [5] = 0.206 + .412 +.206 + .090 +.033 = .947
C_Probability [6] = 0.206 + .412 +.206 + .090 +.033 +.0515 = .9985

By calculating the cumulative probability of selection step using roulette wheel can be done to generate random number Random which range is in between 0–1 as given below

Random [1] = .822	**Random** [4] = 0.943
Random [2] = 0.912	**Random** [5] = 0.201
Random [3] = 0.823	**Random** [6] = 0.610

If for example generated a random number is greater than C_Probability [1] and smaller than C_Probability [3] then select Chromo [3] as a chromosome for next generation in the existing population.

New_Chromo[1] = **Chromo**[3]	**New_Chromo**[4] = **Chromo**[5]
New_Chromo[2] = **Chromo**[4]	**New_Chromo**[5] = **Chromo**[1]
New_Chromo[3] = **Chromo**[3]	**New_Chromo**[6] = **Chromo**[2]

Now, the existing chromosomes in the population look like given below:

Chromo [1] = [6]	**Chromo** [4] = [9]
Chromo [2] = [7]	**Chromo** [5] = [2]
Chromo [3] = [6]	**Chromo** [6] = [4]

4.3 Cross-Over

The crossover process generally helps to cut a chromosome by selecting a cutting point randomly and joining another chromosome at that point. This process is restrained by using a parameter called crossover-rate which is expressed by ρc.

Here "par_chromosome" chromosome will be selected as parent chromosome. Here, the set of randomized numbers Random [par_chromosome] < ρc will be selected. Now, the crossover rate will be set to 35%. Now the process will be initialized as follows.

At first, a random number Random is generated as the number of population

Random [1] = 0.069
Random [2] = 0.172
Random [3] = 0.679
Random [4] = 0.437
Random [5] = 0.312
Random [6] = 0.826

Now it is clear that, as Random [1], Random [2], Random [5] have the values less than ρc. So, Chromo [1], Chromo [2] and Chromo [5] are selected for crossing over process.

Chromo [1] >< **Chromo** [2]
Chromo [2] >< **Chromo** [5]
Chromo [5] >< **Chromo** [1]

Now three crossover constants will be selected randomly for three cutting point of three chromosomes. So,

Cut_point [1] = 0
Cut_point [2] = 0
Cut_point [3] = 0

Then for crossover, crossover, parent's gens will be cut at gen number 1, e.g.

Chromo [1] >< **Chromo** [2] = [6] >< [7] = [7]
Chromo [2] >< **Chromo** [5] = [7] >< [2] = [2]
Chromo [5] >< **Chromo** [1] = [2] >< [6] = [6]

After crossover process, the chromosomes are,

Chromo [1] = [7]
Chromo [2] = [2]
Chromo [3] = [6]
Chromo [4] = [9]
Chromo [5] = [6]
Chromo [6] = [4]

4.4 Mutation

In the mutation process, a significant change in the chromosome has been done.

Total gene = number of genes in Chromosome * the number of populations = 1 * 6 = 6 The mutation is a process of change and so if the mutation rate or changing rate is kept low (in a range of 0.01 to 0.1) than it provides the fittest result. The mutation rate is defined by ρm. Here mutation rate is defined 10% (0.1). So, 10% of the total gen will be mutated. So, number of mutations will be = 0.10 * 6 = .6 ≈ 1

So, after mutation in the 3rd chromosome which was randomly chosen, the chromosomes will look like this,

Chromo [1] = [7] **Chromo** [4] = [9]
Chromo [2] = [2] **Chromo** [5] = [6]
Chromo [3] = **[1]** **Chromo** [6] = [4]

After mutation, the objective function will be again evaluated by following,

For **Chromo** [1] = [7],
Func_ objective [1] = Abs $(7^2 - 8 * 7 + 15) = 8$
For **Chromo** [2] = [2]
Func_ objective [2] = Abs $(2^2 - 8 * 2 + 15) = 3$
For **Chromo** [3] = [1]
Func_ objective [3] = Abs $(1^2 - 8 * 1 + 15) = 8$
For **Chromo** [4] = [9]
Func_ objective [4] = Abs $(9^2 - 8 * 9 + 15) = 24$
For **Chromo** [5] = [6]
Func_ objective [6] = Abs $(6^2 - 8 * 6 + 15) = 3$
For **Chromo** [6] = [4]
Func_ objective [5] = Abs $(4^2 - 8 * 4 + 15) = 1$

From this evaluation is clear that the objective functions are decreasing in some cases and the lowest value of an objective function will be considered much fitter.

Hereafter 1st iteration fitter Chromosome is: **Chromo [6]** = [4]

And this fitter chromosome will undergo the same process of this algorithm. After the next iteration, the value of fitness function will be decreased and after running 6 generations, the fittest chromosome will be obtained for which related objective function becomes 0. So fittest chromosome is: **Chromo** = [5]

After decoding the answer, the result will be transformed like as follows

Chromo = [00000101]

It is expressed that x1 = 5
Now if the value of x is put in the equation
x1 + x2 = −b/a (Where a & b are coefficients of x^2 & x)
or, 5 + x2 = 8 (as b = −8 and a = 1)
or, x2 = 3
Now, (x1, x2) = (5,3)
For justification F(x) = $x^2 - 8x + 15$
Then F(5) = $5^2 - 8 * 5 + 15 = 0$
F(3) = $3^2 - 8 * 3 + 15 = 0$
So it is clear that the value of these variables generated by GA satisfies the mathematical equality.

5 Experimental Result and Complexity Analysis

5.1 Execution Time Comparison

Results obtained by implementing our proposed algorithm are shown in Table 1. Table 1 shows variations in runtime when ran for three consecutive times.

The total number of generations depends on the number of randomly taken chromosomes. In our implementation, the results we found are shown in Table 2. This table shows changes in generations which are depending on the number of random values.

Table 1. Data table for execution time.

Equations	Execution Time 1st run (second)	Execution Time 2nd run (second)	Execution Time 3rd run (second)
$x^2 - 8x + 15$	0.92	3.277	1.028
$x^2 - 7x + 12$	0.934	2.857	1.011
$x^2 - 2.5x + 1$	2.014	2.995	2.012
$x^2 - 3x + 2$	1.384	3.055	1.023
$x^2 - x - 2$	0.873	3.265	2.995

Table 2. Data table for generations.

Number of random values	Generations
6	6
8	8
5	5
4	4
3	3

As the genetic algorithm moves towards the solution by consecutive crossovers and mutations among the chromosomes so it shows variable execution time for a fixed code, the execution time can be much lower or much higher when we run a single time. So as genetic algorithm code has no specific execution time therefore the efficiency of using the algorithm cannot be compared with other existing methods (Fig. 5).

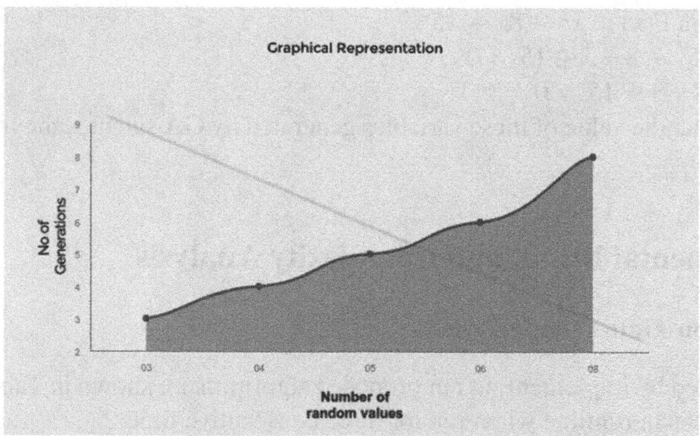

Fig. 5. Graphical representation for given data.

As total no of generation = number of genes in Chromosome * number of populations, a total number of generations and the number of initial population was found the same in our implementation.

5.2 Complexity Analysis

The time complexity of Genetic algorithm depends on three parameters-

1. Fitness function.
2. Selection operator.
3. Variation operator

Among the three parameters, it mainly depends on the fitness function. If the time complexity of GA is evaluated with Big O notation, then it can be O(NG), where N is the size of population and G stands for the number of iterations. On the other hand, if we assume N be the size of the population and L be the length of the genotypes, then for a simple Rastrigin function, the time complexity for the evaluation of the whole generation will be O(NL). If the selection is stochastic then it is needed to sort the population. In this case, time complexity will be O(NlogN), while for tournament selection it will be O(N). If the population is transformed with a crossover and mutation operator, then time complexity will be O(NL).

5.3 Best and Worst-Case Complexity

In Table 1, we have taken several equations and found their computation time. We can see for $x^2 - 8x + 15 = 0$ equation on 1st Run the computation time was least. The reason behind it was the requirement of a few steps of the crossover and mutation process to find out the required root.

On the other hand, in Table 1, for the same equation's 2nd run, the computation time was highest. The only reason was it took a lot of steps in the crossover and mutation process to find the final roots. These were the best and worst time complexity for this implementation.

6 Conclusion

To find an efficient solution of a quadratic equation within acceptable time form was our primary focus of this work. We compared our proposed genetic algorithm approach with an existing method of solving equations. After numerous analysis, we have to come in the conclusion that GAs has an upper-hand for obtaining a solution. After further considering the obtained result and CPU times and comparing them with other based known existing solutions of solving a quadratic equation it can be stated that the GA based proposed approach performs well and much more efficiently.

7 Future Work

In the future, there is a scope for working on crossing over rate. We were not getting expected outcome when both of the roots are imaginary, negative or fractional. So the future recommendation is to implement the solving technique of second and higher-order equations using GA considering these things also.

References

1. Nayak, T.: Solution to quadratic equation using genetic algorithm. In: Proceedings of National Conference on AIRES, Andhra University (2012)
2. Holland, J.H.: Genetic algorithms. Sci. Am. **267**, 66–72 (1992)
3. Li, K., Jia, L., Shi, X.: An efficient hybridized genetic algorithm. In: Proceedings of IEEE International Conference of Safety Produce Informatization (IICSPI 2018), pp. 118–121 (2019)
4. Bapon, S.D, Hossain, M.S., Fahad, M.N.: Improvement of solving first order linear equations by adopting genetic algorithm. Unpublished Undergraduate Thesis, Chittagong University of Engineering & Technology, Chattorgram, Bangladesh, February 2019
5. Rodríguez, A., Mendes, B.: Probability, Decisions and Games. Wiley, Hoboken (2018)
6. Bashir, L.Z.: Solve simple linear equation using evolutionary algorithm. World Sci. News **19**, 148–167 (2015)
7. Chen, T.Y., Chen, C.J.: Improvements of simple genetic algorithm in structural design. Int. J. Numer. Meth. Eng. **40**, 1323–1334 (1997)
8. Janjarassuk, U., Puengrusme, S.: Product recommendation based on genetic algorithm. In: 5th International Conference on Engineering, Applied Sciences and Technology (ICEAST), Luang Prabang, Laos, pp. 1–4 (2019)
9. Uddin, M., Mangla, C., Ahmad, M.: Solving system of nonlinear equations using genetic algorithm. J. Comput. Math. Sci. **10**(4), 877–886 (2019)
10. Grosan, C., Abraham, A.: A new approach for solving nonlinear equations systems. IEEE Trans. Syst. Man Cybern. - Part A: Syst. Hum. **38**(3), 698–714 (2008)
11. Riazi, A.: Genetic algorithm and a double-chromosome implementation to the traveling salesman problem. SN Appl. Sci. **1**, 1397 (2019). https://doi.org/10.1007/s42452-019-1469-1
12. Rovira, A., Valdés, M., Casanova, J.: A new methodology to solve non-linear equation systems using genetic algorithms. Int. J. Numer. Meth. Eng. **63**, 1424–1435 (2005)
13. Zhang, Y., Jin, W., Hu, Z., Chan, C.W.: A genetic-algorithms-based approach for programming linear and quadratic optimization problems with uncertainty. J. Math. Probl. Eng. **12**, 1024–123X (2013)
14. Tsutsui, S., Fujimoto, N.: Solving quadratic assignment problems by genetic algorithms with GPU computation: a case study. In: Genetic and Evolutionary Computation Conference (GECCO 2009), pp. 2523–2530 (2009). https://doi.org/10.1145/1570256.1570355
15. Sheta, A., Turabieh, H.: A comparison between genetic algorithms and sequential quadratic programming in solving constrained optimization problems. ICGST Int. J. Artif. Intell. Mach. Learn. (AIML) **6**, 67–74 (2006)
16. Darwin, C.: On the origin of the species. Darwin **5**, 386 (1859)

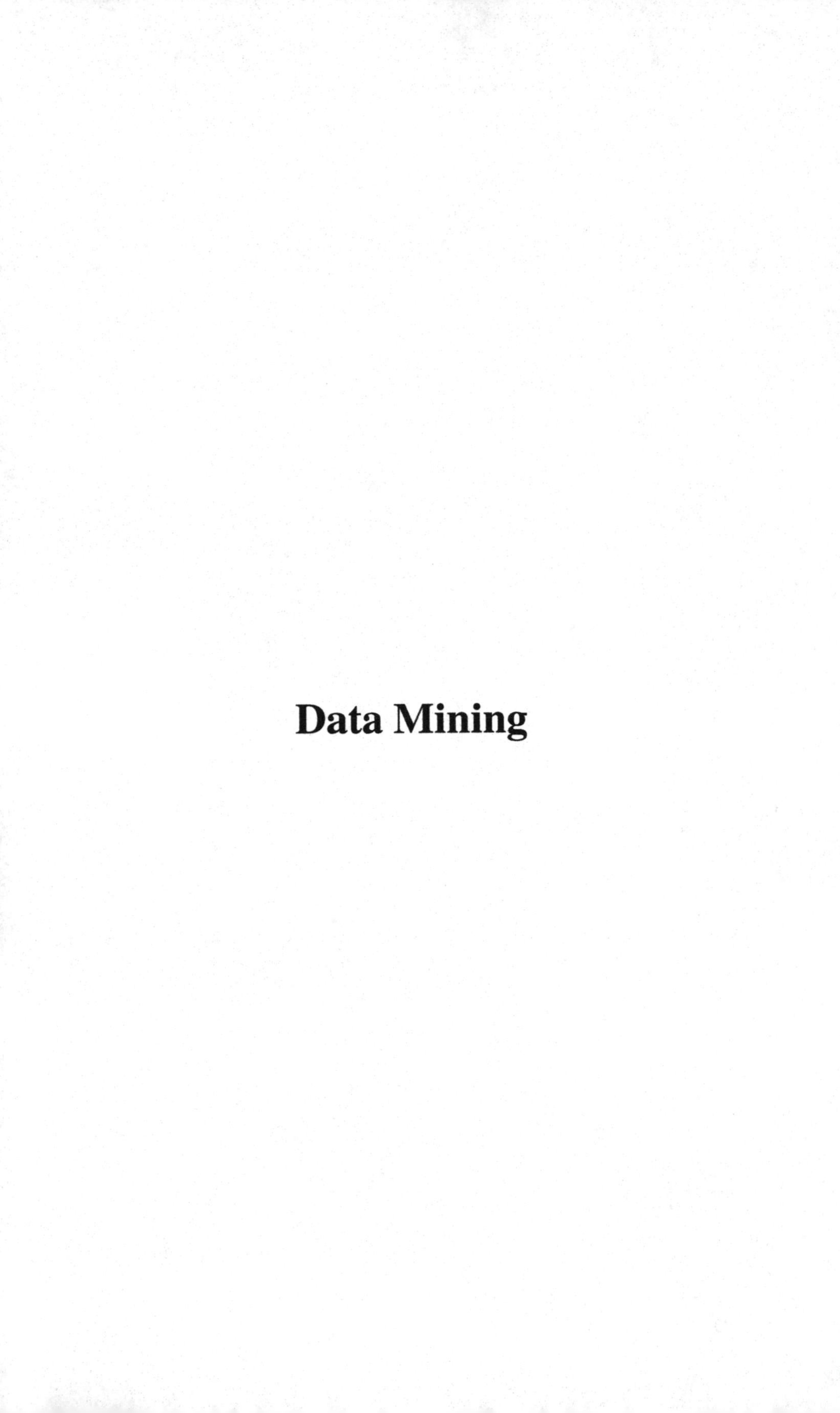

Data Mining

Link Prediction on Networks Created from UEFA European Competitions

Oğuz Findik([✉]) and Emrah Özkaynak

Karabük University, Karabük, Turkey
oguzfindik@karabuk.edu.tr

Abstract. Link prediction is widely used in network analysis to identify future links between nodes. Link prediction has an important place in terms of being applicable to many real-world networks with dynamic structure. Networks with dynamic structure, such as social networks, scientific collaboration networks and metabolic networks, are networks in which link prediction studies are performed. In addition, it is seen that there are few studies showing the feasibility of link prediction by creating networks from different areas. In this study, in order to show the applicability of link prediction processes in different fields link prediction was made by applying traditional link prediction methods in the networks formed from the data of football competitions played after the groups between the years 2004–2017 in the UEFA European League. The AUC metric was used to measure the success of forecasting. The results show that link prediction methods can be used in sports networks.

Keywords: Link prediction · Data mining · Complex network

1 Introduction

Nowadays, the interaction between people, objects and events is increasing due to the increase in the variety and use of communication tools. The components of this interaction that occur in daily life form a network structure. In recent years, complex network science has become one of the popular disciplines, dealing with the analysis of information from the structure of networks. The growing interest in complex network science is rooted in the growing number of applications developed in various biological, sociological, technological and communication fields, and the availability of large amounts of real data suitable for complex network analysis [1–6]. Detection of connection types in the network [7–9], detection of central nodes [10–13] and prediction of possible future links [14–19] are important areas of study in complex network analysis.

The link prediction in the complex networks includes the detection of missing links based on the attributes of the observed links and nodes and the information obtained from the structural features of the complex network, or the prediction of new links that may occur in the future [20, 21].

In complex networks, it is possible to predict the links that are not available, using the properties of the determined nodes. The important point here is to find out the

T. Bhuiyan et al. (Eds.): ICONCS 2020, LNICST 325, pp. 207–217, 2020.
https://doi.org/10.1007/978-3-030-52856-0_16

relationship between the nodes and to determine the effect of the properties of the nodes on the formation of links in the network. Because it is possible that new nodes will be added to the network and there will be ruptures in the existing relations as well as the possibility of new relationships in the network. The dynamic structure of complex networks makes it difficult to make successful prediction procedures [22]. Actually, the link prediction is based on an analysis of the existing network structure. The more accurate this analysis and the relationships between the nodes can be determined as having the correct and distinctive features, the greater the accuracy of the prediction. When analyzing a complex network in terms of link prediction, the accuracy of the prediction of the link between the nodes as well as the occurrence of its type and weight should be taken into account [23]. A number of link prediction methods based on network structures have been proposed in previous years [14–19].

Link prediction methods are applied in the networks created in any area where the components it contains interact with each other. Nowadays, link prediction methods are used for e-commerce suggestion in online shopping sites [26], friendship suggestion in social networks [27, 28] and filtering systems [24, 25] that work like a advice system for the areas that users need. In addition, link prediction can be applied to evaluate the models of a network that is continuously expanding, and successful results are obtained [29]. Another area of study in which link prediction is applied has been to analyze the networks of scientific collaboration and to uncover authors who are eligible to co-author [30, 31].

In this study, unlike the prediction studies in the previous years, the applicability of traditional link prediction methods in the networks formed from football competitions was investigated. Traditional link prediction methods were applied, and networks were predicted from the data of football competitions played after the groups in the UEFA Europa League between 2004 and 2017. The AUC metric was used to measure the success of the predicted results [32]. AUC results show that traditional link prediction methods can be used to predict future events in networks generated from football competitions.

In the second part of the study, the traditional link prediction methods used in the experimental study and the AUC which is the link prediction evaluation criterion are explained. In the third part of the study, the experimental study is explained in detail. In the fourth part of the study, the results of the experimental study are evaluated. In the fifth part of the study, the results are discussed.

2 Methods

In link prediction studies, neighborhood-based methods can be easily applied in many of the complex networks due to the use of information from the common neighbors of the nodes and this can produce successful results, depending on the width of the data sets available. Looking at what some of the criteria used in neighborhood-based link methods mean.

- $\Gamma(x)$ is the cluster of neighbors of the node x in the complex network.
- $|\Gamma(x)|$ is the degree of the node x (number of neighbors) in the complex network.

2.1 Common Neighbor

Suppose Γ(x) is cluster of x's neighbors and Γ(y) is cluster of y's neighbors. This method concludes that the greater the number of common neighbors between the node x and node y, the higher the probability of a link between them [14].

$$S_{xy} = |\Gamma(x) \cap \Gamma(y)| \tag{1}$$

2.2 Jaccard Index

This method is used to predict the link as a method derived from data mining. The probability of the link between the two nodes is calculated by dividing the number of common neighbors of the nodes by the total number of neighbors [15].

$$S_{xy} = \frac{|\Gamma(x) \cap \Gamma(y)|}{|\Gamma(x) \cup \Gamma(y)|} \tag{2}$$

2.3 Preferential Attachment

Preferential attachment index is used in non-scalable growing networks. The probability of a new link to node X is proportional to Γ(x). The probability of link between the node x and node y is proportional to Γ(x) * Γ(y). The higher the number of links for a node, the higher the probability of a new link to that node in the future. The possibility of a link between the two nodes is directly proportional to the number of adjacent nodes in the network [16].

In unweighted networks, Preferential Attachment Index Similarity Criteria are calculated as in Eq. 3:

$$S_{xy} = \Gamma(x) * \Gamma(y) \tag{3}$$

2.4 Adamic-Adar Index

This method calculates the common neighbors by giving more value to less connected nodes. Γ(x) indicates the degree of the common neighbor which means node z, that is how many nodes are bound to the node [17].

In unweighted networks, Adamic-Adar Similarity Criterion is calculated as in Eq. 4:

$$S_{xy} = \sum_{z \in \Gamma(x) \cap \Gamma(y)} \frac{1}{log(|\Gamma(z)|)} \tag{4}$$

2.5 Resource Allocation Index

Resource Allocation Index is used in complex networks to measure links between pairs of nodes that are not directly linked to each other. Although there is no link between the nodes, the nodes provide transmission between their common neighbors. Each node providing the transmission has a resource unit and distributes it to its neighbors evenly. The similarity between these nodes is calculated according to the sources they receive from each other [18].

$$S_{xy} = \sum_{z \in \Gamma(x) \cap \Gamma(y)} \frac{1}{k_z} \tag{5}$$

2.6 Sorenson Index

This method is similar to Jaccard. The Sorensen index is calculated as the ratio of multiplying the sum of the common neighbors (x) and (y) by 2 to the sum of Γ(x) and Γ(y) [19].

$$S_{xy} = \frac{2|\Gamma(x) \cap \Gamma(y)|}{k_a + k_b} \tag{6}$$

2.7 Link Predicted Assessment Criteria (AUC)

Measurements such as success, error, accuracy and error rate are used to measure errors of link prediction methods. Accuracy is determined by the ratio of the correct classified samples to the total number of samples, while the error rate is obtained by dividing the number of errors by the total number of samples.

A ROC curve is a curve in which the ratio of false positives (1-specificity) on the vertical axis and true positives (sensitivity) on the vertical axis for different thresholds. Each point on the ROC curve shows the sensitivity and 1-specificity values corresponding to different threshold values. In general, threshold values giving low false positivity rates also have a low true positivity rate. The results with high true positive rate and low false positive rate are called successful results. The level of success decreases as the ROC curve approaches the 'false positive rate' axis. A single value of the success of the system is expressed by the area under the ROC curve (AUC). The greater the value of this field, the higher the reliability value of the system [32]. The AUC is calculated as in Eq. 7:

$$\frac{n' + 0.5n''}{n} \tag{7}$$

Where n' is the number in which we select a random pair of links from the missing link set and the unconnected link set. If the score is obtained from an independent and the same distribution, the AUC value will be 0.5. Therefore, the degree of AUC exceeding 0.5 indicates how good the predicts are by chance.

3 Experimental Study

Link prediction methods are generally applied intensively on social networks and interaction networks. So, there are few studies that measure the performance of these methods in dynamic networks in different areas. Therefore, evaluation of the performance of link prediction methods in different networks such as sports network [5, 6] is the basis of this study. In addition, another aim of the study is evaluating the usability of link prediction methods against difficulties in calculating the probability of future encounter between teams in sports competitions. The general steps of the experimental study are shown in Fig. 1.

3.1 Dataset and Pre-processing

In the experimental study, in order to measure the applicability of traditional link prediction methods in sports networks, networks were created from the UEFA Europa League matches given in Table 1 with the number of nodes and links. The teams that compete in the created networks form the nodes. The matches that the teams have made with each other form the links. The network formed consists of unweighted and undirect links.

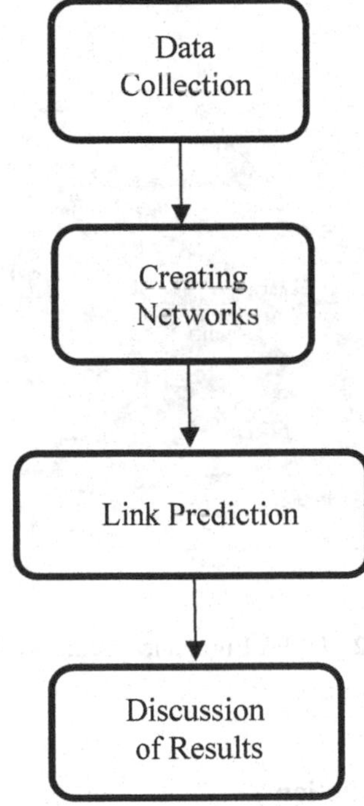

Fig. 1. The general steps of the experimental study

Table 1. Nodes and links for the UEFA Europa league network.

	All rounds
Nodes	154
Edges	388

3.2 Creating Networks

The UEFA Europa League network shown in Fig. 2 was created using the nodes and links given in Table 1. The higher the number of nodes and links in the networks, the more complex the visualization of the network and the intelligibility of the data to be obtained. Therefore, various applications are used in order to make the data obtained from nodes and links accurate and understandable and to visualize the network. Therefore, the data obtained from nodes and links must be accurate and understandable. Various applications are used to visualize the network with these data. In this study, Gephi [33] software was preferred for obtaining data from the network and visualizing the network. Gephi software is one of the most preferred software both in terms of being open source and because of its high performance in analyzing data accurately and comprehensively and in visualizing the network.

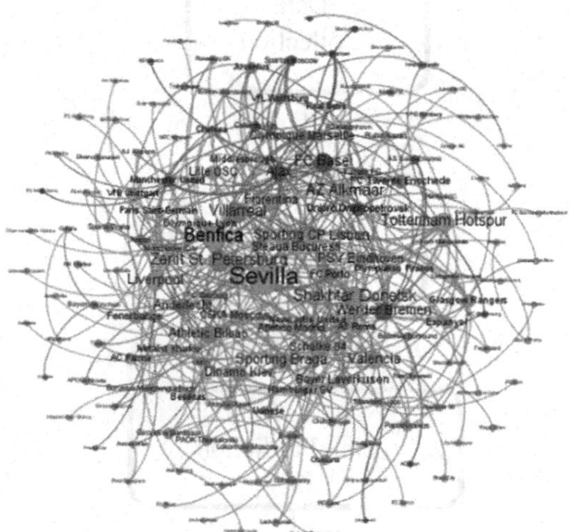

Fig. 2. UEFA Europa league network

3.3 Application of Link Prediction

In the experimental study, 4 different unweighted and undirect networks were formed including the period of 2004–2007, 2007–2010, 2007–2013, 2004–2013 for the training network using the UEFA Europa League [34] football competitions between 2004–2017. For the test networks, the four-year periods following the established networks were used. After establishing training and test networks, Common Neighbor, Jaccard Index, Preferential Attachment Index, Adamic-Adar Index, Resource Allocation Index and Sorenson Index methods were applied.

4 Results and Discussion

4.1 Network Formed Between 2004–2007

While the network established between 2004–2007 was used for training, competitions in 2008, 2009, 2010 and 2011 were used as test networks. The dataset used in the study is shown in Table 2 and the results obtained are shown in Table 3.

Table 2. Nodes and links created for the years 2004–2007 network.

	2004–2007
Nodes	13
Links	20

Table 3. Link prediction AUC results in network created between 2004–2007

	2008	2009	2010	2011
Common Neighbor	0,304	0,437	0,494	0,504
Jaccard Index	0,391	**0,531**	**0,615**	**0,627**
Adamic Adar	0,314	0,491	0,530	0,541
Preferential Attachment	**0,435**	0,470	0,603	0,615
Sorenson Index	0,261	0,390	0,434	0,443
Resource Allocation Index	0,323	0,344	0,432	0,441

Table 3 shows that although the prediction results are not successful enough, the higher the test data, the higher the predictive success. Among the traditional methods of link prediction, the Jaccard Index seems to be more successful than the other methods. The fact that the prediction results are not successful enough is due to the fact that the training and test networks in the data set used are in a short time period.

4.2 Network Formed Between 2007–2010

While the network created between 2007–2010 was used for training, the competitions that took place in 2011, 2012, 2013, 2014 were used as test networks for link prediction. The dataset used in the study is shown in Table 4 and the results obtained are shown in Table 5.

Table 4. Nodes and links created for the years 2007–2010 network

	2007–2010
Nodes	37
Links	26

Table 5. Link prediction AUC results in network created between 2007–2010 years

	2011	2012	2013	2014
Common Neighbor	0,310	0,446	0,504	0,514
Jaccard Index	0,399	**0,542**	**0,627**	**0,640**
Adamic Adar	0,313	0,506	0,546	0,557
Preferential Attachment	**0,443**	0,479	0,615	0,628
Sorenson Index	0,266	0,398	0,443	0,452
Resource Allocation Index	0,310	0,351	0,441	0,450

When we look at Table 5, we can see that the prediction results are similar to those in Table 3. This is due to the fact that the training and test networks in the data set used for both link prediction are formed with similar characteristics and in a short time period. It is understood that Jaccard Index and Preferential Attachment Methods, which are traditional link prediction methods, give more successful results than the others.

4.3 Network Formed Between 2007–2013

While the network created between 2007–2013 was used for training, the competitions that took place in 2014, 2015, 2016 and 2017 were used as test networks. The dataset used in the study is shown in Table 6 and the results are shown in Table 7.

Table 6. Nodes and links created for the years 2007–2013 network.

	2007–2013
Nodes	64
Links	51

When we look at Table 7, it is seen that the prediction results are more successful than Table 3 and Table 5. This is due to the expansion of the networks used for both training and testing, as shown in Table 7. It is understood that Jaccard Index, Preferential Attachment and Adamic Adar methods, which are traditional link prediction methods, give more successful results than the others.

Table 7. Link prediction AUC results in network created between 2007–2013 years

	2014	2015	2016	2017
Common Neighbor	0,373	0,535	0,605	0,617
Jaccard Index	0,479	**0,650**	**0,753**	**0,768**
Adamic Adar	0,376	0,607	0,656	0,669
Preferential Attachment	**0,532**	0,575	0,738	0,753
Sorenson Index	0,319	0,478	0,531	0,542
Resource Allocation Index	0,377	0,421	0,529	0,540

4.4 Network Formed Between 2004–2013

While the network created between 2004–2013 was used for training, the competitions that took place in 2014, 2015, 2016 and 2017 were used as test networks. The dataset used in the study is shown in Table 8 and the results obtained are shown in Table 9.

Table 8. Nodes and links created for the years 2004–2013 network.

	2001–2013
Nodes	154
Links	203

Table 9. Link prediction AUC results in network created between 2004–2013 years

	2014	2015	2016	2017
Common Neighbor	0,609	0,695	0,792	0,903
Jaccard Index	0,703	0,767	0,836	0,911
Adamic Adar	0,616	0,696	0,786	0,888
Preferential Attachment	**0,781**	**0,836**	**0,886**	**0,913**
Sorenson Index	0,509	0,580	0,667	0,773
Resource Allocation Index	0,593	0,676	0,778	0,817

Table 9 shows that the prediction results are more successful than Table 3, Table 5 and Table 7. This is due to the expansion of the networks used for both training and testing, as shown in Table 8. Looking at Table 9, all of the traditional link prediction methods give successful results as the training network expands.

5 Conclusion and Future Work

In this study, unlike the prediction studies in the previous years, the applicability of traditional link prediction methods in the networks formed from football competitions was investigated. Networks of different time periods have been formed by using the teams competing in UEFA Europa League between 2004–2017 and the competitions between these teams. In these networks, link prediction processes were performed by using traditional methods used in link prediction studies. The success of the link prediction operations was obtained by using the AUC metric. As a result of experimental studies, it has been seen that traditional link prediction methods have achieved acceptable success. However, another result obtained from experimental studies was the importance of selection of training and test data to be used in link prediction processes. When Table 3, Table 5 and Table 7 are examined, it is seen that the link prediction results are not successful enough. Because, as shown in Table 2, Table 4 and Table 6, the fact that the training and test networks are in short time periods prevents a successful link prediction. As can be seen in Table 9, if the networks consisting of data used for training and testing are sufficient, link prediction operations are also successful. Therefore, it is important that the training and test data to be used in link prediction processes are prepared in a way that is suitable for a successful prediction process. In future studies, it is aimed to incorporate more features from the structure of networks in link prediction processes in order to increase the success of traditional link prediction methods.

References

1. Newman, M.E.J.: SIAM Rev. **45**, 167 (2003)
2. Dorogovtsev, S.N., Mendes, J.F.: Evolution of Networks. Oxford University Press, Oxford (2003)
3. Dodds, P.S., Muhamad, R., Watts, D.J.: Science **301**, 827 (2003)
4. Watts, D.J., Strogatz, S.H.: Nature (London) **393**, 440 (1998)
5. Fındık, O., Özkaynak, E.: Complex network analysis of players in tennis tournaments. In: International Conference on Advanced Technologies, Computer Engineering and Science (ICATCES 2018), Karabük, pp. 383–388 (2018)
6. Sulak, E.E., Yılmaz, H. Özkaynak, E.: Complex network analysis of UEFA Europe league competitions. In: International Conference on Advanced Technologies, Computer Engineering and Science (ICATCES 2018), Karabük, pp. 389–393 (2018)
7. Watts, D.J., Strogatz, S.H.: Collective dynamics of 'small-world' networks. Nature **393**(6684), 440–442 (1998)
8. Erdős, P., Rényi, A.: On random graphs. I(Pdf). Publications Mathematica **6**, 290–297 (1959)
9. Barabasi, A.-L., Albert, R.: Emergence of scaling in random networks. Science **286**, 509 (1999)
10. Scott, J.: Social Network Analysis: A Handbook. Sage Publications, London (2000). 209 p.
11. Mika, P.: Social networks and the semantic web. In: Jain, R., Sheth, A. (eds.) Semantic Web And Beyond Computing For Human Experience. Springer, New York (2007). https://doi.org/10.1007/978-0-387-71001-3. 234 p.
12. Newman, M.E.J.: Mathematics of networks. In: Durlauf, S.N., Blume, L.E. (eds.) The New Palgrave Dictionary of Economics. Palgrave Macmillan, London (2008). https://doi.org/10.1007/978-1-349-58802-2_1061

13. Ruhnau, B.: Eigenvector centrality: a node-centrality? Soc. Netw. **22**(4), 357–365 (2000)
14. Newman, M.E.J.: Clustering and preferential attachment in growing networks. Phys. Rev. E Stat. Phys. Plasmas Fluids Relat. Interdiscip. Top **64**, 025102 (2001)
15. Paul: Etude De La Distribution Florale Dans Une Portion Des Alpes Et Du Jura. Bull. La Soc. Vaudoise Des Sci. Nat. **37**, 547–579 (1901)
16. Barabasi, A.-L., Reka, A.: Emergence of scaling in random networks. Science (80–) **286**, 509–512 (1999)
17. Barabasi, A.-L., Albert, R.: Statistical mechanics of complex networks. Rev. Modern Phys. **74**(1), 47–97 (2002)
18. Zhou, T., Lü, L., Zhang, Y.C.: Predicting missing links via local information. Eur. Phys. J. B **71**, 623–630 (2009)
19. Sorensen, T.: A Method of establishing groups of equal amplitude in plant sociology based on similarity of species content. Det. Kong. Danske Vidensk, Selesk Biol. Skr. **5**, 1–34 (1948)
20. Liben-Nowell, D., Kleinberg, J.: The link-prediction problem for social networks. J. Am. Soc. Inf. Sci. Technol. **58**, 1019–1031 (2007)
21. Linyuan, L.L., Zhou, T.: Link prediction in complex networks: a survey. Phys. A Stat. Mech. Appl. **390**, 1150–1170 (2011)
22. Liu, Z., Zhang, Q.M., Lü, L., Zhou, T.: Link prediction in complex networks: a local Naïve Bayes model. EPL **96**, 48007 (2011)
23. Huang, Z.: Link prediction based on graph topology: the predictive value of generalized clustering coefficient. SSRN (2010)
24. Resnick, P., Varian, H.R.: Recommender systems Mmende Tems. Commun. ACM **40**, 56–58 (1997)
25. Lü, L., Medo, M., Yeung, C.H., Zhang, Y.-C., Zhang, Z.-K., Zhou, T.: Recommender systems. Phys. Rep. **519**, 1–49 (2012)
26. Huang, Z., Li, X., Chen, H.: Link prediction approach to collaborative filtering. In: Proceedings of 5th ACM/IEEE Joint Conference on Digital Libraries, JCDL 2005 (2005)
27. Kleinberg, J.: Analysis of Large-Scale Social And İnformation Networks Subject Areas. Author for Correspondence (2013)
28. Zhang, Q.M., Lü, L., Wang, W.Q., Zhu, Y.X., Zhou, T.: Potential theory for directed networks. Plos One **8** e55437 (2013)
29. Wang, W.Q., Zhang, Q.M., Zhou, T.: Evaluating network models: a likelihood analysis. EPL **98**, 1–6 (2012)
30. Bürhan, Y., Daş, R.: Akademik Veritabanlarından Yazar-Makale Bağlantı Tahmini. Politeknik Dergisi J. Polytech. **20** 787–800 (2017)
31. Türker, İ., Çavuşoğlu, A.: Detailing the co-authorship networks in degree coupling, edge weight and academic age perspective. Chaos Solitons Fractals **91**, 386–392 (2016)
32. Hanley, J.A., Mcneil, B.J.: The meaning and use of the area under a receiver operating characteristic (ROC) curve. Radiology **143**, 29–36 (1982)
33. Bastian, M., Heymann, S., Jacom, M.: Gephi: an open source software for exploring and manipulating networks. In: Third International AAAI Conference on Weblogs and Social Media. AAAI Publications (2009)
34. Internet: UEFA European Cup Coefficients Database (2018). https://Kassiesa.Home.Xs4all.Nl/Bert/Uefa/Data/Index.Html

Sustainable Rice Production Analysis and Forecasting Rice Yield Based on Weather Circumstances Using Data Mining Techniques for Bangladesh

Mohammed Mahmudur Rahman(✉), Tajnim Jahan, Tanjima Nasrin, Salma Akter, and Zinnia Sultana

International Islamic University Chittagong, Chittagong, Bangladesh
provaiiuc@raudah.usim.edu.my, tajnim94@gmail.com, tanjimanasrin541@gmail.com, imdsalma00@gmail.com, zinniaiiuc@yahoo.com

Abstract. Rice production assumes the most noteworthy part in national economy of Bangladesh. But due to several weather circumstances, rice production is being influenced day by day. In this research work, present a sustainable rice production analysis and forecasting rice yield for Aus, Aman and Boro rice based on weather circumstances. This paper aims to forecast rice production on the basis of weather parameters (Temperature, Rainfall, Humidity) and then predict future rice production based on previous data analysis. This research work has considered here Multiple Linear Regression, Support Vector Machine and Random Forest methods of data mining for selected region of Bangladesh. On the basis of the final calculating result, the analysis will help the farmers to understand which types of rice will be planted in which weather and it will help to achieve greater profit in the economy of Bangladesh.

Keywords: Multiple linear regression · Data mining · Support Vector Machine · Weather parameters · Random forest · Rice production

1 Introduction

Agriculture is Bangladesh's largest services division but Bangladesh is among the most helpless nations to environmental change, which represents a long haul risk to the nation's agrarian segment, especially in regions influenced by flooding, saline interruption, excessive heat and dry spell. For a long time, individuals of Bangladesh are doing agribusiness yet they don't get good monetary outcome as a result of influencing rice yields by different elements. They don't have sufficient information on the adequacy of these elements and better specialized data. Rice production depends on the rate of temperature, amount of rainfall and percentage of humidity. Due to lack of knowledge about this weather circumstances farmers are being failed in case of yield prediction. To analyze the rice

T. Bhuiyan et al. (Eds.): ICONCS 2020, LNICST 325, pp. 218–229, 2020.
https://doi.org/10.1007/978-3-030-52856-0_17

production different method or environment can be used, but in this research data mining will be used which is the most efficient and reliable field for agriculture.

Data Mining is mostly applied to agricultural issues. Data Mining is used to explore huge data set and to create useful characteristics and trends in the information collections. The general aim of the Data Mining process is to extract data from the data set and to turn it into a justifiable framework for further use. The main purpose of this research is to create a comprehensible interface for farmers to evaluate rice production on the basis of weather data using data mining techniques to increase profit rates.

2 Literature Review

Researchers argue that data mining techniques can be useful for agricultural data analysis and prediction [10]. Various data mining techniques, such as DBSCAN, K-means, EM, WEKA, can be useful for predicting and analyzing agriculture. The purpose of this paper was to find useful knowledge from the outcomes of these techniques that would help improve agricultural yield.

Production of crop yields was a topic of enthusiasm for manufacturers, specialists and agrarian associations. Multiple data mining techniques used to produce crop yields. Scientists have focused on different data mining techniques such as K-Means, K-Nearest Neighbor (KNN), Artificial Neural Networks (ANN), and Support Vector Machines (SVM) to solve crop yield output [1, 7].

To establish a new approach for rice yield forecasting in Bangladesh based on algorithms for machine learning the proposed approach uses forecast weather and prior reported rice yield information as the source of data [4]. These proposed approach initially built a model for predicting weather data using neural network and estimating the rice yield applied SVM.

Researchers have developed an information guided model that learns from historic soil just as rainfall data and forecasts crop yields in a few regions over seasons [9]. For this examination rice is considered to be a specific harvest. The standardized neural network hybrid model identifies optimal mixes of soil parameters and blends them with the pattern of rainfall in a chosen area to advance the predicted harvest yield. The basis for the rainfall predictive analysis model relies on the Supervised Learning approach to the Time-Series [13].

Agriculture is the important sector for the economy [5]. This paper can be useful in growing the net rate crop and in recommending the best yield by managing the data sets while improving the quality and gain of the rural area. The parameters for the datasets include soil type, temperature, humidity, water level, rainfall, soil pH etc. This forecast will assist the farmers with choosing whether the specific harvest is reasonable for that particular soil.

Production of agricultural crops depends on the seasonal, biological, and economic causes [8, 15]. In this paper, exhibited the crop yield, pick the most incredible yield, and along these lines Improves the value and increase of data mining methodology development [12].

In [6], this paper aimed at establishing a new approach to the efficiency of rice yields under different climatic conditions that can support ranchers and various accomplices in a better fundamental initiative in terms of agronomy and yield choice.

Analysts concentrated on information from agribusiness information to anticipate harvest yield for real crops in different region [2]. Applying data mining techniques such as K-means; K-NN; linear regression; neural net for predicting annual yield of Bangladesh's major crops [3].

Though it is extremely hard to contrast with others but in this research we attempt to find some related work in this fields. Algorithm of regression analysis that are used for making prediction and give more better result have been evaluated on the dataset. It isn't conceivable to find data of agriculture field in our nation so we have physically gathered all information ourselves and handled them so as to make them appropriate for calculations.

2.1 Research Question

In this research, some questions are appeared about the proposed work. That is "what will be done for improving crop production and how will it be done? How farmers can know about the suitable time or place for planting rice? How future rice production will be predicted?".

2.2 Research Objective

From the research question, the research objective is: rice production will be predicted based on weather data by applying Multiple Linear Regression, SVR (Support Vector regression) and Random forest method. This analysis will help to improve the production, using this rice production analysis farmers will get an idea and understandable scenario that how they should plant rice, which districts will be best for which types of rice. Based on previous data analysis future production will be made to give an idea on how much rice production can be in future, so that farmers can do their work on that perspective.

3 Methodology

In this research work, regression algorithm of data mining have been applied to analyze the rice production of respective districts in Bangladesh. Multiple Linear Regression, Support Vector Machine and Random Forest algorithm have been used to predict the rice production.

3.1 Multiple Linear Regression

Multiple linear regression refers to an accurate framework that uses a couple of illustrative elements to predict the outcome of a response variable. Multiple linear regression aims to display the direct connection between the logical (autonomous) factors and the (subordinate) variable reaction. The purpose of this research work is to predict the dependent variable using a linear function of the independent variables.

The model is:

$$Y = \beta_0 + \beta_1 x_1 + \beta_2 x_2 + \cdots + \beta_p x_p + \varepsilon \quad (1)$$

Here Y denotes the dependent variable, $x_1, x_2, \ldots x_p$ are number of independent variables, ε denotes "noise" variable which is a normally distributed random variable with mean equal to zero and standard deviation σ whose value we do not know. We also do not know the values of the coefficients $\beta_0, \beta_1, \ldots \beta_p$. We estimate all these unknown values from the available data. Beta (β) coefficients are the point estimator of independent variables. Multiple linear regression is used to know if each independent variable predicts the dependent variable significantly.

3.2 Support Vector Regression

SVM is a supervised machine learning algorithm which can be used for classification or regression problems. The segment of this which is use for regression known as "Support Vector Regression or SVR" to predict or explain the values taken by a continuous predicted attribute. There are some differences between SVM and SVR. First of all, the production is a real number which makes it difficult to predict in hand. In the case of regression, a tolerance margin (epsilon) is set in approximation to the SVM that would have already been demanded from the problem [11]. Whatever it is the basic idea, is consistently the same to minimize errors, separating the hyper plane that extends the edge and thinks the piece errors are tolerated. In this proposed work, support vector regression is applied for making prediction and regression of vectors has been implemented on the dataset that works using kernel feature in this research help. The kernel function denotes an internal product in feature space and is generally referred to as:

$$K(x, y) = <\varphi(x), \varphi(y)> \tag{2}$$

A kernel transforms an enter information space into the specified shape. Here, the kernel takes a low-dimensional input place and transforms it right into a better dimensional vicinity. It is most beneficial in non-linear separation trouble. The kernel trick enables the SVR to find a fit, and then mapping data to the original space. The model produced using Support Vector Regression is based on a sub-set of training records as the cost feature for building the version ignores any training facts close to the model prediction. The computational complexity does not rely upon the dimensionality of the input space Moreover, it has brilliant speculation capacity with high prediction accuracy.

3.3 Random Forest

A random forest is a group of choice trees, like other machine learning procedure random forest use preparing information to figure out how to make forecasts. Random forest can be utilized for both classification and regression. It's a generous enhancement for simple decision tree as the name proposes, it makes a forest in arbitrary way. The forest created by this calculation has a decision tree ready for any strategy. In this methodology, forest of multiple trees are produced [14]. From that point, there are combined so as to deliver significantly increasingly exact prediction. The higher the quantity of decision trees that are produced, the higher the strength of the prediction. Random forest is reliable as it can work with missing values and it won't over fit the model.

There are two steps in the algorithm Random Forest, one is random forest creation, the other is to make a prediction of the random forest classification created in the first step. Random forest works as follows:

It randomly pick "K" features from total "m" features where k << m. Among the "K" parameters, calculate the node "d" the use of the great break up factor and then split the node into daughter nodes using the exceptional split. Then it repeats the a to c steps till "l" range of nodes has been reached. Build forest with the aid of repeating steps from a to d for "n" wide variety times to create "n" wide variety of trees.

In the following stage, with the random forest classifier created, prediction with random forest regression is worked on three steps. These are:

Step 1: Sample inputs are taken from the training data set.
Step 2: Bootstrap sample is used to train random forest regression model and a prediction result is created.
Step 3: The ensemble prediction is calculated by averaging the forecasts of the trees which produce the final prediction.

In this research the proposed model is built using supervised machine learning in order to develop an efficient outcome. For this at first data have been collected that are real and raw data from renowned source to get the proper prediction result and better accuracy. Some data preprocessing steps have been applied to remove the noise and redundant data and a standard form has been made to evaluate the process. Figure 1 represents the workflow structure and in Fig. 2 using the flowchart, the whole process is described accordingly.

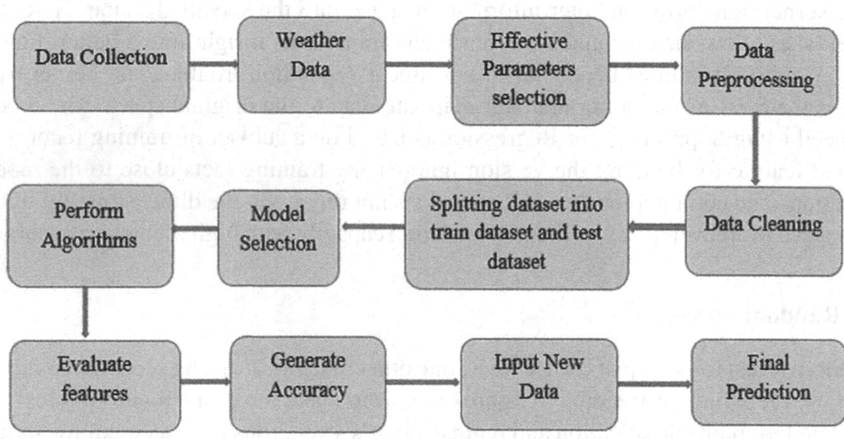

Fig. 1. Workflow structure

Data preprocessing and cleaning were needed to make the data readable by machine that consumes the most of the time of the research. Collected data contain redundant value, null value, some contain conflicting value, some contain different unit factor and has no correlation between them. So it was needed to figure out the reliable value to fill the null value, to filter out the data. Then the all meaningful parameters have been arranged in a readable form which is very important to give the proper accuracy and converted the data in a same unit factor which is also very essential to correlate the data perfectly with each other.

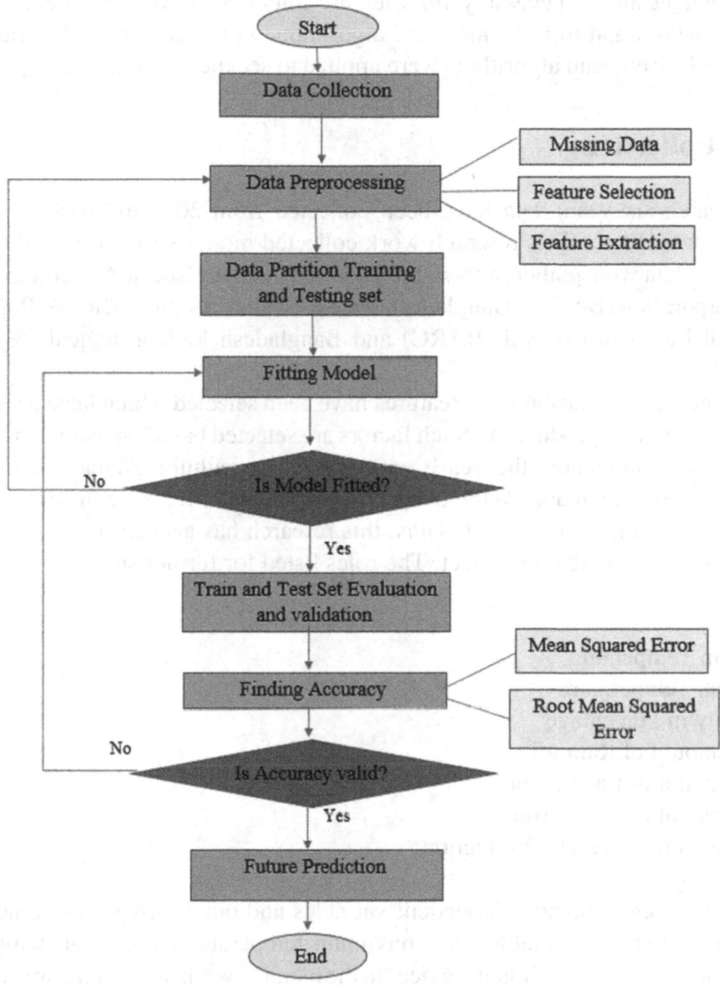

Fig. 2. Flowchart of the research work

After preprocessing and cleaning the collected data, all the data have been set in a form for evaluation. At first all the weather parameters have been arranged in CSV format with production data separately for Aus, Aman and Boro rice. Then data visualization is done using matplotlib library to see the correlation between independent variables and dependent variables and found a proper view that show the dependency of the variables.

In machine learning, data splitting is a significant part to process the big data in a model and in an efficient way. For any supervised machine learning or large statistics application this technique is considered very important because the main output mostly depends on the accuracy of the result given by the machine or model. It is a commonplace strategy that take all available classified information, and divide it into training and testing subsets. By using TrainTestSplit library the dataset has been partitioned with 75:25 ratio. To evaluate the proposed model python environment is used and based on this environment all the necessary libraries are imported from Scikit Learn package to split the dataset and to implement the algorithms with their required library. After splitting the datasets, said algorithms were applied to see the performance of predicting.

4 Data Collection

In this research six years data have been collected from 2013 to 2018 for different districts of Bangladesh. This research work collected month wise weather data for 34 districts. The data were gathered from the yearbook of Bangladesh Agricultural Development Corporation (BADC), Bangladesh Rice Research Institute (BRRI), Bangladesh Agricultural Research Council (BARC) and Bangladesh Meteorological Department (BMD).

For further review, attributes or features have been selected which have a significant impact on agricultural production. Such factors are selected based on annual production, whose changes can change the yearly outcome of agriculture. Actually the selected attributes are basically made on the availability of the data. Because in some cases the right amount of data wasn't found. Thus, this research has avoided the data that were not available or impossible to collect. The roles listed for further study in this research are:

i) Maximum Temperature
ii) Minimum Temperature
iii) Humidity in Percentage
iv) Total Amount of Rainfall
v) Total Amount of Land Area
vi) Total amount of Yield Area
vii) Total amount of Yearly Production

In this research effort five dependent variables and one independent variable have been taken. Dependent variables are maximum temperature, minimum temperature, rainfall, humidity and area of planting rice. In the planned work, maximum and minimum temperature are taken in Degree Celsius, rainfall is taken in Millimeter, Humidity is taken in percentage and area is taken in Hectares. Production data of three types of rice have been taken in Metric Tons which is the independent variable. All the data were placed in CSV format on excel sheet.

5 Experimental Result

In this experimental study, at first separated weather dataset of each parameters with target value have been evaluated to see the dependency on each other and to see the performance of the proposed method. The regression technique: multiple linear regression, support vector regression and random forest have been applied on the dataset. Each method has different performance, because each working process and environment algorithms are different.

Table 1. Accuracy comparison on weather dataset

Dataset	Multiple linear regression	Random forest	Support vector regression
Maximum temperature	15%	54%	42%
Minimum temperature	16%	52%	41%
Humidity	26%	72%	55%
Rainfall	28%	75%	56%

Table 2. Actual production and Predicted value using Support Vector Regression

Year	Districts	Rice type	Actual production value (M.ton)	Predicted production value (M.ton)
2013	Sylhet	Aus	34671	57826
2013	Barishal	Aman	196532	187203
2013	Feni	Boro	121469	121705
2014	Chandpur	Aus	22977	20089
2014	Dinajpur	Aman	474410	477130
2014	Madaripur	Boro	168672	198203
2015	Dhaka	Aus	1545	1282
2015	Rajshahi	Aman	273827	250524
2015	Bogura	Boro	682502	658469
2016	Bhola	Aus	75607	74737
2016	Rangpur	Aman	163600	172671
2016	Cox's Bazar	Boro	565685	581456
2017	Comilla	Aus	63482	75085
2017	Rajshahi	Aman	70130	71142
2017	Jessore	Boro	682506	658469
2018	Chittagong	Aus	81801	102602
2018	Hatiya	Aman	119763	108973
2018	Mymensingh	Boro	1072834	200561

Comparison between the actual value and the expected value was seen after estimation of production value. Then accuracy of those algorithm has been found. The accuracy comparison on different attributes dataset is shown in the Table 1. In the table it has been seen that multiple linear regression has given very poor accuracy than support vector regression and random forest method. Therefore support for vector regression and random forest algorithm were used for further work.

Afterward all the weather attributes data and data of area as inputs have been added in one dataset with rice production data as output. In this study three types of rice (Aus, Aman and Boro) data have been used. That's why three final dataset have been created to see the comparison of the production of each rice in different districts and to predict the rice production for future. In that case, the chosen methods have been applied on dataset of three types of rice and predicted the value of testing set based on training set. The predicted value of production results in very close to the actual value. As the predicted and actual value are very close the two method have given better accuracy.

Table 2 shows the predicted value of rice production for some districts in Bangladesh found by using Support Vector Regression algorithm. Prediction has been made for three types of rice.

Table 3. Actual production and Predicted value using Random Forest

Year	Districts	Rice type	Actual production value (M. ton)	Predicted production value (M. ton)
2013	Sylhet	Aus	34671	32143.75
2013	Barishal	Aman	196532	175858.05
2013	Feni	Boro	121469	133161.55
2014	Chandpur	Aus	22977	24574.00
2014	Dinajpur	Aman	474410	454556.65
2014	Madaripur	Boro	168672	196586.90
2015	Dhaka	Aus	1545	1912.60
2015	Rajshahi	Aman	273827	242375.55
2015	Bogura	Boro	682502	703468.45
2016	Bhola	Aus	75607	62284.40
2016	Rangpur	Aman	163600	177233.55
2016	Cox's Bazar	Boro	565685	581360.90
2017	Comilla	Aus	63482	59629.70
2017	Rajshahi	Aman	70130	82078.40
2017	Jessore	Boro	682506	707468.40
2018	Chittagong	Aus	81801	67924.15
2018	Hatiya	Aman	119763	104691.85
2018	Mymensingh	Boro	1072834	986354.55

Here, Table 3 shows the predicted value of rice production for some districts in Bangladesh found by using Random Forest algorithm. Prediction has been made for three types of rice.

The comparison of accuracy between Random Forest and Support Vector Regression for three types of rice has been shown in Fig. 3.

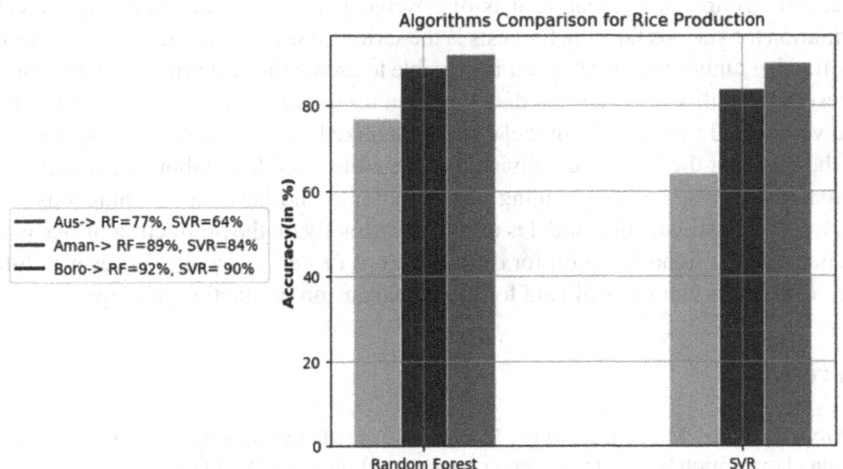

Fig. 3. Accuracy comparison for rice production

From the above figure it can be said that the Random Forest Method worked very well in this research, giving greater accuracy than supporting vector regression. After that prediction for future year has also been made by using input variables of few districts and it is showed in Table 4.

Table 4. Future predicted production value

Region	Year	Rice type	Production (M. ton)
Comilla	2020	Aus	187913
Chittagong	2020	Aman	503212
Mymensingh	2021	Boro	1124565
Sylthet	2021	Aus	129976

This rice production analysis will help the farmers during planting rice in different districts as prediction has been made for 34 districts was so reliable. So it will be easy for farmers to decide which types of rice will grow well in which district by seeing this analysis and then it will help to increase the profit level of economy in Bangladesh.

6 Conclusion

In recent years, the difficult assignment of predicting rice crop yield has been tried with incredible efforts. In this advanced world, every division is being edified by various innovative advancements and findings. Hope this research will be a great helpful for the betterment of agricultural production as in Bangladesh agriculture is a very monumental figure. All through this research, it is discovered that the inaccessibility of expected information for various farming harvests is the serious issue for such scientifically usage. By collecting other crops real data it is possible to create the scenario like mentioned in this research. In this research real data has been used that's why the accuracy has been found very well. In future, this model can be actualized as web and versatile applications with the goal that the agriculture division of the nation and field laborers can utilize the anticipated outcome before planning of a generation and have an advantageous profit edge. In this investigate, the model is executed distinctly on the production of rice in any case, but it is additionally useful for different crops or items as well. However in future work, researchers can use soil data for more analysis on production of crops.

References

1. Arooj, A., Riaz, M., Akram, M.N.: Evaluation of predictive data mining algorithms in soil data classification for optimized crop recommendation. In: ICACS (2018)
2. Mucherino, A., Papajorgji, P., Pardalos, P.M.: A survey of data mining techniques applied to agriculture. Oper. Res. **9**, 121–140 (2009). https://doi.org/10.1007/s12351-009-0054-6
3. Ming, J., Zhang, L., Sun, J., Zhang, Y.: Analysis models of technical and economic data of mining enterprises based on big data analysis. In: 3rd IEEE International Conference on Cloud Computing and Big Data Analysis (2018)
4. Hossain, M.A., Uddin, M.N., Hossain M.A., Jang, Y.M.: Predicting rice yield for Bangladesh by exploiting weather condition. In: IEEE (2017)
5. Preethaa, M.K.R.S., Nishanthini, S., Santhiya, D., Shree, K.V.: Crop yield prediction. Int. J. Eng. Technol. Sci. IJETS™ **3**(3), 111–116 (2016)
6. Gandhi, N., Petkar, O., Armstrong, L.J., Tripathy, A.K.: Rice crop yield prediction in India using support vector machines. In: 13th International Joint Conference on Computer Science and Software Engineering (JCSSE) (2016)
7. Medar, R.A., Rajpurohit, V.S.: A survey on data mining techniques for crop yield prediction. Int. J. Adv. Res. Comput. Sci. Manag. Stud. **2**(9), 59–64 (2014)
8. Sujatha, R., Isakki, P.: A study on crop yield forecasting using classification techniques. In: IEEE (2016)
9. Kulkarni, S., Mandal, S.N., Sharma, G.S., Mundada, M.R.: Predictive analysis to improve crop yield using a neural network model. In. IEEE (2018)
10. Bharadi, V.A., Abhyankar, P.P., Patil, R.S., Patade, S.S., Nate, T.U., Joshi, A.M.: Analysis and prediction in agricultural data using data mining techniques. In: ICEMTE (2017)
11. Sukhadia, K., Chaudhari, M.B.: A survey on rice crop yield prediction in india using improved classification technique. Int. J. Sci. Res. Comput. Sci. Eng. Inf. Technol. **5** (2019). https://doi.org/10.32628/CSEIT1951122. IEEE
12. Sharma, D., Sabitha, A.: Identification of influential factors for productivity and sustainability of crops using data mining techniques. In: 6th International Conference on Signal Processing and Integrated Networks (SPIN), pp. 322–328. IEEE (2019). https://doi.org/10.1109/spin.2019.8711630

13. Palanivel, K., Surianarayanan, C.: An approach for prediction of crop yield using machine learning and big data techniques. Int. J. Comput. Eng. Technol. (IJCET) **10**, 110–118 (2019). Article ID IJCET_10_03_013
14. Hualin, X., Huang, Y., Chen, Q., Zhang, Y., Wu, Q.: Prospects for agricultural sustainable intensification: a review of research. Land Open Access J. (2019). https://doi.org/10.3390/land8110157
15. Delgado, J.A., Short, N.M., Roberts, D.P., Vandenberg, B.: Big data analysis for sustainable agriculture on a geospatial cloud framework. Front. Sustain. Food Syst. (2019). https://doi.org/10.3389/fsufs.2019.00054

Bangladeshi Stock Price Prediction and Analysis with Potent Machine Learning Approaches

Sajib Das, Md. Shohel Arman(✉), Syeda Sumbul Hossain, Md. Sanzidul Islam, Farhan Anan Himu, and Asif Khan Shakir

Department of Software Engineering, Daffodil International University, Dhaka, Bangladesh
sshuvo27@gmail.com

Abstract. Stock price forecasting, is one of the most significant financial complexities, since data are not reliable and noisy, impacting many factors. This article offers a machine learning model for the stock price prediction using Support Vector Machine-Regression (SVR) with two different kernels which are Radial Basis Function (RBF) and linear kernel. This study shows the Prediction and accuracy comparison between Support Vector Regression (SVR) and Linear Regression (LR) and also the accuracy comparison for different kernels of Support vector Regression (SVR). The model has used sum squared error (SSE) to determine the accuracy of each algorithm; which has shown significant improvement than the other studies. This analysis is conducted on the price data of about five years of Grameenphone listed on Dhaka Stock Exchange (DSE). The highest accuracy was found with Linear Regression model in every case with the highest accuracy of about 97.07% followed by SVR (Linear) model and SVR (radial basis function) model with the highest accuracy rate of about 97.06% and 96.82%. In some cases the accuracy of SVR (radial basis function) was higher than SVR (linear). But it was the Linear Regression which had the highest accuracy of all in every case.

Keywords: Machine learning · Stock price prediction · Support vector regression · Linear regression

1 Introduction

The stock market refers to the selection and exchange of stocks in which common shares of public companies are bought, exchanged and issued. The shares of the company are all shares in which the company's ownership is split. In proportion to the number of shares in total, a single share of the stock represents fractional ownership. The prices of stocks shift with market forces every day. This means that share prices are changing due to demand and supply. If more people would like to purchase a stock (demand) than sell it (supply), the price will increase. On the other hand, if more people wanted to sell a stock than purchase it, there would be more supply than demand, and the price would fall [1]. In other words the more a stock has been transacted the more is valuable.

T. Bhuiyan et al. (Eds.): ICONCS 2020, LNICST 325, pp. 230–240, 2020.
https://doi.org/10.1007/978-3-030-52856-0_18

For years, stock price forecasts have focused because they can generate substantial profit. Investors have tried to predict the trends using various methods and bet in the markets. Technical analysis like RSI (Relative Strength Index), MFI (Money Flow Index), MACD (Moving Average Convergence/Divergence) etc. [2] and fundamental analysis like Investor sentiment analysis [3], EPS (Earnings per Share), Net asset value etc. are used in analyzing the trends of stock prices. Different machine learning algorithms have also used in forecasting stock prices. Tough it's a tricky task to as predict stock prices as the prices follow a random pattern.

We have collected the stock price data of GrameenPhone of about last five years (1/1/2014–21/11/2019) form Stock Bangladesh website (stockbangladesh.com). The dataset contains six columns named Date, Open, High, Low, Close and volume. Where the Date stands for a particular date, the Open indicate the opening price of a stock on the particular date, the High and Low stands for the highest and lowest trading price of on that day. The Close indicates the closing price of the day and the volume indicates the numbers of share transacted on the particular day.

We have evaluated the performance of SVR (Support vector machine-Regression) with Linear & Radial Basis Function (RBF) kernels and Linear Regression with the previous price data.

2 Literature Review

Various algorithms for machine learning are used to predict stock price trends. Some of them are ANN (Artificial Neural Networks) [4–7], GA (Genetic Algorithm) [6], LS-SVM (Least Square Support Vector Machine) [2, 8], Trend Estimation with Linear Regression (TELR) [9], SVM (support vector machines) [5, 7, 10] with different kernels, KNN (K Nearest Neighbors) [7] structural support vector machines (SSVMs) [11]. Some statistical analyses are also used like Autoregressive Integrated Moving Average (ARIMA) [12]. But none of them were able to give quite promising prediction due to the non-linearity of the data.

Studies have tried to predict stock prices using Artificial Neural Network. In a study in 2017 [5] on Korean stock market ANN was used to predict the stock price [13] with the highest accuracy of 81.34% for 20 days and 83.01% for 30 days moving average. In another study [7] ANN was used and got 86.69% average accuracy based on experiment carried out on three different stocks. In 2018 this study [4] ANN was used and the best SSE score was 0.6271104815 for Apple, 0.0121281374 for Pepsi, 0.0335425612 for IBM, 0.016770174 for McDonald and 0.0211154625 for LG. In this study [5] author used ANN and achieved 96.10% accuracy for 5-fold average prediction (Mj′). Mj is a model where $1 \leq j \leq J$, for each classifier. And Mj′ is a variant model as a substitution of Mj. 92.81% accuracy was achieved from model Mj.

Least square support vector machine (LS-SVM) is another popular machine learning used to predict stock prices. In this study [8] author a LS-SVM model along with Particle swarm Optimization (PSO) and the accuracy rate of the system was around 90.5–93%. Another research [1] used LS-SVM with PSO optimization and LS_SVM to predict stock prices. The Mean Squared Error (MSE) was 0.5317 for Adobe, 0.6314 for oracle 0.7725 for HP and 0.7905 for American Express with PSO-LS-SVM where MSE was 0.5703 for Adobe, 0.8829 for Oracle 1.2537 for HP and 1.0663 for American Express.

Other potent machine learning algorithms like SVM was used in this study [7] and found average accuracy of 89.33% after applying the algorithm for three company stocks. For BSE-Sensex the accuracy was 90.10% using polynomial kernel where c = 1 and degree = 1 and for RBF kernel the accuracy was 88.08 where c = 1 gamma = 4. For Infosys the accuracy was 89.59% with polynomial kernel where c = 1 and degree = 1 and 87.80% for RBF kernel where c = 5 and gamma = 1.5. Another research [10] that used SVM with RBF kernel has the mean accuracy of 53.3% to 56.8% for 10 days. And the accuracy rate can be lower than 50% for different dataset. A modified linear regression algorithm Trend Estimation with Linear Regression was used in this study [8] and Mean Absolute Percentage Error (MAPE) was 5.41% for bank data and 5.42% for overall stock data. K Nearest Neighbors or KNN is also been used to predict stock prices. A study that used KNN [6] has an accuracy of 83.52% with KNN. Structural support vector machines (SSVMs) is used in a research and the accuracy with training samples was higher than 78% and the accuracy with testing samples was about 50%.

3 Methodology

As our Fig. 1 shows our proposed model has five stages. First we collected the data and pre-process it. Then we optimized the parameters that we are going to use for our training algorithm. Then we tested our dataset with Linear Regression and support vector regression with 2 different kernels using the parameters that we optimized. Then we extracted our output and tested the accuracy of our algorithms with SSE. Finally we visualized the comparison between the actual values and the predicted values.

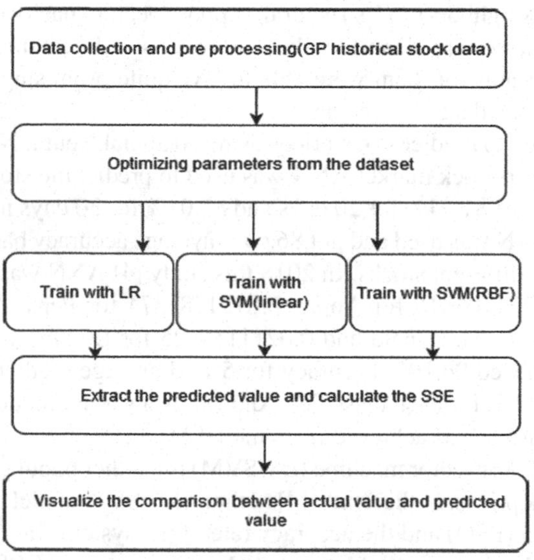

Fig. 1. The proposed model

3.1 Data Collection and Pre-processing

We collected the data form stockbangladesh.com. The website is an open source website and contains the previous price data of all the companies listed in Dhaka Stock Exchange. We have collected the price data of Grameenphone from 1st January 2014 to 21st November 2019 where the data size was 1413 meaning that we have the price information of 1413 days for the stock. We got the dataset in the recent price to the oldest price form. To Process the data to our desired order we had to flip the data to get the oldest price to recent price order. We checked for null values; there was none so we used the dataset as it was (Fig. 2).

Date	Open	High	Low	Close	Volume
1/1/2014	79.5	81.6	79	79.5	210400
2/1/2014	82.5	85.6	80.5	83.8	751200
6/1/2014	85.4	85.4	82.1	83.9	194800
7/1/2014	79.5	85.8	75.5	85.2	377400
8/1/2014	85.9	89	84.9	88	641200
9/1/2014	88.3	90.4	85	86.2	378800
12/1/2014	87.9	89.3	86.5	87.4	368800
13/01/2014	87.5	89.3	83.2	83.4	493400
15/01/2014	83.4	84.8	81	82	540200

Fig. 2. Sample data of GP

3.2 Optimizing Parameters from the Dataset

We have used the Close column of our dataset as the input parameter to predict the stock prices. The close prices for different dates were used as the dependent variable to predict stock prices. We have split the data into 80% test data and 20% train data and stored them into different variables to use them as parameters.

3.3 Linear Regression

We have used linear regression algorithm to train our model. Linear regression is a statistical method for modeling a relationship between two variables that corresponds to the observed data on a linear equation. One variable is regarded as an explanatory variable and the other as a dependent variable. The linear regression method can be used to predict under the assumption that the correlation between the variables will continue in the future. A linear regression Eq. (1) is as follows

$$Y_i = \beta_0 + \beta_1 X_i + \varepsilon_i \tag{1}$$

Here, Y_i is the outcome (predicted output) of the dependent variable for the ith test unit, X_i is the independent variable which is used for prediction for i^{th} test unit. $\beta_0+\beta_1 X_i$ is the linear relation between Y_i and X_i β_0 is the intercept or the mean of Y when X = 0 and β_1 is the slope or the change in mean when X increases by 1. The ε_i represents the error term. In Our model we have used the data close column as our independent variable. So in our model $\text{Close}_i = X_i$.

The β_0 and β_1 parameters are unknown. They are estimated by using least square method. The least square method (2) is as follows:

$$b = \frac{n(\sum XY) - (\sum X).(\sum Y)}{n(\sum X^2) - (\sum X)^2} \quad (2)$$

Considering the least square the best fitted line is taken and uses that as function for the prediction.

3.4 Support Vector Regression

Support Vector Regression (SVR) has the same principal that Support Vector Machine (SVM) uses except for a few minor differences. At first, as output is a real number, the information at hand which has endless possibilities becomes very hard to predict. In the case of regression, the SVM is approximated by a range of tolerance (epsilon), which would already have requested the problem. The main idea, however, is always the same: to mitigate error, to individualize the hyperplane which maximizes the margin, taking into account which part of the error is tolerated.

The fundamental idea behind SVM is for training information from the input field to be transformed into a higher dimension of function Φ and then a separating hyperplane with maximum margin in the function space is constructed as shown in Fig. 3.

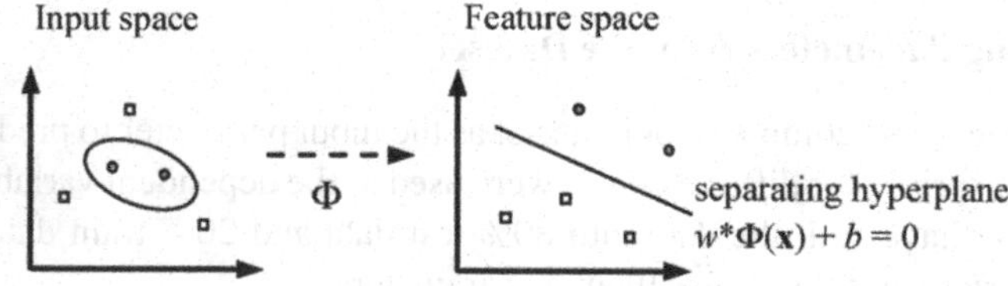

Fig. 3. Using a kernel function SVM mapped the data into a higher dimensional space and separated them using a hyperplane.

When it comes to SVR we can consider a set of training data $\{(x_1, y_1)\ldots(x_l, y_l)\}$ where each $x_i \subset R^n$ which represents the sample input space and has an adequate target value $y_i \subset R$ for $i = 1,\ldots,l$, where l is the size of training data [14]. The standard SVR [16] estimation function (1) is as follows:

$$f(x) = (w \cdot \Phi(x)) + b \quad (3)$$

Where $w \subset R_n$, $b \subset R$ and Φ indicates a nonlinear conversion from R_n to a high-dimensional space. Our objective is to find the value of w and b so that we can determine values of x by reducing the risk of regression.

$$R_{\text{reg}}(f) = C\sum_{i=0}^{l}\Gamma(f(x_i) - y_i) + \frac{1}{2}\|w\|^2 \tag{4}$$

Here Γ() is a cost function C is a constant and the data points vector w may be formulated as:

$$w = \sum_{i=1}^{l}\left(\alpha_i - \alpha_i^*\right)\Phi(x_i) \tag{5}$$

The most widely used cost function is the $\mathscr{E}$-insensitive loss function [15].The function is in this following form:

$$\Gamma(f(x) - y)) = \begin{cases} |f(x) - y| - \varepsilon \\ 0, \end{cases} \tag{6}$$

The regression risk in (4) and the -insensitive loss function (6) can be minimized by solving the quadratic optimization problem.

ς is a slack variable used to calculate errors outside $\mathscr{E}$ tube. In Fig. 4 SVR is fitting a tube with radius $\mathscr{E}$ to the data and positive slack ς is measuring the points that are outside the tube

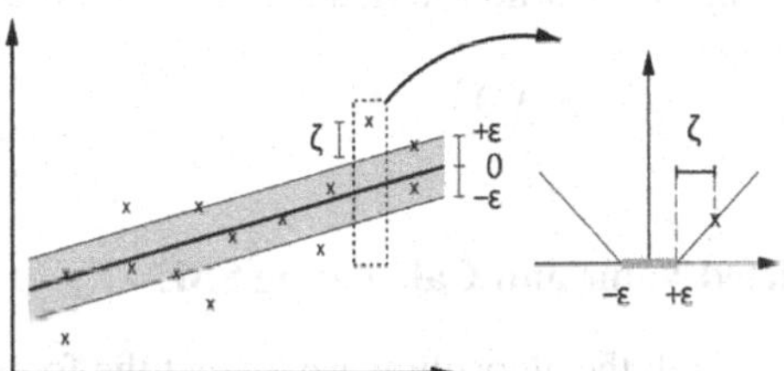

Fig. 4. The configuration of the soft margin loss applies to a linear SV system

The standard formula can be rewritten by substituting (5) to (3):

$$\begin{aligned} f(x) &= \sum_{i=1}^{l}(\alpha_i - \alpha_i^*)(\Phi(x_i)\cdot\Phi(x)) + b \\ &= \sum_{i=1}^{l}(\alpha_i - \alpha_i^*)k(x_i, x) + b. \end{aligned} \tag{7}$$

In (6) the function k (x_i,x) can substitute the dot product known as the kernel function. The kernel function is the idea is to map the non-linear data set into a higher dimensional space where a hyperplane can be found that separates the samples. There are different types of kernels in SVM. The kernels that we used for our model are Radial basis function kernel of RBF and linear kernel.

3.4.1 Radial Basis Function Kernel

The Radial basis function kernel, or RBF kernel also known as Gaussian kernel, is a kernel that is in the form of a radial basis function. The RBF kernel on two samples x and x′, interpreted in some input space as feature vectors, is defined as follows:

$$K(\mathrm{x}, \mathrm{x}') = \exp\left(\frac{\|\mathrm{x} - \mathrm{x}'\|^2}{2\sigma^2}\right) \tag{8}$$

It can also be interpreted as:

$$K(\mathrm{x}, \mathrm{x}') = \exp(-\gamma \|\mathrm{x} - \mathrm{x}'\|^2) \tag{9}$$

Radial basis function takes parameters like gamma and c. The parameter gamma describes the degree to which the effect of a single example of learning exceeds. The C parameter works against maximizing the margin of the decision function from accurate identification of training instances. We have set the values of our parameters by gamma = 0.1 and c = le3.

3.4.2 Linear Kernel

The Linear kernel function is the simplest kernel function. The function is given by the internal product (x, y) and an optional constant C. Algorithms using linear kernel functions are often the same as their non-kernel counterparts. It can be interpreted as:

$$k(x, y) = x^T y + c \tag{10}$$

3.5 Extracting Predicted Value and Calculating SSE

After training our dataset with the algorithms we extract the forecasted values that our algorithms predicted. We calculated the accuracy by calculating the SSE where the value is between 0 to 1. 1 is the best possible value that we can get meaning an accuracy of hundred percent. The formula for calculating SSE is:

$$SSE = \sum_{i=1}^{n} (Y_i - \hat{Y}_i)^2 \tag{11}$$

Where $\mathrm{Y_i}$ is the actual value and $\hat{Y}_i$ is the predicted value.

3.6 Visualizing the Comparison Between Actual and Predicted Values

Finally we plotted our value on a graph and compared the predicted values in respect of the actual values. We have compared the values for 10 days, 20 days and 30 days for linear regression and for SVR with both the RBF and linear kernels.

4 Result and Discussion

After training and test our model we have extracted the predicted value for different days. We have predicted the closing price for a 10 days, 20 days and 60 days period. The accuracy for predicting the price for less number of days was much higher than the accuracy for a higher number of days. The accuracy and predicted price changes after each iteration. We have discussed about the accuracy and the predicted price that we got for a random iteration. After running our program we found an accuracy of 97.07% with linear Regression 97.06 with SVR (RBF) and 96.82 with SVR (linear) for 10 days. We have plotted the comparison between the actual value and predicted value using graphical representations. We have used matplotlib; a python library to visualize the graph for the values. The 10 day comparison graph among the Linear Regression, SVR (RBF) and SVR (linear) is shown below:

Figure 5 shows the comparison between actual value and forecasted value for 10 days with LR. It has a 94.07% accuracy which is pretty high for a continuous valued prediction. The graph shows that the predicted value is almost as same as the actual value which is pretty impressive. In Fig. 6 we can see the graphical comparison between the actual and predicted value for SVR (linear). The accuracy is 97.06% which is pretty similar to the LR prediction and the predicted values are very close to the actual values. In Diagram 6 the graph shows the comparison between actual and predicted values with SVR (RBF). The patterns are quite close for actual and predicted values but still not as accurate as LR and SVR (linear). The accuracy is 96.86% which is still pretty high (Fig. 7).

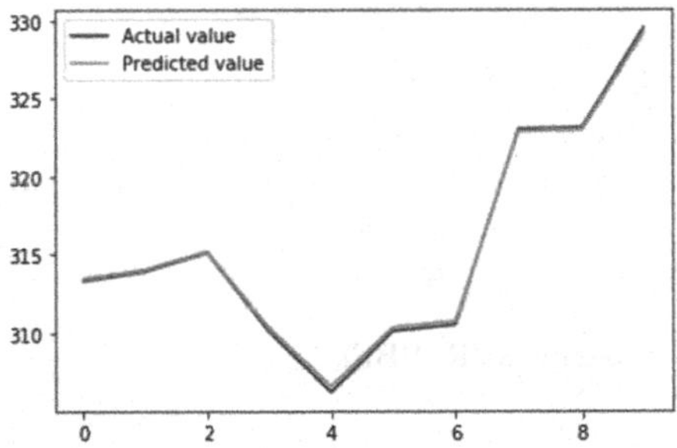

Fig. 5. Comparison for 10 days (LR)

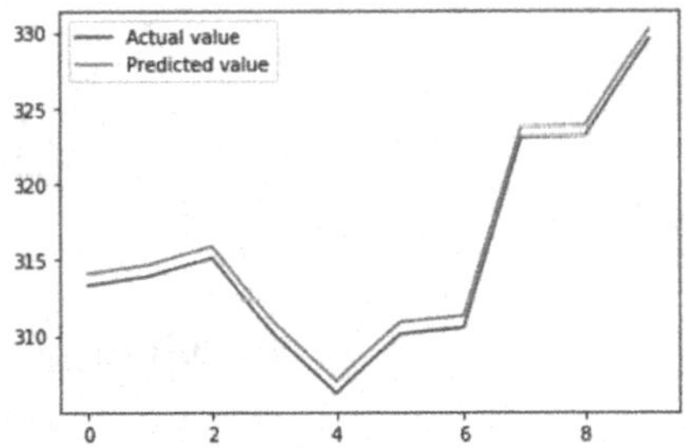

Fig. 6. Comparison for 10 days SVR (linear)

We have predicted the closing price for 30 days period too. For 30 days The Linear regression performed the best with the highest accuracy of 91.22% while the SVR (linear) has an accuracy of about 90.70% and SVR (RBF) has an accuracy of about 87.50%. The accuracy for all of the algorithms are still quite good.

Figure 8 shows that the actual and predict values are very close. Figure 9 shows the predicted prices followed the same trend as the actual prices. In Fig. 10 with SVR (RBF) the prices wasn't quite accurate but still pretty good for a continuous valued prediction.

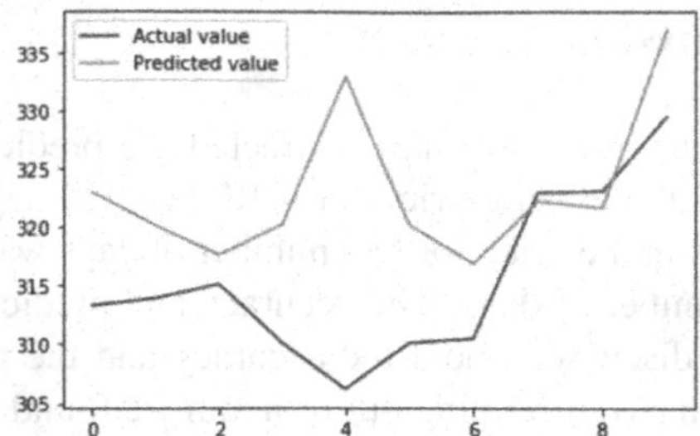

Fig. 7. Comparison for 10 days SVR (RBF)

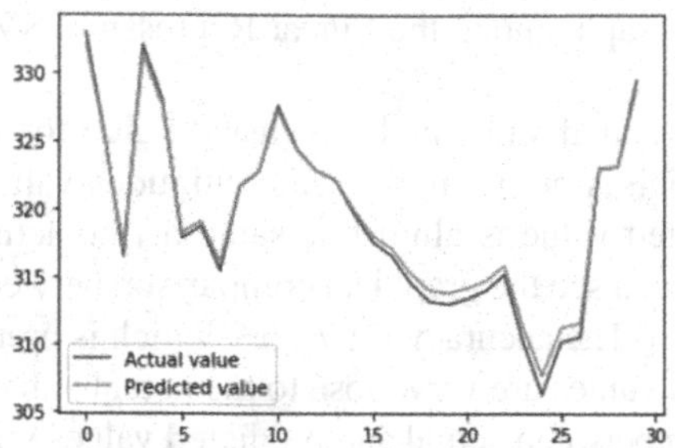

Fig. 8. Comparison for 30 days (LR)

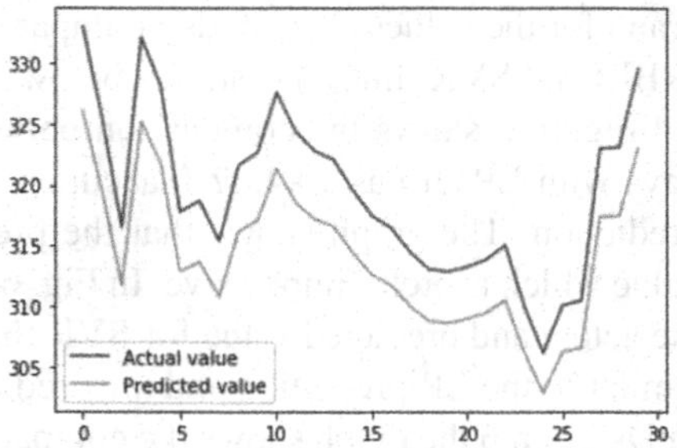

Fig. 9. Comparison for 30 days SVR (linear)

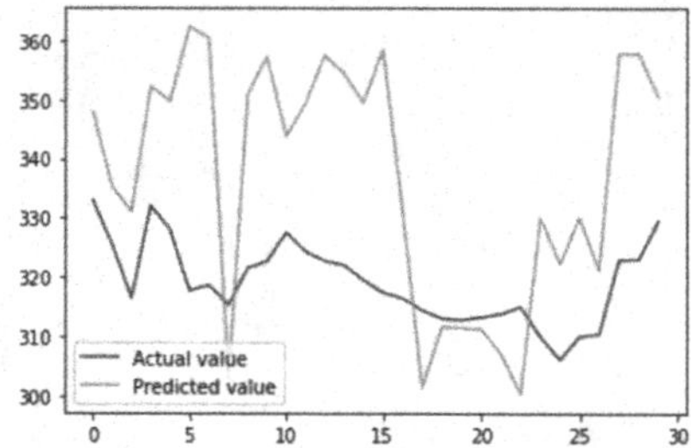

Fig. 10. Comparison for 30 days SVR (RBF)

For 60 days prediction like other prediction LR has the best performance with an accuracy of 79.82% while SVR (RBF) has a better accuracy than SVR (linear) with 78.50% and SVR (linear) have an accuracy of 77.53%. The comparison in graphical representation is shown below:

In Fig. 11 we can see that the predicted price trend followed the actual price trend. The accuracy of linear is much lower than the 10 days or 30 days prediction accuracy but it's still pretty close. For SVR (linear) the trend is similar but the values are a little far from the actual price point. For SVR (RBF) the price point are pretty close in some points but still has a lower accuracy than LR (Figs. 12 and 13).

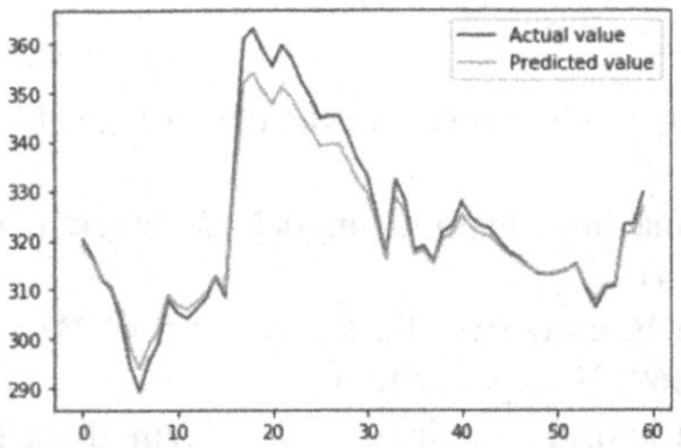

Fig. 11. Comparison for 60 days (LR)

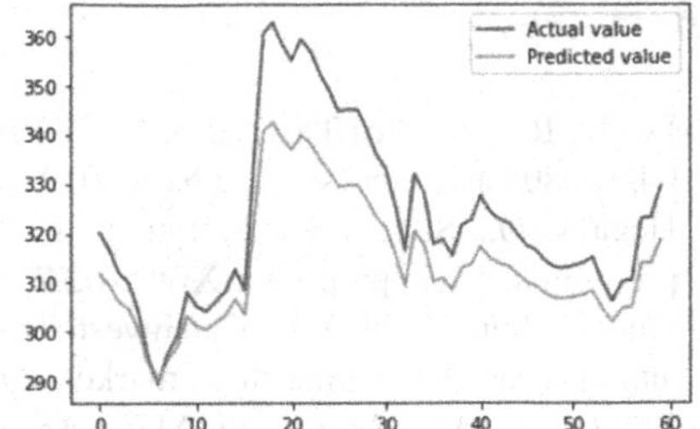

Fig. 12. Comparison for 60 days SVR (linear)

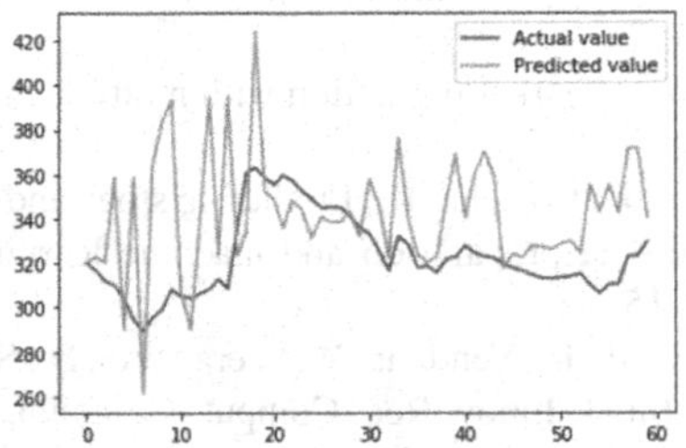

Fig. 13. Comparison for 60 days SVR (RBF)

The accuracy comparison for 10, 30 and 60 days are given at the table:

Days	LR	SVR (linear)	SVR (RBF)
10	97.07%	97.06%	96.82%
30	91.22%	90.70%	87.50%
60	79.82%	77.53%	78.50%

As per our table we can see that Liner Regression algorithm has the best performance among all. SVR (linear) and SVR (RBF) have pretty much similar performance with varying performance for different days.

5 Conclusion

Linear Regression model has performed the best to predict stock price. For fewer days it has a tremendous performance. SVR (linear) and SVR (RBF) has a quite impressive performance too. But with other parameters the performance of SVR may be improved. Using technical and fundamental indicators like RSI, MACD, investor sentiment percentage, company background etc. as parameters might improve the prediction performance as these have an effect on stock price movement. Using these parameters in potent machine learning algorithms might increase the accuracy of price prediction.

References

1. David, R.H.: Forces That Move Stock Prices. https://www.investopedia.com/articles/basics/04/100804.asp. Accessed 20 Nov 2019
2. Hegazy, O., Soliman, O.S, Salam, M.A.: A machine learning model for stock market prediction. arXiv preprint arXiv:1402.7351 (2014)
3. Guo, K., Sun, Y., Qian, X.: Can investor sentiment be used to predict the stock price? Dynamic analysis based on China stock market. Phys. A **469**, 390–396 (2017)
4. Ebadati, O.M.E., Mortazavi, M.T.: An efficient hybrid machine learning method for time series stock market forecasting. Neural Netw. World **28**(1), 41–55 (2017)
5. Pyo, S., Lee, J., Cha, M., Jang, H.: Predictability of machine learning techniques to forecast the trends of market index prices: hypothesis testing for the Korean stock markets. PLoS ONE **12**(11), e0188107 (2017)
6. Qian, B., Rasheed, K.: Stock market prediction with multiple classifiers. Appl. Intell. **26**(1), 25–33 (2007)
7. Patel, J., Shah, S., Thakkar, P., Kotecha, K.: Predicting stock and stock price index movement using trend deterministic data preparation and machine learning techniques. Expert Syst. Appl. **42**(1), 259–268 (2015)
8. Akash, A., Rajaji, S., Aravinth, R., Vendhan, V., Veerapandi, D.: Stock market trend prediction using machine learning. Int. J. Innov. Res. Comput. Commun. Eng. **7**, 1000–1006 (2017). https://doi.org/10.15680/ijircce.2019.0702085
9. Efat, M.I.A., Bashar, R., Uddin, K.I., Bhuiyan, T.: Trend estimation of stock market: an intelligent decision system. In: International Conference on Cyber Security and Computer Science (2018)
10. Madge, S., Bhatt, S.: Predicting stock price direction using support vector machines. Independent work report spring (2015)
11. Leung, C.K.S., MacKinnon, R.K., Wang, Y.: A machine learning approach for stock price prediction. In: Proceedings of the 18th International Database Engineering & Applications Symposium, pp. 274–277. ACM (2014)
12. Müller, K.-R., Smola, A.J., Rätsch, G., Schölkopf, B., Kohlmorgen, J., Vapnik, V.: Predicting time series with support vector machines. In: Gerstner, W., Germond, A., Hasler, M., Nicoud, J.-D. (eds.) ICANN 1997. LNCS, vol. 1327, pp. 999–1004. Springer, Heidelberg (1997). https://doi.org/10.1007/BFb0020283
13. Kamalakannan, J., Sengupta, I., Chaudhury, S.: Stock market prediction using time series analysis. In: 2018 IADS International Conference on Computing, Communications & Data Engineering (CCODE), pp. 7–8 (2018)
14. Müller, K.R., Smola, A., Rätsch, G., Schölkopf, B., Kohlmorgen, J., Vapnik, V.: Using support vector machines for time series prediction. In: Advances in Kernel Methods—Support Vector Learning, pp. 243–254 (2018)
15. Edwards, R.D., Magee, J., Bassetti, W.C.: Technical Analysis of Stock Trends. CRC Press, Boca Raton (2018)
16. Cherkassky, V., Ma, Y.: Practical selection of SVM parameters and noise estimation for SVM regression. Neural Netw. **17**(1), 113–126 (2004)

Machine Learning on Imbalanced Data

Training Data Selection Using Ensemble Dataset Approach for Software Defect Prediction

Md Fahimuzzman Sohan(✉), Md Alamgir Kabir, Mostafijur Rahman, S. M. Hasan Mahmud, and Touhid Bhuiyan

Department of Software Engineering, Daffodil International University, Dhaka, Bangladesh
{sohan35-1284,alamgir.swe,mostafijur.swe}@diu.edu.bd,
{hasan.swe,t.bhuiyan}@daffodilvarsity.edu.bd

Abstract. Cross-project defect prediction (CPDP) is using due to the limitation of within project defect prediction (WPDP) in Software Defect Prediction (SDP) research. CPDP aims to train one project data to predict another project using the machine learning technique. The source and target projects are different in the CPDP setting, because of various structured source-target projects, sometimes it may not be a perfect combination. This study represents a categorical data set ensemble technique, where multiple data sets have been aggregated for source data instead of using a single data set. The method has been evaluated on nine data sets, taken from the publicly accessible repository with two performance indicators. The results of this data set ensemble approach show the improvement of the prediction performance over 65% combinations compared with traditional CPDP models. The results also show that same categories (homogeneous) train-test data set pairs give high performance; otherwise, the prediction performances of different category data sets are mostly collapsed. Therefore, the proposed scheme is recommended as an alternative to predict defects that can improve the prediction of most of the cases compared with traditional cross-project SDP models.

Keywords: Software defect prediction · Cross-project defect prediction · Training data selection · Data set ensemble

1 Introduction

The defect is bug or mistake in the source code of software and can give unexpected results to the developers. Finding and correcting defects are expensive for the development and maintenance of a software [1]. So the ultimate goal of SDP is early defect identification and that can reduce development cost and time. At present software grows vastly and also many challenges and attention are arising about the massive size and complexity of the software projects. Here, the defect

T. Bhuiyan et al. (Eds.): ICONCS 2020, LNICST 325, pp. 243–256, 2020.
https://doi.org/10.1007/978-3-030-52856-0_19

prediction is important to take challenges over big and complex software projects [2]. SDP is an active research topic in software engineering and regarding various techniques, for instance: statistical, machine learning, parametric, mixed model techniques [3].

CPDP is a commonly used theme in SDP. CPDP uses different project data for the train model and validation. In practice, it is needed to build the prediction model with a sufficient number of data to achieve high prediction performance [4]. In some cases CPDP has a limitation, a common problem of CPDP is the heterogeneous[1] data set. Since the training and test data come from different projects that's because there is a chance of dissimilarity between the source and targeted data, it can give unexpected results. Conceptually the expectation is homogeneous test-train combination is a better setting than heterogeneous combination [5]. Because validation data need it's similar category data that is used to prepare the prediction model.

To address this dissimilarity between the training and test data selection, some prior work proposed model ensemble [6] and data set ensemble [7,8] techniques. In the model ensemble technique, they have used multiple project data to produce large scale training data, also they combined multiple defect prediction models. Moreover, He et al. [7] and Jing et al. [8] have used the ensemble data set approach, they combined multiple data sets to prepare the models. After analyzing their results, the highest and lowest f-1 score has been found for the two studies are 0.874 and 0.293, 0.34 and 0.70 respectively. Here, a huge distinction has been observed between the highest and lowest performance. Though, they did not investigate this dissimilarity between performance among the defect prediction models. This investigation has worked over the diversity of various structured data sets and their predicted performance.

However, in this investigation, firstly the traditional defect prediction modeling technique [9] has been used on nine software defect data sets that have been collected from SeaCraft repository [10] (also known as PROMISE data sets) for this study, as historical data. The structure of the data sets is not the same, some mostly defect-prone or defect-free or in average mode. From this variety of data distribution, the collected data sets have been divided into three categories based on their number of non-defective and defective classes, they are Non-defect Majority, Neutral, and Defect Majority. Consequently, the ensemble technique have been conducted using the categorically divided data sets for defect prediction models. Indeed, the experiment result has been divided into two phases: first identifying the problem of cross-project with multi-structured data sets and after that, the comparative discussion has been given between the performance of cross-project and data set ensemble technique with required results analysis data set ensemble technique shows improved results than cross-project technique. In this study, f1-score and accuracy make 108 combinations for data set ensemble setting. Among them, 65% combinations have been able to improve the performance compared with traditional cross-project technique.

[1] For this study homogeneous or heterogeneous being called based on the number of non-defective and defective class in a data set.

The reminder part of this paper is organized as follows. Section 2 represents the related work of this study. The proposed technique has been described in Sect. 3. Section 4 presents the details about the methodology. Result analysis has been allocated in Sect. 5. Lastly, Sect. 6 has concluded the study.

2 Related Work

Software Defect prediction is a popular research area in software engineering. Catal and Diri [11] have a review article on SDP, the first one has been found in 1990 from their considered articles on defect prediction, which was by Porter and Selby [12]. Since then hundreds of defect prediction model has been presented. From the trends and techniques, easily SDP research can be identified by some groups. For example: WPDP [13], CPDP [14], class imbalance learning defect prediction [15], ensembles learning defect prediction [16]. Researchers are also interested in new techniques (i.e., transfer learning [17], bellwethers method [18]). However, the main focus of this study is cross-project with multi-structured data set issues. The next subsection is describing the previous research schemes about software defect prediction with the ensemble data set.

2.1 Defect Prediction with Ensemble Data Set

It has been mentioned previously that some studies have been found where data set ensemble techniques have been used to tackle data heterogeneity problem. He et al. [7] have worked for three questions in their study: firstly they have performed the training data from other projects to predict defects of the target project, then they compared the performance between the same project defect prediction and different projects defect prediction models, and lastly they have tried to find out the impact of various data sets on selecting the suitable training data for defect prediction models. Kamei et al. [6] have combined the defect data sets for just-in-time (JIT) cross-project defect prediction. They have used model selection, data merging, and ensembles of models techniques to optimize the performance. They are telling in the article that a pool of data collected from the different projects can make a model more strong in a cross-project setting. Moreover, they have implemented models ensemble technique for JIT defect prediction to improve the performance. Jing et al. [8] have used 14 project data from four different companies to perform transfer learning approach. Their transfer learning has implemented on one-to-one and many-to-one heterogeneous cross-project defect prediction. They have shown the data set ensemble (many-to-one) can achieve a better result than the traditional approach in cross-project defect prediction manner. These prior works have agreed that data set aggregation can be a robust model fit to apply on the cross-project defect prediction.

3 Proposed Approach

This investigation has two case studies, firstly a problem of traditional CPDP has been identified in the collected data sets and to define the problem a data set ensemble technique has been applied on the data sets. The traditional cross-project approach demonstrates that single project data is used to prepare the prediction models. But under this study, data set ensemble learning has been used for training the models, it aims to aggregate multiple data sets in a new data storage and that will used to prepare prediction models. Fukushima et al. [19] have a relevant setting, they applied it to JIT SDP. They have worked 11 publicly available data sets, where 110 traditional cross-project combinations (11×10) performed. Their investigation indicates that ensemble the data sets (combine historical data from different projects) technique perform well on JIT defect prediction.

In this study, firstly traditional cross-project models have been performed using collected 9 open source project data, which makes 72 combinations (9×8). In Eq. 1, N is the number of data sets used in this cross-project defect prediction models. These nine data sets have created (9-1) models each time and their summation is 72.

$$CPDP(N) = \sum_{d=1}^{N}(N-1) = \sum_{d}^{9}(9-1) \tag{1}$$

But, this approach fails to achieve successive performance, few numbers of combinations have given good result and the rest combinations have fallen. After observing the result it can be pointed that homogeneous train-test data set combinations to perform outstanding and heterogeneous combinations were lower. For this reason, the collected data sets have been divided into three categories based on their similarity of class ratio in the data sets. They are:

- Non-defect Majority: defective classes are 1–30%
- Neutral: defective classes are 31–70%
- Defect Majority: defective classes are 71–100%

Each category contains three homogeneous data sets after distributing the collected data sets into their respective categories. Then every three homogeneous data sets are manually combined, which prepared three new data sets. Besides, these three new data sets have been used to prepare prediction models, which creates new 18 combinations (3×6), Eq. 2 represents the train data selection of ensemble data sets technique. Note that test data sets are no modified, the individual data set has been tested by the required models in this study.

$$\text{Data sets ensemble}\,(N) = \sum_{d=1}^{N}\frac{N}{3}(N-3) \tag{2}$$

4 Methodology

4.1 Data

For this study, nine publicly available data sets have been chosen from nine different projects, everyone is the latest version of the project data sets are collected from SeaCraft repository [10], which are commonly used in SDP. Table 1 represents the details about the data sets. All projects have been developed with Java programming language. Jureczko and Madeyski [20], they have prepared the defect data sets and donated to the repository. Table 1 shows that non-defective and defective modules are not the same for every data set, the structure is different. Where some data sets are highly defected free, some defect-prone. In this study, the investigated data sets have 19 static code metrics, they are reported as good quality indicators and widely used metrics [21]. All metrics are prepared for the size and complexity of a software project. The metrics are calculated using a tool, named Ckjm[2]. The metrics suggested by Chidamber and Kemerer [22]; from here the name adopted, CK metrics. After the value of 19 metrics the final labeling has been placed as the class is defect-free or defective (as a binary value, 0 for defect-free and 1 for defective).

Table 1. Statistics of used data sets in this study

Project	No. of classes	Non-defective	Defective	% of defective
Ant	745	579	166	22
Ivy	352	312	40	11
Jedit	492	481	11	2
Log4j	205	16	189	92
Lucene	340	137	203	60
Poi	442	161	281	64
Synapse	256	170	86	34
Xalan	909	11	898	99
Xerces	588	151	437	74

4.2 Classifier

In this study, Gaussian Naive Bayes classifier has been used. It is a classification based investigation; which is the most used and relatively well performer classifier in the field of SDP [2]. In a prediction model, there are many attributes and they continuously perform one by one. Following a Gaussian distribution, the continuous values have been associated with each distributed class. In this experiment, the training data contains a continuous attribute, x. The first work is to segment the data by the class, then the mean and variance of x have been taken from each class. Let, μ_k be the mean of the value in x associated with class C_k and let σ_k^2 be the variance of the values in x associated with class C_k. If the observer value (test data) is v then the probability distribution of v given

[2] http://gromit.iiar.pwr.wroc.pl/p_inf/ckjm/.

of a class C_k is $P(x = v|C_k)$ can be computed by plugging v into the equation for a normal distribution parameterized by μ_k and σ_k^2. The equation is,

$$P(x_i|y) = \frac{1}{\sqrt{2\pi\sigma_k^2}} e^{-\left(\frac{(x_i-\mu_y)^2}{2\sigma_k^2}\right)} \tag{3}$$

4.3 Performance Evaluation Criteria

How a classifier or classification performed, this calculation conducted by performance metrics. This subsection describes the performance measures used in this investigation. Various performance evaluation metrics have been used in SDP [2,8,23,24]. Performance metrics in SDP come from the confusion matrix, it shows the actual and predicted value from a classification. SDP classification has two outputs, positive and negative [15]. Two commonly selected performance metrics have been used in this study: f1-score and accuracy lifted the correctly classified instances from the whole classification, which means it is the ratio of correctly predicted instances with total instances [25]. The equation of accuracy looks like that: $\frac{TP+TN}{TP+FP+TN+FN}$. To calculate f1-score first need to perform on Precision and Recall [26]. Precision is correctly predicted faulty instances from the total number of faulty instances and Recall is the ratio of faulty instances that are correctly predicted. F1-score is the combined form Precision and Recall: $\frac{2\times Precision \times Recall}{Precision+Recall}$

4.4 Experiment Outline

Dealing with heterogeneous data sets is a challenging task also in defect prediction, for cross-project SDP it is more difficult. The cross-project approach takes a project's data to train a model and use different project data to predict. So, there is a big chance of collision between train and test data combination duo to the variety of project structure. That's why it needs more attention to tackle the issue and it already is in. Figure 1 represents the required steps for this experiment. Firstly, nine defect data sets have been collected from nine different projects and used to build several prediction models. In this study, all prediction models have been build with the Gaussian Naive Bayes classifier. After that f1-score and accuracy have been used to calculate the performance of the classification. These nine data sets have performed as train data individually for nine times. Each time one data set has been used to train a model and the remaining eight data sets have been used to validate the model. This process has been performed nine times and prepared 72 (9×8) combinations of the cross-project model (please see Sect. 3 for the concept). Under this cross-project setting, some prediction was highly accurate and some were a relatively low performer. For this low performer combinations data set ensemble approach has been performed (please see Sect. 3 for details about the approach). Also for this approach Gaussian Naive Bayes classifier; f1-score and accuracy have been used.

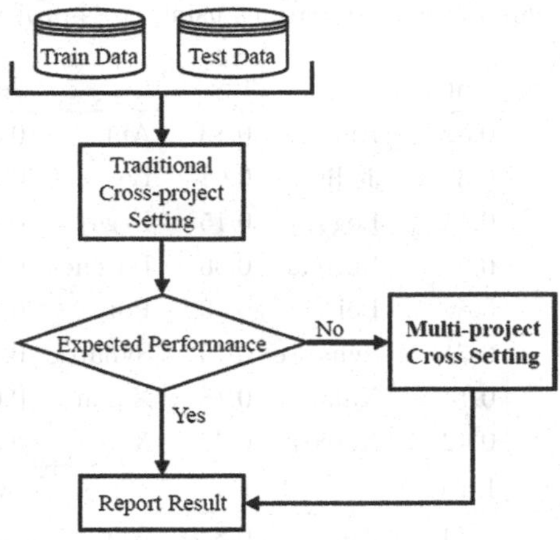

Fig. 1. Steps of the experiment

5 Result Analysis

5.1 Case Study 1

This case study represents the result of the traditional cross-project setting. The traditional cross-project is where the supply of train and test data are from different projects. In this study, nine data sets have been used nine times as train data. Each time one data set used to train a model and other eight have used to test the model. In this way, 72 combinations performed and the performance has been calculated using f1-score and accuracy.

Table 2 shows the f1-score of 72 combinations. The first training data set is Ant, it performs with the other eight data sets. Result shows that Ivy achieves best performer (0.82) against the Ant training model and Xalan was the worst (0.14). Similarly against training data Ivy and Jedit, Ant (0.83) and Ivy (0.92) were the top; Log4j (0.15) and Xalan (0.03) were the worst performers respectively. Then when Lucene and Poi were the training data set also here Ant is the topper for both (0.74 and 0.8 respectively); for train data set Synapse, the f1-score of Poi is highest. Log4j achieves the lowest value against the Lucene, Poi, and Synapse train data sets. Lastly, against train data sets Log4j, Xalan and Xerces the top performer test data sets are Xalan (0.95), Poi (0.75) and Poi (0.78) respectively. For the three models test data set Jedit was the worst performer.

Table 3 shows the prediction performance of classification models using accuracy. This table shows that the result is almost similar to the F-1 score. Against Ant and Jedit training data sets, the best performer test data set is Ivy for both (0.83 and 0.89 respectively) and train data Ivy, Ant outperforms (0.82). For train data Lucene, Poi and Synapse the most performer test data sets are Ant (0.75), Ivy (0.81) and Poi (0.77) respectively; for all these three train data sets most lower performer test data set is Log4j (0.27, 0.2 and 0.29 respectively). Log4j,

Table 2. F1-score of 72 combinations using cross-project technique

Test/Train	Ant		Ivy		Jedit
Ivy	0.82	Ant	0.83	Ant	0.86
Jedit	0.62	Jedit	0.68	Ivy	0.92
Log4j	0.15	Log4j	0.15	Log4j	0.14
Lucene	0.56	Lucene	0.56	Lucene	0.57
Poi	0.54	Poi	0.53	Poi	0.53
Synapse	0.71	Synapse	0.75	Synapse	0.78
Xalan	0.14	Xalan	0.18	Xalan	0.03
Xerces	0.42	Xerces	0.42	Xerces	0.41
Test/Train	Lucene		Poi		Synapse
Ant	0.74	Ant	0.8	Ant	0.66
Ivy	0.7	Ivy	0.79	Ivy	0.72
Jedit	0.54	Jedit	0.62	Jedit	0.47
Log4j	0.21	Log4j	0.17	Log4j	0.21
Poi	0.61	Lucene	0.58	Lucene	0.64
Synapse	0.73	Synapse	0.71	Poi	0.76
Xalan	0.33	Xalan	0.23	Xalan	0.42
Xerces	0.43	Xerces	0.43	Xerces	0.52
Test/Train	Log4j		Xalan		Xerces
Ant	0.36	Ant	0.41	Ant	0.45
Ivy	0.21	Ivy	0.29	Ivy	0.42
Jedit	0.04	Jedit	0.11	Jedit	0.16
Lucene	0.71	Log4j	0.6	Log4j	0.45
Poi	0.76	Lucene	0.71	Lucene	0.7
Synapse	0.5	Poi	0.75	Poi	0.78
Xalan	0.95	Synapse	0.54	Synapse	0.54
Xerces	0.82	Xerces	0.67	Xalan	0.63

Xalan, and Xerces are mostly defect-prone data sets. Against this three train data sets Xalan (0.96), Poi (0.72) and Poi (0.77) respectively. Also, the worst performers are Ivy (0.15), Jedit (0.23) and Jedit (0.3).

5.2 Case Study 2

Case study 2 represents the output of the proposed data sets ensemble technique. Where multiple project data have been used to prepare training models instead of using single project. In this study from collected nine defect data sets, three new data sets have been prepared manually using multiple projects data technique. Each new data set carries three project data out of nine data sets,

Table 3. Accuracy of 72 combinations using cross-project technique

Test/Train	Ant		Ivy		Jedit
Ivy	0.83	Ant	0.82	Ant	0.79
Jedit	0.72	Jedit	0.77	Ivy	0.89
Log4j	0.16	Log4j	0.14	Log4j	0.09
Lucene	0.52	Lucene	0.5	Lucene	0.42
Poi	0.5	Poi	0.46	Poi	0.4
Synapse	0.7	Synapse	0.72	Synapse	0.67
Xalan	0.28	Xalan	0.33	Xalan	0.07
Xerces	0.38	Xerces	0.37	Xerces	0.28
Test/Train	Lucene		Poi		Synapse
Ant	0.75	Ant	0.8	Ant	0.69
Ivy	0.74	Ivy	0.81	Ivy	0.76
Jedit	0.66	Jedit	0.72	Jedit	0.6
Log4j	0.27	Log4j	0.2	Log4j	0.29
Poi	0.61	Lucene	0.56	Lucene	0.64
Synapse	0.72	Synapse	0.71	Poi	0.77
Xalan	0.48	Xalan	0.38	Xalan	0.57
Xerces	0.43	Xerces	0.4	Xerces	0.53
Test/Train	Log4j		Xalan		Xerces
Ant	0.24	Ant	0.4	Ant	0.47
Ivy	0.15	Ivy	0.35	Ivy	0.5
Jedit	0.06	Jedit	0.23	Jedit	0.3
Lucene	0.59	Log4j	0.67	Log4j	0.55
Poi	0.66	Lucene	0.67	Lucene	0.69
Synapse	0.39	Poi	0.72	Poi	0.77
Xalan	0.96	Synapse	0.51	Synapse	0.52
Xerces	0.74	Xerces	0.68	Xalan	0.73

using this way three new data sets (3×3) performed for defect prediction models. The combination of three new data sets are like that (Ant + Jedit + Ivy), (Lucene + Poi + Synapse) and (Log4j + Xalan + Xerces). Similarly, the Gaussian Naive Bayes classifier has been implemented on these three combined data sets, after that f1-score and accuracy have been used for performance evaluation. It makes eighteen data set ensemble combinations.

Table 4 shows the result of the data sets the ensemble approach for this study. For both f1-score and accuracy of (Ant + Jedit + Ivy) train data set, Synapse was a top performer (0.76) and Xalan was the lowest (0.12). In terms of f1-score and accuracy for all settings two test data sets Xalan and Log4j are commonly lower performers. Moreover, Ant and Log4j vale gave the highest (0.76) and lowest f1-score respectively against (Ant + Jedit + Ivy) train data set, under the same train data Ant and Ivy both commonly performed high (0.78) under f1-score and accuracy. Under the same setting Log4j commonly performed worst (0.17 and 0.2) in terms of f1-score and accuracy. Lastly, for train data (Log4j + Xalan + Xerces) highest performer test data set was Poi and the lowest was Jedit in terms of both performance measures.

Table 4. F1-score and accuracy using data set ensemble technique

F1-score					
Test/Train	Ant + Jedit + Ivy		Lucene + Poi + Synapse		Log4j + Xalan + Xerces
Log4j	0.16	Ant	0.78	Ant	0.48
Lucene	0.58	Ivy	0.75	Ivy	0.45
Poi	0.54	Jedit	0.62	Jedit	0.17
Synapse	0.76	Log4j	0.17	Lucene	0.7
Xalan	0.12	Xalan	0.25	Poi	0.77
Xerces	0.41	Xerces	0.43	Synapse	0.56
Accuracy					
Test/Train	Ant + Jedit + Ivy		Lucene + Poi + Synapse		Log4j + Xalan + Xerces
Log4j	0.18	Ant	0.78	Ant	0.5
Lucene	0.58	Ivy	0.78	Ivy	0.53
Poi	0.54	Jedit	0.72	Jedit	0.32
Synapse	0.76	Log4j	0.2	Lucene	0.69
Xalan	0.12	Xalan	0.41	Poi	0.77
Xerces	0.41	Xerces	0.4	Synapse	0.56

5.3 Result Discussion

This section represents the compression after preforming the traditional cross-project and data set ensemble approaches. It is already described that for this study the collected nine data sets have been divided into three categories using their class ratio, then they have performed as the cross-project and data set ensemble approach. Table 2 and 3 is the value of f1-score and accuracy respectively, here single project has been used to cross. Single project crossing has a heterogeneous problem it has been identified previously in this study. Here this ensemble data set technique has been used to overcome the problem. Table 4 shows the result of the data set ensemble technique, where multiple data sets have been used to prepare prediction models. Table 5 and 6 shows the performance comparison between traditional cross-project and data sets ensemble technique in term of f1-score and accuracy respectively. From both tables, 108 combinations performed in this comparison. Tables demonstrate that in most cases data set ensemble technique performs well than traditional cross-project technique. Statistics show that 70 (65%) data set ensemble models have been able to improve the performance, 26 (24%) comparisons show that performance was

Table 5. Competitive analysis between data set ensemble (i.e., combined) and cross-project defect prediction. Total 54 comparisons have been shown for f1-score; where ↑, ↓, and ↕ indicate the improvement, degradation, and unchanged of performance respectively

F1-score						
Test/Train	Combined	Ant	Combined	Ivy	Combined	Jedit
Log4j	↑ 0.16	0.15	↑ 0.16	0.15	↑ 0.16	0.14
Lucene	↑ 0.58	0.56	↑ 0.58	0.56	↑ 0.58	0.57
Poi	↕ 0.54	0.54	↑ 0.54	0.53	↑ 0.54	0.53
Synapse	↑ 0.76	0.71	↑ 0.76	0.75	↓ 0.76	0.78
Xalan	↓ 0.12	0.14	↓ 0.12	0.18	↑ 0.12	0.03
Xerces	↓ 0.41	0.42	↓ 0.41	0.42	↕ 0.41	0.41
	Combined	Lucene	Combined	Poi	Combined	Synapse
Ant	↑ 0.78	0.74	↓ 0.78	0.8	↑ 0.78	0.66
Ivy	↑ 0.75	0.7	↓ 0.75	0.79	↑ 0.75	0.72
Jedit	↑ 0.62	0.54	↕ 0.62	0.62	↑ 0.62	0.47
Log4j	↓ 0.17	0.21	↕ 0.17	0.17	↓ 0.17	0.21
Xalan	↓ 0.25	0.33	↑ 0.25	0.23	↓ 0.25	0.42
Xerces	↕ 0.43	0.43	↕ 0.43	0.43	↓ 0.43	0.52
	Combined	Log4j	Combined	Xalan	Combined	Xerces
Ant	↑ 0.48	0.36	↑ 0.48	0.41	↑ 0.48	0.45
Ivy	↑ 0.45	0.21	↑ 0.45	0.29	↑ 0.45	0.42
Jedit	↑ 0.17	0.04	↑ 0.17	0.11	↑ 0.17	0.16
Lucene	↓ 0.7	0.71	↓ 0.7	0.71	↕ 0.7	0.7
Poi	↑ 0.77	0.76	↑ 0.77	0.75	↓ 0.77	0.78
Synapse	↑ 0.56	0.5	↑ 0.56	0.54	↑ 0.56	0.54
Total	↑ 11, ↑ 5, ↕ 2		↑ 10, ↓ 5, ↕ 3		↑ 11, ↓ 5, ↕ 2	
	↑ 32, ↓ 15, ↕7					

decreased and the other 12 (11%) comparisons show that performance of data set ensemble models have been neutral out of 108 comparisons compared with traditional cross-project technique. After observing these tables some points can be identified:

- A trend has been noticed that same category (homogeneous) train-test data set combinations competitively perform better than different category (heterogeneous) combinations.
- Preparing prediction models using highly imbalance (defect-prone or defect-free) data sets can't be a good choice.
- The result shows that in predictive models, using the data set ensemble technique is better than using a single data set for SDP.

Table 6. Competitive analysis between data set ensemble (i.e., combined) and cross-project defect prediction. Total 54 comparisons have been shown for accuracy; where ↑, ↓, and ↕ indicate the improvement, degradation, and unchanged of performance respectively

Accuracy						
Test/Train	Combined	Ant	Combined	Ivy	Combined	Jedit
Log4j	↑ 0.18	0.16	↑ 0.78	0.14	↑ 0.5	0.09
Lucene	↑ 0.58	0.52	↑ 0.78	0.5	↑ 0.53	0.42
Poi	↑ 0.54	0.5	↑ 0.72	0.46	↓ 0.32	0.4
Synapse	↑ 0.76	0.7	↓ 0.2	0.72	↑ 0.69	0.67
Xalan	↓ 0.12	0.28	↑ 0.41	0.33	↑ 0.77	0.07
Xerces	↑ 0.41	0.38	↑ 0.4	0.37	↑ 0.56	0.28
	Combined	Lucene	Combined	Poi	Combined	Synapse
Ant	↑ 0.78	0.75	↓ 0.78	0.8	↑ 0.78	0.69
Ivy	↑ 0.78	0.74	↓ 0.78	0.81	↑ 0.78	0.76
Jedit	↑ 0.72	0.66	↕ 0.72	0.72	↑ 0.72	0.6
Log4j	↓ 0.2	0.27	↕ 0.2	0.2	↓ 0.2	0.29
Xalan	↓ 0.41	0.48	↑ 0.41	0.38	↓ 0.41	0.57
Xerces	↓ 0.4	0.43	↕ 0.4	0.4	↓ 0.4	0.53
	Combined	Log4j	Combined	Xalan	Combined	Xerces
Ant	↑ 0.5	0.24	↑ 0.5	0.4	↑ 0.5	0.47
Ivy	↑ 0.53	0.15	↑ 0.53	0.35	↑ 0.53	0.5
Jedit	↑ 0.32	0.06	↑ 0.32	0.23	↑ 0.32	0.3
Lucene	↑ 0.69	0.59	↑ 0.69	0.67	↕ 0.69	0.69
Poi	↑ 0.77	0.66	↑ 0.77	0.72	↕ 0.77	0.77
Synapse	↑ 0.56	0.39	↑ 0.56	0.51	↑ 0.56	0.52
Total	↑ 14, ↓ 4		↑ 12, ↓ 3, ↕ 3		↑ 12, ↓ 4, ↕ 2	
	↑ 38, ↓ 11, ↕5					

6 Conclusion

WPDP and CPDP are commonly used theme in defect prediction research. Nowadays, CPDP is using in large range instead of WPDP due to heterogeneous data sets and unavailability of data. But it is challenging also. An ideal training model needs to have a sufficient number of data and their equal presence of different classes. Intemperance of a specific class can negatively influence the performance of a prediction model. This study proposed a data set ensemble approach to deal with multi-structured data sets (i.e., heterogeneous data sets). Initially collected nine data sets have performed as a traditional cross-project technique in this study. In addition, the data sets have been categorically divided into three parts: Non-defect Majority, Neutral Data set and Defect Majority (for details please see Sect. 3). This categorically divided data sets have been combined manually according to their category. Similarly, these combined data sets have been used to prepare defect prediction models. Moreover, the performance of traditional cross-project and proposed data set ensemble approaches have been given in this study. Indeed, the study result shows that the data set ensemble technique can able to improve the performance than traditional cross-project technique in most cases.

This investigation is possible to increase with more classifiers, performance metrics, and various type data sets. In future work, these criteria would also include comparing the study with other relevant works.

References

1. Wahono, R.S., Suryana, N.: Combining particle swarm optimization based feature selection and bagging technique for software defect prediction. Int. J. Softw. Eng. Appl. **7**(5), 153–166 (2013)
2. Wahono, R.S.: A systematic literature review of software defect prediction: research trends, data sets, methods and frameworks. J. Softw. Eng. **1**(1), 1–16 (2015)
3. Gayatri, N., Nickolas, S., Reddy, A.V., Reddy, S., Nickolas, A.V.: Feature selection using decision tree induction in class level metrics data set for software defect predictions. In: Proceedings of the World Congress on Engineering and Computer Science, pp. 124–129 (2010)
4. Ryu, D., Jang, J.-I., Baik, J.: A transfer cost-sensitive boosting approach for cross-project defect prediction. Software Qual. J. **25**(1), 235–272 (2015). https://doi.org/10.1007/s11219-015-9287-1
5. Marjuni, A., Adji, T.B., Ferdiana, R.: Unsupervised software defect prediction using signed Laplacian-based spectral classifier. Soft. Comput. **23**(24), 13679–13690 (2019). https://doi.org/10.1007/s00500-019-03907-6
6. Kamei, Y., Fukushima, T., McIntosh, S., Yamashita, K., Ubayashi, N., Hassan, A.E.: Studying just-in-time defect prediction using cross-project models. Empir. Softw. Eng. **21**(5), 2072–2106 (2015). https://doi.org/10.1007/s10664-015-9400-x
7. He, Z., Shu, F., Yang, Y., Li, M., Wang, Q.: An investigation on the feasibility of cross-project defect prediction. Autom. Softw. Eng. **19**(2), 167–199 (2012)
8. Jing, X., Wu, F., Dong, X., Qi, F., Xu, B.: Heterogeneous cross-company defect prediction by unified metric representation and CCA-based transfer learning. In: Proceedings of the 2015 10th Joint Meeting on Foundations of Software Engineering, pp. 496–507 (2015)
9. Bowes, D., Hall, T., Petrić, J.: Software defect prediction: do different classifiers find the same defects? Software Qual. J. **26**(2), 525–552 (2017). https://doi.org/10.1007/s11219-016-9353-3
10. Menzies, T., Krishna, R., Pryor, D.: The SEACRAFT Repository of Empirical Software Engineering Data (2017). https://zenodo.org/communities/seacraft
11. Catal, C., Diri, B.: A systematic review of software fault prediction studies. Expert Syst. Appl. **36**(4), 7346–7354 (2009)
12. Porter, A.A., Selby, R.W.: Empirically guided software development using metric-based classification trees. IEEE Softw. **7**(2), 46–54 (1990)
13. Liu, M., Miao, L., Zhang, D.: Two-stage cost-sensitive learning for software defect prediction. IEEE Trans. Reliab. **63**(2), 676–686 (2014)

14. Sohan, M. F., Jabiullah, M. I., Rahman, S. S. M. M., Mahmud, S. H.: Assessing the effect of imbalanced learning on cross-project software defect prediction. In: 2019 10th International Conference on Computing, Communication and Networking Technologies (ICCCNT), pp. 1–6. IEEE (2019)
15. Sohan, M.F., Kabir, M.A., Jabiullah, M.I., Rahman, S.S.M.M.: Revisiting the class imbalance issue in software defect prediction. In: 2019 International Conference on Electrical, Computer and Communication Engineering (ECCE), pp. 1–6 (2019)
16. Wang, S., Yao, X.: Using class imbalance learning for software defect prediction. IEEE Trans. Reliab. **62**(2), 434–443 (2013)
17. Ma, Y., Luo, G., Zeng, X., Chen, A.: Transfer learning for cross-company software defect prediction. Inf. Softw. Technol. **54**(3), 248–256 (2012)
18. Krishna, R., Menzies, T.: Bellwethers: a baseline method for transfer learning. IEEE Trans. Softw. Eng. (2018)
19. Fukushima, T., Kamei, Y., McIntosh, S., Yamashita, K., Ubayashi, N.: An empirical study of just-in-time defect prediction using cross-project models. In: Proceedings of the 11th Working Conference on Mining Software Repositories, pp. 172–181 (2014)
20. Jureczko, M., Madeyski, L.: Towards identifying software project clusters with regard to defect prediction. In: Proceedings of the 6th International Conference on Predictive Models in Software Engineering, p. 9. ACM, September 2010
21. Menzies, T., Greenwald, J., Frank, A.: Data mining static code attributes to learn defect predictors. IEEE Trans. Software Eng. **33**(1), 2–13 (2006)
22. Chidamber, S.R., Kemerer, C.F.: A metrics suite for object oriented design. IEEE Trans. Software Eng. **20**(6), 476–493 (1994)
23. Son, L.H., Pritam, N., Khari, M., Kumar, R., Phuong, P.T.M., Thong, P.H.: Empirical study of software defect prediction: a systematic mapping. Symmetry **11**(2), 212 (2019)
24. Özakıncı, R., Tarhan, A.: Early software defect prediction: a systematic map and review. J. Syst. Softw. **144**, 216–239 (2018)
25. Manjula, C., Florence, L.: Deep neural network based hybrid approach for software defect prediction using software metrics. Cluster Comput. **22**(4), 9847–9863 (2018). https://doi.org/10.1007/s10586-018-1696-z
26. Xu, Z., et al.: TSTSS: a two-stage training subset selection framework for cross version defect prediction. J. Syst. Softw. **154**, 59–78 (2019)

Prevalence of Machine Learning Techniques in Software Defect Prediction

Md Fahimuzzman Sohan[1(✉)], Md Alamgir Kabir[1], Mostafijur Rahman[1], Touhid Bhuiyan[1], Md Ismail Jabiullah[1], and Ebubeogu Amarachukwu Felix[2]

[1] Daffodil International University, Dhaka, Bangladesh
{sohan35-1284,alamgir.swe,mostafijur.swe,drismail.cse}@diu.edu.bd, t.bhuiyan@daffodilvarsity.edu.bd

[2] University of Malaya, Kuala Lumpur, Malaysia
felixbosken@siswa.um.edu.my

Abstract. Software Defect Prediction (SDP) is a popular research area which plays an important role for software quality. It works as an indicator of whether a software module is defect-free or defective. In this study, a review has been conducted from January 2015 to August 2019 and 165 articles are selected in the area of SDP to know the prevalence of Machine Learning (ML) techniques. These articles are collected by searching in Google Scholar, and they are published in various platforms (e.g., IEEE, Springer, Elsevier). Firstly the information has been extracted from the collected particles, and then the information has been pre-processed, categorized, visualized, and finally, the results have been reported. The result shows the most frequently used data sets, classifiers, performance metrics, and techniques in SDP. This investigation will help to find the prevalence of ML techniques in SDP and give a quick view to understand the trends of ML techniques in defect prediction research.

Keywords: Software Defect Prediction · Machine Learning techniques · Software defects · Defect prediction technique

1 Introduction

An error or fault can occur in the source code of a software, and causes of the software failure. It is essential to find the error at the early stage of software development. Defect identification before the software release helps to serve quality products and also reduces the development cost. SDP research is dominated by various ML techniques from the beginning of the research history. Generally, the defect prediction using ML refers to that some features are extracted from software code, and then these features are used to create predictive models with various classifiers [1]. The features are chosen from various activities in the source code (e.g., CK metrics [2] have been prepared based on code size and complexity) [3]. As other ML investigations, in SDP data sets are commonly used to train models and validate in defect prediction research. Previously two

T. Bhuiyan et al. (Eds.): ICONCS 2020, LNICST 325, pp. 257–269, 2020.
https://doi.org/10.1007/978-3-030-52856-0_20

types of data sets have been used for defect prediction: publicly available data and private data [4]. Publicly available data sets are openly accessible, available in several data repositories; anyone can easily download and use in their investigation [5–9]. Private data are prepared by individual investigators, they can also use publicly available software project to create their required data sets for the SDP investigation [10,11].

In SDP, the ML algorithms are used widely. Various classifiers are being used in defect prediction models, such as supervised, unsupervised, semi-supervised, ensemble methods. Among them, supervised learning is the most commonly used technique in defect prediction models [12]. Similarly, many performance metrics have been used to assess the performance of the defect prediction models [13]. Furthermore, various research topics have been considered for defect prediction research. In [4], Wahono has described the five commonly considered topics of SDP in his article; estimation, association, classification, clustering, and dataset analysis. Previous SDP review studies have considered 13 to 23 years to conduct their investigation, besides they have considered a relatively small amount of articles from the large territory of defect prediction research.

However, this study is conducted by collecting a competitively large amount of articles from the year 2015 to 2019 in the area of SDP. Some review studies have considered only journal articles [4], some of them have withdrawn papers using exclusion criteria [14,15]. But, in this investigation, conference and journal articles are included, and only a few papers have been excluded using exclusion criteria, where less possibility to leave out the suitable studies. By comparing the most cited studies [4,15,21,26] with our review, we show the domination of ML techniques and its extensive usage in the area of SDP so that researchers can get a quick view to understand the trends of ML techniques used in the SDP research.

Briefly, this review article represents an overall assessment of the recent SDP research activities. More specifically, the trends of using data sets, classifiers, performance metrics, and techniques have been considered in this study. For this investigation, 165 articles have been collected by searching in Google Scholars. Firstly, from the individual selected articles, the raw data have been collected and categorically stored according to their publishing platform. Then the specific information has been extracted from the storage. Finally, the results have been reported. This investigation will help to understand and give the primary idea about the considered techniques for defecting defects in software projects.

The organization of this paper is as follows: Sect. 2 represents the related work. Next Sect. 3 is the review method, where the steps of conducting the whole review process have been described. Then the results and discussions have been presented in Sect. 4. Finally, conclusions and future work have been described in Sect. 5.

2 Related Work

Till to date, one of the relevant work has been presented by Wahono [4] in 2015 where systematic study is conducted in the area of SDP. In this work, 71 articles were collected from different domains between 2000 and 2013. This work has investigated several parameters that are saturated with SDP research. He has shown the trend of using various ML techniques and defect prediction components. Another systematic review article has been presented by Malhotra [15], where SDP using ML and statistical techniques have been discussed. The author has used 61 articles between 1991 and 2013, to estimate the existence of ML for SDP. This analytical article shows the trend of the defect prediction research and performance comparison among the various ML techniques.

Shepperd et al. [16] have investigated over 600 defect prediction results; those have been collected from 42 SDP research articles. They have conducted a meta-analysis between the selected results and tried to find out the influencing factors from the defect prediction models Sing et al. [17] have studied 150 defect prediction articles, from them they have selected 20 relevant sets to analyze in their investigation. This review article contains a discussion about various research trends and techniques of SDP. Catal and Diri [18] have an article on the same topic. A few later, Catal [20] has also published a similar paper on defect prediction. A relatively recent study on this topic has been presented by Özakıncı and Tarhan [21], where 52 articles have been considered from 2000 to 2016. They have provided the overall scenario about the characteristics, performances, and usefulness of the selected defect prediction articles. Hosseini et al. [22] have conducted a Systematic Literature Review (SLR) and meta-analysis to investigate the recent activities in cross-project defect prediction (CPDP). They have considered 30 studies to find the information about metrics, modeling techniques, performance metrics, CPDP approaches, data sets for their review article. The result of the study shows the most used performance metric, modeling technique, data set, and CPDP approach are Recall, Naïve Bayes (NB), PROMISE, and data heterogeneity respectively.

Table 1 presents the details information about previous investigated reviews articles. Where the article name, author name, the period of the collected article, the total number of investigated articles, and major tasks in the article have been presented. This primary investigation is based on 165 defect prediction articles (including preprints and review articles), collected between January 2015 and August 2019. These articles belong to several journals and conference proceedings, also published from different domains. The focus of this review article is to identify and analyze the recent state of SDP research using ML.

Table 1. Existing research on SDP

No.	Article name	Year	Period	Number of investigated articles	Literary tasks
1	A systematic review of software fault prediction studies [18]	2009	1990–2007	74	• Software Metrics • Defect Dataset • Defect Prediction Methods • Performance Evaluation Metrics
2	Software fault prediction: A literature review and current trends [20]	2011	1990–2009	90	• Publication • Defect Prediction Data sets • Software Metrics • Defect Prediction Methods
3	A Systematic Review of Machine Learning Techniques for Software Fault Prediction [15]	2014	1991–2013	64	• Publication • ML Techniques • Software Metrics • Defect Prediction Data sets • Performance Metrics
4	A Systematic Review on Software Defect Prediction [17]	2015	1992–2014	20	• Authors and Publication • Defect Prediction Dataset • Techniques
5	A Systematic Literature Review of Software Defect Prediction: Research Trends, Data sets, Methods and Frameworks [4]	2015	2000–2013	71	• Researcher and Publication • Research Trends and Topics • Defect Prediction Data sets • Software Metrics • Defect Prediction Methods • Defect Prediction Frameworks
6	Early Software Defect Prediction: A Systematic Map and Review [21]	2018	2000–2016	52	• Publication • Defect Prediction Data sets • Software Metrics • Defect Prediction Methods
7	Empirical Study of Software Defect Prediction: A Systematic Mapping [19]	2019	1995–2018	156	• Publication • Defect Prediction Data sets • Software Metrics • Defect Prediction Techniques • Statistical Testing
This Study	**Prevalence of Machine Learning Techniques in Software Defect Prediction**	**2019**	**2015–2019**	**165**	**•Publication Source and Year** **• Defect Prediction Data sets** **• ML Algorithms** **• Performance Evaluation Metrics** **• Defect Prediction Techniques**

3 Review Method

Previously several SLR studies have been presented on SDP research; already those have been discussed in Sect. 2. This study is a primary literature review, where statistical analysis has been conducted among the collected 165 articles. A piece of information about our considered articles is available at: https://figshare.com/s/1f3905e5669048c8323d. Several steps have been performed to complete this review work and Fig. 1 shows the required steps taken for this investigation. Up next: discussion over the driven steps of the review process. Firstly, the necessity of the review article has been identified. Prior literature review articles were mostly published in 2015 or earlier, from this point of view the motivation of collecting data between 2015 and 2019 has arisen. The second step is to identify the suitable keywords that will be used to search and collect the raw articles from the online platform. Three keywords have been chosen, which the most relevant keywords in this field are: 'Software Defect Prediction', 'Software Fault Prediction', and 'Software Bug Prediction'. Then these three keywords have been used to manually search the targeted articles on Google Scholar. Those articles have been collected which are relevant to the three keywords, ensuring by reading the titles and other segments. The next step is data extraction. More than 200 articles were downloaded initially; after that, most relevant 165 articles have been selected for this study. Moreover, six primary components (attributes) have been extracted from each research paper and then stored in different Excel files according to their publication source for further use. In this step, data have been taken from each component for combining them and stored according to their category. Then calculation has been conducted for each component individually and finally, the results have been prepared and presented using different tables and graphs. Hence, this literature review has been conducted on 165 defect prediction research articles. Six common components have been considered from each research article. Consequently, six specific questions have been investigated in each article to collect information about the components. The questions are: what is the publisher of the article, in which year it has

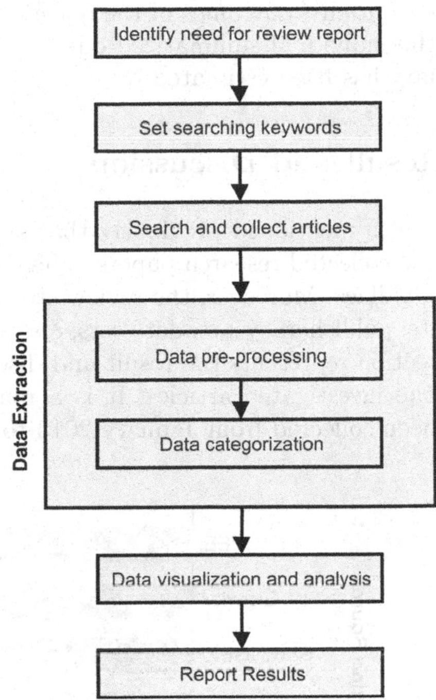

Fig. 1. Considered steps for the review study

been published, which data set(s) have been used, which classifier(s) has been used, which performance metric(s) has been used, which topic(s) has been considered. Initially, outcomes of the questions have been summarized individually, then the individual summarized outcomes have been combined and the overall summary has been estimated.

4 Result and Discussion

It has been mentioned previously that six primary components have extracted from the collected research papers. The components have been shown in Table 2 using boldface. Moreover, the review study has been conducted on the ML components: publishers, years, data sets, classifiers, performance metrics, and topics. This section represents the result and discussion over each component obtained from the investigated articles. It is a reminder that all of the 165 documents have been collected from January 2015 to August 2019.

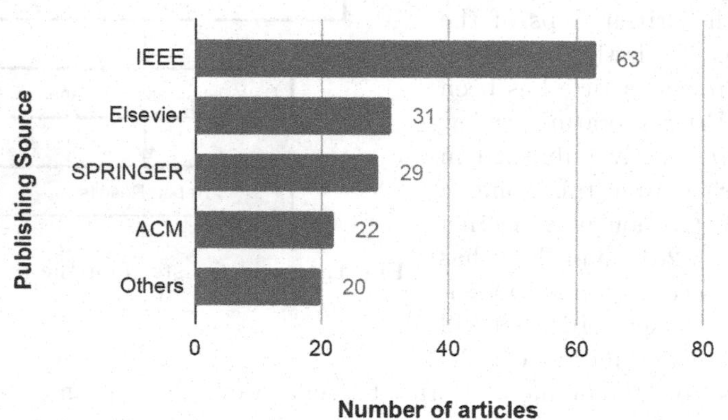

Fig. 2. Top publishers in the field of SDP among the collected articles

Publication Platform: In this study, collected articles have been published from various sources. Figure 2 shows the respective publishers of selected articles. Here, only the publishing platform has been considered, where the journal or conference information has been excluded. Figure 2 shows most of the defect prediction articles came from the IEEE; out of 165 articles, 63 (38.18%) were published from IEEE between the periods.

Publication Year: It has been mentioned previously that the collected articles are published from January 2015 to August 2019. Figure 3 shows the distribution of the investigated articles according to their publishing years. Most of the articles have been published in 2015, 47 (28.48%) articles have been found from the total articles. The figure shows the number of articles is decreasing by years

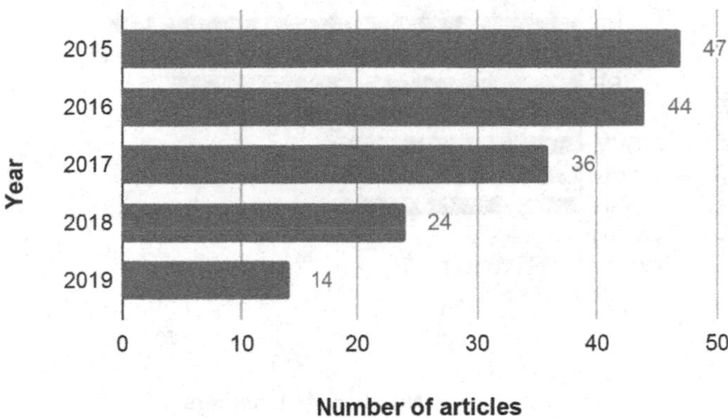

Fig. 3. Published articles by the selected years

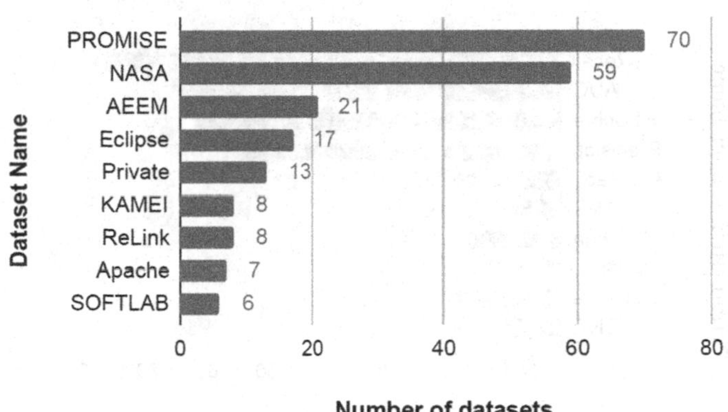

Fig. 4. Most commonly used data sets in the defect prediction research

from 2015, it doesn't mean that the amplification of the research is decreasing (more discussion has been given later about it).

Used Data Sets: Many data sets have been used in defect prediction research, where most of the data sets were public. Figure 4 shows that PROMISE data sets are the most used in the field (PROMISE data and PROMISE repository data sets are different here, the example of PROMISE data can be found in [23]). PROMISE data sets have been used in 70 (42.68%) articles, out of 165. NASA [24] is the second commonly used dataset, in 59 (35.98%) articles out of 165. AEEEM and Eclipse are the next frequently used data sets in the field of SDP.

Used Classifier: This part provides the details about the used classifiers in the considered articles. Figure 5 shows that the most used ML classifier is Naïve Bayes (NB) in defect prediction models. NB used in 68(41.46%) and secondly Decision Tree (DT) has been used in 65 (39.63%) articles out of 165 articles individually.

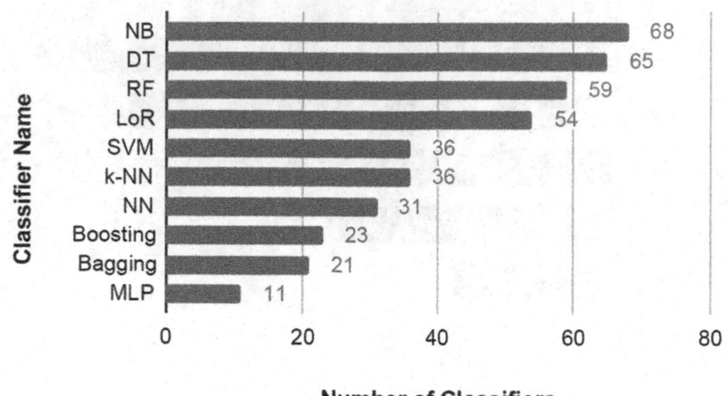

Fig. 5. Most commonly used ML classifiers in defect prediction research

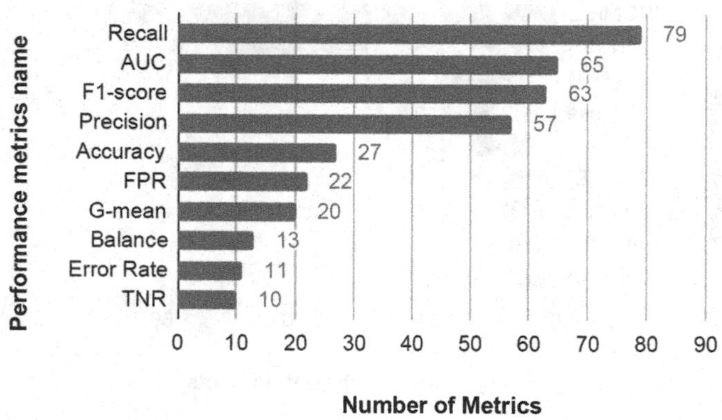

Fig. 6. Most commonly used performance metrics in defect prediction research

Used Performance Metrics: Various performance metrics have been used to measure and compare the performance of defect prediction models. Under this investigation, Recall has been found as the most used performance metrics. Recall has been used in 79 (48.17%), and after that Area Under Curve (AUC) used in 65 (39.63%) articles among the 165, Fig. 6 shows more data about it.

Considered Topic: Figure 7 represents the distribution of the research topics of collected SDP articles. Most of the researchers have been used classification techniques for their defect prediction models. Result shows that 110 (67.07%) articles were based on classification techniques among 165 articles.

Table 2 represents commonly used classifiers, performance metrics, data sets, topics, publishers, and distribution of considered studies by the years in SDP. This data have been partially presented previously using several graphs. In this table, 'Name', 'No', and '%' refer to name of the component, the total number of the article those have used the component, and their percentage. Note that

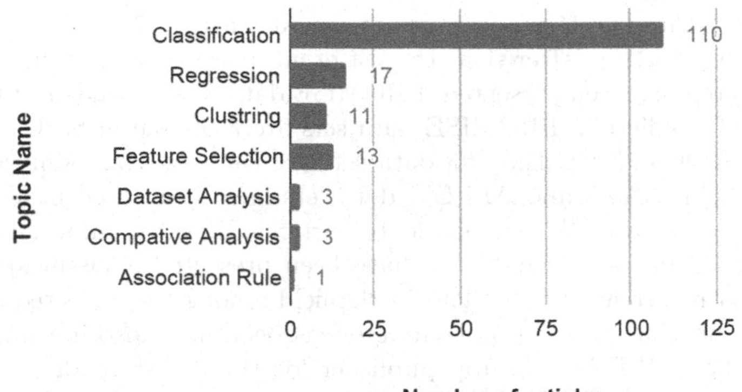

Fig. 7. Topics used in defect prediction research

Table 2. Statistics of most frequently used classifiers, performance metrics, data sets, topics, publishers, and year-wise distribution of selected studies in SDP

Most used classifiers			Most used performance metrics			Most used data sets		
Name	No.	%	Name	No.	%	Name	No.	%
NB	68	41.46	Recall	79	48.17	PROMISE	70	42.68
DT	65	39.63	AUC	65	39.63	NASA	59	35.98
RF	59	35.98	F1-score	63	38.41	AEEEM	21	12.80
LoR	54	32.93	Precision	57	34.76	Eclipse	17	10.37
SVM	36	21.95	Accuracy	27	16.46	Private	13	7.93
k-NN	36	21.95	FPR	22	13.41	KAMEI	8	4.88
NN	31	18.9	G-mean	20	12.2	ReLink	8	4.88
Boosting	23	14.02	Balance	13	7.93	Apache	7	4.27
Bagging	21	12.8	Error Rate	11	6.71	SOFTLAB	6	3.66
MLP	11	6.71	TNR	10	6.1			
Most used topics			Top publishers			Published articles by year		
Name	No.	%	Name	No.	%	Year	No.	%
Classification	110	67.07	IEEE	63	38.18	2015	47	28.48
Regression	17	10.37	Elsevier	31	18.79	2016	44	26.67
Feature Selection	14	8.54	Springer	29	17.58	2017	36	21.82
Clustring	11	6.71	ACM	22	13.33	2018	24	14.45
Dataset	3	1.83	Others	20	12.12	2019	14	8.48
Comparative analysis	3	1.83	*ND*			*ND*		
Association Rule	1	0.61						

NB = Naive Bayes, DT = Decisions Tree, RF = Random Forest, LoR = Logistic Regression, SVM = Support Vector Machine, k-NN = k-Nearest Neighbors, NN = Neural Network, MLP = Multilayer Perceptron, AUC = Area Under the Curve, FPR = False Positive Rate, TNR = True Negative Rate, ND = No Data

all information has been collected from 165 research articles in January 2015 and August 2019. Firstly, the table represents the most used classifiers in defect prediction research. Naive Bayes (NB) is the most used classifier in the field, it has been considered in 41.46% articles by the respective researchers. Second and third used classifiers are Decision Tree (39.63%) and Random Forest (35.98%) respectively. Next is the most used performance metric used in the investigated articles. Most three performance metrics are Recall (48.17%), AUC (39.63%), and F1-score (38.41%). After that, the list of most used data sets in defect prediction research has been presented. PROMISE data sets are the most used data sets in defect prediction; PROMISE data sets are available in SeaCraft repository [25]. NASA and AEEEM [26] data sets are the next commonly used data sets in the field. NASA and AEEEM data sets have been used in 35.98% and 12.8% articles respectively out of the 165 articles. Besides, information about the topics used in the research area have been presented. Classification is the most focused research topic (67.1%) in the field among the collected data sets. Regression and feature selection technique has been used also in some articles. The table shows IEEE is the top publisher for the defect prediction articles, 62 articles have been found and collected from the publisher. The next top two publishers are Elsevier, and ACM respectively. Lastly, the table represents information about yearly published articles from 2015 to 2019. Where the number of articles per year are decreasing. This study has taken a competitively short time, five years; and data of the last year is not consistent, there are a few months left to finish the year. Moreover, journals and conferences take a year or several months to publish their volumes, proceedings [14]. It can be the cause of decreasing the number of papers in the last years.

Results Comparison: Table 3 represents the comparison of outcomes of the study with the most relevant other four studies [4,15,21,26]. The comparison table carries five components: publications, data sets, algorithms, performance metrics, and topics; that are commonly involved in defect prediction research using ML. Top publishers, most frequently used data sets, algorithms, performance metrics, and topics have been sequentially listed out from the four studies. Wahono's [4] investigation shows initially most of the articles have been collected from IEEE. Özakıncı and Tarhan [21] have collected most of the articles from Scopus, and under this study most of the articles have found in IEEE. No specific data was found about the publishers from the first and last studies. Malhotra [15] and D'Ambros et al. [26] both show NASA is the most used data sets in their investigation. However, this study shows that PROMISE is the most used data sets. PROMISE is recently released and vastly used data sets competitively NASA in the defect prediction field. In the comparison table, two of the studies have found Decision Tree (DT) is the most used ML classifier in the area. Moreover, the third and also this study shows Bayesian Learner is the most used classifier. Various performance metrics have been used in SDP research, among them Recall has been found as the most used in this study. Furthermore, Recall is on the most commonly used in the other two studies and ROC (Receiver Operating Characteristic) in another study. Indeed, only Wahono's study has information about 'topics', specific data were not obtained from other studies; the study shows classification is the most considered topic. Lastly, this study shows the same result, classification is the most used topic which is closely followed by regression.

Table 3. The comparison of outcomes of this study with most relevant four studies

Study/Components	Publishers	Data sets	Algorithms	Performance metrics	Topics
Malhotra [15]	*ND*	1. NASA 2. PROMISE 3. Eclipse 4. Open Source Project 5. Student Developed Data	1. DT 2. NN 3. SVM 4. Bayesian Learner 5. Ensemble Classifier	1. Recall 2. Accuracy 3. Precision 4. AUC 5. F-measure	*ND*
Wahono [4]	1. IEEE 2. ACM 3. Springer 4. Elsevier 5. Scopus	*ND*	1. Bayesian Learner 2. DT 3. NN 4. RF 5. LoR	*ND*	1. Classification 2. Estimation 3. Dataset Analysis 4. Association 5. Clustring
Ozakıncı and Tarhan [21]	1. Scopus 2. Springer 3. Web of Science 4. ACM 5. Wiley	*ND*	*ND*	1. ROC 2. Recall 3. Accuracy 4. AUC 5. False Alarms	*ND*
D'Ambros et al. [26]	*ND*	1. NASA 2. PROMISE 3. Eclipse 4. Student Developed Data 5. Apache	1. DT 2. Bayesian Learner 3. Regression 4. SVM 5. NN	1. Recall 2. AUC 3. Precision 4. Accuracy 5. F-measure	*ND*
This Study	1. IEEE 2. Elsevier 3. Springer 4. ACM 5. Others	1. PROMISE 2. NASA 3. AEEEM 4. Eclipse 5. Student Developed Data	1. Bayesian Learner 2. DT 3. RF 4. LoR 5. SVM	1. Recall 2. AUC 3. F-measure 4. Precision 5. Accuracy	1. Classification 2. Regression 3. Feature Selection 4. Clustring 5. Dataset Analysis

ND - No specific data was

5 Conclusions and Future Work

This study represents a scenario about the recent fundamental activities in SDP research. In this study, a review investigation has been conducted over the ML technique in SDP. Initially, more than 200 research articles were downloaded from the Google Scholar between January 2015 and August 2019, 165 have been selected from them to perform this review study. Firstly, some keywords ('Software Defect Prediction', 'Software Fault Prediction', and 'Software Bug Prediction') have been considered, which are most relevant in this field. Then downloaded the articles based on the keywords from Google Scholar. After that, raw data have been extracted from each article and stored individually in an Excel file for further analysis. Then the extracted data have been used to prepare the results. The study results show recent activities and trends in defect prediction research, more specifically about the publications, data sets, classifiers, performance metrics, and topics. This investigation shows most of the articles have been published from IEEE, 68 articles out of 165. Moreover, the most used dataset, classifier and performance metric is PROMISE (70 articles), Naïve Bayes (68 articles), and Recall (79 articles) respectively. Lastly, the most chosen topic in defect prediction is classification, 110 articles were classification based out of 165. Hopefully, this review investigation will help to get an idea about the recent activities of the SDP research.

This study is not an SLR, so there is the opportunity to extend the study based on the criteria. Future work will be more details, where more topics and activities of defect prediction research will be discussed.

References

1. Dam, H.K., et al.: A deep tree-based model for software defect prediction. arXiv preprint arXiv 1802.00921 (2018)
2. Chidamber, S.R., Kemerer, C.F.: A metrics suite for object oriented design. IEEE Trans. Software Eng. **20**(6), 476–493 (1994)
3. Kondo, M., Bezemer, C.-P., Kamei, Y., Hassan, A.E., Mizuno, O.: The impact of feature reduction techniques on defect prediction models. Empir. Softw. Eng. **24**(4), 1925–1963 (2019). https://doi.org/10.1007/s10664-018-9679-5
4. Wahono, R.S.: A systematic literature review of software defect prediction: research trends, datasets, methods and frameworks. J. Softw. Eng. **1**(1), 1–16 (2015)
5. Sohan, M.F., Kabir, M.A., Jabiullah, M.I., Rahman, S.S.M.M.: Revisiting the class imbalance issue in software defect prediction. In: 2019 International Conference on Electrical, Computer and Communication Engineering (ECCE), pp. 1–6. IEEE (2019)
6. Park, B.J., Oh, S.K., Pedrycz, W.: The design of polynomial function-based neural network predictors for detection of software defects. Inf. Sci. **229**, 40–57 (2013)
7. Xu, Z., et al.: Cross version defect prediction with representative data via sparse subset selection. In: Proceedings of the 26th Conference on Program Comprehension, pp. 132–143, ACM (2018)
8. Sohan, M.F., Jabiullah, M.I., Rahman, S.S.M.M., Mahmud, S.H.: Assessing the effect of imbalanced learning on cross-project software defect prediction. In: 2019 10th International Conference on Computing, Communication and Networking Technologies (ICCCNT), pp. 1–6. IEEE (2019)
9. Huda, S., Liu, K., Abdelrazek, M., Ibrahim, A., Alyahya, S., Al-Dossari, H., Ahmad, S.: An ensemble oversampling model for class imbalance problem in software defect prediction. IEEE Access **6**, 24184–24195 (2018)
10. Wong, W.E., Debroy, V., Golden, R., Xu, X., Thuraisingham, B.: Effective software fault localization using an RBF neural network. IEEE Trans. Reliab. **61**(1), 149–169 (2011)
11. Hryszko, J., L., adeyski, M.: Assessment of the software defect prediction cost effectiveness in an industrial project. In: Software Engineering: Challenges and Solutions, pp. 77–90 (2017)
12. Yan, M., Fang, Y., Lo, D., Xia, X., Zhang, X.,: File-level defect prediction: Unsupervised vs. supervised models. In: 2017 ACM/IEEE International Symposium on Empirical Software Engineering and Measurement (ESEM), pp. 344–353. IEEE (2017)
13. Kamei, Y., Shihab, E.: Defect prediction: accomplishments and future challenges. In: 2016 IEEE 23rd international Conference on Software Analysis, Evolution, and Reengineering (SANER), vol. 5, pp. 33–45. IEEE (2016)
14. Radjenović, D., Heričko, M., Torkar, R., Živkovič, A.: Software fault prediction metrics: a systematic literature review. Inf. Softw. Technol. **55**(8), 1397–1418 (2013)

15. Malhotra, R.: A systematic review of machine learning techniques for software fault prediction. Appl. Soft Comput. **27**, 504–518 (2015)
16. Shepperd, M., Bowes, D., Hall, T.: Researcher bias: the use of machine learning in software defect prediction. IEEE Trans. Software Eng. **40**(6), 603–616 (2014)
17. Singh, P.K., Agarwal, D., Gupta, A.: A systematic review on software defect prediction. In: 2015 2nd International Conference on Computing for Sustainable Global Development (INDIACom), pp. 1793–1797. IEEE (2015)
18. Catal, C., Diri, B.: A systematic review of software fault prediction studies. Expert Syst. Appl. **36**(4), 7346–7354 (2009)
19. Son, L.H., Pritam, N., Khari, M., Kumar, R., Phuong, P.T.M., Thong, P.H.: Empirical study of software defect prediction: a systematic mapping. Symmetry **11**(2), 212 (2019)
20. Catal, C.: Software fault prediction: a literature review and current trends. Expert Syst. Appl. **38**(4), 4626–4636 (2011)
21. Özakıncı, R., Tarhan, A.: Early software defect prediction: a systematic map and review. J. Syst. Softw. **144**, 216–239 (2018)
22. Hosseini, S., Turhan, B., Gunarathna, D.: A systematic literature review and meta-analysis on cross project defect prediction. IEEE Trans. Software Eng. **45**(2), 111–147 (2017)
23. Jureczko, M.R., Madeyski, L.: Towards identifying software project clusters with regard to defect prediction. In: Proceedings of the 6th International Conference on Predictive Models in Software Engineering, p. 9. ACM (2010)
24. Shepperd, M., Song, Q., Sun, Z., Mair, C.: Data quality: some comments on the nasa software defect datasets. IEEE Trans. Software Eng. **39**(9), 1208–1215 (2013)
25. Menzies, T., Krishna, R., Pryor, D.: The SEACRAFT Repository of Empirical Software Engineering Data (2017)
26. D'Ambros, M., Lanza, M., Robbes, R.: An extensive comparison of bug prediction approaches. In: 2010 7th IEEE Working Conference on Mining Software Repositories (MSR 2010), pp. 31–41. IEEE (2010)

Software Process Improvement Based on Defect Prevention Using Capability and Testing Model Integration in Extreme Programming

Md. Habibur Rahman[1,2](✉), Ziaur Rahman[1,3], Md. Al - Mustanjid[4], Muhammad Shahin Uddin[1], and Mehedy Hasan Rafsan Jany[1]

[1] Mawlana Bhashani Science and Technology University, Tangail, Bangladesh
mdhabibur.r.bd@ieee.org
[2] Bangabandhu Sheikh Mujibur Rahman Digital University, Kaliakair, Bangladesh
[3] RMIT University, GPO Box 2476, Melbourne, VIC 3001, Australia
rahman.ziaur@rmit.edu.au
[4] Daffodil International University, 102/1 Sukrabad, Dhanmondi, Dhaka 1207, Bangladesh
mustanjid.se@gmail.com, shahin.mbstu@gmail.com, rafsan.mbstu@gmail.com

Abstract. Nowadays, Software Process Improvement popularly known as SPI has been able to receive an immense concern in the continuous process to purify software quality. Several Agile methodologies previously have worked with Extreme programming (XP). Before improving the process, defect prevention (DP) is inevitable. In addition, DP largely depends on defect detection either found earlier in the design and implementation stages or held in the testing phases. However, testing maturity model integration (TMMI) has a crucial aspect in DP as well as process improvement of the software. In particular, when software gets validated by being tested and fixed the defects up, it achieves the maximum capability maturity model integration (CMMI) aiming the process improvement. Here, the article has proposed an improved defect detection and prevention model to enhance the software process following the approach of XP. Besides, as a unique contribution, we have united the capability and testing model integration to ensure better SPI.

Keywords: SPI · CMMI · TMMI · Agile · Defect prevention · Extreme programming

1 Introduction

The Agile development method is pursued on the basis of customer demands and front planning [1]. Evolutionary learning, incremental development, and Agile methodology inclusion increase customer satisfaction [2]. Small to medium-sized companies rely on Agile's light SPI to endure in the globe of competitive development. SPI in Agile gears up the development team to derive the desires of

T. Bhuiyan et al. (Eds.): ICONCS 2020, LNICST 325, pp. 270–279, 2020.
https://doi.org/10.1007/978-3-030-52856-0_21

the organization and prop up software products [3]. This demand encourages researchers to enhance SPI in Agile with stronger accuracy [4]. XP is the most notable software development methodology among several Agile methodologies [5]. XP differs mainly in placing a higher value on adaptability than predictability from traditional methods. XP connects all the practices of the waterfall and iterative model in software development projects [6]. XP prescribes a set of daily procedures from executives and developers. The high expectation within a short time is possible in XP to improve the software process. XP aims to unite humanity and productivity. The customer puts the desirable requirements and the SPI technical team checks the anticipated results based on the perceived criteria of the customer. The ultimate goal of XP is to alleviate modification expenditures [7]. It is undeniable to compromise on quality in the XP. Without DP, software quality cannot be assured. Any inconsistency in the process of software development is classified as a mistake, error or defect [8]. Defects can emerge at any level during the life cycle of software development. For such factors, DP plays a key role in the software system quality refinement. Before making a software, it is best to locate defects. Recognizing defects and triggers of these defects is the most fundamental but mostly overlooked which is essential for quality control [9–11]. DP is a gradual way of finding the root causes of defects and changes the way recurring faults are noticed in SPI [12]. This resistant action cuts development costs and results in higher-quality and reliable software development [13]. Defects must be operated at all steps to preserve customer integrity [14].

Only DP is not adequate to measure SPI empirically. Process management, measurement and other activities need to be concerned along with prevention [13]. CMMI advises organizational interventions, and features to increase product demands, analysis and refurbishment. CMMI software development framework model concentrated on the software development organizations' maturity evaluation [15,16]. CMMI has two parts, one weighing the potential of the process zone as well as the other reflecting organizational maturity at specific levels. CMMI is the SPI initiative that noticeably prevents defects during software development and production life cycle [17]. On the other hand, CMMI is intended to gain high quality by conveying cost optimization, productivity, customer satisfaction and return on investment (ROI) [18]. Further, CMMI requirement implementation guides are conducted by Agile methodology marking the queries which are not marked through the CMMI framework [2].

According to [19], the immature testing process does not efficiently identify defects in SPI. The TMMI is a reference framework and guidance for improving the test process. TMMI attains the concepts of CMMI. In test engineering and development cycle, TMMI uplifts the organization testing process along with software quality and productivity. It is categorized into five stages. The highest satisfaction is mentioned with extremely high maturity level. Satisfying all processes in every maturity level an organization can gain top maturity level step by step [18].

Thus, this paper recommends a model for DP in Agile with XP to deliver SPI more productively. The model standardization is ensured by the combination of CMMI along with TMMI.

The structure of this article is as follows. Section 2 is provided with related works. Section 3 illustrates the proposed model. Section 4 analyzes the results meet up with model. Section 5 concludes the paper with future work.

2 Related Works

The effectiveness of CMMI in the development of Agile software was evaluated in [20] based on a systematic review of the literature published up to 2011. Several criteria were used to measure CMMI adeptness in Agile development. The study also determined that CMMI can be achieved using Agile software development.

The article [17] explored how SPI treats defects of software development. Comparisons between the scrum and XP model explored in [7] placed by their model features that lead to a deep understanding of these models. Authors in [21] deployed an improved model with consideration of XP's weak documentation and architectural design. A new framework tailored by integrating testing phases at each step to tackle the deficiency of the XP criteria outlined in [22].

Authors in [3] investigated 423 detailed articles in consonance with SPI aspects published from 2001 to March 2013. This paper also provided a systematic review of literature on the SPI fields mainly studied in previous research. The research found that new SPI techniques need to be built which really compares traditional techniques to run Agile more fluently. Authors concluded that far more research on Agile strategies is required.

Studies above clearly point out that DP in SPI of Agile methodology, particularly in XP requires a new initiative for progression. Moreover, this paper suggests a model to refurbish SPI through DP in XP. SPI and quality of the software are quantified by the incorporation of CMMI with TMMI.

3 Proposed Model

DP tasks are consistently investigated; these are rolled out by each of the allocated teams. Predetermine the causes of defects as it is required to fully overcome the consequences of defects. Addressed action items and set priorities focused on a causal interpretation throughout the assessments. Thereafter, to prevent the defects, the expense of implementing structural changes is estimated. Finally, the intended influence on software quality is taken into account. Figure 1 signifies the DP strategy of software development process. The critical role in the execution phase is to develop a plan of action. At first, members of the software development group meet to plan for the duties and relevant DP operations. There is a kick-off meeting held to convey information about the implementation process among members of the team. The session outlines the procedures, standards, protocols, techniques, and tools appropriate to the functions of the software. Developers concentrate on the latest modifications based on vibrant specifications. Assumed outcomes and evaluating approaches for evaluation are analyzed. Generic errors and advised corrective efforts are included; and also team assignments, a task scheduler and project targets are instituted.

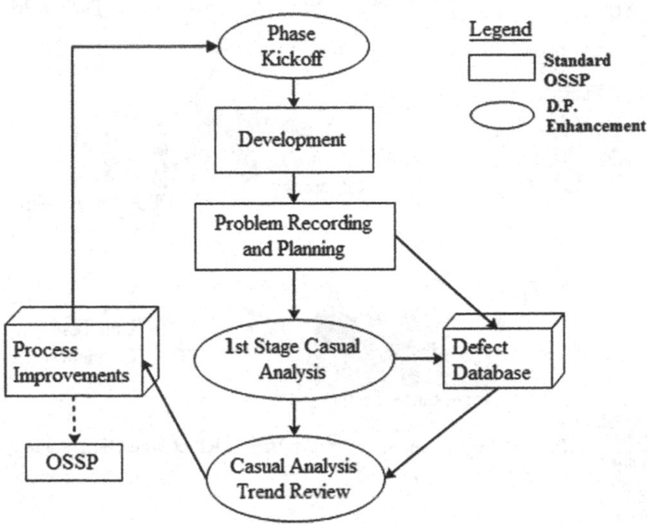

Fig. 1. Defect prevention strategy for software development process; Here in the Figure, OSSO stands for organization standard software process

Management in the IT sector must be committed to practicing a written DP policy at both the organization and project stage presented in Fig. 2. In order to strengthen software processes and items, long-term plans should be adopted for funding, resources and implementation. In Fig. 2 the defect detection and prevention are described in XP. Developers must pay attention to client stories determining their values with all along software development life cycle (SDLC). The acceptance test standards should also be fixed in the iteration plan. In the planning phase, these are conducted. The design has been done based on the software development plan. Coding with pair programming and refactoring are begun after the design phase. Refactoring is accomplished on the basis of the defects encountered in the test stage. Utilizing unit testing, programmers track the output. Testing continues with ongoing integration shortly after the coding. In this stage, the entire acceptance along with the user acceptance test is executed.

According to the SDLC, a whirlpool diagram in Fig. 3 is proposed and tested for DP on a small project. Customers always prefer to satisfy their requirements into 100%. In practice, it is quite impossible to develop that kind of software. Thus, we propose a model in Fig. 3 provides more than 90% defect free software and achieved the highest maturity. In this model, perfection is boosted in anti-proportional rate by limiting the software defects. Hence, after several phases, the model optimizes the defects in the downward cycle.

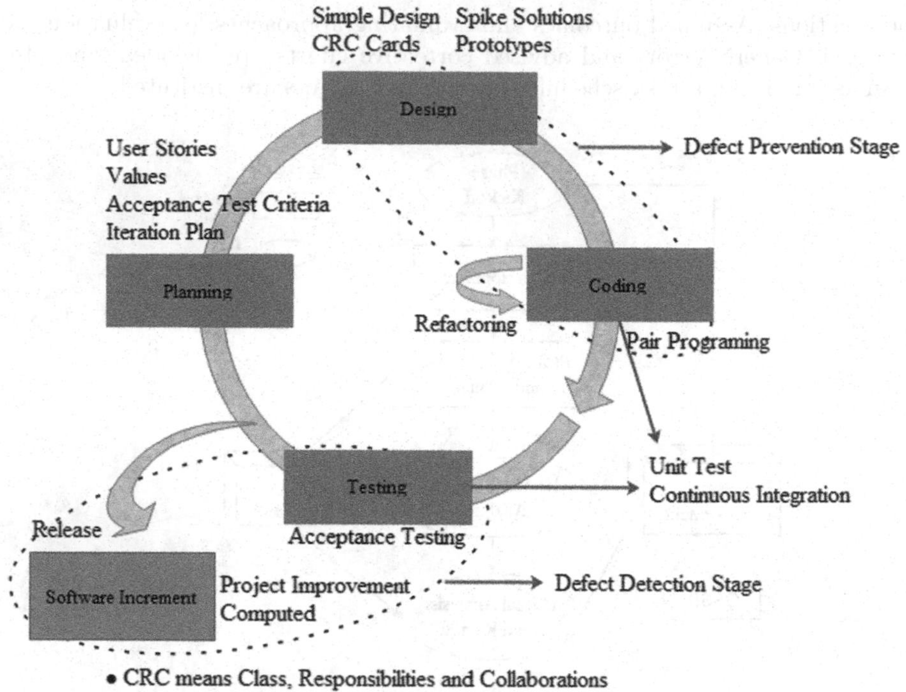

Fig. 2. Defect detection and prevention model in Extreme programming

4 Result Analysis

There are many software process evaluation methods and norms [23,24]. DP is gradually improving the process of production. The preceding Eq. (1) ensures software quality.

$$QA = QC(Defect \quad Identification) + DP \tag{1}$$

where, QA = Quality Assurance; DP = Defect Prevention and QC = Quality Control

Standard quality is upheld using parameters for judging the quality of the software. To enhance the software mechanism and acquire qualified software, the following eight substantial measurement parameters are regarded.

Here,
Q1 = Integrity
Q2 = Correctness
Q3 = Maintainability
Q4 = Efficiency
Q5 = Reliability

Q6 = Modifiability
Q7 = Reusability and
Q8 = Portability

Integrity measures code and information consistency by monitoring an authorized individual's access to software. Correctness examine the expectations of the user in software and how certain requirements are. Maintainability suggests how much effort will be made to address and follow up defects that occurred in the operational processes of software. Efficiency gets to decide what further computing logistics and code a program requires to deliver a function. Reliability ensures that the expected function of a program is performed with the appropriate clarification while it ought to be performed. Especially in packaging and function scopes, a software program performs as needed in another application helps to ensure reusability. The term modifiability defines the adjustment capability of the additional features of the customer requirements. Another term portability indicates the platform independence of the software [25].

A testing and capability maturity model as leveled in Table 1. If the software satisfies the integrity and correctness, the capability maturity will be initiated. The software capabilities will be characterized by modifiability, reusability, and portability. Containing all the quality parameters, the testing maturity will be high, and the ability will be scalable.

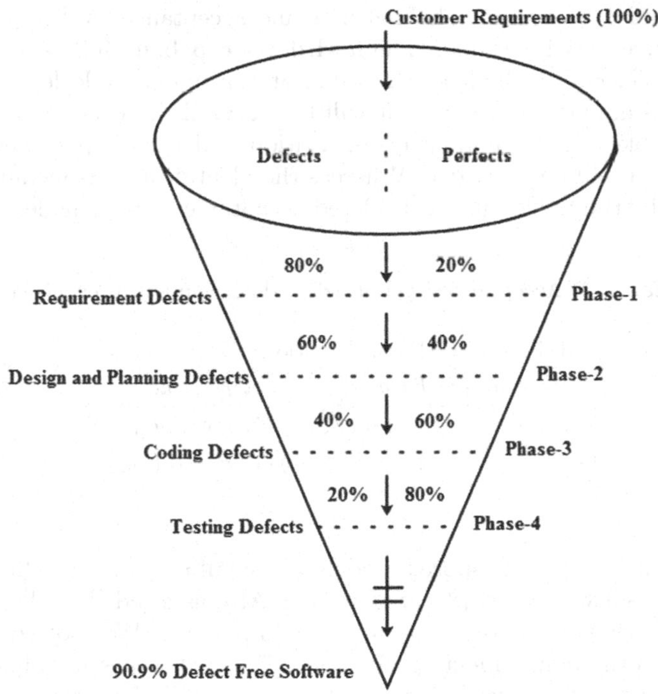

Fig. 3. Software defect prevention whirlpool diagram in Extreme programming in Agile methodology

Table 1. Software process improvement with quality parameters in the CMM and TMM integration

CMM level	Focus	Satisfaction of TMM	Quality parameters
5. Optimizing	Continual SPI	Extremely high	Q1, Q2, Q3, Q4, Q5, Q6, Q7 and Q8
4. Managed	Performance and software quality both are measured	High	Q1, Q2, Q4 and Q5
3. Defined	Well organizational process and support	Medium	Q6, Q7 and Q8
2. Repeatable	Software management process	Low	Q3 and Q6
1. Initial	Ad-hoc and unorganized	Extremely low	Q1 and Q2

Table 2. Maturity level of defect detection and prevention

TMM (Detection)	CMM (Prevention)	
	Optimized	*Managed*
Extremely high	Highly matured (++)	Matured (+×)
High	Matured (×+)	Immature (××)

Table 2 and 3 represented the maturity and acceptance level respectively. In Table 2, the maturity is considered high when the capability fulfills the optimized level. If the defects are high and avoided at the manageable level, it will be acknowledged immature otherwise it will be matured. Levels of acceptance just set out in Table 3. If the amount of recognition of defects is poor and occurred continuously, it will be discarded. Whereas the identification is medium and can be specified by the model, it is considered acceptable or negotiable.

Table 3. Acceptance level of defect detection and prevention

TMM (Detection)	CMM (Prevention)	
	Defined	*Repeatable*
Medium	Acceptable(⊕⊕)	Negotiable (⊕⊗)
Low	Negotiable (⊗⊕)	Rejected (⊗⊗)

By implementing the proposed model on a small project, we achieved 90.9% defect free software [https://github.com/Al-mustanjid/Travellers_Project]. Figure 4 portrays the outcomes of our overall approach. We spotted more than 80% defects in the requirement specification. Forward to passing planning, coding and testing phases, we lower the defects to 20% throughout the testing phase. Software is launched for a short period of time after that alpha version.

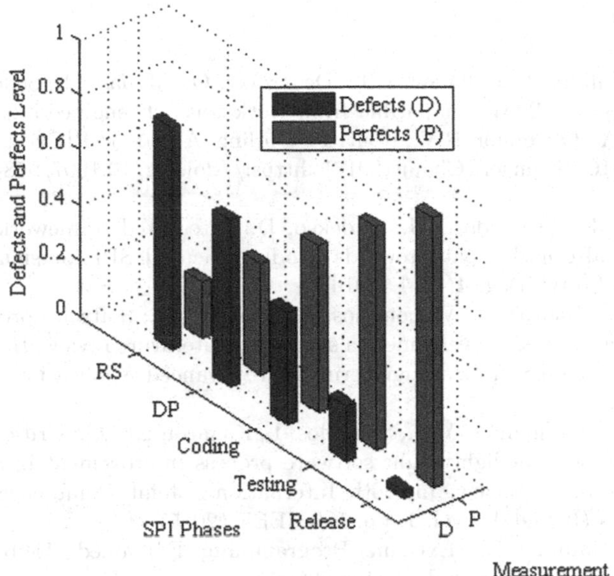

Fig. 4. Expected defects reduction by TMMI Phase; RS stands for Requirement Specification and DP is for Design and Planning

The faults are decreased to more than 90% since obtaining the reviews and customer feedback in circular phases. Finally, we got the highest degree defect free software implemented in XP.

5 Conclusion

XP is one of the most widely used methodologies for small software project development where DP is inevitable towards ensuring quality software delivery. As per our investigation, no defect detection and prevention model in SPI that in particular can solve issues encountering by the industry could desirably reduce the defects step by step in the Agile. As capability based CMMI and testing based TMMI approach measure software standardization, but proposing a novel approach integrating both could envisage a new dimension to encourage industry practicing Agile XP.

In this paper we have observed through the experiments that proposed model applied to the software projects can significantly reduce defects as clarified by the relevant sections. To fulfill the software quality improvement standards, this proposed model is able to achieve the highest level of optimization and detection that can also be considered as a separate contribution to the authors. The future includes experimenting the model with large scale project implementation.

References

1. Torrecilla-Salinas, C.J., Guardia, T., De Troyer, O., Mejías, M., Sedeño, J.: NDT-Agile: an agile, CMMI-compatible framework for web engineering. In: Mas, A., Mesquida, A., O'Connor, R.V., Rout, T., Dorling, A. (eds.) SPICE 2017. CCIS, vol. 770, pp. 3–16. Springer, Cham (2017). https://doi.org/10.1007/978-3-319-67383-7_1
2. Engdashet, T., Machado, R.J., Midekso, D.: Integrated framework of agile and CMMI: an alternative path towards product focused SPI for small companies. Lect. Notes Softw. Eng. **4**(1), 1 (2016)
3. Santana, C., Queiroz, F., Vasconcelos, A., Gusmão, C.: Software process improvement in agile software development a systematic literature review. In: 41st Euromicro Conference on Software Engineering and Advanced Applications, pp. 325–332. IEEE (2015)
4. Kouzari, E., Gerogiannis, V.C., Stamelos, I., Kakarontzas, G.: Critical success factors and barriers for lightweight software process improvement in agile development: a literature review. In: 10th International Joint Conference on Software Technologies (ICSOFT), vol. 1, pp. 1–9. IEEE (2015)
5. Beck, K., Gamma, E.: Extreme Programming Explained: Embrace Change. Addison-Wesley Professional, Boston (2000)
6. Paulk, M.C.: Extreme programming from a CMM perspective. IEEE Softw. **18**(6), 19–26 (2001)
7. Anwer, F., Aftab, S., Shah, S.M., Waheed, U.: Comparative analysis of two popular agile process models: extreme programming and scrum. Int. J. Comput. Sci. Telecommun. **8**(2), 1–7 (2017)
8. Clark, B., Zubrow, D.: How good is the software: a review of defect prediction techniques. In: Software Engineering Symposium, Carreige Mellon University (2001)
9. Narayan, P.: Software defect prevention in a nut shell. iSixSigma LLC., CTO Media LLC., copyright 2007 (2000)
10. Adeel, K., Ahmad, S., Akhtar, S.: Defect prevention techniques and its usage in requirements gathering-industry practices. In: Student Conference on Engineering Sciences and Technology, pp. 1–5. IEEE (2005)
11. Suma, V., Gopalakrishnan Nair, T.: Better defect detection and prevention through improved inspection and testing approach in small and medium scale software industry. Int. J. Prod. Qual. Manage. **6**(1), 71–90 (2010)
12. Chillarege, R., et al.: Orthogonal defect classification-a concept for in-process measurements. IEEE Trans. Softw. Eng. **18**(11), 943–956 (1992)
13. Söylemez, M., Tarhan, A.: Challenges of software process and product quality improvement: catalyzing defect root-cause investigation by process enactment data analysis. Soft. Qual. J. **26**(2), 779–807 (2016). https://doi.org/10.1007/s11219-016-9334-6
14. Noor, R., Khan, M.F.: Defect management in agile software development. Int. J. Mod. Educ. Comput. Sci. **6**(3), 55 (2014)
15. Team, C.P.: Capability maturity model® integration (CMMI SM), version 1.1. CMMI for Systems Engineering, Software Engineering, Integrated Product and Process Development, and Supplier Sourcing (CMMI-SE/SW/IPPD/SS, V1. 1) (2002)
16. Torrecilla-Salinas, C., Sedeño, J., Escalona, M., Mejías, M.: Agile, web engineering and capability maturity model integration: a systematic literature review. Inf. Softw. Technol. **71**, 92–107 (2016)

17. Harter, D.E., Kemerer, C.F., Slaughter, S.A.: Does software process improvement reduce the severity of defects? A longitudinal field study. IEEE Trans. Softw. Eng. **38**(4), 810–827 (2012)
18. Çiflikli, E.G., Coşkunçay, A.: An ontology to support TMMi-based test process assessment. In: Stamelos, I., O'Connor, R.V., Rout, T., Dorling, A. (eds.) SPICE 2018. CCIS, vol. 918, pp. 345–354. Springer, Cham (2018). https://doi.org/10.1007/978-3-030-00623-5_25
19. Garousi, V., Felderer, M., Hacaloğlu, T.: Software test maturity assessment and test process improvement: a multivocal literature review. Inf. Softw. Technol. **85**, 16–42 (2017)
20. Silva, F.S., et al.: Using CMMI together with agile software development: a systematic review. Inf. Softw. Technol. **58**, 20–43 (2015)
21. Qureshi, M.R.J., Ikram, J.S.: Proposal of enhanced extreme programming model. Int. J. Inf. Eng. Electron. Bus. **7**(1), 37 (2015)
22. Hameed, A.: Software development lifecycle for extreme programming. Int. J. Inf. Technol. Electr. Eng. **5**(1) (2016)
23. Unterkalmsteiner, M., Gorschek, T., Islam, A.M., Cheng, C.K., Permadi, R.B., Feldt, R.: Evaluation and measurement of software process improvement–a systematic literature review. IEEE Trans. Softw. Eng. **38**(2), 398–424 (2012)
24. Fenton, N., Bieman, J.: Software Metrics: A Rigorous and Practical Approach. CRC Press, Boca Raton (2014)
25. Gaffney Jr, J.E.: Metrics in software quality assurance. In: Proceedings of the ACM 1981 Conference, pp. 126–130. ACM (1981)

Predicting Fans' FIFA World Cup Team Preference from Tweets

Md. Fazla Rabbi[1(✉)], Md. Saddam Hossain Mukta[2], Tanjima Nasreen Jenia[1], and A.K.M. Najmul Islam[3]

[1] American International University-Bangladesh, Dhaka, Bangladesh
fazlarabbi76@gmail.com, tanjima.nasreen@gmail.com
[2] United International University, Dhaka, Bangladesh
saddam@cse.uiu.ac.bd
[3] University of Turku, Turku, Finland
najisl@utu.fi

Abstract. *FIFA* world cup is the most prestigious football tournament and widely viewed sporting event in the world. People support different teams (countries) of FIFA world cup based on players' skills, number of winning trophies, and deliberate strategies that are applied by these teams during the tournament. These people share their opinion, criticism, love, and affection on the social media, i.e., Twitter. In this paper, we predict users' FIFA world cup supporting preference from their tweets. First, we analyze user's tweets and build two different types of classifiers by using *LIWC* and *ELMo Word Embedding* based techniques. These classifiers predict which team a user prefers from her word usage pattern in tweets. We find that *Random Forest* classifier performs the best for LIWC based model. We also find deep learning based word embedding technique, *ELMo*, achieves decent potential to predict users' team supporting preference. Later, we build a multi-level weighted ensemble model to integrate both of the independent models, i.e., *LIWC* and *ELMo*. Our ensemble model shows substantial prediction potential (average accuracy-83.5%) to predict users' FIFA world cup supporting preference from their tweets.

Keywords: FIFA · LIWC · Word embedding · SMOTE · Classification

1 Introduction

The *Fédération Internationale de Football Association (FIFA)* organizes men's football competition in every four years, which is popularly known as FIFA *world cup*. Currently, a total of 32 nations compete in the tournament phase for winning the championship title. The people from the rest of the nations (i.e., India, China, Bangladesh, and Singapore) also watch the world cup with full warmth and enthusiasm. These people show their passion about their preferred team (e.g., Brazil, France, and Argentina) by wearing jersey or flying the flag of the nation. With the proliferation of social media technologies [9], users' frequently

T. Bhuiyan et al. (Eds.): ICONCS 2020, LNICST 325, pp. 280–292, 2020.
https://doi.org/10.1007/978-3-030-52856-0_22

share their preferences and rivalry about these teams of the world cup on social media such as Twitter and Facebook. In recent studies, researchers have been able to find many interesting insights such as personality, value and preferences of users by analyzing the texts of tweets [15,16]. In this paper, we predict users' FIFA world cup team preferences by analyzing their cognitive attributes derived from tweets.

Preferring a world cup team may depend on many factors. For example, some people like *total football* [18], while others may like individual skill. In recent years, several studies show that human preferences are influenced by her psychological and cognitive attributes [23,26,27]. Weaver et al. [27] find that *personality* influences movie preference of the user since different movies are capable of providing different ranges of stimuli to users, which are directly connected to human psychological state. Personality and preference have profound impact on decision making [23], reading habits [6], and buying products [26]. In recent studies [5,25], researchers find that what people *say* and *write* reflect their individual characterization. In another study [2], authors describe that people actually reveal their preferences on social media. Therefore, we believe that it is also possible to predict users' supporting preferences[1] by analyzing their word usage (*writing*) pattern in tweets.

In recent years, a few studies have been conducted on sports result prediction [12,14] by using different machine learning techniques. Nichols et al. [17] build a sports summarization technique from tweets. Leung et al. [12] predict results of a game based on historical data. In the current literature, we also find users preferences such as food consumption [1], and political support [4] from social media usage. However, none of the previous works predict users' supporting preferences by analyzing their word usage pattern on social media. Identifying the fans' preferences based on tweets can have several real life applications. First, sports manufacturers can estimate their future production about the quantity of sports accessories (i.e., jersey of Brazil, Flag of Argentina, and Bracelet of Germany). Second, it can improve social media marketing as the right ad can be shown to the right fans (i.e., targeted marketing for increasing sales of sports accessories). Third, TVs can take decision on broadcasting programmes based on the fans' demand. Finally, reporters of print media can write articles and features for the world cup playing nation that has greater number of fans.

In our study, we collect data of 376 users who tweet actively in Twitter. We extract a total of 8,05,182 tweets and analyze the data by using *Linguistic Inquiry and Word Count (LIWC)* [19], a popular psycholinguistic text analysis technique. Since users' preferences are influenced by their psychological attributes, we analyze their tweets to understand their psychological features [26]. We consider that LIWC categories of words are independent variables. On the other hand, we manually analyze users' tweets by three different *annotators* to understand their support in the world cup (motivated by the approach of Conover et al. [4]). We collect supporters of 7 different playing nations: *Argentina, Brazil, Croatia,*

[1] For the sake of brevity, we write *supporting preference* instead of *FIFA world cup supporting team preference* throughout the paper.

England, France, Germany, and *Portugal.* We collect users' supporting teams as ground truth data. Then, we build a classification model by using LIWC categories of words. We observe that the highest and the lowest AUC scores of our classifiers are 90.5% and 60.7%, respectively. We mainly analyze users' tweets who are not citizens or immigrants of a country that plays the FIFA world cup tournament. A user from a world cup playing nation likely supports his own team regardless of the current performance and skill set of the team.

We also analyze our dataset by using a pre-trained *ELMo* [21] model. Then, we build another classification model by using deep learning based *Long Short Term Memory (LSTM)* technique [8]. We observe that the highest and the lowest AUC scores of our classifiers are 87.5% and 64.2%, respectively. Finally, we combine both of the approaches (i.e., *LIWC*, and *ELMo*) by using a novel *multi-level weighted ensemble* techniques. Our technique maximizes diversity among the learners and finds a substantially strong prediction potential in all of the 7 class labels. Our ensemble classifier achieves the highest and the lowest AUC scores of 92.5% and 67.7%, respectively.

In summary, we have the following contributions:

- We are the first to predict users' FIFA world cup team preference from their tweets.
- We build two different classification models, i.e., *LIWC* and *ELMo*, to predict users' preferred team.
- We also integrate both of these models by using a multi-level weighted ensemble technique.

2 Methodology

We first crawl users' tweets, then we annotate the users' supporting preferences by analyzing their tweets. Next, we build classification models to predict users' supporting preference. Then, we integrate different models to build a multi-level weighted ensemble model. In this section, we describe different steps to build our classification models to predict users' supporting preferences from their tweets.

- *Crawling dataset*: We crawl the tweets of a user that contain tweets related to FIFA world cup by using Twitter's *advanced search technique.* We consider only English words during our linguistic analysis.
- *User profile creation based on world cup supporting team.* We collect all the tweets of a user in a separate file along with the supporting information. We analyze the users' tweets by using *LIWC* tool [19] and a pre-trained *Word Embedding* technique, *ELMo*. We also manually analyze the users' tweets from three different annotators and *label* the users' by using their preferred *team label.*
- *Building classifiers.* In this module, we present the construction process of our independent classifiers. First, we conduct LIWC based analysis on users' tweets and find relevant features by using *Fisher's linear discriminant analysis (LDA)* [11]. Then, we build classification model by using these correlated

Table 1. Statistics on our dataset.

# of users	376
# of total tweets	805,182
Average # of tweets	2,142
Maximum # of tweets of a user	3,249
Minimum # of tweets of a user	23
Total # of words in tweets	2,44,81,502
Average # of words in tweets	30
Maximum # of words in tweets of a user	6,69,308
Minimum # of words in tweets of user	230

features. We also build another classification model by using deep learning based *ELMo* word embedding technique. Finally, we integrate these two classifiers by using a *multi-level weighted ensemble* technique.

3 Data Collection

In this study, we collect tweets of a total of 376 users. We randomly select users of the countries that are not FIFA world cup playing nations. These countries never participated in a FIFA world cup tournament. We select users from these countries because they are likely not to be biased to support their own country. A Twitter user who is a citizen of a FIFA low ranked country (i.e., *Tunisia-26, and Serbia-29*[2]) prone to support his own nation. We find these Twitter users by using *Twitter advanced search technique*[3].

We set keywords: *worldcup2018*, *fifa*, *fifa2018*, *worldcup*, *wc2018*, *worldcup18*, *fifa18*, and *Russia2018* in Twitter advanced search. We set *India, Malaysia, Vietnam, Sri Lanka, Singapore, Estonia, Finland,* and *Bangladesh* in the *location* of Twitter *advanced search.* We collect the tweets by using *tweepy*[4] Python implementation package. Since we analyze English tweets by using *LIWC* and *ELMo*, we use Python *langdetect*[5] implementation package.

We create an individual file for the tweets of each user. Thus, we have a total of 376 data files that contain tweets of our experiment. Table 1 presents the statistics of our dataset. As a ground truth data, the *annotators* use users' supporting team by analyzing their tweets. We also cross check the tweets of both the FIFA world cups of 2014 and 2018 for confirmation.

We manually study the tweets of the users and check the images (i.e., jersey, flags, and bracelets) to understand which team they support. Some users may

[2] https://www.fifa.com/fifa-world-ranking/ranking-table/men/.
[3] https://twitter.com/search-advanced.
[4] http://www.tweepy.org/.
[5] https://pypi.org/project/langdetect/.

Table 2. Twitter_id, country, tweets, comments, and preference on supporting team.

Twitter_id and user's country	Tweets	Observation/Label
abdulafaan Kashmir, India	1. To all the dumbasses out there who are barking abt Messi's international team break. There's a difference between taking time off and retiring. Messi will not participate in next few friendlies. He will be back for the Copa America. This was decided b/w AFA and Messi 2. Because I don't support you just for winning! I support you because I love you! Because of what you've done for football! For me you'll always be The Greatest	The supporter writes about his affection, love, and criticism for his team. **Argentina (ARG)**
AskarShaikh Dhaka, Bangladesh	1. After #brazil's #secondround #match against #mexico #vaibrazil #worldcup20 #worldcupvibes #instaworldcup #followforlike #followforfollow	The supporter posts a photo with jersey and flag of the supporting team **Brazil (BRA)**
Hasan_Showrav Dhaka, Bangladesh	1. BRAZIL!!!! BRAZIL!!!! BRAZIL!!!! @ Dhaka cantonment 2. #Congratulations BRAZIL... 3. #BRAZIL!!! #Brother... @ Dhaka cantonment 4. Congratulations BRAZIL!!! Well played.. Neymar Jr. 5. #BRAZIL 6. #Then.. #Now.. #Forever.. @ Dhaka cantonment	The supporter posts at least a tweet for every match of the supporting team **Brazil (BRA)**
widluvshanky Kolkata, India	1. #brazil #shanky #SSG @widluvshanky @ Howrah, India 2. 1 min of silence for those who thought that Brazil is going to be eliminated today 3. Into the quarter final Brazil 4. Firmino 5. Brazil Brazil Brazil	The supporter also posts tweet after every match of the supporting team **Brazil (BRA)**

Table 3. Statistics on supporting team.

FIFA playing country	# of users	% of the total users
Brazil	136	36
Argentina	107	28
France	42	11
Germany	31	8
England	28	8
Croatia	21	6
Portugal	11	3

Table 4. Statistics after over sampling.

FIFA playing country	Label	Sample size after SMOTE
Brazil	BRA	136
Argentina	ARG	107
France	FRA	42
Germany	GER	31
England	ENG	28
Croatia	CRO	21
Portugal	POR	22

tweet for a non supporting team for their outstanding or poor performance. We become confirmed about their team preference by checking texts and images in several places. Table 2 presents few *Twitter ID*, *their location*, *tweets for their supporting team*, our observation and finally *label* about their supporting preference. Among the 376 users, we find supporters of a total of 7 different countries. Majority of the users support *Brazil* or *Argentina* (65% of the total instances). Table 3 presents the statistics on the number of supporters on different world cup playing teams.

Table 5. Fisher's linear discriminant function coefficients between LIWC word categories and supporting teams.

Category	Example words	BRA	ARG	FRA	GER	ENG	CRO	POR
affect	happy, cried, abandon	9.53	7.87	2.04	4.34	9.61	2.42	8.50
posemo	love, nice, sweet	2.34	2.65	2.03	2.12	2.47	2.82	2.08
sad	worry, crying, grief	4.65	6.50	5.95	7.08	3.94	2.37	1.85
see	view, saw, seen	7.74	6.56	6.72	6.34	4.90	4.23	3.48
feel	feels, touch	9.07	7.56	4.64	1.09	8.48	7.33	2.22
leisure	cook, chat, movie	5.21	6.11	9.56	5.74	8.72	6.04	6.18
achieve	Earn, hero, win	9.18	4.44	9.09	8.64	8.69	8.79	7.48

4 Building Fans' Preference Prediction Model

In this section, we build models to predict fan's supporting preference from her tweets. First, we apply SMOTE, an oversampling technique to balance our dataset. Then, we analyze users' tweets by using two techniques: i) *LIWC*, and ii) *ELMo*. Later, we build classifiers for supporting preferences by using both of the above techniques. Since *LIWC* and *ELMo* based classifiers show different performances to predict different teams, we integrate both of these models by using a *multi-level weighted* ensemble technique.

4.1 Dealing with Imbalanced Dataset

We observe from Table 3 that we have a few supporters of Portugal in our dataset. Among the supporters of all 7 countries, *Portugal* has only instances of 11 (3%) that makes our dataset imbalanced. The difference of the number of instances with other classes is considerably large. The dataset which has large variance among different class instances is called an imbalanced dataset [13]. Class imbalance problem may lead to poor performance in machine learning prediction. Therefore, we use *Synthetic Minority Over-sampling Technique* (SMOTE) technique, which is powerful and widely used in imbalanced dataset [3]. We use *SMOTE* package by using WEKA [7] machine learning toolkit to increase the imbalanced instances. In our study, we apply the *SMOTE* technique and increase the instance by 200%. Then, we generate new dataset and instances of the minority class (i.e., *Portugal*) to increase from 11 to 22 which is close to the number of instances of Croatia (6%). Table 4 presents the statistics on the supporting team after applying *SMOTE* sampling technique.

Table 6. Accuracy of different LIWC based classifiers to predict FIFA supporting teams.

Label of teams	Highest AUC achieving classifier	AUC	TPR	Accuracy	F-Score
BRA	Random Forest	0.635	0.426	0.592	0.397
ARG	RepTree	0.607	0.308	0.574	0.357
FRA	RepTree	0.815	0.512	0.783	0.500
GER	Random Forest	0.905	0.516	0.876	0.532
ENG	Naive Bayes	0.781	0.28	0.813	0.513
CRO	Random Forest	0.81	0.214	0.753	0.414
POR	Random Forest	0.899	0.675	0.853	0.438

4.2 Classification with LIWC Based Approach

We first select relevant LIWC features to predict users' supporting team preferences. Then, we build a model to predict the users' supporting preferences.

Feature Selection: Users' supporting team preference may depend on their psychological attributes. Some support a team for entertaining representation of skills, while other prefer to watch a match for the holistic strategy of the game. For investigating users' personal attributes, we use LIWC tool [25] to find important psychological features from their tweets. We consider LIWC categories of tweets as independent variables and labels of the supporting team preference as ground truth data (dependent variable).

We use *LIWClite7* [19] a student version of LIWC tool. LIWC analyzes 80 different features of text in different categories. The categories are linguistic processes, psychological processes, personal concerns, and spoken categories. The psychological processes is divided into five categories: social process, affective process, cognitive process, perceptual process, and biological process. In our experiment, we have 80 different numeric independent variables and categorical dependent variable. For identifying relevant independent variables, we use *Fisher's linear discriminant analysis (LDA)* [11] by using SPSS[6]. Discriminant analysis finds correlation between independent variables and dependent variable having more than two class labels. A discriminant analysis calculates the probability of group membership based on a series of independent variables. We compute a multi-level discriminant analysis by using SPSS. Table 5 presents the correlation between LIWC word categories of users' tweets and their team of

[6] https://www.ibm.com/analytics/spss-statistics-software.

support in FIFA world cup. Fisher's LDA coefficient scores are proportional to the coefficients of multiple linear regression with dependent variables, i.e., users' supporting teams. Therefore, predictors with larger (>1.0) scores are better predictors[7]. We find the best subset of 7 LIWC word categories: *affect, posemo, sad, see, feel, leisure,* and *achieve.*

Building Model: We find tweets of a total of 7 popular world cup playing nations in our dataset, so our problem is a 7-class classification problem. We apply *Naive Bayes, Support Vector Machine (SVM), Random Forest, Random Tree* and *RepTree* classifiers in our dataset by using WEKA [7] machine learning toolkit. Table 6 presents the best classifier, its true positive rate (*TPR*), accuracy, area under the ROC curve (*AUC*) and *F-Score* for predicting different supporting team. We compute the performance of the classifiers by using accuracy under the 10-fold cross validation. We find that on an average the accuracy of our classifiers is 74.91%. We use ZeroR classifier as baseline method, which has an accuracy of 14.28%. We observe that our classifiers always outperform the baseline. We also find that average root mean squared error (RMSE) of our classification model is 0.82. We see that *Random Forest* classifier achieves the best result. The classifier finds the best feature among a random subset of features. Then, the tree creates an ensemble of decision trees by using a bagging method. Our classifier for *Germany* (GER) achieves the highest (87.6%) accuracy. Our classifier for *Argentina* (ARG) obtains the lowest (57.4%) accuracy to predict users' world cup supporting preference.

4.3 Classification with ELMo Based Approach

In this approach, we build a deep learning based multi-class classification model. We run our implementation in *google Colaboratory*[8] environment where we use Python *Keras* implementation package. First, we convert our tweets based on a popular pre-trained word vector representation, *ELMo* model, which converts the words into floating point numbers. The floating point representation captures all the information in the sequence of words in the text. We add different layers sequentially by using *Keras* model. We also use dense layer which is fully connected among the neurons with other layers. At the end layer, we use *softmax* activation function for multi-class classification, i.e., *ARG, BRA, ENG, GER,* etc. Our *embedding* dimension is 1,024. We run a total of 70 epochs, and batch size is 10. The model achieves an average *RMSE* score of 0.76. Table 7 presents that the average accuracy of the classifier is 69.5%. The model has a little less accuracy than that of the LIWC based classification model.

[7] https://www.originlab.com/doc/Origin-Help/DiscAnalysis-Result.
[8] https://colab.research.google.com.

Table 7. Model performance with *ELMo* word Embedding.

Measure	BRA	ARG	FRA	GER	ENG	CRO	POR
Accuracy	0.67	0.71	0.62	0.77	0.66	0.70	0.74
F-Score	0.54	0.61	0.48	0.58	0.47	0.49	0.50

4.4 Ensemble of LIWC and ELMo Based Approaches

We find that *LIWC* based classifiers show weak performance (according to Table 6) to predict few teams, i.e., *ARG*, and *BRA*. We observe that majority of the people of FIFA non playing nations support *Argentina* or *Brazil*. A strong rivalry prevails among the supporters of these two nations. They likely tweet frequently after *winning* of the supporting team or defeating of the *rival* team. We find that supporters' *LIWC* categories of these two teams are similar, therefore we find overlapping features among the supporters' tweets of these two teams. Thus, we find weak prediction potential by using *LIWC* based classifiers. *LIWC* word categories are independent to each other. *LIWC* cannot discover relationship among the words in a document. On the other hand, *word embedding technique* is capable of capturing context of words, the technique finds dependency among words. According to the Sect. 4.3, *ELMo* based approach performs better for the nations (i.e., *ARG* and *BRA*) that predict weakly by using *LIWC* based classifiers. Each type of classifier has individual strength over others in learning different properties of the problem. Therefore, diverse classifier can enhance the overall class performance [22]. Towards this direction, we build a multi-level weighted ensemble classifier to maximize the diversity among the classifiers.

To build our multi-level weighted ensemble model, we perform the following two steps: i) computing multi-level weights for each classifier, and ii) building the final ensemble model. Figure 1 presents the architecture of our weighted average ensemble value model.

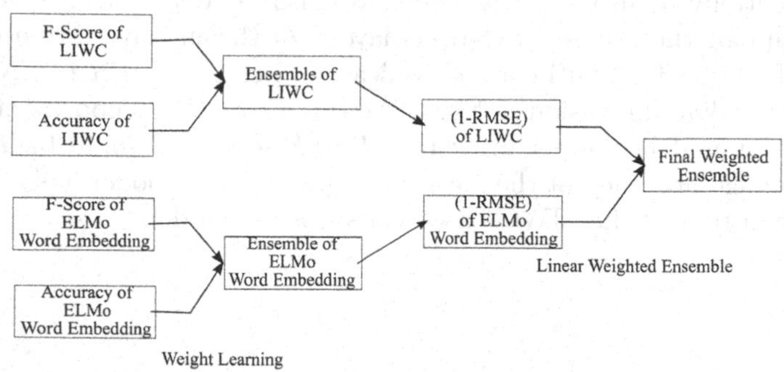

Fig. 1. Ensemble of FIFA supporting preference.

$$E_{LIWC} = \frac{W_{F-LIWC} * Y_{LIWC} + W_{Accuracy-LIWC} * Y_{LIWC}}{W_{F-LIWC} + W_{Accuracy-LIWC}} \quad (1)$$

$$E_{ELMo} = \frac{W_{F-ELMo.} * Y_{ELMo} + W_{Accuracy-ELMo} * Y_{ELMo}}{W_{F-ELMo} + W_{Accuracy-ELMo}} \quad (2)$$

From Eqs. 1 and 2, we build next level of ensemble model, E_{Final}.

$$E_{Final} = \frac{W_{LIWC-RMSE} * E_{LIWC} + W_{ELMo-RMSE} * E_{ELMo}}{W_{LIWC-RMSE} + W_{ELMo-RMSE}} \quad (3)$$

Table 8. Model performance of the multi-level weighted ensemble classifier.

Measure	BRA	ARG	FRA	GER	ENG	CRO	POR
Accuracy	0.72	0.75	0.85	0.92	0.88	0.83	0.90
F-Score	0.58	0.67	0.61	0.72	0.65	0.69	0.75

Learning Weights: To maximize the diversity of the classifiers, we use three different performance metrics: *high F-Score*, *high accuracy*, and *low RMSE*. We train our classifiers in three different levels to determine the weights of LIWC and ELMo based classifiers to predict supporting preference. To this end, we build classification models by using 30% (112 users) of users' tweet. To preserve diversity, we build ensemble of models by using LIWC based approach. In this ensemble model (E_{LIWC}), we use *F-Score* and *Accuracy* as two different weights (according to Eq. 1). Following Eq. 2, we build similar ensemble of classifier by using *ELMo* based approach. We again use *F-Score* and *Accuracy* as two different weights for the ensemble classifier. In the next level, we use low root mean squared error (RMSE) as the weights of the both of ensemble classifiers that we generate in the previous level.

A Weighted Linear Ensemble: We build a weighted linear ensemble model from *LIWC* and *ELMo* based models. We use the rest of the instances of 264 (70% of the total dataset) instances. For each of the ensembles (i.e., LIWC and ELMo) generate a RMSE score, we consider the weight by subtracting the RMSE score from 1. Thus, we generate the final weights following Eq. 3. Finally, we build our multi-level weighted linear ensemble model by using the weights derived from another dataset, so that our models do not get over-fitted. Table 8 presents the supporting preference classification result by using our multi-level weighted ensemble classifier. Our multi-level weighted ensemble model achieves an average accuracy of 83.5%.

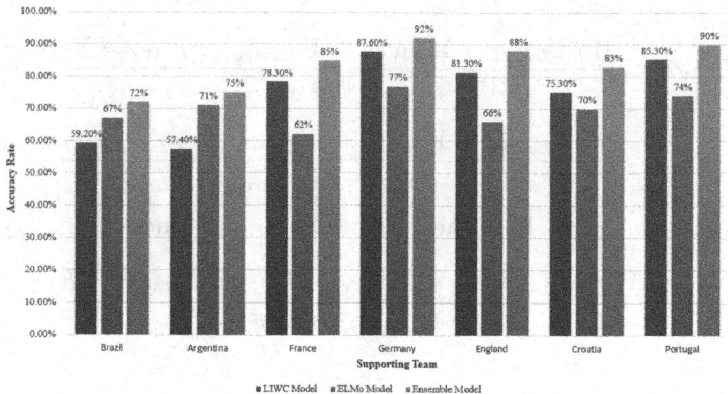

Fig. 2. Comparison of accuracy among different models.

5 Discussion

Our study predicts the world cup team supporting preferences from users' tweets. To the best of our knowledge, no other study attempted before to predict world cup team supporting preferences based on users' tweets.

In contrast to prior literature, identifying insights such as personality and values of users by analyzing the texts from social media [15,16], our study goes beyond and identifies users' world cup supporting team preference. We believe our approach can be followed to predict other types of user preferences such as food, travel, music, movies, etc. from the word usage pattern on social media. All these studies may in fact bring practical contributions for real life applications, especially for targeted marketing on social media. Taken together, our approach opens up opportunities for the researchers and practitioners.

We find that 7 LIWC categories of words are correlated with users' preference of supporting a world cup team in our dataset. These categories are quite intuitive, which further validates the efficacy of our approach. For example, supporters of world cup usually tend to express *affect* category of words about their teams in their tweets. They also write *posemo* category of words (i.e., love, nice, and excellent) in their tweets regarding their teams. Sometimes strong supporters convey *sad* message through their tweets when their team is defeated. We also observe that many of the supporters express their deep love after winning a match and they write *achievement* related words in their tweets.

In this study, we observe that LIWC based model achieves moderate prediction potential (average F-Score 44.72%). Since modeling human preference is difficult, we also use a non-linear model, i.e., *LSTM*. We find that LSTM based classifier has a better F-Score (average F-Score 52.42%) than that of LIWC based model. Though majority of the cases, LSTM is used for time-series and sequence prediction, but we use the model by using a label encoder that performs outstanding in our problem settings. In our study, we could use other word embedding techniques, i.e., *word2vec* [24], *FastText* [10], and *GloVe* [20]. *ELMo* does not create representation for each word, rather it captures context of a word in a sentence through the deep learning model. The other models fail in this aspect where *ELMo* shows superior performance than those models.

We find that our multi-level weighted ensemble classifier has substantial prediction potential. Our classifier for *Germany* (GER) shows the strongest accuracy (92%) and the classifier for *Brazil* (BRA) presents the weakest accuracy (72%) performance. Our ensemble classifier achieves better accuracy of 12.68% and 20% than that of independent *ELMo* and *LIWC* based model, respectively.

6 Conclusion

In this paper, we have built classification models to predict users' preference of FIFA world cup supporting team from their tweets. We have extracted users' psycholinguistic attributes by using *LIWC* and representation of words by using *ELMo* from their tweets. Then, we have annotated popular teams with the help of different annotators. Next, we have applied different classification techniques. Later, we have built a multi-level weighted ensemble approach by using both *LIWC* and *ELMo* based classifiers. Our ensemble classifiers obtain substantial prediction potential for predicting users' preferences of world cup supporting team than that of independent models.

References

1. Abbar, S., Mejova, Y., Weber, I.: You tweet what you eat: studying food consumption through Twitter. In: ACM CHI, pp. 3197–3206. ACM (2015)
2. Back, M.D., et al.: Facebook profiles reflect actual personality, not self-idealization. Psychol. Sci. **21**(3), 372–374 (2010)
3. Chawla, N.V., Bowyer, K.W., Hall, L.O., Kegelmeyer, W.P.: SMOTE: synthetic minority over-sampling technique. J. Artifi. Intel. Res. **16**, 321–357 (2002)
4. Conover, M.D., Gonçalves, B., Ratkiewicz, J., Flammini, A.: Predicting the political alignment of Twitter users. In: PASSAT, pp. 192–199. IEEE (2011)
5. Fast, E., Chen, B., Bernstein, M.S.: Empath: understanding topic signals in large-scale text. In: Proceedings of the 2016 CHI Conference on Human Factors in Computing Systems, pp. 4647–4657 (2016)
6. Gambrell, L.B.: Getting students hooked on the reading habit. Read. Teach. **69**(3), 259–263 (2015)
7. Hall, M., Frank, E., Holmes, G., Pfahringer, B., Reutemann, P., Witten, I.H.: The WEKA data mining software: an update. ACM SIGKDD Explor. Newsl. **11**(1), 10–18 (2009)
8. Hochreiter, S., Schmidhuber, J.: Long short-term memory. Neural Comput. **9**(8), 1735–1780 (1997)
9. Islam, A.N., Mäntymäki, M., Benbasat, I.: Duality of self-promotion on social networking sites. Inf. Technol. People **32**(2), 269–296 (2019)
10. Joulin, A., Grave, E.: FastText. zip: Compressing text classification models. arXiv preprint arXiv:1612.03651 (2016)
11. Lachenbruch, P.A., Goldstein, M.: Discriminant analysis. Biometrics **35**, 69–85 (1979)

12. Leung, C.K., Joseph, K.W.: Sports data mining: predicting results for the college football games. Procedia Comput. Sci. **35**, 710–719 (2014)
13. Menardi, G., Torelli, N.: Training and assessing classification rules with imbalanced data. Data Min. Knowl. Disc. **28**(1), 92–122 (2012). https://doi.org/10.1007/s10618-012-0295-5
14. Miljković, D., Gajić, L., Kovačević, A., Konjović, Z.: The use of data mining for basketball matches outcomes prediction. In: 8th International Symposium on Intelligent Systems and Informatics (SISY), pp. 309–312. IEEE (2010)
15. Mukta, M.S.H., Ali, M.E., Mahmud, J.: User generated vs. supported contents: which one can better predict basic human values? In: Spiro, E., Ahn, Y.-Y. (eds.) SocInfo 2016. LNCS, vol. 10047, pp. 454–470. Springer, Cham (2016). https://doi.org/10.1007/978-3-319-47874-6_31
16. Mukta, M.S.H., Khan, E.M., Ali, M.E., Mahmud, J.: Predicting movie genre preferences from personality and values of social media users. In: Eleventh International AAAI Conference on Web and Social Media (2017)
17. Nichols, J., Mahmud, J., Drews, C.: Summarizing sporting events using Twitter. In: Proceedings of the 2012 ACM International Conference on Intelligent User Interfaces, pp. 189–198. ACM (2012)
18. Ornstein, D.: Dutch substance over style (2008). https://bbc.in/2SaodXq
19. Pennebaker, J.W., Booth, R.J., Francis, M.E.: Linguistic inquiry and word count: LIWC [computer software]. liwc.net, Austin, TX (2007)
20. Pennington, J., Socher, R., Manning, C.: Glove: Global vectors for word representation. In: EMNLP, pp. 1532–1543 (2014)
21. Peters, M.E., Neumann, M.: Deep contextualized word representations. arXiv preprint arXiv:1802.05365 (2018)
22. Polikar, R.: Ensemble learning. In: Zhang, C., Ma, Y. (eds.) Ensemble Machine Learning, pp. 1–34. Springer, Boston (2012). https://doi.org/10.1007/978-1-4419-9326-7_1
23. Rangel, A., Camerer, C., Montague, P.R.: A framework for studying the neurobiology of value-based decision making. Nature Rev. Neuro. **9**(7), 545–556 (2008)
24. Rong, X.: word2vec parameter learning explained. arXiv:1411.2738 (2014)
25. Tausczik, Y.R., Pennebaker, J.W.: The psychological meaning of words: LIWC and computerized text analysis methods. J. Lang. Soc. Psychol. **29**(1), 24–54 (2010)
26. Verplanken, B., Holland, R.W.: Motivated decision making: effects of activation and self-centrality of values on choices and behavior. J. Pers. Soc. Psychol. **82**(3), 434 (2002)
27. Weaver, J.B., Brosius, H.B., Mundorf, N.: Personality and movie preferences: a comparison of american and german audiences. Personality Individ. Differ. **14**(2), 307–315 (1993)

Machine Learning in Health Care

Machine Learning Based Recommendation Systems for the Mode of Childbirth

Md. Kowsher[1(✉)], Nusrat Jahan Prottasha[2], Anik Tahabilder[3], and Md. Babul Islam[4]

[1] Department of Applied Mathematics, Noakhali Science and Technology University, Noakhali 3814, Bangladesh
ga.kowsher@gmail.com

[2] Department of Computer Science and Engineering, Daffodil International University, Dhaka 1207, Bangladesh
nuaratjahan1234561234@gmail.com

[3] School of Engineering + Technology, Western Carolina University, Cullowhee, NC 28723, USA
tahabilderanik@gmail.com

[4] Department of Applied Physics and Electronic Engineering, University of Rajshahi, Rajshahi 6205, Bangladesh
babul.apee@ru.ac.bd

Abstract. Machine learning method gives a learning technique that can be applied to extract information from data. Lots of researches are being conducted that involves machine learning techniques for medical diagnosis, prediction and treatment. The goal of this study is to perform several machine learning actions for finding the appropriate mode of birth (cesarean or normal) to minimize maternal mortality rate. To generate a computer-aided decision for selecting between the most common way of baby birth, C-section and vaginal birth, we have used supervised machine learning to train our classification model. A dataset consists of the information of 13,527 delivery patients has been collected from Tarail Upazilla Health complex, Bangladesh. We have implemented nine machine learning classifier algorithms over the whole datasets and compared the performances of all those proposed techniques. The computer recommended mode of baby delivery suggested by the most convincing method named "impact learning," showed an accuracy of 0.89089172 with the F1 value of 0.877871741.

Keywords: Baby delivery · Impact learning · Artificial neural network · Machine learning classifiers

1 Introduction

According to the World Health Organization, maternal mortality of women in Bangladesh is 194 per 100000 live births [1]. Moreover, Save the Children news reports a 51% increase in unnecessary C-sections within two years in Bangladesh [2]. This rate of maternal death can be reduced by choosing the mode for baby birth more carefully.

T. Bhuiyan et al. (Eds.): ICONCS 2020, LNICST 325, pp. 295–306, 2020.
https://doi.org/10.1007/978-3-030-52856-0_23

There are two common types of baby birth, e.g., vaginal birth and C-Section or cesarean delivery. Usually, women who want less recovery time and willing to reduce the risk of significant surgery adopt vaginal birth. In some other cases, like delivering a large baby compared to the mother's pelvis or if the baby is not in a heads-down position, C section delivery is adopted. Both two procedures have pros and cons based on individual baby birth. Usually, the decision for the process of childbirth is taken by the gynecologist based on the biological factors of mother including age, para, ANC, blood circulation, partograph, AMTSL, birth weight, PNC-1, BP, presentation, membrane, as well as cervix (OS). The aim of this research is to formulate a computerized decision considering the present medical condition as well as earlier medical records of a mother.

There are a lot of classification and decision-making algorithms for clinical decision making, including Naive Bayes, K-NN, Decision Tree, ANN. In our proposed model, we have used the nine most promising decision-making algorithms. To implement the proposed techniques, we have collected data of 13,527 pregnant women having 21 different parameters for each data row for our model. Then we have classified this data into two groups, i.e. training and test data in a proportion of 75:25. The data was preprocessed properly to ensure the highest accuracy including missing value check, features selection, features scaling and so on. We have used training data to train the proposed model and later on, the test data was used to test the performance of the trained model. Among all the proposed algorithms, "Impact Learning" showed the best performance in both accuracy and F1 score.

The contributions of this paper are summarized as:

- We have developed a pipeline of decision making to forecast the most appropriate mode of childbirth (cesarean or normal).
- We have used nine classifiers procedures to execute our work including ANN, impact learning as well as analyzed and compared results performed by all selective algorithms.

The remaining sections are organized as follows: Sect. 2 explains related work of various classification techniques for prediction of baby birth, Sect. 3 describes the methodology and materials used, Sect. 4 discusses evaluated Results and Sect. 5 delineates the conclusion of this research work.

2 Related Works

In 2005, Terhaar [3] claimed that elective cesarean delivery is not yet a reasonable option for mothers as it is still having enough risk of surgery risk of mortality. Karlström, Nystedt and Hildingsson in their research [4] compared the feeling of women who preferred and finally had a vaginal birth vs. who preferred cesarean birth and finally had a cesarean birth. The finding says that women in the first group who choose cesarean birth encountered more degree of fare during baby birth compared to the second group. Moreover, the women who had cesarean delivery was not pleased with the decision-making process. Moffat et al. find that the decision of the mode of delivery is usually taken during the time of pregnancy [5] and the mother is not often involved in decision making. Since some women are not willing to take responsibility for decision making, more importance should be given on an individual's information in case of making the decision. Researchers have started to find a way to make a decision using the help of a computer. Shorten et al. have proposed an internet-based decision-making web for women to choose between these two modes of baby birth in their research [6]. In 2019, Beksac, Mehmet Sinan, et al. have proposed an artificial neural network supervised delivery route recommendation system [7] by analyzing data of 7000 baby births.

Similar classification algorithms have been used successfully in some other biomedical field like disease classification. Deepti et al. proposed a model to identify diabetes at a premature age by applying Decision Tree, SVM and Naïve Bayes on Pima Indians Diabetes Database (PIDD) datasets. They chose sufficient measures for accuracy including precision, ROC, F measure, Recall but Naïve Bayes beat them by acquiring the highest accuracy [8]. Similarly, Kowsher et al. described classification methods for determining T2D medications [9]. Vijayan V. examines various types of preprocessing techniques, which include PCA and discretization. It increases the accuracy of the Naïve Bayes classifier and the Decision Tree algorithm but reduces SVM accuracy [10].

Unlike these works, we have presented the existing classification techniques and neural network model for forecasting the most suitable baby delivery mode. Besides, we have used another captivating and new algorithm, "impact learning" for classification, which has also shown excellent accuracy.

3 Proposed Work

In order to find the optimum mode of baby birth using machine learning algorithm, we went through four major stages, such as data collection, data preprocessing, training data using proposed algorithms, and predictions. The high number of samples and proper diversity is ensuring the quality of the dataset. In addition, data preprocessing has made these data outliers free and more reliable. We have implemented the nine most suitable machine learning classifiers and deep neural networks on the pre-processed data set. Our trained neural network has predicted the most appropriate mode of child birth with a high degree of accuracy and reliability.

The data set has been collected from the Tarail Upazilla Health complex, Tarail, Kishorganj, Bangladesh and has been divided into training data and test data. Training data has been used to train our proposed Artificial Neural Network and the test data has been used to test the performance of the trained ANN. We have considered ten factors, each having different weights on decision making to suggest the suitable most mode of baby birth. The dataset has been preprocessed considering the targeted variable to fit the machine learning classifier and deep mural network. All those classifiers performed well with this preprocessed test data. But the classifier named "impact learning" has revealed the best performance. A figure below describes the workflow of birth classification (Fig. 1).

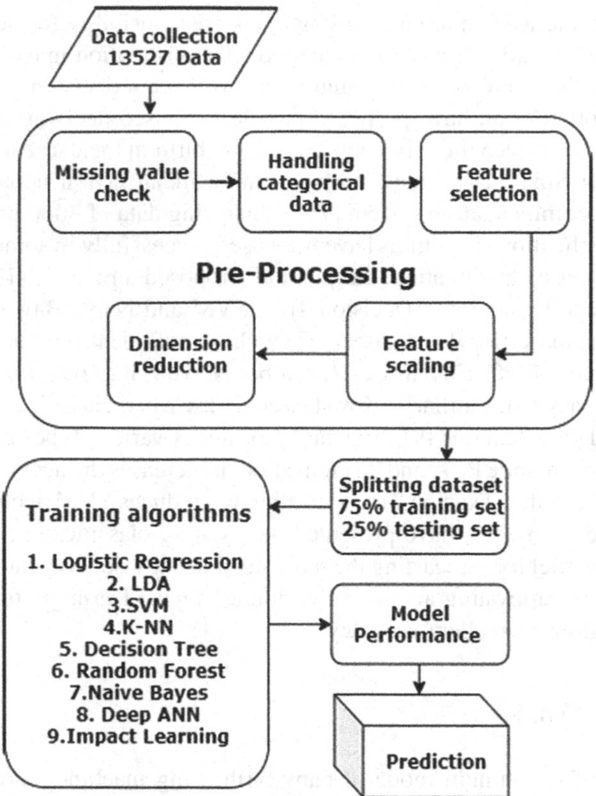

Fig. 1. The workflow of birth classification.

3.1 Introducing Dataset

Our working dataset contains medical information of 13,527 pregnant women having 21 different parameters for each pregnant women including date of admission and time, name, address, age, para, ANC number of eclipses (by medically trained provider), reason of admission, during pregnancy (week), breech delivery, cesarean, blood circulation, partograph, AMTSL, birth weight, PNC1 (postnatal delivery services), PNC-1(postnatal services and status of the mother), BP, presentation, membrane, as well as cervix (OS).

Para refers to the number of pregnancies that a woman has carried past 20 weeks of pregnancy. This number includes both live births and pregnancy losses after 20 weeks. On the other hand, Gravida stands for the total number of confirmed pregnancies a woman has had, regardless of the outcome of the pregnancy. ANC (antenatal check-up) means mother general condition and fetus general condition. ANC is done at step 3 when the baby is in the abdomen, first check-up at 16 weeks, a second checkup at 28–30 weeks, third 36–38 weeks. PNC means postnatal care. After delivery, this is done by checking the normal state of the mother. There are four types of presentation e.g., cephalic, transverse, breach, oblique. Usually, cephalic is for normal delivery, but sometimes there is a breach at multi-case but normal delivery is done. Cesarean delivery occurs for oblique or transverse. Partograph are used to determine the physical condition of the mother and baby. After children's birth, Placenta is extracted in the AMTCL method. Blood circulation is given if the patient is in Anemic. Most of the time, the Membrane stays fully intact. Sometimes it suffers from leaking, rupture. Blood pressure is observed to monitor the normal stage of the mother.

When a patient is admitted to hospital with FTP & LP (full-term pregnancy with labor pain), If the baby can open its mouth about 10 cm or above, it can be delivered in a normal process. On the contrary, if convex (OS) is not 10 cm when it is over 12 h, this patient usually has obstructed labor (prolonged 1st stage of labor) and requires a cesarean delivery.

3.2 Pre-processing

Data preprocessing is a very significant step in the data mining process. It involves converting the raw data from various sources into a recognizable format. Properly pre-processed data ensures the best training of algorithms. To make our system more reliable, we had multi-stage preprocessing of the dataset.

Missing Value Check: Usually, missing values occur when no data value is stored for the variable in an observation. Missing values reduces the accuracy of parameter calculation as well as the accuracy of features. A lot of researchers are using prediction, mean, median, mode method to replace a missing value. But the most promising way of replacing a missing value is the mean imputation method and it has been used to maintain the sample size negotiating the diversity. We have carefully inspected for missing values and finally filled those fields with the mean value of the most similar population. The mean value has been calculated by using the following equation.

$$\bar{x} = \frac{1}{n} \sum x_k \tag{1}$$

Where, $\bar{x}$ denotes the mean and provides the average number of n.

Handling Categorical Value: Most of the machine learning algorithms can't handle categorical variables unless they are converted to numerical values and many algorithm's performances vary based on how categorical variables are encoded. Categorical encoding converts categorical features into numerical values and those values are fed into the model. In our data set, there are three categorical variables names as 'REASON', "PRESENTATION" and "MEMBRANE". Integer encoding and one-hot encoding are two most robustly used ways of encoding into numerical data. In the label encoder, categorical features are an integer value and contain a natural order relationship, but the multiclass relationship will provide different values for various classes. One-hot encoding maps categorical value into binary vectors. Here, we have used one-hot encoding to assign a binary value of 0 or 1 for categorical values and convert it to a binary vector.

Features Selection: Feature selection includes the identification of features and reduction of the features having no significance or having very small significance on the objective function and high impact features are maintained. Our dataset contains 21 types of elements and we have checked p-value for checking the probability for the null hypothesis. The features are taken out whose p-value indicates less than 0.05. After checking multicollinearity, we have avoided those elements which show redundancy and do not support p-value assumption. As we have to handle redundancy, it is essential to choose some methods such as the chi-squared test and the Correlation Coefficient. The Correlation Coefficient can be calculated by numerical data. Assume that A and B are two features and it can be defined as:

$$\sum_{1}^{n} \frac{(a_i - \bar{A}) + (b_i - \bar{B})}{n\sigma_a\sigma_b} \tag{2}$$

After performing both p-value and multicollinearity tests, we came forward with nine features among which AGE, PARA, GRAVIDA, DIASTOLIC, SOISTOLIC, CERVIX(OS), FHR(BPM), REASON, PRESENTATION are independent features and outcome is the dependent feature.

Feature Scaling: In most of the cases, the data of the dataset is not normalized and not even on the same scale. Feature scaling is used to normalize the range of independent variables or features of data. Each feature has been assigned value and has been provided equal weight in order to obtain a consistent scale for all data. However, for feature scaling, different features can have different weights. Standardization, Mean Normalization, Min-Max Scaling, Unit vectors are some of the proven and promising techniques of feature scaling.

As the features are confined within a bounded area, we have used Min-Max Scaling or normalization process. We have chosen the range between 0 and 1 for feature scaling. Mathematically,

$$x' = \frac{x - min(x)}{max(x) - min(x)} \tag{3}$$

When x = max, then y = 1 and x = min, y = 1.

The scaling range belongs between 0 and 1 (positive value) and −1 to 1(negative) and we have taken the value between 0 and 1.

Dimension Reduction: Dimensionality reduction employs minimizing random variables by considering the principal set of variables that avoids overfitting. Dimension reduction becomes essential for a dataset consisting of huge data. Since our independent variables are not too huge, eliminating dimension is not essential. But, in this work, we have performed dimension reduction in order to visualize the dimensional graph and alleviating execution time. If anyone can feel adding more attributes, such as the whole length (9–10 months) reports, then it will obtain a vast dataset and reducing dimension will play a vital role. There exists a lot of methods for reducing dimension including LDA, SVD, NMF, PCA and so forth. Here, we have applied Principal Component Analysis (PCA) which is a linear transformation based on the correlation between features to identify patterns. High dimensional data are estimated into lower or equal dimensions through maximum variance. To visualize the cartesian coordinate system visually, we have taken two components of PCA according to their high variance.

3.3 Training Selective Algorithms

The training data which has been extracted at the first stage was applied to each algorithm to find out the route map of the target variable and the model performance was assessed by obtaining accuracy. To compute the most suitable mode of baby birth, we have implemented eight machine learning classifiers such as Logistic Regression, SVM, Naive Bayes Classifier, k-Nearest Neighbor, Support Vector Machines, Decision Trees, Random Forest and Deep Neural Networks. Apart from these, we have applied the most captivating algorithm is "impact learning" which has shown the best performance.

Machine Learning Classifier: The basis of Logistic regression is a probability model; it is derived from linear regression that mapped the dataset into two categories by considering existing data. First, features are mapped linearly that are transferred to a sigmoid function layer for prediction. It shows the relationship between the dependent and independent variables, but output limits the prediction range on [0, 1]. To suggest the mode of baby birth, we choose a binary classification method [11].

In our work, Linear Discriminant Analysis (LDA) finds out the linear correlation of all the elements to support binary or multiclass classification [12]. The possibility of inserting a new dataset into every class is identified by LDA. Then, the class having the dataset is considered to be the output. It calculates the mean function for each class and it is estimated by vectors for finding group variance.

Support Vector Machine (SVM) is one of the most robustly used classifiers to create decision boundary as hyperplane to keep the widest distance from both sides of points. This hyperplane refers to separating data into two groups in two-dimensional space. It works better with a non-linear classification by the kernel function [13]. Besides, it is capable of separating and classifying unsupported data.

K-nearest neighbors (KNN) for supervised machine learning is an instant learning algorithm in which input labeled data act as a training instance [14]. On the other hand, the output also produces a group of data. When k = 1, 2, 5, it means the class has 1, 2 or 5 neighbors of every data point. Here, we have used k = 5 to ensure five neighbors for every data point. Minkowski distance has been used to provide distance between two points in an N-dimensional vector space to run data. Mathematically, Minkowski distance can be calculated by the equation below:

$$d = \sqrt[p]{(x1 - x2)^2 + (x2 - y2)^2} \tag{4}$$

Here, d denotes Minkowski distance between p1 and p2 point.

Naive Bayes Classifier has been derived from Bayes theorem [15]. But, features are independent of each other in present class and classification that counts the total number of observations. It outperformed with a huge dataset of categorical variables. It involves limited training data to estimate better results. Naive Bayes theorem probability $P(C|X)$. can be calculated from posterior probability, $P(X|C), P(C)$. and P(X). The equation can be written in the following form:

$$P(C|X) = \frac{P(X|C) * P(C)}{P(X)} \tag{5}$$

The decision tree is a decision to support a predictive tool based on tree structure by putting logic to translate the features [13]. It brings a conditional control system and marks red or green for dead or alive leaves. It consists of three types of nodes, e.g., the root node, decision nodes, and leaf nodes. Among them, the root node is the highest node and data are split into choices to find out the result. Decision nodes basically made of decision rules to produce the outcomes by considering the information gain and an oval shape is used to denote it. The terminal node is the step that needs to be taken after getting the outcome of all decisions.

Random forests or random decision forests are an ensemble learning method for classification, regression [16]. Random-forest has been derived from multiple random trees to calculate the elements of molecular structure. A decisione is a collection of results from the random forest algorithm and bagging is applied tit to reduce bias-variance trade-off. It can perform feature selection directly and output represents the mode of all classes.

Artificial Neural Network: An Artificial Neural Network(ANN) is a computing system that is inspired by, but not analogous to, biological neural networks that constitute human brains [17]. It consists of three layers, i.e., input layer, hidden layer, and output layer. The functionality of the input layer is to feed raw data to the network. The hidden layer is the layer which maintains the relation between input and output based on given conditions. Output layers value is determined by activity, weight, and relationship from the second layer.

Since we need to find out the probability of each mode of childbirth and the objective function is binary, so we used sigmoid function instead of softmax between the hidden layer and output layer. There is no rule of thumb to choose the hidden layer in ANN. If our data is linearly separable, then we don't need any hidden layer. Then the average node between the input and output node is preferable.

In this research, we have used four hidden layers between the input node and the hidden layer and 25 epochs to train the neural network. It had no gradient vanishing problem and used the ReLU activation function to train the dataset without pretraining.

Impact Learning: Impact learning is a new supervised and competitive learning algorithm for regression and classification [18]. It fits curve by the impacts of features from the intrinsic rate of natural increase (RNI) and back forces or impact from other independent features. The trained impact learning is also used for checking multicollinearity or redundancy for feature selection.

$$\text{The mathematical expression, } \mathrm{x(t)} = \frac{k\sum_{i=1}^{n} c_i y_i}{r - ak} + \mathrm{b} \tag{6}$$

Where k is carrying capacity and a is the intrinsic rate of natural increase (RNI).

Validation: Validation is the action of verifying the performance of proposed algorithms. It cooperates to test the model and reduce overfitting. There are a lot of validation methods available including Holdout method, K-Fold Cross-Validation, Stratified k-Fold Cross-Validation and Leave-P-Out Cross-Validation. We have applied the k-fold validation and the dataset has been divided into k subsets. One k subset act as a test set and error is estimated by averaging k trails. Therefore, k-1 subsets produce the training set. We prefer k = 10 which contains ten folds, repeat one time and stratified sampling as each fold has a similar number of samples.

4 Experiment

In order to experiment with our proposed techniques, we have first built the model and trained it. Nine classifier algorithms have been used to predict the most suitable mode of childbirth. The preprocessed training dataset has been used to test the performance of the model. Then we have tested the performance of our model using the test dataset. In summary, we elucidated several experiments to compute the accuracy of our model.

4.1 Experimental Setup

We have implemented the whole task in a python programming language having version 3.6 in Anaconda distribution. Python library offers various facilities to build machine learning and deep learning model. The unbeatable library for data representation is pandas that provide huge commands and large data management facility. We have used it to read and analyze data in less code writing. Afterward, sci-kit-learn has features for various classification, clustering algorithms to build models. Also, Keras combines the advantages of Theano and TensorFlow to train a neural network model. We used it to fit and evaluate function to train and assess the neural network model respectively bypassing the same input and output, and then we applied Matplotlib for graphical visualization.

4.2 Model Performance and Final Result

When the model was built, we trained it using the training dataset. While train the model, we tuned the relevant parameter to make the model more accurate. After the model got trained properly, we run our test data set to find the mode of baby birth. For each different algorithm, the value was tabulated, and we found reliable accuracy and F1 value.

For boosting performance, it is always a better idea to increase data size instead of depending on prediction and weak correlations. Also, adding a hidden layer may increase accuracy and speed because of its tendency to make a training dataset overfit. But partially, it depends on the complexity of the model. Contrarily, increasing the epochs number improves performance though it sometimes overfits training data. It works well for the deep network than the shallow network when considering the regulation factor (Table 1, Fig. 2).

The table above compares the performance of all the algorithms mentioned in this model. We have considered accuracy and F1 score as an indicator of performance. Accuracy refers to the closeness of a measured value to a standard or true value. On the other hand, the F1 value can be calculated by the equation

$$F1 = \frac{2 * (precision * recall)}{(precision + recall)} \tag{7}$$

Table 1. Accuracy and F1 score of selective models

Name	Accuracy	F1 score
Logistic Regression	0.842675159	0.832870920
SVM	0.817197452	0.806994760
Naive Bayes	0.874522293	0.870958195
K-NN	0.855414013	0.846528487
LDA	0.835839207	0.820602597
Decision Tree	0.836305732	0.829431859
Random Forest	0.864352273	0.850348735
ANN	0.868152866	0.862268685
Impact Learning	0.890891729	0.877871741

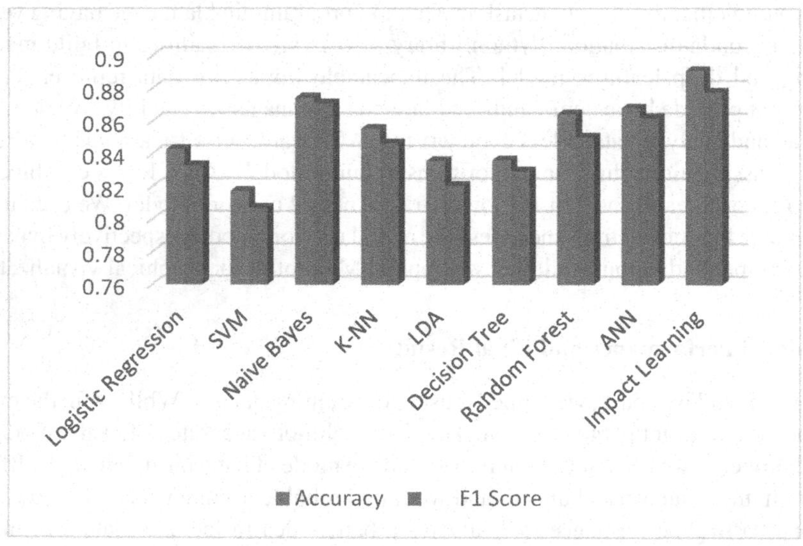

Fig. 2. Graphical representation of Accuracy and F1 score

The higher the accuracy and F1, the better the performance. If accuracy and F1 score both are not measured highest for one algorithm, precedence is always given to the F1 score. Among the eight most-used medical classification algorithms, Naive Bayes shows the highest accuracy of 0.874522293, as well as the highest F1 score of 0.870958195. Moreover, our proposed algorithm Impact Learning exceeded the performance of Naive Bayes with an accuracy value of 0.89089172 and an F1 value of 0.877871741.

After applying feature extraction to the dataset and implementing several types of classification and deep neural network, we found impact learning as the best performer having the best validity, and Random forest classifier are preferable among other machine learning classifiers.

Beksac et al. have displayed vaginal birth versus cesarean birth at their computerized prediction model [7] using Artificial Neural Network. Beksac has shown a performance accuracy of 84.36%, whereas our best selective algorithm impact learning got an accuracy of 89.08%, and ANN got an accuracy of 86.81%.

5 Conclusion and Future Works

Machine learning and intelligent computerized techniques are being used in medical science so frequently. We have used this computer-aided technology to make the baby birth decision making easier. This computerized decision will not replace the decision taken by the doctor rather will help the doctor to get a much better insight into the data and to take the decision in a more scientifically convincing way. As a research work, the whole computation was done in a computer-based programming environment. However, it's possible to make this system available for doctors just by developing an easy graphical user interface of this model, which will be usable for a as a medical device.

In the future, we will work to enhance the accuracy of decision making by considering a greater number of earlier records and features to make the decision much more reliable. Larger dataset leads to the higher training set and it helps to gain better accuracy. Also, we can implement more classifiers to pick up the leading one for record-breaking performance and extend it to automatic analysis. We have plan to apply this system in a real lifes for predicting the necessary steps after a baby delivery. In addition, we have a scheme to collect the data for the full nine months of pregnancy. Eventually, the plan is to design a fully functional graphical interface to decide the mode of childbirth that can be used by doctors and even by the ordinary user without understanding the machine learning classifiers.

References

1. Da, R.N.: Success factors for women's and children's health (2015)
2. BANGLADESH_51 per cent increase in "unnecessary" C-sections in two years_Save the Children International. https://www.savethechildren.net/news/bangladesh-51-cent-increase-"unnecessary"-c-sections-two-years
3. Terhaar, M.: The decision for cesarean birth. J. Nurse Pract. **1**, 141–147 (2005). https://doi.org/10.1016/j.nurpra.2005.09.010
4. Karlström, A., Nystedt, A., Hildingsson, I.: A comparative study of the experience of childbirth between women who preferred and had a caesarean section and women who preferred and had a vaginal birth. Sex. Reprod. Healthc. **2**, 93–99 (2011). https://doi.org/10.1016/j.srhc.2011.03.002
5. Moffat, M.A., et al.: Decision making about mode of delivery among pregnant women who have previously had a caesarean section: A qualitative study. BJOG An Int. J. Obstet. Gynaecol. **114**, 86–93 (2007). https://doi.org/10.1111/j.1471-0528.2006.01154.x
6. Shorten, A., et al.: Developing an internet-based decision aid for women choosing between vaginal birth after cesarean and planned repeat cesarean. J. Midwifery Women's Heal. **60**, 390–400 (2015). https://doi.org/10.1111/jmwh.12298

7. Beksac, M.S., Tanacan, A., Bacak, H.O., Leblebicioglu, K.: Computerized prediction system for the route of delivery (vaginal birth versus cesarean section). J. Perinat. Med. **46**, 881–884 (2018). https://doi.org/10.1515/jpm-2018-0022
8. Sisodia, D., Sisodia, D.S.: Prediction of diabetes using classification algorithms. Proc. Comput. Sci. **132**, 1578–1585 (2018)
9. Kowsher, M., Tithi, F.S., Rabeya, T., Afrin, F., Huda, M.N.: Type 2 diabetics treatment and medication detection with machine learning classifier algorithm. In: Uddin, M.S., Bansal, J.C. (eds.) Proceedings of International Joint Conference on Computational Intelligence. AIS, pp. 519–531. Springer, Singapore (2020). https://doi.org/10.1007/978-981-13-7564-4_44
10. Vijayan, V.V., Anjali, C.: Decision support systems for predicting diabetes mellitus-a review. In: Global Conference on Communication Technologies, GCCT 2015, pp. 98–103 (2015)
11. Bost, R., Popa, R.A., Tu, S., Goldwasser, S.: Machine learning classification over encrypted data. In: iot.stanford.edu (2015)
12. Tharwat, A., Gaber, T., Ibrahim, A., Hassanien, A.E.: Linear discriminant analysis: a detailed tutorial. AI Commun. **30**, 169–190 (2017). https://doi.org/10.3233/AIC-170729
13. Suykens, J.A.K., Vandewalle, J.: Least squares support vector machine classifiers. Neural Process. Lett. **9**, 293–300 (1999). https://doi.org/10.1023/A:1018628609742
14. Harper, P.R.: A review and comparison of classification algorithms for medical decision making. Health Policy (New York) **71**, 315–331 (2005). https://doi.org/10.1016/j.healthpol.2004.05.002
15. Bouckaert, R.R.: Naive bayes classifiers that perform well with continuous variables. In: Webb, G.I., Yu, X. (eds.) AI 2004. LNCS (LNAI), vol. 3339, pp. 1089–1094. Springer, Heidelberg (2004). https://doi.org/10.1007/978-3-540-30549-1_106
16. Ho, T.K.: Random decision forests. In: Proceedings of the International Conference on Document Analysis and Recognition, ICDAR, pp. 278–282 (1995)
17. Nelson, D., Wang, J.: Introduction to artificial neural systems. Neurocomputing **4**, 328–330 (1992). https://doi.org/10.1016/0925-2312(92)90018-k
18. Kowsher, M., Tahabilder, A., Murad, S.A.: Impact-learning: a robust machine learning algorithm. In: Proceedings of the 2020 8th International Conference on Computer and Communications Management, ACM (2020, in press)

EMG-Based Classification of Forearm Muscles in Prehension Movements: Performance Comparison of Machine Learning Algorithms

Sam Matiur Rahman[1(✉)], Omar Altwijri[2], Md. Asraf Ali[1], and Mahdi Alqahtani[2]

[1] Department of Software Engineering, Daffodil International University, Dhaka, Bangladesh
sammatiurrahman@gmx.com

[2] Biomedical Technology Department, College of Applied Medical Sciences, King Saud University, Riyadh, Saudi Arabia

Abstract. This paper aimed to classify two forearm muscles known as Flexor Carpi Ulnaris (FCU) and Extensor Carpi Radialis Longus (ECRL) using surface Electromyography (sEMG) signal during different hand prehension tasks, such as cylindrical, tip, spherical, palmar, lateral and hook while grasping any object. Thirteen Machine Learning (ML) algorithms were analyzed to compare their performance using a single EMG time domain feature called integrated EMG (IEMG). The tree-based methods have the top performance to classify the forearm muscles than other ML methods among all those 13 ML algorithms. Results showed that 4 out of 5 tree based classifiers achieved more than 75% accuracies, where the random forest method showed maximum classification accuracy (85.07%). Additionally, these tree-based ML methods computed the variable importance in classification margin. The results showed that the lateral grasping was the most important moving variable for all those algorithms except AdaBoost where tipping was the most significant movement variable for this method. We hope, this ML- and EMG-based classification results presented in the paper may alleviate some of the problems in implementing advanced forearm prosthetics, rehabilitation devices and assistive biomedical robots.

Keywords: EMG signal · Machine learning · Forearm muscle · Rehabilitation

1 Introduction

Myoelectric control based-prostheses have become a huge area of interest in last few decades as the injuries in the medial elbow have been increased among sportsmen and active individuals [1, 2]. Specifically, Flexor Carpi Ulnaris (FCU) and Extensor Carpi Radialis Longus (ECRL) muscles are the most frequently diagnosed overuse injuries. There are many examples of active applicable field involving the forearm, including rehabilitation [3, 4], physiological exercise [5], sports [6, 7] and prosthesis control [8]. Since these 2 most important forearm muscles are responsible for control wrist movements and act to flex and abduct the hand [9], it remains unclear about its eternal myoelectric signal

T. Bhuiyan et al. (Eds.): ICONCS 2020, LNICST 325, pp. 307–317, 2020.
https://doi.org/10.1007/978-3-030-52856-0_24

patterns. It is well known that surface electromyography (sEMG) is a non-invasive universally applicable technique which have been widely applied to the analysis of forearm muscles pattern. Because, EMG assesses the electrical signals that generated in the skeleton muscles of the human body during muscle fiber contraction, and these signals are constantly arbitrary [10, 11]. Additionally, sEMG signal reflects the activation level of skeletal muscles which become an innovative means for the movement of myoelectrical arm prostheses [12, 13].

Today, state-of-the-art standard machine learning (ML) algorithms are the suitable means to identify muscle patterns based on EMG signal [14]. ML is the popular subfield within artificial intelligence research that is transforming almost everything from legal research to medical diagnostics, depends on three key parts; a model, a dataset, and the hardware that it's backed by [15–17]. In recent years, there has been growing attention in applying ML algorithms to expand the deftness of myoelectric prostheses or any rehabilitation device. Consequently, although characterization of 2 forearm muscles are critical in the diagnosis of any neuromuscular disorders [18], machine-learning based pattern classification algorithms would be beneficial to generate such characterizations [19].

So far, a number of studies have investigated the forearm muscle patterns using EMG signal with a single ML algorithm. For example, support vector machine ML classifier was commonly applied for EMG-based forearm muscles pattern recognition [20–23]. Benalcázar et al., proposed a real time model for recognition of 5 types of hand gesture (fist, pinch, open, wave-in and wave-out) using sEMG while sensors were placed on the forearm and they used k-nearest neighbor ML classifier [24]. Researchers also used some other ML algorithm as a single classifier for EMG-based forearm muscle pattern recognition, like Artificial Neural Network (ANN) [25], random forest [26] and Bayesian classifier [27]. On the other hand, a number of researchers used multiple ML algorithms and EMG signal for upper limb muscles classification [28, 29].

However, the scarcity of literatures pertaining to a proper workout progression relative to the forearm muscles highlights a necessity to study the patterns using sEMG signal and multiple ML algorithms. We applied a broad range of popular as well as novel machine learning classifiers that represent different methods of learning and reasoning. Because, our purpose of this research is to select the best classifier to have a high percentage of classification accuracy to identify 2 important forearm muscles using sEMG Signal during changes in the different prehension movements. Although muscle pattern classification using different EMG features extraction is a well-known technique in research domain. But our current study aimed to identify 2 forearm muscles using only a single time domain variable, called average integrated EMG (IEMG) during changes different prehension movements and the classification performances were compared between multiple machine learning classifiers.

2 Methods

EMG datasets from the UCI Machine Learning Repository was used and those are freely accessible for the academic users [30, 31]. To elaborate how the data was recorded, here we briefly describe the procedure.

2.1 Participants

Six subjects (3 male and 3 female) participated in the experiments within the age range 20 to 22 years. All participants reported no history of upper extremity or other musculoskeletal complaints as per the published paper's methods [31, 32].

2.2 EMG Data Collection and Pre-processing

The study consisted of basic and essential hand movement of grasping. Self-selected speed and force were considered for each subject. There were 2 forearm sEMG electrodes placed by elastic bands as well as the reference electrode in the middle, in order to record the muscle activity. The subjects were asked to repeat the 6 prehension movements as shown in Fig. 1. The movements involved in the study were, *i*) spherical: holding a sphere-shaped apparatuses, *ii*) tip: holding small item, *iii*) palmar: grasping with palm facing the object, *iv*) lateral: holding thin and flat objects (like card), *v*) cylindrical: holding cylinder-shaped tools, and *vi*) hook: holding a heavy load while grasping the handle. For each movement the subject was asked to perform it for 6 s and the entire process was repeated 30 times for each movement. Thus, for each subject a total of 180 six-second long 2-channel EMG signals were recorded. The entire data collection process and protocols has been described in detail in the published manuscripts [31, 32].

National Instrument analog-to-digital converter, NI USB-6009 was used for EMG data acquisition to a personal computer. The signal was recorded by two-channel EMG system called Delsys Bagnoli™ Handheld. The sliding window that was proposed in the study was focused only on the segments where the muscle was contracted [31, 32]. Within a sliding window of 40 ms the average integrated EMG (IEMG) value was calculated as Eq. (1):

$$IEMG = \sum\nolimits_{K=1}^{N} |e_k| \tag{1}$$

The muscle was considered as contracted once the value exceeded a predefined threshold. Note that, pre-processed EMG signal from six movements were used as input to the classifier.

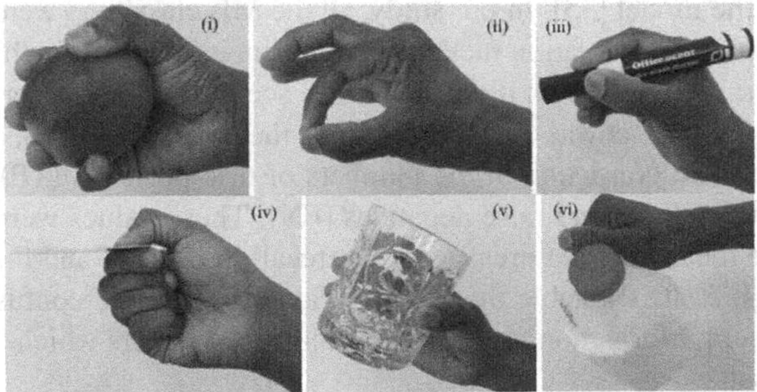

Fig. 1. Six prehension movements

2.3 Classification

Our preliminary objective was to investigate which classifiers are more appropriate and have highest accuracies to classify 2 forearm muscles in terms of EMG activity during different hand prehension tasks. Table 1 presents the list of machine learning algorithms used in the study. The performance metrics of all the classifiers were evaluated using a k-fold cross-validation to make sure that the data were not overfitted. The training set of the individual participant was divided into K equal parts (or folds). Then the model was trained using the data in the k − 1 folds and validateed on the remaining k^{th} fold. All the classification algorithms were evaluated using the standalone Python programming language (version 3.6, www.python.org) script, which consists of python Scikit-learn, NumPy, SciPy, Matplotlib, and pandas libraries [33, 34]. All the major parameters of each ML classifiers were tuned to improve the overall classification accuracy. For example, for the random forest, the *n_estimators*, which refers to the number of trees in the forest and for the K-NN the *n_neighbors*, which refers to the number of neighbors.

Table 1. Machine learning algorithms used in this study

Random Forest (RF)	K-nearest-neighbor (KNN)
Gradient Boosting Tree (GBT)	Gaussian Naive Bayes (GNB)
Extremely Randomized Trees (ET)	Bernoulli Naive Bayes (BNB)
Decision Tree (DT)	Stochastic Gradient Descent (SGD)
Adaptive Boosting (ADB)	Linear Discriminant Analysis (LDA)
Neural Network (NN)	Logistic Regression (LR)
Support Vector Machine (SVM)	

2.4 Performance Evaluation

Cross-validation is a statistical approach that used to assess and compare ML algorithms by dividing data into two segments: one used to learn or train a model and the other used to validate the model [35]. In our study, all the ML classifiers were validated with the default k-fold cross-validation method. Main principle of this method is that entire data was shuffled randomly then divided into k^{th} sections. The learner's classification performance on the test set was compared against the expected values, and a confusion matrix was generated, consisting of the numbers of true positives (TP), true negatives (TN), false positives (FP), and false negatives (FN). These values were used to calculate performance measuring features; accuracy, recall, precision, and F-score, as shown in Eqs. 2 through 5. It is notable that, results calculated by the confusion matrix can generate convenient information for merging multiple classifiers which lead to correctly classifying the patterns.

$$Accuracy = \frac{TP + TN}{TP + TN + FP + FN} \tag{2}$$

$$Recall = \frac{TP}{TP + FN} \tag{3}$$

$$Precision = \frac{TP}{TP + FP} \tag{4}$$

$$F - score = \frac{Precision \times Recall}{Precision + Recall} \tag{5}$$

3 Results

Table 2 presents the performance metrics (accuracy, precision, recall and F-score) of all the 13 classifiers those were calculated based on the Eqs. (2) to (5). The classification accuracy of all classifiers has been illustrated in Fig. 2. As indicated in the Fig. 2 and Table 2, four tree-based classifiers (RF, GBT, ET and DT) gained more than 75% accuracy, interestingly the first three has more than 80% classification accuracy. Four classifiers (ADB, NN, SVM and K-NN) had modest accuracies those ranged between 60 to 70%. Remaining five classifiers namely GNB, BNB, SGD, LDA and LR were showed poor classification performance with less than 60%.

Table 2. Classification accuracies using different machine learning algorithms

ML	Accuracy	Precision	Recall	F-score
RF	85.07	85.01	85.01	85.00
GBT	83.64	84.51	84.08	84.00
ET	82.88	83.01	83.02	83.05
DT	76.41	76.02	76.02	76.43
ADB	68.84	69.01	69.34	69.89
NN	64.29	64.06	64.43	64.65
SVM	63.79	64.03	64.09	64.76
K-NN	60.68	61.51	61.02	61.91
GNB	56.31	58.21	56.55	53.82
BNB	52.38	52.33	52.08	52.73
SGD	50.25	50.07	50.12	36.74
LDA	47.63	47.36	48.22	45.93
LR	47.62	47.78	48.56	45.76

Note: blue and orange shades indicate the best and worst group of classifiers respectively

Table 3 generated variable importance (ranges from 0 to 1) from five tree-based ML classifiers in the classification margin. Here, EMG data from lateral movement played the most important role in the classification margin, where it generated highest importance in all the classifiers except the ADB where it was 2nd most important. Two classifiers (RF and DT) yielded 2nd most important during Cylindrical movement. Additionally, Tip and Palmar movement are the 2nd most important variable in ET and GBT classifiers. In ADB classifier, except Tip and Lateral movements, all other movements have very low importance, even spherical movement has zero importance.

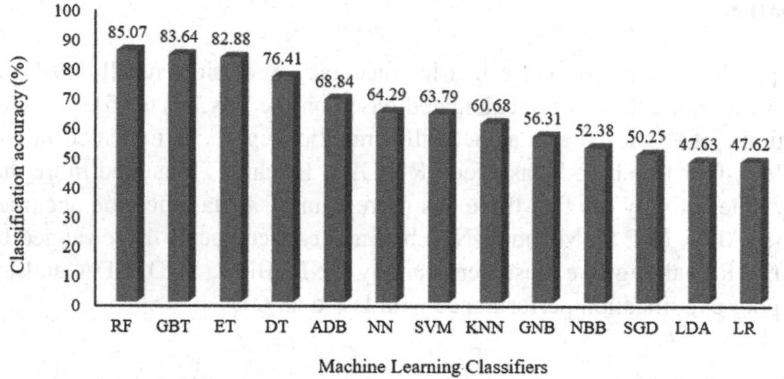

Fig. 2. Graphical representation using bar graph to simply classification accuracies generated by 13 machine learning classifiers.

Table 3. Variable importance from the tree-based algorithm

ML	Cylindrical	Hook	Lateral	Palmar	Spherical	Tip
RF	0.18	0.16	**0.19**	0.16	0.14	0.16
ET	0.16	0.16	**0.19**	0.16	0.16	0.18
GBT	0.16	0.09	**0.24**	0.21	0.09	0.2
DT	0.19	0.16	**0.24**	0.15	0.13	0.14
ADB	0.08	0.04	0.34	0.12	0.00	**0.42**

Note: Bold number represents most important variable in the classification margin

Figure 3 shows the comparison between precision and recall results from each classifier. Precision is a performance measure of positive predictions, whereas recall is a performance measure of the whole positive part of a dataset. The precision and recall values were similar (difference is 0.0) for the following classifiers, GBT, ET, ADB, NN, SVM, BNB, KNN and SGD. Very marginal difference found (difference is ~0.1) in RF, DT, LDA and LR methods. But large differences found for GNB (difference is 0.05) classifiers which indicates that this classifier have week prediction to classify positive and negative values correctly.

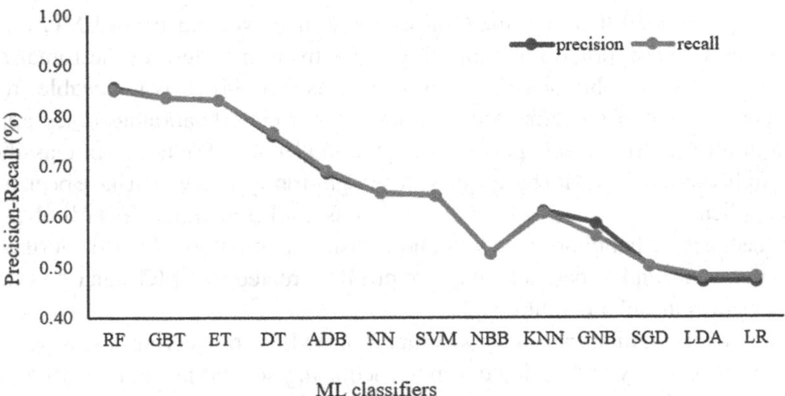

Fig. 3. Differences between the percent of precision and recall values from different classifiers.

4 Discussions

Owing to the recent progress in the field of machine learning algorithms, interest in the field of dynamic exoskeletons and orthoses using electromyographic signal has increased rapidly. Therefore, our objective in this paper was to compare and determine which machine learning classifier learns best to classify 2 important forearm muscles using EMG signal which may lead researchers to understand the patterns to design and develop EMG controlled orthotic exoskeleton for the hand. Our result successfully evaluates the performance of the 13 popular and widely used supervised ML algorithms based on EMG signal. Furthermore, we investigated the importance of a feature by determining the increase in the model's prediction error after permuting the feature. Here the features or variables are 6 types of basic hand movements. More preciously, it assists which variable contributes more or less to predict the outcomes (2 forearm muscles).

Classification accuracy is a measure of showing how well the classifier correctly identifies the objects [36, 37]. In our paper, objects refer to classify 2 most important human forearm muscles, FCU and ECRL. Our results show that 4 tree-based ML classifier have higher classification accuracies (>75%) compare to other supervised learning techniques in this study. Therefore, our findings support previous work where tree-based ensembles ML are becoming well-established as popular and powerful pattern recognition techniques [38]. In addition, our results in accordance with recent work done by Pancholi et al. and Gu et al. where Random forest obtained higher accuracy for EMG signal classification [28, 39].

In our current study, two muscles were classified during six movements based on only EMG variable, called average integrated EMG (IEMG). A number of researchers used only a single EMG variable like IEMG to identify muscle function or patterns [40, 41]. Therefore, we feel that, although we used only a single EMG variable (IEMG), but our methodological approach was in right track. We strongly believe that, our classification results based on IEMG might helpful in the upper limb rehabilitation. Since, sEMG is widely used as a measuring technique to acquire information about the clinical state of the muscles and as a cause of control information for telerobotic and prosthetics [42].

It is hypothesized that classification of forearm movement using EMG measurements would be appropriate for improving the activation pattern of the forearm muscles as well as the rehabilitation/training programs [43, 44]. It is noticeable from the more recent history of movement studies that higher classification accuracy approach is required for forearm muscle pattern recognition [19, 45]. We hope our classification results might helpful for EMG based pattern recognition system which have been broadly used in applications such as powered exoskeletons, multifunctional upper limb prostheses, biofeedback, rehabilitation robots and assistive computers [46–48]. Furthermore, medical personals and researchers may use profiles created by EMG signal to study and diagnose neuromuscular conditions.

The major strength of this study was that it provided a pioneering assessment on the classification accuracy and variable importance using several machine learning classifiers during basic forearm movements. To the authors' knowledge this has not been investigated broadly before. Alternatively, it is also essential to discuss a few points that may be considered as limitations of the proposed research method, including: firstly, we have considered average integrated EMG (IEMG) signal, which is the only feature in the study. Then, we used open access EMG database, but the corresponding data are scientifically valid as its consequences are already published in previous literatures [31, 32].

5 Conclusion

We investigated performance of the machine learning classification techniques to improve the identification of The Flexor Carpi Ulnaris (FCU) and the Extensor Carpi Radialis Longus (ECRL) muscle based on EMG signal. Our findings indicate that tree-based classifiers have the best classification accuracy. We hope our results for the classification of the forearm gestures based on EMG signal will provide a useful foundation for future research in the interfacing and application of medical rehabilitation devices. In future research, this result may apply in real time to myoelectric prostheses or any hand-related assistive device.

References

1. Weeks, K.D., Dines, D.M.: Ulnar collateral ligament: throwing biomechanics. In: Dines, J.S., Altchek, D.W. (eds.) Elbow Ulnar Collateral Ligament Injury: A Guide to Diagnosis and Treatment, pp. 11–16. Springer, Boston (2015). https://doi.org/10.1007/978-1-4899-7540-9_2
2. Islam, A., Sundaraj, K., Ahmad, B., Ahamed, N.U., Ali, A.: Mechanomyography sensors for muscle assessment: a brief review. J. Phys. Ther. Sci. **24**(12), 1359–1365 (2012)
3. Lipinski, C.L., Donovan, L., McLoughlin, T.J., Armstrong, C.W., Norte, G.E.: Surface electromyography of the forearm musculature during an overhead throwing rehabilitation progression program. Phys. Ther. Sport **33**(18), 109–116 (2018)
4. Aktan, M.E., Akdoğan, E.: Design and control of a diagnosis and treatment aimed robotic platform for wrist and forearm rehabilitation: DIAGNOBOT. Adv. Mech. Eng. **10**(1), 1687814017749705 (2018)
5. Islam, A., Sundaraj, K., Ahmad, R.B., Sundaraj, S., Ahamed, N.U., Ali, M.A.: Analysis of crosstalk in the mechanomyographic signals generated by forearm muscles during different wrist postures. Muscle Nerve **51**(6), 899–906 (2015)

6. Ahamed, N.U., Sundaraj, K., Ahmad, B., Rahman, M., Ali, M.A., Islam, M.A.: Surface electromyographic analysis of the biceps brachii muscle of cricket bowlers during bowling. Aust. Phys. Eng. Sci. Med. **37**(1), 83–95 (2014). https://doi.org/10.1007/s13246-014-0245-1
7. Schoeffl, V., Klee, S., Strecker, W.: Evaluation of physiological standard pressures of the forearm flexor muscles during sport specific ergometry in sport climbers. Br. J. Sports Med. **38**(4), 422–425 (2004)
8. Kapelner, T., Negro, F., Aszmann, O.C., Farina, D.: Decoding motor unit activity from forearm muscles: perspectives for myoelectric control. IEEE Trans. Neural Syst. Rehabil. Eng. **26**(1), 244–251 (2018)
9. Islam, M.A., Sundaraj, K., Ahmad, R.B., Sundaraj, S., Ahamed, N.U., Ali, M.A.: Cross-talk in mechanomyographic signals from the forearm muscles during sub-maximal to maximal isometric grip force. PLoS One **9**(5), e96628 (2014)
10. Ahamed, N.U., Sundaraj, K., Ahmad, R.B., Rahman, M., Islam, A., Ali, A.: Analysis of the effect on electrode placement on an adolescent's biceps brachii during muscle contractions using a wireless EMG sensor. J. Phys. Ther. Sci. **24**(7), 609–611 (2012)
11. Frigo, C., Ferrarin, M., Frasson, W., Pavan, E., Thorsen, R.: EMG signals detection and processing for online control of functional electrical stimulation. J. Electromyogr. Kinesiol. **10**(5), 351–360 (2000)
12. Ahamed, N.U., Sundaraj, K., Ahmad, R.B., Nadarajah, S., Shi, P.T., Rahman, S.M.: Recent Survey of Automated Rehabilitation Systems Using EMG Biosensors. J. Phys. Ther. Sci. **23**(6), 945–948 (2011)
13. Ahamed, N.U., Sundaraj, K., Alqahtani, M., Altwijri, O., Ali, M., Islam, M.: EMG-force relationship during static contraction: effects on sensor placement locations on biceps brachii muscle. Technol. Health Care **22**(4), 505–513 (2014)
14. Phinyomark, A., Scheme, E.: EMG pattern recognition in the era of big data and deep learning. Big Data Cogn. Comput. **2**(3), 21 (2018)
15. Ahamed, N.U., Benson, L., Clermont, C., Osis, S.T., Ferber, R.: Using wearable sensors to classify subject-specific running biomechanical gait patterns based on changes in environmental weather conditions. PLoS One **13**(9), e0203839 (2018)
16. Palaniappan, R., Sundaraj, K., Ahamed, N.U.: Machine learning in lung sound analysis: a systematic review. Biocybern. Biomed. Eng. **33**(3), 129–135 (2013)
17. Ahamed, N.U., Benson, L., Clermont, C., Osis, S.T., Ferber, R.: Fuzzy inference system-based recognition of slow, medium and fast running conditions using a triaxial accelerometer. Proc. Comput. Sci. **114**, 401–407 (2017)
18. Islam, M.A., Sundaraj, K., Ahmad, R.B., Sundaraj, S., Ahamed, N.U., Ali, M.A.: Longitudinal, lateral and transverse axes of forearm muscles influence the crosstalk in the mechanomyographic signals during isometric wrist postures. PLoS One **9**(8), e104280 (2014)
19. Gu, Y., Yang, D., Huang, Q., Yang, W., Liu, H.: Robust EMG pattern recognition in the presence of confounding factors: features, classifiers and adaptive learning. Expert Syst. Appl. **96**, 208–217 (2018)
20. Saponas, T.S., Tan, D.S., Morris, D., Balakrishnan, R.: Demonstrating the feasibility of using forearm electromyography for muscle-computer interfaces. In: Proceedings of the SIGCHI Conference on Human Factors in Computing Systems, pp. 515–524. ACM Digital Library, NY, USA (2008)
21. Khokhar, Z.O., Xiao, Z.G., Menon, C.: Surface EMG pattern recognition for real-time control of a wrist exoskeleton. Biomed. Eng. Online **9**(1), 41 (2010)
22. Arjunan, S.P., Kumar, D.K., Naik, G.R.: A machine learning based method for classification of fractal features of forearm sEMG using twin support vector machines. In: Annual IEEE International Conference on Engineering in Medicine and Biology Society (EMBC), pp. 4821–4824. IEEE, Buenos Aires (2010)

23. Yoo, H., Park, H., Lee, B.: Optimized method for surface electromyography classification regarding channel reduction in hand prosthesis: a pilot study. Ann. Phys. Rehabil. Med. **61**, e468 (2018)
24. Benalcázar, M.E., Jaramillo, A.G., Zea, A., Páez, A., Andaluz, V.H.: Hand gesture recognition using machine learning and the Myo armband. In: 25th European Signal Processing Conference, pp. 1040–1044. IEEE, Kos (2017)
25. Uvanesh, K., et al.: Classification of surface electromyogram signals acquired from the forearm of a healthy volunteer. In: Classification and Clustering in Biomedical Signal Processing, pp. 315–333. IGI Global (2016)
26. Su, R., Chen, X., Cao, S., Zhang, X.: Random forest-based recognition of isolated sign language subwords using data from accelerometers and surface electromyographic sensors. Sensors **16**(1), 100 (2016)
27. Chen, X., Zhang, X., Zhao, Z.-Y., Yang, J.-H., Lantz, V., Wang, K.-Q.: Multiple hand gesture recognition based on surface EMG signal. In: 1st International conference on Bioinformatics and Biomedical Engineering, pp. 506–509. IEEE, Wuhan (2007)
28. Pancholi, S., Joshi, A.M.: Portable EMG data acquisition module for upper limb prosthesis application. IEEE Sens. J. **18**(8), 3436–3443 (2018)
29. Kim, K.S., Choi, H.H., Moon, C.S., Mun, C.W.: Comparison of k-nearest neighbor, quadratic discriminant and linear discriminant analysis in classification of electromyogram signals based on the wrist-motion directions. Curr. Appl. Phys. **11**(3), 740–745 (2011)
30. Dua, D., Taniskidou, E.F.: UCI machine learning repository. University of California, School of Information and Computer Science, Irvine, CA. http://archive.ics.uci.edu/ml. Accessed 22 Nov 2019
31. Sapsanis, C., Georgoulas, G., Tzes, A., Lymberopoulos, D.: Improving EMG based classification of basic hand movements using EMD. In: 35th Annual International Conference on Engineering in Medicine and Biology Society (EMBC), pp. 5754–5757. IEEE, Osaka (2013)
32. Sapsanis, C., Georgoulas, G., Tzes, A.: EMG based classification of basic hand movements based on time-frequency features. In: 21st Mediterranean Conference Control & Automation (MED), pp. 716–722. IEEE, Chania (2013)
33. Raschka, S.: Python Machine Learning. Packt Publishing Ltd., Birmingham (2015)
34. Pedregosa, F., Varoquaux, G., Gramfort, A., Michel, V., Thirion, B., Grisel, O., et al.: Scikit-learn: machine learning in Python. J. Mach. Learn. Res. **12**(11), 2825–2830 (2011)
35. Refaeilzadeh, P., Tang, L., Liu, H.: Cross-Validation, Encyclopedia of Database Systems (EDBS), pp. 1–7. Arizona State University, Springer, Heidelberg (2016)
36. Gorunescu, F.: Classification performance evaluation. In: Gorunescu, F. (ed.) Data Mining. Intelligent Systems Reference Library, 12, pp. 319–330. Springer, Heidelberg (2011). https://doi.org/10.1007/978-3-642-19721-5_6
37. Ahamed, N.U., Kobsar, D., Benson, L., Clermon, C.T., Osis, S.T., Ferber, R.: Subject-specific and group-based running pattern classification using a single wearable sensor. J. Biomech. **84**, 227–233 (2019)
38. Auret, L., Aldrich, C.: Empirical comparison of tree ensemble variable importance measures. Chemometr. Intell. Lab. Syst. **105**(2), 157–170 (2011)
39. Gu Z., Zhang K., Zhao W., Luo Y.: Multi-class classification for basic hand movements. https://www.andrew.cmu.edu/user/zijingg/Multi_Class_Classification_for_Basic_Hand_Movements.pdf. Accessed 23 Sept 2019
40. Isakov, E., Keren, O., Benjuya, N.: Trans-tibial amputee gait: time-distance parameters and EMG activity. Prosthet. Orthot. Int. **24**(3), 216–220 (2000)
41. Sypkes, C.T., Kozlowski, B.J., Grant, J., Bent, L.R., McNeil, C.J., Power, G.A.: The influence of residual force enhancement on spinal and supraspinal excitability. PeerJ **6**, e5421 (2018)
42. Parker, P., Englehart, K., Hudgins, B.: Myoelectric signal processing for control of powered limb prostheses. J. Electromyogr. Kinesiol. **16**, 541–548 (2006)

43. Ahamed, N.U., Sundaraj, K., Ahmad, R.B., Rahman, M., Ali, A.: A framework for the development of measurement and quality assurance in software-based medical rehabilitation systems. Proc. Eng. **41**, 53–60 (2012)
44. Klein, C.S., Li, S., Hu, X., Li, X.: Editorial: electromyography (EMG) techniques for the assessment and rehabilitation of motor impairment following stroke. Front. Neurol. **9**, 1122 (2018)
45. Cao, H., Sun, S., Zhang, K.: Modified EMG-based handgrip force prediction using extreme learning machine. Soft. Comput. **21**(2), 491–500 (2015). https://doi.org/10.1007/s00500-015-1800-8
46. Amsuss, S., Goebel, P.M., Jiang, N., Graimann, P.B., Paredes, L., Farina, D.: Self-correcting pattern recognition system of surface EMG signals for upper limb prosthesis control. IEEE Trans. Biomed. Eng. **61**(4), 1167–1176 (2014)
47. Ahamed, N.U., Sundaraj, K., Poo, T.S.: Design and development of an automated, portable and handheld tablet personal computer-based data acquisition system for monitoring electromyography signals during rehabilitation. Proc. Inst. Mech. Eng. Part H: J. Eng. Med. **227**(3), 262–274 (2013)
48. Cipriani, C., Controzzi, M., Carrozza, M.C.: Objectives, criteria and methods for the design of the SmartHand transradial prosthesis. Robotica **28**(6), 919–927 (2010)

Prediction Model for Self-assessed Health Status in Flood-Prone Area of Bangladesh

Md. Kamrul Hossain(✉)

Daffodil International University, Dhaka 1207, Bangladesh
kamrul.ged@diu.edu.bd

Abstract. Bangladesh is a frequently affected by river flood and flash flood because of its geographical location. Along with the number of vulnerabilities, flood is cause sever health related problems. Thus objective of this study was to develop a prediction model for self-assessed health for the people of flood-prone area of Bangladesh. A CHAID technique is applied to predict the self-assessed health status. Data was collected from 883 individuals who were selected applying multistage random from four selected flood affected districts - Sunamgonj, Chattogram, Jamalpur and Gaiandha of Bangladesh. It is observed that more than 54% people of the flood affected area had reported that they were in poor health condition. In addition, food scarcity, worried about future, health awareness, use of hygienic toilet and education level were found the influential factors for self-assessed health status. However, food scarcity was the most influential factors for the prediction model. Accuracy, Precision, Recall and F1 Score for the training model were found 75.1%, 82.01%, 74.5% and 78.1% respectively whereas for test model were 74.1%, 85.5%, 71.0% and 77.6% respectively. The prediction model would assist to identify people who might be under risk in the flood affected area and also can mitigate health related disaster in the area.

Keywords: CHAID technique · Self-Assessed health · Flood-prone area

1 Introduction

Bangladesh is situated in the convergence of Ganges (Padma) – Brahmaputra (Jamuna) – Meghna River which is largest delta in the world [1, 2]. This delta contains 80% rainfall of annual monsoon during June – September and cause overflow of water as well as flood in Bangladesh [3]. Therefore, Bangladesh is experiencing flood in every year. Climate change and global warming are also influencing flood of this area [4]. As a result the frequency of occurring flood is increasing in Bangladesh.

Due to flood, normal living style, agriculture sector, daily activities, health care facilities, food supply, sanitation and economic activities of the affected area had deteriorated [5, 6]. Flood has time varying affect on health. The affect of flood can be classified as physical impacts as well as psychological health impacts [7]. Directly the impact that is physical impact might be include water bone disease, fecal-oral disease, injury, acute

T. Bhuiyan et al. (Eds.): ICONCS 2020, LNICST 325, pp. 318–329, 2020.
https://doi.org/10.1007/978-3-030-52856-0_25

asthma, skin rashes and clusters, outbreaks of gastroenteritis, and respiratory in-fections [8, 9]. Psychological impact of flooding includes post-traumatic stress disor-der, anxiety, depression, distress, insomnia, nightmares and suicidal ideation which are the long term affect [10–12]. The curse of flood effect significantly high on elderly, the family lived in low economic condition, had food scarcity, unhygienic water source and sanitation [13]. Shimi et al. [14] suggested to that education, hygienic sanitation and health awareness can helps to mitigate the disaster of flood affected area.

Bangladesh is severely affected by the natural disaster; a prediction model which can find out people who might be under risk of flood can help to reduce loss. There is surprisingly limited literature about affects of flood on health, specifically in relation to health status and associated factors. This is may be because of getting rigorous controlled epidemiologic data, especially in low or middle income countries. A number of studies [15–20] have been conducted to develop model for predict self-assessed diseases. However, there is no available literature for predict health status in flood affected area. Thus this study aimed to predict health status of flooded affected area based on self-assessed data.

2 Materials and Methods

2.1 Self-assessed Health

Self-assessed health (SAH) measurement is a commonly applied approach for conducting social research. This approach captured the elements of health from a crowded multifactor sample in the cases in which it is not possible to measure health status by specialist. However, SAH depends on the thinking of the respondent which is a limitation of this approach and because of it; influential factors of health status can be missed [21].

2.2 Study Area

Flood Forecasting and Warning Centre had reported that Netrokona, Sunamganj, Sylhet, Chattogram, Cox's Bazar, Bandarban, Lalmonirhat, Kurigram, Jamalpur, Gai-bandha and Bogura districts were the mostly flood affected area in 2019 [22]. There-fore, Sunamgonj, Chattogram, Jamalpur and Gaiandha were randomly selected as study area. Sample size was equally distributed among the flood affected area of selected four districts to determine self-assessed health status and its determinants.

2.3 Sampling Strategy

This study is quantitative and cross section in nature. Multi-stage random sampling was applied to collect data from the respondents. At first among the flood (in 2019) affected areas, four districts were selected randomly. From each districts 2 affected upzila (sub-district) were selected randomly to collect the individuals' response. The required sample size was determine using the following formula (Eq. 1)

$$N = z^2 * p * (1 - p) * D_{eff}/d^2 \quad (1)$$

Where N is the sample size, z is the value of normal score which is 1.96 at 95% confidence interval, p is the prevalence, this study considered p is 0.5 for maximizing the sample, d is the margin of error which is considered as 5%. D_{eff} is the deign effect and 2.18 is considered as D_{eff} for this study because Schwartz [23] showed 2.18 as ratio of disease affected in flood affected and non-affected.

Considering 5.5% sampling error, 884 people of the selected area were interviewed randomly from the selected areas. However, after cleaning data 881 observations were used for predicting disease occurring criteria.

Survey Instrument

A structure questionnaire was developed to collected data from the respondents based on available literature on affect of flood on health status. The questionnaire consist of background characteristics, self-assessed health status, health related factors. Undergraduate level students who belong to same selected district were participated in a training workshop before going for data collection. Before finalize the survey instrument, pilot survey was conducted and revised the questionnaire accordingly.

Data Collection and Process Procedures

Data was collected by face to face interview using the developed structural questionnaire from the randomly selected individuals. The participation of individuals were considered as voluntary and they were allowed to withdrawal themselves from interview any time. Data was collected immediately after the flood in 2019 to minimize the response error. After codding the categorical variables, the data was entry in the SPSS software version 23 for analysis.

2.4 Analytical Tool

Prevalence Rate

Prevalence rate (Eq. 2) is the percentage of observed frequency respect to total frequency of an event [24].

$$\text{Prevalence rate} = (\text{Observed frequency}/\text{Total frequency}) * 100\% \tag{2}$$

Chi Square (χ2)

Finding associated factors using Pearson's Chi Square statistic is a very common method [25] and it identify individual associated factor using the statistic (Eq. 3).

$$\text{Chi Square}\left(\chi^2\right) = \sum\left[(O - E)^2/E\right] \tag{3}$$

Where, O is observed frequency and E is the expected frequency.

Cramer's V

Chi Square can only identify association between categorical variables, however to measure the strength of association Cramer's V (Eq. 4) is applied. Cramer's V lies between zero (0) to one (1) and close to zero indicates weak whereas close to one indicates strong association.

$$\text{Cramer's}V = \surd((\chi^2/n)/(\min(c-1, r-1))) \tag{4}$$

Where, c and r is the number of column and row of cross table respectively.

The value of Cramer's V indicates that >0.05, >0.10, >0.15 and >0.25 are weak, moderate, strong and very strong association between the categorical variables [26].

Chi-square Automatic Interaction Detector (CHAID)

CHAID [27] is a well-known tool to develop a predictive model for categorical data. Among the three decision tree, Quick Unbiased Efficient Statistical Tree algorithms (QUEST), Chi-squared Automatic Interaction Detection (CHAID) and Classification & Regression tree (C&RT); he maximum classification and most prediction accuracy formed by CHAID algorithm [28]. The CHAID is a combination of Chi Square statistic and modified Automatic Interaction Detector [29].This analytical tool recursively splits the observations into distinct segment based on common characteristics. These segments are known as nodes and nodes are constructed to minimize variation within a segment and maximize variation among the segments. In Node 0 (Root node), CHAID shows the classification of the dependent variable based on target group. Then the total observations are divided into the categories of the independent variable which has most significant influence and each of categories is considered as a node (Parent's node). The creation of node (Child's node) is a continuous process from each parent's node until there is significant classification of observations. The last classification of a parent's node is known as Terminal node which is the less influential factors of a model.

Model Evaluation

Model were evaluated using the following equation (Eq. 5–8)

$$\text{Accuracy} = (\text{TP} + \text{TN})/\text{Total observation} \tag{5}$$

$$\text{Precision} = \text{TP}/\text{Total redicted positive} \tag{6}$$

$$\text{Recall} = \text{TP}/\text{Total observed positive} \tag{7}$$

$$\text{F1 Score} = 2 * (\text{Precision} * \text{Recall})/(\text{Precision} + \text{Recall}) \tag{8}$$

3 Result and Discussion

Table 1 presents the association between background characteristics and self-as-sessed health status of flood affected area. The prevalence rate of poor health among the respondents was 54.8%. That is, among the 881 respondents 483 were reported poor health status as affect of flood, whereas Kunii et al. [30] reported more than 98% people suffered from disease in 1998 for flood. Among the male respondent 61.6% had re-ported poor health whereas among them female 43.7% had reported poor health due to flood. The association between gender and self-assessed health status is strong as the Cramer's statistic is less than 0.25, however, the association is significant at 5% level. Among the illiterate respondents, the poor health was more than twice than the literate responded. Kablan et al. [31] also reported that literacy helps to improve coping capacity of flood affected people. The association between education and self-assessed health status is very strong as the Cramer's V is 0.434 and the association is significant at 1% level.

About 54% respondents who were more than 40 years had reported about their poor health whereas more than 62% respondents who were less than 40 years had reported that their health status were poor. There is weak association between self-assessed health status and age in the flood affected area, though the association is not significant. However, Bich et al. [13] mentioned that elderly suffered more due to flood.

The respondents who were suffering from food scarcity more than 77% of them re-ported that they had food healthy status whereas only 30.6% respondent who were not suffered food scarcity had reported for health status. Based on Cramer's V, it can be conclude that there is very strong association between food scarcity and health status at flood affected area.

More than two third of the respondents who were worried about their future had reported for status whereas 42% respondents who are not worried about their future had reported poor health status. Worried about future and self-assessed healthy status are significantly associated at 1% level and Cramer's V statistic representing that there is strong association between these two variables.

Table 1. Association with background with self-assessed health status in flood-prone area

Factors	Categories	Self-assessed health		Chi square	Cramer's V
		Poor health	Good health		
Gender	Male	341 (61.6)	215 (38.7)	47.3**	0.221
	Female	142 (43.7)	183(56.3)		
Education	Illiterate	353 (79.9)	89 (20.1)	166.02***	0.434
	Literate	163 (37.1)	276 (62.9)		
Age	<40 years	282 (62.8)	167 (37.2)	7.06	0.08
	40+ years	234 (54.2)	198 (45.8)		
Food scarcity	Yes	406 (77.8)	116 (22.2)	194.7***	0.47
	No	110 (30.6)	249 (69.4)		
Worried about future	Yes	419 (64.5)	231 (35.5)	35.46***	0.201
	No	97 (42.0)	134 (58.0)		
Total		483 (54.8)	398 (45.2)		

Note. ***, ** and * represents 1%, 5% and 10% level of significant

Table 2 presents association between health's related factors and health status in the flood prone area. It is observed that 43% the respondents who had awareness about flood related disease had reported about poor health, whereas, 67.6% respondents who were not aware about flood related disease had reported about poor health. The association is strong as Cramer's V statistic is 0.24; and the association is significant at 1% level. More than 86% respondents who did not use shop after defecation had reported for suffering from poor health whereas half of the respondents who were users of shop after defecation also suffered from poor health. These two variables were very strongly associated and the association is significant at 1% level. The number of poor health status reported respondents were half in compare between the user of hygienic and non-hygienic sanitation facilities. The association is very strong as Cramer's V is 0.402 and Chi Square statistic is showing that association is significant at 1% level.

Table 2. Association with health related factors and self-assessed health status

Factors	Categories	Self-assessed health		Chi square	Cramer's V
		Poor health	Good health		
Awareness about health	Yes	140 (43.1)	185 (56.9)	50.94***	0.24
	No	376 (67.6)	180 (32.4)		
Use of soap after defecation	Yes	383 (52.7)	344 (47.3)	59.4***	0.26
	No	133 (86.4)	21 (13.6)		
Hygienic	Yes	215 (41.8)	299 (58.2)	142.5***	0.402
	No	301 (82.0)	66 (18.0)		

The 881 observations were divided into two datasets for training model and test model. At first, 80% data that 723 observations were used to train the prediction model of self-assessed health status (Fig. 1) and rest 20% data that is 158 observations were used to test the prediction model (Fig. 2). It is found that both training and test model had identified the same variables in same ordered to predict the health status of flood affected area. That is, the selected influential factors are same for the both model. There is 6 terminate nodes.

It is revealed that food scarcity is the most dominating factors for self-assessed health status in flood affected area. Gaillard et al. [32] also reported that the flood affected area suffered health problem due to food scarcity. In addition to food scarcity, worried about future, health awareness, hygienic sanitation and education are the significant factors to predict self-assessed health status. The individuals who do not have scarcity of food, health awareness is the only indicator of health status. It is found that only 14% people were suffered from poor health who did not have scarcity of food and aware about health whereas about 41% people were suffered from poor health who did not have scarcity of food but were not aware about health. However, worried about future is the best predicting factor of health status for the individuals who have scarcity of foods. More than 94% illiterate respondents had reported poor health who were suffered from scarcity of food as well as were worried about their future days. As most of the people who lived in the river basin are were illiterate or limited education, that is why may be the education is less important among the variables.

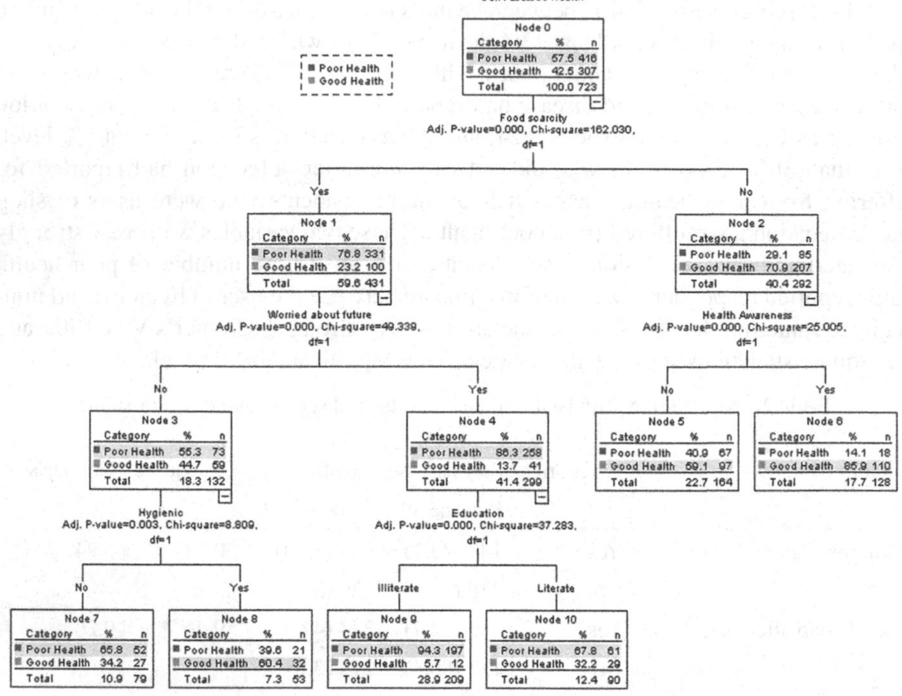

Fig. 1. Training model for self-assessed health status of flood-prone area

Hygienic sanitation is also an influential predictor of health status for the individuals who had food scarcity during flood but were not worried about future days. It is revealed that more than 66% people who had food scarcity as well as used non-hygienic latrine though were not worried about future had reported poor health, however, about 31% people reported poor health who used hygienic latrine as well as were not worried about future though had food scarcity.

The models (training (Fig. 1) and test (Fig. 2)) are explaining that there is higher chance of poor health due to the affect of flood - if an individual has scarcity of food and worried about future days and illiterate. More than 92% people who were illiterate, worried about future days and had food scarcity were reported poor health. In addition, there is less chance to suffer health problem in flood affected area - if an individual has sufficient food and awareness about flood related disease. About 14% and 7% people (in training and test model respectively) were reported poor health who were aware about health and had sufficient food.

Figure 3 presents the gain chart of training and test models which is the Cumulative gains at each node. As the gain rises steeply toward 100%, the model is a good model.

Figure 4 presents the index value of the training and test model. The graph of index value is also showing the estimated model is good to predict self-assessed health status as the index value stated from more than 160% which is above 100% and gradually decreased to 100%.

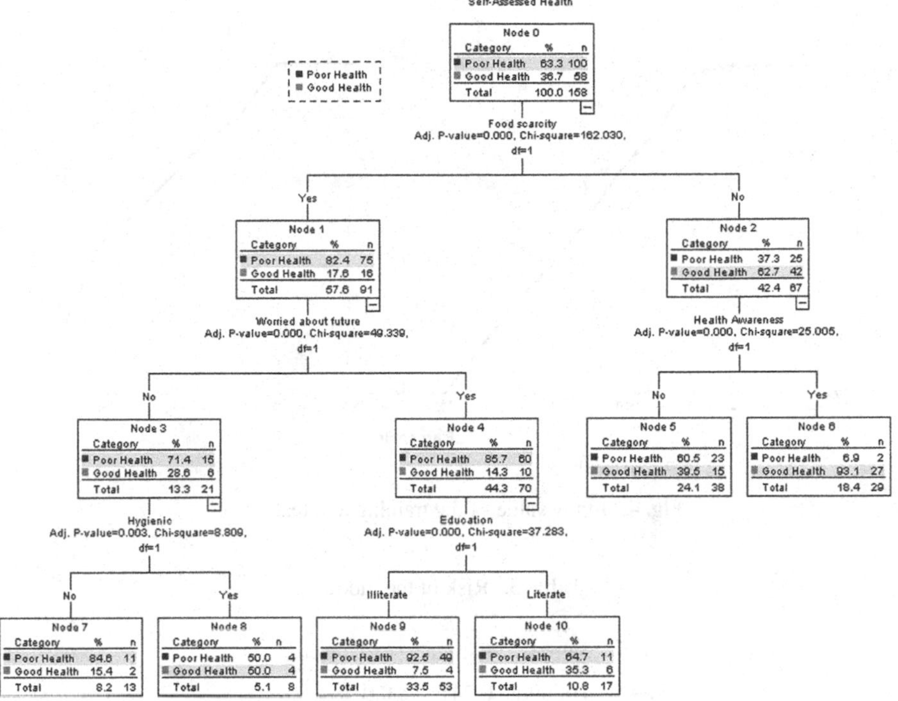

Fig. 2. Test model for self-assessed health status of flood-prone area

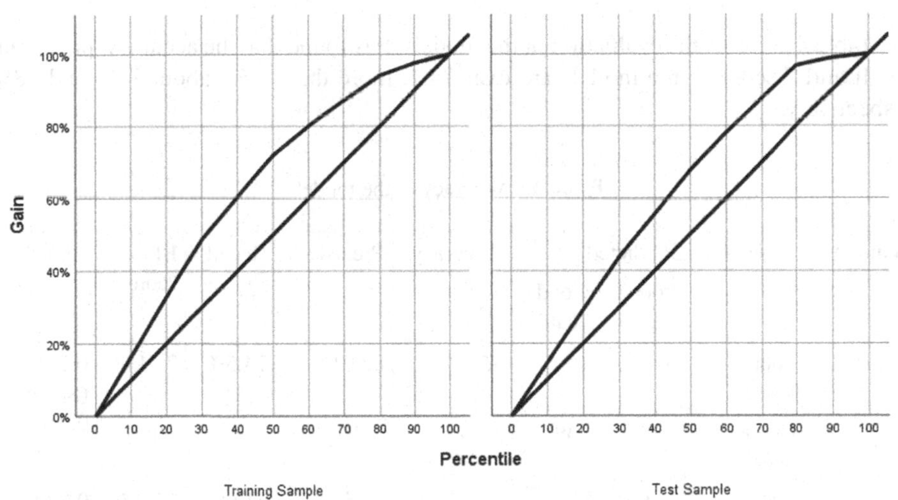

Fig. 3. Gain of the training and test model

Table 3 presents the risk of misclassification at any stage of the models. That is, there is about 25% cases have chance to be misclassified for both training and test model.

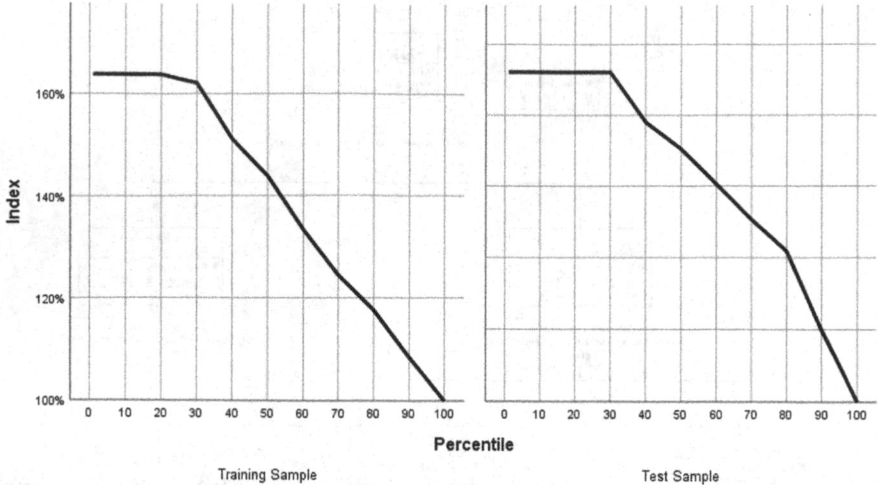

Fig. 4. Index value of the training and test model

Table 3. Risk of the models

Sample	Estimate	Std. error
Training	0.241	0.016
Test	0.259	0.035

Table 4 presents the evaluation of the models. It is found that the accuracy, precision, recall and F score of the models are over 74%, more than 82%, about 71% and 78% respectively.

Table 4. Accuracy of the model

Sample	Observed	Predicted		Accuracy	Precision	Recall	F1 score	Risk
		Poor health	Good health					
Training	Poor health	310	106	75.9%	82.01%	74.5%	78.1%	0.241 (Std. err 0.016)
	Good health	68	239					
Test	Poor health	71	29	74.1%	85.5%	71.0%	77.6%	0.259 (Std. err 0.035)
	Good health	12	46					

4 Conclusion

Because of flood, people faced hardship in their daily and economic activities as well as suffered from health problems. A predicted model of health status can helps to mitigate the suffering of flood affected people. Therefore, this study used CHAID model to find most influential factors to predict self-assessed health status at flood affected area.

Food scarcity is the most influential indicator of self-assessed health status, which is followed by worried about future, hygienic sanitation, health awareness and education. Both training and test model found that more than 92% people reported poor health who were illiterate, had food scarcity along with worried about future days. More than 66% people who reported poor health were using non hygienic latrine and had food scarcity though were not worried about future days. Though the parameters of model evaluation (gain chart, index value chart, accuracy, precision, recall and F1 score) have represent the model as a good predictor of self-assessed health status for flood affected area, there is, 25% chance to be misclassification. Including more variables and increasing sample size, the limitation of misclassification might be overcome.

References

1. Sarker, M.H., Huque, I., Alam, M., Koudstaal, R.: Rivers, chars and char dwellers of Bangladesh. Int. J. River Basin Manag. **1**, 61–80 (2003). https://doi.org/10.1080/15715124.2003.9635193
2. Nicholls, R. J., Goodbred, S. L.: Towards integrated assessment of the Ganges-Brahmaputra delta. In: The 5th International Conference on Asian Marine Geology, and 1st Annual Meeting of IGCP475 DeltaMAP and APN Mega-Deltas, Thailand , pp. 13–18 (2004)
3. Mirza, M.M.Q.: Global warming and changes in the probability of occurrence of floods in Bangladesh and implications. Glob. Environ. Change **12**, 127–138 (2002). https://doi.org/10.1016/s0959-3780(02)00002-x
4. Brammer, H.: Floods, cyclones, drought and climate change in Bangladesh: a reality check. Int. J. Environ. Sci. **73**, 865–886 (2016). https://doi.org/10.1080/00207233.2016.1220713
5. Carroll, B., Balogh, R., Morbey, H., Araoz, G.: Health and social impacts of a flood disaster: responding to needs and implications for practice. Disasters **34**, 1045–1063 (2010). https://doi.org/10.1111/j.0361-3666.2010.01182.x
6. Talbot, C.J., et al.: The impact of flooding on aquatic ecosystem services. Biogeochemistry **141**(3), 439–461 (2018). https://doi.org/10.1007/s10533-018-0449-7
7. Zhong, S., et al.: The long-term physical and psychological health impacts of flooding: a systematic mapping. Sci. Total Environ. **626**, 165–194 (2018). https://doi.org/10.1016/j.scitotenv.2018.01.041
8. Howard, M.J., Brillman, J.C., Burkle, F.M.: Infectious disease emergencies in disasters. Emerg. Med. Clin. North Am. **14**(2), 413–428 (1996). https://doi.org/10.1016/s0733-8627(05)70259-5
9. Reacher, M., et al.: Health impacts of flooding in Lewes: a comparison of reported gastrointestinal and other illness and mental health in flooded and non-flooded households. Commun. Dis. Public Health **7**, 39–46 (2004)
10. Alderman, K., Turner, L.R., Tong, S.: Assessment of the health impacts of the 2011 summer floods in Brisbane. Disaster Med. Public Health Prep. **7**, 380–386 (2013). https://doi.org/10.1017/dmp.2013.42

11. Hetherington, E., McDonald, S., Wu, M., Tough, S.: Risk and protective factors for mental health and community cohesion after the 2013 Calgary flood. Disaster Med. Public Health Prep. **12**, 470–477 (2018). https://doi.org/10.1017/dmp.2017.91
12. Liu, Z.D., et al.: Distributed lag effects and vulnerable groups of floods on bacillary dysentery in Huaihua, China. Sci. Rep. **6**, 29456 (2016). https://doi.org/10.1038/srep29456
13. Bich, T.H., Quang, L.N., Thanh Ha, L.T., Duc Hanh, T.T., Guha-Sapir, D.: Impacts of flood on health: epidemiologic evidence from Hanoi, Vietnam. Glob. Health Action. **4** (2011). https://doi.org/10.3402/gha.v4i0.6356
14. Shimi, A.C., Parvin, G.A., Biswas, C., Shaw, R.: Impact and adaptation to flood: a focus on water supply, sanitation and health problems of rural community in Bangladesh. Disaster Prev. Manag. **19**, 298–313 (2010). https://doi.org/10.1108/09653561011052484
15. Atieh, M.A., et al.: Predicting per implant disease: chi-square automatic interaction detection (CHAID) decision tree analysis of risk indicators. J. Periodontol. **90**, 834–846 (2019). https://doi.org/10.1002/jper.17-0501
16. Chen, W., et al.: Establishing decision trees for predicting successful postpyloric nasoenteric tube placement in critically ill patients. J. Parenter. Enteral. Nutr. **42**, 132–138 (2018). https://doi.org/10.1177/0148607116667282
17. Zhou, H., Wang, Z., Xu, Y.: Risk factors of suicide ideation in Chinese graduate students: CHAID tree analysis. Can. Soc. Sci. **13**, 29–33 (2017). https://doi.org/10.3968/9857
18. Kaya, S., Guven, G.S., Aydan, S., Toka, O.A.: Comprehensive framework identifying readmission risk factors using the CHAID algorithm: a prospective cohort study. Int. J. Qual. Health C. **30**, 366–374 (2018). https://doi.org/10.1093/intqhc/mzy022
19. Ponseti, F.J., et al.: Self-determined motivation and competitive anxiety in athletes/students: a probabilistic study using bayesian networks. Front. Psychol. **10** (2019). https://doi.org/10.3389/fpsyg.2019.01947
20. van Hoffen, M.F., Norder, G., Twisk, J.W., Roelen, C.A.: Development of prediction models for sickness absence due to mental disorders in the general working population. J. Occup. Rehabil. (2019). https://doi.org/10.1007/s10926-019-09852-3
21. Au, N., Johnston, D.W.: Self-assessed health: what does it mean and what does it hide? Soc. Sci. Med. **121**, 21–28 (2014). https://doi.org/10.1016/j.socscimed.2014.10.007
22. WHO: Bangladesh Monsoon Flood 2019: Situation Report #02 (2019). https://reliefweb.int/report/bangladesh/bangladesh-monsoon-flood-2019-situation-report-02-27-jul-2019. Accessed 09 Sept 2019
23. Schwartz, B.S., et al.: Diarrheal epidemics in Dhaka, Bangladesh, during three consecutive floods: 1988, 1998, and 2004. Am. J. Trop. Med. Hyg. **74**, 1067–1073 (2006)
24. Hossain, M.K., Ferdushi, K.F., Khan, H.T.: Self-assessed health status among ethnic elderly of tea garden workers in Bangladesh. Ageing Int. **44**, 385–398 (2019). https://doi.org/10.1007/s12126-019-09354-w
25. Kass, G.V.: An exploratory technique for investigating large quantities of categorical data. Appl. Stat. **29**(2), 119–127 (1980). https://doi.org/10.2307/2986296
26. Akoglu, H.: User's guide to correlation coefficients. Turk J. Emerg. Med. **18**, 91–93 (2018). https://doi.org/10.1016/j.tjem.2018.08.001
27. McHugh, M.L.: The chi-square test of independence. Biochem. Med. **23**, 143–149 (2013). https://doi.org/10.11613/BM.2013.018
28. Lin, C.L., Fan, C.L.: Evaluation of CART, CHAID, and QUEST algorithms: a case study of construction defects in Taiwan. J. Asian Archit. Build. **18**, 539–553 (2019). https://doi.org/10.1080/13467581.2019.1696203
29. Morgan, J.N., Sonquist, J.A.: Problems in the analysis of survey data, and a proposal. J. Am. Stat. Assoc. **58**, 415–434 (1963)

30. Kunii, O., Nakamura, S., Abdur, R., Wakai, S.: The impact on health and risk factors of the diarrhoea epidemics in the 1998 Bangladesh floods. Public Health **116**(2), 68–74 (2002). https://doi.org/10.1038/sj.ph.1900828
31. Kablan, M.K.A., Dongo, K., Coulibaly, M.: Assessment of social vulnerability to flood in urban Côte d'Ivoire using the MOVE framework. Water **9**(4), 292 (2017). https://doi.org/10.3390/w9040292
32. Gaillard, J.C., Pangilinan, M.R., Rom Cadag, J., Le Masson, V.: Living with increasing floods: insights from a rural Philippine community. Disaster Prev. Manag. **17**, 383–395 (2008). https://doi.org/10.1108/09653560810887301

Machine Learning Techniques for Predicting Surface EMG Activities on Upper Limb Muscle: A Systematic Review

Joy Roy[1], Md. Asraf Ali[1(✉)], Md. Razu Ahmed[1], and Kenneth Sundaraj[2]

[1] Department of Software Engineering, Daffodil International University, Dhaka, Bangladesh
asraf.swe@diu.edu.bd

[2] Centre for Telecommunication Research and Innovation (CeTRI), Fakulti Kejuruteraan Elektronik & Kejuruteraan Komputer (FKEKK), Universiti Teknikal Malaysia Melaka (UTeM), Malacca, Malaysia

Abstract. The aim of this review study is to analyze the techniques for predicting the surface EMG activities on upper limb muscles using different machine learning algorithms. In this study, we followed a systematic searching procedure to select articles from four different online databases, i.e. PubMed, Science Direct, IEEE Xplore and Biomed Central (published years between 2010 and 2018). In our searching procedure, we searched by characteristically with two keywords ("EMG" and "Machine Learning") in the above four listed databases to find the related articles in the field of machine learning techniques for predicting surface EMG activities on upper limb muscles. From the searching of this review, we selected total 25 articles for predicting surface EMG signals on upper limb muscles, where 10 articles are provided most efficient and effective classifier of surface EMG signals, 11 articles described different hand gesture recognition using machine learning algorithms, 2 articles explained that the importance of muscles selection, 1 article presented the natural pinching technique and 1 article focus on evaluation error rate of movements. This review presents not only the machine learning techniques for prediction of surface EMG activities on upper limb muscles but also it focuses on the challenge of the machine learning techniques for predicting surface EMG data. In addition, we believe that this review also provides muscle related issues that will impact the prediction of surface EMG activities on muscle.

Keywords: Surface electromyography · Machine learning · Prediction · Muscle activity · Upper limb

1 Introduction

Every year more than 15 million people are affected by stroke according to the World Health Organization (WHO). Currently, stroke is the most familiar disease and the cause of stroke is the interruption of the blood flow within a brain area [1]. Usually, stroke

T. Bhuiyan et al. (Eds.): ICONCS 2020, LNICST 325, pp. 330–339, 2020.
https://doi.org/10.1007/978-3-030-52856-0_26

patients are lost their upper limb muscles control and free movement of muscles [2]. This type of problem for muscle activity is possible to recover by short term rehabilitation system. This rehabilitation is depending on surface electromyography (sEMG) signals because sEMG signals are generated during any types of muscles contraction [3–7]. Recently, sEMG signals are used to recognize the complex pattern for skeletal movements. For example, the hand patterns were used in the rehabilitation system of a stroke patient and as well as used to control robotics hand movement [8, 9]. Moreover, natural hand pinching movement is also an effective rehabilitation technique for a paralyzed patient [8]. To make more efficient rehabilitation system, last few years Machine Learning Techniques are most popular and proved more effective to recover the muscles activity by the classification of sEMG signals. For example, the authors of the study [10] classified the sEMG signals through different machine learning techniques including Support vector machine (SVM), Random forest (RF), K-nearest neighbor (KNN), Naïve Bayes (NB) and Discriminant analysis (DA).

To rehabilitee the upper limb muscle activity, muscles selection is an important factor for recording the sEMG signals because different studies are selected different muscles. For example, the study [11] selected 12 muscles (serratus anterior, anterior deltoid, posterior deltoid, pectoralis major, latissimus dorsi, teres major, biceps brachii, brachialis, brachioradialis, triceps brachii, extensor carpi radialis, and flexor carpi radialis) of the upper limb. On the other hand, the study [1] selected 9 muscle (Brachio Radialis, Protanor Teres, Biceps, Triceps, Anterior Deltoid, Posterior Deltoid, Pectoralis Major, Infra Spinatus and Elector Spinae of the upper limb. Moreover, the study [12] selected 16 muscles (deltoid anterior, deltoid middle, deltoid posterior, teres major, trapezius, biceps brachii, brachioradialis, triceps brachii, flexor pollicis longus, flexor digitorum superficialis, flexor carpi ulnaris, flexor carpi radialis, extensor pollicis longus, extensor indicis, extensor carpi ulnaris, and extensor carpi radialis) of the upper limb.

To recognition the muscle activities, another important task is sEMG parameter which are apply to analyse the role of upper limb muscles. Because, different studies used different parameter including mean absolute value (MAV) [9, 10, 13–15, 24], zero crossing (ZC) [9, 11, 13, 14, 16], waveform length (WL) [2, 9, 10, 13, 15–17, 22], root mean square (RMS) [1, 9, 14, 15, 18].Therefore, the aim of this present study is to review the machine learning techniques for predicting sEMG activities on upper limb muscle.

2 Methods

2.1 Article Searching Procedure

We followed a systematic searching procedure to obtain all related article that discussed the activities of upper limb muscles using sEMG signals and machine learning algorithm. In our searching procedure, we searched into four different online databases (PubMed, Science Direct, IEEE Xplore and Bio-med Center) with two keywords "EMG" and "Machine Learning". Then, we have selected only "conference and journal papers" to find the related articles published in the English Language in the years of 2010 to 2018.

2.2 Article Inclusion and Exclusion Criteria

For the final selection of articles, we considered the upper limb muscle, sEMG signal, and machine learning techniques. We used some criteria to include and exclude studies from the selected articles through our systematic searching process. Then, we read the title, abstract, methodology of each article. For inclusion the articles, we considered those articles that were related to only upper limb classification using machine learning technique. The exclusion processes were the following: (1) articles related to sEMG base lower limb pattern classification and prediction, (2) article that related with automated system, (3) article related to brain stimulation.

2.3 Data Extraction

We carefully studied the selected articles to specify their key information. Then, we followed a standard data extraction procedure in order to summarize for storing data from each article. Each article was evaluated based on some specific information including: (1) Muscle selection (2) sEMG data collection technique (3) sEMG data preprocessing techniques (4) sEMG Parameter for data analysis and (5) Machine Learning technique.

2.4 Research Questions

The final sets of articles were used to provide the answer to the following question: (1) Which machine learning techniques are used to predict the upper limb muscles activities? (2) Which parameter of sEMG signals are used to predict the upper limb muscles activity? (3) Which muscles are used to record sEMG signals for predicting the muscle activities of upper limb?

3 Results

3.1 Article Search Results

Using our systematic searching procedure, we selected 16 articles from the total searched result of four online databases. Those articles were published in English language in the journals and conferences between the years of 2010 to 2018. We investigate the information of each article and found their main fundamentals. We searched with two keywords ("EMG" and "Machine Learning") to find the articles. Total of 651 articles was found from four electronics database (PubMed, Science Direct, IEEE Xplore and Biomed Central). Firstly, the searched result is filtered by journals and conference articles only, and 153 articles rejected by this filtering. Then, we rejected 466 articles because of various reason including automated system, brain stimulation, duplicate articles, Needle EMG and non-related with this study. Further, we read the abstract and methodology of each article. Finally, 25 articles were included in this study for predicting sEMG activities on upper limb muscles using machine learning techniques (Fig. 1).

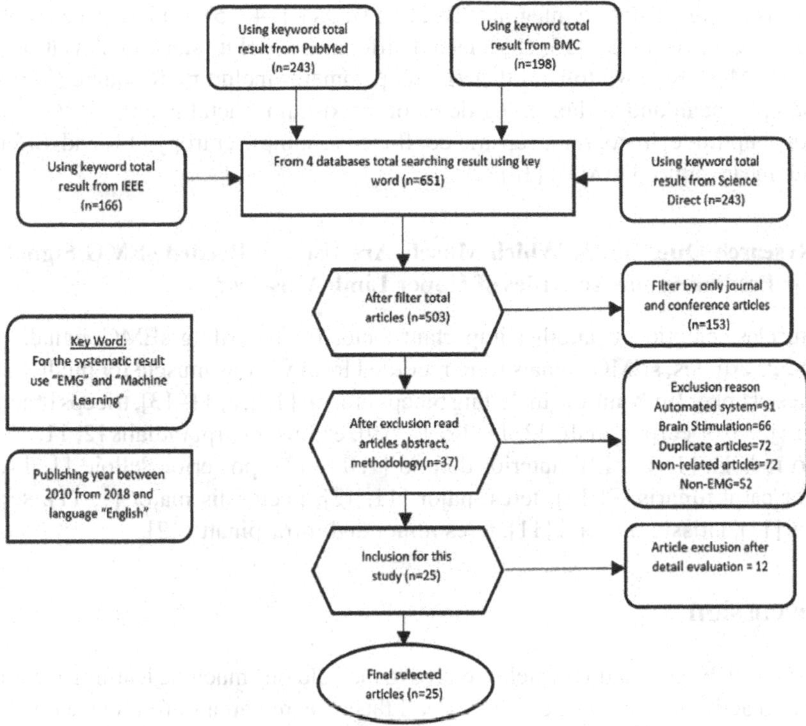

Fig. 1. Flow chart of systematic searching procedure

3.2 Research Question 1: Which Machine Learning Techniques Are Used to Predict the Upper Limb Muscles Activities?

For prediction, classification is a big issue for sEMG signal analysis, but it can handle with machine learning techniques. From selected articles, it is observed that different studies are used different machine learning techniques for classifying the sEMG signals. In 25 selected studies, eleven studies [10, 12, 15, 17, 19, 20, 22, 23, 25, 27, 29] used SVM, six studies [10, 14, 15, 18, 19, 27] discuss with KNN, seven studies [9, 11–13, 24, 27, 28] experiment with ANN, three studies [10, 18, 19] used DA, two studies [10, 19] used NB and three studies [10, 19, 30] discuss with RF.

3.3 Research Question 2: Which Parameter of sEMG Signals Are Used to Predict the Upper Limb Muscle Activity?

sEMG parameter is an important issue for the signal classification in order to predict the muscles activities. We found different studies used different parameters for sEMG signal classification. Within 25 selected articles, twelve studies [2, 9, 10, 13, 15–17, 21, 22, 24, 27, 28] used WL, seven studies [9, 10, 13, 14, 16, 26, 27] applyed ZC, nine studies [9, 10, 13–15, 21, 24, 26, 27] used MAV, seven studies [1, 9, 14, 15, 18, 21, 27] used RMS, seven studies [9, 10, 13, 14, 16, 26, 27] applyed slope sign change (SSC), two studies

[14, 15] used simple square integral (SSI), two studies [14, 15] used average amplitude change (AAC), two studies [15, 18] selected difference absolute standard deviation value (DASDV). Moreover, we found other sEMG parameter including R-square (SD) value [11], sample mean and variance, log detector, maximum fractal length, EMG integral, Willison amplitude, histogram, cepstral coefficients, sample entropy [14] and difference absolute mean value (DAMV) [18].

3.4 Research Question 3: Which Muscle Are Used to Record sEMG Signals for Predicting the Activities of Upper Limb Muscles?

The muscles selection is another important factor for recording sEMG signal. In the selected 25 articles, sEMG signals were recorded from various muscle for predicting the activities of upper limb muscle including biceps brachii [1, 2, 8, 11–13], triceps brachii [1, 2, 11–13], flexor carpi radialis [2, 11, 12, 15, 19], extensor carpi radialis [2, 11, 12, 15], brachio radialis [1, 11, 12], anterior deltoid [1, 11, 12], posterior deltoid [1, 11, 12], extensor carpi ulnaris [2, 12], teres major [11, 12], pectoralis major [1, 11], serratus anterior [11], latissimus dorsi [11], teres minor and infraspinatus [2].

4 Discussion

We studied all the selected 16 articles related to the field on "machine learning techniques and sEMG activities on muscles". To extend this research area in future, we conducted this research and deliberated a summary of the information that focused on sEMG data collection and analysis process to classify the sEMG signals for predicting the activities of upper limb muscle using machine learning techniques. In this regards, the outcome of this review study are presented as follows:

4.1 sEMG Data Collection Techniques for Upper Limb Muscle

To develop a sEMG based muscles classification system where muscles selection is a big challenge [5]. In this work, we only determine for collecting sEMG data from the upper limb muscles. Arjan et al. [21] proposed the movement error rate to forecast delays and calculate mistakes and delays as particular performance features. The most efficient way for recording the sEMG data from upper limb muscles using different type of sensors [19]. For example, the study [14] worked with MYO armband to record the sEMG data. They presented a new system which is able to detect any gesture of the hand with the best performance of 86%. Moreover, Lenny et al. [8] described their experiment for variable and binary control, where they used the touch sensor to record the correlation between the actual pinch and sEMG data. They showed the binary control algorithm is widely used for its speed than variable control algorithm.

4.2 EMG Parameter for Predicting Upper Limp Muscle Activity

sEMG parameter is an essential feature which is extract from raw sEMG signals. Thus, the selection of sEMG parameter is an important factor for muscle classification in order to predict its activities. Regarding this issue, the study [13], extracted various features including IEMF and SSC as sEMG parameter from raw EMG signals. The researchers of another study [9] predict the grasp type recognition rate based on the discrete wavelet transform as a sEMG parameter. They also used different sEMG parameters in their work such as time domain, frequency domain, time-frequency domain, and time scale domain to classify the sEMG signals. Moreover, another researchers of the studies [10, 19] increased their classification accuracy using AUC-RMS techniques as the sEMG parameters. According to the study of [9], the time domain feature of EMG signals are following:

Mean absolute value (MAV): It is a basic time domain feature because it is measured by a function of time domain. MAV value estimates the force that produces by muscles.

$$MAV = 1/N \sum_{i=1}^{N} |x_i| \tag{1}$$

Zero crossing (ZC): Zero crossing measure that a number of EMG raw data crosses the zero line with time feature. It is containing the information of frequency domain properties.

$$ZC = \frac{1}{T-1} \sum_{t-1}^{T-1} 1_{R<0}(s_t s_{t-1}) \tag{2}$$

Waveform length (WL): Waveform length is a basic time domain feature. It is measuring the complexity of raw EMG signals. WL related to the frequency and waveform amplitude.

$$WL = \sum_{x=1}^{N-1} |x_{i+1} - x_i \tag{3}$$

Root Mean Square (RMS): For the analysis of sEMG signals, Root mean square is the most popular feature. It is measuring the power of EMG signals while producing a waveform and easily analyzable by RMS.

$$RMS = \sqrt{\frac{1}{N} \sum_{i=1}^{N} x_{i^2}} \tag{4}$$

4.3 Machine Learning Techniques for Predicting sEMG Activity on Upper Limb Muscle

Support Vector Machine (SVM)

SVM is the prominent machine learning technique for the classification of sEMG signals. In our study, we found several studies they examined the upper limb muscle activities to evaluate the classification performance by SVM. The study [17] used kernel-based SVM classifier and normalized the sEMG of six different grasps. They achieved an average performance rate of 97.5% through 10-fold cross-validation. Junez and Terriza [20] showed in their experiment for SVM classification method to recognize the fifteen different hand gesture with the satisfactory accuracy of those movements. Moreover, we found few articles whereas SVM is compared with other commonly used classifiers. For example, Wahid et al. [19], investigated five different classifiers performance (KNN, DA, NB, RF, and SVM) to recognize different hand gestures. They showed that the SVM gives higher performance com-pared to other classifiers. Another study [15], they compared SVM and KNN to classify the time domain feature of sEMG signals to recognize the hand pattern. They concluded that the SVM achieved better accuracy than KNN.

Random Forest (RF)
RF performs better for many clinical and biomedical problems. It is a supervised based machine learning algorithm that uses for both classification and regression problems in medical care services. This algorithm can handle the missing value problem. Minas et al. [12] used the RF in their experiment to combine N decision trees and assembled each tree with an out-of-bag sample to classification the sEMG signals to reach the grasping movement. They estimated their model to give an accurate performance of the full hand gesture movements. The other studies [10, 19] used the RF to recognize the hand gestures and as well as the shown two different classification accuracy for the normalized sEMG feature and the original sEMG feature. The RF classifier achieved the best performance (i.e. 96.38%) using sEMG features with normalized to the AUC-RMS value [10].

Artificial Neural Network (ANN)
ANN used to classify the sEMG data on upper limb muscle activity. Minas et al. [12] presented a study on the constructed ten hidden unit's neural network with a signal hidden layer. Thus, this neural network classification used to detect the motion with Levenberg-Marquardt backpropagation algorithm. The other study [11] used ANN to predict the sEMG signal on muscles during loaded and unloaded movements. They constructed the ANN classifier with four layers, and they yielded that ANN is the best classification techniques to estimate the complex patterns of muscles stimulation. However, another study [9] showed that the use of back-propagation ANN (success rate of ANN is 88.4%) to recognize the complex pattern for classifying the EMG signals. Moreover, the study [13] presented a comparison study by accuracy for the classification of muscles movement using ANN (i.e. 91.6%) and Random Forest (i.e. 97.7%).

K-Nearest Neighbor (KNN)
From the selected articles, we get several studies where KNN compare with another classification algorithms. Kim et al. [18] presented a comparative study between KNN, quadratic discriminant analysis and linear discriminant analysis to recognize the few wrist-motions directions. They showed KNN achieved the best accuracy for recognition. They also found a significant variance between KNN and other two classification algorithms. But, another study [15] showed that the SVM beat KNN classifier to classify the sEMG signal with seven elementary properties of the time domain feature. Moreover, the study [14] introduced a new strategy for identifying hand gesture patterns based on KNN and dynamic time warping algorithms. The contribution of this study is shown to be accurate and effective prediction results for the classification of sEMG signal analysis on upper limb muscle.

Naïve Bayes (NB)
The researchers of the studies [10, 19] presented a comparative study between SVM, NB, KNN, RF, and DA to classify sEMG data. They normalized the sEMG data using the AUC-RMS and showed that the classification accuracy is difference between normalized sEMG feature and original sEMG feature. Finally, they concluded that the SVM and RF techniques is outperformed than NB in terms of accuracy.

In summary, we painted the research direction and problems in relation to upper limb muscle classification and Bio-medical fields by machine learning techniques, which has an emerging impact in health research fields.

5 Conclusion

We investigated the different machine learning techniques for predicting the sEMG activities on upper limb muscles. Various issues were presented for predicting sEMG activities on upper limb muscle including muscle classification techniques, muscle selection, and sEMG parameter to signify the muscle activities. These outcomes can be apply for predicting the upper limb muscle activities in order to identify the critical situation of neuromuscular disorders patients.

Competing Interest. The authors confirmed that they have no competitive interest.

References

1. Costa, Á., Itkonen, M.,, Yamasaki, H., Alnajjar, F.S., Shimoda, S.: Importance of muscle selection for EMG signal analysis during upper limb rehabilitation of stroke patients. In: Proceedings of Annual International Conference on IEEE Engineering in Medicine and Biology Society, EMBS, pp. 2510–2513. IEEE, Seogwipo (2017)
2. García-Cossio, E., Birbaumer, N.,, Ramos-Murguialda, A.: Facilitation of completely paralyzed forearm muscle activity in chronic stroke patients. In: International IEEE/EMBS Conference on Neural Engineering NER, pp. 1545–1548. IEEE, San Diego (2013)
3. Ali, M.A., Sundaraj, K., Ahmad, R.B., Ahamed, N.U., Islam, M.A., Sundaraj, S.: sEMG activities of the three heads of the triceps brachii muscle during cricket bowling. J. Mech. Med. Biol. **16**(05), 1650075 (2016)
4. Ali, M.A., Sundaraj, K., Ahmad, R.B., Ahamed, N.U., Islam, M.A., Sundaraj, S.: Evaluation of repetitive isometric contractions on the heads of triceps brachii muscle during grip force exercise. Technol. Health Care **22**(4), 617–625 (2014)
5. Ahamed, N.U., Sundaraj, K., Alqahtani, M., Altwijri, O., Ali, M.A., Islam, M.: EMG-force relationship during static contraction: effects on sensor placement locations on biceps brachii muscle. Technol. Health Care **22**(4), 505–513 (2014)
6. Ahamed, N.U., Sundaraj, K., Ahmad, B., Rahman, M., Ali, M.A., Islam, M.A.: Surface electromyographic analysis of the biceps brachii muscle of cricket bowlers during bowling. Aust. Phys. Eng. Sci. Med. **37**(1), 83–95 (2014). https://doi.org/10.1007/s13246-014-0245-1
7. Ali, M.A., Sundaraj, K., Ahmad, R.B., Ahamed, N.U., Islam, M.A.: Surface electromyography for assessing triceps brachii muscle activities: a literature review. Biocybern. Biomed. Eng. **33**(4), 187–195 (2013)
8. Lucas, L., DiCicco, M., Matsuoka, Y.: An EMG-controlled hand exoskeleton for natural pinching. J Robot Mechatron. **16**, 482–488 (2016)

9. Ahsan, M.R., Ibrahimy, M.I., Khalifa, O.O.: Electromyography (EMG) signal based hand gesture recognition using artificial neural network (ANN). In: 2011 4th International Conference on Mechatronics Integrated Engineering for Industrial and Societal Development, ICOM 2011 - Conf Proceedings, pp. 17–19. IEEE, Kuala Lumpur (2011)
10. Wahid, M.F., Tafreshi, R., Al-Sowaidi, M., Langari, R.: Subject-independent hand gesture recognition using normalization and machine learning algorithms. J. Comput. Sci. **27**, 69–76 (2018)
11. Tibold, R., Fuglevand, A.J.: Prediction of muscle activity during loaded movements of the upper limb. J. NeuroEng. Rehabil. **12**, 1–12 (2015)
12. Liarokapis, M.V., Artemiadis, P.K., Kyriakopoulos, K.J., Manolakos, E.S.: A learning scheme for reach to grasp movements: on EMG-based interfaces using task specific motion decoding models. IEEE J. Biomed. Heal Inf. **17**, 915–921 (2013)
13. Jose, N., Raj, R., Adithya, P.K., Sivanadan, K.S.: Classification of forearm movements from sEMG time domain features using machine learning algorithms. IEEExplore.ieee.org (2017)
14. Yang, C., He, S., Wang, M., Cheng, L., Hu, Z.: Hand gesture recognition using MYO armband. In: Proceedings of 2017 Chinese Automation Congress CAC 2017, January 2017, pp. 4850–4855. IEEE, Jinan (2017)
15. Paul, Y., Goyal, V., Jaswal, R.A.: Comparative analysis between SVM & KNN classifier for EMG signal classification on elementary time domain features. In: 4th IEEE International Conference on Signal Process Computing Control ISPCC 2017, January 2017, pp. 169–175. IEEE, Solan (2017)
16. Zia, M., Gilani, S.O., Waris, A., Niazi, I.K., Kamavuako, E.N., Denmark, A.: A novel approach for classification of hand movements using surface EMG signals. Department of Health Sciences and Technology, Centre for sensory motor Interaction, Aalborg University, 2017 IEEE International Symposium Signal Processing and Informaion Technology, pp. 265–269. IEEE, Bilbao (2017)
17. Kakoty, N.M., Hazarika, S.M.: Recognition of grasp types through principal components of DWT based EMG features. In: IEEE International Conference on Rehabilitation Robotics. IEEE, Zurich (2011)
18. Kim, K.S., Choi, H.H., Moon, C.S., Mun, C.W.: Comparison of k-nearest neighbor, quadratic discriminant and linear discriminant analysis in classification of electromyogram signals based on the wrist-motion directions. Curr. Appl. Phys. **11**, 740–745 (2011)
19. Wahid, M.F., Tafreshi, R., Al-Sowaidi, M., Langari, R.: An efficient approach to recognize hand gestures using machine-learning algorithms. In: Middle East Conference on Biomedical Engineering (MECBME), March 2018, pp. 171–176. IEEE, Tunis (2018)
20. Junez, G.P., Terriza, J.H.: Hand gesture recognition based on sEMG signals using support vector machines. IEEE International Conference on Consumer Electronics-Berlin, pp. 174–178. IEEE, Berlin (2016)
21. Gijsberts, A., Atzori, M., Castellini, C., Müller, H., Caputo, B.: Movement error rate for evaluation of machine learning methods for sEMG-based hand movement classification. IEEE Trans Neural Syst. Rehabil. Eng. **22**, 735–744 (2014)
22. Anil, N., Sreeletha, S.H.: EMG based gesture recognition using machine learning. In: Second International Conference on Intelligent Computing and Control Systems (ICICCS). IEEE, Madurai (2018)
23. Arjunan, S.P., Kumar, D.K., Naik, G.R.: A machine learning based method for classification of fractal features of forearm sEMG using Twin Support Vector Machines. In: 32nd Annual International Conference of the IEEE EMBS. IEEE, Buenos Aires (2010)
24. Zhang, B., Zhang, S.: The estimation of grasping force based on the feature extracted from EMG signals. In: IEEE Advanced Information Management, Communicates, Electronic and Automation Control Conference (IMCEC). IEEE, Xi'an (2016)

25. Castiblanco, C., Parra, C., Colorado, J.: Individual hand motion classification through EMG pattern recognition: supervise and unsupervised methods. In: XXI Symposium on Signal Processing, Images and Artificial Vision (STSIVA). IEEE, Bucaramanga (2016)
26. Chen, H., Tong, R., Chen, M., Fang, Y., Liu, H.: A hybrid CNN-SVM classifier for hand gesture recognition with surface EMG Signals. In: International Conference on Machine Learning and Cybernetics (ICMLC), pp. 619–624. IEEE, Chengdu (2018)
27. Kaya, E., Kumbasar, T.: Hand gesture recognition systems with the wearable Myo Armband. In: 6th International Conference on Control Engineering & Information Technology (CEIT), pp. 1–6. IEEE, Istanbul (2018)
28. Luh, G.C., Ma, Y.H., Yen, C.J., Lin, H.A.: Muscle-gesture robot hand control based on sEMG signals with wavelet transform features and neural network classifier. In: International Conference on Machine Learning and Cybernetics (ICMLC), pp. 627–632. IEEE, Jeju (2016). ISSN 2160-1348
29. Amamcherla, N., Turlapaty, A., Gokaraju, B.: A machine learning system for classification of emg signals to assist exoskeleton performance. In: IEEE Applied Imagery Pattern Recognition Workshop (AIPR), pp. 1–4. IEEE, Washington (2018)
30. Rodriguez, D., Piryatinska, A., Zhang, X.: A neural decision forest scheme with application to EMG gesture classification. In: SAI Computing Conference (SAI), pp. 243–252. IEEE, London (2016)

Machine Learning in Disease Diagnosis and Monitoring

Retrospective Analysis of Hematological Cancer by Correlating Hematological Malignancy with Occupation, Residence, Associated Infection, Knowledge and Previous Cancer History in Relatives

Khaled Sohel Mohammad[1(✉)], Nurbinta Sultana[1], Hassanat Touhid[2], and Ashrafia Esha[1,2]

[1] Daffodil International University, Dhaka, Bangladesh
khaledsohel@daffodilvarsity.edu.bd
[2] Gonoshasthaya SamajVittik Medical College, Savar, Bangladesh

Abstract. Cancer incidences are increasing day by day and has become a global burden now. The incidences are frequently occurring in low-income countries like Bangladesh. A retrospective descriptive type of study had been carried out by us over 500 patients of hematological cancer in Bangladesh. The "French American British" classification of hematological cancer is used to carry out the morphological typing. We have correlated Hematological Malignancy (HM) with occupation, residence, associated infection, idea about cause of cancer and previous cancer history in relative. The analysis showed the diagnosed cancers are positively co-related with age, gender, occupation & idea about cause of cancer and negatively co-related with division, previously cancer history in relatives & associated disease. Our study shows the risk factor and the distribution pattern of hematological malignancy in the area of Bangladesh. It presents the distribution pattern of HM according to Age, Gender & correlation of HM with occupation, residence & other factor.

Keywords: Retrospective analysis of hematological malignancy · Hematological cancer in Bangladesh · Blood cancer · Cancer related to gender and occupation · Hematological malignancy

1 Introduction

In western country patient's information are kept properly by the hospitals and health care providers. This is very helpful and standard for collecting data. In Bangladesh some specialized hospital follow this system properly. Moreover there are few cancer specialized hospital in this country. So proper data collection from hospital record is difficult here. Measurement of cancer patients and proper diagnosis of cancer are the essential key attributes in the process. Predicting

T. Bhuiyan et al. (Eds.): ICONCS 2020, LNICST 325, pp. 343–353, 2020.
https://doi.org/10.1007/978-3-030-52856-0_27

current cancer status and the risk factor of cancer occurrence are the objective of this research where SPSS tools is applied and hypothesis testing is used to find a comparative analysis between cancer and different risk factor. To point out the need for further understanding and investigation, we failed to find enough researches for predicting cancer status. Lack of reliable source of data, not having enough data coverage, not considering effective factors as a mean of research are few of the many short comings that can be found in this limited research scope.

1.1 Justification of the Study

Cancer is now becoming a burden for this country. The number of cancer patient is increasing day by day but no proper preventive measures, diagnostic criteria, risk factor & treatment policy have been proved yet. Besides cancer treatment is very costly. There are several researches or studies on cancer. But to be specific, - such Hematological cancer related studies are few. There is a specific hematological cancer study which had been done in 2014. After that no such study has been carried out. The study gives a view of present hematological incidence in Bangladesh. Age-sex ratio, risk factor, occupation related ratio & some others. These collectively gives idea about preventive measure & risk factor. Also the information will be used for further studies.

2 Literature Review

From various researches it has been identified that higher casualties of cancer hits in low-income countries [1]. World-wide number of new cancer cases have risen to 18.1 million and brought the death toll to 9.6 million in 2018. 20% of men and 17% of women experience cancer in their life time and about 12% men and 9% women die from the disease. 5-year prevalence (who are alive within five year of cancer diagnosis), would be 43.8 million [2]. It is projected that by 2030 between 10 and 11 million cancer will be diagnosed each year in lower and middle-income countries and death from cancer worldwide reach over 13 million in 2030 [3]. Despite of taking all kinds of positive steps for now and future, the challenges of facing cancer are ever high, since the incidences of cancer in these setting will continue to rise due to increasing lifespans through better control of communicable disease [1]. Recently Bangladesh has shown huge improvement to manage infectious diseases as highlighted in Lancet [4]. Cancer has never been prioritized as chronic disease [5]. Since there are no standard body of keeping records or registration processes the number is unknown to us. At present there are about 1.3 to 1.5 million cancer patients exist in Bangladesh, where about two lakh patients joins newly as cancer positive each year [6]. According to the statistics of Bangladesh Bureau, the sixth leading cause of death is brought by cancer. The cancer based death would be highly increased from a 7.5% in 2005 to a 13% in 2030 according to International agency for research [5]. The real cancer status may not be reflected by these estimate as many cases go unreported because of lacking of education, poverty, misconception and awareness among all population. Moreover, the cost of cancer treatment is very high and hence in Bangladesh cancer care and management systems, are below international standard. Besides, there are lack of oncologists and sufficient infrastructure to support patients in Bangladesh.

Hematological malignancies are primary cancers originating cells of the bone marrow and lymphatic system. There are three main categories which are Leukemia, Lymphoma, and Multiple Myeloma (MM). Other categories are Myelodysplastic Syndrome (MDS), Polycythemia Vera, and primary Myelofibrosis. The most common type of leukemia are: Chronic Myeloid Leukemia (CML), Chronic Lymphocytic Leukemia (CLL), Acute Myeloid Leukemia (AML), and Acute Lymphoblastic Leukemia (ALL). Lymphomas are two types. They are Hodgkin's Lymphoma (HL) & Non-Hodgkin's Lymphoma (NHL). The Primary causes of hematological malignancy are remain unknown but it is believed to be connected with environmental exposures, ionizing radiation and infectious agent. These includes: x-ray, pesticides, Dye, Benzene vapor, cytotoxic drugs and chromosomal [1]. There is a link in between infectious agent and hematological malignancies in the young. Epstein-bar virus (EBV) is the major cause of Burkett's lymphoma and Hodgkin's disease. Human T cell leukemia virus, herpes virus 6, 7 and 8 also cause different types of hematological malignancy [7]. Information pertaining to the epidemiological aspect of Hematological Malignancy in Bangladeshi population is limited [8]. To identify the risk factor of hematological malignancy, we have to find out the epidemiological aspect of hematological malignancy in the environmental background. In this particular retrospective study, we are providing report on the overall pattern and occupation/knowledge/residence distribution with relationships of proved hematological malignancies in Bangladesh.

3 Methodology

For research methodology, we have used Statistical Package for the Social Sciences (SPSS) to predict the risk factor of hematology cancer. We collect data from the patient by face to face interview through questionnaire from Dhaka Medical college hospital and analysis the data by using SPSS tools. Finally we make combination of analysis data to get a better prediction by using multiple liner regression model (Fig. 1).

Data are collected from diagnosed hematological cancer patients. We visited Dhaka medical college several time and talk with patients and gather information. Thus we collect row data for our research and these data are valid for our research work.

After collecting row data by face to face interview from the patients we process these data according to our research question. We select about 505 patient's data for our research work. We exclude some data due to lack of proper information or dissimilarity among information.

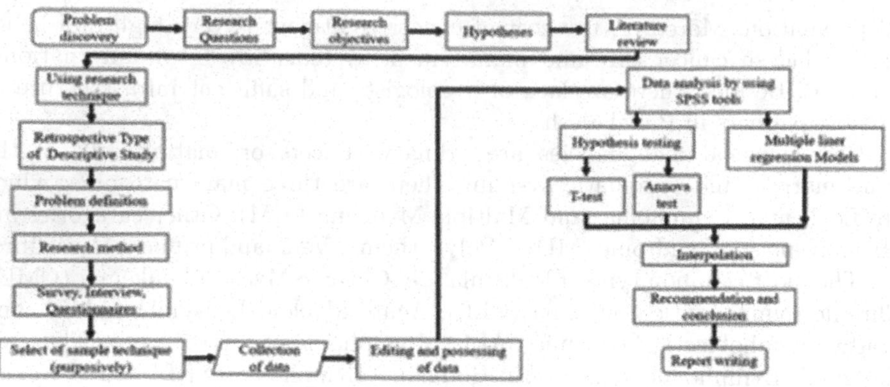

Fig. 1. Research methodology

4 Results

In this study, total 505 diagnosed cases of hematological malignancy which are collected from hospitals were retrospectively analyzed. Among these, 4 to 94 years old patient are included. Males were 321 which means 63.6% and females were 184 which means 36.4% and the ratio between male and female is 1.7:1 (Table 5). Prevalence of Hematological Malignancy was statistically significant (P = 0.012) in case of gender and male are more affected than female. About 29.9% cases of Hematological malignancy were adolescence aged between 10 to 19 years old (Table 1).

Table 1. Age-group specific distribution of hematological malignancy in Bangladesh

	Age	Frequency	Percent	Valid percent	Cumulative percent
Valid	Under 9	8	1.6	1.6	1.6
	10–19	143	28.3	28.3	29.9
	20–29	99	19.6	19.6	49.5
	30–39	91	18.0	18.0	67.5
	40–49	62	12.3	12.3	79.8
	50–59	53	10.5	10.5	90.3
	60–69	42	8.3	8.3	98.6
	70 and older	7	1.4	1.4	100.0
	Total	505	100.0	100.0	

The combined median age at diagnosis for all hematological malignancies was 49 years.

Here, we see that hematological malignancy most frequently occur at the age group of 10–19 in Fig. 2.

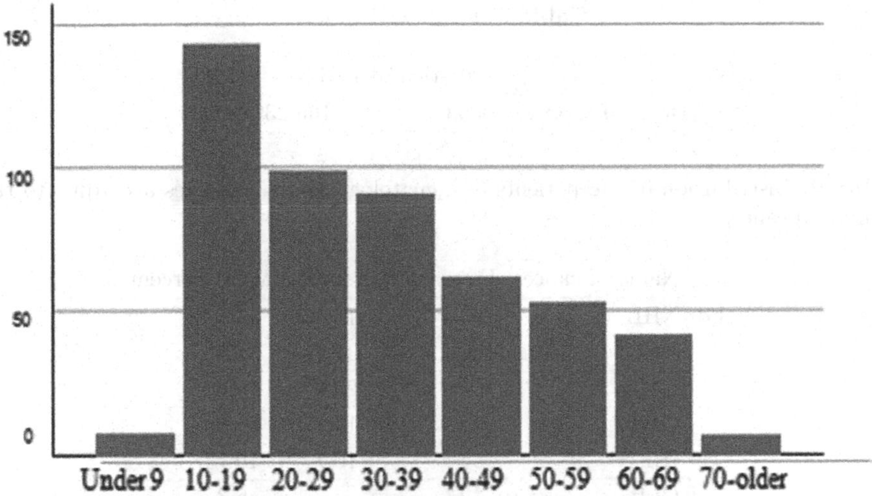

Fig. 2. Graphical presentation of hematological malignancy according to age.

We also performed hypothesis testing on age where our null hypothesis was accepted due to the significance value was under .05. Our null hypothesis was,"age has impact on cancer incidence" (Table 2).

Table 2. Hypothesis test on age (ANOVA)

Diagnosed cancer			Sig.
Between groups	(Combined)		.000
	Linear term	Unweighted	.319
		Weighted	.000
		Deviation	.000
Within groups			
Total			

Here, we see that in our country most frequent hematological malignancy is ALL.

The most frequent hematological Malignancy is ALL (31.7%) which is one third of total hematological malignancy cases where the AML is 20.6% CML is 19.6% NHL is 11.1% HL is 10.7% & CLL is 6.3% (Table 4) (Table 3, Fig. 3).

Moreover, sex-specific analysis was also performed for the overall and individual cancer cases. Most of the patients (63.6%) of hematological malignancies are male (Table 5) (Fig. 4).

We also performed hypothesis testing on Gender where our null hypothesis was accepted due to the significance value was under .05. Our null hypothesis was, "Gender has impact on Cancer Incidence".

Table 3. Diagnosed cancer

	Statistica	df1	df2	Sig.
Brown-Forsythe	8.593	7	166.930	.000

Table 4. Distribution of the patients of hematological malignancies according to the diagnosed cancer

	Name of cancer	Frequency	Percent	Valid percent
Valid	NHL	56	11.1	11.1
	ALL	160	31.7	31.7
	AML	104	20.6	20.6
	CML	99	19.6	19.6
	HL	54	10.7	10.7
	CLL	32	6.3	6.3
	Total	505	100.0	100.0

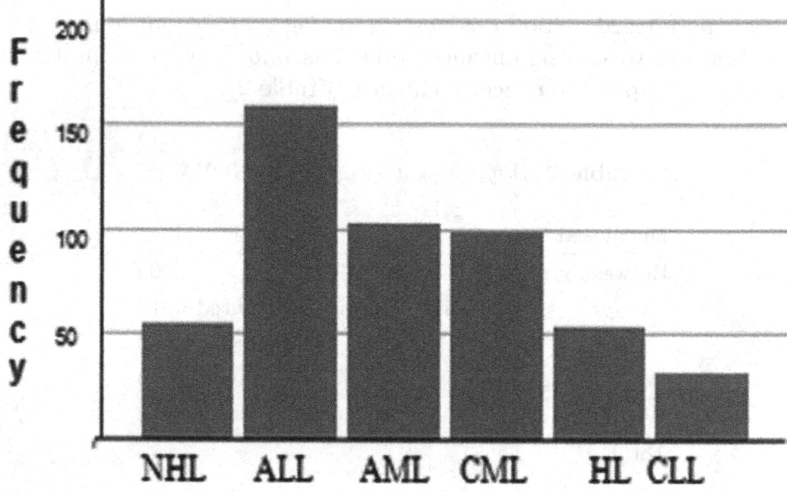

Fig. 3. Graphical presentation of hematological malignancy according to diagnosed cancer

Table 5. Distribution of the patients of hematological malignancies according to Gender.

	Gender	Frequency	Percent
Valid	Male	321	63.6
	Female	184	36.4
	Total	505	100.0

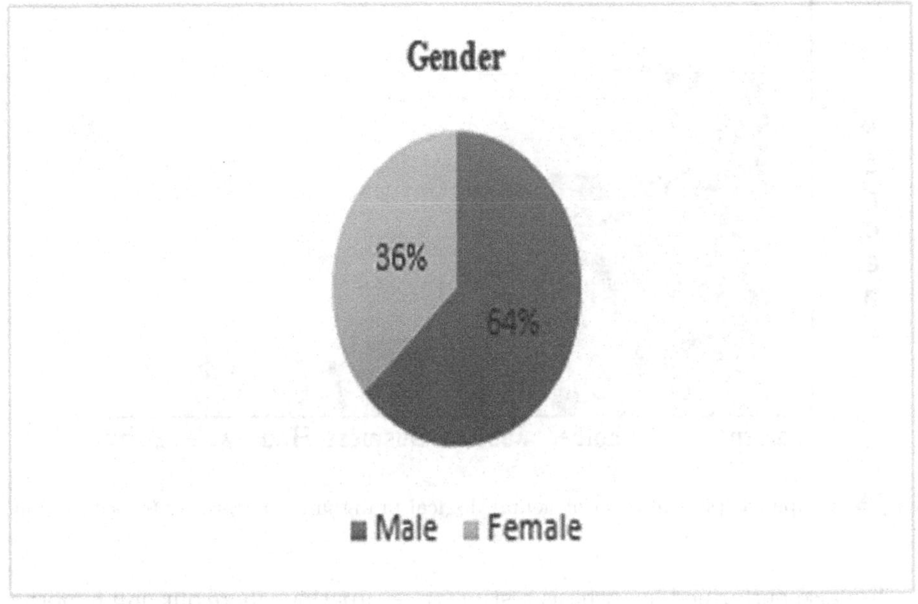

Fig. 4. Graphical presentation of hematological malignancy according to gender

Occupation has statistically significance (P = .001) impact on cancer. Most of the patient of hematological malignance (44%) are student (Table 7) (Table 6, Fig. 5).

Table 6. Variances on diagnosed cancer.

		Sig. (2tailed)	Mean difference	Std. error difference
Diagnosed cancer	Equal variances assumed	.012	−.322	.129
	Equal variances not assumed	.014	−.322	.130

Table 7. Distribution of the patients of hematological malignancies according to their occupation.

	Occupation	Frequency	Percent	Valid percent
Valid	Student	222	44.0	44.0
	Jobholder	154	30.5	30.5
	Jobless	35	6.9	6.9
	Business	48	9.5	9.5
	Housewife	42	8.3	8.3
	Baby	4	.8	.8
	Total	505	100.0	100.0

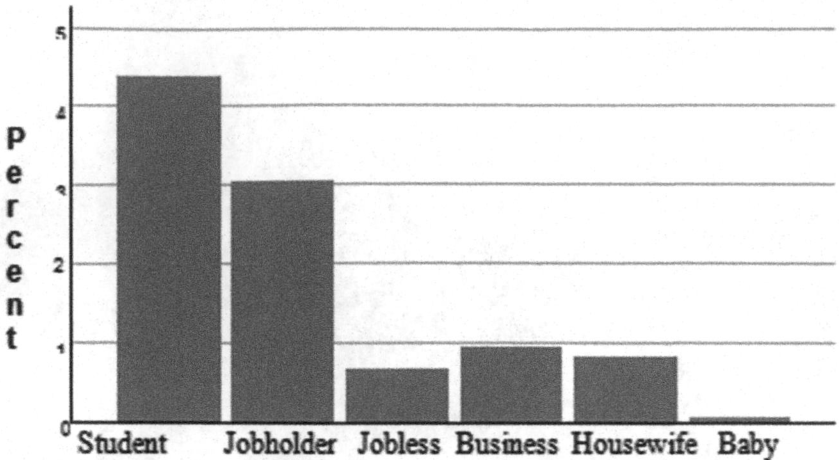

Fig. 5. Graphical presentation of hematological malignancy according to occupation.

We also performed hypothesis testing on occupation where our null hypothesis was accepted due to the significance value was under .05. Our null hypothesis was, "occupation has impact on Cancer Incidence" (Table 8).

Table 8. Hypothesis test (One way ANOVA test)

	Sum-of squares	df	Mean square	F	Sig.
Between groups	39.555	5	7.911	4.175	.001
Within groups	945.542	499	1.895		
Total	985.097	504			

Idea about the cause of cancer has also statistically significant (P = .001) impact on cancer. About 80.6% of the patient of hematological malignancy has no proper idea about the cause of cancer (Table 9).

Table 9. Distribution of the patients of hematological malignancies by having proper idea about the cause of cancer

		Frequency patients	Percent	Valid percent
Valid	No	407	80.6	80.6
	Yes	98	19.4	19.4
	Total	505	100.0	100.0

We also performed hypothesis testing on having proper idea about the cause of cancer where our null hypothesis was accepted due to the significance value was under .05. Our null hypothesis was, "Having proper idea about the cause of cancer has impact on Cancer Incidence" (Table 10).

Table 10. Independent sample test

		Sig. (2-tailed)	Mean difference	Std. error difference
Diagnosed cancer	Equal variances assumed	.006	−.430	.156
	Equal variances not assumed	.006	−.430	.154

In this study we see that there are some potential risk factor of hematological malignancy which are statistically significant. They are age, gender, occupation and Idea about the causes of cancer.

5 Discussion

This is a comprehensive report on the burden of hematological malignancy in Bangladesh. In contrast to WHO estimate our data present a different picture [9,10]. The most frequent hematological Malignancy is ALL (31.7%) which is one third of total hematological malignancy cases where the AML is 20.6% CML is 19.6% NHL is 11.1% HL is 10.7% & CLL is 6.3% (Table 4). According to the prediction of WHO, Non-Hodgkin Lymphoma is the commonest hematological malignancy & the rate of which is 1.9 per 100,000 persons. Chronologically 2nd most is leukemia which rate is 1.7 per 100,000 persons, 3rd is Hodgkin Lymphoma and 4th is multiple myeloma [11]. In Pakistan, NHL is the most prevalent type of HM [11]. In US, NHL is the commonest cancer among HM, which is 1.5 times that of all leukemia [12]. In other Asian countries including Japan, Korea and Singapore, NHL is the most frequent hematological malignancies [11,13]. In our study, there are some unexpected discrepancies. Lacking of proper referral system might be the cause of these discrepancies. Lymphoma is a hematological disorder but a small number of patients might have been admitted to the medical oncology department.

Younger population is seemed to be afflicted by hematological malignancy in Bangladesh which is differ from western countries. At diagnosis, the median age was 48 years. But the real median age can be lower. Acute myeloid leukemia, Acute lymphoblastic leukemia, chronic myeloid leukemia, Hodgkin's lymphoma, Non Hodgkin lymphoma are found to occur in young adults in which the median age is between 27 to 48 years (Table 1). Another side, chronic lymphocytic leukemia & multiple myeloma are frequently occur in childhood age in Bangladesh & also in western counties. Gender is an important risk factor for hematological malignancy. In our study we see that men are more frequent than female in hematological malignancy & the ratio is 1.7:1. In other worldwide study, we also see that hematological malignancy is gender-skewed and men are more frequent than female. It may be due to gender discrimination as considering the socioeconomic status female cases were unreported in low income families. Men get more priority in seeking medical attention which could be another cause of unreported female cases. The higher prevalence of HM in males might be the result of increased exposure to environmental and occupational risk factors, smoking, alcohol consumption as well as different hormonal and genetic background of males and females [14]. Acute Myeloid Leukemia and Acute Lymphoblastic Leukemia are the most frequent HM in Bangladesh and these two constituted 52.3% (n = 505) of leukemia cases (Table 4). The frequency of ALL is one & half times higher than that of AML in Bangladesh. The incidence of ALL is relatively common in Italy, US, Switzerland and Costa Rica [15]. ALL is predominantly a disease of Childhood in western countries. Chronic leukemia constituted 25.9% of all HM in Bangladesh. CLL is the third most common type (19.6% n = 99), while CLL is the least frequent (6.3% n = 32) HM (Table 4). The frequency of CLL is three times higher than CLL.

Working environment & Residual environment are the commonest risk factor for cancer. In our study, we co-relate Hematological Malignancy with respondent occupation and we find that Student (44%) are most vulnerable to Hematological Malignancy (Table 7). Most probably the causes behind this are radiation & radio wave discharge from their cell phone, laptop & other electric device. We also find that most of the cancer patients are from Dhaka which about 35.2% and 2nd most from Chittagong is about 18.8%. We have already known that developed area has more radiation, benzene vapor, radio wave & other carcinogenic factor. So these probably the cause of increasing cancer patients in these two cities.

In this study, we also correlate Hematological Malignancy with Associated infection, previous cancer history in relatives and idea about cause of cancer. We find that associated infection and previous cancer history in relatives have no significant impact on Hematological Malignancy. But Idea about cause of cancer has significant impact on Hematological Malignancy. A large number of HM patient about 80.6% has no idea about the cause of cancer. As a result they were careless about cancer risk factor. So Government can take cancer awareness program in order to decrease cancer incidence in Bangladesh.

6 Conclusion

This study is done on diagnosed hematological cancer patient to understand the patterns and distribution of Hematological cancer in Bangladesh. More investigations are needed to explain the epidemiology and biology of hematological malignancies in Bangladesh. In this research, we analyzed data to predict risk factor of hematological cancer. More investigation are needed to explain the epidemiology, genetics and biology of hematological cancer in Bangladesh.

References

1. Hossain, M., et al.: Diagnosed hematological malignancies in Bangladesh - a retrospective analysis of over 5000 cases from 10 specialized hospitals. BMC Cancer **14**, 438 (2014)
2. WHO—IARC - International Agency for Research on Cancer. https://www.who.int/cancer/PRGlobocanFinal.pdflast. Accessed 08 June 2019
3. WHO—Key statistics. https://www.who.int/cancer/resources/keyfacts/en/. Accessed 12 June 2019
4. Das, P., Horton, R.: Bangladesh: innovating for health. Lancet **382**, 1681–1682 (2013)
5. Hussain, S., Sullivan, R.: Cancer control in Bangladesh. Jpn. J. Clin. Oncol. **43**, 1159–1169 (2013)
6. Hussain, S.: Comprehensive update on cancer scenario of Bangladesh. South Asian J. Cancer **2**, 279 (2013)
7. Lehtinen, T., Lehtinen, M.: Common and emerging infectious causes of hematological malignancies in the young. APMIS **106**, 585–597 (1998)
8. Bhutani, M., Vora, A., Kumar, L., Kochupillai, V.: Lympho-hemopoietic malignancies in India. Med. Oncol. **19**, 141–152 (2002)
9. Cancer prevention. https://www.who.int/cancer/prevention/en/. Accessed 13 June 2019
10. Report, S.: Molecular cancer diagnosis in Bangladesh. https://www.thedailystar.net/health/news/molecular-cancer-diagnosis-bangladesh-1712689. Accessed 15 June 2019
11. Latest world cancer statistics – GLOBOCAN 2012: estimated cancer incidence, mortality and prevalence worldwide in 2012 – IARC. https://www.iarc.fr/news-events/latest-world-cancer-statistics-globocan-2012-estimated-cancer-incidence-mortality-and-prevalence-worldwide-in-2012/
12. Tarver, T.: Cancer facts & figures 2012. American Cancer Society (ACS). J. Consum. Health Internet **16**, 366–367 (2012)
13. Park, H., et al.: Statistics of hematologic malignancies in Korea: incidence, prevalence and survival rates from 1999 to 2008. Korean J. Hematol. **47**, 28 (2012)
14. Lichtman, M.: Battling the hematological malignancies: the 200 years' war. Oncologist **13**, 126–138 (2008)
15. Redaelli, A., Laskin, B., Stephens, J., Botteman, M., Pashos, C.: A systematic literature review of the clinical and epidemiological burden of acute lymphoblastic leukaemia (ALL). Eur. J. Cancer Care **14**, 53–62 (2005)

Performance Comparison of Early Breast Cancer Detection Precision Using AI and Ultra-Wideband (UWB) Bio-Antennas

Bifta Sama Bari[1], Sabira Khatun[1(✉)], Kamarul Hawari Ghazali[1], Minarul Islam[1], Mamunur Rashid[1], Mostafijur Rahman[2], and Nurhafizah Abu Talip[1]

[1] Faculty of Electrical and Electronic Engineering Technology, Universiti Malaysia Pahang, Pekan, Pahang, Malaysia
sabirakhatun@ump.edu.my

[2] Department of Software Engineering, Daffodil International University, Dhaka, Bangladesh

Abstract. Breast cancer is the most common cancer among women and a major cause of death globally. A high percentage of the cancer death can be reduced if it is detected earlier (Stage 1 or 2). Early and non-invasive (health-friendly) diagnosis is the most essential key to detect breast cancer that ensures a fast and effective treatment for reducing women mortality. Ultra-wide band (UWB) technology is considered as an effective technique for breast cancer detection due to its health friendly (non-ionizing) nature to human tissue. The UWB technology uses the scattering or reflected wave/signal from breast tissue for diagnosis. A high-performance bio-antenna plays an important role in transmitting and receiving the UWB signal for this case. In this paper, breast cancer detection performance comparison of two types of UWB bio-antennas (pyramidal shaped UWB patch and the proposed modified T shaped UWB patch) has been investigated depending on accuracy. A system has been developed using a pair of UWB transceivers with bio-antennas and artificial neural network (ANN). The signals are transmitted and received through breast phantom for different arbitrary tumor size and location for considered antennas. The obtained tumor/cancer location and size detection accuracy are approximately 90.27% and 89.91% for pyramidal shaped antenna, whereas, those for the proposed (modified T shaped) antenna are nearly 91.03% and 91.09% respectively. The proposed (modified T shaped) antenna is comparatively better to detect early breast cancer than pyramidal shaped antenna, by showing its suitability for practical use in near future.

Keywords: Breast cancer early detection · Bio-antenna · Ultra-wideband (UWB) · Artificial neural network (ANN)

1 Introduction

Breast cancer is the most frequent diagnosed cancer in women worldwide [1]. It is considered as the second cause of cancer death after lung cancer among women [2]. The statistical view of Canadian Cancer Society exposes that about 26,900 women were

T. Bhuiyan et al. (Eds.): ICONCS 2020, LNICST 325, pp. 354–365, 2020.
https://doi.org/10.1007/978-3-030-52856-0_28

diagnosed and 5,000 women were died with breast cancer in 2019 [3]. As there is no remedy, target is for long-run survival. So, early detection is essential [4]. If breast tumor can be detected early enough, the five-year and ten-year overall survival rate are approximately 91.2% and 84.8% respectively [5]. Ultra-wideband (UWB) technology offers a safe and promising technique for early breast cancer detection without any harmful effect on human health. Compared to other traditional techniques including X-Ray mammography, magnetic resonance imaging, ultrasound, computerized tomography, biopsy and positron emission tomography [6, 7], UWB technology is preferable with its low cost, safety and non-invasive properties [7, 8].

Ultra-wide band (UWB) microwave techniques has added a new dimension for early breast cancer detection [5, 9]. It is beneficial with low power consumption, high data transmission, less complexity, low cost etc. It consists of transmitting signals through the breast tissue and recording the received signals scattered from different locations [10]. In this technique, the tumor/cancer is identified from the processing of the scattered signals collected at the antennas. This technique is conducted by utilizing UWB antennas with a frequency of 3.1 GHz to 10.6 GHz [11]. Thus, an UWB bio-antenna plays an vital role in the UWB radar system for both transmitting and receiving the pulse waves [12]. Various ultra-wideband (UWB) antennas have been proposed for breast cancer detection. For example, [13] developed a UWB microwave system comprising of an array of 16 antennas. The stacked-patch and wide-slot antennas [14] have been designed at the University of Bristol. A micro strip patch antenna with pyramidal shaped patch has been proposed by Reza et al. [15]. All the proposed antennas have their own advantages and drawbacks for early breast cancer detection, leaving a room for further enhancement. Towards this aim, a micro strip bio-antenna with modified T shaped patch has been proposed to achieve wider bandwidth and better cancer detection performance. To evaluate the performance comparison between the proposed (modified T shaped) antenna and the existing (pyramidal shaped) antenna [15], an early breast cancer detection system has been developed using artificial neural network (ANN) and UWB technique. Then, a comparison has been made between two UWB bio-antennas in terms of breast cancer detection accuracy, including tumor/cancer location in 3-dimension (x, y and z-axis) and size. We have collected UWB signals individually for both the existing and the proposed bio-antenna. The collected signals are trained, validated and tested to measure and compare the detection accuracy for both bio-antennas.

This chapter is organized as following sections. The next section presents the methodology including the experimental set-up for data collection, data analysis and artificial neural network. Followed by results and discussions with performance comparison of both bio-antennas in Sect. 3 and finally the conclusion in Sect. 4.

2 System Model and Development Steps

Two different bio-antennas (existing pyramidal and proposed modified T shaped UWB) have been used in this experiment. An Artificial Intelligence (feed-forward back propagation neural network) has been utilized for tumor/cancer detection. The overall process consists of experimental set-up, data collection for both bio-antenna as well as data processing and analysis, and the developed detection system. Finally, we have made a comparison of tumor/cancer detection accuracy using two different bio-antennas. The complete work flow of this paper is shown in Fig. 1.

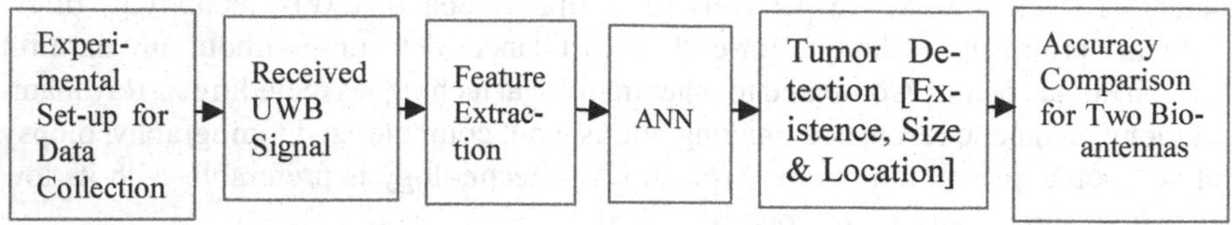

Fig. 1. The block diagram of overall workflow.

2.1 The Experimental Set-up for Data Collection

For data collection, an experimental set-up is required with transmitting and receiving antenna. The experimental set up consists of a breast phantom, breast tumor, computer, transmitting antenna as transmitter, receiving antenna as receiver, UWB transceiver and different connecting cables.

UWB Bio-Antennas. The UWB signal has been collected by using a pair of existing pyramidal shaped UWB antenna [15] at first. Then, the signal has been collected by using a pair of the proposed modified T shaped UWB antenna. Both bio-antennas are constructed with FR-4 substrate and copper is coated on patch. Both types of antenna have high bandwidth, gain and directivity which are able to gather signal within UWB range. A pair of pyramidal shaped patch antenna is used as transmitter and receiver. Similarly, a pair of the proposed antenna is used as transmitter and receiver. The existing pyramidal shaped UWB bio-antenna is shown in Fig. 2. Similarly, Fig. 3 represents the proposed modified T shaped bio-antenna.

Fig. 2. An existing (pyramidal shaped UWB patch) bio-antenna [15].

Breast Phantom and Breast Tumor. A breast phantom and breast tumor with different size has been used. A few researchers have already developed numerous sorts of breast

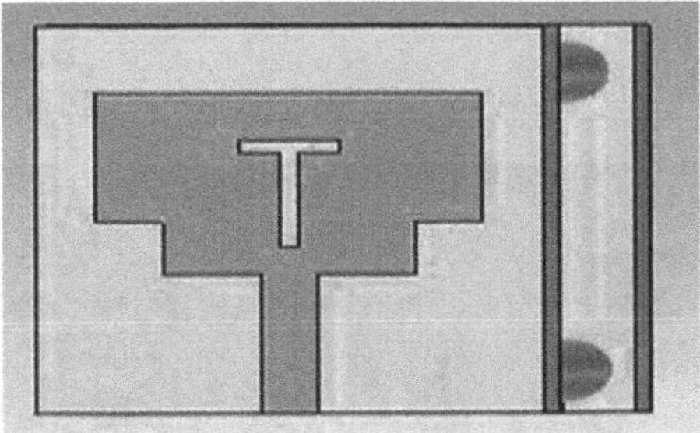

Fig. 3. The proposed (modified T shaped UWB patch) bio-antenna.

phantom to detect the breast cancer [16–18]. An easy way to form breast phantom and tumor has been proposed by Alshehri et al. [16], which is low cost, easily accessible and non-chemical materials. A homogeneous breast phantom has been developed in this research based on Alshehri et al. [16]. The Phantom is constructed using a glass of 1.6 (mm) thickness that is used as skin and pure petroleum jelly is utilized as breast fatty tissue. A mixture of 10 g wheat flour along with 5.5 g water is utilized to construct the tumor with different sizes. Then, the tumor is inserted into the phantom in different location for each experimentation-trial. The breast phantom has been placed in between the transmitter and receiver (Fig. 4).

UWB Transceiver. The UWB pulses are generated in transceiver; transmitted through transmitting antenna, whereas the receiving antenna receives the pulses. The UWB transceiver system P400 RCM from Time domain Co. [19] has been utilized in this experiment. The feeding cable is used here to connect the antenna with UWB transceiver. The Ethernet cable is used to connect the transceiver with computer.

Data Collection. The complete system set-up for data collection is presented in Fig. 4. The UWB transceiver system is utilized to produce the UWB pulses as well as to receive the scattered waveform.

The bio-antennas are connected with UWB transceivers and controlled by a PC. The receiving antenna received the forward scattered signals transmitted by the transmitting antenna and saved in PC for further processing. This procedure is repeated in various times for different tumor sizes and locations (x, y, z). Total 448 data samples were collected for each type of bio-antenna and then used to train, validate and test the detection system. Table 1 represents the received UWB signals with corresponding transmitted signal for various tumor sizes.

Table 1 shows the variation of received UWB signals with respect to tumor sizes for the same transmitted signal. The variations are very minimal and tough to distinguish by human eyes, hence needs ANN to classify and estimate the size. Among them, the received UWB signal for 4 mm tumor shows better performance. Table 2 shows the variation in the received UWB signals for 4 mm tumor placed in different positions.

Fig. 4. Experimental set-up scenario for data collection.

2.2 Data Processing and Analysis

The received signals were processed to attain related discrete 1632 data points for each sample. Among total 448 data samples, 70% data is used for training, 15% is used for validation and 15% is used for testing. The received signals (1632 data points) are processed to obtain essential features (four features: max, min, mean, standard deviation) for each data sample before feeding to the neural network by applying similar process as in [20, 21]. Feature extraction is done to decrease computing time and complexity.

2.3 Artificial Neural Network (ANN) Used for Tumor Detection

Artificial Intelligence (AI) is a technique to emulate human intelligence into computer technology. An Artificial Neural Network (ANN) is one of the powerful AI techniques that have the capability to learn a set of data. It comprises of nodes arranged in two or more layers [22, 23].There are many NN types, in this study, a feed-forward back propagation NN is considered for tumor detection. It was developed by utilizing MATLAB software in which input turns to forward in one direction. Hence, input data goes through some hidden nodes with hidden layer (if exists) and lastly to output node. The performance of the NN module can be expanded by changing the number of hidden neurons. In this system, the number of nodes (neurons) in input layer, hidden layer and output layer is 4, 10 and 4 respectively. The neural network architecture is shown in Fig. 5.

The NN module performance was evaluated with collected data samples. The untrained data samples are tested and their performance accuracy is analyzed based on the performance plots. The net activation equation for a unit of NN is given by Eq. 1 and Eq. 2 [22].

$$net_j = \sum\nolimits_j y_i . w_{ij} \tag{1}$$

$$y_j = f\left(net_j\right) \tag{2}$$

Table 1. Received UWB signal variation for different tumor size.

UWB Transmitted Signal	Tumor Size (mm)	UWB Received Signal
	2	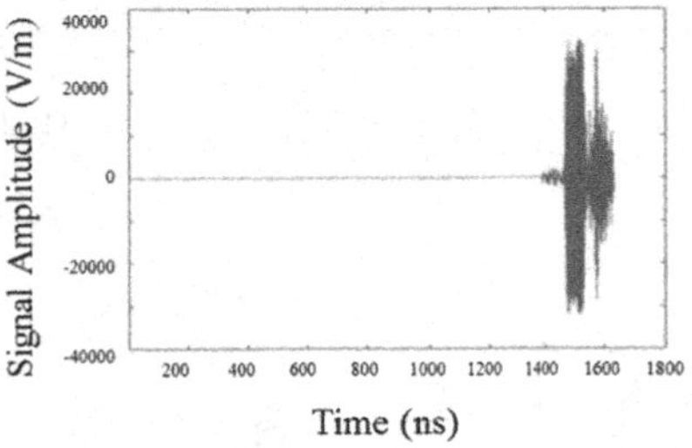
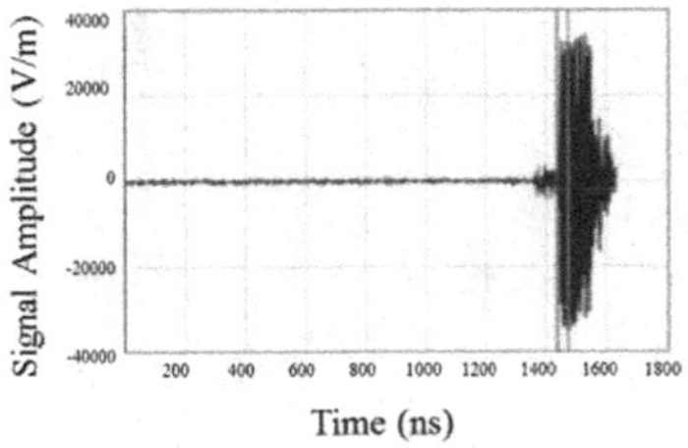	3	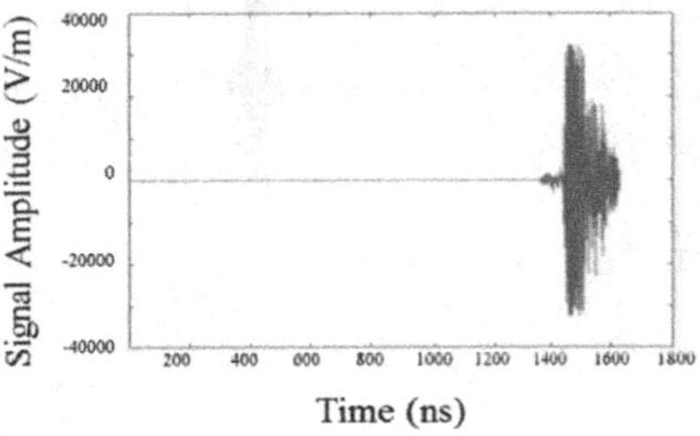
	4	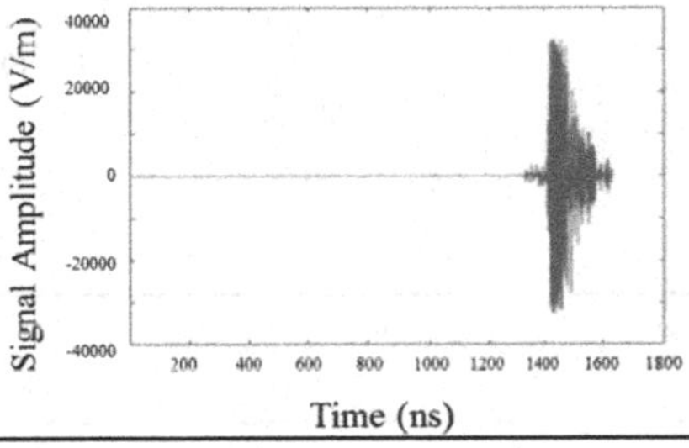

Here, f is a differentiable and nonlinear transfer function. For the best training results, it should produce the output in the range of $[-1, +1]$. The error function E is summed all over the NN nodes which is expressed by Eq. 3,

$$E = \frac{1}{N}\sum (t_n - y_n)^2 \quad (3)$$

where, t_n is the target or actual values and y_n is the predicted values by the NN. N is the number of samples.

Hence, the used formula for relative performance rate is shown in Eq. 4 [24].

$$E = \frac{\max(y_i, t_i) - \min(y_i, t_i)}{\max(y_i, t_i)} \quad (4)$$

where, y_i are the predicted and t_i are the target/actual values.

Table 2. Received UWB signal variation for 4 mm tumor in different positions.

UWB Transmitted Signal	Tumor Positions (x, y, z) (mm)	UWB Received Signal
	(31, 22, 8)	
	(32, 20, 13)	
	(55, 30, 12)	

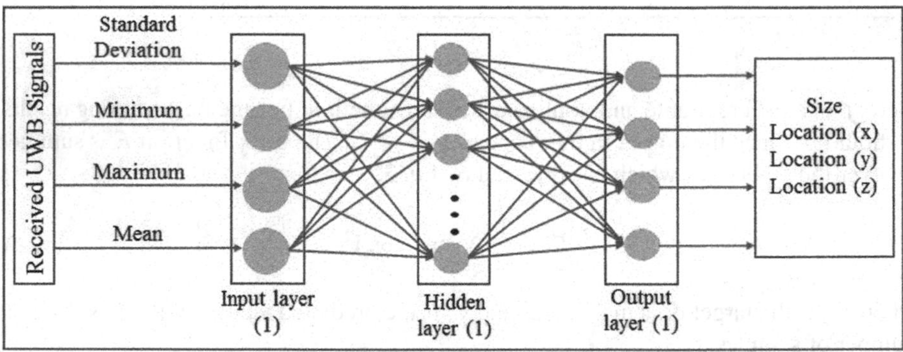

Fig. 5. Neural network architecture.

The predicted output for each data sample is evaluated and compared with the target value in order to get performance accuracy of the system using Eq. 5 [24].

$$\textit{Performance}\ \text{accuracy}(\%) = 100 - E\,(\textit{error}\ \%) \tag{5}$$

The Eq. 4 and Eq. 5 is used to get performance accuracy for both tumor size and location respectively. For tumor existence, any −ve output for an input signal sample, indicates no tumor presence (i.e., healthy breast), otherwise tumor exists (for +ve output). The NN design and performance parameters are shown in Table 3.

Table 3. Design and performance parameters of NN.

NN design parameters	Values
Number of nodes in input layer	4
Number of nodes in hidden layer	10
Number of nodes in output layer	4
Maximum number of epochs	1000
Transfer function	tansig
Training function	trainlm
Minimum performance gradient	1.00e−07
Momentum constant	0.793
Learning rate	0.001

2.4 Tumor Detection Accuracy Comparison

The performance comparison between two bio-antennas has been conducted in terms of early breast cancer detection accuracy. This comparison evaluates that how the bio-antenna plays an important role towards breast tumor detection precision. The antenna with better accuracy in early breast cancer detection precision exposes that it is able to transmit and receive good quality of signal in any data/signal collection system. The detection accuracy evaluated in terms of tumor 3D location and size using Eqs. 4 and 5 respectively.

3 Results and Discussions

The collected signals using the existing (pyramidal shaped) and the proposed (modified T shaped) antennas are used for training, validation and testing the system. The training, testing and validation performance for the ANN network is shown in Fig. 6. It shows that the best validation is occurred at epoch 6 with desired testing and validation results for good network performance. The system with same ANN and both types of bio-antenna exhibits approximately 100% efficiency for the detection of tumor/cancer existence. For tumor position and size detection, different arbitrary locations (x, y, z) and sizes have been used to validate the system accuracy.

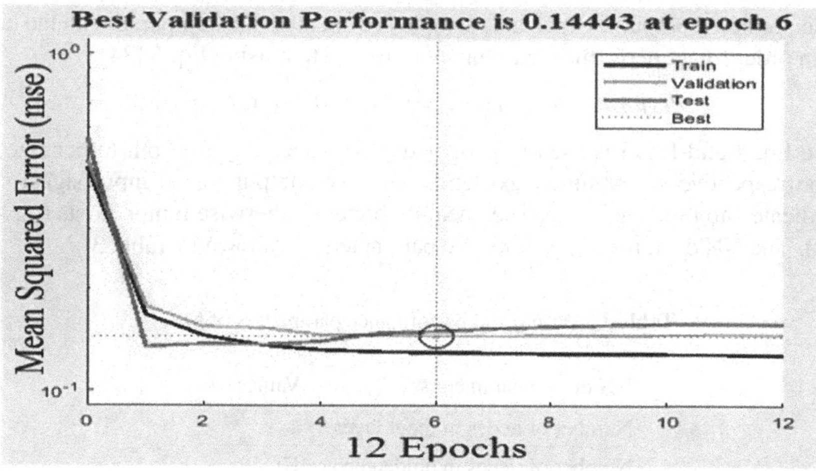

Fig. 6. Neural network performance

Tables 4 and 5 show the detection accuracy of pyramidal shaped UWB patch antenna in terms of tumor location and size respectively. Similarly, Tables 6 and 7 show the detection accuracy of the proposed modified T shaped UWB patch antenna in terms of tumor location and size respectively. The average cancer detection accuracy by using the existing pyramidal shaped antenna [15] is 90.27% and 89.91% for tumor location and size respectively. Whereas those accuracies using our proposed (modified T shaped) antenna are 91.03% and 91.09% for tumor location and size respectively. The comparison shows that breast cancer detection accuracy is bit higher for the proposed (modified T shaped) antenna than the pyramidal shaped antenna. This indicates that the proposed bio-antenna has clear signal reception capability, hence, better breast cancer detection performance than the existing one.

Table 4. Tumor location detection accuracy of the pyramidal shaped UWB antenna [15].

Tumor location (x, y, z)	Target (mm) [actual output]	NN output (mm)	Error, E (%)	Accuracy for each target (%)	Average accuracy for each axis (%)	Overall accuracy (%)
X	49	56.1	10.87	89.13	91.23	90.27
	50	45.25	7.65	92.35		
	31	33.62	7.79	92.21		
Y	32	37.12	13.79	86.21	89.82	
	29	26.91	7.21	92.79		
	22	24.32	9.54	90.46		
Z	10	11.15	10.31	89.69	89.77	
	10	9.20	8	92.00		
	8	9.13	12.38	87.62		

Table 5. Tumor size detection performance of the pyramidal shaped UWB antenna [15].

Target of size (mm) [actual output]	NN output (mm)	Error, E (%)	Accuracy for each target (%)	Overall average accuracy (%)
2	2.11	5.21	94.79	89.91
3	2.69	10.3	89.7	
4	3.41	14.75	85.25	

Table 6. Tumor location detection accuracy of the proposed modified T shaped UWB antenna.

Tumor Location (x, y, z)	Target (mm) [actual output]	NN output (mm)	Error, E (%)	Accuracy for each target (%)	Average accuracy for each axis (%)	Overall Average accuracy (%)
X	49	45.61	6.93	93.07	94.04	91.03
	50	46.22	7.56	92.44		
	31	32.07	3.33	96.67		
Y	32	36.86	13.1	86.9	87.45	
	29	26.22	9.59	90.41		
	22	25.87	14.96	85.04		
Z	10	9.93	0.7	99.30	91.59	
	10	10.19	1.86	98.14		
	8	10.79	25.85	74.15		

Table 7. Tumor size detection performance of the proposed Modified T shaped UWB antenna.

Target of size (mm) [actual output]	NN output (mm)	Error, E (%)	Accuracy for each target (%)	Overall average accuracy (%)
2	1.75	12.5	87.5	91.09
3	3.37	10.98	89.02	
4	3.87	3.25	96.75	

4 Conclusion

The performances of ultra-wideband (UWB) bio-antennas are presented in this chapter with comparison for early breast cancer detection. A modified T shaped UWB patch bio-antenna has been developed. The UWB signals through breast phantom were collected by using two different bio-antennas (namely the 'modified T shaped' and existing 'pyramidal shaped' UWB patch bio-antennas). The collected signals were fed into a developed artificial neural network (ANN) module for training, validation and testing for early breast cancer detection precision. In this way, the performance of both 'pyramidal shaped' and the proposed 'modified T shaped' UWB patch bio-antennas were evaluated and compared according to their tumor detection accuracy. Both of the antennas show good performance in breast tumor/cancer detection in terms of existence, tumor size and location in 3D environment. However, the tumor detection accuracy is bit better for the proposed (modified T shaped UWB patch) antenna than the pyramidal shaped UWB patch antenna due to its wider bandwidth and capability to receive clear signal.

Acknowledgment. This work is supported by Universiti Malaysia Pahang (UMP), Internal Research Grant RDU1703236 and Post-Graduate Research Scheme (PGRS190327). The authors would like to thank the Faculty of Electrical & Electronic Engineering Technology (FTKEE), UMP (http://www.ump.edu.my) for providing the facilities to conduct this work.

References

1. Hammouch, N., Ammor, H.: Smart UWB antenna for early breast cancer detection. ARPN J. Eng. Appl. Sci. **13**, 3803–3808 (2018)
2. Azamjah, N., Soltan-Zadeh, Y., Zayeri, F.: Global trend of breast cancer mortality rate: a 25-year study. Asian Pac. J. Cancer Prev. **20**, 2015–2020 (2019)
3. Breast cancer statistics - Canadian Cancer Society. https://www.cancer.ca/en/cancer-information/cancer-type/breast/statistics/?region=on. Accessed 10 Dec 2019
4. Alshehri, S., Khatun, S.: UWB imaging for breastr cancer detection using neural network. Prog. Electromagn. Res. C **7**, 447–465 (2009)
5. Park, E.H., et al.: Basic facts of breast cancer in Korea in 2014: the 10-year overall survival progress. J. Breast Cancer. **20**, 1–11 (2017)
6. Lakshmi, A.N., Khatun, S., AlShehri, S.A.: A preview study on UWB imaging system to detect early breast tumor. In: Yonazi, J.J., Sedoyeka, E., Ariwa, E., El-Qawasmeh, E. (eds.) e-Technologies and Networks for Development. CCIS, vol. 171, pp. 104–115. Springer, Heidelberg (2011). https://doi.org/10.1007/978-3-642-22729-5_9
7. Kwon, S., Lee, S.: Recent advances in microwave imaging for breast cancer detection. Int. J. Biomed. Imaging **2016**, 1–26 (2016)
8. Hang, J.A., Sim, L., Zakaria, Z.: Non-invasive breast cancer assessment using magnetic induction spectroscopy technique. Int. J. Integr. Eng. **9**, 54–60 (2017)
9. Seidman, H., Stellman, S.D., Mushinski, M.H.: A different perspective on breast cancer risk factors: some implications of the nonattributable risk. CA Cancer J. Clin. **32**, 301–313 (1982)
10. Karli, R., Ammor, H., Shubair, R.M., Alhajri, M.I., Alkurd, R., Hakam, A.: Miniature planar ultra-wide-band microstrip antenna for breast cancer detection. In: 16th Mediterranean Microwave Symposium (MMS). IEEE, 14–16 November 2016
11. FCC (Federal Communications Commission): Ultra-wideband Operation FCC Report and Order.In: Technical Report US 47 CFR Part15 (2002). https://transition.fcc.gov/Bureaus/Engineering_Technology/Orders/2002/fcc02048.pdf. Accessed 29 Mar 2019
12. Guo, Y.X., Khoo, K.W., Ong, L.C.: Wideband circularly polarized patch antenna using broadband baluns. IEEE Trans. Antennas Propag. **56**, 319–326 (2008)
13. Fear, E.C., Bourqui, J., Curtis, C., Mew, D., Docktor, B., Romano, C.: Microwave breast imaging with a monostatic radar-based system: a study of application to patients. IEEE Trans. Microw. Theory Tech. **61**, 2119–2128 (2013)

14. Nilavalan, R., Craddock, I.J., Preece, A., Leendertz, J., Benjamin, R.: Wideband microstrip patch antenna design for breast cancer tumour detection. Microwaves. Antennas Propagat. IET **1**, 277–281 (2007)
15. Reza, K.J., Khatun, S., Jamlos, M.F., Fakir, M.M., Morshed, M.N.: Performance enhancement of ultra-wideband breast cancer imaging system: proficient feature extraction and biomedical antenna approach. J. Med. Imaging Heal. Inf. **5**, 1246–1250 (2015)
16. Alshehri, S.A., Khatun, S., Jantan, A.B., Raja Abdullah, R.S.A., Mahmood, R., Awang, Z.: Experimental breast tumor detection using NN-based UWB imaging. Prog. Electromagn. Res. **111**, 447–465 (2011)
17. Lazebnik, M., Madsen, E.L., Frank, G.R., Hagness, S.C.: Tissue-mimicking phantom materials for narrowband and ultrawideband microwave applications. Phys. Med. Biol. **50**, 4245–4258 (2005)
18. Porter, E., Fakhoury, J., Oprisor, R., Coates, M., Popović, M.: Improved tissue phantoms for experimental validation of microwave breast cancer detection. In: Proceedings of the 4th European Conference on Antennas and Propagation, pp. 1–5 (2010)
19. RCM Pulse-On UWB devices: Time Domain Corporation, Comings Research Park; 330 Wynn Drive, Suite 300, Hantsville, Al 35805, USA (2017)
20. Reza, K.J., Khatun, S., Jamlos, M.F., E-Khuda, I., Ishwar, Z., Khalib, A.: Proficient feature extraction strategy for performance enhancement of NN based early breast tumor detection. Int. J. Eng. Technol. **5**, 4689–4696 (2013)
21. Vijayasarveswari, V., Jusoh, M., Khatun, S.: Experimental UWB based efficient breast cancer early detection. Indian J. Sci. Technol. **10**, 1–6 (2017)
22. Haykin, S., et al.: Neural Networks and Learning Machines, 3rd edn. Pearson Education Inc., Upper Saddle River, New Jersey 07458 (2009)
23. Land, W.H., et al.: PNN/GRNN ensemble processor design for early screening of breast cancer. Proc. Comput. Sci. **12**, 438–443 (2012)
24. Alshehri, S., Jantan, A., Raja Abdullah, R.S.A., Mahmud, R., Khatun, S., Awang, Z.: A UWB imaging system to detect early breast cancer in heterogeneous breast phantom. In: International Conference on Electrical, Control and Computer Engineering, pp. 238–242 (2011)

Processing with Patients' Statements: An Advanced Disease Diagnosis Technique

Shakhawat Hossain[1], Md. Zahid Hasan[2(✉)], and Aniruddha Rakshit[2]

[1] CSE, International Islamic University Chittagong, Chattogram, Bangladesh
shakhawat.cse@outlook.com

[2] CSE, Daffodil International University, Dhaka, Bangladesh
{zahid.cse,aniruddha.cse}@diu.edu.bd

Abstract. This paper represents a novel strategy for developing a disease diagnosis gadget from a patient's statement. For that, the system solely accepts patients' statements in a natural language like English and analyzes the patients' statements to prognosis the symptoms the affected person is presently suffering from. The framework forms the patients' discourse and afterward utilizes Term Frequency (TF) to find the indications of a malady. Cosine Similarity is utilized to settle on a final decision with respect to regarding disease diagnosis task. Cosine Similarity quantifies the similitude between two non-zero vectors in a vector space model where one of the vectors is constructed with the symptoms the patient is encountering and the rest is developed during knowledge base setup. The framework is tested over 1013 patients with various ailments and its accuracy up to 98.3%.

Keywords: Disease diagnosis tool · Patient's statement · Cosine similarity · Term frequency · Diseases' symptoms · Expert system

1 Introduction

Early detection of a disease facilitates a patient with more time to seek medical advice before it gets to an advanced stage. It ensures enough time for the physicians to analyze patients' history and provide treatment to the patients to prevent complication before getting too worse. Every year, a large number of patients' die of different disease because the diseases are not detected in time. So, physicians advise starting treatment at the early stage of any disease. However, it's not always easy to detect disease at its early stage. Detection of disease at the early stage requires a number of confirmatory tests which is not possible for the people from all living standards. Rather, unnecessary tests cost some extra amount of money. So, there should be some systems that detect diseases only by analyzing its symptoms. Researchers have been trying to develop expert systems to detect disease at the early stage and a lot has been developed. Unfortunately, each of these expert systems focuses only on a specific disease by just analyzing the signs and symptoms of that particular disease. So, the developed expert systems can hardly detect a specific disease from its symptoms as many diseases show the same signs and

T. Bhuiyan et al. (Eds.): ICONCS 2020, LNICST 325, pp. 366–375, 2020.
https://doi.org/10.1007/978-3-030-52856-0_29

symptoms. Besides, there are no available expert systems that can analyze a patient's statement provided in his natural language to diagnose any disease.

Disease diagnosis using an expert system has been an important research topic for the last few decades. Researchers have been conducting researches to diagnose different type of diseases using different methodologies. Computer scientists are trying to simplify the disease diagnosis process with the help of many intelligent methodologies. The first medical expert system was developed by Shortliffe at el. (1984) at Stanford University. They developed MYCIN to help the doctors to discover infectious bacteria and provide preventive treatment [1]. A few years later, Harry Pople (1986) proposed CADUCEUS [2] to improve the MYCIN. Harry's proposed methodology covers a wide area of internal medicine rather than a narrow field like blood poisoning. On the other hand, Barnett GO at el. developed DXplain [3] in 1987. DXplain the first web-based clinical decision support system that considers patients signs, symptoms and clinical reports to diagnosis a disease. DXplain is established based on pseudo-probabilistic algorithm [4] that provides differential diagnoses based on a robust knowledge base. In recent years a huge number of Clinical Decision Support System (CDSS) have been developed to diagnosis medical diseases and help the medical experts pro-vide better treatment. These CDSSs can be categorized into two basic types: knowledge base and non-knowledge base [5]. Evidential Reasoning (ER) Approach [6] and Belief rule-base inference methodology using the evidential reasoning Approach-RIMER [7] are being used to develop some Knowledgebase intelligent disease diagnosis and suspicion tools [9–13]. These knowledgebase approaches incorporate an inference engine to diagnosis diseases based on its knowledge base. The basic knowledge base in a rule-based expert system is constructed with some if-then rules [7]. The non-knowledgebase CDSS is a new technique that incorporates some statistical and machine learning algorithms [8] to establish a medical expert system. Genetic algorithm [14], artificial neural network [15], CNN [16–19], RNN [20, 21] and other approaches are nowadays frequently being used to diagnose medical diseases. However, none of these approaches can identify diseases from a patient's verbal statement. Therefore, this paper proposes a novel approach that determines a disease at its early stage by analyzing its symptoms. The proposed system only takes the statement of a patient to diagnose a disease.

2 Methodology

To diagnose a disease at its early stage from its symptoms, cosine similarity (CS) is proposed in this study. Cosine similarity is a measurement approach that determines to what extents two documents are similar [21]. For that purpose, cosine similarity considers two non-zero vectors and finds the cosine of the angle between these vectors in a vector space model [22]. The formal definition of cosine similarity can be stated as,

$$\text{Cosine Similarity} = \frac{\alpha \cdot \beta}{\|\alpha\| \|\beta\|} = \frac{\sum_{i=1}^{N} \alpha_i \beta_i}{\sqrt{\sum_{i=1}^{N} \alpha_i^2} \sqrt{\sum_{i=1}^{N} \beta_i^2}} \tag{1}$$

Here, α and β are two non-zero vectors and

$$\vec{\alpha}.\vec{\beta} = \sum_{1}^{n} \alpha_1\beta_1 + \alpha_2\beta_2 + \alpha_3\beta_3 + \ldots + \alpha_n\beta_n \tag{2}$$

The basic explanation of cosine similarity comes from the geometric definition of the dot product,

$$\alpha.\beta = \|\alpha\|\|\beta\|\cos(\theta) \tag{3}$$

$$\cos(\theta) = \frac{\alpha.\beta}{\|\alpha\|\|\beta\|} = \textit{Cosine Similarity} \tag{4}$$

Where $\|\alpha\|$ and $\|\beta\|$ are the Euclidean norm of vector α and β. This can be written as α = $\alpha = \sqrt{\alpha_1^2 + \alpha_2^2 + \ldots + \alpha_n^2}$ and $\beta = \sqrt{\beta_1^2 + \beta_2^2 + \ldots + \beta_n^2}$. The angle between vectors ranges from 0 to 1. This angle determines the projection of α into the β. If a vector is close to the other vector, the angle between two vectors will be 0, which determines the two sentences are almost similar in case of content. For example, in Table 1 there are four instances of a word 'feel' and two instances of a word 'white'. For these two different types of words, we can count the value as 4 and 2 respectively. Similarly, if we consider two different term-frequency vectors α = (4, 0, 3, 2) and β = (2, 1, 3, 2) can be calculated as following:

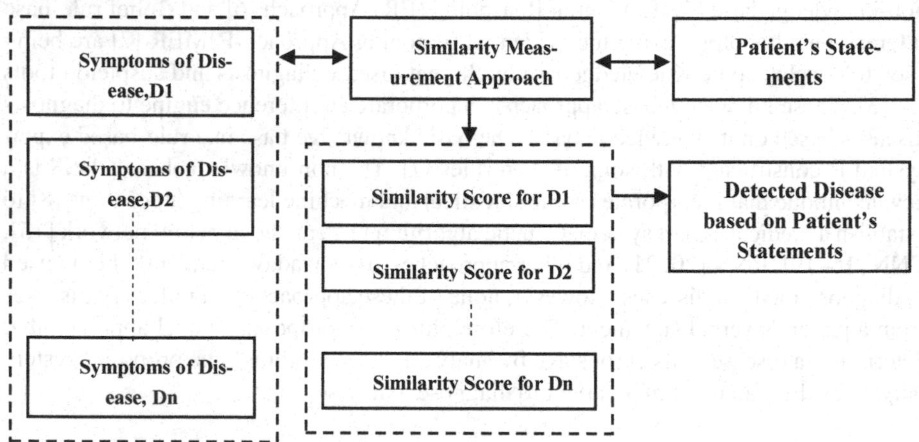

Fig. 1. Disease diagnosis system from patient's statement

$$\alpha, \beta = 4 \times 2 + 0 \times 1 + 3 \times 3 + 2 \times 2 = 21$$

$$\|\alpha\| = \sqrt{4^2 + 0^2 + 3^2 + 2^2} = 5.385$$

$$\|\beta\| = \sqrt{2^2 + 1^2 + 3^2 + 2^2} = 4.243$$

$$\text{similarity } (\alpha, \beta) = 0.92$$

3 System Implementation

The input data need to be well processed to extract the necessary information from a patient's statement. The patient's statement is collected in a natural language which is then processed to extract the symptoms of a particular disease. Simplifying the task, the content of a patient's statement [23] is carefully gone through and only nouns, adjectives and verbs of the sentences are considered. Other parts of speech are being removed as a part of data preprocessing. The Latent Analogy [24] is used in this system to tag the parts of speech. The elimination of article and punctuations makes the data processing task easier. The training process includes only the base form of the verb and noun, pronoun, adjective. The regular expression can be used to remove punctuations from the sentences.

The words of the sentences should be in their base form to enhance the system accuracy. Streamer Porter Algorithm [25, 26] can be used to convert every word into their base forms. In this process, noun, adjective, verb, adverbs are reduced to its base form. The statements are then tokenized to construct the vectors. The final vector construction is accomplished based on the times of appearance of every word in the statement. Term Frequency (TF) [27] is used in the proposed system to count the time a word appears in the statement. TF can be implemented as,

$$tf_{t,d} = \begin{cases} \log(1 + f_{t,d}), \, iff_{t,d} > 0 \\ 0 \end{cases} \tag{5}$$

Here, t defines a word; d is a patient's statement and $tf_{t,d}$ is the frequency of the word in the statement.

After, the final vector construction is done Eq. (1) is used to calculate the similarity scores against each disease. The maximum similarity score defines the disease that a patient is currently suffering from. The resultant value for the disease will be either 1 or near about 1. When the similarities score 1, it is defined that the symptoms the patient is experiencing have a 100% match with the symptoms of the predicted disease. The architectural design for the proposed system is as follows:

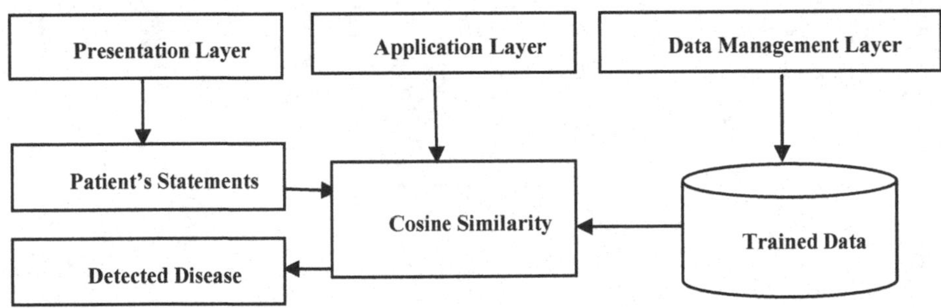

Fig. 2. System architecture of the proposed disease diagnosis tool

The proposed system needs to be trained with a large number of datasets. These datasets state the symptoms of different diseases which literally construct the knowledge base of the proposed system (see Fig. 2).

The proposed system first analyzes the statement of a patient and extracts the important keywords or the symptoms of a disease. The knowledge base contains all the symptoms of corresponding diseases. Data management layer controls all functionality of patient's symptoms say, data processing, word to vector converting, and training the data. Then the system constructs a word vector with these extracted symptoms. To accomplish the final disease detection tasks, the system finds the similarity score of this vector against all the trained data vectors in the knowledge as stated in Fig. 1. The application layer is responsible to find the similarity between two non-zero vectors. The maximum score defines the most probable disease a patient is suffering from. The presentation layer displays the detected disease of the patient using the system. The system has been developed with Java (Spring MVC) and MySQL with HTML and JSP in the front end (see Fig. 3, 4 and 5).

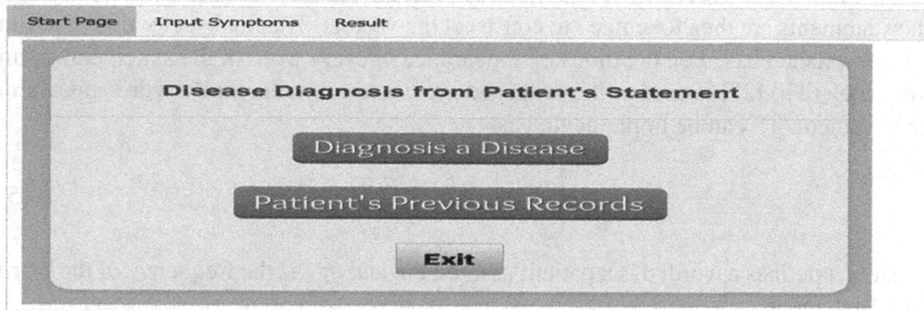

Fig. 3. Main interface of the system

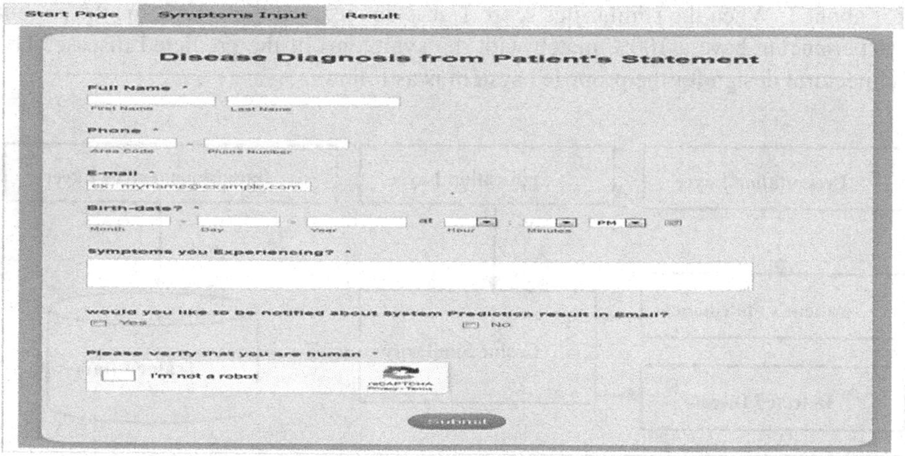

Fig. 4. Interface for symptoms input from patient

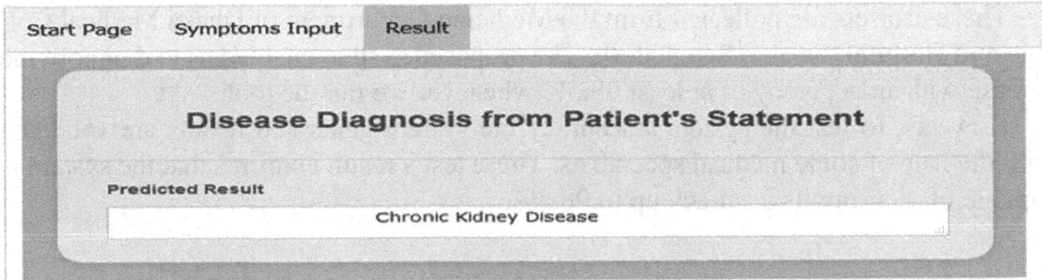

Fig. 5. Result shows the predicted disease from patient's statement

4 Result and Discussion

To analyze the potential outcomes of the proposed system, the system is implemented and tested over 1013 patients. The system was trained with 14 different datasets. Each of these datasets contains the symptoms of a specific disease.

Table 1. System validation with some test results

Test no.	Patient's name	Patient's statement	System suspected disease	Expert's suspected disease
1	Saiful Karim	I feel weak and tired all day. My face, hands, and feet seem to be swollen. I feel my hands and feet are getting white. Sometimes I have bloody and foamy urine	Chronic Kidney Disease	Chronic Kidney Disease
2	SumaiyaFarhana	I have been suffering from high fever with headache. I sometimes have vomiting or nausea. I also have been suffering from diarrhea	Malaria	Malaria
3	Debashis Das	I have serious pain on the left side of my chest. I am feeling tired and I think I can hardly breathe	Heart Attack	Heart Attack
4	Banuj Kumar Datta	I have been suffering from fever for the last few days. I have serious pain in the whole body. I think I am dying from joint pain. I notice thatthe joint areas are swelling	Chikungunya	Chikungunya
5	Moniruzzaman Khan	I have got skin rash on both side of my face. I feel like I am getting white just like losing blood. I have an acute fever and I am losing hair seriously	Lupus	Lupus

These datasets are collected from the Medicine Department of Dhaka Medical College and Hospital, Dhaka, Bangladesh. The proposed system enabled us to diagnose the disease with an accuracy of at least 98.3% whenever we ran the tool.

However, to test the system's accuracy the system-generated results are validated with the help of some medical specialists. These test's result confirms that the system is capable of securing its accuracy up to 98.3%.

Table 2. System accuracy test with 177 CKD patient's data

N = 177	Predicted: yes	Predicted: no
Actual: yes	TP: 97	FN = 4
Actual: no	FP: 3	TN = 73
Accuracy	96%	

Table 3. System accuracy test with 169 Lupus patient's data

N = 169	Predicted: yes	Predicted: no
Actual: yes	TP: 98	FN = 0
Actual: no	FP: 2	TN = 69
Accuracy	99%	

Table 4. System accuracy test with 255 Chikungunya patient's data

N = 255	Predicted: yes	Predicted: no
Actual: yes	TP: 193	FN = 3
Actual: no	FP: 2	TN = 57
Accuracy	98%	

From the above data provided in Tables 2, 3 and 4, it becomes visible that the diagnostic accuracy of the proposed system varies for different diseases. The accuracy of the proposed system mostly depends upon the training datasets. However, the proposed system introduces the state of the art in disease diagnosis from the patients' statement. The existing disease diagnosis systems not only focus solely on a single disease rather than deciding from the problem statement but also hardly achieve the expected accuracy while diagnosing any disease. The following table (Table 5) explains the disease diagnosis accuracy of different prominent expert systems.

Table 5. Comparison among different disease diagnosis methodologies

Author name	Methodology	**Accuracy**
Saifur Rahman et al.	Belief Rule Based Inference Methodology Evidential Reasoning (RIMER) approach to predict Asthma disease	93.2%
Mohammad Shadat Hossain et al.	Belief Rule Based Expert System (BRBES) to detect Tuberculosis	95.25%
Ruoxuan Cui et al.	Combination of Multilayer Perceptron (MLP) and Recurrent Neural Network (RNN) to predict Alzheimer's Disease	89.7%
Tomas Mikolov et al.	Combination of Latent Dirichlet Allocation (LDA) and Latent Semantic Analysis (LSA) using Skip-gram and Recurrent Neural Net Language Model	58.9%
Shakhawat Hossain et al.	Belief Rule Based Inference Methodology Evidential Reasoning (RIMER) for predicting Chronic Kidney Disease (CKD)	92.9%
Edward Choi et al.	Recurrent Neural Network (RNN)	77%
Proposed method	**Term Frequency (TF) and Cosine Similarity**	**98.3%**

5 Conclusion

Disease diagnosis of a patient from his/her problem statement is a challenging task for the researchers. Researchers have been trying to develop a system that is capable of suspecting the actual disease of a patient without the help of any medical expert. This paper proposes such an intelligent methodology that is capable of analyzing a patient's statement to diagnose the disease a patient is currently suffering from. The proposed system accepts a patient's statement in a natural language and conducts a deep analysis of the provided speech to extract the symptoms of the probable disease. Based on the extracted symptoms the system utilizes the cosine similarity approach to measure the similarity-scores performed against different diseases. The maximum similarity score defines the suspected disease for a given problem statement. The accuracy of the proposed system is measured 98.3% based on the tests run on the statements of some 1013 patients in Dhaka Medical College.

References

1. Buchanan, B., Shortliffe, E.: Rule-Based Expert Systems: The Mycin Experiments of the Standford Heuristic Programming Project. Addison-Wesley Longman, USA (1984)

2. Banks, G.: Artificial intelligence in medical diagnosis: the INTERNIST/CADUCEUS approach. Crit. Rev. Med. Inf. **1**(1), 23–54 (1986)
3. Barnett, O., Cimino, J., Hupp, J., Hoffer, E.: DXplain- an evolving diagnostic decision-support system. J. Am. Med. Assoc. (JAMA) **258**(1), 67–74 (1987)
4. Detmer, W., Shortliffe, E.: Using the internet to improve knowledge diffusion in medicine. Commun. ACM **40**(8), 101–108 (1997)
5. Berner, E.: Clinical Decision Support Systems, vol. 233, 2nd edn. Springer, Cham (2016). https://doi.org/10.1007/978-3-319-31913-1
6. Yang, J., Xu, D.: On the evidential reasoning algorithm for multiple attribute decision analysis under uncertainty. IEEE Trans. Syst. Man Cybern. - Part A: Syst. Hum. **32**(3), 289–304 (2002)
7. Yang, J., Liu, J., Wang, J., Sii, H., Wang, H.: Belief rule-base inference methodology using the evidential reasoning approach-RIMER. IEEE Trans. Syst. Man Cybern. - Part A: Syst. Hum. **36**(2), 266–285 (2006)
8. Baig, M., Hosseini, H., Lindén, M.: Machine learning-based clinical decision support system for early diagnosis from real-time physiological data. In: IEEE Region 10 Conference (TENCON), Singapore, pp. 2943–2946 (2016)
9. Hossain, M., Hossain, M., Khalid, S., Haque, M.: A belief rule-based (BRB) decision support system for assessing clinical asthma suspicion. In: Scandinavian Conference on Health Informatics (SHI), pp. 83–89 (2014)
10. Karim, R., Andersson, K., Hossain, M., Uddin, J., Meah, P.: A belief rule based expert system to assess clinical bronchopneumonia suspicion. In: 2016 Future Technologies Conference (FTC), USA, pp. 655–660, January 2017
11. Hossain, S.: An expert system to suspect chronic kidney disease. Int. J. Comput. Sci. Eng. (IJCSE) **8**(8), 307–312 (2016)
12. Hossain, M., Ahmed, F., Johora, F., Anderson, K.: A belief rule based expert system to assess tuberculosis under uncertainty. J. Med. Syst. **41**(3), 43 (2017)
13. Mourya, A., Tyagi, P., Asutosh, D.: Genetic algorithm and their applicability in medical diagnostic: a survey. Int. J. Sci. Eng. Res. **7**(12), 1143–1145 (2016)
14. Amato, F., López, A., Méndez, E., Vaňhara, P., Hampl, A., Havel, J.: Artificial neural networks in medical diagnosis. J. Appl. Biomed. **11**, 47–58 (2013)
15. Singhal, S., Kumar, H., Passricha, V.: Prediction of heart disease using CNN. Am. Int. J. Res. Sci. Technol. Eng. Math. **23**(1), 257–261 (2018)
16. Abiyev, R., Ma'aitah, M.: Deep convolutional neural networks for chest diseases detection. J. Healthc. Eng. **2018**, 1–11 (2018)
17. Ragab, D., Sharkas, M., Marshall, S., Ren, J.: Breast cancer detection using deep comvolutional neural networks and support vector machines. PeerJ **7**, e6201 (2019)
18. Alakwaa, W., Naseef, M., Badr, A.: Lung cancer detection and classification using convolutional neural network. Int. J. Adv. Comput. Sci. Eng. Appl. **8**(8), 409–417 (2017)
19. Cui, R., Liu, M.: RNN-based longitudinal analysis for diagnosis of Alzheimer's disease. Comput. Med. Imaging Graph. **73**, 1–10 (2019)
20. Choi, E., Schuetz, A., Stewart, W., Sun, J.: Using recurrent neural network models for early detection of heart failure onset. J. Am. Med. Inf. Assoc. **24**, 361–370 (2013)
21. Mothukuri, R., Nagaraju, M., Chilukuri, D.: Similarity measure for text classification. Int. J. Emerg. Trends Technol. Comput. Sci. (IJETTC) **5**(6), 16–24 (2016)
22. Mikolov, T., Chen, K., Corrado, G., Dean, J.: Efficient estimation of word representations in vector space. In: International Conference on Learning Representations (ICLR), vol. 3, September 2013
23. Hasan, Z., Hossain, S., Rizvee, A., Rana, M.: Content based document classification using soft cosine measure. Int. J. Adv. Comput. Sci. Appl. (IJACSA) **10**(40), 522 (2019)
24. Bellegarda, J.: Part-of-speech tagging by latent analogy. IEEE J. Sel. Top. Signal Process. **4**(6), 985–993 (2010)

25. Porter, M.: An algorithm for suffix stripping. Program Electron. Libr. Inf. Syst. **40**(3), 211–218 (2006)
26. Joshi, A., Thomas, N., Dabhade, M.: Modified porter stemming algorithm. Int. J. Comput. Sci. Inf. Technol. **7**(1), 266–269 (2016)
27. Yamamoto, M., Church, K.: Using suffix arrays to compute term frequency and document frequency for all substrings in a corpus. Comput. Linguist. **27**(1), 1–30 (2001)

Non-invasive Diabetes Level Monitoring System Using Artificial Intelligence and UWB

Minarul Islam[1], Sabira Khatun[1](✉), Nusrat Jahan Shoumy[2], Md. Shawkat Ali[3], Mohamad Shaiful Abdul Karim[1], and Bifta Sama Bari[1]

[1] Faculty of Electrical and Electronic Engineering Technology, Universiti Malaysia Pahang, Pekan, Pahang, Malaysia
sabirakhatun@ump.edu.my
[2] School of Computing and Mathematics, Charles Sturt University, Wagga Wagga, NSW, Australia
[3] BMTF, Dhaka Cantonment, Dhaka, Bangladesh

Abstract. Diabetes is a silent-killer disease throughout the world. It is not curable, therefore, regular blood glucose concentration levels (BGCL) monitoring is necessary to be healthy in a long run. The traditional way of BGCL measurement is invasive by pricking and collecting blood sample from human arm (or finger-tip), then measuring the level either using a glucometer or sending to laboratory. This blood collecting process produces significant discomfort to the patients, especially to the children with type-A diabetes, resulting increased undetected-cases and health-complications. To overcome this drawbacks, a non-invasive ultra-wideband (UWB) BGCL measurement system is proposed here with enhanced software module. The hardware can be controlled through the graphical user interface (GUI) of software and can execute signal processing, feature extraction, and feature classification using artificial intelligence (AI). As AI, cascade forward neural network (CFNN) and naïve bayes (NB) algorithms are investigated, then CFNN with four independent features (skewness, kurtosis, variance, mean-absolute-deviation) are found to be best-suited for BGCL estimation. A transmit (Tx) antenna was placed at one side of left-earlobe to Tx UWB signals, and a receive (Rx) antenna at opposite side to Rx transmitted signals with BGCL marker. These signals are saved and used for AI training, validation and testing. The system with CFNN shows approximately 86.62% accuracy for BGCL measurement, which is 5.62% improved compared to other methods by showing its superiority. This enhanced system is affordable, effective and easy-to-use for all users (home and hospital), to reduce undetected diabetes cases and related mortality rate in near future.

Keywords: UWB · Non-invasive measurement · Blood glucose concentration level · Cascade forward neural network

1 Introduction

Diabetes occurs, when either human body unable to produce enough insulin, or stop producing insulin. Insulin is a type of hormone produced by pancreas which is utilized

T. Bhuiyan et al. (Eds.): ICONCS 2020, LNICST 325, pp. 376–387, 2020.
https://doi.org/10.1007/978-3-030-52856-0_30

to regulate blood glucose level. Diabetes has no remedy, hence, leading a consistent and systematic healthy lifestyle along with BGCL screening is the only way to keep fit for long run. Failure to control BGCL within healthy range can lead severe life threatening concern, including, kidney failure, stroke, heart attack, lower limb amputation and blindness [1]. In [2], based on the statistics and trends for a period of 1980 to 2014, it was predicted that in year 2030, diabetes can be the seventh leading cause of death. This happens due to the existing way for measuring and monitoring BGCL invasively, where, blood drop is usually drawn from fingertip or arm by pricking with a needle. Resulting, trauma occurs among most of the patients, especially for children (or those with Type-A diabetes) who has to go through this process several times a day. Besides, it incurs costs to test the blood and get BGCL reading through laboratory in hospital and/or using glucometer with measuring-strip at home. Hence, only detected diabetes patients undergo the process as per need, while healthy (or un-diagnosed) people do not examine their blood (health condition) regularly. As a result, undiagnosed cases with severe health concern are in up-rising trend. This problem only can be minimized with a non-invasive, user friendly and affordable blood glucose monitoring system. Most of the proposed/developed non-invasive systems/technics along with their benefits and limitation are analyzed in [3, 4]. Majority of the proposed systems depicted initial success, however, with time they turned to unreliable, along with less-accurate [3–14]. Moreover, those are costly, and required additional enhancements for practical use.

The ultra-wideband (UWB) imaging technique is a potential alternative for non-invasive blood glucose monitoring techniques due to its non-ionizing and health-friendly nature [15]. UWB is convenient for medical purpose uses due to its non-ionizing and health-friendly nature to human body [16]. UWB signals usually reacts on the variation of dielectric properties of body tissues or cells as a function of frequency. This phenomenon is supported in [17] by showing that the dielectric properties decrease with the increase of Glucose Concentration Level (GCL) through sugar syrup phantom, where, the difference is clearly visible for UWB higher frequency range. This idea of GCL detection was adopted in [18–20] to propose non-invasive blood glucose detection strategy through human earlobe and arms utilizing UWB imaging technique. Using UWB and artificial neural network (ANN) a very basic and expert operated system was proposed in [19, 20], with low accuracy, without GUI, and inconvenient for home users.

To overcome these issues, this chapter proposes a user-friendly, and non-invasive BGCL screening strategy utilizing the UWB and an enhanced software system. This software system consists of modules to process and discretise received UWB analogue signals to make it digital for feature extraction, classification and BGCL signature estimation through a graphical user interface (GUI) using a computer. A new feature extraction strategy in terms of four independent features (skewness, kurtosis, variance, mean-absolute-deviation (MAD)) is proposed to enhance BGCL estimation accuracy. Besides, CFNN and naïve bayes (NB) algorithms were used to investigate to find their suitability for feature classification and BGCL estimation accuracy. Finally, CFNN is used as appropriate/better classifier to be used and to compare BGCL estimation performance with other related existing systems. The proposed system with CFNN is light-weight, affordable and reliable besides higher accuracy.

This chapter is organized as follows. Section 2 depicts the system development details including hardware part, software part with GUI, and the full system, Sect. 3 presents results and discussions, followed by the conclusion.

2 The System and Developing Steps

2.1 Overall System Model

The system comprises of a pair of UWB transceiver, two antennas (Tx and Rx antennas), and a software module (for signal processing and classification using CFNN) with a GUI. The left earlobe is considered to collect data signal. The Tx antenna is placed at one side of earlobe, whereas the Rx antenna on the other side connected with respective transceivers. The UWB signal pulse with the center frequency of 4.3 GHz is transmitted by the Tx antenna through earlobe, then, received by the Rx antenna and saved. The received signal is processed, classified and measured the BGCL through the GUI. The BGCL results can also be saved, manipulate and observed through GUI. The Overall system is presented in Fig. 1.

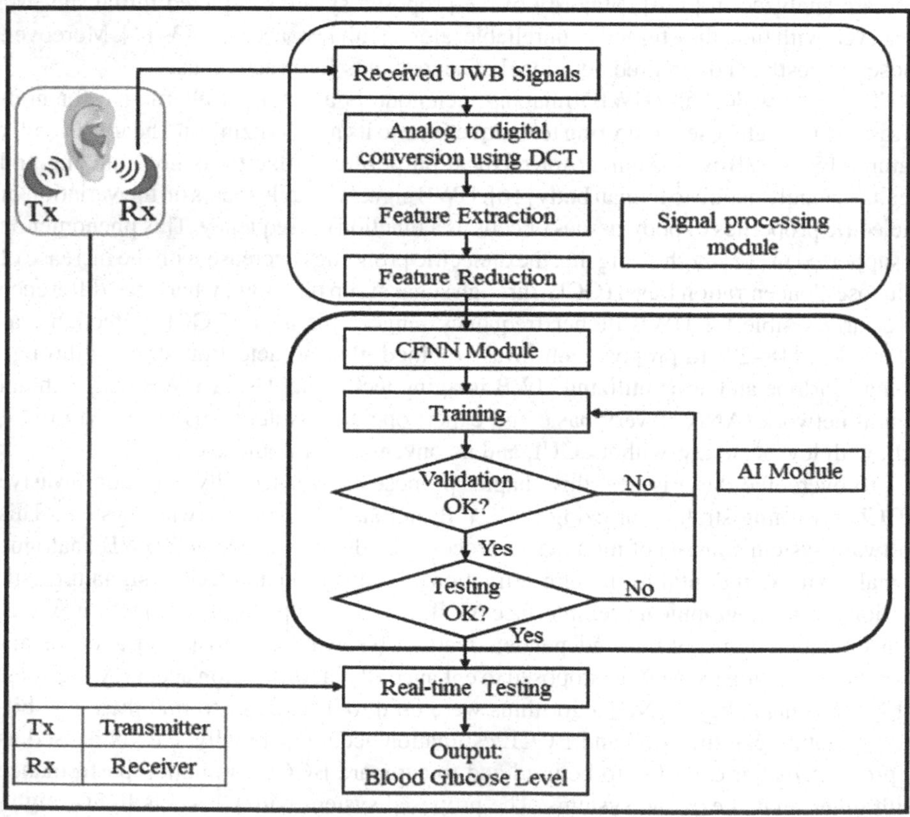

Fig. 1. The overall system.

2.2 System Hardware and Setup

Two UWB bio-antennas (with bandwidth, gain and directivity of around 8.77 GHz, 6.09 dB and 8.15dBi respectively [21]) were connected with corresponding UWB transceivers utilizing 0.5-meter-long SMA connectors. The transceivers were connected to a computer (PC) through ethernet cable in order to transmit and receive the UWB signals as shown in Fig. 2. The signal transmission, reception, saving, processing and analysis were done through the PC using software interface. The experimental system setup and data collection scenarios are presented in Figs. 2 and 3 respectively.

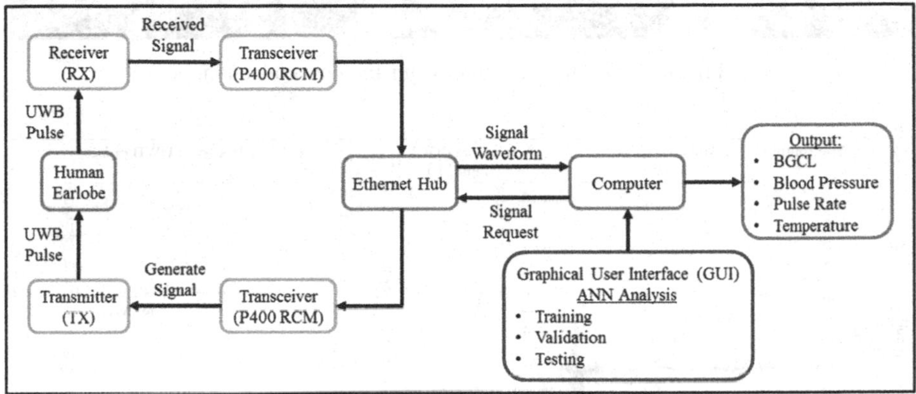

Fig. 2. System block diagram.

2.3 Signal Acquisition

The left earlobe was considered to obtain UWB signal pulses for BGCL investigation, because of its suitability in terms of absence of bone, little fat content, and saturated blood vessels with relaxed blood flow. The collected signal pulses were saved, processed, then used to train, validate, and test both of the AIs (CFNN and NB) individually for BGCL marker classification along with recognition.

We collected a total number of 167 data samples (UWB signals and actual BGCL measurement data using glucometer) from subjects (students and staffs of Universiti Malaysia Pahang as well as some local volunteers) at Universiti Malaysia Pahang (UMP) Health Centre in presence of medical doctors and nurses. The volunteers signed the consent form prior to collect data. Then following health-status were measured by doctors from each volunteer individually: BGCL, systolic blood pressure (SBP), diastolic blood pressure (DBP), pulse rate (PR) and temperature (Temp). Followed by, UWB signals were collected through their left earlobe respectively and saved.

Figure 4 shows the variation of received UWB signals affected by random BGCL for the very same transmitted UWB signal. Their differences are not significant to be identified by human eyes, hence, AI is essential for classification and appropriate BGCL measurement.

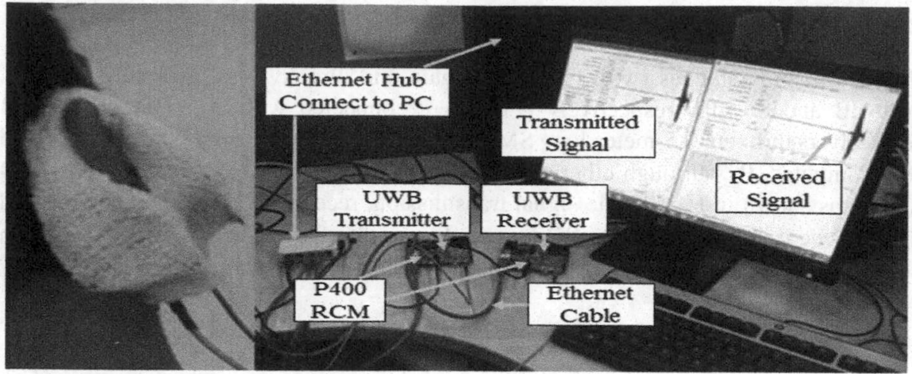

Fig. 3. Experimental system setup and data collection.

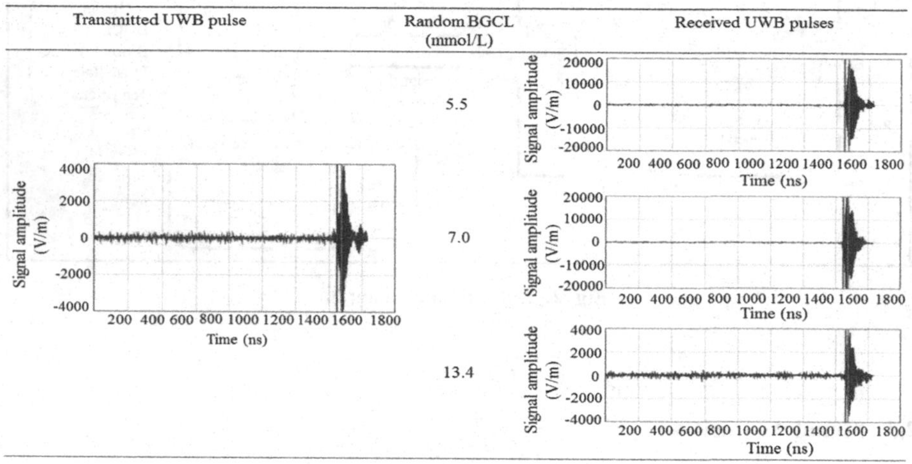

Fig. 4. UWB transmitted and received signal pulses based on random BGCL.

2.4 Signal Processing and Feature Extraction

Discrete Cosine Transform (DCT) is used to convert the received analogue signal to digital form, as a result, 1632 discrete data points were extracted. This huge data points are difficult to handle, besides, if makes the system complicated with intolerable delay and memory consumption. Hence, four independent but prominent feature is proposed, which are skewness, kurtosis, variance and mean absolute deviation (MAD) for improving system performance and increase processing speed. The calculation of these features are shown in Eqs. 1 to 4.

$$Skewness\ (skew) = \frac{1}{N}\sum_{i=1}^{N}\left[\frac{\left(X_i - \bar{X}\right)}{\sigma}\right]^3 \tag{1}$$

$$Kurtosis\ (kurt) = \frac{1}{N}\sum_{i=1}^{N}\left[\frac{(X_i - \bar{X})}{\sigma}\right]^4 \quad (2)$$

$$Variance\left(\sigma^2\right) = \frac{\sum_{i=1}^{N}(X_i - \bar{X})^2}{N} \quad (3)$$

$$MAD = \frac{\sum_{i=1}^{N}|X_i - \bar{X}|}{N} \quad (4)$$

Here, X and N represent the received UWB signal pulses and number of data samples for UWB signals.

2.5 Architecture and Development Details of CFNN

An artificial neural network (ANN) as part of AI, is a computational model based on the structure of biological neurons and their functions. As AI, CFNN algorithm is used to develop part of the proposed software system (after some investigation not presented here due to page limitation) and comparison with NB. The simple nature of CFNN offers the proposed system lightweight with tolerable accuracy level. Figure 5, shows the considered CFNN architecture, consisting of a single input layer with four neurons, one hidden layer with ten neurons and a single output layer with five neurons. Four neurons at input layer and five neurons at output layer correspond to four extracted features (skewness, kurtosis, variance, mean-absolute-deviation (MAD)) and five performance measurement values (BGCL, systolic blood pressure (SBP), diastolic BP (DBP), pulse rate (PR), and Temperature (Temp)) respectively.

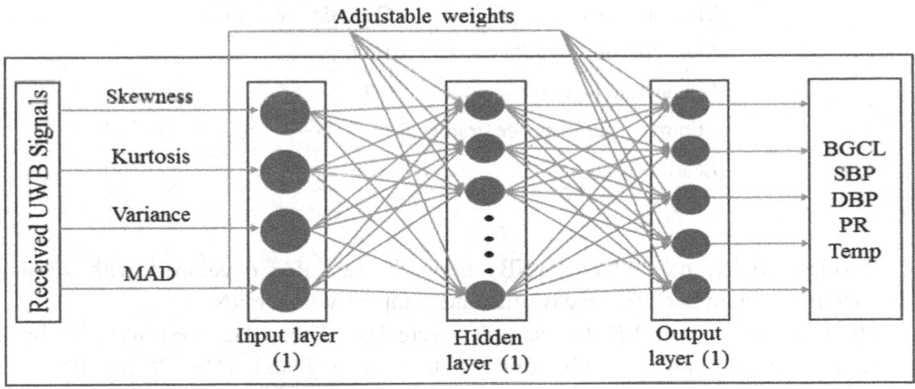

Fig. 5. CFNN architecture.

The additional connections in CFNN help to adjust weights and improve the speed of training and learning. The main learning steps are as follows:

i. Initialization weights with random small values:

$$w_k, k = 1, 2, \ldots, L;\ where\ L\ is\ number\ of\ layer$$

ii. The input, hidden and output layer interconnection for each combination is shown in Eq. 5.

$$X = f_i(w_i x_i + b_i) \tag{5}$$

where, f_i is the input layer activation functions, x_i is input features, w_i is the input weight metrices and b_i is the bias values for $i = 1, 2, 3, \ldots, n$.

iii. For other layers, such as hidden and output layer combination and final output can be obtained from Eq. 6.

$$Y = \left(\sum_{i=1}^{n} f_i w_i x_i + b_i\right) + \left(\sum_{j=1}^{k} f_h w_h x_h + b_h\right) * \left(\sum_{j=1}^{n} f_o w_o x_o + b_o\right) \tag{6}$$

where, f_i, f_h and f_o are the activation functions of input, hidden and output layers respectively; w_i, w_h, and w_o are the weight matrices of input, hidden and output layers respectively.

The CFNN design parameters and functions are shown in Table 1. Using these parameters, the training, testing and validation performance were conducted.

Table 1. CFNN training parameters and functions.

Other training parameters	Value and functions
Transfer function	Transig
Training function	Cascade forwardnet
Max. epochs	1000
Momentum constant	0.9
Minimum performance gradient	1e – 25
Learning rate	0.001

Besides CFNN, naïve bayes (NB) network was also developed with similar parameters to obtain performance results and compare with CFNN.

The total collected UWB data samples were 167. These data were used for both CFNN and NB individually with strategy: 70% (117 signals), 15% (25 signals), and 15% (25 signals) for training, validation, and testing respectively.

The performance evaluation and error calculation were done using Eqs. 7 to 9. Equations 10 and 11 were used to calculate true positive rate (TPR) and false negative rate (FNR).

$$Error = \frac{|actual\ value\ -\ system\ output|}{actual\ value} \times 100\% \tag{7}$$

$$system\ accuracy = 100\% - Error \tag{8}$$

$$Average\ system\ accuracy = \frac{1}{N}\sum_{n=1}^{N} A_{nn} \tag{9}$$

where, N is the total number of data samples, and A_{nn} is the diagonal elements in confusion matrix.

$$TPR = \frac{TP}{TP + FN} \tag{10}$$

$$FNR = \frac{FN}{FN + TP} \tag{11}$$

3 Results and Discussions

The optimum CFNN validation performance (which is 1.9447 mean square error (MSE)) is shown in Fig. 6. The net performance (error and accuracy) are determined by Eqs. 7 and 8 respectively. The average system accuracy (using Eq. 9) for CFNN and NB is around 86.62% and 85.3% respectively as shown in Tables 2 and 3. The CFNN performance accuracy is improved by 1.32% and 5.62% compared to NB and [19] respectively as shown in Table 4.

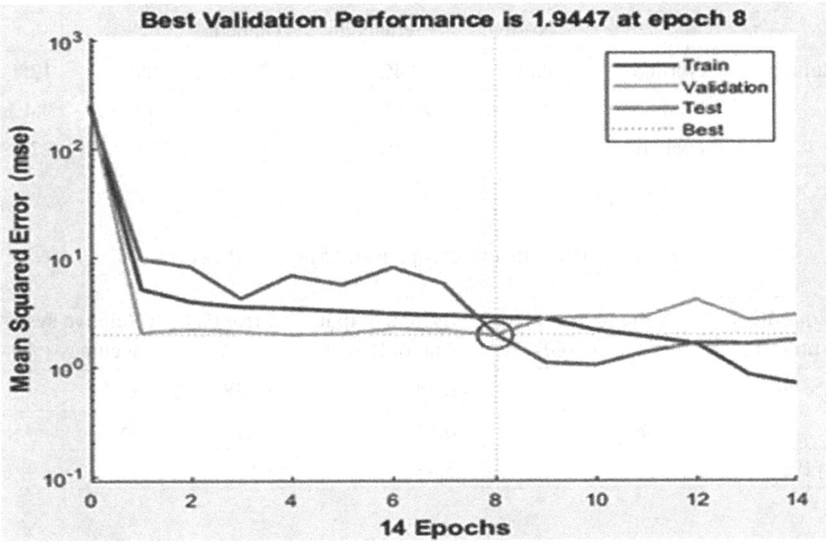

Fig. 6. Best validation performance.

The comparison of CFNN and NB performances to estimate SBP, DBP, PR, and Temp is shown in Table 5. Here, CFNN average actual value of SBP = 121.67 mmHg and system output is 128.82 mmHg; hence, the relative accuracy is 94.12% with error

5.88%. Similarly, the other measurements like DBP, PR and Temp are also shown in Table 2. It shows, CFNN performs better compared to NA for all cases. Hence, CFNN is integrated with GUI and the system for practical use.

For practical measurement of BGCL, SBP, DBP, PR, and Temp (for one specific case) through system with GUI along with the health status is shown in Fig. 7. The 'readings' show BGCL = 6.44 mmol/L with 'status' diabetic; SBP = 128.82 mmHg, DBP = 78.43 mmHg, resulting 'status' pre-high; PR = 86.10 bpm, and Temp = 39.42 °C with 'status' normal by indicating '–'.

Table 2. Accuracy rates of CFNN with TPR and FNR.

		Predicted output			TPR	FNR
		Normal	Prediabetic	Diabetic		
Actual input	Normal	90.6%	7%	2.4%	90.6%	9.4%
	Prediabetic	13%	82%	5%	82%	18%
	Diabetic	7%	7%	86%	86%	14%

Table 3. Accuracy rates of NB with TPR and FNR.

		Predicted output			TPR	FNR
		Normal	Prediabetic	Diabetic		
Actual input	Normal	88%	9.4%	2.6%	88%	12%
	Prediabetic	2.7%	90.6%	6.7%	90.6%	9.4%
	Diabetic	13.3%	9.4%	77.3%	77.3%	22.7%

Table 4. Performance comparison of proposed system.

Random BGCL measurement	Average measured value (mmol/l)	System output (mmol/l)	Error (%)	Relative system accuracy (%)
CFNN	5.68	6.44	13.38	86.62
NB	5.68	6.51	14.7	85.3
Ref. [19]	6.76	5.48	19	81

Table 5. Relative accuracy and system output SBP, DBP, PR and Temp.

Algorithm	Type of measurement	Average measured value (mmol/l)	System output (mmol/l)	Error (%)	Relative system accuracy (%)
CFNN	SBP	121.67 mmHg	128.82 mmHg	5.88	94.12
	DBP	72.48 mmHg	78.43 mmHg	8.21	91.79
	PR	81.34 bpm	86.10 bpm	5.85	94.15
	Temp	37.7 °C	39.42 °C	4.56	95.44
NB	SBP	121.67 mmHg	132.17 mmHg	8.62	91.38
	DBP	72.48 mmHg	81.93 mmHg	13.04	86.96
	PR	81.34 bpm	88.24 bpm	8.48	91.52
	Temp	37.7 °C	40.72 °C	8.02	91.98

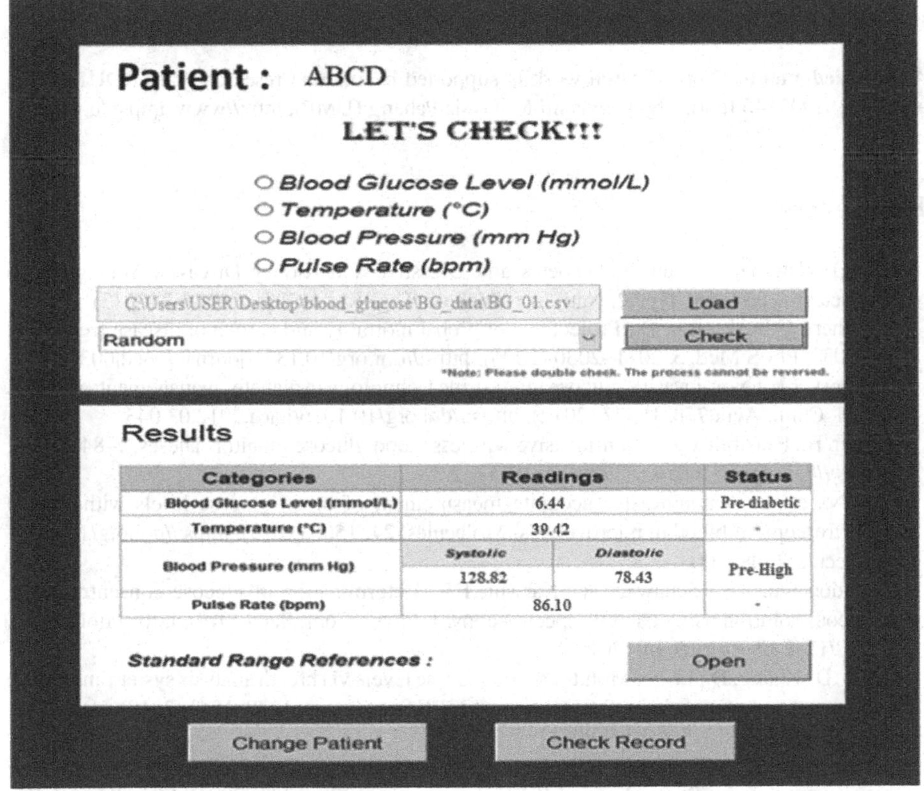

Fig. 7. System health measurement results through GUI.

4 Conclusion

A non-invasive system with enhanced software and GUI for reliable blood glucose concentration level (BGCL) measurement has been presented in this chapter. The UWB transceivers, bio-antennas and software with GUI were used to collect data signal through human ear-lobe. The corresponding physical health status (BGCL, SBP, DBP, PR, and Temp) for each individual were also recorded to determine system accuracy. Four new significant feature vectors (skewness, kurtosis, variance, MAD) were proposed and extracted from received UWB signal to reduce size and related complexity. The extracted features were fed into developed CFNN and NB algorithms individually, and found that CFNN is bit better to enhance BGCL estimation accuracy. Finally, the software with CFNN was integrated with hardware system. It depicts 5.62% higher accuracy compared to similar existing system, by demonstrating its superiority for real-world use. The system is appropriate for domestic-users (at home) due to its user-friendly software module with GUI for regular BGCL monitoring, besides, it is useful in hospitals too. It can measure the BGCL, SBP, DBP, PR, and Temp simultaneously in one go with health status. More data samples and an enhanced deep machine learning is under investigation to further enhance the system efficiency.

Acknowledgments. This research work is supported by internal research grant RDU1703125 and PGRS1903146 funded by Universiti Malaysia Pahang (UMP), http://www.ump.edu.my/.

References

1. (NIH) National Institute of Diabetes and Digestive and Kidney Diseases: Your guide to diabetes; Type 1 and Type 2. Natl. Inst. Diabetes Dig. Kidney Dis. **14**, 1–67 (2013)
2. Mathers, C.D., Loncar, D.: Projections of global mortality and burden of disease from 2002 to 2030. PLoS Med. **3**, 2011–2030 (2006). https://doi.org/10.1371/journal.pmed.0030442
3. Vashist, S.K.: Non-invasive glucose monitoring technology in diabetes management: a review. Anal. Chim. Acta **750**, 16–27 (2012). https://doi.org/10.1016/j.aca.2012.03.043
4. Freer, B.: Feasibility of a Non-invasive wireless blood glucose monitor. Theses. 1–84 (2011). https://doi.org/10.1007/s13398-014-0173-7.2
5. Li, N., et al.: A noninvasive accurate measurement of blood glucose levels with Raman spectroscopy of blood in microvessels. Molecules. **24**, 1500 (2019). https://doi.org/10.3390/molecules24081500
6. Rondonuwu, F.S., Setiawan, A., Karwur, F.F.: Determination of glucose concentration in aqueous solution using FT NIR spectroscopy. J. Phys.: Conf. Ser. (2019). https://doi.org/10.1088/1742-6596/1307/1/012019
7. Guo, D., Zhang, D., Li, N.: Monitor blood glucose levels via breath analysis system and sparse representation approach. In: Proceedings of IEEE Sensors, pp. 1238–1241 (2010). https://doi.org/10.1109/ICSENS.2010.5690611
8. Domschke, A., et al.: Holographic sensors in contact lenses for minimally-invasive glucose measurements. In: Proceedings of IEEE Sensors, pp. 1320–1323 (2004). https://doi.org/10.1109/icsens.2004.1426425
9. Osiecka, I., Pałko, T.: Overview of some non-invasive spectroscopic methods of glucose level monitoring (2016). https://www.infona.pl/resource/bwmeta1.element.baztech-0da018fd-b2ae-4dd6-b9c3-95e925c4ab3b

10. Pickup, J.C., Hussain, F., Evans, N.D., Rolinski, O.J., Birch, D.J.S.: Fluorescence-based glucose sensors. Biosens. Bioelectron. **20**, 2555 (2005). https://doi.org/10.1016/j.bios.2004.10.002
11. Osiecka, I., Pałko, T., Łukasik, W., Pijanowska, D., Dudziński, K.: Impedance spectroscopy as a method for the measurement of calibrated glucose solutions with concentration occurring in human blood. In: Jabłoński, R., Szewczyk, R. (eds.) Recent Global Research and Education: Technological Challenges. AISC, vol. 519, pp. 211–216. Springer, Cham (2017). https://doi.org/10.1007/978-3-319-46490-9_30
12. Arakawa, M., et al.: Red blood cell aggregation measurement with 40-MHz ultrasound has a possibility for noninvasive evaluation of blood glucose level in patients with diabetes. In: IEEE International Ultrasonics Symposium, IUS. IEEE Computer Society (2018). https://doi.org/10.1109/ULTSYM.2018.8580086
13. Li, R., Liu, G., Xia, X., Liu, T., Hu, Z.: The studies of noninvasive blood glucose monitoring using optical coherence tomography. In: Ma, X., Wu, F., Fan, B., Li, X., Zhang, Y. (eds.) 9th International Symposium on Advanced Optical Manufacturing and Testing Technologies: Optical Test, Measurement Technology, and Equipment, p. 44. SPIE (2019). https://doi.org/10.1117/12.2505124
14. Yeh, S.J., Hanna, C.F., Khalil, O.S.: Monitoring blood glucose changes in cutaneous tissue by temperature-modulated localized reflectance measurements. Clin. Chem. **49**, 924–934 (2003). https://doi.org/10.1373/49.6.924
15. FCC News Release. https://transition.fcc.gov/Bureaus/Engineering_Technology/News_Releases/2002/nret0203.html. Accessed 10 Dec 2019
16. Lim, E.G., Wang, Z., Lei, C.U., Wang, Y., Man, K.L.: Ultra wideband antennas - past and present. IAENG Int. J. Comput. Sci. **37**, 1–12 (2010)
17. Topsakal, E., Karacolak, T., Moreland, E.C.: Glucose-dependent dielectric properties of blood plasma. In: 2011 30th URSI General Assembly and Scientific Symposium, URSIGASS (2011). https://doi.org/10.1109/URSIGASS.2011.6051324
18. Xiao, X., Li, Q.: A noninvasive measurement of blood glucose concentration by UWB microwave spectrum. IEEE Antennas Wirel. Propag. Lett. **16**, 1040–1043 (2017). https://doi.org/10.1109/LAWP.2016.2618946
19. Ali, M.S., Shoumy, N.J., Khatun, S., Kamarudin, L.M., Vijayasarveswari, V.: Non-invasive blood glucose measurement performance analysis through UWB imaging. In: 2016 3rd International Conference on Electronic Design, ICED 2016, pp. 513–516. Institute of Electrical and Electronics Engineers Inc. (2017). https://doi.org/10.1109/ICED.2016.7804698
20. Ali, M.S., Khatun, S., Kamarudin, L.M., Shoumy, N.J., Islam, M.: Non-invasive ultra-wide band system for reliable blood glucose level detection. Int. J. Appl. Eng. Res. **11**, 8373–8376 (2016)
21. Reza, K.J., Khatun, S., Jamlos, M.F., Fakir, M.M., Morshed, M.N.: Performance enhancement of ultra-wideband breast cancer imaging system: proficient feature extraction and biomedical antenna approach. J. Med. Imaging Heal. Inf. **5**, 1246–1250 (2015)

Text and Speech Processing

An Investigation and Evaluation of N-Gram, TF-IDF and Ensemble Methods in Sentiment Classification

Sheikh Shah Mohammad Motiur Rahman[1(✉)], Khalid Been Md. Badruzzaman Biplob[1], Md. Habibur Rahman[2], Kaushik Sarker[1], and Takia Islam[1]

[1] Department of Software Engineering, Daffodil International University, Dhaka, Bangladesh
{motiur.swe,takia35-1014}@diu.edu.bd,
{khalid,kaushik.swe}@daffodilvarsity.edu.bd

[2] Department of Information and Communication Technology, Mawlana Bhashani Science and Technology University, Santosh, Tangail, Bangladesh
mdhabibur.r.bd@ieee.org

Abstract. In the area of sentiment analysis and classification, the performance of the classification tasks can be varied based on the usage of text vectorization and feature extraction methods. This paper represents a detailed investigation and analysis of the impact on feature extraction methods to attain the highest classification accuracy of the sentiment from user reviews. Unigram, Bigram and Trigram are applied as n-gram vectorization models with TF-IDF features extraction method individually. Accuracy, misclassification rate, Receiver Operating Characteristics (ROC) and recall-precision are used in this study to evaluate which are counted as the most important performance measurement parameters in machine learning based approaches. Parameters are measured by the output obtained from Bagged Decision Tree (BDT), Random Forest (RF), Ada Boost (ADA), Gradient Boost (GB) and Extra Tree (ET). The outcomes of this study is to find out the best fitted combination of term frequency–inverse document frequency (TF-IDF) and n-grams for different data size.

Keywords: Sentiment classification · N-gram techniques · TF-IDF · Ensemble methods

1 Introduction

The process of identifying the user opinion based on their feedback is termed as sentiment analysis. Behind the concept, the sentiment analysis is to analyze the user feedback and explore the information [1]. Politics, Games, movie industry and healthcare institutions are the application areas of sentiment analysis. In the healthcare industry, the quality of patient care and the supports are analyzed [2].

T. Bhuiyan et al. (Eds.): ICONCS 2020, LNICST 325, pp. 391–402, 2020.
https://doi.org/10.1007/978-3-030-52856-0_31

In terms of politics, public's sentiments are analyzed the result prediction of election towards the candidate selection of political parties [3–5]. Movie industries are trying to find out the strength and weaknesses of the movies based on the viewer's comment by collecting it [6]. Several machine learning algorithms are used to evaluate the performance to find out the optimum result from people's sentiment. Dataset is labeled into numerical values either zero or one while preprocessing in supervised learning. Soon after the preprocessed data has trained the machine to decide and retrieved the significant information, it helps to make the decision [7]. It's much harder to obtain acceptable result in unsupervised learning than supervised learning because of unlabeled data. Several clustering methods are used to provide acceptable result in unsupervised learning [7]. Averaging, boosting and stacking are applied as supervised machine learning approaches to enhance the robustness of supervised learning [8,9]. Aspect level, sentence level and document level classifications are used to investigate the sentiment analysis [10]. Aspect level classification is focused on the whole presented expressions within a document. When sentences are treated as positive and negative review it will be considered as sentence level classification [10]. Every single document containing either a positive or negative review is termed as document level classification. In this work, ensemble machine learning algorithms are used to analyze the performance and find out the best fitted vectorization methods combining with TFIDF feature extraction model for both small and large data size. However, document level classification is focused on the Ensemble Machine Learning Classifiers in this study. This paper is structured as follows: Sect. 2 describes the background and recent research work based on the sentiment analysis. Research methodology is presented in Sect. 3. Results and performances are evaluated in Sect. 4. Finally, Sect. 5 provides the conclusion of the results with future scope.

2 Background and Related Work

In this section, a detailed discussion to the earlier research work on the supervised machine learning algorithms for sentiment classification has been discussed. SVMperf and word2vec method is compared in article [3]. Around 87.10% accuracy achieved in word2vec while 90.30% is found for SVMperf. Lexicon-based and part-of-speech feature selection methods have been used on clothing products dataset in Chinese comment. Valdivia et al. [11] applied the Voting and stacking concept with machine learning algorithm. NRC hashtag sentiment lexicons (HS AffLex and HS NegLex) and NRC sentiment140 lexicons (S140 AffLex and S140 NegLex) are used in manuscript [12]. Document and sentiment classification implemented in Bayesian Logistic Regression (BLR), Support Vector Machine, Naïve Bayes and C4.5. MuchoCine (MC) and Spanish Corpus dataset are used to found the accuracy 88.27%, 88.31%, 88.5%, and 87.66% respectively for the above algorithms. Naïve Bayes, Support Vector Machine and Maximum Entropy classification found 82.7%, 86.1% and 84.85% accuracy respectively [13]. The frequently used movie review dataset is considered the Cornell movie review dataset. Word similarity mapping and Part-of-speech (POS) are considered for selecting features set. Matsumoto et al. [14] used the Polarity and Internet Movie Database (IMDb). For the sentiment classification, document level sentiment analysis is used. Support vector machine (SVM) is applied on those datasets and found 84.6% classification accuracy for Unigram + Bigram while Bigram and Unigram attained 80.4% and 83.7% accuracy respectively. Tripathy et al. [7] have considered CountVectorizer combining with TF-IDF for document label classification for weighted value for the text. Linear Discriminant Analysis (LDA), Random Forest, Support Vector Machine (SVM) and Naive Bayes (NB) machine learning algorithms are used for classifying the sentiment. Accuracy around 92.0%, 95.0%, 94.0% and 89.5% are found respectively for the above mentioned algorithms. Polarity movie review and aclIMDb dataset are used for their achieved accuracy [15,16]. Furthermore, in most of the cases highest accuracy is found into 100% for several classification algorithms. This study tried to find out the highest accuracy on the large and small data size for sentiment classification. Python programming is used to test the accuracy level of Gradient Boost (GB), Ada Boost (ADA), Bagged Decision Tree (BDT), Random Forest (RF) and Extra Tree (ET) machine learning algorithms.

2.1 Unigram

Unigram is the simplest form of language model in which all conditioning context are simply thrown away. Each term is estimated independently. This kind of model is named as unigram language model [17]. Context is ignored by Unigram model:

$$P(w_1 w_2 ... w_n) = P(w_i) \tag{1}$$

Where, w_1 $w_2 ... w_n$ is a sequence of words and P indicates the probability [18].

$$P_{uni}(t_1 t_2 t_3 t_4) = P(t_1)P(t_2)P(t_3)P(t_4) \tag{2}$$

Where, t_1, t_2, t_3, t_4 represent a sequence of terms and P is a symbolic representation of probability [17].

2.2 Bigram

Bigram is much more complex language models which conditions are on the unigram models term [17]. This model adds one word of context:

$$P(w_i | w_1 w_2 ... w_{n-1}) = P(w_i | w_{I-1}) \tag{3}$$

Where, w_1 $w_2 ... w_n$ is a sequence of words and P indicates the probability [18].

$$P_{bi}(t_1 t_2 t_3 t_4) = P(t_1)P(t_2 | t_1)P(t_3 | t_2)P(t_4 | t_3) \tag{4}$$

Where, t_1, t_2, t_3, t_4 represent a sequence of terms and P is a symbolic representation of probability [17].

2.3 Trigram

Trigram is many more complex language models which condition are on the bigram models term. This model adds two words of context:

$$P(w_i|w_1w_2...w_{n-1}) = P(w_i|w_{I-2}|w_{I-1}) \tag{5}$$

Where, w_1 w_2...w_n is a sequence of words and P represents the probability [26].

$$P_{tri}(t_1t_2t_3t_4) = P(t_1)P(t_3|t_2|t_1)P(t_4|t_3|t_2)P(t_5|t_4|t_3) \tag{6}$$

Where, t_1, t_2, t_3, t_4 represent a sequence of terms and P is referred to a representation of probability.

2.4 TF-IDF

TF-IDF (TID) can be formulated by term frequency X inverse document frequency. For producing a composite weight for each term in each of the documents TF-IDF has been used [24]. Term Frequency (TF): The measurement of how continually a term occurs in one document [20].

TF(t) = (The number of times of one term that appears in one document)/(Total number of terms in that document).

Inverse Document Frequency (IDF): It measures how important a term is. All terms are considered equally important during computing TF [21].

IDF(t) = log_e(Total number of documents/Number of documents with term t in it).

$$TF\text{-}IDF = TF(t) * IDF(t) \tag{7}$$

3 Methodology

Sentiment classification has are two types of process: one is binary classification and another is multiclass [4]. In binary classification, each document d_i in D, where D = $d_1, d_2, d_3, ...,d_n$ is classified. A predefined set of reviews category is labeled as R where R = Positive, Negative = 1, 0. In multiclass classification, each document d_i is classified and labeled as R_* where, R_* = strongly positive, positive, neutral, negative, strongly negative [6]. Binary classification has been considered during this investigation. The methodology has been depicted at Fig. 1

3.1 Dataset Used

There are two datasets used in this study. One is collected by Andrew Maas named "Large Movie Review Dataset" [18–22] containing a collection of 50000 IMDb [15] movie review. The movie categories are horror, funny, action, romantic, comedy, fantasy, adventure and science fiction. Maximum 30 reviews per movie are collected in this dataset and an equal number of negative and positive reviews are considered. Less than or equal 4 out of 10 from user rating, is classified as a Negative review and classified as Positive reviews which are greater than or equal 7. Another is "Sentiment polarity datasets" collected by Bo Pang, Lillian Lee [16] consists of a collection of 2000 movie reviews. Neutral reviews are ignored in this dataset.

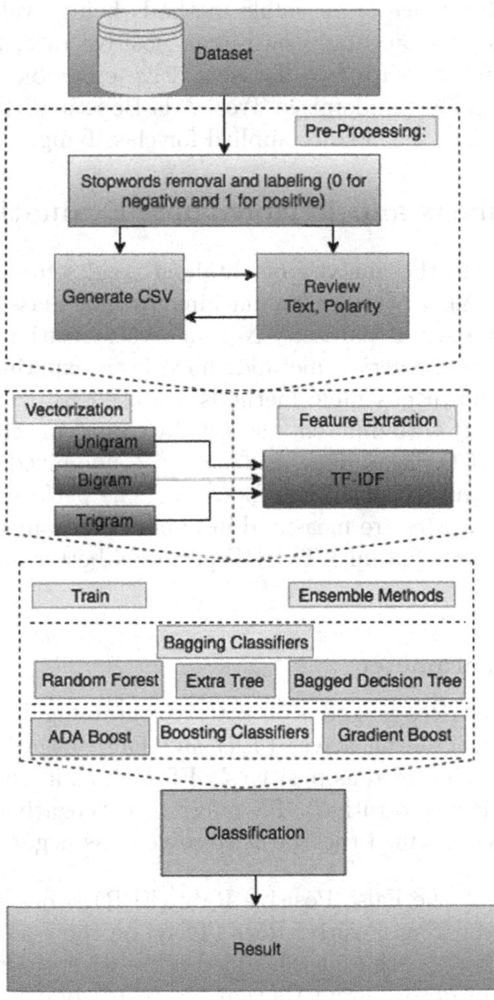

Fig. 1. Overview of investigation and evaluation approach

3.2 Data Preprocessing

Data preprocessing is needed for the performance improvement of classification [23]. In this phase, the stopwords and special characters have been removed. Every document is labeled as positive or negative and generate a CSV file.

3.3 Vector Generation and Feature Extraction

Vector generation of each review using unigram, bigram and trigram (n-gram) and extract features with TF-IDF are performed in this stage. A series of tokens, length n is defined as n-gram [23].

3.4 Train and Classify with Ensemble Methods

After that, the performance of ensemble methods being evaluated by training them and calculating the accuracy rate, true positive rate, false positive rate and misclassification rate with two datasets. Five ensemble methods (Bagged Decision Tree, Extremely Randomized Tree, Ada Boosting, Random Forest and Gradient Tree Boosting) [28–30] are applied for classifying.

4 Result Analysis and Performance Evaluation

This section represents the analysis of obtained results from experiments and evaluates the performance of ensemble machine learning classifiers with the perspective of different sizes of datasets. N-grams vectorization techniques along with TF-IDF (feature extraction method) have been experimented and implemented. Five well-known ensemble methods are used to evaluate the n-grams techniques in this study with different datasets by classifying the sentiment. Used classifiers are Bagged Decision Tree, Extremely Randomized Tree, Ada Boosting, Random Forest and Gradient Tree Boosting. The performances of ensemble machine learning classifiers are measured in paper. Unigram + TF-IDF perform better with ADABoost. Bigram + TF-IDF performs better with the rest of the methods [27].

4.1 Evaluation Parameter

One of evaluation matrices is confusion matrix containing True positives (TP), False positives (FP), True negatives (TN) and False negatives (FN). TP are defined as "correctly identified as positives". FP defined as the "classifiers identified a negative review as positive". TN referred to "negative reviews are identified correctly". FN identified the "positive reviews as negative" [25].

ROC Curve: In ROC, the False Positive Rate (FPR) is one plot on the x-axis and another plot is the True Positive Rate (TPR) on the y-axis. The fraction or the rate of negative reviews that are classified as positive is defined as FPR. The rate or the fraction of positive reviews that are correctly classified is defined as TPR.

Precision-Recall Curve: In Precision-Recall, the x-axis contains one plots called Recall and on the y-axis contains Precision. Recall is defined as same as the TPR. Precision represents the measures of that fraction or rate of reviews classified as positive which are truly positive.

Accuracy: Correctly classified total number of data (ratio) is defined as accuracy.

$$Accuracy = (TP + TN)/(TP + TN + FP + FN) \tag{8}$$

Misclassification Rate: Misclassification Rate is the error rate which is calculated by 1-Accuracy or 100-Accuracy (in percentage).

4.2 Result Analysis

Figure 2, 3 and 4 depict the ROC curve obtained from the Unigram + TF-IDF, Bigram + TF-IDF and Trigram + TF-IDF with ensemble techniques on 2000 data. Figure 5, 6 and 7 represent the Precision-Recall curve of same sequence with 2000 data. Figure 8, 9 and 10 depict the ROC curve obtained from the Unigram + TF-IDF, Bigram + TF-IDF and Trigram + TF-IDF with ensemble techniques on 50000 data. Figure 11, 12 and 13 represent the Precision-Recall curve of same sequence with 50000 data. From these figures, it's been observed that Extra Tree classifier provides 100% accuracy, TPR and Recall. Even Extra Tree classifier provides 0% error rate or misclassification rate with all combinations.

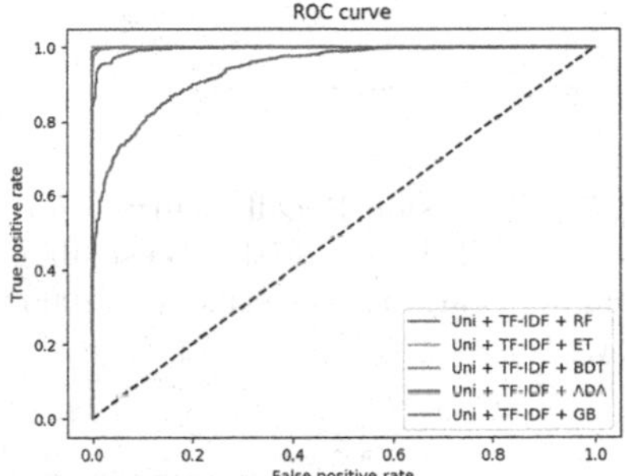

Fig. 2. ROC curve for Unigram + TF-IDF with ensemble machine learning classifiers (2000 Data)

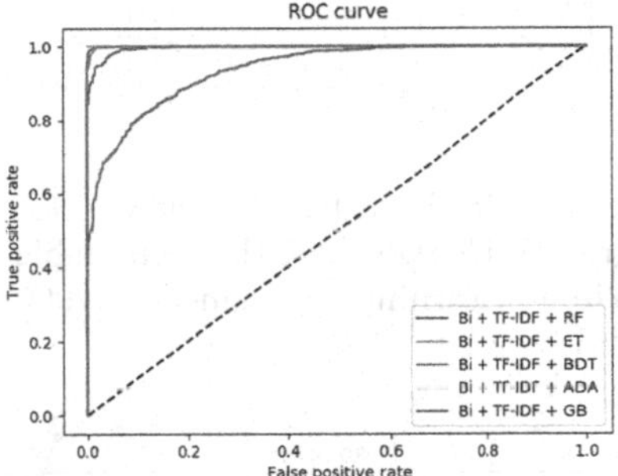

Fig. 3. ROC curve for Bigram + TF-IDF with ensemble machine learning classifiers (2000 Data)

From ROC, Precision-Recall, Accuracy (Table 1 and Table 2), it's been observed that RF classifier provides same performance with unigram + TF-IDF for both datasets. For large dataset, bigram and trigram with RF provides highest outcome. BDT performs almost same with unigram and trigram along with TF-IDF for both datasets. For brigram + TF-IDF, BDT perform better with small dataset. ADA and GB both perform better with small dataset than large dataset. Table 3 and Table 4 represent the comparison of misclassification rate for 2000 and 50000 data respectively.

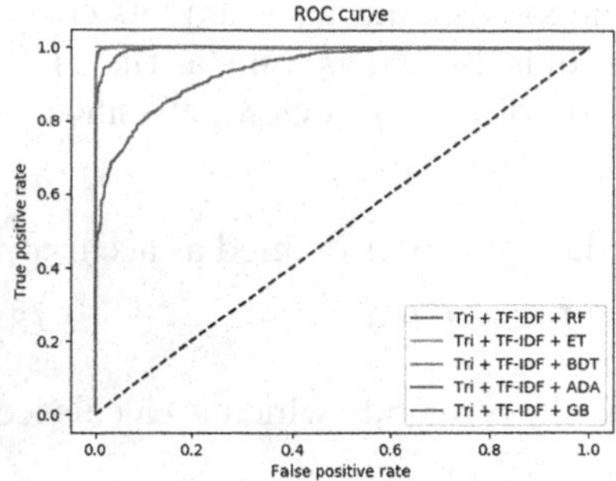

Fig. 4. ROC curve for Trigram + TF-IDF with ensemble machine learning classifiers (2000 Data)

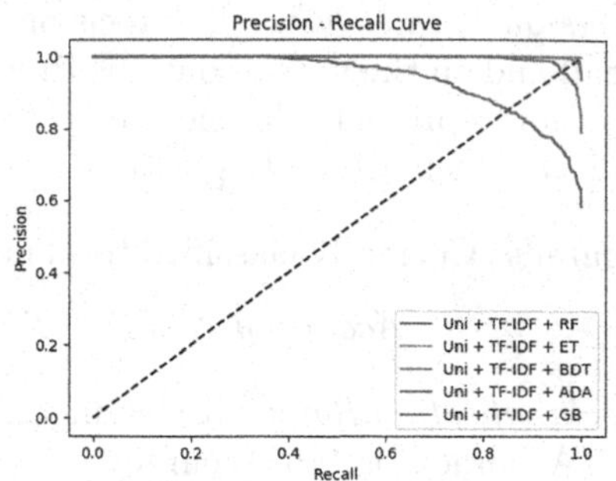

Fig. 5. Precision-Recall curve for Unigram + TF-IDF with ensemble machine learning classifiers (2000 Data)

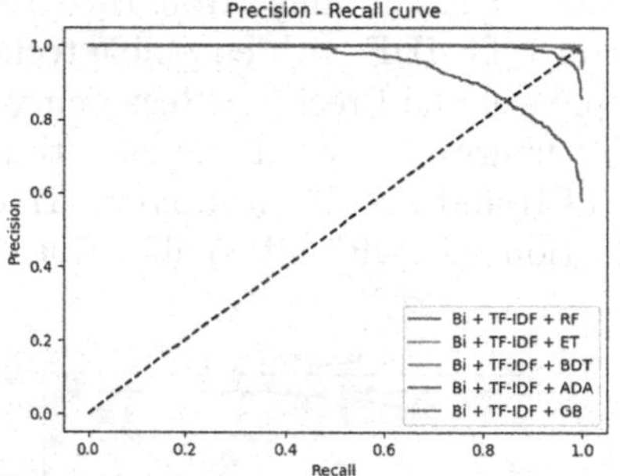

Fig. 6. Precision-Recall curve for Bigram + TF-IDF with ensemble machine learning classifiers (2000 Data)

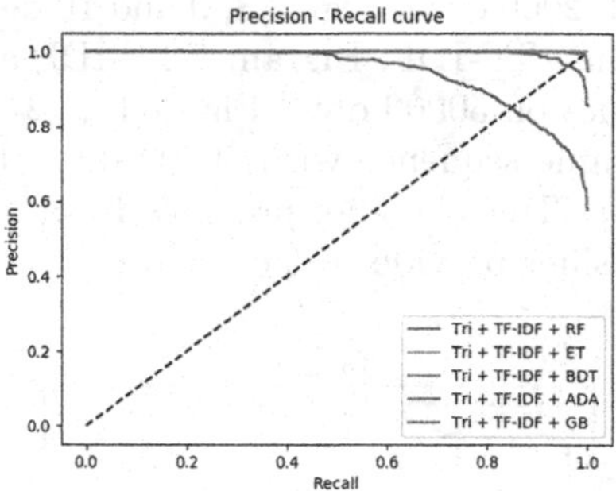

Fig. 7. Precision-Recall curve for Trigram + TF-IDF with ensemble machine learning classifiers (2000 Data)

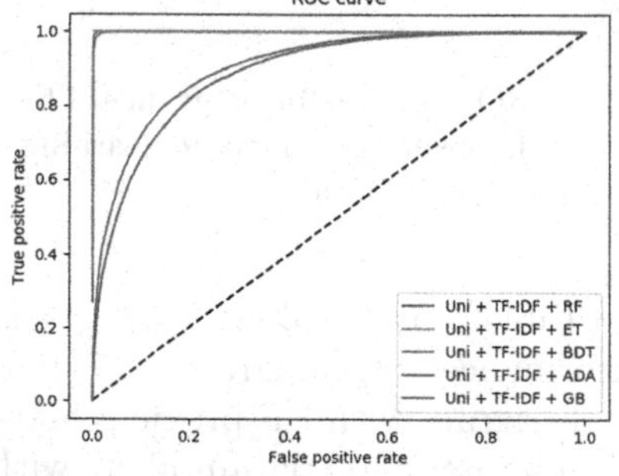

Fig. 8. ROC curve for Unigram + TF-IDF with ensemble machine learning classifiers (50000 Data)

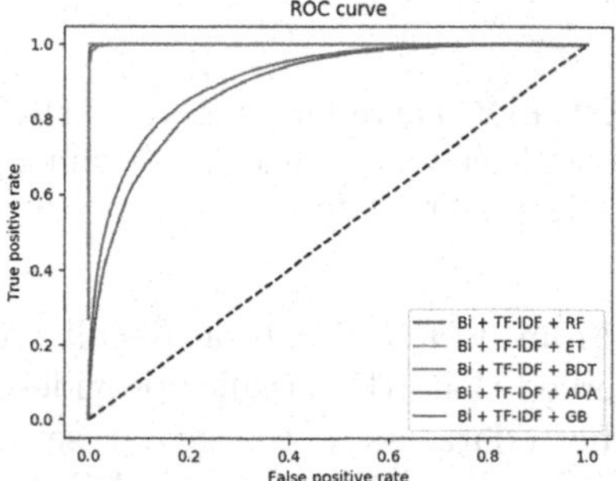

Fig. 9. ROC c3urve for Bigram + TF-IDF with ensemble machine learning classifiers (50000 Data)

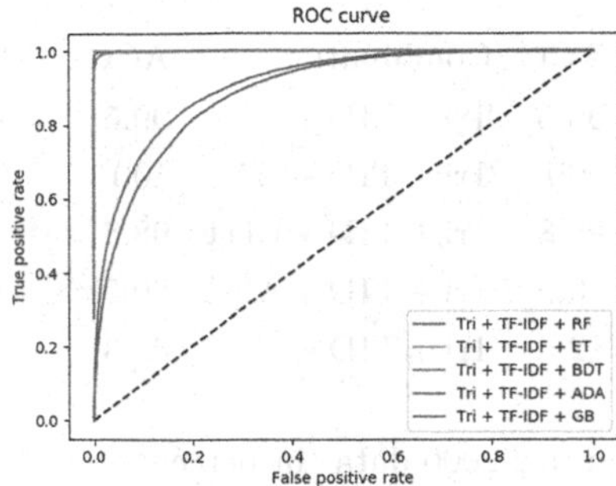

Fig. 10. ROC curve for Trigram + TF-IDF with ensemble machine learning classifiers (50000 Data)

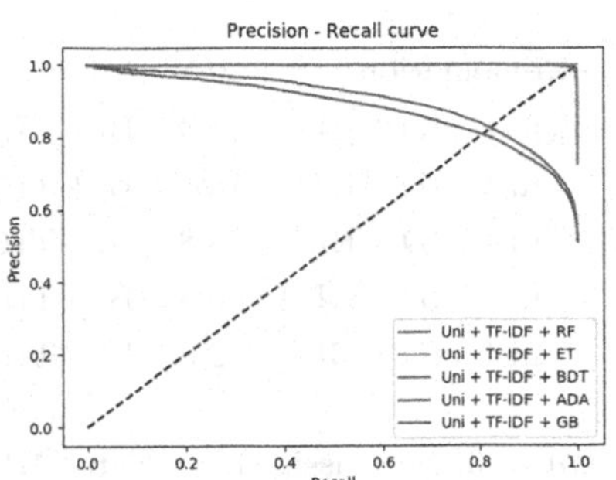

Fig. 11. Precision-Recall curve for Unigram + TF-IDF with ensemble machine learning classifiers (50000 Data)

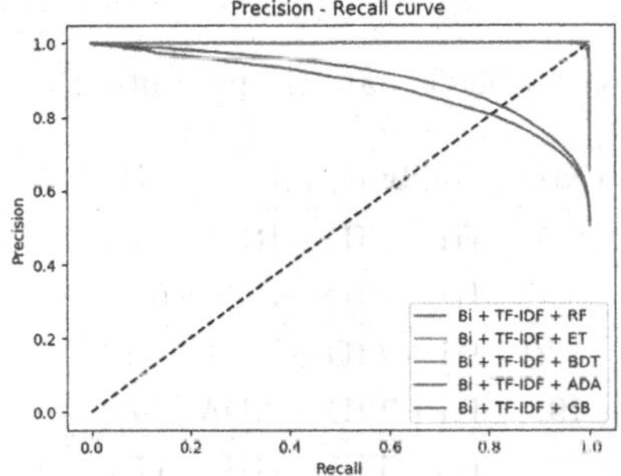

Fig. 12. Precision-Recall curve for Bigram + TF-IDF with ensemble machine learning classifiers (50000 Data)

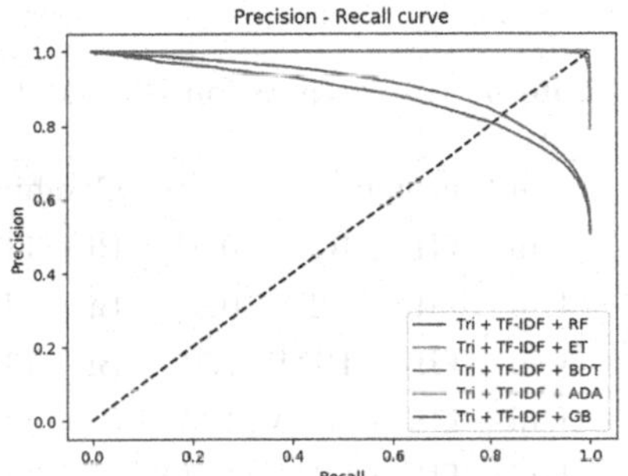

Fig. 13. Precision-Recall curve for Trigram + TF-IDF with ensemble machine learning classifiers (50000 Data)

Table 1. Accuracy-ACC comparison for 2000 data (in percentage).

Combination	ACC	Combination	ACC	Combination	ACC
Uni + TID + RF	99.4	Bi + TID + RF	99.1	Tri + TID + RF	99.2
Uni + TID + ET	100	Bi + TID + ET	100	Tri + TID + ET	100
Uni + TID + BDT	98.3	Bi + TID + BDT	99.2	Tri + TID + BDT	98.8
Uni + TID+ ADA	85.1	Bi + TID + ADA	84.5	Tri + TID + ADA	84.5
Uni + TID + GB	95.5	Bi + TID + GB	96.3	Tri + TID + GB	96.3

Table 2. Accuracy-ACC comparison for 50000 data (in percentage).

Combination	ACC	Combination	ACC	Combination	ACC
Uni + TID + RF	99.4	Bi + TID + RF	99.5	Tri + TID + RF	99.5
Uni + TID + ET	100	Bi + TID + ET	100	Tri + TID + ET	100
Uni + TID + BDT	98.8	Bi + TID + BDT	98.8	Tri + TID + BDT	98.8
Uni + TID + ADA	80.8	Bi + TID + ADA	80.5	Tri + TID + ADA	80.5
Uni + TID + GB	82.0	Bi + TID + GB	82.3	Tri + TID + GB	82.3

Table 3. Misclassification Rate-MR comparison for 2000 data (in percentage).

Combination	MR	Combination	MR	Combination	MR
Uni + TID + RF	0.65	Bi + TID + RF	0.9	Tri + TID + RF	0.85
Uni + TID + ET	0	Bi + TID + ET	0	Tri + TID + ET	0
Uni + TID + BDT	1.75	Bi + TID + BDT	0.8	Tri + TID + BDT	1.2
Uni + TID + ADA	14.9	Bi + TID + ADA	15.5	Tri + TID + ADA	15.5
Uni + TID + GB	4.1	Bi + TID + GB	3.7	Tri + TID + GB	3.7

Table 4. Misclassification Rate-MR comparison for 50000 data (in percentage).

Combination	MR	Combination	MR	Combination	MR
Uni + TID + RF	0.61	Bi + TID + RF	0.53	Tri + TID + RF	0.52
Uni + TID + ET	0	Bi + TID + ET	0	Tri + TID + ET	0
Uni + TID + BDT	1.19	Bi + TID + BDT	1.21	Tri + TID + BDT	1.19
Uni + TID + ADA	19.2	Bi + TID + ADA	19.5	Tri + TID + ADA	19.5
Uni + TID + GB	19.98	Bi + TID + GB	17.7	Tri + TID + GB	17.7

5 Conclusion

The evaluation of n-gram methods with TF-IDF (TID) has been implemented and broadly experimented along with ensemble methods. Figure 1 represents the overview of proposed approach. Figure 2, 3, 4, 8, 9, 10 represent the ROC curve with unigram + TF-IDF, bigram + TF-IDF, trigram_TF-IDF along with the ensemble methods for 2000 and 50000 dataset respectively. The Precision-Recall curve with unigram + TF-IDF, bigram + TF-IDF, trigram_TF-IDF along with the ensemble methods are represented in Fig. 5, 6, 7, 11, 12, 13 represent for 2000 and 50000 dataset respectively. Table 1 and Table 2 represent the comparison of accuracy. Table 3 and 4 represent the error rate. ADA boost and Gradient Boost performs better with small data classification. Random Forest with bigram + TF-IDF and trigram + TF-IDF provide better performance with large dataset. Bagged Decision Tree performs almost the same in all the cases. In future, the scope of this study can further be enhanced by applying the stacked and voting classifier.

References

1. Gautam, G., Yadav, D.: Sentiment analysis of Twitter data using machine learning approaches and semantic analysis. In: Seventh International Conference on Contemporary Computing (IC3), pp. 437–442. IEEE (2014)
2. Elnagar, A., Khalifa, Y.S., Einea, A.: Hotel Arabic-reviews dataset construction for sentiment analysis applications. In: Shaalan, K., Hassanien, A.E., Tolba, F. (eds.) Intelligent Natural Language Processing: Trends and Applications. SCI, vol. 740, pp. 35–52. Springer, Cham (2018). https://doi.org/10.1007/978-3-319-67056-0_3
3. Zhang, D., Xu, H., Su, Z., Xu, Y.: Chinese comments sentiment classification based on word2vec and SVMperf. Expert Syst. Appl. **42**(4), 1857–1863 (2015)
4. Wang, H., Can, D., Kazemzadeh, A., Bar, F., Narayanan, S.: A system for real-time Twitter sentiment analysis of 2012 US presidential election cycle. In: Proceedings of the Association for Computational Linguistics System Demonstrations, pp. 115–120 (2012)
5. Liu, B.: Sentiment analysis and opinion mining. Synth. Lect. Hum. Lang. Technol. **5**(1), 1–167 (2012)
6. Sorostinean, M., Sana, K., Mohamed, M., Targhi, A.: Sentiment analysis on movie reviews (2017)
7. Tripathy, A., Rath, S.K.: Classification of sentiment of reviews using supervised machine learning techniques. Int. J. Rough Sets Data Anal. (IJRSDA) **4**(1), 56–74 (2017)
8. Pedregosa, F., et al.: Scikit-learn: machine learning in Python. J. Mach. Learn. Res. **12**(Oct), 2825–2830 (2011)
9. Ensemble methods. http://scikit-learn.org/stable/modules/ensemble.html
10. Feldman, R.: Techniques and applications for sentiment analysis. Commun. ACM **56**(4), 82–89 (2013)
11. Martín-Valdivia, M.T., Martínez-Cánara, E., Perea-Ortega, J.M., Ureña-López, L.A.: Sentiment polarity detection in Spanish reviews combining supervised and unsupervised approaches. Expert Syst. Appl. **40**(10), 3934–3942 (2013)
12. Arif, M.H., Li, J., Iqbal, M., Liu, K.: Sentiment analysis and spam detection in short informal text using learning classifier systems. Soft. Comput. **22**(21), 7281–7291 (2017). https://doi.org/10.1007/s00500-017-2729-x
13. Xia, R., Zong, C., Li, S.: Ensemble of feature sets and classification algorithms for sentiment classification. Inf. Sci. **181**(6), 1138–1152 (2011)
14. Matsumoto, S., Takamura, H., Okumura, M.: Sentiment classification using word sub-sequences and dependency sub-trees. In: Ho, T.B., Cheung, D., Liu, H. (eds.) PAKDD 2005. LNCS (LNAI), vol. 3518, pp. 301–311. Springer, Heidelberg (2005). https://doi.org/10.1007/11430919_37
15. Large movie review dataset. https://ai.stanford.edu/~amaas/data/sentiment/
16. Movie review data. http://www.cs.cornell.edu/people/pabo/movie-review-data/
17. Types of language models. https://nlp.stanford.edu/IR-book/html/htmledition/types-of-language-models-1.html
18. Language modeling. https://web.stanford.edu/class/cs124/lec/languagemodeling.pdf
19. Tf-idf. http://www.tfidf.com/
20. Croft, W.B., Metzler, D., Strohman, T.: Search Engines: Information Retrieval in Practice, vol. 283. Addison-Wesley, Reading (2010)
21. Manning, C.D., Raghavan, P., Schütze, H.: Introduction to Information Retrieval, vol. 1, no. 1, p. 496. Cambridge University Press, Cambridge (2008)

22. Tang, H., Tan, S., Cheng, X.: A survey on sentiment detection of reviews. Expert Syst. Appl. **36**(7), 10760–10773 (2009)
23. Maas, A.L., Daly, R.E., Pham, P.T., Huang, D., Ng, A.Y., Potts, C.: Learning word vectors for sentiment analysis. In: Proceedings of the 49th Annual Meeting of the Association for Computational Linguistics: Human Language Technologies, vol. 1, pp. 142–150. Association for Computational Linguistics (2011)
24. Ahmad, F.K.: Comparative analysis of feature extraction techniques for event detection from news channels' Facebook page. J. Telecommun. Electron. Comput. Eng. (JTEC) **9**(1–2), 13–17 (2017)
25. Davis, J., Goadrich, M.: The relationship between Precision-Recall and ROC curves. In: Proceedings of the 23rd International Conference on Machine Learning, pp. 233–240. ACM (2016)
26. N-gram language models. http://lintool.github.io/UMD-courses/CMSC723-2009-Fall/session9-slides.pdf
27. Rahman, S.S.M.M., Rahman, M.H., Sarker, K., Rahman, M.S., Ahsan, N., Sarker, M.M.: Supervised ensemble machine learning aided performance evaluation of sentiment classification. J. Phys: Conf. Ser. **1060**(1), 012036 (2018)
28. Rana, M.S., Rahman, S.S.M.M., Sung, A.H.: Evaluation of tree based machine learning classifiers for android malware detection. In: Nguyen, N.T., Pimenidis, E., Khan, Z., Trawiński, B. (eds.) ICCCI 2018. LNCS (LNAI), vol. 11056, pp. 377–385. Springer, Cham (2018). https://doi.org/10.1007/978-3-319-98446-9_35
29. Motiur Rahman, S.S.M., Saha, S.K.: StackDroid: evaluation of a multi-level approach for detecting the malware on android using stacked generalization. In: Santosh, K.C., Hegadi, R.S. (eds.) RTIP2R 2018. CCIS, vol. 1035, pp. 611–623. Springer, Singapore (2019). https://doi.org/10.1007/978-981-13-9181-1_53
30. Sohan, M.F., Rahman, S.S.M.M., Munna, M.T.A., Allayear, S.M., Rahman, M.H., Rahman, M.M.: NStackSenti: evaluation of a multi-level approach for detecting the sentiment of users. In: Prateek, M., Sharma, D., Tiwari, R., Sharma, R., Kumar, K., Kumar, N. (eds.) NGCT 2018. CCIS, vol. 922, pp. 38–48. Springer, Singapore (2019). https://doi.org/10.1007/978-981-15-1718-1_4

Aspect Based Sentiment Analysis in Bangla Dataset Based on Aspect Term Extraction

Sabrina Haque[1(✉)], Tasnim Rahman[1(✉)], Asif Khan Shakir[1(✉)], Md. Shohel Arman[1], Khalid Been Badruzzaman Biplob[1], Farhan Anan Himu[1], Dipta Das[1], and Md Shariful Islam[2]

[1] Department of Software Engineering, Daffodil International University, Dhaka, Bangladesh
{haque35-1235,tasnim.swe,asif.swe,arman.swe, himu.swe}@diu.edu.bd, Khalid@daffodilvarsity.edu.bd, diptadas73@gmail.com

[2] Institute of Information Technology, University of Dhaka, Dhaka, Bangladesh
shariful.islam@iit.du.ac.bd

Abstract. Recent years have seen rapid growth of research on sentiment analysis. In aspect-based sentiment analysis, the idea is to take sentiment analysis a step further and find out what exactly someone is talking about, and then measuring the sentiment if she or he likes or dislikes it. Sentiment analysis in Bengali language is progressing and is considered as an important research interest. Due to scarcity of resources like proper annotated dataset, corpora, lexicon such as part of speech tagger etc. aspect-based sentiment analysis hardly has been done in Bengali language. In this paper, we have conducted our experiments based on a recent work from 2018 using conventional supervised machine learning algorithms (RF, SVM, KNN) to perform one of the ABSA's tasks - aspect category extraction. The work is done on two datasets named – *Cricket* and *Restaurant*. We then compared our results with the existing work. We used two traditional steps to clean data and found that less preprocessing leads to better F1 Score. For Cricket dataset, SVM and KNN performed better, resulting F1 score of 37% and 27%. For Restaurant dataset, RF and SVM achieved improved score of 35% and 39% respectively. Additionally, we selected two more algorithms LR and NB, LR achieved best F1 score (43%) for Restaurant dataset among all.

Keywords: Supervised machine learning · Sentiment analysis · Aspect Based Sentiment Analysis (ABSA) · ABSA dataset in Bangla · Aspect category extraction

1 Introduction

We are in the age of internet where every day we generate over 2.5 quintillion of data [1] and sentiment analysis has become one of the key tools for making sense of these user generated data. Sentiment Analysis (SA) (or Opinion Mining) is a field regarding NLP (Natural Language Processing) that builds systems which generally tries to extract

T. Bhuiyan et al. (Eds.): ICONCS 2020, LNICST 325, pp. 403–413, 2020.
https://doi.org/10.1007/978-3-030-52856-0_32

opinions within text in natural language understanding [2]. Even SA has occupied a wide area in the real-world applications and both business importance and academic interest [3]. The typical sentiment analysis generally focuses on predicting the overall polarity (positive or negative or neutral) of the given sentence.

If we imagine having a large dataset that contains feedbacks of customers from various sources like social media, online reviews or customer's online surveys. e.g. "Food is decent but service is so bad", it is evident that the sentiment towards food is positive however contains a powerful negative sentiment towards facet service. So, after classifying the overall sentiment, existence of a strong negative sentiment would neglect the positive fact that food was actually good [3]. But to make the information more helpful and get a complete picture, the nitty-gritty of each feedback must be retrieved. To solve this issue Aspect Based Sentiment Analysis (ABSA) comes up being an advanced tool to make it possible to analyze these reviews and predict opinions not only for an overall feedback, but also on an aspect-level [4].

ABSA task has been added since 2014 in the annual SemEval (Semantic Evaluation, a reputed workshop in the NLP domain) competition [3]. SemEval has introduced a complete dataset in English for the ABSA task and later they expanded it in multi-lingual datasets in which eight languages over seven domains were included [5]. Datasets of several languages, such as Arabic, Czech, and French were created to perform ABSA. Moreover, there are plenty of powerful libraries like NLTK, Textblob and Spacy that have become major part while performing SA or ABSA. Also, they've published benchmark datasets Restaurant and Laptop [6] with gold annotations.

In SemEval 2014 [7] ABSA's task was divided into four subtasks-

Aspect term Extraction - An aspect term refers to a particular aspect of the target entity [8]. Aspect term extraction is returning a list containing all distinct aspect terms from a set of sentences with pre-identified entities (E) e.g., (restaurants; laptop) by identifying the aspect terms e.g. (delicious; hard-disk).

Aspect Term Polarity - From a given set of aspect terms within a sentence, determining whether the polarity of each aspect term is positive, negative, neutral or conflict [8].

Aspect Category Detection - From a predefined set of aspect categories e.g. (food, display), identifying the aspect categories discussed in a given sentence [8]. Aspect categories are typically crude comparing with the aspect terms of and they do not necessarily occur as terms in the given sentence.

Aspect Category Polarity - From a set of pre-identified aspect categories e.g. (food; display), determine the polarity (positive, negative, neutral or conflict) of each aspect [8].

While performing ABSA, it involves around two crucial tasks – 1) extracting the specific areas or aspects, 2) identifying the polarity for every aspect. As one sentence or review might contain different polarities [5], an overall decision will not be beneficial every time. Aspect extraction is necessary to first deconstruct sentences into product features and after the task is done only then assign a separate polarity value to each of these features. There are several approaches in previous studies that has already been developed to perform ABSA in English and some other languages that includes supervised, semi supervised, unsupervised approaches, rule-based approaches and more. Most of the approaches were machine learning centric [3, 9].

In early 2010 ABSA was introduced as a framework titled "aspect-based sentiment analysis" [10] address the problem of getting only the overall sentiment from a sentence where aspect refers to a component or attribute of an entity.

One of the first studies for both explicit and implicit aspects extraction from product reviews, proposed a rule-based approach [11]. Two popular review datasets (Restaurant and Laptop) were used for evaluating the system where the proposed framework achieved highest precision of 94.15% among their five kind of review categories.

In SemEval 2014 ABSA's task is divided into before mentioned four subtasks [7]. Also, they've published benchmark datasets Restaurant and Laptop with gold annotation [6]. With continuation of SemEval 2014, in 2015 an aspect category extraction was modeled as a multiclass classification problem with features based on n-grams, parsing, and word clusters. SVM with a linear kernel was trained for category extraction [4]. The highest F-1 scores in both datasets are 50.86% and 62.68% respectively.

In another work CNN has been adopted in work of Wang's aspect-based sentiment analysis [3]. They have introduced a combined model with aspect prediction and sentiment prediction that left behind the highest scores achieved by the wining team in SemEval 2015. There F1 score was 51.3%.

Above discussed reviews are done regarding English language. If we highlight some other languages for ABSA then language, Arabic [12], Czech [13], French [14], Hindi [15] can be mentioned. Czech language is progressing very successfully in ABSA and several label corpora has been built both for supervise and unsupervised training, morphological tools and lexicons. For aspect term extraction both rule-based and machine learning algorithms were applied on the new dataset that consists of segments from user reviews of IT products [13]. 65.70% and 30.27% F1 score were achieved for short-term and long-term reviews. In another work the authors introduced two new corpora in Czech language to attempt ABSA for both supervised and unsupervised training [16]. The four subtasks of ABSA have been done where word clusters are created and used as features. F1 score came out of 71.4% and 71.7% for aspect term and aspect category extraction.

Regarding Hindi language a new dataset has introduced that includes several domains [15]. CRF and SVM are used for aspect term extraction and sentiment analysis. The average F1-score is 41.07% for aspect term extraction and accuracy is 54.05% for sentiment classification.

Bengali is the 7th most spoken languages in the world [17]. People are using it frequently over the social media for expressing reviews, sentiments or feedbacks. But there is no proper dataset available and very few works have been done regarding ABSA. Very recently in 2018, an annotated dataset to perform ABSA has been published in Bengali language where the authors have "extracted aspects", one of the SemEval 2014 tasks [5, 7]. The dataset contains two domains - Cricket and Restaurant. SVM, RF and KNN classifiers has been used and highest F1 score of 34% and 42% has been achieved from Cricket and Restaurant domains. Bengali language is far behind and remains un-explored due to very less availability and lack of various resources and tools such as annotated corpora, lexicons, Part-of-Speech (PoS) tagger etc. that plays vital role while performing ABSA. Therefore, the concentration of this paper is to use the annotated dataset from [5] and perform ABSA's aspect extraction task to take ahead the possibilities of ABSA's aspect category extraction in Bengali language. We have used supervised machine learning algorithms SVM, RF, KNN, LR, and NB. We have also compared our results with the previous work by [5] (Table 1).

Table 1. Example of aspect based sentiment analysis (cricket & restaurant dataset)

	Review Text	Aspect Category	Polarity
Original Text	বোলাররা যে পরিমানে শর্ট বল দিচ্ছে তাতে রান কত বেশি হয় সেটাই দেখার বিষয়	**Bowling**	**Negative**
Translated	It is a matter of watching how much runs the bowler is making in the short ball	**Bowling**	**Negative**
Original Text	যদিও খাদ্য ভালো ছিল পরিবেশনা ছিল বিশ্রী	**Service**	**Negative**
Translated	Although the food was good, the serving was awkward	**Service**	**Negative**

Rest of the paper is organised as follows: Sect. 2 presents the proposed model, Sect. 3 depicts the experimental results and discusses on the major findings based on the experimental results. Finally, Sect. 4 concludes the paper with future research leads with some future indications.

2 Methodology

The methodology proposed on this paper is divided into following sections: data collection, data preprocessing, data analysis and visualizing the outcome. The proposed model of this research is shown in Fig. 1 where the steps are introduced respectively.

2.1 Dataset Collection

We have used the datasets created for ABSA and specially designed for aspect term and polarity extraction for the first time in Bengali [5] by Md. A.R and Emon K.D, 2018 (https://github.com/AtikRahman/Bangla_ABSA_Datasets). The two different datasets, are named, Cricket dataset and Restaurant dataset.

Cricket dataset consists of human-annotated user comments with five different aspect categories - bowling, batting, team, team management, and other. On the other hand, Restaurant dataset is an abstractly translated in Bengali form of the SemEval 2014's

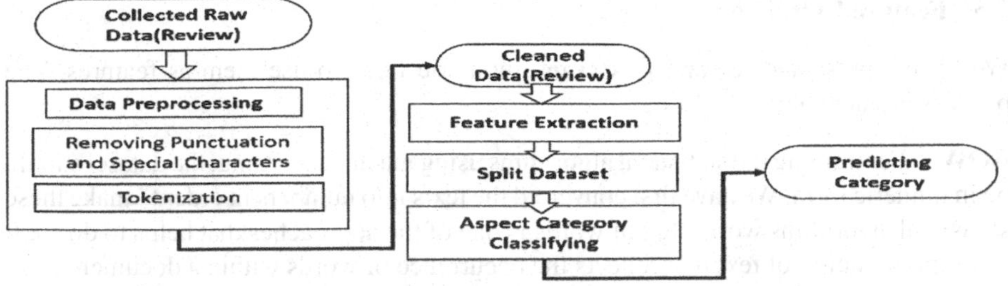

Fig. 1. Proposed model for aspect based sentiment analysis

English dataset [4], consisting five aspect categories-Food, Price, Service, Ambiance, and Miscellaneous. To make the overall of understanding of the datasets (Cricket and Restaurant) a complete statistic has been presented in Table 2.

Table 2. Overall statistics of both datasets

Dataset	No. of reviews	Aspect category	Polarity
Cricket	2979	Batting Bowling Team management Other	Positive (19%) Negative (72%) Conflict (9%)
Restaurant	2059	Food Price Service Ambiance Miscellaneous	Positive (59%) Negative (23%) Conflict (12%) Neutral (6%)

2.2 Data Preprocessing

Data preprocessing plays a vital role on text analysis to make the model understand the data. Text data contains a lot of noise and as a result, it's a challenge to clean the texts. Data pre-processing reduces the size of the input text documents significantly and is done by various steps:

1) ***Removing special characters:*** Removed the special characters as they sometime create confusion, we feel in these kind of Bengali datasets special characters will lead to complexity for classification.
2) ***Removing punctuations:*** One of the very popular and often applied preprocessing is removing punctuations. Even the full-stop "." in Bengali language refers to "।" sign. So, we have removed punctuations.

2.3 Feature Extraction

We have represented reviews (texts) into numeric form to use them as features. The process is stated here:

BOW - For training the statistical algorithms using machine learning, the dataset should be in numeric form. We have first converted the texts into numbers in order to make these statistical algorithms work. Bag of words is one of the approaches that helps to do so. It is a representation of text that reflects the occurrence of words within a document [18].

TF-IDF - It is almost a similar approach like BOW but has little different idea behind it. It is evident that it has two terms, where TF (Term Frequency) refers to the number of times a word occurs in a document and IDF (Inverse Document Frequency) refers to how important the word is in the document [19]. The equation for TF and IDF given bellow-

$$\mathbf{TF(t)} = (\text{Number of times term t appears in a document}) / (\text{Total number of terms in the document})$$

$$\mathbf{IDF(t)} = \text{log\_e (Total number of documents} / \text{Number of documents with term t in it)}.$$

We have used sklearn library [20] that contains the TFiDfVectorizer class which has been used to convert the features into TF-IDF feature vectors. We have set the limitation of maximum features to 2500. It only uses the 2500 most frequently occurring words to create BOW feature vector. For classification we have passed the known label corresponding to the review (Table 3).

Table 3. Sample Bengali pre-processed data

Original Review	সময় বাংলাদেশের ভাগ্য ড্র রেখেছে, নাহয় হার চাড়া উপায় ছিলোনা.!!
Processed Review	সময় বাংলাদেশের ভাগ্য ড্র রেখেছে নাহয় হার চাড়া উপায় ছিলোনা
Tokenization	‘সময়’ ‘বাংলাদেশের’ ‘ভাগ্য’ ‘ড্র’ ‘রেখেছে’ ‘নাহয়’ ‘হার’ ‘চাড়া’ ‘উপায়’ ‘ছিলোনা’
Uni-gram	সময়’ ‘বাংলাদেশের’.‘ভাগ্য’ ‘ড্র’ ‘রেখেছে’ ‘নাহয়’ ‘হার’ ‘চাড়া’ ‘উপায়’ ‘ছিলোনা’

2.4 Fitting Algorithm to Train

Finding a well-performing machine learning algorithm for a particular dataset is a challenging task. We went through "Trial and Error" process to determine a sufficient list of algorithms that works on these datasets. We studied several algorithms that has been using for ABSA [5, 7, 21–23]. Finally, we have selected frequently used following algorithms for classifying-

1. As we want to compare result with [5] we used same algorithms SVM (Support vector machine), RF (Random Forest) and KNN (K-Nearest Neighbor)
2. Algorithms not used in [5], LR (Logistic Regression) and NB (Naïve Bayes).

Logistic Regression (LR) is an appropriate regression analysis to act on dichotomous variable (binary variable). To describe data and to explain the relationship between one dependent binary variable and one or more nominal, ordinal even interval level independent variables we have used logistic regression [24].

On the contrary, Naive Bayes classifier is surprisingly a powerful algorithm for predictive modeling. We selected NB as it has often been used in sentiment analysis as it remains less affected by data scarcity and text classification tasks [25, 26].

2.5 Languages and Tools

The system is implemented using Python 3 (Jupyter NoteBook) in Anaconda. The Python modules skLearn - which provides a set of modules for machine learning and data mining [16] is used. For NLP tasks NLTK (A leading platform for building Python programs and rich with libraries to perform NLP tasks [27]) has been used.

3 Results and Discussion

3.1 Split Dataset

Working with supervised machine learning requires the dataset to be split into two parts, training set and testing set. In this work the data split has been done by a split function named Train_test_split function which is imported from scikit-learn library [16]. We used 80% of dataset for training and 20% for testing.

3.2 Aspect Category Classifying

We have provided the experimental average results of precision, recall, and F1 score for the classification task using supervised machine learning algorithms SVM, RF, KNN, LR and NB, calculating from both of the dataset's different aspect categories, in Table 4. To represent the results, precision, recall and F1-score terms have been used and the measurements are done using four parameters - true positive (tp), true negative (tn), false positive (fp) and false negative (fn).

Table 4 denotes the overall confusion matrix of the experimental results for aspect category extraction using RF, SVM, KNN, LR and NB for both Cricket and Restaurant

Table 4. Results experiments using RF, SVM, KNN, LR & NB

Dataset	Algorithm	Precision	Recall	F1 score
Cricket	RF	0.39	0.36	**0.37**
	SVM	0.40	0.35	0.35
	KNN	0.27	0.27	0.27
	LR	0.41	0.34	0.34
	NB	0.23	0.27	0.18
Restaurant	RF	0.70	0.27	0.35
	SVM	0.79	0.30	0.39
	KNN	0.39	0.38	0.38
	LR	0.42	0.43	**0.43**
	NB	0.25	0.26	0.17

datasets. From this the experimental results can be depicted from five algorithms performed on Cricket and Restaurant dataset. For Cricket dataset, the precision rate from Logistic regression is highest, which is 41%, and the recall rate from Random Forest is highest, 36%. As in this particular problem for aspect category extraction, both precision and recall are important, thus, we can see Random Forest has given the highest F-1 score, 37%.

Similarly, for the Restaurant dataset, both Logistic Regression provided the highest precision score, 42% and recall score 43% resulting highest F-1 score of 43%. The other algorithms such as RF, SVM and KNN also performed well with F1-Score of 35%, 39% and 38%.

For both of the Cricket and Restaurant dataset, NB algorithm performed significantly low with the F1-Score of 18% and 17%.

It is apparent that in Cricket dataset the scores for RF, LR and SVM are comparatively better in overall. KNN and NB performed less comparative to other algorithms.

Conversely, in the case of Restaurant dataset results, SVM, and LR provided the highest result for the Restaurant dataset.

Table 5 and Table 6 shows the comparison among our experimental results and the results achieved from [5] for both cricket and restaurant dataset on different algorithms. For Cricket dataset, the F1 score from our experiment is 35% from SVM and 27% from KNN resulting higher score than [5], where the previous results for both algorithms were 34% and 25% respectively. However, RF provided same result as [5], which is 37%.

From Table 5, the results for restaurant dataset can be outlined. SVM and RF algorithms has given better F1 Score than previous one, 39% and 35%, where the previous results were 38% and 33% for these algorithms. In this case, KNN performed less than the previous one resulting F1 score of 38%, lower than 42%.

From the experimental results and discussions we can conclude that our experiments have provided improved results than the previous work [5] and we have eliminated some preprocessing steps. As a result this less preprocessing leads to better F1 score in both dataset. Aspect category extraction is a multi-label classification problem [5] where one opinion might carry several categories. Hence, our supervised classifiers might skip some

Table 5. Model performance comparison of cricket dataset

Model	Precision (previous result)	Precision (our result)	Recall (previous result)	Recall (our result)	F1 score (previous result)	F1 score (our result)
SVM	.71	.40	0.22	0.35	0.34	0.35
KNN	.45	.27	0.21	0.27	0.25	0.27
RF	.60	.39	0.27	0.36	0.37	0.37

Table 6. Model performance comparison for restaurant dataset

Model	Precision (previous result)	Precision (our result)	Recall (previous result)	Recall (our result)	F1 score (previous result)	F1 score (our result)
SVM	0.77	0.79	0.30	0.30	0.38	0.39
KNN	0.54	0.39	0.34	0.38	0.42	0.38
RF	0.64	0.70	0.26	0.27	0.33	0.35

of these aspect categories. Better results can be attained, if we can train the datasets in more advanced way using POS tagging.

4 Conclusions and Recommendations

In this study we have used conventional supervised aspect category model of machine learning with less preprocessing. We used two traditional steps to clean data and achieved better results comparing ABSA Bangla dataset's paper for both of the dataset. The advanced researchers use better and detailed dataset for ABSA these days which results high accuracy. More detailed annotated dataset like SemEval for Bengali language can lead to impressive results.

Moreover, sentiment analysis is getting popular for spam review/comment detection and fraud app detection these days. So, increasing research with more non-English languages and aspects can lead to more precise notion about users and their reviews that can help to make better business decision as well as improve cyber security.

Besides, unsupervised approaches have been seen to build good enough impact on ABSA even in different language like Czech. However, in this trend, very effective deep learning powerful neural networks model can lead to more satisfying work and results in ABSA proven in the paper comparing with SemEval 2015 task. In future, we would like to explore more advanced techniques of deep learning (CNN) applied in NLP for ABSA for both aspect category and sentiment analysis extraction. Also, we would like to use Bangla POS tagger to train model in aspect term extraction and train classifier with more preprocessing steps.

References

1. Data never sleeps 5.0. https://www.domo.com/learn/data-never-sleeps-5
2. MonkeyLearn. https://monkeylearn.com/sentiment-analysis/#what-is-sentiment-analysis
3. Wang, B., Liu, M.: Deep learning for aspect-based sentiment analysis. Report cs224, Stanford University (2015)
4. Pontiki, M., Galanis, D., Papageorgiou, H., Manandhar, S., Androutsopoulos, I.: SemEval-2015 task 12: aspect based sentiment analysis. In: 9th International Workshop on Semantic Evaluation (SemEval 2015), pp. 486–495. Association for Computational Linguistics, Denver (2015). https://doi.org/10.18653/v1/s15-2082
5. Rahman, M.A., Dey, E.K.: Datasets for aspect-based sentiment analysis in Bangla dataset. MDPI J. **3**(2), 15 (2018). https://doi.org/10.3390/data3020015
6. Pontiki, M., Bakagianni, J.: SemEval-2014 ABSA Test Data (Gold Annotations Corpus). http://metashare.elda.org/repository/browse/semeval-2014-absa-test-data-gold-annotations/b98d11cec18211e38229842b2b6a04d77591d40acd7542b7af823a54fb03a155/
7. Pontiki M., Galanis, D., Pavlopoulos, J., Papageorgiou H., Androutsopoulos I., Manandhar S.: SemEval-2014 task 4: aspect based sentiment analysis. In: 8th International Workshop on Semantic Evaluation (SemEval 2014), pp. 27–35. Association for Computational Linguistics (2014). https://doi.org/10.3115/v1/s14-2004
8. Hercig, T., Brychc, T., Svoboda, L., Konko, M., Konko, M.: Unsupervised methods to improve aspect-based sentiment analysis in Czech. Comput. Sist. **20**(3), 365–375 (2016). https://doi.org/10.13053/cys-20-3-2469
9. Hasib, T., Rahin, S.A.: Apsect-based sentiment analysis using Semeval and Amazon datasets. Academic thesis Paper, BRAC University (2017)
10. Thet, T.T., Na, J.C., Khoo, C.S.G.: Aspect-based sentiment analysis of movie reviews on discussion. J. Inf. Sci. **36**(6), 823–848 (2010). https://doi.org/10.1177/0165551510388123
11. Poria, S., Cambria, E., Ku, L.W., Gui, C., Gelbukh, A.: A rule-based approach to aspect extraction from product reviews. In: 2nd Workshop on Natural Language Processing for Social Media (SocialNLP), pp. 28–37. Association for Computational Linguistics and Dublin City University, Ireland (2014) https://doi.org/10.3115/v1/w14-5905
12. Smadi, M.A., Qawasmeh, O., Talafha, B., Quwaider, M.: Human annotated arabic dataset of book reviews for aspect-based sentiment analysis. In: 3rd International Conference on Future Internet of Things and Cloud, pp. 726–730. IEEE, Italy (2015). https://doi.org/10.1109/ficloud.2015.62
13. Tamchyna, A., Fiala, O., Veselovská, K.: Czech aspect-based sentiment analysis: a new dataset and preliminary results. In: Information Technology Application Theory (ITAT 2015), vol. 1422, pp. 95–99. CEUR-WS, Slovakia (2015)
14. Apidianaki, M., Tannier, X., Richart, C.: Datasets for aspect-based sentiment analysis in French. In: Tenth International Conference on Language Resources and Evaluation (LREC 2016), pp. 1122–1126. European Language Resources Association (ELRA), Portorož (2016)
15. Akhtar, M.S., Ekbal, A., Bhattacharyya, P.: Aspect based sentiment analysis in Hindi: resource creation and evaluation. In: Tenth International Conference on Language Resources and Evaluation (LREC 2016), pp. 2703–2709. European Language Resources Association, Portorož (2016)
16. Sklearn. https://pypi.org/project/sklearn/
17. Bengali Language. https://en.wikipedia.org/wiki/Bengali_language
18. Gentle introduction to the bag-of-words model. https://machinelearningmastery.com/gentle-introduction-bag-words-model/
19. Panchal, A.: Text Summarization using TF-IDF. Towards Datascience. https://towardsdatascience.com/text-summarization-using-tf-idf-e64a0644ace3

20. Sklearn.feature_extraction.text.TfidfVectorizer. https://scikit-learn.org/stable/modules/generated/sklearn.feature_extraction.text.TfidfVectorizer.html
21. Hamdan, H., Bellot, P., Bechet, F.: Lsislif: CRF and logistic regression for opinion target extraction and sentiment polarity analysis. In: 9th International Workshop on Semantic Evaluation (SemEval 2015), pp. 753–758. Association for Computational Linguistics, Denver (2015). https://doi.org/10.18653/v1/s15-2128
22. Mubarok, M.S., Adiwijaya, Aldhi. M.D.: Aspect-based sentiment analysis to review products using Naive Bayes. In: AIP Conference, vol. 1867 (2017). https://doi.org/10.1063/1.4994463
23. Chowdhury, S., Chowdhury, W.: Performing sentiment analysis in Bangla microblog posts. In: 2014 International Conference on Informatics, Electronics & Vision (ICIEV), pp. 1–6, IEEE, Dhaka (2014). https://doi.org/10.1109/iciev.2014.6850712
24. Korkmaz, M., Güney, S., Yigiter, S.Y.: The importance of logistic regression implementations in the Turkish livestock sector and logistic regression implementations/fields, Turkey (2012)
25. Ismail, H., Harous, S., Belkhouche, B.: A comparative analysis of machine learning classifiers for Twitter sentiment analysis. Res. Comput. Sci. **110**, 71–83 (2016). https://doi.org/10.13053/rcs-110-1-6
26. Jurafsky, D.: Language modeling, index of class cs124/lecture. Stanford University (2018)
27. NLTK 3.4.4 documentation. https://www.nltk.org/. Accessed 22 May 2019

Development of a Tangent Based Robust Speech Feature Extraction Model

Mohammad Tareq Hosain[1], Abdullah Al Arif[1], Ahmed Iqbal Pritom[1(✉)], Md Rashedur Rahman[2], and Md. Zahidul Islam[1]

[1] Green University of Bangladesh, Dhaka, Bangladesh
mtareqhosain@gmail.com, arif.cse.gub@gmail.com, {iqbal,zahid}@cse.green.edu.bd

[2] Islamic University of Technology, Gazipur, Bangladesh
bishad19@iut-dhaka.edu

Abstract. An accurate speech recognition system requires close observation of the selection of an error-free speech feature extraction model. This paper describes a prominent solution to obtain robust features from the sound spectrum and ensures the easy recognition of speech. The proposed architecture uses Tangent based (TB) auditory feature extraction that aims to find and process robust features from the sine wave of auditory signal data. This experiment suggests that every specific tune carries distinguishing signal patterns in the spectrum diagram and hence does the tangent of the amplitude of the same signal. To recognize the sound, a single attribute had been used rather than using multiple attributes where the slope of the sound spectrum being calculated.

Keywords: Tangent based (TB) feature extraction · Sound spectrum · Signal processing · Speech recognition

1 Introduction

Humans have an unparalleled physical ability to be engaged in sophisticated vocal communication. Our vocal folds, combined with the articulators, produces a perplexing arrangement of the tune, namely “Speech”, which can be considered as information if interpreted correctly. The speech production process includes vent, voice and elocution [6]. Undoubtedly, speech is the most contributing factor in linguistic messaging. It should be noted that the ingenuousness with which humans speak is in contrast to the complication of the process.

Voice spectrogram, commonly known as voiceprint is a sophisticated way to display speech signal which can differ by a wide margin due to different attitude of voiced and fricative sounds [1]. The complex process of analyzing voiceprint generally gets subdivided into a Front-End and a Back-End process. The Front-End process deals with necessary prepossessing and feature extraction modules while Back-End handles the classification of sound [16].

Supported by Green University of Bangladesh.

T. Bhuiyan et al. (Eds.): ICONCS 2020, LNICST 325, pp. 414–425, 2020.
https://doi.org/10.1007/978-3-030-52856-0_33

A good combination of these two processes ensures improved accuracy for several look-alike tasks associated with signal recognition i.e. differentiating isolated and connected words, analyzing spontaneous vs. discrete signals and distinguishing between speaker-independent and dependent voices [12].

Because of their complex computational model, several feature extraction models couldn't gain extensive pragmatic use even after presenting a sound solution to accomplish almost identical tasks performed by traditional methods [10,11]. Momentous performance boost of neoteric processors opens possibilities for the re-evaluation of the customary solutions while electing application-specific speech features. These features can be categorized into four groups namely Continuous, Qualitative, Spectral and Teager energy operator (TEO) based [14].

Every individual word spoken by humans has a specific pattern of the spectrum and none of these spectra has an exact match with each other. Moreover, their tangent between the average amplitude throughout time is also similar and can be used as a distinct feature. In this paper, several words and their spectrum have been analyzed. Some general steps such as filtering, framing and leveling were followed before going through feature extraction. Based on the spectrum and following these general steps, a novel feature extraction algorithm has been proposed. Finally, the values retrieved from the Tangent based feature extraction method were used to determine the accuracy of the system.

This paper is organized as follows. Section 2 presents the background analysis on the domain knowledge. The system recognition process and proposed methodology are illustrated in Sect. 3. In Sect. 4, we presented several performance evaluation techniques. We concluded the paper with some valuable discussions in Sect. 5.

2 Related Works

Proposing a new speech feature extraction technique requires meticulous attention to details in the previously established solutions. In this section, we have gone through both conventional and contemporary feature extraction models along with their area of applicability, advantages, and drawbacks.

Mel frequency cepstral coefficients (MFCC) is the most supreme and comprehensively used method for feature extraction that mainly represents the vocal belt data. It is well known for its wide range of applications in speech recognition and speaker identification. Mel-Scale generates two different types of frequency spacing scheme namely Linear spacing for below 1000 Hz and Logarithmic spacing for above 1000 Hz [3].

Although logarithmic frequency spacing enables MFCC to provide the most precise approximation than other feature extraction techniques, it gets seriously exposed to dealing with continuous, intermittent and low-frequency noises [2,8].

Regression oriented sound features can be generated by a prediction based feature extraction method called Linear Predictive Coding (LPC). This technique not only shows great prudence in approximating an incoming sample by observing the linear combination of previously examined n-samples but also provides accurate parameters of speech with good computational speed [5].

In [13], authors provided strong evidence that without finding an optimal order of LPC for frames like music, silence and background noises, the basic task of speech to frame conversion can be turned into a cumbersome process. Moreover, research has shown that without integrating a weighting function with conventional LPC or LPCC, extracting features from stuttered speech can be highly error-prone and time consuming [7]. Several other drawbacks of LCP like the occurrence of residual error and incapability to analyze local events demand an alternative Spectral speech feature extraction technique.

The success rate of Pattern recognition heavily depends on transformation invariance. Often it becomes tremendously difficult for Principal Component Analysis (PCA) to model several instances of a single character because of variation in shape, size, and orientation of an object, the diabolo network of PCA is utterly forced to learn the pattern of each instance separately. Tangent distance analysis between net input can resolve the issue by generating an objective function that guarantees efficient incorporation of transformation invariance [6].

Passing a normalized image as input through the system and extracting comparatively difficult features like hybrid curves is a challenging issue in image processing. Addressing this issue, a novel idea of tangent and secant based structure construction was proposed to recalculate hybrid curve information in terms of angle [15].

Tangential vectors play a significant role in Pitman Stroke Pattern recognition [9]. This Text Identification System requires straight and quarter circle strokes discrimination to recognize a shorthand language. The tangent based approach came in handy in such a case where a series of tangent feature values (TFV) were combined to form derived feature value (DFV) in identifying shapes in a stroke.

3 Proposed System

This section explicitly illustrates the speech recognition process along with our proposed feature extraction method. The system process block diagram is shown in Fig. 1. There are many procedural actions in this system and every action has an essential part in this system as well. The procedural actions are recording speech, initial processing, feature extraction, and finally classification to justify the accuracy of speech recognition.

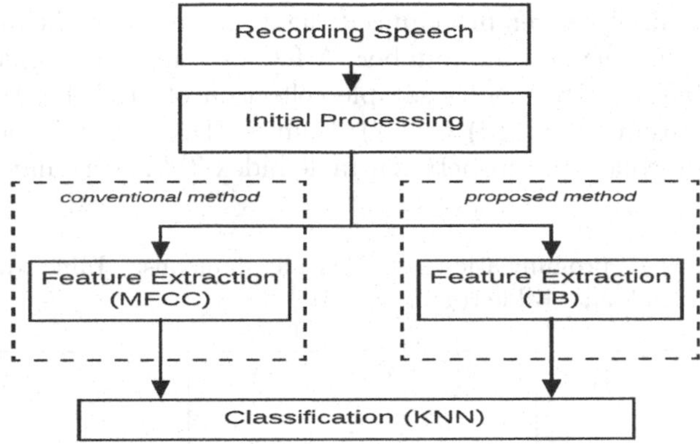

Fig. 1. Conceptual block diagram of proposed speech feature extraction system

3.1 MFCC

Many feature extraction models are being used for speech recognition. In this study, Mel Frequency Cepstral Coefficients (MFCC) was used. MFCC represents a human's speech signal as a feature vector and it has established its effectiveness. The basic computation steps of MFCC is portrayed in Fig. 2.

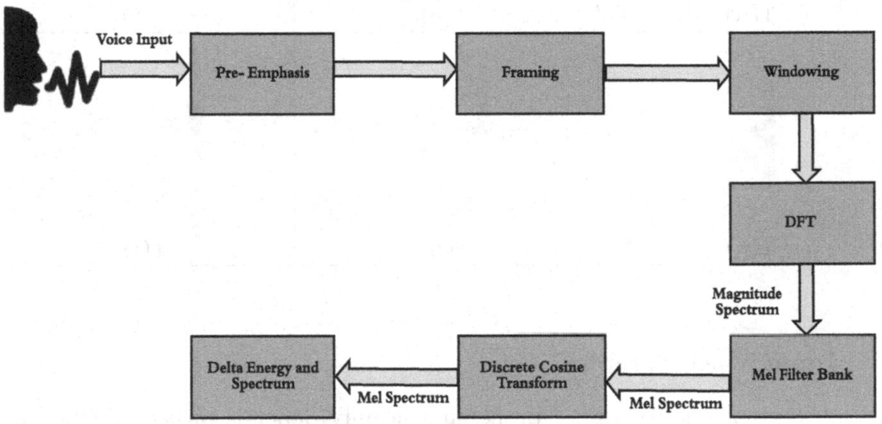

Fig. 2. Block diagram of computation steps in MFCC

3.2 Proposed Methodology

Every specific speech shows a tangible pattern in signal spectrum. Our elementary target was to find robust features through rigorous analysis of some selective Bengali tunes. That's why we primarily collected auditory samples of first 3 Bengali numerals. '1', '2' and '3' are pronounced as **"Ek"**, **"Dui"** and

"Tin" in Bengali. Whoever pronounced the numbers, it explicates nearly the same paradigm for the specific number. A few of collected samples are shown in Table 1. Table 1(a)–1(c) shows sample collection of "Ek" i.e. '1' in Bengali. Similarly, data from Table 1(d) to 1(f) delimits "Dui" i.e. '2' and Samples of "Tin" i.e. '3' are collocated in between table index Table 1(g) and 1(i).

Table 1. Iterative pronunciation of Bengali numerals: Table 1(a)–1(c) "Ek", Table 1(d)–1(f) "Dui" and Table 1(g)–1(i) "Tin"

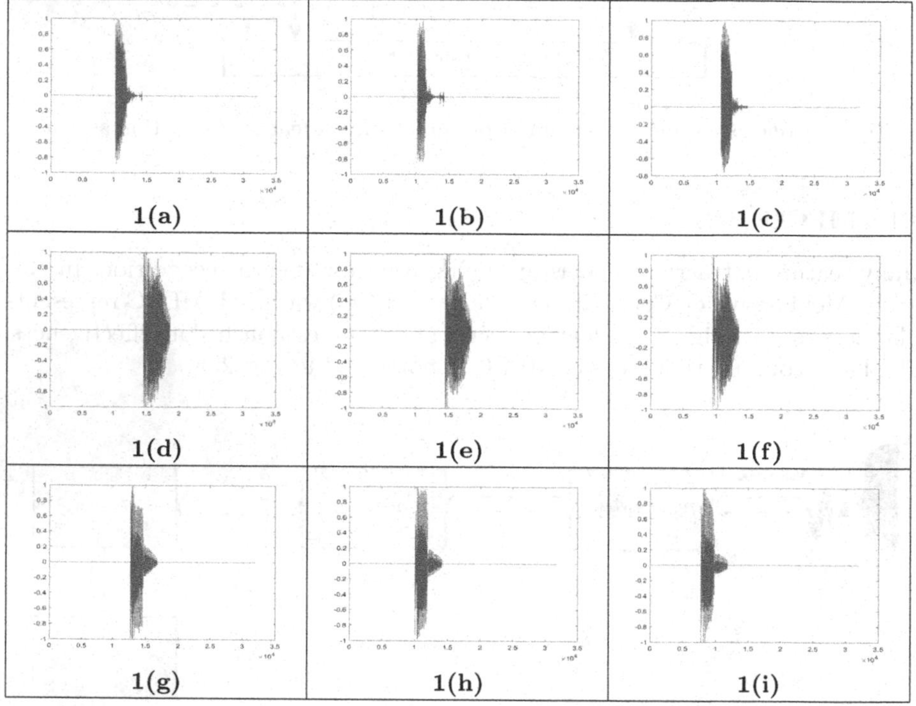

1(a)	1(b)	1(c)
1(d)	1(e)	1(f)
1(g)	1(h)	1(i)

3.3 Input Voice Samples

The strategy of quality signal processing heavily depends on well-defined and pre-packaged data sets. Subtle misleading features that may have a significant negative impact in resolving challenging issues like simultaneous recognition of speech and speaker, may be resulted if data extraction and classification procedure are not accompanied by a large data set to learn from. Analyzing the possible scenario, we determined to develop a mid-scale dataset. We considered the dataset establishment section as the initial stage of this methodology.

The unavailability of the audio dataset for Bengali numerals forced us to generate a new dataset to work with. In this process, we collected analog signal data from 400 participants (ages in between 21 and 45) who were engaged in 3 sessions to provide sample input of 3 numerals i.e. **"Ek"**, **"Dui"** and **"Tin"** in Bengali. From each participant, we collected 4/5 samples on average for every single numeral and discarded all accept one, considering issues like signal strength and noise. Thus our final data set consisted of 1200 samples and 400 for each numeral.

3.4 Filtering

In Fig. 3, a sample filtered spectrum of 3 different tones has been displayed. The audio spectrum is presented as a continuous signal where X-axis denotes the required time for complete signal acquisition and Y-axis represents the amplitude of a signal. This step takes the input data set to refine data from noises. The sample voice was taken within 2 s up to 16 khz using the mono channel and 8 bits per sample data. Though the duration of time was too short still there were so many noises in the sample data. To collect noise-free auditory samples, the starting point started with a higher amplitude of input sample voice data and the ending point ended until that amplitude dropped significantly. The speaker spoke "1", "2" and "3" (in Bengali) which has shown in three different spectra. In the first spectrum, the recording of sample audio data started at point A and ended at point B. The duration was also 2 s from point A to B. So, X is a point when the amplitude started to become high and Y is another point when the amplitude started to become low. Here X to Y is a raw data set which is filtered data set and this filtered data set is used in the following process of framing.

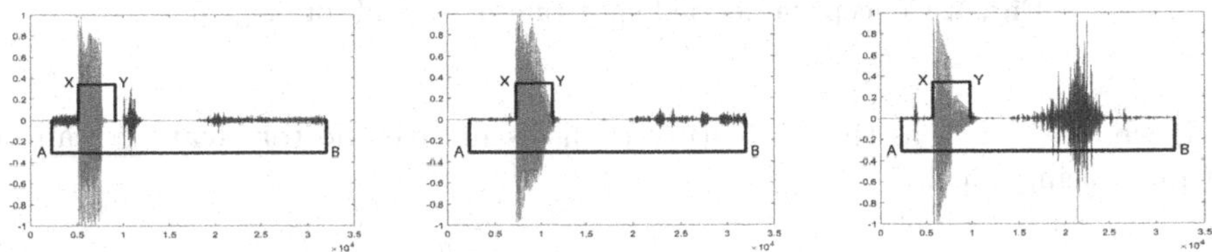

Fig. 3. Filtered spectrum of 1, 2 & 3 (in Bengali)

3.5 Framing

In the framing process, the filtered data were partitioned into successive shorter segments of the one-dimensional array as a cohesive unit of values. As the amount of frames increases, the dimension of both accuracy and function increases as well. In this study, the number of frames is chosen with our expedient number.

3.6 Leveling

The average of data throughout the frames of the filtered audio data is level. And then we got the level of the spectrum. The number of stairs and the number of frames are the same. Let us consider y_i is the level and there are k samples per frame. So we can present the average of i iterations using Eq. 1.

$$y_i = \sum_{j=k*i}^{\{k*(i+1)\}-1} \frac{rD(j)}{k} \qquad [i = 0, 1, 2, 3...] \tag{1}$$

Here, rD is the array of filtered raw data and j is the index of this array.

3.7 Tangent Determining

This is the final stage of our methodology to extract feature and the features are tangents between the levels of the spectrum.

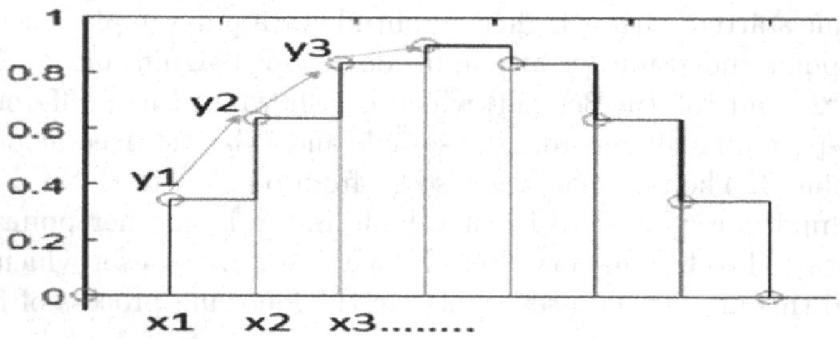

Fig. 4. Conceptual leveled spectrum of an auditory signal

If we consider f_i as the ith feature then distinctive auditory features can be obtained using Eq. 2.

$$f_i = (\tan\theta)_i = \frac{y_{i+i} - y_i}{x_{i+i} - x_i} \tag{2}$$

After placing the value of y_i from (1) into (2) we get,

$$f_i = \frac{\sum_{j=k*(i+1)}^{\{k*(i+2)\}-1} \frac{rD(j)}{k} - \sum_{j=k*i}^{\{k*(i+1)\}-1} \frac{rD(j)}{k}}{x_{i+1} - x_i} \tag{3}$$

Here, $x_{i+1} - x_i$ is the number of samples per frame, k.

Hence, replacing $x_{i+1} - x_i$ with k offers us to finalize a complete equation to generate robust tangent based features.

$$f_i = \frac{\sum_{j=k*(i+1)}^{\{k*(i+2)\}-1} \frac{rD(j)}{k} - \sum_{j=k*i}^{\{k*(i+1)\}-1} \frac{rD(j)}{k}}{k} \tag{4}$$

Based on the calculations, we finally proposed a new algorithm based on tangent calculation. The flowchart of this algorithm is shown in Fig. 5.

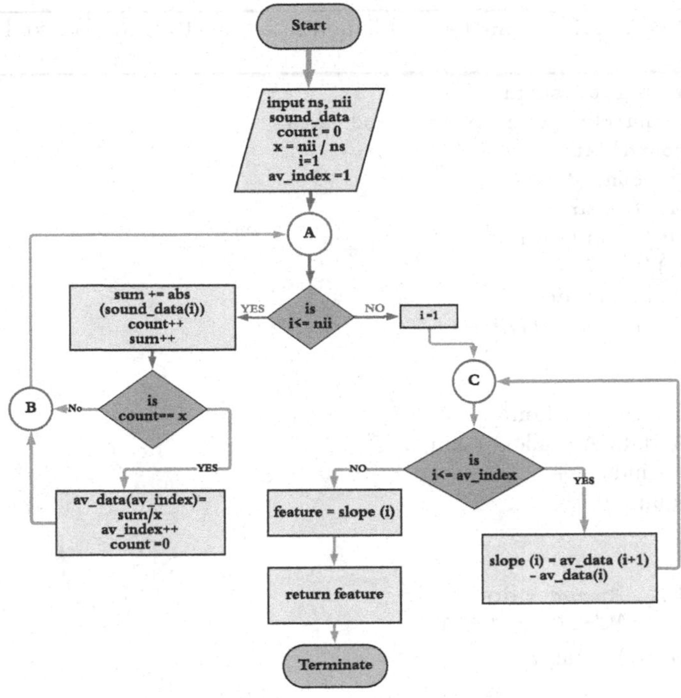

Fig. 5. Proposed TB algorithm

3.8 Proposed Algorithm

Algorithm 1 can be considered as an epitome to illustrate the sequential processes undertaken to design our feature extractor. Here, nf denotes the intended number of frames. The number of frames influences the classification accuracy of input sound data. If the result is not up to the mark or in case the system does not give a good accuracy then we need to increase the number of frames to retrieve more features which will help to classify with more accuracy. $n(rD)$ is another variable that contains the number of the index of filtered sound data. It depends on the input audio. rD refers to input filtered audio. It is a linear array. It stores all the amplitude values over the input period sequentially. The variable count is used as a counter of the index. And *Avindex* is used to store the index number of *Avdata*. Variable *Avdata* is used to store the total average of data throughout the frames of the filtered audio data. Consequently, *Avdata* simply denotes the average of the amplitude of input audio data of each $n(rD)/nf$ index. Therefore, we obtained a one-dimensional array of homogeneous auditory information.

There are two loops in this algorithm. The first loop iterates till the last index of audio data and calculates *Avdata*. The second loop works until the last index of *Avindex* and determines tangent values. So this segment of code should be considered cardinal for our feature extraction model.

Algorithm 1: Algorithm for Implementation of Tangent Based Feature Extraction

```
/* nf=number of sample                              */
/* n(rD)=number of index of sound data              */
/* rD=sound data                                    */
/* input sound data                                 */
/* output feature                                   */
count = 0, Av_index=1
k = n(rD)/nf
for i = 0.........nii do
    sum=sum+ abs (rD(i))
    count++
    i++
    if (count==x) then
        Avdata(Av_index)=sum/x
        Av_index++
        count=0
    end
end
for i = 1.......Av_index do
    tan(i) = (Avdata(i+1)-Avdata(i))/k
    feature(i) = tan(i)
    i++
end
```

4 Performance Evaluation and Result

To analyze the performance of different classifiers on the sample audio data set, experiments were conducted with 10 fold cross-validation method using open-source data mining tool WEKA. The dataset was further justified by MFCC after being single-handedly evaluated by an independent classifier. Meticulous attention to detail was required to find the best suited classifying algorithm for proper justification. We settled upon Naive Bayes as the independent classifier while KNN was selected to perform a comparative study between conventional feature extractor and our proposed tangent based feature extractor. The comparison between feature extraction method MFCC and our proposed tangent based method will be discussed in this section.

4.1 Naive Bayes Analysis

The evaluation process involves the Naive Bayes classifier as an independent classifier. This classifier worked way better for this data set. The accuracy we found using this classifier is 84.67% over 140 instances and three classes. To get accuracy, 10 fold cross-validation was used. The accuracy of 84.67% is a good performance for a novel method in general.

4.2 Comparison with an Existing Method

The feature extraction using MFCC found 13 feature dimensions accompanied by 13 delta coefficients from each MFCC feature dimensions which resulted in a total of 26 dimensions for each speech signal. In order to perform feature data classification process using a computationally intensive KNN algorithm, we were in need to determine k amount of closest neighbor or if explicitly stated, the value of K to justify the accuracy of our feature extraction process. The determination of the exact k value would influence the accuracy of the speech recognition system. The determination of k value was set using cross-validation in the dataset by trying some k values (3–32) to the system, and then we observed the accuracy which is elucidated in Table 2.

Table 2. The effect of k values on accuracy using TB proposed method and KNN classifier

Value of K	Accuracy of MFCC (%)	Accuracy of TB (%)
3	86.43	88.67
4	84.29	85.34
5	84.29	85.34
8	85.0	76.67
12	83.57	76.0
16	82.41	75.34
20	83.57	71.34
24	80.71	70.67
28	80.0	71.34
32	81.43	71.34

MFCC would increase the accuracy system of the speech recognition system so that the feature amount used was 26 dimensions. System testing is done by dividing the dataset into training data and test data using k-fold cross-validation. The best accuracy result of Tangent based method is 88.67%. The accuracy has increased comparing the usual conventional MFCC method with the proposed TB method. It also could decrease the feature data dimension. Because the TB method used only 20 feature dimensions.

Figure 6 showed the comparison result among tow methods; those are the usual conventional MFCC method with 26 feature dimension data and TB with 20 feature dimension data. TB improves the accuracy of the conventional MFCC method from 86.43% to 88.67% with decreasing data dimensions from 26 to 20.

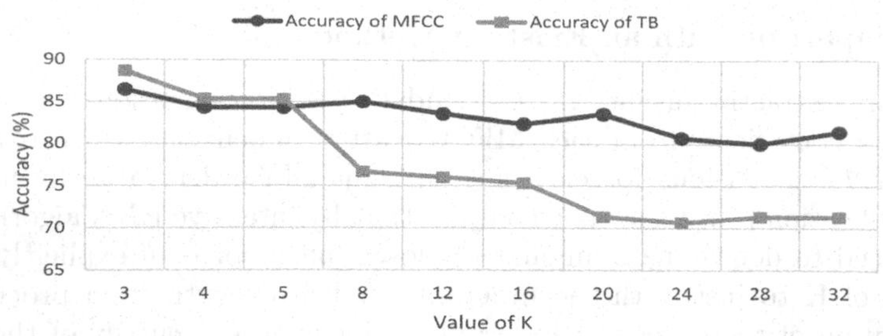

Fig. 6. Comparison between MFCC method and TB method

5 Conclusion and Future Works

Our model proposes the extraction of features as a part of the dimensionality reduction method based on the tangent value of the auditory spectrum. Extracted features play a significant role in speech classification in terms of improving accuracy. The more we use a generalized feature from the original data set, the more we increase the probability to obtain the best performance from the classifier. Tangent value calculation for sound spectrum generated appropriate characteristics for model building thereby decreases training times and avoids overfitting. This system aims to extract multiple features from a spectrum of a specific speech. A small value of k implies that noise will have a greater impact on the outcome and therefore in Fig. 6, compared to MFCC, the accuracy of Tangent based approach has suddenly fallen down when the value of K was set to 8 and above. We investigated the startling incident and found ***curse of dimensionality*** [4] as the leading cause behind the outcome. The performance of the classifier decreases when the dimensionality of the problem becomes too large. The smaller the size of the training data, the fewer features should be used. But in this system, extracted features were so many and on the other hand training data were not so many. This system would give better accuracy if the curse of dimensionality was avoided. Though it's a new approach of feature extraction it has satisfying accuracy over other algorithms with limited training data. This proposed methodology will surely come up with better efficiency when a higher number of incidents are considered along with a limited number of classes to operate with. Emphasizing on establishment of a robust algorithm and for the simplification of process, we focused on some basic Bengali literal samples instead of dealing with large scale auditory dataset. In future, we will investigate the performance of our algorithm on a large scale dataset considering all possible exceptions including uni-gram analysis for Bengali alphabets. Moreover, tangent based pithy approaches like Inflection point calculation may bring noteworthy contribution in recognizing shapes with specified geometric properties. Replacing missing and misleading features with features obtained by calculation of the change in tangents can be highly beneficial to the advancement of Intelligent character recognition as well.

References

1. Speech synthesis and recognition. https://www.dspguide.com/ch22/6.htm
2. What are the different types of noise? https://www.cirrusresearch.co.uk/blog/2015/01/4-different-types-noise/. Accessed 21 July 2019
3. Alim, S.A., Rashid, N.K.A.: Some commonly used speech feature extraction algorithms. In: From Natural to Artificial Intelligence-Algorithms and Applications (2018)
4. Bellman, R.E.: Adaptive Control Processes: A Guided Tour, vol. 2045. Princeton University Press, Princeton (2015)
5. Gupta, D., Bansal, P., Choudhary, K.: The state of the art of feature extraction techniques in speech recognition. In: Agrawal, S.S., Dev, A., Wason, R., Bansal, P. (eds.) Speech and Language Processing for Human-Machine Communications. AISC, vol. 664, pp. 195–207. Springer, Singapore (2018). https://doi.org/10.1007/978-981-10-6626-9_22
6. Hariharan, M., Vijean, V., Fook, C., Yaacob, S.: Speech stuttering assessment using sample entropy and least square support vector machine. In: 2012 IEEE 8th International Colloquium on Signal Processing and its Applications, pp. 240–245. IEEE (2012)
7. Hariharan, M., Chee, L.S., Ai, O.C., Yaacob, S.: Classification of speech dysfluencies using LPC based parameterization techniques. J. Med. Syst. **36**(3), 1821–1830 (2012)
8. Magre, S.B., Deshmukh, R.R., Shrishrimal, P.P.: A comparative study on feature extraction techniques in speech recognition. In: International Conference on Recent Advances in Statistics and Their Application (2013)
9. Nagabhushan, P., Murali, S.: Recognition of pitman shorthand text using tangent feature values at word level. Sadhana **28**(6), 1037–1046 (2003). https://doi.org/10.1007/BF02703814
10. Pritom, A.I., Munshi, M.A.R., Sabab, S.A., Shihab, S.: Predicting breast cancer recurrence using effective classification and feature selection technique. In: 2016 19th International Conference on Computer and Information Technology (ICCIT), pp. 310–314. IEEE (2016)
11. Sabab, S.A., Munshi, M.A.R., Pritom, A.I., et al.: Cardiovascular disease prognosis using effective classification and feature selection technique. In: 2016 International Conference on Medical Engineering, Health Informatics and Technology (MediTec), pp. 1–6. IEEE (2016)
12. Saini, P., Kaur, P.: Automatic speech recognition: a review. Int. J. Eng. Trends Technol. **4**(2), 1–5 (2013)
13. Sankar, A., et al.: Speech sound classification and estimation of optimal order of LPC using neural network. In: Proceedings of the 2nd International Conference on Vision, Image and Signal Processing, p. 35. ACM (2018)
14. Sezgin, M.C., Gunsel, B., Kurt, G.K.: Perceptual audio features for emotion detection. EURASIP J. Audio Speech Music Process. **2012**(1), 16 (2012)
15. Usha, K., Ezhilarasan, M.: Hybrid detection of convex curves for biometric authentication using tangents and secants. In: 2013 3rd IEEE International Advance Computing Conference (IACC), pp. 763–768. IEEE (2013)
16. Washani, N., Sharma, S.: Speech recognition system: a review. Int. J. Comput. Appl. **115**(18), 7–10 (2015)

Semantic Sentence Modeling for Learning Textual Similarity Exploiting LSTM

Md. Shajalal[1(✉)] and Masaki Aono[2]

[1] Department of Computer Science and Engineering,
Hajee Mohammad Danesh Science and Technology University, Dinajpur, Bangladesh
shajalal@hstu.ac.bd

[2] Department of Computer Science and Engineering, Toyohashi University of Technology, Toyohashi, Aichi, Japan
aono@tut.jp

Abstract. Finding the semantic similarity between texts is not trivial and is an indispensable task in many NLP and information retrieval tasks. In this paper, we introduced a semantic sentence modeling approach for learning the similarity between sentences using long-short-term-memory (LSTM) networks. First, sentences are represented with high dimensional vectors based on the word-embedding model that encodes the semantic meaning of the sentences. Then the encoded sentences are used to train the siamese LSTM model. The trained model builds a structured high dimensional space and can predict the semantic similarity between sentences. We applied our proposed method on two benchmark datasets on semantic textual similarity. The experimental results exhibited the efficiency of our method and outperformed some know related methods with 82% and 83% accuracy in terms of Pearson's r and Spearman's ρ, respectively.

Keywords: Sentence modeling · Word semantics · Semantic modeling · Semantics

1 Introduction

Semantic similarity between a pair of sentences/texts is absolutely indispensable form many tasks. The applications of semantic textual similarity ranges from natural language processing to information retrieval, machine translation, web search, text classification, etc. [1–3]. The list will just go on. The typical approach to calculate the textual similarity is the trivial lexical measure that consider the number of overlapping lexical items between texts [4]. But lexical similarity functions can compute the similarity within a certain level. Moreover, similarity measure using only the content of the text-pairs can capture textual similarity but not semantic. In some circumstances, these measures might lead

T. Bhuiyan et al. (Eds.): ICONCS 2020, LNICST 325, pp. 426–438, 2020.
https://doi.org/10.1007/978-3-030-52856-0_34

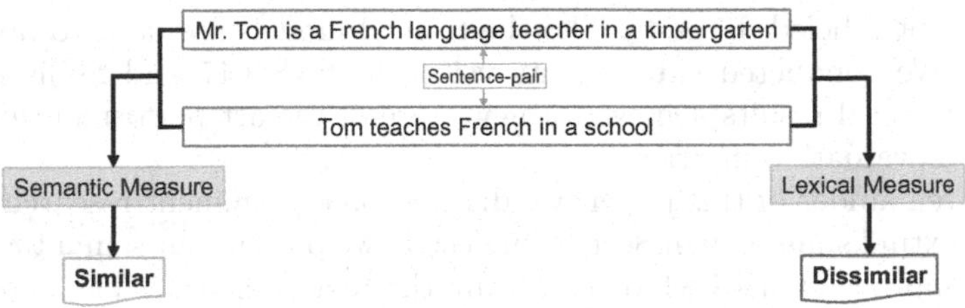

Fig. 1. An example sentence-pair where traditional lexical similarity is unable to capture the semantic similarity

the similarity score towards negative direction. To understand the shortcomings of such kind of lexical measures, lets take an example sentence-pair illustrated in Fig. 1. We can see that lexical measure can not always capture the similarity.

However, the applications of semantic textual similarity does not only rely on these simple lexical measures. Researchers proposed different similarity measures exploiting the semantic information from multiple structure knowledge bases [5–11]. Both the word and sentence-level semantics are utilized to compute the similarity between sentences [6,12–16]. WordNet is one of the most usual resources from where different methods estimate the similarity using the word's senses [17,18]. In other words, the meanings of each words from WordNet are applied to calculate the similarity. The distributed representation of words, word-embedding [19,20] is widely used to extract semantic information of words as well as sentences. The variants of word-embedding models such as sentence to vector [21], tweet to vector [22], document to vector [21] etc. are also utilized for estimating textual similarity. Corpus-based methods are also available for capturing semantic similarity [6]. Semantic meaning of sentences are also identified by top retrieved web documents, top retrieved tweets and so on. In the recent past, semantic textual similarity (STS) has gained a considerable attention in the research community [5–10]. SemEval[1] organized some multilingual and cross-language tasks on STS in the recent past [5,7,10].

Different deep learning based methods [23–26] were proposed to learn the semantic similarity from the sentences' context. The methods varies widely that used different variants of techniques such as recurrent neural networks (RNNs) [24,26], convolutional neural networks (CNNs) [24], long-short-term-memory networks (LSTMs) [26], etc. In this paper, we proposed a LSTM based technique that learns text similarity by modeling sentence semantically. Word-embedding is a prominent approach to represent words in a high dimensional space where the text can be convert into a vector. The vector representation of a particular word also indicate the semantics. Using the help of word embedding, we first model each sentence by vector representations of its words. Then, we feed the sentence semantics into siamese LSTM model. We train the models by using

[1] SemEval: https://en.wikipedia.org/wiki/SemEval.

three different labeled datasets. The the trained models are used to predict the similarity. We conducted experiments using the STS2017 and SICK datasets. The experimental results achieved a new state-of-the-art performance in terms of standard evaluation metrics.

In the remainder of this paper, we discuss some prominent research work on semantic textual similarity in Sect. 2. In Sect. 3, we present our semantic sentence modeling approach with LSTM to capture the text similarity. The experiments and evaluation results are described in Sect. 4. Section 5 presents some conclusion remarks and future directions.

2 Related Work

Researchers proposed different methods which relied on handcrafted features extracted from the content information of sentences, WordNet, and some other resources [5,7,9,10,18]. Some prior methods utilized the word-level semantics to calculate sentence-level similarity [15,16]. Different types of corpus-based and knowledge-based similarity measures were also introduced for the same purpose [6]. The semantic information from some external structured knowledge base such as Wikipedia and WordNet are employed to estimate the similarity. In some prior works [27–29], the proposed methods identified the semantic meaning of words from WordNet and applied that word-level semantic information to compute the similarity between texts. Researchers also proposed corpus-based methods combining with WordNet-based measures [6,30]. Recently, researchers tried word-embedding based techniques which are also used for semantic similarity [14,31,32].

Tai et al. [26] proposed Tree-LSTMs that generalize the order-sensitive chain-structure of standard LSTMs to tree-structured network topologies [23]. Their method first builds up a parse tree for the corresponding sentence and then used those tree in the LSTM network. The skip-thoughts model was proposed to extend the skip-gram approach of *word2vec* from the word to sentence level [25]. The model feeds every sentence into a recurrent neural network that tries to reconstruct the immediately preceding and following sentences in that context.

3 Semantic Sentence Modeling with LSTM

This section presents our proposed method for learning textual similarity utilizing semantic sentence modeling with long-short-term-memory networks. The individual sentence is prone to have limited content information that they can not represent the semantic meaning. Word-embedding is a remarkable technique to capture the semantics of each word in a very high dimensional space. Therefore, we hypothesis that the semantic information (i.e. word vector) return by pre-trained word-embedding model might be a better approach to represent sentences. The semantic information for each sentence is then fed into the LSTM network for training the model. The trained model is then used for predicting the

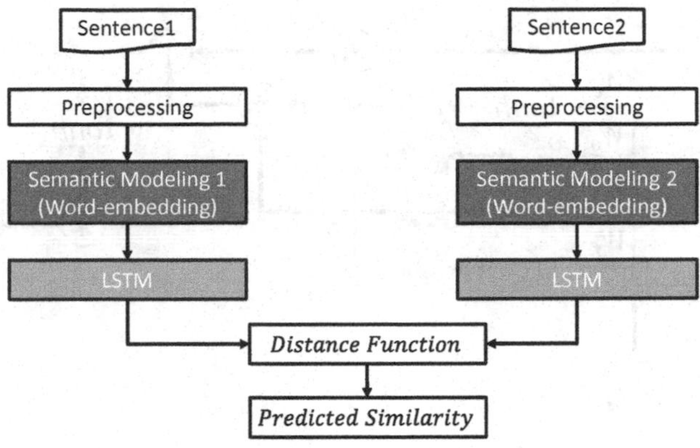

Fig. 2. An overview of semantic sentence modeling with LSTM.

similarity between two sentences. The high-level building blocks of our proposed approach is given in Fig. 2.

Our method can be divided into three phases including i. Preprocessing ii. Sentence modeling and iii. Training the siamese LSTM model. In the preprocessing phase, different punctuation marks have been filtered out from the sentences. The sentence is then tokenized to convert into a list of words. We also remove the stop words from the texts. Then lemmatization is applied to convert each word into its root form.

Let a sentence S contains n words except stopwords. The semantic information of each individual word is returned by the word-embedding model. A T dimensional vector corresponding to each word represents the semantic information. The pre-trained word vector model trained with *google news corpus* is used to represent words into vectors. The dimension of the word vector model is 300 (i.e $T = 300$). The sentences are represented as a sequence of word vectors. Each sentence makes a matrix by exploiting n vectors which express the semantic meaning. The matrix can be denoted as followings:

$$M(S) = \begin{bmatrix} w_{11} & w_{12} & w_{13} & \cdots & w_{1T} \\ w_{21} & w_{22} & w_{23} & \cdots & w_{2T} \\ w_{31} & w_{32} & w_{33} & \cdots & w_{3T} \\ \vdots & \vdots & \vdots & \ddots & \vdots \\ w_{n1} & w_{n2} & w_{n3} & \cdots & w_{nT} \end{bmatrix}$$

where each row indicates the corresponding T dimensional vector representation returned by a pre-trained word-embedding model.

Inspired by the success of long-short-term-memory networks in different NLP tasks [33,34], we exploit LSTM to capture the better semantic similarity between texts. The matrix representations for sentences are then used as the input in the LSTM which is a special kind of recurrent neural network (RNN) capable of learning long-term dependencies [35]. The LSTM networks are designed

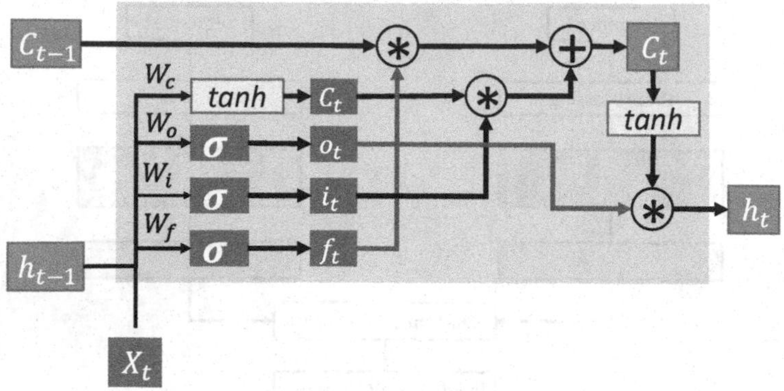

Fig. 3. The execution flow of LSTM networks

explicitly to mitigate the long-term dependency problem. They can remember information for long periods of time and eventually learn from the previous contexts. The LSTM update the hidden state vector h_t by adapting standard feed-forward neural networks for sequence data $(x_1, \cdots, x_T)$ as followings:

$$h_t = \sigma(W[x_t, h_{t-1}])$$

The LSTM sequentially updates a hidden state representation relying on a memory cell consisting of four components, namely *input gate* i_t, *forget gate* f_t, *output gate* o_t and *memory state* c_t. These all are real-valued vectors. The memory state c_t and the output gate o_t determines the way by which the other units are being affected. On the other hand, the input gate i_t and the forget gate f_t decide whether the gates store or omit information in the memory on each new input and the current state.

The overall execution flow of each state and gate has been illustrated in the Fig. 3. Let the weight matrices for input gate, forget gate, state and output gate be W_i, W_f, W_c, W_o respectively and their corresponding bias vectors are b_i, b_f, b_c and b_o. The LSTM updates state and gates at each $t \in \{1, \cdots, T\}$ as the following:

$$i_t = \sigma(W_i[C_{t-1}, h_{t-1}, x_t] + b_i) \quad (1)$$

$$f_t = \sigma(W_f[C_{t-1}, h_{t-1}, x_t] + b_f) \quad (2)$$

$$o_t = \sigma(W_o[C_{t-1}, h_{t-1}, x_t] + b_o) \quad (3)$$

$$\widetilde{C_t} = tanh(W_c[C_{t-1}, h_{t-1}, x_t] + b_c) \quad (4)$$

$$C_t = \widetilde{C_t} \cdot i_t + f_t \cdot C_{t-1} \quad (5)$$

$$h_t = o_t \cdot tanh(C_t) \quad (6)$$

We leverage siamese networks consisting of two similar LSTM networks corresponding to each sentence. Each of them processes one sentence in a given pair. Our network learns the sentence mapping utilizing the space of variable-length sequences of T dimensional vectors. This sentence representation is passed through the LSTM where the hidden states h_t are being updated using the equations noted in Eqs. 2–6. The representation is used to train a given context in each hidden state. At last, the final representation is encoded in the last state. In this work, the number of hidden states is 150. We utilize the Manhattan distance function applied on left and right LSTM networks to estimate the similarity.

4 Experiment Results and Evaluation

4.1 Dataset Collection

The performance of our proposed method has been validated by conducting the experiments on two benchmark dataset for semantic textual similarity. The first dataset is provided by the organizer of the SemEval STS2017[2] [7]. There are 250 pairs of sentences in the dataset. They also provided the gold-standard judgment for each sentence-pair. The gold standard similarity scores were computed considering human assessors' judgment. The score ranges in [0, 5]. We also applied our method on Sentences Involving Compositional Knowledge (SICK[3]) dataset consists of about 10,000 English sentence pairs, generated starting from two existing sets: the 8K ImageFlickr data set and the SemEval 2012 STS MSR-Video Description data set. There similarity score for each sentence-pair in this dataset is also ranged in [0, 5]. The larger the score, the more similar the sentence pair is. The pre-trained word-embedding (word2vec[4]) models trained on *Google News Corpus* is employed in our proposed LSTM-based method.

4.2 Evaluation Metric

The performance of our method has been tested in terms of different evaluation metrics including *Pearson Correlation Coefficient*[5] r, Spearman Correlation Coefficient ρ, *mean squared error*[6], MSE. These evaluation metrics has also been used as an official metric to test the performance of a method in SemEval STS2017 [7]. Given that $X = \{x_1, x_2, x_3...x_n\}$ and $Y = \{y_1, y_2, y_3...y_n\}$ be the two sets of scores for n sentence-pairs estimated by the system and gold-standard, respectively. Each x_i (or y_i) in X (or in Y) indicates the semantic similarity of i-th sentence-pair. The higher the value of correlation coefficients (both Pearson's r and Spearman's ρ) between X and Y, the better the system is. On the other hand the lower the value of MSE, the better the system is and vice versa.

[2] STS2017: http://alt.qcri.org/semeval2017/task1/.
[3] SICK dataset: http://marcobaroni.org/composes/sick.html.
[4] Word2Vec: https://code.google.com/p/word2vec/.
[5] https://en.wikipedia.org/wiki/Pearson_correlation_coefficient.
[6] https://en.wikipedia.org/wiki/Mean_squared_error.

4.3 Preparing Training Set

Training set always be a scare in the field of learning sentence similarity. Though the bag-of-words, TF/IDF, etc. work well in other natural language processing tasks, but it does not work well in this field [23]. We train the LSTM network with different training set consisting of labeled sentences pairs. The Stanford natural language inference corpus [36] consists of 367K sentence-pairs. Each sentence-pair is labeled by a binary value, 1 indicates both sentences are similar and 0 indicates dissimilarity. The model is also trained with 404K Quora question pairs [23] and 10k SICK sentence-pairs. This training set is labeled using the same procedures as the previous one. We prepare another training set using sentence pairs provided by SemEval STS task organizers from 2012–2016. The following Table 1 presents summary of the training sets.

Table 1. The summary of training sets

Training set	Sources	Size
Stanford NLI corpus	Stanford NLP	367K
SICK dataset	Flickr & SemEval	10k
Qoura question-pairs	Qoura	404K
STS training set	STS task organizer	3K

4.4 Experimental Setup

We conducted experiments using different experimental settings. Since we model sentences semantically with the help of word-embedding and trained the model using LSTM network feeding different training sets, we conducted experiment with all the trained models. The experiment with Stanford NLI training set is denoted as LSTM_SNLI. In LSTM_SICK, the model is trained with the 70% sentence-pairs of SICK dataset and 30% ware used for testing. Then we applied the trained model with Quora question-pairs and this setting is referred as LSTM_Quora. The model also is trained exploiting our prepared training set using STS (2012–2016) sentence-pairs. This setting is denoted as LSTM_STS12-16. We trained LSTM with 150 hidden layer. The experiment using the traditional handcrafted features is used as the baseline in this research. The summary of experimental settings are given below:

- **LSTM_SNLI:** The experiments were conducted exploiting the trained LSTM model to predict the sentence similarity. The LSTM model were trained with the stanford natural language inference corpus.
- **LSTM_Quora:** We carried out experiments with Quora question-pairs and trained the model in this setting. Mueller and Aditya [23] prepared a big labeled training set for learning sentence similarity.

- **LSTM_SICK:** The experiments were conducted using the LSTM model trained with SICK dataset.
- **LSTM_STS12-16:** In this setting, we prepare a new training set utilizing the previous STS task dataset from 2012–2016.
- **Baseline:** This setting used the linear ranking of different hand crafted features.

4.5 Results and Discussion

The performance of the different experimental settings on SemEval STS2017 dataset is reported in the Table 2. The results conclude that LSTM_SNLI achieved the best performance in terms of Pearson's r and Spearman's ρ. However, the model trained with SICK sentence-pairs performed better according to the MSE measure. The settings LSTM_Quora also performed competitively as compared to LSTM_SNLI and LSTM_SICK. The plausible reason is that the previous two settings trained the model with SNLI corpus and SICK datasets. These two datasets have a huge number of sentence-pairs. The SNLI corpus comprises of 367K sentences. On the other hand, Quora dataset only has question-pairs and the testing dataset hardly have the question-pairs. Therefore LSTM_SNLI and LSTM_SICK can predict the sentence similarity better than LSTM_Quora. On contrary, LSTM_Quora might capture better similarity for question-pairs [23]. The LSTM_STS12-16 trained the network using our prepared training set contains only 3K sentence-pairs. This model is suffered for the small-sized training set. Though the training set is smaller in size as compared to the other two settings, this method also performed competitively. The baseline which used different handcrafted features performed poorly as compared to the other settings.

Table 2. The performance of different experimental settings on SemEval STS2017 dataset in terms of Pearson's r, Spearman's ρ and mean squared error, MSE. The best result is in **bold**.

Dataset	Method	Pearson's r	Spearman's ρ	MSE
STS2017	LSTM_SNLI	**0.8215**	**0.8301**	0.1523
	LSTM_SICK	0.7948	0.7820	**0.1329**
	LSTM_Quora	0.7641	0.7619	0.1549
	LSTM_STS12-16	0.7415	07325	0.1723
	Baseline	0.5612	0.5748	0.5254

Similarly, our methods almost have the same kind of performance on the SICK dataset and the results are reported in the Table 3. In that case, LSTM_SICK was the number one in terms of all evaluation measures. However, the model trained using our prepared dataset LSTM_STS12-16 performed better in the STS2017 dataset as compared to the performance on the SICK dataset. STS17 and the training dataset provided by the same organizers. We think this can be one of the plausible reasons. The performance of our method is also consistent with two different kinds of datasets. However, the experimental results clearly demonstrated the effectiveness in predicting sentence similarity in two benchmark datasets.

Table 3. The performance of different experimental settings on SICK dataset in terms of Pearson's r, Spearman's ρ and mean squared error, MSE. The best result is in **bold**.

Dataset	Method	Pearson's r	Spearman's ρ	MSE
SICK	LSTM_SNLI	0.7258	0.7149	0.1884
	LSTM_SICK	**0.7875**	**0.7798**	**0.1411**
	LSTM_Quora	0.7179	0.7018	0.1983
	LSTM_STS12-16	0.6215	0.6201	0.2349
	Baseline	0.5087	0.5091	0.5714

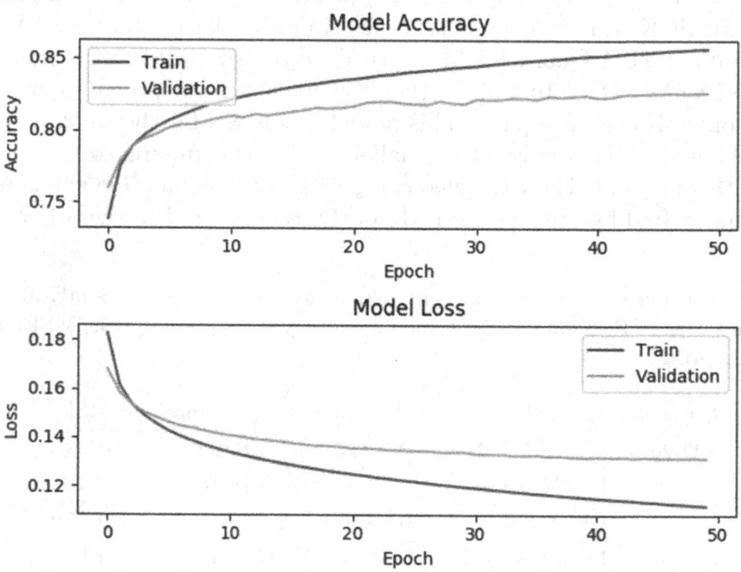

Fig. 4. The accuracy and loss curve of the LSTM model. The X-axis represents the epoch and the Y-axis represents the accuracy and loss in two diagrams respectively.

The curve for the accuracy and loss of our proposed LSTM model for learning semantic textual similarity is illustrated in Fig. 4. This model was trained using the SNLI dataset. We can see that the accuracy and loss of both training and validation data are consistent. The performance comparison of our methods with

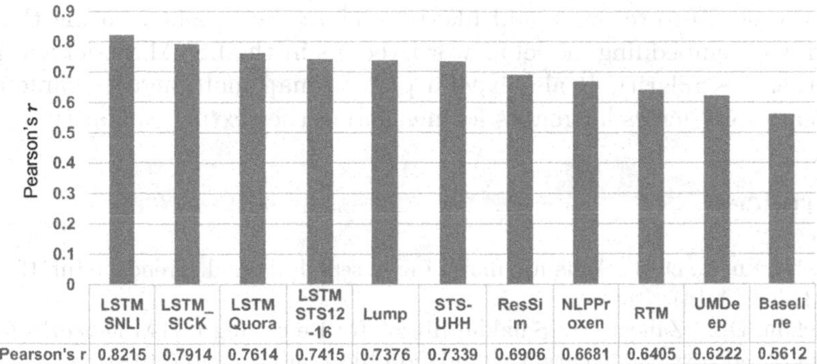

	LSTM SNLI	LSTM_ SICK	LSTM Quora	LSTM STS12 -16	Lump	STS-UHH	ResSi m	NLPPr oxen	RTM	UMDe ep	Baseli ne
Pearson's r	0.8215	0.7914	0.7614	0.7415	0.7376	0.7339	0.6906	0.6681	0.6405	0.6222	0.5612

Fig. 5. The performance comparison of our methods with some other known related methods [7,37–39]. The X-axis represents different methods and Y-axis represents the performance of them in terms of Person's r.

some known related methods [7,37–39] in terms of Pearson's correlation coefficient r in Fig. 5. These relevant methods were submitted in the SemEval STS task 2017. Our proposed LSTM_SNLI method clearly outperformed other known related methods in terms of Pearson's r. In addition, our another experiment with the trained model using Quora question-pairs LSTN_Quora also got better accuracy as compared to the related methods. The proposed LSTM network-based model trained with two different training sets has got the best accuracy that reflects that our method is consistent. The participating team *Lump* computed the similarity score with the help of different lexical, syntactic, context-based and word-embedding based features. The multilingual word-embedding model was used by *ResSim* team. *UMDeep* also predicted the sentence-similarity exploiting deep LSTM model but our method performed better than their approach. The experimental results and this comparison clearly demonstrated the effectiveness of our proposed method in predicting semantic textual similarity.

5 Conclusion

In this paper, we have modeled sentences semantically with the help of word-embedding and predict the similarity using the trained model applying a long-short-term-memory network. Our method trained the LSTM network with four different labeled training sets. The training sets are composed of sentence-pairs with their similarity labels. We found that the model trained with a big training set performed better. The conclusion about the training set is that the bigger the training set in terms of the number of human assessors' annotated sentence-pairs, the better the LSTM model to predict the similarity is. Our proposed semantic sentence modeling-based methods outperformed some known related methods on two benchmark datasets. We found that the performance was consistent over different datasets. Therefore we can conclude that our method is efficient to measure the semantic textual similarity between two sentences.

In the near future, we would like to explore the benefit of using the multilingual word-embedding model as word vectors in the LSTM model and predict the sentence similarity. It also have a plan to map multilingual character-level representations across languages for measuring the textual similarity.

References

1. Li, H., Xu, J., et al.: Semantic matching in search. Found. Trends® Inf. Retr. **7**(5), 343–469 (2014)
2. Sachan, D.S., Zaheer, M., Salakhutdinov, R.: Revisiting LSTM networks for semi-supervised text classification via mixed objective function (2018)
3. Song, W., Liu, Y., Liu, L.Z., Wang, H.S.: Semantic composition of distributed representations for query subtopic mining. Front. Inf. Technol. Electron. Eng. **19**(11), 1409–1419 (2018)
4. Bertero, D., Fung, P.: HLTC-HKUST: a neural network paraphrase classifier using translation metrics, semantic roles and lexical similarity features. In: Proceedings of the 9th International Workshop on Semantic Evaluation (SemEval 2015), pp. 23–28 (2015)
5. Agirre, E., et al.: SemEval-2016 task 1: semantic textual similarity, monolingual and cross-lingual evaluation. In: Proceedings of the 10th International Workshop on Semantic Evaluation (SemEval-2016), pp. 497–511 (2016)
6. Mihalcea, R., Corley, C., Strapparava, C., et al.: Corpus-based and knowledge-based measures of text semantic similarity. In: AAAI 2006, pp. 775–780 (2006)
7. Cer, D., Diab, M., Agirre, E., Lopez-Gazpio, I., Specia, L.: SemEval-2017 task 1: semantic textual similarity-multilingual and cross-lingual focused evaluation. arXiv preprint arXiv:1708.00055 (2017)
8. Zhang, Z., Saligrama, V.: Zero-shot learning via semantic similarity embedding. In: Proceedings of the IEEE International Conference on Computer Vision, pp. 4166–4174 (2015)
9. Šarić, F., Glavaš, G., Karan, M., Šnajder, J., Bašić, B.D.: TakeLab: systems for measuring semantic text similarity. In: Proceedings of the First Joint Conference on Lexical and Computational Semantics-Volume 1: Proceedings of the Main Conference and the Shared Task, and Volume 2: Proceedings of the Sixth International Workshop on Semantic Evaluation, pp. 441–448. Association for Computational Linguistics (2012)
10. Agirre, E., et al.: SemEval-2015 task 2: semantic textual similarity, English, Spanish and pilot on interpretability. In: Proceedings of the 9th International Workshop on Semantic Evaluation (SemEval 2015), pp. 252–263 (2015)
11. Hassanzadeh, H., Groza, T., Nguyen, A., Hunter, J.: UQeResearch: semantic textual similarity quantification. In: Proceedings of the 9th International Workshop on Semantic Evaluation (SemEval 2015), pp. 123–127 (2015)
12. Karpathy, A., Joulin, A., Fei-Fei, L.F.: Deep fragment embeddings for bidirectional image sentence mapping. In: Advances in Neural Information Processing Systems, pp. 1889–1897 (2014)
13. Rychalska, B., Pakulska, K., Chodorowska, K., Walczak, W., Andruszkiewicz, P.: Samsung Poland NLP team at SemEval-2016 task 1: necessity for diversity; combining recursive autoencoders, WordNet and ensemble methods to measure semantic similarity. In: Proceedings of the 10th International Workshop on Semantic Evaluation (SemEval-2016), pp. 602–608 (2016)

14. Shajalal, M., Aono, M.: Semantic textual similarity in Bengali text. In: 2018 International Conference on Bangla Speech and Language Processing (ICBSLP), pp. 1–5. IEEE (2018)
15. Shajalal, M., Aono, M.: Semantic textual similarity between sentences using bilingual word semantics. Progr. Artif. Intell. **8**(2), 263–272 (2019). https://doi.org/10.1007/s13748-019-00180-4
16. Shajalal, M., Aono, M.: Sentence-level semantic textual similarity using word-level semantics. In: 2018 10th International Conference on Electrical and Computer Engineering (ICECE), pp. 113–116. IEEE (2018)
17. Wei, T., Lu, Y., Chang, H., Zhou, Q., Bao, X.: A semantic approach for text clustering using WordNet and lexical chains. Expert Syst. Appl. **42**(4), 2264–2275 (2015)
18. Bär, D., Biemann, C., Gurevych, I., Zesch, T.: UKP: computing semantic textual similarity by combining multiple content similarity measures. In: Proceedings of the First Joint Conference on Lexical and Computational Semantics-Volume 1: Proceedings of the Main Conference and the Shared Task, and Volume 2: Proceedings of the Sixth International Workshop on Semantic Evaluation, pp. 435–440. Association for Computational Linguistics (2012)
19. Bojanowski, P., Grave, E., Joulin, A., Mikolov, T.: Enriching word vectors with subword information. Trans. Assoc. Comput. Linguist. **5**, 135–146 (2017)
20. Mikolov, T., Sutskever, I., Chen, K., Corrado, G.S., Dean, J.: Distributed representations of words and phrases and their compositionality. In: Advances in Neural Information Processing Systems, pp. 3111–3119 (2013)
21. Le, Q., Mikolov, T.: Distributed representations of sentences and documents. In: International Conference on Machine Learning, pp. 1188–1196 (2014)
22. Li, Q., Shah, S., Liu, X., Nourbakhsh, A., Fang, R.: Tweet topic classification using distributed language representations. In: 2016 IEEE/WIC/ACM International Conference on Web Intelligence (WI), pp. 81–88. IEEE (2016)
23. Mueller, J., Thyagarajan, A.: Siamese recurrent architectures for learning sentence similarity. In: AAAI 2016, pp. 2786–2792 (2016)
24. He, H., Gimpel, K., Lin, J.: Multi-perspective sentence similarity modeling with convolutional neural networks. In: Proceedings of the 2015 Conference on Empirical Methods in Natural Language Processing, pp. 1576–1586 (2015)
25. Kiros, R., et al.: Skip-thought vectors. In: Advances in Neural Information Processing Systems, pp. 3294–3302 (2015)
26. Tai, K.S., Socher, R., Manning, C.D.: Improved semantic representations from tree-structured long short-term memory networks. arXiv preprint arXiv:1503.00075 (2015)
27. Lintean, M.C., Rus, V.: Measuring semantic similarity in short texts through greedy pairing and word semantics. In: FLAIRS Conference (2012)
28. Ferreira, R., Lins, R.D., Freitas, F., Simske, S.J., Riss, M.: A new sentence similarity assessment measure based on a three-layer sentence representation. In: Proceedings of the 2014 ACM Symposium on Document Engineering, pp. 25–34. ACM (2014)
29. Fernando, S., Stevenson, M.: A semantic similarity approach to paraphrase detection. In: Proceedings of the 11th Annual Research Colloquium of the UK Special Interest Group for Computational Linguistics, pp. 45–52 (2008)
30. Li, Y., McLean, D., Bandar, Z.A., Crockett, K., et al.: Sentence similarity based on semantic nets and corpus statistics. IEEE Trans. Knowl. Data Eng. **8**, 1138–1150 (2006)

31. Han, L., Kashyap, A.L., Finin, T., Mayfield, J., Weese, J.: UMBC_EBIQUITY-CORE: semantic textual similarity systems. In: Second Joint Conference on Lexical and Computational Semantics (*SEM), Volume 1: Proceedings of the Main Conference and the Shared Task: Semantic Textual Similarity, vol. 1, pp. 44–52 (2013)
32. Kenter, T., De Rijke, M.: Short text similarity with word embeddings. In: Proceedings of the 24th ACM International Conference on Information and Knowledge Management, pp. 1411–1420. ACM (2015)
33. Guo, D., Zhou, W., Li, H., Wang, M.: Hierarchical LSTM for sign language translation. In: Thirty-Second AAAI Conference on Artificial Intelligence (2018)
34. Howard, J., Ruder, S.: Universal language model fine-tuning for text classification. In: Proceedings of the 56th Annual Meeting of the Association for Computational Linguistics (Volume 1: Long Papers), vol. 1, pp. 328–339 (2018)
35. Hochreiter, S., Schmidhuber, J.: Long short-term memory. Neural Comput. **9**(8), 1735–1780 (1997)
36. Bowman, S.R., Angeli, G., Potts, C., Manning, C.D.: A large annotated corpus for learning natural language inference. arXiv preprint arXiv:1508.05326 (2015)
37. España-Bonet, C., Barrón-Cedeño, A.: Lump at SemEval-2017 task 1: towards an interlingua semantic similarity. In: Proceedings of the 11th International Workshop on Semantic Evaluation (SemEval-2017), pp. 144–149 (2017)
38. Duma, M.S., Menzel, W.: SEF@UHH at SemEval-2017 task 1: unsupervised knowledge-free semantic textual similarity via paragraph vector. In: Proceedings of the 11th International Workshop on Semantic Evaluation (SemEval-2017), pp. 170–174 (2017)
39. Bjerva, J., Östling, R.: ResSim at SemEval-2017 task 1: multilingual word representations for semantic textual similarity. In: Proceedings of the 11th International Workshop on Semantic Evaluation (SemEval-2017), pp. 154–158 (2017)

Bangla Language Processing

A Study of fastText Word Embedding Effects in Document Classification in Bangla Language

Pritom Mojumder[1(✉)], Mahmudul Hasan[2], Md. Faruque Hossain[1], and K. M. Azharul Hasan[2]

[1] Department of Electronics and Communication Engineering, Khulna University of Engineering & Technology, Khulna 9203, Bangladesh
pritom@ieee.org, fhossain@ece.kuet.ac.bd

[2] Department of Computer Science and Engineering, Khulna University of Engineering & Technology, Khulna 9203, Bangladesh
{mahmudul,az}@cse.kuet.ac.bd

Abstract. Natural language processing is the current topic due to many important tasks like document classification, named entity recognition, opinion mining, sentiment analysis, textual entailment, etc. Such types of task in the Bangla language is also important. This research work endeavored to find out the word embedding of the Bengali language. Leveraging the fastText word embedding, it has shown significant performance in Bangla document classification without any prepossessing like lemmatization, stemming, and others. For the extrinsic evaluation of our word vectors, a classification problem-solving strategy has been used which showed an outstanding result. In the classification module, attempts have been made to classify 40 thousand News samples into 12 categories. For this purpose, three deep learning techniques have been used: Convolutional Neural Network (CNN), Bi-Directional LSTM (BLSTM) and Convolutional Bi-Directional LSTM (CBLSTM) along-side fastText. From the analogous study of all the parameters of every classifier implemented here, we found that the BLSTM technique is the most promising technique for this task. This technique achieved 91.49%, 87.87%, and 85.5% accuracies for Training, Testing, and Validation set, respectively.

Keywords: Natural language processing · Word embedding · Deep learning

1 Introduction

In natural language processing (NLP), document classification is a problem of assigning a document to one or more classes or categories. The approach for automatic document classification has a long history. These approaches involve the one-hot vector, co-occurrence matrix-based method [7], term frequency-inverse

T. Bhuiyan et al. (Eds.): ICONCS 2020, LNICST 325, pp. 441–453, 2020.
https://doi.org/10.1007/978-3-030-52856-0_35

document frequency (tf-idf) method [20], singular value decomposition (SVD) method [13], and more others.

The deep learning-based approach is the recent trend in the NLP task [22]. Training a deep learning model for NLP tasks requires pre-processed features that are represented in vector space. Previously this representation used to be done using term frequency-inverse document frequency (tf-idf) technique [20]. The constraint of this pretty old technique is that it does not subsist the semantic context of the sentence. On the other hand, the contemporary word embedding technique developed by Mikolov et al. [17] tries to retain this semantic context of the sentence. Figure 1 illustrates the distinction between these two techniques. In Fig. 1 (A), though word "Hospital" has a semantic relation with the word "Patient," but tf-idf can not manifest this in vector space. In the case of word embedding, this relation is shown in Fig. 1 (B) using the edges.

Another word embedding technique, fastText, which is considered in this work, has a stable version, robust performance, can be easily implemented, and one of the de-facto standard methods for the present time. The main contribution of this paper is to demonstrate the implication of fastText word embedding[3] in Bangla document classification. The dataset that has been used in our research contains 12 classes, whereas most of the works in Bangla document classification have considered a few number of classes. We have compared the performance with three different neural network models. We have also presented a comparative study with previously done Bangla document classification tasks by various researchers.

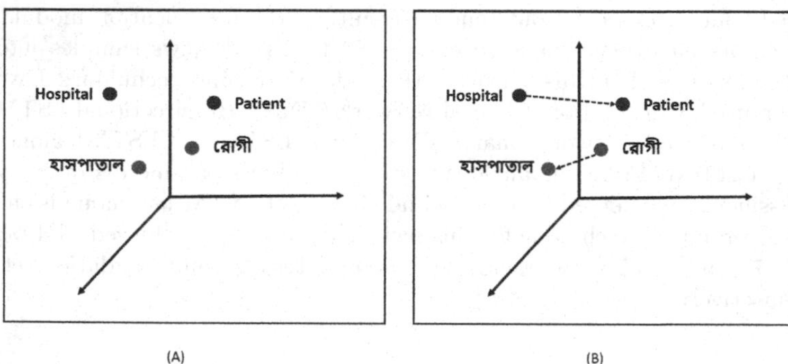

Fig. 1. Words in vector space (A) for tf-idf (B) for word embedding

2 Related Works

There are many word embedding techniques like word2vec, GloVe, fastText, etc. Popular word embedding word2vec by Mikolov et al. [16] has been used in many NLP tasks such as document classification [14] and sentiment analysis [23].

The authors in [16] have introduced two model architectures: Continuous Bag-of-Words (CBOW) and Continuous Skip-grams. These two models enable us to learn a distributed representation of words from a large dataset. According to [16], CBOW architecture works better on the syntactic task, and the Skip-grams architecture works better on the semantic tasks. Sumit et al. [21] showed that Skip-grams based method outperformed CBOW in Bangla sentiment analysis tasks due to better word representation.

Convolutional neural networks (CNN) based approach has been taken in sentence classification by Kim [11]. The author has archived superior performance using word2vec. Long Short Term Memory (LSTM), which is a variant of Recurrent Neural Network (RNN), is being used in many NLP tasks [22]. It has been proved that LSTM performs well on sequence data [9]. The hybrid architecture of bidirectional LSTM and CNN discussed by Chiu and Nichols for name entity recognition [5]. However, these methods have analyzed for the processing of English and other languages, whereas, there are a limited number of works in Bangla language.

Several works have been found in the literature on the Bangla document classification task. Decision Tree (DT), K-Nearest Neighbour (KNN), Naïve Bayes (NB), and Support Vector Machine (SVM) based classification methods have been mentioned by Mandal and Sen (2014) [15]. They have used tf-idf for feature extraction on a small dataset and only for five classes. In this work, the best performance has demonstrated for SVM with 89.14% accuracy. In another work, SVM based approach achieved 91% F1-score, researched by Ahmed and Amin [1]. In this work considered word embedding technique word2vec developed by Mikolov et al. [16]. The work suggests that word embedding can significantly improve the accuracy of the classification. In such a classification task, the largest dataset of Bangla articles was used by Alam et al. [2], where the articles were labeled into five categories. The work utilized word2vec and tf-idf with several machine learning approaches and showed that network based approach performs better (F1-score 95%). However, in our work, articles are labeled into twelve categories and the fastText word embedding technique has been used.

3 Methodology

3.1 fastText Word Embedding

Word embedding is a distributional representation of words where each word should be mapped to a shared low dimensional space, and each word will be associated with a d-dimensional vector [8]. Unlike many word embeddings, fastText does not ignore the morphology of words. This method is based on continuous skip-grams. Here each word is represented as character n-gram. So for $n = 3$, the word *quick* will be represented as:

$$<qu, qui, uic, ick, ck>$$

This approach preserves subword information and can compute valid word embedding for out-of-vocabulary words [3]. So, it can give the vector for unseen words during training the word embeddings.

To learn word representations, fastText follows the continuous skip-grams introduced by Mikolov et al. [16], which is a simple model and works well with a small amount of the training data. However, this model ignores the internal structure of words. The authors of fastText proposed different scoring functions to preserve the subword information.

Given the word w, the set of n-grams appearing in w will be $N_w \subset \{1, ..., N\}$, Where N is the dictionary size of n-grams. Vector representation Z_g is assigned for each n-gram n. Thus the driven scoring function becomes:

$$s(w, c) = \sum_{n \in N_w} Z_g^T V_c$$

here, c = context word, V_c = context vector

3.2 Bi-directional Long Short Term Memory (LSTM)

When a deep learning models tends to be deeper then vanishing gradient problem arises. LSTM models can resolve this problem by saving past context and use it any time. For this reason LSTM are widely used for sequential data structure. In the sequential data structures, data can be three dimensional where first two dimensions capture the context of the sentence using samples and words, and the last dimension captures the notion of time. In unidirectional LSTM the network captures chronological order of the data where older past data have impacts on hypothesis. But in the case of Bi-Directional LSTM the network captures both chronological and reverse chronological pattern where both older past and recent

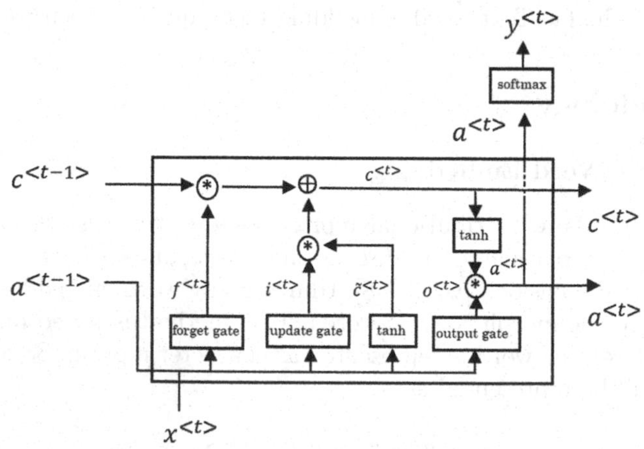

Fig. 2. A simple LSTM cell (Source: [18])

past impacts the hypothesis. For this reason Bi-Directional LSTM works very efficiently on Natural Language. Figure 2 depicts a single LSTM cell [6]. The equation for full LSTM cell is as following [18]:

$$C^{\tilde{<t>}} = \tanh(W_c[A^{<t-1>}, X^t] + b_c)$$
$$\Gamma u = \sigma(W_u[A^{<t-1>}, X^t] + b_u)$$
$$\Gamma f = \sigma(W_f[A^{<t-1>}, X^t] + b_f)$$
$$\Gamma o = \sigma(W_o[A^{<t-1>}, X^t] + b_o)$$
$$C^t = \Gamma u * C^{\tilde{<t>}} + \Gamma f * C^{<t-1>}$$
$$A^{<t>} = \Gamma o * C^{<t>}$$

Where,

$C^{\tilde{<t>}}$ = Candidate Value for Memory Cell, C.
$C^{<\tilde{t}-1>}$ = Candidate Value for Previous Memory Cell, C.
Γu = Update Gate
Γf = Forget Gate
Γo = Output Gate
W_c, W_u, W_f, W_o = Weights for the Candidate Cell, Update Gate, Forget Gate and Output Gate respectively
b_c, b_u, b_f, b_o = Bias for the Candidate Cell, Update Gate, Forget Gate and Output Gate respectively
$A^{<t>}$ = Activation Function
$A^{<t>}$ = Previous Cell Activation Function
$\sigma(x) = \frac{1}{1+e^{-x}}$
$\tanh(x) = 2g(2x) - 1$

3.3 Convolutional Neural Network (CNN)

Usually, a convolutional neural network (CNN) consists of two primary layers named convolution and pooling layer. CNN works best for Image type data, which are mostly three-dimensional. In our case, the word embedding vector is three dimensional, which we can easily fit in the CNN. CNN can seize local spatial patterns in each of its convolutional layers. With the help of pooling layers, it lowers the spatiality of each dimension. CNN uses filters in convolution layers to adapt the weights of the network according to the loss using sliding. From the response of each filter, feature maps are created in each layer. In most cases, the filter size is taken to be 3×3 or 5×5.

3.4 Evaluation Metrics

For the performance analysis of the word to vector model skip-grams, we used the classification task as an extrinsic evaluation technique. For this reason, we need standard metric values by which we can make a comparative analysis. So our work is indirectly focused on classification, and we have used the following evaluation metrics for the evaluation of the classification:

Confusion Matrix. The dimension of the confusion matrix is N × N, where N denotes the number of classes or labels. In this matrix, the rows represent the number of samples which model has predicted, and the columns represent the number of actual sample values. Hence, the number of samples in the diagonal of the confusion matrix means the better performance of the deep learning model. From the confusion matrix, we can calculate the other metrics. The confusion matrix helps us to visualize the complete performance of the model. It represents a summary of prediction results on a classification task.

TP(S_i) = All the predicted cases are S_i and those are really S_i.
TN(S_i) = All the predicted cases are non S_i and those are really non S_i.
FP(S_i) = All the predicted cases are S_i, but those are not S_i.
FN(S_i) = All the predicted cases are non S_i, but those are S_i.

It is useful for measuring accuracy, sensitivity, Recall and AUC-ROC curve.

Accuracy. It is the measure of correct prediction against total samples.

$$\text{Accuracy} = \frac{TP + TN}{TP + TN + FP + FN}$$

Precision. It means the rate of correctly predicted positives against the total number of predicted positives.

Recall. It represents the actual positive rate claimed by the model, which means the number of correctly claimed positives compared to the actual number of positives in the dataset.

F1 Score. F1 Score is the weighted average of Precision and Recall.

3.5 Dataset Preparation

The open-source dataset has been used here is collected from Kaggle[1]. It contains 3999 Bangla news articles in 12 different categories. Maintaining the ratio of 87.5%:10%:2.5%, the whole dataset is split into Training Set, Validation Set, and Testing Set consisting of 35000, 4000, and 1000 samples, respectively. Dataset overview is shown in Table 1.

3.6 Architecture of the Work

In this project, raw Bangla text data is filtered with regular expression. With this filtering, common Bangla stopwords and noisy characters were removed. After filtering, each sample is tokenized into words. After tokenization, 100 words are

[1] https://www.kaggle.com/zshujon/40k-bangla-newspaper-article.

Table 1. Dataset overview

Categories	Frequencies	% Ratio of total
Art and literature	368	0.92
Bangladesh	12239	30.60
Durporobash	176	0.44
Economy	4771	11.93
Education	774	1.93
Entertainment	2448	6.12
International	1835	4.59
Life-style	1121	2.80
North America	189	0.47
Opinion	10611	26.53
Sports	3354	8.39
Technology	2113	5.28
Total	**39999**	100

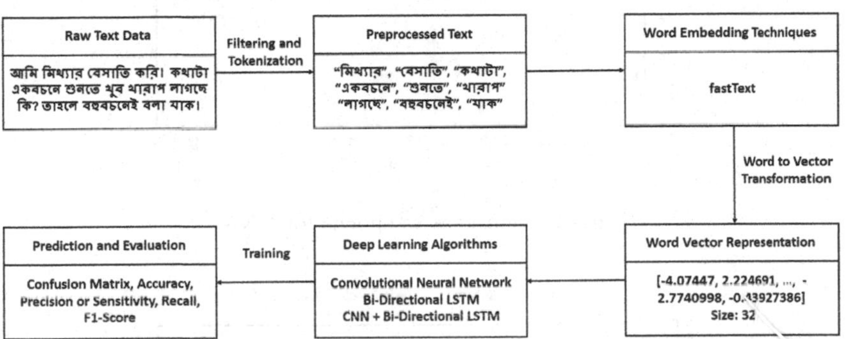

Fig. 3. Proposed architecture of the work

taken for each article or sample. If any sample were lacking 100 words, then the remaining words were padded. These tokenized words are then represented in vector space using word embedding techniques fastText. Each word is represented into 32 sized word vector. Hence each sample contains 100×32 word vectors. These word vectors of each sample are trained with Deep Learning techniques such as CNN, BLSTM, and CBLSTM. With the combination of embedding techniques and deep learning techniques totally, three models are trained with features. After training, each model is evaluated with the accuracy value. Other metrics: Confusion Matrix, Precision or Sensitivity, Recall, and F1-Score are shown in Sect. 4.2. The overall work-flow or architecture of this work is represented in Fig. 3.

4 Experimental Setup and Result Analysis

4.1 Experimental Setup

In this work, 32-dimensional word vectors were trained using Gensim fastText implementation [19]. Neural networks are implemented using Keras [6]. We have used Adam optimizer [12] for optimization of the loss or cost function. For the classification task, all the neural network models are trained in Google Colab. Colab offers 1xTesla K80 GPU, having 2496 CUDA cores, compute 3.7, 12 GB (11.439 GB Usable) GDDR5 VRAM for leveraging deep learning techniques. Besides Gensim and Keras, we have also used numpy and matplotlib library for numerical computation and data visualization, respectively.

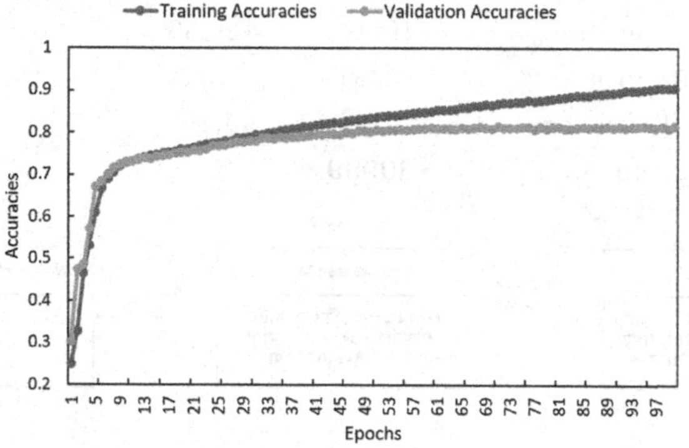

Fig. 4. Accuracies vs epochs for CNN

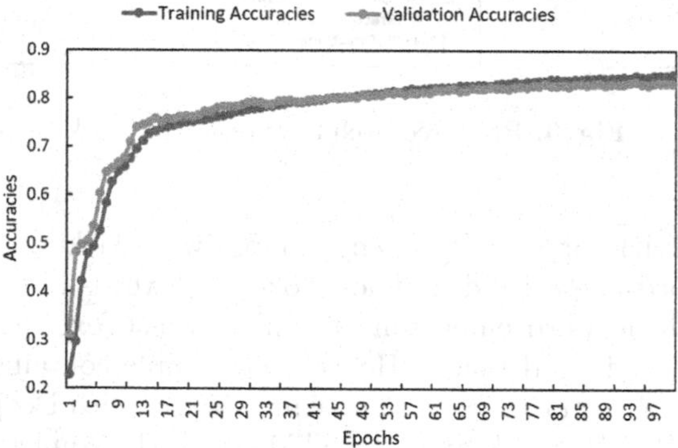

Fig. 5. Accuracies vs epochs for CBLSTM

4.2 Result Analysis

In this section, we present performance measures from three models to evaluate the impact of fastText word embedding on document classification. Besides, the results have been compared with previous works.

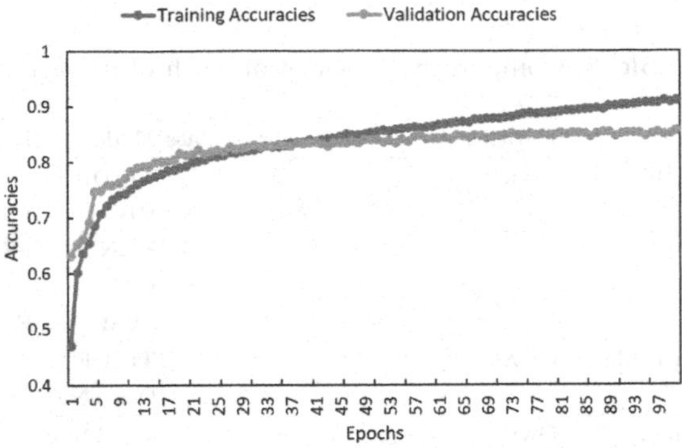

Fig. 6. Accuracies vs epochs for BLSTM

The first model is CNN, which acquires 80.2% testing accuracy. From the observation of the train vs validation accuracy in Fig. 4, in the beginning, training and validation accuracies sharply increased, and validation accuracies were slightly higher. After 12 epochs, validation accuracy started to increase slowly than training accuracy, and in the end, there is a clear difference between training accuracy and validation accuracy (Table 2). That means the model losing the ability to predict new data, which is indicating the over-fitting problem.

The second model is CBLSTM, which acquires 84.3% testing accuracy. From Fig. 5 we see that training and validation accuracy curves are overlapped. Training accuracy (85.01%) is also close to testing accuracy (84.3%). It indicates that the model is not losing the ability to predict new data.

Our third model is BLSTM, which acquires 85.5% testing accuracy, and in terms of testing accuracy, this is the best. But if we see Fig. 6 validation accuracy is not increasing with testing accuracy after 29 epochs. At the end of the training, validation accuracy is less than the testing accuracy. It indicates the model is suffering over-fitting. Comparisons among models have been shown in Table 2.

In terms of bias-variance, the second model (CBLSTM) is the best. However, in terms of testing accuracy, the third model (BLSTM) is the best. For the third model confusion matrix have been shown in Table 4 and evaluation metrics in Table 5. In the work [15], it has been suggested that stemming is an important part of reducing dimension. In our work, fastText word embedding facilitates

Table 2. Comparative analysis on different models

Network type	Training accuracy	Validation accuracy	Testing accuracy
CNN	0.9146	0.8080	0.802
CBLSTM	0.8501	0.8323	0.843
BLSTM	0.9149	0.8787	0.855

Table 3. Comparative description with other works

Author and year	Dataset	Number of class	Model	Evaluation metric
Mandal and Sen [15]	Own	5	TFIDF	
			NB	FS 85.22
			KNN	FS 74.24
			DT	FS 80.65
			SVM	FS 89.14
Chakraborty and Huda [4]	Own	16	TFIDF	
			DenseNN	FS 84.0
Ahmed and Amin [1]	Own	7	Word2vec	
			SVM	FS 91.0
Kabir et al. [10]	Own	9	SGD	N/A
Alam et al. [2]	BARD	5	Word2Vec	
			LR	FS 95.0
			NN	FS 96.0
Our Study	40k News Article	12	fastText	
			CNN	FS 80.0
			CBLSTM	FS 84.0
			BLSTM	FS 85.0

FS = F1-Score, SGD = Stochastic Gradient Decent
LR = Linear Regression, NN = Neural Network, N/A = Not Available
CBLSTM = CNN + Bi-directional LSTM, BLSTM = Bi-driectional LSTM

Table 4. Confusion Matrix of Testing Set using fastText + Bi-Directional LSTM

	ARL	BND	DUR	ECO	EDU	ENT	INT	LIF	NRA	OPN	SPR	TEC
ARL	4	0	0	0	0	2	0	0	0	2	0	0
BND	1	252	0	6	3	3	2	0	0	20	1	1
DUR	1	1	0	0	0	1	1	1	0	3	0	0
ECO	0	9	0	101	0	0	0	0	0	9	0	4
EDU	2	2	0	4	12	0	0	0	0	1	0	1
ENT	0	1	0	0	0	62	1	0	0	1	1	0
INT	0	5	0	0	0	2	42	0	0	8	0	1
LIF	0	2	0	0	1	2	0	28	0	4	0	0
NRA	0	0	0	0	0	0	1	0	0	2	0	0
OPN	1	10	0	0	1	1	1	3	0	237	2	0
SPR	0	2	0	0	1	1	0	0	0	2	73	0
TEC	0	1	0	3	1	0	1	1	0	0	0	44

ARL = Art & Literature, BND = Bangladesh, DUR = Durporobash, ECO = Economy,
EDU = Education, ENT = Entertainment, INT = International, LIF = Life-Style
NRA = North America, OPN = Opinion, SPR = Sports, TEC = Technology

Table 5. Evaluation Metrics of Testing set for FastText + Bi-Directional LSTM

Labels	Precision $\frac{TP}{FP+TP}$	Recall $\frac{TP}{FN+TP}$	F1-score $\frac{2(Recall * Precision)}{(Recall + Precision)}$	Support
Art and literature	0.44	0.50	0.47	8
Bangladesh	0.88	0.87	0.88	289
Durporobash	0.00	0.00	0.00	8
Economy	0.89	0.82	0.85	123
Education	0.63	0.55	0.59	22
Entertainment	0.84	0.94	0.89	66
International	0.86	0.72	0.79	58
Life-style	0.85	0.76	0.80	37
North America	0.00	0.00	0.00	3
Opinion	0.82	0.93	0.87	256
Sports	0.95	0.92	0.94	79
Technology	0.86	0.86	0.86	51

dimensional reduction and lessen the task of stemming. We have presented comparisons with previous works in Table 3.

5 Conclusions

This work presents the effective Bangla document classification method with the fastText word embedding technique. A relatively large dataset was used in this work where articles are classified into 12 classes. The work shows that with fastText word embedding significant performance can be gained without some preprocessing like lemmatization, stemming and others. The results from three different models (CNN, CBLSTM, BLSTM) show that the LSTM based approach can gain better performance (CBLSTM 84.3%, BLSTM 85.5%) than the other approach (CNN 80.2%). The over-fitting problem was encountered for the first and the third model due to class imbalance in the dataset. In the future, to improve the performance, other better word embedding techniques with a different deep learning approach need to investigate for Bangla document classification.

References

1. Ahmad, A., Amin, M.R.: Bengali word embeddings and it's application in solving document classification problem. In: 2016 19th International Conference on Computer and Information Technology (ICCIT), pp. 425–430. IEEE (2016)

2. Alam, M.T., Islam, M.M.: Bard: Bangla article classification using a new comprehensive dataset. In: 2018 International Conference on Bangla Speech and Language Processing (ICBSLP), pp. 1–5. IEEE (2018)
3. Bojanowski, P., Grave, E., Joulin, A., Mikolov, T.: Enriching word vectors with subword information. Trans. Assoc. Comput. Linguist. **5**, 135–146 (2017)
4. Chakraborty, M., Huda, M.N.: Bangla document categorisation using multilayer dense neural network with TF-IDF. In: 2019 1st International Conference on Advances in Science, Engineering and Robotics Technology (ICASERT), pp. 1–4. IEEE (2019)
5. Chiu, J.P., Nichols, E.: Named entity recognition with bidirectional LSTM-CNNs. Trans. Assoc. Comput. Linguist. **4**, 357–370 (2016)
6. Chollet, F.: Deep Learning with Python, 1st edn. Manning Publications Co., Greenwich (2017)
7. Figueiredo, F., Rocha, L., Couto, T., Salles, T., Gonçalves, M.A., Meira Jr., W.: Word co-occurrence features for text classification. Inf. Syst. **36**(5), 843–858 (2011)
8. Goldberg, Y.: Neural network methods for natural language processing. Synth. Lect. Hum. Lang. Technol. **10**(1), 117–118 (2017)
9. Jozefowicz, R., Zaremba, W., Sutskever, I.: An empirical exploration of recurrent network architectures. In: International Conference on Machine Learning, pp. 2342–2350 (2015)
10. Kabir, F., Siddique, S., Kotwal, M.R.A., Huda, M.N.: Bangla text document categorization using stochastic gradient descent (SGD) classifier. In: 2015 International Conference on Cognitive Computing and Information Processing (CCIP), pp. 1–4. IEEE (2015)
11. Kim, Y.: Convolutional neural networks for sentence classification. arXiv preprint arXiv:1408.5882 (2014)
12. Kingma, D.P., Ba, J.: Adam: a method for stochastic optimization. arXiv preprint arXiv:1412.6980 (2014)
13. Li, C.H., Park, S.C.: An efficient document classification model using an improved back propagation neural network and singular value decomposition. Expert Syst. Appl. **36**(2), 3208–3215 (2009)
14. Lilleberg, J., Zhu, Y., Zhang, Y.: Support vector machines and Word2vec for text classification with semantic features. In: 2015 IEEE 14th International Conference on Cognitive Informatics & Cognitive Computing (ICCI*CC), pp. 136–140. IEEE (2015)
15. Mandal, A.K., Sen, R.: Supervised learning methods for Bangla web document categorization. arXiv preprint arXiv:1410.2045 (2014)
16. Mikolov, T., Chen, K., Corrado, G., Dean, J.: Efficient estimation of word representations in vector space. arXiv preprint arXiv:1301.3781 (2013)
17. Mikolov, T., Sutskever, I., Chen, K., Corrado, G.S., Dean, J.: Distributed representations of words and phrases and their compositionality. In: Advances in Neural Information Processing Systems, pp. 3111–3119 (2013)
18. Olah, C.: Understanding LSTM networks (2018). http://colah.github.io/posts/2015-08-Understanding-LSTMs/
19. Řehůřek, R., Sojka, P.: Software framework for topic modelling with large corpora. In: Proceedings of the LREC 2010 Workshop on New Challenges for NLP Frameworks, pp. 45–50. ELRA, Valletta, May 2010. http://is.muni.cz/publication/884893/en
20. Salton, G., Buckley, C.: Term-weighting approaches in automatic text retrieval. Inf. Process. Manag. **24**(5), 513–523 (1988)

21. Sumit, S.H., Hossan, M.Z., Al Muntasir, T., Sourov, T.: Exploring word embedding for Bangla sentiment analysis. In: 2018 International Conference on Bangla Speech and Language Processing (ICBSLP), pp. 1–5. IEEE (2018)
22. Young, T., Hazarika, D., Poria, S., Cambria, E.: Recent trends in deep learning based natural language processing. IEEE Comput. Intell. Mag. **13**(3), 55–75 (2018)
23. Zhang, D., Xu, H., Su, Z., Xu, Y.: Chinese comments sentiment classification based on Word2vec and SVMperf. Expert Syst. Appl. **42**(4), 1857–1863 (2015)

A Hybrid Approach Towards Two Stage Bengali Question Classification Utilizing Smart Data Balancing Technique

Md. Hasibur Rahman(✉), Chowdhury Rafeed Rahman, Ruhul Amin, Md. Habibur Rahman Sifat, and Afra Anika

United International University, Dhaka, Bangladesh
{mrahman161260,msifat152028,aanika161034}@bscse.uiu.ac.bd, rafeed@cse.uiu.ac.bd, ruhulamin6678@gmail.com

Abstract. Question Classification (QC) system classifies the questions in particular classes so that Question Answering (QA) System can provide correct answers for the questions. We present a two stage QC system for Bengali. One dimensional convolutional neural network (CNN) based model has been constructed for classifying questions into coarse classes in the first stage which uses word2vec feature representation of each word. A smart data balancing technique has been implemented in this stage which is a plus for any training dependent classification model. For each coarse class classified in the first stage, a separate Stochastic Gradient Descent (SGD) based classifier has been used in order to differentiate among the finer classes within that coarse class in stage two. TF-IDF representation of each word has been used as feature for each SGD classifier separately. Experiments show the effectiveness of this two stage classification method for Bengali question classification.

Keywords: Question Classification (QC) · Natural Language Processing (NLP) · Stochastic Gradient Descent (SGD) · Convolutional Neural Network (CNN) · Word2Vec · TF-IDF

1 Introduction

Question Classification (QC) system categorizes questions asked in natural language into different classes. With the increasing significance of information, people are using search based tools more robustly than ever before. These search based and knowledge based tools often retrieve appropriate information using some sort of QA system. The precondition of a sound QA system is a sound QC system. Different algorithms have been proposed in [3–5,15] and [23] for Bengali question classification task.

We propose a two stage approach for Bengali QC. Our approach shows superior performance compared to state-of-the-art Bengali question classifiers. We also propose a natural language related sample augmentation technique in order to remove class imbalance by generating theoretical samples. Such augmentation

T. Bhuiyan et al. (Eds.): ICONCS 2020, LNICST 325, pp. 454–464, 2020.
https://doi.org/10.1007/978-3-030-52856-0_36

technique can be of use when training deep learning based data hungry classifiers related to natural language.

In the first stage, we classify the given question into one of the six coarse classes of our dataset. In the next stage, we classify the question sample into one of the finer classes existing within the coarse class obtained from stage one. We have class imbalance among stage one coarse classes which we resolve by constructing samples using SMOTe (Synthetic Minority Oversampling Technique). We implement this technique on a special vector representation of our question samples in order to gain theoretical representative samples for the minority classes. Our Experimental results show that our approach is successful in creating representative theoretical samples from existing minority class samples. Such a balanced dataset has helped our 1D CNN based model of stage one to gain excellent results. 1D CNN works with the help of word2vec representation of each word. For each coarse class, we have a separate SGD classifier to classify the question sample into one of the finer classes within that coarse class. We have used TF-IDF representation of question words as source of features for our SGD classifiers. We keep stop words of question samples while classifying. In [1], the authors showed superior performance of different classifiers when stop words were not removed.

2 Literature Review

2.1 Existing Question Answering Systems

The oldest QA system named 'BASEBALL' [11] was developed in 1961. This system answers questions only related to baseball games. Another old QA system is 'LUNAR' [28]. It was developed in 1972 and could answer questions about soil samples. Different QA Systems have been developed in different languages such as Arabic QA system named 'AQAS' [21], Arabic factoid question answering system [10], Chinese QA system [30], Hindi QA system for E-learning Documents [16] and Hindi - English QA system [25]. Various analysis procedures for QA system exist such as morphological analysis [13], syntactical analysis [32], semantic analysis [27] and expected answer Type analysis [6]. Other popular QA systems are Apple Siri, Amazon Alexa and IBM Watson.

2.2 Research Works on Question Classification System

Question classification (QC) can be performed using two approaches such as rule-based approach and machine learning based approach [3]. Grammar coded rules are used to classify the questions to appropriate answer type in rule-based approach [24,26]. Harish Tayyar Madabushi and Mark Lee also proposed a rule-based approach [20] for QC. At first, based on a question structure they extracted relevant words. Then they classified questions based on rules that associated these words to concepts. Different types of classifiers have been used to categorize each question into a suitable answer type in machine learning based approach.

Some of the examples are - Support Vector Machine (SVM) [23,31], Support Vector Machines and Maximum Entropy Model [14], Naive Bayes (NB), Kernel Naive Bayes (KNB), Decision Tree (DT) and Rule Induction (RI) [3]. In [2], the authors proposed an approach for QC that combined SVM model and CNN model. In [8], the authors proposed an integrated genetic algorithm (GA) and machine learning (ML) approach for question classification in English-Chinese cross-language question answering. The authors of [22] analyzed and marked out different patterns of questions based on their grammatical structure and used machine learning algorithms to classify them. In [18], the authors proposed a kind of semi-supervised QC method that was based on ensemble learning. Information gain and sequential pattern for feature extraction to classify English questions were used in [19]. QC systems have been developed for different languages such as Chinese language [29,30,33], Spanish language [7], Japanese language [9], Arabic Language [12] and so on.

2.3 Question Classification Systems in Bengali Language

The authors extended their work done in [3] from single layer taxonomy to two-layer taxonomy using 9 coarse-grained classes and 69 fine-grained classes for Bengali question classification [5]. In [15], the authors used 6 coarse classes and 50 finer classes following the method proposed in [17]. Lexical features and syntactical features were used to classify questions into appropriate classes [23]. In [1], the authors provided a comparison of machine learning-based methods based on performance and computational complexity. They used 7 different classifiers to conduct comparison where Stochastic Gradient Descent (SGD) performed the best.

3 Our Dataset

We have used the same dataset as [15]. There are 3333 "wh" type of questions in the dataset. The two types of classes making up this dataset are - coarse class and finer class (within each coarse class). This aspect has been shown in Table 1. The maximum word number of a question is 21.

4 Proposed Methodology

4.1 Method Overview

Fig. 1 shows the complete high level overview of our proposed technique for Bengali question classification (QC). At first, we construct word2vec representation for all words of our question corpus. Using these vector representations, we perform class balance on our six coarse class QC data. We use 1D CNN based model in order to classify a question into one of the six coarse classes in the first stage using word2vec representation as feature. In the next stage, we use a separate SGD classifier for each separate coarse class in order to classify the question into

Table 1. Coarse and fine grained question categories

Coarse class	Finer class
ENTITY (482)	SUBSTANCE (10), SYMBOL (11), CURRENCY (24), TERM (10), WORD (10), LANGUAGE (30), COLOR (10), RELIGION (15), SPORT (10), BODY (10), FOOD (11), TECHNIQUE (10), PRODUCT (10), DISEASE (10), OTHER (22), LETTER (10), VEHICLE (11), PLANT (12), CREATIVE (216), INSTRUMENT (10), ANIMAL (10), EVENT (10)
NUMERIC (889)	COUNT (213), DISTANCE(13), CODE(10), TEMPERATURE (13), WEIGHT (20), MONEY (10), PERCENT (27), PERIOD (33), OTHER (34), DATE (452), SPEED (10), SIZE (54)
HUMAN (651)	INDIVIDUAL (610), GROUP (18), DESCRIPTION (13), TITLE (10)
LOCATION (611)	MOUNTAIN (23), COUNTRY (105), STATE (88), OTHER (121), CITY (274)
DESCRIPTION (198)	DEFINITION (141), REASON (26), MANNER (12), DESCRIPTION (19)
ABBREVIATION (502)	ABBREVIATION (489), EXPRESSION (13)

one of the finer classes residing within that coarse class. As source of feature, we use TF-IDF (Term Frequency Inverse Data Frequency) of the words residing in the question samples of each coarse class.

Figure 2 shows the data processing steps of our system. In the **filtration** step, we remove all the punctuation [ex: ',', '.', '?' ...] from the dataset. We now take two different routes of data preprocessing for our stage one and stage two classifier as shown in the figure. These steps are described in Subsect. 4.2 and 4.3.

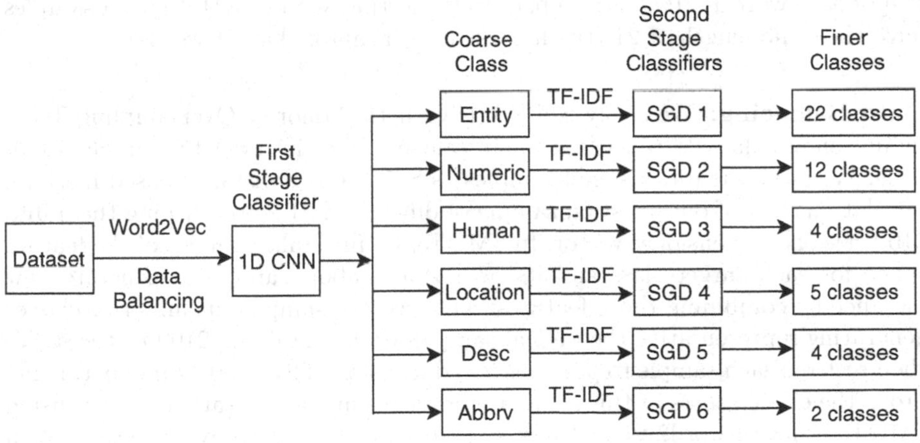

Fig. 1. System high level overview

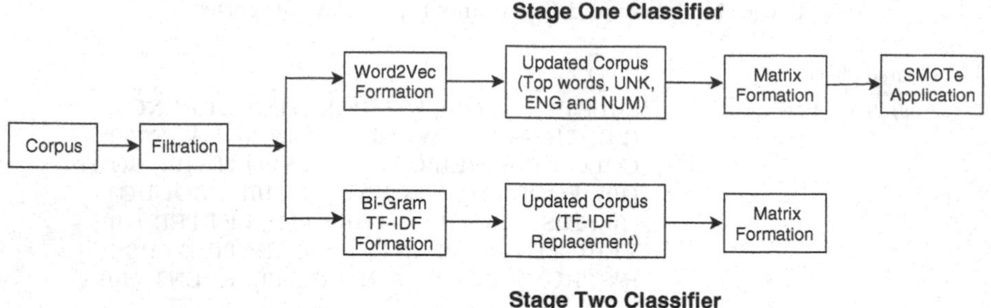

Fig. 2. Data preprocessing overview

4.2 Coarse Class Classification

Data Preprocessing: We need appropriate numeric representation of each word in order to train and test any deep learning based model. We use **word2vec** representation of each word as feature for the stage one classifier. For constructing word2vec of a particular word, a neural network hidden layer is trained such that the input is one hot vector of that word and target output is the probability distribution of all words being neighbour of our word of interest. The goal is to have similar vector representation for words of similar meaning.

We learn unique word2vec representation of only those words which appear at least 15 times in our corpus. We call these words our **top words**. There are 163 such words in our corpus. The learning process of word2vec would fail if we took non-frequent words as well. If a word represents numeric value, we replace that word with special keyword NUM. We also replace English words with ENG. Apart from these two kinds of words, words appearing less than 15 times are replaced with UNK keyword. Finally, we form word2vec of size 100 for each of the 163 top words, UNK, NUM and ENG. We store up the vectors in a new updated corpus. Each question sample is now of dimension 21×100 as vector size of each word is 100, and we pad each question sample such that all samples have the same length of 21 (the highest length sample has 21 words).

Data Balancing: We apply SMOTe (Synthetic Minority Oversampling Technique) on our dataset consisting of six coarse classes in order to gain class balance. We need one dimensional samples as SMOTe is a distance based method. We flatten each of our question sample of dimension 21×100 turning them into 2100 size one dimensional vector. In SMOTe, we first take samples of the feature space for each target class and its nearest neighbors, and then generate new instance by combining those features. Thus we oversample our minority classes generating representative theoretical samples each containing 2100 features. We then reshape each sample to previous two dimension of 21×100. Our experiments prove the effectiveness of this smart theoretical sample generation process using SMOTe utilizing word2vec features. It is to note that we apply SMOTe only on training data. All of our validation samples come from the actual dataset. Such oversampling helps our data hungry convolutional neural network based model to learn class discriminating features.

CNN Model: Figure 3 shows the architecture of our 1D CNN. This is a typical 1D CNN architecture consisting of some convolution layers as the first few layers and dense layers coming at later stages. We do not use any pooling layer as we have found out a decrease of validation accuracy while using such layers. It is probably because of the loss of some useful local features while pooling. We have used dropout layers after every convolution and dense layers in order to reduce overfitting. Except for the last layer, we use **relu** activation function in each layer. In the final output layer, we use **softmax** activation function. We use **Adam** optimizer for parameter update and **Categorical Crossentropy** loss function for performing multi-class classification. CNN can extract features from local input patches allowing for data efficiency and representation modularity. These same properties make them highly significant to sequence processing.

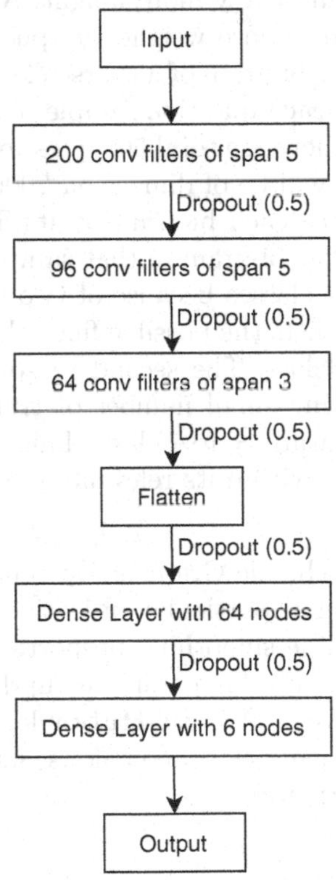

Fig. 3. Architecture of 1D convolutional neural network

4.3 Finer Class Classification

Data Preprocessing: We use TF-IDF representation for numeric representation of each word in order to train and test our finer class classifiers. TF-IDF indicates Term Frequency - Inverse Data Frequency. We use bi-gram for TF-IDF construction. The goal of bi-gram TF-IDF is to assign higher weights to the word couples that are more significant for our classification process. Generally, the word couples that appear many times in one class of data and have very low frequency in other classes are the most significant. Word couples that appear frequently in samples of all classes are generally insignificant. TF-IDF is used as feature with classifiers that have low number of parameters capable of learning even from small number of training samples.

Each of the six coarse classes of our dataset are divided into finer classes. For example, **Entity** coarse class is divided into 22 finer classes. We implement TF-IDF separately for the question samples of each separate coarse class as we have separate SGD model for each separate coarse class. The words which are not frequent among all class samples are the ones that actually help in distinguishing between the classes and should carry more weight. As a result, TF-IDF ensures less weight for stop words and more weight for special keywords. We calculate TF-IDF score for each unique bi-gram of a coarse class. Then we construct a one dimensional score vector for each question sample of that coarse class. Suppose, in a particular coarse class, there are total 500 question samples and 2000 unique bi-grams. Now, each sample will be of dimension 2000 for that particular coarse class. It is because we replace each bi-gram by its TF-IDF score according to the presence or absence of that bi-gram in that sample. We do not use any data balancing technique for finer classes because of two reasons. The first reason is that stage one classifier shortlists the possible finer classes by allowing us to look into the appropriate coarse class. The second reason is that we have separate SGD classifier (can learn using small number of training samples) working on the finer classes of each separate coarse class. This allows each SGD model to specialize on the finer classes within its relevant coarse class.

SGD Classifier: SGD (Stochastic Gradient Descent) is an iterative algorithm which is used for optimizing a particular objective function. It optimizes an unbiased function with suitable smoothing properties. For each iteration, a set of instances are chosen randomly for parameter update instead of choosing all instances in a dataset all at once. We use **Huber** loss function instead of mean squared error as it is less sensitive to anomalous data points. To reduce overfitting, we use **L2 regularization**.

5 Results and Discussion

We have used 10 fold cross validation for evaluating our proposed methods, as it prevents the rise or fall of validation accuracy by chance. For performance evaluation, we use **precision**, **recall** and **f1 score**. We calculate these measures as follows:

$$Precision = \frac{TruePositive}{TruePositive + FalsePositive} \quad (1)$$

$$Recall = \frac{TruePositive}{TruePositive + FalseNegative} \quad (2)$$

$$f1 - Score = 2 * \frac{Precision * Recall}{Precision + Recall} \quad (3)$$

It is to note that we have not eliminated stop words. In [1], all the machine learning based algorithms performed better when stop words were not eliminated. Table 2 shows the average result of precision, recall and f1-score after 10 fold cross-validation for coarse class classification. The validation accuracy for coarse class classification in our case is close to 95% which is significantly higher compared to validation accuracy of 89% obtained from the application of SGD. 1D CNN successfully learns discriminating features for coarse class classification with the help of data balancing technique.

Table 2. Experiment results of coarse class classification

Precision	0.9310
Recall	0.9344
F1 Score	0.9325

Table 3 shows the precision, recall and f1 score of all six SGD based models and the average of those scores. It is to note that Model 1 of the table is the SGD model used for classifying the finer classes within coarse class one (Entity coarse class). Similar implications are applicable for the other five models. Our method shows superior performance when it comes to finer class classification compared to the finer class classification results provided in [1] (Results provided in Table 4). This has been possible, because each of our six SGD models has the advantage of specializing on the finer classes of only one coarse class.

Table 3. Experiment results of finer class classification

	Model 1	Model 2	Model 3	Model 4	Model 5	Model 6	Average
Precision	0.9198	0.7693	0.8033	0.9035	0.9513	0.9282	0.8792
Recall	0.9404	0.7586	0.8371	0.9035	0.9641	0.9048	0.8847
F1 Score	0.9297	0.7404	0.8091	0.8964	0.9565	0.9018	0.8723

In natural language based classification tasks where there are main classes and sub-classes within each main class, such two stage approach can be a good way of boosting performance. Our proposed data balancing technique can be used with any imbalanced natural language based classification dataset where data hungry deep learning based models are to be implemented. It is to note that deep learning based 1D CNN model has given poor accuracy while trained and validated on the finer classes, as number of samples of each of these classes is insufficient to train data hungry deep learning based model. In such cases, models such as stochastic gradient descent which have low number of parameters to learn should be used.

Table 4. Finer class classification performance of state-of-the-art approaches

	MLP	SVM	NBC	SGD	GBC	KNN	RF
Accuracy	0.83	0.801	0.789	0.832	0.792	0.781	0.816
F1 Score	0.810	0.765	0.759	0.808	0.775	0.755	0.783

6 Conclusion

We have introduced a two stage approach for Bengali question classification - a deep learning based approach in the first stage and a gradient descent based approach in the second stage. We have also introduced a way of creating new representative theoretical samples for each coarse class which assists in maintaining class balance in training set. We have shown the effectiveness of our approach through experiments. Researchers working on building Bengali question answering system can follow this work as part of their question classification module. Our finer class classifiers are expected to show better performance provided that more training data per finer class is collected. We leave this as part of future work.

References

1. Anika, A., Rahman, M., Islam, D., Jameel, A.S.M.M., Rahman, C.R., et al.: Comparison of machine learning based methods used in Bengali question classification. arXiv preprint arXiv:1911.03059 (2019)
2. Aouichat, A., Hadj Ameur, M.S., Geussoum, A.: Arabic question classification using support vector machines and convolutional neural networks. In: Silberztein, M., Atigui, F., Kornyshova, E., Métais, E., Meziane, F. (eds.) NLDB 2018. LNCS, vol. 10859, pp. 113–125. Springer, Cham (2018). https://doi.org/10.1007/978-3-319-91947-8_12
3. Banerjee, S., Bandyopadhyay, S.: Bengali question classification: towards developing QA system. In: Proceedings of the 3rd Workshop on South and Southeast Asian Natural Language Processing, pp. 25–40 (2012)

4. Banerjee, S., Bandyopadhyay, S.: An empirical study of combing multiple models in Bengali question classification. In: Proceedings of the Sixth International Joint Conference on Natural Language Processing, pp. 892–896 (2013)
5. Banerjee, S., Bandyopadhyay, S.: Ensemble approach for fine-grained question classification in bengali. In: 27th Pacific Asia Conference on Language, Information, and Computation, pp. 75–84 (2013)
6. Benamara, F.: Cooperative question answering in restricted domains: the WEBCOOP experiment. In: Proceedings of the Conference on Question Answering in Restricted Domains, pp. 31–38 (2004)
7. Cumbreras, M.Á.G., López, L., Santiago, F.M.: BRUJA: question classification for Spanish. using machine translation and an English classifier. In: Proceedings of the Workshop on Multilingual Question Answering, pp. 39–44. Association for Computational Linguistics (2006)
8. Day, M.Y., Ong, C.S., Hsu, W.L.: Question classification in English-Chinese cross-language question answering: an integrated genetic algorithm and machine learning approach. In: IEEE International Conference on Information Reuse and Integration, pp. 203–208. IEEE (2007)
9. Dridan, R., Baldwin, T.: What to classify and how: experiments in question classification for Japanese. In: Proceedings of the 10th Conference of the Pacific Association for Computational Linguistics, pp. 333–341 (2007)
10. Fareed, N.S., Mousa, H.M., Elsisi, A.B.: Syntactic open domain Arabic question/answering system for factoid questions. In: 9th International Conference on Informatics and Systems, pp. NLP-1. IEEE (2014)
11. Green Jr, B.F., Wolf, A.K., Chomsky, C., Laughery, K.: Baseball: an automatic question-answerer. In: Papers Presented at the May 9–11, 1961, Western Joint IRE-AIEE-ACM Computer Conference, pp. 219–224. ACM (1961)
12. Hasan, A.M., Rassem, T.H., Noorhuzaimi, M., et al.: Combined support vector machine and pattern matching for Arabic Islamic hadith question classification system. In: Saeed, F., Gazem, N., Mohammed, F., Busalim, A. (eds.) IRICT 2018. Advances in Intelligent Systems and Computing, vol. 843, pp. 278–290. Springer, Cham (2018). https://doi.org/10.1007/978-3-319-99007-1_27
13. Hovy, E., Gerber, L., Hermjakob, U., Junk, M., Lin, C.Y.: Question answering in webclopedia. In: TREC, vol. 52, pp. 53–56 (2000)
14. Huang, Z.: Question classification using head words and their hypernyms. In: Proceedings of the Conference on Empirical Methods in Natural Language Processing, pp. 927–936 (2008)
15. Islam, M.A., Kabir, M.F., Abdullah-Al-Mamun, K., Huda, M.N.: Word/phrase based answer type classification for Bengali question answering system. In: 5th International Conference on Informatics, Electronics and Vision (ICIEV), pp. 445–448. IEEE (2016)
16. Kumar, P., Kashyap, S., Mittal, A., Gupta, S.: A Hindi question answering system for e-learning documents. In: 3rd International Conference on Intelligent Sensing and Information Processing, pp. 80–85. IEEE (2005)
17. Li, X., Morie, P., Roth, D.: Semantic integration in text: from ambiguous names to identifiable entities. AI Mag. **26**(1), 45 (2005)
18. Li, Y., Su, L., Chen, J., Yuan, L.: Semi-supervised learning for question classification in CQA. Natural Comput. **16**(4), 567–577 (2017)
19. Liu, Y., Yi, X., Chen, R., Zhai, Z., Gu, J.: Feature extraction based on information gain and sequential pattern for English question classification. IET Softw. **12**(6), 520–526 (2018)

20. Madabushi, H.T., Lee, M.: High accuracy rule-based question classification using question syntax and semantics. In: Proceedings of COLING 2016, the 26th International Conference on Computational Linguistics: Technical Papers, pp. 1220–1230 (2016)
21. Mohammed, F., Nasser, K., Harb, H.: A knowledge based Arabic question answering system (AQAS). ACM SIGART Bull. **4**(4), 21–30 (1993)
22. Mohasseb, A., Bader-El-Den, M., Cocea, M.: Question categorization and classification using grammar based approach. Inf. Process. Manag. **54**(6), 1228–1243 (2018)
23. Nirob, S.M.H., Nayeem, M.K., Islam, M.S.: Question classification using support vector machine with hybrid feature extraction method. In: 20th International Conference of Computer and Information Technology (ICCIT), pp. 1–6. IEEE (2017)
24. Prager, J., Radev, D., Brown, E., Coden, A.: The use of predictive annotation for question answering in trec8. In: In NIST Special Publication 500–246: The Eighth Text REtrieval Conference (TREC 8). Citeseer (1999)
25. Sekine, S., Grishman, R.: Hindi-english cross-lingual question-answering system. ACM Trans. Asian Lang. Inf. Process. **2**(3), 181–192 (2003)
26. Voorhees, E.M., et al.: The TREC-8 question answering track report. In: TREC, vol. 99, pp. 77–82. Citeseer (1999)
27. Wong, W.: Practical approach to knowledge-based question answering with natural language understanding and advanced reasoning. arXiv preprint arXiv:0707.3559 (2007)
28. Woods, W.: The lunar sciences natural language information system. BBN report (1972)
29. Xu, W., Yu, Z., Ting, L., Jinshan, M.: Syntactic structure parsing based Chinese question classification. J. Chin. Inf. Process. **2** (2006)
30. Yu, Z., Ting, L., Xu, W.: Modified Bayesian model based question classification. J. Chin. Inf. Process. **19**(2), 100–105 (2005)
31. Zhang, D., Lee, W.S.: Question classification using support vector machines. In: Proceedings of the 26th Annual International ACM SIGIR Conference on Research and Development in Information Retrieval, pp. 26–32. ACM (2003)
32. Zheng, Z.: AnswerBus question answering system. In: Proceedings of the Second International Conference on Human Language Technology Research, pp. 399–404. Morgan Kaufmann Publishers Inc. (2002)
33. Zheng-tao, Y., Xiao-zhong, F., Jian-yi, G.: Chinese question classification based on support vector machine. J. South China Univ. Technol. **33**(9), 25–29 (2005)

An Empirical Framework to Identify Authorship from Bengali Literary Works

Sumnoon Ibn Ahmad, Lamia Alam, and Mohammed Moshiul Hoque(✉)

Department of Computer Science and Engineering (CSE), Chittagong University of Engineering and Technology (CUET), Chattogram 4349, Bangladesh
sumnoon52@gmail.com, lamiacse09@gmail.com, mmoshiulh@gmail.com

Abstract. Authorship attribution is the process of identifying the probable author of an unknown document. This paper proposes a neural network based framework, which identifies the authorship from Bengali literary documents. For this purpose, a corpus consisting of 12,142 text documents of 23 writers/bloggers is built. A static dictionary is used to count vectorization and important features are selected using information gain. The proposed system is trained with 9099 documents and tested with 3043 documents. The experimental result shows that neural network with n-gram and parts of speech (PoS) features achieved 94% accuracy on developed corpus.

Keywords: Bangla language processing · Authorship attribution · Feature extraction · Machine learning

1 Introduction

Due to the rapid growth in the use of internet and its effortless access via digital devices a substantial contents are uploaded enormously and quickly on the web as digital form. Also increasing popularity of text digitization and online documentation has made it very difficult to detect the authorship of a digital text. Therefore, automatic authorship detection or attribution has gained much attention in recent years to identify the original author from a huge amount of digital contents. Authorship detection is conducted mainly to verify authorship of a particular text. It is conducted by comparing works of other authors with the author in question. There are many application of authorship attribution such as plagiarism detection, resolving ownership dispute of unknown text, forensic linguistics etc. [6,14,18].

Authorship detection is one of applied field of Natural Language Processing (NLP), which utilizes the stylometric approach to determine authorship of unknown text. The stylometric approach refers to the statistical approach to differentiate writing styles of different authors [9]. Most of the authors tend to follow unique behavior in their text whether it is the use of certain word or collection of words or sometimes it maybe certain style of writing. Stylometry helps in determining these behaviors of the author. In order to do that, multiple texts

T. Bhuiyan et al. (Eds.): ICONCS 2020, LNICST 325, pp. 465–476, 2020.
https://doi.org/10.1007/978-3-030-52856-0_37

with known authors are used to extract stylometric features and using these features the text of unknown author is compared with text of known authors.

Although a substantial amount of works have been conducted on authorship attribution in English and other European languages, no remarkable work has been done yet on authorship attribution for text written in Bengali language. The major barrier of performing research on authorship attribution in Bengali due to the lack of linguistic resources in digital form and inadequate corpora. There are many well-known writers in Bengali literature and important properties can be discovered from their writing variations. These properties can be useful for literary, history, social and cultural studies respectively.

An author usually follows an unique writing style or feature which may be utilized to identify authorship of a particular writing. Stylometry concerns the writing style and it investigates the writing to find the specific pattern or characteristics of that writer. The major contributions of this work is that, we proposed a neural network based authorship identification system for Bengali texts using feature extraction method to extract n-gram and parts of speech (PoS) features to improve accuracy. In order to train and test our system we developed a Bengali text corpora including 23 authored texts which contains about 12,142 texts files. Also, we evaluated the proposed framework against two other algorithms-Random-forest and Support Vector Machine (SVM) are implemented and tested on our developed dataset. The experimental finding reveals that, the proposed neural-network based framework with PoS features achieved the higher accuracy than other algorithms in detecting authorship.

2 Related Work

Automatic identification of authorship is a long studied research issue for well resourced languages like, English. However, it is in preliminary stage till now with respect to Bengali literature. A character-level CNN method was proposed in [15], which identifies authorship and achieved 96% accuracy for 6 authors and 69% accuracy for 14 authors respectively. Marouf et al. proposed a technique that used BanglaMusicStylo dataset and gained 86.29% accuracy on 1470 Bengali songs of Rabindranath Tagore and Kazi Nazrul Islam [11,17]. A hierarchical classifier based method was developed to detect authorship of unknown text [7]. A neural network based approach was proposed, which achieved 85% accuracy for 5 writers in Bengali languages. They used word length, and Wh words as features with small dataset [12]. Islam et al. is used n-grams, conjunction, pronoun features to detect authorship of 10 authors, which gained 96% accuracy [13]. Hossain et al. used word frequency, modified word frequency, spelling of word features and gained 90.67% accuracy 6 Bangladeshi writers [10]. Chakraborty et al. investigated the ten-fold cross-validation and concluded that SVM is better than decision tree and neural network for small dataset [6]. Phani et al. [18] had devised a process with character bi-grams and tri-grams and word uni, bi and tri-grams. They have also used a corpus of three thousands text from three prominent Bengali authors. Instead of using literature of Bengali authors as corpus, Das et al. [8] have used text from four Bengali blog writers. They have used different feature count, such as length of different word, sentence, number of parts of speech used in sentence and number of words used in a certain position of the sentence. Saha et al. used multi-layer perceptron to correctly attribute short text to their authors using a twitter dataset of four authors and 400 tweets for each author with accuracy of 96.44% [21].

Most of the works stated above had very small dataset and less variation in author categories or limited writing styles. In contrast to these, we developed a neural network based system for Bengali authorship attribution that is trained and tested with larger dataset.

3 Proposed Methodology

Proposed authorship detection system is divided into two phases- training phase and testing phase. At first, machine learning model has been trained using the training dataset and classification accuracy of the model is evaluated using the testing dataset in testing phase. Around 75% of prepared dataset is used in training and 25% is used in testing. As our primary dataset was raw and full of noises, we have to perform some data cleaning and remove noises. Then, the normalized data is used to extract features. After extracting the features, most useful features are selected using information gain (IG) value of the features. Then, final dataset was prepared and used to train classifier model. We used three classification algorithms and prepared four models. Neural network model was prepared in two ways, in one model we did not use parts of speech features and in other model we have used parts of speech features. Then, we have compared both model with our test set which was unknown to our models during training period. A schematic representation of our proposed authorship detection system is illustrated in Fig. 1.

3.1 Input

We have collected text from 23 writers which includes various writing styles. We have used hold-out method for training and testing our model as it is very good on large dataset and needs less computational power. For training, text of a certain writer was stored in a folder with his name and compressed for training set. For testing, a collection of text which was unknown to the model during training is used and the authorship detection was done with the help of previous knowledge and characterising the writing style of the text. Figure 2 shows an sample of raw data.

3.2 Pre-processing of Raw Data

Raw data is not suitable for training purpose due to noises. Sometimes words from foreign languages are introduced into writings and these words help to detect authorship of particular text (e.g. literature of Kazi Nazrul Islam used

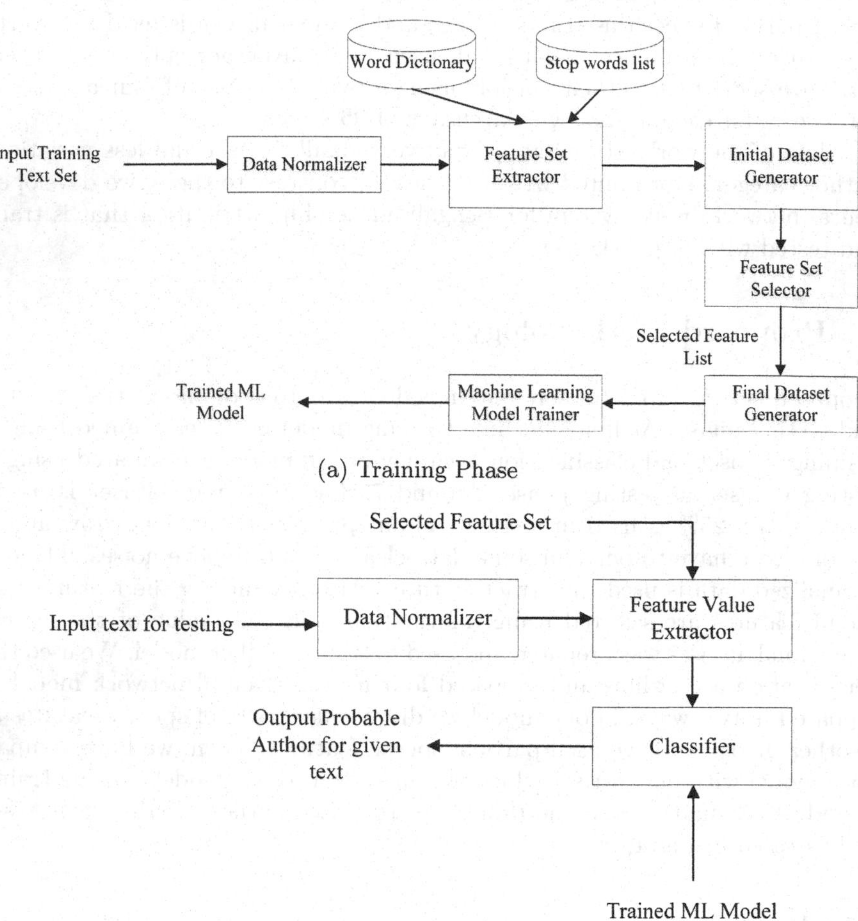

Fig. 1. Proposed authorship detection system

আজ মহাবিশ্বে মহাজাগরণ, আজ মহামাতার মহা আনন্দের দিন, আজ মহামানবতার মধ্যযুগের মহা উদ্‌বোধন! আজ নারায়ণ আর ক্ষীরোদসাগরে নিদ্রিত নন। নরের মাঝে আজ তাঁহার অপূর্ব মুক্তি-কাঙাল বেশ। ওই শোনো, শৃঙ্খলিত নিপীড়িত বন্দিদের শৃঙ্খলের ঝনৎকার।

Fig. 2. Sample text

Urdu words in his literature) or produces unwanted noise in other cases. Therefore, pre-processing is used to reduce error rate. Each text can be divided into multiple sentences. The end or beginning of a sentence is determined with punctuation. A collection of Bengali and English punctuation mark has been used to decompose the text into sentence. After the decomposition, the punctuation are removed as they don't have any significance. A dictionary of stop words are used to remove unrelated words from the text. A pre-processed text is shown in Fig. 3 as an example.

আজ মহাবিশ্বে মহাজাগরণ আজ মহামাতার মহা আনন্দের দিন আজ মহামানবতার মধ্যযুগের মহা উদ্ বোধন ।
আজ নারায়ণ আর ক্ষীরোদসাগরে নিদ্রিত নন ।
নরের মাঝে আজ তাঁহার অপূর্ব মুক্তি কাঙাল বেশ ।
ওই শোনো শৃঙ্খলিত নিপীড়িত বন্দিদের শৃঙ্খলের ঝনৎকার ।

Fig. 3. Pre-processed sample text

3.3 Feature Extraction

N-gram and PoS features are used to observe in the corpus. We have verified with uni-gram, bi-gram and tri-gram of word because increased grams do not give any significant information about authors. The training set is tokenized into uni-grams. Then we combined them to create word bi-gram and tri-gram. A PoS tagger is used to identify token from each sentence. This tagger takes text as input and detects each word from the text and assign them with relative parts of speech. A modified PoS tagger is used to tag other words outside of parts of speech. Due to lack of proper dynamic PoS tagger in Bengali, we had to create our own static PoS tagger which can detect nouns, pronouns, adjectives, verbs, adverbs and conjunctions. The Pos tagger utilizes a dictionary of words which is consist of more than 50 conjunctions, 30 pronouns, 23000 nouns, 1100 adjectives, 70000 verbs and 16000 adverbs. Conjunctions and Pronouns were collected from [5]. Frequency of each features is calculated from the text, which is used to find the important features. Figure 4 shows a set of sample features. With the help of word dictionary and n-gram extractor, a large number of feature words are found from the training data. These features can be reduced by the information gain (IG). IG is used to determine how much information can be extracted using a feature and how important is the feature to contribute in overall prediction system. The information gain (IG) is calculated by Eq. 1.

$$IG(S,T) = E(S) - \sum_{t \in T} p(t) \times E(t) \tag{1}$$

সাথে	কোন	কিন্তু	না	করিয়া
0	1	12	28	1

Fig. 4. Sample text after feature extraction

where, $E(S)$ is defined as entropy which is the opposite of probability and it is directly related to the information gain in such a way that the more the entropy of an event the more information can be gained from that event. Entropy is calculated by Eq. 2.

$$E(S) = -\sum_{x \in S} p(x) \times \log_2 p(x) \tag{2}$$

3.4 Final Dataset Generation

With the help of information gain calculation and stop word dictionary we have selected most important features from our primary dataset and removed unnecessary words and stop words from the text and prepared our final dataset. The final dataset is generated in .csv format.

3.5 Classifier

A neural network model is trained with developed dataset [22]. The propose neural network consist of three hidden layer with 128, 64 and 32 nodes in each layer. An activation function [20] is used to find the output from a node. In the proposed model, the rectified linear unit function a.k.a *ReLU* is used. Figure 5 illustrates the neural network model. The proposed neural network model have used three hidden layer and one input and one output layer. In each hidden layer number of nodes or neurons were 128, 64 and 32 respectively. Each neurons, also known as perceptron [19], acts as a simple learner that takes one or multiple inputs and process them with a weight given on each of the input. Than it generates a binary decision. Using multiple similar neurons a layer of multi-layer perceptron is created. For weight optimization we have used Adam stochastic gradient-based optimization [16] and number of epoch was 3000.

The training procedure consists of three major steps:

- **Step 1: Forward Pass.** In forward pass we run the sample vector from input layer to output layer through multiple hidden layers. The input value is multiplied with weight and a bias is added. Then the output is applied through a activation function in our case ReLU function. Suppose, w denotes the vector of weights, x is the vector of inputs, b is the bias and ϕ is the activation function, then for the $i_t h$ neuron the output y would be given by Eq. 3.

$$y = \sum_{i=1}^{n} w_i x_i + b = \phi(w^x + b) \tag{3}$$

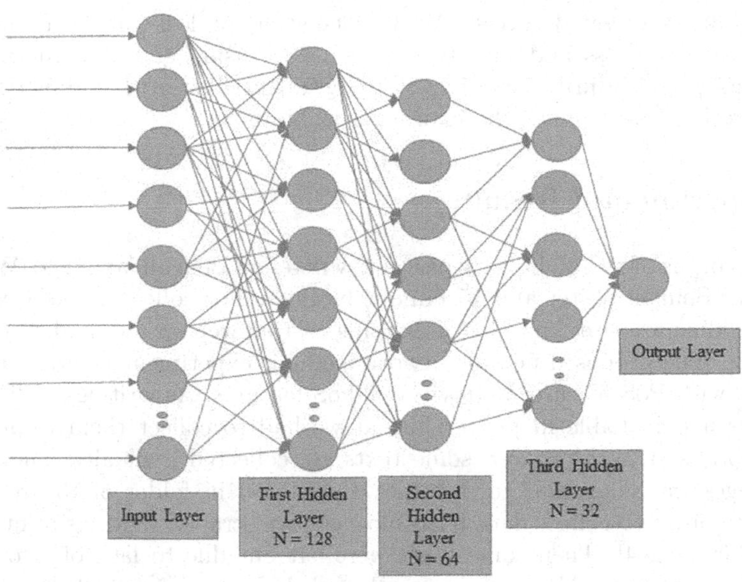

Fig. 5. Multilayer perceptron model having three hidden layers

Activation Function: It is used to determine the output of neural network like yes or no. Depending on the function the value results from 0 to −1 or −1 to 1 etc. In our system, we have used Rectified Linear Unit (*ReLU*) activation function, which is given by Eq. 4.

$$\phi(x) = max(0, x) \tag{4}$$

It is one of the most simplest and popular activation function. The biggest advantage of *ReLU* is the non-saturation of its gradient, which improves the acceleration of Adam stochastic optimization more than any other activation function.

- **Step 2: Calculation of loss function.** After the forward pass we would get some output from our model which refers as predicted output. Using predicted output and real output we calculate loss that we need to propagate using back-propagation algorithm. We have used cross-entropy as loss function in our system. The calculation of loss function is performed by calculating loss for each label separately and then summing the result [Eq. 5].

$$loss = -\sum_{c=1}^{M} y_{o,c} \log(p_{0,c}) \tag{5}$$

where, M is the number of classes, y is the binary indicator (0 or 1) of classification and $p_{0,c}$ is the predicted probability observation (o) of class c

- **Step 3: Backward Pass.** After calculation of loss function, we back-propagate the loss and update the model by using gradient. In this step, weights would adjust according to the gradient flow in that direction. The process is repeated until the final error is minimum.

4 Experimental Results

We used corpus of 12,142 literary passages written in Bengali language. We chose 8 eminent Bengali writer and 15 famous bloggers. For collecting data, we have scraped online websites and blog sites using custom web scraper and saved them in doc file. The proposed neural network model is experimented in two types of datasets: with PoS features and without PoS features. As writings of literature writers is not available in proper format we had to collect them from books, online portals [1,3]. Moreover, some texts are collected manually. The data in later stages was converted to .txt files and stored in folder of the respective author. In order to collect data from bloggers, we scraped writings of numerous bloggers from [2,4]. Then some texts were left out due to lack of information and volumes of text. Also, we have collected data from [5] which have a good collection of writings from various bloggers. Table 1 represents the summary of dataset.

Table 1. Data summary

Number of documents	12142
Number of sentences (approx.)	607050
Number of words (approx.)	1214100
Total unique words (approx.)	29000

In order to classify the texts, we have to feed our collected documents to our classifier model. Table 2 shows the summary of dataset used for our classification process.

Table 2. Data summary for train and test phase

	Training	Testing
Number of class	23	23
Number of documents	9099	3043
Average word per documents	50	52

4.1 Evaluation Measures

Confusion matrix is used to evaluate our model against test data. Confusion matrix of proposed approach with parts of speech feature is shown in Fig. 6.

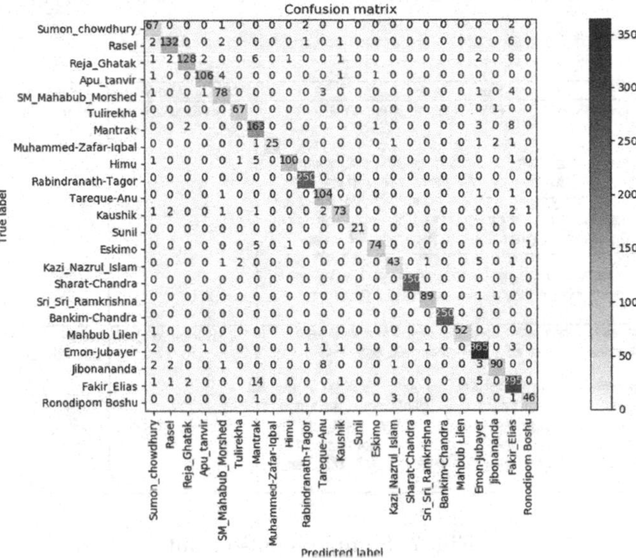

Fig. 6. Confusion matrix of proposed approach with PoS features

Figure 6 shows that 250 texts of Rabindranath Tagor, 250 text of Sarat Chandra and 250 text of Bankim Chandra are detected correctly. Precision, recall, F_1 score and accuracy measures are used as per Eq. 6 – Eq. 9 respectively.

$$\texttt{Precision} = \frac{TP}{TP + FP} \tag{6}$$

$$\texttt{Recall} = \frac{TP}{TP + FN} \tag{7}$$

$$F_1 = \frac{2 * precision * recall}{precision + recall} \tag{8}$$

$$\texttt{Accuracy} = \frac{TP + TN}{TP + TN + FP + FN} \tag{9}$$

Here, TP, TN, FP and FN stands for true positive, true negative, false positive and false negative respectively. In Table 3 shows the precision, recall and F_1 and accuracy of different classification algorithms used based on our dataset.

4.2 Sample Input and Output

Figure 7 shows the sample input and corresponding output as examples. First example indicates the incorrect prediction of author and second shows the correct

Table 3. Comparison of results

	Precision	Recall	F_1	Accuracy
Neural Network (without PoS feature)	0.92	0.90	0.91	91.62
Neural Network (with PoS feature)	0.94	0.94	0.94	94.25

Sample Input	Real Author	Probable Author
তৃতীয় পরিচ্ছেদ বিজয় — বদ্ধজীবের মনের কি অবস্থা হলে মুক্তি হতে পারে? শ্রীরামকৃষ্ণ — ঈশ্বরের কৃপায় তীব্র বৈরাগ্য হলে, এই কামিনী-কাঞ্চনে আসক্তি থেকে নিস্তার হতে পারে। তীব্র বৈরাগ্য কাকে বলে? হচ্ছে হবে, ঈশ্বরের নাম করা যাক — এ-সব মন্দ বৈরাগ্য। যার তীব্র বৈরাগ্য, তার প্রাণ ভগবানের জন্য ব্যাকুল; মার প্রাণ যেমন পেটের ছেলের জন্য ব্যাকুল। যার তীব্র বৈরাগ্য, সে ভগবান ভিন্ন আর কিছু চায় না। সংসারকে পাতকুয়া দেখে: তার মনে হয়, বুঝি ডুবে গেলুম। আত্মীয়দের কাল সাপ দেখে, তাদের কাছ থেকে পালাতে ইচ্ছা হয়; আর পালায়ও। বাড়ির বন্দোবস্ত করি, তারপর ঈশ্বরচিন্তা করব — এ-কথা ভাবেই না। ভিতরে খুব রোখ।......	Sri Sri Ramakrishna	Jibonananda
অষ্টম পরিচ্ছেদ সকলে আনন্দ করিতেছেন। ঠাকুর কেশবকে বলিতেছেন, "তুমি প্রকৃতি দেখে শিষ্য কর না, তাই এইরূপ ভেঙে ভেঙে যায়। "মানুষগুলি দেখতে সব একরকম, কিন্তু ভিন্ন প্রকৃতি। কারু ভিতর সত্ত্বগুণ বেশি, কারু রজোগুণ বেশি, কারু তমোগুণ। পুলিগুলি দেখতে সব একরকম। কিন্তু কারু ভিতর ক্ষীরের পোর, কারু ভিতর নারিকেলের ছাঁই, কারু ভিতর কলায়ের পোর। (সকলের হাস্য) "আমার কি ভাব জানো? আমি খাই-দাই থাকি, আর সব মা জানে। আমার তিন কথাতে গায়ে কাঁটা বেঁধে। গুরু, কর্তা আর বাবা।	Sri Sri Ramakrishna	Sri Sri Ramakrishna

Fig. 7. Sample input-output

prediction of author. The reason behind the incorrect prediction is that certain text of the author Sri Sri Ramakrishna and the author Jibonanada are almost similar and frequency of PoS features are also similar.

4.3 Comparison with Existing Techniques

In order to measure the effectiveness, we compare the proposed method with the available techniques. Table 4 shows the summary of the comparison.

Table 4 reveals that the proposed system has performed very well compared to other systems. The previous approaches used their own dataset. A recent method proposed by Khatun et al. achieved the higher accuracy (96%) than others [15]. However, they used only 6600 text documents written by 6 authors. Another method [13] also found the 96% accuracy for 10 authors with very small text documents (only 3125). Accuracy may vary due to the writing styles. Therefore, accuracy may comes naturally higher for small dataset and limited number of authors due to less variation of writing styles. The proposed system considered the larger number of text documents (12,142) and authors (23) than the existing approaches. The system achieved a reasonably good accuracy which amount to 94% in terms of number of documents and authors.

Table 4. Comparison with previous approaches

	Total Authors	No. of documents	Accuracy (%)
Khatun et al. [15]	6	6600	96
Chowdhury et al. [7]	6	2,400	92.9
Islam et al. [12]	5	1,973	85
Islam et al. [13]	10	3,125	96
Hossain et al. [10]	6	2,764	90.5
Proposed System	23	12,142	94.12

5 Conclusion

This paper introduced a neural network based approach for identifying authorship from Bengali literary or blog texts. The proposed system can identify authorship of 23 authors in Bengali literature. To build the framework a self-developed dataset is used for training and testing with 12,142 text documents. The neural network approach with n-gram and parts of speech features provided the better accuracy than the existing techniques. The proposed system is not tested with standard dataset and not validate with the standard technique which are the main limitations of the system. The accuracy may be improved with more label data. K-fold cross validation technique may be used for training phases for better training accuracy. These are left as future issues.

References

1. Ebanglalibraray. https://www.ebanglalibrary.com
2. Sachalayatan. https://en.sachalayatan.com
3. Society for natural language technology research. https://nltr.org/index.php
4. Somewhere in blog. https://www.somewhereinblog.net
5. Stylogenetics. https://github.com/olee12/Stylogenetics
6. Chakraborty, T.: Authorship identification in Bengali literature: a comparative analysis. CoRR abs/1208.6268 (2012). http://arxiv.org/abs/1208.6268
7. Chowdhury, H.A., Imon, M.A.H., Islam, M.S.: Authorship attribution in Bengali literature using fasttext's hierarchical classifier. In: 2018 4th International Conference on Electrical Engineering and Information & Communication Technology, iCEEiCT, pp. 102–106. IEEE (2018)
8. Das, P., Tasmim, R., Ismail, S.: An experimental study of stylometry in bangla literature. In: 2015 2nd International Conference on Electrical Information and Communication Technologies, EICT, pp. 575–580. IEEE (2015)
9. Holmes, D.I.: The evolution of stylometry in humanities scholarship. Literary Linguist. Comput. **13**(3), 111–117 (1998)
10. Hossain, M.T., Rahman, M.M., Ismail, S., Islam, M.S.: A stylometric analysis on Bengali literature for authorship attribution. In: 2017 20th International Conference of Computer and Information Technology, ICCIT, pp. 1–5. IEEE (2017)

11. Hossain, R., Al Marouf, A.: Banglamusicstylo: a stylometric dataset of bangla music lyrics. In: 2018 International Conference on Bangla Speech and Language Processing, ICBSLP, pp. 1–5 (2018)
12. Islam, M.A., Kabir, M.M., Islam, M.S., Tasnim, A.: Authorship attribution on Bengali literature using stylometric features and neural network. In: 2018 4th International Conference on Electrical Engineering and Information & Communication Technology, iCEEiCT, pp. 360–363. IEEE (2018)
13. Islam, N., Hoque, M.M., Hossain, M.R.: Automatic authorship detection from Bengali text using stylometric approach. In: 2017 20th International Conference of Computer and Information Technology, ICCIT, pp. 1–6. IEEE (2017)
14. Juola, P.: Rowling and Galbraith: an authorial analysis. Language Blog (2013)
15. Khatun, A., Rahman, A., Islam, M.S., Marium-E-Jannat: Authorship attribution in Bangla literature using character-level CNN. arXiv preprint arXiv:2001.05316 (2020)
16. Kingma, D.P., Ba, J.: Adam: a method for stochastic optimization. arXiv preprint arXiv:1412.6980 (2014)
17. Marouf, A., Hossain, R.: Lyricist identification using stylometric features utilizing banglamusicstylo dataset. In: 2nd International Conference on Bangla Speech and Language Processing (ICBSLP2019) (2019)
18. Phani, S., Lahiri, S., Biswas, A.: A supervised learning approach for authorship attribution of bengali literary texts. ACM Trans. Asian and Low-Resour. Lang. Inf. Process. (TALLIP) **16**(4), 28 (2017)
19. Rosenblatt, F.: The perceptron: a probabilistic model for information storage and organization in the brain. Psychol. Rev. **65**(6), 386 (1958)
20. Rumelhart, D.E., Hinton, G.E., Williams, R.J.: Learning internal representations by error propagation. California Univ San Diego La Jolla Inst for Cognitive Science, Technical report (1985)
21. Saha, N., Das, P., Saha, H.N.: Authorship attribution of short texts using multilayer perceptron. Int. J. Appl. Pattern Recogn. **5**(3), 251–259 (2018)
22. Wilson, E., Tufts, D.W.: Multilayer perceptron design algorithm. In: Proceedings of IEEE Workshop on Neural Networks for Signal Processing, pp. 61–68. IEEE (1994)

Supervised Machine Learning for Multi-label Classification of Bangla Articles

Dip Bhakta[1](✉), Avimonnu Arnob Dash[1], Md. Faisal Bari[1], and Swakkhar Shatabda[2]

[1] Department of ICT, Bangladesh University of Professionals (BUP), Dhaka, Bangladesh
bhaktadip@gmail.com, info@bup.edu.bd

[2] Department of Computer Science and Engineering, United International University (UIU), Dhaka, Bangladesh
swakkhar@cse.uiu.ac.bd

Abstract. Multi-label text classification has been a key point of research in the area of text classification latterly. But to the best of our knowledge, there have been very few research on multi-label text classification for Bangla text. There is also inadequacy of proper dataset for multi-label classification on Bangla text. Multi-label classification has many applications in the real world. One of them is automated labeling of articles of online news portals so that readers can easily look up other news articles on similar topics by clicking on hyperlinks. We applied supervised multi-label classification techniques on Bangla news articles for automated tag generation to predict related topics. We have built a new dataset from scratch and applied various problem transformation methods for multi-label classification with naive bayes classifier, logistic regression and SVM. We have analyzed the performance of these algorithms on Bangla news articles with precision, recall, f1-score and hamming loss. The dataset and the analysis of the results can be valuable for further research on multi-label text classification of Bangla text. We have open-sourced the dataset and the source code of this work (http://bit.ly/34cSNCR).

Keywords: Multi-label classification · Supervised · Bangla text · SVM · Naive bayes · Logistic regression · F1-score

1 Introduction

Extensive amount of works have been done on text classification. Many works have also been done on Bangla text classification. It has been an admired research area in Bangla natural language processing latterly. Usually a text classification process classifies a text to a single class from a set of classes. If the set of classes consists of only two classes, then this is called binary classification, in contrast, it is called multiclass classification if the set of classes consists of more than two classes. But many real world applications need prediction of more than one class from a set of classes. One of these applications is to predict the tags from news articles of online news portals [1]. Tags are used in online news articles so that readers can easily find the related articles on the similar topics.

T. Bhuiyan et al. (Eds.): ICONCS 2020, LNICST 325, pp. 477–487, 2020.
https://doi.org/10.1007/978-3-030-52856-0_38

When one or more than one classes are to be predicted from a set of classes, this is called multi-label classification. Multi-label learning also has applications in functional genomics, improving text search results etc. [2, 3]. There are several other interesting applications of multi-label classification that includes music categorization into emotions [4–6], semantic video annotation [7, 8] and direct marketing [9].

There have been many works on multi-label text classifications too [10, 11]. But most of them have been done on English literature. Though text classification of Bangla text has been developed through frequent studies and many state of the art methods have been applied for this purpose, we have found very few works on multi-label text classification for Bangla literature. Many comprehensive datasets are also available for Bangla text classification. But to the best of our knowledge, there is no dataset available for multi-label classification of Bangla articles.

We have built a dataset appropriate for multi-label text classification from scratch. We have collected the data from 'Sports' section of online news portal of the Prothom Alo[1]. 9,815 articles of this section have been used to build this dataset which contains 45,146 words after preprocessing. Labels for these articles have also been included in the dataset from the 'Related topics' section below the news articles. There are 415 unique labels in the dataset.

Multi-label classification problems face many challenges unlike single label classification problems [12]. Usually, multi-label text classification is implemented using two ways. One is problem transformation method and another is algorithm adaptation method. In problem transformation methods, a multi-label classification problem is transformed into many single label classification problems. Then single label classifier algorithms e.g. naive bayes, logistic regression are applied on those single label classification problems. In algorithm adaptation methods, classification algorithms are adapted for multi-label classification. Various problem transformation methods and adapted algorithms have been developed over the past years [10]. We have applied binary relevance method, classifier chains method and label powerset method as problem transformation methods with classification algorithms i.e. naive bayes classifier, logistic regression and SVM. After application of these algorithms, we have got a quite satisfactory result on our dataset. Using micro average of F1-score, the best result we have got from the predictions of the algorithms is 71.15%. Using hamming loss, the best result we have got is 0.90%. We have also used precision and recall as performance metrics.

The contributions made by this work are - 1) As to the best of our knowledge, there are no dataset available for Bangla multi-label text classification, we have built a new open-source dataset for Bangla multi-label text classification and 2) As to the best of our knowledge, no work has been done on Bangla multi-label text classification for Bangla articles, we have provided an insight of the performances of machine learning algorithms on Bangla multi-label text classification for Bangla articles. In the subsequent sections of this paper, we briefly describe the preliminary studies for multi-label classification, present a view of related works in this area, materials and methodology where we describe our processes, analysis of the result of our experiment and then we conclude the work in the conclusion section.

---

1 www.prothomalo.com/sports.

2 Preliminaries

We have used several problem transformation methods in our work. Here at first, we discuss these problem transformation methods.

2.1 Binary Relevance Method

In this method, an ensemble of single-label binary classifiers is trained, one for each class. Here each classifier predicts *yes* or *no* for its class. *Yes* means the class is included in the predicted set of labels while *no* means the class is not included in the predicted set of labels. The output set of labels from the classifier consists of all the predicted classes. Suppose, there are l labels in a dataset. So l classifiers will be constructed from the dataset which will answer if the class should be included in the predicted set of labels or not. The problem of this method is that if there are correlations between labels, then the correlations between labels are ignored by this method.

2.2 Classifier Chains

In this method, a chain of binary classifiers is constructed from the dataset. It also produces l binary classifiers if there are l labels in the dataset. But in this method, each classifier takes into account the predictions of all of the classifiers before it. That means if the class i has been predicted before class j, the classifier of class j uses the prediction of class i to make its prediction. This method can take label correlations into consideration.

2.3 Label Powerset

This method considers every possible combination of classes in the set of classes. It actually predicts any one element from the power set of classes. If there are l classes in the dataset, it converts the dataset such that it contains $2\hat{}l$ classes. This method also considers label correlations. We face problems with this method when there are too many classes in the dataset.

In case of evaluation metrics, we cannot use the same performance metrics as the single label classification. Here we discuss the techniques for evaluation metrics of multi-label classification problems that have been proposed in literature.

2.4 Hamming Loss

Hamming loss basically refers to the ratio of incorrectly predicted labels to the total number of labels. If D is the dataset and L is the set of labels, then

$$Hamming\ loss\ (D) = \frac{1}{|D|.|L|} \sum_{i=1}^{D} \sum_{j=1}^{L} xor(y_{i,j}, z_{i,j}) \quad (1)$$

Here $y_{i,j}$ is the target and $z_{i,j}$ is the prediction.

2.5 Micro-averaging and Macro-averaging

For micro-averaging, we add True Positives, True Negatives, False Positives and False Negatives for all the labels individually.

$$Precision^{micro}(D) = \frac{\sum_{l_i \in L} TPs(l_i)}{\sum_{l_i \in L} TPs(l_i) + FPs(l_i)} \quad (2)$$

$$Recall^{micro}(D) = \frac{\sum_{l_i \in L} TPs(l_i)}{\sum_{l_i \in L} TPs(l_i) + FNs(l_i)} \quad (3)$$

Micro-averaging F1-score will be the harmonic mean of Eqs. (2) and (3). Macro-averaging is the average of precisions and recalls of the dataset for all the labels.

$$Precision^{macro}(D) = \frac{\sum_{l_i \in L} Precision(D, l_i)}{|L|} \quad (4)$$

$$Recall^{macro}(D) = \frac{\sum_{l_i \in L} Recall(D, l_i)}{|L|} \quad (5)$$

Macro-averaging F1-score will be the harmonic mean of Eqs. (4) and (5).

3 Related Works

3.1 Bangla Text Classification

Some interesting works have been accomplished on Bangla text. Mansur M. (2006) implemented n-gram based learning techniques to validate Zipf's law with Bangla text [13]. They used character level n-gram so that the redundancy in the dataset from various forms of the same word gets eliminated and the sliding window technique can capture the context of the word. Mandal A.K. and Sen R. (2014) built a corpus named BD corpus and applied NB, KNN, DT and SVM on their dataset [14]. Their results show that SVM outperforms other algorithms on average and DT takes much time than other algorithms. They used precision, recall and F-measure as evaluation metrics. Chy A.N. et al. (2014) built full text RSS from different newspapers [15]. They preprocessed the dataset and applied naive bayes classifier on that. Kabir F. et al. (2015) designed an algorithm based on stochastic gradient descent (SGD) and used TF-IDF as feature extraction technique [16]. Their study shows that SGD gives a better result than SVM and naive bayes classifier with the dataset they built from BDNews24. Alam M.T. and Islam M.M. (2018) built the largest dataset available for Bangla text classification containing 3,76,226 articles [17]. They built the trainset with TF-IDF features along with word2vec. They applied logistic regression, neural networks, naive bayes, random forest, Adaboost and analyzed the results with precision, recall and F1-score. They achieved a quite satisfactory result.

There have been some comparative studies on Bangla text classification too. Islam M. et al. (2017) compared the performance of SVM, naive bayes and stochastic gradient descent on Bangla text classification [18]. They used both Chi square distribution and TF-IDF as feature extraction methods. Dhar A. et al. (2018) used 'term association' and 'term aggregation' feature extraction methods and applied multi-layer perceptron (MLP), random forest (RF), support vector machine (SVM), naive bayes multinomial (NBM) and KStar (K*) on 8000 Bangla text documents [19]. They achieved an accuracy of 98.68%. Again, Dhar A. et al. (2018) used inverse class frequency along with TF-IDF as feature extraction method and applied different classification algorithms [20]. They got an accuracy of 98.87%.

3.2 Multi-label Text Classification

We can get an overview of multi-label text classification from [10, 11]. Katakis I. et al. (2008) tried to solve various limitations of user-tagging in user-centric content publishing and management web application [1]. They used binary relevance method with naive bayes classifier as base learner. Read J. (2008) addressed the problem of label co-occurrences method that it increases the complexity since it produces sparse set of labels [21]. They observed that very few label co-occurrences are frequently repetitive. Therefore, they pruned the label sets, co-occurrences between whom are not frequently repetitive. This paper shows that this method not only reduce complexity but also increases the accuracy metrics. Tsoumakas G. et al. (2010) tried to reduce computation complexity and increase performance measures by taking k subsets randomly from the set of labels [22]. Read J. (2010) solved the multi-label classification problem using pruned sets method and also with classifier chain method [23]. Here, he compared the methods with respect to random K label sets. Abe S. (2015) proposed fuzzy SVM to address the problem that a data sample may be classified into a multi-label class that is not pre-defined or a data sample may be classified to no class [24]. Liu J. et al. (2017) stated different challenges in extreme multi-label text classification [25]. They proposed a new deep learning method, XML CNN, which takes multi-label co-occurrences into account. They used a dynamic max pooling scheme, binary cross entropy loss and a hidden bottleneck layer.

Ahmed N.A. et al. (2015) addressed problem of lack of enough datasets and research on multi-label text classification in Arabic language [26]. They made a comprehensive dataset and tested accuracy and runtime of different problem transformation (PT) methods.

In Sect. 3.1, researchers worked on Bangla text classification, but those works were for single label text classification and we have worked on multi-label text classification of Bangla articles. In Sect. 3.2, all of the works for multi-label text classification were on other languages than Bangla. We have found only one study on multi-label text classification of Bangla language. Hasan M.N. et al. (2017) worked on multi-label classification of Bangla sentences [27]. They have collected 10,000 crime related sentences and tagged them as victim, suspect, crime type, crime place, crime time, hospital, police station and neutral. They collected the sentences from different newspapers and preprocessed the data using word embedding model and made clusters of different types. They used LibSVM and Scikit- learn. One of the main differences of their work and our work is that they used word embedding model to classify the sentences and we have used TF-IDF vectors to classify the articles. They worked on Bangla sentences of crime type and we have worked on Bangla news articles of 'Sports' section. They worked with only 8 classes in their dataset, but we have worked with 415 unique classes in our dataset.

4 Methodology

The steps of our method is represented by a block diagram below (Fig. 1).

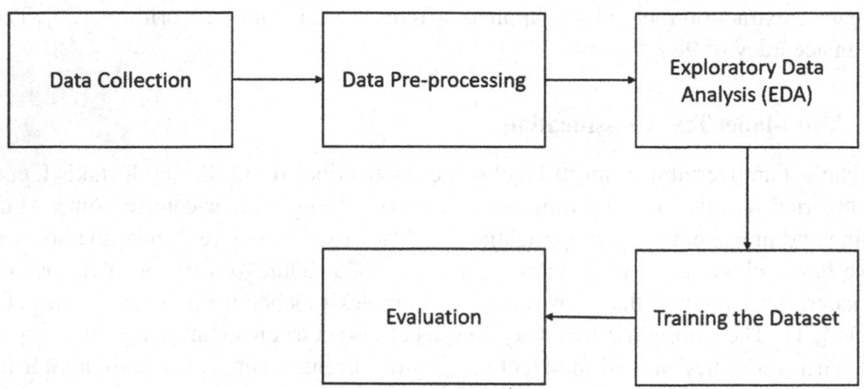

Fig. 1. Steps of the methodology

At first, we have collected the data for applying multi-label classification. Since real world data is often inconsistent and inappropriate for applying classification algorithms, we have pre-processed the data. Then we have performed some exploratory data analysis (EDA) to understand the perspectives of the characteristics of the data. Then we have trained the data samples and evaluated the predictions of unseen data samples.

4.1 Data Collection and Pre-processing

We have collected 9,815 articles from 'Sports' section of online news portal of the Prothom Alo, a leading newspaper of Bangladesh. At first, we have collected source codes of the article pages. Then we tokenized the articles and counted the term frequencies of all the words. During tokenization process, we eliminated the punctuations, numbers and stop words like 'ও,' 'এবং', 'অথবা'etc. Then we have performed stemming operation on the tokenized documents. At this step, we have had 45,146 words in the corpus. Then we have calculated the TF-IDF of all the words in the corpus. By doing this, we have found out the most important words for our classification tasks. Then we have got the tags associated with each article.

4.2 Exploratory Data Analysis (EDA)

We have already mentioned that there are 9,815 articles with 45,146 words in the corpus. There are 415 unique labels associated with the articles. The frequency distribution of labels in the articles is shown below (Figs. 2 and 3).

The graph given above is representing the number of labels per article. We have observed that 97.28% data samples lies within the first 180 labels. There are at most 9 labels in an article and there is at least one label for each article. The average number of labels associated with each article is 3.21.

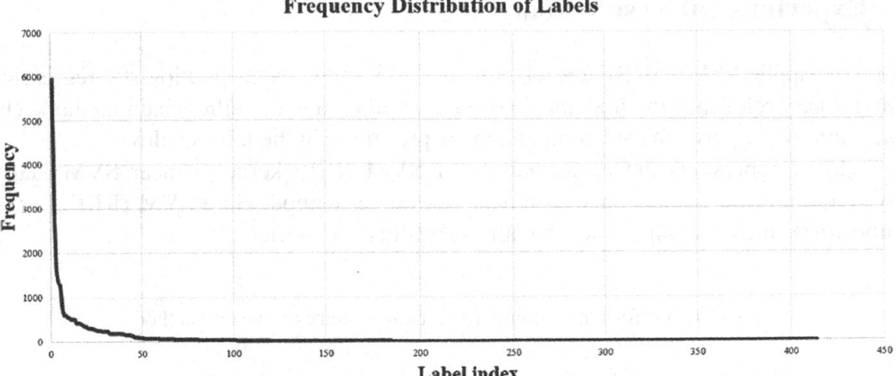

Fig. 2. Frequency distribution of labels in articles

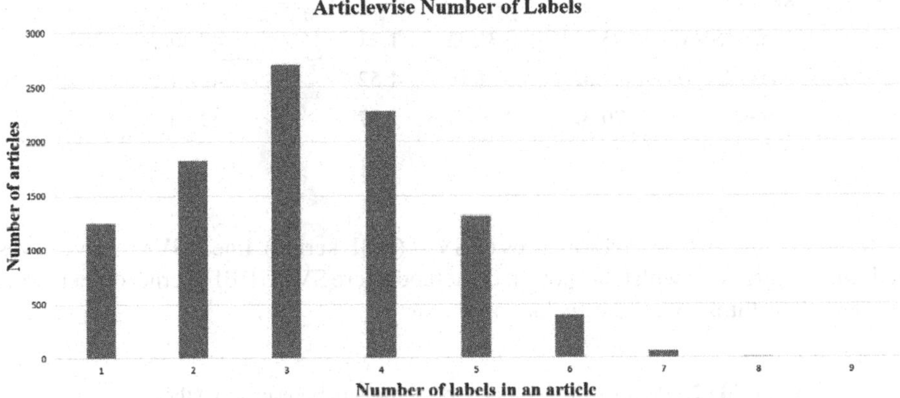

Fig. 3. Articlewise number of labels

We have taken first 40,000 words from the corpus according to their TF-IDF values and converted them into TF-IDF vectors.

4.3 Training and Evaluation Process

We have split our dataset and used 80% of data samples for training process and used 20% of data samples for evaluation purpose. We have performed 5-fold cross validation for validation purpose and calculated the mean average of the performance metrics. We have used Jupyter Notebook[2] to train our data samples. We imported the multi-label learning methods and different classification algorithms from Scikit-learn[3] and applied them to train our dataset. We have also imported the packages for precision score, recall score, hamming loss, f1 score and used them for evaluation process.

[2] https://jupyter.org/.
[3] https://scikit-learn.org/.

5 Experimental Result Analysis

We have applied SVM (RBF kernel), linear SVM, naive bayes and logistic regression using binary relevance method, label powerset method and classifier chain method. The summary of the performance comparisons is presented in the tables below.

Table 1 represents the performances of SVM (RBF kernel), linear SVM, naive bayes and logistic regression with binary relevance method. Here SVM (RBF) kernel outperforms the other algorithms for all the evaluation metrics.

Table 1. Performance comparison using binary relevance method

Classification algorithm	Precision	Recall	Hamming loss	F1-score
SVM (RBF kernel)	98.85	55.57	0.90	71.15
Linear SVM	95.76	31.32	1.21	47.20
Naive Bayes	69.02	31.59	1.52	43.34
Logistic regression	70.67	20.77	1.57	32.10

Table 2 represents the performances of SVM (RBF kernel), linear SVM, naive bayes and logistic regression with label powerset method. Here SVM (RBF) kernel outperforms the other algorithms for all the evaluation metrics.

Table 2. Performance comparison using label powerset method

Classification algorithm	Precision	Recall	Hamming loss	F1-score
SVM (RBF kernel)	85.89	52.57	1.07	65.22
Linear SVM	80.19	33.80	1.34	45.90
Naive Bayes	77.53	26.87	1.52	39.91
Logistic regression	36.27	11.41	1.90	17.36

Table 3 represents the performances of SVM (RBF kernel), linear SVM, naive bayes and logistic regression with classifier chain method. Here SVM (RBF) kernel outperforms the other algorithms for all the evaluation metrics.

From the performance comparisons, we can observe that SVM (RBF kernel) with binary relevance method has given the best performance with all evaluation metrics on our dataset though the time for training and evaluation is much higher than other

Table 3. Performance comparison using classifier chain method

Classification algorithm	Precision	Recall	Hamming loss	F1-score
SVM (RBF kernel)	95.57	32.89	1.20	48.94
Linear SVM	94.32	31.73	1.23	47.49
Naive Bayes	70.31	20.47	1.55	31.71
Logistic regression	69.97	22.64	1.52	34.21

algorithms. Here, the performance of algorithms with label powerset method is not quite impressive. This means there is less correlation among labels in our dataset. Classifier chain method takes more time for training and evaluation than the other two methods. RBF kernel of SVM has performed better than the other algorithms.

6 Conclusion

We have tried to build a new comprehensive dataset using Bangla articles to work on multi-label text classification. We hope that further researches on multi-label text classification of Bangla articles will be facilitated by the dataset. We have tried to automate the tagging process of Bangla news articles. We have applied several methods and algorithms on our dataset. The results are satisfactory but the results show that multi-label classification on Bangla text is quite challenging and the results can be improved through further research on this area. We hope our work will be able to provide an insight into this topic. We also want to work further on this topic and try to get better results. We want to build an extremely large dataset to work on extreme multi-label text classification of Bangla articles in future.

References

1. Katakis, I., Tsoumakas, G., Vlahavas, I.: Multilabel text classification for automated tag suggestion. In: Proceedings of the ECML/PKDD, vol. 18, p. 5 (2008)
2. Zhan, M.L., Zhou, Z.H.: Multilabel neural networks with applications to functional genomics and text categorization. IEEE Trans. Knowl. Data Eng. **18**(10), 1338–1351 (2006)
3. Wei, Z., Zhang, H., Zhang, Z., Li, W., Miao, D.: A naive Bayesian multi-label classification algorithm with application to visualize text search results. Int. J. Adv. Intell. **3**(2), 173–188 (2011)
4. Li, T., Ogihara, M.: Toward intelligent music information retrieval. IEEE Trans. Multimedia **8**(3), 564–574 (2006)
5. Wieczorkowska, A., Synak, P., Raś, Z.W.: Multi-label classification of emotions in music. In: Kłopotek, M.A., Wierzchoń, S.T., Trojanowski, K. (eds.) Intelligent Information Processing and Web Mining. Advances in Soft Computing, vol. 35, pp. 307–315. Springer, Heidelberg (2006)

6. Trohidis, K., Tsoumakas, G., Kalliris, G., Vlahavas, I.P.: Multi-label classification of music into emotions. In: ISMIR, vol. 8, pp. 325–330 (2008)
7. Qi, G.J., et al.: Correlative multi-label video annotation. In: Proceedings of the 15th ACM International Conference on Multimedia, pp. 17–26. ACM (2007)
8. Snoek, C.G., Worring, M., Van Gemert, J.C., Geusebroek, J.M., Smeulders, A.W.: The challenge problem for automated detection of 101 semantic concepts in multimedia. In: Proceedings of the 14th ACM International Conference on Multimedia, pp. 421–430. ACM (2006)
9. Zhang, Y., Burer, S., Street, W.N.: Ensemble pruning via semi-definite programming. J. Mach. Learn. Res. **7**(Jul), 1315–1338 (2006)
10. Tsoumakas, G., Katakis, I.: Multi-label classification: an overview. Int. J. Data Warehouse. Min. (IJDWM) **3**(3), 1–13 (2007)
11. Madjarov, G., Kocev, D., Gjorgjevikj, D., Džeroski, S.: An extensive experimental comparison of methods for multi-label learning. Pattern Recogn. **45**(9), 3084–3104 (2012)
12. Alazaidah, R., Ahmad, F.K.: Trending challenges in multi label classification. Int. J. Adv. Comput. Sci. Appl. **7**(10), 127–131 (2016)
13. Mansur, M.: Analysis of n-gram based text categorization for Bangla in a newspaper corpus (Doctoral dissertation, BRAC University) (2006)
14. Mandal, A.K., Sen, R.: Supervised learning methods for Bangla web document categorization. arXiv preprint arXiv:1410.2045 (2014)
15. Chy, A.N., Seddiqui, M.H., Das, S.: Bangla news classification using naive Bayes classifier. In: 16th International Conference on Computer and Information Technology, pp. 366–371. IEEE (2014)
16. Kabir, F., Siddique, S., Kotwal, M.R.A., Huda, M.N.: Bangla text document categorization using stochastic gradient descent (SGD) classifier. In: 2015 International Conference on Cognitive Computing and Information Processing (CCIP), pp. 1–4. IEEE (2015)
17. Alam, M.T., Islam, M.M.: BARD: Bangla article classification using a new comprehensive dataset. In: 2018 International Conference on Bangla Speech and Language Processing (ICBSLP), pp. 1–5. IEEE (2018)
18. Islam, M., Jubayer, F.E.M., Ahmed, S.I.: A comparative study on different types of approaches to Bengali document categorization. arXiv preprint arXiv:1701.08694 (2017)
19. Dhar, A., Mukherjee, H., Dash, N.S., Roy, K.: Performance of classifiers in Bangla text categorization. In: 2018 International Conference on Innovations in Science, Engineering and Technology (ICISET), pp. 168–173. IEEE (2018)
20. Dhar, A., Dash, N.S., Roy, K.: Classification of Bangla text documents based on inverse class frequency. In: 2018 3rd International Conference on Internet of Things: Smart Innovation and Usages (IoT-SIU), pp. 1–6. IEEE (2018)
21. Read, J.: A pruned problem transformation method for multi-label classification. In: Proceedings of 2008 New Zealand Computer Science Research Student Conference (NZCSRS 2008), vol. 143150, p. 41 (2008)
22. Tsoumakas, G., Katakis, I., Vlahavas, I.: Random k-label sets for multilabel classification. IEEE Trans. Knowl. Data Eng. **23**(7), 1079–1089 (2010)
23. Read, J.: Scalable multi-label classification (Doctoral dissertation, University of Waikato) (2010)
24. Abe, S.: Fuzzy support vector machines for multilabel classification. Pattern Recogn. **48**(6), 2110–2117 (2015)
25. Liu, J., Chang, W.C., Wu, Y., Yang, Y.: Deep learning for extreme multi-label text classification. In: Proceedings of the 40th International ACM SIGIR Conference on Research and Development in Information Retrieval, pp. 115–124. ACM (2017)

26. Ahmed, N.A., Shehab, M.A., Al-Ayyoub, M., Hmeidi, I.: Scalable multi-label Arabic text classification. In: 2015 6th International Conference on Information and Communication Systems (ICICS), pp. 212–217. IEEE (2015)
27. Hasan, M.N., Bhowmik, S., Rahaman, M.M.: Multi-label sentence classification using Bengali word embedding model. In: 2017 3rd International Conference on Electrical Information and Communication Technology (EICT), pp. 1–6. IEEE (2017)

Computer Vision and Image Processing in Health Care

Ulcer Detection in Wireless Capsule Endoscopy Using Locally Computed Features

Md. Sohag Hossain[1], Abdullah Al Mamun[2(✉)], Tonmoy Ghosh[3], Md. Galib Hasan[1], Md. Motaher Hossain[1], and Anik Tahabilder[4]

[1] Department of Electrical and Electronic Engineering, Pabna University of Science and Technology, Pabna 6600, Bangladesh
msh22eee@gmail.com

[2] Faculty of Engineering and Technology, Multimedia University, 75450 Melaka, Malaysia
mamun130203@gmail.com

[3] Department of Electrical and Computer Engineering, The University of Alabama, Tuscaloosa, AL 35487, USA

[4] School of Engineering + Technology, Western Carolina University, Cullowhee, NC 28723, USA

Abstract. WCE (Wireless Capsule Endoscopy) has become one of the most significant inventions for detecting different types of digestive tract diseases of humans. Distinct types of abnormalities like polyps, ulcer, tumor and intestine cancer are diagnosed by the clinicians with the implement of WCE in a convenient way. In order to deduce the incubus of the physicians an automated and efficient recognition system is required. In this paper, an advanced method for automatically detecting ulcers in the images of the WCE video record is proposed using the HSV color model. Region of interest (ROI) was identified applying a threshold on images that were extracted from the video of WCE. Local features have been extracted only from the ROI which is usually a small part of an image that offers a low computational cost. Linear discriminant analysis has been used for the separation of ulcer and non-ulcer images. The proposed algorithm was tested on a publicly available database. The performance has obtained accuracy 87.55%, sensitivity 94.70%, specificity 83.30%, precision 75.00% and F1 score 83.70%. Hence, the proposed method outperforms an efficient method that will create a great impact in this research arena.

Keywords: Wireless Capsule Endoscopy (WCE) · Linear discriminant analysis · Ulcer detection · HSV

1 Introduction

A lot of people are suffering from different types of diseases throughout of the world which are related to the gastrointestinal tract. Around 27.8% people from Bangladesh faced the death due to the intestine infectious diseases [1]. Whereas 1.6 million people from America are persisting by inflammatory bowel disease (IBD) and it has increased

T. Bhuiyan et al. (Eds.): ICONCS 2020, LNICST 325, pp. 491–502, 2020.
https://doi.org/10.1007/978-3-030-52856-0_39

up to 200,000 since 2011. Among the 70,000 IBD diagnosis process, majority of the portion was for the children whore are attacked by the Crohn's disease and ulcerative colitis [2] which is now rising globally [3]. The particular problem should be detected as early as possible if we want to get the remedy from the diseases. That's why researchers are seeking for the up gradation of the technology to detect the diseases symptoms. Consequently, different types of medical diagnosis process have been developed like CT scan, endoscopy, X-ray, etc. Since these processes have many disadvantages including side effect, researcher are trying to find a suitable layout in order to remove the side effect and difficulties. After that researchers introduced a noble technology of WCE which is easily swallowed and painless as well which includes transmitter, camera, light and battery. It transmits the captured video to the receiver which will be converted into pixel image for evaluating and detecting the problems on the cells to detect the abnormalities like polyps, ulcer, tumor and intestine cancer [4]. Our main concern is to detect the ulcer portion in this particular paper.

There are three major components in the WCE such as a capsule, sensing system with data recording unit and battery reservation cell and a computer to inspect and clarification which allow examining the images during the WCE whole process [4]. The patient need to eat the capsule with a glass of water and image recorder will record the image by different varieties of sensor which are connected to the waist and abdomen. The capsule will travel the whole digestive tract to capture the videos of the entire tract which will be transmitted to the receiver wirelessly through a transmitter. It can be identified From Fig. 1(b) how the sensors are connected to the body and capsule layout look like. It will take almost eight hour to complete the whole tract which will dispose and pass within 24–72 h and will capture around 50,000 images.

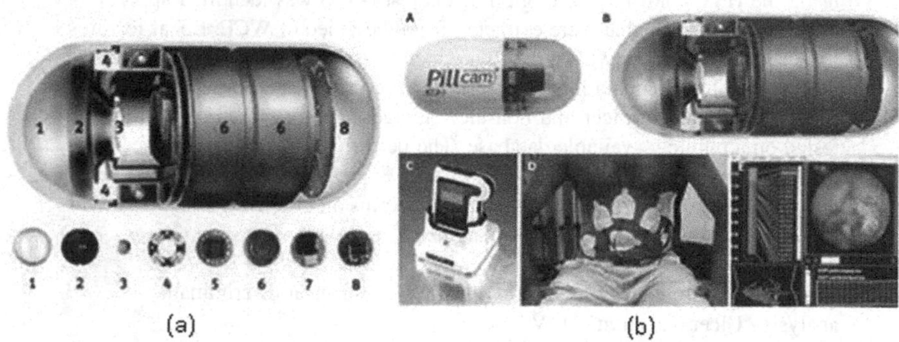

Fig. 1. (a) Interior construction of CE and (b) Image capturing process using CE

It the initial stage the software was developed for only recognizing the bleeding potion and the sensitivity and specificity that were obtained are only 21.5% and 41.8% respectively [5]. In order to recognize abnormalities such as bleeding, polyps, ulcer, tumor and intestine cancer feature extraction process has been designed [6]. By using Hue-Saturation-Intensity color model ulcer and bleeding portion is detected from the video of the WCE [7] whereas statistical feature framework is used in [8]. Curvelet dependent textural features are used for ulcer detection [9] whereas histogram [10] is used for bleeding portion detection from the converted images. In [11] pathology detection and color segmentation technique proposed for recognizing the image from the WCE video. For detecting the ulcer, Color Coherence Vector introduced in [12] whereas histogram based technique employed in [4]. In addition color and statistical based ulcer and bleeding detection technique also used in [13–15].

In this paper, a technique has been proposed using HSV color model with a linear discriminant analysis classifier. First of all, the video was converted into images. Then, enhancement has been applied to the image for highlighting the actual information of ulcer. After that, color threshold has been applied at HSV color space to get the region of interest (ROI). Then, the images have been converted into binary images, adjustment of the intensity and sharp the images and also filter has been used for ruining the unwanted pixels. Then, several local features have been extracted from the ROI. Using these features, a classifier was developed and tested on a publicly available WCE database.

2 Ulcer Property in WCE Images

The normal and ulcer regions in WCE images can be segregated using color features because the color intensity is the basic property to analyze by the clinicians. According to Fig. 2, the ulcer regions in WCE images show more or less inequality in color compared to its surrounding regions [7]. Actually, Ulcer is usually pinkish or white pinkish color than the surroundings, while ulcers exhibit high intensity hues [4]. The ulcer portion contains higher pixel intensities and the non-ulcer portion contains lower pixel intensities [16].

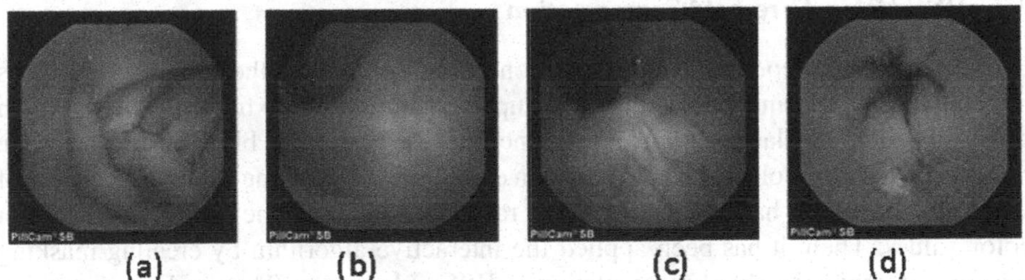

Fig. 2. Capsule endoscopy images of non-ulcer (a, b) and ulcer (c, d)

3 Proposed Method

For removing non-ulcer portion color threshold has been applied on the WCE images and only consider the abnormal portion which is ulcer for this paper. Normally ulcer portion is a tiny portion of the ulcer image frame. Here operation has performed only on that small portion so the calculation is easy. The flow diagram of the proposed method is shown in Fig. 3.

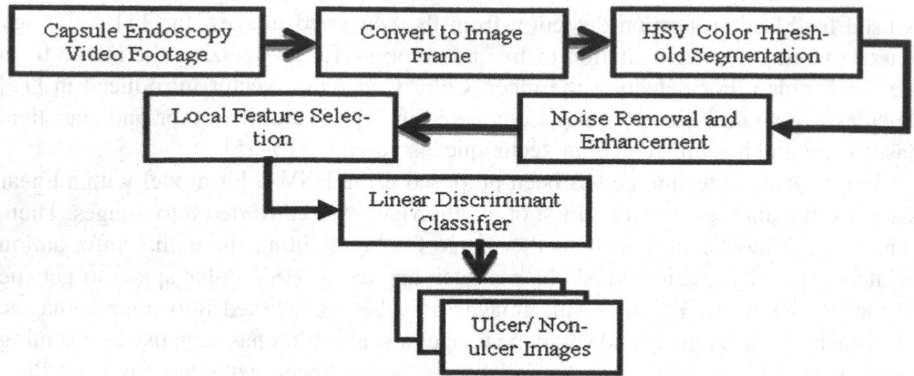

Fig. 3. Pictorial representation of the proposed method

3.1 Database

At the beginning stage of the research is to covert the video frame from the WCE into image regarding to the rate of frame which are indicated on the capsule specification to further process like color threshold, segmentation, feature extraction, and classification. In our experiment, we examined WCE of PillCam®SB of frame rate per 2 per second which obtained a huge amount of data for evaluating. In this research work, we evaluated around 244 color images in which 110 were ulcer and 134 were non-ulcer images which are available in [17].

3.2 HSV Color Threshold Segmentation

Each image frame contains a black portion at the corner and the black portion does not contain any information and may interrupt the nature of the extracted features which drives to poor ulcer classification performance. So, the borderline black portion has been removed. Then, the color threshold has been employed for avoiding the non-ulcer area of the images and there have a specified color range and detecting the objects of consistent color values. Then, it has been applied the interactive algorithm by creating masking for the soft image threshold segmentation in HSV color space. The geodesic distances-based segmentation with robustness triangle inequality algorithm has manipulated in [18]. By using this masking color threshold segmentation method, we have obtained the ROI pixels.

3.3 Morphological Erosion and Dilation

After the color threshold segmentation, we get the binary image. The binary image is containing 0 and 1 of the 2D matrix. In binary image 1 illustrates white portion and 0 illustrates the black portion. Then fill the holes in that binary image of a specified range from the border of the image using Soille's method [19]. Let consider pixel p should be deleted which is undesirable which means non-ulcer portion. It will be deleted in two steps [20].

Step-1: After fulfilling conditions G_1, G_2 and G_3
Step-2: After fulfilling conditions G_1, G_2 and G_3'
Condition G$_1$:

$$X_H(p) = 1$$

Where,

$$X_H(p) = \sum_{i=1}^{4} b_i$$

$$b_1 = \begin{cases} 1, \text{ if } X_{2i-1} = 0 \\ 0, \text{ Otherwise} \end{cases}$$

Condition G$_2$:

$$2 \le \min\{n_1(p), n_2(p)\} \le 3$$

Where,

$$n_1(p) = \sum_{k=1}^{4} X_{2k-1} \vee X_{2k}$$

$$n_2(p) = \sum_{k=1}^{4} X_{2k} \vee X_{2k+1}$$

Condition G$_3$:

$$(X_2 \vee X_3 \vee \bar{X}_8) \wedge X_{1=0}$$

Condition G_3':

$$(X_6 \vee X_7 \vee \bar{X}_4) \wedge X_5 = 0$$

These two steps make an iteration of the algorithm.

The RGB color image is reconstructed from the binary image. Then the images are converted into grayscale for adjusting and sharpen the image. For adjusting the images 1% of the contrast value is saturated at low and high intensities. For sharpening the images unsharp masking technique is used where the blurred portion is rejected.

3.4 Noise Removal and Morphological Operation for Structuring Elements

We remove the noise by using N_D filer in multidimensional images. After removing the noise using the filters has been applied global image threshold as Otsu's method. In this method, a level is chosen to lower the intraclass variance of the white and black pixels [21]. After creating a level Bradley's method [22] is applied for creating binary images. Bradley's method uses a neighborhood image size of around 1/8th of the image and produces a binary image as a local matrix of the same size as its input. Fernand Meyer algorithm is applied to those binary images [23]. This method returns a level matrix that represents the watershed regions of its input matrix. If the output of this method is j, $j \ge 0$

When,
j = 0; No watershed region
j = 1; First watershed region
j = 2; Second watershed region etc.

Then morphological dilation and erosion have applied the images where predefined pixels are dilated and eroded. The binary dilation of P and Q are denoted by P ⊕ Q [24],

$$P \oplus Q = \left\{ z | \left(\hat{Q} \right)_z \cap P \neq \emptyset \right\}$$

The binary erosion of P and Q are denoted by P ⊖ Q [24],

$$P \ominus Q = \left\{ z | \left(\hat{Q} \right)_z \subseteq P \right\}$$

Where, $\hat{Q}$ is the reflection of the structuring element of Q.

After performing these operations on the images, we reconstruct the binary image into an RGB color image. Then those RGB images have been transformed into HSV color model to extract features. These steps have been shown in Fig. 4. Where upper contains for an ulcer image frame and lower contains for a non-ulcer image frame.

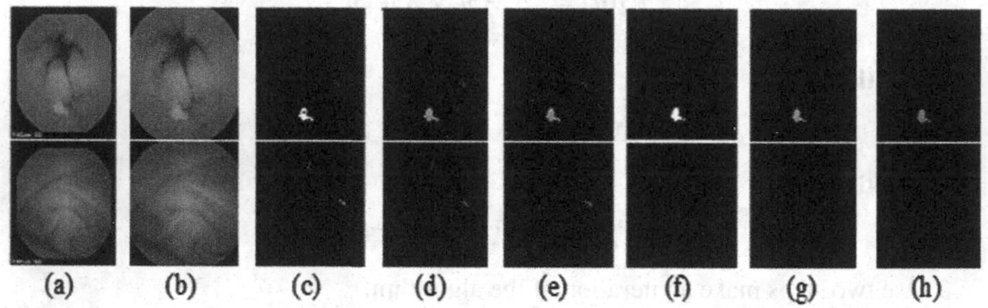

Fig. 4. (a) Source image Ulcer (upper) and Non-ulcer (lower); (b) After removing borderline black portion; (c) HSV color threshold segmented image; (d) Adjust the intensity and sharpen image after converting to grayscale; (e) After noise removed; (f) After morphological operation; (g) Reconstructed RGB image; (h) Converted to HSV color space

3.5 Ulcer Feature Selection

RGB color image consists of three color channels named Red (R), Green (G) and Blue (B). These color channels are the functions of the image coordinate (x, y). A matrix of a pixel is [R (x; y) G (x; y) B (x; y)]. Each pixel component represents 8-bit integer numbers which vary from 0 to 255. In this method, the RGB images have been transformed into an HSV color image from where ulcer features have been computed by using statistical values like the mean and local standard deviation of the images. In HSV color space, each pixel is represented by hue, saturation, and value. Hue, saturation, the value can be calculated using the following equations from the pixel values of R, G and B [25]:

$$H = \cos^{-1} \frac{\frac{1}{2}[(R-G)+(R-B)]}{\sqrt{(R-G)^2+(R-B)(G-B)}} \tag{1}$$

$$S = 1 - \frac{3}{R+G+B}(\min(R,G,B)) \tag{2}$$

$$V = \frac{1}{3}(R+G+B) \tag{3}$$

From the values of H, S, and V here taken for statistical feature values for the classification.

3.6 Linear Discriminant Classifier

In order to classify ulcer and non-ulcer images for the proposed method linear discriminant classifier has been used. This classifier technique belongs to the arena of pattern recognition which will calculate the maximum value of the division of projected class and the class variance. Consequently, maximizing the ration will surcharge the projected class and lessen the class variance. The ration may be defined as for the vector T.

$$J(T) = \frac{T^P M_B T}{T^P M_W T} \tag{4}$$

Where M_W and M_B represent the within and between matrices of the classes [26]. The classification performance is appreciated by the 10 fold cross-validation technique.

4 Result and Discussion

In the case of classification of the images, there are four different types of occurrences may happen which are true ulcer detection (T_U), true non-ulcer detection (T_N), false ulcer detection (F_U) and false non-ulcer detection (F_N). The performance of the proposed ulcer detection technique is calculated by five parameters that are accuracy, sensitivity, F1 score [27, 28] etc. Calculation using the following equations:

$$\text{Accuracy} = \frac{\sum T_U + \sum T_N}{\sum T_U + \sum T_N + \sum F_U + \sum F_N} \tag{5}$$

$$\text{Sensitivity} = \frac{\sum T_U}{\sum T_U + \sum F_N} \tag{6}$$

$$\text{Specificity} = \frac{\sum T_N}{\sum T_N + \sum F_U} \tag{7}$$

$$\text{Precision} = \frac{\sum T_U}{\sum T_U + \sum F_U} \tag{8}$$

$$\text{F1Score} = \frac{2 \times Sensitivity \times Precision}{Sensitivity + Precision} \tag{9}$$

Table 1 represents the accuracy, sensitivity, F1 score etc. of the proposed method when classification is done using linear discriminant classifier and taking the features of the source images only after removing the borderline black portion. At this, the proposed method shows performance with accuracy 76.00%, sensitivity 73.00%, specificity 78.50%, precision 73.16% and F1 score 73.08%. Table 2 illustrates the performance results of the HSV color threshold segmentation where accuracy 85.45%, sensitivity 92.00%, specificity 81.50%, precision 73.25% and F1 score 81.56%.

Table 1. Performance result of classification using features of the source image

Performance parameter	Value
Accuracy (%)	76.00
Sensitivity (%)	73.00
Specificity (%)	78.50
Precision (%)	73.16
F1 Score (%)	73.08

Table 2. Performance after color threshold segmentation

Performance parameter	Value
Accuracy (%)	85.45
Sensitivity (%)	92.00
Specificity (%)	81.50
Precision (%)	73.25
F1 Score (%)	81.56

It represents that using HSV color threshold segmentation performance has been improved with accuracy 9.45%, sensitivity 19.00%, specificity 3.00%, precision 0.09% and F1 score 8.48%. Table 3 represents the performance after applying the image adjustment and sharpen step with filling the small holes which upgrade accuracy 0.85%, sensitivity 0.05%, precision 1.25 and F1 score 0.46%. Then has been applied to the morphological operation and used filters for removing the non-ulcer portions. That's performance has been shown in Table 4. The application of this step has enhanced the performance with accuracy 1.25%, sensitivity 2.20%, specificity 0.80%, precision 1.00% and F1 score 1.68%.

In Table 5 the performance comparison of the proposed method with different color spaces. In this proposed method HSV color space has been used which provides the best performance over the color spaces RGB, L*a*b* and YCbCr. The five parameters accuracy, sensitivity, specificity, precision, and f1 score are higher for all the color spaces. Then Table 6 shows the comparison results by varying the features. It can be observed that using all features mean hue, saturation, value and local standard deviation of hue,

Table 3. Performance after morphological erosion and dilation

Performance parameter	Value
Accuracy (%)	86.30
Sensitivity (%)	92.50
Specificity (%)	82.50
Precision (%)	74.00
F1 Score (%)	82.02

Table 4. Performance after removing noise and morphological operation

Performance parameter	Value
Accuracy (%)	87.55
Sensitivity (%)	94.70
Specificity (%)	83.30
Precision (%)	75.00
F1 Score (%)	83.70

Table 5. Comparison of performance with different color space

Color spaces	Acc. (%)	Sen. (%)	Spe. (%)	Pre. (%)	F1 Score (%)
RGB	84.32	90.40	81.00	72.00	80.15
HSV	**87.55**	**94.70**	**83.30**	**75.00**	**83.70**
L*a*b*	85.15	91.20	81.20	73.50	81.39
YCbCr	84.24	90.40	80.80	72.00	80.15

saturation, value for the proposed method offers the best performance with accuracy 87.55%, sensitivity 94.70%, specificity 83.30%, precision 75.00% and F1 score 83.70%. Table 7 shows the performance of the proposed technique compared with various types of classifiers named logistic regression, linear discriminant, and SVM using linear and quadratic kernel. Among this linear discriminant analysis exposes the best performance for the proposed method.

Lastly, the classification performance of the proposed method has been compared with the results obtained by the other methods of [16, 29, 30] and [31]. In [29] a segmentation technique is applied for extracting color information from the significant regions using Log Gabor filter in H plane. DCT-LAC method in YCbCr color space has used in [30] for ulcer detection. Whereas, in [16] color histogram of the asymmetric indexed image has used for automatic ulcer detection. Another method described in literature

Table 6. Comparison of the variation of features

Feature	Acc (%)	Sen (%)	Spe (%)	Pre. (%)	F1 Score (%)
M_H, M_V and Sd_H	86.50	92.00	83.00	61.00	73.35
M_H, M_V and Sd_S	86.10	91.00	86.00	75.00	82.22
M_H, M_V and Sd_V	84.80	91.00	81.00	75.00	82.22
M_H, Sd_H and Sd_V	83.60	92.00	79.00	69.00	78.85
M_H, M_S, M_V and Sd_H	87.30	94.60	83.00	75.00	84.05
M_H, M_S, M_V and Sd_S	86.90	93.00	83.00	75.00	83.03
M_H, M_S, M_V and Sd_V	**87.55**	**94.70**	**83.30**	**75.00**	**83.70**
M_S, M_V, Sd_H and Sd_S	85.70	93.00	82.00	71.00	80.52
M_H, M_S, M_V, Sd_H and Sd_S	86.10	94.00	82.00	70.00	80.24
M_H, M_S, M_V, Sd_H and Sd_V	84.40	93.00	80.00	74.00	82.41
M_S, M_V, Sd_H, Sd_S and Sd_V	84.80	93.00	81.00	72.00	81.16
M_H, M_S, M_V, Sd_H, Sd_S and Sd_V	84.80	93.00	81.00	72.00	81.16

Mean of Hue = M_H; Mean of Saturation = M_S; Mean of Value = M_V; Standard deviation of Hue = Sd_H; Standard deviation of Saturation = Sd_S and Standard deviation of Value = Sd_V.

Table 7. Performance comparison with different classifiers

Classifiers	Acc (%)	Sen (%)	Spe (%)	Pre (%)	F1 Score (%)
Logistic regression	85.61	88.28	83.57	78.00	82.82
Linear discriminant	**87.55**	**94.70**	**83.30**	**75.00**	**83.70**
SVM (Linear kernel)	86.84	90.00	82.42	74.66	81.61
SVM (Quadratic kernel)	85.30	90.00	82.43	75.33	82.01

Table 8. Comparison with others literature

Methods	Accuracy (%)	Sensitivity (%)	Specificity (%)
Log Gabor filter [29]	74.80	75.00	73.15
DCT-LAC [30]	86.54	84.51	88.56
Color histogram [16]	87.09	84.08	90.93
Y-plane histogram [31]	87.49	83.68	91.08
Proposed method	**87.55**	**94.70**	**83.30**

[31] where for ulcer detection the Y plane histogram of a CE image has been implemented. Finally, it is mentioned that our method offers the best performance over each method unlike the other color and statistical methods [13–15]. The comparison has been shown in Table 8.

5 Conclusion

The proposed method uses the HSV color threshold segmentation for extracting the region of interest (ROI) in WCE images. Features have been extracted only from the region of interest which is usually a small part of an image that offers a low computational cost that it is not biased by the normal regions of an image. Linear discriminant analysis has been used for the separation of ulcer and non-ulcer images using those extracted local features. The effective local features to identify ulcer images are the mean of Hue, saturation, and value and standard deviation of value in the HSV color domain. The method has been applied for manifold frames of capsule endoscopic images and found effectiveness. The performance has obtained accuracy 87.55%, sensitivity 94.70%, specificity 83.30%, precision 75.00% and F1 score 83.70%. Hence, the proposed method outperforms the state of art methods in terms of accuracy and specificity. Hence, it is expected that the proposed ulcer detection technique will ease the diagnosing process for the physician in examining a large number of WCE images for detecting the ulcer portions.

References

1. Death in Different Diseases. http://www.healthdata.org/bangladesh
2. Kaplan, G.G., Ng, S.C.: Understanding and preventing the global increase of inflammatory bowel disease. Gastroenterology **152**, 313–321.e2 (2017). https://doi.org/10.1053/j.gastro.2016.10.020
3. Kaplan, G.G., Jess, T.: The changing landscape of inflammatory bowel disease: East meets West. Gastroenterology **150**, 24–26 (2016). https://doi.org/10.1053/j.gastro.2015.11.029
4. Ghosh, T., Das, A., Sayed, R.: Automatic small intestinal ulcer detection in capsule endoscopy images. Int. J. Sci. Eng. Res. **7**, 737–741 (2016)
5. Francis, R.D.: Sensitivity and specificity of the red blood identification (RBIS) in video capsule endoscopy. In: 3rd International Conference on Capsule Endoscopy 2004 (2004)
6. Coimbra, M.T., Cunha, J.P.S.: MPEG-7 visual descriptors—contributions for automated feature extraction in capsule endoscopy. IEEE Trans. Circuits Syst. Video Technol. **16**, 628–637 (2006). https://doi.org/10.1109/TCSVT.2006.873158
7. Li, B., Meng, M.Q.-H.: Computer-based detection of bleeding and ulcer in wireless capsule endoscopy images by chromaticity moments. Comput. Biol. Med. **39**, 141–147 (2009). https://doi.org/10.1016/j.compbiomed.2008.11.007
8. Ghosh, T., Bashar, S.K., Alam, Md.S., Wahid, K., Fattah, S.A.: A statistical feature based novel method to detect bleeding in wireless capsule endoscopy images. In: 2014 International Conference on Informatics, Electronics & Vision (ICIEV), pp. 1–4. IEEE (2014)
9. Ghosh, T., Fattah, S.A., Shahnaz, C., Wahid, K.A.: An automatic bleeding detection scheme in wireless capsule endoscopy based on histogram of an RGB-indexed image. In: 2014 36th Annual International Conference of the IEEE Engineering in Medicine and Biology Society. pp. 4683–4686. IEEE (2014)
10. Li, B., Meng, M.Q.H.: Texture analysis for ulcer detection in capsule endoscopy images. Image Vis. Comput. **27**, 1336–1342 (2009). https://doi.org/10.1016/j.imavis.2008.12.003
11. Szczypiński, P., Klepaczko, A., Pazurek, M., Daniel, P.: Texture and color based image segmentation and pathology detection in capsule endoscopy videos. Comput. Methods Programs Biomed. **113**, 396–411 (2014). https://doi.org/10.1016/j.cmpb.2012.09.004

12. Yeh, J.-Y., Wu, T.-H., Tsai, W.-J.: Bleeding and ulcer detection using wireless capsule endoscopy images. J. Softw. Eng. Appl. **07**, 422–432 (2014). https://doi.org/10.4236/jsea.2014.75039
13. Hossain, M.S., Al Mamun, A., Hasan, M.G., Hossain, M.M.: Easy scheme for ulcer detection in wireless capsule endoscopy images. In: 2019 1st International Conference on Advances in Science, Engineering and Robotics Technology (ICASERT), pp. 1–5. IEEE (2019)
14. Al Mamun, A., Hossain, M.S.: Ulcer detection in image converted from video footage of wireless capsule endoscopy. In: 2019 1st International Conference on Advances in Science, Engineering and Robotics Technology (ICASERT), pp. 1–4. IEEE (2019)
15. Al Mamun, A., Hossain, M.S., Hossain, M.M., Hasan, M.G.: Discretion way for bleeding detection in wireless capsule endoscopy images. In: 2019 1st International Conference on Advances in Science, Engineering and Robotics Technology (ICASERT), pp. 1–6. IEEE (2019)
16. Kundu, A.K., Fattah, S.A.: An asymmetric indexed image based technique for automatic ulcer detection in wireless capsule endoscopy images. In: 2017 IEEE Region 10 Humanitarian Technology Conference (R10-HTC), pp. 734–737. IEEE (2017)
17. The capsule endoscopy website. https://www.capsuleendoscopy.org
18. Protiere, A., Sapiro, G.: Interactive image segmentation via adaptive weighted distances. IEEE Trans. Image Process. **16**, 1046–1057 (2007). https://doi.org/10.1109/TIP.2007.891796
19. Soille, P.: Morphological Image Analysis: Principles and Applications. Springer, Heidelberg (2013). https://doi.org/10.1007/978-3-662-05088-0
20. Lam, L., Lee, S.-W., Suen, C.Y.: Thinning methodologies-a comprehensive survey. IEEE Trans. Pattern Anal. Mach. Intell. **14**, 869–885 (1992). https://doi.org/10.1109/34.161346
21. Otsu, N.: A threshold selection method from gray-level histograms. IEEE Trans. Syst. Man. Cybern. **9**, 62–66 (1979). https://doi.org/10.1109/TSMC.1979.4310076
22. Bradley, D., Roth, G.: Adaptive thresholding using the integral image. J. Graph. Tools. **12**, 13–21 (2007). https://doi.org/10.1080/2151237X.2007.10129236
23. Meyer, F.: Topographic distance and watershed lines. Signal Process. **38**, 113–125 (1994). https://doi.org/10.1016/0165-1684(94)90060-4
24. Gonzales, R., Woods, R., Eddine, S.: Digital Image Processing using MATLAB 2nd edn. (2009)
25. Kaur, S., Banga, D.V.K.: Content Based Image Retrieval: Survey and Comparison between RGB and HSV Model (2013)
26. Fattah, S.A., et al.: An approach for formant based speech recognition in noise. In: TENCON 2012 IEEE Region 10 Conference, pp. 1–4. IEEE (2012)
27. Altman, D.G., Bland, J.M.: Statistics notes: diagnostic tests 1: sensitivity and specificity. BMJ **308**, 1552 (1994). https://doi.org/10.1136/bmj.308.6943.1552
28. Sasaki, Y.: The Truth of the F-measure. Teach Tutor Mater (2007)
29. Karargyris, A., Bourbakis, N.: Identification of ulcers in wireless capsule endoscopy videos. In: 2009 IEEE International Symposium on Biomedical Imaging: From Nano to Macro, pp. 554–557. IEEE (2009)
30. Eid, A., Charisis, V.S., Hadjileontiadis, L.J., Sergiadis, G.D.: A curvelet-based lacunarity approach for ulcer detection from Wireless Capsule Endoscopy images. In: Proceedings of the 26th IEEE International Symposium on Computer-Based Medical Systems, pp. 273–278. IEEE (2013)
31. Kundu, A.K., Bhattacharjee, A., Fattah, S.A., Shahnaz, C.: An Automatic Ulcer Detection Scheme Using Histogram in YIQ Domain from Wireless Capsule Endoscopy Images (2017)

Human Age Estimation and Gender Classification Using Deep Convolutional Neural Network

Md. Khairul Islam[1] and Sultana Umme Habiba[2](✉)

[1] Department of Computer Science and Engineering, Khulna University of Engineering and Technology, Khulna, Bangladesh
mdkislam27@gmail.com

[2] Green University of Bangladesh, Dhaka, Bangladesh
suhabiba12@gmail.com

Abstract. At present age estimation and gender classification task has achieved a great importance due to analyzing the category of people in social media, business, customers' choice etc. Automatic age and gender classification task from analyzing facial images has become a concern to this competitive world. In this paper, we have proposed to apply transfer learning technique on facial images of people of different ages and gender. Age and gender are special attributes which can be extracted from facial images. A deep convolutional neural network is trained using our target dataset to achieve a good classification performance. We have evaluated the classification performance on Adience benchmark for age and gender estimation using ResNet50, VGG16, VGG14 and VGG17 deep CNN models. Using an ensemble technique (majority voting) of these (VGG) classifiers, we have found approximately 90% classification accuracy on age estimation task. We have also found 94% 1-off age classification accuracy using VGG14.

Keywords: Deep convolutional neural network · Age estimation · Gender classification · Ensemble classifier

1 Introduction

1.1 Age Estimation

Age estimation from facial images has become a challenging classification task in the present world due to many applications. Sentiment analysis, emotion detection in social media, contextual advertising for a special customer group (at different age level), creating a control over watched media on the basis of viewer's gender and age – all these applications are dependent on the performance of age and gender classification task. For this reason estimation of the age of a person from his or her face, has become an interesting task and challenging also.

Automatic age estimation faces some difficulties which should be considered to determine one's age, especially the age group (age range). The age estimation task is

T. Bhuiyan et al. (Eds.): ICONCS 2020, LNICST 325, pp. 503–514, 2020.
https://doi.org/10.1007/978-3-030-52856-0_40

quite different on the basis of some characteristics like aging is a continuous process. We can never make this process slower or faster. Even this aging is not reversible at all. We cannot find age changes through facial attributes in one or two years gap only. Rather aging process and characteristics vary from person to person due to their lifestyle, healthy or unhealthy food habits, weather and physical exercise. All these contributes to the key challenges in the task of age estimation using computer vision technology. To achieve a good performance in this task, the algorithm should be able to perform better using an incomplete database since the database may not contain the image of a fixed age person rather the images of people who belongs to a particular age group. Since aging is a sequential process, the images of people in different age groups are temporal data. So the class labels in predicting the age of people should follow an order of time. Each class label follows an ordered ranking with respect to time. For this reason an enriched database with corresponding class labels is mandatory to accomplish the task of age estimation.

1.2 Related Works

Recently many researchers have initiated computer vision and machine learning based approaches to the task of age and gender classification. Zakariya [1] et al. proposed a VGG face model which was a deep convolutional neural network model pre trained to do the task of face detection automatically. Before they had trained the VGG face model with the Adience dataset for age and gender classification, this model was pre trained to recognize face to improve age estimation performance. This VGG Face model consisted of eight convolution layers and three fully connected layers. They had used max pooling layer to reduce the number of training parameters so that the model would not get overfit. These three fully connected layers were followed by a drop out and rectification layer so that the model would generalizes well and the output of the fully connected layers would be mapped to the number of classes. They had shown the age and gender classification accuracy approximately 59.9%. They had also compared the performance using the same dataset in GoogleNet model also. GoogleNet was not better than VGG Face model where it had shown 45% classification accuracy on the task of age and gender classification. Haibin [2] et al. proposed to use an age estimation deep convolutional neural network on the basis of regression. To improve the convergence rate they used batch normalization in the network. They trained the model in two phases where firstly, they had trained the model to recognize faces identity and then training was done with age estimation data. They measured the performance of the model on the basis of MAE. They had improved the MAE at 4.32 which was comparatively good than another estimator using SVM showing an MAE of 5.83 on the same FGNet dataset. Ranjan [3] et al. proposed an estimation method on the basis of analyzing wrinkle area of the face. Since wrinkle features are found in the especial geographical area of the face, they had detected those areas and extracted wrinkle features from face images. They extracted wrinkle features from images basically in the forehead, eyelids, eye corners, and chin areas. They made clusters using Fuzzy c-means clustering on the basis of wrinkle features. Age classification is done depending on the degree of membership of the clusters of a face image on which age class label it belongs to. All these techniques kept many issues for further improvement, especially the performance of this task. Many feature extraction algorithms like Local Binary Pattern (LBP) [4], Bio-inspired features (BIF) [5], Wavelet transformation etc. were used for face feature extraction in previous works. Many dominant classifiers like Support Vector Machine (SVM) [6], Multiple Linear Regression [7, 8], K Nearest Neighbor (KNN), shallow convolutional neural network [9], Support Vector Regression (SVR) [10] etc. have been used. But all these faced challenges to do classification using an unconstrained database having images of low resolution, noise, facial expression etc. [11, 12]. We have proposed to use, transfer learning approach to train VGG16 and ResNet50 deep convolutional neural network with an augmented large data set to achieve a good classification performance. Deep learning based classification methods outperform all other techniques in the field of classification tasks.

Now a days the importance of age and gender classification cannot be denied at all. In different applications like human machine interaction, targeted advertisement, biometrics, surveillance system, security, customer satisfaction and preference analysis all these require to detect the gender and age of users.

2 Methodology

We have proposed to use deep convolutional neural network as a classifier. To achieve satisfactory result on age estimation, transfer learning technique is followed to train the model with our work dataset. To train the pretrained models with a new data, we have tuned the model. In the following section we have described transfer learning, deep convolutional neural network and fine tuning of the model.

2.1 Transfer Learning

Conventional machine learning algorithms usually work for a specific task in isolation. If the classification task differs in feature distribution, we have to rebuild the model. Transfer learning removes the isolated paradigm of machine learning rather opens the way so that the previous knowledge of any related classification task can contribute to the new classification problem. This actually involves the model to learn a feature which relates to the previous learning. This process can make the model faster, more accurate and also lower the required number of training samples. Sometimes this transfer may worse the model performance, which is called negative transfer. We should always use this approach so that the transfer of previous knowledge about the related works will improve the performance of the new model. In deep learning, this transfer learning is known as inductive learning. The model learns to map the input features with corresponding class labels. This mapping will be efficient if the model initiates the distribution of weights related to the target classification task which is called inductive bias.

2.2 Deep Convolutional Neural Network

Deep convolutional neural network consist of a group of convolution and pooling layers. Convolution layers extract features from images. This network works as a classifier when all extracted features through the convolution layers using activation function are connected through a fully connected layer. The output from the fully connected layers are mapped to the required number of classes to accomplish the target task. In a deep convolutional layer, lower layer extract general features which are not unique for a specific task. Rather the extracted features in the last layer are task relevant and most responsible for doing the classification task. A transitions of features during training time pushes the network to be able to do the target classification task.

We have used VGG16 [13] and ResNet50 [14] deep convolutional neural network as classifier to estimate age and gender of a person. VGG16 is pre-trained with ImageNet [15] dataset containing 1000 classes to classify. Using transfer learning method, a target dataset for age and gender classification is trained on a pre-trained VGG16 model. VGG16 was introduced by Simonyan et al. [13] where the variant 16 indicated the number of convolution layers. First two layers consisted of 64 convolution filters having a size of $3 \times 3 \times 3$ an $3 \times 3 \times 64$ and stride with value 1 in all directions. These two layers are followed by a max pooling layer of size 2×2 with stride 2. Max pooling layers reduces the number of parameters which converges the model faster and generalizes well. Max pooling causes drop out of the training parameters so that the trained model will be able to do the classification task successfully on the unseen samples beyond the training dataset. The next convolution layers are also followed by max pooling layer after a fixed number. And all these extracted features are flattened and the network passes through the fully connected layers. A one dimensional feature vector is generated by the last layer which is mapped with the class labels to classify.

2.3 Fine Tuning the Model

Since VGG16 is a pre-trained model, fine tuning of the model is required to do a new classification task with a new dataset. In deep network initial layers learn general features rather the task specific features are learnt in deeper layers. During training time, we initialize the model with the pre-trained weights and make trainable parameter false for initial layers. To train the model with our work dataset, we freeze the initial layers and retrain the deeper layers with new data. Since VGG16 was pre-trained to classify 1000 classes, we have to replace the last layer output with our target number of classes. Thus the output of fully connected layers is mapped to our required eight numbers of classes (Fig. 1).

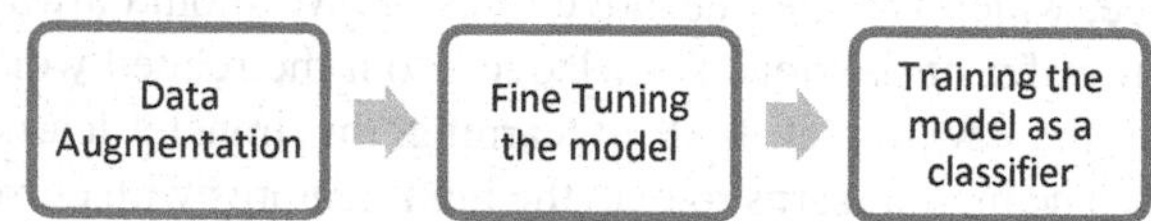

Fig. 1. Transfer learning in VGG16 using Adience benchmark.

2.4 Dataset

We have trained our model using Adience [1] benchmark dataset to estimate age and gender of people from images. This dataset contains images collected from Flickr which were uploaded through mobiles. That's why these datasets contain unconstrained images having lower resolution, variety of poses, unwanted background, different lighting condition etc. All real world difficulties to estimate age and gender from images are present in this dataset. Besides these images are like images in social media or web contents which is relevant to achieve our application purpose. Since it is sometimes too hard to identify a person's age, giving a look to him, it will be a challenging task to estimate the exact age of a person using his facial image. So we have classified the age of people in several groups. Eight age groups are available to classify using our model where the groups are in sequential order – (0–2), (4–6), (8–13), (15–20), (25–32), (38–43), (48–53), (60–). We have augmented the data applying different orientation, contrast, flipping etc. for achieving better classification performance. In our work dataset each class contains 5004 images where the total number of classes are eight. So the total number of images (both train and test) is 40032 after augmentation. We have found unbalanced data where the number of images per class is not same. Over sampling technique is applied to balance the data (Fig. 2).

Fig. 2. Images of different age groups from Adience database

3 Experimental Result

To train pre-trained VGG16 and Resnet50 models with our work dataset, we have used hold out cross validation to partition total data into training samples, validation samples and test set. 80% of the total data was used for training the model, 10% was used for measuring validation accuracy and 10% was used as test samples. Following this proportion, each class contains 500 samples as test images. Validation accuracy is a measurement to evaluate the performance of the model so that how much the model works well at unseen samples. Validation accuracy measures how the model generalizes and training accuracy measures how the model learns feature during training time. We have also measured the performance of the VGG16 model lowering the convolution layers also. Keeping the three fully connected layers unchanged, we have removed the last two convolution layers from last block which is named as VGG14 in this paper. Since deep layers learn complex and specific features well, we also increased one convolution layer in the last block and mentioned in this paper as VGG17. We have tried to focus on which model performs better with our work dataset. We have used Adam optimizer for classification and learning rate was fixed to 0.00001.

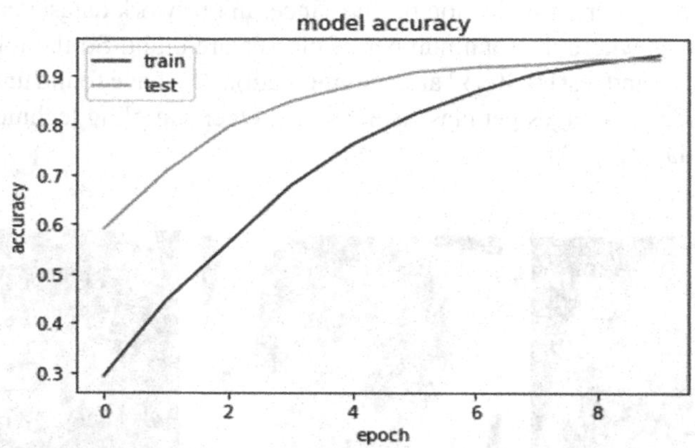

Fig. 3. Training and validation accuracy for VGG16 (Age estimation)

From Fig. 3 the relation between the number of epochs of training and both validation and training accuracy can be explained. The model generalizes well if validation accuracy is higher than training accuracy during training time. This figure notifies that the model converges to learn and validate samples at 5–6 epochs of training. The validation accuracy is always higher than the training accuracy, so that we can get a generalized model which is not confined in classifying only training samples. For age estimation we have found validation accuracy up to 99% where training accuracy is 96%. From Fig. 4 we have found validation accuracy 97% and training accuracy 91% at 3–4 epochs of training for gender classification task.

From Fig. 6 it is clear that most of the test samples are positioned diagonally so that the model performs well to classify the data. The maximum classification accuracy is shown in the age group (0–2). Since children in this age group have some especial facial attributes to differentiate them successfully from others. From Fig. 5 we have found that (0–2) is mostly error predicted by class (4–6) which is adjacent to this age group. If we take one off accuracy (if error predicted class label is adjacent to actual class) for this label, we get an accuracy of 98% for this class. Sometimes it becomes a great challenge to estimate the age of people only looking him. So a machine finds similar difficulties in doing this classification. The worst classified two groups are (38–43) and (48–53) having an accuracy of 77% and 77%. Both classes are mostly misclassified by predicting themselves as in age group (25–32). Since growing age is a continuous

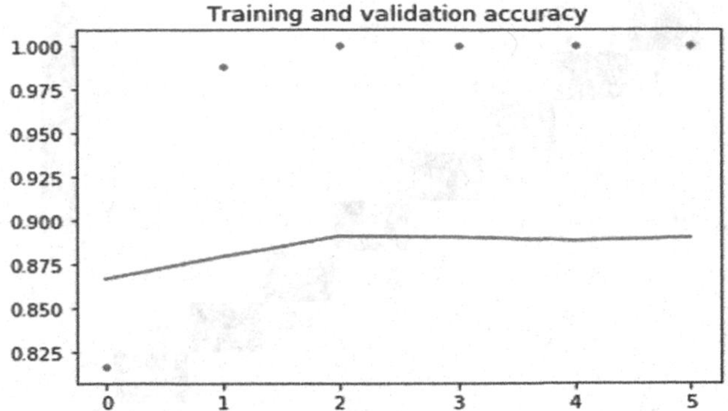

Fig. 4. Training and validation accuracy for VGG16 (Gender classification)

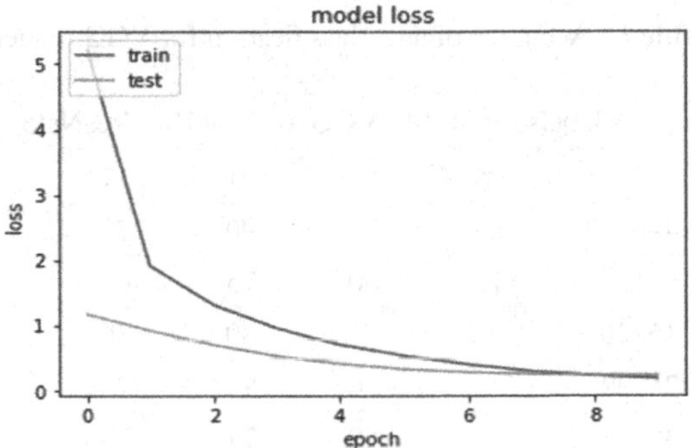

Fig. 5. Training Vs Validation Loss in VGG16 for age estimation

process, changes because of aging are continuous also. So the aging features for people at (25–48) are so much confusing depending on gender, style, genetic materials etc. If we take one off accuracy for these lower classification groups with respect to (25–32) age group, the classification accuracy increases up to 92% and 84%. Overall, this classification accuracy is satisfying to do such challenging task of age estimation from facial images having noise, motion, pose, different facial expression, styles, make over etc (Table 1).

Since we have found three trained classifier to a specific task on age estimation, we have improved the overall performance to do age classification applying simple neural network ensemble technique on these three classifiers. Three deep convolutional neural networks are trained with same training dataset and initialized with same training weights during training time. From Table 2. VGG14 and VGG17 are found showing better classification accuracy than VGG16. Generally in most cases, VGG16 shows better performance than others like VGG16 or VGG17. The reason behind this different situation is using dropout layer. Since we have used a large dataset, we have used a dropout layer with a value of 0.5 to avoid over fitting of the model. This dropout layer reduces number of trainable parameters at every fully connected layers. In VGG16, the network has three fully connected layers before the last softmax layer. [13]. When we

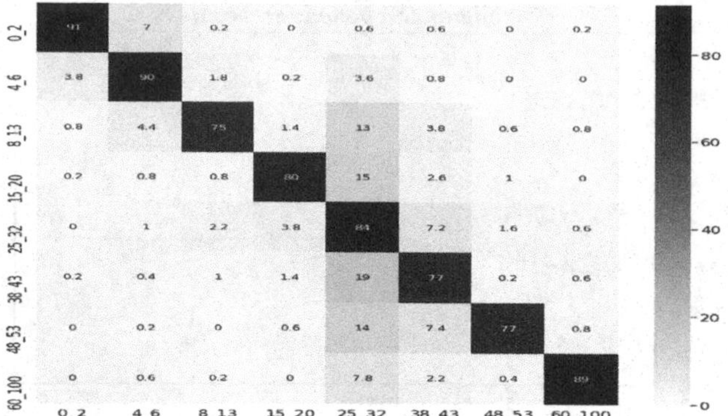

Fig. 6. Confusion matrix for age estimation using VGG17

Table 1. Accuracy of age classification for VGG models

Class labels	VGG14	VGG16	VGG17	ResNet5
0–2	95	89	91	77
4–6	85	82	90	70
8–13	72	60	75	65
15–20	93	76	80	86
25–32	81	76	84	73
38–43	61	59	77	78
48–53	73	63	77	78
60–	88	83	89	53
Average	81	74	83	72.5

have taken the first fully connected layer removing the second and third at VGG16 (we mention this as VGG14), the reduction of trainable parameters is less than VGG16. Similarly the dropout layer causes less reduction in learnable values in VGG17 which has two less fully connected layers than VGG19. But in VGG16, dropout occurs in all three fully connected layers. At each training epoch the output from fully connected layers were passed in base model. This causes a little fall in classification performance in VGG16. Applying the majority voting technique to classify a person's age with these three classifiers, we have found approximately 90% classification accuracy (Table 3). We have made a comparison of our method with previous work (VGG Face Model and GoogleNet classifier) used in [1] using the same Adience Benchmark Database (Fig. 7).

From Table 4 we have found that VGG14 performs better than VGG16 or VGG17 to classify gender depending on our test samples. Applying an ensemble technique among these three classifiers, the ensemble network shows approximately 91% classification accuracy to classify gender of people at different ages and lifestyles (Fig. 8).

Table 2. 1-Off accuracy of age classification for three models

Model	Original accuracy	1-off accuracy
ResNet50	72.5	84
VGG14	81	94
VGG16	74	88
VGG17	83	93

Table 3. Comparison of age classification accuracy

Class labels	Ensembled VGG networks	ResNet50	VGG face model [1]	GoogleNet [1]
0–2	98	77	93.17	86.75
4–6	92	70	62.11	27.89
8–13	85	65	42.06	21.47
15–20	95	86	24.23	14.10
25–32	96	73	86.17	76.6
38–43	91	78	8.88	12.03
48–53	81	78	38.17	7.05
60–	84	53	60.70	34.63
Average	90	72.5	59.90	45.07

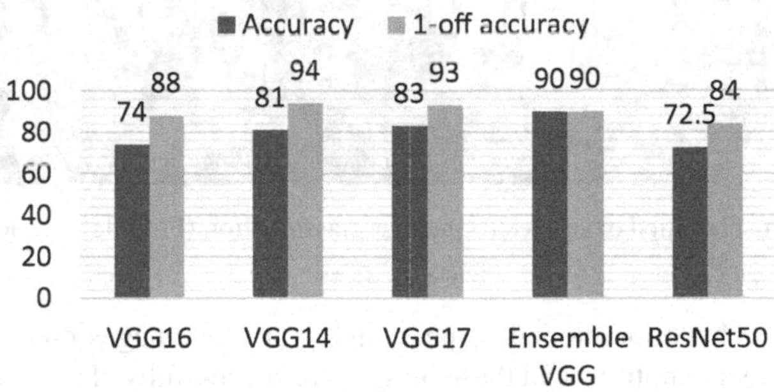

Fig. 7. Classification accuracy (Original and one – off)

In Fig. 9 some misclassified examples for gender classification. Gender detection from facial attributes faces some difficulties with resolution, noise, pose, emotions etc. in Fig. 9, (a) and (b) are misclassified by predicting themselves as male by the classifier. Due to excessive noise (blur image) misleading output is given by the classifier. Again in (c), the male is erroneously classified a female due to pose and facial expression. All these classification faces challenges to classify gender from real life data. Although

Table 4. Gender classification accuracy

Class labels	ResNet50	VGG14	VGG16	VGG17	Ensembled networks
Male	85	89	87	85	90
Female	87	88	85	89	91
Average	86	89	86	87	91

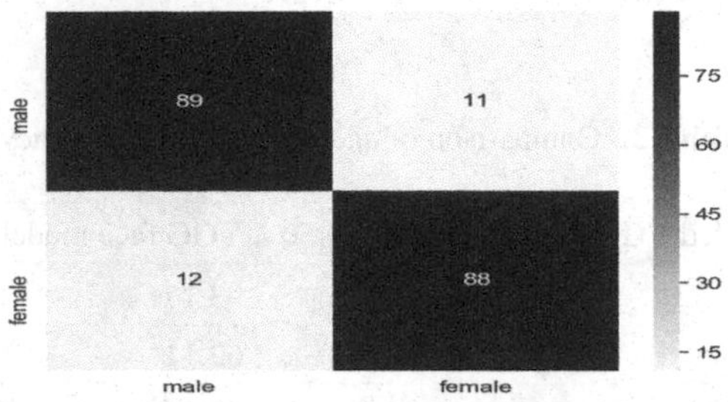

Fig. 8. Confusion matrix for gender classification using VGG14

we have found some misclassified samples in our work, most of the data are classified successfully having low resolution, motion effect, unnecessary background, different pose etc.

Fig. 9. Some misclassified examples for gender classification (From left sequentially a, b, c)

In Fig. 10 we have mentioned some samples of blur images containing different pose, lighting effect, emotions and these images are successfully classified by our model for age group classification task (Fig. 11).

 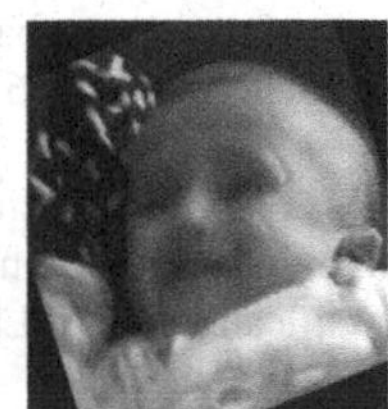  

Fig. 10. Successfully classified samples for age estimation

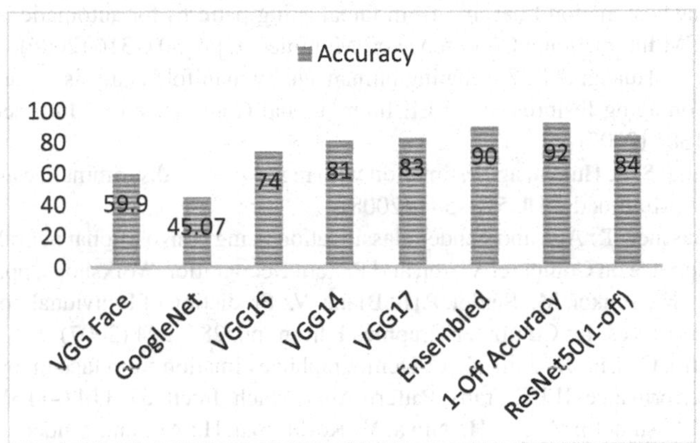

Fig. 11. Comparison with other methods in [1] and our proposed ensembled classifier

4 Conclusion

Age and gender classification task has achieved a circle of concern at present world. Security control, social sentiment analysis, context based advertisement, surveillance system, monitoring customers' choice and requirements, crime content analysis all these applications demand an automated system which can successfully estimate age and classify gender of different people from their images. These images may vary in pose, resolution, occlusion, lighting conditions etc. which are available in real world unconstrained images. In our proposed work, we have done this classification task using transfer learning approach. We have used ResNet50 and VGG16 deep convolutional neural network and changed layers in its original architecture to achieve a good performance. Finally, applying simple ensemble technique we have achieved overall classification accuracy up to 90%.

Acknowledgement. This paper is partially funded by Green University of Bangladesh.

References

1. Qawaqneh, Z., Mallouh, A.A., Barkana, B.D.: Deep convolutional neural network for age estimation based on VGG-face model. In: IEEE Conference on Computer Vision and Pattern Recognition (2017)

2. Liao, H., Yan, Y., Dai, W., Fan, P.: Age estimation of face images based on CNN and divide and rule strategy. Math. Probl. Eng. **2018** (2018). Article ID 1712686 https://doi.org/10.1155/2018/1712686
3. Jana, R., Datta, D., Saha, R.: Age estimation from face image using wrinkle features. In: International Conference on Information and Communication Technologies (2014)
4. Gunay, A., Nabiyev, V.V.: Automatic age classification with LBP. In: Computer and Information Sciences (2008)
5. Fu, Y., Guo, G., Huang, T.S.: Age synthesis and estimation via faces: a survey. IEEE Trans. Pattern Anal. Mach. Intell. **32**, 1955–1976 (2010)
6. Geng, X., Zhou, Z.H., Zhang, Y., Li, G., Dai, H.: Learning from facial aging patterns for automatic age estimation Learning from facial aging patterns for automatic age estimation. In: 14th ACM International Conference on Multimedia, pp. 307–316 (2006)
7. Fu, Y., Xu, Y., Huang, S.T.: Estimating human age by manifold analysis of face pictures and regression on aging features. In: IEEE International Conference on Multimedia and Expo, pp. 1383–1386 (2007)
8. Fu, Y., Huang, S.T.: Human age estimation with regression on discriminative aging manifold. IEEE Trans. Multimedia **10**, 578–584 (2008)
9. Levi, G., Hassner, T.: Age and gender classification using convolutional neural networks. In: IEEE Conference on Computer Vision and Pattern Recognition Workshops, pp. 34–42 (2015)
10. Scherbaum, K., Sunkel, M., Seidel, P.H., Blanz, V.: Prediction of Individual non-linear aging trajectories of faces. In: Computer Graphics Forum, pp. 285–294 (2007)
11. Han, H., Otto, C., Liu, X., Jain, K.A.: Demographic estimation from face images: Human vs. machine performance. IEEE Trans. Pattern Anal. Mach. Intell. **37**, 1148–1161 (2015)
12. Hayashi, J., Yasumoto, M., Ito, H., Niwa, Y., Koshimizu, H.: Age and gender estimation from facial image processing. In: SICE 2002. Proceedings of the 41st SICE Annual Conference, pp. 13–18 (2002)
13. Simonyan, K., Zisserman, A.: Very deep convolutional networks for large scale image recognition. In: International Conference on Learning Representations (ICLR) (2015)
14. He, K., Zhang, X., Ren, S., Sun, J.: Deep residual learning for image recognition. In: IEEE Conference on Computer Vision and Pattern Recognition (2016)
15. Krizhevsky, A., Sutskever, I., Hinton, E.G.: Imagenet classification with deep convolutional neural networks. In: Advances in Neural Information Processing Systems, pp. 1097–1105 (2012)
16. Hayashi, J., Yasumoto, M., Ito, H., Koshimizu, H.: Method for estimating and modeling age and gender using facial image processing. In: Proceedings of the Seventh International Conference on Virtual Systems and Multimedia (2001)

Diagnosis of Acute Lymphoblastic Leukemia from Microscopic Image of Peripheral Blood Smear Using Image Processing Technique

Sadia Narjim[1(✉)], Abdullah Al Mamun[2], and Diponkar Kundu[1]

[1] Department of Electrical and Electronic Engineering, Pabna University of Science and Technology, Pabna 6600, Bangladesh
sadianarjim700@gmail.com

[2] Faculty of Engineering and Technology, Multimedia University, Melaka 75450, Malaysia

Abstract. At present, cancer is a second leading cause of death which rises the global burden. Among them acute lymphoblastic leukemia is a subtype of blood cancer which is most common in child as well as adults. It occurs when the number of lymphoblast is more producing from stem cells. Over time the accumulation of this abnormal cells in bone marrow prevents to produce other healthy blood cells in our body which is very dangerous. So, early detection is one of the most important which can increase patient's survivability and treatment options. For cancer diagnosis, Ultrasound, Mammogram, MRI and microscopic images are some common methods used in medical science. Some basic detection processes of leukemia are CBC, PBS test and bone marrow test based on microscopic images. For blood cancer diagnosis, microscopic images are used manually which is time consuming and less accurate and can produce non standardized reports. So, it needs to detect leukemia automatically. Recently some computer aided methods are generated to diagnosis leukemia which are more reliable, more accurate, more precise and faster than manual diagnosis methods. In this paper a new automatic system has been proposed to detect all based on several image processing techniques from microscopic image of blood smear such as, segmentation, preprocessing, enhancement for getting better performance. To, classify blast cells and healthy cells ensemble classifier has been used with several types of feature such as, texture features, geometric features, statistic features. In this paper 99.1% accuracy, 98% Sensitivity have been achieved.

Keywords: Acute Lymphoblastic Leukemia (ALL) · WBCs count · Segmentation · Enhancement techniques · Feature extraction · Classification · MATLAB

1 Introduction

Diagnosis of blood cancer is considered as one of the vital problems in the medical science as it's depend on the ability of the hematologist which take long time to diagnosis. But it is very essential to detect cancer as soon as possible for rapid reaction and better

T. Bhuiyan et al. (Eds.): ICONCS 2020, LNICST 325, pp. 515–526, 2020.
https://doi.org/10.1007/978-3-030-52856-0_41

opportunities of treatment. So, for improving accuracy CAD (computer-aided diagnosis) systems have been applied. To minimize any type of lesion for doctor tiredness and diminish the ballast of data overloading and workload CAD systems are used. By advancing the perfection of the image using these systems, the medical images are correctly interpreted and processed to highlight the obvious parts [1]. The identification of paranormal signs as soon as possible which a physician fails to detect is the prime purpose of CAD systems [2]. Escalante et al. used ensemble particle swarm model selection (EPSMS), to detect acute leukemia from digitized bone marrow images. For similar dataset the performance of the classification of acute leukemia by using EPSMS was better than the performance of manually designed classifiers. The obtained results was 97.68% for classification of 2 type problems and for more than 2 type problems it was 94.21% [3]. Rawat et al. proposed a computer aided diagnostic (CAD) system to detect the presence of blood cancer (ALL) based on gray level co-occurrence matrices (GLCM) and shape based features. After extracting features auto support vector machine (SVM) is used to classify unhealthy images and healthy images from dataset. The classification accuracy of combined by using texture-shape feature is 89.8% [4]. According to [5] the proposed method is to identify and classify acute lymphoblastic leukemia (ALL) automatically from microscopic images using several classifier to compare the best one. By using SVM classifier with a Gaussian radial basis kernel the supreme result had been attained which was 93% accuracy and 98% sensitivity [5]. Another research by Mohapatra et al. [6] developed an automatic leukemia detection system based on Fuzzy based Blood Image Segmentation. Classification achieved 93% accuracy by using the Support Vector Machine (SVM). Again in [7], SVM classifier has been used to classify the cells into normal and blast using shape and color features. Overall accuracy of 93.7%, sensitivity of 92% and specificity of 91% have been achieved by testing the proposed algorithm over the ALL-IDB-1 dataset [7]. In [8], a CAD framework has been applied on blood smear images to diagnose the cases as normal or abnormal for Acute Lymphoblastic Leukemia (ALL) cases. Then different classifiers have been applied and compare between them. The framework has been yielding promising results which reached 96.25% accuracy, 97.3% sensitivity, and 95.35% specificity using decision tree classifier. In this paper an automated process is used for detecting leukemia from microscopic images in Ycbcr color space. Techniques like fluorescence in situ hybridization (FISH), immunophenotyping, cytogenetic analysis and cytochemistry are also employed for detecting specific leukemia which are time consuming and costly. So, in order to detect leukemia a low cost and an effective solution is to use image analysis which is a quantitative examination of stained blood microscopic images [9]. In [10], ALL-IDB-1 dataset have been used for research obtaining from online which is a public dataset. It consists of total 108 images where 59 images are from healthy patients and 49 images are affected with leukemia. This proposed system can distinguish acute lymphoblastic leukemia (ALL) cells contained images from healthy lymphocytes contained images. The proposed CAD system consists of some stage i.e. preprocessing, segmentation, post processing, feature extraction and classification. For segmenting WBC color thresholder is used from image processing toolbox in MATLAB. To extract feature some statistical, shape, geometrical features are used to classify ALL affected image from healthy images. However, selecting the effective features to classify cancer cases and healthy cases is still a complex issue [11, 12]. Color and statistical based ulcer and bleeding detection technique also used in [13, 14] and [15].

2 Proposed Method

This method is an incomparable method that has been used to detect acute lymphoblastic leukemia (ALL) from the microscopic images of peripheral blood smear. The block diagram of the proposed methodology is shown in Fig. 1. In the proposed method, color threshold has been used to separate white blood cells (WBCs) or lymphocytes (which are one kind of WBC) from the microscopic images of blood smear. At first only the white blood cells have been segregated and has been removed the other blood cells (like RBCs, PLT) because acute lymphoblastic leukemia (ALL) is produced by the immature lymphocyte cells (called lymphoblast) which is a type of WBC. So, the several operation has applied only the WBCs which are affected by ALL. The method has been used in this work is simple, easy to understand, easy to calculate, fast and more accurate. The system has developed in MATLAB R2018a.

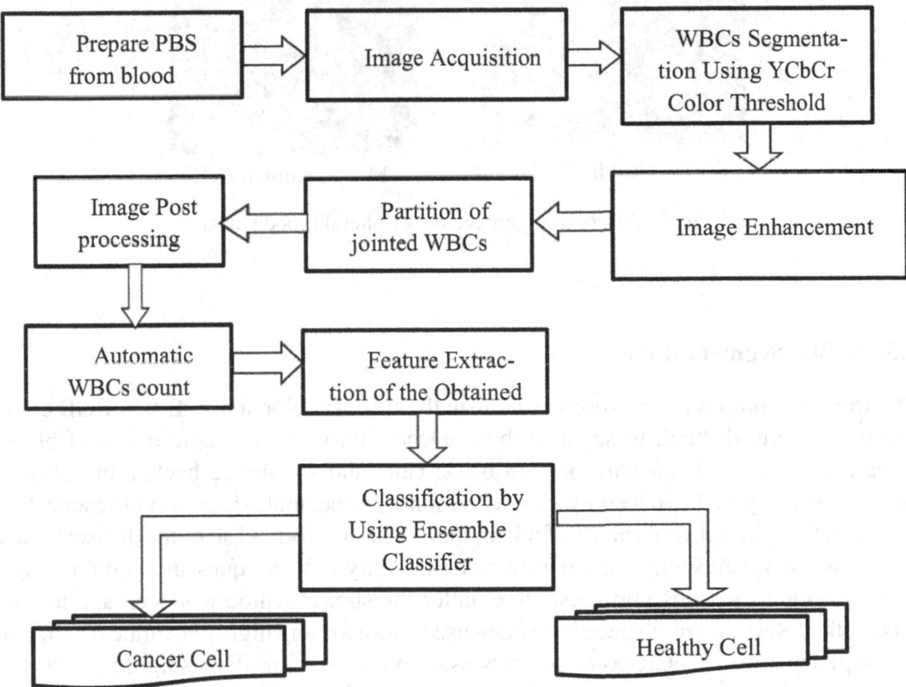

Fig. 1. Block diagram of proposed method

2.1 Prepare PBS

The first step of this research work is collecting dataset including both cancerous and non-cancerous. To collect the required dataset at first it's needed to prepare peripheral blood smear (PBS) or bone marrow smear then by keeping blood smear under microscope with a digital camera which is placed at the eye piece and microscopic images are collected. The dataset should be with high resolution, enough clear and proper brightness at the time of obtaining images.

2.2 Image Acquisition

In this work the dataset of ALL-IDB has been used which was collected from Dr. Fabio Scotti and Dr. Donida Labati after fulfilling ALL-IDB License Agreement and Terms of Use. It is a publicly open to download the dataset available in online [10]. They provide high quality images. ALL-IDB1 dataset contains total 108 image where 59 images are non-cancerous and 49 images are affected by leukemia with 24-bit color, resolution 2592 × 1944 (for healthy images) and 1712 × 1368 (for cancerous images) (Fig. 2).

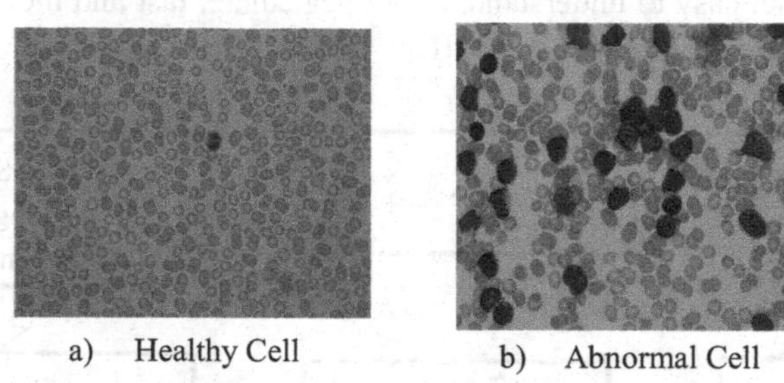

Fig. 2. Microscopic image of peripheral blood smear

2.3 WBCs Segmentation

The images captured by microscope are usually in RGB color space. But in RGB color space it is quite difficult to segment these. Generally, in microscopic image of blood smear, the color and intensity of both blood cells and the image background differs highly. This may be happened by various reasons. For accurate detection of leucocytes, segmentation plays a vital role. To find out the essential information of the dataset with a great efficient result segmentation must be best. Plenty of techniques are used for image segmentation in various purposes. Here, color threshold method has been applied. In this method, several color space have been used for searching highly accurate result. For this segmentation YCbCR color space is used to create mask. By using this, only the leucocyte cells of the image have been separated which is the informative portion for my research work and have removed the non-informative portion (Fig. 3).

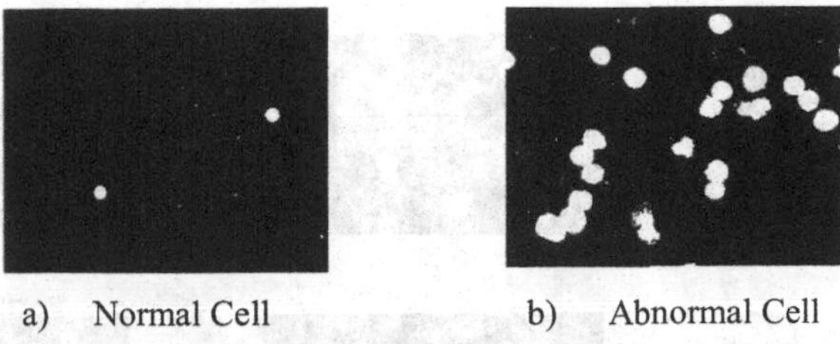

a) Normal Cell b) Abnormal Cell

Fig. 3. WBCs segregated using color threshold

2.4 Image Enhancement

To make the image more suitable for the next step image enhancement is needed. To advance the quality, brightness and contrast characteristics of an image these techniques are applied which can also sharpen image details [16]. After segmenting WBCs, there are many noises and unwanted region of hole which have to be distinguished. In this paper three steps to make the image more appropriate for next processing. These are (Fig. 4):

- median filtering,
- area opening and
- morphological reconstruction

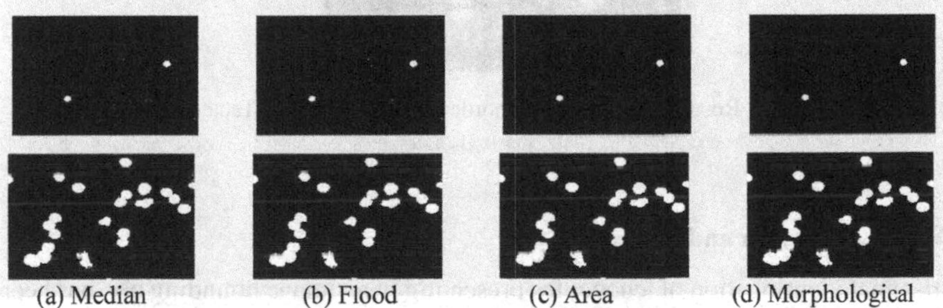

(a) Median (b) Flood (c) Area (d) Morphological

Fig. 4. Enhanced image, up: Non-cancerous, Down: Cancerous

2.5 Separation of Joined WBCs

After the image enhancement operation, watershed segmentation has been used to separate the connected cells (Fig. 5).

As there are many WBCs presented in the image so it is possible to connect with each other. As a result, to count WBCs accurately it's needed to separate them. Here in the proposed methodology, watershed segmentation has been applied using distance transform. The goal of this method is to detect connected objects to apply a boundary line. The concept of distance transform is very simple. It is the distance of nearest non-zero valued pixel from each pixel.

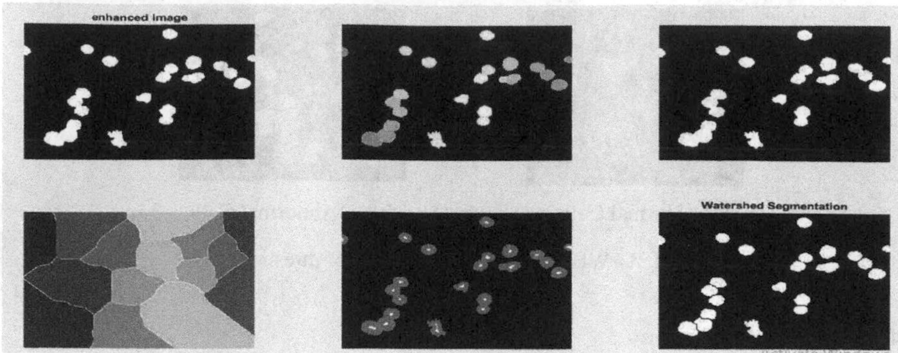

Fig. 5. Watershed segmented image (ALL affected)

2.6 Image Post-processing

In the dataset, there is a possibility of the presence of leucocytes on the edges of the image. So, to remove this border objects imclearborder function is used in the work. It also reduces the error of leucocytes identification (Fig. 6).

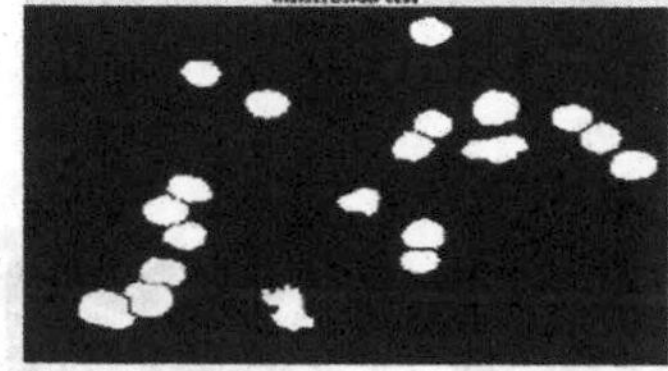

Fig. 6. Resultant image after border cleaning (ALL affected)

2.7 WBCs Detection and Count

After the final identification of leucocytes presenting in an image bounding box has been used to detect the cells individually and also count the number of the cells automatically. The final image of detecting leucocytes is shown in Fig. 7.

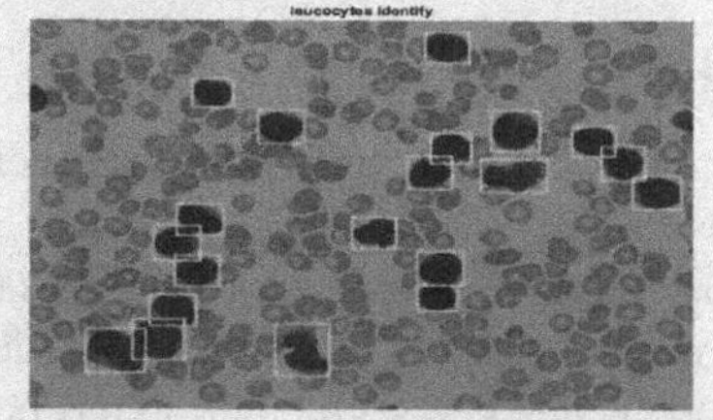

Fig. 7. Leucocytes identification (ALL affected)

2.8 Feature Extraction

Feature extraction is the process of extracting informative data from the image to classify the cancerous and non-cancerous image. Converting the extracted data into a set of features is known as feature extraction. Classifier performance mostly depends on feature selection

Among the features several types of features have been used such as shape features, statistical features, texture features, geometric features which are including several parameters like, area, perimeter, solidity, elongation, mean, standard deviation, rectangularity, variance, eccentricity, minor axis length, major axis length, compactness and form factor. So, the total features extracted is 26 and the feature vector size is 26*108. These parameters are calculated by the following equations

Form factor $= \frac{4 \times \text{pi} \times \text{Area}}{\text{Perimeter}^2}$

Eccentricity $= \frac{\sqrt{a^2 - b^2}}{a}$ (a = major axis length, b = minor axis length)

Solidity $= \frac{\text{Area}}{\text{Convex Area}}$

Compactness $= \frac{\text{Perimeter}^2}{\text{Area}}$

Elongation $= 1 - \frac{\textit{minor axis}}{\textit{major axis}}$

Rectangularity $= \frac{\text{Area}}{\textit{major axis} \times \textit{minor axis}}$

Mode: It is defined as most frequent value of the pixel's intensity of the ROI.

Mean: It is the average value of the pixel's intensity of the ROI.

Standard deviation: Standard deviation is a standard express how much pixel's intensity differ from the mean of pixels' intensities of the ROI.

Variance: It is the Variance value of the pixel's intensity of the ROI. The variance is the square of the standard deviation, the second central moment of a distribution, and the covariance of the random variable with itself.

2.9 Classification

Classification is a theoretical approach to identify definite class of images. There are several methods are used for classifying dataset for a specific purpose. In this paper ensemble classifier has been used for classifying the healthy and cancerous images. It gives a satisfying result. It is a set of classifiers whose purpose is to adjoin particular decisions in various way (typically by voting) for classifying new examples. So, it combines the predictions of multiple classifiers. One of the most active areas of research in supervised learning has been to study methods for constructing good ensembles of classifiers. It is also known as a multiple-classifier system (MCS). That is why ensemble methods placed first in many prestigious machine learning competitions. It is highly desirable to maintain a very high recognition and a low error rate in all automated disease recognition systems. It is difficult to classify lymphoblast by a single classifier as the complex pattern recognition. So, an ensemble classifier is more appropriate as it is a combination of several classifiers

3 Result and Discussion

As usual the classification of leukemia and non-leukemia images, four occurrences may possible to create which shown in Table 1.

Table 1. Possible occurrence in classification

Possible occurrence	Explanation
True leukemia detection (TP)	Prediction and in actual is leukemia
True non-leukemia detection (TN)	Prediction and actual is non-leukemia
False leukemia detection (FP)	Prediction is leukemia but in actual it's non-leukemia
False non-leukemia detection (FN)	Prediction is non-leukemia but in actual it's leukemia

Only accuracy can't represent the performance of a method. There are some other parameters also such as sensitivity, specificity, precision, negative predicted value (NPV) and F1 score to predict the actual result

Accuracy: It denotes the measurement result of accurate diagnosis test. It defined as,

$$\text{Accuracy} = \frac{TP + TN}{(TP + TN + FP + FN)}$$

Sensitivity: It is the ratio of quantity of actual effectual positive prediction to the number of true positive.

$$\text{Sensitivity} = \frac{TP}{(TP + FN)}$$

Specificity: It can be defined as the ratio of quantity of actual negative prediction to quantity of actual negatives. It can be defined as,

$$\text{Specificity} = \frac{TN}{(TN + FP)}$$

The higher specificity shows more accurate non-leukemia detection.

Precision: It measures the proportion of proposed work with positive results which are identified accurately.

$$\text{Precision} = \frac{TP}{(TP + FP)}$$

F1 Score: It is a harmonic mean of sensitivity and precision.

$$\text{F1 Score} = \frac{2 \times Precision \times Sensitivity}{Precision + Sensitivity}$$

Table 2 shows the results of several sample combination of features and using mean, variance and standard deviation of all attributes for the proposed method gives the upmost performance with accuracy 99.1%, sensitivity 98%, specificity 100%, precision 100% and F1 score 99%. As this framework utilized the simplest layout to identify the particular segments, it will take less computational time to evaluate and make the framework more efficient.

Table 2. Performance analysis varying features

Features	Acc (%)	Sen (%)	Spec (%)	FPR (%)	FNR (%)	Pre (%)	F1 score (%)
Solidity	53.3	95	4	96	5	54	69
Major axis	73.8	81	65	35	19	73	77
Standard deviation, variance	86	84	88	12	16	89	86
Standard deviation	83.2	86	80	20	14	83	84
Form factor	43.9	71	12	88	29	49	58
Mean, standard deviation	97.2	95	100	0	5	100	97
Mean, standard deviation	97.2	95	100	0	5	100	97
Mean, standard deviation, variance	99.1	98	100	0	2	100	99

Then Fig. 8 illustrates the performance comparison of the proposed method with different color spaces. In this proposed method color thresholder has been used in YCbCr color space which provide the best performance over the color spaces RGB, L*a*b* and HSV.

Figure 9 shows performance of the proposed method compared with different types of classifiers namely logistic regression, linear discriminant analysis, SVM, QSVM, ensemble subspace discriminant, linear discriminant and quadratic discriminant. Among this ensemble subspace discriminant analysis exposes the best performance for the proposed method.

The performance of the proposed method is compared with the results obtained by the other existing methods such as [5, 7, 8] and [17] in the Fig. 10 where SVM, Decision tree, KNN classifiers have been used. It is seen that our proposed method provides the best possible result.

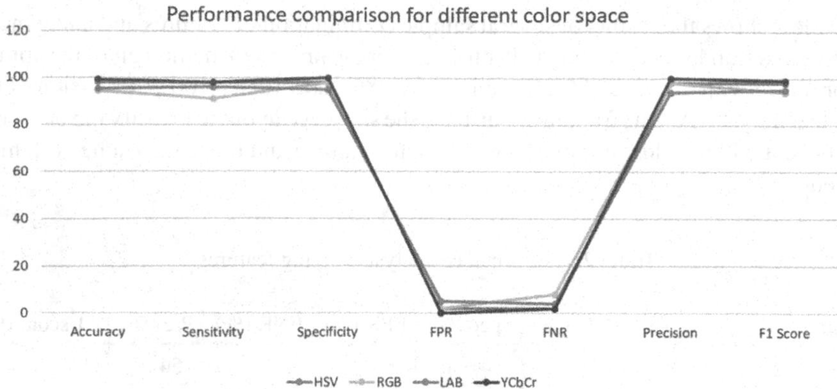

Fig. 8. Performance comparison for several color spaces

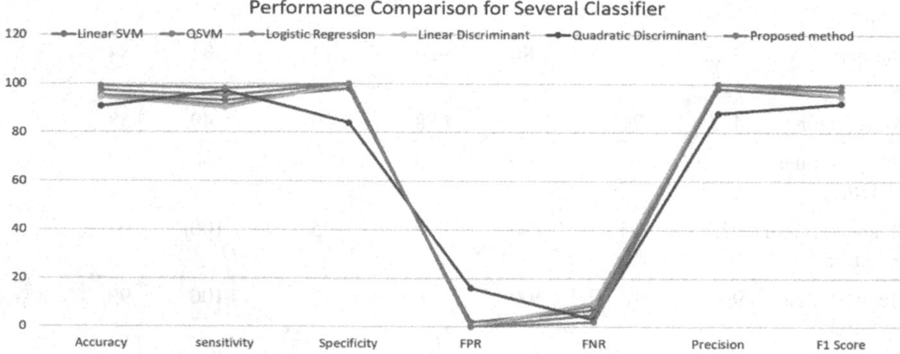

Fig. 9. Comparison of several classifier

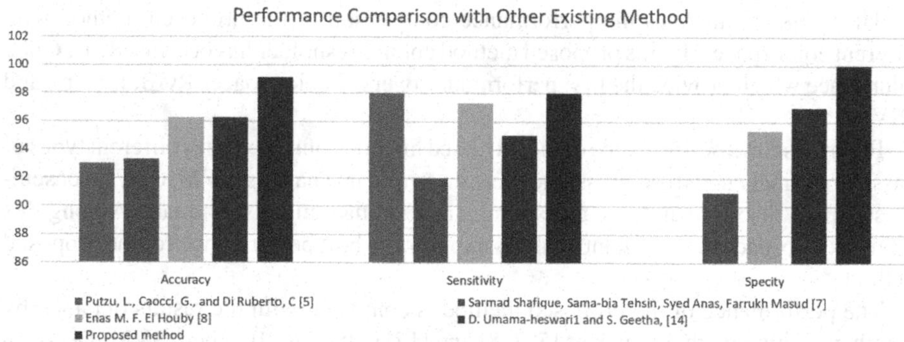

Fig. 10. Performance comparison with other existing methods

4 Conclusion

At present Acute Lymphoblastic Leukemia (ALL) has become a one of the popular fetal disease for both child and adults. Accurate and more efficient diagnosis of ALL is more important matter for the patient's treatment. The main goal of this paper is to diagnosis ALL accurately than hematologist without consuming much time. Consequently, a new CAD system has been proposed based on image processing techniques applying microscopic images of blood smear. Initially, color thresholder in YCbCr color space has been used for leucocyte segmentation. After then some pre-processing, post-processing operations are applied on segmented images for getting the more accurate result. Finally several types of feature such as, texture features, geometric features, statistic features are extracted. Then using ensemble classifier classify healthy and cancerous images on the basis of obtained feature vector. This gives the performance result i.e. 99.1% accuracy, 98% Sensitivity, 100% specificity, 99% F1 score, 53% RPP, 46% RNP, 2% FNR, 0% FPR, 100% precision. So, it is obvious that the proposed method is able to detect leukemia and non-leukemia images successfully.

References

1. Chen, C.-M., Chou, Y.-H., Tagawa, N., Do, Y.: Computer-aided detection and diagnosis in medical imaging. Comput. Math. Methods Med. **2013** (2013). https://doi.org/10.1201/b18191
2. Computer Aided Diagnosis - Medical Image Analysis Techniques|IntechOpen. https://www.intechopen.com/books/breast-imaging/computer-aided-diagnosis-medical-image-analysis-techniques
3. Escalante, H.J., Montes-y-Gómez, M., González, J.A., Gómez-Gil, P., Altamirano, L., Reyes, C.A., Reta, C., Rosales, A.: Acute leukemia classification by ensemble particle swarm model selection. Artif. Intell. Med. **55**, 163–175 (2012). https://doi.org/10.1016/j.artmed.2012.03.005
4. Rawat, J., Singh, A., Bhadauria, H.S., Virmani, J.: Computer aided diagnostic system for detection of leukemia using microscopic images. Procedia Comput. Sci. **70**, 748–756 (2015). https://doi.org/10.1016/j.procs.2015.10.113
5. Putzu, L., Caocci, G., Di Ruberto, C.: Leucocyte classification for leukaemia detection using image processing techniques. Artif. Intell. Med. **62**, 179–191 (2014). https://doi.org/10.1016/j.artmed.2014.09.002
6. Mohapatra, S., Samanta, S.S., Patra, D., Satpathi, S.: Fuzzy based blood image segmentation for automated leukemia detection. 2011 International Conference on Devices and Communications ICDeCom 2011 - Proceedings (2011). https://doi.org/10.1109/icdecom.2011.5738491
7. Li, Y., Zhu, R., Mi, L., Cao, Y., Yao, D.: Segmentation of white blood cell from acute lymphoblastic leukemia images using dual-threshold method. Comput. Math. Methods Med. **2016** (2016). https://doi.org/10.1155/2016/9514707
8. El Houby, E.M.F.: Framework of computer aided diagnosis systems for cancer classification based on medical images. J. Med. Syst. **42**(8), 1–11 (2018). https://doi.org/10.1007/s10916-018-1010-x
9. Mohapatra, S., Patra, D., Satpathi, S.: Image analysis of blood microscopic images for acute leukemia detection. In: International Conference on Industrial Electronics, Control and Robotics Image (2010)

10. Labati, R.D., Piuri, V., Scotti F.: ALL-IDB : the acute lymphoblastic leukemia image database for image processing. IEEE International Conference on Image Processing, Department of Information Technology, Università degli Studi di Milano, pp. 2089–2092 (2011)
11. Mohanty, A.K., Senapati, M.R., Lenka, S.K.: An improved data mining technique for classification and detection of breast cancer from mammograms. Neural Comput. Appl. **22**, 303–310 (2013). https://doi.org/10.1007/s00521-012-0834-4
12. Xie, W., Li, Y., Ma, Y.: Breast mass classification in digital mammography based on extreme learning machine. Neurocomputing **173**, 930–941 (2016). https://doi.org/10.1016/j.neucom.2015.08.048
13. Al Mamun, A., Hossain, M.S.: Ulcer detection in image converted from video footage of wireless capsule endoscopy. In: 1st International Conference on Advances in Science, Engineering and Robotics Technology ICASERT 2019, pp. 1–4 (2019). https://doi.org/10.1109/icasert.2019.8934597
14. Hossain, M.S., Al Mamun, A., Hasan, M.G., Hossain, M.M.: Easy scheme for ulcer detection in wireless capsule endoscopy images. In: 1st International Conference on Advances in Science, Engineering and Robotics Technology ICASERT 2019, pp. 1–5 (2019). https://doi.org/10.1109/icasert.2019.8934510
15. Al Mamun, A., Hossain, M.S., Hossain, M.M., Hasan, M.G.: Discretion way for bleeding detection in wireless capsule endoscopy images. 1st International Conference on Advances in Science, Engineering and Robotics Technology ICASERT 2019, pp. 1–6 (2019). https://doi.org/10.1109/icasert.2019.8934589
16. Shaikh, N., Rajaput, K., Pawar, R., Vibhute, D.A.S.: Counting of RBC's and WBC's using image processing technique. Int. Res. J. Eng. Technol. **6**, 1948–1950 (2019)
17. Umamaheswari, D., Geetha, S.: A framework for efficient recognition and classification of acute lymphoblastic leukemia with a novel customized-KNN classifier. J. Comput. Inf. Technol. **26**, 131–140 (2018). https://doi.org/10.20532/cit.2018.1004123

Computer Networks

Analysis of Software Defined Wireless Network with IP Mobility in Multiple Controllers Domain

Md. Habibur Rahman[1,2(✉)], Nazrul Islam[1], Asma Islam Swapna[3], and Md. Ahsan Habib[1]

[1] Mawlana Bhashani Science and Technology University, Tangail, Bangladesh
{mdhabibur.r.bd,m.a.habib}@ieee.org, nazrul.islam@gmail.com

[2] Bangabandhu Sheikh Mujibur Rahman Digital University, Kaliakair, Bangladesh

[3] Universidade Estadual de Campinas, Barão Geraldo 13083-970, Brazil
asma0swapna@gmail.com

Abstract. Software Defined Networking (SDN) approach is a generalized concept that de-couples software plane from the hardware plane of a network. SDN can be an alternative to well-defined protocol stack, scalability, and full resource management capabilities. SDN for wireless environment became a popular research field for future deployment. Therefore, performance issues of Software Defined Wireless Networking (SDWN) have become important in order to study and analyze the underlying network design, scope, and capabilities. This research work represents the performance analysis of SDWN for multiple domains and inter-controller communication. Integration of IP mobility with the Mobile Nodes (MN) affects TCP throughput, bandwidth, transmission jitter and latency of underlying SDWN. This paper concludes that SDWN has both integrated performance in efficient handoff through IP mobility solution and somewhere penalties as well in terms of inter-controller communication. In the end, a comparative study with distributed mobility solutions is performed against an IP based model.

Keywords: SDWN · Performance analysis · Wireless mobility · Mininet Wi-Fi · Mobile IP

1 Introduction

Software Defined Networking (SDN) offers a lot of possibilities to the network industries. It provides the advance features like programmable controller, flexible and scalable network architecture for the future Internet. The Open Network Foundation (ONF) deploys the OpenFlow protocol in SDN as the part of gradual research results [1]. SDN physically separates the data plane from the control plane that are existing together in the current network. The SDN moves the control plane in a central controller and forwards decision to the data plane. OpenFlow provides the facility of splitting the control plane and forwarding plane [2].

T. Bhuiyan et al. (Eds.): ICONCS 2020, LNICST 325, pp. 529–538, 2020.
https://doi.org/10.1007/978-3-030-52856-0_42

OpenFlow is a standard, adopted especially for the SDN architecture. According to OpenFlow specification in [3], any OpenFlow switch holds flow entries in itself that contains incoming packet header information. The OpenFlow protocol moves the control from the switches to the Open Flow controller [4,5]. Phemius et al. [6] proposed an extensible DIstributed SDN Control (DISCO) for the SDN topology. Software Defined Wireless Networking (SDWN) [6] is a branch of Software Defined Network (SDN). SDWN becomes most adaptable technology for the proper management of the densely populated cellular network [7,8]. This technology assures simple and scalable network architecture and effective mobility management of the IP networks. The SDWN programmatically centralizes and separates the control plane from the data plane. The Programmatic control plane is responsible for the Access Points (APs) to choose the flow table algorithm and the data plane is responsible for the traffic transmission and reception over the wireless link [6,9]. Since the widespread adoption of the SDWN, the Software Defined Mobility Management (SDMM) gets attention by the cellular company and the researchers. Researchers pay much more attention for the mobility management.

IP mobility refers to the set of mechanisms to keep ongoing sessions continuity while a mobile user changes its mobility anchor point in the network [10]. In SDN-related Mobility Protocols, IP mobility functions commonly adopted by existing mobility protocols [11]. While existing mobility protocols paid more attention to adding new features, such as multicast, to basic mobility functions. SDN based communication between two mobile hosts and handling the movement are described in paper [11]. This paper represents the performance analysis of SDWN with IP mobility in the multiple controller domains.

However, in Software Defined Mobility Management architecture, consisting of several collaborating domains. Each confederation is useful to densely populated mobility management. Every domain contains at least one controller and a mobility management application in the control plane. In paper [12], the authors implemented and deployed a software-defined IP mobility architecture in Mininet WiFi platform. Mobility management on both the Inter-domain and Intra-domain scenario has been focused in [12]. In this paper, the RYU component based framework is used in the mobility solution for a multiple controller domain. This paper is deployed in the Inter-domain scenario for the mobility management. Qualities of Service (QoS) performances are measured of the proposed design. TCP throughput, bandwidth, latency, and transmission jitter are the QoS parameters. These offer better solutions for the mobility management of the IP networks in multiple controller domains.

The structure of this paper is as follows. In Sect. 2, related works are described. Section 3, describes the research methodology. Section 4, design and implementation are illustrated. Section 5, evaluates the performance to show that results meet up with designs objectives. Section 6, conclude the paper with future work.

2 Background and Related Work

Software Defined Wireless Networking (SDWN) architecture is composed of both North-South and East-West network dimension. East-West network interface operates for wireless and mobile devices using inter-controller protocols. Border Gateway Protocol (BGP) is used for the wireless and mobile devices in East-West network interface [13]. Previous researches [3,8,13] have been performed on OpenFlow switches, heterogeneous network customization, splitting effect of control and data plan in network dynamicity and so on. OpenRoad was the first work in the history of SDWN where an OpenFlow based network was proposed with wireless compatibility [14]. Wang et al. in paper [12] used Mininet platform and a cross-domain SDN testbed for the mobility management of the network. The authors in paper [12] focused on the intra-domain scenarios in SDN. The IP mobility based on inter-domain in SDWN has been little studied before. However, this paper is proposed a SDWN in inter-domain scenario and evaluates the performance in the Mininet Wi-Fi [15] platform.

OpenFlow (v 1.4) is used for simulating the Software Defined Wireless Network model in Mininet Wi-Fi testbed. When the OpenFlow approach is used in SDN design, the switches are placed after the controller layer and between southbound APIs and physical devices. Using OpenFlow protocol in SDN architecture the mobility management becomes a challenging issue. Mobility management for inter-domain communication between two hosts for single controller is illustrated in paper [12]. Wang et al. [12] described the session initialization and the handoff management for both single and multiple controllers. Yet, to our best knowledge there are no performance analyses of a SDWN network; that are deployed with multiple east-west controller interface and a profound impact of that on network parameters.

Thereby, this study shows up with such an SDWN, where multiple controllers share and update the flow tables. Controllers also update the transmission session for the mobility movement of the wireless and radio accessed devices in the network. Mobility management is performed with IP mobility solution. The emulation stage based on random way point model is taken in concern for mobility model [16]. In the inter-controller communication, controller exchange information. Controllers also update the entity reachability, flow setup, tear down and update request and at last update their capability information. In this related deployment scenario, network traffic is orchestrated across inter-domain SDWN network domains. As reference [17], RYU controller is adapted in this research work. Using controller's defined policy, east-west interface enables communication among the controllers. Exchange of research parameters impacts overall network performance. The outcome of this study is to capture and analyze overall performance of this network.

3 Research Methodology

A literature review has been performed to analyze the proposed mobility management solution for IP networks. In Software Defined Mobility Management

(SDMM), the confederation of collaborating multiple controller domains are studied before. The mobility management application is used for analyzing the performance of the proposed architecture. Before this, a simulation or emulation tool needs to choose to analyze the performance. Among Mininet Wi-Fi [15], NS-3 [18], EstiNet [19], OpenNet [20], Mininet Wi-Fi is chosen for OpenFlow Version, Wireless Functionality, Controller Compatibility and Extendibility. Mininet Wi-Fi is an emulation tool which can assign the packet loss, channel bandwidth, and delay etc. to the proposed architecture link. Basic Linux TC tools are used to emulate the network architecture by the Mininet Wi-Fi. The Mininet Wi-Fi is installed in Ubuntu operating system having core i5 processor. Wireshirk [21] is used for capturing the data of the proposed SDWN topology. The Mininet Wi-Fi and Wire-shirk are easier to install as well as to use for simple command line prompt.

The proposed design is tested repeatedly assigning different values such as packet loss, channel bandwidth and delay to the link. The emulated data are collected appropriately. Different graphs are plotted to represents the performance of proposed mobility management solution of IP network using MATLAB tool.

4 Design and Implementation

This section describes the design of the mobility architecture. Several mobile hosts are connected into the three distinct domains. Three distinguished controllers are connected by the inter-controller channel. Every controller contains four access points (AP). The hosts are connected in wireless medium. The host could move from one domain to another domain. At the time of random mobility, hosts may be connected with any APs in any controller. The controllers A, B and C handovers their session through the inter-controller channel. The mobile hosts can move from one domain to the other. The routing table information of the host should be hand-off to the newly connected controller.

Figure 1 depicts the testbed wireless SDN topology with three domains having one RYU controller on each domain. The mobility solution for the mobile hosts is highly reliable in the RYU controller. The packets are transmitted and received between the Correspondent Nodes (CNs) and the Mobile Nodes (MNs) via the communication channel. The MNs randomly move from one AP to another AP in the domains of different controllers through the inter controller channel. The RYU controller framework helps MN to move rapidly. RYU exchange information between domains and transfer routing table information to the controllers. There are several mobility management controllers. Here we integrated the RYU framework controller for the mobility management. The Mobile Nodes (MN) functions mobility by detaching from current AP and getting attached to the nearby one. This mobility model in Mininet Wi-Fi emulators follows Random Way Point (RWP) to move around the testbed. Mutiple controllers with different domain use Inter-Controller channel that satisfies the controller policy of RYU framework. MN in the SDWN testbed connects the next access point or OpenFlow switch in the same or different domain according to the reachability and capability of the controller.

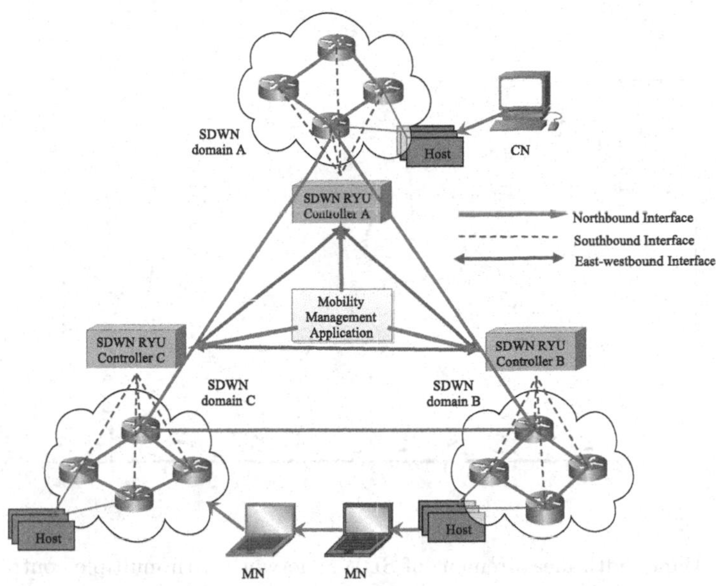

Fig. 1. Software Defined Wireless Networking (SDWN) topology with multiple controller domains.

The northbound interface communicates through SDN devices between the controllers and mobility management applications. The east/west bound interface is a medium between the two controllers in different domain. And the southbound interface is a medium between the control plane and data plane. The southbound interface is used to train the controllers to collect the information about the Mobile Nodes (MNs). It is also responsible for functioning the packet operation among the MNs using the SDN devices. Mapping functionality is done by the control plane and data plane using SDN devices

5 Results and Analysis

This section illustrates the performance analysis of SDWN based on Mobile IP (MIP) mobility; also, the research work compares the performance parameters against distributed mobility solutions. MIP model redirects all the CN-to-MN traffic once MN moves to a new switching AP. The session handover is performed both in data plane and control plane. With is network status the simulation is performed for 5 times each for 15 s and the average outcome is recorded to analyze the following network parameters and represent the performance of the whole.

5.1 Bandwidth

For the bandwidth measurements, two different hosts (h1 and h4) from each of the controller domains is chosen and ping test is performed. The resultant throughput vs. time graph is shown in Fig. 2.

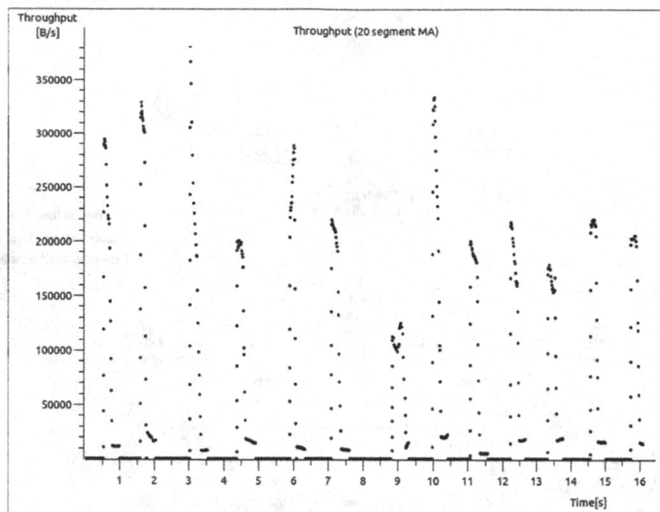

Fig. 2. Bandwidth measurement of SDWN network with multiple controllers.

Figure 2. Depicts that, during changing the domain of attachment, h1 provides less throughput. The query or response packets is therefore delayed for flow update and impacts on session handover to the newly attached domain controller. However, after the handover, the immediate packet statistics showed highest throughput among the rest controller duration.

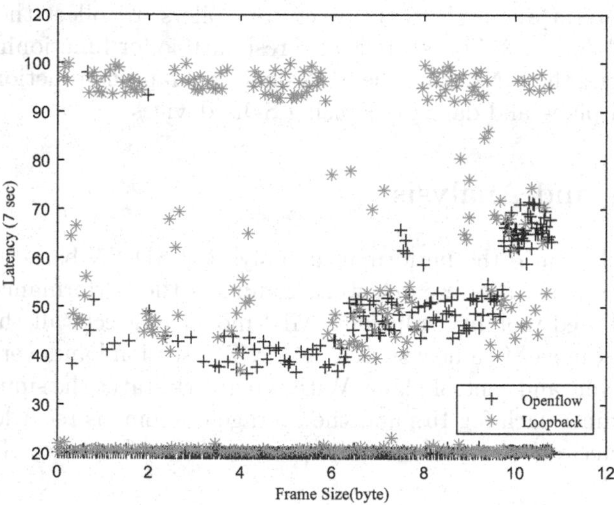

Fig. 3. Latency Measurement in OpenFlow and loopback interface during handoff situations

5.2 Latency

Delay measurement in terms of packet frame size is discussed in this subsection. Figure 3 represents the latency in microseconds in terms of each frame byte fractions for each packets. Both loopback and OpenFlow packets are captured in the simulation and compared in the graphical representation.

The result showed loopback packets taking large latency hence more time to reach from one node to another entity than OpenFlow packets in the network. The reason of such behavior is the flow entry and the session handling mechanism in the controller policy that took less time for matched packet entries.

5.3 Jitter

Packet delay variations throughout the whole experimentation time turned out impactful on different packet sizes. Figure 4 shows the delay variation for different packet sizes in the transmission process. The figure represents higher variations for smaller packet size hence high jitter in packet seizes less than 3 bytes.

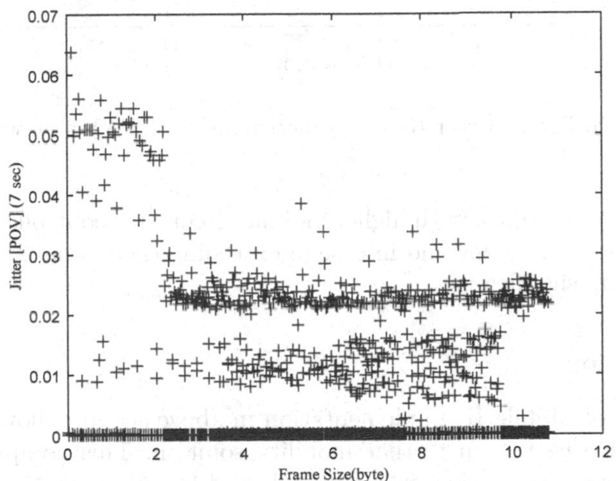

Fig. 4. Jitter (Packet Delay Variations) measurement of SDWN network.

Lower sized packets create high values in TCP timeouts throughout the transmission process and thus decrease overall throughput as well. On the other hands, higher packets in size 3 bytes or larger has less TCP timeouts and higher throughput.

5.4 Packet Error Rate (PER)

Packet-in messages in the controllers can be a successful packet, or broken forwarded TCP packets. While handling session handovers by the controller in wireless SDN, for different mobility frequency among the host nodes, the ratio of error packets with respect to total received packets varies and increases with higher frequency. This packet error rate represented in Fig. 5, for different mobility frequency.

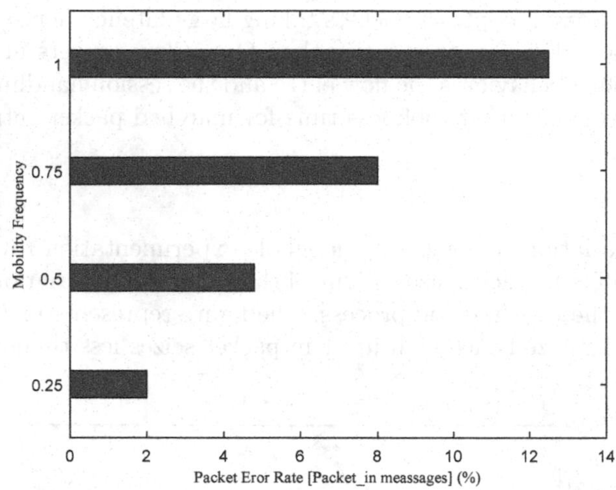

Fig. 5. Packet Error Rate (%) measurement of SDWN network.

This behavior clarifies, with higher mobility frequency controller get less time for transferring flow entries and in case of exceeding their capabilities error rate starts increasing significantly.

5.5 Evaluation

The outcomes of Mobile IP implementation in above section allows to compare the performance issues with other mobility solution. This comparative study will allow understanding the efficiency and need for applying Mobile IP rather than other mobility solution such as Distributed Mobility Management (DMM).

Table 1. Comparative study among DMM and mobile IP mobility solution applied in SWDN

Mobility solution	Scalability option	Handoff efficiency	Optimization aspect
Mobile IP (our proposed)	Large complex inter-domain	Seamless-like (User not perceivable)	Air link
DMM [10]	Limited	Seamless for certain duration	VoIP session

Researcher Luca Valtalina in paper [10] represented DMM to be the solution for low scalability potential single point of failure and suboptimal routing in SDN. The paper depicted expected level of QoS and enhanced performance on certain parameter for DMM adopted SDN.

DMM requires a prediction function to cope with high latency where Mobile IP has solution for seamless performance in inter-controller wireless domain. DMM solution can support continuity of session and handover to new AP only for session bounded to 150 ms [10]. Table 1 in the following depicts the comparative study performed among DMM and Mobile IP applied in SDWN.

6 Conclusion

In this paper, a performance analysis on SDWN is conducted with integration of Mobile IP mobility management for inter-controller communication. The outcomes from Mininet Wi-Fi test bed demonstrated a visible state in terms of performance parameters and scalability. Mininet Wi-Fi simulation evaluated that, single controller centralized OpenFlow communication results in higher jitter and latency. On the other hand, for more complex inter-controller communication, throughput increases for IP based session handover among controllers. The reason of such difference is the efficient handoff, MIP based mobility solution for wireless SDN. MIP mobility model takes less timeout, lower retransmission time and scalability in controller performance. A comparative study in terms of handoff efficiency is performed between Mobile IP and distributed mobility solution, i.e. DMM. The study resulted in more seamless handover in IP based mobility of inter-controller network, scalability, and mobility optimization than DMM does.

In future, we will try to implement the network in real time setup. It would be very interesting to evaluate performance analysis in Software Defined Wireless Mobile Network.

References

1. Open Networking Foundation (2013). https://www.opennetworking.org/?lang=en. Accessed 28 July 2018
2. Medved, J., Varga, R., Tkacik, A., Gray, K.: Opendaylight: towards a model-driven SDN controller architecture. In: Proceeding of IEEE International Symposium on a World of Wireless, Mobile and Multimedia Networks 2014, pp. 1–6. IEEE (2014)
3. Specification, O.S.: Open networking foundation. Version ONF TS-015 **1**(3), 1–164 (2013)
4. Jammal, M., Singh, T., Shami, A., Asal, R., Li, Y.: Software defined networking: state of the art and research challenges. Comput. Netw. **72**, 74–98 (2014)
5. van der Pol, R.: D1.2 openflow (2011). https://kirk.rvdp.org/publications/RoN-2011-D1.2.pdf. Accessed 7 Aug 2018
6. Phemius, K., Bouet, M., Leguay, J.: Disco: distributed multi-domain SDN controllers. In: 2014 IEEE Network Operations and Management Symposium (NOMS), pp. 1–4. IEEE (2014)

7. Costanzo, S., Galluccio, L., Morabito, G., Palazzo, S.: Software defined wireless networks: Unbridling SDNs. In: 2012 European Workshop on Software Defined Networking, pp. 1–6. IEEE (2012)
8. Bernardos, C.J., De La Oliva, A., Serrano, P., Banchs, A., Contreras, L.M., Jin, H., Zúñiga, J.C.: An architecture for software defined wireless networking. IEEE Wirel. Commun. **21**(3), 52–61 (2014)
9. Sama, M.R., Contreras, L.M., Kaippallimalil, J., Akiyoshi, I., Qian, H., Ni, H.: Software-defined control of the virtualized mobile packet core. IEEE Commun. Mag. **53**(2), 107–115 (2015)
10. Valtulina, L., Karimzadeh, M., Karagiannis, G., Heijenk, G., Pras, A.: Performance evaluation of a SDN/OpenFlow-based distributed mobility management (DMM) approach in virtualized LTE systems. In: 2014 IEEE Globecom Workshops (GC Wkshps), pp. 18–23. IEEE (2014)
11. Wang, Y., Bi, J.: A solution for IP mobility support in software defined networks. In: 2014 23rd International Conference on Computer Communication and Networks (ICCCN), pp. 1–8. IEEE (2014)
12. Wang, Y., Bi, J., Zhang, K.: Design and implementation of a software-defined mobility architecture for IP networks. Mob. Netw. Appl. **20**(1), 40–52 (2015)
13. Jagadeesan, N.A., Krishnamachari, B.: Software-defined networking paradigms in wireless networks: a survey. ACM Comput. Surv. (CSUR) **47**(2), 1–11 (2014)
14. Yap, K.K., et al.: Openroads: empowering research in mobile networks. ACM SIGCOMM Comput. Commun. Rev. **40**(1), 125–126 (2010)
15. Fontes, R.R., Afzal, S., Brito, S.H., Santos, M.A., Rothenberg, C.E.: Mininet-wifi: emulating software-defined wireless networks. In: 2015 11th International Conference on Network and Service Management (CNSM), pp. 384–389. IEEE (2015)
16. Bettstetter, C., Resta, G., Santi, P.: The node distribution of the random waypoint mobility model for wireless ad hoc networks. IEEE Trans. Mob. Comput. **2**(3), 257–269 (2003)
17. Component-based software defined networking framework. https://osrg.github.io/ryu/. Accessed 25 Oct 2019
18. Henderson, T.R., Lacage, M., Riley, G.F., Dowell, C., Kopena, J.: Network simulations with the ns-3 simulator. SIGCOMM Demonstr. **14**(14), 527 (2008)
19. Wang, S.Y., Chou, C.L., Yang, C.M.: Estinet openflow network simulator and emulator. IEEE Commun. Mag. **51**(9), 110–117 (2013)
20. Chan, M.C., Chen, C., Huang, J.X., Kuo, T., Yen, L.H., Tseng, C.C.: Opennet: a simulator for software-defined wireless local area network. In: 2014 IEEE Wireless Communications and Networking Conference (WCNC), pp. 3332–3336. IEEE (2014)
21. Wireshark-go deep. https://www.wireshark.org/. Accessed 12 Dec 2019

An SDN Based Distributed IoT Network with NFV Implementation for Smart Cities

Bivash Kanti Mukherjee[1(✉)], Sadiqul Islam Pappu[2], Md. Jahidul Islam[1], and Uzzal Kumar Acharjee[1]

[1] Jagannath University, Dhaka, Bangladesh
mshunnohridoy@gmail.com, jahidul.jnucse@gmail.com, uzzal@cse.jnu.ac.bd
[2] Daffodil International University, Dhaka, Bangladesh
sadiqul15-9769@diu.edu.bd

Abstract. The Internet of Things (IoT) is an arrangement of connected numerous digital devices usually contained Unique Identifiers (UIDs) and have the capability to exchange data over a network without any human interaction. Another new paradigm Software-Defined Networking (SDN) comes in for the organization and control of the large amount of data produced by IoT devices. It separates the data plane from the control plane of network devices which enables easy configuration and management of those devices. Furthermore, Network Function Virtualization (NFV) is emerged to optimize and secure the SDN-IoT network. It enables network devices to be deployed as virtualized components via software. In this research, the authors have proposed an SDN based distributed IoT network with NFV implementation for smart cities. Where smart city is a residential area which utilizes Information and Communication Technology (ICT) as well as IoT network to develop the standard of living of its residents. The integration of NFV in the SDN-IoT network improves the network performance by increasing throughput, and time sequence while mitigating the round trip time as well. Moreover, the authors have used multiple distributed controllers and a clustering scheme to improve load balancing, scalability, availability, integrity, and security of the whole network.

Keywords: IoT · SDN · NFV · Smart City · OpenFlow · Controller · Cluster etc

1 Introduction

Nowadays, a rapid evolution of IoT is seen with plenty of physical objects connected to the Internet. IoT technology can connect each and everything throughout the world via the internet [1]. It can sense or monitor surroundings through sensor networks and can identify things by scanning an RFID tag [2]. Potential areas where IoT technology is utilized include home automation, industrial

T. Bhuiyan et al. (Eds.): ICONCS 2020, LNICST 325, pp. 539–552, 2020.
https://doi.org/10.1007/978-3-030-52856-0_43

automation, health care, smart grid, smart cities, etc. As the number of connected objects to the internet are rising day by day so the management and control of IoT becomes a very challenging task. Here, SDN comes in to give the flexibility and programmability of the IoT network instead of modifying the structure of existing implementations. Moreover, it can simplify network operations, reduce cost and accelerate service delivery by separating the control plane from the data plane of traditional network devices. In addition, NFV is introduced to develop the flexibility of network service provisioning and to diminish the time to market the latest services [3]. It also reduces Operating Expenses (OpEx) and Capital Expenses (CapEx) significantly.

A recent survey says that over 50% of the world's population now living in towns [2] that has a significant impact on city resources and infrastructure. For the proper utilization of city resources as well as to improve the quality of life for all inhabitants smart cities are now becoming IoT dependent. Because of the rising acceptance of IoT system, multiple challenges have arisen in terms of security, availability, and management. Common security mechanisms i.e. firewalling, intrusion detection system, etc. are no longer enough to secure the vast IoT network. Billions of devices are now connected to the IoT network and sharing sensitive data so they are becoming more vulnerable to security attacks. Moreover, any delay in response time through the communication will be resulting in a negative impact on the overall performance and accuracy of the network system, especially in cases of real-time transaction. To minimize the response time while improving the security system SDN is used in IoT applications. Recently, multiple controllers are used in SDN instead of using a centralized controller which helps to distribute traffic loads of IoT devices among the controllers. Resources will be available instantly when they are required by the user by means of SDN-IoT network. Furthermore, using an SDN controller a network can be configured in a dynamic way. One of the most common protocols used by SDN is OpenFlow [4]. In recent years, NFV is introduced as a promising technology that has the ability to virtualize the network functions replacing traditional network devices like switches, routers, firewalls, etc. with software running on commercial off-the-shelf servers [5]. So it enables service providers to implement network functions in virtual server rather than in conventional hardware. Therefore, it improves network scalability, load balancing, and power consumption as well.

In this research, the authors have proposed a distributed SDN-IoT network with NFV implementation for smart city usage. Besides, to develop cost-effective, scalable, reliable, and resilient smart cities the authors have implemented NFV in that SDN-IoT network. The authors have also introduced a clustering approach for the efficient management of large IoT network which will enable reliable communications while consuming less power. Besides, for the proper distribution of communication traffic at the same time improving security in SDN-IoT environment, the authors have proposed multi-functional distributed controllers in the network. Moreover, the implementation of NFV in SDN-IoT architecture increases the overall network efficiency which will give more flexibility to the network operators to control their networks dynamically.

The authors have organized the paper as follows: Authors discuss related works in Sect. 2. Section 3 introduces the proposed NFV implemented SDN-IoT Network architecture and also explains the working principle of it. After that, simulation results and findings are illustrated in Sect. 4. Section 5 includes the conclusion of the research with future research scopes.

2 Related Works

Several researches have carried out in this field. Some of them are listed below:

The research in [6] provides a detail view of different SDN-IoT frameworks and security solutions, current trends in research and therefore the futurist contributory factors. However, no new methodology had been proposed. Further, three architectures are proposed in [7] which are designed to work with all existing platforms like OpenFlow, OpenStack, and OpenDaylight. The authors focused on controller security throughout the research but couldn't give any solution for the challenging management task of vast IoT devices. A comprehensive survey presents in [1] showing the security mechanisms that SDN technology can serve for the IoT environment. The authors also proposed a role-based security controller architecture (called Rol-Sec) for the SDN-IoT environment. But they didn't simulate it in an SDN environment and also not provided any performance analysis of the proposed architecture. Another survey in [8], the authors introduced the software-defined NFV architecture as the state of the art of NFV and presented relationships between NFV and SDN. They also provided a historic view of the involvement from the middlebox to NFV. The authors discussed various challenges and problems of NFV but didn't provide any suitable solution in their research. The research in [9] focused on driving mobile network evolution towards cost-efficient IT-based solutions using standardized hardware and software-based ideas like SDN and NFV. The authors also highlighted some other limitations for integrating IT concepts in telecommunication networks. However, more granular and customizable network architecture is needed to deal with the challenge of network service automation through softwarization and cloudification.

Further, in the research [10,11], the authors introduced a highly secured SDN called Black SDN and designed an NFV integrated distributed IoT network with that SDN for more efficient network performance and security. Though the authors didn't provide any simulation data and also not clarified performance analysis information. Besides, in the research [12], the authors concentrated on investigating the security issues of SDN along with the limitations of the proposed solutions. Another group of researchers in [13] used an SDN gateway for monitoring the traffic originating from and directed to IoT based devices. But still, energy-efficient better routing mechanism is required for IoT nodes to minimize resource usage. Moreover, researchers in [14] analyzed the challenges associated with IoT technology and proposed a software model based on SDN that can prevent different attacks in the IoT environment. However, implementation of the proposed algorithm and the result analysis for different security attacks was not shown. Furthermore, in the research [15], authors presented a study that is focused on an efficient method to build a cluster network using SDN, network virtualization, and OpenFlow technologies. But the performance of the proposed clustered routing approach for SDN-IoT network is not measured.

Moreover, authors in the research [16] presented a framework to exploit security features of SDN/NFV and made efficient integration with existing IoT security methods. They also explored the opportunities that NFV and SDN jointly offer in coping with security threats against IoT services. An SDN/NFV packet/optical transport network named ADRENALINE testbed was proposed in [17] and the authors also figured out an edge/core cloud platform for end-to-end 5G and IoT services. Similarly, the authors in the research [18] focused on investigating the roles of SDN/NFV in deploying IoT services and proposed an SDN/NFV architecture for applying in IoT framework. Where the components of the proposed architecture are physically used and some of them are accessed from the local server instead of deploying them in the cloud. Furthermore, a new approach was presented in [19] for comprehensive monitoring of software-defined 5G mobile network by using IoT based framework which provides easier implementation of a monitoring system for mobile network operators. In another research [20], the authors discussed major security challenges in IoT networks and also presented two secured SDN-IoT integration technique termed as loosely and tightly coupled. The security framework of the proposed SDN integrated networks should be improved to develop more efficient IoT networks that can be applied in real industrial applications. A network slicing concept was presented in [21], which had a particular focus on its application to 5G systems. The authors also gave a short overview of the SDN architecture proposed by the Open Network Foundation (ONF) and additionally presented a scenario that couples SDN and NFV technologies to address network slices. However, any analysis of the security and privacy concerns that are risen from 5G slicing has not been seen. Besides, in the research [22], a comparison was conducted in between a proposed SDN/NFV network and a typical 4g network that was represented through mathematical illustration. However, no new theory has been given on how to reduce cost and save energy in the SDN/NFV based IoT networks.

Most of the research works focused on improving IoT security and controller security for the SDN-IoT network. Several researches are done on NFV implementation in SDN-IoT architecture to give more flexibility to network operators in controlling their network while reducing the capital and operational expenses as well. Different researchers proposed many SDN-IoT architecture with NFV implementation but very few of them are presented simulation works in this field. To solve various challenges in the IoT network many researchers are still trying to find optimal solutions for providing smart citizens with a network that will be more secure, handy and optimized.

3 Proposed SDN-IoT Network with NFV Implementation

The authors have designed an IoT network for smart city applications. To build a dynamic, programmatically efficient IoT network Software-defined Networking (SDN) technology is used in the network. Moreover, to simplify the architecture of physical networks and at the same time to improve the scalability and adaptability of the network, the authors have also implemented Network Functions Virtualization (NFV) method in these proposed network architecture.

The authors have divided the entire network scenario into four layers. They are-

- Infrastructure Layer
- Control and Virtualization Layer
- Application Layer
- NFV Management and Orchestration

3.1 Infrastructure Layer

The infrastructure layer is divided into two parts. One is the clustered IoT nodes and another is the data plane. Handling a large IoT network efficiently is a very challenging task without any properly organized structure. So the authors have

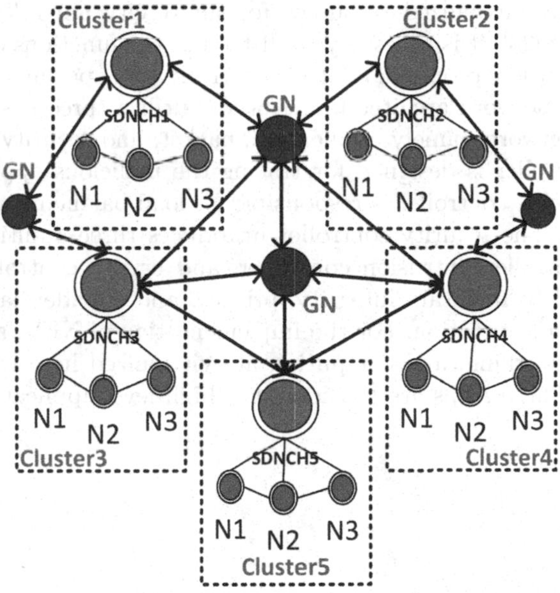

Fig. 1. IoT clustering

proposed a clustering method to organize the IoT nodes in an efficient way. A cluster consists of several IoT nodes (N1, N2, N3..., n). These IoT nodes have the sensing capability to collect data from their surroundings. Every cluster is managed by a Cluster Head (CH). Cluster heads are selected randomly by the respective cluster's IoT nodes based on the highest energy presented in the node. To develop this design authors tend to place an SDN controller within each cluster head (SDNCH) [15]. The main purpose of SDNCH is to control and monitor the cluster domains. Moreover, it secures all cluster domains from internal and external threats. Several nodes are selected as common nodes in between the clusters called Gateway Nodes (GNs). GNs are used to maintain communication between the cluster domains.

The graphical illustration of these clustering scheme is depicted in Fig. 1. Further, the data plane involves a group of basic network devices including router, switch, firewall, and cloud infrastructure. The data communication between the cluster heads and the control plane is maintained by some SDN-IoT gateways over the data plane. After a complete routing on the data plane, the traffic is passed to the control and virtualization layer through SDN OpenFlow routing protocol.

3.2 Control and Virtualization Layer

This layer consists of a group of multi-functional controllers and virtualized resources which is shown in Fig. 2. It provides the control of the forwarding data behavior and the virtualized resources for smart city apps. To eliminate the bottleneck issues [23], it is necessary to distribute the functions of the SDN controller. So, the authors proposed multiple controllers for specific roles to play [1,7] in the proposed network architecture. Authors utilize three basic types of controllers in the network namely application, packet, and security controller. The application controller is designed for tracing the malicious applications within the network. Packet controller is responsible for load balancing and packet security monitoring. The security controller introduces three additional controllers such as key controller, intrusion controller, and crypto controller. These controllers are used to maintain integrity, privacy, and confidentiality throughout the whole network operation. For the implementation of NFV, all the resources e.g. storage, networking, and computing are virtualized here which are known as NFV Apps. These Apps are considered as high-level applications.

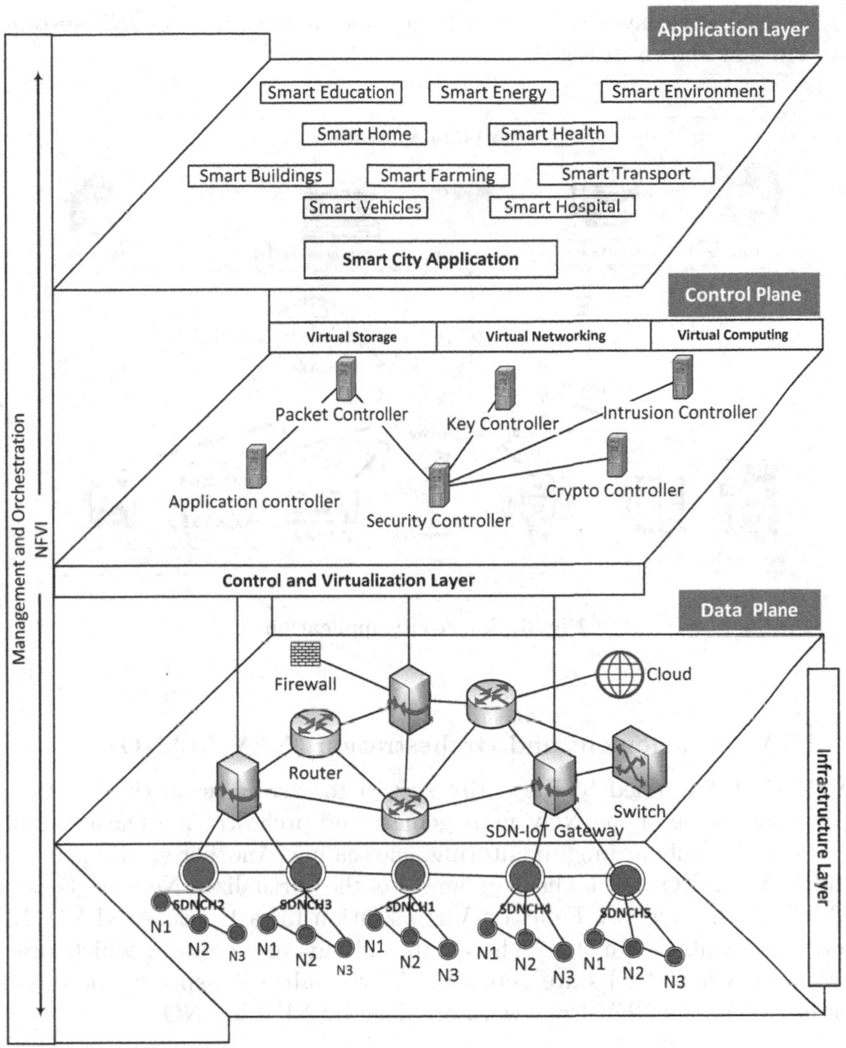

Fig. 2. Proposed network architecture

3.3 Application Layer

This is the upper layer of the network architecture where the application fields of the developed network are enlisted. The authors have proposed this network architecture, especially for smart city applications. This layer covers an array of smart city applications like smart home, smart vehicle, smart education, smart healthcare, smart transportation, etc. Moreover, it includes server and cloud infrastructures that share content and provide real-time services to the user. Data processing and providing services are also the most vital functions of this layer. Overall, this layer provides a large-scale management of IoT system for smart cities as shown in Fig. 3.

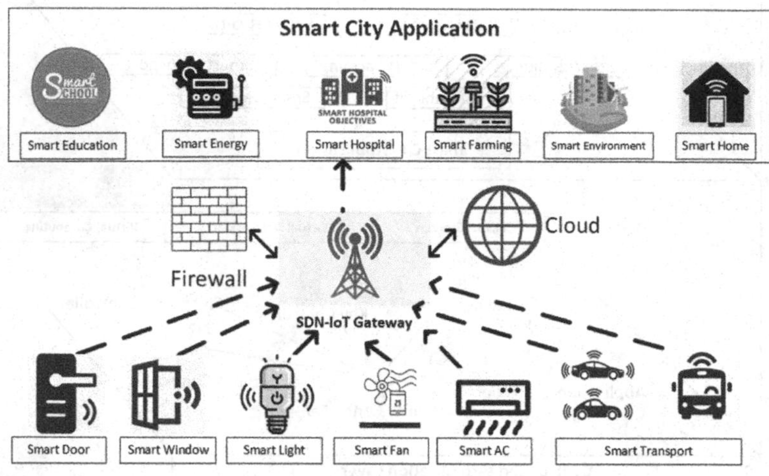

Fig. 3. Smart city application

3.4 NFV Management and Orchestration (NFV MANO)

NFV MANO is applied to the entire system to virtualize all the functions of the network. Some of the NFV management and orchestration features include network service onboarding, monitoring, and scaling. Another vital role is played by the NFV MANO that is the deployment of the Virtualized Network Functions (VNFs) over the Network Function Virtualization Infrastructure (NFVI). NFVI includes the combination of both hardware and software resources which form the environment where VNFs are deployed. All virtualization-specific management tasks needed in the NFV framework are done by NFV MANO.

4 Results and Discussions

The authors have built three network topology with 10, 20, and 50 IoT nodes. Entire simulation is done on Mininet-WiFi, a tool to emulate wireless OpenFlow scenarios allowing high-fidelity experiments that replicate real networking environments. Moreover, the authors have used the Wireshark packet analyzer for analyzing network packets and determining throughput, round trip time, and time sequence (tcptrace) of the three network topologies respectively. In this section, at first, the authors have compared their three network topologies with respect to three simulation parameters i.e throughput, round trip time, and time sequence (tcptrace). Then, the authors have compared their best efficient network topology with another two reference papers performance regarding the simulation parameters and present the analysis result.

4.1 Throughput for Different Number of Nodes

Figure 4 shows that the average throughput of 10, 20, and 50 nodes topology is approximately similar during 0–5 s. But after 6s the average throughput for 10 and 20 nodes topology drops while throughput for 50 nodes topology grows identically. As the cluster heads can utilize multiple gateways to pass the data traffic to the control plane, it significantly lessens the possibility of traffic congestion or bottlenecks in a single gateway even if the number of nodes increases. For this reason, 50 nodes topology comparatively gives better throughput delivery compared to others.

Further, the authors take the best performer in throughput comparison (50nodes) and compare it with an extended version of the Multinetwork Information Architecture (MINA) [24]. Figure 5 shows that the average throughput

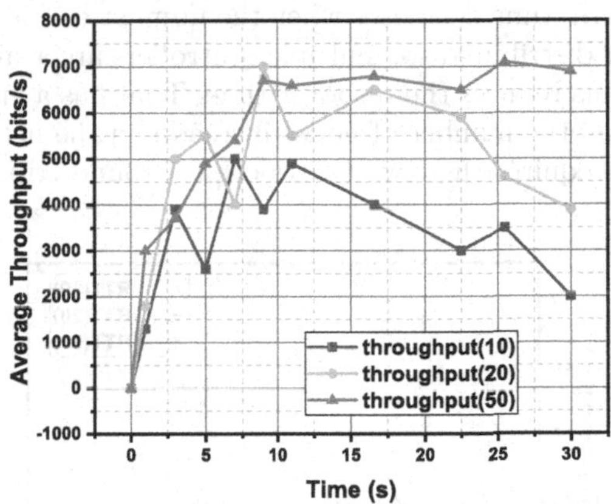

Fig. 4. Average throughput comparison (10, 20, 50 nodes)

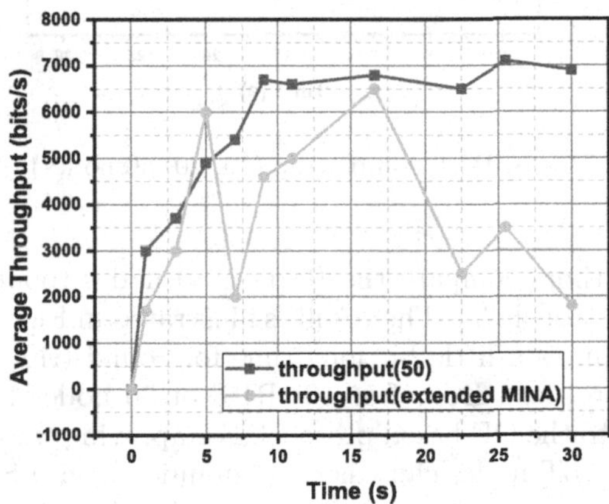

Fig. 5. Average throughput comparison (50 nodes vs extended MINA)

of both networks increases identically until they reach 6000bits/s but after 5s the throughput of extended MINA suddenly falls down meanwhile the throughput of 50 nodes topology progresses similarly. As the authors have used multiple controllers in the proposed network architecture for proper distribution of network traffic among respective controllers, it minimizes the delay time and improves network performance. Besides, the management and orchestration of network functions virtualization improves the load balancing of the network resulting in a greater throughput delivery.

4.2 Round Trip Time for Different Number of Nodes

Round-Trip Time (RTT) is the time that need for a signal to be sent plus the time it takes for an acknowledgment of that signal to be received. At first, the authors compare their three build topology with each other. From Fig. 6 it is shown that round trip time decreases when the number of nodes increases. Since the network is fully distributed so, multiple controllers are available for handling specific task and thus reduces the response time. That has a great impact on the round trip time even the number of nodes increases in the network. As a result, 50 nodes topology requires the lowest period for a round trip.

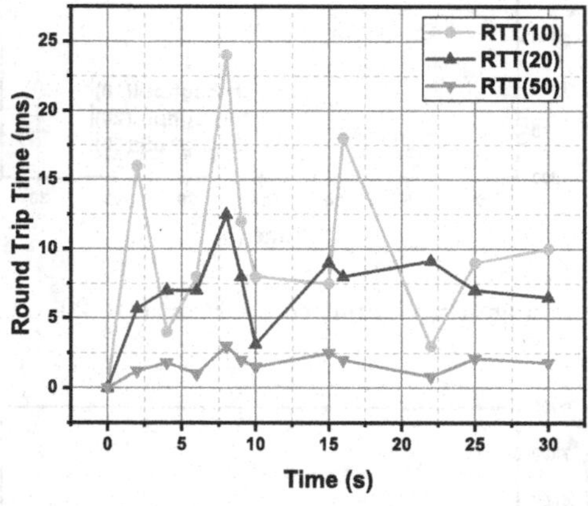

Fig. 6. RTT comparison (10, 20, 50 nodes)

Further, the authors compare the RTT of 50 nodes topology with another OpenFlow-based protocol [25]. The result is illustrated in Fig. 7. It shows that 50 nodes topology requires a little bit long time for round trip before 9s compare to the OF-based protocol. But after 10s RTT of 50 nodes topology decreases smoothly compare to the OF-based protocol. For applying the clustering method in the network, the IoT nodes can easily communicate with SDN-IoT gateways via multiple cluster heads preventing network congestion. As a result, it reduces the network latency and improves the round trip time as well.

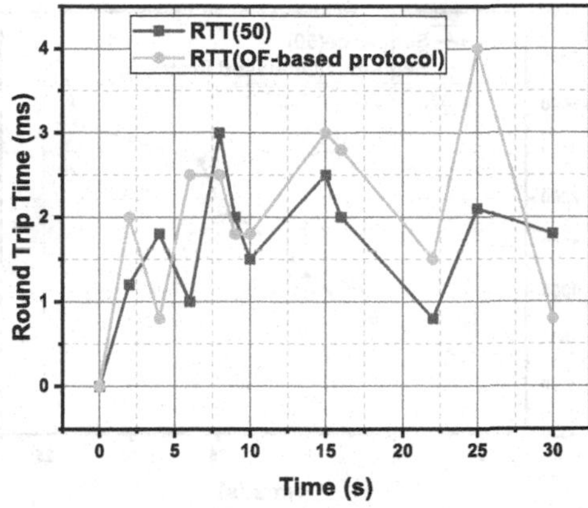

Fig. 7. RTT comparison (50 nodes vs OF-based protocol)

4.3 Time Sequence (tcptrace) for Different Number of Nodes

Time Sequence (tcptrace) illustrates the TCP metrics including forwarded segments and acknowledgments. Figure 8 indicating that sequence number increases with time if the number of nodes increases. For this reason, the increment of sequence number for 50 nodes topology is greater than 10 and 20 nodes topology. As we know that time sequence indicates the TCP flows so this tcptrace comparison symbolizes the progress of TCP flows in the particular network. Moreover, this comparison is performed to show how the TCP flow behaves for a varying number of nodes.

Further, the authors have compared the time sequence of 50 nodes topology with the OpenFlow-based protocol once again. The result is depicted in Fig. 9. From Fig. 9, it is easily noticeable that 50 nodes topology gives a smoother time

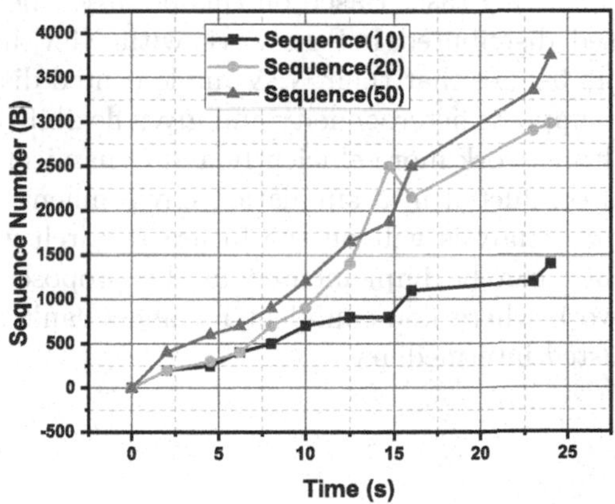

Fig. 8. Time sequence comparison (10, 20, 50 nodes)

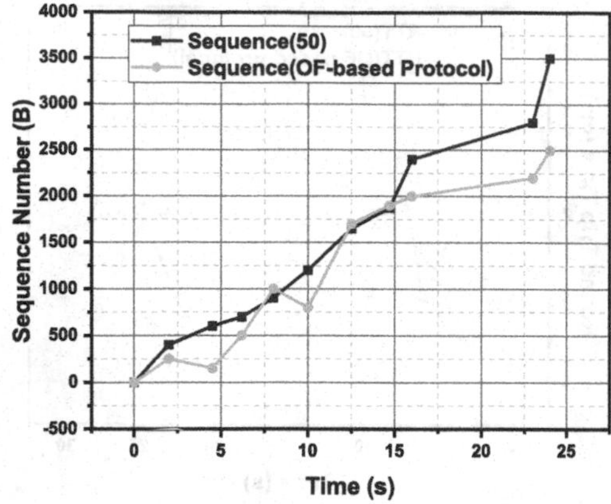

Fig. 9. Time sequence comparison (50 nodes vs OF-based protocol)

sequence increment compared to the OF-based protocol. In the proposed network multipurpose distributed controllers are used to accept and transfer data packets via multiple gateways that diminish the possibility of single-point failure in the network resulting in a higher data transmission rate. That's why the TCP flow of the 50 nodes topology comparatively higher and smoother than the conventional OF-based protocol.

5 Conclusion

The implementation of NFV is essential for the balance and orchestration of virtual resources in SDN-IoT environment. Despite the immense speed at which NFV is being accepted by both academia and industry, it is still in the early stage. Besides, the optimization of algorithms for real streaming in SDN/NFV architecture is a challenging task. Based on this premise, the authors have proposed an SDN based distributed IoT network with NFV implementation for smart cities. Authors believe that their NFV implemented distributed SDN-IoT network inherently supports heterogeneity and gives flexibility to smart citizens to manage IoT multi-network more efficiently and dynamically.

This research is conducted in a simulation environment. Practical application and performance analysis will be the future research work. Additionally, blockchain technology can be implemented in the proposed network to have a peer-to-peer network where non-confident members can't interact with each other without a trusted intermediary.

References

1. Kalkan, K., Zeadally, S.: Securing internet of things with software defined networking. IEEE Commun. Mag. **56**(9), 186–192 (2017)
2. Chakrabarty, S., Engels, D.W.: A secure IoT architecture for smart cities. In: 2016 13th IEEE Annual Consumer Communications & Networking Conference (CCNC), pp. 812–813. IEEE (2016)
3. Han, B., Gopalakrishnan, V., Ji, L., Lee, S.: Network function virtualization: challenges and opportunities for innovations. IEEE Commun. Mag. **53**(2), 90–97 (2015)
4. McKeown, N., et al.: Openflow: enabling innovation in campus networks. ACM SIGCOMM Comput. Commun. Rev. **38**(2), 69–74 (2008)
5. Rahman, A., Islam, M.J., Sunny, F.A., Nasir, M.K.: Distblocksdn: a distributed secure blockchain based SDN-IoT architecture with NFV implementation for smart cities. Technology (ICIET) **23**, 24 (2019)
6. Tayyaba, S.K., Shah, M.A., Khan, O.A., Ahmed, A.W.: Software defined network (SDN) based internet of things (IoT): a road ahead. In: Proceedings of the International Conference on Future Networks and Distributed Systems, p. 15. ACM (2017)
7. Chourishi, D., Miri, A., Milić, M., Ismaeel, S.: Role-based multiple controllers for load balancing and security in SDN. In: 2015 IEEE Canada International Humanitarian Technology Conference (IHTC 2015), pp. 1–4. IEEE (2015)
8. Li, Y., Chen, M.: Software-defined network function virtualization: a survey. IEEE Access **3**, 2542–2553 (2015)
9. Hoffmann, M., et al.: SDN and NFV as enabler for the distributed network cloud. Mob. Netw. Appl. **23**(3), 521–528 (2018)
10. Islam, M.J., Mahin, M., Roy, S., Debnath, B.C., Khatun, A.: Distblacknet: a distributed secure black SDN-IoT architecture with NFV implementation for smart cities. In: 2019 International Conference on Electrical, Computer and Communication Engineering (ECCE), pp. 1–6. IEEE (2019)
11. Chakrabarty, S., Engels, D.W., Thathapudi, S.: Black SDN for the internet of things. In: 2015 IEEE 12th International Conference on Mobile Ad Hoc and Sensor Systems, pp. 190–198. IEEE (2015)
12. Feghali, A., Kilany, R., Chamoun, M.: SDN security problems and solutions analysis. In: 2015 International Conference on Protocol Engineering (ICPE) and International Conference on New Technologies of Distributed Systems (NTDS), pp. 1–5. IEEE (2015)
13. Bull, P., Austin, R., Popov, E., Sharma, M., Watson, R.: Flow based security for IoT devices using an SDN gateway. In: 2016 IEEE 4th International Conference on Future Internet of Things and Cloud (FiCloud), pp. 157–163. IEEE (2016)
14. Al Shuhaimi, F., Jose, M., Singh, A.V.: Software defined network as solution to overcome security challenges in IoT. In: 2016 5th International Conference on Reliability, Infocom Technologies and Optimization (Trends and Future Directions) (ICRITO), pp. 491–496. IEEE (2016)
15. Gonzalez, C., Charfadine, S.M., Flauzac, O., Nolot, F.: SDN-based security framework for the IoT in distributed grid. In: 2016 International Multidisciplinary Conference on Computer and Energy Science (SpliTech), pp. 1–5. IEEE (2016)
16. Farris, I., et al.: Towards provisioning of SDN/NFV-based security enablers for integrated protection of IoT systems. In: 2017 IEEE Conference on Standards for Communications and Networking (CSCN), pp. 169–174. IEEE (2017)

17. Muoz, R., et al.: The adrenaline testbed: an SDN/NFV packet/optical transport network and edge/core cloud platform for end-to-end 5G and IoT services. In: 2017 European Conference on Networks and Communications (EuCNC), pp. 1–5. IEEE (2017)
18. Sinh, D., Le, L.V., Lin, B.S.P., Tung, L.P.: SDN/NFV–a new approach of deploying network infrastructure for IoT. In: 2018 27th Wireless and Optical Communication Conference (WOCC), pp. 1–5. IEEE (2018)
19. Maksymyuk, T., Dumych, S., Brych, M., Satria, D., Jo, M.: An IoT based monitoring framework for software defined 5G mobile networks. In: Proceedings of the 11th International Conference on Ubiquitous Information Management and Communication, p. 105. ACM (2017)
20. Krishnan, P., Najeem, J.S., Achuthan, K.: SDN framework for securing IoT networks. In: Kumar, N., Thakre, A. (eds.) UBICNET 2017. LNICST, vol. 218, pp. 116–129. Springer, Cham (2018). https://doi.org/10.1007/978-3-319-73423-1_11
21. Ordonez-Lucena, J., Ameigeiras, P., Lopez, D., Ramos-Munoz, J.J., Lorca, J., Folgueira, J.: Network slicing for 5G with SDN/NFV: concepts, architectures, and challenges. IEEE Commun. Mag. **55**(5), 80–87 (2017)
22. Almustafa, K., Alenezi, M.: Cost analysis of SDN/NFV architecture over 4G infrastructure. Procedia Comput. Sci. **113**, 130–137 (2017)
23. Ojo, M., Adami, D., Giordano, S.: A SDN-IOT architecture with NFV implementation. In: 2016 IEEE Globecom Workshops (GC Wkshps), pp. 1–6. IEEE (2016)
24. Qin, Z., Denker, G., Giannelli, C., Bellavista, P., Venkatasubramanian, N.: A software defined networking architecture for the internet-of-things. In: 2014 IEEE Network Operations and Management Symposium (NOMS), pp. 1–9. IEEE (2014)
25. Wang, Y., Bi, J.: A solution for IP mobility support in software defined networks. In: 2014 23rd International Conference on Computer Communication and Networks (ICCCN), pp. 1–8. IEEE (2014)

On the Energy Efficiency and Performance of Delay-Tolerant Routing Protocols

Md. Khalid Mahbub Khan[1], Sujan Chandra Roy[2], Muhammad Sajjadur Rahim[2(✉)], and Abu Zafor Md. Touhidul Islam[1]

[1] Department of Electrical and Electronic Engineering, University of Rajshahi, Rajshahi 6205, Bangladesh
khalidmahbub.khan@yahoo.com, touhid.eee@ru.ac.bd

[2] Department of Information and Communication Engineering, University of Rajshahi, Rajshahi 6205, Bangladesh
sujan.007.ice@gmail.com, sajid_ice@ru.ac.bd

Abstract. Delay-Tolerant Network (DTN) is a resource-bound networking system which consists of many intermittently connected, movable devices known as nodes. Energy can be considered as an important resource for DTN scenarios since these nodes have limited energy. In order to perfect network enforcement, it is necessary to exploit the energy of the nodes efficiently. In DTN, most of the node energy is consumed because of mobility, scanning neighbors to deliver message and message transmission. Node energy has a significant role for successful transmission of messages. Higher energy of a node means that it has a high possibility to route its message with success across the network. So, for effective message routing it is mandatory to select an energy efficient routing mechanism in DTN environment. This point makes us interested to study the consumption of node energy in DTN scenarios. Within this research, the study of energy issue is focused for DTN routing approaches: Epidemic, Resource Allocation Protocol for Intentional DTN (RAPID), MaxProp, Probabilistic Routing Protocol using History of Encounters and Transitivity (PRoPHET), Spray and Wait, and Spray and Focus with their comparative performance analysis on behalf of four performance criteria: average remaining energy of node, delivery ratio, average latency, and transmission cost. Simulations are performed in Opportunistic Network Environment (ONE) simulator by varying node density while keeping message Time-To-Live (TTL) fixed and further, message TTL is changed while node density is kept fixed. We have found that Spray and Wait is the most energy efficient DTN routing scheme, whereas Spray and Focus yields the best performance in terms of delivery ratio, average latency and transmission cost.

Keywords: Delay-Tolerant Network · Routing protocol · Energy efficiency · Performance evaluation · Opportunistic Network Environment (ONE) simulator

1 Introduction

Due to the expeditious adaptation of small, lighter, energy constrained and portable devices in modern communication field, the networking scenario has been changed,

T. Bhuiyan et al. (Eds.): ICONCS 2020, LNICST 325, pp. 553–565, 2020.
https://doi.org/10.1007/978-3-030-52856-0_44

and often suffers from lack of fixed infrastructure support. Because people of a particular region build a network, they demand faster data communication to share their data among themselves. They also desire connectivity while they are moving from one region to another. So, such network has an unstable network topology and routing paths are repeatedly detached. Existing TCP/IP routing technique cannot perform data communication efficiently since source to destination connectivity is the major requirement in this case. To overcome such situation, Delay-Tolerant Network (DTN) employs sporadic node connectedness. It has a wide implementation in wireless sensor networks (WSNs), vehicular networks, airborne networks, underwater networks, etc. DTN architecture utilizes "Store-Carry-and-Forward" approach to route data. In this strategy, a message carrying node forwards the message to the encountered node if the connectedness between them is available. Message would be stored for a momentary time if there is no connectivity, and that message is not disregarded by the source [1–4].

There are many routing techniques that have been recommended to handle recurrent disconnectedness, larger delays, unpredictable node mobility, and finite resources of DTN architectures. These protocols are generally categorized into two major groups: one is replication based where multiple replicas of a message are forwarded through the entire network and they can create many redundant message replicas. So, a high probability of flooding is assumed. That is why, these routing strategies are also admitted as "Flooding" based techniques. Another group of routing techniques consider network's historical knowledge to forward restricted copies of message towards elected nodes which adopt collected network's knowledge effectively. All forwarding techniques of DTN were developed to improve successful data forwarding in the network [5, 6].

However, nodes in DTN environment are battery driven. They are generally powered by lithium-ion batteries. They have a limited lifetime because their batteries stock restricted amount of energy. Moreover, nodes use Bluetooth, Wi-Fi, and such wireless technology in order to get connected. In this case, the quantity of energy that is spent for sending, receiving and storing message can be regarded as a crucial factor for the network. So, optimization of energy is essential for forwarding data in opportunistic environment. Furthermore, nodes also consume their energy to scan their nearest nodes to send their message. As energy is considered a key network resource, it should be utilized effectively and less consumed for better performance as well as longevity of the network [7, 8]. So, routing techniques should be designed in such a manner so that nodes consume less energy while they are working in the network. Thus, energy efficient routing protocol is required in DTN to forward data effectively [9].

In most cases, it is seen that the investigations [2, 3, 6, 10] related to DTN routing protocols going on evaluating the performance of existing routing techniques focused on various aspects such as delivery ratio, average latency, transmission cost, count of hop, etc. Usually, a DTN scheme should pursue to attain higher probability of delivery, minimum latency, hop count and cost of transmission for a successful packet delivery. But to fulfill all these requirements is very difficult in reality, regarding the system is constrained on behalf of energy consumption. In addition, in many studies authors compare the performance of their forwarding algorithm to the existing others to demonstrate the effectiveness of their proposed approach without considering the network's energy issue [4, 5]. However, in [11] the authors have simulated the performance of a group of

DTN routing protocols for an environmental data gathering application considering the issue of energy consumption of mobile nodes with a view to find out the most-suited routing strategy for their application scenario. Within this research, we represent a performance evaluation of several DTN routing techniques as well as considering energy aspects of the network. The performance investigation of this research work extensively reflects how remaining energy of the selected forwarding techniques influences their performance after simulating them using Opportunistic Network Environment (ONE) simulator. The arrangement of remaining paper is: a brief overview of the investigated DTN routing approaches is given in Sect. 2. Later, Sect. 3 explains about the necessary simulation environment. A relative discussion of the simulation outcomes along with two comparison tables are provided in Sect. 4 and finally, Sect. 5 gives the conclusions as well as some future planning about this research.

2 Investigated DTN Routing Protocols

This section includes a brief explanation with basic routing mechanism of several DTN routing strategies: Epidemic, RAPID, MaxProp, PRoPHET, Spray and Wait (SNW), and Spray and Focus (SNF). These are considered in this research to analyze their performance.

Epidemic routing approach is the primitive routing approach among the other DTN routing techniques. In this case, message replication is the main concern. Here, source node frequently replicates its message and transmits the message duplicate for recently encountered nodes that do not receive any copy of message. Hence, message is spreading through the entire network to confirm that destination would be able to receive it. This strategy assures the successful conveyance of message without concerning message's transmission delay, buffer size, network congestion, etc. So, this unconsciousness about network resource makes it a poor choice for data forwarding in DTN environment. Because of uncontrolled replication of messages, congestion and flooding can arise into the network [6, 10].

Resource Allocation Protocol for Intentional DTN (RAPID) technique focuses on resource allocation problem during data transmission in DTN environment. In this forwarding technique, DTN architecture is considered as utility-driven scheme and it attempts to optimize a particular forwarding parameter like average latency, missed time period, or maximum latency. Here, a utility function is maintained and it refers to a utility value U_i for each data packet based on the routing parameter. U_i represents the predicted contribution of packet i toward the considered forwarding parameter. The packets which locally outcome in highest increase within the utility, RAPID copies those earlier. Whether the network resources (e.g., bandwidth) admit, this routing strategy aims to make copy of all the packets [12].

MaxProp routing strategy introduces schedule-based forwarding mechanism. This strategy specifies and prioritizes schedule for forwarding data packets. An ordered list of packets that are gathered in transmitting end depending on a cost authorized toward every target. This cost reflects the calculation of delivery ratio. This routing technique fixes a maximum priority for data packets depending on minimum hop counts as well as avoiding the multiple receptions of same packet [13].

Probabilistic Routing Protocol using History of Encounters and Transitivity (PRoPHET) routing technique makes appropriate usage of network resource. In this routing mechanism, a set of probabilities is preserved for ensuring satisfied message transfer in the direction of recognized targets. This protocol adopts likelihood of the node's actual-world encounter for message routing instead of blind copying. After the encounter, message would be forwarded to the target from source node according to the higher probability of delivery to destination. The node that has higher delivery probability would be able to receive the message [10].

Spray and Wait (SNW) restricts the amount of message copy along with keeping the resource usage minimum. In this strategy, only L copies of message are propagated through the entire network. Here, L means maximum allowable number of the message replicas. This value is preferred depending on node quantity and expected average time [10]. There are two stages that form this protocol [14]:

Stage 1: Within this stage source node routes L copies of its message intended to the first L number nodes that are encountered with source. These nodes are identified as L distinct relays. This is recognized as "Spray".
Stage 2: Whether the target is not achieved in previous "Spray" stage, each of the L nodes that accepted a message replica has to wait until their confrontation with the target node so that they can forward their message directly toward the target. For this reason, this stage is known as "Wait".

Spray and Focus (SNF) exploits an improved single-copy strategy. Here, after receiving only single replica of message by a relay, this single message version would be retransmitted rather than direct transmission. This routing approach is quite similar to Spray and Wait approach in "Spray" stage. The major difference between two are involved in the second stage. In Spray and Focus, instead of waiting to encounter with target by each relay node they simply forward their message copy toward a more relevant relay in accordance with a precisely formed utility-driven model, and whenever any relay along with a single transmission token remains for a particular message, it switches into "Focus" stage. Thus, in "Focus" stage a distinct relay node can get a message copy unlike the target nodes get it via the direct forwarding that are performed in "Wait" stage of Spray and Wait [15].

3 Simulation Settings

In this research, Opportunistic Network Environment (ONE) simulator [16] is adopted to simulate experimented routing protocols in an energy module. This simulator is basically Java based where source codes are written in Java programming language and the script of simulation is written in plain text. Necessary parameters for the simulation and routing strategies are given in Table 1 and Table 2, respectively.

Table 1. General parameters of simulation.

Parameter	Value
Simulation duration	6 h
Node density	25, 30, 35, 40, 45, 50
Interface type	Bluetooth
Transmission rate	250 kbps
Transmission range	100 m
Routing protocols	Epidemic, RAPID, MaxProp, PRoPHET, Spray and Wait, Spray and Focus
Buffer capacity (MB)	4
Message generation rate (per minute)	1
Message TTL (in minutes)	120, 150, 180, 210, 240, 270
Message size (KB)	400
Mobility model	Shortest path map-based movement
Simulation area size	4500 m × 4000 m

Table 2. Parameters for routing protocols.

Routing algorithm	Parameter	Value
Epidemic	N/A	N/A
RAPID	Utility algorithm	Average delay
MaxProp	N/A	N/A
PRoPHET	Seconds in time unit	30
Spray and Wait	No. of copies (L)	8
Spray and Focus	No. of copies (L)	8

Table 3 represents some parameters those are related to node's energy setting. "Capacity of Battery" is the energy which is given to each node before starting simulation. "Scan Energy" determines the amount of energy that is spent for every scanning in order to discover a device. "Transmit Energy" means the energy consumption per second during transmitting. "Receive Energy" is the amount of energy that is spent during receiving. "Interval of Energy Recharge" specifies the interval time during which node can recharge their power. In order to evaluate the energy efficiency of the DTN routing protocols, we have set the value of "Interval of Energy Recharge" to 28,000 s (about 7.77 h) which is approximately 1.77 h more than the simulation duration. This ensures that the battery-driven mobile nodes are charged only once at the start of the simulation, and these nodes will not be recharged during the simulation time.

Table 3. Parameters related to energy of node.

Parameter	Settings
Capacity of battery	4800 J
Scan energy	0.92 mW/s
Transmit energy	0.08 mW/s
Receive energy	0.08 mW/s
Interval of energy recharge	28,000 s

4 Analysis of Simulation Results

After finishing simulation successfully of the inquired DTN routing protocols in ONE simulator, we find the simulation results oriented report on behalf of four performance indicating metrics: Average Remaining Energy, Delivery Ratio, Average Latency, and Transmission Cost. This section provides a brief review about those metrics as well as a comparative analysis of the simulation outcomes.

4.1 Average Remaining Energy

This performance criterion can be defined as average of the node energy that is remaining after simulation is finished. It is expected for a node to be higher in value so that the node is alive for an extended time. When a node's energy level turns to zero, it is known as dead node. Figure 1 and Fig. 2 are illustrating node's average remaining energy with the increasing of both node density and message TTL. If node density is increased, the amount of scanning and transmitting activities of nodes is also increased. As a result, more power is consumed so as the remaining energy would decrease. It would also decrease if TTL is rising since message would be alive for more time. So, more message delivery would take place in the network and expenditure of node's energy will increase. From Fig. 1, it is clear that Spray and Wait protocol attains the highest value of remaining energy among the others and almost keeping constant value with the rise of node density by exploiting limited number of message replication in forwarding mechanism. So, in this case it is energy efficient than other routing techniques. Here, limited energy will spend for limited copy of message conveyance. In Fig. 2, Spray and Wait as well as RAPID shows the highest energy remaining in the node with the increasing TTL. In RAPID it seems that after making the copy of earlier message within the utility, they will be active for more time with increasing their TTL value which prevents further message replication and expenditure of node's energy will be reduced. So, both Spray and Wait and RAPID are energy efficient in this case. However, MaxProp routing approach exhibits the lower energy efficiency in both cases since the amount and the lifetime of message grow into the schedule that is determined by it for message forwarding, while Spray and Focus, PRoPHET and Epidemic show inferior performance than Spray and Wait.

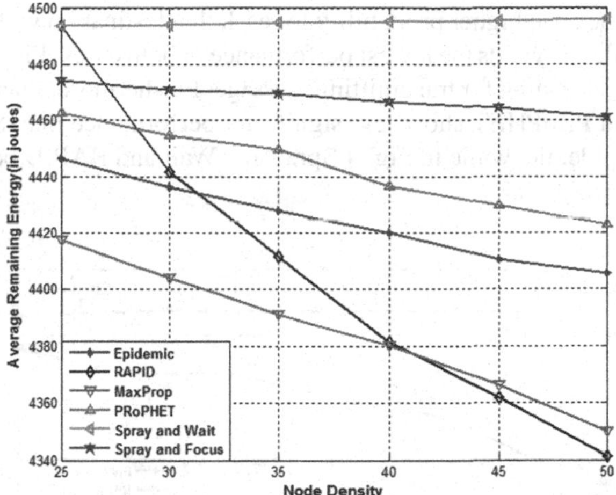

Fig. 1. Average remaining energy with varying number of nodes.

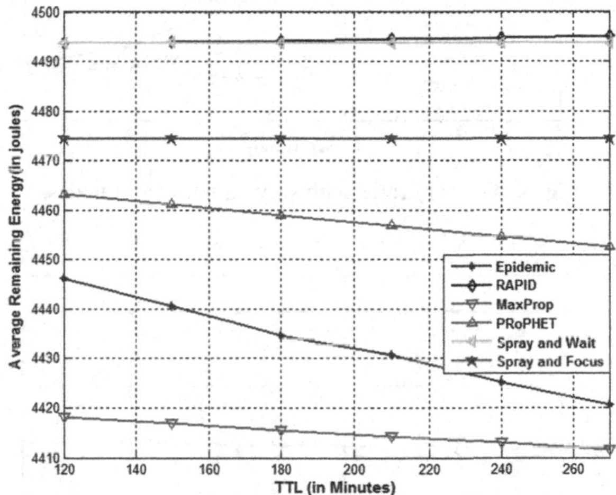

Fig. 2. Average remaining energy with the variation of TTL.

4.2 Delivery Ratio

This metric can be specified as the ratio of message amount that completely reached toward destination to the amount of message produced by originating node. This ratio is desired to be high and influenced by energy of nodes as dead nodes will no longer contribute to message delivery. Figure 3 and Fig. 4 demonstrate that how variation of node density and TTL affect delivery ratio, respectively. From both figures, it can be decided that Spray and Focus shows the superior performance than other protocols on behalf of delivery ratio. This technique involves improved single-copy forwarding strategy to take routing decision which limits the failure rate to reach destination of messages and increases the success rate. Moreover, within this approach, messages with larger validity time have higher probability to reach the destination within that time. On the contrary, Epidemic yields the lowest performance in both cases (Fig. 3 and Fig. 4) due to its uncontrolled flooding for transmitting message. Furthermore, MaxProp, Spray and Wait, RAPID and PRoPHET show less significant performance than Spray and Focus and more than Epidemic, while in Fig. 4 Spray and Wait and RAPID both display quite same performance.

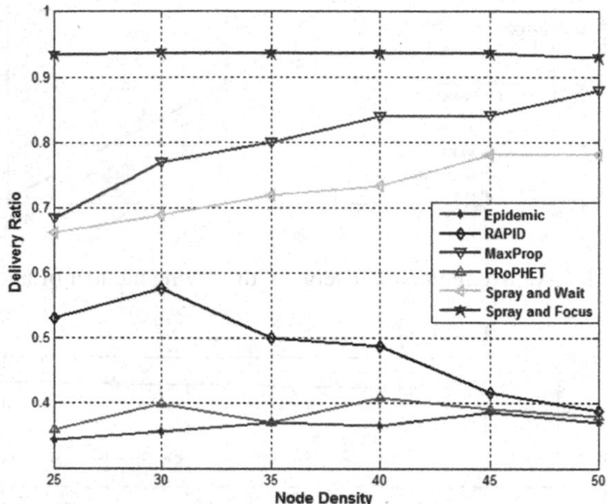

Fig. 3. Delivery ratio with varying number of nodes.

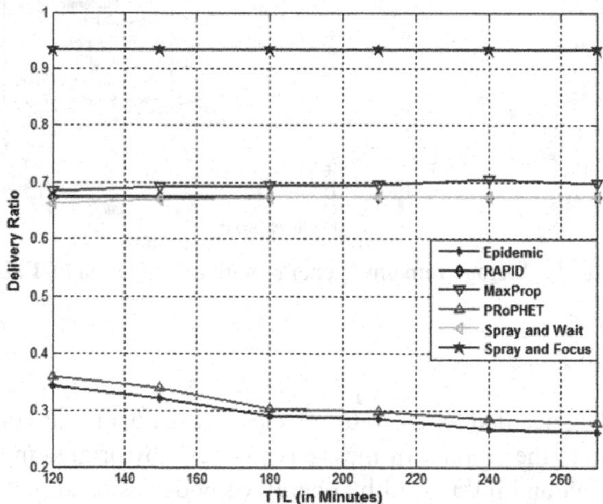

Fig. 4. Delivery ratio with the variation of TTL.

4.3 Average Latency

This parameter can be illustrated as the average delay time that is needed between the generation of a message by its producer node and absolute reception by its destination node. For efficient networking environment this parameter is supposed to be small in value. Figure 5 represents average latency with respect to node density where Spray and Focus exhibits the lowest latency compared to others. Messages would be reached successfully with minimum delay because a single copy of message transmitted again by relay node in the "Focus" stage of this technique. So, destination will be able to receive it more early than other routing strategies. On the other hand, although the line indicating RAPID in Fig. 5 begins with highest latency but after increasing node density (above 30 nodes) the RAPID's value of latency is decreasing and PRoPHET's line initiates bellow RAPID but rises above the other with the increasing of node density. Furthermore, Fig. 6 represents that Spray and Focus displays the lowest latency for expanding TTL while MaxProp provides the poorest performance for average latency in this case. PRoPHET, Epidemic, RAPID, and Spray and Wait provide transitional performance between Spray and Focus and Epidemic. So, according to Fig. 5 and Fig. 6, Spray and Focus has the best performance for average latency.

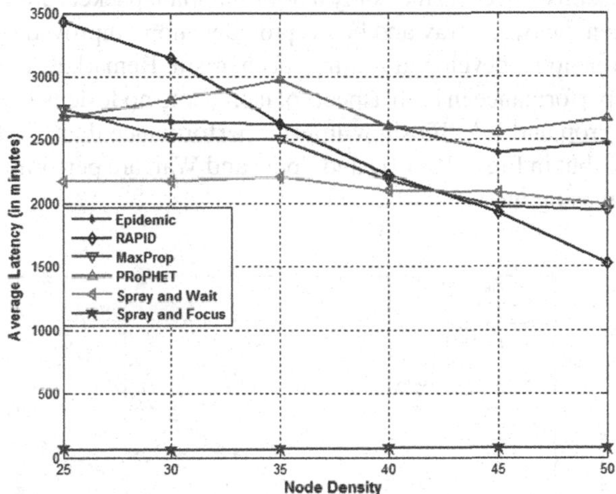

Fig. 5. Average latency with varying number of nodes.

4.4 Transmission Cost

It is the measure which represents the total amount of unnecessary packets that are relayed to convey a single packet. This metric computes the efficiency of transmission and its value is wanted to be small for effective networking operation. It is realized from both Fig. 7 and Fig. 8 that Epidemic has more transmission cost than other routing approaches to deliver a single packet as it replicates many unnecessary packets with both increasing of node density and TTL. So, it shows the worst performance among the

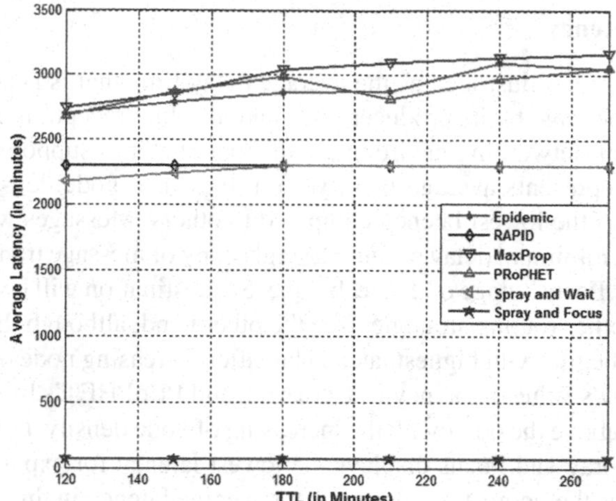

Fig. 6. Average latency with the variation of TTL.

other forwarding techniques. On the contrary, both Spray and Focus and Spray and Wait represent less transmission cost since only a few redundant packets are generated in both cases. But between the two, Spray and Focus provides more improved performance than Spray and Wait due to its developed routing mechanism. Remarkably, Spray and Focus exhibits the best performance in both aspects of increasing node density and TTL. Again, PRoPHET, MaxProp and RAPID show inferior performance than the best performing protocol in Fig. 7, but in Fig. 8 RAPID and Spray and Wait are performing in the similar fashion with increasing message TTL.

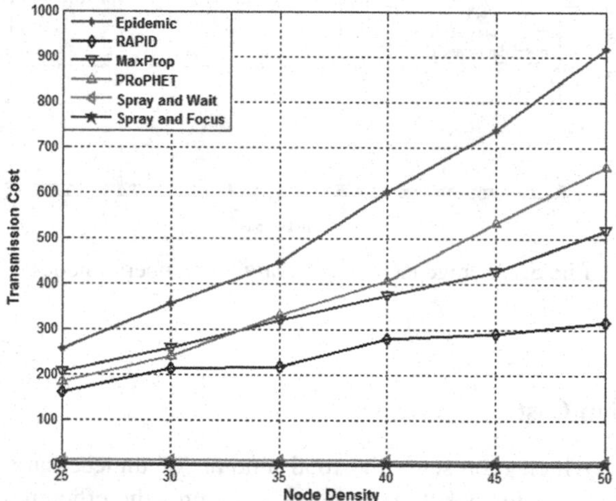

Fig. 7. Transmission cost with varying number of nodes.

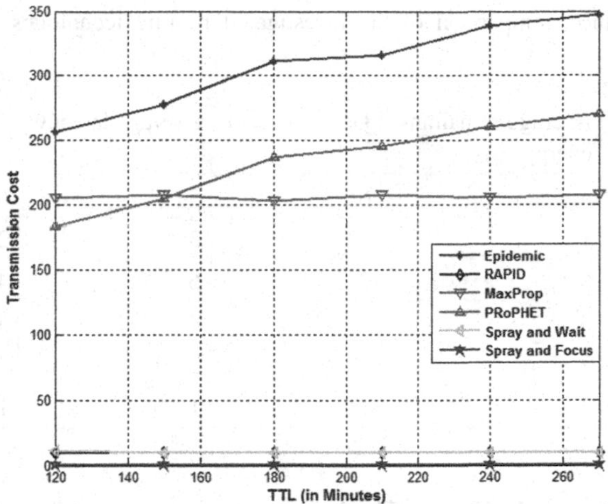

Fig. 8. Transmission cost with the variation of TTL.

4.5 Summary

In order to summarize the obtained simulation results, we provide the following comparison tables, where better performances are indicated by lower integer numbers and worse performances are marked by higher integer numbers (Tables 4 and 5).

Table 4. Performance comparison of the investigated DTN routing techniques (with variation of node density).

Routing protocol	Average remaining energy	Delivery ratio	Average latency	Transmission cost
Epidemic	4	6	5	6
RAPID	5	4	4	3
MaxProp	6	2	3	4
PRoPHET	3	5	6	5
SNW	1	3	2	2
SNF	2	1	1	1

Table 5. Performance comparison of the investigated routing techniques (with variation of message TTL).

Routing protocol	Average remaining energy	Delivery ratio	Average latency	Transmission cost
Epidemic	5	6	5	6
RAPID	1	3	3	2
MaxProp	6	2	6	4
PRoPHET	3	5	4	5
SNW	2	4	2	3
SNF	3	1	1	1

5 Conclusions and Future Endeavors

In this research, we have investigated the energy efficiency of various DTN routing techniques: Epidemic, RAPID, MaxProp, PRoPHET, Spray and Wait and Spray and Focus. Besides, we also try to explore their corresponding routing performance. From all of the outcomes we found that Spray and Wait is the most energy efficient approach than other simulating approaches with the increasing density of nodes. But when we evaluate their performance with expanding TTL, both Spray and Wait and RAPID have the same level of energy efficiency; while in both cases, MaxProp shows lowest energy efficiency. However, Spray and Focus exhibits the best performance for other metrics: delivery ratio, average latency, and transmission cost. Epidemic indicates the lowest performance for delivery ratio, and transmission cost under the consideration of TTL variation. MaxProp also has the highest average latency when it is simulated with TTL variation. On the other hand, RAPID and PRoPHET have the highest latency with changes in node density. In future, the impact of other aspects, such as buffer size, mobility models, message generation rate, etc. on the DTN routing protocols would be considered with a view to design an energy efficient improved routing scheme for Delay-Tolerant Network.

References

1. Cao, Y., Sun, Z.: Routing in delay/disruption tolerant networks: a taxonomy, survey and challenges. IEEE Commun. Surv. Tutor. **15**, 654–677 (2013)
2. Moreira, W., Mendes, P., Sargento, S.: Opportunistic routing based on daily routine. In: IEEE International Symposium on a World of Wireless, Mobile and Multimedia Networks, San Francisco, USA, pp. 1–6 (2012)
3. Zhang, Y., Gao, W., Cao, G., Porta, T.L., Krishnamachari, B., Iyengar, A.: Social-aware data diffusion in delay tolerant MANETs. In: Thai, M., Pardalos, P. (eds.) Handbook of Optimization in Complex Networks. Springer Optimization and Its Applications, vol. 58. Springer, New York (2012). https://doi.org/10.1007/978-1-4614-0857-4_15
4. Xia, F., Jedari, B., Das, S.K.: PIS: a multi-dimensional routing protocol for socially-aware networking. IEEE Trans. Mob. Comput. **15**, 2825–2836 (2016)

5. Socievole, A., Marano, S.: Evaluating the impact of energy consumption on routing performance in delay tolerant networks. In: Wireless Communications and Mobile Computing Conference, Cyprus, pp. 481–486 (2012)
6. Alaoui, E.A.A., Agoujil, S., Hajar, M., Qaraai, Y.: The performance of DTN routing protocols: a comparative study. WSEAS Trans. Commun. **14**, 121–138 (2015)
7. Ababou, M., Bellafkih, M., El Kouch, R.: Energy efficient routing protocol for delay tolerant network based on fuzzy logic and ant colony. Int. J. Intell. Syst. Appl. **10**(1), 69–77 (2018)
8. Cabacas, R.A., Nakamura, H., Ra, I.: Energy consumption analysis of delay tolerant network routing protocols. Int. J. Softw. Eng. Appl. **8**(2), 1–10 (2014)
9. Bista, B.B., Rawat, D.B.: Energy consumption and performance of delay tolerant network routing protocols under different mobility models. In: International Conference on Intelligent Systems, Modelling and Simulation, Bangkok, Thailand, pp. 326–330 (2016)
10. Khan, M.K.M., Rahim, M.S.: Performance analysis of social-aware routing protocols in delay tolerant networks. In: International Conference on Computer Communication, Chemical, Material and Electronic Engineering, Rajshahi, Bangladesh, pp. 1–4 (2018)
11. Spaho, E.: Energy consumption analysis of different routing protocols in a delay tolerant network. J. Ambient Intell. Humaniz. Comput. (2019). https://doi.org/10.1007/s12652-019-01604-8
12. Balasubramanian, A., Levine, B.N., Venkataramani, A.: DTN routing as a resource allocation problem. In: SIGCOMM, Kyoto, Japan, pp. 373–384. ACM (2007)
13. Burgess, J., Gallagher, B., Jensen, D., Levine, B.N.: MaxProp: routing for vehicle-based disruption-tolerant networks. In: International Conference on Computer Communications, Barcelona, Spain, pp. 1–11 (2006)
14. Spyropoulos, T., Psounis, K., Raghavendra, C.S.: Spray and wait: an efficient routing scheme for intermittently connected mobile networks. In: WDTN, Philadelphia, PA, pp. 252–259. ACM (2005)
15. Spyropoulos, T., Psounis, K., Raghavendra, C.S.: Spray and focus: efficient mobility-assisted routing for heterogeneous and correlated mobility. In: Fifth Annual IEEE International Conference on Pervasive Computing and Communications, White Plains, NY, pp. 79–85 (2007)
16. Opportunistic Network Environment (ONE) simulator project page. https://www.netlab.tkk.fi/tutkimus/dtn/theone. Accessed 10 Nov 2019. 11:53:38 AM, Bangladesh Standard Time

Conic Programming Approach to Reduce Congestion Ratio in Communications Network

Bimal Chandra Das[1(✉)], Momotaz Begum[2], Mohammad Monir Uddin[3], and Md. Mosfiqur Rahman[1]

[1] Daffodil International University, Dhaka, Bangladesh
bcdas@daffodilvarsity.edu.bd, mosfiqur.ged@diu.edu.bd

[2] Dhaka University of Engineering and Technology, Dhaka, Bangladesh
momotaz.2k3@gmail.com

[3] North South University, Dhaka, Bangladesh
monir.uddin@northsouth.edu

Abstract. This research introduce a robust optimization model to reduce the congestion ratio in communications network considering uncertainty in the traffic demands. The propose formulation is depended on a model called the pipe model. Network traffic demand is fixed in the pipe model and most of the previous researches consider traffic fluctuation locally. Our proposed model can deal with fluctuation in the traffic demands and considers this fluctuation all over the network. We formulate the robust optimization model in the form of second-order cone programming (SOCP) problem which is tractable by optimization software. The numerical experiments determine the efficiency of our model in terms of reducing the congestion ratio compared to the others model.

Keywords: Conic programming · Ellipsoid · Pipe model · Traffic demand · Robust optimization

1 Introduction

The ratio of traffic flow through a link and its capacity is the network link utilization rate. In a network, the maximum value of all links employment rates is called the network congestion ratio [1,2]. Congestion is occurred when some nodes or links in network transmit too much information, it takes more time to send data from source to destination and decreases the network performance. Congestion also reduces the throughput or makes packet loss [3]. Nowadays, in information and communications technology (ICT) sector, how to reduce the network congestion is a major concern for better performance of network. More traffic can be allowed in the network by minimizing congestion ratio in the network.

T. Bhuiyan et al. (Eds.): ICONCS 2020, LNICST 325, pp. 566–577, 2020.
https://doi.org/10.1007/978-3-030-52856-0_45

To minimize the congestion ratio in networks, there are several researches have been presented in the history. For internet traffic engineering, Wang and Wang [4] introduced a explicit routing problem in the form of a linear programming (LP) problem. Minimizing congestion ratio is the objective of this research. The traffic demand d_{pq} for each pair (p, q) is explicitly given in their research. This research achieves the sufficient routing attainment than the Multi-Protocol Label Switching (MPLS) standard due to the known traffic matrix, $T = \{d_{pq}\}$. Their proposed model for internet traffic which is performed by the given traffic demand is known as the pipe model [5–7]. But in real life, the network traffic demands fluctuates depending on many situation and we don't know our traffic demand in advance. It may vary time to time, situation to situation or in any prospect of activities. Besides, it is a difficult work for any network operator to determine the exact requirement of network traffic. The performance of network is also depends on congestion ratio and traffic flow over the nodes or links [2]. Traffic fluctuations in the network causes congestion and it degrade the network performance.

In this work, to reduce congestion ratio in communications network, we introduce a robust optimization model considering traffic fluctuation. We suppose that the operators can measure the demand of traffic matrix. In the measured traffic demand matrix, there may have some errors or fluctuations, but the total volume of fluctuations is circumscribed by a preassigned parameter. The introduced parameter in the ellipsoidal uncertainty set shows the total traffic fluctuations over the network. In this case, for robust optimization, the ellipsoidal uncertainty set is considered to allow errors or fluctuations in the measured traffic demands matrix of the pipe model depending on a parameter. We construct the second-order cone (SOC) constraints applying robust optimization technique and finally develop our recommended model in the form of SOCP which is the major contribution of our research in communication sectors. The model demonstrates the volume of allowed fluctuations in traffic. The introduced model for communications network also permits the network operator to approximately guess the traffic demand. The main advantage is that we do not need exact traffic demand like pipe model but approximately guess the demands. Based on the approximate data of demands, we can make fluctuations in traffic demand over the network.

2 Network Model and Backbone Network

The directed graph $G(V, A)$ is known as a network where A is the set of links and V is the set of vertices (nodes).In a network, a link from source node $i \in V$ to destination node $j \in V \setminus \{i\}$ is expressed as $(i, j) \in A, i \neq j$. The traffic or information is enter into and moving outside the network through the set of edge node $Q \subseteq V$. The pair of edge node is denoted by $(p, q) \in W$, where $p \in Q$ and $q \in Q$, and $p \neq q$. The set of pairs of edge node (p, q) is denoted by W. The traffic portion from node $p \in Q$ to node $q \in Q$ using the link $(i, j) \in A$ is denoted by x_{ij}^{pq} and the links capacity for the link $(i, j) \in A$ is indicated by c_{ij}.

By reducing the congestion ratio, r the allowable traffic in the network can be maximized. The allowable traffic in the network is welcomed up to the present traffic amount times $1/r$. we also can uphold the performance of the network by minimizing the congestion in the network [8].

To transfer data between different LANs or subnetworks, the network or backbone network prepares paths for interconnecting various pieces of network. The backbone network can attach together distinct networks over wide areas, in different areas, or in the same area. In a large association that have areas may have a network backbone which links all the areas together. To construct the network or backbone network, the network congestion ratio is usually taken into attention. Network congestion is also depends on the traffic variation and routing management in the backbone network [9]. The objective of this paper is to minimize the network congestion ratio with routing control and traffic variation.

3 Pipe Model

The traffic demand data $T = \{d_{pq} : (p, q) \in W\}$ between source and destination nodes are considered to be explicitly know in the pipe model. In order to reduce the congestion in network, the routing management for the pipe mode is given below:

$$\min r \tag{1a}$$

$$\text{s.t.} \sum_{j:(i,j)\in A} x_{ij}^{pq} - \sum_{j:(j,i)\in A} x_{ji}^{pq} = 1, \qquad i = p, \forall (p,q) \in W \tag{1b}$$

$$\sum_{j:(i,j)\in A} x_{ij}^{pq} - \sum_{j:(j,i)\in A} x_{ji}^{pq} = 0, \qquad \forall i \in V \setminus \{p,q\}, \forall (p,q) \in W \tag{1c}$$

$$\sum_{(p,q)\in W} d_{pq} x_{ij}^{pq} \leq c_{ij} r, \qquad \forall (i,j) \in A \tag{1d}$$

$$0 \leq x_{ij}^{pq} \leq 1, \qquad \forall (i,j) \in A, \forall (p,q) \in W \tag{1e}$$

$$0 \leq r \leq 1. \tag{1f}$$

The traffic flow control constraints are represented by the constraints (1b) and (1c) in the above formulation. The Eq. (1b) shows that the total flow of traffic passing from node $i (= p)$ is equal to 1. If the node i is neither a source or destination node, the constraint (1c) means that the total amount of traffic entering to node i must be equal as the total amount passing from node i. The relation (1d) represents that the addition of the part of demands of traffic broadcasted through the link (i, j) is less than or equal to the capacity of that link times the congestion ratio of that network. The objective function described by (1a) provides that r is the congestion ratio of the network and it is found if an optimal solution is attained. The pipe model typically attains a high routing achievement correlated to the others model; however, the pipe model desires the extract information of traffic demands T, but, in reality, the network operators can not measure the extract information of traffic demand easily because demand of traffic fluctuates due to many reasons.

4 Hose Model

In this model, the authors presume that the network operators could freely specify the total outgoing/incoming data from/to node p and node q rather than to measure the actual information of traffic. In hose model formulation, the total passing information from node p in the network is denoted by

$$\sum_q d_{pq} \le \alpha_p,$$

here α_p is the maximum volume of information that node p can deliver. In the same way, if β_q is the maximum volume of information that node q can collect from the network, then the total entering information to node q is described by

$$\sum_p d_{pq} \le \beta_q.$$

This formulation for traffic model is recognized as the hose model [5–7, 10] which are bordered by β_q and α_p. The optimal routing management of this kind of formulation to reduce the congestion ratio in network is described as follows Chu et al. [11]

$$\begin{aligned}
&\min\ r \\
&\text{s.t.} \sum_{j:(i,j)\in A} x_{ij}^{pq} - \sum_{j:(j,i)\in A} x_{ji}^{pq} = 1, \qquad i = p, \forall (p,q) \in W && \text{(2a)}\\
&\quad \sum_{j:(i,j)\in A} x_{ij}^{pq} - \sum_{j:(j,i)\in A} x_{ji}^{pq} = 0, \qquad \forall i \in V \setminus \{p,q\}, \forall (p,q) \in W && \text{(2b)}\\
&\quad \sum_{q\in Q} d_{pq} \le \alpha_p, \quad \forall p \in Q && \text{(2c)}\\
&\quad \sum_{p\in Q} d_{pq} \le \beta_q, \quad \forall q \in Q && \text{(2d)}\\
&\quad \sum_{(p,q)\in W} d_{pq} x_{ij}^{pq} \le c_{ij} r, \quad \forall (i,j) \in A && \text{(2e)}\\
&\quad 0 \le x_{ij}^{pq} \le 1, \qquad \forall (i,j) \in A, \forall (p,q) \in W && \text{(2f)}\\
&\quad 0 \le r \le 1. && \text{(2g)}
\end{aligned}$$

The important note compared to the pipe model is that the traffic matrix $T = \{d_{pq} : (p,q) \in W\}$ is considered as variable. In the pipe model, the constraints (2c) and (2d) are incorporated to formulate the hose model. Since the constraint (2e) consists the products of two variables hence is not an LP and it is not easy to solve by optimization software. However, to overcome this difficulty,

Chu et al. [11,12] developed a technique using dual of the subproblems to convert the problem into an LP problem and final form of hose model is expressed by

$$\min r \tag{3a}$$

$$\text{s.t.} \sum_{j:(i,j)\in A} x_{ij}^{pq} - \sum_{j:(j,i)\in A} x_{ji}^{pq} = 1, \qquad i = p, \forall (p,q) \in W \tag{3b}$$

$$\sum_{j:(i,j)\in A} x_{ij}^{pq} - \sum_{j:(j,i)\in A} x_{ji}^{pq} = 0, \qquad \forall (p,q) \in W, \forall i \in V \setminus \{p,q\} \tag{3c}$$

$$\sum_{p\in Q} \alpha_p \pi_{ij}(p) + \sum_{q\in Q} \beta_q \lambda_{ij}(q) \le c_{ij} r, \qquad \forall (i,j) \in A, \tag{3d}$$

$$x_{ij}^{pq} \le \pi_{ij}(p) + \lambda_{ij}(q), \quad \forall (i,j) \in A, \forall (p,q) \in W \tag{3e}$$

$$\pi_{ij}(p), \lambda_{ij}(q) \ge 0, \quad \forall (i,j) \in A, \forall (p,q) \in W \tag{3f}$$

$$0 \le x_{ij}^{pq} \le 1, \qquad \forall (i,j) \in A, \forall (p,q) \in W \tag{3g}$$

$$0 \le r \le 1. \tag{3h}$$

In the hose model, there is an opportunity to choose the parameters to bound the total volume of outgoing/incoming data. The hose model is recognized as more adaptable. On the other hand, there is an opportunity to allow big fluctuation in the hose model. Nonetheless, the routing achievement is much lower than the pipe model. The advantage of the hose model is that we can allow big amount of fluctuation using the hose technique. There is no traffic limit for each link just total passing and entering data limit for every node in the network.

5 Robust Optimization

If the values of some parameters of an optimization problem are not given directly or they have uncertainty then optimization problem is said to be a robust optimization problem if in the worst case, we want to solve the problem with respect to the uncertainty [13,14]. Optimizing the problem wherein the problem data belongs to the set is the objective of robust optimization. The uncertainty set of an optimization problem is a set where the parameters are apparent to fall in. In robust case, this kind of uncertainty set consist of unbelievably several points.

In our research, we introduce a distinct type of hypothesis on errors. In the network, for each source-destination pair, our proposed model can express deviations of traffic demand. Specially, we introduce to constrained the total volume of squared errors by a positive constant, ϵ for all $(p,q) \in W$ in $\bar{d}_{pq}$, and the actual demand of traffic belongs to

$$\Theta_\epsilon = \left\{ \mathbf{d} : \sqrt{\sum_{(p,q)\in W} (d_{pq} - \bar{d}_{pq})^2} \le \epsilon \right\}, \tag{4}$$

The ϵ represents a single network-wide parameter in our research [15]. In Sect. 6, we introduce the optimization model in robust form depends on the error (4) to the pipe model.

It is noted that we need the *estimated value* of traffic demand expressed by $\bar{d}_{pq}$ explicitly for each $(p, q) \in W$ in our model.

6 Robust Optimization Model

To formulate our proposed model, robust optimization approach is applied to the pipe model. We have the following inequality since the Eq. (1d) should be valid for each $\mathbf{d} \in \Theta_\epsilon$:

$$\max_{\mathbf{d}\in\Theta_\epsilon} \left(\sum_{(p,q)\in W} d_{pq} x_{ij}^{pq} \right) \leq c_{ij} r. \tag{5}$$

To obtain a second-order cone constraint for our model, now we rewrite the constraint (5). The following lemma takes an essential role in calculating the left hand side of (5).

Lemma 1. *Let $\Omega_\theta = \{\boldsymbol{x} \in \mathbb{R}^n : ||\boldsymbol{x}|| \leq \theta\}$, where $|| \cdot ||$ is the Euclidean norm. For given $\boldsymbol{a} \in \mathbb{R}^n$ and $\theta > 0$, we have*

$$\max_{\boldsymbol{x}\in\Omega_\theta} \boldsymbol{a}^T \boldsymbol{x} = \theta ||\boldsymbol{a}||.$$

Proof. For our optimization problem, the Lagrangian function can be represented as follows:

$$\max_{\mathbf{x}\in\Omega_\theta} \mathbf{a}^T\mathbf{x}, \text{ s.t. } \quad ||\mathbf{x}|| \leq \theta, \quad \forall \mathbf{x} \in \Omega_\theta \text{ is}$$
$$F(\mathbf{x}, \lambda) \equiv \mathbf{a}^T\mathbf{x} + \lambda(\theta - ||\mathbf{x}||).$$

The Karush Kuhn Tucker (KKT) conditions are (at the optimal point).
(*i*) $\nabla_{\mathbf{x}} F(\mathbf{x}, \lambda) \equiv \mathbf{a} - \lambda \nabla_{\mathbf{x}} ||\mathbf{x}|| = 0,$
(*ii*) $\lambda(\theta - ||\mathbf{x}||) = 0,$
(*iii*) $\theta - ||\mathbf{x}|| \geq 0,$
(*iv*) $\lambda \geq 0$ From condition (i), we can write

$$\mathbf{a} - \lambda \nabla_{\mathbf{x}} ||\mathbf{x}|| = 0 \Leftrightarrow \mathbf{a} - \lambda \frac{\mathbf{x}}{||\mathbf{x}||} = 0 \Leftrightarrow \mathbf{a}||\mathbf{x}|| = \lambda \mathbf{x} \Leftrightarrow \mathbf{a}\theta = \lambda \mathbf{x}$$

$\Leftrightarrow ||\mathbf{a}||\theta = \lambda||\mathbf{x}|| \Leftrightarrow ||\mathbf{a}||\theta = \lambda\theta \therefore \lambda = ||\mathbf{a}||$
Again, $\mathbf{a}\theta = \lambda\mathbf{x} \Leftrightarrow \mathbf{x} = \theta.\frac{\mathbf{a}}{||\mathbf{a}||} \Leftrightarrow \mathbf{a}^T\mathbf{x} = \theta.\frac{\mathbf{a}^T\mathbf{a}}{||\mathbf{a}||}$
$\Leftrightarrow \mathbf{a}^T\mathbf{x} = \theta.\frac{||\mathbf{a}||^2}{||\mathbf{a}||} \Leftrightarrow \mathbf{a}^T\mathbf{x} = \theta||\mathbf{a}||.$
Here $\mathbf{x}$ is the optimal solution of the above optimization problem, which indicates that $\max_{\mathbf{x}\in\Omega_\theta} \mathbf{a}^T\mathbf{x} = \theta||\mathbf{a}||.$

We introduce a variable for each $(p, q) \in W$ to use Lemma 1 to evaluate the left-hand side of the constraint (5):

$$v_{pq} = d_{pq} - \bar{d}_{pq}.$$

It is easily clear that

$$\mathbf{d} \in \Theta_\epsilon \Leftrightarrow \mathbf{v} \in \Omega_\epsilon.$$

We have for every $(i,j) \in A$, using Lemma 1,

$$\begin{aligned} &\max_{\mathbf{d}\in\Theta_\epsilon} \left(\sum_{(p,q)\in W} d_{pq} x_{ij}^{pq} \right) \\ &= \max_{\mathbf{v}\in\Omega_\epsilon} \left(\sum_{(p,q)\in W} v_{pq} x_{ij}^{pq} \right) + \sum_{(p,q)\in W} \bar{d}_{pq} x_{ij}^{pq} \\ &= \epsilon \sqrt{\sum_{(p,q)\in W} \left(x_{ij}^{pq}\right)^2} + \sum_{(p,q)\in W} \bar{d}_{pq} x_{ij}^{pq}. \end{aligned} \tag{6}$$

We get the identical inequality for every $(i,j) \in A$ substituting the left-hand side of (5) by (6):

$$\sqrt{\sum_{(p,q)\in W} \left(x_{ij}^{pq}\right)^2} \le \frac{1}{\epsilon} \left(c_{ij} r - \sum_{(p,q)\in W} \bar{d}_{pq} x_{ij}^{pq} \right). \tag{7}$$

Now, we propose a SOCP problem.

The $1+r$ dimensional *second-order cone* is defined as

$$\mathrm{SOC}(1+r) = \left\{ \mathbf{x} \in \mathbb{R}^{1+r} : x_0 \ge \sqrt{\sum_{j=1}^{r} x_j^2} \right\}.$$

When a subvector is restricted in a convenient dimensional second-order cone (SOC), such a constraint is known as a SOC constraint. The SOC is a closed convex cone. An problem is said to be a SOCP problem if it has only a linear objective function, second-order cone constraint, and linear constraints. The primal-dual interior-point methods can solve an SOCP problem very methodically [16,17]. However, the modern optimization softwares such as Gurobi, SCIP, or CPLEX [18–20] can handle SOCP.

By using the second-order cone, the constraint in (7) involving square root can be stated as:

$$w_{pq}^{ij} = x_{ij}^{pq} \tag{8}$$

$$w_0^{ij} = \left(c_{ij} r - \sum_{(p,q)\in W} \bar{d}_{pq} x_{ij}^{pq} \right) / \epsilon \tag{9}$$

$$\begin{pmatrix} w_0^{ij} \\ \mathbf{w}^{ij} \end{pmatrix} \in \mathrm{SOC}(1+|W|), \tag{10}$$

where $\mathbf{w}^{ij} = (w_{pq}^{ij})_{(p,q)\in W}$. Here it is clear that the constraints (8) and (9) are linear constraints and the constraint (10) is a SOC constraint. Therefore, we formulate our proposed model in the form of SOCP which is a robust model:

$$\min r \tag{11a}$$

$$\text{s.t.} \sum_{j:(i,j)\in A} x_{ij}^{pq} - \sum_{j:(j,i)\in A} x_{ji}^{pq} = 1, \qquad \forall i = p, \forall (p,q) \in W \tag{11b}$$

$$\sum_{j:(i,j)\in A} x_{ij}^{pq} - \sum_{j:(j,i)\in A} x_{ji}^{pq} = 0, \qquad \forall i \in V \setminus \{p,q\}, \forall (p,q) \in W \tag{11c}$$

$$\sqrt{\sum_{(p,q)\in W} \left(x_{ij}^{pq}\right)^2} \leq \frac{1}{\epsilon}\left(c_{ij}r - \sum_{(p,q)\in W} \bar{d}_{pq}x_{ij}^{pq}\right), \qquad \forall (i,j) \in A \tag{11d}$$

$$0 \leq x_{ij}^{pq} \leq 1, \qquad \forall (i,j) \in A, \forall (p,q) \in W \tag{11e}$$

$$0 \leq r \leq 1. \tag{11f}$$

The network operators can manage the operations without recognizing the specific traffic demand by permitting them to total error in the estimated traffic demand by using our proposed SOCP model. The objective of our proposed model is to reduce the congestion ratio of network allowing fluctuations in the traffic demands. The major advantage of our model is that we can allow many fluctuations in the estimated traffic demand over the network. In our model, there is no link's traffic fluctuation limit or any node's traffic fluctuation limit. We allow the total amount of fluctuations for the whole network. Each link of the network has an opportunity to choose the amount of fluctuation independently. In the hose model, they also have the same opportunity for each link but they have the boundaries for total passing and entering volume of traffic for each node.

7 Numerical Experiments

7.1 Experiments Settings

The network congestion ratios obtained by the ellipsoid model is compared against the model where the data of traffic-demand matrix is exactly given, called the pipe model. We also compare our proposed model with the hose model where total volume of outgoing/incoming amount from/to every node is known. The networks applied in this experiments are demonstrated in Fig. 1. The Networks 1, 2, and 3 are referenced typical backbone networks used in [21]. The another network (JPN12) is a Japan photonic network-12 which is a real network in Japan. In the experiment, the capacities of the network links are considered in the range of (2000, 3000) for all considered sample networks. We set the traffic demands $\bar{d}_{pq}$ randomly generated with a uniform distribution in the range of (0, 100). In the hose model, bounds are set as follows:

$\alpha_p = \sum_{q \in Q} \bar{d}_{pq}$, $\forall p \in Q$, $\beta_q = \sum_{p \in Q} \bar{d}_{pq}$, $\forall q \in Q$. The Python language is used to write the experiments program and the professional optimization software Gurobi, version 7.0.1 (October Sky 2016) [10] is used to solve the optimization problems. Windows based computer with 16 GB memory, Intel(R) Core(TM) i7-4790 CPU @ 3.60 GHz is used to run the experimental program.

Theoretically, we explain the efficiency of our proposed model in Sect. 6. The purpose of conducting the numerically experiment is to show whether the proposed model is run by modern software or not. The another purpose is to prove the efficiency of our contribution numerically (Table 1).

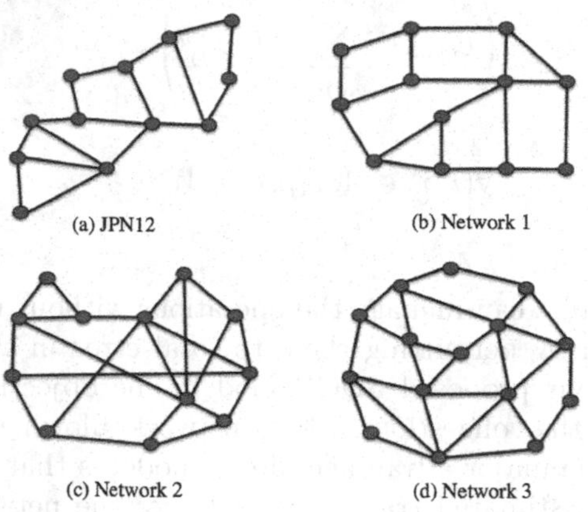

Fig. 1. Fixtures of consider networks

Table 1. Considered network used in the experiment.

Network type	No. of nodes considered	No. of links considered
JPN12	12	17
Network 1	12	18
Network 2	12	22
Network 3	15	27

7.2 Experiments Results

The network congestion ratios obtained by the ellipsoid model is compared with the hose and pipe models for $\epsilon = 20$ and 50. We solve the LP problems of the pipe and hose models and SOCP problems for the ellipsoid model and compare their achievement. To evaluate the performances of the considered models, we generate 100 random problems for each model and for each considered network to compare their performance. The comparisons of average congestion ratios for $\epsilon = 20$ and $\epsilon = 50$ are reported in Fig. 2 and Fig. 3, respectively.

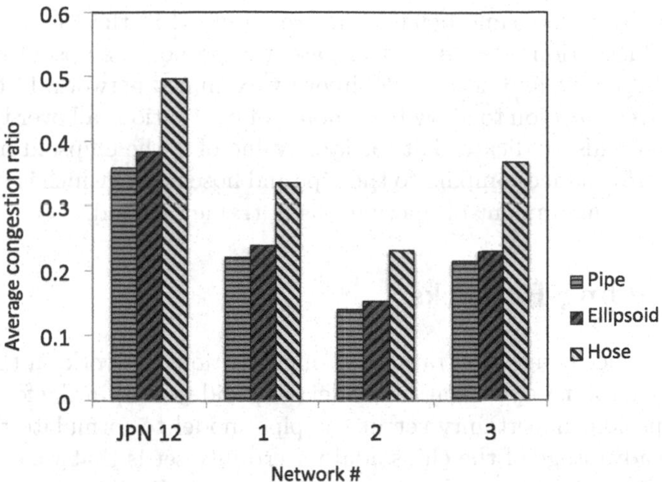

Fig. 2. Comparison of average congestion ratio for $\epsilon = 20$.

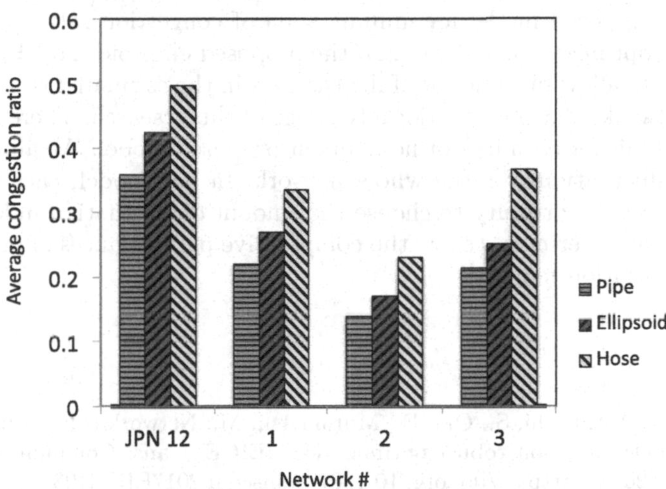

Fig. 3. Average congestion ratio comparison for $\epsilon = 50$.

Figure 2 shows that the average congestion ratios achieve by our recommended model (ellipsoid model) always lies between the pipe and hose models in all considered networks. From the figure, it is noted that, when fluctuate the traffic with $\epsilon = 20$, the average congestion ratio for the ellipsoid model lies between 38.24% to 15.23%, whereas this ratio for the hose model lies between 49.66% to 23.09% in the four sample networks. It is already proved that due to known traffic demand the pipe model obtains the highest routing achievement compared to others.

Figure 3 shows the same behavior as we observed in the Fig. 2 although we allow total fluctuation, $\epsilon = 50$. In this case, the proposed ellipsoid model again lies between the pipe and hose model in every examined network. In the ellipsoid mode, we have an option to allow big amount of fluctuations all over the network. Figures 2 and 3 also indicate that for large value of ϵ, the ellipsoid model shows the better performance compare to the pipe and hose model which is the practical contribution of big amount of fluctuations in traffic demand.

8 Concluding Remarks

In order to reduce congestion ratio in communications network, in this research, we introduce a robust optimization model (ellipsoid model) in the form of SOCP. We use ellipsoidal uncertainty set in the pipe model to formulate the ellipsoid model. The advantage of the ellipsoidal uncertainty set is that we can deal with total fluctuation of traffic demands over the network. By introducing the SOCP model, the network operators can deal without knowing the exact traffic demand by permitting them to total error in the estimated traffic demand. The problems of the proposed model for minimization of congestion ratio is run by the professional optimization software. In the proposed ellipsoid model, we have an opportunity to allow big amount of fluctuations in the estimated traffic demands in whole network, which is a major advantage of this research. There is no traffic fluctuation limit for each link or node in our proposed model. We allow the total amount of fluctuations for the whole network. In our model, each link in the network has an opportunity to choose the amount of fluctuation independently. The numerical experiments show the comparative performances of our proposed robust optimization model.

References

1. Das, B.C., Takahashi, S., Oki, E., Muramatsu, M.: Network congestion minimization models based on robust optimization. IEICE Trans. Commun. **E101-B**(3), 772–784 (2018). https://doi.org/10.1587/transcom.2017EBP3193
2. Oki, E., Iwaki, A.: Performance comparisons of optimal routing by pipe, hose and intermediate models. In: Proceedings of IEEE Sarnoff Symposium (Sarnoff 2009), pp. 1–5, March/April 2009. https://doi.org/10.1109/SARNOF.2009.4850317
3. Xu, J., Yang, J.Z., Guo, C., Lee, Y.-H., Lu, D.: Routing algorithm of minimizing maximum link congestion on grid networks. Wireless Netw. **21**(5), 1713–1732 (2014). https://doi.org/10.1007/s11276-014-0878-8
4. Wang, Y., Wang, Z.: Explicit routing algorithms for internet traffic engineering. In: IEEE International Conference on Computer Communications and Networks (ICCCN) (1999). https://doi.org/10.1109/ICCCN.1999.805577
5. Juttner, A., Szabo, I., Szentesi, A.: On bandwidth efficiency of the hose resource management model in virtual private networks. In: IEEE Infocom 2003, pp. 386–395, March/April (2003). https://doi.org/10.1109/INFCOM.2003.1208690

6. Duffield, N.G., Goyal, P., Greenberg, A., Mishra, P., Ramakrishnan, K.K., Merwe, J.E.: Resource management with hose: point-to-cloud services for virtual private networks. IEEE/ACM Trans. Netw. **10**(5), 679–692 (2002). https://doi.org/10.1109/TNET.2002.803918
7. Kumar, A., Rastogi, R., Silberschatz, A., Yener, B.: Algorithms for provisioning virtual private networks in the hose model. IEEE/ACM Trans. Networking **10**(4), 565–578 (2002). https://doi.org/10.1109/TNET.2002.802141
8. Li, C., Xie, R., Huang, T., Liu, Y.: Jointly optimal congestion control, forwarding strategy and power control for named-data multihop wireless network. IEEE Access **5**, 1013–1026 (2017). https://doi.org/10.1109/ACCESS.2016.2634525
9. Singhal, P., Yadav, A.: Congestion detection in wireless sensor network using neural network. In: International Conference for Convergence for Technology-2014, April 2015. https://doi.org/10.1109/I2CT.2014.7092259
10. Das, B.C., Oki, E., Muramatsu, M.: Comparative performance of green pipe, green hose, and green hose-rectangle models in power efficient network. In: IEEE ComSoc International Communications Quality and Reliability Workshop, pp. 1–6 (2018). https://doi.org/10.1109/CQR.2018.8445921
11. Chu, J., Lea, C.: Optimal link weights for maximizing QoS traffic. In: IEEE ICC 2007, pp. 610–615 (2007). https://doi.org/10.1109/ICC.2007.105
12. Chu, J., Lea, C.: Optimal link weights for maximizing QoS traffic. IEEE/ACM Trans. Netw. **17**(3), 778–788 (2009)
13. Boyd, S., Vandenberghe, L.: Approximation and Fitting in Convex Optimization, pp. 318–324. Cambridge University Press, Cambridge (2005)
14. Pedroso, J.P., Rais, A., Kubo, M., Muramatsu, M.: Second-order cone optimization. In: Mathematical Optimization: Solving Problems Using Gurobi and Python, pp. 108–115, September 2012
15. Das, B.C., Oki, E., Muramatsu, M.: A simple SOCP formulation of minimization of network congestion ratio, RIMS Kokyuroku 2027, Kyoto University, Kyoto, Japan, vol. 2027, pp. 52–59, April 2017
16. Nesterov, Y., Nemirovsky, A.: Interior-point polynomial methods in convex programming. Studies in Applied Mathematics, vol. 13. SIAM, Philadelphia (1994)
17. Boyd, S., Vandenberghe, L.: Interior-point methods. In: Convex Optimization. Cambridge University Press, Cambridge (2005), chap. 11, sect. 11.7, pp. 609–614 (2005)
18. Gurobi Optimization. Verison: 6.5.2, October Sky (2015). http://www.gurobi.com
19. Solving Constraint Integer Programs. http://scip.zib.de
20. Explore IBM software and Solutions. https://www-01.ibm.com/software/commerce/optimization/cplex-optimizer/
21. Ouedraogo, I.A., Oki, E.: A green and robust optimization strategy for energy saving against traffic uncertainty. IEEE J. Sel. Areas Commun. **34**(5), 1405–1416 (2016). https://doi.org/10.1109/JSAC.2016.2545378

Future Technology Applications

Sightless Helper: An Interactive Mobile Application for Blind Assistance and Safe Navigation

Md. Elias Hossain(✉), Khandker M Qaiduzzaman, and Mostafijur Rahman

Department of Software Engineering, Daffodil International University, Dhaka, Bangladesh
elias35-1426@diu.edu.bd

Abstract. This paper proposes a mobile application named "Sightless Helper", for assisting blind or visually impaired people. The application uses footstep counting and GPS for indoor and outdoor navigation. It can detect objects and unsafe areas to ensure safe navigation. The system consists of voice recognition, touchpad, button and shaking sensor for easy interaction between the user and the system. During any kind of accident, it can detect unusual shaking of the user, and send his/her location to some emergency contacts. "Sightless Helper" pro-vides several useful additional features such as calendar, news reading, barcode reading, battery monitoring, etc. The performance of the application is tested considering voice recognition time and location sending time. The experimental result shows that the voice recognition time of the application is around 6.303 ms and 6.375 ms for male and female voices respectively. The average location sending time is nearly 7.629 ms to any distance. The usability test result reveals that the proposed application has an average 72.2% System Usability Scale (SUS) score, showing its suitability for practical implementation.

Keywords: Android application · Visually Impaired people · Object identification · GPS navigation

1 Introduction

Living in a society and performing daily work like normal people is a challenge to the Visually Impaired (VI) people. Around 20 million individuals in the USA live with visual disabilities [1]. 285 million people are affected by visual impairment. The geographical distribution of Visual Impairment is uneven in the world [1]. Another major issue for the VI people is to connect with the world to share information. Nowadays modern innovations are making a difference for them to overcome the troubles to some degree. Numerous equipment or program instruments are designed to assist them [2]. They face numerous problems every day among which the major problems understand the self-position, determining the heading and the movement directions, and understanding the locations of the objects [3]. Especially, smartphones are being used as a multi-functional device to assist the Visually Impaired (VI), people. Since smartphones have several useful

T. Bhuiyan et al. (Eds.): ICONCS 2020, LNICST 325, pp. 581–592, 2020.
https://doi.org/10.1007/978-3-030-52856-0_46

sensors, software developers are focusing to design effective applications for Visually Impaired people. One of the most popular platforms for designing mobile applications is An-droid. In the late years, the Android application has turned out to be a basic piece of present-day innovation in the field of restorative, bio-innovation, bioinformatics, prudent area, social issues and diversion purposes. In some developed nations portable application is being used as a weapon in the field of security for visually impaired individuals. It would be an extraordinary thought whether the Android application is utilized as the arms of visually impaired people. According to the opinion of some visually impaired individuals, their major problem is to locate a place precisely. Most of the time they count the foot-steps to determine the location of a place but it is cumbersome to memorize the number of footsteps for thousands of places. Sometimes they also fall in danger while they move in risky places like stairs; the edge of the balcony, busy roads, muddy and sleepy places, etc. Even during the danger, some of them cannot contact their parents or trustworthy persons because it is really difficult to use any mobile application for a Visually Impaired person. That is why it is important to configure the touchpad of the mobile phone in such a way that they can quickly access some essential applications. In the present form, the use of the touchpad or keypad is a difficult task for visually impaired individuals. An effective tool to interact with the smartphone could be the voice command. The motivation of this work is to design an effective android mobile application that can provide all-in-one facilities for the visually impaired (VI) people. Over the last few years, researchers have emphasized mobile applications rather than traditional tools to assist VI people. Some of the researchers gave concentration on indoor navigation whereas some of the researchers choose outdoor navigation for the experiment. Very few researchers have given concentration on both indoor and outdoor navigation. Additionally, most of the systems are more concerned about navigational issues. Most of the systems gave less attention to safety, usability, communication, and gadget usage and system interaction issues. Therefore, it is of great need to design such a system that can provide all of the features simultaneously without interrupting each other. The sightless based application developed based on the smartphone in recent years are as follows. Turn-by-turn is an effective method for assisting blind people, proposed in paper [4] and [5]. A smart navigation system named NavEye was proposed in paper [6] for university students. The paper [7] design and developed of an Electronic Travelling Aid (ETA) kit to help the visually impaired people to find obstacle free path. The paper [8] proposed a Screen Magnifier system that represents the enlarged form of the screened context. A modification of an existing blind assisting system named smart backpack was presented in paper [9]. In paper [10], a mobile application is introduced that can assist the VI people in an outdoor environment. Another application named Blind Reader is proposed in paper [11] that helps the visionless people read any book or document. In Paper [12], a smartphone application named NavCog3 is proposed that can assist blind people in navigating in the large indoor environment. The proposed system will assist education process for visually impaired with an easy-to-use interface and a number of built-in learning materials [13]. In paper [14], a mobile application named BLaDE is developed for VI people to read product barcodes. The application uses a camera or webcam to find a product with a barcode. Another research [15] essential target is to help an outwardly impeded or dazzle client in exploring from guide A toward point B through solid bearings given from an online network. In this paper, we have designed and developed a system based on the sightless helper. The solution is very effective than any of the above mentioned research work. The proposed system is very much user-friendly to the visually impaired people. In Sect. 2, the Methodology is described. In Sects. 2.1 and 2.2 the blind channel control system is described. In Sect. 2.3, the indoor and outdoor navigation system is described. Section 2.4 shows the voice recognition algorithm step. In Sect. 2.5 shows the user interface design of this proposed system. Section 3 described the Result and Discussions, system usability scale (SUS) and comparison with the existing system. In Sects. 4, conclusion and future work are described.

2 Methodology

In our application, most of the challenges of VI people are considered and solved one by one. To interact with the mobile phone both touchpad and voice command is used. One of the strong sides of the developed application is that it does not require any pedometer for step counting. Since pedometer is not available in most of the smartphones, we used an accelerometer instead. Another unique feature of the application is that it can detect unusual shaking. As a result, if the VI person falls accidentally it can detect that. The application immediately calls and sends the location of the VI person via text message to some pre-stored mobile numbers. Moreover, to avoid accidents, the application notifies the VI person whenever she/he enters in an unsafe area. To assist the blind people, the application can provide direction of any pre-stored location offline. Besides, it can also provide direction from online to navigate safely. Apart from these the application also assists to perform some daily works including, using the calendar, reading news, reading barcode, monitoring the battery level. This section discusses the design of the proposed solution "Sightless Helper". The system has a Blind channel that controls the workflow of the individual modules of the system, and it is divided into two parts. The first one is the Blind Assistant Section (BAS) and the other one is the Blind People Section (BPS) as shown in Fig. 1. The target user of BAS is the human assistant of the VI people and the target user of BPS are the VI people themselves. BAS consist of several other modules such as Contact module, Permission module, Pedometer module, and Area module. On the other hand, BPS consist of five modules, Speaking scanning module, Touch module, Jolt module, Required module, and Indication module. The detailed system architecture of the proposed system is shown in Fig. 1. The whole system is controlled from the Blind channel centrally. Section 2.1 and 2.2 presents the details of BAS and BPS.

2.1 Blind Assistant Section (BAS)

As discussed above, the BAS is divided into four modules, Contact module, Permission module, Pedometer module, and Area module. The primary focus of BAS is to provide safety and assisted movements to the VI people. The description of each module of BAS is described in the following subsections.

Contact Module. This module provides communication facilities for the VI people. A human assistant of a blind person can input some trusted contact numbers through this module. Whenever the human assistant provides the contact numbers, are stored in an offline database.

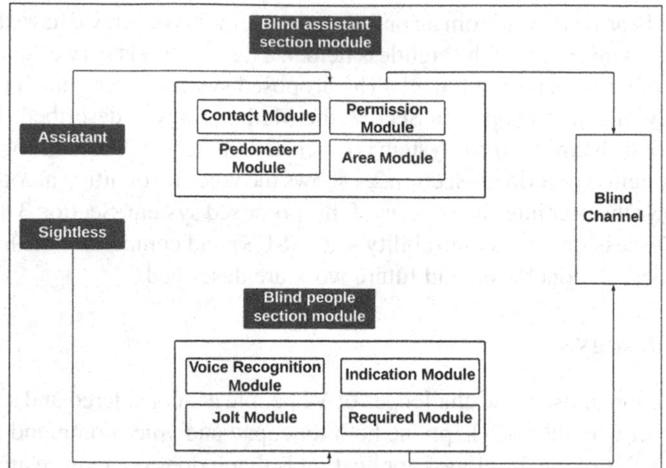

Fig. 1. The architectural design of the proposed Sightless Helper system.

Permission Module. This module ensures permission for the system. Since the application runs in the background continuously, it is the first and foremost need to ensure permission to run in the background. After installing the application, the assistant of the blind person ensures all of the required permissions for this system.

Pe2dometer Module. It is seen that most of the smartphones do not have an inbuilt pedometer sensor for footstep monitoring and calculating. This module uses the accelerometer sensor which is inbuilt in almost all of the Smartphones for counting the foot-steps. This module is set by a human assistant of the blind person. First, the assistant saves the footstep count for the usual daily activities of the user, including places such as the bathroom, kitchen, dining table, etc. By this, if the VI people want to go to the washroom, they can easily understand their destination by footstep count, provided by the system. The workflow of the Pedometer module is shown in Fig. 2.

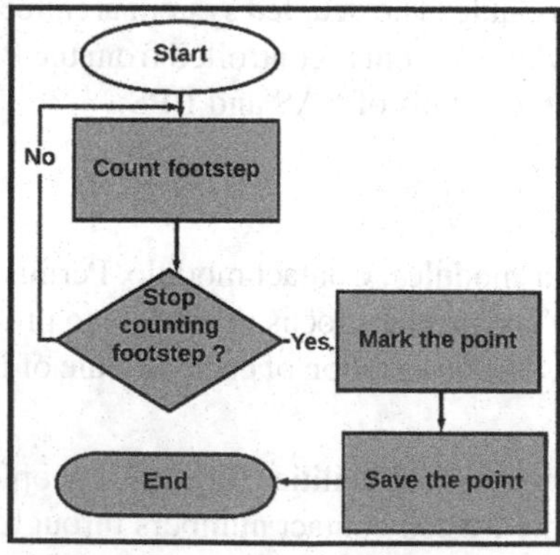

Fig. 2. Pedometer module flow chart

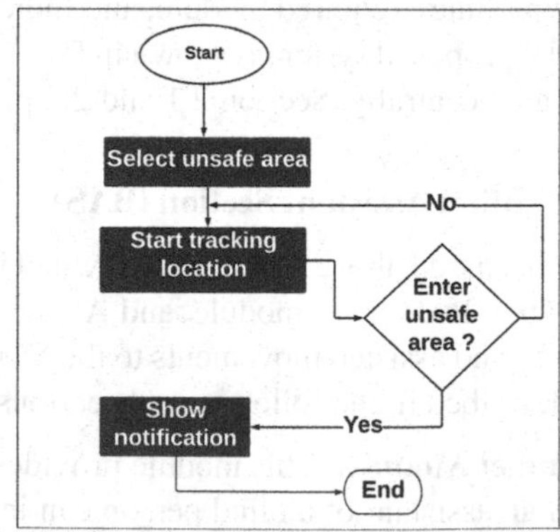

Fig. 3. Area module flow chart

Area Module. This module is designed to store some specific locations. The human assistant of a blind person sets some specific locations that are stored in the database. Besides, the assistant can also set some unsafe locations so that the VI person stays safe. Whenever the blind individual enters in an unsafe place, the system automatically notifies that you entered in an unsafe area, please be safe. The flowchart of the area module is shown in Fig. 3.

2.2 Blind People Section (BPS)

Blind People Section is used by the VI people. As discussed earlier, this module consists of five modules. The Speaking Scanning module this module starts by voice command. Whenever gives a voice command such as "HELP", "Call to father", "Call to mother", "Send location", "Police", "Barcode", "Go to washroom", "Go to the kitchen room", "Go to the dining table", "Go to Toilet" the system can detect the command by searching in a predefined dictionary. After detecting the predefined commands, the system can perform some actions according to the type of command. There may have several actions such as, activating the automatic navigation and starting to guide the blind person to reach the destination. When the blind person starts the navigation, the system guides the direction through voice, based on the current location point of the user. After reaching the destination, the system notifies the user by saying, Please stop, you reached your destination. This system can detect obstacles too. This module also has barcode scanning capability. When the system receives specific commands like Barcode, it automatically opens the camera and notifies by saying the user, please put your phone and scan the barcode. The working procedure of the speaking scanning module is shown in Fig. 4 and the workflow of the touch modules shown in Fig. 5.

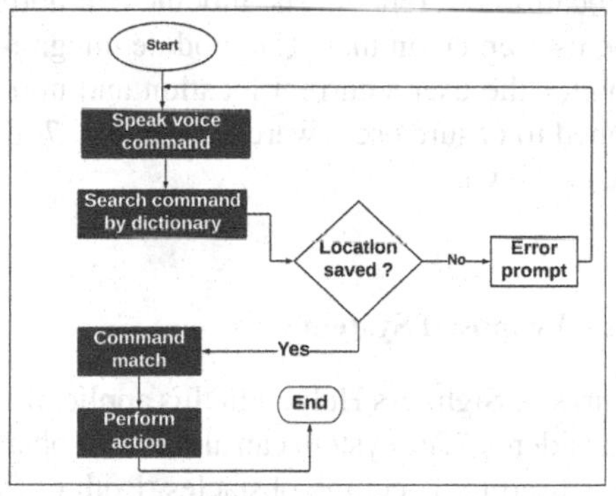

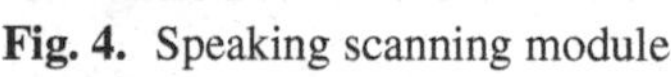
Fig. 4. Speaking scanning module

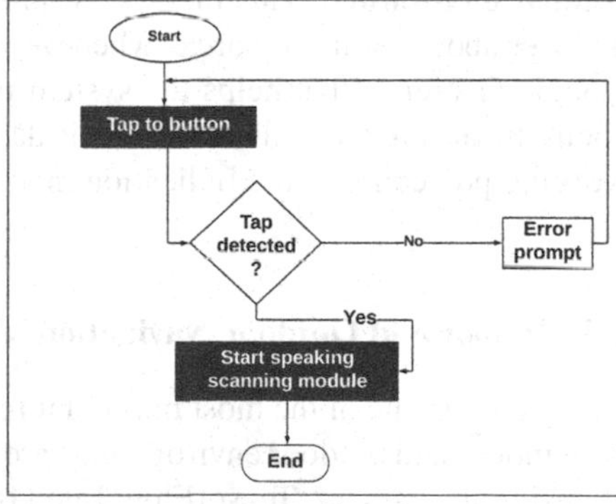

Fig. 5. Touch module flow chart

Jolt Module. Jolt module commonly called a shaking module. This module starts by shaking the phone. This module utilizes the advantages of phone shaking using the accelerometer sensor. An accelerometer is an electromechanical device used to measure acceleration forces. Such forces may be static, like the continuous force of gravity or dynamic to sense movement or vibrations. Acceleration is the measurement of the change in velocity or speed divided by time. In unwanted circumstances, if the phone shakes more than three times, the phone sends the current location of the blind person to the selected contact number automatically. It also calls one of the trusted numbers. When the phone shakes continuously, the trusted person receives notifications automatically and can see the user movement. In Fig. 6, the working procedure of 6 the jolt module is shown.

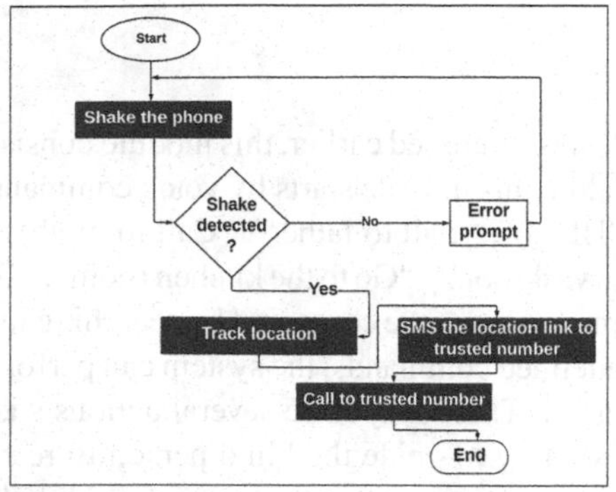

Fig. 6. Jolt module flow chart

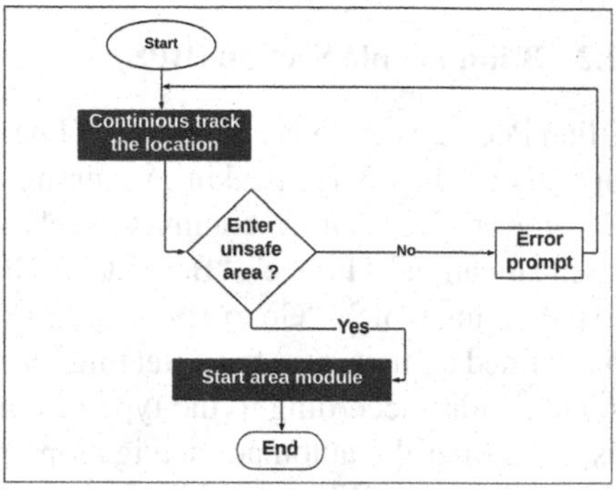

Fig. 7. Indication module flow chart

Required Module. The Required module can notify about battery level, current time, current date, latest news, etc. Blind people need a lot of things. If a blind person wants to see time, date or battery level then it's very complex. This system automatically notifying about latest news if the user wants to know.

Indication Module. This module ensures location awareness. The module can notify the user about the unsafe areas whenever the user enters in that. The module integrates Google Geofence that helps the system monitor the user's current location and notify about the unsafe areas. This module is designed to ensure user awareness. In Fig. 7, the working procedure of the Indication module is shown.

2.3 Indoor and Outdoor Navigation of the Proposed System

Navigation is one of the most important features of Sightless Helper. In this application, both indoor and outdoor environments are considered. The system can also detect obstacle using the camera. TensorFlow Lite [16] is used to detect the obstacles. Both of the navigation systems are shown in Fig. 8.

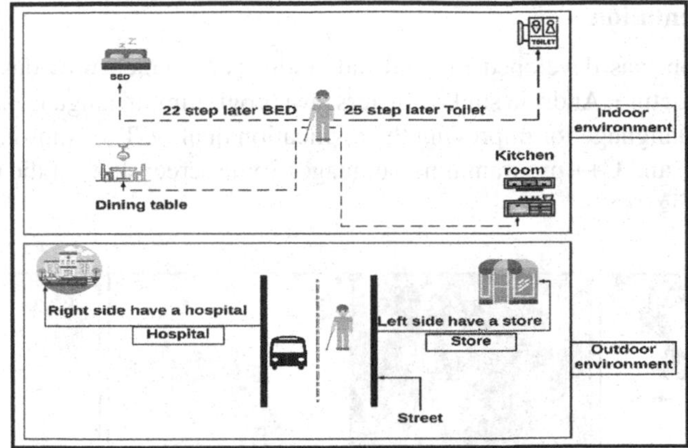

Fig. 8. Navigation on indoor and the outdoor environment.

2.4 Voice Recognition Algorithm

Algorithm 1 shows the voice recognition algorithm. Sightless Helper performs actions through voice command. The voice recognition sys-tem has an imported dictionary that stores the action words. Also, the system can import mobile numbers from the database. Whenever the VI person gives a voice command, the command is recognized by the help of the dictionary. The details sequence are shown in Algorithm 1.

Algorithm 1: VOICE RECOGNITION

```
import the dictionary of action words and the list of mobile
numbers
while true do
  input voice command
  tokenize the keywords from the voice command
    if mobile GPS is enabled then
      if keyword exists in the dictionary as action word then
        Trigger following actions according to the action words:
        Call ();
        SMS ();
        Navigate ();
        BatteryLevelNotifier();
        FootStepNotifier ();
        BarcodeReaderHelper ();
        NewsHelper ();
      else
        Notify wrong command
      end
    else
      enable the mobile GPS
    end
end
```

2.5 Implementation

The application was developed by Android studio [17], which provides a prominent application structure. Android studio bolsters java programming language and the Kotlin programming language for improving the application quality. The Android libraries are composed of C and C++ programming language. Some screenshots of the user interface are shown in Fig. 9.

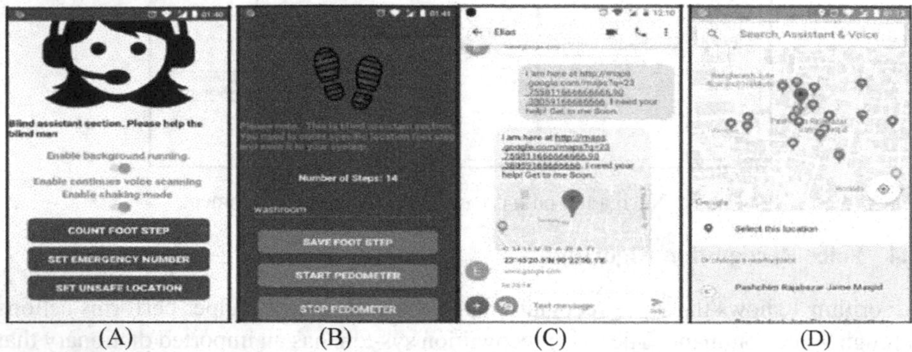

Fig. 9. "Sightless Helper": (A) shows the user interface of BAS, (B) shows the input panel of the footstep counting module, (C) shows an SMS, sent from the VI persons mobile in unwanted situation and (D) shows the Google API for selecting unsafe area.

3 Result and Discussions

3.1 Performance Testing

Since voice command and location sending are the major tools for interacting with the Sightless Helper, performance testing is done on voice recognition and location sending time considering 10 pairs of male and female voices. Partial test results are shown in Table 1.

For Test case 9, each person gave the same voice command to the system for 30 times and the best (B), worst (W), average (A) response time and the standard deviation (SD) were recorded. From the experimental result, it is seen that on average the system takes 6.303 ms (ms) for male voices, and 6.375 ms (ms) for female voices to respond. It indicates that the system can detect both types of voices within a similar amount of time. The best response time found for male and female voices were also the same, which is 5.1 ms (ms). The worst response time for male and female voices was recorded 11.2 ms (ms) and 12.60 ms (ms) respectively. On the other hand, for male and female voices, the average standard deviations were found 0.928% and 1.05%, indicating that the system shows almost negligible fluctuations for voice recognition time. Table 2 shows, the response time (millisecond), distance (km) and GPS coordinate of the sender and the receiver. For testing Location Sending Time in Sightless Helper, an experiment was done to inspect how much time it takes to send the location to a specific number. The experiment consisted of 10 test cases, shown in Table 2. The location was sent to 10 distinct locations and response time was recorded at the receiver's end.

Table 1. Voice command test results of sightless helper on 10 men and women

Test	Male				Female			
	B	W	A	S	B	W	A	S
1	5.2	6.5	6	0.39	5.1	6.5	5.97	0.36
2	5.9	6.9	6.44	0.3	5.1	6.97	5.91	0.52
3	5.7	9.1	6.28	0.96	5.1	11.9	7.03	2.27
4	5.1	10.5	6.9	1.62	5.2	6.2	5.3	0.44
5	5.1	9.6	6.62	1.58	5.1	10.2	6.54	1.37
6	6.1	9.2	6.77	0.85	5.7	12.6	6.76	1.99
7	5.1	8.5	5.86	0.94	5.97	6.9	6.44	0.28
8	5.5	6.4	5.95	0.29	6.1	10.3	6.91	1.16
9	5.1	11.2	6.07	1.73	5.4	6.9	6.1	0.48
10	5.2	6.9	6.14	0.62	5.2	11.6	6.79	1.69
			6.303	0.928			6.375	1.05

Table 2. Performance measurement of data transaction between sender and receivers.

Test no	Response time (MS)	Distance (Km)	Sender(GPS)Receiver(GPS
1	6.2	3.3	23.75, 90.38 23.73, 90.39
2	6.2	2.54	23.75, 90.3824.37, 88.60
3	7.4	20.4	23.75, 90.3823.87, 90.39
4	5.87	13.62	23.75, 90.3824.46, 89.71
5	8.97	3.3	23.75, 90.3823.76, 90.37
6	11.45	242	23.75, 90.3822.34, 91.82
7	8.2	244.2	23.75, 90.3824.89, 91.88
8	8.6	204.6	23.75, 90.3824.41, 88.97
9	4.2	1.5	23.75, 90.3823.76, 90.37
10	9.2	33	23.75, 90.3823.99, 90.42
Average Response time	7.629		
Standard Deviation (SD)	1.98		

3.2 Usability Testing

There were 30 participants whose response was recorded based on the questionnaire of the SUS method [18]. From Fig. 10, it is seen the average SUS score is 72.27 which indicates that according to the [18], this system is suitable for practical implementation. To assess the usability of the proposed system, testing is done based on the System Usability Testing Score (SUS) method [19].

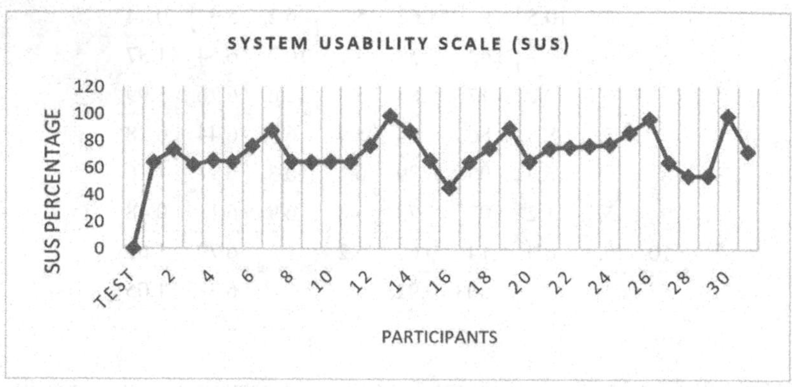

Fig. 10. Usability testing score of sightless helper on 30 users

3.3 Comparison Table

The proposed system provides several useful features. All of the useful features are summarized with some unique contributions and shown in Table 3. It shows the features that are matched or unmatched with the existing applications.

Table 3. Feature comparison of "Sightless Helper" with existing applications.

App name	Key features	Platform	Matches feature
NavEye [6]	Navigational help	Android	Yes
Screen magnifier [8]	Enlarged screened context	Android	No
Smart backpack [9]	Assist blind people	Android	Yes
Blind reader [11]	Read document	Android	No
NavCog3 [12]	Assist blind people in navigating in the large indoor environment	Android	Yes
BLaDE [14]	Reading barcode	Android	Yes

4 Conclusion and Feature Work

In this work, a mobile application is designed in such a way that it can work as a hand to the VI people. Since the Smartphone has become a part and parcel in our life, it is beneficial to Smartphones for developing assistance tools to solve the problems of the disabled 7 people. We concentrated on every aspect of design issues so that the application becomes more usable. Since interaction with the application is a big issue, we considered voice command as the primary interaction method whereas touch screen, hotkey buttons and shaking are used as the alternative. Moreover, the touch screen is designed by audio feed-back so that the VI person can understand what command is he touching on the screen. Shaking and hotkey buttons provide rapid action in dangerous situations. As a result, usability testing of the application provided a satisfactory result. From the experimental result of the voice recognition module, it is seen that the application is very responsive to the voice command. In the case of navigation, we provided both indoor and outdoor navigation facilities. The application also provides online and offline navigation facilities. One of the strong parts of the application is that it concerns the safety of blind people. It can make the VI person cautious about some dangerous areas, and in a dangerous situation, it can send feedback to trusted people in no time. The experimental result shows that the application can successfully send SMS and location to the trusted people. Besides all these features, the application can be used for some daily utilities such as phone calls, news reading, using calendars, barcode reading, battery monitoring. Etc. The plan for this application is to make it learn from the environment. In the future, we have a plan to make the local navigation module more accurate using machine learning algorithms. Besides, a hardware integration with the application might improve the obstacle avoidance capability. Another feature that can be integrated with the system is designing a reader module through a screen touch. Testing the application in real-life for a long time might reveal more problems, faced by the VI people. Solving each of the problems using the available resource of a smartphone will be the future challenge for this application.

References

1. Visual impairment and blindness 2010, August 2016. http://www.who.int/blind-ness/data_maps/VIFACTSHEETGLODAT2010full.pdf
2. Hersh, M., Johnson, M.A.: Assistive Technology for Visually Impaired and Blind People. Springer, London (2010). https://doi.org/10.1007/978-1-84628-867-8
3. Hub, A., Diepstraten, J., Ertl, T.: Design and development of an indoor navigation and object identification system for the blind. In: ACM SIGACCESS Accessibility and Computing, no. 77–78, pp. 147–152. ACM (2004)
4. Ahmetovic, D., Gleason, C., Kitani, K.M., Takagi, H., Asakawa, C.: NavCog: turn-by-turn smartphone navigation assistant for people with visual impairments or blindness. In: Proceedings of the 13th Web for All Conference, p. 9. ACM (2016)
5. Ahmetovic, D., Gleason, C., Ruan, C., Kitani, K., Takagi, H., Asakawa, C.: NavCog: a navigational cognitive assistant for the blind. In: Proceedings of the 18th International Conference on Human-Computer Interaction with Mobile Devices and Services, pp. 90–99. ACM (2016)

6. AlAbri, H.A., AlWesti, A.M., AlMaawali, M.A., AlShidhani, A.A.: NavEye: smart guide for blind students. In: 2014 Systems and Information Engineering Design Symposium (SIEDS), pp. 141–146. IEEE (2014)
7. Vijayalakshmi, N., Kiruthika, K.: Voice based navigation system for the blind people. Int. J. Sci. Res. Comput. Sci. Eng. Inf. Technol. IJSRCSEIT **5**, 256–259 (2019)
8. Blenkhorn, P., Evans, G., King, A., Kurniawan, S.H., Sutcliffe, A.: Screen magnifiers: evolution and evaluation. IEEE Comput. Graphics Appl. **23**(5), 54–61 (2003)
9. Cruz, F., Yumang, A., Mañalac, J., Cañete, K., Milambiling, J.: Smart backpack for the blind with light sensors, ZigBee, RFid for grid-based selection. In: AIP Conference Proceedings, vol. 2045, p. 020054. AIP Publishing (2018)
10. El-Behiery, H., Abdel-Wahab, M.: Smart touch phones blind assistant system. Am. J. Syst. Softw. **2**(3), 72–80 (2014)
11. Sabab, S.A., Ashmafee, M.H.: Blind reader: an intelligent assistant for blind. In: 2016 19th International Conference on Computer and Information Technology (ICCIT), pp. 229–234. IEEE (2016)
12. Sato, D., Oh, U., Naito, K., Takagi, H., Kitani, K., Asakawa, C.: Navcog3: an evaluation of a smartphone-based blind indoor navigation assistant with semantic features in a large-scale environment. In: Proceedings of the 19th International ACM SIGACCESS Conference on Computers and Accessibility, pp. 270–279. ACM (2017)
13. Ranjan, A., Navamani, T.M.: Android-based blind learning application. In: Hu, Y.-C., Tiwari, S., Mishra, K.K., Trivedi, M.C. (eds.) Ambient Communications and Computer Systems. AISC, vol. 904, pp. 247–255. Springer, Singapore (2019). https://doi.org/10.1007/978-981-13-5934-7_22
14. Tekin, E., Vásquez, D., Coughlan, J.M.: SK smartphone barcode reader for the blind. In: Journal on Technology and Persons with Disabilities: Annual International Technology and Persons with Disabilities Conference, vol. 28, p. 230. NIH Public Access (2013)
15. Olmschenk, G., Yang, C., Zhu, Z., Tong, H., Seiple, W.H.: Mobile crowd assisted navigation for the visually impaired. In: 2015 IEEE 12th International Conference on Ubiquitous Intelligence and Computing and 2015 IEEE 12th International Conference on Autonomic and Trusted Computing and 2015 IEEE 15th International Conference on Scalable Computing and Communications and Its Associated Workshops (UIC-ATC-ScalCom), pp. 324–327. IEEE
16. Tensor flow. https://www.tensorflow.org/lite. Accessed 24 Nov 2019
17. Android studio. https://developer.android.com/studio. Accessed 25 Nov 2019
18. Bangor, A., Kortum, P., Miller, J.: Determining what individual SUS scores mean: adding an adjective rating scale. J. Usability Stud. **4**(3), 114–123 (2009)
19. Brooke, J., et al.: SUS-a quick and dirty usability scale. Usability Eval. Ind. **189**(194), 4–7 (1996)

IoT Based Smart Health Monitoring System for Diabetes Patients Using Neural Network

Md. Iftekharul Alam Efat[1(✉)], Shoaib Rahman[2], and Tasnim Rahman[2]

[1] Institute of Information Technology, Noakhali Science and Technology University, Noakhali, Bangladesh
iftekhar.efat@gmail.com

[2] Department of Software Engineering, Daffodil International University, Dhaka, Bangladesh

Abstract. In improvement of the quality of health care services, Internet of Things (IoT) has evolved rapidly for monitoring patient from distance. However, notifying health status based on continuous change of health condition for immediate healing to patient, existing systems has some limitations. In this paper, we demonstrate a smart health monitoring technology for diabetic patients which follows up their health condition depending on sugar level, heart pulse, food intake, sleep time and exercise. To illustrate, this technology takes the variables (data) as input through sensors continuously and process with neural network to evaluate the data, resulting four modes of health risk status: low, medium, high and extreme. The range of the risk status can differ based on patient's type and previous histories of their health. In addition, an automatic phone call and/or SMS notification is being sent to patient's relative along with patient's location if his/her health condition is at high or extreme risk. Besides, it also calls patients nearest hospital in case of extreme risk. However, the system provides allied instruction as voice command to patient's mobile in both cases. This technology has been experimented on 25 diabetic patients successfully and achieved 84.29% accuracy to identify the proper risk level, which is a highly acceptable level of identifying health risk status.

Keywords: Internet of Things (IoT) · Diabetes management · mHealth · Patient monitoring · Neural network

1 Introduction

In this age of Internet of Things (IoT), even now longer waiting time and longer patient monitoring system are common issues. The diabetic patients have to wait in the hospitals and diagnostic centres for hours for fasting glucose test, oral glucose tolerance test and blood pressure check-up. It has become a necessity to develop smart health monitoring system for the diabetic patients, which can be used for daily routine diabetes monitoring. Alongside of monitoring, the system should be able to analyse the patients' current health status and contact the patients' doctors and family members in emergency basis whenever the diabetic condition is deteriorating.

T. Bhuiyan et al. (Eds.): ICONCS 2020, LNICST 325, pp. 593–606, 2020.
https://doi.org/10.1007/978-3-030-52856-0_47

Enormous amount of solutions for diabetic patient monitoring has been developed till today. With the help of Internet of things these solutions can solve diabetic patient monitoring problem easily and remotely while helping massive number of people in the world. In this paper, we have highlighted our system, which is able to provide an automatic monitoring and alert giving system-using sensors, for the patients suffering from diabetes. We have studied and compared current implemented systems and explored the gaps in different systems in order to make a better solution for diabetes patients.

The continuous health monitoring system of any individual using Internet of Things (IoT) and technology has become a foremost requirement these days. In the area of healthcare, these systems need to be easy to use for the user patients and faster to analyse the data. Besides, the system should be able to monitor the health condition of patients anytime, anywhere. As one of the major concerns is diabetes in health care area, development of diabetic monitoring system for diabetic patients demands a smarter way to support them.

In this advanced time, people are using all the smart devices and technology for any problem, but still they need to go to the physicians to diagnose their health conditions manually. Smart solutions for this problem can reduce stress related to journey, save time to meet the doctor and save cost for the patient rather than manual support at clinic.

However, the smart health care system should provide better service for remote health care. Our system and architecture are designed for individual patients or hospitals for monitoring and measuring different parameters and risk factors for diabetics. Along with tracking down the previous health monitoring data, our system also implements easy visualization of patient data.

Another major concern of this system is analysing the data and identifying risk levels for the individual patient. Aside from all these features, our system provides alert to doctors and family members based on the analysed result and identified risk level of any diabetic patient.

In this paper we will discuss our solution based on diabetes patient's food intake, sugar level, heart pulse, and exercise status, risk status with conjunction to SMS and email services, various sensors, parameters for patient's data analysis that implements the drawbacks of most of the existing systems.

Rest of the paper is organised as follows: Sect. 2 describes state-of-art heath status monitoring system related methods, Sect. 3 presents the proposed model, Sect. 4 depicts the experimental results and discussion and major findings based on the experimental result. Finally, Sect. 5 concludes the paper with future research leads.

2 Related Works

Extensive amount of work has been done on the area of smart health monitoring system for various health conditions. In paper [1], the authors have studied on wearable sensor-based systems for health monitoring and prognosis. The maximum number of patients in the clinics was ambulatory and suitable to monitor by sensors, which are wearable. The proposed architecture takes the physiological signals from the patient body with the help of sensors and sends to the nearly central node, which can be any smart device or smart phone having GUI, alarm signal, logical database and sensor control unit. The central node sends the signal or alarm to ambulance and medical centre by monitoring the data.

A review has been done on modelling and designing on mobile health monitoring system [2]. Over fifty different health-monitoring systems were taken in to account, and major advantage of design level, current issues, critical analysis of efficiency and clinical acceptance on the existing smart health monitoring systems were reviewed.

In IoT based Healthcare Monitoring System [3] authors described the working process of a wireless based temperature and heartbeat monitoring system using sensors measuring heartbeat and body temperature of a patient controlled by the microcontrollers which can help a patient in their emergency situation.

For helping the patients on their mental status and physical health IoT has been used in [4]. For remote health care the authors have presented architecture using IoT [5]. They have considering body sensors using devices Electro-cardiogram Sensor, thermometer, Sphygmomanometer, Wi-Fi-module, Arduino. In paper [6], the authors has made an IoT Based Smart Health Care Monitoring System which considers the rural and remote areas people's health related issues like diabetics, Pulse rate and kidney functioning, body temperature, heart health [7].

Machine learning based classification methods are being proposed to test diabetes patient data to provide early prediction of diabetes [8]. It also provides personalized diet control list and activity suggestion to reduce risk. Modalities and components from different impactful intervention are discussed in [9] for management of insulin, self-monitoring and prevention, diabetes education.

A case study on evaluation of experience of continuous monitoring of diabetes patient and variables monitoring using biomedical sensors is proposed in [10] for type 1 diabetes mellitus. In [11], the authors have considered Type 1 diabetes and continuous glucose monitoring for various age women resulting system of insulin informed advisory proved safe and feasible. Type 1 and type 2 diabetes, insulin therapy and remote monitoring for diabetes patients are considered in [12] for cloud system. However, they focused on telemedicine system for the mobile application and health care provider.

A remote patient monitoring system architecture is proposed by [13] for decision support system using electronic health record. A discussion on evolution of inpatient diabetes management is covered in [14] to make a model of remote patient monitoring and management from the formal consultations.

3 Methodology

3.1 Decision Support System

Diabetics' patients are not constantly watched like in a hospital, but are dealing with their disease essentially by themselves and therefore they regularly have to concern about the status of their health condition. The core architecture of the proposed decision support system depends on various IoT devices and sensors that are connected with the mobile application using Bluetooth network.

To illustrate, the system takes sugar level, heart pulse, food intake (in kilo calorie), sleeping time (in hours), work or exercise (burning kilo calorie), GPS information with different sensors by wireless or wired devices [15]. Mobile device integrates all the health information in an application and sends all these to the webserver, which store the data into the database.

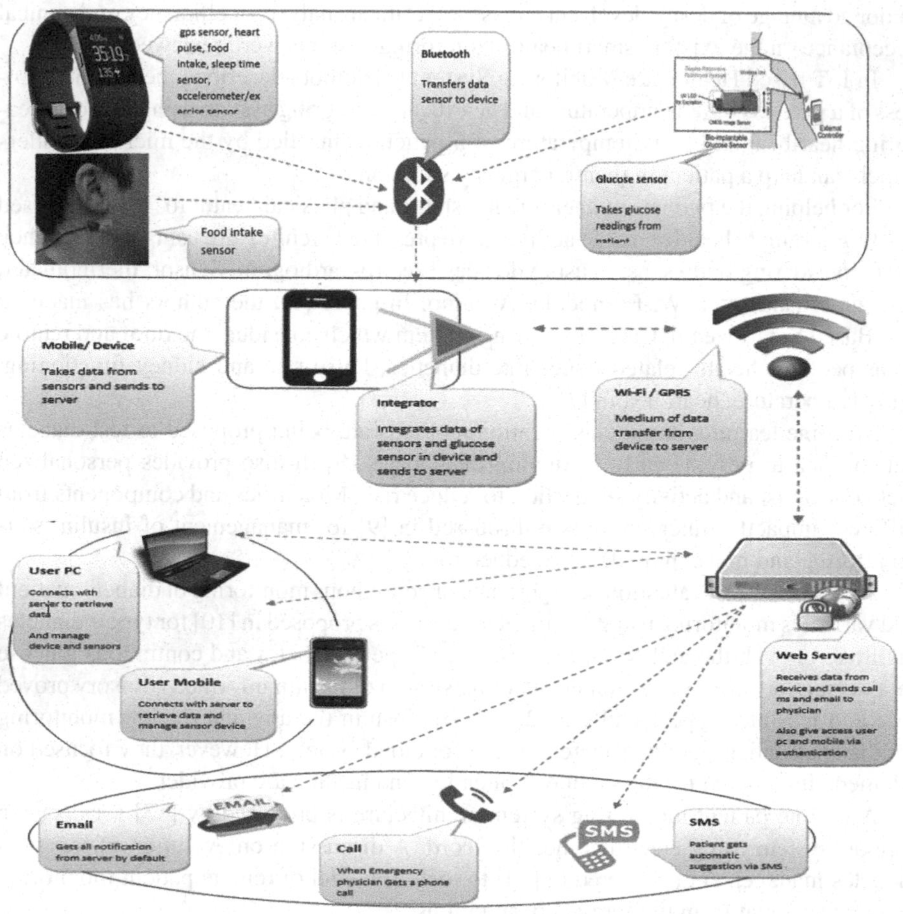

Fig. 1. The proposed architecture for health status monitoring system

The webserver process individual patient data with the proposed neural network (briefly described in Sect. 3.2) and identify the risk level accordingly. For data processing it considers each individual patient's previous history (record) to train the neural network as well as dynamically fix the danger range for that respective patient. However, this danger range will be adjusted later on with consultation of the expert doctor manually considering the patient's overall condition.

This decision support system also integrated with email, phone call and/or SMS system to inform the health condition of the patient to the respective relative and/or nearest hospital. Generally, it stores patient data in six (6) or more timestamp and process the report through mobile application to the patient; therefore s/he can be aware about his/her condition. However, for high or extreme case, the system will automatically give phone call and/or send SMS notification to patient's relative along with patient's current location. Also, the system will send to the nearest hospital of that patient (GPS location), for emergency treatment in extreme case.

The overall framework of the proposed model of diabetes patient health monitoring system is illustrated as in Fig. 1.

User PC and User mobile device can communicate with the server to retrieve data and it can control the sensor and device using Wi-Fi or internet. Users can visit and retrieve data anywhere anytime from the database about their previous and current health condition and sensors status when they are not able to delete or modify any of the information due to their health security reason. Physicians and relatives are allowed to retrieve data from their database and suggest individuals about their status.

3.2 Risk Classifying Using Neural Network

In the field of machine learning, artificial neural networks are statistical learning model, which is inspired by biological neural network. The networks are interlinked set of neurons, sending messages to each other. Based on the inputs and outputs the network can be adopted consistently, making them suitable for supervised learning.

A neural network is a collection of "neurons" with "synapses" bridging them. The collection is ordered in to three leading parts: the input layer, the hidden layer, and the output layer. The hidden layers can have multiple hidden layers up to n hidden layers and are used to get on something critical and complicated. These three layers in the network are called dense layers. These layers do not interact with the external environment, but they have enormous impact on the final output.

In our proposed system, there are seven neurons in the input layer: patient's age, sex, sugar level (mg/dL), blood pressure (mmHg), food intake amount (Kilo Calorie), sleep time (hours) and exercise or calorie burn. However, in our output layer, we have four neurons that will identify the risk level of a patient, which are: extreme, high, medium and low.

Determining an acceptable number of neurons to use in the hidden layers, the following rules have been considered:

- The number of hidden neurons should be between the size of the input layer and the size of the output layer
- The number of hidden neurons should be two-third of the size of the input layer, plus the size of the output layer
- The number of hidden neurons should be less than twice the size of the input layer

However, using too few neurons in the hidden layers will result in something called under fitting. Under fitting occurs when there are too few neurons in the hidden layers to adequately detect the signals in a complicated data set. Similarly, using too many neurons in the hidden layers may result in over fitting. Over fitting occurs when the neural network has so much information processing capacity that the limited amount of information contained in the training set is not enough to train all of the neurons in the hidden layers.

The neural network is then weighted using two key steps: forward propagation and back propagation. In forward propagation, we applied a set of weights to the input data and calculate an output. For the first forward propagation, the set of weights is selected randomly. Correspondingly, in back propagation, we measured the margin of error of the output and adjust the weights accordingly to decrease the error.

In forward propagation, we applied the sigmoid activation function to the hidden layer sums to get the final value. This function actually transformed the input signal into an output signal and is necessary for neural networks to model complex non-linear patterns that simpler models might miss. Then, we sum the product of the hidden layer results with the second set of weights (also determined at random the first time around) to determine the output sum (Fig. 2).

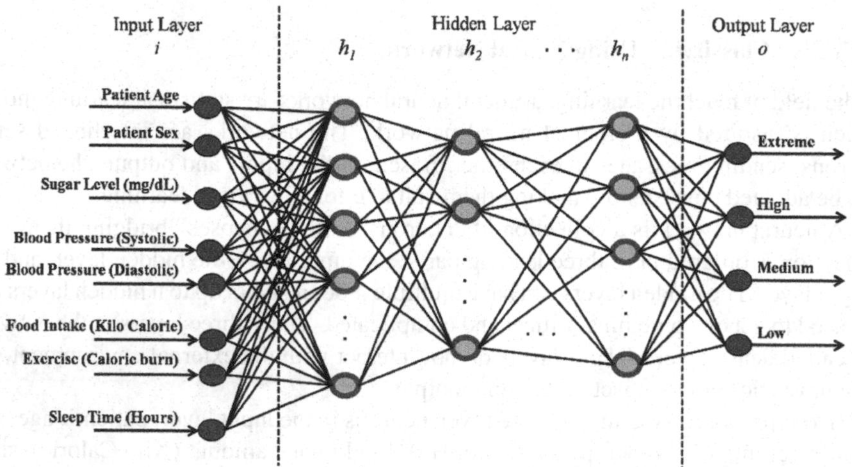

Fig. 2. Proposed neural network to identify patient's risk level

To improve our model, we first have to quantify just how wrong our predictions are. Then, we adjust the weights accordingly so that the margin of errors is decreased. Similar to forward propagation, back propagation calculations occur at each "layer". We begin by changing the weights between the hidden layer and the output layer. Calculating the incremental change to these weights happens in two steps: 1) we find the margin of error of the output result (what we get after applying the activation function) to back out the necessary change in the output sum and 2) we extract the change in weights by multiplying delta output sum by the hidden layer results.

$$Output\ SUM\ margin\ of\ Error = target - calculated$$

To calculate the necessary change in the output sum, we take the derivative of the sigmoid function and apply it to the output sum. Therefore, the derivative of sigmoid, will give us the rate of change of the activation function at the output sum:

$$S' = \frac{d_{sum}}{d_{result}}$$

Since the output sum margin of error is the difference in the result, we can simply multiply that with the rate of change to give us the delta output sum:

$$\frac{d_{sum}}{d_{result}} \times (target\ result - calculated\ result) = \Delta\ sum$$

Once we arrive at the adjusted weights, we started again with forward propagation. Finally, a quick forward propagation has been executed, which yields the final output very much closer to the expected output.

4 Result and Discussion

4.1 Data Collection and Processing

Smart health monitoring system is an IoT (Internet of Things) based system; therefore, we have used various sensors and IoT devices to collect raw data. To examine the system, we have taken 25 sample diabetics patient and did continuous monitoring to collect data. These sample patients were chosen considering the variety of age and gender, who are suffering from diabetics at least for five years. However, 2 months data have been collected, from that we have taken 6 (six) significant timestamp data for a particular day of each patient.

In this data collection process, various sensors and IoT devices give the inputs: sugar level, blood pressure, exercise (calorie burn) and sleep hours. However, in our proposed system we used some more features (data) to prepare the Decision Support System; those data were collected manually from survey. For example, the food intake data was collected from the patients' daily routine and then converted it to numeric Kilo-Calorie value for further process.

Next, we did some data cleaning and processing to prepare a proper format for neural network. Like, the sex has been considered at 1 and 0 for men and women respectively. In this approach, we have prepared a large number of data for our proposed system, with approximate 9000 tuple, one portion of that is shown in Table 1.

In the next stage, specialized doctors' consultation was merged with each patient data. To illustrate, for each particular patient these data was examined by expert doctors to identify the risk level for that particular patient considering those seven types of input data. Finally, a complete set was prepared to train the neural network. A glimpse of data has been illustrated in Table 2, which belongs to a particular patient of 52 years old and female, with different risk level.

However, to test the system, next we took 10 random patient's 7 random days data, excluded from the train set. Then, do the similar process of identifying risk level by expert doctor. Those 70 tuples were examined through our neural network which result has been discussed briefly in Sect. 4.4.

Table 1. Experimental data for health status monitoring system

Patient	Day	Timestamp	Age	Sex	Sugar level (mg/dL)	Blood pressure		Food intake (Kcal)	Sleep (Hrs.)	Exercise (Kcal)
						Systolic (mmHg)	Diastolic (mmHg)			
P1	D1	07:30:25	39	F	87	140	69	200	7	250
		12:22:00			90	146	77	0	0	150
		17:15:26			76	161	75	120	2	300
	D4	06:30:23			81	145	72	0	6	200
		14:22:56			91	140	76	50	0	0
		18:17:32			97	162	68	100	0	240
		21:43:23			79	152	65	0	0	170
P7	D2	06:12:17	45	M	189	138	68	60	6	200
		10:16:56			199	143	65	200	2	0
	D5	07:24:24			172	167	67	0	8	200
		14:53:35			300	164	68	300	0	0
		18:26:42			218	168	69	0	2	350
	D7	06:46:35			102	162	56	0	7	240
		11:46:53			110	158	64	120	0	0
		13:42:23			150	156	76	250	0	0
		18:43:29			180	146	69	50	0	500
	D9	08:30:24			91	148	69	100	8	250
		10:23:57			82	140	71	250	0	0
		16:34:45			78	147	80	0	1	200
P15	D16	08:32:13	56	M	50	141	67	0	8	250
		10:02:54			67	146	65	240	0	600
	D23	09:45:17			56	133	84	370	8	350
		14:17:23			62	153	77	0	0	0
		19:14:26			68	157	69	50	1	50
		21:46:12			57	143	68	0	0	315
	D24	07:56:53			57	146	78	0	7	200
		09:57:25			69	151	67	200	0	0
P20	D11	06:46:43	29	F	58	136	64	0	8	200
		12:24:32			62	140	62	0	0	0
		19:43:23			57	138	68	120	0	120
	D17	08:31:20			62	140	72	220	9	0
		13:42:20			67	148	62	300	0	0

(*continued*)

Table 1. (*continued*)

Patient	Day	Timestamp	Age	Sex	Sugar level (mg/dL)	Blood pressure		Food intake (Kcal)	Sleep (Hrs.)	Exercise (Kcal)
						Systolic (mmHg)	Diastolic (mmHg)			
P23	D25	06:54:31	47	M	51	139	86	0	6	260
		10:00:01			68	143	72	200	0	0
		12:51:53			59	136	68	0	0	0
		15:52:23			56	142	69	300	1	0

Table 2. A particular patient data with risk level

Sugar	Systolic BP	Diastolic BP	Food intake	Exercise	Sleep	Risk
75	141	69	0	300	8	L
134	165	68	220	50	6	M
142	161	67	350	0	5	H
85	155	65	200	240	6	L
57	140	72	0	200	6	L
106	153	69	240	0	7	M
139	145	68	290	0	6	M
75	139	76	50	250	9	L
134	143	63	150	100	7	M
196	145	68	350	50	5	H
57	137	76	80	0	8	L
179	142	66	250	280	6	M
120	120	84	30	90	7	M
152	155	87	350	0	4	H
199	163	76	260	0	5	H
135	127	68	100	250	7	M

4.2 Implementation

The overall system has two different layers: mobile application (patient end) and web application (consultant end). However, this web application is directly operate the decision support system as well as the neural network to process data. This application has been designed to be compliant with the Model-View-Control (MVC) pattern, which improves system security through isolating the model (system data) from direct users. Also, considering the scalability issue for an IoT based software system, MVC will perform better than other state-of-art patterns. More than that, this system can adopt more IoT device or sensor smoothly handling millions of data for the decision support system.

Similarly, the mobile application portion was implemented for Android OS, using Java and SQLite to store the data collected from the patient and his/her medical sensors. Data synchronization between the local smartphone database and the remote health portal database is performed through sending HTTP requests from the smartphone to the health portal server which in turn responds with JSON formatted acknowledge message.

The dashboard for the users is illustrated in Fig. 3 where users can see and control the things. For example, heart rate of a patent is recorded into the webserver that can be seen by the user with the current and previous data with a clear visual representation. Also, glucose data is represented in glucose data page, which can be viewed, by patient or physician. Similarly, positioning and exercise data are recorded in GPS data page, where the patient's each movement of human body wearing the device can be traced for calculating exercise or calorie burn data.

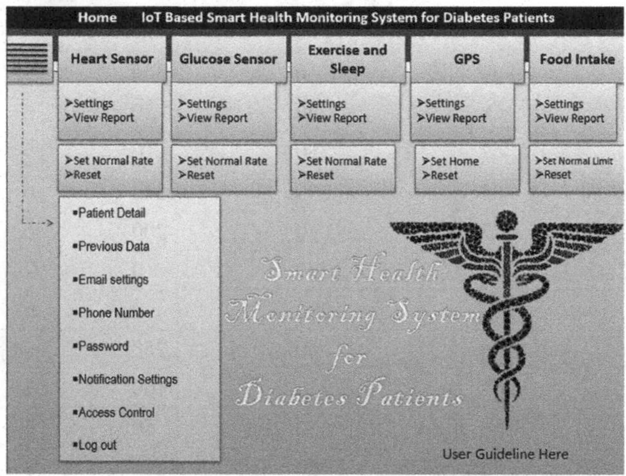

Fig. 3. Online view and control page for user

Location data useful for the excise rate time and patients position record to trace him/her. Steps counted by the sensor are viewed on the steps page and the physical condition of the patient at a particular time. Sleeping time data of the patient is recorded on a regular basis to determine the health condition relation with the defined body is on the trace for treatment. The major information for the food intake and rate of intake with the time and health condition associated with the prescribed patient is generated in the food info page with all the vital information to analyse the physical condition and the amount of ingredients need and present into the body.

Risk level based on the parameters is taken manually from the doctor to identify individual record and condition of health. Decision making process is also considered from the doctor's advice. Client gets user data from the server for specific user and sensor, which can also be viewed, in web. Server can be a windows or Linux server which can communicate with the smart device to store data and represent in front of the user in need as well as previous data and analysis report and the information related to that specific patient and data.

4.3 Experimental Protocol

For identifying the risk levels from the dataset, we have used artificial neural network in this work. We have divided the dataset in to two classes: upper class, containing all the data with extreme and high-risk levels, and lower class, containing all the data with medium and low risk levels.

We then trained our neural network with 9000 data which are acquired from 25 patients. We randomly took 10 patients' data for random 7 days and made them as the test data. To lessen the effect of randomly selected examples to the results, we have continued our experiments 10 times. After that, we have taken the average of performance data in terms of accuracy, sensitivity and specificity.

4.4 Classification Results

We tested our network with total 70 data records. Out of 70 data records, 59 results were predicted correctly. For each of the risk levels our network provided significant results. For the extreme risk level, the network predicted 5 out of 6 correct extreme cases. 23 out of 28 high risk levels where correctly identified for the case of High-risk levels. Regarding medium risk level 11 out of 14 cased were detected. And finally, for the low risk levels 20 out of 22 cases were correctly identified. Table 3 depicts the number of actual diagnosis by doctor and predictions by proposed NN.

Table 3. Numbers of actual and predicted risk levels

	Actual diagnosis by doctor	Prediction by proposed method
Extreme	6	5
High	28	23
Medium	14	11
Low	22	20

From the Fig. 4(a), we can see, the low risk level have been correctly identified with the highest rate of 90%. On the other hand, for the cases extreme and high, the correctly identified rate is 83% and 82% respectively. Medium correctly identified risk levels have the moderate prediction rate of 78%. For our two classes defined in Sect. 4.3 we have identified the True positive, True negative, False positive and False negative cases. Table 4 shows the numbers of identified cases.

In the case of risk level prediction for health issue, these measurements are crucial. The predicted results for each person may or may not match with the person's actual health status. For our experiment, the true positive cases correctly identify both of the higher class and lower-class cases for the persons who actually have those risk levels. From the Table 4, we can see that, our network has identified 28 True Positive cases having the highest number of identifications. True Negative cases are those where the

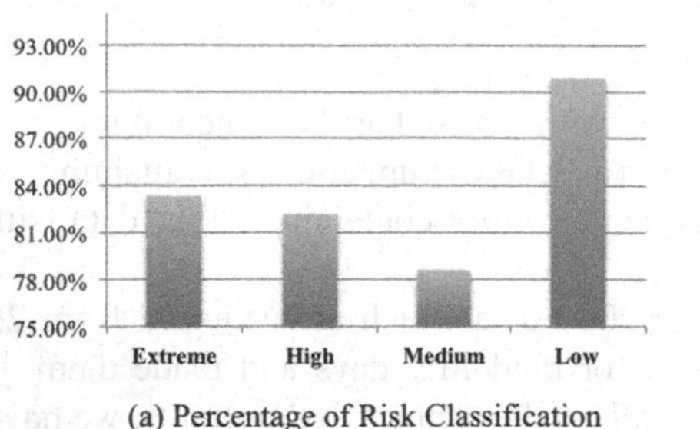

(a) Percentage of Risk Classification

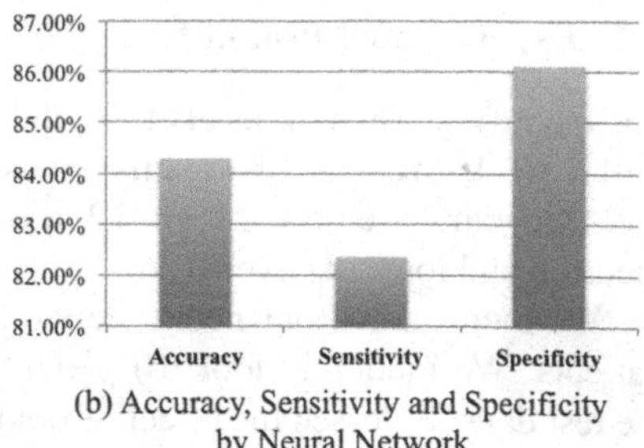

(b) Accuracy, Sensitivity and Specificity by Neural Network

Fig. 4. Performance evaluation of neural network

Table 4. Confusion matrix

TP 28	FP 5
TN 6	FN 6

persons do not have any health issues, and our network predicted 6 true negative cases. False Positive cases confirm the cases were healthy people actually has health issues, where False Negative cases confirm that the healthy person actually has health issue. Both of the predictions can be life threatening for the patients. Our network predicted lowest numbers of false positive and false negative cases resulting 5 and 6 cases out of 70 respectively.

For measuring the performance of our network, we have also identified the sensitivity, specificity and accuracy for the outcomes. The accuracy of the test is defined by the ability of the test to differentiate the patient and health issues correctly. Sensitivity and specificity refer to the correct prediction of positive and negative cases, in our case higher class and lower class. In this case, the performance of the networks considers being satisfactory if these measurements are high. From the Fig. 4(b), it can be depicted that our network provides 84.29% accuracy, 82.35% sensitivity and 86.11% of specificity, which is quite high.

5 Conclusion and Future Scope

Continuous monitoring of health status for diabetic's patient is medically challenged and costly. However, using Internet of Things (IoT) doctors can monitor their patients outside the hospital and also apart from their consulting hours. Connecting smart health status diagnosis devices exploit resources to provide an improved feature of care, which leads to better clinical outcomes. Also, achievement of this system reduces clinic visits, bed days of care and length of stays in hospitals.

In this paper, we proposed an IoT-based health status monitoring system for diabetes patients with the aim of shifting the prominence from a conventional clinician-cantered approach to a patient-cantered one. Nevertheless, the main contribution of this research is the new architecture of a Decision Support System and a Neural Network to identify risk level. This is achieved through remote collection of patients' data using various IoT devices and sensors, and then identifies patient specific risk level through decision support system.

The results obtained from a pilot software system considering end-to-end functionality with a seamless, secure and accurate data transfer from the IoT devices to the server and an effective risk level based decision taken by the system. Although the full extent of the clinical impact on the patients' quality of life should be assessed prior to potential future commercialization, and lessons are constantly being learnt from this work as it progresses. These suggested improvements and further studies are currently part of the authors' on-going research.

References

1. Pantelopoulos, A., Bourbakis, N.: A survey on wearable sensor-based systems for health monitoring and prognosis. IEEE Trans. Syst. Man Cybern. Part C (Appl. Rev.) **40**, 1–12 (2009). https://doi.org/10.1109/tsmcc.2009.2032660
2. Baig, M., Gholamhosseini, H.: Smart health monitoring systems: an overview of design and modeling. J. Med. Syst. **37**(2), 9898 (2013). https://doi.org/10.1007/s10916-012-9898-z
3. Gundre, S., Kamble, S., et al.: IoT based healthcare monitoring system. Int. J. Res. Appl. Sci. Eng. Technol. **7**(6), 988–993 (2019). https://doi.org/10.22214/ijraset.2019.6171
4. Ramya Sri, I., Konduru, S., Madiraju, P., et al.: IoT based health monitoring system. Int. J. Sci. Res. Comput. Sci. Eng. Inf. Technol. **5**(2), 501–504 (2019). https://doi.org/10.32628/cseit195273
5. Warsi, G., Hans, K., Khatri, S.: IoT based remote patient health monitoring system. In: 2019 International Conference on Machine Learning, Big Data, Cloud and Parallel Computing (COMITCon), pp. 295–299 (2019). https://doi.org/10.1109/comitcon.2019.8862248
6. Dinesh, K., Vijayalakshmi, K., et al.: IoT based smart health care monitoring system. Int. J. Inst. Ind. Res. **3**(1), 22–24 (2018)
7. Gupta, N., Chahande, M., Pandey, S.: Study of IoT based health monitoring devices. Int. J. Eng. Technol. **9**, 451–456 (2017). https://doi.org/10.21817/ijet/2017/v9i3/170903s070
8. Alfian, G., Syafrudin, M., Ijaz, M., et al.: A personalized healthcare monitoring system for diabetic patients by utilizing BLE-based sensors and real-time data processing. Sensors **18**(7), 2183 (2018). https://doi.org/10.3390/s18072183
9. Shan, R., Sarkàr, S., Martin, S.S.: Digital health technology and mobile devices for the management of diabetes mellitus: state of the art. Diabetologia **62**(6), 877–887 (2019). https://doi.org/10.1007/s00125-019-4864-7
10. Rodríguez-Rodríguez, I., Rodríguez, J., Zamora-Izquierdo, M.: Variables to be monitored via biomedical sensors for complete type 1 diabetes mellitus management: an extension of the "on-board" concept. J. Diab. Res. **2018**, 1–14 (2018). https://doi.org/10.1155/2018/4826984
11. Breton, M., Patek, S., Lv, D., et al.: Continuous glucose monitoring and insulin informed advisory system with automated titration and dosing of insulin reduces glucose variability in type 1 diabetes mellitus. Diab. Technol. Ther. **20**(8), 531–540 (2018). https://doi.org/10.1089/dia.2018.0079
12. Joubert, M., Benhamou, P., Schaepelynck, P., et al.: Remote monitoring of diabetes: a cloud-connected digital system for individuals with diabetes and their health care providers. J. Diab. Sci. Technol. **13**(6), 1161–1168 (2019)

13. Ahmad, B., Ayu, M., Abdullahi, I., Yakubu, Y.: Remote patient monitoring system architecture for diabetes management. In: 2017 International Conference on Computing, Engineering, and Design (ICCED), pp. 1–6 (2017). https://doi.org/10.1109/ced.2017.8308120
14. Rushakoff, R.J., Rushakoff, J.A., Kornberg, Z., MacMaster, H.W., Shah, A.D.: Remote monitoring and consultation of inpatient populations with diabetes. Curr. Diab. Rep. **17**(9), 1–8 (2017). https://doi.org/10.1007/s11892-017-0896-x
15. Sreevallabhan, K., Chand, B.N., Ramasamy, S.: Structural health monitoring using wireless sensor networks. In: IOP Conference Series: Materials Science and Engineering (2017). https://doi.org/10.1088/1757-899x/263/5/052015

Parking Recommender System Using Q-Learning and Cloud Computing

Md. Omar Hasan[1], Khandakar Razoan Ahmed[1], and Md. Motaharul Islam[2(✉)]

[1] BRAC University, Dhaka, Bangladesh
omarhasan115@gmail.com, razoanahmed421@gmail.com
[2] United International University, Dhaka, Bangladesh
motaharul@cse.uiu.ac.bd

Abstract. Artificial Intelligence (AI) based recommender systems help to make our life easy and comfortable. From simple chatbot to YouTube recommendation, AI is used to recommend news, videos, etc. which provide us more information and saves our time. In big cities, parking seems to be a major problem where commuters need to find a suitable parking space among many parking areas which cause wastage of time and fuel. Our paper proposes a parking recommender system where commuters will be suggested a parking area to a nearby place for helping them to save time, parking cost and ensure high security. To collect data of parking spaces, we propose a Cloud architecture where we use the concept of Edge and Cloud computing to collect and process data smoothly and reduce latency. To deal with bigger amounts of data we use Data Streaming Pipelining to process and analyze those data. We use Amazon Web Services (AWS) to implement our proposed Cloud architecture. For creating the AI based recommender system, we propose the Q-learning algorithm with ε-soft policy to suggest nearby parking areas. Our novel approach will be helpful for both local and global citizens to find an ideal parking area close to their working place, home, etc. Our proposed Cloud architecture is able to reduce latency and make data transferring system faster. Also the Q-learning algorithm can outperform in terms of both certain and uncertain situations.

Keywords: Parking recommender system · Edge Computing · Data Streaming Pipelining · Q-learning · Cloud · AWS

1 Introduction

Nowadays, parking has become a major challenge for modern cities due to the increasing number of private cars. In developing countries such as India, Bangladesh, etc. face a lot of problems due to a lack of parking systems. In Bangladesh, commuters face a lot of problems while navigating to these parking areas because the roads are very narrow and unauthorized parking creates traffic

T. Bhuiyan et al. (Eds.): ICONCS 2020, LNICST 325, pp. 607–618, 2020.
https://doi.org/10.1007/978-3-030-52856-0_48

congestion. Due to lack of parking management system, they spend hours and hours to find a parking area and a free parking space which waste their valuable time. Even, sometimes they park their car in an open space without proper security. Parking has become a challenging issue for developed countries where lots of parking areas exist but people waste their time to find or navigate to a parking area and a free parking space. The concept of the Internet of Things (IoT), Cloud and Machine Learning brings light to this current challenge.

IoT is an idea where all the sensors of our personal computers, mobiles, etc. are connected together and by developing IoT based solutions, our life is improving day by day. To make an IoT based solution we need a large storage system where all our data can be securely maintained. That is why Cloud and IoT are used together. In a parking system, sensors are used to collect data of free parking spaces. These sensors give information about whether a parking space is full or empty. Ultrasonic and Infrared (IR) sensors are used most of the time in parking areas to check parking status [15,16]. To collect data from these sensors we need Edge server and by using Cloud where we can process, analyse and store these data.

Edge computing is an idea where we process and analyse the data as close as possible to the devices where the data is generated. It process and analyse the data locally in real-time. It does process locally at multiple decision points so that it can reduce network traffic. The process of data near Edge devices can reduce the large number of data that are being transferred which helps to get structured data only to Cloud for analysis. It is stored for the further process so that the Cloud has to deal only the data when it needs. In this way, it decreases precious bandwidth, associated cost and server resources. Also, it decreases latency that occurs on other Cloud systems. Edge devices collect large amounts of data as it also handles high-data-rate devices. This amount of raw data is sent to cloud for analysis and inference which can cost a huge number of bandwidth that is precious and sometimes quite tough in many situations. AWS provides AWS Greengrass core service which gives us all the services that we can get from Edge computing. AWS Greengrass is called the forefront of Edge Computing and we use this service for Edge Computing.

As we need to set up edge server, MQTT broker and AWS IoT Greengrass core SDK need to be configured in our computer. The MQTT broker will collect data and send it to SDK and then SDK will send it to Greengrass service. Now, we need Amazon FreeRTOS or AWS IoT Device SDK to be configured with the sensors to interact with AWS Greengrass Core service using local network so that the AWS IoT Greengrass Core SDK will send data to AWS IoT Greengrass service. The AWS IoT Greengrass Core SDK enables Lambda functions to communicate with the Greengrass core service, send messages to AWS IoT, communicate with the local shadow service, invoke other deployed Lambda functions, and access secret resources.

Reinforcement Learning (RL) is an area of Artificial Intelligence. RL gives a better performance where uncertainty exists. In RL, there is an agent who performs action in the environment and based on that action the agent will receive rewards or penalty. The agent will do more actions in order to maximize rewards. The policy defines the learning way of our agent where policy can be different in terms of different scenarios. According to the policy, the agent performs action and changes its states in the environment. Rewards are based on the agent's action in the environment. In [20], the authors first describe the concepts of RL and the implementation of RL in different areas. RL is used in different types of recommender systems [13,19] and these systems perform very well than the traditional systems. Q-learning is a very famous off-policy reinforcement learning algorithms. Q-learning is performed on a Q-table which is basically a matrix. The agent of Q-learning will take random actions by changing its state and learn from both positive and negative actions.

Our proposed system aims to achieve two goals. First, our proposed Cloud architecture will reduce the latency than the other systems. Secondly, the Q-learning algorithm that we use for recommendations will provide better performance in uncertain situations. Our main contributions are listed here:

- We have proposed a Cloud architecture to reduce latency and make data transferring process faster.
- We have proposed an Android application to show the recommendation result through an User Interface.
- We have applied Q-learning using a custom data set with our parameters and our algorithm performs well based on the parameters.
- We have also shown how our proposed Cloud architecture will outperform better.

The rest of the paper is organized with different sections. Section 2 discusses about the previous research works. In Sect. 3, we describe our system architecture. Section 4, we apply and describe Q-learning with epsilon-soft policy. Section 5 is about experimental evaluations and finally, Sect. 6 puts conclusion to our research work.

2 Related Works

The authors introduce a new algorithm called the Parking rank algorithm to recommend a parking area based on public information [1]. They were inspired by the old Page rank algorithm and they introduce their algorithm. First, their parking rank algorithm sorts those places where parking areas exist and they proposed the way to recommend the parking area.

In [2] authors design a parking lot recommendation algorithm where the algorithm uses the minimum short distance to recommend the users. They provide a smart parking system where users can book, navigate to the parking areas and pay their bills online. This novel approach can work in general situations but some uncertain cases where many parking lots exist and security will be a concern this system will not work properly.

In [3] a server-based system is proposed by authors to recommend the parking places according to user distance. They use K-medoid clustering and Conditional

Random Fields to detect user parking. Their approach is unique but for multiple parking areas it might get slow to take data from sensors and the clustering method is not fully accurate sometimes.

Authors in [4] proposed some IoT-based contextualization techniques to reduce the complexity of data processing. Their approach is to collect data from sensors and using a server-based system the data will be contextualized. This will be beneficial for the parking recommender system.

In [5] the authors approached a periodical recommendation using a mobile parking system. They focused on mobile communication such as GPS, NFC, etc. to provide an ideal parking recommender system. In fact, they approached different types of periodical recommendations based on different scenarios. Their novel approach is effective to reduce parking conflict.

The authors in [6] proposed a recommender system for taxi drivers where they can pick up the passengers quickly which helps them to increase profit. They use GPS trajectories of taxis to find the probability of parking places where passengers likely to wait for a taxi. Their recommender system helps both passenger and taxi drivers to find themselves in a quick manner.

In [7] the authors proposed a parking recommendation model based on reservation. Their proposed selection method helps to calculate the optimal objective parking lot. They aim to reduce the waiting time, cost and improve the facilities of parking utilization.

3 System Architecture

3.1 Cloud Architecture

We have proposed a cloud architecture in Fig. 1. Multiple parking areas are shown with sensors e.g. S1, S2, S3, etc. which change its value when the parking space is full or empty. MQTT (Message Queuing Telemetry Transport) broker will collect those data from these sensors and send it to AWS IoT Greengrass core SDK using MQTT protocol which is a Bi-directional process. MQTT broker is a software that runs on our computer and it eliminates the insecure connections, scales, manages all the client's connection states and reduces network strain. MQTT broker can work as one to many or many to one connection and it will send data to AWS IoT Greengrass core Software Development Kit (SDK). Then it will send data upwards where we need AWS IoT Greengrass Core service to process and analyze data in real-time.

AWS IoT Greengrass helps us to run the local computation, messaging, data sync and ML inference capabilities on connected devices in a secure way. With the help of AWS IoT Greengrass, connected devices can run AWS Lambda functions, execute predictions based on machine learning models, keep device data in sync, and communicate with other devices securely – even when they are not connected to the internet. This service will also ensure that the sensor responds quickly to local events. We will apply Data Streaming Pipeline to process the data from Greengrass service which will be bigger and critical during the time to time.

The data steaming pipeline helps to make a smooth automated flow of information from one point to another. This software can handle millions of data at scale in real-time and also it analyzes and stores these data. This large amount of data can be in various formats so it transfers those in one common format. Then it analyzes those data and sends them only if it is necessary. And then the data are stored in the same format. Now for the data streaming pipeline, we have used Amazon Kinesis Data Streams which is a real-time service. This service can capture large amounts of data from thousands of sources. The collected data will be available in milliseconds for real-time processing. Then the Amazon Kinesis Data Analytics service will do the rest of the analyzing part. Amazon Kinesis Data Analytics service is the easiest way to analyze streaming data, gain actionable insights, and respond to user needs in real-time. This service reduces the complexity of creating, handling, and integrating streaming applications with other AWS services. After getting a standardized version of the analyzed data we need to go for the execution part. Therefore we need AWS Lambda which is a server-less service that runs our given code in response to events and automatically manages all the resources for computing. Lambda service will execute the algorithm with all the underlying resources and then send it to the Amazon S3 (Simple Storage Service) for storing data. In this service, we can store and retrieve any amount of data anytime from anywhere on the internet. After the analysis part, all the data we need to store will be stored in this service. Finally, we need the Amazon DynamoDB service which is a NoSQL database service that works fast. By using this service we can create database tables that can store and retrieve any amount of data and can serve any level of request traffic. It provides an on-demand backup capability and also allows us to create a full backup of the created table for long term retention. Now all the analyzed data we need will be available in the database in a standardized version.

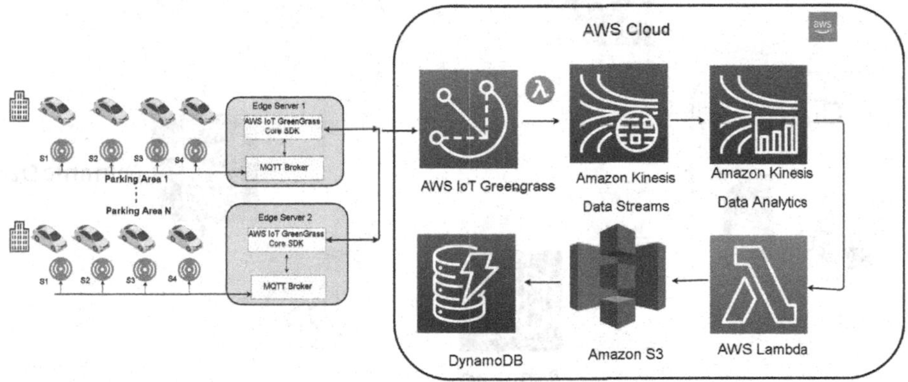

Fig. 1. Integration of cloud and edge computing for recommender system

3.2 Use Case Architecture

In Fig. 2 depicts how the data travel from the DynamoDB to clients webpages or applications screen. Here this architecture is based on Three-tier architecture which is a type of software architecture that used in the Client-Server system. It has basically consisted of 3 tiers or 3 layers. The first part of this architecture is the Presentation layer where this data will be on the client's screen. This tier will interact with the second tier.

The second part of this architecture is the part of the Application layer or we can call logic tier. All the data that the client wants to see on his application which needs to travel through a server-less logic tier. In this logic tier, here we are using Amazon API Gateway and Amazon Lambda for the backend task. Amazon API Gateway and AWS Lambda services can have the most impact compared to a traditional, server-based implementation in this Application tier. The features of these two services will allow us to build a server-less application that is highly available, scalable, and secure. In a traditional model, the application might require thousands of servers. However, by leveraging Amazon API Gateway and AWS Lambda services we will not be responsible for server management in any capacity. In addition, by using these managed services we do not need any operating systems to choose, secure, patch, or manage. So it will reduce risk to your cost from over-provisioning and also reduce the risk of performance from under-provisioning. The last part is the data tier where we are already using DynamoDB. When the client will want to see some data in the presentation tier, our application tier will try to do the backend task and try to bring those data from the data tier and present it to client's application.

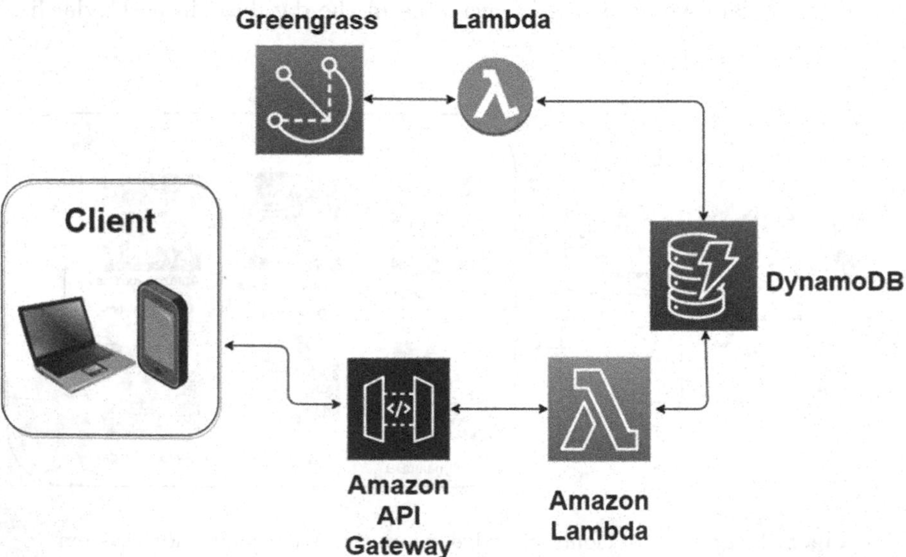

Fig. 2. Use case architecture of AWS services

Figure 2 shows the data collected from sensors will process locally through the AWS IoT Greengrass Core service and store into DynamoDB for reducing latency. In addition, it will also help to do some process locally and people will get their desired information in a secure and faster way.

3.3 Recommender System Architecture

In Fig. 3, the user will be connected with a simple Android application. Through a User Interface (UI) the user can give input to a parking location. The user data will be sent to the AWS services as depicted in Fig. 3. The Amazon Lambda will execute the algorithm using the Q-table and send the results to the user. The table in Fig. 3 shows the free parking spaces in different parking areas e.g. P1, P2, etc. The Q-learning agent will do both explore and exploit and find the best suggestions for the users. The user will see the results or recommendations through the android application.

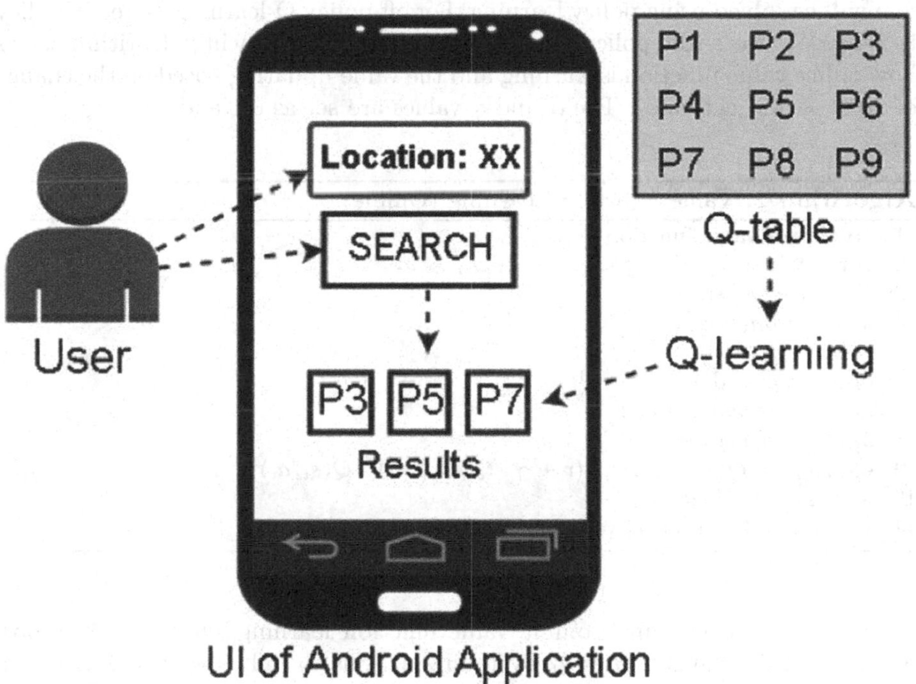

Fig. 3. Visualization of the Q-learning algorithm for recommender system

4 Algorithmic Analysis of Q-Learning

To implement Q-learning, first we design a finite Markov Decision Process (MDP) where states and actions are defined by S and A. We define the reward function as,

$$R_a(s, s') = E(r_{t+1} | s_t = s, s_{t+1} = s', a_t = a) \quad (1)$$

the state transition probability function defined as,

$$P_a(s, s') = P_r(s_{t+1} = s' | s_t = s, a_t = a) \quad (2)$$

and, the goodness of an action depends on the value function $Q(s, a)$ which is,

$$Q(s_t, a_t) = Q(s_t, a_t) + \alpha * (r + \gamma * Q(s_{t+1}, a_t) - Q(s_t, a_t)) \quad (3)$$

We choose four parameters such as 1. distance, 2. time, 3. cost, and 4. security. So, based on parameters $(P_i, ...P_n)$, we can define our following states of the agent:

$$S_{rcp} = (r_i c_i, p_i, ..., r_n c_n, p_n) \quad (4)$$

To define rewards, if our agent directly reaches to goal position we give him reward +10 and for negative action −5. The exploration and exploitation problem will be solved using policy learning. For off policy Q-learning ε-greedy policy is used. We use ε-soft policy for our algorithm. The following algorithm shows how online value function is learning and the value updating based on the change of state s_t and action a_t. The α and γ values are set as 0.1 and 0.9.

Algorithm 1. Value Function Learning (Online)

Initialize value function table
repeat
$s_t = current\_state();$
$a_t = action(s_t);$
reconfig(a_t);
observe_reward();
$s_{t+1} = current\_state();$
$a_{t+1} = get\_action(s_{t+1});$
$Q(s_t, a_t) = Q(s_t, a_t) + \alpha$ *(r + γ *$Q(s_{t+1}, a_t)$ - $Q(s_t, a_t)$);
$s_t = s_{t+1}$, $a_t = a_{t+1}$;
until value function converges

The above algorithm is online value function learning where we show how our agent will change states s_t by taking actions a_t. The agent will get both positive or negative rewards based on the actions taken.

5 Experimental Evaluations

5.1 Q-Learning Agent vs Server-Based Method

We evaluate our proposed Q-learning agent with server-based approach. By using a server system, user request for parking space then the server search for the free parking area and reply to the user. This is time consuming and it can not provide proper recommendation. For our Q-learning agent it will do both explore and exploit to search for best parking areas according to the parameters. We choose some parameters to evaluate the performance and in both certain and uncertain situations our proposed Q-learning agent performs very well.

The comparison table shows some parameters for evaluation and Fig. 4 shows our result. Q-learning agent performs very well that it quickly calculates the distance of the user and based on the selection criteria it suggests user to the parking area. But the server-based method takes request from the user, checks availability and then sends back to user (Table 1).

Table 1. Comparison table

Parameters	Q-learning agent	Server-based method
No. of parking areas (m^2)	10	10
No. of requests (per min.)	5	5
GPS access	Yes	No
No. of free spaces	20	20
Explore or exploit	Both	Exploit only

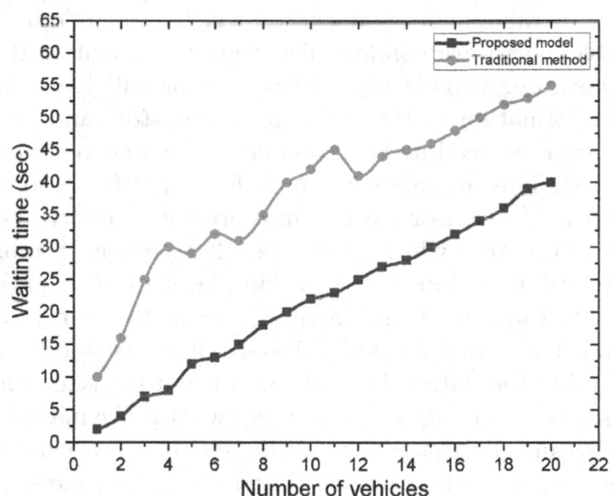

Fig. 4. Comparison of waiting time for recommendation between proposed model (Q-learning agent) and traditional method (server-based method)

Our Q-learning agent performs well in terms of recommendation because the agent makes a balance in both exploitation and exploration. But, the server-based system only calculates the shortest path algorithm which is not an optimal way. Finally, the agent is a pre-trained model based on the parameters that is why it takes less time where the server-based system becomes slow here.

5.2 Simulation of Data Processing of Cloud Architecture

The table below shows a data table where the DynamoDB shows the parking status of multiple parking areas (Table 2).

Table 2. Data table

Sensor no.	Sensor ID	MsgID	Status	Time	Location	Vehicle type	Parking SpotNo.	Other info.
DkU12B1L1EP1S1	S23100	M28122	Empty	02/01/20 18.20.56	UTT-12	–	East Pillar1	On service
DkB2B1L2EP2S3	S23110	M39132	Full	02/01/20 20.20.16	BAN	SUV	West Pillar1	On service
DkG2B1L1EP3S5	S53111	M44142	Empty	02/01/20 10.22.26	GUL2	–	East Pillar3	On service
DkG2B1L1EP2S7	S53222	M45152	Full	02/01/20 12.20.36	GUL-2	SUV	North Pillar2	Out of service

As our ultrasonic sensors will collect data from time to time and we will get all the valuable data through edge server. Through the Edge server, we will get our desired parking lot status and these data will travel trough Greengrass service, Amazon Kinesis Data streams and lastly Amazon Kinesis Data Analytics for processing and analyzing. Then we will get the Data table where all the information regarding parking spots and sensors will be available in a standardized way. In this table, there are columns like Sensor No, Sensor ID, Message-ID, Status, Time, location, Vehicle type. Every sensor will have their unique No and unique ID information so that we can collect, store and then can retrieve these data whenever we need it. For example, in the first row first Sensor, no is DkU12B1L1EP1S1. This unique sensor no is for a specific sensor so that we can trace exactly where this sensor exists. Dk represents a district which is Dhaka then U represents the area which is Uttara, 12 represents Sector/Block which means Sector 12, B1 is building no 1 parking level L1 (Ground), E represents East P1 represents Pillar no 1 and lastly S1 for spot 1. Now, We can say this sensor is from no. 1 spot of Ground-level first pillar Eastside Building 1, Sector 12, Uttara. By using the data table, we can know if the sensor has any unique ID or not or it sends any message or not, if yes what is the message-id which will also be unique because by this id we will be able to know what is the message and what is the current status, when is last time it send message where is the location, etc. By the sensor Id, we will be able to know which type of sensor it is and what is the advantages of it. All this information that we can see in this table mainly process and analyze through the software and then stored in DynamoDB. Now, whenever any data we need we will get from DynamoDB. So, these kinds of tables from thousands of edge servers are coming for processing and in that part services like Data Streams and Data Analytics will help us to easily do that.

6 Conclusions and Future Works

In this paper, we have proposed a recommender system that will help people to find a parking area without wasting time in a nearby location. Our goal is to minimize the data transferring time and make the process faster that is why we approach the concept of Edge Computing, data streaming pipelining and AWS. We apply the Q-learning algorithm to suggest users a parking area in a nearby location. We use minimum distance, time, low cost, and security as our parameters. However, our future plan is to take data of parking space from the real-time scenario and apply advance RL algorithms to enhance the performance.

References

1. Dong, S., Chen, M., Peng, L., Li, H.: Parking rank: a novel method of parking lots sorting and recommendation based on public information. In: 2018 IEEE International Conference on Industrial Technology (ICIT), Lyon, pp. 1381–1386. IEEE Press (2018). https://doi.org/10.1109/ICIT.2018.8352381
2. Fang, J., Ma, A., Fan, H., Cai, M., Song, S.: Research on smart parking guidance and parking recommendation algorithm. In: 8th IEEE International Conference on Software Engineering and Service Science (ICSESS), Beijing, pp. 209–212. IEEE Press (2017). https://doi.org/10.1109/ICSESS.2017.8342898
3. Srisura, B., Wan, C., Sae-lim, D., Meechoosup, P., Mar Win, P.: User preference recommendation on mobile car parking application. In: 6th IEEE International Conference on Mobile Cloud Computing, Services, and Engineering (MobileCloud), Bamberg, pp. 59–64. IEEE Press (2018). https://doi.org/10.1109/MobileCloud.2018.00017
4. Yavari, A., Jayaraman, P.P., Georgakopoulos, D.: Contextualised service delivery in the internet of things: parking recommender for smart cities. In: IEEE 3rd World Forum on Internet of Things (WF-IoT), Reston, VA, pp. 454–459. IEEE Press (2016). https://doi.org/10.1109/WF-IoT.2016.7845479
5. Srisura, B., Avatchanakorn, V.: Periodical mobile recommendation toward parking conflict reduction. In: IEEE 6th International Conference on Industrial Engineering and Applications (ICIEA), Tokyo, Japan, pp. 397–402. IEEE Press (2019). https://doi.org/10.1109/IEA.2019.8715025
6. Yuan, N.J., Zheng, Y., Zhang, L., Xie, X.: T-finder: a recommender system for finding passengers and vacant taxis. IEEE Trans. Knowl. Data Eng. **25**, 2390–2403 (2013). https://doi.org/10.1109/TKDE.2012.153
7. Fu, J., Chen, Z., Sun, R., Yang, B.: Reservation based optimal parking loT recommendation model in internet of vehicle environment. China Commun. **11**, 38–48 (2014). https://doi.org/10.1109/CC.2014.6969792
8. Koster, A., Oliveira, A., Volpato, O., Delvequio, V., Koch, F.: Recognition and recommendation of parking places. In: Bazzan, A.L.C., Pichara, K. (eds.) IBERAMIA 2014. LNCS (LNAI), vol. 8864, pp. 675–685. Springer, Cham (2014). https://doi.org/10.1007/978-3-319-12027-0_54
9. Hasan, M.O., Islam, M.M., Alsaawy, Y.: Smart parking model based on internet of things (IoT) and TensorFlow. In: 7th International Conference on Smart Computing & Communications (ICSCC), Sarawak, Malaysia, pp. 1–5. IEEE Press (2019). https://doi.org/10.1109/ICSCC.2019.8843651

10. Shinde, S., Patil, A., Chavan, S., Deshmukh, S., Ingleshwar, S.: IoT based parking system using Google. In: International Conference on I-SMAC (IoT in Social, Mobile, Analytics and Cloud) (I-SMAC), Palldam, pp. 634–636. IEEE Press (2017). https://doi.org/10.1109/I-SMAC.2017.8058256
11. Rummery, G.A., Niranjan, M.: On-line Q-learning using connectionist systems. Department of Engineering, University of Cambridge (1994)
12. Resnick, P., Varian, H.R.: Recommender systems. Commun. ACM **40**(3), 56–58 (1997)
13. Chi, C.Y., Tsai, R.T.H., Lai, J.Y., Hsu, J.Y.J.: A reinforcement learning approach to emotion-based automatic playlist generation. In: 2010 International Conference on Technologies and Applications of Artificial Intelligence, pp. 60–65. IEEE (2010)
14. Konstan, J.A., Riedl, J., Borchers, A., Herlocker, J.L.: Recommender systems: a grouplens perspective. In: Recommender Systems: Papers from the 1998 Workshop (AAAI Technical Report WS-98-08), pp. 60–64 (1998)
15. Wu, T., Tsai, P., Hu, N., Chen, J.: Research and implementation of auto parking system based on ultrasonic sensors. In: International Conference on Advanced Materials for Science and Engineering (ICAMSE), Tainan, pp. 643–645. IEEE Press (2016). https://doi.org/10.1109/ICAMSE.2016.7840267
16. Shao, Y., Chen, P., Cao, T.: A grid projection method based on ultrasonic sensor for parking space detection. In: IGARSS 2018–2018 IEEE International Geoscience and Remote Sensing Symposium, Valencia, pp. 3378–3381. IEEE Press (2018). https://doi.org/10.1109/IGARSS.2018.8519022
17. Sutton, R.S., Barto, A.: Reinforcement Learning: An Introduction. MIT Press, Cambridge (1998)
18. Islam, M.M., Khan, Z., Alsaawy, Y.: An implementation of harmonizing internet of things (IoT) in cloud. In: Pathan, A.-S.K., Fadlullah, Z.M., Guerroumi, M. (eds.) SGIoT 2018. LNICST, vol. 256, pp. 3–12. Springer, Cham (2019). https://doi.org/10.1007/978-3-030-05928-6_1
19. Taghipour, N., Kardan, A., Ghidary, S.S.: Usage-based web recommendations: a reinforcement learning approach. In: Proceedings of the 2007 ACM Conference on Recommender Systems, pp. 113–120. ACM (2007)
20. Bu, X., Rao, J., Xu, C.: Coordinated self-configuration of virtual machines and appliances using a model-free learning approach. IEEE Trans. Parallel Distrib. Syst. **24**, 681–690 (2013). https://doi.org/10.1109/TPDS.2012.174
21. Oshii, K., Goto, M., Komatani, K., Ogata, T., Okuno, H.G.: Hybrid collaborative and content-based music recommendation using probabilistic model with latent user preferences. In: ISMIR, vol. 6, p. 7 (2006)
22. Song, Y., Dixon, S., Pearce, M.: A survey of music recommendation systems and future perspectives. In: 9th International Symposium on Computer Music Modeling and Retrieval (2012)
23. Shani, G., Heckerman, D., Brafman, R.I.: An MDP-based recommender system. J. Mach. Learn. Res. **6**(Sep), 1265–1295 (2005)
24. Suhr, J.K., Jung, H.G., Bae, K., Kim, J.: Automatic free parking space detection by using motion stereo-based 3D reconstruction. Mach. Vis. Appl. **21**(2), 163–176 (2010)
25. Elliott, R.J., Aggoun, L., Moore, J.B.: Hidden Markov Models. Springer, Heidelberg (1995). https://doi.org/10.1007/978-0-387-84854-9
26. Amazon Homepage. https://aws.amazon.com
27. Towards Data Science. https://towardsdatascience.com

Advanced Artistic Style Transfer Using Deep Neural Network

Kabid Hassan Shibly(✉), Sazia Rahman, Samrat Kumar Dey, and Shahadat Hossain Shamim

Dhaka International University, Dhaka, Bangladesh
khshibly00@gmail.com

Abstract. At present, neural style transfer technique is gaining more and more popularity in different fields like sports and entertainment. During the artistic style transfer of an image, style loss and content loss occurs. Several research works are being performed in present with a view to reduce the rate of both style and content loss, but some of these processes require much time for style transfer. In this paper, we propose a style transfer method using convolutional neural network that minimizes the rate of style and content loss in a minimal time compared to some other works. The proposed method is applied on different images and artworks. The results are compared with some recent research works related to this method and the proposed method is found to be 5–7% more efficient and faster than those related works.

Keywords: Neural network · Deep Neural Network (DNN) · Convolutional Neural Network (CNN) · Visual Geometry Group (VGG) · Neural Style Transfer (NST)

1 Introduction

Neural style transfer of image is a technique that is used to optimize image. Using this technique, the artistic style of one image can be adopted into another different image. To recreate any painting by following its original version requires a large amount of time and artistic skill. NST technique was proposed by Gatys et al. [1] used Convolutional Neural Network (CNN) to capture the style of an artwork and to pass it to other images. In their proposed technique CNN is able to store both style information and the content information of the art.

In NST technique; a content image, a style image from artwork and an input image is provided. After style transferring, the style of the input image changes according to the artistic image style and it is provided as the generated result image. Thus, NST easily applies the style of an artwork on another image.

There have been several works on NST technique in recent years. Various types of convolutional neural networks are used in these works such as deep convolutional neural network, feed-forward convolutional network, compact

T. Bhuiyan et al. (Eds.): ICONCS 2020, LNICST 325, pp. 619–628, 2020.
https://doi.org/10.1007/978-3-030-52856-0_49

feed-forward convolutional network. [2–4] Throughout the process of style transferring, content loss or style loss can occur. Content loss function and style loss function is used to express the measurement of loss through the transfer process. Although different works on NST assure minimal loss of content and style, many of them require a vast amount of time for style transfer of image which can be a drawback of work.

The purpose of our work is to assure neural style transfer within minimal time along with minimizing style loss and content loss of an image. We have used CNN for neural style transfer of image. Here, feature layers are used to calculate feature loss by which the loss rate of style and content can be easily found and minimized. After the regeneration process, the styled images are provided as output. In Sect. 2, we have discussed about some works which are related to NST. The proposed methodology and result is presented in Sect. 3 and 4. And finally, the article is concluded in Sect. 5.

2 Related Work

In recent times, there have been multiple number of research works based on NST for image, video, text and so on. In this section, some research works based on neural style transfer technique are discussed.

An NST algorithm is proposed in [2] that is based on the Markov random field model and trained by deep convolutional neural network. They stated that NST method with summary cannot constrain spatial layout which provides less visually plausible result. They applied the Markov random field method on both photographic and non-photo realistic synthesis tasks which increases visual plausibility.

Feed-forward convolutional network was used in [3] for NRT of real-time videos. They proposed a hybrid loss to capitalize the content information, style information and temporal information. They also proposed a two-frame synergic training mechanism to calculate temporal loss.

Compact feed-forward convolutional networks were used by authors of [4] to generate multiple samples of the same arbitrary size texture and to transfer artistic style from given image to any other image. They showed that generative approach can produce quality texture than descriptive method. They proposed a generative method which is faster and more memory efficient than descriptive method. They also proposed a multi-scale generative architecture for their task.

The authors of [5] used the dual-stream deep convolutional network and edge-preserving filter in image style transfer process. They used an additional similarity loss function to constrain reconstruction and style transfer procedures.

Neural style transfer was treated as a domain adaptation problem by authors [6]. In their work, they showed theoretically that Gram matrices of feature map is equivalent to minimize the Maximum Mean Discrepancy with the second order polynomial kernel. They also extended the original NST method with different distribution algorithms.

An algorithm for photographic style transfer using deep learning approach was proposed in [7]. They also applied their method for different applications such as alternation of weather or time of the day of an image or transferring artistic edits from one image to another.

Authors of [8] proposed a style transfer network called StyleBank which consists of multiple convolution filter banks and each of these filters represents a style for neural image transfer. They compared their method with different methods and displayed that their result is easy to use and qualitatively better than existing methods.

A Trained convolutional neural network was used by [9] authors for solving the problem of face swapping in images. They tried to capture the appearance of the target identity from an unstructured collection of images. They devised a new loss function so that the network can produce highly photorealistic results.

A comparison among different methods and algorithms of NST qualitatively and quantitatively in [10]. They also proposed a taxonomy of current algorithms related to NST and discussed various applications of NST.

A technique was proposed in [11] that can transfer the painting from a head portrait onto another. They used convolutional neural networks and presented an extension to video. They stated that their approach transfers the painting style while maintaining the input photograph identity and significantly reduces facial deformations over state of the art.

A method was proposed by authors of [12] to tackle the limitations of universal style technique by whitening and coloring feature transform. To generate the effectiveness of their algorithm, they generated high quality stylized images and compared them with different methods.

The authors of [13] presented a method that takes raster image and provides painting-like image. They discussed the steps of their method where the images are segmented for computing brush stroke paths if any holes on regions are filled and the axis of the regions are pieced together then sorted the spatial order. Then the brush paths are provided brush strokes which makes the image look like a painting.

A neural style transfer algorithm was presented in [14] to resolve the flexibility speed problem of the feed-forward method. They used adaptive instance normalization layer to align the mean and variance of the content features with the mean and variance of the style feature. They also compared their result with different style transfer methods.

An optimization objective is presented in [15] that can combine the content structure and style textures in a single layer of the pre-trained network. Their proposed optimization objective is dependent on one layer of the CNN while existing methods that use multiple layers. They also showed that the results images of their work were better than the results of similar methods.

An approach to capture particularities and variations of different styles and contents was proposed in [16]. Fixpoint triplet style loss and disentanglement loss concept was introduced in their work in order to present these variations. Again various evaluation methods were proposed to measure the importance of these two losses. A qualitative result also was provided to show the importance of their approach.

A content transformer module between encoder and decoder was presented in [17]. Along with this, a normalization layer was also present for synthesis of higher resolution images. Qualitative and quantitative evaluations of their work was also presented.

3 Methodology

The proposed method is implemented using Python language on a computer system of Windows 10 64 bit operating system with 2.10 GHz processor speed and 4 GB RAM. We have used the VGG network to perform object recognition and localization. The 19 layer VGG network's feature space has been used in its normalized version. Here, we have scaled the weight of convolutional filters over images and positions. Though the same scaling or re-scaling can be done with 19 layer VGG network, it can be done without significant change with the output. Because this network contains no normalization over features, we prefer not to use any fully connected layers. For synthesizing images, we found better results using average normalization rather than fully normalization. Figure 1 displays the graphical representation of our proposed method.

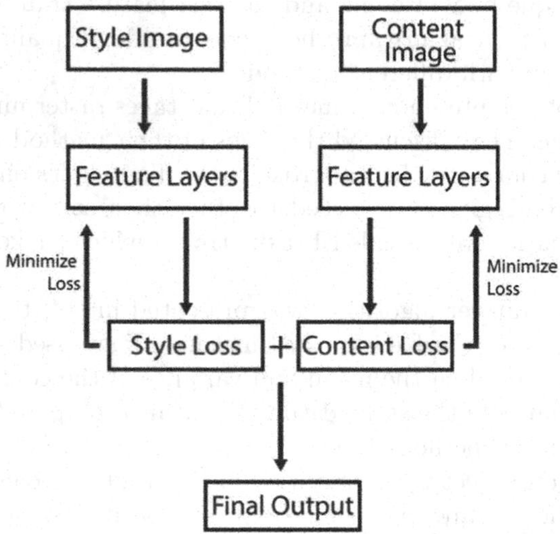

Fig. 1. Graphical representation of our proposed method

Here, starting with content, each image given in encoded in each layer of the Convolutional Neural Network. A layer with distinct filters with feature maps. The responses of a layer can be fixed in a matrix.

The image that is encoded in multiple layers, to visualize that image can perform gradient descent to find a similar image matched feature with the original image. We have defined the squared-error loss between the two feature representations in Eq. (1).

$$L_{content}(\overrightarrow{p}, \overrightarrow{x}, l) = \frac{1}{2} \sum_{i,j} F^l_{ij} - P^l_{ij} \tag{1}$$

The derivative of this loss with respect to the activations in layer equals in Eq. (2),

$$\frac{\delta L_{content}}{\delta F^l_{ij}} = \begin{cases} (F^l - P^l)_{ij}, & \text{if } F^l_{ij} > y0 \\ 0, & \text{if } F^l_{ij} < 0 \end{cases} \tag{2}$$

From this, the image can be computed using standard error backpropagation. This will make changes in the initial image and will generate a response in a certain CNN layer as the original image. Along with the processing of the network going up order, the input image converts into an image that is increasingly sensitive to the actual content of the image. But it changes reasonably its exact aspects. The high-level or high-valued contents like objects and their arrangements are captured in higher layers. The pixel values of the reconstructed image were not restrained by the input image. So, the lower-level layers are can reproduce the original image pixels. By this mean higher layers of the network can be referred for content representation.

To capture style and apply that to the reconstructed image, a feature space design is used. It sums up an interaction between filter responses and the supposition is dominated in the feature maps as shown in Eq. (3),

$$G^l_{ij} = \sum_k F^l_{ik} F^l_{jk} \tag{3}$$

When we added the feature interactions in different layers, a static, different scale rendition of the input image, which captures its texture information. We can visualize the information captured by the style feature spaces which is built on different layers that match the input image style. We used gradient descent from a white noise image. It minimizes the mean-squared distance between the values of the Gram matrices from the original image and the Gram matrices of the image to be generated as shown in Eq. (4),

$$E_l = \frac{1}{4N_l^2 M_l^2} \sum_{i,j} (G^l_{ij} - A^l_{ij})^2 \tag{4}$$

$$L_{style}(\overrightarrow{a}, \overrightarrow{x}) = \sum_{l=0}^{L} w_l E_l \tag{5}$$

The total loss is shown in Eq. (5). So, the derivative with activations in layer can be calculated with Eq. (6).

$$\frac{\delta E_l}{\delta F^l_{ij}} = \begin{cases} \frac{1}{N_l^2 M_l^2}((F^l)^T(G^l - A^l))_i j & \text{if } F_i j^l > 0 \\ 0 & \text{if } F_i j^l < 0 \end{cases} \tag{6}$$

To transfer the style we have to consider both content and style. The captured content and style we have to represent these in the input image. The content and style feature represents in many layers in the CNN. The loss function we can portray in the Eq. (7),

$$L_{total}(\overrightarrow{p}, \overrightarrow{a}, \overrightarrow{x}) = \alpha L_{content}(\overrightarrow{p}, \overrightarrow{x}) + \beta L_{style}(\overrightarrow{a}, \overrightarrow{x}) \tag{7}$$

The gradient with respect to the pixel values can be used as input for some numerical optimization strategy. To get information from image we need to match the image sizes. We resize the style image exactly to the size of content image. Then we go for computing the feature. The texture or style feature of the lower layer performs like a specific image for the style image.

4 Result Analysis

To demonstrate both content and style in the CNN we mix these two features from two different images and represent in a single image. Here, for experiment purpose, we use a photograph of a random Bangladeshi Photographer and a famous art named "Two Faces" by Zainul Abedin in Fig. 2. We tried to manipulate both content and style in a new independent, meaningful image.

But, we cannot extract content and style from an image completely. Working on this we tried to keep the content of one image and style of another image. But, in a term of conventional way the perfect image cannot exist. During the procedure, we tried to minimize the loss using the loss function. And worked on both content and style features. We have the power to control the focus, the content or style which will get more preference.

Figure 3 displays the result of style transfer using different arts by various artists of Bangladesh (Zainul Abedin, Rafiqun Nabi, Saiful Islam, Shahbuddin, Shidhir Bhattacharjaa) with a single source image.

Most of the cited articles in Table 1 used VGG networks except Huang et al. [14]. VGG network is a widely used network. Though it is a bit challenging to train this network, it provides significant results after being trained. In ImageNets such as VGGNet, ResNet, Inception, Xception, ResNet provides more accurate result but, VGGNet provides better results in terms of performance and speed [18,19].

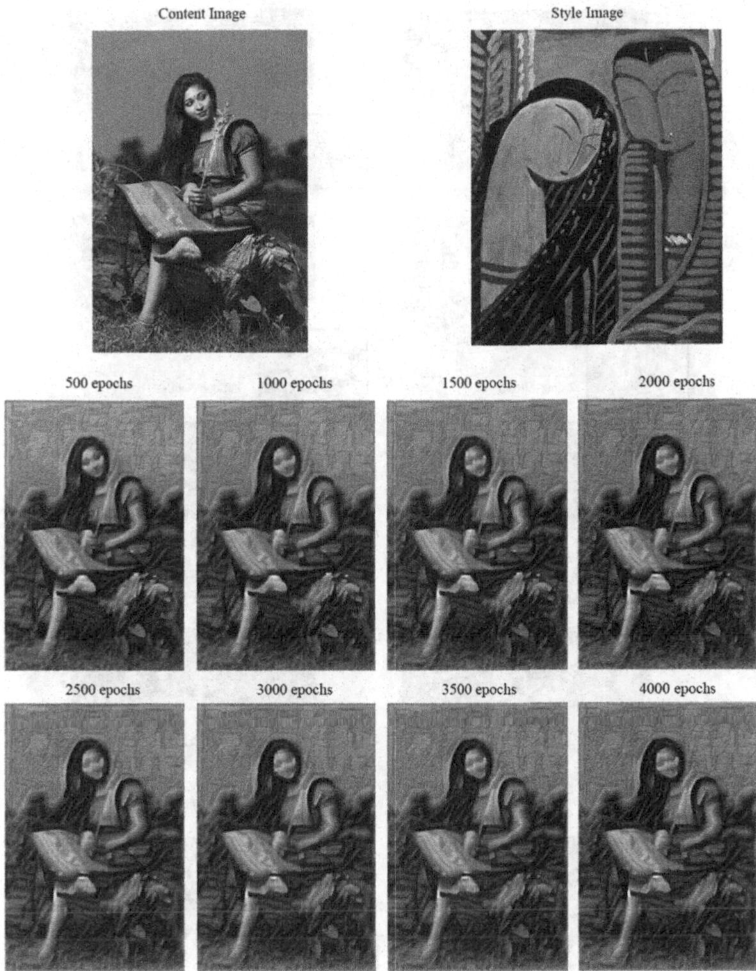

Fig. 2. Style transfer of an image by our proposed method

Figure 4 displays the result of style transfer using different methods along with our proposed method. From this figure, it can be seen that the loss rate of both content and style of the image styled by our proposed method is quite less compared to other methods cited in the paper. In Table 1 we showed the result of Log (Ls), Preference (%) and Time/sec compared with some other style transfer methods. The comparison result among the proposed method and some other related works are displayed in Fig. 5.

From the comparison, it can be seen that the time requirement of our proposed system is quite lower compared to other related works along with assuring minimal amount of style and content loss.

Fig. 3. Artistic transformation based on arts by various artists of Bangladesh

Table 1. Comparison among different styling transfer methods

	Chen et al. [15]	Huang et al. [14]	T. Net [13]	Gatys et al. [1]	Li et al. [9]	Proposed method
Log(Ls)	7.4	7.0	6.8	6.7	6.3	6.7
Preference%	15.7	24.9	12.7	16.4	30.3	15.2
Time/sec	2.1	0.20	0.18	21.2	0.83	0.91

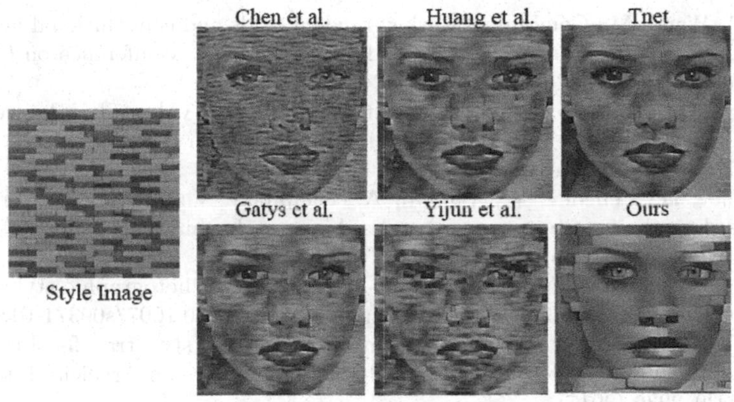

Fig. 4. Style transfer of an image by different methods

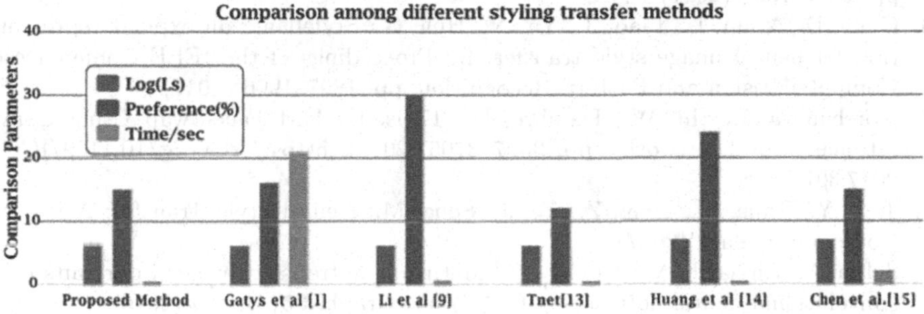

Fig. 5. A comparison among different styling method with proposed method

5 Conclusion

Though style transfer of image is a popular technique nowadays, a higher loss rate of content or style is a limitation of it. In this paper, we have used the VGG network to extract content and style from image and calculated the content and style loss. In order to do that we have applied feature analysis technique on the layers of CNN. And after minimizing the loss, the generated styled image is delivered as output which has a lower rate of content and style loss. This method is simpler compared to different methods of styling. Therefore, it might be proved beneficial for minimizing the loss rate while style transferring of an image.

References

1. Gatys, L.A., Ecker, A.S., Bethge, M.: Image style transfer using convolutional neural networks. In: Proceedings of the IEEE Conference on Computer Vision and Pattern Recognition, pp. 2414–2423 (2016)

2. Li, C., Wand, M.: Combining Markov random fields and convolutional neural networks for image synthesis. In: Proceedings of the IEEE Conference on Computer Vision and Pattern Recognition, pp. 2479–2486 (2016)
3. Huang, H., et al.: Real-time neural style transfer for videos. In: Proceedings of the IEEE Conference on Computer Vision and Pattern Recognition, pp. 783–791 (2017)
4. Ulyanov, D., Lebedev, V., Vedaldi, A., Lempitsky, V.: Texture networks: feed-forward synthesis of textures and stylized images. In: International Conference on Machine Learning, pp. 1349–1357 (2016)
5. Wang, L., Wang, Z., Yang, X., Hu, S.-M., Zhang, J.: Photographic style transfer. Vis. Comput. **36**(2), 317–331 (2018). https://doi.org/10.1007/s00371-018-1609-4
6. Li, Y., Wang, N., Liu, J., Hou, X.: Demystifying neural style transfer. In: Proceedings of the Twenty-Sixth International Joint Conference on Artificial Intelligence, pp. 2230–2236 (2017)
7. Luan, F., Paris, S., Shechtman, E., Bala, K.: Deep photo style transfer. In: Proceedings of the IEEE Conference on Computer Vision and Pattern Recognition, pp. 6997–7005 (2017)
8. Chen, D., Yuan, L., Liao, J., Yu, N., Hua, G.: Stylebank: an explicit representation for neural image style transfer. In: Proceedings of the IEEE Conference on Computer Vision and Pattern Recognition, pp. 1897–1906 (2017)
9. Korshunova, I., Shi, W., Dambre, D., Theis, L.: Fast Face-Swap Using Convolutional Neural Networks, pp. 3697–3705 (2017). https://doi.org/10.1109/ICCV.2017.397
10. Jing, Y., Yang, Y., Feng, Z., Ye, J., Song, M.: Neural Style Transfer: A Review. Computer Science (2017)
11. Selim, A., Elgharib, M., Doyle, L.: Painting style transfer for head portraits using convolutional neural networks. ACM Trans. Graph. **35**(4), 129 (2016)
12. Li, Y., Fang, C., Yang, J., Wang, Z., Lu, X., Yang, M.H.: Universal style transfer via feature transforms. In: Advances in Neural Information Processing Systems, pp. 385–395 (2017)
13. Gooch, B., Coombe, G., Shirley, P.: Artistic vision: painterly rendering using computer vision techniques. In: Proceedings of the 2nd International Symposium on Non-Photorealistic Animation and Rendering. ACM (2002)
14. Huang, X., Belongie, S.: Arbitrary style transfer in real-time with adaptive instance normalization. In: Proceedings of the IEEE International Conference on Computer Vision, pp. 1501–1510 (2017)
15. Chen, T.Q., Schmidt, M.: Fast patch-based style transfer of arbitrary style. In: Proceedings of the NIPS Workshop on Constructive Machine Learning (2016)
16. Kotovenko, D., Sanakoyeu, A., Lang, S., Ommer, B.: Content and style disentanglement for artistic style transfer. In: The IEEE International Conference on Computer Vision, pp. 4422–4431 (2019)
17. Kotovenko, D., Sanakoyeu, A., Ma, P., Lang, S., Ommer, B.: A content transformation block for image style transfer. In: 2019 IEEE/CVF Conference on Computer Vision and Pattern Recognition (CVPR), pp. 10024–10033 (2019)
18. Wei, T., Wang, C., Rui, Y., Chen, C.W.: Network morphism. In: International Conference on Machine Learning, pp. 564–572 (2016)
19. Simonyan, K., Zisserman, A.: Very deep convolutional networks for large-scale image recognition. arXiv preprint arXiv:1409.1556 (2014)

Block Chain Applications

Examining Usability Issues in Blockchain-Based Cryptocurrency Wallets

Md Moniruzzaman(✉), Farida Chowdhury, and Md Sadek Ferdous

Shahjalal University of Science and Technology, Sylhet, Bangladesh
monirulhasann@gmail.com, {farida-cse,sadek-cse}@sust.edu

Abstract. Blockchain has emerged as a revolutionary technology that has been envisioned to disrupt several industries, including financial domains with its decentralised and highly-secure design. However, since the beginning of its evolution, it has been highly criticised for the difficulties in dealing with it properly. As cryptocurrency is the most successful application of blockchain, we aim to identify the potential obstacles and usability issues, which might hinder its wide-scale adoption, of five applications (i.e., wallets) that are used to manage cryptocurrencies. Applying the analytical cognitive walk-through usability inspection method, we investigate common usability issues with desktop and mobile-based wallets. Our results reveal that both wallets lack good usability in performing the fundamental tasks which can be improved significantly. We summarise our findings and point out the aspects where the issues exists so that improving those areas can result in better user experience and adoption.

Keywords: Usability · Human computer interaction · Cryptocurrency · Blockchain · Cognitive walk-through · User-interface · User-experience

1 Introduction

With the inception of Bitcoin in 2008 [1] a new form of digital currency called cryptocurrency has come into existence. The primary goal of such a digital currency is to carry out financial transactions among respective parties without any trusted intermediaries. This is fundamentally different to the existing financial transactions systems which rely on a single or group of trusted organisations for any financial transaction to happen. This strong property of a cryptocurrency is often regarded as a fundamental breakthrough in financial technology domains.

A cryptocurrency is underpinned by this novel technology called Blockchain which is an ordered data structure consisting of consecutive blocks of transactions linked together with a strict set of rules. These chained blocks are then distributed and stored by the nodes in a peer-to-peer network where each new block of transactions is created and appended at a predefined interval in a decentralised fashion by means of a consensus algorithm.

T. Bhuiyan et al. (Eds.): ICONCS 2020, LNICST 325, pp. 631–643, 2020.
https://doi.org/10.1007/978-3-030-52856-0_50

Blockchain exhibits several sought-after properties such as distributed consensus and the immutability and irreversibly of the blockchain state. It is even envisioned that blockchain technology will effectively disrupt several existing application domains and there have been huge interests among the practitioners to explore this avenue. However, as of today, cryptocurrency has remained the most successful application of blockchain technology and because of the worldwide popularity, Bitcoin has become its poster-boy. Driven mostly by speculation and a hype-cycle, the price of a single Bitcoin even reached 19, 783USD in December, 2017 [2]. Following the footsteps of Bitcoin, there are other cryptocurrencies which serve different purposes and target different applications domains. However, the common undertone among all these digital currencies is to either complement or supplement the fiat-currency based traditional monetary systems in different application scenarios. This can only be possible with a wide-scale adoption of these cryptocurrencies.

One of the crucial barriers for the wide-scale adoption of any novel technology is the issues in usability. Usability is the degree to which a software is easy to use and a good fit for the audience. A cryptocurrency heavily relies on cryptographic mechanisms which are often difficult to utilise in an effective manner, even for experienced security programmers [3]. Therefore, it is imperative to investigate how a general user can effectively use a cryptocurrency.

A cryptocurrency use asymmetric cryptography for security through a pair of keys: the private and public. A private key is a secret number that allows a user to use the currency. It must remain secret at all times as revealing it to third parties is equivalent to giving them control over the corresponding currency. As such, these keys are fundamental to manage and transfer the ownership of a cryptocurrency to another user. To facilitate the management of such keys, a software called *Wallet* is used to create and store the required cryptographic keys and hence, plays a vital role in all use cases of a cryptocurrency. If a user loses a wallet due to theft, hard disk crashes or malware, the user loses all the associated keys and hence, the cryptocurrencies. Unfortunately, if this happens, there is no way to recover the lost currencies. Another concern is that these keys are often encrypted with a password. If the user forgets the associated password, there is no way to decrypt and recover the private keys. Hence, there is no other recovery mechanism, provided that the backup is not taken. A wallet is essentially the interface by which a user interacts with the associated cryptocurrency and the underlying blockchain. Therefore, its usability must be studied to find out any usability issues in those wallets, which might be the key obstacles behind any global adoption.

Towards this aim, there have been a few studies, elaborated in the subsequent section. Unfortunately, all these studies focused only on Bitcoin. There are other popular cryptocurrencies which were mostly overlooked in those studies. We tackle this issue in this paper by presenting a usability study, based on a popular analytical method called *Cognitive Walkthrough*, of three popular cryptocurrencies, namely Bitcoin [1], Ethereum [4] and Ripple [5], and their different popular wallets. We provide a short background of these cryptocurrencies and their wallets in Sect. 2 along with a discussion of different usability study methods. Then, in Sect. 3, we analyse the existing works in relation to our current papers.

For each of the selected wallets, recruited participants have been asked to carry out a series of vital tasks which in a way represent the general use-cases of such wallets. We present the description of these tasks and other experimental setups in Sect. 4. Once completed, we have measured and analysed the rate of success and failure of completing the tasks and identified several crucial issues while using these cryptocurrency wallets. The findings of our analysis and a brief discussion are presented in Sect. 5. Finally, we conclude in Sect. 6 with a hint of the future work in this field.

2 Background

In this section, we present a brief description of the selected cryptocurrencies (Sect. 2.1) and their different types of wallets (Sect. 2.2). In addition, we present short introduction to the usability testing and its different aspects (Sect. 2.3).

2.1 Selected Cryptocurrencies

For this study, we have selected 3 cryptocurrencies, namely Bitcoin, Ethereum, and Ripple (a.k.a. XRP). The selected currencies represent the top-three cryptocurrencies in terms of their total market capital (a popular metric in the cryptocurrency sphere) as of 27 October, 2019 [6]. A brief introduction of the selected currencies are presented below.

- **Bitcoin** [1] is the first cryptocurrency to utilise a public blockchain system secured via a novel consensus algorithm called *Proof of Work* (PoW). It is currently the most popular virtual currency. Despite its technological breakthrough, it suffers from severe limitations such as transaction speed, issues of scalability and exorbitant energy consumption [7].
- **Ethereum** [4] is often regarded as Blockchain 2.0 as it showcases the next evolution of the blockchain technology. It facilitates the deployment and execution of computer programs, known as smart-contracts, on top of its public blockchain and thus, promotes the notion of blockchain as a platform. It also has similar limitations as Bitcoin [7].
- **Ripple** [5] is a public blockchain platform that has been created mainly to be integrated with financial institutions to facilitate instant payment, possibly in cross-border scenarios utilising its underlying protocol. It is gaining popularity because of its scalability and transaction speed.

2.2 Wallets

Bitcoin Core was the first wallet implemented by the bitcoin developers for desktop computers [8]. Since then there are several forms of wallets now. Next, we provide a brief discussion on different forms of wallets available on the market.

Desktop Wallet: Desktop wallets for cryptocurrencies are software that are available for most of the desktop operating systems such as Mac, Windows, Linux. In desktop wallets, private keys are stored in the computer. Some of the desktop wallets are targeted for a single cryptocurrency such as Bitcoin Core while other wallets (e.g. Exodus [9]) support multiple currencies. The User Interface (UI) of Exodus wallet is shown in Fig. 1.

Fig. 1. User Interface of Exodus wallet.

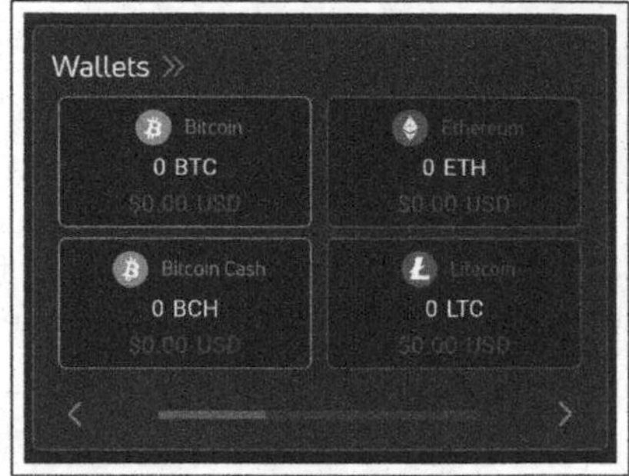

Fig. 2. User Interface of Jaxx wallet.

Mobile Wallet: Mobile wallets are mobile apps (applications) whose popularities are increasing day by day with the increase of smartphone uses. Figure 2 shows the UI of Jaxx Liberty, a mobile based Multi-currency Wallet [10].

Hardware Wallet: Hardware wallets are hardware devices built specifically for handling private keys. It provides a better security option with its support for strong cryptographic mechanisms by which the keys are stored in such devices. Examples of hardware wallets are Ledger [11] and Trezor [12].

Paper Wallet: Paper wallet is simply the private keys printed on a paper, mostly used as a form of backup. As it keeps the private keys offline, it provides a way of storing and keeping cryptocurrencies safer from cyber-attacks, malware, etc. Figure 3 represents a typical paper wallet of Ethereum.

Fig. 3. Ethereum paper wallet

Web Wallet: Web wallets are internet-based wallets which can be accessed via different internet browsers, such as Google Chrome, Firefox, and so on, by visiting the websites of some specific service providers. The private keys are generally stored on the server of the respective service providers and hence, many do not consider it a safe practice to store respective keys in the server as online servers are often target for hackers. However, we have seen the emergence of some web wallets (e.g. Metamask [13]) which are browser extension or add-on and does not require any key storage in the server.

2.3 Usability and Cognitive Walkthrough

Usability is the degree to which a software is easy to use, making sure that the functionalities help a user of average ability to achieve their intended purpose [14]. J. Nielsen defined usability with the following 5 components: Learn-ability, Efficiency, Memorability, Errors and Satisfaction [15].

To evaluate the usability of a system, it is important to analyse the system, utilise the resources available and select the appropriate inspection methods, which are crucial for the desired output and greatly reduces the risk of coming out with the limited set of findings.

There are mainly two types of methods, *Analytical* and *Empirical*, which are used to evaluate any usability related issues in a system. In usability testing, an empirical method means performing a test with the real users of the product while being observed by usability experts [16]. That is, it is based on experience or direct observation rather than any quantitative analysis or pure logic. On the other hand, an analytical approach tries to simulate people using a system, typically a software or a hardware, and then uses design principles, models or guidelines by experts as participants to judge and predict likely problems. An analytical usability testing is relatively easy to perform as it only requires several usability experts to find out the most of the usability problems, thus the overhead to perform a test is minimal.

Cognitive Walk-through (C.W.) is a usability inspection method which relies on the analytical approach to carry out a usability testing. It focuses on the ease of use and learn-ability of a product from a new user's perspective, usually performed by one or more expert [17]. In cognitive walk-through, a participant evaluates the user-interface of the corresponding application and carries out a series of tasks. The tasks allow the evaluator to assess different usability aspects corresponding to the particular application. In general, a cognitive walk-through process consists of three parts:

- Pointing out the intended target.
- Identifying the tasks essential to achieve the goal.
- Evaluating the interface and reporting the usability problems.

3 Related Work

There have been a few existing works which studied the usability issues related to cryptocurrency wallets. For example, Kazerani et al. performed a study using

Changetip and Coinbase to investigate what degree usability and user experience were a factor for bitcoin [18]. In their study, participants were beginner level bitcoin users and were asked to provide commentary while completing a provided task. They found that about half of the participants were unable to understand the concepts and were confused about their actions.

On the other hand, Krombholz et al. presented the first large scale survey to investigate how users experience the Bitcoin ecosystem in terms of security, privacy and anonymity [19]. They found that many users did not use all security capabilities of their selected Bitcoin management tool and had significant misunderstanding on how to remain anonymous and protect their privacy in the bitcoin network. They also found that 22% of their participants had lost their money due to security breaches or self-induced errors.

S. Eskandari et al. first evaluated the usability and security issues in bitcoin key management and summarised the bitcoin key management approaches analysing 6 representative bitcoin clients and found that users performing tasks involving key management can be stuck with complex security issues [20]. They also applied a cognitive walk-through inspection method along with a set of guidelines with four fundamental tasks for bitcoin but didn't showed any stats or numerical representation regarding the usability issues in bitcoin wallets.

As we can see, most usability testing for cryptocurrencies so far are based on Bitcoin. There are other significant cryptocurrencies offering a wide range of possibilities, unfortunately, there usability analysis has not been publicly reported. We aim to fill in this gap in this study where we have measured the usability of both desktop and mobile based wallets for the selected cryptocurrencies in all notable platforms applying an analytical usability inspection method, the cognitive walk-through method.

4 Experiment Setup

In this section, we present the experimental setup. In particular, we discuss about the selected wallets (Sect. 4.2), associated tasks (Sect. 4.1) and the participants (Sect. 4.3).

4.1 Experimental Tasks

To investigate the usability issues faced by the cryptocurrency users and to measure the effectiveness and satisfaction level, the cognitive walk-through inspection method has been selected, focusing on the essential tasks to be performed by a cryptocurrency user. The design of analytical cognitive walk-through for this study is summarised next.

For our experiment, we have selected 4 major tasks which are sub-divided into 13 sub tasks. For each sub-task, participants have been required to answer the following four standard questions which was first mentioned on the usability book by C. Wharton et al. [21] and currently is considered as standard procedures in the cognitive walk-through questionnaires. These questions essentially require each participant to answer in a binary *yes/no* fashion where a *yes* signifies that the user has been able to perform the respective task whereas a *no* signifies the user has failed.

Q1 Will the user understand how to start the task? (understanding that the action is needed)
Q2 Is the control (e.g. button) for the action clearly visible?
Q3 Will the user associate the correct action with the outcome they expect to achieve? (link of the control with the action)
Q4 If the correct action is performed, will the user see that progress is being made towards their intended outcome?

Eskandari et al. [20] in their study determined four vital tasks a cryptocurrency user needs to know while dealing with the wallets. We have reviewed those tasks and come up with a few modifications for this study. The tasks selected for our experiment are presented below.

T1: Configure - Starting a wallet for the first time in a new device, creating a new account (sub-task *t1*) and checking its balance (sub-task *t2*).
T2: Spend - Making a transaction of a given amount of cryptocurrencies to a valid receiving address. Thus, this task involves finding the transaction functionalities (send-receive) (sub-task *t3*), entering information such as receiver's address (sub-task *t4*), amount (sub-task *t5*) and finally, submitting the transaction (sub-task *t6*).
T3: Spend in Secondary Device - Spending the given amount on a secondary device but from the same wallet (account) and to the same address as *T2*. This task requires taking a backup (sub-task *t7*) via a wallet from the primary device and restoring to the secondary device (sub-task *t8*) and then making the transaction (sub-tasks *t9*, *t10* and *t11*) following the steps of Task *T2*.
T4: Recover - Recovering after losing the principal credential (e.g. hard drive crash). This task will require getting the right option to restore from backup to the correct state while having a backup (sub-task *t12*) or getting the verdict when the backup is not available (sub-task *t13*).

4.2 Selected Wallets

Next, in order to select the corresponding wallets, a small case study was conducted. Our goal has been to select a set of cryptocurrency wallets which covers the majority of the desktop and mobile platforms for these cryptocurrencies. The selected wallets are presented in Table 1.

These wallets represent the most widely used wallets in desktop/laptop computers and mobile devices. Some of them are used as desktop wallets for a single cryptocurrency (e.g. Bitcoin Core and Ethereum Wallet for Bitcoin and Ethereum respectively) while others are multi-currency wallets, supporting different cryptocurrencies. Finally, Coinomi is a mobile-based XRP Wallet.

Table 1. Selected wallets for the study

No.	Wallet name	Platform & type
1	Exodus	Desktop-based multi-currency wallet
2	Bitcoin core	Desktop-based bitcoin wallet [8]
3	Jaxx	Cross platform multi-currency wallet [10]
4	Ethereum wallet	Desktop-based ethereum wallet
5	Coinomi	Mobile-based XRP wallet

4.3 Participants

There were 5 participants in this study. It is widely accepted that testing with five participants is capable of finding almost as many usability problems as testing with many participants [22]. An analytical cognitive walkthrough is more favorable as it requires expert users to simulate the evaluation from the eye of a novice user. The mean participant age in years is 30 and standard deviation is 5.98. All participants had minimum qualifications of B.Sc. in computer science with 1 year of research experience in blockchain areas and familiarity in usability. The mean experience in blockchain is 1.6 in years, standard deviation is 1.2 and each of the participants is a blockchain researcher at Shahjalal University of Science and Technology, Sylhet, Bangladesh.

Prior to the evaluation, each participant was supplied with the documentation of our designed cognitive walk-through method and other necessary tutorials. Each participant was asked to carry out the above-mentioned tasks for the selected wallets and answer 4 usability questions (Q1–Q4). Each participation lasted 80 min in average which was conducted in a distraction free room while all the participants evaluated the desktop wallets on a Windows-10 laptop with Intel core-i5 processor and 8 GB of RAM and the mobile wallets on a Asus Zenfone 5 Android phone, with a screen recorder application running in the background during the evaluation. While carrying out the experiment, the number of *yes* and *no* for the selected tasks was recorded. At the end of the experiment, each participant also had the opportunity to provide verbal feedback.

5 Findings and Discussion

Since there were 4 significant tasks (T1–T4) broken down to 13 sub-tasks and 4 usability questions for each sub-task, an evaluator actually had submitted 52 answers in a yes-no fashion. The total number of failed steps (signified by a *no* answer) for each wallet by all the 5 participants are presented in Table 2 which also includes the average of failed steps out of 52 by all participants.

As we can see, no wallet is without any failed steps, meaning novice users failed to perform some fundamental tasks in every wallet. To be more specific, about 47% of the steps to complete the fundamental tasks are failed on bitcoin core, which is the first appeared, one of the most popular bitcoin wallet. For other

Table 2. The rate of failed steps by the participants.

Evaluator no.	Exodus	Bitcoin core	Ethereum	Jaxx	Coinomi
E1	6	22	8	2	0
E2	26	31	9	7	5
E3	9	25	10	4	2
E4	6	22	8	2	0
E5	4	22	12	4	0
Avg. failed steps out of 52	10.2	24.4	9.4	3.8	1.4
% of usability problems	19.62%	46.92%	18.08%	7.3%	2.69%

desktop wallets, the average rate of failure are 19.62% and 18.08% respectively for Exodus and Ethereum wallet. The failure rate on the mobile wallets are 3.8% and 2.69% for Jaxx and Coinomi respectively which is much better compared to the result of desktop versions while the rate of usage of mobile based wallets are notably lower than that of desktop based wallets. The rate of success for these tasks are shown in Fig. 4 along with their standard deviations.

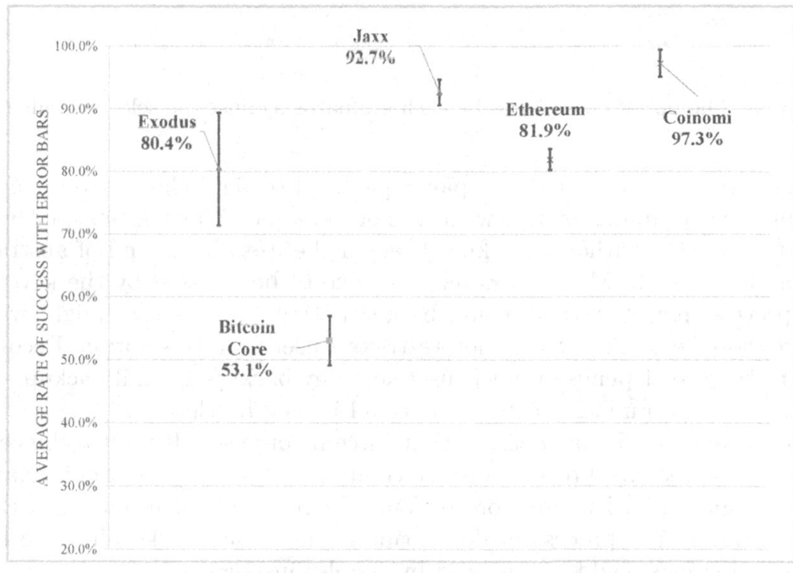

Fig. 4. The success rate of the fundamental tasks.

Figure 5 better represents the difficulties faced while completing the tasks for all the selected wallets where the bars signifies the number of failed steps out of 52 grouped by participants. It also shows the symmetry of evaluation records of the participants. The percentage of failed steps against the 4 fundamental tasks are represented in Fig. 6 which shows that spending and receiving coins (T2) were the most easy task to accomplish by the participants while the remaining other tasks were difficult to complete. In particular, Task T4 (recovering a lost credential) was the most difficult task to complete. This shows that all essential tasks except spending a cryptocurrency are proven to be extremely difficult for new cryptocurrency users.

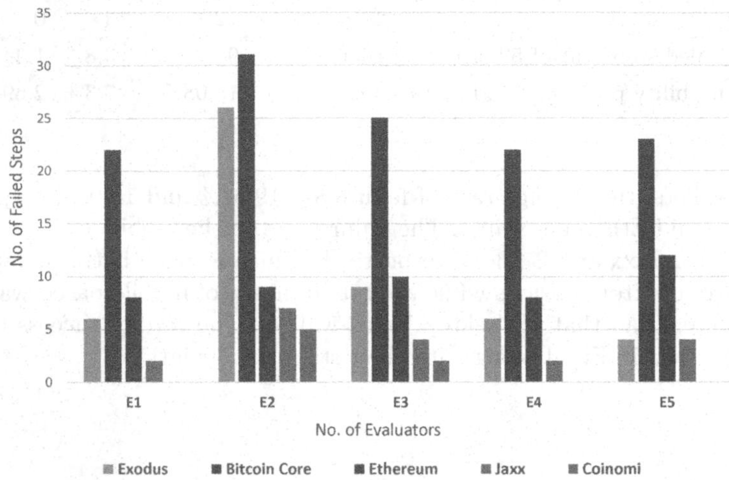

Fig. 5. The no. of failed steps by each evaluator against the selected wallets.

The verbal session with the participants also highlighted several aspects regarding the usability of the wallets. For example, 3 of the selected wallets generate key pairs without any knowledge of the user. This kind of abstraction is debatable though. Many users may not like to be stressed by the key generation process, however, there could be a situation where a user might want to manage those keys. The abstraction restricts a user from this option. Recovering from the key loss depends on if the user kept any backup. Even if backup sounds like an easy task, finding the right file could be is a hassle.

One of the participant reported that Bitcoin core used difficult technical languages. These technical terms must be complicated to the new users. Examples of such languages in Bitcoin Core is "out of sync" or "synchronizing with network", meaning the process of downloading the whole blockchain. The highly technical language could be replaced by simpler instructions.

Ethereum wallet improved upon the difficulties of Bitcoin Core. For example, upon launching the wallet, it asks the user to create a new account or to restore an old one. It also notifies the user to keep a copy of the folder *KeyStore* for backup. The backup procedure of Ethereum wallet is also simple because it has a drop-down option of backup inside the file menu. The backup procedure maps to a folder named KeyStore and if that file is kept safe in a secondary device, then restoring the account to a new device is hassle-free.

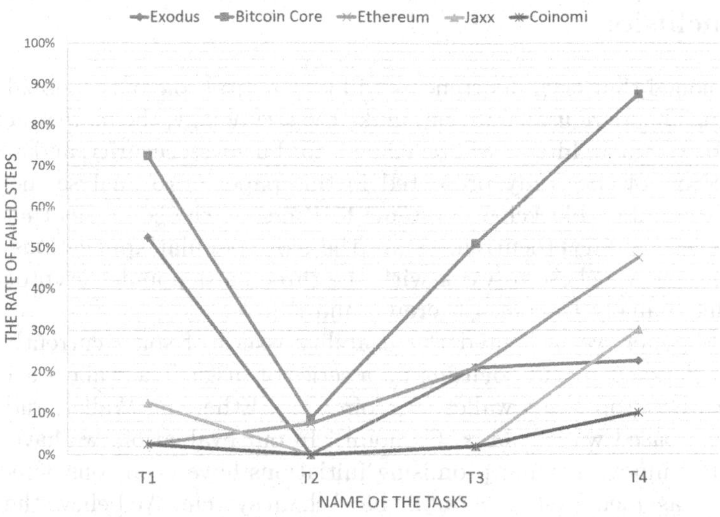

Fig. 6. The percentage of failed steps against each task for the selected Wallets

As per the evaluation, Bitcoin Core wallet failed to answer the question "Will the user associate the correct action with the outcome they expect to achieve?" the highest number of times. The wallet lack interface cues and features like tool help, wizards, or any action guides. Conversely, the Ethereum wallet is more flexible in the sense that the new users can explore effortlessly.

Exodus shows the two main options, "Send Assets to Wallet" and "Restore from Backup" which is vital for any users starting to use the wallet. It comes with the simple sidebar making it easy to swap between the functionalities along with the latest price of popular cryptocurrencies. This wallet emphasises on taking offline backup and follow the state-of-art backup procedure. This was the most usable desktop based wallet in the study but still the participants failed a few sub tasks in T1, T3, and T4.

We selected two popular mobile based wallets: Coinomi and Jaxx Liberty. Mobile based wallets have more attractive interfaces with the interface cues enabling new users to get comfortable with the wallet. The backup procedure is relatively simple in such wallets. The wallets also notify the user about the risks of not taking a backup. The average rate of success in completing the fundamental tasks for Jaxx and Coinomi was 92.7% and 97.3% respectively which is pretty good compared to the desktop wallets where the success rate of Exodus, the most usable desktop wallet was around 80.4%.

Even though the Cognitive Walkthrough is quite flexible, it has some pitfalls too. The learn-ability error bars presented as the standard deviation in Fig. 4 represents that the value of standard deviation was reducing while the evaluators was gradually coming to the end of the assessment. Still, the findings on this study is clear enough to identify the usability issues in fundamental tasks in cryptocurrency wallets. Resolving these issues will significantly improve the user acceptance and global adoption of cryptocurrencies.

6 Conclusion

It is envisioned that cryptocurrencies will play a vital role in the global currency ecosystem. The more usable we can make the technology, the more practitioners, users, and system architects will be using it for business, security, and anonymity. The objective of the study presented in this paper is to analyse the usability issues of the public blockchain systems focusing on the key tasks that must be accomplished on. Cryptocurrencies are the most popular applications based on blockchain and we chose to work with the three most popular cryptocurrencies at the time, namely Bitcoin, Ethereum and Ripple.

In this paper we presented the usability issues of some currently popular wallets of these currencies focusing on a series of tasks. The wallets can be categorised as: Desktop based wallet (Bitcoin Core, Ethereum Wallet, and Exodus) and Mobile based wallet (Jaxx, Coinomi). In our evaluation, we have observed that a lot of innovative and promising initiations have been considered to solve the key management system of public blockchain system. We believe the security-usability trade-off applies to blockchains too as the key idea is to make the system secure, anonymous, and reliable. However, as our findings suggest that the software (wallets) used to access any cryptocurrency suffer from serious usability issues, in particular for general users.

A set of usability guidelines need to be developed especially for cryptocurrency wallets so as to enable the development of more usable cryptocurrency wallets and other applications. We plan to work on this in the continuation of this study in future.

References

1. Nakamoto, S.: Bitcoin: A Peer-to-Peer Electronic Cash System (2008)
2. Morris, D.: Bitcoin Hits a New Record High, But Stops Short of $20,000. https://fortune.com/2017/12/17/bitcoin-record-high-short-of-20000/
3. Acar, Y., et al.: Comparing the usability of cryptographic APIs. In: IEEE Symposium on Security and Privacy, pp. 154–171 (2017)
4. Ethereum: A global, open-source platform for decentralized applications. https://www.ethereum.org/
5. Instantly Move Money to All Corners of the World - Ripple. https://ripple.com/
6. CoinCap.io - Reliable Cryptocurrency Prices and Market Capitalizations. https://coincap.io/
7. Chowdhury, M.J.M., et al.: A comparative analysis of distributed ledger technology platforms. IEEE Access **7**, 167930–167943 (2019)
8. Bitcoin Core Desktop Wallet. https://bitcoincore.org/
9. Exodus Multicurrency Wallet. https://exodus.io/
10. Jaxx Liberty: Secure Blockchain Wallet, Exchange and Portfolio. https://jaxx.io/
11. Hardware Wallet - State-of-the-art security for crypto assets. https://www.ledger.com/
12. Trezor Hardware Wallet - The original & most secure bitcoin wallet. https://trezor.io/
13. MetaMask: A crypto wallet & gateway to blockchain apps. https://metamask.io/

14. Krug, S.: Don't Make Me Think: A Common Sense Approach to Web Usability. Pearson Education India (2000)
15. Nielsen, J.: Usability 101: Introduction to Usability. https://www.nngroup.com/articles/usability-101-introduction-to-usability/
16. Bridgman, P.: Empirical Method. https://www.accessscience.com/content/empirical-method/231000/
17. Mahatody, T., Sagar, M., Kolski, C.: Cognitive Walkthrough for HCI evaluation: basic concepts, evolutions and variants, research issues. In: Proceedings of EAM (2007)
18. Kazerani, A., Rosati, D., Lesser, B.: Determining the usability of bitcoin for beginners using change tip and coinbase. In: Proceedings of the 35th ACM International Conference on the Design of Communication (2017)
19. Krombholz, K., Judmayer, A., Gusenbauer, M., Weippl, E.: The other side of the coin: user experiences with bitcoin security and privacy. In: Grossklags, J., Preneel, B. (eds.) FC 2016. LNCS, vol. 9603, pp. 555–580. Springer, Heidelberg (2017). https://doi.org/10.1007/978-3-662-54970-4_33
20. Eskandari, S., Clark, J., Barrera, D., Stobert, E.: A first look at the usability of bitcoin key management. NDSS Workshop on Usable Security (USEC) (2018)
21. Wharton, C., Rieman, J., Lewis, C., Polson, P.: The cognitive walkthrough method: a practitioner's guide (1994)
22. Nielsen, J.: How Many Test Users in a Usability Study? https://www.nngroup.com/articles/how-many-test-users

Algorithm Design, Bioinformatics and Photonics

Efficient Query Processing for Multidimensional Data Cubes

Rejwana Tasnim Rimi and K. M. Azharul Hasan(✉)

Department of Computer Science and Engineering,
Khulna University of Engineering & Technology, Khulna 9203, Bangladesh
rejwana@kuet.ac.bd, az@cse.kuet.ac.bd

Abstract. Data cubes come up with a suitable paradigm for storing, accessing, processing and analysis multidimensional data. Conventional Multidimensional Arrays (CMA) are the basic data structure to process such multidimensional data. But the performance of the MDAs degrades when the number of dimension increases. In this paper, we propose a new approach for computing multidimensional data cube using conversion of dimensions of the multidimensional array. We design efficient algorithms for Multidimensional On Line Analytical Processing (MOLAP) operations using the Converted two dimensional Array (C2A). We represent the MOLAP array as a Converted two dimensional Array where n-dimension is converted into two dimension. Then we apply the operations of data cube namely slice and dice on both CMA and C2A. We calculate the time for slice and dice operations for CMA and C2A. The proposed model requires less time for index computation when number of dimension is high. The cache miss rate is also lower for C2A based implementation. Therefore, our proposed algorithm shows superior performance than the traditional scheme.

Keywords: Data cube · MOLAP · Query processing · Cache miss · Dimension conversion · Slice · Dice

1 Introduction

The research on data cube computation is gaining more and more attention of data scientists when dealing with Big Data challenges specially for decisions making based on aggregation for variety of domains such as remote sensing, climate simulations, geographic information systems, medical imaging or astronomical observations [1]. The industries namely manufacturing, finance make their decisions based on aggregation of data over multiple dimensions [2]. The data cube technology such as Multidimensional On-Line Analytical Processing (MOLAP) plays the vital role for data analysis and decision making for the enterprise based on their historical structured data [3]. Efficient building of data cube requires a good data structure which has been recognized as one of the most important and essential issue for MOLAP [4,5]. Relational data

T. Bhuiyan et al. (Eds.): ICONCS 2020, LNICST 325, pp. 647–658, 2020.
https://doi.org/10.1007/978-3-030-52856-0_51

are mainly used for efficient computation of data cube [6]. The data cube is built by storing it into a multidimensional array facing from the Relational Database (RDB). The Multidimensional arrays (CMA) are the basic data structure for MOLAP computation [4]. The multidimensional query such as slice and dice is the retrieval of desired summery data from a multidimensional structure based on aggregation operation. The multidimensional query is well defined from MOLAP structure as MOLAP operations [6]. A typical MOLAP cube is defined as $Q(D_1, D_2, ..., D_n : M_1, M_2, ..., M_k)$ where $D_i(n \leq i \leq 1)$ are attributes or dimensions to be aggregated and $M_j(k \leq j \leq 1)$ are the measure values to be summarized. Due to wide acceptance of main memory database [8], the proposed system is built on main memory system. In this research, we proposed a new model for multidimensional query processing. In our model, at first evaluate a multi-dimensional sparse array from RDB. Then design our algorithm and show the effectiveness and superiority of the model for data cube operations namely slice and dice for in-memory system. The model can be applied not only to data cube computation [4,6] but also multidimensional databases [12,13], data mining [14] and multiway data analysis [15].

2 Related Works

Many techniques have been proposed in the literature for data cube computation based on high dimensional array [2,4,7]. [2] introduce the of HaCube which designed for efficient parallel data cube analysis on large-scale data by taking advantages from both MapReduce and parallel DBMS. They also generate data cube materialization algorithm which is able to facilitate the features in MapReduce-like systems towards an efficient data cube computation. A star-cubing method that performs aggregations on multiple dimensions simultaneously is presented in [3]. It utilizes a star tree structure, extends the simultaneous aggregation methods, and enables the pruning of the group-bys that do not satisfy the iceberg condition. The percentage cube is proposed in [6] which takes percentages as the fundamental aggregated measure. [9] presents a MOLAP data structure based on extendible array where the multidimensional cube operations are defined and shows the effectiveness of dynamic dataset. A multidimensional database implementation is proposed in [13] and shows the fundamental database operation for future data maintenance. The model is effective for large duplicate values. [1] proposes a massive data cube computation scheme in distributed environment. Mapreduce based data cube computation on tensor structure is proposed in [16] to reduce the cube computation time by sharing sorts cost and input data scan. A rank aware cube computation is proposed in [17] to answer the top k queries. A virtual denormalization for main memory OLAP is presented in [5] and shows some superiority of the scheme. But the scheme uses a CMA as data structure. All the models applies conventional array operations for data cube computation. We retrieve the operations by dimension conversion and found better result for data cube computation.

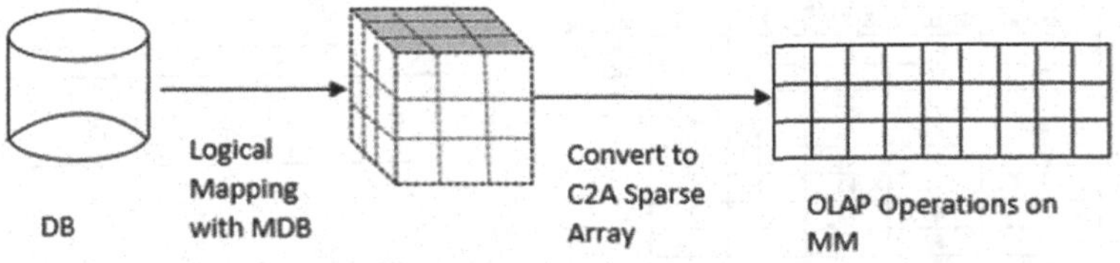

Fig. 1. The data cube computation model.

3 Dimension Conversion

The Multidimensional arrays (CMA) are transformed to a Converted two Array [10,11] and are used as the basic data structure to compute the data cube. The Converted two Array (C2A) is a two dimensional abstraction of a n ($n \geq 2$) dimensional array where the odd dimensions contribute along row direction and even dimensions contribute along column direction. Let $x_1, x_2, ..., x_n$ be the index of an element of a CMA $A[l_1][l_2]...[l_n]$ where $l_1, l_2, ..., l_n$ are the length of each dimension $d_1, d_2, ..., d_n$ and $x_i = 0, 1, 2, 3, ..., l_{i-1}$ where $0 \leq i \leq n$. Any element of A can be found by the addressing function.

$$f(x_1, x_2, ..., x_n) = x_1, l_2, l_3, ..., l_n + x_2, l_3, l_4, ..., l_n + ... + x_{n-1}, l_n + x_n$$

We construct a two dimensional array C2A $A'[X'][Y']$ of size L'_1, L'_2 and subscripts $X'(0 \leq X' \leq L'_1)$ and $Y'(0 \leq Y' \leq L'_2)$. Where, $L'_1 = l_1 \times l_3 \times ... \times l_{n-1}$ and $L'_2 = l_2 \times l_4 \times ... \times l_n$. The X' and Y' are calculated as follows

$$X' = \begin{cases} x_1 l_3 l_5 ... l_{n-3} l_{n-1} + x_3 l_5 l_7 ... l_{n-3} l_{n-1} + ... + x_{n-3} l_{n-1} + x_{n-1}, & when\ n\ is\ even. \\ x_1 l_3 l_5 ... l_{n-2} l_n + x_3 l_5 l_7 ... l_{n-2} l_n + ... + x_{n-2} l_n + x_n, & when\ n\ is\ odd. \end{cases}$$
$$Y' = \begin{cases} x_2 l_4 l_6 ... l_{n-3} l_{n-1} + x_4 l_6 l_8 ... l_{n-3} l_{n-1} + ... + x_{n-3} l_{n-1} + x_{n-1}, & when\ n\ is\ even. \\ x_2 l_4 l_6 ..... l_{n-2} l_n + x_4 l_6 l_8 ... l_{n-2} l_n + ... + x_{n-2} l_n + x_n, & when\ n\ is\ odd. \end{cases} \quad (1)$$

For example, the conversion of a CMA of dimension 6 to a C2A is

$$X' = x_1 l_3 l_5 + x_3 l_5 + x_5,\ and \\ Y' = x_2 l_4 l_6 + x_4 l_6 + x_6 \quad (2)$$

4 Query Processing for Multidimensional Data cube

4.1 The Computation Model

We load data from a RDB. Figure 1 shows the logical view of the proposed computational and Fig. 2 shows the implementation view. The measure value is stored in the array. Figure 2(a) shows a RDB where there are 4 dimension attributes and one measure attributes remains. Therefore, we need a 4 dimensional array as shown in Fig. 2(b). The 4 dimensional structure is then converted

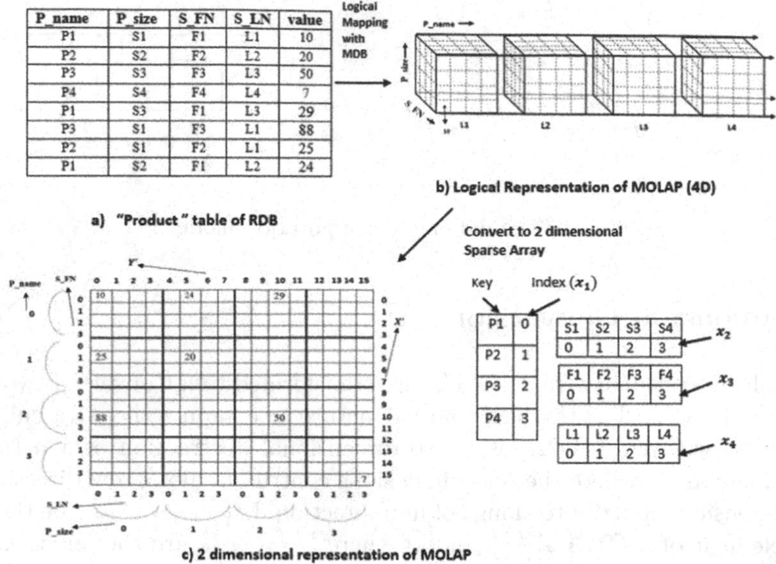

P_name	P_size	S_FN	S_LN	value
P1	S1	F1	L1	10
P2	S2	F2	L2	20
P3	S3	F3	L3	50
P4	S4	F4	L4	7
P1	S3	F1	L3	29
P3	S1	F3	L1	88
P2	S1	F2	L1	25
P1	S2	F1	L2	24

Fig. 2. Logical realization of the proposed data cube computation model

to a 2 dimensional C2A. According to the computation technique Sect. 3, the C2As are created and mapped shown in Fig. 2(c).

The measure value is stored as the cell value in the array. In Fig. 2(a) the "Product" table contain five columns where P_name, P_size, S_FN,S_LN columns are dimensions and value column is measure. We retrieve the data to a CMA as well as to C2A. These two arrays contain measure. For example, Fig. 2(a) 1(a), the location of the value "50" in CMA is A[2][2][2][2] and in C2A it will be $A'[10][10]$ $(2 \times l_3 + 2 = 10, 2 \times l_4 + 2 = 10)$ by Eq. 2.

4.2 Slice Operation

Slice is a common data cube operation which pick the subset of a multi-dimensional cube by choosing a single value for one of its dimensions. One of the slice query based on Fig. 2(a) is as follows:

```
SELECT sum(value)
FROM product
WHERE P_name = 'P2';
```

The above statement can be transformed as $x_i = v_1$ where x_i is the index value corresponding to P2 and v_1 ='P2'. Therefore the candidate tupples become <$x_1 = v_1, ..., x_4$>. Let the length of the dimension l_1, l_2, l_3 and l_4.

Algorithm 1. Slice for MDA(n)

for $x_2 \leftarrow 0$ to $l_2 - 1$ **do**
    for $x_3 \leftarrow 0$ to $l_3 - 1$ **do**
        ....
        for $x_n \leftarrow 0$ to $l_n - 1$ **do**
            $A[v_1][x_2][x_3]...[x_n]$
        end for
    end for
end for

CMA Algorithm. The algorithm for slice using CMA is shown in Algorithm 1 where the tuple $<x_1 = v_1, ..., x_n>$ is known and $x_1 = v_1$. We need $n-1$ loops to carry out the search.

C2A Algorithm Development. To retrieve an element from C2A we need the following parameters

- Start Index (SI) for X' (or Y')
- Total number Target Rows (TR) (or columns)
- Striding values to continue the loop.

There are three types of indices of CMA that are important for C2A algorithm development. These are inner index, outer index and intermediate index. For 6D, according to row x_1 is the outer index, x_3 is intermediate index and x_5 is inner index as shown in Eq. 2. For a MDA(4) the intermediate index is void. Figure 3 shows the inner and outer index for 4D.

4D. For slice, suppose we want to find the values from C2A for P2. Here, $x_1 = 1$ for example $<1, *, *, *>$ as shown in Fig. 3(a) (the outer index). The candidate rows are $X' = <4, 5, 6, 7>$. Hence the SI and TR are 4. And the striding value is 1 (i.e. unit striding). In general for 4D case the $SI = x_i \times l_3 = 4$ and $TR = \prod_{p=1,3} l_p (p \neq i)$ where i is the known dimension for the query. In case of tuple $<*, *, 1, *>$ (see Fig. 3(b)) where x_3 is known which is the inner index of C2A, the SI for C2A will be 1 (i.e x_3) because x_3 is an inner index. The stride value is l_3. Therefore the row indexes will be $X' = <1, 5, 9, 13>$. If we consider the following query

```
SELECT sum(value)
FROM product
WHERE P_size = 'S2';
```

The index of 'S2' is 1. So,the $<*, 1, *, *>$ tuple, (see Fig. 3(c)). The SI for C2A will be $x_2 \times l_4 = 1 \times 4 = 4$ and stride value is 1. The target column indices are $Y' = <4, 5, 6, 7>$. For the tuple $<*, *, *, 1>$ (Fig. 3(d)) is the fourth index of MDA which is the inner index of C2A. Here stride value is l_4. Therefore, the target column indices are $Y' = <1, 5, 9, 13>$. The algorithm for C2A of MOLAP

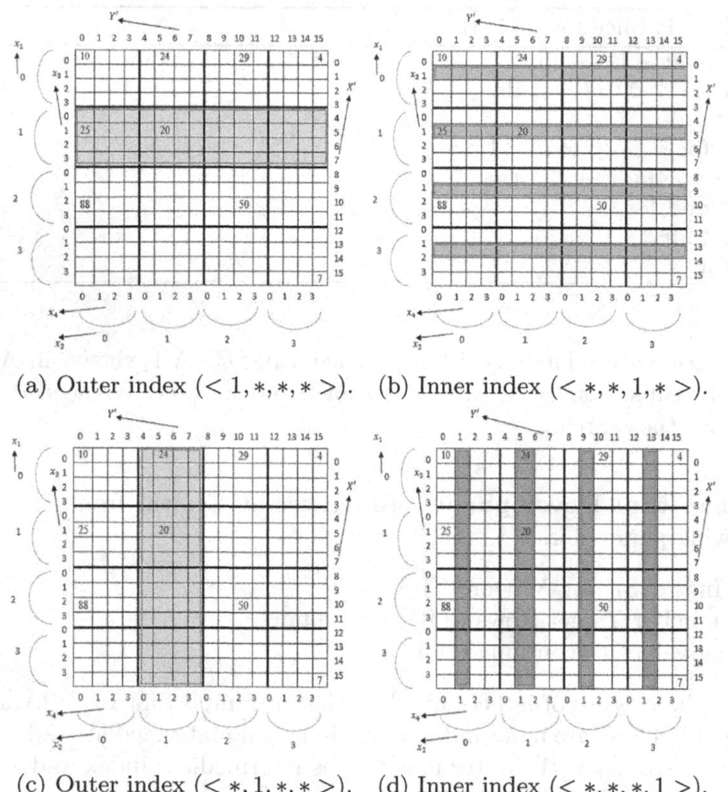

(a) Outer index ($<1, *, *, *>$). (b) Inner index ($<*, *, 1, *>$).

(c) Outer index ($<*, 1, *, *>$). (d) Inner index ($<*, *, *, 1>$).

Fig. 3. Slice realization for C2A.

is summarized in Algorithm 1 for row indices X'. Algorithm for Y' can also be developed in the same way.

6D. The subscript of a tuple $x_1, x_2, x_3, x_4, x_5, x_6$ is x_1, x_3, x_5 contributes for row direction X' and x_2, x_4, x_6 contributes for column direction Y' for MDA(6). In case of the query $<*, *, 1, *, *, *>$where x_3 is known, the period between two consecutive rows is determined by $p_i = l_5 \times (l_3 - 1) + 1$.

nD. Let $A[l_1][l_2]...[l_n]$ be a CMA(n) of size $[l_1 l_2 ... l_n]$. The values for SI for C2A are as follows

$SI = x_i$ for inner index
$SI = x_i \times l_3 \times l_5 \times ... \times l_{n-1}$ for outer index
$SI = x_i \times l_5 \times l_7 \times ... \times l_i$ for intermediate index and i is the known dimension.

Algorithm 2. Slice for C2A of four dimensional MOLAP

procedure C2A OF FOUR DIMENSION
  if $i = 1$ **then**
    $SI \leftarrow x_i \times l_3; stride \leftarrow 1;$
  else
    $SI \leftarrow x_i; stride \leftarrow l_3;$
  end if
  $TR \leftarrow \prod_{p=1,3} l_p (p \neq i);$
  $Count \leftarrow 0; k \leftarrow 0;$
  while $(Count \leq TR)$ **do**
    for $j \leftarrow 0$ to L_2' **do**
      $print(A'[k][j])$
    end for
    $k \leftarrow k + stride; count \leftarrow count + 1;$
  end while
end procedure

The values for stride values are $stride = l_{n-1}$ for inner index, $stride = 1$ for outer index, and long stride for intermediate index is $ld = (l_3 - 1) \times l_5 \times ... l_{n-1} - 1$. Algorithm 3 shows the summarization of the query process.

4.3 Dice Operation

The dice operation is a form of range key query where two or more dimensions values are known and creates sub-cube. Consider the following query.

```
SELECT sum(value)
FROM product
WHERE  P_name = 'P2'  and P_size= 'S2';
```

The above query can be transformed as $x_1 = 1$ and $x_2 = 1$ where x_1 is the index value corresponding to P2 and x_2 is the index value corresponding to S2. Therefore the candidate tuples become $<x_1 = 1, x_2 = 1, *, *...>$. Figure 4 shows the candidate records for the above query corresponding to a C2A. Like silce, the searching of dice also depends on the position of x_i. If position of all inputs are odd (value of i) the searching perform along with X axis and for all even positions the searching perform along with Y axis. In above query the dice operation perform in 2 directions. So, unlike slice, here both row and column-wise searching is required. At first, we have to calculate the first index of both row and column. From the X axis the first index will be $x_1 \times l_3 = 1 \times 4 = 4$ and stride value is 1. The target rows indices are $X' = <4, 5, 6, 7>$. Similarly, Y axis the first index will be $y_1 \times l_4 = 1 \times 4 = 4$ and stride value is 1. The target rows indices are $Y' = <4, 5, 6, 7>$. the candidate area for dice is shown in Fig. 4(a). The coordinates are (4, 4), (4, 5), (4, 6), (4, 7), (5, 4), (5, 5), (5, 6), (5, 7), (6, 4), (6, 5), (6, 6), (6, 7), (7, 4), (7, 5), (7, 6), (7, 7). If we consider the following query

Algorithm 3. Slice for C2A of CMA(n)

procedure C2A OF MDAN
    if i is inner index **then**
        $SI \leftarrow x_i; stride \leftarrow l_{n-1};$ ▷ if, $i = n - 1$
    else if i is outer index **then**
        $SI \leftarrow x_i \times l_{n-1} \times l_{n-3} \times ...l_3; stride \leftarrow 1;$ ▷ if, $i = 1$
    else
        $SI \leftarrow x_i \times l_{n-1} \times l_{n-3} \times ...l_{i+2}; stride \leftarrow 1;$
    end if
    $TR \leftarrow \prod_{p=1,3,5} l_p(p \neq i);$ ▷ For outer index, $TR \leftarrow l_3 \times ... \times l_{n-1};$
    $ld \leftarrow l_{n-1} \times ln - 3 \times ... \times (l_i - 1) + 1;$
    $Count \leftarrow 0; k \leftarrow 0; m \leftarrow 0;$
    while $(Count \leq TR)$ **do**
        for $j \leftarrow 0$ to L'_2 **do**
            $print(A'[k][j])$
        end for
        if $m\%(l_{i+2} \times l_{i+4} \times ... \times l_{n-1}) = 0$ **then**
            $k \leftarrow k + ld; count \leftarrow count + 1;$
        end if
    end while
end procedure

```
SELECT sum(value)
FROM product
WHERE  S_FN = 'F2'  and S_LN= 'L2';
```

The index of P2 and F2 will be 2. For the tuple $<*, *, 2, 2>$ as shown in Fig. 4(b) which corresponds to the inner index of C2A. Here stride value is l_3 and l_4 for the X and Y axis. Therefore, the target row indices are $X' = <2, 6, 10, 14>$ and the target column indices are $Y' = <2, 6, 10, 14>$. The candidate query region is shown in Fig. 4(b).

The data cubes are decision making database and its volume is large with respect to traditional database. From organizational point of view, the major advantages of the proposed system are in two folds. Firstly it is easy to design query algorithms that improves the data locality and cash miss rate. Therefore, algorithms will be fast for large scale data and secondly it is possible to allocate large MOLAP arrays by two pointers only by dynamic memory allocation. Therefore, with a single C2A array large data can be handled for decision making.

5 Performance Analysis

In this section we compare the execution performance for Slice and dice operation both for CMA and C2A based algorithm. We consider the row major order looping for both queries. The performance of both the system depend on number of addition and multiplication operation needed for nD array. For example, if α

Algorithm 4. Dice for C2A of four dimensional MOLAP

```
procedure C2A OF FOUR DIMENSION
    if i = 1 then
        SI ← x_i × l_3; stride_x ← 1;                    ▷ Starting index of row
    else
        SI ← x_i; stride_x ← l_3;
    end if
    if j = 1 then
        SI ← y_i × l_4; stride_y ← 1;                    ▷ Starting index of column
    else
        SI ← y_i; stride_y ← l_4;
    end if
    TR_x ← ∏_{p=1,3} l_p(p ≠ i);
    TR_y ← ∏_{p=2,4} l_p(p ≠ j);
    Count_x ← 0; k_x ← 0;
    while (Count_x ≤ TR_x) do
        while (Count_y ≤ TR_y) do
            print(A'[k_x][k_y])
            k_y ← k_y + stride_y; count ← count_y + 1;
        end while
        k_x ← k_x + stride_x; count ← count_x + 1;
    end while
end procedure
```

and β are the cost of addition and multiplication operation, then for 6-D array the cost for TMA is $(15\alpha + 5\beta)l^5$ and for C2A is $(\alpha + \beta)l^5$. The conversion cost for C2A is $(6\alpha + 4\beta)$. Therefore, the improvement of C2A over TMA, $\eta = 1 - \frac{((\alpha+\beta)l^5+6\alpha+4\beta))}{((15\alpha+5\beta)l^5)}$. If n increases the η increases.

The RDB data are taken from database both for CMA and C2A. We calculate the execution time in main memory for different dimensions and for different slice and dice operations. We show the average result here. We retrieved the data to a dense array. Figure 5 and Fig. 6 shows the comparison and improvement of CMA versus C2A for slice and dice operation respectively for varying number of dimension $n(n = 4D \sim 10D)$. The execution time of C2A has clear improvement over CMA. Both figures show when the dimensions increases the execution time of C2A decrease. This is because, the index computation for C2A based algorithms has advantages over the CMA based algorithms. Therefore, the CMA based algorithms needs $(n - 1)$ for nested loops for slice and n nested loops for dice operation. But the C2A based algorithms needs two nested loops irrespective of the values n. This gives the facility for better data locality for retrieval. Therefore, cache miss rate for CMA based algorithms is higher than C2A based algorithms. Hence we can conclude that the C2A based data cube computation has better performance than the CMA based algorithms for large number of dimensions.

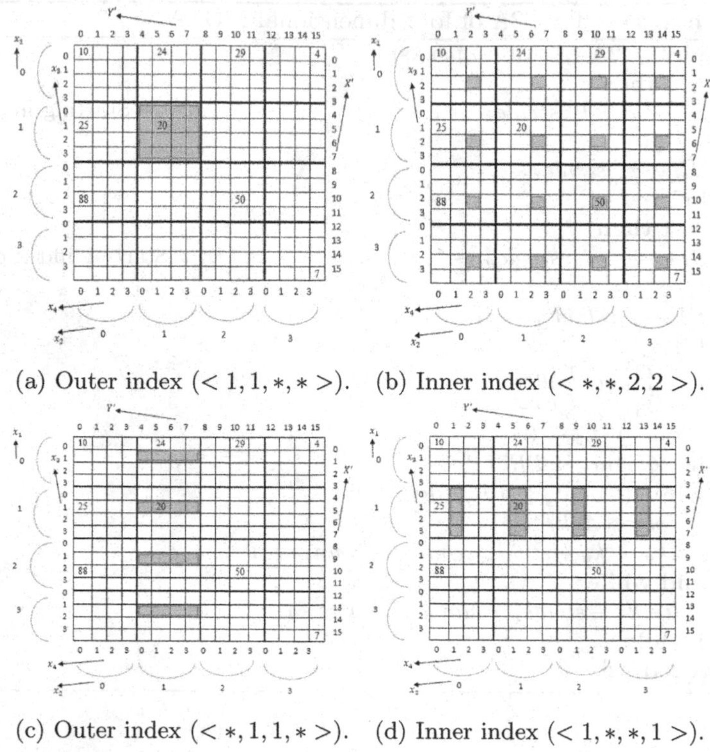

(a) Outer index ($< 1, 1, *, * >$). (b) Inner index ($< *, *, 2, 2 >$).

(c) Outer index ($< *, 1, 1, * >$). (d) Inner index ($< 1, *, *, 1 >$).

Fig. 4. Dice realization for C2A.

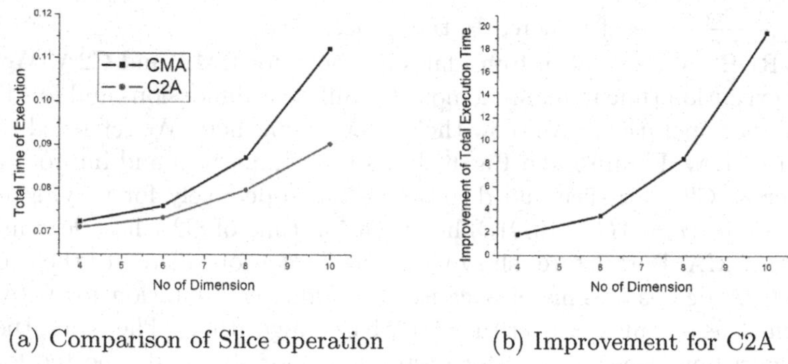

(a) Comparison of Slice operation (b) Improvement for C2A

Fig. 5. Performance analysis of MDA and C2A for slice.

6 Conclusion

Query processing for decision making database is very important task. Therefore improved query processing is desirable for MOLAP database. In this research our purpose was to improve the MOLAP operations using converted MDA. We

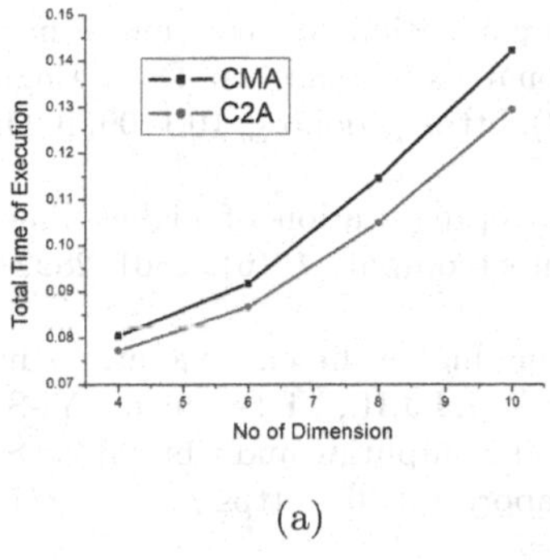

(a)

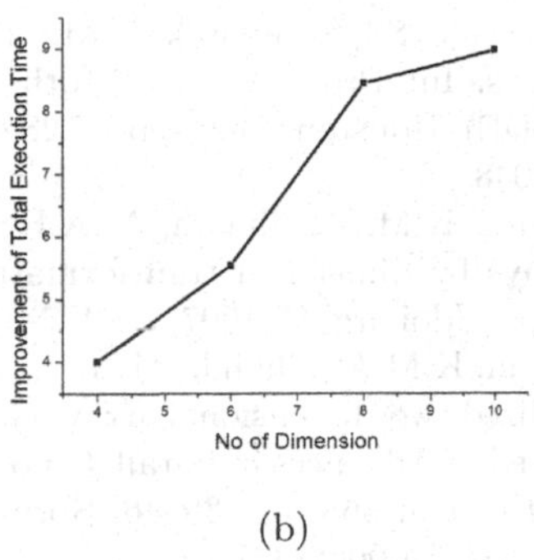

(b)

Fig. 6. Performance analysis of MDA and C2A for dice.

develop and analyze an efficient algorithm for MOLAP query processing. We calculate the retrieval time of both CMA and C2A. C2A based algorithm shows superiority than the CMA based algorithms. The reason for the better performance is that C2A requires less loop and fewer cache miss rate. The scheme can easily be implemented in parallel and distributed environment for parallel processing.

References

1. Merticariu, V., Baumann, P.: Massively distributed data cube processing. In: IEEE International Geoscience and Remote Sensing Symposium (2019). https://doi.org/10.1109/IGARSS.2019.8900432
2. Wang, Z., Chu, Y., Tan, K.L., Agrawal, D., Abbadi, A.E., Xu, X.: Scalable Data Cube Analysis over Big Data. Published in arXiv (2013)
3. Xin, D., Han, J., Li, X., Shao, Z., Wah, B.: Computing iceberg cubes by top-down and bottom-up integration: the starcubing approach. IEEE Trans. Knowl. Data Eng. **19**(1), 111–126 (2007). https://doi.org/10.1145/1807167.1807271
4. Hasan, K.M.A., Tsuji, T., Higuchi, K.: An efficient implementation for MOLAP basic data structure and its evaluation. In: Kotagiri, R., Krishna, P.R., Mohania, M., Nantajeewarawat, E. (eds.) DASFAA 2007. LNCS, vol. 4443, pp. 288–299. Springer, Heidelberg (2007). https://doi.org/10.1007/978-3-540-71703-4_26
5. Zhang, Y., Zhou, X., Zhang, Y., Zhang, Y., Su, M., Wang, S.: Virtual denormalization via array index reference for main memory OLAP. IEEE Trans. Knowl. Data Eng. **28**(4), 1061–1074 (2016). https://doi.org/10.1109/KDE.2015.2499199
6. Zhang, Y., Ordonez, C., García-García, J., Bellatreche, L., Carrillo, H.: The percentage cube. Inf. Syst. **79**, 20–31 (2019)
7. Zhao, Y., Deshpande, P.M., Naughton, J.F.: An array-based algorithm for simultaneous multidimensional aggregates. In: Proceedings of SIGMOD Conference, pp. 159–170 (1997). https://doi.org/10.1145/253260.253288
8. Plattner, H.: SanssouciDB: an in-memory database for processing enterprise workloads. In: Datenbanksysteme for Business, Technologie und Web (BTW). Gesellschaft for Informatik, Bonn, pp. 2–21 (2011)

9. Sarawagi, S., Stonebraker, M.: Efficient organization of large multidimensional arrays. In: Proceedings of 10th International Conference on Data Engineering (ICDE), Houston, Texas, pp. 328–386 (1994). https://doi.org/10.1109/ICDE.1994.283048
10. Hasan, K.M.A., Shaikh, M.A.H.: Efficient representation of higher-dimensional arrays by dimension transformations. J. Supercomput. **73**(6), 2801–2822 (2017). https://doi.org/10.1007/s11227-016-1954-x
11. Hasan, K.M.A., Shaikh, M.A.H.: Representing higher dimensional arrays into generalized two-dimensional array: G2A. In: Park, J.J.J.H., Yi, G., Jeong, Y.-S., Shen, H. (eds.) Advances in Parallel and Distributed Computing and Ubiquitous Services. LNEE, vol. 368, pp. 39–46. Springer, Singapore (2016). https://doi.org/10.1007/978-981-10-0068-3_5
12. Deshpande, P., Ramasamy, K., Shukla, A., Naughton, J.F.: Caching multidimensional queries using chunks. In: Proceedings of the ACM SIGMOD Conference on Management of Data, pp. 259–270 (1998). https://doi.org/10.1145/276305.276328
13. Hasan, K.M.A., Kuroda, M., Azuma, N., Tsuji, T., Higuchi, K.: An extendible array based implementation of relational tables for multi dimensional databases. In: Tjoa, A.M., Trujillo, J. (eds.) DaWaK 2005. LNCS, vol. 3589, pp. 233–242. Springer, Heidelberg (2005). https://doi.org/10.1007/11546849_23
14. Yan, J., et al.: Trace-oriented feature analysis for large-scale text data dimension reduction. IEEE Trans. Knowl. Data Eng. **23**(7), 1103–1117 (2011)
15. Sun, J., Tao, D., Papadimitriou, S., Yu, P.S., Faloutsos, C.: Incremental tensor analysis: theory and applications. ACM Trans. Knowl. Discov. Data **2**(3), 1–37 (2008)
16. Kim, S., Lee, S., Kim, J., Yoon, Y.-I.: MRTensorCube: tensor factorization with data reduction for context-aware recommendations. J. Supercomput. (6), 1–11 (2017). https://doi.org/10.1007/s11227-017-2002-1
17. Miranda, F., Lins, L., Klosowski, J.T., Silva, C.: TOPKUBE: a rank-aware data cube for real-time exploration of spatiotemporal data. IEEE Trans. Vis. Comput. Graph. **24**, 1394–1407 (2018)

Proposal of a Highly Birefringent Bow-Tie Photonic Crystal Fiber for Nonlinear Applications

Md. Moynul Hossain[1], Md. Anowar Kabir[1], Md. Mehedi Hassan[1], Md. Ashikur Rahman Parag[1], Md. Nadim Hossain[1], Bikash Kumar Paul[1,2,3], Muhammad Shahin Uddin[1,3], and Kawsar Ahmed[1,3](✉)

[1] Department of Information and Communication Technology, Mawlana Bhashani Science and Technology University, Santosh, Tangail 1902, Bangladesh
moynul.ict15031@gmail.com, anowarkabir.mbstu@gmail.com, mehedihassan.mbstu@gmail.com, porag15002@gmail.com, nadimmbstuict@gmail.com

[2] Department of Software Engineering, Daffodil International University, Sukrabad, Dhanmondi, Dhaka 1207, Bangladesh
bikash.swe@diu.edu.bd

[3] Group of Bio-photomatix, Mawlana Bhashani Science and Technology University, Santosh, Tangail 1902, Bangladesh
shahin.mbstu@gmail.com, kawsar.ict@mbstu.ac.bd, k.ahmed.bd@ieee.org

Abstract. In this letter, a bow-tie-type photonic crystal fiber (PCF) with high birefringence (Hi-Bi) has been proposed. The core of the PCF is elliptical with Chalcogenide glass ($Ga_8Sb_{32}S_{60}$) material. The whole analysis of the PCF is finished by the finite element method (FEM) for wavelength ranging from 2,000 nm to 3,000 nm to obtain some optical parameters like birefringence, beat length, power fraction, numerical aperture, effective refractive area, and nonlinearity. Therefore, a perfectly matched layer (PML) is also used to throw out unwanted radiation directed as an absorbing boundary condition (ABC). It has generated high birefringence (Hi-Bi) of 0.287 at 2,975 nm wavelength, the highest power fraction of 89.39% at 2,000 nm wavelength, the higher numerical aperture of 0.86, and the better nonlinearity of $6.10 \times 10^3\ W^{-1}Km^{-1}$. Hence, the proposed PCF plays a significant role in PCF areas with the better polarization filter, cross talk (CT), sensing, and nonlinear applications.

Keywords: Photonic crystal fiber (PCF) · Perfectly matched layer (PML) · Finite element method (FEM) · High birefringence (Hi-Bi) · Absorbing boundary condition (ABC) · Birefringence · Nonlinear coefficient

T. Bhuiyan et al. (Eds.): ICONCS 2020, LNICST 325, pp. 659–670, 2020.
https://doi.org/10.1007/978-3-030-52856-0_52

1 Introduction

Photonic crystal fiber (PCF) is an exclusive section of optical fiber. The PCFs or fibers with microstructure hole present some special characteristics which provide some new applications including fiber sensors, broadband dispersion controlling, super continuum generations, and capacity to maintain high polarization and so on [1]. Nowadays, microstructure fiber presents some excellent optical profiles such as high birefringence, extreme-high nonlinearity, high numerical aperture, high power fraction, lower dispersion variation, ultra-low confinement loss compared to any other traditional optical devices [2].

Nonlinearity is one of the indispensable parameters of the PCFs which yields some useful applications, for example, optical generation, optical properties amplification, optical switching, optical wavelength adjustment, optical regenerations, and many others [3–5]. PCFs have various tunable characteristics, for example, background material, cladding, pitch, doping core of PCF, and so on. These properties provide better discipline over nonlinearity, loss, and birefringence and many others. Nowadays, the PCF is an attractive device to recognize data for its better performance profile and different study of applications like telecommunication [6], sensors [7], medicine [8], and spectroscopy [9]. Birefringence is also an important parameter of a PCF. Besides, some PCFs were proposed to achieve high birefringence property.

Recently, Chalcogenide glasses can be applied to on-chip combined photonic devices, since they provide a larger band mid-infrared transmission bandwidth with the utmost operating wavelength is up to 2,500 nm and with insignificant two-photon saturation [10–12].

Accordingly, Zhang et al. [13] reported a PCF with a birefringence of 10^{-3} at 1,550 nm wavelength. Moreover, Agrawal et al. [14] presented a spiral PCF having maximum birefringence 1.16×10^{-2} at the following wavelength. Therefore, Wang et al. [15] designed a rectangular PCF with a higher birefringence profile of 1.83×10^{-2} at the same wavelength. Nonetheless, Revathi et al. [16] designed a spiral PCF with elliptical air holes and provide birefringence 2.56×10^{-2}. Then it was renovated 2.97×10^{-2} by using soft glass as the base materials [17]. In comparison, Yang et al. [18] displayed a PCF with a smaller air hole in the core area with nonlinearity $68\,W^{-1}Km^{-1}$ and birefringence of 2.22×10^{-2}. However, Hasan et al. [19] represented a composite PCF providing better optical performance such as birefringence of 3.45×10^{-2} with dispersion $39\,W^{-1}Km^{-1}$. In addition, Liao et al. [20] introduced a microfiber supporting birefringence of 2.1×10^{-2}, the broad effective area of $1.48 \times 10^{-12}\,m^2$, and nonlinearity of $156.74\,W^{-1}Km^{-1}$ with negative dispersion. In the meantime, Hui et al. [21] designed a PCF and improved a nonlinear coefficient of $3{,}726\,W^{-1}Km^{-1}$. Therefore, Ohishi et al. [22] presented a PCF with a nonlinearity of $5{,}700\,W^{-1}Km^{-1}$. From the following studies, it is still needed to design a PCF with better nonlinearity, high birefringence, better beat length, high power fraction, and other optical profiles.

In this paper, a bow-tie-type structure of PCF is proposed, simulated and analyzed. The core of the PCF is elliptical which is composed of Chalcogenide glass ($Ga_8Sb_{32}S_{60}$). The finite element method (FEM) and perfectly matched layer (PML) are used for investigating the optical parameters of the proposed PCF. The high birefringence of 0.287 and beat length of 11.57 μm is obtained at operating wavelength 2,975 nm and 2,000 nm. Thus, the proposed PCF is a strong candidate for high birefringence. The PCF has also achieved a better nonlinearity and numerical aperture. So, proposed PCF may be useful for optical properties amplification and nonlinear applications.

2 Design Methodology and Theoretical Analysis

The cross-section of the proposed PCF is shown in Fig. 1 with a brief diagrammatical description. The PCF is designed with an elliptical core. The major and minor axis of the ellipse is b = 0.6 μm and a = 0.3 μm. Thus, the eccentricity of this elliptical core is 0.87. The Chalcogenide glass ($Ga_8Sb_{32}S_{60}$) is used as a core material. The refractive index of this following material is calculated by Eq. 1. The silica glass is used as the background material of the cladding section of the PCF. The well patterned symmetrical air hole is made this PCF about a bow-tie-type structure. This type of air hole is improved the optical parameters. The measurement of diameter and pitch of the air hole is d = 1.0 μm and Λ = 1.1 μm, respectively. Therefore, the external structure is represented as a perfectly matched layer (PML) boundary condition with a width of 0.86 μm. The radius of the inner and outer circle of the PCF is r1 = 8.6 μm and r2 = 9.46 μm, respectively.

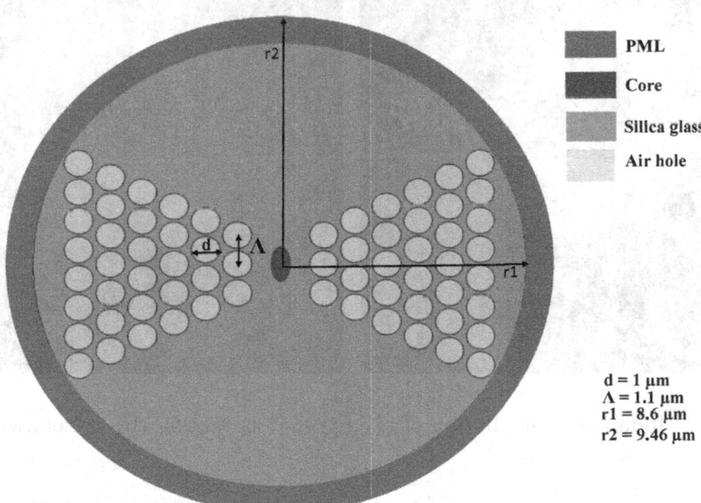

Fig. 1. Basic cross-sectional structure of the proposed PCF.

The refractive index of the Chalcogenide glass ($Ga_8Sb_{32}S_{60}$) and silica glass is calculated by the Sellmeier equation (1) [23].

$$n(\lambda) = \sqrt{1 + \sum_{i=1}^{m} \frac{A_i \lambda^2}{\lambda^2 - B_i^2}} \quad (1)$$

Where, A_i, B_i is Sellmeier coefficients and λ represents the operating wavelengths of the PCF. For Chalcogenide glass, m = 2, and $A_1 = 6.2563$, $A_2 = 2.9444$, $B_1 = 0.3425\,\mu\text{m}$, and $B_2 = 34.28\,\mu\text{m}$ [23]. And for silica glass, m = 3, and $A_1 = 0.696166$, $A_2 = 0.4079426$, $A_3 = 0.8974794$, $B_1 = 0.00467914826\,\mu\text{m}$, $B_2 = 0.0135120631\,\mu\text{m}$, and $B_3 = 97.9340025\,\mu\text{m}$ [24]. Therefore, all the numerical analyses are performed and done by the finite element method (FEM) for wavelength ranging from 2,000 nm to 3,000 nm. The COMSOL Multiphysics software is used for designing the proposed PCF and collecting necessary data for evaluating the optical parameters. In this paper, some important optical parameters like mode field distribution, birefringence, beat length, power fraction, numerical aperture, effective area, and nonlinearity are described with an appropriate figure and its applications. The distribution of the electric mode field is evaluated in two way, these are X-polarization and Y-polarization. The mode field distribution of these two polarization is shown in Fig. 2.

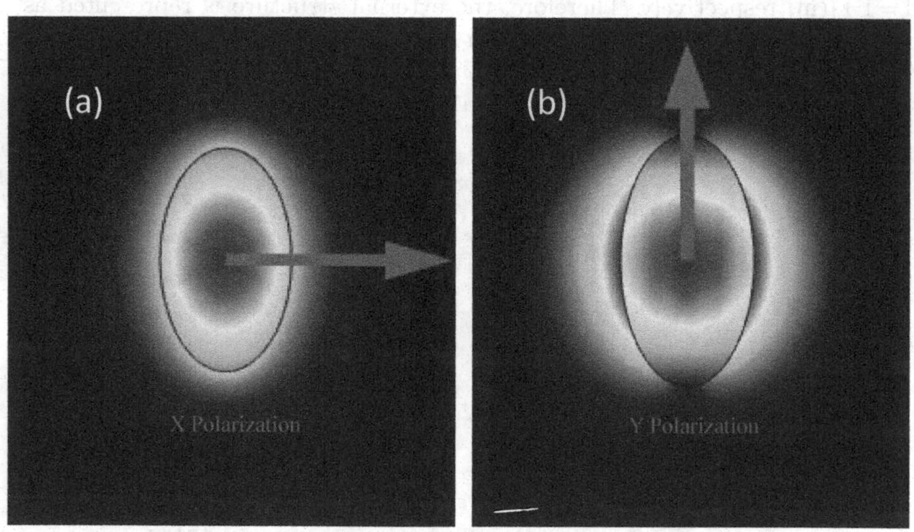

Fig. 2. Mode field distribution of the (a) X-Polarization (b) Y-Polarization

The birefringence of two adjacent states of polarization is estimated by Eq. (2) [10].

$$B(\lambda) = \left| Re\left[n_{eff}^{x}(\lambda) - n_{eff}^{y}(\lambda) \right] \right| \quad (2)$$

Here, n_{eff}^{x} and n_{eff}^{y} are the effective refractive index of Chalcogenide in X and Y polarization. And the Re defines the real part. The performance of polarization is evaluated by the beat length. It is the ratio of birefringence and wavelength. The beat length of the designed PCF is determined by Ref. [10].

$$L_B = \frac{\lambda}{B} \tag{3}$$

Here, L_B and B are represented as the beat length and birefringence. The power fraction of a PCF is the percentage of the ratio of core power and total power of the PCF. It is estimated by Eq. 4 [25].

$$P_f(\%) = \frac{\int_x S_z dA}{\int_{All} S_z dA} \times 100 \tag{4}$$

Here, the nominator and denominator represent the current and total region of interest and S_z defines the pointing vector in the z-direction. The total light acceptance or numerical aperture (NA) is determined through Eq. 5 [25].

$$NA = \left[1 + \frac{\pi A_{eff}}{\lambda^2}\right]^{-\frac{1}{2}} \tag{5}$$

Here, A_{eff} defines the effective refractive area. This area is calculated by Eq. 6 [26].

$$A_{eff} = \frac{(\int\int |E(x,y))|^2 \, dxdy)^2}{\int\int |E(x,y))|^4 \, dxdy} \tag{6}$$

Here, E(x, y) is orthogonal electric field. However, rectangular polarization, mobility, and stability of the proposed PCF may be evaluated by the nonlinear coefficient that is calculated through Eq. 7 [15].

$$\gamma = \frac{2\pi n_2}{\lambda A_{eff}} \tag{7}$$

Here, n_2 and A_{eff} are represented as a nonlinear coefficient and effective area.

3 Result Discussion and Analysis

The proposed PCF is described with several optical parameters like birefringence, beat length, power fraction, numerical aperture, effective mode area and nonlinear coefficient with their explanation, interpretation, diagrammatical definition and optical applications.

Birefringence: Birefringence is a double refraction of light in a lucid, molecular orientation, and it is extremely capable of polarization-maintaining fiber. It is considered as fateful characteristics of PCFs. The birefringence of the proposed PCF is calculated among the difference between the effective refractive indices of the X and Y polarization through the Eq. (2) and also displays in Fig. 3.

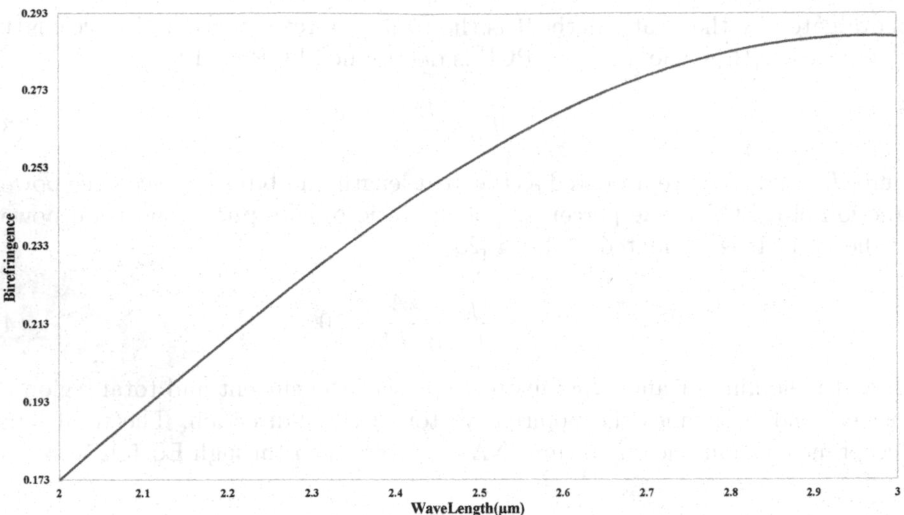

Fig. 3. Investigation of birefringence with respect to the operating wavelength.

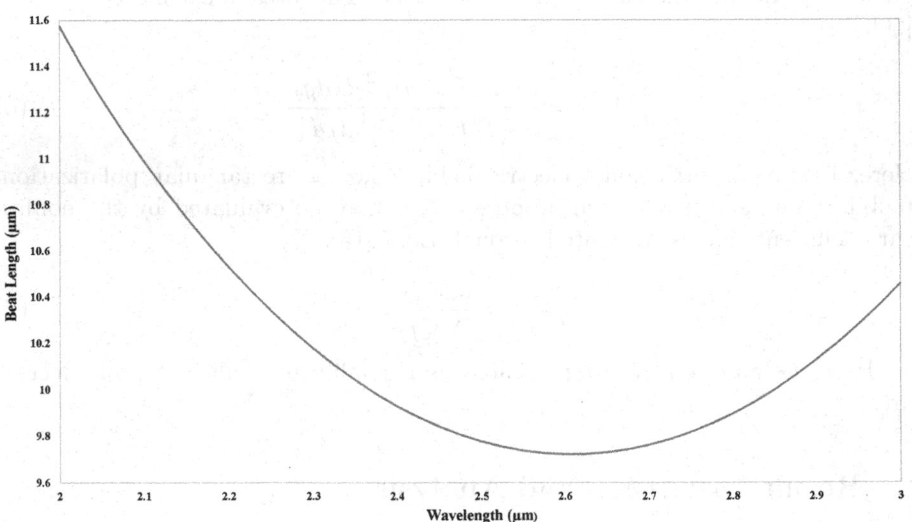

Fig. 4. Analysis of beat length with respect to the wavelength ranging from 2.00 µm to 3.00 µm.

The birefringence of the PCF is gently increased by increasing wavelength. In this scenario, the maximum birefringence is 0.287 at 2.975 µm wavelength and it would be improved than previous work which is shown in Table 1.

Beat Length: Polarization-conserving performance can be achieved by the beat length of the PCF. The fiber with the higher beat length will maintain polarization further strongly than the fiber with the shorter beat length. It is the optical signal dispatch length towards the fiber so that the phase differences of X and Y polarization states fluctuate 2π radians or 360°. Beat length is depended on the operating wavelength and the birefringence. In the proposed PCF, the beat length has been investigated through the mathematical expression (3) and plotted in Fig. 4. In this scenario, the slope of the beat length is gently decreased with wavelength ranging from 2.00 µm to 2.60 µm, and then abruptly increased by increasing wavelength.

Power Fraction: Figure 5 describes the power fraction conversion with respect to wavelength ranging from 2,000 nm to 3,000 nm. It is a percentage of core power with a total power of the PCF. In addition, it characterizes a downward sloping curve that is reversely proportional to raising wavelength from 2.00 µm to 3.00 µm. Nonetheless, power fraction of X and Y polarization can be flattened in a specific range 70.24–89.40% and 43.89–87.29%, respectively from 2.00 µm to 3.00 µm wavelength. Here, the X-polarization is achieved a better the power fraction rather than Y-polarization. The best power fraction for the proposed PCF is 89.40% at 2,000 nm wavelength for the X-polarization. The light is smoothly confined over the core, because up to 80% power entering through the core. The high power fraction is greatly useful for the high bit rate transmissions and high power communications.

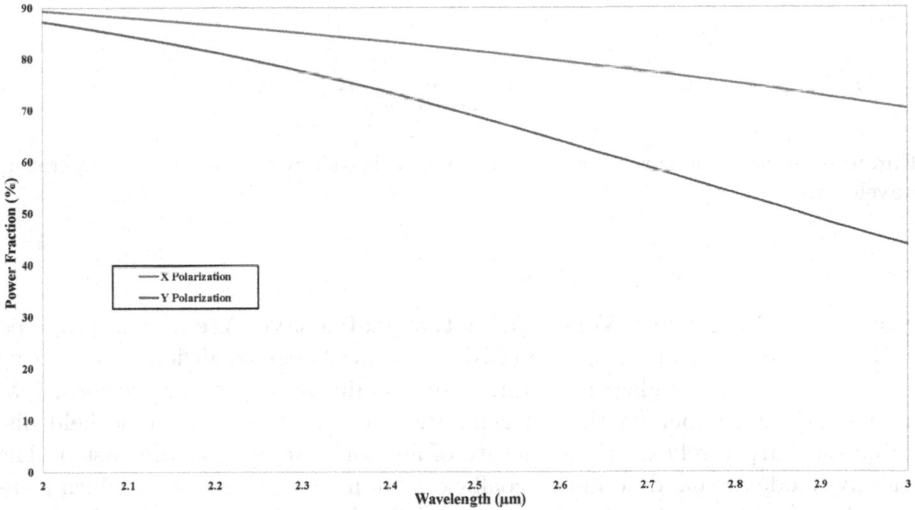

Fig. 5. Power fraction for X and Y polarization for operating wavelength 2.00 µm to 3.00 µm.

Numerical Aperture: The total optical light-receiving at the receiver sight is fully faithful to the numerical aperture (NA) of the proposed PCF. It is calculated through the mathematical expression (5). The NA is a dimensionless parameter. It is dependent on the operating wavelength and effective mode area. The NA of the orthogonal polarization (X and Y polarization) with respect to the wavelength is depicted in Fig. 6. Furthermore, in this Fig. 6, the highest NA achieved by the X-polarization is 0.8602 at 3.00 µm. However, the highest values of the NA, fibers will collect more light (totally enter into the core region) than the lowest values of the NA. The highest value of the proposed PCF is the most suitable in distinct operative applications such as medical imaging and optic coherence tomography (OCT).

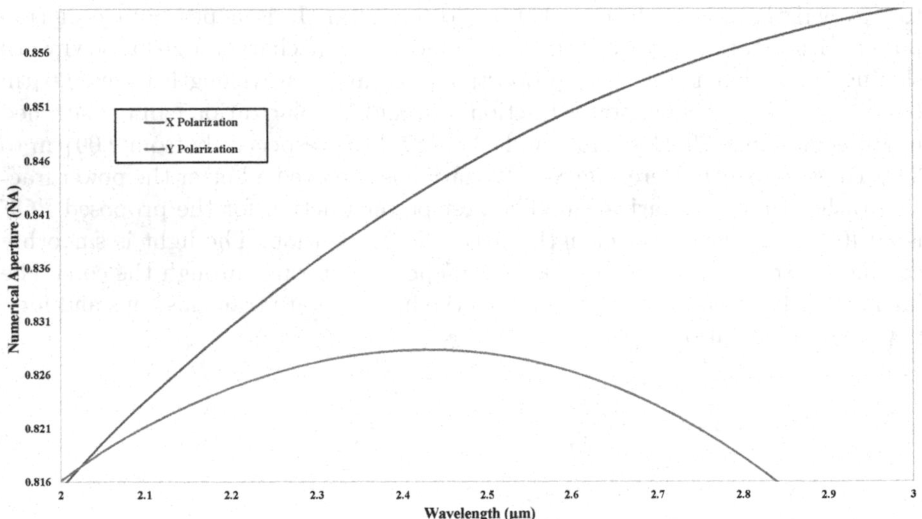

Fig. 6. Numerical aperture of two orthogonal polarization with respect to the operating wavelength.

Nonlinear Coefficient Versus Effective Refractive Area: The proposed PCF produces high birefringence (Hi-Bi) and nonlinear coefficient from a tiny area of ($Ga_8Sb_{32}S_{60}$) glass core. Immensely nonlinear PCFs may necessary for high power and super continuum generation. In addition, the mode field distribution sharply rely on the structure of air holes, shape and dimension. The effective mode area and nonlinear coefficient are inversely associated which mentioned in Eq. (6) and (7). For the proposed PCF, we observe an effective mode area versus nonlinear coefficient profile for the wavelength ranging from 2.00 to 3.00 µm. Hence, the outcome has been mentioned in Fig. 7 and 8 for corresponding modes of X and Y polarization respectively. From the Figs. 7 and 8, it shows the mode area raises for increasing wavelength, on the contrary, nonlinear

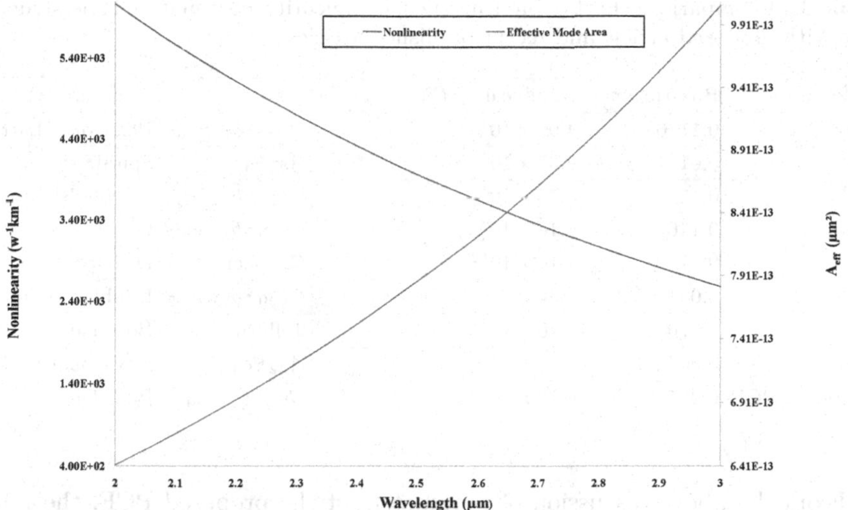

Fig. 7. Nonlinear coefficient and effective mode area of the proposed PCF of X-polarization with wavelength.

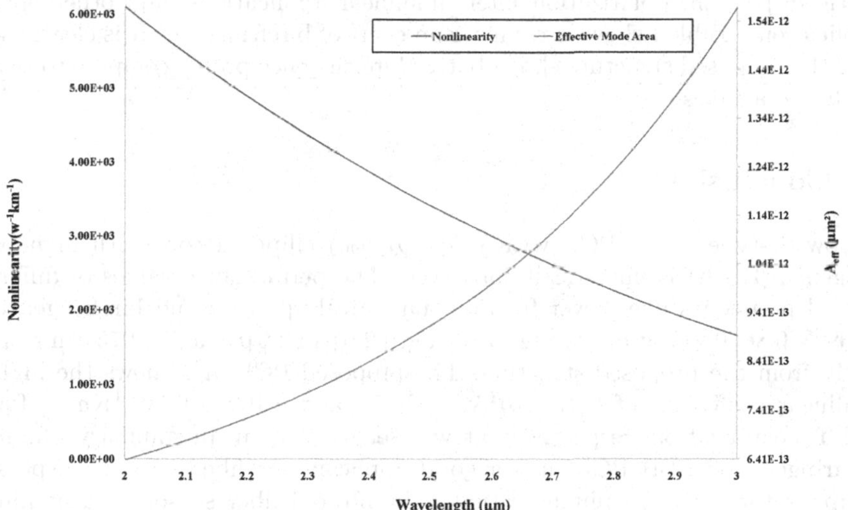

Fig. 8. Nonlinear coefficient and effective mode area of the proposed PCF of Y-polarization with wavelength.

coefficient falls for increasing wavelength. The cause is the field slowly expanses into the cladding region.

Table 1. A comparison chart of birefringence, nonlinearity, core material and structure type with proposed article and recent published articles.

References	Birefringence	Nonlinearity ($W^{-1}Km^{-1}$)	Material	Structure type
[10]	0.1176	4.97×10^4	$Ge_{20}Sb_{15}Se_{65}$	Hexagonal Lattice
[16]	0.01	2.67×10^4	As_2S_3	Spiral
[21]	0.151	3.73×10^3	$Ge_{20}Sb_{15}Se_{65}$	Double-Rhombic
[24]	0.146	6.16×10^3	$Ge_{20}Sb_{15}Se_{65}$	Quasi
[25]	0.17	7.10×10^{12}	Graphene	D-shape
[27]	0.041	4.38×10^3	$Ge_{20}Sb_{15}Se_{65}$	Double-Rhombic
[28]	0.076	3.40×10^3	Tellurite	Bow-Tie
[29]	0.0022	–	As_2Se_3	Hexagonal Lattice
Proposed PCF	0.287	6.10×10^3	$Ga_8Sb_{32}S_{60}$	Bow-Tie

From the above discussion of parameters of the proposed PCF, the power fraction, numerical aperture, nonlinear coefficient are better for the optical performance. Therefore, the birefringence of the PCF is so much higher than previous articles. Thus for the high birefringence of the proposed PCF is useful for gentle dispersion, polarization filter, nonlinear applications, and other optical applications. Table 1 shows a comparison chart of birefringence. It is clearly seen that the proposed structure shows better birefringence profile compare to recent published articles.

4 Conclusion

A bow-tie-type based PCF with ($Ga_8Sb_{32}S_{60}$) elliptical core with high birefringence (Hi-Bi) is numerically observed. The performance values of different optical properties like power fraction, numerical aperture and birefringence of 89.39%, 0.86, 0.287 at operating wavelength 2.0 µm 3.0 µm and 2.975 µm respectively from the proposed structure. The proposed PCF also shows the highest nonlinear coefficient of $6.07 \times 10^3\,W^{-1}Km^{-1}$ and $6.10 \times 10^3\,W^{-1}Km^{-1}$ for X and Y polaraization, respectively at wavelength 2.0 µm. In summary, the high birefringence (Hi-Bi) PCF may a good applicant for fiber sensors, dispersion compensator, optical communication, mid-infrared fiber sensor, and nonlinear applications.

References

1. Paul, B.K., Moctader, M.G., Ahmed, K., Khalek, M.A.: Nanoscale GaP strips based photonic crystal fiber with high nonlinearity and high numerical aperture for laser applications. Results Phys. **10**, 374–378 (2018)
2. Sonne, A., Ouchar, A., Sonne, K.: Improving of high birefringence with negative dispersion using double octagonal lattice photonic crystal fiber. Optik **127**(1), 8–10 (2016)

3. Wang, A., et al.: Visible supercontinuum generation with sub-nanosecond 532-nm pulses in all-solid photonic bandgap fiber. IEEE Photonics Technol. Lett. **24**(2), 143–145 (2011)
4. Yatsenko, Y.P., Pryamikov, A.D.: Parametric frequency conversion in photonic crystal fibres with germanosilicate core. J. Opt. A: Pure Appl. Opt. **9**(7), 716 (2007)
5. Ahmed, F., Roy, S., Paul, B.K., Ahmed, K., Bahar, A.N.: Extremely low loss of photonic crystal fiber for terahertz wave propagation in optical communication applications. J. Opt. Commun. (2018). https://doi.org/10.1515/joc-2018-0009
6. Habib, M.S., Ahmad, R., Habib, M.S., Hasan, M.I.: Residual dispersion compensation over the S+ C+ L+ U wavelength bands using highly birefringent octagonal photonic crystal fiber. Appl. Opt. **53**(14), 3057–3062 (2014)
7. Emiliyanov, G., Hoiby, P., Pedersen, L., Bang, O.: Selective serial multi-antibody biosensing with TOPAS microstructured polymer optical fibers. Sensors **13**(3), 3242–3251 (2013)
8. Woodward, R.M., Wallace, V.P., Arnone, D.D., Linfield, E.H., Pepper, M.: Terahertz pulsed imaging of skin cancer in the time and frequency domain. J. Biol. Phys. **29**(2–3), 257–259 (2003)
9. Zhang, J., Grischkowsky, D.: Waveguide terahertz time-domain spectroscopy of nanometer water layers. Opt. Lett. **29**(14), 1617–1619 (2004)
10. Zhanqiang, H., Zhang, Y., Zhou, H., Wang, Z., Zeng, X.: Mid-infrared high birefringence bow-tie-type Ge20Sb15Se65 based PCF with large nonlinearity by using hexagonal elliptical air hole. Fiber Integr. Opt. **37**(1), 21–36 (2018)
11. Eggleton, B.J., Luther-Davies, B., Richardson, K.: Chalcogenide photonics. Nat. Photonics **5**(3), 141 (2011)
12. Eggleton, B.J.: Chalcogenide photonics: fabrication, devices and applications Introduction. Opt. Express **18**(25), 26632–26634 (2010)
13. Zhang, M.Y., Li, S.G., Yao, Y.Y., Zhang, L., Fu, B., Yin, G.B.: Influence of microstructured core on characteristics of photonic crystal fibers. Acta Phys. Sinica **59**(5), 3278–3285 (2010)
14. Agrawal, A., Kejalakshmy, N., Chen, J., Rahman, B.M.A., Grattan, K.T.V.: Golden spiral photonic crystal fiber: polarization and dispersion properties. Opt. Lett. **33**(22), 2716–2718 (2008)
15. Wang, W., Yang, B., Song, H., Fan, Y.: Investigation of high birefringence and negative dispersion photonic crystal fiber with hybrid crystal lattice. Optik-Int. J. Light Electron Opt. **124**(17), 2901–2903 (2013)
16. Revathi, S., Inbathini, S.R., Saifudeen, R.A.: Highly nonlinear and birefringent spiral photonic crystal fiber. Adv. OptoElectronics **2014**, 464391 (2014)
17. Revathi, S., Inabathini, S., Sandeep, R.: Soft glass spiral photonic crystal fiber for large nonlinearity and high birefringence. Opt. Appl. **45**(1), 15–24 (2015)
18. Yang, T., Wang, E., Jiang, H., Hu, Z., Xie, K.: High birefringence photonic crystal fiber with high nonlinearity and low confinement loss. Opt. Exp. **23**(7), 8329–8337 (2015)
19. Hasan, M.I., Habib, M.S., Habib, M.S., Razzak, S.A.: Design of hybrid photonic crystal fiber: polarization and dispersion properties. Photonics Nanostruct. Fundam. Appl. **12**(2), 205–211 (2014)
20. Liao, J., et al.: Ultrahigh birefringent nonlinear slot silicon microfiber with low dispersion. IEEE Photonics Technol. Lett. **27**(17), 1868–1871 (2015)
21. Hui, Z.Q., et al.: Midinfrared high birefringence $Ga_{20}Sb_{15}S_{65}$-based photonic crystal fiber with large nonlinearity using dual-rhombic air hole. J. Nanophotonics **12**(1), 016018 (2018)

22. Ohishi, Y.: New prospect of soft glass highly nonlinear microstructured optical fibers. In: Conference on Lasers and Electro-Optics/Pacific Rim. Optical Society of America, TuA4_2 (2013)
23. Chauhan, P., Kumar, A., Kalra, Y., Saini, T.S.: Design and analysis of photonic crystal fiber in Ga-Sb-S chalcogenide glass for nonlinear applications. In: AIP Conference Proceedings, vol. 2009, no. 1, p. 020047 (2018)
24. Amiri, I.S., et al.: Design of $Ga_{20}Sb_{15}S_{65}$ embedded rectangular slotted quasi photonic crystal fiber for higher nonlinearity applications. Optik **184**, 63–69 (2019)
25. Ahmed, K., Paul, B.K., Jabin, M.A., Biswas, B.: FEM analysis of birefringence, dispersion and nonlinearity of graphene coated photonic crystal fiber. Ceram. Int. **45**(12), 15343–15347 (2019)
26. Hassan, M.M., Kabir, M.A., Hossain, M.N., Biswas, B., Paul, B.K., Ahmed, K.: Photonic crystal fiber for robust orbital angular momentum transmission: design and investigation. Opt. Quantum Electron. **52**(1), 8 (2020)
27. Hui, Z., Zhang, Y., Soliman, A.H.: Mid-infrared dual-rhombic air hole $Ga_{20}Sb_{15}S_{65}$ chalcogenide photonic crystal fiber with high birefringence and high nonlinearity. Ceram. Int. **44**(9), 10383–10392 (2018)
28. Wei, S., et al.: Design on a highly birefringent and highly nonlinear tellurite ellipse core photonic crystal fiber with two zero dispersion wavelengths. Opt. Fiber Technol. **20**(4), 320–324 (2014)
29. Dabas, B., Sinha, R.K.: Design of highly birefringent chalcogenide glass PCF: a simplest design. Opt. Commun. **284**(5), 1186–1191 (2011)

A Bioinformatics Analysis to Identify Hub Genes from Protein-Protein Interaction Network for Cancer and Stress

Md. Liton Ahmed[1], Md. Rakibul Islam[1], Bikash Kumar Paul[1,2,3(✉)], Kawsar Ahmed[2], and Touhid Bhuyian[1]

[1] Department of Software Engineering, Daffodil International University, Sukrabad, Dhanmondi, Dhaka, Bangladesh
{liton35-114,bikash.swe}@diu.edu.bd

[2] Department of Information and Communication Technology (ICT), Mawlana Bhashani Science and Technology University (MBSTU), Santosh, Tangail 1902, Bangladesh

[3] Group of Bio-photomatix, Santosh, Tangail, Bangladesh

Abstract. Cancer is a disease involving the uncontrollable growth of cells with potential strafe to other organs of the body. Stress is a state of the body a non-specific response to any demand for change. Cancer had a deep relation with stress. Activation of the stress response and exposure to the associated hormones could promote the growth and spread of tumors. The immune system can be important for finding and eliminating cancer cells. This study is based on Cancer and Stress. In this study, we collect responsible genes from NCBI's Gene database individually for stress and cancer. After that, common responsible genes were collected by using Venny online tools. From the common genes, we had constructed a protein-protein interaction network using the STRING database. Afterward, the top 10 hub genes were identified by using CytoHubba. Hub genes were identified based on their degree value where degree value more than or equal 72 are considered as hub gene. These hub genes may use to design a potential drug for cancer and stress combine. We have collected 3264 and 9433 human genes for Cancer and Stress respectively. 2477 common genes are found through Venny. We have been identified the UBC, TP53, RPS3, RPL5, RPL11, RPS27A, RPL19, RPL3, RPS7, and CTNNB1 as targeted hub genes by using the CytoHubba plugin of Cytoscape.

Keywords: PPI network · Gene regulatory network · Cancer · Stress · Computational biology

1 Introduction

Cancer is a term which is familiar to explain a physical process, in which the body cell increases uncontrollable and irregular process to the extent that create a form

T. Bhuiyan et al. (Eds.): ICONCS 2020, LNICST 325, pp. 671–679, 2020.
https://doi.org/10.1007/978-3-030-52856-0_53

of a tumor [1]. The rate of mortality of human for cancer is increasing day by day. According to the World Health Organization (WHO), Cancer is the second main cause of the death of people worldwide. One out of 5 men and one of every 6 women overall create cancer growth in their lifetime and one out of 8 men and one of every 11 women dies of cancer. The worldwide cancer burden has increased to 18.1 million new cases and 9.6 million deaths in 2018 [2]. In 2012, there were 14,100,000 new cases and 8,200,000 deaths for cancer worldwide. The lung cancer was 1,820,000, breast cancer was 1,670,000 and colorectal was 1,360,000 and the most widely recognized reasons for cancer death were lung cancer 1,600,000 deaths, liver cancer 745,000 deaths and stomach cancer 723,000 deaths [3]. By subgroup investigations, they found that North America populations and male laborers are at higher danger of cancer than Europeans and female laborers. In their research, they found that the increased risk is higher in men than women for lung and colorectal cancer [4]. Among the total population of Bangladesh, the death rate of lung cancer (per 1 million population) for men was 1591 and women were 231 [5].

Stress is also increasing rapidly day by day. It is increasing worldwide. The word stress was coined by Hans Selye, who defined it as "the non-specific response of the body to any demand for change". Stress is a major threat to human beings because these daily needs can't be managed satisfactorily and it is at risk of health and social aspects of life [6]. According to the American Institute of Stress, the top causes of stress are job pressure, Money, Health, Relationships, Poor Nutrition, Media Overload and Sleep Deprivation in the U.S. As a result of stress, psychological turmoil, loss of mood in a short time, tetchy mood, avoiding the work, losing encouraged in the work, avoiding duties, mistakes in the work even self-injury or suicide thoughts may come.

In this study, we constructed a protein-protein interaction network by using the common genes of cancer and stress through the help of Cytoscape software. Oxidative stress reason of DNA destruction in genes that is related to colon cancer of human [7]. There is a deep relation between Cancer and stress. This study will show how much the relationship is between cancer and stress. Their analysis showed that the important risk factor for lung cancer, colorectal cancer, esophagus cancer, and overall cancer is work stress. There are various biological processes whereby stress at work can lead to cancer [4].

In recent years, cancer and stress patients have been growing unbelievably. In this study, they compared the performance of network-based methods using protein expression profiles for cancer protein ranking. Jie Ren told that Global network-based ranking is more efficient for proteomics data in cancer protein identification [8]. In this research, Chao Wu had improved a method which name was NGP (Networked Gene Prioritizer) to prioritize cancer-associated genes and contrast the deeds of NGP with HKR (Heat Kernel Ranking), the Taylor method and RIF (Regulatory Impact Factor) [9]. The analysis proved that the performance of NGP was better than another method [9]. Nobody has yet created a PPI network for cancer and stress. This will give a revolutionary change in Bio-medical and it will add a new dimension to medical science.

2 Proposed Methodology

See Fig. 1.

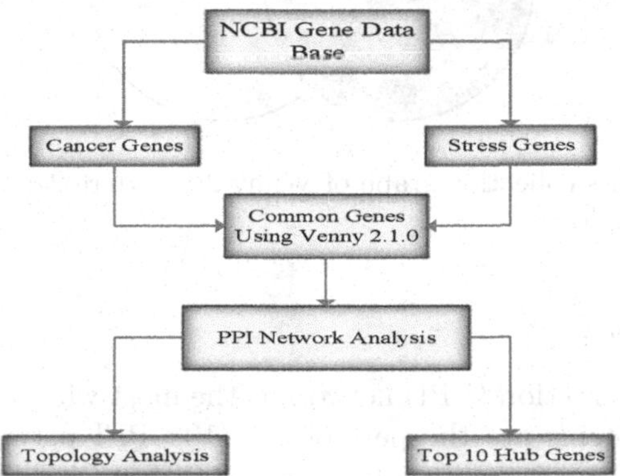

Fig. 1. The flowchart of working procedure of this study.

2.1 Gene Collection, Filtering and Common Genes Finding

The associated genes of Cancer and Stress are collected from the NCBI's (National Center for Biotechnology Information) gene database. NCBI is a trusted vast gene repository. It stores genes, DNA and protein sequence data for human and other animals. It also provides a different kind of databases that help to analyze the biological processes. Only human genes are collected as a filter. There were many common genes between two selected disease, we used Venny 2.1.0 (https://bioinfogp.cnb.csic.es/tools/venny/) to identify the common genes between cancer and stress (Table 1 and Fig. 2).

Table 1. Gene collection table for Cancer and Stress.

Name of disease	No. of gene for human	Common genes between cancer and stress only for human
Cancer	9433	
Stress	3264	2477

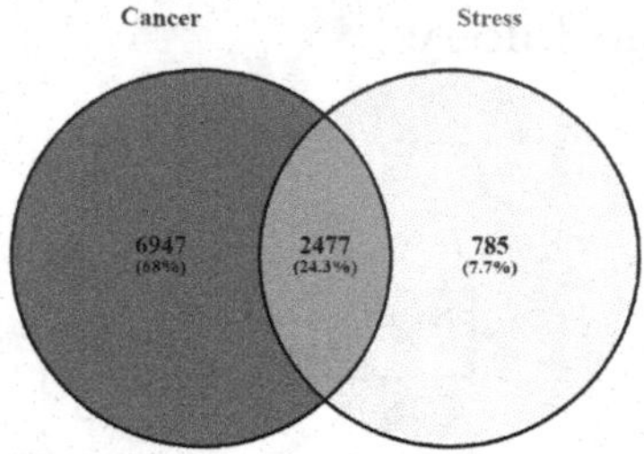

Fig. 2. Common genes collection graph of Venny 2.1.0. Here 24.3% genes are common between Cancer and Stress.

2.2 PPI Network

Protein-protein Interaction (PPI) network is the most widely recognized natural systems where proteins are the part of cell [10]. PPI network recapitulates a huge number of protein-protein interaction data from individual small experiments [11]. We had constructed a PPI network by using an online tool STRING database with a 990-confidence score. Currently, the STRING database covers 24.6 million proteins from the 5090 organisms [12]. We had collected the sif file of the PPI network from NetworkAnalyst online tool, where it uses the STRING database to generate a PPI network by using gene information [13]. Afterward, we visualize the sif file and construct the PPI network with Cytoscape software, which is a popular open-source biological software [14].

2.3 Topological Analysis

NetworkAnalyzer enumerates the topological network properties for directed and undirected networks which is a plugin of Cytoscape [15]. CytoHubba is used to explore the important hub genes in a PPI network [16]. It provides 11 topological analysis methods including Degree, Edge Percolated Component, Maximum Neighborhood Component, Density of Maximum Neighborhood Component, Maximal Clique Centrality and six centralities (Bottleneck, EcCentricity, Closeness, Radiality, Betweenness, and Stress) based on shortest paths [16].

3 Results and Discussion

The findings are described in the below sub-section respectably. The main goal of this study is to create PPI network and then analyze the network.

3.1 Common Genes Finding and PPI Network Construction

We collected genes from the NCBI Gene database. For stress and cancer, we had collected 3264 and 9433 human genes respectively. Using Venny, we were found 2477 common genes between the two selected diseases. A PPI network is constructed using those common genes where the number of nodes (genes) are 3009 and the edge number is 7580. The PPI has been built by Cytoscape with STRING database.

3.2 Topological Analysis of PPI Network

In undirect network, NetworkAnalyzer plugin can compute the various topological parameters. NetworkAnalyzer calculate the parameters of this undirect PPI network, where 0.233 is clustering coefficient, Network diameter is 13, Network centralization is 0.178, Shortest paths are 8495452 (93%), Network density is 0.002, Network heterogeneity is 2.579 and the radius of the network is 1.

In the undirected network, node degree represents the number of interactions connecting with other nodes. Such as UBC is interconnected with other 541 nodes/proteins. The betweenness centrality of a node reflects the amount of control that this node exerts over the interactions of other nodes in the network [17]. Closeness centrality is a quantity of how shortly information is transmitted from a given node to other available nodes in the network. The neighborhood connectivity gives the average connectivity of all neighbor's node. In directed and undirected networks, the clustering coefficient is a ratio N/M, where N is the number of edges between neighbors of n, and M is probably the maximum number of neighbor's edge of n [17]. It discerns commensurate to the size of the node. The topological coefficient is a comparative quantity for the boundary in which one node imparts neighbors with other nodes (Table 2 and Fig. 3).

Table 2. Topological analysis result table of Cancer and Stress genes using NetworkAnalyzer plugin.

Name of gene	Node degree	Betweenness centrality	Closeness centrality	Topological coefficient	Neighborhood connectivity	Stress centrality
UBC	541	0.63020811	0.42527729	0.00617573	10.65988909	35287354
TP53	129	0.09867435	0.35334061	0.01590495	19.04651163	6000302
RPS3	95	0.00992221	0.30741639	0.03277625	20.8	911062
RPL5	92	0.00654576	0.30532272	0.03456416	21.34782609	697860
RPL11	88	0.00489242	0.30500314	0.03573273	22.01136364	603740
RPS27A	84	0.01050204	0.32067789	0.03462774	26.17857143	887090
RPL19	82	0.00609683	0.30699536	0.03742773	23.85365854	679740
RPL3	80	0.00445669	0.30693069	0.03812696	24.325	658304
RPS7	76	0.00325889	0.30474796	0.04036936	24.90789474	415384
CTNNB1	72	0.04426593	0.33676182	0.02378177	24.04166667	2897114

Figure 4 is constructed using the CytoHubba that is a plugin of Cytoscape. And the degree value is greater than or equal to 72. Ten genes are found as hub gene. Those ten genes are UBC, TP53, RPS3, RPL5, RPL11, RPS27A, RPL19, RPL3, RPS7 and CTNNB1. Rakib et al. shows that UBC is a key gene of stress [18]. Ten Different color nodes represent the high node degree value in Fig. 4. Where red to green colors represent high to low degree value.

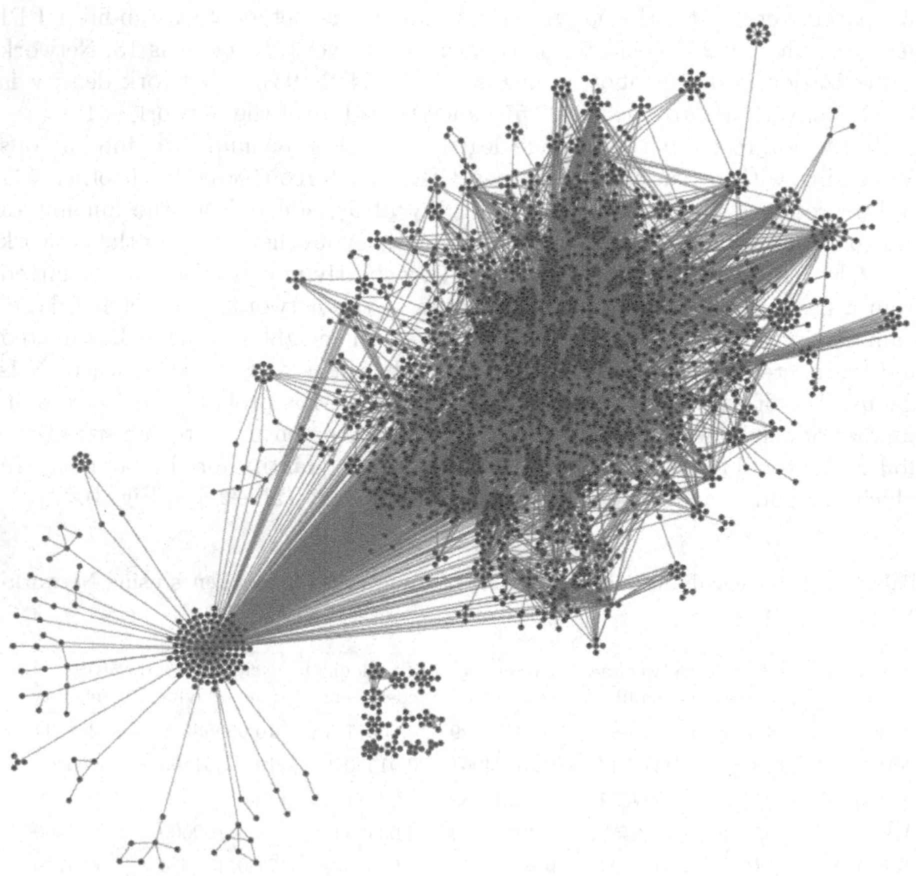

Fig. 3. Protein-protein interaction (PPI) network of Cancer and Stress. Each node represents a protein and edges represents protein interactions. The network is created by Cytoscape software. The network consists of 3009 nodes and 7580 edges.

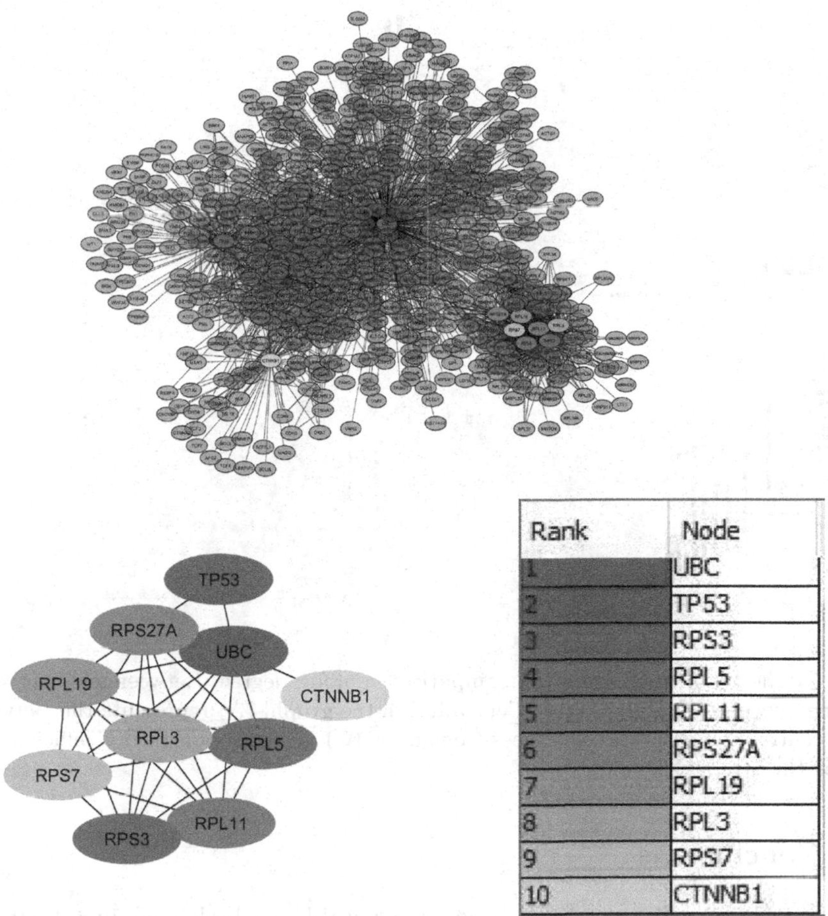

Rank	Node
1	UBC
2	TP53
3	RPS3
4	RPL5
5	RPL11
6	RPS27A
7	RPL19
8	RPL3
9	RPS7
10	CTNNB1

Fig. 4. PPI network of Cancer and Stress using the CytoHubba. Color node indicates that the top ten nodes according to their degree value. (Color figure online)

The scatter plots of Fig. 5 have been generated by NetworkAnalyzer that is a plugin of Cytoscape. Figure 5 (A) was created using the values of betweenness centrality and number of neighbors. It indicates that a limited number of hubs (high interaction) control the lower interaction nodes [19]. Figure 5 (B) computes the closeness centrality of all nodes against the number of neighbors. Figure 5 (C) represents that, how many neighbors are shared with other nodes by the topological coefficient. Figure 5 (D) shows the measure of the shortest path that passes through the nodes. A node has a high stress When a high shorest path passes through a node.

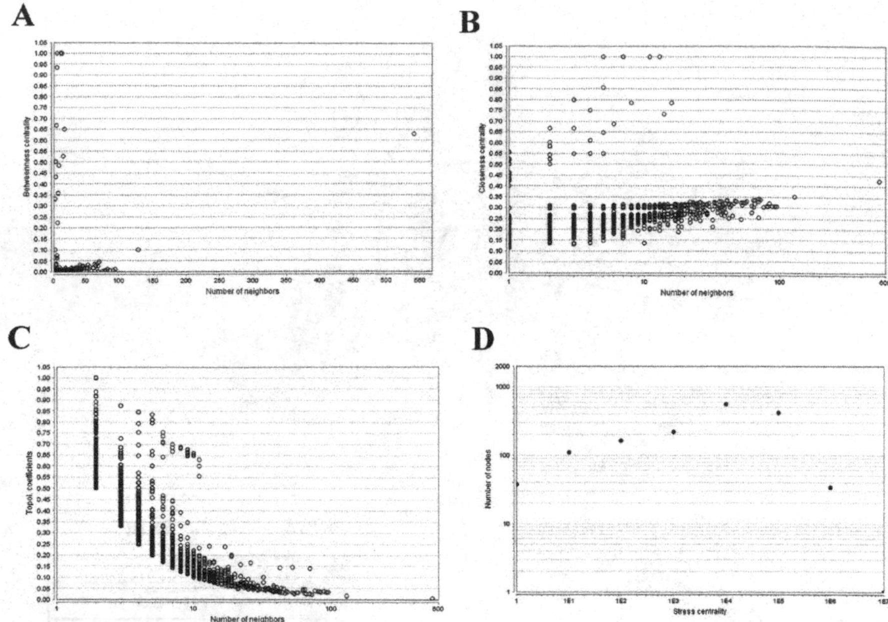

Fig. 5. The graph represents the comparisons among degree, Betweenness centrality, Closeness Centrality, and Stress Centrality. In the graph, (A) represents the Betweenness centrality, (B) is the Closeness Centrality, (C) is the Topological Coefficient and (D) is the Stress Centrality.

4 Conclusions

Computational methods have become inevitable to biological investigations. Basically, exhibited for the biological analysis of sequences, Bioinformatics now surrounded by a wide range of subject areas with structural biology, genomics, and gene expression studies. In present Bioinformatics arrange data in a way that allows researchers to entrance existing information and to commit new entries as they are grown. In this study, we got 10 hub genes UBC, TP53, RPS3, RPL5, RPL11, RPS27A, RPL19, RPL3, RPS7, and CTNNB1. These 10 genes have a significant role in progression of Cancer and Stress. Using 10 genes, potential drugs may build to cure these two diseases. Our future analysis will be on to design a potential drugs for Cancer and Stress.

References

1. Kangas, M., Henry, J.L., Bryant, R.A.: Posttraumatic stress disorder following cancer: a conceptual and empirical review. Clin. Psychol. Rev. **22**(4), 499–524 (2002)
2. Ferlay, J., et al.: Estimating the global cancer incidence and mortality in 2018: GLOBOCAN sources and methods. Int. J. Cancer **144**(8), 1941–1953 (2019)

3. Ferlay, J., et al.: Cancer incidence and mortality worldwide: sources, methods and major patterns in GLOBOCAN 2012. Int. J. Cancer **136**(5), E359–E386 (2015)
4. Yang, T., Qiao, Y., Xiang, S., Li, W., Gan, Y., Chen, Y.: Work stress and the risk of cancer: a meta-analysis of observational studies. Int. J. Cancer **144**(10), 2390–2400 (2019)
5. Ahmed, K., et al.: Early detection of lung cancer risk using data mining. Asian Pac. J. Cancer Prev. **62**(4) (2013)
6. Sharma, N., Gedeon, T.: Objective measures, sensors and computational techniques for stress recognition and classification: a survey. Comput. Methods Programs Biomed. **108**(3), 1287–1301 (2012)
7. Glei, M., et al.: Comet fluorescence in situ hybridization analysis for oxidative stress-induced DNA damage in colon cancer relevant genes. Toxicol. Sci. **96**(2), 279–284 (2006)
8. Ren, J., Shang, L., Wang, Q., Li, J.: Ranking cancer proteins by integrating PPI network and protein expression profiles. BioMed Res. Int. (2019)
9. Wu, C., Zhu, J., Zhang, X.: Integrating gene expression and protein-protein interaction network to prioritize cancer-associated genes. BMC Bioinform. **13**(1), 182 (2012)
10. Cheng, L., Liu, P., Wang, D., Leung, K.S.: Exploiting locational and topological overlap model to identify modules in protein interaction networks. BMC Bioinform. **20**(1), 23 (2019)
11. Bork, P., Jensen, L.J., Von, M.C., Ramani, A.K., Lee, I., Marcotte, E.M.: Protein interaction networks from yeast to human. Curr. Opin. Struct. Biol. **14**(3), 292–299 (2004)
12. Szklarczyk, D., et al.: STRING v11: protein-protein association networks with increased coverage, supporting functional discovery in genome-wide experimental datasets. Nucleic Acids Res. **47**(D1), D607–D613 (2018)
13. Murray, P., McGee, F., Forbes, A.G.: A taxonomy of visualization tasks for the analysis of biological pathway data. BMC Bioinform. **18**(2), 21 (2017)
14. Yeung, N., Cline, M.S., Kuchinsky, A., Smoot, M.E., Bader, G.D.: Exploring biological networks with cytoscape software. Curr. Protoc. Bioinform. **23**(1), 8–13 (2008)
15. Assenov, Y., Ramírez, F., Schelhorn, S.E., Lengauer, T., Albrecht, M.: Computing topological parameters of biological networks. Curr. Protoc. Bioinform. **24**(2), 282–284 (2007)
16. Chin, C.H., Chen, S.H., Wu, H.H., Ho, C.W., Ko, M.T., Lin, C.Y.: cytoHubba: identifying hub objects and sub-networks from complex interactome. BMC Syst. Biol. **8**(4), S11 (2014)
17. Doncheva, N.T., Assenov, Y., Domingues, F.S., Albrecht, M.: Topological analysis and interactive visualization of biological networks and protein structures. Nat. Protoc. **7**(4), 670 (2012)
18. Islam, M.R., Ahmed, M.L., Paul, B.K., Bhuiyan, T., Ahmed, K.: Potential therapeutic drugs for ischemic stroke and stress disorder: a bioinformatics analysis. Inf. Med. Unlocked **17**, 100259 (2019)
19. Najafi, A., Masoudi, N.A., Ghanei, M., Nourani, M.R., Moeini, A.: Pathway reconstruction of airway remodeling in chronic lung diseases: a systems biology approach. PLoS ONE **9**(6), e100094 (2014)

Innovative Automation Algorithm in Micro-multinational Data-Entry Industry

Nuruzzaman Faruqui[1](✉), Mohammad Abu Yousuf[1], Partha Chakraborty[2], and Md. Safaet Hossain[3]

[1] Institute of Information Technology, Jahangirnagar University, Savar, Dhaka, Bangladesh
faruquizaman27@gmail.com

[2] Department of Computer Science and Engineering, Comilla University, Comilla, Bangladesh

[3] Department of Computer Science and Engineering, City University, Dhaka, Bangladesh

Abstract. Data have ascended a place among capital, labor and land in production. The emerging data-driven economy has facilitated the scope of growth of data-entry industry – an industry equipped with modern computing and communication infrastructure enriched with specialized software interface allowing data-entry professionals to look into the source, collect and store target data. These data are used in business intelligence and analytics for value creation. By nature, data-entry is a tedious and repetitive task. It not only hampers creativity of the operators but also leave a possibility of wrong entry. In this paper, an innovative algorithm has been proposed which can automate the date entry industry with above 97% accuracy, more than 15 times faster than existing speed with no additional cost apart from the cost of existing infrastructure. The proposed algorithm has been tested and compared with several data-entry focused companies which demonstrate that it outperforms current manual data-entry approach and it has the potential to revolutionize the data-entry industry.

Keywords: Automation · String matching · Root inspection · String replacement · Mapping matrix · Local server

1 Introduction

The digital transformation is changing the way of operating business; the way economies work and humans interact [1]. The life on social media has added a new dimension to human life [2]. The emergence and acceptance of virtual social life are fueling the need of migrating to online business model. Here, physical form of each individual, their behavior and activities are a set of data. The analysis of these data can be used to predict market demands, make intellectual decisions and prepare guideline for sustained innovation. Which has underpinned the emergence the data-driven economy where data are at the core [3]. The internet is a vast source of data. It is possible to mine these data, extract knowledge, and utilize them to develop tactical business strategies and stay ahead in competition of seizing the larger market share. Many micro-multinational

T. Bhuiyan et al. (Eds.): ICONCS 2020, LNICST 325, pp. 680–692, 2020.
https://doi.org/10.1007/978-3-030-52856-0_54

companies have emerged lately to fill the demand of data [4]. The business model is simple – collecting, processing, storing and delivering data to the clients. The clients mine the data, extract knowledge and use them the way they are intended to. However, this emerging data-entry industry is mostly powered by manual labor.

The manual data-entry process is slow and there are possibilities of making mistakes [5]. Although there are software interface designed to reduce the number of wrong inputs, guarantee of 100% accuracy cannot be promised. Moreover, data-entry is a tedious task. In their research, S. Shukla, S. Salve and P. Y. Yavar have shown that monotony can hamper the concentration and thus lead to speed-accuracy reduction [6]. On the contrary, B. Laursen, B. R. Jensen and G. Sjøgaard suggested that the speed of human repetitive action becomes faster with more iterations [7]. However, human capability has limit. Employing more operators can faster the process with additional cost. There are several options to minimize the cost. Outsourcing the data-entry responsibility in underdeveloped or developing countries is one of them. Low wages, low employment to graduation ratio, high unemployment rate have fostered an economy in these countries where it is possible to get qualified data-entry operators at a low wage. Thus, data-entry centric micro-multinational companies are growing in underdeveloped and developing part of the world [8].

Another way of reducing the cost, enhancing the accuracy and speeding up the process is automation. Machine learning algorithms may be an option to automate the process. However, to train a model to collect data from heterogeneous source such as the web, a very large volume of data with proper quality [9] is required. In fact, the data required to train a model are the data the data-entry professionals collect. After collecting the data through operators, machine-learning approach may be a convenient solution. However, if the data-source changes, the accuracy of the existing model will be compromised [10]. Data-entry automation through string-matching algorithm is another option [11]. However, pattern-matching algorithms match exact case [12]. There may be multiple variations in the data and the data may vary from source to source. That is why; designing an algorithm to automate the data-entry process leveraging a well performing string-matching algorithm is a challenging task. Through proper data processing, establishing the relation between data and their pattern of distribution, it is possible to overcome the challenges and use string-matching algorithms to automate the data-entry process. Such an algorithm has been developed, applied and tested in this paper.

The rest of the paper is organized as follows – The background study, related and relevant researches have been highlighted in Sect. 2. The methodology has been demonstrated in Sect. 3. The Sect. 4 contains the implementation process. The experimental data and performance analysis are in Sect. 5. Finally, the paper has been concluded in Sect. 6.

2 Background

Pattern-matching algorithms find out presence of the target string within source string.

The traditional string-matching approach before 1977 used to start matching characters from the beginning of a string and when the characters of substring used to match sequentially, it used to be considered as a match. However, for a target pattern $a^n b$ and in $a^{2n}b$ string, a total number of $(n + 1)^2$ comparisons are necessary. Moreover, the traditional approach used to involve backing up the input text as a search progress. It introduces additional complexity. Which is not an efficient approach. D. E. Knuth, J. H. Morris, Jr., and V. R. Pratt have developed an algorithm which finds all of the occurrences of a pattern of m length within a text of n length. Their algorithm performs the search in $O(m + n)$ time without any backing up complexity [13] and thus improves the accuracy while reduces the time required to find a match. With reduced complexity and better accuracy, the string-matching algorithm becomes a good fit for data-entry automation.

Another string-matching algorithm was proposed by R.S. Boyer and J.S. Moore which searches the location of the target string in the source string. Instead of starting from the beginning of the string, they started from the end of the pattern which leads to an unusual yet effective characteristics. In their research, it has been demonstrated that the algorithm often overlooks large portion of the text being searched and makes the algorithm faster. The number of the characters to be inspected is a function of the length of the target string. If a string written in English alphabet has five characters, and the match found at i^{th} position, then the algorithm will check i/4 characters. That means, the number of characters to be inspected decreases. As a result, for large pattern, the inspection time reduces and the location of the character is tracked faster [14]. When the location of the target string is tracked, it becomes easier to scrape the target from the source.

The approaches of both [13] and [14] includes the location of the starting point of characters of the target string. The proposed algorithm of this paper requires an approach where no particular direction such as starting from beginning or starting from end is mandatory. Because the data-source are the web where billions of valuable data are mixed with data having little or no value. Algorithm requires to start from beginning or end will end up in scanning a large amount unwanted data to look for the desired one. In 1990, D.M. Sunday proposed a string-matching algorithm which can match pattern without requiring any particular direction. The proposed method addresses the limitations of KMP and BM algorithms [14, 15]. The capability of searching for target string in any direction paves the way of developing an automatic system using string-matching algorithm to scrape thousands of data in less amount of time.

The D.M. Sunday' string matching algorithm is an improvement of BM algorithm.

BM algorithm for English text is several times faster than KMP algorithm [15]. However, it has some limitations. The limitations of BM algorithm has been addressed and eliminated in D.M. Sunday's algorithm. It has three variations. The first variation is the quick search algorithm which is easy to code, execute and performs faster. It adopts the scanning direction of straight-forward (SF) algorithm. However, one of the variations of D.M. Sunday's algorithm, maximal shift (MS) algorithm, maximizes the shift through the characters while searching for specific pattern. It increases the speed of searching. The third variation of D.M. Sunday's algorithm is optimal mismatch (OM) algorithm, which uses a string-pattern scan order that optimizes the possibility of getting a mismatch at inspecting positions [16]. The speed, efficiency and robustness of D.M. Sunday's algorithm can be used to automate data-entry process. The FS algorithm performs very fast searching whereas the MS algorithm further enhances the speed by shifting the current inspecting position by maximum shift. For very large volume of data the OM algorithm can inspect the mismatching elements faster. Combining the variations of Sunday's string-matching algorithm, a fast, efficient and accurate data-entry automation algorithm can be developed.

3 Applied Methodology

The innovative data-entry automation algorithm scrapes data from web, has been developed using Sunday's string-matching algorithm [16]. However, it is not possible to directly apply the algorithm and achieve expected result. At the very beginning, the pattern among data are analyzed. The patterns are divided into two classes - (1) Information Pattern (I_P) and (2) Tag Pattern (T_P). The web is source of bullions of data mixed together [17]. The system needs to be able to include the target data only while excluding the rest of the part of the source. It is possible to do it by establishing a relation between I_P and T_P. To established the relation, the source is transformed into three forms – (1) Original Document (D_o), (2) Document with HTML Tags (D_t) and (3) Unformatted Document (D_u). The source transformation helps establishing the relation between I_P and T_P. It is possible to relate I_P and T_P without the transformation. However, it becomes more time consuming and complex. It is easier to identify the target data from source data when the tags enclosing the target data are visible. The styling IDs and classes are also easier to identify from D_t. Complexities arise when distinguishable features are not present among two or more tags enclosing target data. In this case, parts of D_u are used which enclose the target data.

Different parts of the data based on their significances, locations and impacts, may contain different styling classes and IDs in the html tags. The purpose of the algorithm is to scrape target data through repetitive same operation. The variations among classes and IDs impose complexity in repetitive operation and require artificial intelligence. However, by simplifying the html tags into their base forms, it is possible to avoid the complexities, reduce computational cost and scrape desire data without using artificial intelligence. By inspecting the D_t an array of styling classes (Eq. 1) and IDs (Eq. 2) are formed. Then using Sunday's string-matching algorithm (SMA), classes and IDs of the array are matched. If the match is found, an XOR operation is performed between the tag elements (T_E) and the matrix elements which eliminates the classes and IDs and leave the based html tags (Eqs. 3 and 4).

$$C = [C_1, C_2, C_3, \ldots C_n] \tag{1}$$

$$I = [I_1, I_2, I_3, \ldots I_n] \tag{2}$$

$$T_{EC} := SMA(\sum\nolimits_{i=1}^{n} C_i) \oplus C_i \tag{3}$$

$$T_{EI} := SMA(\sum_{i=1}^{n} I_i) \oplus I_i \tag{4}$$

After the operations of Eq. 3 and 4, the data-source contains data and base html tags only. The target data are already marked on D_o and the enclosing simplified tags are on

D_t. At this stage, a mapping matrix is formed using the required data and enclosing tags. The enclosing tags play the vital role in separating the target data. Whatever data fall in between the html tags in the mapping-matrix are the target data. The target data vary from source to source. However, the tags remain the same. By utilizing this relation, whatever fall in between the common tags can be copied. The methodology has been illustrated in Fig. 1.

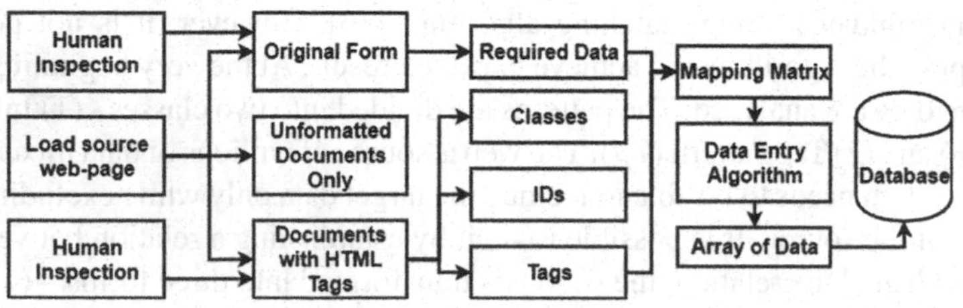

Fig. 1. Methodology of data entry automation

The data entry algorithm takes the mapping matrix as input, simplify the tags by removing classes and ids, and replace the starting tags with double quote mark and ending tags with double quote mark with commas. The entire comma separated document is enclosed in first brackets to form an array of data. Finally, the data from the array are stored in the database.

3.1 Forming the Mapping Matrix

Forming the mapping matrix is a preprocessing step of the proposed algorithm. The source of the data is web. Different websites have different data-patterns. That is why same mapping matrix is not applicable to all of the websites. However, the structure of the matrix remains the same. Only the values change.

The first step of forming the mapping matrix is to inspect D_O, D_t, and D_u. These three are generated using three PHP functions (Eq. 5, 6 and 7).

$$D_O = \mathit{get\_file\_contents}(\text{"}\mathit{source}\text{ ulr"}) \tag{5}$$

$$D_t = \mathit{htmlspecialchars}(\mathit{Original\ Document}) \tag{6}$$

$$D_u = \mathit{strip\_tag}(\mathit{Original\ Document}) \tag{7}$$

From D_O the target data are highlighted and stored in the matrix in the first column. The starting and ending tags are marked by inspecting D_t and assigned to second and third column of the matrix. In the fourth and fifth column, the classes and IDs are assigned. The mapping matrix is defined by,

$$\mathit{Mapping\ Matrix} = \sum_{i=1,}^{n} (R_{i1}, OT_{i2}, CT_{i2}, I_{i3}, C_{i4}) \tag{8}$$

Here, *R*, *OT*, *CT*, *I* and *C* represent required data, opening tags, closing tags, ids and classes respectively. The *i* represents the row of the matrix. If some matrix value is missing, it is replaced by null value. Several attempts have been taken to automate the mapping matrix. However, the required data depends on the demand of the clients and vary for every new data-entry project. Moreover, the names of the classes and the IDs depend on the developer of sources and vary from source to source. As a result, no strategy could be developed in this paper to automate the mapping matrix formation.

3.2 Applied Algorithm

The data-entry automation algorithm is an application of Sunday's string-matching algorithm combined with repetitive bitwise 2D matrix XOR operation. The string-matching algorithm looks for $R_{i1}, OT_{i2}, CT_{i2}, I_{i3}$ *and* C_{i4} in the source. When a match is found, the algorithm generates a temporary source data matrix (SDM). The row index of the SDM is the number of iterations in the algorithm. The SDM is superimposed on the mapping-matrix and an XOR operation is performed. The target data vary for each row of the matrix but tags remain the same. As a result, the tags are eliminated. Then the empty OT_i is replaced by double opening quotes and the empty CT_i is replaced by double quote followed by a comma. The ID_i and C_i are eliminated by repetitive self-XOR operation. The entire process is repeated until all of the sources are scanned. Finally, the entire comma separated double quote enclosed data are stored in database maintaining CSV standard. The algorithm 1 demonstrate the steps of the proposed algorithm.

Algorithm 1. Data-entry automation

```
L_A ← URL Inspection(Root domain)
for (int j = 1, j <= size of (L_A), j++) {
S_o ← load from web (L_A[j])
store (S_o) → local directory}
for (int i = 1, i <= size of (L_A), i++)
S_o ← load from local directory (L_A[i])
if (SMA (S_o, OT_i2)) {
if (SMA (S_o, CT_i2)) {
OT_i2 := ( OT_i2 ⊕ OT_i2), CT_i2 := ( CT_i2 ⊕ CT_i2) }
OT_i2:= "; OT_i2:= ",;
Self-XOR (I_i3, C_i4)
int r = 1, i = 1,
while (R_i1 exists){
Database [row[r]] ← Mapping Matrix (R_i1) i++
if (r % Number of Field per Row) (r++)}
```

The algorithm locates the target data; eliminates rest of the part the source including the html tags, IDs and classes. The final output of the algorithm is all of the target data isolated from the source, organized in CSV standard, and stored in the database.

4 Implementation

The proposed system has been implemented in local server running in Microsoft Windows 10 operating system, powered by Intel(R) Core (TM) i3-6100 CPU @ 3.70 GHz (4 CPUs) with 8192 MB primary memory. A dedicated five MBPS broadband internet connection has been used as communication medium. The code has been written in

PHP. The platform has been executed in Google Chrome, Mozilla Firefox, Microsoft Edge and Opera browser. No significant variation in performance has been noticed for different browser. The root inspection has been performed using Xenu's Link Sleuth, a program to check broken link of website, also capable of inspecting and saving all of the links by root domain inspection. All of the available links of the source website were inspected and saved in spreadsheet using this program.

It is possible to scrape target data directly from the source website. However, it is very time-consuming process. Because each page contains multiple data and for each data the algorithm performs all of the operations. As a result, a single page is called for multiple times, which not only create additional computational burden on the server, but also generates DOS attack alarm in the server. It may cause refusal of further connection requests at the middle of the progress of data scraping resulting in incomplete operation. To avoid such complexities, the source website is mirrored in the local storage as static website. Each page of the source website is stored in the local storage in separate directory named according to the meta-title. The link to the webpages to local storage remain the same as the source website. That is why the previously stored URLs still work.

The URLs are used to load in a variable, the variable is used to store the static webpages in local storage using the file_get_contents() function. Then, the variable is transferred to proposed algorithm. The algorithm performs the string-matching, replaces the matched tags with predefined values and eliminates the IDs and classes. All of these operations are based on Sunday's string matching algorithm. In the implementation, the SMA has not been re-implemented, instead the 'str_replace()' function of PHP language has been used. This function uses optimized SMA and replace the sub-string as per input arguments. The implementation of the system has been demonstrated in Fig. 2.

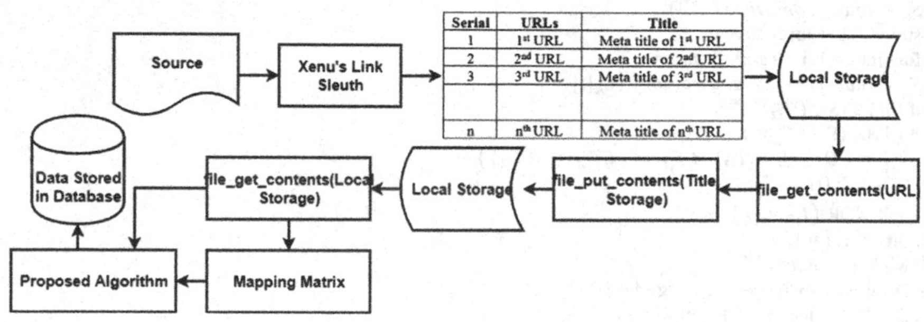

Fig. 2. Implementation of the proposed model

In this paper, the data are stored in database. However, before that, the data are formatted in CSV, which is a globally accepted data format. It ensures the robustness of the scraped data and make the system platform independent.

5 Experiment and Performance Analysis

The performance of the system has been analyzed by evaluating execution time and cost. To compare the performance, a survey has been conducted on existing solution of data-entry process. To ensure confidentiality, the name of the companies and individuals, who were surveyed have not been disclosed.

To perform the experiment, we requested webmasters of 10 different websites. Of which, eight of the webmasters responded back and three of them granted us with the permission to conduct the experiment imposing the condition of complete anonymity and deletion of data after scraping. By accepting the condition, the experiment has been performed.

Website data are private property and govern by the privacy policy, copyright law and terms and conditions. Without the permission of the owners, we cannot apply the algorithm to websites we do not own. That is why, 17 dummy websites with similar data field were developed in local server to evaluate the performance of the proposed algorithm.

5.1 Field Selection

The experiment is conducted on 3 live websites and 17 dummy websites (built in local server for experimental purpose). All of the experimenting websites contain university ranking and admission related data. Each of the universities has been considered as individual source in the experiment. The structure of the webpages are different. However, there are 16 common fields for each university in all of the websites. The Table 1 contains these 16 fields.

Table 1. The fields of data

Serial	Category	Datatype	Element(s)
1	Name	Text	1
2	Acronym	Text	1
3	Founded	Numeric	1
4	Tuition Fee	Currency	4
5	Number of students	Numeric	4
6	Number academic staff	Numeric	2
7	Control type	Text	1
8	Entity type	Text	1
9	Campus location	Text	1
10	Library	Text	1
11	Housing	Text	1
12	Sports	Text	1
13	Financial aid	Text	1
14	Acceptance rate	Percentage	1
15	Selection process	Text	1
16	List of Degree Offered	Text	4

5.2 Market Analysis

The cost and time required to collect the data mentioned in Table 1 from three source websites were calculated though manual inspection. For other 17 dummy sites, the cost and time were inferred based on the observation on market analysis. First, four local companies were requested to send proposal mentioning the tentative time and cost required to collect these data along with the accuracy. Later, the same proposal were sent to five freelancers and requesting for the same information. The responses from the four companies and five freelancers have been presented in Table 2.

Table 2. Cost of data collection manually

Type	Price (BDT)	Time (days)	Confidence
Company	2,00,000	30	100%
Company	1,80,000	45	99%
Company	1,80,000	40	99%
Company	1,25,000	60	98%
Freelancer	3,45,000	15	100%
Freelancer	1,50,000	50	100%
Freelancer	1,25,000	45	95%
Freelancer	1,20,000	40	90%
Freelancer	1,20,000	50	90%

The companies and freelancers were requested to disclose their data collection process. Upon their denial, the surveyor group further persuaded highlighting the concern of the quality of data. It was assured by them that the data are collected with direct human inspection, reviewed for multiple times and thus quality is never compromised. All of the companies and freelancers provided similar response which proves that the data are collected by manual inspections of data-entry operators.

5.3 Confidence Rate Analysis

The cost analysis shows that the accuracy-confidence is not less than 90% for any of the companies or freelancers. The total number of individual experimental data element is 3,79,536. Because of this large number of data element, even at 90% accuracy the number of wrong entry cumulates to large number. Using Eq. 9 the number of unintentional modification of data element are calculated, where D_{te} stands for total number of data element and C_r represents confidence rate.

$$Number\ of\ Modified\ Field = D_{te} \times \frac{100 - C_r}{100} \tag{9}$$

In the experimental source, at 90% confidence rate, the number of modified data element is 37,953, which is not acceptable. At 98%, confidence rate the number of modified elements is 7590. It clearly shows that for small number of data, the 98% confidence rate is acceptable, not for large amount of data. A 100% accuracy is mandatory for such cases. Which is not a feasible expected result of manual data-entry. The time required to collect the data is too long. It is evident that if the time is reduced, the confidence rate reduces (Fig. 3).

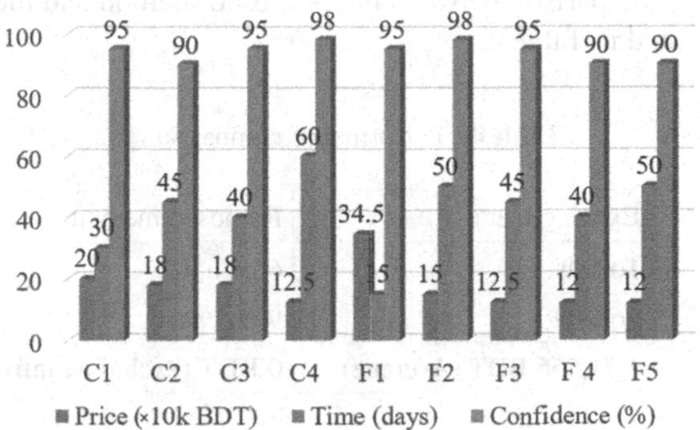

Fig. 3. Cost, time and confidence rate

5.4 Performance Analysis and Comparison

The same amount of data, which were proposed to four companies and five freelancers, were collected using the algorithm proposed in this paper. No new infrastructure is brought to perform the experiment. As a result, there is no infrastructural cost. At the same time, the algorithm collected data automatically. That is why there is no cost of employee. The time required to collect the data has been segmented into two categories – mapping matrix preparing time and data collection time. The individual and overall time duration, accuracy and expenditure have been demonstrated in Table 3.

Table 3. Performance observation on live websites.

Source	Mapping matrix preparation time	Data collection time	Accuracy (%)	Cost (BDT)
Site 1	4 h	2.1 h	100	0
Site 2	9 h	4.8 h	94	0
Site 3	38 h	7.6 h	99	0

The time taken to collect all of the data by the proposed system is 65.5 h. The average accuracy is 97.67%. The average time required and accuracy remain almost same for the 17 dummy websites. The average time required to perform the same task using existing method is 1000 h with an average accuracy of 96.67%. For the proposed method, there is no cost involved, considering that, the infrastructure has already been built. The average cost of collecting the same amount of data through manual method is 1,71,666 BDT. The comparison between the proposed method and the existing method has been demonstrated in Table 4.

Table 4. Performance comparison

Evolution criteria	Existing method	Proposed method
Average Time	1000 h	65.5 h
Average Accuracy	96.67%	97.67%
Expenditure	1,71,666 BDT (Average)	0 BDT (excluding infrastructural cost)

Because of being an automatic system, the proposed method outperforms the existing manual process.

5.5 Accuracy Deviation

Theoretically, the accuracy of the proposed method should be 100%. However, in experiment, for site 2, the accuracy is 94%. The reason behind this deviation is 'connection timeout' for several pages. The data to of those pages were null in the database. For site 3, the accuracy is 99%. The reason behind the deviation is mapping matrix mismatch. The source website has several webpages where the template is different. The mapping matrix created for one web-template does not provide accurate result for different templates. That is why the accuracy for the third site became 99%. If there is no 'connection timeout' and no template variation among the webpages, the algorithm will ensure 100% accuracy.

6 Conclusion

There are several limitations of the proposed method. The first limitation is the manual process of mapping matrix formation. The overall accuracy of the system depends on the accuracy of the mapping matrix. If the mapping matrix is not correct, the accuracy may fall to 0%. Careful inspection is mandatory to generate the mapping matrix, which require both time and effort. Moreover, the server downtime and connection request timeout can cause significant reduction in accuracy. In the proposed method, no prevention mechanism of server downtime or connection request time out was developed. However, it is possible to include these features in the algorithm. The proposed method scan all of the webpages of the source and send request for each of the pages. If there are too many requests in short span of time, the server may consider the request as DOS attack and thus block further requests. As a result, the algorithm will keep adding null values, which will reduce the accuracy drastically. However, it can be prevented by adding random time delay in between two requests which may increase the average time required to collect the data. The proposed algorithm has the capability to revolutionize the data-entry industry by reducing the cost to almost zero while ensuring more than 15 times faster data-collection capability. A careful inspection during mapping matrix design can ensure 100% accuracy. No doubt that the demand of data in emerging data-driven economy is rising faster than ever. This rising demand is creating opportunities for data-entry industry. The proposed algorithm will make the data-entry based companies faster, more accurate and more profitable.

References

1. Aaronson, S.A.: Why the world needs a new approach to governing cross-border data flows. In: Centre for International Governance Innovation (2018). https://www.cigionline.org/publications/data-different-why-world-needs-new-approach-governing-cross-border-data-flows. Accessed 18 Sep 2019
2. Berman, P.S.: Legal Jurisdiction and Virtual Social Life. Cath. UJL Tech. **2**(27), 103 (2019)
3. Al-Rawi, A.: Viral news on social media. Digital Journalism **1**(7), 63–79 (2017)
4. Bhattacharjeea, D., Ghoshb, T., Bholaa, P., Martinsenb, K., Dana, P.K.: Data-driven surrogate assisted evolutionary optimization of hybrid powertrain for improved fuel economy and performance. Energy **187**, 235–248 (2019)
5. Autor, D.H., Dorn, D., Katz, L.F., Patterson, C., Reenen, J.V.: The fall of the labor share and the rise of superstar firms. In: CEPR Discussion (2017). https://ssrn.com/abstract=2968382. Accessed 19 Sep 2019
6. Barchard, K.A., Paceb, L.A.: Preventing human error: the impact of data entry methods on data accuracy and statistical results. Comput. Hum. Behav. **5**(27), 1834–1839 (2011)
7. Shukla, S., Salve, S., Yavar, P.Y.: Does emotion modulation influence speed-accuracy trade-off in numerical data entry task? Res. Des. Connected World **135**, 497–507 (2019)
8. Laursen, B., Jensen, B.R., Sjøgaard, G.: Effect of speed and precision demands on human shoulder muscle electromyography during a repetitive task. Eur. J. Appl. Physiol. Occup. Physiol. **78**, 544–548 (1998)
9. Maskell, P., Pedersen, T., Petersen, B., Dick-Nielsen, J.: Learning paths to offshore outsourcing: from cost reduction to knowledge seeking. Ind. Innov. **14**, 239–257 (2007)
10. Cortes, C., Jackel, L.D., Chiang, W.P.: Limits on learning machine accuracy imposed by data quality. In: Proceeding KDD 1995 Proceedings of the First International Conference on Knowledge Discovery and Data Mining, Montréal, Québec, Canada, pp. 20–21 (1995)
11. Doan, A., Domingos, P., Halevy, A.: Learning to match the schemas of data sources: a multistrategy approach. Mach. Learn. **50**, 279–301 (2003)
12. Tsuruoka, Y., Tsujii, J.: Improving the performance of dictionary-based approaches in protein name recognition. J. Biomed. Inf. **37**, 461–470 (2004)
13. Franek, F., Jennings, C.G., Smyth, W.F.: A simple fast hybrid pattern-matching algorithm. In: Apostolico, A., Crochemore, M., Park, K. (eds.) CPM 2005. LNCS, vol. 3537, pp. 288–297. Springer, Heidelberg (2005). https://doi.org/10.1007/11496656_25
14. Knuth, D.E., Morris Jr., J.H., Pratt, V.R.: Fast pattern matching in strings. SIAM J. Comput. **6**, 323–350 (1977)
15. Boyer, R.S., Moore, J.S.: A fast string searching algorithm. Commun. ACM **20**, 762–772 (1977)

16. Smit, G.D.V.: A comparison of three string matching algorithms. Wiley Online Libr. **12**, 57–66 (1982)
17. Sunday, D.M.: A very fast substring search algorithm. Commun. ACM **33**, 132–142 (1990)
18. Sharma, K., Shrivastava, G., and Kumar, V.: Web mining: today and tomorrow. In: 3rd International Conference on Electronics Computer Technology, Kanyakumari, India, pp. 8–10 (2011)

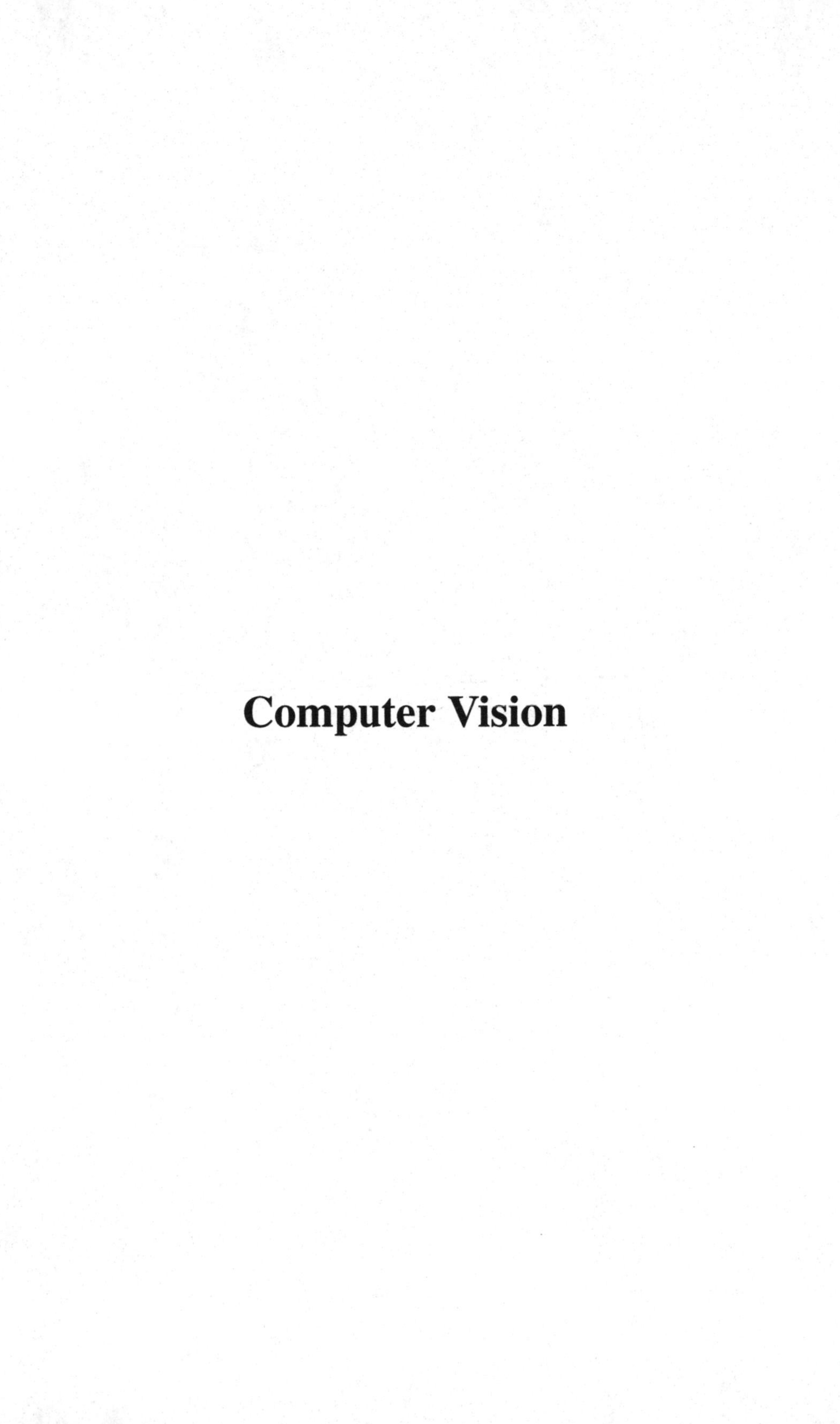

Computer Vision

Classification of Succulent Plant Using Convolutional Neural Network

Ashik Kumar Das(✉), Md. Asif Iqbal, Bidhan Paul, Aniruddha Rakshit, and Md. Zahid Hasan

Department of Computer Science and Engineering, Daffodil International University, Dhaka, Bangladesh
{kumar15-7210,asif15-7407,bidhan15-6786,aniruddha.cse, zahid.cse}@diu.edu.bd

Abstract. Machine learning methods such as deep neural networks have remarkably improved plant species classification in recent years. It is very challenging task to classify plant species based on their categories. In this work, deep learning approach is explained to identify and classify succulent plant species using VGG19, three layers CNN and five layers CNN network on our dataset. The proposed architecture achieved a significant result from VGG19 and three layers CNN model. In succulent plant image dataset, there are 10 different classes of succulent and non-succulent plants. The dataset consists of 3632 succulent plant images and 200 non-succulent plant images. The model achieved 99.77% accuracy which performs better than VGG19 and three layers CNN model.

Keywords: Succulent plant · Convolutional Neural Network · Augmentation · Adam optimizer

1 Introduction

Plants are very useful for us in many ways they give us oxygen through photosynthesis process. They also provide us with food and many other things. Plant reducing causes certain levels of pollutants, such as benzene and nitrogen dioxide and keep the air temperature down not just that reduce noise from a busy road. There are many types of plants but we chose succulent plant because it looks very beautiful, grow slowly so space is usually not a problem, medically uses, and purifies air rapidly, and also removes formaldehyde. Most plants release oxygen during the day and at night they release carbon dioxide but succulent plant keep releasing oxygen all night [1]. A research of NASA found that succulent plant like snake plant and aloe vera are capable of removing 87% of volatile organic compounds (VOC) [1]. In the library and study environment, they are extra helpful because VOC element like benzene and formaldehyde are found in books and ink [1]. Succulent plant-like aloes have many medical uses. They use as a laxative, to treat joint pain, skin inflammation, conjunctivitis, hypertension, stress, etc. [2]. They offer us a positive example by saving water and prospering in troublesome conditions,

T. Bhuiyan et al. (Eds.): ICONCS 2020, LNICST 325, pp. 695–704, 2020.
https://doi.org/10.1007/978-3-030-52856-0_55

advising us that we are more grounded than we understand and even the most exhausting circumstances are not the stopping point [3].

Succulent plants have a worldwide conveyance and they normally come from the dry areas. It may store water in different structures, for example, leaves stems and roots [4]. It has a reputation for being easy to grow. In Africa, Cotyledon Orbiculata is known as "kanniedood", which means "cannot die" [5]. There are more than 30 botanical families of succulent plant from small and large trees [6]. Three types of succulent plants are used for trading, those are Cacti, Aloe and Euphorbia [7]. Because of their capacity to endure dry season conditions and the coming of reasonable warming required to develop these plants outside their regular range, succulent plants are especially supported as house plants [7]. They are popular for house gardening and prized by many plant gatherers because of their irregularity in nature. Identifying a succulent plant is very challenging for non-expert because there are many species that look similar [8]. There are some identification techniques like Visual Identification, Chemical Identification, and Genetic Identification. For Visual Identification plant's characteristics such as size, color, presence of spines, flower or leaf shape are used [7]. Characteristics of a flower is very important because sometimes using other features we can classify to genus or family level. Analyzing the Chemical synthesis of a plant it is possible to classify the plant as mass level. For Genetic Identification DNA pattern is used and it is possible to classify plant to species level [7].

Nowadays, computer vision based techniques like CNN has been playing an important role to classify plant like objects. The point of this research is the proposed CNN technique to identify and classify the succulent plant. This paper is composed as follows: Sect. 2, discusses some previous work-related to plant classification. In Sect. 3, dataset and method have been discussed. Section 4 contains result and discussion of result. Finally, Sect. 5 is the conclusion of the work.

2 Literature Review

There are many researchers work to classify plant through leaf image and flower image and some researchers classify leaf disease but there is no one work with succulent plant image to classify and identify. Belal A.M. Ashqar et al. present plant seedlings classification approach with a dataset. Convolutional Neural Network (CNN) algorithms, a deep learning technique extensively applied to image recognition [9]. Nowadays many researchers using CNN [12] as a classifier and their accuracy is good. N. Valliammal et al. classify plant through leaf image recognition. They converted images from RGB to gray then preprocess the images. For feature extraction, they use border tracing algorithm and for image segmentation, use Preferential Image Segmentation (PIS) method [10]. Shanwen et al. and his co-authors proposed a semi-supervised locally linear embedding (SALLE) to classify plant based on leaf image. They used Manifold learning method for feature extraction and selection & LLE method for avoiding the local minima problems. Used KNN as a classifier and achieve 90% accuracy [11]. K-Nearest Neighbors (KNN) is another popular classification technique. Researchers have used KNN to classify plant type [14], to identify the plant leaves [15]. M.E. Nilsback et al. develop a visual vocabulary as object classifier that explicitly represents the various aspects like color, shape, and texture that distinguish one flower from another [13]. Enes Yigit et al. used support vector machine (SVM) to design an automatic identifier for the plant leaves and gain 94.2% accuracy [15]. Another author used WPROP method and PROP density estimator method and gain 96.69% and 96.82% accuracy [16]. Guillaume Cerutti et al. used some image processing technique like image segmentation, contour detection, image rotation to differentiate among different parts of a tree. To differentiate between foreground and Background used Naive Distance-based Classification for classification purposes [17]. Anxiung et al. worked with flower image and to characterize the color features from flower image they proposed color histogram of ROI and two features sets like Centroid-Contour-Distance (CCD) and Angle Code Histogram (ACH) to characterize the shape features of a flower [18]. Marco Seeland et al. investigates from detection, extraction, fusion, pooling, encoding of local features for quantifying shape and color information of flower images. Scale-Invariant Feature Transform (SIFT), Histogram of Oriented Gradients (HOG) methods, Opponent SIFT and C-SIFT, SVM, MKL also used and gained 94% accuracy [19]. M. Turkoglu et al. extracted features from leaves. Color features, vein feature, Fourier Description, Gray-Level Co-occurrence Matrix are calculated by Extreme Learning Machine (ELM) classifier and achieve 99.10% accuracy on Flavia leaf dataset [20]. Another author has discussed many types of research Like ResNet, AlexNet, VGG 16, VGG 19, DenseNet, SqueezeNet, MXNet [21].

Numerous specialists have just achieved to group various kinds of plant leaf pictures through AI approach. Thus, it is important to classify the succulent plant by image dataset.

3 Methodology

In this paper, our methodology contains few stages of workflow such as data collection, data processing, divide the dataset in train set and test set, evaluation of data, identification, classification and accuracy. Figure 1 is showing our workflow diagram.

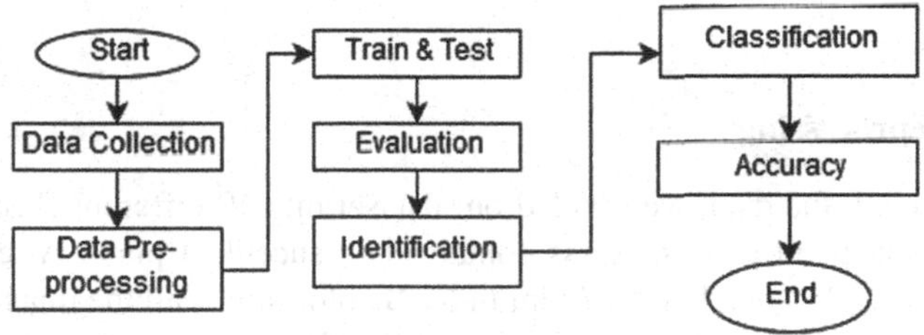

Fig. 1. Workflow diagram

3.1 Dataset

We have made a dataset of succulent plant. We have collected all data from different nurseries from inside and outside Dhaka city. Our data set contains 10 different classes of succulent plant those are Acanthocereus tetragonus, Euphorbia lacteal, Euphorbia trigona, Haworthiopsis limifolia, Hoya Kerrii, Sansevieria trifasciata, Gymnocalycium mihanovichii, Huernia macrocarpa, Mammillaria compressa and others. Our dataset contains 3632 images total. We took 2776 images in the training set and 856 images in the test set. Figure 2 shows different types of data with class name.

Fig. 2. Images of succulent plant and non-succulent plant

3.2 Data Preprocessing

After collecting all the data, we divided our dataset into 10 different classes. 9 classes contain succulent plant and one class contains non-succulent plant. After resizing all images into 240 × 240 pixels with 72dpi in RGB color mode, all the image data are fed to our model. To reduce unnecessary objects from the background, image cropping is done on our images. Adobe Photoshop tools are used for pre-processing our data.

Data augmentation technique is employed to avoid overfitting and expand the dataset artificially. It increases the value of base data by including data got from inside and outside sources within a venture. It helps to get better result by increasing data of the dataset. Figure 3 shows an example of a succulent plant that are augmented.

Fig. 3. Augmented image data of succulent plant.

3.3 Proposed Architecture

In the computer vision field, CNN is one of the most productive deep learning algorithms. CNN mostly used for image recognition, image classification, etc. We have proposed a CNN model to classify our succulent plant dataset. CNN contains two diverse significant parts: feature extraction and classification. In convolutional layers feature extraction performs and in the fully connected layer classification performs. There are five convolutional layers, four pooling layers and one fully connected layer in our proposed architecture. Our first convolutional layer is input layer and its padding is same, the filter size is 32 with 3 × 3 kernel and its input size is 240 × 240 with RGB color mode. In this layer, ReLU activation function is used and max-pooling layer with pool size 2 and stride 2 is used to reduce the parameter with 25% dropout. Filter size of the second convolutional layer is 64 filter size with 3 × 3 kernel with same padding and strides 1. To increase the stability of the convolutional network batch normalization is used in this layer. Our third convolutional layer is 64 filter size with 3 × 3 kernel and its padding are same and strides 1 with batch normalization and the result go through next max-pooling layer and dropout layer. The output of the third layer is the input of the fourth layer. Our fourth convolutional layer is 64 filter size with 3 × 3 kernel, same padding with 1 × 1 strides and the output goes through batch normalization, ReLU, max-pooling layer and dropout layer as like the previous layer. Filter size of our fifth convolutional layer is 256 with 3 × 3 kernel, same padding with 1 × 1 strides. The output goes through batch normalization and ReLU and max-pooling layer as like a previous layer than goes through another 25% dropout layer. After all, five-layers, there is a fully connected layer or dance layer. Our fully connected layer has 512 hidden nodes with batch normalization, ReLU and activation with a 50% drop out with softmax activation (Fig. 4).

3.4 Performance of Proposed Architecture

For training the model, we input our training data and test data into the model. We have used 76% of data for training the model and rest of the data is used for testing purpose.

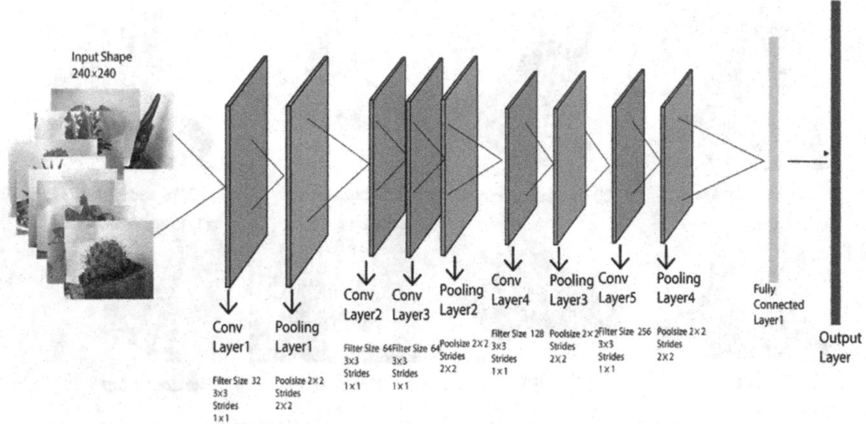

Fig. 4. The architecture of the proposed CNN model.

Fixed sized of 240 × 240 image is the input of the model and applied 5 convolutional layers, four max-pooling layers respectively and a fully connected layer in the network. While training all images from training set the image data is also used to fix 240 × 240 pixel ratio into the first layers. While training, the model pooling layers help to gradually reduce the spatial size of the representation for minimizing the number of parameters of the network. Adam Optimizer is used to compile our model. We fixed value of learning rate 0.000001, our proposed method uses Adam optimizer. From test set and train set we get some data in the validation set. We have run 40 epochs in our model. We used the same dataset in other two model which are VGG19 and another CNN and this CNN network were based on four convolutional layers, three max-pooling layers and one fully connected layer. Table 1 shows the accuracy of the different model which was applied to our dataset.

Table 1. Accuracy comparison of three models

Model	Accuracy
VGG19	95.86%
Three layers CNN	97.66%
Proposed CNN model	99.77%

4 Experimental Result and Analysis

We separated our dataset into two sets like the training set and test set. There are 76% data of our dataset in the training set and the rest of the data is in the test set. From test set and training set, some images are taken and made the validation set of data for validation purposes. An error of the training set of data is called training loss. After running the validation set of data through the trained network, we get some error. This error is called validation loss. Train error and validation error drop with the increasing epochs. With the drop of train loss and validation loss, train accuracy and validation accuracy increase rapidly. In Fig. 5 training loss vs validation loss and training accuracy vs validation accuracy can be noticed.

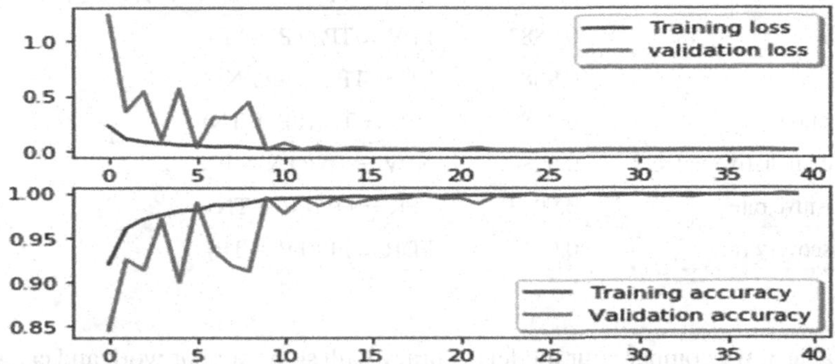

Fig. 5. Training loss vs validation loss, training accuracy vs validation accuracy.

A survey of prediction results on a classification problem is called a confusion matrix. The number of correct and incorrect prognostications are reviewed by each class with count values and broken down. After completing our work, we get our confusion matrix in Fig. 6.

true label \ predicted label	0	1	2	3	4	5	6	7	8	9
0	114	0	0	1	0	0	0	0	0	0
1	0	146	0	0	0	0	0	0	0	0
2	0	0	35	0	0	0	0	0	0	0
3	0	0	0	41	0	0	0	0	0	0
4	0	0	0	0	75	0	0	1	0	0
5	0	1	0	0	0	45	1	0	0	0
6	0	0	0	0	0	0	77	1	0	0
7	0	0	0	0	0	0	0	167	0	0
8	0	0	0	0	0	0	0	0	68	0
9	0	0	0	0	1	0	0	1	3	78

Fig. 6. Confusion Matrix

We have used the average accuracy performance metric based on the confusion matrix. Confusion Matrix has four components True Positive (TP), False Positive (FP), False Negative (FN) and True Negative (TN). From our confusion matrix (Fig. 6), we have calculated our total TP = 846, TN = 7693, FP = 10, FN = 10 values.

Accuracy can be measured from TP, FP, TN and FN values. Table 2 is showing the classification performance of the proposed architecture based on the confusion matrix.

Table 2. Classification performance of the proposed architecture.

Measure	Value	Derivation
Accuracy	0.9977	ACC = (TP + TN)/(TP + TN + FP + FN)
Precision	0.9883	PPV = TP/(TP + FP)
Recall	0.9883	RC = TP/(TP + FN)
Specification	0.9987	SPC = TN/(FP + TN)
Negative predictive value	0.9987	NPV = TN/(TN + FN)
False positive rate	0.0013	FPR = FP/(FP + TN)
False discovery rate	0.0117	FDR = FP/(FP + TP)

In Table 3, we compare our model accuracy with some similar work and can see our result is better than other methodologies.

Table 3. Comparison result with existing models.

Author name	Category	Algorithm	Accuracy
Ashqar, B.A.M., AbuNasser, B.S., Abu-Naser, S.S (2019)	Plant seedlings classification	CNN	99.48%
Zhang, S., Chau, K.W. (2009)	Plant leaf classification	SALLE, K-NN	90%
Siraj, F., Salahuddin, M.A., Yusof, S.A.M. (2010)	Digital image classification for Malaysian blooming flower	CNN	67%
Yigit, E., Sabanci, K., Toktas, A., Kayabasi, A. (2019)	Plant leaf identification	SVM	94.2%
Proposed architecture	Classification of succulent plant	CNN	99.77%

5 Conclusion and Future Work

In this paper, we proposed a deep learning approach to classify 10 different classes of succulent plants through the CNN model. Five convolutional layers, four max-pooling layers are considered for building our network model. Dropout layer is imposed in each fully connected layer for reducing the overfitting in the system. Rotation, Shifting, Scaling, Shearing and Flipping data augmentation approaches are employed for augmenting the dataset. After successful completion of 40 epochs, the model achieves 99.77% accuracy with the dataset. In this study, we consider total 9 classes of succulent plants which is insufficient to optimize the model or make difficulty to other unknown succulent species. Therefore, our future aim is to augment number of succulent plant classes for better optimization and make an android app which will help the user to identify succulent plant.

References

1. 5 health benefits of having succulents in your home. https://www.redonline.co.uk/interiors/homeware/a526209/five-health-benefits-ofhaving-succulents-in-your-home. Accessed 20 Oct 2019
2. Succulents offer magical healing powers. https://www.dailyrepublic.com/all-drnews/solano-news/local-features/local-lifestyle-columns/succulents-offer-magicalhealing-powers. Accessed 20 Oct 2019
3. The Symbolic Meaning Behind Succulent Arrangements - Plant The Future. https://www.plantthefuture.com/the-symbolic-meaning-behind-succulentarrangements. Accessed 20 Oct 2019
4. Succulent Plant Site - Information on the cultivation of succulents. http://www.succulents.co.za. Accessed 20 Oct 2019
5. Succulent Plant Site - Information on the cultivation of succulents. http://www.succulents.co.za
6. Oldfield, S.: Cactus and succulent plants: status survey and conservation action plan. In: International Union for Conservation of Nature and Natural Resources (IUCN) (1997)
7. Rutherford, C., Groves, M., Sajeva, M.: Succulent Plants A Guide to CITES-Listed Species (2017)
8. Identifying Types of Succulents - with Pictures|The Succulent Eclectic. https://thesucculenteclectic.com/identifying-types-of-succulents-pictures. Accessed 20 Oct 2019
9. Ashqar, B.A.M., Abu-Nasser, B.S., Abu-Naser, S.S.: Plant seedlings classification using deep learning. Int. J. Acad. Inf. Syst. Res. (IJAISR) **3**(1), 7–14 (2019)
10. Valliammal, N., Geethalakshmi, S.N.: Automatic recognition system using preferential image segmentation for leaf and flower images. Comput. Sci. Eng. Int. J. (CSEIJ) **1**(4), 13 (2011)
11. Zhang, S., Chau, K.-W.: Dimension reduction using semi-supervised locally linear embedding for plant leaf classification. In: Huang, D.-S., Jo, K.-H., Lee, H.-H., Kang, H.-J., Bevilacqua, V. (eds.) ICIC 2009. LNCS, vol. 5754, pp. 948–955. Springer, Heidelberg (2009). https://doi.org/10.1007/978-3-642-04070-2_100
12. Siraj, F., Salahuddin, M.A., Yusof, S.A.M.: Digital image classification for Malaysian blooming flower. In: Second International Conference on Computational Intelligence, Modelling and Simulation, pp. 33–38 (2010)
13. Nilsback, M.-E., Zisserman, A.: A visual vocabulary for flower classification. In: Proceedings of IEEE Computer Society Conference on Computer Vision and Pattern Recognition, pp. 1447–1454 (2006)
14. Saleem, G., Akhtar, M., Ahmed, N., Qureshi, W.S.: Automated analysis of visual leaf shape features for plant classification. Comput. Electr. Agric. **157**, 270–280 (2019)
15. Yigit, E., Sabanci, K., Toktas, A., Kayabasi, A.: A study on visual features of leaves in plant identification using artificial intelligence techniques. Comput. Electr. Agric. **156**, 369–377 (2019)
16. Mallah, C., Cope, J., Orwell, J.: Plant leaf classification using probabilistic integration of shape texture and margin features. In: Proceedings of Computer Graphics Imaging/798: Signal Processing Pattern Recognition Application, pp. 279–286 (2013)

17. Cerutti, G., et al.: Late Information Fusion for Multi-modality Plant Species Identification (2013)
18. Hong, A., Chi, Z., Chen, G., Wung, Z.: Region-of-interest based flower images retrieval. In: IEEE International Conference on Acoustics, Speech, and Signal Processing (ICASSP), vol. 3, pp. III-589 (2003)
19. Seeland, M., Rzanny, M., Alaqraa, N., Wäldchen, J., Mäder, P.: Plant species classification using flower images—a comparative study of local feature representations. PLoS ONE **12**(2) (2017)
20. Turkoglu, M., Hanbay, D.: Recognition of plant leaves: an approach with hybrid features produced by dividing leaf images into two and four parts. Appl. Math. Comput. **352**, 1–14 (2019)
21. Wäldchen, J., Rzanny, M., Seeland, M., Mäder, P.: Automated plant species identification—trends and future directions. PLoS Comput. Biol. **14**(4), e1005993 (2018)

Smoke Detection from Different Environmental Conditions Using Faster R-CNN Approach Based on Deep Neural Network

Sumayea Benta Hasan, Shakila Rahman, Md. Khaliluzzaman(✉), and Siddique Ahmed

Department of Computer Science and Engineering, International Islamic University Chittagong (IIUC), Chittagong 4318, Bangladesh
sumayeahasan05@gmail.com, arianarahman80@gmail.com, khalilcse021@gmail.com, drsiddiqueahmed@gmail.com

Abstract. From the last few decades, smoke detection performed for noble purposes like to rescue people from fire, make wood-land or wildlife safe from fire disaster and so on. Most of those detections were sensor based where detectors detect smoke optically or by physical processes and which causes false alarm most of the time. By the passing time, the author's tries to overcome those false alarm rates by introducing hand-featured methods. From this perspective, those established systems performed better than sensor based tools. However, coming towards a significant point, in most instances, only one or two certain areas like forest were considered in addressing smoke. Now, moving on this research, we aimed to experience indeed with detecting diverse circumstances smoke by the Faster R-CNN approach based on the Inception-V2 deep neural network. We focused on the single class, i.e., smoke and training the method with images of our own combined extracted image frames. The proposed method achieves 97.31% detection accuracy and is compared to previous approaches to show higher detection accuracy over recent works.

Keywords: Smoke detection · Faster R-CNN · DNN · Inception-V2 · Hand-featured methods

1 Introduction

To diminish losses due to fire, different devices, methods, networks, etc. are being initiated from the earliest era to identify smoke as a symbol of fire. However, most of them are environment restricted, and upgrading the accuracy level in detecting smoke from an image is still an enormous want. It is not a minor task to detect smoke from various surroundings, as smoke shows different features in different circumstances. Dust, fog, temperature extremes, sunlight, etc. looks like smoke, hence it is a task not to recognize these environmental conditions as smoke. For trying to overcome the drawbacks of previous techniques, this paper proposed a deep neural network with Faster R-CNN based on Inception-V2, for detecting smoke from different environmental conditions.

T. Bhuiyan et al. (Eds.): ICONCS 2020, LNICST 325, pp. 705–717, 2020.
https://doi.org/10.1007/978-3-030-52856-0_56

In the last few decades, a large number of works have carried out for smoke detection based on handcrafted features and deep neural networks. Such as, in [1], the authors basically used the Faster R-CNN for detecting wildland forest fire smoke. By including two kinds of smoke into forest background, synthetic forest smoke images were produced. These were done because of the limited training deep models, where results showed the feasibility of accomplishing. These were finished by discussing the boost performance, which could be possible by the improvement of the synthetic process for images of forest smoke or consideration of the answer on video sequences. In [2], the authors proposed a combination of CNN and RNN for detecting smoke in both space and time domain. Input frames were passing through the convolutional layers, and in next, the fully connected layer was used for feeding the results to GRU. Each data set consists of at least 64 frames. Finally, accuracy was evaluated by Inception-V4 and Xception models. The accuracy of Inception-V4 was 58.75%, 59.18% on test data and train data respectively. In Xception, the extreme version of Inception shows 41.25% for test accuracy and 41.82% for train accuracy. In [3], the authors described the fast smoke detection for surveillance cameras, which relies on smoke region's shape features with color information. Background subtraction was used for assessing the probability of being a pixel in smoke regions. After uniting the separated pixels, roughness of boundary were analyzed for confirmation of smoke region. Comparison between initial frames and processed frames finalized the results. Parallel processing of some steps were done by CUDA GPUs. In [4], a method was proposed for implementing the classification and automatic feature extraction by means of a novel deep normalization and convolutional neural network (DNCNN) to improve smoke detection performance. This method achieved the false alarm rate below of 60% and 96.37% detection accuracy. In [5], fire and smoke were detected from video images. ViBe method and frame-by-frame differences were respectively used for extracting background and updating the proper motion area. Then the Caffe model and algorithm of adaptive weighted direction were exercised. Video frames were divided into 16*16 grids for further reduction of false alarm rate. All the clues were summarized for gaining final results. An adaptive method was proposed in [6]. Here, adequate synthetic images of smoke were introduced. For confusing the distributions of extracting features, the authors built the proposed architecture. The offered architecture could show robustness with optimal results. A deep neural approach based on convolutional neural networks was proposed in [7]. The proposed network was utilized for extracting features and classification beneath the same architectural view. After testing on video, the outcomes indicated that treating CNN in the video is immensely promising. In [10], the authors proposed a method with a combination of dual-threshold AdaBoost with the staircase searching approach. Statistical and extended Haar-like features were extracted from integral images. For the classification of smoke features, the proposed combination was performed. Finally, for further validation of smoke existence, dynamic analysis was proposed. This handcrafted featured method, needed for more optimization for enhancing the lower power equipment's processing speed.

Since the deep neural network has a great accuracy level [12, 14] in image recognition, sound recognition, natural language processing, etc. and has exceptional better performance in the context of blobs of the pixel. Aiming on to gain a greater accuracy, in this paper, a deep neural network (DNN) is chosen. Furthermore, as the Faster R-CNN being one of the better performers in objects detecting algorithms is chosen in this work, which is actually based on deep neural network. Faster R-CNN shows better performance through its region proposal learning in its network instead of using selective search methods, and it shows good accuracy than most of newer deep neural approaches of object detection.

The rest of the paper is organized as follows. The methodology of the proposed smoke detection is presented in the next Section. The experimental results are demonstrated in Sect. 3. The paper is concluded in Sect. 4.

2 Methodology

In this section, we have described the research implementation procedure. In this work, a smoke region detection and localization framework is established based on the deep convolutional neural network architecture. The architecture automatically extracted various features of smoke to detect and localize the candidate region accurately from an input image.

2.1 Workflow Diagram

For a better analysis of this paper concept, a workflow diagram for whole approaches to detect smoke is presented in Fig. 1.

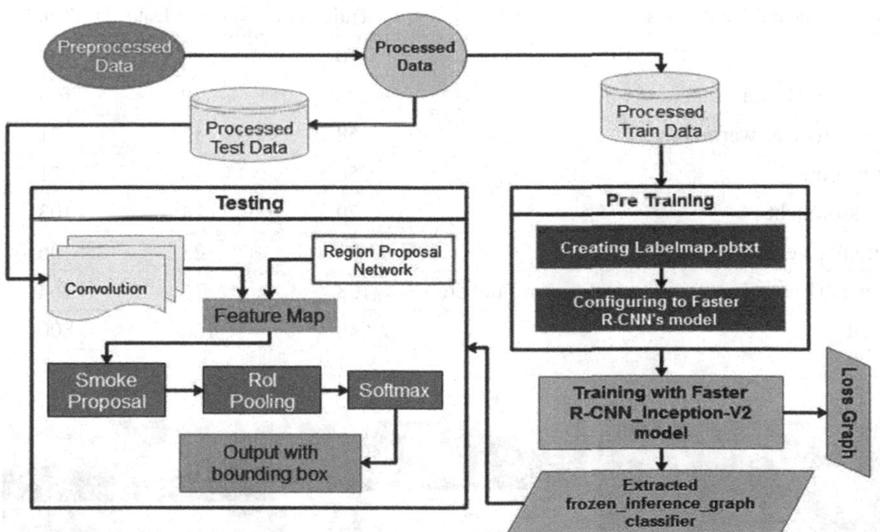

Fig. 1. Workflow diagram for the whole detection procedure.

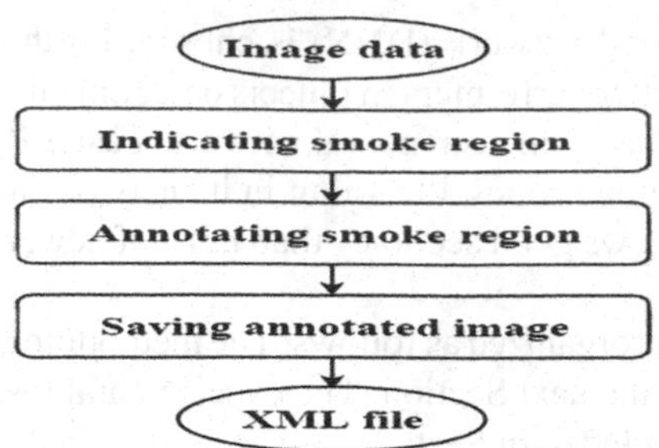

Fig. 2. Flowchart for labeling the resized images.

Data Pre-processing. To complete the preprocessing task, firstly, data must be collected according to the desired environmental conditions. The detailed procedures of data preprocessing steps are described in the next sections.

Data Collection. Data of different environmental conditions were collected from the video (converted into frames), self-captured images, and online sources. The dataset statistics is shown in Table 1, where it represents that train and test dataset were followed according to the measurement of 80% and 20% respectively. Some sample of the dataset is shown in Fig. 3.

Table 1. Dataset statistics

Environmental Categories	Train Data	Test Data	Total
Forest	110	20	130
Residential area	126	29	155
Warm food & warm drinks	58	13	71
Transport	56	15	71
Dark or night	79	24	103
Ritual's created	83	23	106
Others (Dust, Cigarette, Flamethrower, Fuel etc.)	128	36	164
Total	640	160	800

Fig. 3. Some sample collected image of different shapes.

Resizing Collected Image Data. The resized image refers to turning all the images into the same shape. So, after collecting raw images, to working favor, we resized those images into a fixed size. We fixed images with 800*600, and this can be different per choice. Resized images are shown in Fig. 4.

Fig. 4. Resized images of Fig. 2.

Labeling or Annotating. Firstly, the desired resized image was selected through labeling software. After that, by the option named 'create rectangle box', the smoke region of image data was indicated and labeled as 'smoke'. Finally, the XML file, which contains the detailed about chosen somke region, was created by the term 'save'. Figure 2 shows the flowchart for labeling the images and labeling portions of sample data are shown in Fig. 5.

Fig. 5. Sample labeled image data.

Data Processing. In this context, two steps are considered that are generating comma separated value (CSV) and generating TFRecords.

Generating Comma Separated Value (CSV). In this regard, a file of plain text was created in a tabular format for exporting data easily and import in a structured manner.

Generating TFRecords. For storing a sequence of binary records, different records file were created.

Workflow Diagram for Data Pre-processing and Processing. Workflow diagrams of data pre-processing and processing at a glance are presented in Fig. 6.

Pre-training Process.

Creating Labelmap. In this context, a graph file text type document was created known as Label map, where the label map tells where each object is actually exist and this is done through defining a mapping of class names to class ID numbers. As in our work, we have one label 'smoke' so the ID number is 1.

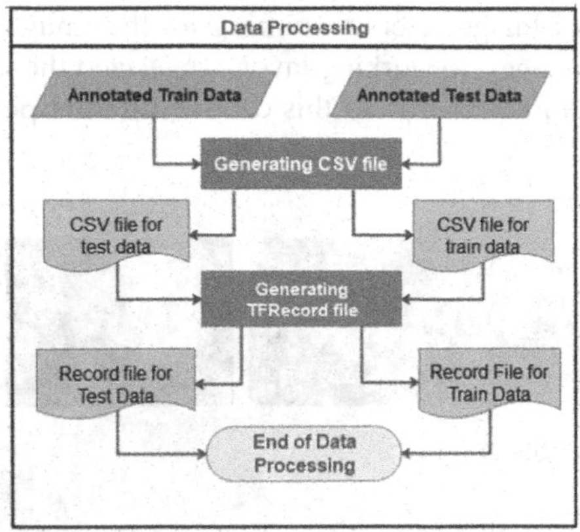

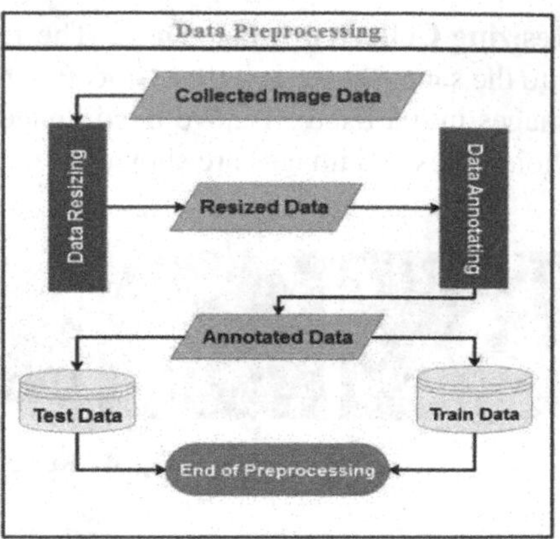

Fig. 6. Workflow diagrams of data pre-processing and processing: a) data processing, and b) data preprocessing.

Configure Training. This step defines which model and what parameters will be used for training. In this paper, we considered the inception-v2 for feature extraction, and for region proposal, we considered Faster R-CNN. Inception-V2 and Faster R-CNN are described in the next section.

Inception-V2: In image recognition performance, deep convolutional networks [11] have been centralized to the largest advancement within recent years. For example, the architecture of Inception has been shown for reaching at a better performance level in relatively low computational cost. In deep learning, inception-V2 is familiar for its performance. Factorization was introduced through inception-v2. It has two 1*1 filters from the base, and there exist three 3*3 filter. All these sum up with a final concatenation. There are few more versions for inception, like: version-1, version-3, and version-4. In inception-v1, there was a 5*5 filter, whereas inception-v2 removes it with two 3*3 filters, which boost the performance, and it should point out that 5*5 filter is more costly than 3*3.

Faster R-CNN: Region with Convolutional Neural Network (R-CNN) and Fast R-CNN [13] is the ancestor of Faster R-CNN. Selective search (SS) [15] is used in those approaches, which is a slow and time-consuming process. Hence, the authors introduced Faster R-CNN, where the region proposals are not exercised by the selective search method; instead, it lets the network learned about the region proposals [9]. Here, the feature map of any input is extracted by the convolutional neural network, and the region proposal is done by Faster R-CNN. Then, the smoke proposal is obtained and go through the region of interest pooling (ROI) for reshaping all the proposals. Finally, passing through a softmax, the smoke region is detected. The architecture of Inception-V2 and Faster R-CNN are shown in Fig. 7.

Training Procedure. For training procedure required the training data, learning rate, and optimizer. The learning rate is selected from the empirical value, which is 0.0002. For optimizer, the SGD is utilized with momentum 0.9. Training is continued till getting

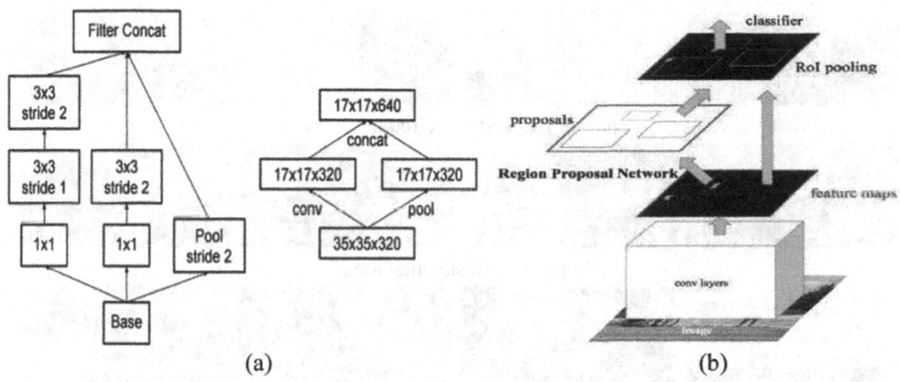

Fig. 7. (a) Architecture of Inception-V2 [8], and (b) Architecture of Faster R-CNN [9].

the average stable loss value, and in this research training, this value is on average 0.15, which takes a long time to train the classifier. The training steps was 36700. For better understanding, the loss curve is as follows in Fig. 8.

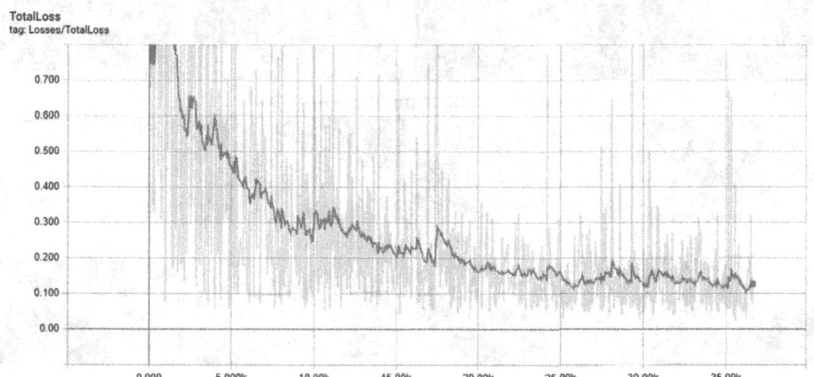

Fig. 8. Loss curve of Inception-V2 network.

3 Experimental Results

3.1 Categorized Data

The categorized data set is discussed in this section, which is pointed out in the previous section. Smoke, visible suspension of different particles which is actually floated in air, have variations in speed, shape, color, density, etc. So, for recognizing smoke from any different circumstances, the dataset is categorized because we tried to experiment the smoke detection for different environmental conditions. The different environmental categories of dataset are shown in Fig. 9.

Sample 1:Forest fire circumstances

Sample 2: Residential area

Sample 3:Warm foods and drinks

Sample 4: Transport fire smoke

Sample 5: Dark or night environment

Sample 6: Ritual's created

Sample 7: Others environmental conditions like: dust, cigarette, flamethrower, fuel

Fig. 9. Different environmental categories dataset.

3.2 Performance Measurement Tools

Performance of proposed approach according to accuracy measurement procedure has been analyzed by true positive (TP), true negative (TN), false positive (FP), false negative (FN), intersection over union (IoU), precision, and recall.

The true positive refers to the portion that belongs to the original smoke region and correctly detected. True negative refers to the portion that doesn't belong to the smoke region and thus not detected. False positive refers to the portion that is detected; however, it is not a part of the original smoke region. And false negative refers to the portion that is not detected however it is a part of the original smoke region. Since we know the coordinates of the original region area, we can calculate true positive by considering the amount of area detected correctly. Similarly, we can calculate the other measurements accordingly. The IoU is defined in Eq. (1). Precision or specificity refers to the percentage of correct positive predictions among all which is calculated by Eq. (2). Percentage of total positive cases that classifiers can catch correctly refers to the recall, also known as sensitivity, which is calculated by Eq. (3). The accuracy is calculated by the Eq. (4).

$$IoU = \frac{Area\ of\ Overlap\ between\ Ground\ truth\ and\ Predicted\ crosswalks\ (Gt \cap P)}{Area\ of\ Union\ between\ Ground\ truth\ and\ predicted\ crosswalks\ (Gt \cup P)} \tag{1}$$

Here, Gt refers to ground truth value and P refers to predicted crosswalks.

$$Precision = \frac{TP}{TP + FP} \tag{2}$$

$$Recall = \frac{TP}{TP + FN} \tag{3}$$

$$Accuracy = \frac{TP + TN}{TP + TN + FP + FN} \tag{4}$$

3.3 Experimental Outputs

In this section, some experimental results are demonstrated from different environments and lighting conditions. Figure 10 shows the single sample image from every different environmental condition which represented the output of that environment. In those figures, Fig. 10(a) represents the input image, Fig. 10(b) refers to a labeled image, Fig. 10(c) represents the predicted output and Fig. 10(d) refers to output with IoU.

In Fig. 10, Sample 1 shows the detection result of smoke from forest environment. Sample 2 presents the smoke detection from residential areas. Sample 3 shows the experimental results from the warm foods and drinks. The transport fire-smoke experimental result is shown in Sample 4. Sample 5 presents the experimental result for dark and night environments. Ritual's created smoke is detected in Sample 6. Finally, the Sample 7 shows the experimental result of smoke detection from smoking.

Challenging Data. Experimenting some images of sunlight, dust, fog which look like smoke in most of the aspects, however, those are not originally smoke. The challenging images are shown in Fig. 11. Some sample images which probably look like smoke. These images contain no smoke, and experimental results show no smoke detection region in the image by Faster R-CNN.

3.4 Performance Statistics

The performance statistics, which is evaluated on test dataset and measured by the machine learning matrices are presented in Table 2. From the table it is summarized that the accuracy performed by proposed model is 97.31%. The detection error of the smock region is presented with FP and FN values. The performance of the model is also justified with respect to the intersection over union (IoU), precision and recall.

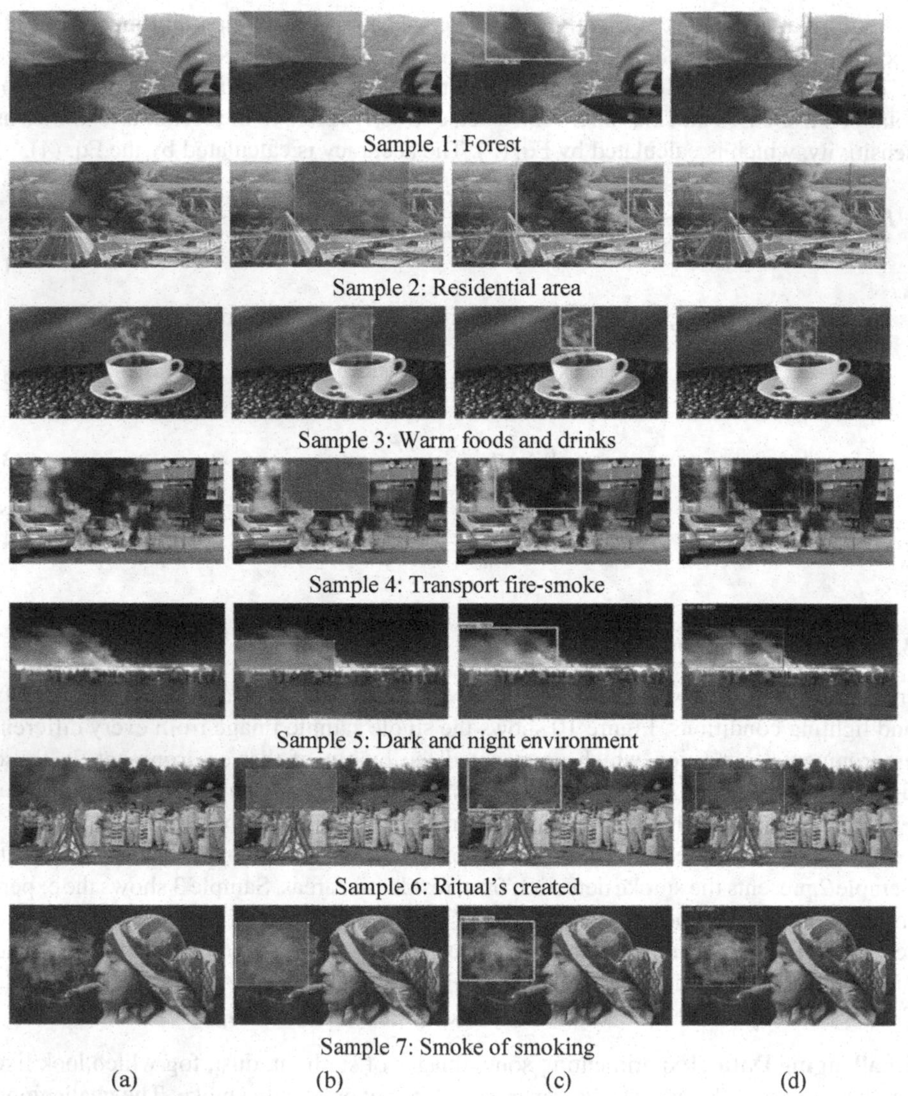

Fig. 10. Experimental outputs for different circumstances: (a) refers to input, (b) refers to labeled image, (c) refers to predicted output, and d) refers to output with IoU.

3.5 Comparison and Discussion

The proposed method's efficiency is further proved while it is compared with the current states of the art that are [2], and [4]. Our method has a better accuracy of 97.31% over different environmental situations which are the most diverse weather conditions shown in Fig. 10. The comparison of the proposed method with [2] and [4] is presented in Table 3.

Fig. 11. Sample challenging dataset which looks contain smoke, however there is no smoke in the environment.

Table 2. Performance of the proposed method for different circumstances

Samples	Detection error		IoU (%)	Precision (%)	Recall (%)	Detection accuracy (%)	Average detection accuracy (%)
	FP (%)	FN (%)					
Forest	3.50	3.20	80.36	96.51	96.80	96.65	97.31
Residential area	2.85	1.50	85.55	97.19	98.50	97.83	
Warm food and drinks	3.89	2.68	80.58	96.16	97.32	96.72	
Transport	2.34	1.30	88.03	97.68	98.7	98.18	
Dark or Night	3.82	1.85	84.25	96.25	98.15	97.17	
Ritual's created	2.40	2.10	85.03	97.61	97.90	97.75	
Others	3.30	2.95	82.29	96.71	97.05	96.89	

Table 3. Comparison of the proposed method

Method	Detection accuracy (%)
Proposed method	97.31
Inception-V4 [2]	58.75
Xception [2]	41.25
DNCNN [4]	96.37

From the experimental results, it is revealed that the proposed method has the best accuracy of 97.31% over different environmental situations, which are the most diverse weather conditions. This research proposed a sequential approach of feature extraction by the Inception-V2 deep neural network and region proposal network for indicating the smoke region by Faster R-CNN. While in [2], the method shows the detection accuracy of 58.75% for the Inception-V4 and 41.75% for the Xception networks respectively. The accuracy is measured with the four matrics, i.e., TP, TN, FP, and FN. However, authors did not described the process of extracting these matrices specifically. Moreover, in [4], the method shows the smoke detection accuracy of 96.37%. Where, the dataset images are not diverse itself. The size of the data set is too small. The image number is increased by the augmented procedure. Whereas, our dataset contains eight hundred images that are taken from different environmental conditions. Our proposed method can both classify and detect smoke regions in diverse and complex scenarios with the proposed network, as shown in Fig. 10, and Fig. 11. These images show the robustness of the model in different environmental conditions.

4 Conclusion

In this paper, a method is proposed to detect and localize the smoke region via a deep neural network and Faster R-CNN. Here, the method detects and localizes the smoke in diverse weather and lighting conditions. The DCNN and Faster R-CNN show the detection accuracy of 97.31%. The image dataset used in this work is our won dataset that are collected from online sources, some of the images are taken from video frames, and many of the images are self-captured images captured by camera. The proposed method uses Faster R-CNN Inception-V2, where Inception-V2 works by going wider to reduce bottlenecks without hurting accuracy. There are certainly scopes of improvement in our model. Future work would be done to implement the system in real-time environments in complex scenarios and improve the accuracy.

References

1. Zhang, Q.X., Lin, G.H., Zhang, Y.M., Xu, G., Wang, J.J.: Wildland forest fire smoke detection based on faster R-CNN using synthetic smoke images. Procedia Eng. **211**, 441–446 (2018)
2. Filonenko, A., Kurnianggoro, L., Jo, K.-H.: Smoke detection on video sequences using convolutional and recurrent neural networks. In: Nguyen, N.T., Papadopoulos, G.A., Jędrzejowicz, P., Trawiński, B., Vossen, G. (eds.) ICCCI 2017. LNCS (LNAI), vol. 10449, pp. 558–566. Springer, Cham (2017). https://doi.org/10.1007/978-3-319-67077-5_54
3. Filonenko, A., Hernández, D.C., Jo, K.H.: Fast smoke detection for video surveillance using CUDA. IEEE Trans. Ind. Inf. **14**(2), 725–733 (2017)
4. Yin, Z., Wan, B., Yuan, F., Xia, X., Shi, J.: A deep normalization and convolutional neural network for image smoke detection. IEEE Access **5**, 18429–18438 (2017)
5. Wu, X., Lu, X., Leung, H.: An adaptive threshold deep learning method for fire and smoke detection. In: 2017 IEEE International Conference on Systems, Man, and Cybernetics (SMC), pp. 1954–1959. IEEE (2017)
6. Xu, G., Zhang, Y., Zhang, Q., Lin, G., Wang, J.: Deep domain adaptation based video smoke detection using synthetic smoke images. Fire Saf. J. **93**, 53–59 (2017)
7. Frizzi, S., et al.: Convolutional neural network for video fire and smoke detection. In: IECON 2016-42nd Annual Conference of the IEEE Industrial Electronics Society, pp. 877–882. IEEE (2016)
8. Szegedy, C., Vanhoucke, V., Ioffe, S., Shlens, J., Wojna, Z.: Rethinking the inception architecture for computer vision. In: Proceedings of the IEEE Conference on Computer Vision and Pattern Recognition, pp. 2818–2826. IEEE (2016)

9. Ren, S., He, K., Girshick, R., Sun, J.: Faster R-CNN: towards real-time object detection with region proposal networks. In: Advances in Neural Information Processing Systems, pp. 91–99 (2015)
10. Yuan, F., Fang, Z., Wu, S., Yang, Y., Fang, Y.: Real-time image smoke detection using staircase searching-based dual threshold AdaBoost and dynamic analysis. IET Image Process. **9**(10), 849–856 (2015)
11. Simonyan, K., Zisserman, A.: Very deep convolutional networks for large-scale image recognition. arXiv preprint arXiv:1409.1556 (2014)
12. Szegedy, C., et al.: Going deeper with convolutions. In: Proceedings of the IEEE Conference on Computer Vision and Pattern Recognition, pp. 1–9. IEEE (2015)
13. Girshick, R.: Fast R-CNN. In: Proceedings of the IEEE International Conference on Computer Vision, pp. 1440–1448 (2015)
14. Zeiler, M.D., Fergus, R.: Visualizing and understanding convolutional networks. In: Fleet, D., Pajdla, T., Schiele, B., Tuytelaars, T. (eds.) ECCV 2014. LNCS, vol. 8689, pp. 818–833. Springer, Cham (2014). https://doi.org/10.1007/978-3-319-10590-1_53
15. Uijlings, J.R., Van De Sande, K.E., Gevers, T., Smeulders, A.W.: Selective search for object recognition. Int. J. Comput. Vis. **104**(2), 154–171 (2013)

Convolutional Neural Networks Based Bengali Handwritten Character Recognition

Sudarshan Mondal and Nagib Mahfuz(✉)

Department of Computer Science and Engineering, North Western University, Khulna, Bangladesh
sudarshaana@gmail.com, ren3336@gmail.com

Abstract. With the increment of computation power, recognizing handwritten Character has become popular and significant improvement has been achieved for most of the major languages. But Bengali character recognition system is not well enough because of the presence of perplexing character and excessive cursive in its characters. Although several research works have been conducted for recognizing the Bengali characters, an efficient procedure is yet to discover. As the number of datasets is inadequate, most of these studies could not achieve a satisfactory level. So we propose here to train a Convolution Neural Network (CNN) and tune the parameters for better accuracy. This procedure is applied to CMATERDB 3.1.2 dataset with 15000.

Keywords: Handwritten Character Recognition (HCR) · Image processing · Convolution Neural Network (CNN) · Parameters tuning

1 Introduction

Optical Character Recognition (OCR) is a process where the computer can automatically recognize handwritten characters. OCR is one of the foremost challenging processes in the field of pattern recognition with a lot of practical applications. Many types of researches are still performing within the field of OCR, especially in Handwritten Character Recognition (HCR). Automatic HCR has many commercial and academic interest in recent years as it has various potential applications. HCR makes an easy interface between man and machine and helps in automation with a huge saving of time. Nowadays, deep learning techniques excel in HCR [1]. Handwriting styles vary from person to person in a different language. Moreover, a few of the complex penmanship scripts contain diverse styles for composing words. Printed shapes of character are easier to classify compared to Handwriting Character Recognition. Most of the Handwriting Character Recognition issues are complex and deal with a huge number of character classes. The similarities in several character formation, the overlaps, and the interconnections of the neighboring characters lead the problem to be more complicated. HCR becomes a helping hand on various real-life applications like automation of the postal system, analysis of passports and travel document analysis, automatic bank-cheque processing and fraud

T. Bhuiyan et al. (Eds.): ICONCS 2020, LNICST 325, pp. 718–729, 2020.
https://doi.org/10.1007/978-3-030-52856-0_57

detection, and also the identification of car's number plate [2, 3]. With the help of HCR bank check fraud can be reduced with higher accuracy and in a short time. Car's number plate detection will be helpful for controlling traffic, implying traffic law as well as reducing unwanted traffic jam and accidents. For digitalizing content, OCR can play an important role by converting existing books and documents into digital content. Portable OCR devices can be the first step for building handwritten-to-speech converting devices.

In the last decade, OCR of handwritten characters has been for the most part found to recognize Roman script, English and a few European related languages, and Asian continental languages like Korean, Chinese, and Japanese. On the contrary, recognition of handwritten Bengali alphabet is not well developed although it is the main language of Bangladesh and is a major language in the Indian subcontinent having fifth-ranked in the world. Over 242 million people from all over the world use Bengali. The Bengali language has a rich heritage of sacrificing life for the mother tongue in 1952. No other nation sacrifices their life for their mother tongue. Its writing style is horizontal and left to right. There is no upper or lower case concept in this language. The Same or distinct consonant characters form a compound character. There are 50 characters and 260 compound characters present in the Bengali language.

Despite the complexity problem of handwritten Bangla character recognition, it is becoming more important [4] as the application of HCR is getting popular day by day. Convolutional Neural Network (CNN) has brought a breakthrough in image classification and image recognition as well as in the core of computer vision. The feature extraction process is not used in CNN like other recognition approaches [5, 6]. There are a few prominent works available that use CNN to recognize Bangla handwritten. Some works have been done in the past few years [7–9]. This encourages us to work with Bengali Handwriting Character Recognition.

2 Related Works

Various types of techniques have been proposed within the process of recognizing handwritten characters. But few comparable works have been carried out recently for recognizing Bengali HCR that have accuracy above 90%. Previously, HMM and SVM based approaches got popularity as they have the potential of unconstrained handwriting character recognition. But recently CNN is proved to be very efficient in image recognition tasks as it does not requires any feature selection process. In the overall recognition scheme, there are three steps (i) pre-processing, (ii) proper feature selection, (iii) relevant post-processing. Normalization, slant correction, data augmentation, etc. are done in the pre-processing step. Using contextual information post-processing reduces the error that contributes most significantly to improve final accuracy.

Most of the researches in the Bengali language are conducted for the Bengali numeral recognition system [3, 10, 11]. Dutta and Chaudhuri [12] proposed to use neural network based model to recognize isolated Bengali handwritten alphabets and numeric characters. Basu et al. [13] introduced a hierarchical method to isolate characters from words then utilizing MLP they classify the classes. Three separate techniques have used in the segmentation stage to extract feature but character patterns have reduced to 36 classes combining similar characters into a single class. Bhowmik et al. [14] introduced a fusion classifier that uses Multilayer Perceptron (MLP), RBF network along with SVM. They used wavelet transform for extracting features from character images and designed a hierarchical classification architecture with SVM. In classification, some visually similar characters have considered as a single class then they trained the classifier to classify 45 different classes. The formation of classes has done in an ad hoc manner. Battacharya et al. [15] break the process into two-stage for recognition of 50 basic alphabet classes. The feature vector is used during the first stage of classification is computed by overlapping a uniform rectangular grid on the bounding box of the character. The response of the first classifier was used is to identify where it is confused to separate the difference between a pair of visually similar shaped characters. To resolve confusion, a second stage of classification is used at that point then a feature vector is calculated by overlaying a separate rectangular grid but comprising of irregularly spaced horizontal alone with vertical lines over the box that bounds the character. This step helps to identify where the regions have more similarities and where there is a lot of differences. They utilized Modified Quadratic Discriminant Function (MQDF) model in the first stages and MLP to classify in the second stages. Recently, Rahman et al. [9] have employed a convolutional neural network-based approach to the Bengali character set and achieved 85.96% accuracy on their own dataset. They normalized the written character images and after that utilize CNN to identify individual characters. 4 feature maps were used to extract local features.

3 Methodology

The process of this research work is to select a benchmark dataset, prepare the dataset if necessary for better accuracy. After selecting a state-of-art algorithm that performs better on recognition, a better architecture of the algorithm needs to be constructed and tune the parameters of the model. Selecting dataset and model construction will be discussed in this section and parameter tuning will be discussed in the "Implementation" selection.

3.1 Dataset

In this research, we've used a benchmark dataset named CMATERDB 3.1.2 [16]. This dataset consists of 15000 sample images of 50 handwritten character classes. It contains 12000 images of 50 characters (240 images for each character) for training and 3000 images of 50 characters (60 images for each character). Some of those images have complexity in shape and have similarities with others. Figure 1 shows randomly pick one image from each class of the handwritten character dataset. This dataset contains very few salts as well as paper noise but has some desired noise in the form of obscuring and lost pixel. Figure 2 is the visualization of 202 no folder of the dataset containing a character named "ন" (Moddhennô) that shows variations in size, shape, rotation, and orientation.

3.2 Dataset Preparation

Pre-processing makes the arbitrary sample data into a common form or shape that makes the dataset appropriate to train the classifiers. This dataset contains a large variety of

Fig. 1. Random character from each character set

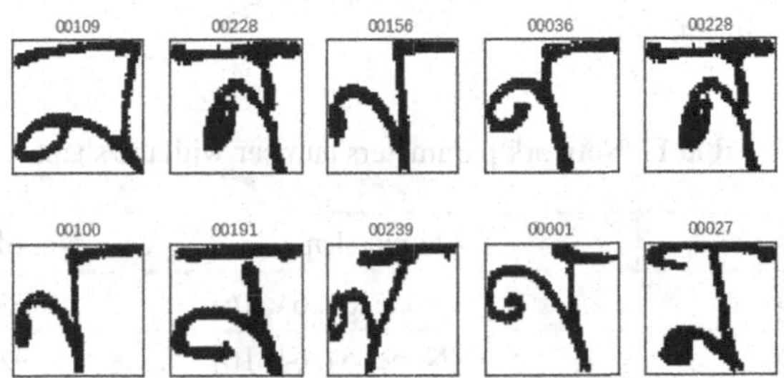

Fig. 2. Random characters in the folder no 202 (ন)

distinct characters because a different person has a different writing style. The original images have different sizes, resolutions, and shapes. A convolutional neural network cannot take different shaped images, so we need to resize all the images into a fixed dimension. That will make the images eligible to feed them into the network. The selected resolution is 64 × 64 for the character image. We rescale the images by dividing every pixel in every image by 255. So the scale is now 0–1 instead of 0–255. That will reduce calculation overhead and takes less time to train the model and it would reduce the use of memory. Then we divide take 20% of the training dataset for validation of the model.

3.3 Convolutional Neural Network (CNN)

In 1980, Fukushima introduced the network model called CNN. As this model requires high computational power, it was not used widely. In 1998, applying gradient-based learning method LeCun et al. [17] reported higher supremacy in digit recognition. As CNN is found to be superior to traditional approaches in different scenarios, several types of CNN have been proposed. Ciresan et al. used CNN that contains multi-column was used to digits recognition, Chinese alphabets, alpha-numerals, finding objects in the image, and a traffic sign. They reported that this method produces superior results and beat conventional methods on various public datasets, such as the MNIST digit dataset, CASIA Chinese character images dataset. Besides, the CNN approach has been designed in such an approach that mimics human visual processing. It handles 2D images in a highly optimized way. Furthermore, CNN has the ability to learn effectively the extraction of 2D features as well as abstraction. The max-pooling layer of CNN absorbs shape variation very effectively. In CNN, fewer parameters are required to train than a fully connected network of similar size. It can produce highly optimized weight. Moreover, the gradient-based algorithm can be used to train a CNN and it doesn't suffer much from the vanishing of gradient problem.

Table 1 shows the overall number of parameters of the CNN used in the research work. It has mainly two parts such as features extractor and classifier. Basically, CNN is consists of three main layers: convolution, max-pooling, and classification. Sometimes a dropout layer is used for regularization parameters. In the basic architecture, the layers that are in even position work for convolution and odd-numbered layers perform the max-pooling operation. But we have altered the sequence and made the first two one as convolution layer and the third one as a max-pooling layer. In our model, we use only the previous layer output as input.

Table 1. Network parameters number with the shape

Layer	Output shape	No. of parameters
conv2d_1 (Conv2D)	(None, 64, 64, 16)	2368
conv2d_2 (Conv2D)	(None, 64, 64, 16)	9232
max_pooling2d_1 (MaxPooling2)	(None, 32, 32, 16)	0
conv2d_3 (Conv2D)	(None, 32, 32, 32)	18464
conv2d_4 (Conv2D)	(None, 32, 32, 32)	25632
max_pooling2d_2 (MaxPooling2)	(None, 16, 16, 32)	0
conv2d_5 (Conv2D)	(None, 16, 16, 64)	51264
conv2d_6 (Conv2D)	(None, 16, 16, 128)	131200
max_pooling2d_3 (MaxPooling2)	(None, 8, 8, 128)	0
conv2d_7 (Conv2D)	(None, 8, 8, 256)	295168
flatten_1 (Flatten)	(None, 16384)	0
dense_1 (Dense)	(None, 256)	4194560
dropout_1 (Dropout)	(None, 256)	0
dense_2 (Dense)	(None, 50)	12850

The planes of a previous layer that are connected to one another are also connected to the next plane node though a small region. All the node that forms the convolution layer automatically extracts the necessary features from the input images data by applying convolution operation. The convolutional and max-pooling masks reduce the dimension of the features based on their size as the features propagate to the final layer. Moreover, the classification accuracy can be improved by increasing the number of feature map that helps to select or map extremely suitable features.

Finally, a Softmax layer or normalized exponential function layer was used at the very end of the model architecture. The score of the respective class has been calculated in the top classification layer through propagation. After the completion of propagation, based on the highest score of the softmax or other function, the classifier generates its outputs for the specific class. For an input instance x, the equation of Softmax function can be written for the i'th class as follows:

$$(y = i|x) = \frac{e^{x^T w_i}}{\sum_{k=1}^{K} e^{x^T w_f}} \tag{1}$$

Where, w = weight vector and f = distinct linear functions

4 Implementation

A Convolution Neural Network has been built with Keras (using Tensor Flow Backend). Several experiments have been conducted to select the best parameters for the model. Initially, the image size is taken as 128 × 128, the number of epochs is 80, 128 batch size and the learning rate is 0.001.

4.1 Image Size

For Convolution Neural Network, Image size is a vital element as all the images must be the same and image size cannot be changed during training or test time. A higher resolution image helps to achieve higher accuracy, but it is computationally costly while in others, the lower resolution is desired. So, the optimal size needs to be determined during training time. Different image size starting from 32 × 32 to 256 × 256 is tested for getting optimal image size. In total 15000 image dataset has been created containing 9600 training images, 2400 validating images and 3000 test images. The experimental result is shown in Table 2:

Table 2. Accuracy variation with a different image size

Image size	Test accuracy	Validation accuracy (%)	No of error
32 × 32	92.13	91.62	136
64 × 64	97.02	96.01	72
128 × 128	95.43	95.5	136
256 × 256	85.06	85.58	448

From the experiment, it is found that the 64 × 64 image size performs better than other sizes.

4.2 Batch Size

The Batch size is a hyper-parameter that defines the number of data to train before applying backpropagation to tune the internal model parameters. When all the training data is used to create a batch, it is called Gradient Batch Descent. When the number of instances in a batch is equal to one, it is called Stochastic Gradient Descent. When the sample in a batch is greater than one but less than the number of samples a dataset, it is known as mini-batch Gradient Descent.

Table 3 showed that the batch size of 64 performs better than others.

Table 3. Variation of accuracy with batch size variation

Batch variation	Valid accuracy	Test accuracy (%)	No of error
64	97.69	96.26	67
80	95.60	95.18	119
128	94.67	94.67	177
256	95.79	96.30	111

4.3 Learning Rate

The learning rate, another hyper-parameter that controls the number of weights is going to be adjusted of the network with respect to the loss gradient. For a lower value of the learning rate, it will go slowly towards the downward slope. The small learning rate can take a long time to converge, especially if the model stack on a plateau region. The learning rate helps to adjust the weight of the model. The learning rate can be fixed or variable during the training session. Different learning rates have been tested for getting the optimal learning rate for this model. The result is shown in Table 4:

Table 4. Accuracy variation with different learning rates

Learning rate	Valid accuracy	Test accuracy (%)	No of errors
0.1	0.02	2	2940
0.01	0.02	2	2940
0.001	96.50	96.30	68
0.0001	90.51	90.02	295

With the learning rate of 0.1 and 0.01, the model does not converge. The experiment showed that with the learning rate 0.001 leads towards the higher accuracy.

4.4 Dropout

Srivastava et al. [18] proposed a new technique to regularize the neural network in 2014 that prevent the model from being over-fitted.

In the Dropout technique, a number of neurons are randomly selected and ignored during the training process. They are “dropped-out” randomly. This means that the contribution of the selected neurons to the next activation layer is removed temporally and no weight will be updated during the backpropagation step.

It helps to prevent the over-fit of a neuron. A further experiment has been conducted if the model accuracy can be improved by using dropout. And using dropout, the accuracy has been improved (Table 5).

The selected parameters have scored an accuracy of 97.8% with 64×64 image size, 128 batch size 64, learning rate 0.001, and with the dropout.

Table 5. Effect of dropout on accuracy

Dropout	Valid accuracy	Test accuracy (%)	Error
Yes	97.8	96.46	66
No	92.94	92.60	222

5 Result Analysis

After getting the optimized value of the model parameters that make the best recognition accuracy. With the parameters, we have trained our model with 200 epochs. The final model can recognize with an accuracy of 97.8%. The learning graph is shown in Fig. 3.

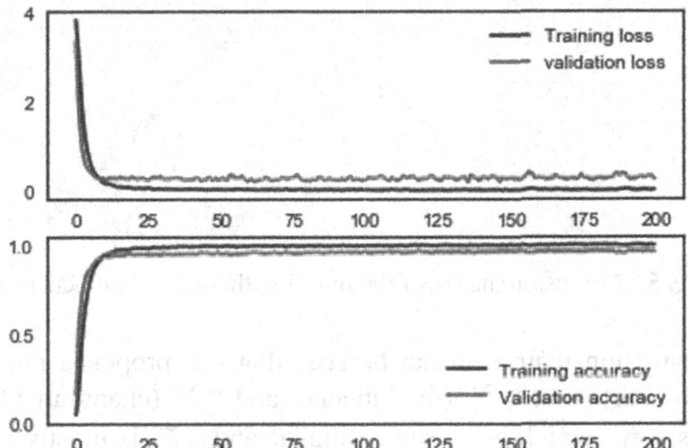

Fig. 3. Graph of training and validation loss, Training and Validation Accuracy

The error recognition list is shown in Fig. 4. The incorrect recognition number is 66.

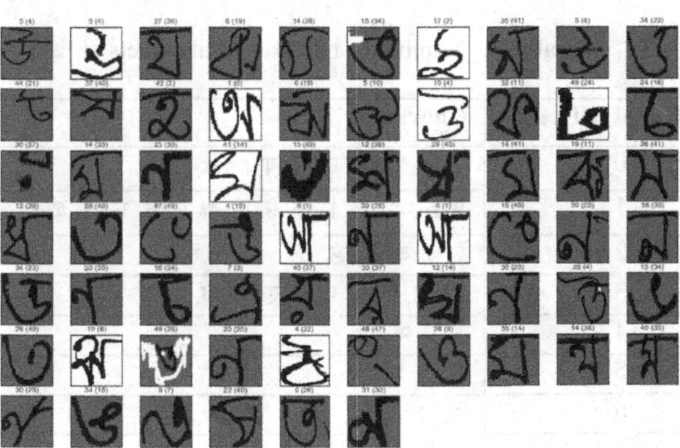

Fig. 4. The error recognition [Predicted level (True Level)]

The confusion matrix of the model with raw data is shown in Fig. 5.

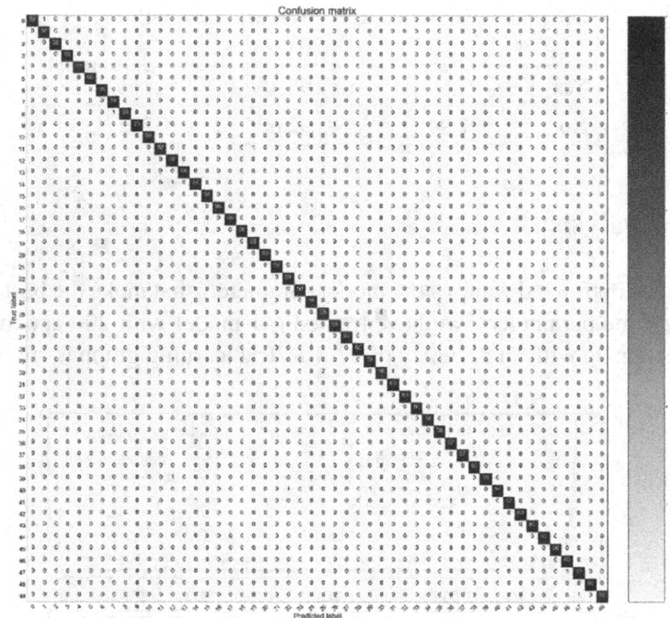

Fig. 5. Confusion matrix of the model without data augmentation

From the confusion matrix, it can be seen that our proposed model made eight mistakes on two characters: " ণ" (moddhennô) and " ঁ" (chandrabindu) where " ণ" is recognized as " ন" which are visually similar and " ঁ" is mostly recognized as " ত", they are also similar in shape. 6 and 5 mistakes have done for 2 and 3 characters, respectively. 4 wrong recognition has been done for 3 characters, 3 wrong recognition for 11 characters. Our model has done 3, 2, and 1 mistakes for 11, 5, and 15 characters. Nine characters are all recognized correctly without a single mistake (Table 6).

Table 6. Number of mistakes of alphabets

Number of Mistakes	Character
0	অ, ঈ, ঞ, ব, ড়, ঢ়, য়, ং, ঃ
1	এ, ঐ, ঔ, ক, চ, জ, ট, ত, থ, দ, প, ফ, শ, হ, ৎ
2	ই, ছ, ঝ, ন, ভ
3	আ, ঋ, খ, গ, ঘ, ঙ, ড, ঢ, ধ, র, ল
4	ঠ, ম, ষ
5	উ, ও, স
6	ঊ, য
8	ণ, ঁ

Table 7 shows the Precision, Recall, and f1-score of each character. From this table, it can be visualized how stable the model is. The precision score is the ability not to label a character that is not the character. And the recall is the ability to recognize a character of a class that has the true label of the class. Considering both the precision and recall, the f1-score is measured. The best value is 1 and the worst is 0 for all of the scores.

Table 7. Precision, Recall, and f1-score of the recognizer model

Character	Preci-sion	Recall	f1-score	Character	Preci-sion	Recall	f1-score
অ	0.97	0.98	0.98	ণ	0.96	0.88	0.92
আ	1	1	1	ত	0.92	0.97	0.94
ই	1	0.95	0.97	থ	1	0.97	0.98
ঈ	1	1	1	দ	0.98	1	0.99
উ	0.97	0.97	0.97	ধ	0.98	1	0.99
ঊ	0.93	0.96	0.94	ন	0.86	0.95	0.9
ঋ	0.97	0.98	0.98	প	0.98	1	0.99
এ	0.98	0.98	0.98	ফ	0.98	1	0.99
ঐ	1	0.98	0.99	ব	1	1	1
ও	1	0.95	0.97	ভ	0.98	1	0.99
ঔ	1	0.98	0.99	ম	0.97	0.98	0.98
ক	1	0.98	0.99	য	0.92	0.97	0.94
খ	0.97	1	0.98	র	0.98	1	0.99
গ	1	1	1	ল	1	0.98	0.99
ঘ	0.98	0.98	0.98	শ	0.98	1	0.99
ঙ	0.95	0.95	0.95	ষ	1	0.97	0.98
চ	0.98	1	0.99	স	0.98	0.97	0.97
ছ	0.98	0.98	0.98	হ	0.98	1	0.99
জ	0.98	1	0.99	য়	1	1	1
ঝ	1	0.98	0.99	ড়	1	1	1
ঞ	1	1	1	ঢ়	1	1	1
ট	0.98	0.98	0.98	ৎ	0.98	1	0.99
ঠ	1	0.97	0.98	ং	1	1	1
ড	0.97	1	0.98	ঃ	1	1	1
ঢ	1	0.97	0.98	ঁ	0.96	0.88	0.92
Avg. Precision = 0.98, Avg. Recall = 0.978 , Avg. f1-score = 0.978							

6 Comparison with Related Works

By comparing the performance of the existing research works in Table 8, our proposed model performs notably better than all the models. All the models except Taufique *et al.*, our model performs better in this field. Taufique *et al.* have used Inception Convolutional Neural Network, a well-developed CNN model but our parameters tuning lead our model to a better recognition accuracy in Bengali HCR.

Table 8. The comparison result of related works

Existing works	Total class	Accuracy (%)
Bhowmik *et al.* [14]	50	84.33
Basu *et al.* [19]	50	75.05
Bhattacharya *et al.* [20]	50	84.33
Bhattacharya *et al.* [21]	50	92.14
Rahman *et al.* [9]	50	85.96
Taufique *et al.* [22]	50	96.70
Proposed method	50	97.80

7 Conclusion

Although character recognition in many languages is performing well, it is not well enough to use in day-to-day life because Bengali characters have many confusing, complex and excessive Characters that leads to low accuracy. In spite of performing outstanding performance of CNNs in handwritten character recognition, the prediction is not errorless. In this research, we investigated the Handwritten Bengali Character (alphabets) recognition approach using CNNs with data augmentation and tried to improve the recognition accuracy. The recognition result is compared to similar works in this field. The experiment results showed that our proposed model achieved the highest known recognition accuracy until the date. In the future, we would like to work by augmenting the dataset that will make more variations in the training data. It can be said that the work of this research is another step in the right direction to make Bengali Character Recognition usable in the real-life application in the near future.

References

1. Kim, I.-J., Xie, X.: Handwritten Hangul recognition using deep convolutional neural networks. IJDAR **18**, 1–13 (2014). https://doi.org/10.1007/s10032-014-0229-4
2. Senior, A., Robinson, A.: An off-line cursive handwriting recognition system. IEEE Trans. Pattern Anal. Mach. Intell. **20**, 309–321 (1998)
3. Kim, D., Bang, S.-Y.: A handwritten numeral character classification using tolerant rough set. IEEE Trans. Pattern Anal. Mach. Intell. **22**, 923–937 (2000)

4. Pal, U., Chaudhuri, B.: OCR in Bangla: an Indo-Bangladeshi language. In: Proceedings of the 12th IAPR International Conference on Pattern Recognition (Cat. No.94CH3440-5) (1994)
5. Unsupervised Feature Learning and Deep Learning Tutorial. http://deeplearning.stanford.edu/tutorial/supervised/ConvolutionalNeuralNetwork
6. CS231n Convolutional Neural Networks for Visual Recognition. http://cs231n.github.io/convolutional-networks
7. Kumar, P., Sharma, N., Rana, A.: Handwritten character recognition using different kernel based SVM classifier and MLP neural network (A COMPARISON). Int. J. Comput. Appl. **53**, 25–31 (2012)
8. Das, N., Sarkar, R., Basu, S., Saha, P., Kundu, M., Nasipuri, M.: Handwritten Bangla character recognition using a soft computing paradigm embedded in two pass approach. Pattern Recogn. **48**, 2054–2071 (2015)
9. Rahman, M., Akhand, M., Islam, S., Chandra Shill, P., Hafizur Rahman, M.: Bangla handwritten character recognition using convolutional neural network. Int. J. Image Graph. Sign. Process. **7**, 42–49 (2015)
10. Fukushima, K.: Neocognitron: a self-organizing neural network model for a mechanism of pattern recognition unaffected by shift in position. Biol. Cybern. **36**, 193–202 (1980). https://doi.org/10.1007/BF00344251
11. Wen, Y., Lu, Y., Shi, P.: Handwritten Bangla numeral recognition system and its application to postal automation. Pattern Recogn. **40**, 99–107 (2007)
12. Dutta, A., Chaudhury, S.: Bengali alpha-numeric character recognition using curvature features. Pattern Recogn. **26**, 1757–1770 (1993)
13. Basu, S., Das, N., Sarkar, R., Kundu, M., Nasipuri, M., Basu, D.: A hierarchical approach to recognition of handwritten Bangla characters. Pattern Recogn. **42**, 1467–1484 (2009)
14. Bhowmik, T.K., Bhattacharya, U., Parui, Swapan K.: Recognition of bangla handwritten characters using an MLP classifier based on stroke features. In: Pal, N.R., Kasabov, N., Mudi, R.K., Pal, S., Parui, S.K. (eds.) ICONIP 2004. LNCS, vol. 3316, pp. 814–819. Springer, Heidelberg (2004). https://doi.org/10.1007/978-3-540-30499-9_125
15. Bhattacharya, U., Shridhar, M., Parui, S., Sen, P., Chaudhuri, B.: Offline recognition of handwritten Bangla characters: an efficient two-stage approach. Pattern Anal. Appl. **15**, 445–458 (2012). https://doi.org/10.1007/s10044-012-0278-6
16. Center for Microprocessor Application for Training Education and Research (CMATER). Computer Science and Engineering Department, Jadavpur University, Kolkata, India. https://code.google.com/archive/p/cmaterdb
17. Lecun, Y., Bottou, L., Bengio, Y., Haffner, P.: Gradient-based learning applied to document recognition. Proc. IEEE **86**, 2278–2324 (1998)
18. Srivastava, N., Hinton, G., Krizhevsky, A., Sutskever, I., Salakhutdinov, R.: Dropout: a simple way to prevent neural networks from overfitting. J. Mach. Learn. Res. **15**, 1929–1958 (2014)
19. Basu, S., et al.: Handwritten Bangla alphabet recognition using an MLP based classifier. In: Proceedings of the Second National Conference on Computer Processing of Bangla, pp. 285–291 (2005)
20. Bhattacharya, U., Parui, S.K., Sridhar, M., Kimura, F.: Two-stage recognition of handwritten Bangla alphanumeric characters using neural classifiers. In: Proceedings of the Second Indian International Conference on Artificial Intelligence (IICAI), pp. 1357–1376 (2005)
21. Bhattacharya, U., Shridhar, M., Parui, S.: On recognition of handwritten Bangla characters, pp. 817–828. Comput. Vis., Graphics and Image Processing (2006)
22. Adnan, M., Rahman, F., Imrul, M., Nasib, A.L., Shabnam, S.: Handwritten Bangla character recognition using inception convolutional neural network. Int. J. Comput. Appl. **181**, 48–59 (2018)

Detection and Classification of Road Damage Using R-CNN and Faster R-CNN: A Deep Learning Approach

Md. Shohel Arman(✉), Md. Mahbub Hasan, Farzana Sadia, Asif Khan Shakir, Kaushik Sarker, and Farhan Anan Himu

Department of Software Engineering, Daffodil International University, Dhaka, Bangladesh
sshuvo27@gmail.com

Abstract. Road surface monitoring is mostly done manually in cities which is an intensive process of time consuming and labor work. The intention of this paper is to research on road damage detection and classification from road surface images using object detection method. This paper applied multiple convolutional neural network (CNN) algorithm to classify road damage and discovered which algorithm performs better in road damage detection and classification. The damages are classified in three categories pothole, crack and revealing. For this research data was collected from street of Dhaka city using smartphone camera and prepossessed the data like image resize, white balance, contrast transformation, labeling. This study applies R-CNN and faster R-CNN for object detection of road damages and apply Support Vector Machine (SVM) for classification and gets a better result from previous studies. Then losses are calculated using different loss functions. The results demonstrate the highest 98.88% accuracy and the lowest loss is 0.01.

Keywords: Road damage identification · Road damage classification · R-CNN · Faster R-CNN

1 Introduction

The city road network is the core system of transportation. Many road accidents happened every day. The World Health Organization 2016 report showed that death rate in Bangladesh is 15.5 because of road accident. Safety of transportation systems is a matter of concern for the government and for the general people with the comprehensive construction of roads [1]. To overcome such terrible situations the most important duties is to repair roads in order to avoid road accidents and ensure road safety. Road networks must be checked regularly in order to identify potential dangers and risks to maintain safety of road network [2]. In reality, experienced workers are usually responsible for the detection of road diseases which highly time consuming and costly. For this reason, a low-cost automated system is needed to identify road damage. There are lots of automated systems to identify road damage based on sensors which are costly. Laser scanning continues to be the key technology for the acquisition of 3D road data [3]. Through this

T. Bhuiyan et al. (Eds.): ICONCS 2020, LNICST 325, pp. 730–741, 2020.
https://doi.org/10.1007/978-3-030-52856-0_58

paper a research has been done on road damage detection and classification using image processing which low-cost intelligence system.

In recent years, deep education in the field of computer vision has achieved remarkable results and has shown great effectiveness in many fields of research. In this study, convolutional neural network algorithms have been applied for road damage object detection and SVM is used for classification. Previously many works had been done on road damage detection using image processing they use different algorithms. Here, R-CNN and faster R-CNN is used for this work by comparing which algorithm works better for road damage detection. Data was collected from the streets of Dhaka city using smartphone camera. And also, data have been preprocessed like image resize, white balance, contrast transformation, labeling.

The remaining paper was organized in the following manner: In Sect. 2 we presented the previous related papers. Section 3 outlines the technical details of the work that has been done, including how the data has been gathered, the structure and the training of the design. Section 4 showed the results of our experiments. We described our conclusion at the Sect. 5.

2 Literature Review

Multiple number of articles based on the task of road surface and road damage publishing and continuing to increase. A standard machine learning approach focused on Support Vector Machine (SVM) [4] has been developed for road pothole detection tasks. They extracted the image region function in this experiment focusing on the histogram and added non-linear SVM kernel to detect the target. The result showed that the pothole can be well and easily recognized in this study.

On paper while [5], a deep learning based, specifically Convolutional Neural Network was used as a classifier to detect road crack damage from images. They build a classifier that is less influential by the noise from lighting, dark casting, etc. The benefits of this study are that it the current method, used by humans to perform the audit of road potholes [6] learning the feature automatically without carrying out any extraction and calculation process compared with conventional methods.

For automated crack detection a low-cost sensor and a deep Convolutional Neural Network [7] were proposed. This experiment showed a Convolutional Neural Network model that can learn from the features automatically without the extraction procedure of any feature. Before the model feed, the input images were annotated manually. Deep learning-a low cost strategy for the identification of road potholes to solve the problem.

N. Hoang developed an intelligence system [8] for pothole identification and tested it using two machine learning algorithms, including the least square support vector machine (LSSVM) and the Artificial Neural Network (ANN). The classification accuracy of LSSVM algorithm was approximately 89% and the use of ANN was approximately 86%.

A pothole detection system was developed by Ryu [9] to read images from an optical device installed in a car and a methodology was then proposed for detecting pothole from the collared data. The suggested method is used first for the removal of dark regions for the pothole using a histogram and the closing process with a morphology filter.

The nominee pothole regions are then selected with different features, such as volume and compactness. Ultimately, when contrasting pothole and context, it is determined whether or not the applicant regions are potholes. With this method, the rating reliability of 73.5% was obtained.

Pothole identification vision-based approach is proposed by A. Akagic et al. [3]. The method first separates the damaged areas from the color space of RGB and then segments the object on them. The quest then only takes place in the area of value derived (ROI). Their approach is appropriate for other supervised methods as a pre-processing stage. The reliability of their system relies on ROI exactness being obtained and 82% are correct.

3 Methodology

The methodology proposed in this article is split into the following segments data collection, data preprocessing, model building and analysis, visualization and result discussion. The proposed working methodology of the study are shown in Fig. 1.

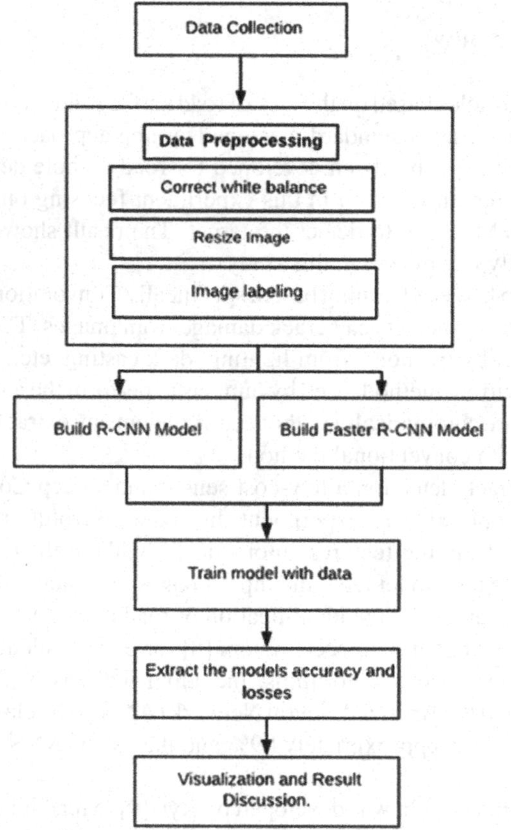

Fig. 1. Working methodology

3.1 Data Preparation

In the road damage detection, there is no large-scale common dataset like other object detection dataset [10]. A dataset was developed by us with 1100 images. In this study we collected data from the streets of Dhaka city using smartphone camera then we corrected the image white balance and contrast transformation. Then resized image into 200 × 200 pixel. After that we labeled our image data with three category Crack, Pothole and Rivaling. Here is our sample data in Fig. 2.

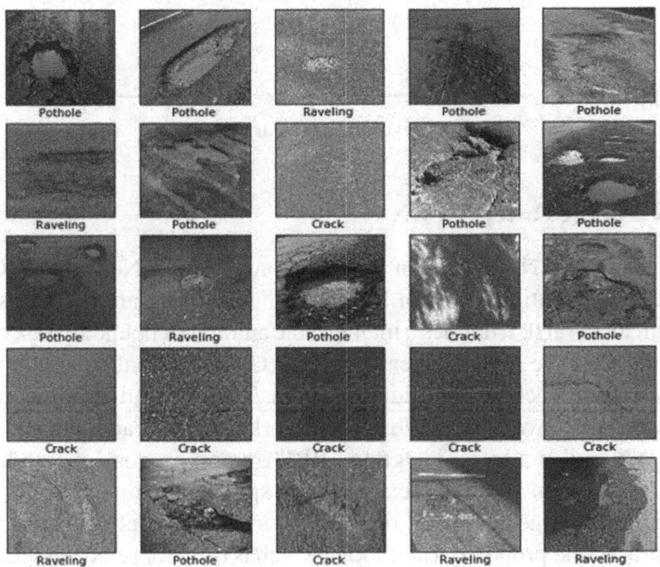

Fig. 2. Sample data

3.2 Deep Learning Based Classification

Artificial Neural Network classification is an incredibly popular way to solve the problem of pattern recognition. A fully connected neural network called a Convolutional Neural Network (CNN) was one of the essential components contributing to these tests. CNN's main advantage is that the important features are automatically detected without any human instruction. CNN model has two parts; the first part is for feature extraction and the second part works for classification. The first layer will attempt to identify edges and shape a model to detect the edge. Then instead layers may try to combine them in simpler ways. In first layer, filter is added to the image and tried to extract the image edges. Second layer is polling layer also added a filter to the image. This layer finds features more deeply from the image and each layer has RelU functionality which helps to connect to the next neuron. Then flatten layer convert 3D image data to 2D data for classification (Fig. 3).

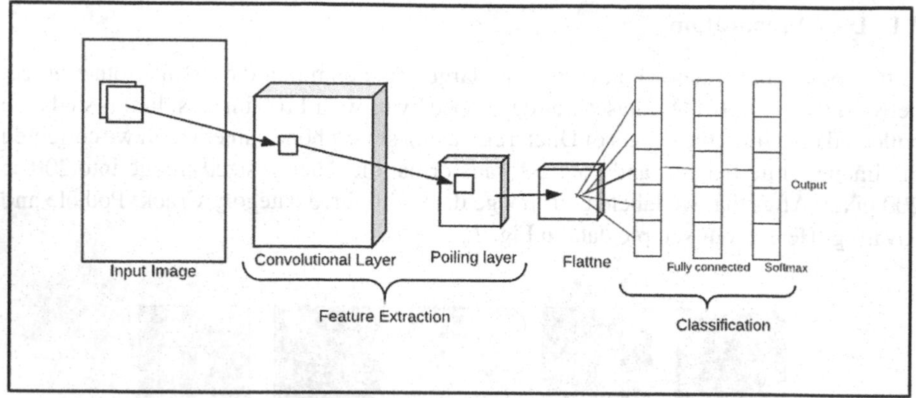

Fig. 3. Convolutional Neural Network

3.3 R-CNN and the Faster R-CNN

R-CNN and faster R-CNN based on Convolutional Neural Network. R-CNN means "Region-based Convolutional Neural Networks" [11]. There are two steps that implements the main idea. First, it defines a manageable amount of boundary box object region applicants with selective search. Then it collects Convolutional Neural Network functions separately from each field for identification. The integration of the area proposal algorithm with the Convolutional Neural Network model is an adaptive acceleration solution. R-CNN builds a large, integrated RPN (region proposal network) and Faster R-CNN with mutual convolutional feature levels specifically this. In order to avoid the problem of picking a large number of regions, Ross Girshick, Jeff Donahue, Trevor Darrell and Jitendra Malik. proposed a method in which is used for selective search to extract 2000 regions from the image and he called them regional proposals. So now only 2000 regions will be operated rather than trying to identify a large number of regions. The selective search algorithm generates these 2000 region proposals. These proposals for 2000 candidate regions are twisted into a square and fed into a convolutional neural network that generates an output of 4096 features. The CNN is an extractor of features and the output layer includes the features collected from the picture then features extracted are fed into the SVM in order to identify the object's existence in the proposal for the applicant area. Similar to the R-CNN, the picture is presented as a convolutional network input that gives a convolutional feature map. A different network is being used to predict regional proposals, in place of using a selective search method on the function graph. Then the predicted regional proposals are shaped using a RoI bundling layer to identify the object in the potential area and forecast the offset values for the border boxes (Figs. 4 and 5).

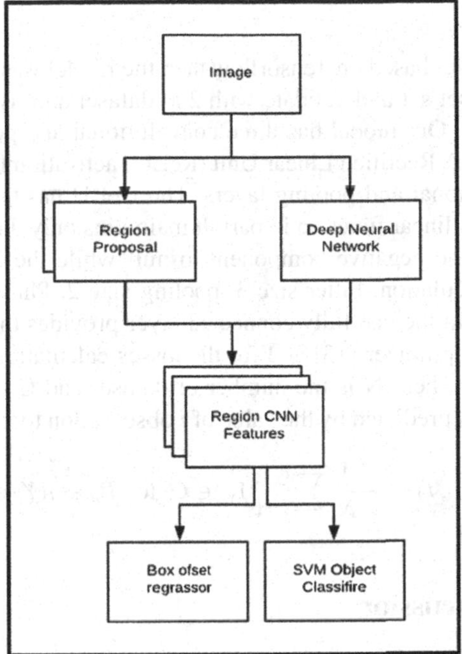

Fig. 4. R-CNN workflow

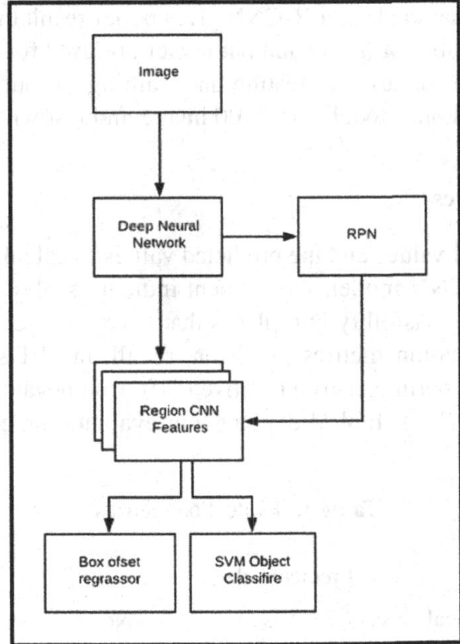

Fig. 5. Faster R-CNN workflow

3.4 Experiment

Our implemented model based on Tensorflow then the model was trained for 50 epochs 1100 of training dataset set and validate with 200 dataset and use optimizer to reduce the cost function [12], Our model has three convolutional and pooling layers and one fully connected layer. A Rectified Linear Unit (ReLU) activation function [8] is implied between the convolutional and pooling layers. The ReLU has the simplification form R[i] = max (i, 0) in its linear function in part. It maintains only the beneficial activation value by decreasing the negative component to null while the built-in max operator facilitates quicker calculation. Filter size 3, pooling size 2, Phase 1 and zero-padding are hyperparameters. In the last fully connected layer provides the classification of the input. We use Adam optimizer [13] and for the losses calculation we used categorical cross-entropy function, here N is the number of dataset and C is the total number of classes and probability predicted by the value of ***i*** observation to the value of ***c*** category.

$$SGC(p,t) = -\frac{1}{N}\sum\nolimits_{c=1}^{c} 1_{y_i} \in C_c \log P_{model}(Y_i \in C_c) \tag{4}$$

4 Result and Discussion

The analysis was done using python and numerical computation library by google TensorFlow and machine learning library scikit learn and as an IDE we used Jupyter Notebook. Convolutional Neural Network method is used for this research. From our experiment we have shown that the Faster R-CNN gives better result the basic R-CNN. Same data, optimizer and number of layers and parameter are used for both models.

We need to split our dataset for testing and training. In our dataset we have total 1300 images we trained our model with 1100 image and test with 200 images.

4.1 Evaluation Metrics

We compared the actual values and the predicted values to calculate the accuracy of the R-CNN and Faster R-CNN model. Assessment indicators play a key role in building a model because it gives visibility into places that need change. We evaluated our two model with three evaluation metrics precision, recall and F1 score. This evaluation process done with four perimeter-true positive (TP), true negative (TN), false positive (FP) and false negative (FN). Table 1 denotes four evaluation metrics parameters.

Table 1. Evaluation metrics

	Predicted class		
Actual class		Yes	No
	Yes	True positive	False negative
	No	False positive	True negative

Here is how calculated Precision, Recall and F1 score

$$Precision = TP \div TP + FP$$

$$Recall = TP \div TP + FN$$

$$F1\,Score = 2 * (Recall * Precision) \div (Recall * Precision)$$

Table 2 denotes this full evaluation metrics of the experimental result of R-CNN and faster R-CNN model for our database. For the faster R-CNN precision result is highest, which is 99% and recall rate is highest for the faster-RCNN which is 97% and f1 score is also highest for the faster R-CNN, F1 score is 98%.

Table 2. Evaluation matrices result

Algorithm	Accuracy	Validation accuracy	Loss	Validation loss
Faster R-CNN	98.02%	99.80%	0.03	0.01
R-CNN	71.44%	76.01%	0.70	0.63

Figure 6 display the graphical representation of precision, recall and F1 score result of the two model, this graph show that all evaluation metrics result best for faster R-CNN.

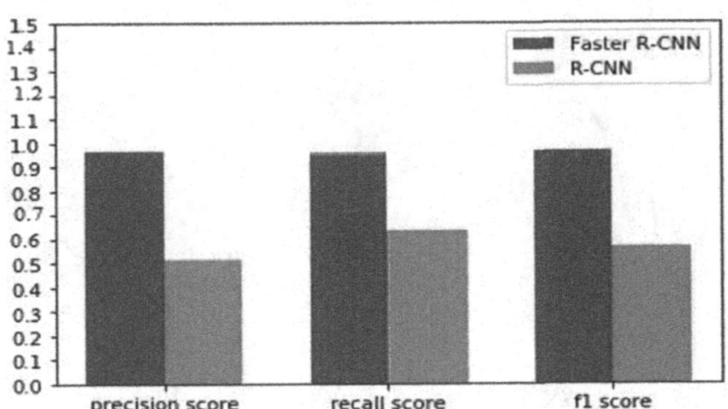

Fig. 6. Evaluation result of the two model

4.2 Accuracy

Accuracy is the most natural indicator of performance. It is simply a ratio of correctly predicted observation to the total observations. Table 3 represent the accuracy and loss of test dataset and training dataset for booth model. Accuracy on training and test data is highest for faster R-CNN, where accuracy is 98.02% and validation accuracy is 99.80% and loss on training and test data is lowest also for faster R-CNN, which is 0.03 and 0.01.

Table 3. Accuracy result of two model

Algorithm	Accuracy	Validation accuracy	Loss	Validation loss
Faster R-CNN	98.02%	99.80%	0.03	0.01
R-CNN	71.44%	76.01%	0.70	0.63

Figure 7 showed the graphical representation of accuracy of faster R-CNN where in x axis represent the number of epoch and y axis represent the accuracy where 1.0 is the highest value of accuracy.

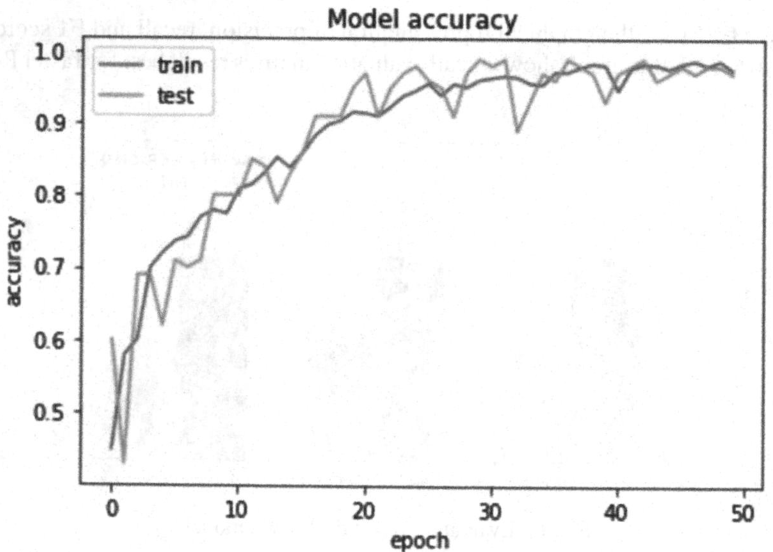

Fig. 7. Accuracy result of faster R-CNN

In Fig. 8 presents the loss function result of faster R-CNN model. In the increase of the number of epochs continuously decrease the loss value of the model.

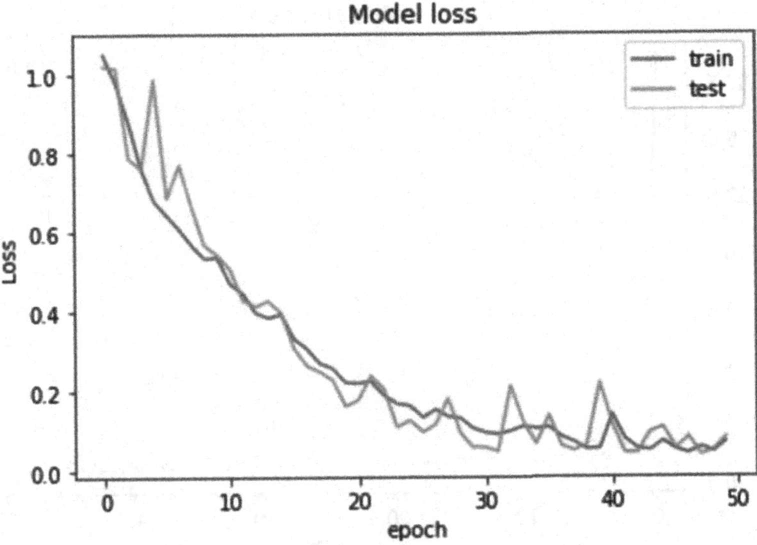

Fig. 8. Loss result of faster R-CNN

Figure 9 display the graphical representation of accuracy of R-CNN where in x axis represent the number of epoch and y axis represent the accuracy where 1.0 is the highest value of accuracy but this mode is not properly fit for the road damage detection.

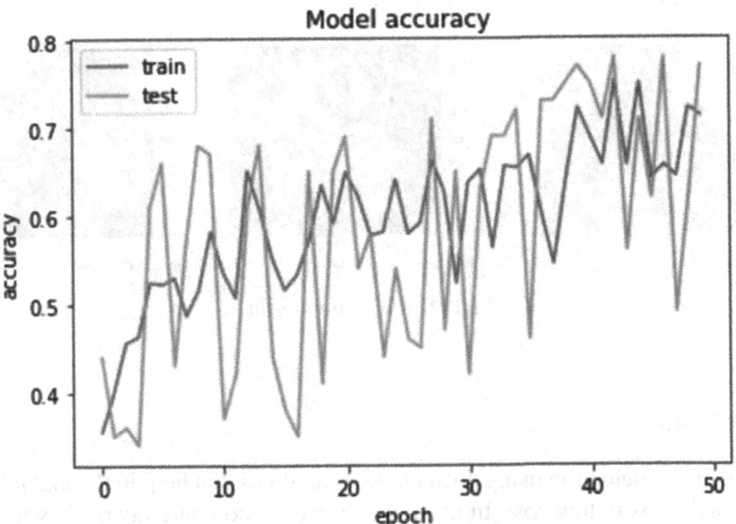

Fig. 9. Accuracy result of R-CNN

In the figure below (Fig. 10) display that R-CNN had higher rate of loss then the faster R-CNN.

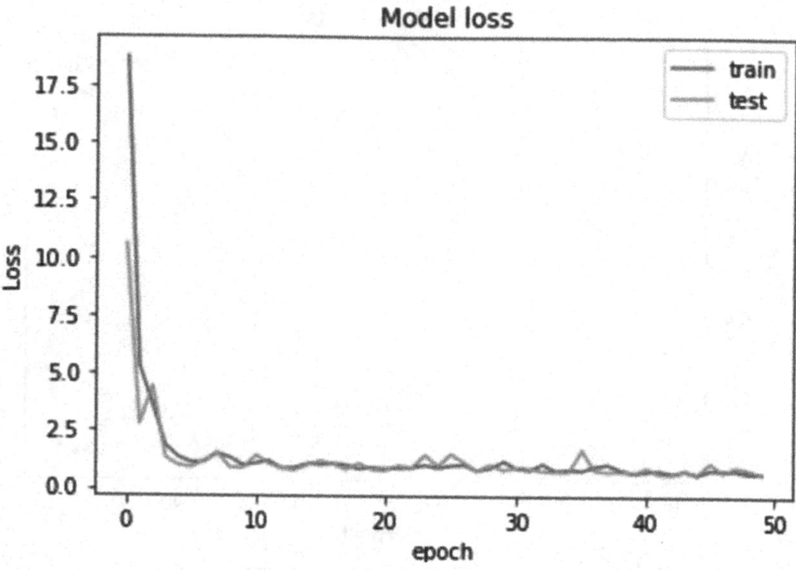

Fig. 10. Loss result of R-CNN model.

After the evaluation result and the accuracy, we can decide that faster R-CNN is better than the R-CNN model. So, after being our model is ready, we provide our model some test images to predict the class of our image. In Fig. 11 display the prediction result of our faster R-CNN model.

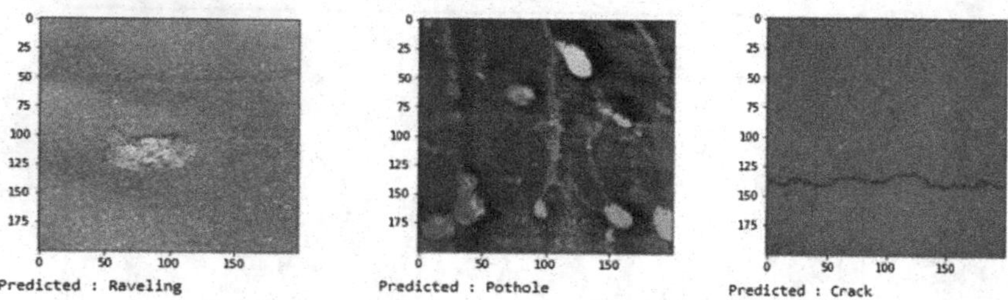

Fig. 11. Prediction result

5 Conclusion

The road damage detection using deep learning methods can help in the maintenance of the road conditions in low cost. In this paper, we have compared two CNN methods to identify which work better for road damage detection and we developed a new dataset on specifically road damage image, hope this will help on future work on this field. In Further, this work can be implemented to transportation system. Extend parameters to predict the repairing cost of road damage and which it can be figured out which area requires urgent repair work.

References

1. Fan, R.: Real-time computer stereo vision for automotive applications. Dissertation, University of Bristol (2018)
2. Kim, T., Ryu, S.K.: Review and analysis of pothole detection methods. J. Emerg. Trends Comput. Inform. Sci. **5**(8), 603–608 (2015)
3. Mathavan, S., Kamal, K., Rahman, M.: A review of three-dimensional imaging technologies for pavement distress detection and measurements. IEEE Trans. Intell. Transp. Syst. **16**(5), 2353–2362 (2015)
4. Lin, J., Liu, Y.: Potholes detection based on SVM in the pavement distress image. In: 2010 Ninth International Symposium on Distributed Computing and Applications to Business, Engineering and Science, pp. 544–547 (2010)
5. Cha, Y.J., Choi, W., Büyüköztürk, O.: Deep learning-based crack damage detection using convolutional neural networks. Comput. Aided Civ. Infrastruct. Eng. **32**(5), 361–378 (2017)
6. Koch, C., Georgieva, K., Kasireddy, V., Akinci, B., Fieguth, P.: A review on computer vision-based defect detection and condition assessment of concrete and asphalt civil infrastructure. Adv. Eng. Inform. **29**(2), 196–210 (2015)
7. Zhang, L., Yang, F., Zhang, Y.D., Zhu, Y.J.: Road crack detection using deep convolutional neural networks. In: 2016 IEEE International Conference on Image Processing (ICIP), pp. 3708–3712 (2016)
8. Hoang, N.D.: An artificial intelligence method for asphalt pavement pothole detection using least squares support vector machine and neural network with steerable filter-based feature extraction. Adv. Civ. Eng. **2018**, 12 (2018)
9. Akagic, A., Buza, E., Omanovic, S.: Pothole detection: an efficient vision-based method using RGB color space image segmentation. In: 2017 40th International Convention on Information and Communication Technology, Electronics and Microelectronics (MIPRO), pp. 1104–1109 (2017)
10. Maeda, H., Sekimoto, Y., Seto, T., Kashiyama, T., Omata, H.: Road damage detection and classification using deep neural networks with smartphone images. Comput. Aided Civ. Infrastruct. Eng. **33**(12), 1127–1141 (2018)
11. Ren, S., He, K., Girshick, R., Sun, J.: Faster r-cnn.: Towards real-time object detection with region proposal networks. In: Advances in Neural Information Processing Systems, pp. 91–99 (2015)
12. Girshick, R., Donahue, J., Darrell, T., Malik, J.: Rich feature hierarchies for accurate object detection and semantic segmentation. In: Proceedings of the IEEE Conference on Computer Vision and Pattern Recognition, pp. 580–587 (2014)
13. Kingma, DP., Ba, J.: A method for stochastic optimization. arXiv preprint arXiv:1412.6980 (2014)
14. Xia, W.: An approach for extracting road pavement disease from HD camera videos by deep convolutional networks. In: 2018 International Conference on Audio, Language and Image Processing (ICALIP), pp. 418–422 (2018)
15. Wang, W., Wu, B., Yang, S., Wang, Z.: Road damage detection and classification with Faster R-CNN. In: 2018 IEEE International Conference on Big Data (Big Data), USA, pp. 5220–5223 (2018)
16. Fan, R, Liu, M.: Road damage detection based on unsupervised disparity map segmentation. arXiv preprint arXiv:1910.04988 (2019)
17. Bhatia, Y., Rai, R., Gupta, V., Aggarwal, N., Akula, A.: Convolutional neural networks-based potholes detection using thermal imaging. J. King Saud Univ. Comput. Inf. Sci. **11**, 1–11 (2019)

Author Index

Printed in the United States
by Baker & Taylor Publisher Services